THE SWEDISH HERITAGE IN AMERICA

THE SWEDISH HERITAGE IN AMERICA

THE SWEDISH ELEMENT IN AMERICA
AND AMERICAN-SWEDISH RELATIONS
IN THEIR HISTORICAL PERSPECTIVE

Allan Kastrup

SWEDISH COUNCIL OF AMERICA
1975

Library of Congress Catalog Card Number: 75-24881

Second printing 1975

Printed in the United States of America
by the North Central Publishing Company, St. Paul, Minnesota

★

Contents

CONTENTS

CONTENTS

★

Foreword

IT IS with great pride that Swedish Council of America makes this noteworthy book available to the general public. Our pride stems from the fact that the book represents one of the first major undertakings of the Council as well as from the achievements of Americans of Swedish background which the publication chronicles. We believe that as Americans of Swedish background it is most appropriate that we sponsor as part of this country's celebration of its Bicentennial a record of the impressive contributions of such Americans toward making this country what it is today.

NILS Y. WESSELL
President, Swedish Council of America

★

Preface

THE SCOPE of this book is larger than its main title at first seems to indicate. It tries to cover not only the story of Swedish emigration to America, the history of the Swedes in the New World and their contributions to the building of the new nation since the modest but significant beginnings in 1638, but also the nearly three and a half centuries of cultural, religious, commercial and political relations between the two countries, as well as the historical background of these events and relationships in Sweden.

In this context, a certain emphasis may first be laid upon the word *contributions*. By the middle of this century a Swedish-born scholar, the late Adolph B. Benson, wrote in an introduction to a book about Swedish pioneers in America: "Despite the labors of several historians, educators, journalists, and historical societies, the general public knows little about Swedish contributions to America. Even the Swedish Americans themselves fail to realize the full magnitude and significance of their accomplishments. Historians — wisely perhaps — deal largely with special topics, and seldom treat the subject as a whole. As a result, we rarely obtain a comprehensive perspective or evaluation of the Swedish influences in our American civilization. We see neither the woods clearly, nor all the trees."

What Dr. Benson wrote in 1948 seems to have lost nothing of its validity, and the present book represents a determined attempt to "treat the subject as a whole." Risks of various kinds are involved in such a venture, but only one will be mentioned here: a substantial volume largely devoted to the immigrants from Sweden and their descendants might finally convey an impression that the Swedish contributions in America carry more weight than they actually do.

On the American side of the Atlantic, however, misconceptions of this type can hardly be long-lived. From Sweden's viewpoint, an American resident of Sweden wrote not so long ago, it is easy to exaggerate the Swedish experience in the United States, which seems to simmer with noteworthy achievements. But looked at from the American end, the Swedish contribution is just as likely to be regarded as a drop in the bucket.

If the present book should lead readers to the lasting conclusion that in the big American bucket there are, in fact, quite a few drops of Swedish origin, and at the same time leave a better understanding of these contents, it will have served one of its objectives. While the book naturally was written primarily for Americans — and not only for those of Swedish ancestry, although large parts are of special interest to them — it is also aimed at students in Sweden. A tendency to "exaggerate the Swedish experience in the United States" may, after all, be less serious than widespread ignorance about the Swedes in America and their accomplishments. And as the history of the Swedes in America becomes better known in Sweden, the American people as a whole will also, inevitably, be better understood.

The great majority of the immigrants from Sweden and their descendants who are described in the book may have become more or less successful, but numerous destinies of other kinds are outlined or indicated, and the author has obviously not aimed at a success story. Fundamentally, the most powerful theme in the history of the Swedish immigrants and their children, as in the history of other immigrant groups, is one of hardships or trials, courage, and strength.

The historical background in Sweden has received more space than in previous books of a similar type, and there are several reasons for this. During the 17th and 18th centuries Sweden was by European economic and cultural standards a rather primitive country, and during the 19th century it was definitely, as the protracted mass emigration showed, overpopulated in relation to its developed resources.

But as an underdeveloped country — to use a modern although already obsolete term — Sweden was always something of a paradox.

Sweden's old traditions of mining, ironmaking and metallurgy, the flowering of scientific research in the 1700s, the relatively high standards of education even before the modern reform work began by the middle of the 1800s — these and other conditions did not indicate underdevelopment, and they promised a rapid advance once Sweden earnestly entered the industrial era. They are, we believe, important for an understanding of the contributions made in America by Swedish immigrants and the first American-born generations.

These contributions are particularly noticeable within the realms of industry, technology, and science, which helps explain the prominence the book gives to such accomplishments. The parts played in such spheres as education, religion, the arts, and public service have, on the other hand, also been regarded as significant. Farming, forestry and construction of various kinds, which were the leading specialties of the immigrant generation, have not been neglected.

To a certain extent, the book also tries to cover cultural, economic and even diplomatic relations between America and Sweden, in both directions. The American impact on Sweden has, of course, been much stronger than the Swedish influences in the New World, and a few brief surveys could not possibly do it justice. A concentrated focus on some specific fields, such as the interchange in the science of economics and American literary repercussions in Sweden, may on the other hand lead to somewhat exaggerated ideas concerning the American-Swedish relationship as a whole. From the Swedish side, the United States looks at least twenty-five and perhaps fifty times larger than Sweden does from the American end, and in this imbalance there are, for both parties but perhaps in particular for the United States, drawbacks as well as advantages. Allergy to bigness, for instance, is not uncommon in Sweden and other small countries.

For prospective readers, a few guidelines of a technical nature. Many emigrants from Sweden changed their names when they came to America, and in the book this process is consistently summarized in the briefest possible way: the original name is given first, being followed immediately by the new one, as for instance in "Johan August

PREFACE

Åkesson or John Augustus Ockerson," or "Gustaf Henning Lindström or Gus Higgins." The diacritical marks of the Swedish
letters å, ä and ö have caused the author more trouble, but in the text
they are, as a rule, dropped when the emigrants settle down in
America.

The author alone is responsible for the contents in this book. He
has had the advantage of being close to American-Swedish cultural
and economic relations in his daily work during three decades but did
not, on the other hand, become seriously interested in the history of
the Swedes in America until it was almost too late. Among those
whose contributions to the book he would like to acknowledge are two
secretarial associates, Tilly Carlborg Rinehart and Mildred Sydlow
Sands, without whose cooperation, actually dating back to 1943, this
project may never have been undertaken. In a related category is Dr.
Nils William Olsson, executive director of Swedish Council of
America, for without his interest and resolution the project would
probably not have resulted in a book, at least not in 1975 or 1976.

Among those who read the whole manuscript, without assuming
any responsibility whatsoever, were Dr. Sten Carlsson of Uppsala
University, Tell G. Dahllöf, Stockholm, whose library of Swedish-
Americana has become widely known among scholars, and Dr.
Franklin D. Scott of Claremont, California, noted historian of Scan-
dinavia. All three offered valuable advice, and so did Dr. Esther
Chilstrom Meixner of Philadelphia, a leading specialist on the history
of the Swedes in the Delaware Valley and herself one of their descend-
ants. Those who have contributed special information, many of
whom are mentioned in the bibliography, include Signe Karlstrom,
Detroit, Einar Viren of Omaha, Nebraska, Carl T. Widen of Austin,
Texas, and Bror H. Grondal of Seattle. Leonard J. Arrington,
Church Historian at Salt Lake City, Utah, R. E. Anderson of Gustavus
Adolphus College, various departments of Yale University, and Re-
gina M. Hanretta of the U.S. Military Academy Archives may also be
mentioned in this connection. On the other side of the Atlantic, Dr.
Wilhelm Odelberg of the Swedish Academy of Sciences and Sigvard
Strandh of the Museum of Technology in Stockholm have been
equally helpful. Much research for the book was conducted in the
New York Public Library, justly described as one of the great cultural
institutions of the United States.

PREFACE

For copy editing the author is especially indebted to Erik J. Friis, long-time director of publications of The American-Scandinavian Foundation. Stylistic advice has often been sought and obtained from Eli Weisman of Swedish Information Service in New York. For help with illustrations we are grateful to the Allhem Publishing Company in Malmö, Sweden, W. Porter Ware of Sewanee, Tenn., Olle Ollén of the Swedish American Line, New York, and several others.

During the first two years of the work on the manuscript consistent encouragement was offered by Dr. Naboth Hedin, then of West Dennis, Massachusetts. Similar support was received throughout from Tore Tallroth and other Swedish representatives, and from Franklin S. Forsberg of Greenwich, Connecticut — one of the millions of Americans of Swedish ancestry who are not mentioned in the text.

The book is, of course, not a biographical reference work. Most of the early pioneers mentioned, and many of the more or less outstanding Americans of Swedish descent briefly described, would have to be included in any sizable book dealing with the history and achievements of the immigrants from Sweden and their descendants, but numerous persons are mentioned primarily as significant examples. Other names could also have been given, but only in a book of even larger dimensions.

By the author as well as by the publisher, the book is hopefully regarded as a contribution to continued research in the history of the Swedes in America and relations between the United States and Sweden. If reading the book should breed a desire to furnish some additional information, such communications should be addressed to "The Swedish Heritage," Swedish Council of America, 2600 Park Avenue, Minneapolis, Minn. 55407, or, in Sweden, to Emigrantinstitutet, Box 201, 351 04 Växjö.

★

Acknowledgments

SWEDISH COUNCIL OF AMERICA takes this opportunity to acknowledge the financial support of all its friends, who by their donations have helped to make the publication of this work possible. To all — Benefactors and Patrons alike — goes the Council's deep and warm appreciation.

Benefactors

Carl A. and Eda A. Anderson Foundation, Inc., Omaha, NE; Robert O. Anderson, Roswell, NM; Lucille E. and Lawrence E. Benson, Minneapolis, MN; Carl A. Berg, Minneapolis, MN; Paul W. Brandel, Chicago, IL; Mr. and Mrs. Curtis L. Carlson, Minneapolis, MN; Dr. Linneus G. Idstrom, Minneapolis, MN; The Jonsson Foundation, Dallas, TX; Sigurd S. Larmon, New York, NY; Maebel and Bertil B. H. Larson, St. Paul, MN; Lilly and Erick La Vine, Minneapolis, MN; Lutheran Brotherhood, Minneapolis, MN; Gudrun and Axel H. Ohman, Minneapolis, MN.

Patrons

Frances and Vince Abramson, Minneapolis, MN; Sonja and Björn Ahlgren, Minneapolis, MN; American Defibrator, Minneapolis, MN; American-Scandinavian Travel Service, New York, NY; American SF Products, Inc., Ft. Lauderdale, FL; Mr. and Mrs. Westen H. Anderberg, Los Angeles, CA; Pia and Burnett Anderson, Paris, France;

ACKNOWLEDGMENTS

Edith and Fred G. Anderson, Minneapolis, MN; Lorraine and A. Harold Anderson, Chicago, IL; Mr. and Mrs. Hugo Anderson, Chicago, IL; Dr. and Mrs. Ingel L. Anderson, Phoenix, AZ; Mr. and Mrs. Marvin R. Anderson, Grosse Pointe Park, MI; Dr. and Mrs. John Rutherford Anderson, Minneapolis, MN; Mr. and Mrs. Westen H. Anderson, Minneapolis, MN; Wilma and Ernest R. Anderson, Minneapolis, MN; Gunnar Back, Philadelphia, PA; Esther and Edward Backstrand, Portland, OR; Barbara and Clifford Benson, Seattle, WA; Marion and Philip Benson, Portland, OR; Edgar Bergen Foundation, Hollywood, CA; Judith and Robert Bergsten, Los Angeles, CA; Grace and Morris Besner, Minneapolis, MN; Blackstone Corporation, Jamestown, NY; Herbert and Carol Bloomberg, Chanhassen, MN; Richard S. and Oliva Bloomberg, Chaska, MN; Edna and Fred W. Broberg, Minneapolis, MN; Mr. and Mrs. Edwin Broden, St. David's, PA; Dr. and Mrs. Harold F. Buchstein, Edina, MN; Eva and Andrew G. C. Bystrom, Minneapolis, MN; Harriet and Mikeal G. Bystrom, Minneapolis, MN; Mr. and Mrs. Einar G. Carlson, Cleveland, OH; Esther and Harry G. Carlson, Edina, MN; Pat and Bob Carlson, Minneapolis, MN; Nelly and Bernard Citron, Los Angeles, CA; Mr. and Mrs. Kenneth A. Cronstrom, Minneapolis, MN; Dr. and Mrs. Donald D. Dahlstrom, Minneapolis, MN; Mary Jean and Irv Dahlstrom, Minneapolis, MN; Bernice Danielson, Topeka, KS; Patricia and John Danielson, Los Angeles, CA; Beryl and Walter G. Danielson, Los Angeles, CA; Helen and Leonard Eck, Minneapolis, MN; Mr. and Mrs. William H. Eckholdt, Minneapolis, MN; Eklund Clothing Co., Minneapolis, MN; Coy G. Eklund, New York, NY; Siri and Sven A. Eliason, Rancho Palos Verdes, CA; Donna and Lynn Elling, Minneapolis, MN; Consul and Mrs. Arthur E. Engdahl, Boston, MA; Mr. and Mrs. Elmer W. Engstrom, Hightstown, NJ; Mr. and Mrs. Alfred W. Erickson, Minneapolis, MN; E. Arthur Erickson, Minneapolis, MN; Gunnar and Alice Erickson, Minneapolis, MN; Mr. and Mrs. Hugo G. Erickson, Roseville, MN; Myrtle and J. Irving Erickson, Chicago, IL; Roland A. Erickson, Greenwich, CT; Mr. and Mrs. Arne Falk, Redwood City, CA; Flygt Corporation, Norwalk, CT; Mr. and Mrs. H. Ellis I. Folke, New York, NY; Gudrun and Harold G. Franzen, Minneapolis, MN; Vivian and Robert Freund, Minneapolis, MN; Brita and Olov G. Gardebring, Bismarck, ND; Louise and Henry Granat, Portland, OR; Hazel and Nels A. Gronquist, Minneapolis,

ACKNOWLEDGMENTS

MN; Annette Grosse, Minneapolis, MN; Doris and Harry Gustafson, Edina, MN; Melba and Walter C. Gustafson, Edina, MN; Gösta B. Guston, Scarsdale, NY; Emily and F. Harold Gyllensward, Richmond, VT; Linn C. and Paul D. Hagstrum, Edina, MN; Shirley and H. Vincent Hagstrum, St. Paul, MN; Dorothy and Bernie Hanson, Minneapolis, MN; Patricia and Nils Hasselmo, Golden Valley, MN; Lorraine S. and Maynard B. Hasselquist, Edina, MN; Dr. James R. Hawkinson, Evanston, IL; Ruth and Raymond P. Hawkinson, Edina, MN; Ellen and Eugene E. Hedlund, Minneapolis, MN; Marion and Donald Hogeland, Philadelphia, PA; Nels M. Hokanson, Pomona, CA; Ruth and Stan Hokanson, Golden Valley, MN; Doris and Philip Hovander, Hopkins, MN; Mary and Paul Hultman, Minneapolis, MN; Mr. and Mrs. Nils R. Johaneson, Grosse Pointe, MI; A. Johnson and Co., Inc., New York, NY; Dorothy and Algot F. Johnson, Minneapolis, MN; Mr. and Mrs. Carl W. Johnson, Washington, DC; Cecil A. Johnson, Omaha, NE; Ethel and Charles V. Johnson, Saratoga, CA; Emily B. and George R. A. Johnson, Minneapolis, MN; Mr. and Mrs. Gustave F. Johnson, Edina, MN; Eva and Hallick B. Johnson, Edina, MN; Florence and Julius A. Johnson, Minneapolis, MN; Mr. and Mrs. Russell M. Johnson, Minneapolis, MN; Vilas Johnson, Chicago, IL; Ruth and Walter G. Johnson, Clinton, WA; Orpha and Francis Scott Keye, Rockford, IL; Florence and Rolf K. Lamborn, Winter Park, FL; Lillie and G. Sigurd Larson, Wausau, WI; Christine B. and Helmer M. Larson, Minneapolis, MN; Robert E. Larson, St. Paul, MN; Mr. and Mrs. David A. La Vine, Wayzata, MN; Dagne and Bernhard W. Le Vander, St. Paul, MN; Iantha and Harold Le Vander, South St. Paul, MN; Dean Melva Lind, St. Peter, MN; Dr. and Mrs. Winston R. Lindberg, Wayzata, MN; Mr. and Mrs. Lawrence Lindgren, Kingsburg, CA; Audrey and Russell C. Lindgren, Minneapolis, MN; Mrs. Grace O. Lindquist, Minneapolis, MN; Evodia and John H. Linner, Minneapolis, MN; Inger and Gunnar Lonaeus, Brasilia, Brazil; Mr. and Mrs. Sigfrid K. Lonegren, Greensboro, VT; Mrs. Gertrude Sidener Lord, Los Angeles, CA; G. Hilmer Lundbeck, New York, NY; Mr. and Mrs. Lester A. Malkerson, Shakopee, MN; Verna and Allan C. Mallquist, Rockford, IL; Dr. and Mrs. Gunard A. Nelson, Minneapolis, MN; Elveda and Harry Morgan Nelson, Golden Valley, MN; Dr. and Mrs. K. Dexter Nelson, Princeton, IL; Dr. and Mrs. Karl M. Nelson, Princeton, IL; Dr. and Mrs. O. L. Norman

ACKNOWLEDGMENTS

Nelson, Minneapolis, MN; Birger Nordholm, Weston, CT; Lorraine C. and Clifford S. Nyvall, Minneapolis, MN; Maxine and Earl E. Olson, Duluth, MN; Mary and Ray Olson, Kingsburg, CA; D. Sally and Karl A. Olsson, Columbia, MD; Dagmar and Nils William Olsson, Minneapolis, MN; Oriflame Corporation, Santa Monica, CA; Hildur and Emil A. Ostrom, Minneapolis, MN; Susan and E. Theodore Palm, Minneapolis, MN; Kerstin and Per Palm, Minneapolis, MN; Mr. and Mrs. James E. Pearson, Minneapolis, MN; Dr. Neville P. Pearson, Minneapolis, MN; Estate of Sigurd G. Pearson, Minneapolis, MN; Meredith and Don Peterson, Minneapolis, MN; Elinor and Glenn D. Peterson, Denver, CO; Claretta and Gordon Peterson, Edina, MN; Dr. and Mrs. Oliver H. Peterson, Minneapolis, MN; Ronald W. and Rosalee H. Peterson, Kingsburg, CA; Barbara and Rudolph A. Peterson, Piedmont, CA; Joyce and Russell G. Peterson, Minneapolis, MN; Mr. and Mrs. Waldemar Peterson, Minneapolis, MN; Mrs. Walfrid H. Peterson, Minneapolis, MN; E. F. Pierson, Kansas City, KS; Lawrence J. Plym, Niles, MI; Products-From-Sweden, Inc., White Plains, NY; Consul Elmer E. Rasmuson, Anchorage, AL; Mary G. Roebling, Trenton, NJ; Peter Rundquist, Eau Claire, WI; Bertil and Carol Sandberg, St. Paul, MN; Dr. and Mrs. K. O. William Sandberg, Chicago, IL; Nels and Hilda Sandberg, St. Paul, MN; Mr. and Mrs. Nels H. Sandberg, Minneapolis, MN; Robert Sandberg, St. Paul, MN; Anne and John B. Sander, Minneapolis, MN; Dr. Glenn T. Seaborg, Lafayette, CA; Mrs. Harold L. Schaefer, Edina, MN; Beverley and Richard L. Schillinger, Minneapolis, MN; H. Åke and Margit Schott, Eden Prairie, MN; Elaine and Roy Schuessler, New Brighton, MN; Sandra and Chet Schwamb, Minneapolis, MN; Harvey Schweers, Kingsburg, CA; Dr. and Mrs. William S. Shaw, Edina, MN; SKF Industries, Philadelphia, PA; Alpha and Elton Strand, Sun City, CA; Mrs. Arthur W. Swanson, Bloomington, MN; Mr. and Mrs. H. R, Swanson, Minneapolis, MN; Eileen and Lloyd O. Swanson, Hopkins, MN; Agatha and O. Harold Swanson, Minneapolis, MN; Swedish American Line, New York, NY; Ellen and Herbert Tellfors, North Freedom, WI; Trelleborg Rubber Co., Inc., Solon, OH; Trollebo Productions, Inc., Los Angeles, CA; Edna and Roy W. Truelson, Minneapolis, MN; Amanda and Stanley A. Uggen, St. Paul, MN; Helen and Paul A. Varg, East Lansing, MI; Viking Sewing Machine Co., Inc., Minneapolis, MN; Dr. and Mrs. Carl B. Walden, Min-

ACKNOWLEDGMENTS

neapolis, MN; Ida and N. Theodore Waldor, St. Paul, MN; Martha and Al Wallen, Edina, MN; Wasa Ry-King Inc., Stamford, CT; Mr. and Mrs. Richard J. Werner, White Bear Lake, MN; Marian S. and Nils Y. Wessell, New York, NY; Lorraine and Wesley M. Westerberg, Minneapolis, MN; Mr. and Mrs. Harold J. Westin, St. Paul, MN; Evelyn and Robert W. Wheeler, Minneapolis, MN; Carl T. and Lucy Widen, Austin, TX; Wigh-Gustafson Properties Co., Kingsburg, CA; Evelyn and Gus Young, Edina, MN; Gus and Eunice Younger, Scottsdale, AZ; Herbert G. Carlson, Omaha, NE; Mr. and Mrs. Clifford Johnson, Golden Valley, MN; Mr. and Mrs. Woodrow C. Lindstrom, Minneapolis, MN; Evald L. Swanson, San Diego, CA.

THE SWEDISH HERITAGE IN AMERICA

★ 1

Sweden and America

A close relationship, based on common ideals and personal ties

A VIRTUAL identity of ideals and aspirations and the existence of millions of Americans of Swedish ancestry are the basic factors in the relations between Sweden and the United States. The values and goals of both nations, like those of other democratic countries, are focused on the rights of the individual, freedom of thought and expression, social justice, and the rule of law. Nearly half of Sweden's some eight million people are aware of having, or at least having had, relatives in America.

Swedes have helped populate and develop America ever since the 17th century. The first landings on the lower Delaware, where a colony was established in 1638 and landmarks of Swedish origin are still to be found, made Sweden one of the three European mother countries of the thirteen original states, preceded only by the much more numerous English and Dutch. In the 1700s most of the Swedes who came to America were seamen. In the early 1800s there were also many craftsmen and merchants among them.

In the 1840s, when America began to attract the Swedish farm population, immigration from Sweden became a continuous stream, and in the late 1860s crop failures temporarily swelled it to a torrent. Incessant migration on a massive scale began ten years later, and it lasted about 35 years, or until the outbreak of the First World War. From 1879 to 1914 about 900,000 Swedes entered the United States.

In relation to the population of their native countries, the Irish, the Norwegians, and the Swedes topped the immigration records during the latter part of the 19th century.

From 1840 down to 1930, when the economic conditions that caused the migration from Sweden had ceased to exist, about 1,300,000 Swedes came to the United States as immigrants; sooner or later, over 200,000 returned to their native country. During the same period the total immigration to America reached about 37 million. From Norway came some 750,000 and from Denmark, today next to Sweden the most populous of the Scandinavian countries, about 375,000. For Finland the total was approximately 350,000; some 70,000 of these were members of the country's Swedish-speaking population.

The great majority of the immigrants from Sweden came from poor homes, in the rural districts or in the cities. In the 19th and early 20th centuries, farming became their leading occupation, and the total area they and their children put under the plow in America was as large as the whole territory cultivated by their kinsmen in Sweden. Their most vital contributions were made in areas intersected by the Mississippi and Missouri river systems — in Minnesota, Illinois, Iowa, Nebraska, the Dakotas, and Kansas. But Swedish immigrants also contributed, for instance, to the development of fruitgrowing on the West Coast and in Florida, to the earliest large-scale potato farming in Idaho and Maine, to the growing of sugar beets in Colorado, and to the raising of cotton and cattle in Texas. About one-third of the emigrants from Sweden moved directly from Swedish to American farms.

Tens of thousands of early comers from Sweden became loggers, miners, or railroad-construction workers. Both in the Middle West and in other sections of the country, large numbers engaged in activities related to building and construction. In relation to their numerical strength, no other ethnic group has produced as much housing of different types as have the Swedes.

To the development of the American manufacturing industry, Swedish immigrants and their sons made highly important contributions as workers, foremen, engineers, inventors, managers, and entrepreneurs. By the middle of the 20th century such activities seemed, in fact, to add up to something that was of even greater significance

4

than the achievements of the farmers of Swedish birth or parentage. Nothing of what the first two generations of Swedish stock did in helping to build the American economy would probably be missed more than the fruits of their labors in industry. Their role was particularly important in steel production, in the making of wood pulp and paper, and in engineering and metalworking. Many inventions and technical improvements made in Sweden have reached American industry via Swedish immigrants.

In the long run, the activities and achievements in the realms of education and science may weigh even more heavily in the balance. The history of the Swedes in America shows that they have always attached great importance to education, and numerous careers have been made in that field as well as in science. Lists of faculty members of American universities and colleges contain thousands of Swedish names, or names of other types whose bearers hail from Sweden. Of the Carlsons, Olsons or Olssons, and Swansons listed in American books of reference, for instance, a remarkably large number describe themselves, directly or indirectly, as educators. Sciences in which Americans of Swedish birth or descent have won distinction include agriculture, biology, botany, chemistry, electronics and other engineering, geography, geology, mathematics, medicine, meteorology, physics, and psychology. In a comprehensive biographical dictionary listing specialists in the physical and biological sciences, there were in the early 1970s over 2,000 Andersons, Bensons, Carlsons, Ericksons or Ericsons, Gustafsons, Hansons, Johnsons, Nelsons, Olsons, Petersons, and Swansons or Swensons, most of whom belonged to the second or third generation. Many of them had, of course, other national origins. Most Americans of Swedish stock have, on the other hand, family names of other types.

The impact made by Swedish immigration on American life may also be studied in the field of public service, in religion, in literature, painting and sculpture, and in music and the other performing arts. As the greatest contributions Swedish and other Scandinavian immigrants have made, some historians have in a more general way mentioned respect for law, stamina and industry, thrift, ambition, and the traditional interest in education; such qualities helped the newcomers and their children build substantial homes and furthered a wholesome community spirit as well as the general welfare.

5

In Sweden, the departure year after year of tens of thousands of men and women in their most productive ages was naturally regarded as a serious, perhaps almost disastrous, loss; especially during the first decade of the 20th century there was much bitterness among those who remained at home. Such feelings, however, have long been completely overcome. More and more Swedes have realized that during the 19th century their country was seriously overpopulated in relation to its developed resources, and that emigration, therefore, served as a human safety valve.

That emigration also resulted in positive and permanent gains for Sweden has likewise been recognized. The newer agricultural, industrial, social, and political ideas and methods of America could hardly have become known in Swedish circles as quickly and effectively had it not been for the personal contacts across the Atlantic which the emigrants created. In the continued exchange of knowledge and experience between the two countries, the Swedish element in America has also been a powerful medium. American influences have, of course, also reached Sweden through numerous other channels.

In 1938, when the Swedish delegates to the celebration of the 300th anniversary of the founding of the Delaware colony returned home, one of them was quoted as having said, "We have conquered America." He did not, of course, have any aggressive inferences, but his statement was overenthusiastic and did not remain unanswered. "You have conquered nothing," replied one of Sweden's most popular writers and humorists. "It is America that has conquered us. Instead of having a New Sweden in America, we now have a New America in Sweden. The whole American civilization seems to have invaded our country — from breakfast foods to mystery stories that put us to sleep at night."

Since then, Swedish imports of American products of various kinds have expanded considerably, and after the middle of this century it has been often said, on both sides of the Atlantic, that Sweden has become the most "Americanized" country in Europe. This is probably true, but it seems to overstate somewhat the actual conditions.

Sweden has always been open to cultural and economic influences from abroad. Many have hardly more than rubbed the surface, but many others have been gradually assimilated, that is, adapted to the

6

nation's own traditions and needs. Most of the oldest and strongest of the numerous American influences are actually often rather hard to identify, for they are incorporated in Sweden's democratic institutions, in its religious and other popular movements, in its schools and libraries, and in its industrial and other economic activities. Much that in the middle of this century seemed to speak of an advanced "Americanization" had, on the other hand, not necessarily an American origin but owed more to the fact that Swedish living standards approached those of the United States, or that economic competition in Sweden was more reminiscent of America than of many countries in Europe. Such things as supermarkets, motels, and drive-in banks had grown up as a result of the high automobile density, but they were, of course, largely based on American models. Frequent offerings of American plays, films, and TV programs as well as displays of American books and magazines added to a certain atmosphere of "Americanization."

Being "Americanized" is obviously not the same as being pro-American. There is no question that the Swedish people as a whole take a very friendly attitude toward the American people, or that the Swedes with few exceptions wish the United States a future of happiness, health, and prosperity. But in the middle or late 1900s America was, nevertheless, a controversial subject, as it had been to varying degrees ever since the early 1800s. Many well-informed and basically pro-American persons regarded it as still a country of extremes, or, in a more modern terminology, as overdeveloped in some respects and underdeveloped in others. In somewhat radical intellectual circles, skeptical views of America often seemed related to a reaction against the U.S. impact on Sweden. Members of the New Left, who, in Sweden as in other countries, in the early 1960s had begun to take an active part in public discussions, went of course farther and looked upon America as a bulwark of an antiquated capitalism. They were as a rule familiar with the social criticism voiced within the United States, but that was also true of moderate groups. Sweden has long been receptive even to such influences from the New World. During the three decades following the Second World War, Swedish newspaper, radio, and TV correspondents in New York and Washington have played a vital role in providing the Swedish public with a balanced view of American developments and tendencies. So have the great majority of the impressive number of Swedes who have visited the United States. In the 1950s Sweden became, in relation to its population, one of the leading generators of transatlantic travel, a development made possible by the direct air traffic between Scandinavia and America.

Longtime Swedish observers of the United States agree that at least since the First World War the land and people of Sweden have, on the whole, been treated in a decidedly fair and generous way by the American press and other media. At times, reports and comments have even seemed too positive. Since the 1920s or 1930s, Sweden's coordination of private, cooperative, and public enterprise, its advances or experiments in economic policies, social welfare, labor relations, housing, architecture, the decorative arts, the sciences, technology, industry, and other fields have received more space in American newspapers, magazines, and books than in any other country outside Scandinavia. During certain periods, however, Sweden has so often been described as remarkably advanced or even as some kind of model that its problems, when they later became more apparent or seemed more complicated, have sometimes been magnified. And "Trouble in Paradise" seems more interesting than the natural conclusion that Sweden has, after all, never been a paradise, even though, as most American commentators agreed, its efforts are worth studying. Conservative publications, in particular, often conveyed the impression that Sweden had quietly become a wholly socialist country and therefore was bound to run into trouble. On both sides of the Atlantic, people obviously have a tendency to shape their picture of the other country to fit their own beliefs, moods, or prejudices.

While Sweden and the United States are largely alike in the basic political structure of society, there are many more or less significant differences in their governmental systems, public institutions, and social developments. Since the First World War a political party supported by a great majority of the industrial workers has been the largest in Sweden, and this faction, the Social Democrats, has governed the country most of the time, either alone or as part of a coalition. Swedish observers adhering to other political beliefs have agreed that another regime would have charted a different course, but that the divergencies would not have been very great.

Direct comparisons between political attitudes and actions east and west of the Atlantic are often dubious, but in Sweden as in the other Scandinavian countries the course set during most of the 20th century has been more to the left than in the United States. Sweden's dependence on foreign trade, based on one of the lowest tariff levels in the world, is both a dynamic and a stabilizing element in the country's development. The Swedes have become used to rapid economic and social change, but they must always be careful to maintain or improve their capacity for industrial achievement and commercial competition. About one-fourth of their production of goods and services is exported, and the volume of imports is about the same as that of sales abroad.

Open doors, constant interchange, and free discussion have been the essence of relations between America and Sweden. An extensive network of close cultural, commercial, and personal links has thus been created. It is not exclusive or unique by any means. All scientific, cultural, and economic exchanges are parts of a worldwide traffic, and immigrants from many countries have, of course, helped build the United States. But from a Swedish viewpoint it is, nevertheless, a special relationship. The large-scale emigration to America was one of the most important events in Sweden's history, and one aspect of American history has deep roots in Sweden.

Our survey will begin with the distant Viking period, which resulted in the first personal contacts between the North of Europe and North America and in various ways has influenced cultural relations between the American and Scandinavian peoples.

★ 2

The Scandinavian Vikings

*A furious outburst of worldwide activity based on
advanced shipbuilding skills*

DURING the Viking Age, from about 800 to 1050, the Norsemen
played a part in European and world history that was far out of
proportion to their numerical strength, their political organization,
and their resources. Scandinavia became, in fact, the leading sea
power of Europe.

At brief intervals, trading, colonizing, and raiding expeditions
poured forth from Denmark, Norway, and Sweden or from Viking
encampments in other lands, and at the end of the period few parts of
Europe that could be reached via the waterways remained untouched.
Smaller groups or entire colonies of settlers had sprung up in the
British Isles and in France, in Russia, and in Iceland and Greenland,
and numerous towns, including Hamburg, London, Paris, Lisbon,
Seville, and Pisa, had been sacked or temporarily conquered. Constantinople, the capital of the Byzantine or Greek Empire, had been
attacked, as well as Baku on the Caspian Sea and Moslem centers
farther south, and Viking traders had often been seen in Baghdad,
the capital of the Arab Caliphate. In the west, the New World had for
some time become known to people of Scandinavian stock. In this as
in many other cases, the dream of better pastures and more fertile
land helped drive the Norsemen overseas, as it did about 1,000 years
later when nearly three million Scandinavians moved to America.

This outburst of activity was made possible by the high standard of shipbuilding skills in Scandinavia which, together with daring seamanship, gave the Vikings the command of the sea and a mobility that was unique. They did not by any means win all battles, but their vessels were by far the best, and they were used with a new, imaginative boldness. One of the best preserved Viking ships was found near Oslo in 1880, sealed in the blue clay of a burial mound, and in 1893 a copy of it crossed the Atlantic under sail in four weeks. This vessel was, however, a longship built for speed, while the Vikings for all longer expeditions depended on another type, a shorter and heavier trading ship able to carry large amounts of supplies. The competence of the Viking naval architects is even today greatly admired by experts.

In Sweden as well as in Denmark and Norway, a central kingdom emerged during the Viking Age, but nationality still meant little or nothing to the Norsemen. Their family, clan, or chieftain, or the valley where they were born or had settled, seemed far more important. Their tongues differed very little, and they understood each other without difficulty. When their interests clashed, however, the Danish, Norwegian, and Swedish Vikings fought even among themselves.

As early as around A.D. 500, the nucleus of a Swedish realm existed in the districts washed by Lake Mälaren, led by Uppland to the north. This is a region of streams and narrow straits, of sheltered bays and islands extending east into the Baltic, and its growing power was largely based on these natural features which were favorable from a military standpoint and fostered seamanship and commercial initiative. The people called themselves Svear, and their gradually expanding dominion became the Svea realm, that is, Sverige or Sweden.

Most of the Swedish Vikings sailed, as was to be expected, eastward across the Baltic to Russia, in search of new trade channels and markets. An extensive network of routes was gradually established, running down either via the Dnieper River to the Black Sea and the Byzantine Empire, or via the Volga to the Caspian Sea and the Arabian lands. Along the rivers the Swedes became known as Rus, a designation which lives on both in the name Russia and in the Finnish name for Sweden, Ruotsi.

If the Swedish leaders aimed at developing trade between Eastern and Western Europe on a large scale and by way of their own land, which seems most likely, they were well along toward that goal in the early 900s. Even a trading town in southern Denmark, named Hedeby, came temporarily into Swedish hands. At the center of the Swedish realm, on an island in Mälaren 15 miles west of the point where that lake meets an inlet from the Baltic and where Stockholm was to be built, the town of Birka played a leading role in the rapidly growing flow of trade. This commerce included silver from the Arabian world, silks and brocades from Byzantium, glass from the Rhineland, textiles from the Frisians on the North Sea, and Frankish ornaments and weapons. In the late 900s, however, the transit trade which had made Birka prosper began to decline, and the town was abandoned by its inhabitants who seem to have moved to still-existing Sigtuna, 20 miles to the north. Birka's ruins have yielded more artifacts and other finds than any other comparable site from the same period. Nearer Stockholm is the site of a town called Helgön, which flourished in the period 400–800, before Birka.

Instead of commerce, plunder and conquest of land became the leading objectives of the Viking expeditions in Western Europe, and permanent settlements were established on a much larger scale than in Eastern Europe. By and large, the Danes concentrated on the North Sea coast to the south and on England and France, while the Norwegians directed their voyages to Scotland and its rugged islands, Ireland, Iceland, and Greenland. From Ireland, however, Norwegians invaded eastern England as well as Wales, and France was also visited by warriors from Norway. Many adventurers from the center of the Swedish realm sought their fortune in the west, particularly in England, and the southern and western sections of present-day Sweden helped recruit expeditions which were mainly Danish or Norwegian. The people in the present Swedish provinces of Skåne, Halland, and Blekinge in the south had much closer contact with Denmark than with the distant Lake Mälaren region, and the west-coast province of Bohuslän had more in common with southern Norway. In the mountainous northwest of Sweden, an old settlement existed in the province of Jämtland, and an inlet of the Atlantic Ocean in Norway, only 100 miles away, was its main link with the outside world. These five provinces did not, in fact, become definitively Swedish until the 17th century.

In the 9th century the Frankish realm was repeatedly ravaged, but during the some 250 years of the Viking Age the British Isles were the scene of more raids for plunder and military campaigns than any other territory. Resistance, however, grew under this pressure, and Norsemen who seemed to aim at real conquest were often overthrown. When the first large assault was made upon England in 866 and some years later seemed headed for complete success, the unification of the English petty kingdoms had already made headway under the kings of Wessex in the south. In 877 even that kingdom, then ruled by Alfred who became known as the Great, was overrun by Danish invaders, but these were defeated the following year, in a battle which may have influenced the course of history.

From Wessex the Danish bands moved to East Anglia, the large peninsular region northeast of London; there the warriors settled and became farmers in a kingdom of their own which had been begun by members of earlier expeditions from Scandinavia. At that time Danes had already established themselves in the eastern and central districts farther north, and all eastern England from the Thames to the river Tees some 75 miles south of the Scottish border became known as the Danelaw (Minnesota has sometimes been called the "American Danelaw," a reference to the Swedish, Norwegian, and Danish immigration in the 1800s and early 1900s). The northern section of this area was the Viking kingdom of York, the end of which did not come until the middle of the tenth century. The Danish settlers and their descendants had by then accepted Christianity and at least begun to recognize the head of the Wessex royal house as their king. Many of the Norsemen had settled on empty land, and their relations with their English neighbors were as a rule friendly.

The Scandinavian speech left a permanent impression on the dialects of eastern and north-central England, and numerous place-names in the old Danish region, such as the ones ending in *by*, *thorpe*, and *toft*, which also are found in America, likewise date from the English Viking period. The northwest of England was influenced in similar ways by Norwegian settlers who had come over from Ireland. Over Erin, according to a contemporary chronicle, "the Ocean poured torrents of foreigners," and a Viking kingdom was established at Dublin, but many Norsemen soon became Irishmen, and in 1014 a decisive battle was won by native forces. On the Isle of Man in the

Irish Sea, strong echoes of the Viking Age are still heard not only in Norwegian-type place-names and landmarks but also in the system of government, the laws, and the courts. Norwegians also settled on the islands and fringes of Scotland, and the Orkneys and Shetlands, which became wholly Norse in speech, remained under Norway into the 15th century.

Toward the end of the tenth century a new Viking storm, led by Olav Tryggvason, later king of Norway, broke over England. The Scandinavian countries were now united realms, and powerful leaders brought organized fleets to the English coasts. Many attacks were, after some time, bought off with huge payments in silver, so-called Danegelds, and substantial parts of these tributes ended up in Scandinavia. In Sweden, for instance, there are more English silver coins from the tenth and eleventh centuries than in all England. The Viking assaults on England, however, did not cease. In 1013 King Svein Forkbeard of Denmark conquered London, and was then recognized as king. After his death the next year his son, the famous Knut or Canute, had to fight hard to break down the resistance to him, but in late 1016 he was elected king of all England. His position was consolidated with support from his half-brother, King Olof of Sweden, who had become the country's first Christian ruler. Many of Sweden's runestones from the 11th century tell of Vikings who took part in campaigns in the west. After Greece, the most common geographical name on such stones is England.

For almost a generation England formed part of a dominion which included Denmark with southwestern Sweden and, temporarily, the kingdom of Norway. England's resiliency was, however, much greater than during the early Viking Age, and Canute the Great ruled as an English king in the first place. His reign is still regarded as a period of unusual order and security.

Seven years after King Canute's death in 1035, the Anglo-Scandinavian empire fell apart. Just before the Norman invasion of England began in 1066, King Harald Hard-Ruler of Norway tried to conquer the country but met defeat and death at Stamford Bridge, just outside the old Norse center of York. It was a significant part of the final act of the Viking Age, for Harald had seen much of its dramatic expansion and confused struggle: he had fought in a famous battle in Norway with the then king, St. Olaf, he had led Norwegian bands in frequent raids on Denmark, and in between he had, like many Swedish Vikings, enrolled in the imperial guard in Constantinople, fighting with it in Italy, North Africa, and Palestine. His wife was the granddaughter of King Olof of Sweden; her father was the ruler of Kiev in Russia and a descendant of Swedish Vikings.

When William of Normandy, a descendant of a Danish or Norwegian Viking named Rolf or Rollo who in 911 had received the duchy of Normandy from the Frankish king, invaded England in 1066 and his Normans then settled there, the farmers and fishermen of Danish and other Scandinavian stock put up particularly stiff resistance. In the long run, however, the kinship between conquerors and conquered won out. Of a different character was the Norman conquest of Sicily, completed in 1090. On this Mediterranean island, the center of a kingdom which included southern Italy, Viking descendants from France set up one of the most brilliant courts in Europe, ruling over a population of many different origins and creeds.

Iceland was, according to legend, drawn into the Viking sphere of interest by two seafarers who were blown off their course, one a Norwegian from the Faroe Islands farther south in the Atlantic Ocean, the other a cosmopolitan Swede who owned land in Denmark. A steady flow of settlers, most of them from Norway and Norwegian centers in the British Isles, began about 870, and a new nation of largely Scandinavian stock was thus created. Many immigrants were undoubtedly Irish. A national assembly, composed of all free landowners and known as the Althing, met for the first time in 930. By 950 the population numbered about 30,000, and in relation to its resources the island must already have seemed overpopulated. The population growth was later slowed down by internal strife, volcanic eruptions, and disease. Iceland was annexed by Norway in 1262.

In the field of literature, Iceland almost immediately became a towering leader among the Nordic nations. The poems and sagas produced in this island in the period 900–1200 remain a vital part of the Scandinavian cultural heritage. The heroic aspects of Viking activities were overemphasized in the sagas, probably because the Icelanders needed dramatic inspiration in their struggle for survival. Unlike Norwegian, Danish, and Swedish, the Icelandic language has not changed very much during the last one thousand years, and the Icelanders of today are often familiar with the original versions of the early poems and sagas.

Many American poets and scholars have become interested in Scandinavia via Old Icelandic literature. In the 19th century the Viking Age at one time or another inspired all the New England poets, as well as Sidney Lanier, regarded as the finest poet of the South. Today, numerous American companies, restaurants, shops, etc., use the appellation Viking, and many of them have no Scandinavian background at all. Major football teams in Minnesota have also been named for the Vikings, and so has an American space program.

The world's largest island was named Greenland by one of its first visitors, Erik the Red, a Norwegian who sailed there from Iceland in 983 and who wanted to make as many Icelanders as possible join him when he returned to it. This piece of travel and emigration promotion worked relatively well, and in 986 two colonies began to spring up in the valleys of southwest Greenland, where grass was plentiful in summer. Some 300 farmsteads were founded, and nearly twenty churches, including a cathedral, were built. In 1124 a deputation was sent to the king of Norway and the archbishop of Scandinavia, who resided in the now Swedish city of Lund. In the 14th century, however, the climate of Greenland deteriorated, contacts with Scandinavia became more difficult and were finally broken, and by 1500 the settlements had become extinct. Two centuries later the Danish recolonization of Greenland began.

The east coast of North America was explored by Norsemen from Greenland, and some of them at least tried to settle there. Leif Eriksson, a son of Erik the Red, was probably the first to reach America, in the year 999 or 1000. Labrador, about 600 miles from the settlements in Greenland, was called Helluland, "Land of Flat Stones," and the territory farther south, probably Newfoundland, was named Vinland, meaning a fruitful land, rich in good pastures. If it had not been for the Indians, who sometimes appeared in large numbers, many more Greenlanders may have come to North America. The first Viking site in America was discovered in 1960 by Norwegian archeologists at L'Anse aux Meadows in northern Newfoundland, facing southern Labrador. Their excavations revealed the sites of two long-houses, the foundations of several smaller buildings and the remains of a smithy and a steam bath.

Because of the Vikings' appetite for silver and successful efforts to satisfy it, their era has sometimes been called the Silver Age of Scandinavia. In the form of coin, bullion, and adornments, huge quantities of the white metal flowed into the Scandinavian countries, first mostly from the Moslem world and later from Western Europe. The Swedish island of Gotland has yielded more silver than any other part of Scandinavia, over half of the known hoards having been dug up there. Most of them were deposited in the first half of the 11th century, which must have been a period of great unrest in the Baltic.

Gold objects from the Viking period are distributed in Scandinavia in approximately the same way as the silver, Gotland being the richest area. Numerous other gold finds date from the fifth century and the beginning of the sixth, which have been called the Golden Age of Scandinavia. In many primitive workshops in Sweden, Denmark, and Norway, gold was then fashioned into ornaments of outstanding beauty. In 1965 a large collection of Swedish Golden Age and Viking art was shown in the United States for the first time. "It was a long wait, but worth it," wrote an art critic in Chicago.

The Viking Age ended by the middle of the 11th century. At that time, Christianity had triumphed in Scandinavia. The history of the following centuries in Sweden is, in large part, a record of both internal and external strife. Among other significant developments were an artistic flowering and the creation of the national assembly, the Riksdag. Around 1400 an attempt was made to unite the Scandinavian countries under one ruler. This led to a bitter struggle between the Danes and the Swedes and finally to Sweden's continued independence as a national state under Gustav Eriksson Vasa (1496–1560), a Swedish nobleman who was elected king in 1523. Between Denmark and Norway, however, the union lasted until 1814.

★ 3

Swedes on the Delaware

*An American colony founded in 1638 by Sweden, then
a great military power*

THE history of Swedish settlement in the New World begins in 1638,
when Sweden, though heavily engaged in the Thirty Years' War,
founded a colony on the Delaware River.

Inspiration for this venture had come from King Gustavus Adolphus of Sweden (1594–1632), who saw the vital need for a growing
overseas trade, and from Dutchmen who already had been active in
transatlantic shipping and colonization and had thereby become interested in an expansion of Swedish commerce. In 1626 a company
with the objective of establishing trading posts or settlements in the
New World was organized in Stockholm under the leadership of Gustavus Adolphus and Willem Usselinx, a Dutch merchant who had
been the real founder of the Dutch West India Company. The new
Swedish company, however, never began to function, the main reason
being the war in Europe.

Under Gustavus Adolphus, who ascended the throne in 1611,
Sweden was recast in a more modern mold, but a large part of his
enormous capacity for achievement was devoted to wars — first with
the Danes, then with the Russians and the Poles, and finally with the
Catholic princes of the Holy Roman Empire. His intervention in the
European continental war began in 1630, when the imperial armies
had almost crushed the Protestant German states and had also in-

vaded Denmark. His victorious progress in Germany ended two years later with his death on the field of battle, but his revolutionary, boldly offensive strategy was emulated by his generals, and France intervened on the same side. In 1648, the armed conflicts that have become known as the Thirty Years' War were finally terminated, and Sweden extended its Baltic empire to ports and territories in northern Germany.

In the early 1600s, as Holland rose to economic and naval power, Dutch capital and enterprise played an increasingly important part in Sweden. The city of Göteborg, or Gothenburg, founded by Gustavus Adolphus, was fashioned by Dutch town planners and merchants, and its layout, with canals and tree-lined avenues, therefore resembles that of tropical Jakarta, now the capital of Indonesia, which the Dutch East India Company established at about the same time. Two other immigrants from the Netherlands, Louis De Geer (1587–1652) and his older partner, Willem de Besche (1573–1629), became pioneers in the modernization of the Swedish iron industry and arms manufacturing, and from their Walloon homeland, the district of Liége in present-day Belgium, they brought to Sweden a large number of skilled ironworkers. The immigration of ironmaking experts from Germany, which had begun earlier, was also important.

As a source of income for the Swedish government, copper from an ancient mine at Falun in the province of Dalarna was even more vital than iron. The annual output reached only a few thousand tons, but without it Sweden's participation in the Thirty Years' War and its emergence as a great military power would hardly have been possible. Without the red metal, moreover, Sweden may never have sent colonists to America: one reason why the Swedish statesmen supported this venture was that they were anxious to open up new markets for their copper overseas. Louis De Geer was the country's foremost copper exporter, as well as its leading financier, but he did not take an active part in the new colonial project. The city of Norrköping, in the province of Östergötland, was the center of his far-flung activities.

A few years after Gustavus Adolphus's death in Germany in 1632, the plans for a Swedish colony on the other side of the Atlantic began to take definite shape under the leadership of Chancellor Axel Oxenstierna (1583–1654), who had been the monarch's trusted adviser and now became his real successor. England's Oliver Cromwell called him "the great man of the continent." Other leading promoters of the colonization scheme were a naturalized Dutchman, Peter Minuit (1580–1638), now famous, above all, for his purchase of Manhattan Island from the Indians in 1626 for merchandise valued at 60 guilders, and Admiral Klas Fleming (1592–1644), who under Gustavus Adolphus had reorganized the Swedish navy. Fleming was born in Finland, which for centuries had been part of the Swedish realm and had a large population of Swedish origin.

After having been discharged by the Dutch as governor of New Amsterdam, Peter Minuit entered Swedish service, and early in 1637 he was appointed leader of an expedition to the Delaware Valley, a region he had already recommended as suitable for a Swedish trading colony. One-half of the venture capital was subscribed by Dutchmen, and most of the goods to be bartered to the Indians for furs and tobacco had been bought in Holland. A merchant ship called *Kalmar Nyckel* (Key of Kalmar, then Sweden's most important stronghold on its southeast coast) was obtained, and as its escort the Swedish government provided a naval vessel, *Fogel Grip* (The Griffin), with 23 soldiers on board. About half of the crews were Dutch, and the navigators of both ships were Dutchmen, the Swedes at that time having had no experience in transatlantic travel.

First land purchases for New Sweden — No reinforcements until 1640

LATE in the fall of 1637 *Kalmar Nyckel* and *Fogel Grip* set sail from Gothenburg, and via the West Indies they reached the American mainland in the spring of 1638. By the middle of March they cruised up the Delaware River until they found the mouth of a western tributary called Minquas Kill, and about two miles upstream they dropped anchor. A Swedish salute boomed out but died away unanswered in the wilderness, and on a large, flat-topped boulder Peter Minuit went ashore with some of his men.

At a conference with five Indian chiefs on board the *Kalmar Nyckel*, probably on March 29 according to the old style, Minuit bought land along the west bank of the Delaware, northward as far as the river's confluence with the Schuylkill, where the city of Philadelphia now sprawls, and southward as far as Bombay Hook. The colony was, as planned, named New Sweden. Near the rocks where the colonists had landed they built a little stronghold which they called Fort Christina in honor of Gustavus Adolphus's 11-year-old daughter (1626–89), who was to succeed him on the throne.

The village which grew up around the fortress, and which became the beginning of the city of Wilmington, was named Christinehamn, or Christina Harbor. It was the first permanent white settlement in the entire Delaware Valley. Dutchmen had already made two attempts to establish themselves in the same area, but had failed. The tributary that makes up most of Wilmington's harbor is still known as the Christina River. In the traditional Swedish manner the colonists built simple but snug log cabins, these being their first lasting contribution to the developing American culture. From New Sweden, the art of log construction gradually spread throughout the colonies.

Already after a few months the Swedish colony lost its energetic and experienced leader, thus suffering a serious setback. In June the *Kalmar Nyckel* was sufficiently stocked to return to Europe, and among its passengers was Peter Minuit, who was expected to report to his sponsors in both Holland and Sweden. In the West Indies, however, he visited a Dutch ship which during a storm blew out to sea and disappeared. The *Kalmar Nyckel*, on the other hand, reached Sweden safely toward the end of 1638, and the *Fogel Grip* followed half a year later. The most valuable article brought back from the Delaware Valley was the title to the land, the beauty and fertility of which the returning men described in enthusiastic terms. From a commercial viewpoint the expedition was a failure. About 2,000 beaver, otter, and bear skins were sold in Holland and some tobacco in Sweden.

In 1639 Admiral Fleming planned to send a large expedition to New Sweden but this proved impossible, and the colony did not receive reinforcements and new supplies until the spring of 1640 when the *Kalmar Nyckel* returned. Among the newcomers were a Dutchman, Peter Hollender Ridder, who had lived in Sweden for several years and now assumed the leadership of the settlement, for which he was well qualified, and a Swedish clergyman, Reorus Torkillus (1608–43), the first Lutheran pastor to serve within the present territory of the United States. A chapel for him was erected at Fort Christina. Torkillus was also a scientist, and he has been called the first meteorologist in America.

In the late fall of 1640 a Dutch ship brought some 50 colonists from Holland, most of whom eventually joined their countrymen farther north. This is regarded as the third expedition to New Sweden. At about the same time the Dutch partners withdrew from the commercial organization sponsoring the colony, and the following expeditions were wholly Swedish, although most of the navigators still came from Holland. At Fort Christina nothing happened until the late fall of 1641, when the faithful *Kalmar Nyckel* and another ship, the *Caritas*, cast anchor. Together they brought about 35 colonists and soldiers, including some Finns, as well as horses, cattle, geese, seeds, farm implements, and merchandise for the Indian trade. In the meantime the limits of the Swedish domain had been greatly extended by purchases from the Indians along the west bank of the Delaware, northward as far as the falls at present-day Trenton in west-central New Jersey and southward down to Cape Henlopen on the Atlantic. A title to land on the east side of the Delaware had also been secured.

With the Indians the Swedes remained, as a rule, on the best of terms, but sometimes they had trouble with Englishmen from the New England colonies and with the leaders of New Netherland. These regarded New Sweden as an intrusion on their own territory, which had expanded southward from the Hudson River Valley. Subsequently, however, the Swedes and the Dutch were for some time drawn closer together as a result of English activities in the Delaware area. A number of Swedish immigrants had already settled in New Amsterdam, the capital of the Dutch colony, and there were also Swedes in the English settlements, but little is known about them.

New life infused into the colony by Governor Printz —
The capital is moved north

NO SHIP arrived from Sweden in 1642, but on February 15, 1643, two vessels, *Fama* and *Svanen* (The Swan), reached Christina Harbor, and this was the beginning of a new era for the colony. New Sweden now received its first full-fledged governor, Lieutenant-Colonel Johan Printz (1592–1663), a veteran of the Thirty Years' War and a seasoned military administrator. From Stockholm he brought detailed instructions concerning the economic, legal, military, and religious activities in the Swedish settlement, a document which has been called the first constitution of both Delaware and Pennsylvania.

Johan Printz was a native of Småland, a Swedish province that in the 19th century was to furnish more emigrants to the United States than any other. For leaving the theater of war in Germany without permission he had been dismissed from active service in the Swedish army, but was then given a chance of rehabilitation on the other side of the Atlantic. With him came his wife and children, two new clergymen, Johannes Campanius (1601–83) and Israel Fluviander, and a small number of colonists, again including some Finns. Printz himself had once served with the army in Finland and had learned the Finnish language.

The new governor was to suffer many bitter disappointments, but with great energy he set about directing the development of New Sweden. One of his first acts was the construction of a fortress, named Nya Elfsborg or New Elfsborg, 15 miles south of Fort Christina but on the east bank of the Delaware, now a part of New Jersey. An officer by the name of Sven Skute, who at this time was next in rank to Printz himself, and who like numerous other Swedish colonists still has descendants in the United States, was placed in command of the new stronghold. Just north of New Elfsborg, a village had been founded two years earlier by a group of disaffected Puritans from New England, who now took an oath of allegiance to the Swedish Crown. Several years later, Governor Printz pushed close to a Dutch post farther north on the New Jersey side of the Delaware.

Most of New Sweden's economic and military expansion under Governor Printz took place on the west bank of the Delaware and north of Fort Christina; the southeastern part of present-day Pennsylvania became the center of the Swedish population. As early as 1643 Printz moved the capital from Fort Christina to the island of Tinicum at the mouth of the Schuylkill River, near the present site of Philadelphia, to be founded by William Penn four decades later. Here the Swedish governor erected a fort called Nya Göteborg, or New Gothenburg, and within it he built a two-story log house named Printzhof for himself and his family, as well as a brewery and probably a chapel for the Reverend Campanius. Gardens and orchards were laid out. Two years later, in November of 1645, an explosion of the powder magazine destroyed the buildings, but with characteristic energy Printz rebuilt the fort and his mansion, which survived until early in the 19th century. A church, next to the original chapel the oldest house of worship of any denomination in Pennsylvania, was also constructed. Dedicated on September 4, 1646, the church remained in use for more than fifty years.

Johannes Campanius, whose father, Jonas Persson, had been a bell ringer in Klara Church in Stockholm, is regarded as the foremost of the Swedish clergymen who served New Sweden in its early days. He became the spiritual guide of the entire colony and traveled frequently to the widely scattered settlements. Simultaneously with his ecclesiastical work he studied the country, made astronomical and climatic observations, collected facts concerning the flora and the fauna, and interested himself in the customs and language of the Delaware Indians. Campanius was a graduate of the University of Uppsala.

Most of the forts, blockhouses, and settlements founded by Governor Printz, with names such as Nya Korsholm, Nya Vasa, and Mölndal, were near present-day Philadelphia. Farther south, between the villages of Upland (now Chester) and Finland (Marcus Hook), which had been started in the early 1640s, he selected a site for a country estate of his own, which he called Printztorp. Other plantations for the raising of crops, cattle, hogs, and sheep were also established.

Agriculture increasingly important — Scant assistance from hard-pressed Sweden

UNDER Governor Printz, the Swedish domain finally comprised most of the present-day state of Delaware, southeastern Pennsylvania, and the southwestern section of New Jersey. In this region the Swedes introduced European civilization, including churches, schools, and law courts as well as modest beginnings of industrial activities, such as flour mills and boat yards. Near Tinicum, Printz constructed a water-powered grist mill, the first mechanical plant within the confines of modern Pennsylvania. "It was a splendid mill which ground both fine and coarse flour, and was going early and late," wrote the Reverend Campanius. In 1644 two "large, beautiful boats" were built near Christina, the first ones on the Delaware. A sloop, which was used by Printz on official business, followed a few years later, and the hull for a ship of about 200 tons was launched in 1652.

There were, obviously, competent carpenters, blacksmiths, and other craftsmen among the settlers.

While the Swedish colony thus began to flourish under Governor Printz, its principal weakness, the shortage of manpower, remained and was never overcome. A census after the new leader's arrival in 1643 showed an adult male population of only 135, and of these 26 died the following year. Many of the original colonists had already passed away, and some had returned to Sweden. The great majority of the settlers and soldiers had not come voluntarily but had been sent over after committing petty crimes, such as failure to pay debts, desertion, poaching, and illegal timber burning. In Finland, especially, forests were often cleared by burning, and Finnish-speaking people who had migrated to northern and western Sweden still followed this custom.

Despite their motley origin the colonists of New Sweden proved, on the whole, to be resourceful pioneers, and under Governor Printz's efficient if often stern leadership they accomplished more than it seemed reasonable to expect. With few exceptions they were people of the soil, and even the soldiers often wanted more time for farming. Gradually, therefore, New Sweden became an agricultural settlement instead of the trading colony that its sponsors in Stockholm had wanted in the first place. During Johan Printz's governorship, the uncertain and often nonexistent communications with Sweden helped to make such a development inevitable.

Two months after his arrival in 1643 Governor Printz wrote to the government in Stockholm that New Sweden was a "remarkably beautiful country, with all the glories that a person can wish on earth," and that he was certain that "in time it would become one of the brightest jewels of the Swedish Crown." He had then good reason to expect that colonists would soon be sent over in larger numbers. The Thirty Years' War was still going on, however, and in the summer of 1643 a new conflict concerning the supremacy in the Baltic broke out between Sweden and Denmark. All Swedish ships, including the *Kalmar Nyckel* and some others which had sailed to the Delaware, were pressed into service. Denmark was invaded by a Swedish army from Germany and finally sued for peace, but in 1644 Admiral Fleming was killed in a naval battle, and New Sweden thus lost its most active supporter. Of even greater importance was probably Queen Christina's assuming royal power toward the end of the same year. She took little interest in the affairs of the Swedish colony in America, and her impulsive interference hampered the activities of Chancellor Oxenstierna, who worked hard to bring Sweden's participation in the continental thirty-year war to a successful conclusion.

In the spring of 1644 the *Fama* brought building materials and other supplies as well as some colonists to New Sweden. In the fall of 1646 another ship, *Gyllene Hajen* (The Golden Shark), came with large quantities of goods, and early in 1648 *Svanen* arrived with a few passengers and a huge cargo of iron and iron articles, but that was all the assistance that Governor Printz obtained from Sweden, despite increasingly desperate appeals for more men. Following the shipment of 1648, he waited in vain for more than five years.

As a result of one of Governor Printz's first requests, made in 1644, a plan to send over about 1,000 soldiers and colonists, including women and children, was discussed in Stockholm, but it had no real chance of fruition. In 1649, on the other hand, when Sweden had come out of the Thirty Years' War as one of the victors, a well-stocked ship, *Kattan* (The Tabby Cat), was dispatched from Gothenburg. It foundered, however, on a reef near Puerto Rico, and after unspeakable miseries most of the seamen and passengers met death in the West Indies, while a small group managed to return to Sweden. About 75 colonists had sailed on this ship but many more, in particular Finns from the Swedish province of Värmland, had wanted to go. By this time, the news of the fertility of the Delaware Valley had spread among the large destitute groups in Sweden, and there was no lack of people willing to brave the dangers of the transatlantic voyage.

Printz leaves in 1653 — New upswing but the colony is lost to the Dutch in 1655

IF THE expedition of 1649 had reached New Sweden, it might have had some influence on the history of the Delaware Valley, but the Swedish dominion was now approaching its end. Its continued expansion had increased the concern of the Dutch, whose leaders, on the other hand, realized that the Swedes had spread themselves too thin.

In 1651, the governor of New Netherland, Peter Stuyvesant, abandoned two Dutch outposts in the northeastern part of New Sweden, which already had been neutralized by the Swedish forts Nya Göteborg and Nya Korsholm; Stuyvesant built a new fortress, Fort Casimir, some five miles south of Fort Christina. Nya Elfsborg, farther south and on the other side of the Delaware, was thus outflanked, and it was given up by the Swedes. In the fall of 1653, when the hard-driven Swedish colonists had begun to revolt, Governor Printz found his position untenable, and via New Amsterdam he sailed for Sweden, leaving his son-in-law, Lieutenant Johan Papegoja, in temporary command. His wife, four of their five daughters, and about 25 settlers and soldiers left the colony at the same time.

Another expedition was, however, being prepared in Sweden when Governor Printz decided to return home. A man-of-war named Örnen (The Eagle), the largest ship used so far, had been selected, and in Gothenburg more than 250 emigrants went on board, while many others, who also had sold all their property, remained on the pier. For the first time "America fever" had gripped poverty-stricken people in Sweden. Some 50 soldiers were under the command of Sven Skute, who had returned to his native country in 1650 and had become its first emigration agent from America. A student of military engineering from Uppsala, Pehr or Peter Mårtensson Lindeström (1632–91), was also among the passengers. The leader of the expedition was a brilliant but inexperienced young economist, Johan Rising (1617–72).

After an exceedingly adventurous and difficult voyage, during which nearly a hundred of the travelers died, Örnen reached the Delaware in May of 1654. Johan Rising, who had been sent to assist Johan Printz but now became acting governor, immediately attacked and seized the Dutch stronghold south of Christina, Fort Casimir, and since this was done on Trinity Sunday, May 23, the fortress was renamed Fort Trefaldighet, or Fort Trinity. In order to strengthen the Swedish hold on the lower Delaware, Rising then decided to establish his headquarters at Fort Christina, which thus again became the capital of the colony. Somewhat farther north he built a two-story executive mansion, and most of the newcomers settled on plantations near Christina.

Although no diplomat, Johan Rising managed the Swedish settlement remarkably well. By the summer of 1655 its cultivated area had increased considerably, and the colonists were more prosperous and contented than ever before. They lacked, however, some vital supplies including munitions. In the fall of 1654 the Swedish ship *Gyllene Hajen* had, after mistakes of navigation, ended up at New Amsterdam, where the cargo was unloaded and most of the passengers from Sweden were persuaded to remain.

The Dutch had not forgotten the seizure of Fort Casimir, as a result of which the control of the whole Delaware region was at stake. After having obtained reinforcements from Holland, Governor Peter Stuyvesant sailed up the river in the summer of 1655 with seven armed ships and a force of several hundred men, perhaps as many as 700. On September 1, he took possession of Fort Trefaldighet, which once more became Fort Casimir.

At Fort Christina, the last stronghold to fly the Swedish flag, Governor Johan Rising parleyed for several days with the Dutch leader, but on September 15 he signed the capitulation papers. Fearing an Indian insurrection and probably also an eventual English intervention, Governor Stuyvesant offered him the right to remain and help develop the colony under joint Dutch-Swedish jurisdiction, but Rising rejected this proposal, adding that his government would surely avenge the Dutch aggression. Sweden, however, was involved in new wars, and no effective action could be taken in far-off America.

On the day when the Dutch recaptured Fort Trefaldighet, a Swedish army led by King Charles X Gustav (1622–60), who had succeeded his cousin Queen Christina after her abdication in 1654, marched into Warsaw, the capital of Poland, and two weeks later, when Fort Christina capitulated, he closed in on Cracow, 150 miles farther south. In 1657, when Denmark declared war on Sweden, he executed a rapid march from the interior of Poland through northern Germany, attacked the Danes from the south and, after having crossed the frozen Danish straits, forced his adversary to sign a costly peace treaty. The war's lasting result was Sweden's achieving her natural boundaries in the south; King Charles himself, however, dreamed of a powerful North European kingdom under Swedish rule. For some time he seemed determined to go to battle against the Dutch, but death overtook him after he had unsuccessfully tried to bring all of Denmark under his rule.

Johan Rising, the last governor of New Sweden, never found any permanent employment after having returned to his native country, but he was the first Swedish writer of importance on economics and commerce. Johan Printz, on the other hand, became governor of the district of Jönköping in northern Småland, where he was born. As governor of New Sweden for ten years he was one of the most picturesque and forceful characters of the American colonial period. He is said to have tipped the scales at about 300 pounds, and the Indians respectfully called him "Big Belly" or, according to another translation, "Big Guts." In 1938, when the 300th anniversary of the arrival of the first Swedish colonists was celebrated, President Franklin D. Roosevelt read a little rhyme about him: "No Gov. of Del., before or since, has weighed as much as Johan Printz."

Swedish-Finnish population grows under Dutch regime, soon followed by British

NEW Sweden's historic significance, from the American as well as from the Swedish viewpoint, is to a high degree based on developments that took place after Sweden had lost political control over the colony.

Most of the Swedish officials returned home after the Dutch conquest, and one group of colonists moved to New Amsterdam, but a large majority of the settlers remained. They had become strongly attached to the land, and under the new administration they carried on their peaceful occupations, little affected by their rulers. A court of law was established at Upland by Swedish settlers and existed for several decades. In 1664 the Dutch ceded the New Sweden colony, as well as their other American possessions, to the British. The first English Pilgrims had arrived in New England in 1620, 18 years before the Swedes began to settle in the Delaware Valley, and Englishmen had begun to establish themselves in Virginia in 1607.

Among the Swedes who saw the Swedish territory pass first into Dutch and then into British hands was Governor Johan Printz's daughter Armegott (1626–96). Her husband, Johan Papegoja, and their four sons settled in Sweden, but she remained at Tinicum or Printztorp, her father's plantation near Upland, until 1676, when she returned to her native country for good. Before that she had visited Sweden twice, in 1663 for her father's funeral. Tinicum was finally sold by her to a Swedish settler. An independent and determined person like her father, she has been claimed to have been one of the first champions of women's rights in America. Through his daughter and her husband, there are numerous descendants of Governor Printz, including some in the United States.

Without the friendly relations existing between the Swedish settlers and the Indians, Armegott Printz-Papegoja would probably not have remained alone on the Delaware as long as she did. This friendship also proved to be a great asset first to the Dutch administrators and then to their British successors. William Penn, who arrived in the Delaware Valley in 1682, in his negotiations with the Indians employed Swedes as interpreters, among them a prominent citizen by the name of Lasse or Lawrence Cock (1646–99), whose father had come to New Sweden in 1641. Another large landowner, Captain Israel Helm, who seems to have arrived from Sweden in 1656, also became an Indian interpreter, as well as a judge. Pennsylvania, Delaware, and New Jersey were never the scene of serious Indian uprisings.

Most of the farmers in the Delaware Valley had large families, and its Swedish-Finnish population also increased as a result of continued immigration. In March of 1656 a Swedish ship, the *Mercurius*, which had sailed from Gothenburg with some 110 colonists before the loss of New Sweden became known, cast anchor near Fort Casimir. This was the 12th expedition sent by the Swedes to the Delaware Valley, and the tenth to reach its destination. Its leader, Johan Papegoja, was told to proceed to New Amsterdam or return to Sweden, but when the Indians threatened to revolt unless the newcomers remained, the ship sailed up the river to Tinicum, where the passengers were allowed to go ashore.

More Swedish and Finnish immigrants arrived from time to time, and a contingent of some 140 Finnish men, women, and children came in 1664. They had begun their long journey by trekking hundreds of miles from the forests of Medelpad in north-central Sweden to a port in Norway. Among the few newcomers toward the end of the century was Baron Isak or Isaac Banér, who had been in English service. He married a farmer's daughter of French origin. Many years after his death in 1713, their two sons were sent to Sweden.

Gradually, during the Dutch and British eras, the geographical distribution of the Swedish-Finnish population in the Delaware Valley changed considerably. In the 1650s some Swedes went to the eastern shore of Chesapeake Bay, in the present state of Maryland, and others moved to Virginia. Later, more Swedish and Finnish farmers settled on the eastern or New Jersey side of the lower Delaware, and many Swedish families moved from the Philadelphia area to farms or villages father north along the rivers. Several colonists followed the Schuylkill River as far up as present Berks County, and some settled as far to the northwest as present-day Harrisburg. The Delaware Valley up to the falls at Trenton, northeast of Philadelphia, had been part of the Swedish colony almost from its beginning.

Even after the British in 1664 had assumed political control over the New Sweden territory, many districts and villages continued to flourish as predominantly Swedish settlements, and in some of them the Swedish language remained in use for another hundred years. In 1683, 924 persons were listed as Swedish, and 14 years later a clergyman in Pennsylvania, Andreas Rudman, wrote in a report to Sweden: "We live scattered among the English and Quakers, yet our language is preserved as pure as anywhere in Sweden. There are about 1,200 persons who speak it." As late as 1725, when English had long been the principal tongue, the number of Swedish-speaking people was estimated at more than 1,500. By the middle of the century the language used by the older settlers was a quaint mixture of Swedish and English, but a visitor from Sweden, a naturalist by the name of Pehr or Peter Kalm, found one village, Repaupo in New Jersey, south of Philadelphia, where the Swedish language had survived practically unchanged. They may still have used a booklet containing eight Swedish songs by the Reverend Andreas Rudman, titled *Svenska Visor*, which had been published in 1701 — one of the very earliest works in any language printed in Philadelphia.

During most of the 18th century strong religious and intellectual ties were maintained between Sweden and its former colony, and this helps explain the vitality of the Swedish language in the Delaware Valley. It is one of the most significant aspects of the entire history of New Sweden.

Sweden resumes religious contacts with the Delaware
settlers in the late 1600s

AFTER 1655, the year Governor Rising surrendered to the Dutch, Sweden for decades did little or nothing to keep in touch with the

Swedes and their descendants on the Delaware. Two clergymen left with Rising, and the Reverend Lars Karlsson Lock, or Laurentius Carolus Lokenius (d. 1688) as he had Latinized his name, was then the only remaining Swedish pastor. Lokenius, a Swede from Finland, had arrived in 1648. His children, by two successive wives, used the name Lock.

At Crane Hook, or in Swedish, Tranudden, on the south side of the Christina River, near its confluence with the Delaware, a log church was built in 1667, and for more than thirty years the settlers in the present Wilmington area assembled there for divine services. During long periods Pastor Lokenius preached on alternate Sundays at Crane Hook and at Tinicum, where services had been held since 1643. When he died in 1688, a German clergyman by the name of Jacob Fabritius was the only Lutheran minister in the Delaware Valley, and he survived Lokenius by only three years. In 1677 Swedish settlers had invited him to preach in a blockhouse which eight years earlier had been built at Wicaco, then a separate village on the banks of the Delaware and now in the southern part of Philadelphia. Wicaco and Tinicum were actually regarded as one congregation, the upper one. Both there and at Crane Hook the settlers later depended on lay readers for their religious services.

In 1696, however, the Church of Sweden began to offer the settlements on the Delaware religious assistance, and this was to assure the perpetuation of the Swedish parishes in America for almost a hundred years. A visit that Andrew Printz, a nephew of the governor, made to the former Swedish colony in 1691–92, and a subsequent letter to Sweden which 30 settlers signed in the spring of 1693, helped bring about the change.

The letter to Sweden, written 55 years after the arrival of the first Swedish colonists, read in part: "Most of us are husbandmen. We plough and sow and till the ground; and as to our meat and drink, we live according to the old Swedish customs. This country is very rich and fruitful, and here grow all sorts of grain in great plenty. . . . We send out yearly to our neighbors on this continent and the neighboring islands bread, grain, flour, and oil. . . . Our wives and daughters employ themselves in spinning wool and flax, and many of them in weaving: so we have great reason to thank the

Almighty for his manifold mercies and benefits. God grant that we may also have good shepherds. . . ."

The actual composer of the letter was the lay reader at Crane Hook near Christina, Carl or Charles Christopherson Springer (1658–1738), whose life had been unusually dramatic. The son of a well-to-do government official in Stockholm, he was, at the age of about 18, sent to the Swedish ambassador in London to complete his studies, but one evening he was kidnapped and carried on board a merchant vessel bound for Virginia. There he was sold as an indentured servant for five years, "like a farm animal" as he later wrote his mother in Stockholm, and at the end of this period he made his way to the Swedes on the Delaware, whom he joined in 1684. For many years he served as a judge, being the best educated person in the community. His grave is under a wall of the Old Swedes Church, Holy Trinity, at Wilmington. Charles Springer's descendants have been numerous, and they are today spread throughout America. Some of them are familiar with the letter their ancestor wrote to his mother in Sweden on June 1, 1693, and which seems to have reached her shortly before she died toward the end of the same year.

In Sweden, the cause of the Swedish settlers in America found an enthusiastic supporter in Jesper Swedberg (1653–1735), who in 1702 was appointed bishop of Skara in the western province of Västergötland and at that post remained in charge of the religious activities in the Swedish settlements on the Delaware. He also championed greater religious freedom, virtually the only Swede of significance to do so at that time. Part of his active life coincided with the reign of King Charles XII (1682–1718), whose wars, first against Denmark-Norway, then against Russia and Poland, and finally once more against the Danish-Norwegian monarchy, ended with the downfall of Sweden's Baltic empire. For nearly another century, however, Finland remained part of the Swedish realm.

In 1696 three divinity students at Uppsala, Eric Björk (1668–1740), Andreas Rudman (1668–1708), and Jonas Aurén (d. 1713), were selected to serve in the Delaware Valley under the auspices of the Church of Sweden. Aurén was actually sent temporarily as an observer, and the other two were told that their careers in the state church would be resumed when they returned to Sweden. After being ordained in the Uppsala Cathedral, the three left for America via England, and by the middle of October they arrived in London. In the party was Andrew Printz, who had been appointed as their guide, and who had decided to settle among the Swedes on the Delaware, but before their ship sailed, in early February of 1697, he disappeared without a trace. Another Swede who had been to America, Jonas Bjurström, was appointed in his place as guide for the voyage.

The Swedish parishes on the Delaware needed not only clergymen but also religious literature as well as elementary textbooks, and considerable efforts were made in Sweden to meet this demand. They included a truly remarkable move, although of little practical importance. The Reverend Johannes Campanius, who had come to the Delaware colony with Governor Printz in 1643 and returned to Sweden five years later, had during his stay in America prepared not only the first known vocabulary of the Indian tribes on the Delaware but also the first translation of the Lutheran Catechism into an Indian tongue, the Lenape language. In 1696 the catechism was finally printed in Stockholm, and of the original edition of about 600 copies, 500 were sent to America with the three young clergymen. In 1938, as part of the New Sweden tercentenary celebration, a facsimile edition of 3,000 copies was printed in the Swedish capital, primarily for distribution in the United States. Johannes Campanius is buried in the church at Frösthult in the Swedish province of Uppland, under a stone slab containing what is probably the only American-Indian epitaph in Europe.

Primers, hymnbooks, and other materials were also sent from Sweden to the Delaware Valley. A special octavo edition of the Bible for the Swedish settlers was printed at Skara in 1727–28.

Churches built at Wilmington and Philadelphia in late 1600s are now national shrines

THE three young clergymen from Sweden, Eric Björk or Biork, Andreas Rudman, and Jonas Aurén, arrived in America on Midsummer Day, June 24, 1697. On the Delaware they were joyfully received by the settlers.

A few months later Pastor Rudman wrote in a letter to Uppsala: "The churches are old and dilapidated, therefore we are eager, with

God's help, to build new ones. The lower one will be at Christina (Wilmington) and the upper at Wicaco or Passayunk." Only a few weeks after the arrival of their new pastor, Eric Björk, the leaders of the Crane Hook congregation had, in fact, decided to build a new church of a more permanent type, and to place this building on a hillock near the site of the old Fort Christina, where a cemetery had been laid out by the first colonists. Under the leadership of Andreas Rudman, the upper congregation of Tinicum-Wicaco started planning for a similar church at Wicaco.

At Christina, or Wilmington, the foundation stone was laid on May 28, 1698, and on Trinity Sunday, June 4, 1699, the edifice, built of bluish stone, was consecrated as Helga Trefaldighets Kyrka, or Holy Trinity Church, a name it still bears. It is one of the oldest Protestant churches now in use in America, and some authorities contend that it is the oldest church in the United States standing almost as originally built and still used for regular services.

Holy Trinity is rich in objects that date from its origin or remind visitors of its Swedish ties. Its most precious historical document is the church book, begun by Pastor Björk. The original altar is preserved within a later one of marble, and the aged pulpit, carved in 1698, is still in use. Portraits of Eric Björk and other early Swedish pastors, some of whom are buried beneath the church, are displayed in the vestry. A silver communion service which the ancient Swedish copper-mining company at Falun in Dalarna donated in 1718, when Björk was rector at the Falun church, is used on special occasions. Other gifts from Sweden include an altar cloth, embroidered by King Gustav V and presented by him just before he died in 1950 at the age of 92, and a scale model of the ship *Kalmar Nyckel*, which was added in 1963 when Wilmington and Kalmar in southeastern Sweden established a family relationship as "friendship towns." Beneath the church and in the cemetery adjacent to it rest the remains of hundreds of early Swedish settlers, many in unmarked graves. The church records were kept in Swedish until 1773. In 1890 they were published in English by the Historical Society of Delaware, in a book of 772 pages.

Today Wilmington boasts an even older building, the Hendrickson House, which stands on the grounds of Holy Trinity. It was built of stone about 1690 by a Swedish farmer farther north on the Delaware

River, and in the late 1950s it was moved to Wilmington where it serves as a museum and a library devoted to Swedish colonial life in America.

North of Wilmington, on Naaman's Creek just south of the Delaware-Pennsylvania stateline, is a two-story stone structure known as the Swedish Blockhouse; it was erected in 1654 by Johan Rising, the last governor of New Sweden. Dutch soldiers took over this building in 1655, and 16 years later it was attacked by the Indians. During the War of Independence it changed hands twice. Another of the few remaining Swedish houses from the colonial period, a one-room log cabin, stands within the confines of Fort Christina State Park, near the rocks where in 1638 the first Swedish colonists landed in America.

At Wicaco in what became the southern part of Philadelphia, a red-brick church, the present Gloria Dei, was built in the late 1600s on the site of the old blockhouse. Dedicated the first Sunday after Trinity in 1700, it is the oldest church now standing in Pennsylvania and the oldest public building in Philadelphia. The congregation has been in continuous existence since the 1640s and is, therefore, the oldest in America. The remains of Andreas Rudman, who preached in this church in 1700–02, are under its chancel, and many of the original settlers lie buried in the adjoining cemetery. Like Holy Trinity at Wilmington, Gloria Dei is now a national shrine. Both churches are also known as "Old Swedes."

The bell of the Gloria Dei, as well as a baptismal font and a wood carving representing the Bible, were brought from Sweden by the early settlers and first used in the church at Tinicum. Models of the first two New Sweden ships and a Swedish chandelier, gifts of the late artist Carl Milles, are suspended from the ceiling. There are also many relics and documents from the English colonial period and the War of Independence. The first lightning rods for the edifice were supplied by Benjamin Franklin. Betsy Ross, who is said to have fashioned the Stars and Stripes for George Washington, was married there in 1777, and she has had numerous emulators. Americans of Swedish ancestry assemble in this church annually on the Sunday nearest April 8, which in 1938, in commemoration of the arrival of the first Swedish colonists 300 years earlier, was designated as Forefathers Day in the commonwealth of Pennsylvania.

The site of the Gloria Dei was donated by three Swedish settlers,

Sven, Ole, and Andreas Swenson, who were the largest landowners in the Wicaco district. From the same three brothers an agent for William Penn bought some of the nearby land for the city of Philadelphia, including what is now Independence Square, with Independence Hall, the "Cradle of American Liberty," in its center. When William Penn himself arrived in America in the fall of 1682, he landed at New Castle on the Delaware, six miles south of Wilmington, that is, at the old Dutch Fort Casimir which for some time had been the Swedish Fort Trefaldighet or Trinity. He spent the first winter farther north at Upland, the old Swedish settlement which he renamed Chester. A few miles upstream he founded Philadelphia, buying large land areas from Swedish settlers who then acquired holdings farther north on the Delaware.

Other Swedish churches and landmarks in the Delaware Valley

IN ADDITION to the Holy Trinity at Wilmington and the Gloria Dei in Philadelphia, three "Old Swedes" churches remain in the region settled by Swedes in the 17th century. Two more churches have strong Swedish or Finnish traditions.

The most imposing of the five "Old Swedes" is the St. James Church in West Philadelphia, which was completed in 1762 when the surrounding village was known as Kingsessing. In part, at least, it was built as a result of the arrival three years earlier of the Reverend Carl Magnus Wrangel, one of the most significant members of the Swedish Lutheran mission on the Delaware, whom we shall meet again. St. James's was originally a daughter church of Gloria Dei. Its transepts and tower were added when the church was rebuilt in 1854.

In Upper Merion, at present-day Bridgeport, Pennsylvania, and on the Schuylkill River in the northwest section of the territory once known as New Sweden, a stone building named Christ Church replaced in 1760 the original structure. It was dedicated by Dr. Wrangel. During the winter of 1777, when George Washington's army was encamped at nearby Valley Forge, he and his officers came occasionally to this church. In 1886 a baptismal font, carved out of Swedish black granite, was presented to the congregation by Prince Oscar of Sweden (later Prince Oscar Bernadotte, 1859–1953), a son of King Oscar II, who in 1876 had become the first member of the Swedish royal family to visit the United States. The twelve stained-glass windows, which were completed in the early 1940s, depict scenes relating to the history of the Swedes in America. Christ Church, which also was an off-shoot of Gloria Dei in Wicaco, stands on land long owned by descendants of Peter Gunnarsson Rambo, who came to New Sweden in 1640 with the second expedition.

The fifth of the remaining old Swedish churches is the Trinity Church at Swedesboro, which the Swedes first called Sveaborg, near Raccoon Creek on the eastern or New Jersey side of the Delaware River. This area was long known as Raccoon. By the turn of the century the schoolmaster there, Hans Stålt, was given permission by Pastor Eric Björk of Christina to hold services. In 1704 a log cabin was dedicated by a clergyman from Sweden, Laurentius Tollstadius, who had come to the Delaware Valley on his own, and who died by drowning two years later. In 1706, the Reverend Jonas Aurén became the first ordained minister at Raccoon. After the War of Independence, the present handsome brick-and-stone edifice was constructed under the direction of one of the last clergymen sent over from Sweden, Nicholas Collin. The church was dedicated by him in 1784. Today, the parish registers and a silver communion service of 1730, as well as tombstones in the churchyard, attest to the Swedish heritage. In 1964, when New Jersey celebrated its tercentenary, the site of the original log church at Swedesboro was dedicated as New Sweden Park.

A log cabin stands just north of Swedesboro, on land that in 1685 was purchased by Mårten Mårtensson, or Morten Mortenson (d. 1706), who had come to New Sweden with Governor Johan Rising in 1654. Near Repaupo, three miles farther north, where many prominent Swedes lived and, as already observed, flawless Swedish was spoken as late as 1750, there is a building known as the Nothnagle House which in part dates from the early Swedish period.

Twelve miles southwest of Swedesboro, on the New Jersey shore of the Delaware and near Pennsville, is Churchtown, the origin of which, called Penn's Neck, was the center of a Swedish-Finnish settlement. A log structure named Sankt Görans Kapell, or St. George's Chapel, was built there in 1717, and this was the beginning of the present St. George's Church, which was erected in 1811, when the Swedish congregation no longer existed. At the New Sweden tercentenary celebration in 1938, a delegation from Finland set up a marker in its churchyard. Not far from the church, where little remains to indicate its Swedish-Finnish roots, is a community called Finn's Point.

In the early 1700s Swedish settlers at Morlatton, or present-day Douglassville on the Schuylkill River some 40 miles northwest of Philadelphia, built their first log church. The first clergyman to serve there was Andreas Rudman of the Wicaco or Gloria Dei congregation, and among his successors was Gabriel Falk, who came in 1733 and almost immediately became engaged in a hand-to-hand struggle with a Moravian emissary for the pulpit. In 1760 the congregation joined the Episcopal Church. The present church edifice, known as St. Gabriel's, was dedicated in 1884. Families of partly Swedish descent who have made significant contributions to the life of the congregation include the Yocoms, who until the early 1900s often supplied at least one of the two wardens. Douglassville boasts the oldest house in Berks County, built in 1716 by Mounce Jones, or, in Swedish, Måns Jonason.

Aside from the Holy Trinity Church with the Hendrickson House at Wilmington and the Gloria Dei in Philadelphia, all built of stone or bricks in the late 1600s, the best preserved and most carefully documented of the remains of Swedish settlements in the 17th century is the Morton Homestead, also known as the Swedish Cabin, in Prospect Park near Darby Creek Bridge, southwest of Philadelphia. Its oldest part was erected by Mårten Mårtensson shortly after he arrived from Sweden in 1654, while two others were added in 1698 and 1806, respectively. Mårtensson's great-grandson John Morton, who became one of the signers of the Declaration of Independence, was probably born in this house. Today many of his descendants still assemble for a reunion at the old homestead. In the same district is a town named Morton. Six miles farther north, near Darby Creek, stands a well-preserved old dwelling known as the Lower Swedish Cabin. It dates from the period 1640–50.

Aside from some Swedish plantations in the Upland area, the New Sweden capital that Governor Johan Printz established on Tinicum Island shortly after his arrival in 1643 was the first permanent white settlement in what became Pennsylvania. The site of the Swedish executive's home and headquarters, which he named Printzhof, is therefore one of the most notable places relating to the early history of the Swedes in America. The foundations of Printzhof, which together with numerous artifacts of Swedish origin were uncovered by an archeological team in 1937, are the only visible remains of the Tinicum settlement. Its present seven acres are known as Governor Printz Park, a national historic landmark. A statue of Johan Printz was unveiled there in 1972. A boulevard running from Philadelphia to Wilmington has been named for Governor Printz, who built the first roads in this region.

Governor Printz's house at Tinicum was one of the best-equipped executive mansions in colonial America, containing, for instance, a valuable library. His yacht seems to have been the first boat of its kind in the New World, and a tablet in the Corinthian Yacht Club, near the site of Printzhof in the southern part of Philadelphia, actually proclaims that he was America's first yachtsman. Although his domain comprised only a small part of Pennsylvania, he has often been called the first governor of the Keystone State. His portrait, a copy of one that hangs in the church at Bottnaryd in northern Småland where he was born and buried, is found in the State House at Harrisburg among those of Pennsylvania's chief executives.

Two monuments of the modern era on historic grounds in Wilmington and Philadelphia

SINCE 1938, when the 300th anniversary of the founding of New Sweden was celebrated, the rocks where the Swedish colonists stepped onto American shores in present-day Wilmington has been marked by a monument in Swedish black granite, designed by Carl Milles and presented by the Swedish nation to the state of Delaware and the people of the United States. At its top, the ship *Kalmar Nyckel* rides on a high-rolling wave under full sail, while scenes on the supporting shaft tell the story of the settlement, beginning with a welcoming committee of wild animals and a group of colonists buying land from the Indians. The monument stands in an enclosed area of two acres, named the Fort Christina Monument after the little stronghold built by the first colonists. It is a national historic site. A memorial wreath is placed there each year on March 29, the day when Peter Minuit and his associates bought land from the Indians. This ceremony is sponsored by the Delaware Swedish Colonial Society.

In his address at the 300th-anniversary festivities in Wilmington in 1938, President Franklin D. Roosevelt observed that the governor of

Delaware holds office in direct succession from the governors of New Sweden. He also recalled that one of his ancestors was an early Swedish settler in New Amsterdam. Sweden's foremost representative on this occasion was 26-year-old Prince Bertil, his father, Crown Prince Gustav Adolf, being compelled by illness to stay on board the ship that had brought the Swedish delegates. The New Sweden tercentenary helped stimulate interest not only in the history of the Swedes in the New World but in all the cultural backgrounds of America. On a much smaller scale, the 325th anniversary of the founding of the Swedish colony was celebrated in 1963. The city of Wilmington then adopted an official flag patterned on the Swedish emblem. The colors of Philadelphia have always been yellow and blue, the same as Sweden's.

In Franklin Delano Roosevelt Park in South Philadelphia, on ground which also belonged to New Sweden, stands the American Swedish Historical Museum, a memorial to that aspect of American history which has its roots in Sweden. In 1926, Crown Prince Gustav Adolf, who 24 years later succeeded his father Gustav V as king, laid the cornerstone of this building, which was modeled after a Swedish manor house, and in 1938 it was formally dedicated by him as part of the tercentenary celebrations. The museum was founded by Dr. Amandus Johnson, author of the first comprehensive history of New Sweden and many other books about early relations between Sweden and America. In the 1970s the museum's location seemed less attractive than before, and new plans were considered.

A few hundred yards from the American Swedish Historical Museum stands a three-story brick house, which was built as a country home about 1740. The history of the site begins with a royal Swedish grant of 1653 to Lieutenant Sven Skute, and the structure is known as "The House on Queen Christina's Land Grant."

In the Delaware Valley there are numerous geographic names of Swedish origin but several are not as easy to identify as Christina, Governor Printz Boulevard, Morton, or Swedesboro. Longacre Boulevard in Philadelphia's western suburb of Yeadon has its name from a Swedish family which became known as Långåker. Mullica Hill, a town near Swedesboro in New Jersey, as well as the Mullica River and the Mullica Inlet were named for a settler of Finnish origin, Erik Pålsson Mollicka, who was born in the Swedish province of

Hälsingland and came to the Delaware Valley in 1664. Other names from the Swedish-Finnish era in the southern part of New Jersey include Elsinborough Township, Rambo Station, Dalbo's Landing, and Helm's Cove.

Thirty-odd Church of Sweden ministers to Delaware — Also other pastors and teachers

INCLUDING the first three pastors who arrived in 1697, about 30 clergymen who had been sent over by the Church of Sweden were active in the Delaware Valley during the 18th century. The last ones arrived in the late 1770s. Other young men came to serve the Swedish congregations as teachers, and a small number of Lutheran ministers arrived without having any official commission. There were also Swedish clergymen of other denominations in America, and some of them tried to win proselytes in the old Swedish settlements on the Delaware.

Practically all of these clergymen and teachers were well educated — the Lutheran ministers were, without exception, university graduates — and they played a leading part in the slowly growing exchange of ideas and experience between Sweden and America, for the benefit of both countries. In America, they helped raise educational standards and lay foundations for rapid economic and cultural progress. They also offered new immigrants and visitors from Scandinavia valuable aid, while authorities and people in Sweden were kept informed by them about conditions in America. Many of those who returned to their native country became leading sources of information about the New World. This early cultural contact with America was, in fact, Sweden's most important gain from its colonial venture on the Delaware.

Of the Swedish clergymen who came in 1697, both Andreas Rudman and Jonas Aurén died in America at a relatively early age. When Rudman, founder of Gloria Dei, passed away in 1708, he was associated with the Christ Episcopal Church in Philadelphia, while Aurén remained as pastor at Raccoon until his death in 1713. Eric Björk of Christina was named provost of the Swedish congregations in 1713, but the next year he moved back to Sweden with his family and became rector at Falun, the ancient industrial and cultural center of the province of Dalarna. His wife, Kristina Stalcop, was the granddaughter of one of the New Sweden soldiers, Johan Andersson, who was dubbed with the nickname Stålkofta, meaning steel jacket. Their son Tobias E. Björk is mentioned in American history books as the author of the first doctor's dissertation about Pennsylvania by a native Pennsylvanian. Written in Latin and submitted at the University of Uppsala in 1731, it dealt with the Swedish Lutheran mission on the Delaware and its relations with other churches.

Eric Björk's successor at Christina, Andreas Hesselius (1677–1733), who came in 1712 and served until 1723, is also one of the best-known members of the Swedish Lutheran mission. His first impressions of America, and especially of living standards and religious conditions in the Delaware Valley, were discouraging. He then began to travel through his territory on foot once a week, teaching old and young, and his more elaborate sermons finally totaled about 750. Like some other Swedish Delaware pastors during the first part of the 1700s, when relations between the religious leaders of Sweden and England were particularly friendly, he received a special compensation for his work among settlers hailing from the British Isles. Hesselius was also a devoted naturalist, and his observations were recorded in a delightful diary. On his way back to Sweden he lost his American-born wife, Sarah Wallrave, as well as a large collection of material for a book about America. In 1724 he read to German-born King Fredrik I and his council in Stockholm a report on the religious conditions in the Delaware Valley, which was published the following year. He described the Indians as practically immune to conversion but "sincere, loyal, honest, and chaste." Hesselius was named rector at Gagnef in his native province of Dalarna. One of his sons, Anders Hesselius "Americanus," became instructor of English at the University of Uppsala.

At Christina, Andreas Hesselius was succeeded by his brother Samuel Hesselius (1692–1753). Another brother, Gustavus Hesselius, who had come to America with Andreas, became an artist, and will be dealt with later. The three brothers were first cousins of Emanuel Swedenborg, the famous scientist and religious seer, their mother being a sister of Bishop Jesper Swedberg, who was Swedenborg's father. Long after his return to Sweden, Samuel Hesselius supplied the Swedish Academy of Sciences with books about America and other material.

43

After Anders Rudman, Andreas Sandel (1671–1744) served as pastor of the Gloria Dei Church near Philadelphia for 17 years, or until 1719, when he was appointed rector at Hedemora in Dalarna. His letters from America to relatives in Sweden were, at his own request, copied and widely circulated. He married Maria Dahlbo, the descendant of an early Swedish colonist from the Baltic island of Gotland, and one of their ten children became the ancestor of a well-known Swedish family by the name of Sandels. One of its members, Count Johan August Sandels (1764–1831), won fame as a general in Finland in the war with Russia of 1808–09 and ended as a field marshal, the last one appointed in Sweden.

One of the most popular pastors of the Wicaco congregation was Johannes Dylander (1709–41), who often offered an early morning service in German, high mass in Swedish, and a vesper in English. In 1741 he had Benjamin Franklin print a 16-page pamphlet, *Free Grace in Truth*, where, in footnotes to an English translation of one of the German theologian Johann Gerhard's meditations in Latin, he expounded on some of his religious beliefs. Dylander died after only four years of service and was buried in Gloria Dei. When he came in 1737, he was accompanied by a teacher, Olof Malander (d. 1744), who for about a year preached at Raccoon and Penn's Neck in New Jersey and later joined the Moravian Brethren. After having been taken to Philadelphia on account of his debts, he worked for some time in Benjamin Franklin's printing office, where he produced a Swedish translation of a Moravian catechism.

Raccoon and Penn's Neck in New Jersey had been united into one pastorate in 1714, and the Reverend Abraham Lidenius, who arrived from Sweden in 1712 together with Andreas Hesselius, had been named its first pastor. The first church at Penn's Neck, St. George's Chapel, was consecrated by him in 1717. Together with his wife, who was of Dutch extraction, and their children he returned in 1724 to Sweden, where he had been appointed rector at Umeå in the far north. His son Johan Abraham Lidenius, who was born at Raccoon, came back to the Delaware Valley in 1751 and was appointed pastor at Raccoon-Penn's Neck four years later. In 1761, when he had been placed in a debtor's prison, he was called back to Sweden, but died in America seven years later.

The life of the Swedish clergymen in the Delaware Valley was always complicated, and most of the time they must have had a strong feeling of struggling for the survival of their congregations. In their eagerness to preserve Lutheran unity, some became passionately orthodox. Others took a dim view of everything, and a few gradually sank into misery.

In the 1730s and 40s, when a religious revival known as the Great Awakening swept through the American colonies, many of the Swedish descendants associated themselves with the English Episcopal Church, the Quakers, the Methodists, or the Catholics. At one time the Swedish Lutherans seemed threatened in particular by the Moravian Brethren, whose American center, the town of Bethlehem in Pennsylvania, was founded in 1741 by exiles from Bohemia and Moravia. Several Swedes who had joined or planned to join the Moravians arrived at about the same time, and three of them, Paul Daniel Brytzelius (1713–73), Lars Nyberg, and Abraham Reinke (1712–60), seem to have been regarded by the Swedish Lutheran ministers on the Delaware as the leading Moravian preachers. Brytzelius was welcomed in many Swedish homes at Raccoon and Penn's Neck, where the pastor's office remained vacant for many years in the 1740s. A minister of the Church of Sweden, Johan Sandin, who also was named provost of the Delaware congregations, came in 1748 but died after six months. During the following winter a visiting Swedish naturalist from Uppsala, Pehr Kalm, preached at Raccoon almost every Sunday, although he had not been ordained.

The inroads made by the Moravians among the Swedes in the Delaware Valley were, however, halted, probably in part because of friendlier relations between the Moravians and some of the Lutheran clergymen. In 1760 one of the leading Swedish Moravians, Paul D. Brytzelius, who had the support of the Lutheran provost Carl Magnus Wrangel, was ordained a minister in the Lutheran church. Later he joined the Episcopalians and was sent to Nova Scotia.

Schoolmasters had assisted the Swedish clergymen ever since the Lutheran mission of the English colonial era was established. At Christina, Eric Björk employed two young men, Sven Colsberg (d. 1710) and John Göding, who also served under Björk's successor. In 1714, Bishop Jesper Swedberg sent out Arvid Hernbom or Bohn, a student from the old cultural center of Skara in Västergötland.

Somewhat later Bishop Swedberg dispatched one of his own sons,

45

Jesper Swedenborg (1694–1771), whose conduct as a young man had caused his father some concern. He was, therefore, sent first to the Swedish army in northern Germany and then to the Delaware Valley, where for nine years he taught in the Swedish parish schools, primarily at Raccoon. After a visit to Sweden he came back "to spend the rest of his days serving countrymen," but remained only a year. All present-day members of the Swedenborg family are his descendants, his elder brother Emanuel Swedenborg having left no children. Another Swede, Nicholas Forsberg from Gothenburg, who after studies at the University of Lund had tried his fortune in other parts of the world, came to the Delaware Valley at the middle of the 1700s and began as a schoolteacher at Christina. He finally served Gloria Dei in Philadelphia, primarily as a parish clerk, and died in a yellow-fever epidemic in 1793.

Swedish church mission on the Delaware reaches a high point toward its end

FOR the Holy Trinity congregation at Christina, a happy period of seven years began in 1749 with the arrival of the Reverend Israel Acrelius (1714–1800), who also was named provost of the Swedish churches in the valley. While decidedly orthodox, he did much to bring about greater harmony everywhere. He became, moreover, the foremost early historian of the New Sweden colony, with a book that will be described shortly. After his return to Sweden, Acrelius was appointed to a rectorship at Fellingsbro in the central province of Närke. As provost in the Delaware Valley he was succeeded by Olof Parlin (1716–57) of Gloria Dei, who died one year later.

Carl Magnus Wrangel (1727–87), who came three years after Acrelius's departure, was one of the best qualified of the Lutheran clergymen sent over from Sweden, representing a rare combination of learning, eloquence, realism, and will power. The remarkable old family or group of families to which he belonged had medieval roots in an estate in Estonia, which had been annexed to Sweden in the middle 1500s. Seventy Swedish officers by the name of Wrangel had fallen during the campaigns of King Charles XII in the early 1700s, and several others, including Carl Magnus Wrangel's grandfather, had for years been prisoners of war in Russia.

After having obtained a doctor's degree at a German university and served as a chaplain at the court in Stockholm, Carl Magnus Wrangel came to the Delaware Valley in the spring of 1759 as provost of the Swedish congregations. He was then only 31 years old, but a religious revival soon developed under his inspired and increasingly unorthodox leadership. At open-air meetings he preached to some of the largest throngs seen in the Delaware River area. On other occasions too he spoke, as a rule, in English, realizing that the younger generations could no longer be reached in the Swedish language. His base of operations was Kingsessing, west of Philadelphia, where the impressive St. James Church was built under his direction in the early 1760s, but he often visited other congregations. An inspection trip in 1764 took him to Great Egg Harbor, a Swedish settlement on the Atlantic coast about 60 miles southeast of Philadelphia, where no Lutheran minister had been for 20 years. It had been founded by Jacob or James Steelman, who also owned land somewhat farther north on Absecon Island, where Atlantic City was built. The Swedish clergyman found the name Steelman well represented in the Egg Harbor area, and it survives in Steelmanville, Steelman's Landing, and other place-names in southern New Jersey. From Philadelphia Dr. Wrangel also traveled 40 miles to the northwest, to Morlatton on the Schuylkill River, the present Douglassville near Dottstown, where a church had been built of oak logs in 1736.

Dr. Wrangel did more for the improvement of education than any other Swedish clergyman in the Delaware Valley. The Lutheran congregation at Wicaco received its first school building, and a new school was established at Kingsessing. In his remarkable directives for the schoolmasters, the first of their kind in Pennsylvania, he stressed the need for good instruction in the English language. Other initiatives by Wrangel included an attempt to obtain an expert from Sweden as manager for a new ironworks in the Philadelphia area. In a letter to a Swedish mineralogist regarding this problem, written in 1763, he described the country people in the Delaware Valley as well-to-do and contented.

At the University of Uppsala the Swedish clergyman had been a pupil of Linnaeus, the famous naturalist, and during his nine years in America he pursued his studies of botany and natural history in general. Upon his advice, a young man by the name of Adam Kuhn, partly of Swedish descent, left for Uppsala in 1761 to study with

47

Linnaeus, and he finally became professor of botany and medicine in what is now the University of Pennsylvania. Among Wrangel's friends were John Bartram, who has frequently been called the "Father of American botany," and Bartram's son William, who also became a noted traveler and naturalist. In 1728 John Bartram had founded the first botanical garden in America at Kingsessing, and he became an ardent student of Linnaeus, to whom he often sent plant specimens. In 1766, Wrangel tried to get the Swedish Academy of Sciences to subscribe money for one of Bartram's trips, and get collections in exchange. Three years later the American botanist was elected a member of the same academy, and Dr. Wrangel, who had then returned to Sweden, was the first to notify him.

Wrangel's relations with some of his Swedish colleagues in America were full of friction, but he and the leader of the German Lutheran congregations in Pennsylvania, Dr. Heinrich Mühlenberg or Henry Muhlenberg, became, on the other hand, close associates and friends. Muhlenberg had arrived in 1743, and already Israel Acrelius had often met him. In 1763, Wrangel and Muhlenberg invited the English evangelist George Whitefield, the first great preacher to travel widely in the American colonies, to a Swedish-German synod.

In 1763 the other Swedish clergymen on the Delaware sent to Sweden a formal protest against their provost, Dr. Wrangel, accusing him of having engaged as his assistant a young runaway pastor, Nils Hörnell from the village of Höör in southern Sweden, who had come to America in late 1762. After having served as a minister in Philadelphia and York, Pennsylvania, the Reverend Nils Hornell became a farmer. One of his grandsons, Judge George Hornell, founded the city of Hornell in New York State some 50 miles south of Rochester. Among his later descendants was Albert Bushnell Hart of Harvard, noted educator and historian.

Dr. Wrangel was recalled to Sweden in 1765, but he answered that he would leave his post only at the express order of the King. Most of the Swedish Delaware congregations as well as Muhlenberg intervened to support him. When Wrangel finally left America in the fall of 1768, he realized that the days of the Swedish Lutheran mission on the Delaware were numbered. The religious needs of people of Swedish descent could, he felt, no longer be met by clergymen who were sent over from Sweden and perhaps planned to stay for only a few years. Instead, an attempt must be made to obtain young men who were born in America but would receive their final training in Sweden, or perhaps, to begin with, from Swedish clergymen in the Delaware Valley. Wrangel himself tried, in fact, to put such ideas into practice before leaving the New World. A few young men studied theology with him, among them a brother of the above-mentioned Adam Kuhn by the name of Daniel, who in 1771 went to Sweden to complete his studies. In 1775 he was appointed pastor at Christina, but died in London before taking up his post.

On his way back to Sweden via England, Dr. Wrangel met John Wesley, the founder of Methodism. This experience, and above all his impressions from America, had a decisive influence when a few years later Wrangel formed an association aimed at improving religious conditions in his native country, the still existing *Pro fide et christianismo*. The Uppsala Cathedral chapter exonerated him in regard to the charges leveled against him as provost of the Swedish Lutheran mission in the Delaware Valley, but he was reprimanded and had to wait nearly four years for a rectorate based in the old silver-mining town of Sala, northwest of Stockholm. Before this appointment, on the other hand, he was named chief chaplain at the Swedish court and preached to large crowds in many of Stockholm's churches. In the beginning he felt very hopeful about the new monarch, Gustav III, who ascended the throne in 1771 and soon increased his own power at the expense of a deteriorating parliament, but after a few years his attitude became more and more negative vis-à-vis the King.

One of Wrangel's antagonists in the Delaware mission, the Reverend Johan Wicksell (1727–1800), served from 1763 to 1773 as minister at Raccoon and Penn's Neck. At that time, about one-half of the congregation at Raccoon was still able to understand Swedish. Wicksell preached constantly in three languages, Swedish, English, and German, and he too gave much attention to education.

In the spring of 1770 Pastor Wicksell received an assistant from Sweden, the Reverend Nils, or Nicholas, Collin. On Whitsunday, June 3, he preached in Swedish at Raccoon, the present Swedesboro, and on the following Sunday in the Old Swedes Church at Wilmington, Holy Trinity. On July 8, 1770, he preached in English at Raccoon, and on July 15 at Penn's Neck. Collin was not the last clergyman sent by the Church of Sweden to the Delaware Valley, but because of the length of his service, together with his qualities, he became the most important of the Swedish ministers who were sent to America in the 18th century.

First Swedish books about America based on experiences of Delaware pastors

IN THE early 1700s, publishing activities in Sweden began to reflect the need for better information about conditions and events on the other side of the Atlantic. The first book about America, titled *A Short Description of the Province of New Sweden*, appeared in Stockholm in 1702. It consisted of selections from Johannes Campanius's American papers, which had been edited by his grandson, Tomas Campanius Holm (1670–1702). A translation was published in Philadelphia in 1834.

Some other documents dating from the time of the Swedish colony on the Delaware were not published until much later, but as a rule they became available for research. The first Swedish engineer in America was Pehr Mårtensson Lindeström, who came to New Sweden with Johan Rising in 1654 and returned with him to Europe the following year. A specialist in fortifications, he drew the first map of the lower Delaware Valley and described this region in a journal which he called *Geographia Americae*. In an English translation by Dr. Amandus Johnson, it was published for the first time in Philadelphia in 1925, but even early Swedish writers, including Tomas Campanius Holm, had been able to draw upon Lindeström's manuscript.

Bishop Jesper Swedberg collected reports from Swedish clergymen in America as well as his own experiences in a large handwritten work, a condensed version of which was published at Skara in 1732 under the title *America Illuminata*. In the editing he had the help of his son Jesper Swedenborg who, after many years as a schoolteacher on the Delaware, became first a minister and finally an estate owner in Sweden.

In the 1750s two important books by Swedes who had studied or worked in America were published in Stockholm. The largest and by far most influential was written by the naturalist Pehr, or Peter, Kalm, about whom more will be said later. His first volume appeared in

1753. The other author was the Reverend Israel Acrelius, who in 1749–56 had served as provost of the Swedish congregations on the Delaware. His book, entitled *A Description of the Swedish Parishes on the Delaware* and published in 1759, is still regarded as an excellent source of information about the New Sweden colony. Acrelius also wrote about the Swedish, Dutch, and English administrations in the Delaware Valley, and about the culture of the people. A translation, entitled *A History of New Sweden; or, the Settlements on the River Delaware,* was published in Philadelphia in 1874 under the joint auspices of the historical societies of Pennsylvania and Delaware.

Through the books and other activities of Acrelius and Kalm, Benjamin Franklin became the first American to be widely known in the Swedish world of learning. Acrelius, who took part in the Riksdag sessions about 1770, paid special attention to Franklin's educational ideas and commended his plan for a more practical school than the conventional type. However, he encountered powerful opposition, as did, in fact, Franklin himself in Philadelphia. Both Acrelius and Kalm favored British rule in America, but the latter was one of the first travelers to mention the possibility that the colonies might some day form an independent nation.

After the publication of Acrelius's and Kalm's books about America, a Stockholm journal, *Lärda Tidningar,* wrote in 1759 that in Sweden "we now have the best, the most reliable, and the most up-to-date information about this distant part of the world." This was a somewhat extravagant statement, for there were valuable works about America in other languages, and the more important ones became known in Sweden. In 1759, for instance, another Swedish periodical, *Den swänska Mercurius,* published long reviews of two French books on America.

Interest in the New World had been awakened and grew slowly but irresistibly. During the first part of the 1700s, when Sweden's relations with the Swedish parishes in the Delaware Valley had become much more active than in the late 17th century, these outposts were often treated in sermons, essays, and pamphlets. By the middle 1700s, moreover, Swedish newspaper and magazine editors began to realize that America as a whole deserved more attention. The wars between the British and the French also brought the New World into greater prominence.

*Pioneer artist and other Americans from Sweden, now in
new phase of progress*

THE number of Swedes who came to America as visitors or immigrants
in the 1700s before the Revolution was larger than generally believed
today, though without doubt the total was modest.

Many of those who became permanent settlers were former sailors
who had tasted or at least observed higher living standards than they
were used to in Sweden. By the middle of the century, Swedes often
served on Dutch or English ships, as gunners, carpenters, mates, or
ordinary seamen, and Pehr Kalm, who met many such people in
Philadelphia, wrote in his diary that most of them had "neither
thought nor desire of ever returning to Sweden." Their native country, they felt, offered them small chance of promotion or even of a
decent livelihood. Among former sailors or merchant marine officers
who seem to have settled in America for other reasons was Peter Kock
(1703–49), a native of the Swedish naval base at Karlskrona, who,
when Kalm made his acquaintance in Philadelphia, had become "one
of the wealthiest of merchants" and a pillar of the Swedish congregation. He was well educated and corresponded with relatives and
friends in his native land.

Three brothers by the name of Hesselius, sons of a minister in the
province of Dalarna and first cousins of Emanuel Swedenborg, came
as already mentioned to the Swedish settlements on the Delaware in
the early 1700s. The youngest, Gustavus Hesselius (1682–1755), remained in America and became the first notable artist of the colonial
period.

Hesselius had studied art during visits to relatives in Stockholm,
and in America he specialized in portraits and religious subjects. An
altarpiece, "The Last Supper," which he completed in 1721 for the St.
Barnabas Church in Queen Anne's Parish in Maryland, is regarded as
his most important work, and it was probably the first public art
commission in the colonies. It is now in private possession at East
Chatham, Virginia. One of his early portraits, that of 89-year-old Ann
Galloway, is in the Metropolitan Museum of Art in New York. A
number of later ones, including two of Indian chiefs, one of his wife,
and a self-portrait, belong to the Historical Society of Pennsylvania. A
large canvas, "The Crucifixion," which was exhibited in Philadelphia
in 1748, hangs in the famous St. Mungo's Cathedral at Glasgow in

Scotland. Hesselius is also represented in the Maryland Historical Society and the Cleveland Museum of Art. In 1938 the Philadelphia Museum of Art showed a large collection of his paintings in connection with the 300th anniversary of the landing of the first Swedes on the Delaware.

Also skilled in mechanical construction, Hesselius built an organ for a Moravian church at Bethlehem, Pennsylvania, one of the first such instruments known to have been made in America. The last 20 years of his life he lived in Philadelphia, and he was buried at Gloria Dei. He left three daughters and one son, John (1728–78), who became a portrait painter. Charles Willson Peale, celebrated especially for his portraits of George Washington, received his first art instruction from John Hesselius.

Of the clergymen and religious teachers of other denominations than the Lutheran who came to America from Sweden in the 1700s, Sven Rosén (1708–50) is today best known. A member of a large family raised in a parsonage in the province of Västergötland, he became, after university studies at Uppsala, one of Sweden's first pietist leaders. He was then accused of heresy, and although an extremely sensitive person leaning toward mysticism, he defended himself brilliantly. Under Sweden's at that time extremely rigorous religious legislation he was exiled in 1741, and the next few years he spent in England and Germany where he joined the Moravian Brethren. Being in frail health he asked for permission to return to Sweden, but this was refused, and at the end of 1746 he came to America, where Philadelphia and Bethlehem were his first destinations. As a Moravian social worker he visited settlements and congregations in Pennsylvania, New Jersey, and Maryland, preaching in German, English, or Swedish. After a particularly strenuous trip to Maryland he died in late 1750 at the age of 42, leaving a German-born wife and a baby daughter. He lies buried at Emmaus, Pennsylvania, which, like Bethlehem, was founded by Moravians. Today, Sven Rosén is regarded as a martyr for the cause of religious liberty. He was, in fact, Sweden's first outspoken champion of modern religious freedom. One of his brothers, known as Nils Rosén von Rosenstein, became a medical pioneer and is regarded as the "Father of Swedish medicine."

Among the Swedish Moravians who remained in America was also Abraham Reinke, a native of Stockholm. Many of his descendants served the Moravian Church as pastors, bishops, or educators. During a visit to Bethlehem, Pennsylvania, in 1754, the Reverend Israel Acrelius met a coppersmith by the name of Hasselberg, who had left his native Sweden in 1749.

Swedish Baptists have been active in America ever since the 1600s, which saw the beginnings of this religious denomination. In the latter part of that century, a Swede by the name of Robert Nordin was ordained a Baptist minister in London and then left for America where, in Prince George County in Virginia, he organized a Baptist congregation and served as its pastor until his death in 1725. Another Baptist minister by the name of Richard Nordin came to Virginia in 1727, but soon returned to England. He may have been a son of Robert Nordin.

One of the few Swedes who are known to have settled in America outside the English colonies was a former army officer of Baltic or North German origin by the name of Carl Fredrick Arensburg (1693-1777), who in 1721 arrived in Louisiana on a French ship with a large group of mostly German immigrants. For over 40 years he served as judge and civic leader of a German settlement on the Mississippi River about 30 miles north of New Orleans. His descendants married into some thirty prominent French families in Louisiana, and keepsakes of his, all concerning Charles XII of Sweden, have been preserved to this day.

A number of Swedish military men, most of them adventurous or restless members of the nobility, visited England's American colonies in the early or middle 1700s, and some became permanent settlers. Among these was Adolph Benzelstierna or Benzel (1718-74), who arrived in 1750 and, except for at least one visit to Europe, spent the rest of his life in America. According to some reports he became a fortification officer and finally an inspector of forests in the English service, while other sources have described him as chief land surveyor and a justice of the peace.

Little is known about Adolph Benzel's life in America, but his Swedish origin was anything but obscure. His mother was a daughter of Bishop Jesper Swedberg, without whose efforts the Swedish settlers in the Delaware Valley probably would have received much less assistance from Sweden. His paternal grandfather ended as

54

archbishop at Uppsala, and his father as well as two of his uncles reached the same position.

Adolph Benzel's father, Eric Benzelius the Younger (1675–1743), was above all an unusually proficient scholar, who, by his enterprise and his close contacts with men of learning in other countries, helped initiate one of the most constructive periods in Sweden's cultural history. Via him, Emanuel Swedenborg became interested in natural science, but this was a special case, Swedenborg being his brother-in-law. His relations with England, at this time a fountainhead of scientific progress, were particularly extensive, and he had a legion of followers in Sweden. In the fields of natural science and medicine, Swedish contacts and exchanges with England reached, in fact, an intensity during the 1700s which was not exceeded until the 20th century. This was, of course, of some significance even from an American viewpoint. Swedish achievements often became known in America via England or through Englishmen, but there were also direct contacts. Many of the Swedes who visited or settled down in the New World in the 18th century had, as already indicated, close personal ties with leaders in science and discovery in their native country.

The emigration from Sweden in the 1700s, most of which flowed toward other European countries, was modest by 19th-century standards, but the first study of the causes of emigration in the nation's history was launched in the 1760s under the auspices of the newly founded Academy of Sciences. Some of those taking part in the discussion maintained that the problem had its roots in unemployment and in feelings of insecurity, while others regarded a lack of economic freedom, resulting from the mercantilistic regulation of industry and trade, as the principal cause of emigration.

The Linnaean Age

Sweden's grim early 1700s — *Harbingers of a new era,
among them Swedenborg*

THE first quarter of the 1700s was one of the most trying periods in
Sweden's history. In 1709, Charles XII's campaign in Russia ended
with a catastrophic defeat in the Ukraine, and while the King himself
managed to escape to Turkey, thousands of Swedish officers and
soldiers were carried off to captivity in Siberia. In 1710–11 the plague
stalked the homeland, killing about one-third of Stockholm's inhabitants and even larger proportions in some smaller towns. After King
Charles's death in a military operation against Denmark-Norway in
1718, large sections of Sweden's eastern coast, including some of its
most valuable ironmaking districts north of the capital, were ravaged
by Russian forces. Its Baltic provinces were ceded to Russia and most
of its possessions in Germany to Prussia and Hanover.

The population of Sweden proper in 1720 was estimated at 1.4
million, and this figure the parliament tried to keep secret, fearing
that the nation's prestige would be damaged further if it became
known abroad. The infant mortality rate was about 25 percent, that is,
one out of every four newborn children did not survive the first year
of age, and even for those who did, life was full of danger, in particular up to the age of ten. Crop failures occurred frequently, and in
many districts starvation was never far away. In Finland, which was to
remain part of the Swedish realm until 1809, at least one-fourth of

the people had perished in the famine of 1696–97, one of the most dreadful disasters of its kind in Europe's history. During the next two decades both Swedes and Finns suffered other serious crop failures, the worst ones in 1717–18.

Sweden was, however, not completely exhausted, and under the influence of a relatively long period of peace and a new intellectual and political climate, an economic and cultural revival developed with surprising speed. In part, it was a direct consequence of consistent government encouragement of commercial and industrial expansion, a policy which favored particularly the applied sciences and also stimulated basic research, but the scientific upsurge was nevertheless miraculous. Even an unrealistic war of revenge with Russia in 1741– 43, which resulted in the temporary occupation of large sections of Finland, could not halt it. On the whole, a peaceful although often adventurous spirit of progress prevailed, and new creative impulses came from abroad, particularly from England but also from the European mainland.

Only a few decades after the collapse of its Baltic empire, Sweden became, in fact, one of Europe's leading research nations, a development which fundamentally was more important than the country's rise to a precarious military great-power position in the early 17th century. It assumed, of course, an international significance regardless of national boundaries, but cultural relations between Sweden and America were also directly affected.

Urban Hjärne (1641–1724), Christopher Polhem (1661–1751), and Emanuel Swedenborg (1688–1772) may be regarded as the great forerunners of the large-scale scientific upswing. All three received inspiration from Sweden's most remarkable scholar of the great-power period, Olaus Rudbeck (1630–1702), who at the age of 22 had begun an extraordinary career with the discovery of the lymphatic system, later demonstrated in a magnificent anatomical theater in a still-standing university building at Uppsala.

Hjärne was born on the eastern border of the Swedish empire and spent most of his childhood in a town which was the beginning of present-day Leningrad. Extended studies in Sweden and abroad and restless activities in various fields, including the medical and literary, made him a man of encyclopedic learning; above all he helped pave the way for modern chemistry. While many of Sweden's best-known scientists and explorers of the following era died as bachelors, Hjärne married three times and had 26 children, the youngest of whom lived until 1805, no less than 164 years after his father's birth. Like numerous other Swedes who have won distinction in the course of the centuries, Urban Hjärne has a large number of descendants even in the United States.

Polhem, who came from the Baltic island of Gotland, was also a polyhistor but first of all a mechanical genius. He became a pioneer in replacing manual operations with machinery as a prerequisite of mass production, and was probably the first to use gages to control mass-produced articles. A book titled *Christopher Polhem: The Father of Swedish Technology*, was published in 1963 by the trustees of Trinity College at Hartford, Connecticut, under a grant from an American industrialist of Swedish origin.

Swedenborg, whose father had organized in the early 1700s Sweden's religious contacts with the settlers in the Delaware Valley, was as a scientist ahead of his time in almost every department, although not all of his conclusions proved accurate. His geological and metallurgical writings alone would, according to experts of today, assure him of a place in the history of natural science, and his findings in physiology were equally far advanced. He was, for instance, the first scholar to localize correctly the motor area in the brain. Swedenborg was also an outstanding mechanical engineer. An airplane sketched by him, a model of which hangs in the Smithsonian Institution in Washington, D.C., is said to contain the first embodiment of the aerodynamic features essential to successful flight. He traveled extensively in Europe and died in London, where in his younger days he had lived for a few years. His remains were interred in the small Swedish church in London, but in 1908 they were transferred to Uppsala Cathedral.

Plumbing the secrets of the universe, Swedenborg looked ever more deeply into the spiritual world, and the last three decades of his long life were devoted to theological studies and writings which finally filled 30 volumes. Eternal life he regarded as an inner condition, a continuation of personal existence on a spiritual plane. He never attempted to found a sect, but in 1787 a religious community based on his ideas and visions was organized in England, and on the other side of the Atlantic churches grew up in Baltimore, Philadelphia,

Cincinnati, Boston, and New York. Today, the United States and England still have the largest congregations, but there are also religious followers of Swedenborg in Sweden and many other countries.

On a much larger scale, Swedenborg's influence has been felt outside the church organization. In America, George Washington, Benjamin Franklin, and Thomas Jefferson were among the first to become interested in him and his writings, and a great many of the leading literary figures of the 19th century, including Ralph Waldo Emerson and Walt Whitman, are known to have studied him. In 1842, Abraham Lincoln received a set of Swedenborg's writings. A message from President Franklin D. Roosevelt in 1938 in connection with the 250th anniversary of Swedenborg's birth said that, "in a world in which the voice of conscience too often seems still and small there is need of that spiritual leadership of which Swedenborg was a particular example."

The best known of the 50-odd Swedenborg church buildings in the United States are the beautiful Cathedral at Bryn Athyn, Pennsylvania, and the Wayfarer's Chapel in Portuguese Bend, California. A Swedenborg School of Religion is at Newton, Massachusetts. The Swedenborg Foundation in New York publishes and distributes the writings of Swedenborg as well as studies of his life and work. A Swedenborg bust was unveiled in Chicago's Lincoln Park in 1924.

A golden age of scientific research in Sweden begins in 1730s

AFTER 1730 the scientific revival began to unfold on a broad front, and the next half-century became a golden age in Swedish research. Ten new chemical elements, or a majority of those discovered during this era, were pinned down or first identified in Sweden, and its scientists made numerous other contributions to progress in chemistry and physics, mineralogy, astronomy, biology, medicine, and other branches of investigation and learning.

Distant parts of the world, including North and South America, the Far East and the Pacific area, were also explored. Several decades earlier, Swedish interest in geographical and other scientific exploration had been stimulated by army officers who returned from Siberia and had become pioneer cartographers of the interior of Asia and even the Far East. Many of the some 3,000 Swedish officers in Siberia lived at Tobolsk in the south, where they built a church and a school as well as a fortress which still stands, and from there some of them pushed to the east of Asia.

The 50-year period of scientific flowering in Sweden has been called the Linnaean Age, for its most inspiring and illustrious figure was Carl von Linné, or Linnaeus (1707–78), the greatest naturalist of his time and the father of modern botany. His first important work, *Systema Naturae*, was published in 1735. Other members of the same generation of scientists included Samuel Klingenstierna (1698–1765), Sweden's first great mathematician and now best known for his successful work on achromatic lenses, and Anders Celsius (1701–44), who before his death at the age of 42 won international fame as an astronomer. His name lives on in the Celsius or centigrade thermometer, which Linnaeus helped to develop.

Another outstanding astronomer, Pehr Wargentin (1717–83), conducted studies of lasting significance concerning the movements and eclipses of the moons of the planet Jupiter. He became, moreover, a pioneer of international consequence in the field of statistics. Sweden has had reliable and well-organized vital statistics ever since 1749, or longer than any other country, and a large part of the credit goes to Wargentin who was the first to organize and analyze the statistical material compiled by the clergy. His life-expectancy and mortality studies attracted attention abroad, and an English philosopher and economist, Richard Price, used them for a modernization of the calculations on which insurance premiums and benefits were based. Price, who became identified with the cause of American independence, later discussed the same subject in his correspondence with Benjamin Franklin — an example of how Swedish scientific achievements reached America via England.

From 1749 until his death 34 years later, Wargentin served as secretary of the Swedish Academy of Sciences, which largely thanks to him developed into a center of scientific research and related activities. For the first time Sweden now became engaged in an intensive exchange of ideas, books, and other publications with England, France, Germany, Holland, Italy, and Russia. Wargentin himself carried on a voluminous correspondence, and more than 4,000 letters to him from learned societies in Sweden and abroad are preserved in the library of the Academy of Sciences in Stockholm. He was elected a member of all leading societies of research and learning in Europe, and like Linnaeus and Celsius he has given his name to a formation on the moon.

In 1781 the Swedish Academy of Sciences received a letter from the newly founded American Academy of Arts and Sciences in Boston, and an exchange of publications began between these two institutions. Wargentin was elected a member of the academy in Boston, which already had invited two other Swedes, Peter Jonas Bergius and Samuel Gustaf Hermelin, who will be mentioned again later.

As secretary of the Academy of Sciences, Wargentin was succeeded by Johan Carl Wilcke (1732–96), who had won European fame as one of the era's leading experimental physicists. Much of his research covered two separate fields, the study of phenomena associated with stationary electricity and the science of heat. Wilcke also conducted magnetic measurements and published the first world map of magnetic inclination. Benjamin Franklin's first paper on electricity, published at London in 1751, Wilcke translated into German, with extensive notes.

Vital importance of agricultural progress — Advances in medicine and public health

THE Swedish Academy of Sciences was founded in 1739, and its first president was Linnaeus, a constant source of inspiration and initiative. Two of the other four founders were Mårten Triewald (1691–1747), who in 1728 had constructed Sweden's first steam engine, based on a system invented in England, and Jonas Alströmer (1685–1761), an industrialist as well as an experimental farmer. In the beginning, the Academy of Sciences saw as its primary objective the promotion of industry and, above all, of agriculture and animal husbandry, which occupied an overwhelming majority of the Swedish people.

Much was actually done to improve the productivity of agriculture, by individuals as well as by authorities and institutions, but in retrospect the progress seems slow, even if the formidable basic difficulties, the scarcity of fertile land and the traditional strip farming, are taken into consideration. Jonas Alströmer's best-known effort offers an example — perhaps by far the most striking one.

After 17 years in London as a businessman, Alströmer established a large woolen factory in his home town Alingsås, in the province of Västergötland, northeast of Gothenburg, and in 1724, at one of his experimental farms, he introduced the potato as a food crop in Sweden. He pushed the root as vigorously as his manufactures, but only members of the upper classes were ready to listen to him, while the farmers and their laborers with few exceptions offered stubborn resistance. Not until the beginning of the 19th century was potato growing generally adopted, and even then potatoes were, to begin with, used primarily as cattle feed and for distillation into liquor. In the late 1700s, badly needed agricultural reforms were introduced in the southern province of Skåne by Rutger Maclean (1742–1816), a descendant of one of the many Scottish businessmen who in the 17th century had settled in Gothenburg. In Sweden as a whole, however, the landless agricultural population increased during the 18th century, the beginning of a development that would add fuel to the coming large-scale Swedish migration to America.

Throughout the 1700s, most people in Sweden still lived so close to a subsistence minimum that a poor harvest immediately resulted in an increase in mortality, and the worst crop failures of the latter part of this century, in 1772–73, caused the death of some 75,000, mostly elderly and sick people and infants. Such hazards, together with the frequent occurrence of smallpox epidemics, underlined the vital importance of rapid progress in medicine and health care, and in this respect, as in many others, the Linnaean Age made its mark.

In medical research, the leading pioneers were Nils Rosén von Rosenstein (1706–73) and Olof af Acrel (1717–1806). The former has been called the "Father of Swedish medicine" and is widely regarded as the founder of pediatrics, that branch of medical science which treats of the hygiene and diseases of children. In this field he was far ahead of his time, for the special problems of child health were not given consistent attention until the 20th century. In 1764, Rosén's essays on these subjects, written for the almanacs of the Swedish Academy of Sciences, were published in extended form in a work titled *Instruction on Childhood Diseases and Their Treatment*, which still is considered one of the most influential medical books ever written. It was translated into English, French, German, Danish, Dutch, and Hungarian, and many universities used it for more than half a century.

Some of the first successful inoculations against smallpox in Sweden, with live virus, were made by Nils Rosén, who during the great plague of 1710, when he was four years old, had become so ill that he was once pronounced dead. For him and one of his brothers, also a highly respected physician, a group of herbs has been named Rosenia. Another brother, Sven Rosén, was, as already mentioned, exiled from Sweden as a heretic and died as a social worker in Pennsylvania.

As professor of medicine at the University of Uppsala, Nils Rosén von Rosenstein was succeeded by his son-in-law, Samuel Aurivillius (1721–67), whose father, an eminent clergyman, had been King Charles XII's spiritual guide during his campaign in Russia. A son of his, and thus grandson of the "Father of Swedish medicine," was one of many Swedish naval officers who took part in the American War of Independence.

In the history of Swedish medicine, Olof af Acrel holds a position similar to that of Nils Rosén von Rosenstein, being regarded as the founder of scientific surgery in Sweden. About 1750, when he had studied not only in his native country but also in England and Germany and had been in charge of a French field hospital in the Rhineland, he helped found the public Seraphim Hospital in Stockholm, where he remained as chief surgeon until 1800. It was Sweden's first general hospital in the modern sense. Olof af Acrel was a brother of the Reverend Israel Acrelius who in 1757 returned to Sweden after seven years in the Delaware Valley.

A leading part in the founding of the Seraphim Hospital in Stockholm was also played by Linnaeus's closest personal friend, Abraham Bäck (1713–95), whose subsequent activities led to numerous improvements in Sweden's public-health services and medical system. The number of regional and local health officers, for instance, increased considerably, and a first foundation was laid for the Caroline Institute in Stockholm, which today awards the Nobel prize in physiology or medicine. In Gothenburg, a modest hospital was opened in 1782. Named the Sahlgren Hospital after its first donor, a wealthy businessman, it is now one of Sweden's foremost medical centers.

Sweden leading producer of iron — Nickel and other metals discovered

MANY of the most significant Swedish contributions to scientific progress in the 18th century were made in chemistry and the closely related field of mineralogy. In the 1770s Sweden's chemists won international fame for the first time, but important foundations had been laid by its mineralogists during the preceding decades. Their activities, in turn, may be seen against the background of the leading Swedish industry, mining and ironmaking. Several mineralogists made their discoveries working for the Board of Mines in Stockholm, the laboratory of which became Sweden's foremost center of analytical chemistry.

During the first half of the 18th century Sweden produced about one-third of all the iron made in Europe, and the country was by far the leading exporter of this metal. England, in particular, depended on Swedish iron and steel, and finished products were shipped to its American colonies. Sweden's dominating position was based on its ample resources of unusually pure ore, water power, and timber for the making of charcoal, but its metallurgical and technological advances were also of great importance, and consistent attention was paid to the quality of the iron. The meticulous precision that still characterizes Sweden's steelmaking, one of the reasons why its specialty steels today have steady customers in the United States and most other industrial countries, is a heritage of the 18th century. Although the Swedish ironmasters of the 1700s, many of whom were of Walloon or German origin, as a rule jealously guarded their secrets of production, these gradually spread to other countries, in the first place to England and Russia which became an important exporter of iron. In the early 1700s Swedish prisoners of war had helped to introduce Western technology at the new ironworks in the Ural Mountains in eastern Russia.

After the middle of the 1700s, when the English had begun to smelt with coke and thus made mass production possible, Sweden began to lose its supremacy in iron, but the second half of the century was, nevertheless, one of the great periods in the history of its iron industry. Its central figure was Sven Rinman (1720–92), who had a thorough knowledge of metallurgy both at home and abroad, and whose activities ranged from scientific research and technical invention to industrial construction and management. It was largely because of him that theoretical progress almost immediately was followed by practical applications. At the same time, specialists in mineralogy, chemistry, and physics received valuable impulses from him.

Ironmaking and related research, together with the long experience in copper mining, helped activate the interest in other ores and metals. In 1735 Georg Brandt (1694–1768) discovered a new metallic element, cobalt, in 1751 Axel Fredrik Cronstedt (1722–65) isolated nickel, and in 1752 Henrik Teofilus Scheffer (1710–59) became the first scientist to describe "white gold" or platinum, which in small quantities had been introduced into Europe from South America. All three worked for the Board of Mines in Stockholm, and it has been said that "together they represented the largest fund of knowledge in chemistry and mineralogy" at that time. In Germany both cobalt and nickel had previously been mistaken for copper ore, and since they refused to yield copper, they were thought to be possessed by evil spirits and given the names of Kobold, or goblin, and Kupfernickel, or Old Nick's copper. Cronstedt's findings were later confirmed by another Swedish chemist, Torbern Bergman, and the name nickel became, like cobalt, generally accepted.

Together with Sven Rinman and another outstanding mineralogist, Anton von Swab (1702–68), Cronstedt introduced the blowpipe into chemical research, and somewhat later other Swedish scientists, including Bergman, made extended use of this method and effected many improvements. Cronstedt's principal work in mineralogy was translated into English, French, German, Italian, and Russian, and several minerals, including zeolite, were named by him. One of his teachers, Johan Gottschalk Wallerius (1709–85), published a comprehensive book dealing with the chemical foundations of agriculture, which also was translated into many languages, including English and Spanish. It became a widely used international handbook and gave Wallerius the honorary title "Father of agricultural chemistry." He applied his ideas practically at a model farm near Uppsala.

Chemical research in full bloom with Torbern Bergman and Carl Scheele

THE flowering of chemical research in Sweden reached its height in the early 1770s, when two of the country's greatest scientists, Torbern Bergman (1735–84) and Carl Wilhelm Scheele (1742–86), were active at Uppsala. The latter was not attached to the university but earned his living as an assistant in a pharmacy. Among their students and friends were Johan Gottlieb Gahn (1745–1818) and Peter Jacob Hjelm (1746–1813), both eminent mineral chemists.

As a young man Bergman had studied insects, a butterfly being named for him by Linnaeus, and somewhat later he did remarkable work in astronomy, physics, and physical geography. In 1767 he became professor of chemistry at Uppsala, and after a few years he was recognized as one of Europe's foremost chemists. His laboratory, in a deplorable condition when he took over, was developed into a model research center, in a beautiful building which still survives.

Through innumerable experiments Bergman worked out a systematic procedure for qualitative analysis of substances in solutions, the basic principles of which are still used in laboratories all over the world, and he was also a pioneer in the field of quantitative analysis. He studied the properties of carbonic acid and the carbon content in iron and steel, analyzed numerous minerals, and created a new and more convenient chemical nomenclature. His international fame rested, above all, on his theory of chemical affinity, which prevailed for almost a century, but today he is best known as the founder of chemical analysis. He is also regarded as one of the two fathers of the carbonated-water industry, the other being Joseph Priestley of Pennsylvania and England.

Like other Swedish scientists of the 18th century, Bergman received flattering offers from abroad, first from Russia, then from Spain, and finally from King Frederick the Great of Prussia. In the Swedish Academy of Sciences he made his entrance in 1764 with an address about thunder and the lightning rod, which had been invented 12 years earlier by Benjamin Franklin. He became one of the most successful academic teachers of his era, and many scientists from other countries attended his courses and seminars.

One of his students was a young Swede from Finland, Johan Gadolin (1760–1852), who later, as a university professor in his native country, did pioneer work concerning the chemistry of rare earths and in physics helped place the science of heat on modern foundations. The first rare-earth element, now of particular interest in nuclear fission, was named gadolinium in his honor. The mineral studied by Gadolin came from Ytterby in the Stockholm archipelago, for which in the 19th century four rare-earth elements were named.

Torbern Bergman played a significant part in discovering Carl Wilhelm Scheele, who, although largely self-taught, became one of the greatest experimental chemists of all time. During his relatively brief life, and despite years of near-poverty and primitive laboratory conveniences, he discovered more new substances of fundamental importance than any other chemist. Much of his work centered on the nature of combustion, in which the foundations of all physiology were also involved.

In the 1770s Scheele discovered three new chemical elements, oxygen, fluorine, and chlorine, and he helped to identify four others, barium, manganese, molybdenum, and tungsten or wolfram. Joseph Priestly has also been credited with the discovery of oxygen, in 1774, since Scheele was late in publishing his findings. Manganese was recognized by Scheele to be an important component of the oxide of a distinctive metal. At about the same time, in 1774, it was isolated by Johan Gottlieb Gahn, who shares the honor of the discovery. Gahnite, a mineral of the spinel group, found in Scandinavia and at Franklin Furnace in New Jersey, has been named in his honor.

Scheele's experiments also indicated the existence of molybdenum, while the metal itself a few years later, in 1782, was prepared in an impure form by Peter Jacob Hjelm, who is regarded as codiscoverer. The element tungsten, after the Swedish "tung sten" or heavy stone, was named by Axel Fredrik Cronstedt, who discovered nickel. Scheele proved that this heavy mineral contained a previously unknown metal, today generally called tungsten in America, which in 1783 was obtained by a Spanish mineralogist who had studied with Torbern Bergman at Uppsala. The heavy mineral itself is now known as scheelite.

Other important research by Scheele concerned nitric and sulfurous acids as well as arsenic and phosphorus and their compounds. From Prussian blue he obtained hydrocyanic acid, previously unknown, and he also discovered copper arsenite, still sometimes called

Scheele's green. He was the first to produce photographic printing paper, although he did not anticipate the art of photography. A number of vegetable acids were also isolated and investigated by him; and glycerol, a component part of all animal and vegetable fats and oils, was obtained for the first time in 1779, an event which has been celebrated as a milestone by the chemical industry in the United States. Many other substances discovered by Scheele have become vitally important in industrial production or in medical and other scientific research; but his work was of particular significance as one of the principal foundations for the subsequent rapid progress of chemistry.

Scheele was born in a Swedish possession in northern Germany but, in contrast to most of Sweden's other leading scientists of the 1700s, he never studied abroad. In 1775 he was invited to membership in the Swedish Academy of Sciences, a unique distinction for a young pharmacist without a diploma. Somewhat later he moved to Köping, a small town southwest of Uppsala, and there he obtained a pharmacy of his own. In 1777 King Frederick the Great offered him a professorship in Berlin, and a similar invitation came from England. His health was gradually undermined by the conditions under which he worked, including frequent handling of the most toxic materials, and he died at the age of 43.

In more detailed biographies of numerous Swedish scientists and other specialists of the 18th century the name Linnaeus appears again and again, and even Carl Wilhelm Scheele's career was indirectly influenced by him. In the late 1760s, when Scheele worked in a pharmacy at Malmö in the south, he won the lasting support of Anders Jahan Retzius (1742–1821), a young professor at the University of Lund, who later became a famous naturalist and a close friend of Linnaeus. A plant genus as well as a group of animal fossils were named Retzia after him. In Stockholm, where Scheele lived in 1768–70, he found some influential new supporters, including Abraham Bäck, the noted physician, and Peter Johan Bergius (1730–90), a botanist and medical specialist, both of whom owed much to inspiration from Linnaeus. Bergius's personal relations with his somewhat domineering master became, on the other hand, strained. Today he is known above all as the founder of the Bergian scientific collections and experimental gardens in Stockholm, which belong to the

Academy of Sciences. Many North American plants were first grown by him in Stockholm, and by Retzius in the botanical garden at Lund in southern Sweden.

New foundations for study of living things laid by Linnaeus and others

LINNAEUS, who in Sweden is known as Carl von Linné, amassed more knowledge of living nature than any scientist before him and became the principal architect of modern systematic biology. He was the first to assign successfully every known animal and plant to its class, order, genus, and species, and the broad outline of this system of classification has remained. His simple but revolutionary method of arranging living things into genera and species, and naming them accordingly, even including Homo sapiens, has long been universally accepted. Today, a third Latin term indicating subspecies, or geographic races, is added when required.

In his botanical classification Linnaeus used the sex differences in plants, which were virtually discovered by him, but he realized that the goal must be a natural system based on true plant relationships, about which comparatively little was known at the time. Many of the basic rules set forth by him remain valid today; he helped lay the groundwork for economic botany, plant ecology, and plant geography. He may also be regarded as one of the first champions of both conservation and environmental health, although the problems of waste and pollution had not become acute during his lifetime. Some of the larger cities in Europe were, however, extremely unsanitary, and Linnaeus was harsh in his descriptions of them.

As a systematizer Linnaeus also made lasting contributions to zoology, including the departments dealing with birds, insects, and shells or mollusks. The foundations he laid for systematic entomology, or insect biology, which now handles some 800,000 different species, were particularly important. Significant entomological studies were also conducted by another Swedish scholar of the 18th century, Charles De Geer (1720–78), whose main work, in the French language, was published in seven volumes in 1752–78. A great-grandson of the famous Louis De Geer of the 17th century, he developed a family estate in the province of Uppland, north of Stockholm, into Sweden's largest producer of iron and became, like his Dutch-

Swedish ancestor, the country's wealthiest man. Another entomologist, Carl Alexander Clerck (1709–65), who had no financial resources but was encouraged by Linnaeus, became a pioneer in the study of spiders.

Fishes were also classified by Linnaeus, and in this case he adopted a system introduced by a close friend from his student years at Uppsala, Peter Artedi (1705–35). It is still in use today, having been laid down in international agreements. Artedi, who at the age of 30 died in an accident in Amsterdam, is regarded as the founder of ichthyology, the scientific study of fishes.

The son of a Lutheran minister, Linnaeus was born in the southern province of Småland on May 23, 1707, "in the most beautiful springtime when the cuckoo was heralding summer," as he writes in his autobiography. After university studies at Lund and Uppsala, he spent the years 1735–38 abroad — in Germany, Holland, England, and France. In Holland he took his doctor's degree, many of his books were first published there, and his international fame was established before he returned to Sweden. For a few years he practiced medicine in Stockholm, and in 1741 he was appointed professor of medicine and botany at Uppsala, where he taught until a few years before his death in 1778. He lies buried in Uppsala Cathedral.

Because of Linnaeus, Uppsala became for several decades the international center of botany and other studies having to do with living nature. Hundreds of students attended his lectures and took part in his excursions, and many of these came from other European countries. Russia, for instance, was well represented, and the famous naturalist also had pupils from America and Africa. Sometimes he lectured on public-health subjects, such as dietary practice and sex education. As a medical expert he was also a pioneer in nautical medicine, in pointing out that living organisms are responsible for many diseases, and in stressing the need for regular physical exercise.

Linnaeus's literary production was prodigious, comprising a large number of enormous scientific works in Latin and hundreds of smaller books and essays in Latin or Swedish. Under the auspices of the parliament he traveled widely in Sweden to take stock of its natural resources. His travel reports, which were highly personal accounts, helped fashion modern Swedish prose.

He was a man of great simplicity, with a deep, religious devotion to nature and a sound outlook on life, but toward the end he was in poor health, having worked beyond his strength, and dark moods prevailed. Fundamentally he was, in fact, a more complex genius than his contemporaries with some exceptions realized. Parallels have, for instance, been drawn between him and another famous Swede, August Strindberg, who began his stormy career several generations later. Strindberg had a profound admiration for Linnaeus. Before that, the Swedish naturalist had won enthusiastic admirers among the great in other countries, including Rousseau in France, Goethe in Germany, and Charles Darwin in England.

In 1784, when Linnaeus's son and successor at Uppsala had died, his library and famous herbarium with some 19,000 plant sheets, as well as large collections of insects and shells, were offered for sale. Numerous manuscripts and about 3,000 letters to Linnaeus, most of them from correspondents outside Sweden, were also included. Everything was purchased by a young English medical student and naturalist, James Edward Smith, and since his death in 1828 the treasures have been in the possession of the Linnean Society of London, which Smith had helped found in 1788. This association has been of untold importance to the study of Linnaeus, to research concerning the history of natural science and even to the interest in botany and nature, especially in the English-speaking world, including America. At an early stage, a previously unpublished travel diary by Linnaeus as well as a selection from his correspondents, in two volumes, were made available in English translations.

It was at a meeting of the Linnean Society of London in 1858 that Charles Darwin first announced the theory of evolution by natural selection, and his famous *Origin of Species* was published the following year. Linnaeus could not foresee the scientific revolution launched by Darwin, but in his later years he had begun to search in new directions, considering the possibility of new species arising out of older ones.

The greatest collections of Linnaeana after those in Burlington House in London are in the university library at Uppsala. Linnaeus's house in Uppsala, moreover, appears today essentially as it did in the 18th century. It adjoins the old university botanical garden, which was laid out in 1657 by Olaus Rudbeck. Six miles from Uppsala, at Hammarby, is Linnaeus's beloved country home, with traditions from the

14th century, which one of his great-grandsons in 1879 sold to the University of Uppsala.

Linnaeus's impact on scientific progress was multiplied by his numerous pupils, and a number of his Swedish ones will be mentioned in the following section, after which we come to some other aspects of his work, especially his direct influence in America.

Linnaeus's "apostles" help explore the world, pioneering botanical research

AT UPPSALA, which despite its fruitful intellectual activities remained a primitive university town with meager resources, Linnaeus mapped out a sweeping program of biological investigation of the earth, and from 1746 one after another of his disciples became cogs in an international research machine with few parallels in the history of science.

Linnaeus himself regarded the travelers, or at least most of them, as his "apostles." The first to set out from Sweden were Christopher Tärnström (1711–46), who en route to China died on an island near Cambodia, and Pehr, or Peter, Kalm (1716–79), who spent two and a half years in North America, and about whom more will be said shortly. These two were followed by at least a dozen other naturalists, who helped explore the Middle East, Africa, the East Indies, the east coast of Australia, New Zealand and the smaller islands of the South Pacific, China, Japan, the north of South America, Siberia, and parts of the Arctic and Antarctic regions.

One of the last traveling naturalists trained by Linnaeus, Carl Peter Thunberg (1743–1828), became the greatest botanical explorer of the 18th century, and has been called the "Father of South African botany" as well as the "Linnaeus of Japan." At that time Japan was closed to all foreigners except merchants of the Dutch East India Company, who were confined to an emporium on an island near Nagasaki, and Thunberg therefore entered Dutch service. To begin with he spent nearly three years in South Africa, and via Java he moved to Japan where he lived for 16 months. He was on friendly terms with the Japanese, especially physicians and scientists who were eager to learn about the Western world, and managed to collect nearly 2,000 plants which were new to science and later were described in his principal work, *Flora Japonica*. A monument to him is to be found at Nagasaki. Thunberg's travel diaries in four volumes, which contain the first more exhaustive information about Japan available in the West, were translated into English, French, and German. During the last 50-odd years of his life he was professor of medicine and botany at the University of Uppsala, which received his large collections.

Two other "apostles," Olof Torén (1718–53) and Pehr Osbeck (1723–1805), also went to the Far East, including China. Daniel Solander (1733–82) sailed around the world on Captain James Cook's first voyage of exploration in 1768–71, and Anders Sparrman (1748–1820), who already had visited South Africa and China, took part in Cook's second expedition in 1772–75, when the Antarctic Circle was crossed for the first time in history. In 1787 Sparrman and two other Swedes were sent to Senegal in West Africa, where they tried to find an area suitable for a Swedish colony without slavery.

While Sparrman later pursued his scientific work in Stockholm and wrote one of the more entertaining travel reports of the 1700s, Solander remained in England where he was regarded as a leading authority in the fields of botany and zoology. Today he is, in the first place, recognized as a pioneer in the botanical exploration of the South Pacific. Solander Island south of New Zealand's South Island was named for him, a monument in Swedish granite stands on Botany Bay at Sydney, Australia, and he is also commemorated in Cape Solander north of that city. In England and other English-speaking countries, Solander's name lives on in the term solander or solander box, that is, a box in the shape of a book which is used for keeping pamphlets, maps, etc. His foremost English patron was Sir Joseph Banks, who also joined Captain Cook's first expedition and later for more than four decades served as president of England's illustrious Royal Society. He was also one of the founders of the Linnean Society of London. Like Solander he was honored with the name of a plant genus, Banksia, which is well known in America. Botany Bay at Sydney was so named because of the many plants Solander and Banks found there.

Three of Linnaeus's most promising pupils died, like Tärnström, before they had completed their explorations: Fredrik Hasselquist (1722–52) in Turkey, Pehr Löfling (1729–56) in the jungles of Venezuela, and Peter Forsskål (1732–63) in Arabia. During their brief lives, however, all three made significant contributions to natural sci-

73

ence. Forsskål's Egyptian-Arabian flora is regarded as a work of the highest merit, and Löfling, whom Linnaeus mourned as his "dearest and best disciple," helped introduce a new epoch in the scientific exploration of South America. Before going there he spent two years in Spain and was named professor of botany by the government at Madrid. His letters and plant descriptions were published by Linnaeus and translated into English, German, and Spanish.

Surinam or Dutch Guiana in northeastern South America was explored by Daniel Rolander (1725–93). One of Linnaeus's disciples, Georg Rothman (1739–78), went to Tripoli in northern Africa and another, Adam Afzelius (1750–1837), brought back rich collections from Sierra Leone on Africa's west coast. Anton Martin (1729–85) became in 1758 the first Scandinavian to make a scientific exploration of arctic regions. After having been recommended by Linnaeus, Johan Peter Falck (1732–74) was appointed professor of botany and medicine in St. Petersburg, the capital of Russia, and later he took part in the first comprehensive scientific survey of the vast Russian territory, including Siberia. A significant role in the exploration of Siberia was also played by a Swede from Finland, Erik Laxman (1737–96), for many years professor at the Russian Academy of Science, who carried on a lively correspondence with Linnaeus. He died during an expedition to Japan to which the Swedish Academy of Sciences had contributed funds.

Sven Waxell (1701–62), who had no connection with Linnaeus, helped explore northeastern Asia and discover the American shores to the east, that is, Alaska. After having left Sweden as a young man and served in the British navy, he came to Russia at the age of 24. In 1733 he joined the second expedition conducted by Vitus Bering, a Danish officer and navigator who had entered the Russian navy, and after whom the Bering Sea and Strait, which separate Asia and Alaska, were named. On July 16, 1741, the explorers sighted a summit in southern Alaska which they called Mount St. Elias, and four days later a landing was made on an island now known as Kayak Island. At this time the command of Bering's ship was turned over to Waxell. After Bering and many other participants had succumbed on the return voyage, Waxell led the survivors, including one of his own sons and two Swedish sailors, back to Asia and ultimately to St. Petersburg. Important scientific collections and findings were also rescued as a result of his efforts. He was, a Russian scientist has observed, the only member of the Bering expedition who took part in this grandiose venture from its beginning until its end 16 years later. Waxell finally became a captain in the Russian navy.

Beginning of Linnaeus's influence in America —
Kalm's scientific tour

AFTER Isaac Newton and other Englishmen, Linnaeus was the first scientist to become widely known in America. The interest in him began soon after the publication of his first important work, *Systema Naturae*, in Holland in 1735, and by the middle of the century it was stimulated by Peter Kalm's American tour. Linnaeus's influence and his disciple's visit contributed greatly to the growing enthusiasm for botany and a systematic study of nature in 18th-century America.

Kalm was sent to North America by the Academy of Sciences in Stockholm on Linnaeus's recommendation, and he was accompanied by an expert gardener, Lars Jungström. His methodical studies on this continent were begun in September of 1748, and when he left for Europe in February of 1751 he had covered parts of Pennsylvania, New Jersey, New York, and New England, as well as southern Canada. To Sweden he sent or brought a large collection of plant specimens, as well as seeds which he thought might be usefully grown in Northern Europe. The results of his botanical explorations were utilized by other botanists, chiefly Linnaeus.

In Philadelphia, where the tour began, Kalm met "the learned Mr. Benjamin Franklin," who became his "very special friend" and in 1750 had a letter from him about the Niagara Falls published in a local journal. This was the first eyewitness account of Niagara to appear in print. At this time Franklin had begun his experiments with electricity, which won him an unusual reputation in Sweden. His subsequent political career and progressive ideas added greatly to his fame.

Among other American friends of Kalm were John Bartram of Pennsylvania, who has been mentioned above, and Cadwallader Colden, physician and botanist, who in 1761–66 served as lieutenant governor of New York. Colden played a leading part in introducing the Linnaean system of classification into America, and he furnished Linnaeus with descriptions of several hundred American plants. His daughter Jane followed in his footsteps and became the first great woman botanist in America.

In his travel diary Kalm mentions several other American colonists who were students of Linnaeus and, as a rule, corresponded with him. James Logan, an Irish-born jurist who had read Linnaeus's *Systema Naturae* immediately after its publication, became chief justice of Pennsylvania and founder of its first university. John Clayton and John Mitchell, both natives of England, explored the plant life of Virginia and Maryland, and the former made vital contributions to a book, *Flora Virginiana*, which with Linnaeus's assistance was published in Holland.

In 1753–61 Kalm's report on his American explorations, titled *Travels in North America, 1748–51*, was published in Stockholm in three volumes, which almost immediately were translated into German, and then into French, English, and Dutch. He did not have Linnaeus's gift of expressive presentation, but his work has won appreciation because of its honesty and wealth of interesting facts. It was the first comprehensive natural history of the New World, and reviews, comments, and quotations appeared in numerous languages. Conditions in America, which, as Kalm wrote, many Europeans regarded as "almost wholly inhabited by savage or heathen nations," thus became much better known. The most recent edition of Kalm's book in the English language is a two-volume paperback published in New York, Toronto, and London in 1966.

One of the most widely read books in America by the middle of the 18th century was, according to Kalm's impressions, Voltaire's *History of Charles XII*, which immediately after its publication in 1731 had been translated into English. Traveling on a boat on the Hudson River, Kalm found that the passengers had brought this book about the Swedish warrior king "to help while away the time." Large parts of his report were, as was to be expected, devoted to plants, animals, and natural phenomena, but he also described in detail economic, religious, and social conditions. On several occasions he expressed strong opinions of his own, and he warned, for instance, against ruthless deforestation and carelessness in agriculture. The "easy method of getting a rich crop" had, he felt, spoiled the settlers, and in another entry in his diary he wrote: "We can hardly be more hostile toward our woods in Sweden and Finland than they are here: their eyes are fixed upon the present gain, and they are blind to the future." Old Swedish settlers told him that in the Delaware Valley there was much less fowl and fish than 50–75 years earlier, and similar observations were made in Canada.

Kalm was born in northern Sweden of parents who had fled there from Finland because of the wars. From 1751, when he came back from his American tour, he served as professor of natural history in the Swedish university at Åbo (or Turku) in Finland, and at this post he spread valuable information about the New World. He sponsored 146 doctoral dissertations, including six on American topics. In 1750 he had married the widow of the pastor of the Swedish congregation at Raccoon (now Swedesboro) in New Jersey, and at one time he hoped to make a second visit to America, earning his living as a clergyman in the Delaware Valley.

Many plant names dating from Linnaeus widely used in America

SINCE Linnaeus created the modern biological terminology and, in particular, botanical nomenclature, he has directly or indirectly contributed many more new words to the English language than any other individual. Such plant names as dahlia, forsythia, gardenia, kalmia, rudbeckia, and zinnia are in daily use in America and other English-speaking countries, and numerous others are well known not only by botanists but also by gardeners, florists, and amateur flower lovers. The botanical Latin created by Linnaeus led to the introduction into English of such words as petal and stamen.

A great many plant groups of Europe, the Americas, Africa, and Asia were named by the Swedish naturalist for other botanists and scholars, and his disciples and successors followed his example. A genus of some 30 North American perennials Linnaeus called Rudbeckia, in honor of both Olof Rudbeck the Younger (1660–1740), who was his predecessor in the chair of botany at Uppsala, and the latter's father, Olaus Rudbeck. This group includes the black-eyed Susan, state flower of Maryland.

The whole American pineapple family, provided by nature with a built-in water system that creates its own humidity, was named for Olof Bromelius (1639–1707), one of Sweden's foremost botanists before Linnaeus. Its more than 2,000 varieties have become known as bromeliads, and in the United States there is a national association with headquarters in Los Angeles, The Bromeliad Society. One of the numerous groups of this family, Bromelia, was also named for Bromelius, and another Linnaeus called Tillandsia in honor of Elias Tillandz (1640–93), a Swedish-born physician who, as professor at the University of Åbo, became Finland's first scientific botanist. A third genus of the pineapple family was later named Billbergia in honor of a Swedish naturalist, Gustaf Johan Billberg (1772–1844).

Since then, three more groups of the pineapple family, Mosenia, Wittrockia, and Lindmania, have been named for Swedish botanists. Most of these plants are found in South America, and in the 19th century Swedish scientists were able to explore the flora of this continent thanks to generous support from Anders Fredrik Regnell (1807–84), who, after studies of medicine and botany at Uppsala, for reasons of health moved to Brazil at the age of 33, and by a successful medical practice, shrewd investments, and unusual frugality became a very wealthy man. Regnell made large donations to the University of Uppsala, in fact, the largest this institution had received since King Gustavus Adolphus in 1624 presented it with a substantial share of his personal land holdings. Two plant groups, one of them the orchid genus Regnellia, have been named for Dr. Regnell.

A genus of tropical American annuals of the potato family Linnaeus named Browallia in honor of his pupil Johan Browallius (1707–55), who, as a university professor at Åbo from 1737, introduced the exact sciences into Finland. One member of this genus, often simply called browallia, is a familiar sight in American summer gardens or on porches.

For Pehr Kalm, who later joined the university at Åbo, Linnaeus named a small genus of North American evergreen shrubs Kalmia. The best-known species of this group is the mountain laurel or Kalmia latifolia, state flower of both Connecticut and Pennsylvania. Plants or flowers of this genus are often called kalmias. Another Linnaeus pupil who finally also taught at Åbo, Anders Dahl (1751–89), gave his name to a genus of Mexican and Central American herbs of the thistle family which have become as popular in Europe as they are in the United States. This generic term, Dahlia, was chosen by a Spanish botanist.

Including Pehr Kalm, the names of no less than twelve of Linnaeus's traveling "apostles" live on in the names of herbs, shrubs, and trees. A tropical African climber which, like a Rudbeckia species, has become known in the United States as black-eyed Susan, is a member of the genus Thunbergia, another widely used name. The African hemp, also often cultivated, belongs to the group Sparmannia, and the scarletseed to the genus Ternstroemia. At least one species of the group Torenia of African and Asiatic herbs has also become popular in America. The other generic plant names recalling Linnaeus's traveling Swedish disciples of the 18th century are Afzelia, Falckia, Forsskalea, Loeflingia, Osbeckia, Rolandra, and Solandra.

A group of well-known ornamental shrubs, Forsythia, Linnaeus named for William Forsyth, a Scotsman who had brought back the first specimens from China, and another has become known as Deutzia, after Johann van der Deutz of Holland who was a friend and patron of Linnaeus's disciple Carl Thunberg, the great botanical explorer. A genus of flowering shrubs of tropical Africa and Asia, including the crape myrtle which is commonly planted in the southern United States, Linnaeus named Lagerstroemia for Magnus von Lagerström (1691–1759), a Gothenburg merchant and patron of science. Zinnia, a genus of American annuals including the garden zinnia which is the state flower of Indiana, derives its name from Johan Gottfried Zinn, a German botanist who corresponded with Linnaeus.

Chiefly because of Linnaeus, the names of his correspondents and friends in America continue to live in the world of flowers and plants. The best known of all the groups concerned, Gardenia, was named by the Swedish naturalist for Alexander Garden of Charleston, South Carolina, who for a time served as professor at King's College in New York, now Columbia University. In 1761 he wrote to the Swedish botanist that he was dreaming of a heaven "where Linnaeus is explaining the wonders of the world to legions of white candid spirits."

A group of North American herbs of the thistle family, Linnaeus named Kuhnia in honor of Adam Kuhn, who had studied with him at Uppsala and became professor of botany and medicine in what is now the University of Pennsylvania. In honor of John Clayton, a genus of mainly North American spring-blooming perennials, among them the common spring beauty, was named Claytonia, and John Mitchell, who also explored the flora of Virginia, gave his name to the small genus Mitchella, which includes the evergreen trailing partridgeberry. Isaac Lawson, a wealthy Scotsman who had helped Linnaeus in

Holland and had written a book titled *Travels in North Carolina*, was honored with the genus Lawsonia, the only species of which is the henna plant. The names of Bartram, Colden, and Logan also live on in the world of nature.

About 8,000 species of plants from all over the earth, including nearly 800 from North America, were described and named by Linnaeus, and most of his terms are still in use. Not only his feelings of friendship and respect but also his humor and irony were often expressed even in his plant names, or in his descriptions and comments. A group of evergreen palm-like plants of Florida and tropical America he named Zamia, not after another botanist but because of the barren appearance of the male cones, the Latin zamia meaning damage or loss. The lovely twin-flower Linnaea borealis, the only plant named for Linnaeus himself, he described as "a plant of Lapland, lowly, insignificant, disregarded, flowering but for a brief space — from Linnaeus, who resembles it." During his travels in America, Kalm found this flower in the herbarium of John Bartram.

In the naming of the plants, Linnaeus kept many of the old generic terms. He approved, for instance, of names taken from mythology or poetry, such as Anemone, which in ancient Greece was the name of the daughter of the winds. Anemones are also known as windflowers. American trees permanently classified and named in Latin by Linnaeus include, for instance, the red cedar, the smooth sumac, and the persimmon.

Linnaeus and the birds' "light cavalry" — Fifty-eight
societies named for him

THOMAS JEFFERSON, who won a reputation as a naturalist a few years after he had drafted the Declaration of Independence, was invited in 1824, two years before his death, to a meeting of the Linnean Society of New York celebrating the anniversary of Linnaeus's birth in 1707. In answer, the former President wrote: "It would certainly be a great enjoyment to be present. . . . As that prospect, however, recedes from my view, another advances with steady and not distant steps, that of meeting the great naturalist himself, and of assuring him in person of the veneration and affection with which his memory is cultivated here."

While Linnaeus became known in America as a botanist in the first place, the study of birds was also stimulated by him and his work. In the early 1800s, one of his most enthusiastic admirers in the United States was John James Audubon, whose bird portraits had a lasting impact on natural science. One of the rare birds which the experts of the National Audubon Society have tried to save from extinction, the white whooping crane or Grus americana, was identified by Linnaeus, who classified and named numerous other North American birds. A contemporary of Audubon in the study of American birds, Alexander Wilson, who first taught school in Pennsylvania and New Jersey, was also influenced by Linnaeus, probably in part via the last Swedish clergyman in the Delaware Valley, Nicholas Collin. Wilson's classic work *American Ornithology* was continued after his death by George Ord, who was of Swedish ancestry. Both were buried at Gloria Dei in Philadelphia.

Linnaeus's own writings in the ornithological field included a remarkably up-to-date thesis on the migration of birds, based in part on an early American ornithologist's observations, and essays describing such birds as the Indian sparrow, the golden oriole, and the fulmar. He spoke with tenderness about birds, which toward the end of his life he described as "cavalry, light, nimble, resplendently clad."

At his home in Uppsala the Swedish naturalist kept a number of exotic pets, including parrots and peacocks as well as a South American agouti and two raccoons from North America. The raccoons were among his favorites, and for the Swedish Academy of Sciences he wrote a report entitled *Description of an American Animal*, which is regarded as one of his best accounts dealing with mammals.

No less than 58 societies in 42 cities on four continents have been named for Linnaeus, and the foremost is, of course, the Linnean Society of London, founded in 1788. The year before a French botanist established Société Linnéenne de Paris, which in the early 1800s became the center of a romantic worship of Linnaeus in many parts of the world. The Philadelphia Linnean Society, founded in 1806, was the first association of its kind in the United States, and among the cities that followed were Boston and New York. The American societies were much more active in the old days than they have been in recent decades.

At least 100 towns, lakes, forests, rivers, streets, etc. in the world bear Linnaeus's name, although the spelling varies somewhat. In the

United States, there are Linneus townships in Maine and Missouri. The land in Maine was granted in 1804 to establish a professorship in botany at Harvard, while Linneus, Missouri, was named in 1841. Illinois has a forest preserve called Linné Woods, and Chicago a Carl von Linné Elementary School, founded in 1895. For many years, New York had a Linnaeus Bridge over the Bronx River. At least 11 vessels have borne Linnaeus's name. The first was built in Flushing, New York, in 1829, and one of the latest was a Russian refrigeration ship commissioned in 1964.

Medals with Linnaeus's portrait have been struck in nine countries, the total of such items being about 70. Monuments have been erected in at least 12 countries, and the city of Edinburgh in Scotland seems to have been first in 1778. At the entrance to the Linnean Plant House in the Missouri Botanical Garden at St. Louis there is a bust of marble dating from 1882. In 1885, a large statue of Linnaeus was unveiled in a park near the center of Stockholm, some 30,000 people headed by King Oscar II attending the ceremony. In 1891, Lincoln Park in Chicago received a copy of this statue. A ceremony has been held there annually on Linnaeus's birthday, May 23.

On the moon, the pioneer naturalist is represented by a mound with a crater in the eastern part of Mare Serenitatis. On the side of the moon facing the earth, six other formations, all of them relatively modest, have been named for Swedish scientists. When the hidden side of the moon was mapped in the 1960s, 13 Swedish names were included.

In America as well as in England, newborn boys were sometimes christened Charles Linnaeus or simply Linnaeus, which does not seem to have happened in Sweden. Charles Willson Peale, who began his career as a saddlemaker and in the 1770s became America's leading portrait painter, named several of his numerous sons after famous painters, such as Raphael, Rembrandt, and Rubens, but toward the end he had two boys christened after Charles Linnaeus and Benjamin Franklin. In Sweden, Linnea has been a popular girl's name.

When the University of Uppsala celebrated the 250th anniversary of Linnaeus's birth in 1957, the speakers used the same lectern from which the naturalist delivered his lectures, and the traditional laurel wreaths for the new doctors were from the laurel tree the great botanist himself planted in his Uppsala garden. Among the foreign scientists and humanists honored for their work in connection with Linnaeus were three Americans. The Linnean Society of London observed the jubilee by exhibiting choice objects from its rich collections, among them Linnaeus's own specimen of the Linnea borealis, the flower he picked during his journey through Swedish Lapland in 1732.

In the United States, a large memorial exhibition was organized in 1957 by the University of Kansas libraries at Lawrence. Their Linnaean collections rank among the largest in the country, and they include nearly all of Linnaeus's major works in many editions, of which at least a hundred are firsts. Originally, most of the material was assembled by the late Ralph N. Ellis and Thomas Jefferson Fitzpatrick, said to have been the leading private collectors of works by and about Linnaeus in the United States. The Strandell Room of the Hunt Institute at the Carnegie-Mellon University in Pittsburgh, an international center for the history of botany, has nearly 4,000 volumes by and about Linnaeus. They were acquired from Dr. Birger Strandell (b. 1901) in Stockholm, a descendant of Linnaeus in the sixth generation and for many years a pillar of the Swedish Linnean Society, who had built up the largest private collection of Linnaeus's writings. The Strandell Room was dedicated in 1973 when a large Linnaeus symposium was held at the Hunt Institute in Pittsburgh.

★ 5

The Gustavian Era
and the American Revolution

Swedes gain greater equality under Gustav III —
Arts and letters flourish

SWEDEN'S golden age of science did not, of course, come to an abrupt end, but it was on the wane in the 1780s, when Linnaeus had died and both Torbern Bergman and Carl Wilhelm Scheele passed away.

A new cultural and political era had actually dawned in 1772, when the 26-year-old King Gustav III (1746–92) assumed the leadership of an army revolt against the parliamentary regime and enlarged the royal power. Not a drop of blood was spilled. The experience in parliamentarism gained during the preceding decades would prove valuable later on, but most people were tired of the party feuds and other political excesses, and they looked to the new King for improvement. After two successive unusually bad harvests and a drastic inflation, the economic conditions were desperate, and bands of starving beggars roamed the country. The population of Sweden proper had increased to about 2 million, and that of Finland to nearly 600,000.

The monarch was filled with enthusiasm for the welfare and potential greatness of his country, and many constructive reforms were effected during the first 10–15 years of his reign. The monetary system and the public finances as well as the administration were set in better order, and the tariffs were lowered. A measure of religious freedom was introduced, and torture as an instrument of legal investigation was abolished. The King even wanted to do away with capital punishment, the application of which was restricted.

The defense system was also modernized; the navy especially was strengthened considerably. Under Fredric Henric af Chapman (1721–1808), who had studied shipbuilding in England, France, and Holland, naval construction was raised to a science, and series-produced vessels were launched for the first time. One of Sweden's most competent and imaginative engineers of this era, Johan Erick Norberg (1749–1818), who had studied at Uppsala, made a successful career in the naval engineering corps but later on spent most of his time in Russia. In 1800, when he lived in Sweden, he made a remarkable attempt to propel a ship by means of steam; he received much encouragement from King Gustav III's son and successor but stubborn resistance from sailing-ship skippers and other people who feared that steam-driven vessels would result in destructive competition. In Russia, where he died after having received unusual official recognition, his activities ranged from mining and metal engineering in Siberia to construction work in arctic Archangel and at Tallinn, the capital of Estonia. Norberg, who for a while tried his fortune in Denmark, was Sweden's first significant international engineer.

Swedish army officers were encouraged to spend some years of service abroad, especially in France, where a regiment with traditions from the late 1600s, known as the Royal Suédois, had Swedish commanders at all levels. In 1783 Count Axel von Fersen, who had just returned to Europe from the American War of Independence, became the last leader of this unit. New military experience was thus brought to Sweden, which, in turn, exported fresh ideas of its own. Some of the troop transports which Napoleon in the early 1800s built for his planned invasion of England were, for instance, based on drawings which had been picked up by a Dutch naval officer in Swedish service.

In the 1780s, new famines and the King's increasingly despotic government caused growing discontent in Sweden, but the most important political development was the widening gap between Gustav and the noblemen, who in the beginning had been his allies. In 1789, when Sweden had become involved in war with both Russia and Denmark, the monarch promulgated a new constitution which further extended the royal authority and curtailed the privileges of the nobles. The other three estates in the parliament, that is, clergy, burghers, and farmers, sided with the King.

The war with Russia brought, at first, serious reverses, but in 1790 the Swedish navy won one of its greatest victories, at Svensksund not far from the Russian capital, St. Petersburg. Peace was signed without territorial changes, and a period of friendly relations with Russia began. New internal problems, including another severe inflation, beset the Swedish government, but the King had begun to dream of a crusade against the French revolutionary government. Some of the projects he considered, such as a Swedish-Russian invasion of Normandy, were probably camouflage for more realistic ambitions, but two army officers were actually sent to France for a survey of the area from Le Havre to Paris.

In the spring of 1792, King Gustav was assassinated by a member of the aristocratic opposition, a fanatic who regarded the monarch as his personal enemy. The attack was made at a masked ball in the Opera House of Stockholm, which is the historical basis for the plot of an opera by Verdi, *Un Ballo in Maschera*, or *The Masked Ball*.

Despite his weaknesses, which were complicated by a personal crisis, Gustav III is widely regarded as one of the greatest sovereigns of the 18th century in Europe. Through his domestic policies he ushered in a social transformation which in other countries was accompanied by violent upheavals. A born aristocrat, he started undermining the ancient privileges of the nobility and opened the gates to the middle class and the farmers, two groups which in the 19th century would become more and more influential. The number of farm laborers, crofters, and farmers' sons without a prospect of land of their own was, however, growing — a problem which eventually would be solved by emigration to America.

The two decades when Gustav III ruled Sweden were an era of sharp contrasts, of distress and misery, on the one hand, and of healthful social change and cultural progress or at least splendor, on the other. Like his uncle, Frederick the Great of Prussia, the Swedish monarch was a great admirer of French civilization, and he fostered arts and letters with passionate interest. The Academy of Music in Stockholm was founded by him in 1771, the Royal Opera in 1773, the Swedish Academy, which today awards the Nobel prize in literature, in 1786, and the Royal Dramatic Theater in 1788. The unique Court

Theater at Drottningholm near Stockholm, where plays and operas are now staged during the summer season with the same costumes, scenery, and effects as in the 18th century, was also, essentially, King Gustav's creation. The operatic and theatrical traditions established by him have, in many ways, influenced personal relations and cultural exchanges between Sweden and America.

Of the eminent Swedish painters who added luster to King Gustav's era, Alexander Roslin (1718–93) is best known in America. He spent most of his life in Paris, where he had made his success in the 1750s. Toward the end of the century, a Swedish sculptor and draftsman, Johan Tobias Sergel (1740–1814), who had won fame in Rome, was one of the central figures in European art. His statue of Gustav III stands near the Royal Palace in Stockholm, which was built in 1697–1754 on the site occupied by a 13th-century castle known as Three Crowns and later destroyed by fire. A Swedish painter who finally settled in America, Adolf Ulric Wertmüller, studied drawing with Sergel in Paris, and there he also received instruction from his relative, Alexander Roslin, who introduced him to French masters.

The greatest poets of the Gustavian Age were Johan Henric Kellgren (1751–95), who as an outstanding liberal journalist helped pave the way for a better understanding of the ideas on which the American republic was founded, and Carl Michael Bellman (1740–95), who also was a composer of great merit. His songs about 18th-century life in Stockholm are both gay and melancholy, love, drinking, death, and the beauty of nature being their most common themes. They are still very popular, and several of them have often been heard in America. To a higher degree than most poets, Bellman defies translation, but some attempts have been made to interpret him in the English language.

In the writings of Carl Michael Bellman, there is at least one evidence of the lively interest with which the American struggle for national freedom was discussed in Sweden: the "hero" in some of his songs, he relates, went, as he often did, to a tavern in Stockholm, where he "found as usual the Society Pro Vino sitting with long Holland pipes and wise perukes by their glittering pear-glasses, constantly arguing about the good of the city, the English colonies, Washington, the price of hay, the scarcity of money, and similar subjects."

A TREATY WITH AMERICA

*Sweden signs a treaty of friendship and commerce with
the newborn American republic*

IN THE late summer of 1776, the American Declaration of Independence caused a stir in political and literary circles in Stockholm, and at first even King Gustav III reacted with enthusiasm.

From historic Gripsholm castle, on Lake Mälaren west of Stockholm, he wrote on October 18 to a French friend that observing how a state, so to speak, creates itself was indeed interesting, and that if he had not been what he was, that is, a ruling monarch, he would have gone to America himself "to follow, first-hand, all the aspects of the birth of this new republic." Perhaps, he added, this was the century of America, but however that may be, he could not help but admire the courage of the revolutionists and applaud their audacity.

Fundamentally the King was of two minds, for he also feared that the American rebels were setting a dangerous precedent that concerned all monarchs. He had, however, an instinctive feeling for the historic importance of the American fight for independence, and once the autonomy of the former colonies had been won, he hastened to recognize the new republic by concluding with it a treaty of friendship and commerce.

King Gustav naturally wanted Sweden to share in the trade with the New World, the control of which England was about to lose. American imports of Swedish iron had, in fact, increased during the war and had been of considerable assistance to the revolutionists. In his decision to make a pact with the United States the monarch was also, inevitably, influenced by his relations with the French, whose friendship was his principal international asset, and on whose financial support he depended for Sweden's rearmament.

France had, of course, welcomed the American revolution, but its leaders realized that recognizing the independence of the Thirteen Colonies would mean instant war with England, and for that they were not prepared. After the British defeat at Saratoga in the fall of 1777, however, they began to fear an American accommodation with London, and in February of 1778 Benjamin Franklin led them into two treaties with the revolutionists, one of friendship and commerce, and one of outright alliance. A few months later, France was at war with Britain.

In the spring of 1782, when news of the British surrender at

Yorktown had reached Europe, King Gustav instructed his ambassador in Paris to negotiate a treaty of friendship and commerce with the American envoy, Benjamin Franklin, and his government in Philadelphia. The Swedish ambassador, Count Gustaf Philip Creutz (1731–85), had supported the American cause from the beginning, and the first suggestion of an early Swedish recognition of the new state probably came from him. He had served in the French capital since 1766 and had become one of its most respected and successful envoys. Before Franklin arrived, nobody could match him in popularity.

Relations between Creutz and Franklin were extremely cordial, but in background and manners the two men were quite different. The Finnish-born Swedish diplomat had written graceful and sensuous poetry which still is regarded as one of the finest expressions of the rococo era in Sweden. In Paris he had a literary salon of his own, and when he gave balls and banquets, the fountains of his embassy palace spouted wine instead of water. After Franklin's arrival in Paris at the end of 1776, Creutz wrote that "never did a queerer figure appear in society." He knew, of course, that the American already had many friends in France, in particular scientists and philosophers, but he could hardly foresee the impression Franklin would make even on the ladies. Both envoys spent more money than they could afford, and Creutz amassed tremendous debts. In 1783 he became president of the King's Council in Stockholm and chancellor of the University of Uppsala.

Just before the end of 1782, an American agent called at the Swedish legation at The Hague, the Dutch capital, and reported as follows the contents of a letter from John Adams, who was to become the second President of the United States: "The King of Sweden has chosen to become the first power to offer a treaty with the United States. . . . Tell [the ambassador] privately that we shall see to it that we remember that it was his sovereign who was the first to do us this honor."

After having spent some time in Holland, which in 1780 had followed France into the war with England as a result of British interference with neutral shipping, John Adams had obtained from the Dutch in October of 1782 a treaty of amity and commerce, the second of its kind. Sweden seemed, therefore, to have been the first country to offer the Americans a pact of friendship and trade without special efforts by them. There was, on the other hand, a direct connection between the Swedish monarch's overtures to the United States and his political and financial relations with France, and John Adams may not have been aware of this. Without any doubt, however, Sweden became the third power to make a treaty with the United States, and the first country not engaged in the conflict to recognize the new republic.

The first draft of the treaty between Sweden and the United States was signed by Creutz and Franklin early in January of 1783, and one month later they affixed their signatures to a second version. On March 5, the treaty was finally concluded, but the document was postdated April 3. In view of Sweden's relations with Great Britain, the government in Stockholm proceeded with caution. The preliminary articles of the Anglo-American settlement had been signed on November 30, 1782, but the peace terms were not published until early the next year. The definitive treaty was signed in Paris on February 3 and ratified on September 3, 1783.

In Sweden as in other European countries including England, the outcome of the American War of Independence was hailed by liberal elements as a triumph of liberty and reason over antiquated tradition and arbitrary power. An eccentric but gifted Swedish poet, Bengt Lidner (1757–93), wrote a song, "The Year 1783," in which he saluted the American people who had enlivened the spirit of freedom, and added: "Thou wilt become everything with freedom, and thou hast deserved it all." In 1776 he had published a dissertation, *De jure revolutionis Americanorum*, which enthusiastically defended the American Revolution.

Despite the strains of the war period, Sweden had been able to maintain its friendly relations with Britain, and its ties with France had been strengthened. Two months after the conclusion of the Swedish treaty with the United States, the French government agreed to extend the payment of subsidies to Sweden for four years. In 1784 King Gustav III himself went to Paris and acquired from France a little island in the West Indies, St. Barthélemy. In return, Sweden granted French vessels certain commercial privileges in the harbor of Gothenburg. The acquisition of the island caused no enthusiasm in Sweden, but its leaders hoped that the colony would become an important base for a growing trade with the New World, and American merchants were delighted.

Sweden's struggle to protect neutral rights at sea significant for Americans

SWEDEN'S treaty of friendship and commerce with the United States was not, in itself, of very great value, but it represented a significant initial relation with a burgeoning independent nation and helped the prestige of the new republic. Sweden, on the other hand, won American good will for its commerce.

The treaty, which was ratified by Congress on July 27, 1783, was to be in force for 15 years. The first of its 29 articles proclaimed that "there shall be a firm, inviolable, and universal peace and a true and sincere friendship" between Sweden and the United States. The two countries further agreed on reciprocal most-favored-nation treatment, applied for the first time in the Franco-American commercial agreement of 1778.

Much of the treaty was devoted to commerce and shipping in times of war, and here it was based on principles in the defense of which the Swedes had played a prominent part during the worldwide conflict just terminated. From an American viewpoint this had been of greater value than the Swedish contributions of men and supplies to the Revolutionary cause. In Europe, Swedish ships were captured on the high seas, Sweden then became the first country to convoy merchant shipping in order to protect neutral rights, and gradually many other countries followed suit. Sweden's subsequent diplomatic relations with the United States were often influenced by a common interest in liberal maritime practices and the rights of neutrals.

The treaty of 1783 has been commemorated by the two countries on several formal occasions, and the emphasis has always been on the spirit in which it was reached, rather than on its contents. On April 3, 1956, the Franklin Medal, authorized by the 84th Congress to celebrate the 250th anniversary of Benjamin Franklin's birth, was presented to the Swedish government at a ceremony in the Foreign Office in Stockholm. "Franklin once wrote," American ambassador John Moors Cabot observed in his address, "that friendship between peoples created stronger ties than any treaties could make. We believe sincerely in that philosophy. We have been privileged to enjoy that kind of friendship with Sweden since our new country was born." Similar comments were made in 1958 in connection with the 175th anniversary of the signing and ratification of the treaty. In an address at the Skansen open-air museum and folk park in Stockholm on the Fourth of July, the Swedish foreign minister, Östen Undén (1886–1974), said: "Sweden has a long tradition of freedom, and we have always with sympathy followed the struggles of other peoples for national independence. This undoubtedly lay behind the interest that Sweden showed in the new North American republic and which, among other things, was expressed in its early recognition of that state."

The island of St. Barthélemy in the West Indies, which Sweden won almost as a by-product of the treaty with the United States, had a fine harbor, and there the Swedes founded the capital, Gustavia, which was named after King Gustav III. During the Napoleonic Wars and other struggles of the early 1800s the colony began to prosper, and at one time its population, which had been about 750 when the Swedes came, reached some 5,000, one-half of whom were slaves. The island did very little to promote Swedish-American commerce, but it became important for the American trade with the British and French West Indies, and during the War of 1812 for trade relations between the United States and Europe.

After 1830, St. Barthélemy, or St. Barts, as the island is called by the English-speaking inhabitants of the Caribbean, became an increasingly heavy burden on the Swedish budget. Slavery was abolished in 1847, but in reports to Stockholm the governors complained of growing poverty and distress, and the inhabitants seemed, with few exceptions, opposed to the Swedish rule. In 1878 the island was finally sold to France for 400,000 francs, which included compensation for Swedish property and pensions for Swedish officers. Later on, many inhabitants appeared to cherish their memories from the old era. In Sweden, the interest in St. Barts's Swedish period has been reactivated in recent decades.

As a result of a treaty of alliance with Great Britain in 1813, Crown Prince Carl Johan of Sweden received the much larger island of Guadeloupe, located in the same area, but this old French possession was repurchased by France the following year.

JOHN HANSON AND JOHN MORTON

*John Hanson, Morton, and other Swedish descendants
in the American struggle for freedom*

WHEN Sweden in 1782 opened the negotiations about a friendship treaty, John Hanson (1721–83), elder statesman of Maryland, was President of the United States in Congress Assembled, the first person elected with this title. His term had begun on November 5, 1781, and on November 28 he welcomed General Washington and introduced him to the Congress in Philadelphia.

John Hanson's Swedish ancestry has not been definitely established, but most authorities believe that his great-grandfather, Johan Hansson, was killed with King Gustavus Adolphus in a battle in Germany in 1632, and that his grandfather, who had the same name, came to New Sweden in 1643 at the age of 13 and moved to Maryland ten years later. Like the sons of many other well-to-do colonial families, John Hanson was probably educated in England.

In 1775, at the beginning of the Revolution, John Hanson played a leading part in rallying the colonists of Maryland, and the first troops sent to George Washington's assistance from the South were organized under his direction. As a member of the Continental Congress in 1780–81 he led the fight to vest title to the Western lands, west of the original colonies, in the new national government instead of dividing them, as had been begun, among individual states. Hanson's determined stand strengthened the union and is regarded as his most far-reaching contribution.

Under the Articles of Confederation, John Hanson was chief executive for one year, ending November 4, 1782. He had few of the powers of the President as defined by the Constitution of 1789, but the country's first cabinet was formed during his term of office, a consular system was established, and the postal service was expanded. Hanson also issued the first Thanksgiving Proclamation, fixing the last Thursday in November as a national day of prayer and expression of gratitude. The National Seal of the United States was first used by him on an official commission to General Washington to arrange for the exchange of prisoners of war with Great Britain.

John Hanson's portrait was painted by two artists, John Hesselius, who was born of Swedish parents, and Hesselius's former disciple, Charles Willson Peale, who did many portraits of George Washington. In 1903 a statue of John Hanson was erected in Statuary

Hall in the Capitol in Washington. In 1959 a monument of crimson Swedish granite, donated by a fraternal organization named the Vasa Order of America, was dedicated at his birthplace, Mulberry Grove at Port Tobacco, Maryland. In 1967 a memorial called the Seven-Johns Monument, with a bust of John Hanson as the top figure, was erected at Gloria Dei in Philadelphia by the Swedish Colonial Society and the Vasa Order Lodges of Sweden. U.S. 50, running from Washington to Annapolis, has been named the John Hanson Highway. In Maryland his birthday, April 14, has been declared John Hanson Day.

A grandson of John Hanson, Alexander Contee Hanson, became a U.S. senator, and a nephew, Thomas Stone of Maryland, was among the signers of the Declaration of Independence. Another signer of partly Swedish ancestry was Benjamin Harrison of Virginia, whose son William Henry Harrison became the ninth President of the United States, and whose great-grandson and namesake Benjamin Harrison was elected the 23rd President.

Of the signers of the Declaration of Independence, John Morton (1724–77) of Pennsylvania holds a special position in the history of the Swedish element in America. In the decisive Congress session July 2–4, 1776, his vote tipped the balance in favor of separation from England. It has been claimed that it was this action that gave Pennsylvania the name of the Keystone State. Morton's great-grandfather, Mårten Mårtensson, or Morten Mortenson, had joined the Swedes on the Delaware in 1654.

John Morton's grave is at Chester, Pennsylvania, the old Swedish settlement of Upland, and a monument there has this inscription: "John Morton, being censured by some of his friends for his boldness in giving his casting vote for the Declaration of Independence, his prophetic spirit dictated from his deathbed the following message: 'Tell them they will live to see the hour when they shall acknowledge it to have been the most glorious service I ever rendered my country.'" Morton died in 1777. The American Swedish Historical Museum in Philadelphia was planned as a memorial to him.

Toward the end of 1776 the military campaigns of the Revolution reached the Delaware Valley, and some people of Swedish stock were, in all likelihood, among the farmers who rowed George Washington and his men across the river for his surprise attack on the English and their Hessian mercenaries on Christmas Day. This success and its sequence in January of 1777 had, of course, strong psychological effects, although pacifists and supporters of England were still found everywhere.

Even in the largely Swedish communities in the Delaware region, old loyalties were being torn apart, and in February of 1777 one of their pastors, Nicholas Collin at Raccoon in New Jersey, was accused of spying and in danger of being shot. His close friendship with the Anglican ministers, who were sympathetic toward England, had made him suspect, but like many other clergymen he actually tried to be neutral. He was, above all, active in alleviating the suffering, which, he wrote in his diary, "could move a heart of stone." The great majority of the settlers of Swedish descent remained loyal to the Revolutionary cause, and the able-bodied men are said to have fought in large numbers. The regiments from Delaware and Maryland were regarded as the best in the American army.

One of the recent immigrants from Sweden known to have taken part in the war, Colonel John Christian Senf (1754–1806), served as a captain of engineers in the South Carolina line of the Continental Army. He has been described as a "strongminded but somewhat autocratic and eccentric genius." In the late 1700s he designed and led the construction of the Santee Canal, which connects Charleston with an extensive river system. He finally became chief engineer of the state of South Carolina.

Swedish naval officers, including nine future admirals, in the American war

SOME Swedes joined the Americans in their struggle for independence at an early stage, and when France in 1778 became involved in the war, nearly a hundred Swedish officers applied for foreign leave and enlisted in the French forces. A few years later, an even larger number of young men with military training served in the Dutch navy. There were also Swedish officers on the British side, but when the war broke out between England and France, many of them resigned and transferred, if they could, to the French fleet. Sweden's relations with France were particularly close at that time.

The great majority of the Swedes in the French, Dutch, and

American forces served at sea, most of them as artillery officers or gunners, and there they made contributions of real significance. Without the intervention of the French navy in America and the Dutch and Spanish actions in European and other waters, Britain's naval supremacy might, of course, have been decisive. The West Indies, then one of the world's richest commercial regions, became the scene of large-scale naval war, and the sea battle off Chesapeake Bay helped bring about the surrender of Yorktown.

Most of the Swedish officers who saw action under the French or American flags were noblemen, and ideologically they were not revolutionists, although they believed in the principle of national freedom. About 50 fought in American waters or on American soil. After the war all the survivors returned to Sweden, and many took part with honor in the naval battles with the Russians in 1788–90. Nine finally became admirals of various grades. The titles used below and indicating their ranks of nobility were, with some exceptions, conferred during their Swedish careers.

Ambassador Gustaf Philip Creutz in Paris, who knew most of the Swedes in French service, regarded Gustaf Rehbinder (1745–82) as the foremost of the Swedish officers in the French navy. In operations off Newport, Rhode Island, he fought with such bravery and resourcefulness that he became second in command of his ship, the highest honor a foreigner in French naval service could reach. After having survived numerous engagements, he was killed in the battle of April 12, 1782, in the West Indies, the "most severe, the longest, and most murderous of the century," where the English were victorious. A distant cousin who also was in French service, Carl Gustaf Rehbinder (1764–82), met death in the West Indies the same year, while a younger brother, Fredrik Gustaf Rehbinder (1754–78), died in 1778 on a British ship riding at anchor on the Delaware.

Adolf Fredrick Pettersén, or Rosensvärd (1753–99), who entered French service in 1777, is probably the best-known Swedish naval officer in the American war. In May of 1781 he was wounded outside the fort of Pensacola in Florida, where he led both infantry units and a brigade of artillery, but took part in the battle until the end. King Louis XVI of France sent a personal letter about him to King Gustav III in Stockholm, and he was immediately ennobled by the Swedish monarch, assuming the name of Rosensvärd. He served later under

Admiral De Grasse in American waters. In Sweden he rose to the rank of rear admiral.

Baron Magnus Palmquist (1761–1834) was, like Pettersén, a commoner when he enlisted in French service in 1778. He distinguished himself in several naval operations in America, including the blockade of Yorktown, and in Sweden he finally became an admiral. Magnus Aurivillius Rosén von Rosenstein (1755–1801), who was a grandson of the "Father of Swedish medicine," also conducted himself bravely. In the battle in the West Indies on April 12, 1782, he was, like Admiral De Grasse himself, taken prisoner by the English, but was exchanged after a short time. Seven years later, when he had rejoined the Swedish navy, he was captured by the Russians in a battle in the Gulf of Finland. His final rank was that of a rear admiral.

Count Claes Adam Wachtmeister (1755–1828) entered French naval service as early as 1776 and then took part in the whole war, fighting both in the West Indies and in Europe. Later he served with distinction in the Swedish navy, spent some time in Russia as a prisoner of war, and was finally promoted to admiral. Baron Otto Henrik Nordenskjöld (1747–1832), of another eminent Swedish family and born in Finland, was one of Sweden's most experienced younger naval officers when he joined the French navy in 1778. After having fought in the West Indies and at Savannah and Chesapeake, he was called back to Sweden in 1781 to become chief of a squadron fitted out to protect neutral rights in European waters. During the war with Russia in 1788–90, he was the real commander of the Swedish navy, although his wise counsel was not always followed. He left active service as a vice-admiral. A close friend, Baron Henrik Johan Nauckhoff (1744–1818), also took part in many naval engagements in America, including the battle of April 12, 1782, in the West Indies, where he was severely wounded and became a prisoner. Later he too suffered Russian imprisonment, but finally he became a commanding admiral in Sweden.

Count Johan af Puke (1751–1816) fought with bravery on many occasions, both in Europe and in American waters. In 1788–90 he took a particularly brilliant part in Sweden's war with Russia, and he reached a higher position than any other Swedish navy veteran of the American war, that of grand admiral and commander-in-chief of Sweden's naval forces. Baron Salomon Mauritz von Rajalin (1757–

1825) fought in the West Indies, and in the Swedish navy he reached the rank of admiral. Count Nils Bielke (1763–82), of one of the oldest families of the Swedish nobility, took part in the capture of Pensacola in 1781. The next year he was killed in a naval action against the English in the East Indies, which also became involved in the war.

Georg Frese (1751–1807) won honors at the capture of Grenada in the West Indies in 1779, and in Sweden he finally became a rear admiral. A younger brother, who had hoped to be sent to America, was killed in the East Indies. Zacharias Schultén (1749–1824) fought in many battles in American waters and has been mentioned as one of the bravest Swedish officers in French service.

One of the most enthusiastic supporters of the American cause among the Swedish naval officers was Baron Georg Carl von Döbeln (1758–1820), who volunteered for the war in 1780. From France he was to have sailed on an American privateer as commander of artillery, but he ended up in the East Indies as an army officer. For his exploits during the Swedish-Finnish war with Russia in 1808–09 he was several decades later immortalized by Johan Ludvig Runeberg (1804–77), Finland's national poet, who wrote in the Swedish language. General Von Döbeln is one of the most famous military men in the annals of both Sweden and Finland, and his motto, "Honor, Duty, Resolution," is still well known.

There were quite a few Swedes among the crews of John Paul Jones, the famous naval hero of the Revolution. Some served on the *Ranger* during the spectacular expedition to the Irish Channel in the spring of 1778. On September 23, 1779, when Captain Jones won his greatest victory off England's east coast, at least seven native Swedes seem to have fought on *Bon Homme Richard*, named in honor of Benjamin Franklin and his *Poor Richard's Almanack*. One of them, Peter Nolde or Nolte, is said to have won "undying glory." A former university student at Uppsala, Bengt Axel Gartman (b. 1748), was one of the gunners. *Bon Homme Richard* had a complement of some 380 officers, men and boys, representing about ten different nationalities. In April of 1788 John Paul Jones spent nine days traveling through Sweden on his way to St. Petersburg and from there to the Black Sea, where he successfully fought the Turks as commander of a Russian squadron. After leaving Russia in the summer of 1789 he visited Warsaw, where

General Kosciusko, another hero of the American War of Independence, proposed that he should help the Swedish navy in its struggle against the Russians. Swedish representatives became involved in the discussions, but the plan failed.

Several naval officers in British service won commendations from their superiors, but only two, Harald Cristiernin (1751–99) and Carl Olof Cronstedt (1756–1820), reached as high positions in the Swedish military organization as did many of those who had fought with the French in America. The former, who distinguished himself in a battle with the Russians in 1788 and somewhat later was taken prisoner, served finally as a rear admiral. Cronstedt became a prisoner of war in America in the fall of 1776 but was allowed almost complete freedom to move about and went, for instance, sightseeing in Philadelphia. After further service on English ships and many adventures, he returned to Sweden in 1779 and requested permission to enlist with the French. He was, however, needed at home, and in 1790 he played a prominent part in the Swedish naval victory at Svensksund in the Gulf of Finland. In the war of 1808–09, on the other hand, he became responsible for the most perplexing surrender in the history of Sweden and Finland. He then held the rank of a vice-admiral.

Another competent naval officer, David Staare (1755–1800), served first with the British and then with the French. In early 1783, when he had come to London in a flight from his rising debts, he married a young American girl, Eloise Hick, who had been sent to England some years earlier. In Sweden they had, at first, a difficult time, for Staare had been stricken from the navy rolls and disowned by his parents in the naval town of Karlskrona, but their problems were solved during a visit to Stockholm, where Mrs. Staare, as one of her admirers wrote, "set fire to all hearts." King Gustav himself invited her to the Opera, and as a result of their conversation she received an annual pension to eke out her husband's salary. In 1797 she obtained a divorce from him, but a year later she married a member of one of the leading families in the Karlskrona district, and they lived happily ever after. Eloise Hick is said to have been "one of those women who appear in this world but once in a century." Her memory lived at Karlskrona for two generations, and she has been called the first ambassador of good will from America to Sweden.

Two Swedish army officers, Fersen and Stedingk,
receive rare American honor

OF THE Swedish army officers who crossed the Atlantic, Georg Gustaf Uggla (1742–1825) joined the American forces after having been in the Dutch service. In 1778–79 he fought in Count Casimir Pulaski's legion, and he distinguished himself during the siege of Savannah and the following attack on the city on October 9, 1779, when the Polish commander was mortally wounded and most of his men were killed. Uggla later served as a staff officer under General Horatio Gates, and after the fierce battle at Camden in South Carolina on August 16, 1780, which finished Gates's army career, he was taken prisoner by the British. Baron Johan Henrik Fock (1753–1817), who came to America in 1781 after having entered French service, is said to have shown unusual bravery at Yorktown. After some years in Sweden, he settled first in London and finally in Ireland under the name of Johan Henrik de Robeck. A great-grandson won fame in the First World War as a British admiral.

Count Curt von Stedingk (1746–1837), who was born in the Swedish province in northern Germany, participated in several engagements in the West Indies, and at the siege of Savannah he commanded a division. In the assault on that city he was severely wounded, and because of his injuries he had to return to Europe, where he planned to recruit an entire regiment of Swedes for the war in America. From 1790 to 1808 he served as Swedish ambassador to Russia, and in 1813 he was in command, under Crown Prince Carl Johan, the former French Marshal Bernadotte, of the Swedish forces in Germany which took part in the final coalition against Napoleon. After the Battle of Nations at Leipzig, he was one of the signers for Sweden of the 1814 peace treaty with France. When he died at the age of 90, he held the rank of a field marshal.

For his service in America, Curt von Stedingk was made a member of the Society of the Cincinnati, a rare honor for a foreigner. This group was formed in 1783 by former officers in the American Revolutionary army, and George Washington was its first president-general. The name Cincinnati was adopted in honor of a famous Roman citizen-soldier, and the city in Ohio was, in turn, named after the society. Membership is hereditary, and the insignia may still, therefore, be worn by the head of the Stedingk family in Sweden.

One more Swedish veteran of the Revolutionary War, and the most prominent of all, Count Hans Axel von Fersen (1755–1810), became a member of the Order of the Cincinnati, but he died a bachelor.

A gallant young man of the world and a favorite at the French court in Paris and Versailles, Count von Fersen became a close friend of Queen Marie-Antoinette. To escape an embarrassing emotional dilemma, he enlisted in the French expeditionary forces, and in July of 1780 he landed in Rhode Island as first aide-de-camp to the commander-in-chief, General Rochambeau. In the beginning he liked New England and its people, but later, under the influence of the enforced inactivity at Newport and probably also disagreeable personal experiences, he became quite critical. Profiteering and lack of determination and patriotism were his principal complaints in letters to his father, Field Marshal Count Axel von Fersen (1719–94), who as a political leader in Sweden vigorously defended the constitutional powers of parliament against the king and sometimes voiced almost republican ideas, although he also fought for the privileges of the nobility. Writing to him from Virginia in the spring of 1782, his son wondered how "the lordly planters . . . were ever induced to form part of a confederation or accept a government founded on perfect equality of rights."

Being one of the few members of the French staffs who had a good command of English, Count Von Fersen often served as a liaison officer between General Rochambeau and George Washington, who won his unqualified respect and admiration. The American leader's "majestic, handsome countenance," he wrote after their first meeting, "is stamped with an honesty and a gentleness which correspond with his moral qualities." At Yorktown Von Fersen distinguished himself in the field, and he was one of the officers present when General Cornwallis surrendered. In the Capitol at Washington his picture appears in the famous painting of this scene by John Trumbull.

After the war, Count Von Fersen became a roving ambassador for King Gustav III of Sweden and, finally, a general and marshal of the realm. During the revolution in France he tried to save the French royal family from execution. In both ideas and manners, he then seemed more and more like a relic of l'ancien régime. In Sweden he was a staunch supporter of the Gustavian monarchy, and at a royal funeral in Stockholm in 1810, the year after King Gustav's son and successor had been driven away in a bloodless revolution, he was beaten and trampled to death by an excited mob. An inscription on a monument at his estate Steninge near the capital, which in 1932 was acquired by an American family, reads in part: "Truth, called forth by time, shall protect his memory and do justice to his virtue."

★ 6

In America: Bridging Two Epochs

Last Swedish clergyman on the Delaware —
Manifold cultural activities

AFTER 1791 the Reverend Nils, or Nicholas, Collin (or Colleen, 1746–1831) was the only Swedish-born clergyman in the Delaware Valley. To cultural relations between Sweden and the United States he contributed more than any other 18th-century Swedish immigrant or visitor. The key role that he played in the growing exchange between the two countries has, in fact, never been equaled.

The son of a Lutheran dean near Uppsala and a student of theology, foreign languages, and mathematics at the university, he dreamed of serving for some time in America, and after having been ordained a minister he received his appointment. In 1770 he arrived in Philadelphia via London, and remained on the Delaware until the end of his life 61 years later. At first, he was assigned to the old Swedish congregations in lower New Jersey, which then included members of many other national origins. In 1786 he took over the rectorship of the three Swedish churches in Philadelphia and its vicinity — Gloria Dei, St. James, and Christ Church at Upper Merion.

A harmonious but sensitive person, Collin often felt bitterly homesick, and several times he seemed about to return to Sweden, but he could never quite make up his mind. While he remained a Swedish citizen and even patriot, he became deeply concerned with the welfare and future of America, first of all his home communities.

After his wife, who was of German stock, had died in 1797, he had periods of intense dejection, but he overcame them by hard work, often taxing his energies to the limit.

Collin's 16 years in New Jersey, which comprised the long war period, were particularly strenuous, but it was in Philadelphia that he made his most significant contributions of lasting interest. When he had settled there in 1786, preparations for the Constitutional Convention began, and arguments for or against a centralized form of government were heard everywhere. The Swedish clergyman had become more and more interested in public affairs, and finally he decided to enter into the discussion. A strong supporter of firm organization, he wrote a series of articles in favor of the new constitution, and the first one appeared in the weekly *Pennsylvania Gazette* on August 8, 1787, six weeks before the convention adjourned. Six other installments followed. The articles were not signed, but it was said that they had been written "by a foreign spectator." Those who knew Collin must have realized that he was the author.

From the beginning Collin took an active part in the civic life of Philadelphia, and he gave much of his time to educational institutions. From 1788 to 1791 he served as a trustee of the University of Pennsylvania, which honored him with a doctor's degree. He also supported other academies and schools in the Philadelphia district and delivered lectures before the students.

In 1789 Dr. Collin was elected a member of the American Philosophical Society. Hardly anybody presented as many papers as he did and on as great a variety of subjects, ranging from natural science, mechanics, and inventions to history, government, and politics. In his inaugural address, which was printed by the society, he outlined, for instance, a method of plowing on hilly land to prevent erosion, and regretting the destruction of American forests, he proposed remedies leading to the preservation and increase of timber. In 1794, he received the society's gold medal for one of his own inventions, a "speedy elevator," probably a fire ladder. The next year he was elected a vice president.

The American Philosophical Society had been founded in 1743 by Benjamin Franklin for the promotion of useful knowledge in the colonies. Before the Revolution, four Swedish scholars, Peter Jonas Bergius, Torbern Bergman, Carl Linnaeus, and the Reverend Carl

Magnus Wrangel, were elected members, and at least eight more were admitted during the following decades, after having been proposed or recommended by Dr. Collin. In 1788, the Swedish Academy of Sciences in Stockholm received the first volumes of the *Transactions* of the Philosophical Society, together with a letter signed by Benjamin Franklin, and a regular exchange of publications was eventually ensured as a result of Collin's efforts.

In the fall of 1793, the yellow fever spread terror in Philadelphia, and other epidemics followed. Visiting and comforting the sick and dying, Dr. Collin wished he could also offer medical assistance and began, therefore, to study medicine. During the years 1802–04, when he had pursued this task with even greater energy after his wife's death, he published a number of newspaper articles to counteract unfounded fears and help the citizens of Philadelphia combat the disease. A few years later, however, he seemed to have lost all ambition, and he asked a Swedish friend, the painter Adolf Ulric Wertmüller, to look after his affairs in case of his death. Another test came in 1808–09 when Collin read about Sweden's war with Russia and loss of Finland, where one of his brothers had settled.

During a journey through New England in the summer of 1794 Dr. Collin was very favorably impressed by this part of the country, and its schools he always regarded as the best in America. In Boston and at Harvard and Yale he met many prominent personalities or future leaders. During a visit to New York he made the acquaintance of Joseph Priestley, the famous English chemist, who also was a nonconformist preacher and had just begun a new life in America. Both Priestley, who had discovered oxygen at about the same time as Scheele in Sweden, and Dr. Collin were at that time members of the Swedish Academy of Sciences.

At one time Collin planned to write a comprehensive book about America for Swedish readers, and existing fragments indicate what he had in mind. Many people in Europe had begun to look upon the United States as at least the beginning of paradise, but they were, he thought, as wrong as those who regarded America as a wild and miserable country. Newcomers should never expect prompt prosperity, and, on account of the language barrier, Swedish immigrants could not compete successfully with the English and the Irish. They should, at any rate, be laborers and not educated people, a theme that also was heard in many of Collin's letters to Sweden and would be voiced again by other Swedes throughout the 1800s. Collin himself had often helped stranded countrymen, the first Swede in America to offer such service on a relatively large scale. The American governmental organization he regarded, on the other hand, as "really splendid," and he believed that "under a strong union and a wise government" the nation would be headed for a great future.

In America, or at least in the Philadelphia area, Dr. Collin gradually became known as an authority on Sweden, and there is good reason to regard him as the first important source of information about Sweden in America. To a geography book he contributed a long article about his native country, which, in part, seemed to explain the homesickness he often felt. "Fondness for convivial pleasures, music and dancing," he wrote for instance, "is a leading feature in the Swedish character; and no nation has better mingled festive joy with moral sentiment." Although a staunch Lutheran, Collin was decidedly tolerant and broadminded, and sometimes he was even criticized for paying too much attention to secular things. A friendlier and more joyous spirit would, he felt, be good for Philadelphia, his home town.

Before leaving Sweden, Collin had visited Swedenborg, and in 1801 he wrote five articles about him for the *Philadelphia Gazette*, the daily to which he usually sent his contributions. They were reprinted by the *American Daily Advertiser*. The General Convention of the New Jerusalem Church, founded by followers of Swedenborg, was organized at Philadelphia in 1817.

Botany and horticulture were among Collin's leading hobbies, and he did much to further such interests in the Delaware Valley. To institutions and scholars in Sweden he sent many collections of specimens of natural history, as well as books and maps, and as a rule he received something in return, such as new literature and seeds which were planted at farms or in experimental gardens that he had helped establish. The rutabaga, or Swedish turnip, for instance, seems to have been introduced in America by him. In 1822, when he was 73 years old, the Academy of Sciences in Stockholm published in its *Transactions* an article by him about North American trees that should be introduced in Sweden. A direct exchange of letters between American and Swedish scientists was also brought about by Dr. Collin.

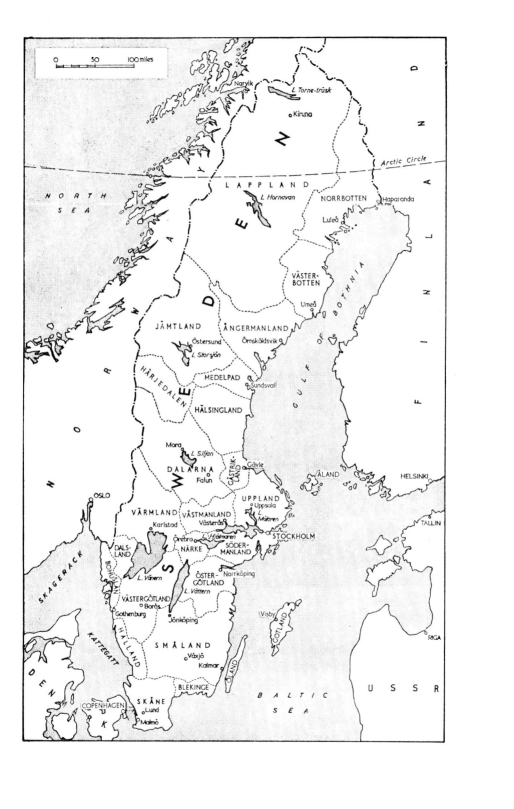

Visby on the Baltic island of Gotland is one of Europe's most picturesque remnants of the early Middle Ages. During that era the city, with its turreted wall and 17 churches, must have made an impression on approaching visitors similar to that of the Manhattan skyline on the travelers of our time. About 14,000 persons have emigrated to America from Gotland, which today has a population of 54,000.

Sweden's most notable runestone, at Rök in Östergötland, dates from the early part of the Viking Age, the ninth century. It has the longest runic inscription known, alluding to heroic ballads and legends now lost. Many of Sweden's 3,000 runic inscriptions are memorials to men who sailed away never to return (p. 14).

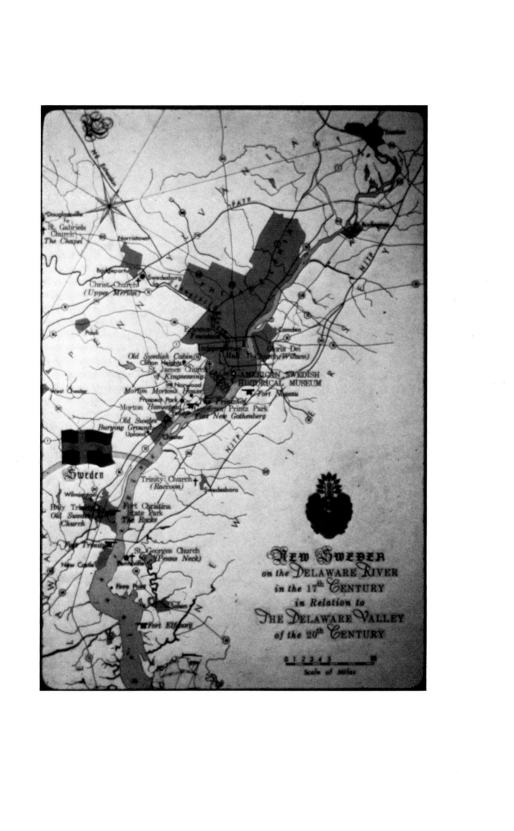

New Sweden
on the Delaware River
in the 17th Century
in Relation to
The Delaware Valley
of the 20th Century

0 1 2 3 4 5
Scale of Miles

1. The first Swedish ships to sail to America, *Kalmar Nyckel* and *Fogel Grip*, were relatively small schooner-rigged pinnaces. *Kalmar Nyckel* (Key of Kalmar) brought to New Sweden not only the first colonists in the spring of 1638 but also reinforcements and supplies in 1640 and 1641. Using a scale model in the Maritime Museum at Gothenburg, Danish-born J. C. Andrésen in 1938 recreated in an oil painting the first Swedish expedition to the Delaware (pp. 20–22). 2. An artistic and somewhat romantic attempt to reconstruct the arrival of the first Swedish colonists in 1638 and their first meeting with Indian chiefs. Christian von Schneidau painted this fresco for the American Swedish Historical Museum in Philadelphia (p. 20).

1. One of the two "Old Swedes" churches in Philadelphia, Gloria Dei, dedicated in 1700, is the oldest church now standing in Pennsylvania. Its congregation, which dates back to the 1640s, is the oldest in America (p. 36). 2. After King Gustavus Adolphus's death on a battlefield in Germany in 1632, his chancellor or prime minister, Count Axel Oxenstierna, became Sweden's real leader. He took an active interest in the Swedish colony on the Delaware, but the war in Europe required more attention (pp. 19, 26). 3. Lieutenant Colonel Johan Printz, a veteran of the Thirty Years' War, ruled New Sweden as governor from early 1643 until the autumn of 1653. Nearly seven feet tall and weighing about 300 pounds — or even, according to a Dutch chronicler, close to 400 — he was easily the first "Big Swede" in America. This portrait hangs in the church at Bottnaryd in the province of Småland, where Printz was born and buried (pp. 22–27, 29–30, 39–40).

Emanuel Swedenborg, an American scholar has written, could on one and the same day "lead the conversation with geologists, physicists, physiologists, metallurgists, engineers, statesmen, philosophers — and angels." Americans known to have been influenced by Swedenborg the philosopher and seer include Benjamin Franklin, Thomas Jefferson, and Abraham Lincoln. The largest of some fifty Swedenborgian churches in the United States is the Cathedral at Bryn Athyn north of Philadelphia (pp. 58–59, 568–570).

1. Linnaeus, the "Flower King," brought order to both botany and zoology by developing the two-name system of nomenclature. His influence and his disciple Pehr Kalm's visit in 1748–51 helped arouse in America a growing enthusiasm for a systematic study of nature. This portrait was painted in 1775 by the Swedish artist Alexander Roslin. The original is at Versailles (pp. 69–83). 2. Carl Wilhelm Scheele, who died eight years after Linnaeus at the age of 43, is regarded as one of the greatest experimental chemists of all time (pp. 67–68). 3. Anders Celsius, Swedish physicist and astronomer of the early 1700s, gave his name to the centigrade thermometer (p. 60).

George Washington posed for a portrait by Adolph Ulric Wertmüller in Philadelphia in 1794 when the Stockholm-born artist, a member of the French and Swedish academies of art, had just arrived from Europe. In America, Wertmüller became more widely known because of a painting with a motif from Greek mythology which many regarded as frivolous, but which was successfully exhibited. The artist finally settled as a farmer on the Delaware (pp. 108–109).

The beginning and the end of the treaty of friendship and commerce which was signed in the spring of 1783 by the Swedish ambassador to France, Count Gustav Philip Creutz, and the American ambassador, Benjamin Franklin. At an early stage of the War of Independence, King Gustav III of Sweden had expressed admiration for the courage of the revolutionists. In 1783 America's white population was a little more than three million, or not much greater than Sweden's (pp. 88–92).

His own correspondence with Sweden was lively, and the one he had with Carl Thunberg of Uppsala, the botanical explorer, became particularly extensive. At times it concerned the problem of slavery. Collin became a member of two American abolitionist societies, and Thunberg had seen slavery in South Africa. The Swedish clergyman's far-ranging interests included history as well as art, and he was one of the founders of the Pennsylvania Historical Society.

Dr. Collin was elected a member of the Swedish Academy of Sciences at Stockholm in late 1793. The next year he was followed by Benjamin Rush, one of the signers of the Declaration of Independence and professor of medicine in the University of Pennsylvania. Dr. Rush, who also became known for his fight against slavery and capital punishment, and for improved education, had been introduced to the academy by Dr. Collin, who ten years later proposed another noted Philadelphian, Benjamin Smith Barton, physician and botanist, and also professor in the University of Pennsylvania. Dr. Barton was finally elected in 1812. The number of native Americans who had become members of the Academy of Sciences in Stockholm thus reached three, which represented only a few percent of the total foreign membership. In the early 1800s, French scientists made up the largest group of foreign members, followed by Germans and Englishmen. The first American member of the Swedish academy was, as already mentioned, John Bartram of Pennsylvania, the pioneer botanist.

Quite a few immigrants from Sweden and their children received from Dr. Collin assistance that furthered their careers, some such cases being mentioned in the following. Among his best American friends were Benjamin Franklin and Thomas Jefferson, David Rittenhouse, astronomer and mathematician, Charles Willson Peale, the portrait painter, who founded the first art museum in America, and John Bartram's son William. He also knew George Washington.

Nicholas Collin, who died in 1831 at the age of 85, was interred in the Gloria Dei Church. His memory is said to have lived on in Philadelphia for two generations. A biography by Dr. Amandus Johnson was published in that city in 1936. It includes part of the diary Collin kept during the period 1770–86 when he served the Swedish congregations in New Jersey.

*Swedish artist portrays George Washington and ends up
as a farmer on the Delaware*

ADOLF ULRIC WERTMÜLLER (1751–1811) was already an artist of distinction when he came to America in 1794. In Paris he had won
recognition in 1783 with the painting *Ariadne on Naxos*, which had
been commissioned by the Swedish ambassador, Gustaf Philip Creutz.
It now hangs in the National Gallery in Stockholm. Somewhat later he
also painted Queen Marie Antoinette and two of her children.

Soon after his arrival in Philadelphia, Wertmüller obtained the
consent of President Washington for a sitting, and the result was a
portrait which at first was received with mixed feelings but gradually
became widely known and appreciated. One of the artist's best friends
in Sweden, a leading architect, congratulated him on having had "the
good fortune to paint the man who for eternity will be famed in world
history," and an American who much later acquired a copy of the
painting wrote that "gentlemen who remember the illustrious original
say that of all the portraits they have ever seen of Washington, none
brings home to their memory so much of truthfulness and accuracy."
The original canvas is now in the possession of the Metropolitan
Museum of Art in New York, while one of several replicas hangs in
the White House.

In 1796 Wertmüller went back to Europe, but after a few years in
Sweden he returned to America in 1800, and married a granddaughter of Gustavus Hesselius, the pioneer Swedish painter of the colonial
era; he bought a farm in the Delaware Valley, on Naaman's Creek,
where today the blockhouse built in 1654 by New Sweden's last governor is the only structure remaining of the original Swedish settlement.
He continued to paint, mostly portraits, but during his last ten years he
was first of all a farmer, and he had, he said, never been happier. His
diary, which was written in French and has been translated into English, is a movingly simple record of his struggle with cows and pigs,
plowing and harvesting.

Wertmüller has been described as a mild and amiable man of
simple tastes, but his European career had not prepared him for the
Puritan traditions in the New World, and he became the first Swedish
artist to be charged with a lack of propriety in his production. One of
his best-known works of the Paris period was *Danaë and the Golden
Rain*, and this canvas he brought to America. It was successfully exhi-

bited in Philadelphia and other cities in Pennsylvania but shocked many people because of its nudity and its motif, the Greek legend about Zeus descending to Danaë in a shower of gold. In 1812, when the artist had died, the painting was sold for $1,500, and in 1850 it was displayed in New York, where at least one art expert welcomed it. After forty years of seclusion, a *New York Times* critic wrote, "the Danaë of Wertmüller has flashed upon New York . . . as fresh and bright and irresistible a vision of loveliness as she was when she turned the heads of our respectable grandfathers in the days before Waterloo." No art museum seemed to want the canvas, however, and in 1913 it was finally presented to the National Gallery in Stockholm by its American owner, who had first discussed his donation on the French Riviera with King Gustav V of Sweden.

Wertmüller was buried in the churchyard of Philadelphia's Gloria Dei. A posthumous exhibition was held in New York in 1815, and a booklet with text by the Reverend Nicholas Collin was published for the occasion. In 1951 the National Gallery in Stockholm opened its doors to a 200th-anniversary show, and, as a result of it, Wertmüller's art won deeper appreciation in Sweden. He is also represented in the Pennsylvania Academy of Fine Arts and the Historical Society of Pennsylvania in Philadelphia, in the Augusta Art Gallery in Augusta, Georgia, and in many museums on the European mainland, including the Prado in Madrid.

From 1790 to 1794 Wertmüller lived in Spain, and when leaving for America he was accompanied by a Swedish friend, Henrik Gahn.

Assimilation of New Sweden descendants completed —
Modern interest in ancestors

THE REVEREND Nicholas Collin became a bridge between two epochs in the history of the Swedes in America: he saw the end of the old Swedish settlements on the Delaware and of their direct religious contacts with Sweden, and he also witnessed the arrival of new immigrants in larger although still modest numbers. His experience and active interest was of great help to the newcomers.

The last Swedish rector at Holy Trinity in Wilmington was Lars or Lawrence Girelius, who had come to the Delaware Valley in 1767. Like Nicholas Collin he received an honorary doctorate from the University of Pennsylvania. Early in 1791 he sailed for Europe, and

Collin was the only Swedish clergyman left. The year before, the jurisdiction over the Swedish churches had been transferred by the archbishop of Sweden to the American Protestant Episcopal Church, but Gloria Dei and St. James in the Philadelphia area as well as Christ Church at Upper Merion remained nominally Lutheran until after Collin's death in 1831.

In the Raccoon district, many old people were still able to understand Swedish when the American Revolution began, and even in 1786, which was his last year there, Collin offered services in Swedish every four, five, or six weeks, as well as on the great religious holidays. After having moved to Philadelphia he seems to have preached exclusively in English, and perhaps on some occasions in German. In the early 1800s, on the other hand, the immigrants from Sweden in the Philadelphia area had become so numerous that Collin began to conduct special services in the Swedish language.

In 1775, descendants of the original Swedish settlers on the Delaware seem to have numbered approximately 15,000, but most of them can hardly have been aware of their Scandinavian origin, even if the river valley retained much of its old atmosphere. Frequent intermarriage with other nationalities had contributed to their assimilation, young people had begun to move to other areas, and many Swedish family names had been Anglicized.

Since the beginning of the 20th century more and more Americans have become interested in their ancient Swedish ancestry. The histories of families hailing from such pioneers as Göran Kyn, Peter Gunnarson Rambo, Sven Skute, Timon Stidden, and Olof Stille are today relatively well known.

Göran Kyn, who came to New Sweden as a soldier with Governor Printz in 1643, became the first large landowner at Upland, or Chester, in Pennsylvania. Many of the colonists were dubbed with nicknames, and Kyn's was "Snövit," or Snow White, a reference to his complexion. In contrast to many other settlers he had a small family, but the number of his descendants born before the Revolution was about 400, and today thousands of Americans, as well as many families in Europe, can claim him as one of their ancestors. In 1913 Dr. Gregory B. Keen published a genealogical study entitled *The Descendants of Göran Kyn of New Sweden*, which, as he wrote in the foreword, he regarded "not merely as a record of a particular family but also a striking example of the wide diffusion of the blood of an early Swedish settler on the Delaware through descendants of other surnames and other races residing both in the United States and in Europe."

The great majority of Göran Kyn's descendants have entirely different surnames, but the original Swedish name lives on in such forms as Keen, Keene, and Kean. The best-known lineal descendant was Dr. William W. Keen (1837–1932) of Philadelphia, who has been called the "Father of American surgery." A specialist in the surgery of the brain and nervous system, he was among the first in the United States to perform successful operations in this field. In the late 1800s he was elected president of the American Surgical Association and the American Medical Association, and in the early 1900s he served for ten years as president of the American Philosophical Society. In 1907 he attended at Uppsala University in Sweden the 200th-anniversary celebration of Linnaeus's birth, and was given an honorary degree. In 1920, at the age of 83, he presided over the International Congress of Surgery in Paris. Being fully aware of his Swedish ancestry, he sometimes said in answer to questions that "it must be my Viking blood that gives me my strength." Other descendants of Göran Kyn have become bankers, industrialists, inventors, educators, judges, and army or navy officers.

Peter Gunnarson Rambo, who came to the Delaware Valley in 1640, has descendants named Rambo, but those with other family names are much more numerous. His descendants of the eighth generation included Harold L. Ickes, who from 1933 to 1946 served as secretary of the interior under Franklin D. Roosevelt and Harry S. Truman. The Swedish colonial strains in President Roosevelt's own ancestry, which already have been mentioned, were well known to him. Sven Skute, who came to New Sweden with Governor Johan Printz in 1643, had at least three children, including a daughter who married one of Peter Rambo's sons. He too has many descendants.

Timon Stidden was one of the passengers on the ill-fated ship *Kattan*, which in 1649 foundered on a reef near Puerto Rico, but he managed to return to Sweden and sailed again for America in 1654. The first medical practitioner in the Delaware Valley, known as "Timon Stidden the surgeon," he purchased at Christina a large part of the land on which the city of Wilmington was built. His sons and grandsons changed the family name to Stedham or Stidham. One of the numerous families hailing from Timon Stidden has preserved the metal case in which he carried his surgical instruments, and upon which his name and title are engraved.

Olof Stille, born on a farm in the Roslagen district northeast of Stockholm, who came to New Sweden in 1641 with his wife and two children, left an only son, but his descendants, like those of Göran Kyn, wrote their old family name into the annals of American medicine and education. Dr. Alfred Stillé (1813–1900) of Philadelphia ranked high both as a practitioner and as a teacher, and seems to have been the first to define the difference between typhus and typhoid fever. He was one of the founders of the American Medical Association, became its first secretary and was elected president in 1867, when he had been named professor at the University of Pennsylvania. A younger brother, Charles Janeway Stillé (1819–99), who was professor of history, served from 1868 to 1880 as president of the University of Pennsylvania, which under his leadership was transformed into one of America's major universities. Upon his retirement he made two visits of exploration to Sweden, and in 1888 he discovered new records of the Swedish colonists on the Delaware. A third brother, Dr. Moreton Stillé (1822–55), made pioneering contributions to medical jurisprudence. Some female descendants of Olof Stille have also distinguished themselves in the field of education and learning.

Sven Gunnarson, who joined the New Sweden colonists in 1640, seems to have been the father of Sven, Ole, and Andreas Swenson, mentioned previously as large landowners in the Philadelphia area. Andreas Swenson's descendants of the sixth generation included Henry Algernon du Pont, who became a U.S. senator from Delaware. At least one of the sons or grandsons of the Swenson brothers moved south, and in the 1700s there were Swenson or Swanson families in Virginia and North Carolina. One of their descendants, Claude Augustus Swanson, served in the U.S. Congress for 35 years, the last 23 as senator, and then as secretary of the navy in the Franklin D. Roosevelt administrations of the 1930s. He was born at Swansonville, Virginia. For four years he served as governor of his home state. Another descendant of Sven Gunnarson, Edward Swanson, is regarded as one of the original pioneers who in 1779–80 with James Robertson founded Nashville, Tennessee.

Current American family names dating from the Swedish settlements on the Delaware include Coxe (originally Cock), Dalbo, Henderson (Hindrickson or Hinderson), Jones (Jonason), Longacre, Morton or Morten, Peterson, Springer, Steelman, and Yocom or Yocum. The great majority of the numerous Yocums in America descend from Peter Jochim or Jochimson of New Sweden. Jonas Nilsson, from whom several Philadelphia families claim descent, arrived with Governor Printz in 1643 and became a successful businessman. He died in 1693, leaving four daughters and seven sons, who used the family name Jonason or Jones. Some members of the Peterson family will be mentioned later.

A family of French-Dutch origin named Bayard, which by marriage became connected with Delaware Swedes, contributed no less than five U.S. senators from the state of Delaware, the last ones being Thomas F. Bayard, who held the office from 1869 to 1885, and his son by the same name, who served from 1923 to 1929. In 1876, the Centennial year, the elder Senator Thomas F. Bayard tried to interest the Swedish government in a monument at Wilmington commemorating the arrival of the first Swedish colonists in 1638, but the answer from Stockholm was negative. Sweden's ambitious participation in the Centennial Exposition at Philadelphia may have influenced the decision. Both in 1880 and in 1884 Senator Bayard became one of the leading candidates for the Democratic Presidential nomination. Later he served as secretary of state in the first Cleveland administration and as the first American representative to the Court of St. James's with the rank of ambassador.

Several scholars with family roots in the Delaware colony have made contributions to historical research concerning the Swedes in America. In 1835 the rector of Gloria Dei Church in Philadelphia, Jehu Curtis Clay, who was a great-grandson of one of the early Swedish settlers, published a book entitled *Annals of the Swedes on the Delaware*, which focused on the ecclesiastical side of the history. A second edition was published in Philadelphia in 1858, a third in Chicago in 1914, and a fourth in Chicago in 1938. Dr. Clay served as rector of Gloria Dei from 1831 to 1863, succeeding Nicholas Collin whose term had begun in 1786. Colonel Henry D. Paxson of Philadelphia, who in 1926 published a book entitled *Where Pennsylvania History Began*, was a descendant of Jonas Nilsson. Albert Bushnell Hart, a famous historian and Harvard professor, and a descendant of the Reverend Nils Hornell who came to the Delaware Valley in 1762, took an active interest in American-Swedish affairs. At the age of nearly 80 he spent a summer in Sweden visiting the homes of his ancestors.

For obvious reasons, families who remained based in the Delaware Valley have had, as a rule, less difficulty in identifying their Swedish origin than those who at an early stage moved to other sections of America. A Swedish Colonial Society, with headquarters at Philadelphia, was organized in 1909, and since 1937 the Swedish descendants in the state of Delaware have a similar association of their own. Both work for the preservation of Swedish landmarks and records and may also publish books and documents relating to the early history of Swedes in America.

Father of famous inventor among new immigrants from Sweden — First consuls named

THE sporadic flow of Swedes into America increased after the War of Independence, probably to some extent as a consequence of the treaty of friendship and commerce. Many of the newcomers were unable to find suitable employment, but craftsmen and others with special training had, as a rule, no such difficulties. Several made successful careers in business. Most of the Swedes naturally settled along the Eastern seaboard, principally in Philadelphia, New York, and Boston, but some went to the South, and in the early 1800s a few traders and hunters found their way to the Middle West.

Shortly after his arrival in Philadelphia in the spring of 1794, Henrik Gahn (1774–1834) went on an exploratory trip through New York State and New England in the company of Dr. Nicholas Collin. He planned to buy vast areas of land and to organize immigration from the Swedish province of Dalarna, where he was born. At an early stage, however, he settled in the city of New York as a businessman, married an American girl, and became a citizen. In 1797 he was appointed the first Swedish consul in New York, and as such he kept in close contact with immigrants and visitors from his native country.

The first Swedish consuls in America, Richard Söderström (d. 1815) in Boston and Carl Hellstedt in Philadelphia, were appointed by King Gustav III in the fall of 1783, following the ratification of the treaty of friendship and commerce. Söderström later moved to Philadelphia, and the two consulates were consolidated under him. He had arrived from Gothenburg in 1780 and seems to have meant much to the promotion of commercial relations between the United States and Sweden. In 1797 he received the title of consul general. Early the same year President George Washington, in one of his last official acts, appointed a Swedish-Finnish businessman, Elias Backman, consul at Gothenburg. The U.S. consulate in Sweden's "Gateway to the West," which from 1802 was directed by Americans most of the time, was the first in the North of Europe.

The United States and Sweden did not exchange diplomatic representatives in the 18th century, but at one time they seemed ready to do so. In 1782 a Swedish mining expert and industrialist, Baron Samuel Gustaf Hermelin (1744–1820), was sent to America to investigate economic and political conditions, and in his pocket he carried credentials as Sweden's first minister to the United States. In a commission signed on September 17, 1782, by John Hanson, then chief executive under the Articles of Confederation, Benjamin Franklin had been designated the first American minister to Sweden, but he never went to Stockholm, and no one was appointed to replace him. Hermelin, who remained in the United States for about two years, was elected a member of the American Philosophical Society in Philadelphia, as well as of the American Academy of Arts and Sciences in Boston. In the early 1800s he tried to develop the mineral resources in Sweden's arctic North, but the long distances and other difficulties proved insuperable. He completed, on the other hand, the first cartographic survey of all of Sweden and Finland.

In Philadelphia Dr. Nicholas Collin was the center of Swedish activities, and he seems to have known all the immigrants from his native country. One of his best friends was Bernard Ulrik Dahlgren (1784–1824), whose father, a disciple of Linnaeus, had been a prominent physician in Sweden and Finland. As a student at the University of Uppsala, Bernard Ulrik was accused of propagating republican ideas, and he then left Sweden, spent two years traveling in Europe, and sailed for America in late 1806. In Philadelphia he became a successful and respected businessman, and in 1809 he was appointed Swedish consul.

Dahlgren's children received, as there was reason to expect, a good education, and his son John (1809–70), who was to become a famous naval officer and inventor and a favorite of President Lincoln, showed great promise from the beginning. He was encouraged in his studies by Dr. Collin, who after his father's death took a special interest in the young boy and often invited him to his home. On November 15, 1825, for instance, John Dahlgren wrote in his diary: "In the evening Dr. Collin gave a party, to which I was invited, and of course was present. The old man was very lively; sang a song and told anecdotes; will be 80 years of age next July." At that time, John had already had some training at sea, on board a brig with a Swedish captain, Charles Sandgren.

One of the Swedish immigrants in Philadelphia, Gustaf Risberg, who had fought in the War of Independence, worked for the Bank of the United States, which had been established by the Federal government to serve as a central bank. Other Swedes who lived in this city during Dr. Collin's long service there had such family names as Afzelius, Bergström, Börjesson, or Borgeson, Carlson, Ekman, Hagström, Hall, Hedelius, Johnson, Lundgren, Mellander, Mellin, Olson, Sallin, Strömberg, and Svanberg.

Some Swedes are known to have lived in Boston even in the 17th century, and in the late 1700s there were small groups of recent immigrants. In 1817 Stockholm-born Johan Hauff, who had become an official translator, wrote the Swedish Academy of Sciences that from its *Transactions*, available in the American Academy of Arts and Sciences, he had made translations which had been published in American magazines or read at meetings of the Linnean Society of Boston. Other Swedes settled in the ports of Rhode Island, which also had entered trade relations with Sweden.

Among the early Swedish immigrants in the South was John Asplund, who, after deserting from the British merchant marine, settled in North Carolina, was converted to Baptism, and finally was ordained a minister in Virginia. After an extensive European tour, he visited in the period 1791–94 some 200 Baptist churches in America, traveling about 7,000 miles on foot or by wagon, and the material he thus collected was published in a book. In 1808, when he had conducted unsuccessful land speculations in Maryland, he was drowned during a canoe trip in Virginia. In his Baptist register, which has become a rare collector's item, an American scholar found 19 names of Baptist ministers who seemed to be descendants of early Swedish colonists on the Delaware.

Many immigrants from Sweden arrived in America after having lived, like Wertmüller, Gahn, and Dahlgren, in other European countries, and others came via the West Indies, in particular the Swedish-owned island of St. Barthélemy.

★ 7

The Era of Bernadotte and Berzelius

Sweden loses Finland in 1809 — New constitution and dynasty, union with Norway

A NEW epoch in Swedish history began in the early 1800s: the period of Gustavian monarchy ended in disaster but was followed by another national regeneration.

King Gustav III's son, Gustav IV Adolf (1778–1837), assumed the reins of government in 1796, when all Europe was about to be set aflame by the Napoleonic wars. Sweden's trade relations with England impelled it to side with that country against Napoleon; in addition the young monarch felt he had a divine mission to oppose the French conqueror. In 1805 he joined England and Russia in a coalition, which, however, soon foundered on the might of the French armies. In early September, 1807, when the British navy bombarded Copenhagen and Denmark was forced into an alliance with Napoleon, the Swedish King sailed home from northern Germany, where his small forces had been defeated.

In the summer of 1807 Russia and France had become engaged in a temporary cooperation, which made Sweden's position extremely dangerous. The following year the Russians invaded Finland with Napoleon's approval, and while the Finnish army fought bravely, the armed forces of Sweden proper were not able to offer effective assistance. Denmark too declared war and a French army under the command of Marshal Jean-Baptiste Bernadotte of France began to gather there in preparation for an assault on Sweden from the south. This threat failed to develop, but in 1809, when the Russians had begun to attack the Swedish mainland on several fronts, Sweden was forced to cede to Russia all of Finland, including the Åland Islands — an archipelago situated 75 miles northeast of Stockholm, which had been Swedish since prehistoric times — as well as the northeasternmost strip of Sweden itself. At first the Russians wanted a larger slice of the Swedish North, including the Lapland ore fields the value of which hardly anybody then realized, but they waived this claim after tough negotiations. A new northern boundary was finally drawn along a mighty river, and it has remained unchanged ever since.

The loss of Finland, which represented more than one-third of the Swedish territory and for six centuries had been part of the realm, caused bitter grief and indignation. "As Heaven is my witness, I would rather have signed my own death sentence," said one of the Swedish signers of the peace treaty, General Curt von Stedingk, who 30 years earlier had fought in the American War of Independence and as ambassador to Russia had tried to alert Stockholm to the gathering storm.

As an autonomous Russian grand duchy, Finland was able to retain its own laws, including the Swedish constitution of 1772, for almost a century. After a few decades Swedish literature in Finland reached its peak in the poetry of Johan Ludvig Runeberg, and one of his songs became the national anthem of the Finnish people.

The war had revealed both inefficiency and defeatism in Sweden's civilian and military administration, but King Gustav Adolf was made the scapegoat for the country's misfortunes, and even before the peace treaty with Russia had been signed he was deposed in a bloodless revolution. After months of imprisonment in Gripsholm castle, in which two royal princes, one a dethroned king and the other a future monarch, had been locked up in the 16th century, he was exiled with his family, and spent the rest of his life wandering about Europe. At first acclaimed both in Germany and in England as one of Napoleon's staunchest opponents, he died in obscurity and poverty.

The deposition of the King was immediately followed by the adoption of a new Swedish constitution. It restored the balance between government and parliament, in accordance with both native political tradition and French 18th-century ideas which also had influenced the American constitution; though frequently amended and modified by custom, it remained in force for 165 years. Freedom of the press was guaranteed, and although the government in 1812 received certain powers of confiscation, in effect until 1845, it became a wellspring of reform and progress. Of great importance was also a stipulation that every citizen was entitled to gain access to the records of the public authorities. Another article provided for a parliamentary ombudsman who would investigate private complaints against abuses of power by public servants — an institution which by the middle of the 20th century would be introduced in several English-speaking countries, and the Swedish name of which is widely used in America. As the first ombudsman the Riksdag elected Baron Lars August Mannerheim (1749–1835), who served with competence and integrity, although liberal critics wanted him to be more active in the performance of his duties. The new constitution, however, left the monarch as the political chief executive, and the organization of the Riksdag continued to be based on the four estates, nobles, clergy, burghers, and farmers. A system of two houses without formal class distinctions was not adopted until 1865.

On the Swedish throne Gustav IV Adolf was succeeded by his uncle, Carl XIII (1748–1818), who, however, was aging rapidly and had no legitimate heirs. A member of the Danish royal family, who was first chosen as crown prince, died suddenly in 1810, and 47-year-old Jean-Baptiste Bernadotte (1763–1844) became the leading candidate. His name was launched as a result of an impromptu action by a young Swedish army officer who visited the celebrated field marshal in Paris where he lived in semi-retirement, and the fact that Napoleon, who approved of the candidature, was then at the height of his power had vital importance. In the late summer of 1810, the Riksdag elected Bernadotte crown prince. In Sweden he was received into the Lutheran faith and took the name of Carl Johan.

The former French marshal almost immediately became the real leader of the Swedish nation, and he began with a determined reversal of its foreign policy, aiming at friendship with Russia. In Norway, for centuries united with Denmark, he hoped to obtain compensation for Finland, which many Swedes had expected him to try to win back with French consent. In 1812 an alliance was made with Russia, where Napoleon the same year lost half a million men, and in 1813, when universal military service had been introduced in Sweden, Bernadotte led a Swedish army in the historic battle of Leipzig. He contributed, however, mostly artillery support, and he did not join in the following drive on Paris, in part because he was dreaming of succeeding Napoleon on the French throne, but first of all because he wanted to proceed against Denmark, which remained allied with France. Toward the end of 1813 the Danes were attacked by the Swedes from the south, and early the next year they surrendered Norway, receiving in return Sweden's last possession in northern Germany, which they soon lost.

As there was good reason to expect, the Norwegians objected to being thus transferred and they declared their own independence. When Bernadotte, however, in the summer of 1814 appeared with an army and England enforced a blockade of the Norwegian coast, the Norwegians, after a few skirmishes with the Swedes, agreed to negotiations and accepted the Swedish King as their monarch. Sweden, on the other hand, recognized Norway's national home rule under its new constitution, which had been adopted on May 17, and the two countries were defined as being independent realms under one king. Norwegian foreign relations, however, were to be handled by the government in Stockholm, an arrangement that seemed natural from a Swedish viewpoint but later would cause increasing friction and contribute to the ultimate dissolution of the union in 1905.

In 1814 Norway had a population of about 900,000 and Sweden nearly 2.5 million. In the negotiations with Norway Crown Prince Carl Johan had pursued a more moderate course than had generally been expected. He thus laid the foundation for a considerable popularity among the Norwegians, and in Sweden he was highly regarded as a statesman. The rather loose union with Norway could not fill the place of the old unity with Finland, but the Swedish nation had overcome the threat of internal chaos and won new international prestige. The eventful period of 1812–14 remained, on the other hand, the high point of Bernadotte's political career.

Swedish poetry flowers, reaching even America —
Longfellow visits Sweden

FROM about 1810 and for two or three decades Swedish poetry blossomed as never before, and this period has appropriately been called

its golden age. German philosophical idealism and Romantic literature were powerful influences, but Sweden's or Scandinavia's own
history, including the distant era of the Vikings, became a main
source of inspiration. A group called the Gothic Society aimed ex-
pressly at bringing about a national regeneration by reviving the old
spirit of freedom and unselfish patriotism.

The leading figures, not only as poets and prose writers but also
because of the strength of their personalities, were Esaias Tegnér
(1782–1846) and Erik Gustaf Geijer (1783–1847). Both were born in
the western province of Värmland, which now became known as a
land of poetry and imagination. Tegnér, who like Linnaeus and
Strindberg was a complicated genius and once was described by his
friend Geijer as "a series of contrasts," was long regarded as Sweden's
foremost poet.

Tegnér's early patriotic songs, which sprang from his anger and
bitterness over the humiliating loss of Finland, electrified the Swedish
public. In one of them, titled "Svea," he first dreamed about recon-
quering Finland, but in the final and less militant version he proposed
instead "to reconquer Finland within the boundaries of Sweden." In
one brief line, one of many winged phrases created by him, he thus
anticipated and defined Sweden's future course and development.
Tegnér himself remained, however, anti-Russian all his life.

A lyrical epic in 24 cantos, based on an old Norse saga, became
Tegnér's most popular work. Published in its entirety in 1825 and
titled *Fritiof's Saga*, it was translated into nearly every European language, and the number of interpretations in English finally reached
15. In 1837 Longfellow wrote an enthusiastic article about it with
specimen translations for the *North American Review*, which had become the leading literary magazine in the United States. Two years
earlier he had made a tour of central Sweden, but he did not meet
Tegnér, who at that time was bishop of the Växjö diocese in southern
Sweden. Later, however, the two poets exchanged letters, and other
poems by Tegnér were translated by Longfellow. When the Swedish
bard died, the American poet composed in his honor a commemorative ode in the old Scandinavian style. The first complete American
translation of *Fritiof's Saga* was published in 1877. Directly or indirectly, American interest in the Viking era and in old Norse literature
was greatly stimulated by Tegnér's epic. By the turn of the century,

adornments of Swedish assembly halls and other buildings in the United States were often inspired by it.

Long before Tegnér passed away in 1846, Longfellow seemed to have only pleasantly romantic memories of Sweden, but his and his wife's visit there in the summer of 1835, and in particular their two months' stay in Stockholm, had on the other hand been very disappointing. Most of the time, Sweden lacked the romantic atmosphere that Longfellow had expected, and the literary life of the capital was, moreover, at its lowest ebb during the summer months, but there must also have been other reasons for his dissatisfaction. In Stockholm, he wrote in one of his more pessimistic letters, there was "no spirit — no life — no enterprise — in a word 'no nothing.'" Among the things he liked in Sweden were the long twilights, the pastoral simplicity of the countryside, the Midsummer celebration, and the Göta Canal, via which he and his wife traveled from the east coast back to Gothenburg. Mary Longfellow, who a few months later died in Rotterdam in complications after childbirth, wrote that she found Gothenburg "much preferable as an abiding place to Stockholm." In 1847, romantic memories of Sweden became the basis for the famous beginning of Longfellow's poem "Evangeline," and as late as 1870 he read a Swedish novel in the original. His knowledge of Swedish also enabled him to read Danish literature. His relationship with Sweden has been described as a hobby rather than a vital, intellectual interest, and even his insight into Tegnér remained rather limited. In Sweden he became, on the other hand, the best-known and most widely translated American poet of the 19th century.

Tegnér's poetry covered a wide range of subjects, and his mood varied from one of indomitable belief in the ideals of beauty, justice, and truth to deep pessimism. On several occasions he expressed his admiration for Napoleon as a hero and man of destiny, but on others he denounced him scathingly as a despot. Tegnér was also a great master of Swedish prose, and in 1817, when he was professor of Greek at Lund, he made one of his most celebrated public addresses at the observance of the 300th anniversary of the Reformation. Napoleon, he said, fell because he struggled with a stronger force, the genius of freedom, which undoubtedly would prevail in the long run. And, he added, "if it should be true what so many say, that the day darkens for old Europe: far to the West beyond the sea, where the sun sets for us, there does it rise on a happier world. There Europe has already sent many of her best hopes; there shall mankind save her penates, as Eneas rescued his from falling Ilion."

Another popular and highly respected poet, Johan Olof Wallin (1779–1839), became one of Sweden's greatest psalmists, and many of his hymns have often been sung in Swedish churches in the United States. Best known is the majestic "All Hail to Thee, O Blessed Morn," traditionally the opening psalm at the early-morning Christmas Day service throughout Sweden. Toward the end of his life, and just before he was elected archbishop at Uppsala, Wallin wrote a glowing poetic tribute to George Washington, the "Citizen-general" and "King without a court." It was read by the poet himself at a dinner given by the American minister in Stockholm on Washington's birthday in 1837.

Because of their preoccupation with a great or mysterious past, most Swedish poets of the early 1800s became more and more conservative in both their political and religious attitudes. Among the exceptions was Geijer, who in 1838 caused a sensation by aligning himself with the liberal opposition. The period of poetic exuberance ended with Carl Jonas Love Almqvist (1793–1866), who not only is regarded as a literary genius but also as the most enigmatic figure in Swedish letters. At first he, too, tried to contribute to a moral rejuvenation of the Swedish nation. After the publication of a modernistic novel in which the heroine was critical of the institution of marriage, his financial position became more and more difficult, and in 1851, when he was suspected of forgery and attempted murder by poisoning his creditor, he fled to the United States, where he lived for 14 years. Traveling as far west as St. Louis and south to Texas, he finally settled in Philadelphia and married an elderly widow, although his first wife still lived. He died, broken and destitute, in a German port. In his youth he and some of his friends had dreamed of emigrating to America in order to realize the ideal life as farmers and philosophers.

One of the literary patriots of the early 1800s, Per Henrik Ling (1776–1839), failed as a poet but became the "Father of Swedish gymnastics." In 1813 he founded the Gymnastic Central Institute in Stockholm, which today attracts many students from abroad, and after the middle of the century similar schools were established in other countries and continents, including North and South America. Among the early promoters in the United States was a widely read poet and prose writer, Bayard Taylor, who in 1857 studied medical gymnastics in Stockholm with a pupil of Ling, Lars Gabriel Branting (1799–1881), whose son Hjalmar became Sweden's first internationally known statesman of modern times. In a book titled *Northern Travel*, the first comprehensive American travel report from Scandinavia, Taylor wrote enthusiastically about his experience with the Ling system, ending: "One thing at least is certain — that in an age when physical training is most needed and most neglected, this system deserves to be introduced in every civilized country, as an indispensable part in the education of youth." Modern Swedish gymnastics differs considerably from the system introduced by Ling, but he was the first champion of universal physical training and of cooperation between teachers of gymnastics and medical science.

The Romantic era also produced one of Sweden's greatest composers, the symphonist Franz Berwald (1796–1868), whose father had moved to Stockholm from a Swedish possession in Germany. Unable to earn his living as a musician, he turned to therapeutic gymnastics, glass blowing, and the manufacture of bricks. The symphony which is regarded as his masterpiece did not receive its first performance until the early 20th century. In 1838, when Berwald lived in Berlin, 17-year-old Jenny Lind made her debut at the Stockholm Opera, but six years later she left Sweden to begin her fantastic international career, and she returned to her native country only for occasional guest appearances. Born of unmarried parents in a penny-pinching home in Stockholm, she had begun studying and dancing at the Opera at the age of nine. Kristina Nilsson, who also would make highly successful American tours, studied for some time with Berwald, before leaving for Paris where she won her first laurels. Her father was a crofter in southern Småland, and as a child she sang and played the violin at parties and country fairs.

In the long history of Swedish folk art, the early 1800s was a period of rich flowering. Especially in the northern province of Hälsingland, in Dalarna around Lake Siljan, and in the southwestern province of Halland as well as the adjoining sections of Småland and Västergötland, the farmers adorned their timber cottages or brick

houses with rustic but colorful wall paintings, most of them with biblical motifs. All three districts became, at one time or another, centers
of emigration to America.

Berzelius lays new foundations for chemistry — Progress in medicine and botany

THE intellectual climate in Sweden during the first part of the 1800s
did not favor the natural sciences, but significant advances were
nevertheless made, especially in chemistry, botany, and medicine. By
1820 Jöns Jacob Berzelius (1779–1848) became a leading figure in the
chemical world, and after Linnaeus he remains Sweden's most illustrious scientist.

By determining on the basis of an enormous amount of analytical
work the atomic weights and the valences of nearly all the known
elements, Berzelius laid a solid foundation for the further development of chemistry. This effort alone could, according to modern
scientists, have kept a whole research institution busy for a considerable time, and yet Berzelius's equipment was almost incredibly primitive even by the international standards of his own era. In order to be
able to present conveniently the results of his analyses, he introduced
in 1814 a new and simple system of chemical symbols, which still is
used by chemists and students all over the world. Iron, for instance,
became Fe after the Latin ferrum, and silver Ag after argentum.
Berzelius's chemical language has been compared to Linnaeus's contribution to the systematic classification of plants and other living
things.

Berzelius's work covered the most different subdivisions of his
science, and he was probably the last chemist in command of all contemporary chemical knowledge. Four chemical terms now in more or
less common use, catalysis, protein, isomeric, and polymeric, were
coined by him. Young and eventually famous chemists from other
countries, in particular Germany, worked in his laboratory, and during his travels he also met the scientific leaders of England and
France, the research facilities of which impressed him immensely. His
textbook of chemistry, published in Stockholm in six volumes, was
translated into five languages and became for decades a primary
source of chemical knowledge. As permanent secretary of the
Swedish Academy of Sciences from 1819 he wrote annual surveys of

the progress of science, which were issued in 27 volumes, and his scientific correspondence fills six large tomes.

About 25 new chemical elements were discovered in the period 1800–50, and ten of them were first identified in Sweden. The traditions established by Swedish mineral chemists of the 18th century were thus carried on successfully, which, above all, was Berzelius's achievement. In 1803 the great chemist discovered cerium, in 1818 selenium, and ten years later thorium. The latter, one of the principal elements from which nuclear energy can be derived by fission, was named after a mineral which Berzelius called thorite for Thor, the old Norse god of thunder. In 1817 a young chemist, Johan August Arfwedson (1792–1841), who worked in Berzelius's laboratory, discovered lithium, and in 1831 one of his former students, Nils Gabriel Sefström (1787–1845), identified vanadium, which Berzelius named after Vanadis, the Norse goddess of love and beauty. During the years 1839–43 another outstanding disciple, Carl Gustaf Mosander (1797–1858), discovered lanthanum, erbium, and terbium, as well as didymium which later was shown to contain two components. The rare-earth elements erbium and terbium were named after Ytterby in the Stockholm archipelago.

A metallic element of the vanadium family, named tantalum after Tantalus of the Greek mythology, was discovered in 1802 by an assistant professor of chemistry at Uppsala, Anders Gustaf Ekeberg (1767–1813). Berzelius, who was born in the ancient Väversunda parsonage in the province of Östergötland, was then a student at the same university, but he could not afford to attend Ekeberg's course, for which there was a special charge. At school he had shown more interest in collecting butterflies and plants than in conventional studies, and the principal's final judgment on him was "a youth with good natural talents but with poor habits and dubious prospects." He did leave Uppsala with a doctor's degree in medicine, but as a chemist he was, on the other hand, largely self-taught.

In 1807 Berzelius was appointed professor of medicine and pharmacy at the School of Surgery in Stockholm, which somewhat later became the Caroline Institute, but he did not obtain a decent income until 12 years later when he also took over as secretary of the Academy of Sciences. At about the same time he was raised to noble rank by King Carl XIV Johan in connection with his coronation, and in 1835, when he finally married at the age of 56, the monarch presented him with a barony. He was elected a member of 85 learned societies in other countries, and various chemical associations and chemistry buildings, such as Berzelius Hall at Yale University, are named in his honor. In 1948 scientists from some 40 countries, including the United States, attended the observance in Stockholm of the 100th anniversary of his death. In 1965 Cornell University's John M. Olin Library at Ithaca, New York, acquired all of Berzelius's manuscripts on microfilm. Many American students and scholars have visited the Berzelius Museum of the Swedish Academy of Sciences at Stockholm.

Berzelius's most significant direct contribution to his native country was probably his stubborn fight, against the opposition of leading literary personalities, for the introduction of chemistry, physics, and natural history into the curriculums of secondary schools. This educational reform, effected at a relatively early stage, would gradually enable Sweden to hold its own in the scientific and technological revolution taking place in Europe and North America.

After Berzelius, Sweden's most renowned scientist of the early–to–middle 1800s was Anders Retzius (1796–1860), the son of an eminent naturalist of the Linnaean era. Anatomy was his leading specialty, and his name lives on in two international anatomical terms, Retzius's veins and the Space of Retzius. As an anthropologist, he laid the foundation for the present system of classification. Together, Retzius and Berzelius reorganized the Caroline Institute, the equipment of which was greatly improved, and helped modernize the medical training in Sweden. These and other efforts brought slow but constant advances in health standards. In the period 1800–10 the infant mortality rate was about 20 percent, compared with 15 in 1850 and 1.1 today.

As secretary of the Academy of Sciences, Berzelius had been preceded by Olof Swartz (1760–1818), who began his studies of botany and medicine at Uppsala the year Linnaeus died and in the early 1800s, with the exception of the much older Carl Peter Thunberg, the botanical explorer, was Sweden's internationally best-known botanist. Among his correspondents were several Americans. His reputation had been made during four years abroad, 1783–87, when his principal goal was to study tropical flora. After a few months in Boston and

Philadelphia, he spent more than two years in Jamaica in the West Indies, living "like a snow bunting among thousands of black birds," and if he had wanted to, he could have stayed there forever as "the King's Botanist on the Island." Other parts of the West Indies were also visited, and via London he returned to Sweden in the fall of 1787, loaded with botanical treasures which resulted in some 850 new plant descriptions. His principal work, *Flora Indiae occidentalis* in three volumes, was completed in 1806. Five years later he was elected secretary of the Academy of Sciences, and in 1813 he was appointed professor at the Caroline Institute. A genus of tropical trees has been named Swartzia after him. His leading botanical specialties were the cryptogams, such as ferns and mosses. A contemporary, Erik Acharius (1757–1819), who has been called Linnaeus's last pupil, won international recognition as the founder of the scientific study of lichens, of which there are at least 35,000 different types. He practiced medicine at Vadstena on Lake Vättern, being this little town's first celebrity since Saint Birgitta or Bridget, the foremost religious and literary personality of Sweden's Middle Ages, lived there about 1350.

As professor of botany at Uppsala, Linnaeus's disciple Carl Peter Thunberg was succeeded in 1829 by Göran Wahlenberg (1780–1851), who broke new ground for Swedish botanical research and is regarded as one of the two founders of modern plant geography. A well-known plant genus, Wahlenbergia, as well as a bay and a glacier in Spitzbergen in the Arctic Ocean are named for him. His colleague at the University of Lund, Carl Adolph Agardh (1785–1859), who became a liberal politician but ended as an ultra-conservative bishop, won a European reputation as a pioneer in the study of the primitive and vitally important plants known as algae, of which he collected nearly 50,000 varieties.

Elias Fries (1794–1878), who in 1814 became an assistant professor of botany at Lund and later moved to Uppsala, has been called the "Linnaeus of the 19th century." Like the father of modern botany he grew up in a vicarage in southern Småland, and at Uppsala he attracted devoted disciples from many countries and received collections and specimens from all parts of the world. His foremost specialty was mycology, and he is regarded as the founder of this science, which deals with the huge group of plants known as fungi and indirectly, at least, has great economic and medical significance. Like

Linnaeus, Fries was much interested in the utilitarian phase of botany, and some of his more popular works were addressed primarily to agronomists and farmers.

In Scandinavia, Russia, and other temperate regions of the earth, hundreds of edible mushrooms grow wild and are picked for the table on a large scale, but even in Sweden few people realize that Elias Fries was the first great instructor in this field. Some plant groups were named for him, but subsequent research resulted in new classifications. In America the name Freesia is sometimes thought to have been coined in his honor, but this is not correct. Many of his descendants also became noted botanists, creating a unique family tradition. One of his contemporaries at Lund, Sven Nilsson (1787–1883), made lasting contributions to archeology, geology, and zoology.

When Elias Fries and Sven Nilsson died, at the respective ages of 83 and 96, Sweden was being transformed into an industrial country, and gradually the natural sciences again began to prosper on a broader front.

Economic betterment but serious social problems and growing political strife

KING CARL XIV JOHAN, who ascended the throne in 1818, became the first monarch in Sweden's long history under whom the country never was involved in war, and this fact alone indicates that his reign must have been a period of steady recovery and unusual contentment for the Swedish nation. There were, on the other hand, serious economic and social problems. A race between population growth and the development of national resources had begun in the 1700s, and it would cast its shadow not only over the era of the first Bernadotte on the Swedish throne but over the whole 19th century.

The construction of the Göta Canal, the last section of which was opened in 1832, may be mentioned as an example of the technological progress. Traversing central Sweden via lakes and rivers and requiring some 60 locks because of the differences in altitude, this waterway enables small vessels to cross the country from Gothenburg to the Baltic, and vice versa. New mechanical workshops and temporary training centers were needed for the time-consuming project, more valuable engineering experience was thus obtained, and this again would soon have an effect also in America. To a young boy named John Ericsson, for instance, the canal opened up a new world of mechanical interest and schooling. Today the Göta Canal is a great attraction for tourists who like to travel at leisure by ship through the Swedish countryside.

The ironworks were gradually modernized, but the beginning industrial revolution did not yet touch Sweden. The pace of agricultural reforms was, on the other hand, stepped up, and both the cultivated area and the productivity of farming increased considerably. Living standards in the rural districts were thus improved, but crop yields varied greatly according to the weather, and relatively large destitute groups were underfed even in normal years. Especially serious was, therefore, the continued growth of the landless agricultural population, which by the middle of the century was to make up no less than 40 percent of the Swedish people.

Realistically although somewhat cynically, Esaias Tegnér saw the rapid increase in population as a result of "the peace, the vaccine, and the spud." The potato had, at last, come into its own, and to most families it became vitally important. In part, however, its zooming popularity among the farmers was based on the fact that it could also produce liquor, and the consumption of alcohol per inhabitant began to rise steeply, reaching levels 5–8 times higher than today's. The reckless abuse of liquor caused, however, a growing reaction, and many temperance societies were formed in the 1830s. King Carl Johan himself took an active part in this campaign, and so did his French-born son, Crown Prince Oscar, who was to succeed him on the throne. From the beginning the Swedish temperance movement was stimulated by influences from the United States, and it would, in turn, affect the emigration to America. The most vigorous temperance advocate, the Reverend Peter Wieselgren (1800–77), who favored religious renewal, is also regarded as a pioneer in adult education.

King Carl Johan and his advisers ruled the country with both authority and efficiency, but the former revolutionary general and republican followed, like other European leaders, a conservative course. After another revolution in France, in July, 1830, he became more afraid of change, and the gap between his bureaucratic regime and the liberal opposition widened. The middle classes were advancing rapidly, and their spokesmen, who included businessmen and industrialists, intellectuals and farmers, knew on the whole what they wanted: constitutional government and a one- or two-chamber parliament instead of the four-estate Riksdag, a more liberal economic legislation and lower tariffs, freedom of the press and of worship, improved elementary education, and closer political relations with England, which, because of its parliamentary system, was regarded as a far more suitable ally than Russia. Some groups wanted King Carl Johan to abdicate in favor of Crown Prince Oscar, who was regarded as liberal, and there were also republican sentiments, but the tension eased during the monarch's last years. A typical representative of the new middle-class ideology was the jurist Johan Gabriel Richert (1784–1864), who has been called the "Father of Swedish liberalism."

While the Riksdag was the principal arena of the political debates, the press joined vigorously in the battle, especially after 1830 when a well-educated businessman, Lars Johan Hierta (1801–72), who was born into the nobility, founded the Stockholm *Aftonbladet*, which became Sweden's first popular newspaper and the main middle-class organ. Under a censorship regulation of 1812 the government tried to suppress it, but by successively changing the heading of his journal, finally reaching *The Twenty-third Aftonbladet*, Hierta was able to carry on without interruption. In 1832 a radical daily, later known as *Handelstidningen*, began to appear in Gothenburg. In the larger cities the liberal papers were much more effective than their conservative adversaries. Their influence on the coming emigration to America, as well as on the whole transformation of Sweden, was to be considerable.

8

Growth of Relations and American Influence in Sweden

First envoys in Washington and Stockholm — U.S.A. largest market for Swedish iron

THROUGHOUT the turmoil and confusion of the Napoleonic era relations between Sweden and the United States remained friendly, although at times it was difficult for the government in Stockholm to maintain harmony both with the American republic and with England, whose goodwill became vital to Swedish policies.

In 1812 an experienced diplomat and commercial agent, Johan Albert Kantzow (1759–1825), was sent to America via London as the first Swedish minister in Washington. Since the war that had just begun between England and the United States was regarded as unpopular in both countries and clashed with Bernadotte's and Sweden's political objectives in Europe, the new envoy was instructed to help bring about an Anglo-American settlement. In this he was not successful, but early in 1814 the American government accepted his offer of mediation, and it was agreed that a peace conference should be held at Gothenburg.

Five American delegates were named, and two of them, Henry Clay and Jonathan Russell, arrived in Sweden, but Napoleon's empire had then collapsed and the Anglo-American peace negotiations were transferred to Ghent in present-day Belgium. At that time, moreover, Sweden was about to take military action against Norway with English naval cooperation, and when Bernadotte received Jonathan Russell, who had been appointed the first American minister in Stockholm, he assured him of his friendship for the United States but made no offer of aid in the complicated peace talks. When Russell returned to Stockholm in the spring of 1815, Sweden had become less dependent on Britain, and with the American envoy he discussed future cooperation against English maritime practices.

When the American declaration of war against England became known in Sweden in the summer of 1812, some 40 American ships were in Gothenburg within reach of British guns, but at the direction of the American consul they were moved into the inner harbor under the protection of Swedish shore batteries. During the war English vessels were not permitted to enter Swedish ports to dispose of American prizes, and merchantmen from the United States joined Swedish convoys while passing through the straits separating Sweden and Denmark.

In the early 1800s, trade between Sweden and the United States began to assume real importance, and during the first half of the century diplomatic and cultural relations between the two countries were largely based on an expanding commerce. America needed more Swedish iron for its industrial development, and since England's import requirements rapidly declined as a result of the substitution of coal for charcoal, the transatlantic market became essential to Sweden and its iron producers. Without it, the gradual reorganization of the Swedish mills and their increasing concentration on high-quality specialties would have been even more difficult than they actually were. In maintaining and expanding their production without access to domestic mineral fuel, Sweden's ironmasters were practically unique in the world.

Sweden's trade and friendship pact with the United States of 1783 was, with certain modifications, reactivated by a commercial ten-year treaty of 1816, which went into effect two years later. It tore down antiquated trade barriers, provided for reciprocal treatment, encouraged direct commerce between American and Swedish ports, and was followed by a steady increase in trade. The United States had already become the largest importer of Swedish iron, and now it obtained from Sweden more than one-third of its purchases of this metal. American vessels carried most of the direct trade, and in Swedish ports they enjoyed greater privileges than those of any other country.

At Gothenburg, cargoes bound for or arriving from the United States made up the largest proportion of the freight handled.

A new treaty of the same type, concluded in 1827 and ratified the following year, extended the application of reciprocity and mutual free trade, and until the early 20th century it remained the basis for American commerce with the united kingdoms of Sweden and Norway. The treaties of 1816 and 1827 are regarded as milestones in the gradual breaking down of restrictions on international commerce and navigation.

In the 1830s, when shipments were also made via German and English ports, direct exports of Swedish bar iron to America reached an annual average of 25,000 metric tons, which was approximately 40 percent of the iron shipped from Sweden and 25 percent of its total sales abroad. The United States still met no less than one-fourth of its need of imported iron by purchases from Sweden. Though by the middle of the century these proportions had declined considerably, the United States remained the best customer of the Swedish iron and steel industry. Bar iron was then gradually replaced by other products, and the Swedish iron stamps, which for two centuries had been leading international trademarks and become highly respected also in the New World, vanished from the scene.

Sweden's transatlantic imports consisted mostly of raw materials and foodstuffs, such as cotton, tobacco, sugar, and rice. Despite increasing purchases of these and other American staples, trade between the two nations resulted in a Swedish export surplus up to the Civil War. At that time transoceanic shipping had already been changed by the abolition of maritime restrictions and by technical advances. In the early 1830s the number of American vessels that came to Sweden began to decrease, and somewhat later Swedish ships transported more than three-fourths of the direct trade. Many of them carried emigrants as well as iron. Gradually, however, Swedish transatlantic shipping began to decline, being unable to compete with the larger and faster vessels built abroad, and by 1860 American ships again accounted for a major part of the direct trade between the United States and Sweden.

After John Paul Jones, who had made a dash through Sweden in 1788, the first famous American to visit the country was not Henry Clay but his former friend Aaron Burr, lawyer, politician, and adven-

turer, who came in early May of 1809, five years after his duel with
Alexander Hamilton and two years after his trial for treason and final
acquittal. In the year 1809 Sweden ceded Finland to Russia and received a new constitution, after King Gustav IV Adolf had been deposed. Burr remained in Sweden for nearly six months which were
crowded with sightseeing, studies of Swedish culture, laws, language,
and other subjects, and meetings and parties with celebrities of various kinds, and in contrast to many other visitors of the same era he
was as a rule impressed by what he saw or heard. In a letter to his
friend Henry Gahn, the Swedish consul in New York who seems to
have suggested that he visit Sweden, he wrote that "there is no country with whose jurisprudence I am acquainted in which personal liberty is so well secured," and in a letter to his daughter the honesty of
the Swedish people became one of the leading themes. In the *Private
Journal of Aaron Burr*, containing his diary and correspondence, and
published two years after his death, his Swedish record occupies
about 100 pages.

*Pro-and-con debate about U.S.A. begins — Swedish reforms
and emigration involved*

THE first part of the Romantic era in Scandinavian literature and
philosophy was a turning point in the history of Swedish attitudes
toward America.

While an instinctive admiration for the young republic had been
predominant in the late 18th and early 19th centuries, poets and
historians then began to question the reasons for this frame of mind,
and in the 1820s they were inclined to look upon the United States as
a country without established traditions and whose future therefore
seemed uncertain. Almost immediately, however, they ran into violent opposition, and a battle which would continue for decades was
thus joined. It would, in fact, never cease, although its themes as well
as the line-up would change. Fundamentally, the developing controversy in Sweden was a European rather than a national phenomenon. Swedish opinion was always greatly influenced by that in other
countries, and in the beginning such influences were of overriding
importance.

The Swedish discussion about the United States that began in the
1820s may, with some simplification, be regarded as one phase of the

ideological and political dialogue between conservatives and liberals. The former took, on the whole, a skeptical view of the American republic, while the latter consistently stood up for it; their convictions were, in both cases, based on political philosophies rather than personal feelings. But the front was, of course, always somewhat fluid. Journalists and other writers could, for instance, feel inspired by American ideas without being liberals, or they could admire the principles on which the United States was founded but might feel disappointed by later developments. George Washington and Benjamin Franklin remained shining symbols even to many traditionalists, but both they and more progressive observers were taken aback by the contrasts and paradoxes of American politics, including the nature of some election campaigns and the beginning spoils system in so far as it became known in Sweden. Much of the criticism or disappointment expressed in Sweden had previously been voiced in the United States itself.

Because of its constitution and the opportunities it could offer its citizens the United States was, according to a liberal publication in the middle of the 1820s, a unique creation. To this, conservative spokesmen answered that a genuine national unity was lacking, and that the federation would be able to survive only as long as the economic expansion continued across the virgin territory. In the 1830s the liberal *Aftonbladet* became the most widely read newspaper in Sweden, and it played a leading part in defending and explaining the United States and its institutions. When Andrew Jackson had become president as the champion of the "common people," conservatives maintained that all nations without an aristocratic elite had sooner or later degenerated, but *Aftonbladet* regarded the absence of a traditional aristocracy as one of the most encouraging aspects of America. Its expectations were, on the other hand, based primarily on an increasingly influential middle class. Liberal writers might, of course, admit that political and social evils existed in the United States as well as in other countries, but these, they added, did not affect basic American principles, and slavery, for instance, was actually a heritage from the colonial powers.

The temperature in the conservative camp climbed when more and more liberals began to regard the United States as the best model for Sweden's own political and social transformation. Democracy, they claimed, was the key to the future, and the American system of government by the people must be carefully studied. Sweden should also look to the United States for guidance in its humanitarian and economic advances. Some conservative commentators were rather moderate in their retorts; while expressing admiration for the American people, they remained convinced that Sweden must continue to build on its own foundations, without importing ideas and practices intended for entirely different conditions. By conservative sharp-shooters, on the other hand, the United States was ironically called the "Liberal Canaan," the lofty ideals of which had inflamed too many Swedes, although they actually were little more than stars on a distant horizon. In 1835, one of the more extreme Romantic poets, P.D.A. Atterbom (1790–1855), saw America as "a gigantic commercial, industrial, and agricultural corporation." A conservative paper said it had heard rumors that a bust of one of *Aftonbladet's* writers would be placed in the American Hall of Fame between pictures of George Washington and Benjamin Franklin.

From the other side of the Atlantic the conservative critics received support which, although not made public, may have had some effects on the continued discussion. In 1841, when European diplomats still regarded the American capital as one of the more unattractive assignments, the Swedish-born chief of its Swedish-Norwegian mission wrote to a high government official and future foreign minister in Stockholm that if the Swedish liberals could spend six months in the United States, they would return home completely cured of their infection. Comments of this particular type may have been unusual, but up to the Civil War all the Swedish-Norwegian representatives in Washington would send more or less negative reports to the government in Stockholm, although they always felt encouraged when American conservatism and "common sense" seemed to be gaining ground. They did, however, also transmit objective information, for instance about economic and technical progress, and some of them admitted that the United States regardless of its politics offered immigrants of the lower classes in Scandinavia certain advantages or at least opportunities.

Although there was only a sporadic emigration from Sweden to the United States in the 1830s, the question of how the country would be able to provide better living standards for its growing population began, during that decade, to play a part in the discussion centering on America. Without more comprehensive political reforms and a more rapid economic growth, large groups of people, the liberals warned, would have no choice but to join in the migration to the New World. This problem would soon become one of the leading themes in the Swedish public debate, and visitors to the United States would supply more and more pertinent material. By 1840, many travelers had, in fact, already contributed to the Swedish symposium on America, although they merely touched upon its possible attractions for immigrants from Scandinavia.

U.S.A. visitors laud inventors, schools, and prisons, fear a coming union breach

SWEDISH study and business trips to the United States began in earnest after the end of the second American war with England in late 1814. The resulting books and other detailed reports helped enliven the discussion at home, and, on the whole, they gradually contributed to more realistic attitudes toward America.

Most of the Swedish travelers in the New World became, essentially, exhilarated and hopeful, while others found more to criticize than to praise. To some degree the reactions varied according to the political beliefs of the observers, but at times liberals and progressive conservatives felt disenchanted. The American republic had, after all, been extolled as the land of the future. At close range many of its problems seemed more serious than expected, and there were, of course, even symptoms of a cleavage both between East and West and between North and South.

In 1818 a widely traveled naval officer, Baron Axel Klinkowström (1775–1837), was sent over the Atlantic to study economic and industrial conditions, with emphasis on shipbuilding and the new use of steam. Throughout his tour, which was limited to the Eastern states, he viewed the American scene with unusual understanding. Among the many political, industrial, and professional leaders he met was President James Monroe, who, in contrast with the city of Washington, won his heart. When the chief executive said that it would please him very much if a foreigner could find anything new and instructive in so young a country as the United States, Klinkowström answered according to his own summary that "the time was near when Europeans would travel to America less for the purpose of introducing their own ideas than to gather information about things that were either imperfectly known or wholly new to Europe."

The Swedish traveler was greatly impressed by the variety of new inventions in America. Its prisons and reformatories aroused similar feelings, and at least one such institution he studied in detail. He then became one of the first Europeans to report favorably on the humane treatment of criminals, and his comments, which soon would be followed by other Swedish eyewitness accounts of the same type, played a part in the prison-reform movement in Scandinavia. In 1820, on his way back to Stockholm, the Swedish baron spent some time in Paris discussing and writing essays on various American subjects, and one of them dealt with the new prisons. Eleven years later the French government sent Count Alexis de Tocqueville to the United States to report on the penal system, and this trip resulted in his famous analysis of American democracy. In 1839, or four years after its first publication in Paris, the book began to appear in a Swedish translation, which was to have effects on the emigration movement of the next decade. The name of one of the emigrants directly influenced by it was Gustaf Unonius, of whom we shall hear more.

A comprehensive report which Klinkowström wrote in French for King Carl XIV Johan was full of praise for the American people, and his conclusion was that Sweden would do well to use the United States as a model in its efforts to achieve technical progress and social betterment. In 1819, however, he also saw America in a state of panic and depression, and he felt disturbed by what he described as excessive speculation and a lack of stability in the banking system. Greater authority for the central government he regarded, therefore, as necessary. Subsequent financial panics and economic depressions in America would always have a strong impact on Sweden and affect the emigration to the West.

Another of Klinkowström's negative observations in America concerned the great variation in income among the states, which, he wrote, "creates many inconveniences for the government and makes it impossible to pursue plans for national improvement." While deploring the evils of slavery, the Swedish nobleman remained skeptical about Americans of African origin, but he also feared that many of the new immigrants from Europe would become a source of trouble.

Without anticipating a larger immigration from Sweden, he remarked that "it is the man with average means, the able and industrious or the persecuted, who will here find the peace he missed in Europe." In New York he met several Swedish settlers, including a wealthy businessman named Charles G. Smedberg, born at Stockholm in 1784. Among the latter's descendants was Vice Admiral William R. Smedberg III, whose career as a naval officer comprised the years 1926–64.

Klinkowström obviously believed in the future of the American nation, but in the last of his 25 long letters to Sweden, all intended for publication, he wrote after having voiced his deep respect for the foresight of the founding fathers: "But America's statesmen, with the best will in the world, could not avoid all the natural circumstances which in the future will have their effect upon the constitution of this country, and that one day will cause a breach between the states." The same report he ended by saying that he left with regret "this country that is still incompletely known among us." He did not pretend that his own interpretation was faultless.

In 1824 Klinkowström's letters were published in Stockholm in two volumes, with a supplementary atlas folio containing maps and pictures, and 21 of them are available in an American edition of 1952, titled *Baron Klinkowström's America 1818–20*. Several of the original pictures were drawn by Klinkowström himself, and copies are in American museums as well as in private possession. One of his best known sketches shows New York's City Hall and Broadway, with fine carriages and at least one roaming pig.

Another naval officer, Carl August Gosselman (1800–1843), made several journeys to North and South America, and in 1835 he published, in two volumes, an objective and favorable account of the United States. Without going overboard, he expressed his appreciation of the American system of government and the progress it had helped bring about. One of the most fascinating aspects of the country was, he thought, the frontier, the possibility of ever moving on, a theme that would be set forth by native historians in the 20th century. The Americans had, consequently, become a people always on the move. Their women he observed with particular interest, quite a few of them being among the most beautiful he had ever seen.

The owner of one of Sweden's leading export and import houses,

Olof Wijk (1786–1856) from Gothenburg, who visited America in 1829, liked much of what he saw and heard, but not enough to be willing to stay for ever. About President Jackson, whom he met, and Jacksonian Democracy he had strong reservations. Like some other Swedish travelers of this era he found, at the same time, unexpected class distinctions. In Sweden he became a conservative member of the four-estate parliament. He was also a champion of temperance and a progressive force in his home town, and in its business life he introduced new American methods. With many other citizens of Gothenburg, Wijk and his descendants made Sweden's "Gateway to the West" more oriented toward the English-speaking world than any other Swedish city.

A wholesale merchant from Stockholm, Carl David Arfwedson (1806–81), who had earned a doctor's degree with a dissertation on Sweden's 17th-century colony on the Delaware, spent two years in the United States and Canada in the early 1830s. After having traveled in the South and Middle West he attended Andrew Jackson's second inauguration in 1833, and the next year he married the daughter of a Philadelphia merchant. He admired the American constitution but feared, like Wijk, that democracy would degenerate because of the electoral system, this despite the fact that he was impressed by the public schools and the ever improving instruction provided. About his travels in the New World he wrote three books, one of which, *The United States and Canada in* 1832, 1833, 1834, was first published in London and still is regarded as an excellent portrayal of life in America.

Arfwedson, who returned to the United States twice, served as American consul in Stockholm 1838–55. In the early 1840s he issued a pamphlet directed to Swedes and Norwegians who considered emigration to the United States. This was, he emphasized, a hazardous step, and everybody should stay at home if possible, but those who nevertheless wanted to leave could turn to him for advice.

The most controversial of the books about the United States published in Sweden in the 1830s was produced by a businessman and former government employee, Carl Ulric von Hauswolff (1791–1843), who had served in the tiny Swedish colony in the West Indies and also spent some years in South America. Printed in 1835 in two volumes and largely based on German writings, it may be regarded as the Swedish beginning of an approach which already had been tried in other countries and later would becloud the exchange of opinions across the Atlantic, in both directions: it was a determined attempt to influence the political discussion at home by painting conditions on the other side in as dark colors as possible.

Hauswolff might, of course, have answered that liberal devotees already had done their best to gild the American lily for purposes of their own, and indirectly, at least, he did exactly that in his foreword: he was fighting against the "preposterous enthusiasm" with which a certain party in Sweden, that is, the liberals, looked toward America. *Aftonbladet* characterized his work as "persistent slander of a great and respectable nation," and added that against this background the dignity of the United States actually stood out in sharper relief. Some conservative publications disagreed, but the counteroffensive continued, and it was resumed as late as 1842 when Gustaf Unonius took Hauswolff to task in a long letter from Wisconsin which was published in *Aftonbladet* in several installments.

An American traveler, Unonius wrote, might arrive in Stockholm in horrible weather, and wading in filth he might hear bawdy songs and curses from taverns and drunkards, be cheated out of money and property, and perhaps finally become overrun by beggars. A report concentrating on such experiences would not, of course, do justice to Sweden, but, Unonius added, it was on the basis of similar negative and fragmentary impressions that Hauswolff had judged the United States.

Sweden's pioneer banker begins his career as a seaman and stevedore in America

IN THE early to middle 1800s, as already indicated, Swedish naval officers played a rather prominent part in the expanding personal, economic, and cultural relations between Sweden and the United States. Most of those who came to America went back to their native country, while others joined the ranks of the immigrants. Among the visitors in the 1830s were André Oscar Wallenberg (1816–86), who came first as an ordinary seaman and later returned as an ensign but worked as a sailor, and his friend Henrik Sundewall (1814–84), who

also was a budding naval officer. These two young men did not publish their impressions of the New World, but their visits assumed
significance for other reasons.

Oscar Wallenberg's father, Marcus Wallenberg (1744–1833), who
became bishop at Linköping in the province of Östergötland, had in
his radical youth been expelled from the University of Uppsala for
one year because of his participation in a music demonstration directed against King Gustav IV Adolf. In 1832, at the age of 16, his son
Oscar sailed to New Orleans and back, as a seaman on a Swedish ship.
In the fall of 1835, when he had graduated from the school that was
the beginning of the Swedish naval academy, he again left for the
United States, and after a month in Boston, where his cash resources
ran out, he spent the next two years working as a seaman on commercial vessels, most of them American. Seaports from Nova Scotia to the
Mexican Gulf became familiar to him, and as some of his ships were
river transports, he was also able to visit such cities as Albany, Buffalo,
Cleveland, and Chicago. For a while he earned his living as a stevedore under the name Andrew Watson.

Wherever he went, young Wallenberg was an attentive observer,
and often he spent his leisure hours reading books and periodicals.
Gradually he became more and more interested in economics and
finance, and finally received a highly instructive object lesson concerning such matters — the commercial and financial crisis of 1837, when
a great many banks and mercantile houses failed and there were
serious riots in New York and other cities. During this confusion
much was written and said about the deficiencies of the American
banking system, and Wallenberg seems to have absorbed the essen-
tials. Toward the end of his life he wrote that it was in America that he
began to think of the various forms of banking, and that his observations there gave him a first insight into the question of how a bank
should not be managed.

Wallenberg returned to Sweden in the late fall of 1837. After
service in the navy and studies in Western and Southern Europe, he
captained a commercial vessel, Sweden's first propeller-driven ship, in
1846–47 and then established himself as a businessman and shipbuilder at Sundsvall, some 200 miles north of Stockholm. He was,
however, soon ready for his principal contribution, a leading role in
the creation of an efficient banking system that would further Swe-

den's economic progress. In 1856 he founded Stockholms Enskilda Bank, which he led until his death three decades later, and in 1863 he was one of the more active founders of Skandinaviska Banken, which also became one of Sweden's foremost commercial banks. In 1971 the two were merged. As a member of parliament for 30 years, Wallenberg helped bring about many reforms which directly or indirectly stimulated Sweden's commercial and industrial development. Some of his initiatives contributed greatly to improvements in the legal status of women and to the introduction of the metric system (1879–88).

During his two years in America, Oscar Wallenberg met several young naval officers from Sweden, among them Henrik Sundewall, a son of the business manager of two large estates in the province of Skåne. After graduation from the naval school at Karlskrona in the southeast of Sweden in 1835, he came to the United States as an ordinary seaman on an American brig. He then served on a naval schooner for 18 months, finally as a noncommissioned officer, and after that he sailed with American merchant vessels until 1840. After several years as an officer in the Swedish navy, two or three in the British navy, and a brief period as a skipper on the Göta Canal, he accepted an offer of employment from Prussia which, after a successful Danish blockade of German ports in the war of 1848–49, had started aiming at larger and more efficient naval forces. The unusually experienced Sundewall was placed in charge of the practical training of Germany's naval personnel, and since he succeeded well in this post he has sometimes been described as the real founder of the German navy. During the years 1859–62 he took a Prussian squadron, with diplomats as well as scientists on board, on a tour of the Far East. The next year he left German service with the rank of rear admiral, and the last two decades he lived at Karlskrona, Sweden's naval base on the Baltic.

Anglo-American influences spur temperance and
revivalist movements in Sweden

DESPITE the animated discussion about America in the 1830s, the Swedish press had not yet become important in arousing an interest in emigration. The circulation of even the leading newspapers and magazines was quite modest, and the rural districts were seldom reached by articles and news reports about the New World. Many other influences were, however, also at work.

New moral and religious impulses from America and England helped prepare the way for the coming migration, as well as for Sweden's own modernization. A pamphlet containing an essay by Benjamin Franklin became, for instance, one of Sweden's first modern best sellers. Entitled *The Way to Wealth, or the Best Sermon ever Preached on Industry and Frugality*, it was published in a score of editions. A dissertation on the effects of alcohol by Benjamin Rush, the American physician who in 1794 had been elected a member of the Swedish Academy of Sciences, was translated by Peter Wieselgren, and six famous sermons on temperance by one of the greatest American preachers of his time, the Reverend Lyman Beecher, were also published in translation. The temperance movement became an integral part of the religious revival that began to sweep the country.

Sweden's old laws of religious compulsion, introduced to maintain the spiritual unity of a small and homogeneous nation whose survival at times seemed threatened, were preserved longer than those in other Protestant countries, or until the late 1850s. A spirit of tolerance prevailed during the first part of the 1800s, but after some new experiences, including extraordinary outbursts of religious fervor, the climate changed temporarily. On the whole, however, it was not so much the lack of religious freedom in Sweden as the great variety of churches in America that would make large groups of people decide to leave for the New World, or would at least contribute to such decisions.

The first noted Methodist in Sweden was an Englishman, James Owen (1774–1854), who in the early 1800s settled in Stockholm and there became an industrial pioneer, especially in the construction of steam engines and steamships. Significant experiments with propellers were also made by him. For his English workmen he invited Methodist ministers from Britain.

In 1830 came the Reverend George Scott (1804–74), a native of Scotland, who was expected to cooperate with Samuel Owen in his work for temperance, or rather complete abstinence, among the Swedish people. Soon fluent in its language, he remained in Sweden for 12 years and assumed an importance far beyond Owen's expectations or hopes. While today little known among the general public, he has, in fact, long been regarded by historians as one of the leading pioneers of the temperance movement in Sweden and as the progenitor of its free churches and 19th-century revivalist activities, which helped bring about a growing release of spiritual forces in the Swedish nation and via the immigrants had far-reaching effects in America.

Scott himself did not found any new religious order in Sweden. After nine years in Stockholm he tried to form a Methodist congregation with Swedish members; this may have been a mistake in view of the existing legislation, but he was actually not aiming at a separatist group, and on the whole he worked for a religious revival within the framework of the Church of Sweden. He was extremely critical of the spiritual conditions in the country, which in letters to his principals in London he described as "a moral wilderness." Several times he undoubtedly went too far in his public statements, but quite a few Swedish leaders were almost equally censorious, in particular so far as the people's attitude toward liquor was concerned.

For ten years George Scott used as his chapel a small summerhouse near the fashionable Kungsträdgården, a park at the center of Stockholm; it was placed at his disposal by Count Carl De Geer (1781–1861), a grandson of the eminent entomologist of the 18th century and, like him, one of Sweden's wealthiest men. De Geer's home in the Swedish capital, which included a garden, became in the 1830s a center of society life in Stockholm, and while Scott may not have taken part, the location of his chapel seemed significant. At an early stage he established close relations with Crown Prince Oscar, who came to one of his first temperance meetings, and he had several audiences with King Carl Johan. Among his protectors and supporters were also Sweden's foremost cabinet minister, Count Mathias Rosenblad (1758–1847), who became one of the leaders of a missionary society founded by Scott, and Bishop, finally Archbishop, Carl Fredrik af Wingård (1781–1851), a conservative friend of temperance and pietism. Their feelings for Scott, however, cooled toward the end.

In the summer of 1836 Scott was joined by a young Presbyterian temperance missionary from America, the Reverend Robert Baird (1798–1863), who returned four years later and may be regarded as one of the most important visitors from the United States that Sweden has had. By Scott he was introduced to King Carl Johan, and to him he presented a copy of a French translation of a book he had written about the temperance movement in the United States. The monarch was so impressed that he had the volume translated into Swedish, published at his own expense, and sent to every parish priest in the country. Popularly known as "The King's book" or "Baird's book," it promoted both temperance and, indirectly, emigration.

Baird believed that the United States was destined to become the religious and moral leader of the world. He had also written an emigrant and travel guide to the Middle West, entitled *View of the Valley of the Mississippi*. There, he said, "the finest land in the world may be purchased at the sum of one dollar and a quarter per acre." Especially during his second visit to Sweden he helped develop an almost utopian image of America.

Religious tracts and temperance pamphlets, some of them containing Scott's own sermons and lectures, were spread by the Methodist missionary by the hundreds of thousands, since 1837 with financial support from the American Tract Society. These activities were also extended to Norway and Finland. In England Scott managed to raise money for a new and much larger chapel, and in 1839–40 a church seating about 1,200 was built at Stockholm's Haymarket, near the site of the present Concert House in which each December 10 the Nobel prizes, except the one for peace work, are distributed.

When Robert Baird returned to Stockholm in 1840, he had become widely known because of "The King's book," and his portrait was found in many homes in Sweden and Norway. He was now secretary of the Foreign Evangelical Society in New York, and temperance promotion remained his primary objective. In late summer he and Peter Wieselgren spoke to several hundred university students and faculty members at the University of Uppsala, and after that they and George Scott made a propaganda tour of the provinces of Gästrikland and Hälsingland farther north. The latter province, in particular, was full of pious Lutheran dissenters known as *läsare* or readers, that is, Bible readers. At the old city of Hudiksvall Baird and his associates spoke to about 5,000 people, including 34 clergymen, and meetings were also held at Njutånger, Norrala, Söderala, Skog, Hamrånge, Hille, and Gävle, names that a few years later would be heard in the settlements of the American Middle West.

The preachers during the trip included a young state-church

minister, Lars Paul Esbjörn, who in 1849 would lead a flock of emigrants from his home district in Hälsingland to the Midwest and become the Swedish Lutheran pioneer pastor of the 19th century in America. Among the farmers Baird met was Olof Olsson of Söderala, who already had listened to Scott in Stockholm, and who in 1846 in western Illinois would buy the first land for a new religious sect which drew most of its strength from the province of Hälsingland.

George Scott was also in close touch with the religious work at Jönköping, the largest city in the northern part of the province of Småland, which would become a center of the free-church movement and sometimes be called "Sweden's Jerusalem." In the early 1840s Småland was the scene of a religious phenomenon called the "preaching sickness." To a friend in America Scott wrote that hundreds or thousands gathered to hear the "preachers," and that some were immediately converted, returned stolen property, and became teetotalers.

In the summer of 1841 George Scott visited America to collect more funds both for his church building in Stockholm and for the prosecution of his work in Sweden. During his tour he preached 61 sermons and delivered 84 addresses, and for various publications he wrote articles about Sweden and his work there. Among the churches he visited were two of the "Old Swedes" in the Delaware Valley, Holy Trinity in Wilmington and Gloria Dei in Philadelphia. After having seen the Wilmington temple, he wrote in his diary: "Felt a glow in my heart while viewing this ancient structure, which proved that . . . Sweden fills a deep and tender place in my heart." In Washington he was, together with some other visitors, received by President John Tyler in the White House. Being very puritanical both in his views and in his habits, he objected to the living standards of well-to-do people, and one day he confided to his diary: "If I am killed in America it will be by soft beds and luxurious living; it is really alarming."

In 1841 the United States had not yet recovered fully from the panic of 1837, and the traveling campaigner from Stockholm felt that in his sermons and addresses he had to use pretty strong language to loosen the purse strings. He was, in fact, rather successful both in the raising of cash and, especially, in securing yearly grants from American societies for his associates in the religious work in Sweden. However, summaries of some of his talks, as well as comments said to have been made in America, were published in the Swedish press. A letter which sounds as if it had been fabricated in Sweden asserted that as a result of Scott's visit the Americans had become convinced that "the Swedish nation was little better than the savages in the deserts of Africa or the cannibals on the islands of the Pacific."

Returning to Sweden in late fall, Scott seems to have expected to spend the rest of his life there, but he soon realized that he was being accused of defaming the Swedish people before American audiences, and that a strange alliance against him had been formed by his old adversaries of the orthodox clergy and the influential liberal press, which disliked the Methodist preacher's relations with the court and conservative leaders, and also felt disturbed by what it regarded as excessive religious zeal. Scott's friends feared that riots would begin as soon as he resumed his preaching by the middle of November, but nothing serious happened until Palm Sunday, March 20, 1842, when the church at the Haymarket was invaded by a howling mob which broke up the meeting. Conservative newspapers described the incident as scandalous and liberal writers expressed disapproval, but new disorders, together with the attitude of the public authorities, compelled Scott to discontinue his Swedish services. On April 30 he left for England, and his family followed two months later. Five of his nine children were born in Stockholm.

Scott followed from England with active interest the religious developments in Sweden, and on the whole he felt quite pleased. A publication which he had established early in 1842, named *Pietisten* but representing the new evangelism rather than pietism, was edited by his foremost disciple and friend, Carl Olof Rosenius, and it has been said that it exercised an influence in Sweden comparable to that of Martin Luther's 95 theses in Germany. In the period 1841–63 Rosenius received an annual stipend from the Foreign Evangelical Society in New York, which in 1849 merged with the American and Foreign Christian Union. During the latter part of the 1800s the religious life in all Scandinavia, as well as among Scandinavian immigrants in America, reflected deep influences from Rosenius. Another friend of Scott, Anders Wiberg, who after some years in the United States became the leading founder of Swedish Baptism, was for some time in charge of a missionary periodical founded by Scott in 1834.

Scott's church at Stockholm's Haymarket continued as an English church under his direction. In 1854 it was reopened for free services, and the voice of Rosenius was often heard from its pulpit. When Scott in 1859 came to Stockholm for a short visit, he was received by the ecclesiastical authorities as an old friend.

When Swedish newspapers thundered against Scott in 1841–42, he was also accused of having helped inspire a Scotsman named Samuel Laing, who had published a book, entitled *A Tour in Sweden in 1838*, which Swedes with good reason regarded as largely anti-Swedish and intensely pro-Norwegian. An early dissolution of the Scandinavian union seemed, in fact, to be his fondest dream. It is true that he had found the ability to read and write to be more general in Sweden than in any other European country with the possible exception of Denmark, and that on some occasion he seemed inclined to believe that the people fundamentally was "as simple in their habits, tastes, and mode of living as any in Europe." But despite their agricultural or pastoral setting the Swedes were actually "in a more de-moralised state than any nation in Europe," and the population of Stockholm was utterly depraved. The main cause was "a radical defect in the construction of society": "the mass of the nation is in a state of pupillage, living like soldiers in a regiment, under classes or oli-garchies of privileged bodies," including the established church, the most powerful such institution in Europe.

Some of Laing's themes would be heard again in both English and American books. The Reverend Robert Baird was, to begin with, influenced by them when he wrote two massive volumes about his tours of Scandinavia, entitled *Visit to Northern Europe* and published in New York in 1841. He had, of course, many other sources, including his own observations, and probably did his best to draw his own con-clusions. His attitude toward the Swedish people was very friendly, and he was impressed by its cultural and political progress. Like Laing he had found an appalling crime rate, but felt that an improvement was near because of the advance of the temperance cause. A more genuine Christian spirit was also necessary, and Sweden should, therefore, have churches which were independent of the state. While regarding Norway as the political pioneer of the North, Baird rec-ommended Copenhagen as the capital of an all-Scandinavian union.

Sweden's penal code listed according to Baird an amazing number of crimes as punishable by death, and it should be revised as soon as possible. After all, he added, "we live in the 19th century." During the period 1800–30 executions in Sweden totaled about 550, or an average of 18 a year, but a marked decline began in the 1830s. During the preparatory work on the new penal code, adopted in 1864, it seemed at one time as if capital punishment would be abolished. From 1865 until 1910, when such punishment was exacted for the last time, there were 15 executions.

Robert Baird made his third and last visit to Sweden in the summer of 1846, when he attended an international temperance conference in Stockholm.

American novelists popular in Sweden — Restrictions on emigration eased in 1840

THE agitation against alcohol was the first of the great popular movements which helped convert Sweden into a modern democracy, but its effects on emigration were to begin with more far-reaching. Close ties were formed with the new noncomformist religious groups, and these were less opposed to emigration than the Lutheran state church. Within this organization, moving away from one's native country was regarded as a form of rebellion, especially when the goal was the faraway New World. An exodus to European territories seemed more natural, and times of economic distress had long caused some Swedish migration, in particular to Denmark and Germany.

By the end of the 1830s the new American literature, represented by James Fenimore Cooper and Washington Irving, had become known in Sweden. People who knew English had started reading Cooper soon after the publication of his first books in the early 1820s, and in the period 1825–33 seven of his novels were issued in Swedish translations. About a dozen more followed during the next few decades. The teller of the Leatherstocking tales became, in fact, one of the most popular foreign authors in the history of reading in Sweden, and he probably even played a part in pulling people over the Atlantic. The romantic aspects of America often added something to its drawing power. James Fenimore Cooper was born in the Delaware Valley, and via his mother, Elizabeth Fenimore, he was of Swedish colonial descent. In the spring of 1826 he seems to have been offered the post of American minister in Stockholm, but while looking for an assignment in Europe at that time, he did not want to shoulder any diplomatic responsibilities.

Washington Irving, who did go to Europe on a diplomatic mission, was also a great favorite with book readers in Sweden. In 1827 no less than eight of his works were brought out in Swedish translations, and the total of such editions finally reached 15. In his comic *History of New York from the Beginning of the World to the End of the Dutch Dynasty* he satirized Swedes as well as Dutchmen and Yankees.

The continued growth of the agricultural population and the slow industrialization, with a subsequent lack of occupational opportunity in the cities, would become much more important than anything else as long-range factors in the Swedish emigration to America, but the problem of taxation had greater immediate significance. A foundation for the modern income tax was laid in 1861, but by 1840 an impost on land was still the foremost source of government revenue, and the farmers demanded a more equitable distribution of the burden.

The indignation among the farmers was also directed against the remaining privileges of the nobility, which represented less than one-half of one percent of the total population. Most of its members had, however, no feeling of being favored, and they would help recruit the ranks of the emigrants to America, as they had done even in the 17th and 18th centuries. Samuel Laing may not have been one of the more reliable observers, but he was close to the truth when he wrote that far from "living like the Russian nobles, in a kind of Asiatic magnificence," as he had imagined, the Swedish nobles were, with few exceptions, "extremely poor, living from civil or military employment with small pay, or on their farms in great obscurity and poverty."

In 1840 the legislation concerning emigration from Sweden was revised by the Riksdag. Although always difficult to enforce, a drastic restriction law had been in effect since the middle of the 18th century, and one of its stipulations, according to which a certain amount of money must be deposited before travel abroad, was now removed as contrary to the spirit of the times. The remaining restrictions were not to be repealed until 1860, but their practical importance was limited, and already the change of 1840 helped set the stage for a growing migration. Gustaf Unonius was one of the first to take advantage of the new legislation, and somewhat later enterprising Swedish sea captains began to offer more or less regular transatlantic services.

At first nobody could tell whether the new emigration to the United States was a temporary phenomenon or if it would continue and gradually increase. In fact, not until the late 1870s or early 80s would it be plain that the Swedish emigration to America had become a long-lived mass movement.

9

Swedish-American Pioneers of the 1840s and 1850s

Growing American immigration from Sweden led by seamen,
liberals, and dissenters

DURING the first part of the 19th century the United States received a small but increasing flow of immigrants from Sweden. Against the background of the gigantic trek in the late 1800's, the scope of this early immigration has often been underestimated.

A large proportion of the Swedish immigrants consisted of seamen who had deserted their ships or had become shipwrecked, or who already had tasted life in America and decided to return as permanent settlers. Legal restrictions on emigration from Sweden could hardly ever be applied to seafaring people.

The great number of sailors who jumped Swedish ships to sign on American vessels was a serious problem from a Swedish viewpoint, as it had been already in the 18th century. In 1804, the Swedish consul in Philadelphia reported to Stockholm that at least 1,000 Swedes were serving in the American merchant marine, and two decades later the number seems to have been about 1,500. Many of them finally entered the United States, and quite a few of these enlisted, to begin with, in the U. S. Army. In the period 1800–1850, the total of Swedish enlistments seems to have been about 200, but not all of them were sailors.

Until about 1845, most of the other Swedes who came to the United States were persons of good social and educational backgrounds, who wanted a more progressive political climate and greater personal and religious freedom than their native country seemed able to provide. In Sweden they had supported the liberal opposition, and often they had, in turn, been aroused by the sustained criticism of political and social conditions, finally making the decision to seek their future beyond the Atlantic. The situation was similar in other European countries.

Other influences behind the slowly growing migration from Sweden were personal problems, a spirit of adventure, and, of course, the hope for better economic opportunities. Many of those who joined the U. S. Army were typical adventurers, while others must have regarded their military service as good preparatory training for life in the New World. Titled army officers were among those who enlisted in the early to middle 1800s.

From 1846 to 1850 about 3,300 Swedish citizens, most of them immigrants, went ashore in New York, which was and remained the leading port of arrival; this number represented an almost tenfold increase over the preceding five-year period. Common people from the Swedish countryside were now for the first time in the majority, and during the next half-century they would play a dominating part in the trek from Sweden. Around the middle of the 1800s, relatively well-to-do farmers who were opposed to the political and religious regime in Sweden made up a much larger proportion of the emigrating country people than they would later on.

Group travel was typical during the first period of sizable migration, and it would continue on a larger scale until the end of the 1860s. The groups were, as a rule, based on strong leadership or at least on family ties and common roots in a certain region of Sweden. From New York and other ports most of the immigrants finally made their way to the Middle West where, they knew, richer land than they had ever seen in Sweden was to be had for the dream price of a dollar or two per acre. Many, however, did not pick the best land available, for they were instinctively drawn to sites which reminded them of their wooded and often lake-studded homeland. The great majority of the immigrants were used to backbreaking and patient work, and whether they went to the Middle West, to New England, or to other parts of the country, they served well in the swelling army of pioneers.

But farming was not the only occupation of the newcomers from Sweden. A relatively large proportion settled in towns or villages as craftsmen, workers, and businessmen.

Almost from the beginning, religious unrest played a significant role in the departure of the Swedish groups. After a few decades the situation would be different, but in the meantime the ferment in Sweden mushroomed when early emigrants returned from America as temporary or permanent missionaries. Some of the visitors were former sailors, who had been converted in the United States and went back to tell people about their new faith and the democratic spirit of the dynamic New World. One became the first Baptist preacher in Sweden, and the Swedish Methodist church as well as the less important Mormon sect were also founded by men who had lived in America. On both sides of the Atlantic, the growth of the new church organizations was stimulated by close contacts.

At an early stage the Swedish Lutheran forces in America became much stronger than the other denominations, but their leaders had also been influenced by the new moral and religious movements in Sweden. The organization which they started building up in the Middle West was a more spontaneous product than the Swedish Lutheran state church. As the immigration from Sweden subsequently increased, a declining proportion of the settlers became active church members, but all were, directly or indirectly, helped by schools, hospitals, and other welfare centers which the religious groups founded. Many such institutions still serve their respective communities and the whole nation.

One of the characteristics of the Swedish settlers in America by the middle of the 1800s seems to have been that in letters to relatives and friends in Sweden they seldom complained of their lot. They had often been warned of the dangers of the New World, and the reality may have turned out to be as grim as it had been painted, but in reports home most of the immigrants passed over their hardships and misfortunes, either because they did not want to admit them or because they regarded them as self-evident at least in the beginning. There were, to be sure, notable exceptions, but numerous letters to Sweden described only the brighter side of life in America, and they were, of course, eagerly read. Later, as more and more immigrants came into their own, their letters would have a tremendous impact in Sweden, overshadowing the flow of people, who, homesick or disillusioned, returned to their native country.

In 1850, according to the U. S. census, about 3,600 Swedish-born people lived in the United States. Illinois topped the list of the states with some 1,100, followed by New York, 750, Massachusetts and Louisiana, about 250 each, and then Iowa and California. Most of those registered in Louisiana were actually headed north along the Mississippi River, and New York, of course, was also a transit area. Ten years later, according to the same source, the number of U.S. residents born in Sweden was nearly 19,000. The trend toward the Middle West had then become much more accentuated.

While the U. S. census figure for 1850 undoubtedly was too low, the actual total of Swedish-born people living in the United States at that time was obviously modest. It represented, however, a significant beginning. Many of the early 19th-century Swedish settlers influenced the subsequent course of events both by letters or visits to their native land and by establishing bases in America where inexperienced newcomers could move in or receive temporary assistance. Many of these immigrants were also helped by settlers from other Nordic countries. In the early and middle 1800s the Norwegian language, which Swedes have no difficulty in understanding, was heard in the Midwest more often than Swedish. The 19th-century immigration from Norway gained momentum earlier than the one from Sweden, and until the 1870s the Norwegian-born people in the United States outnumbered the Swedish immigrants.

The first new Swedish settlements in the East and, above all, the Middle West were particularly important as bases for the growing immigration from Sweden, but even the strange history of the Swedes in Texas offers an instructive example. Our survey of Swedish 19th-century contributions to America's population and growth will begin there, although a brief summary makes the migration from Sweden appear as a less complicated and painful process than it actually was.

Early Swedish settler in Texas generates
the immigration of thousands

ROVING Swedes may have been in Texas at the beginning of the 1800s, and at least one Swedish immigrant, who settled there permanently, is reported to have arrived as early as 1822. He became known as Joe Smith but said that his real name was Jan Jacob Lundquist, and that he was born in the city of Halmstad in southwestern Sweden in 1794. If this should be true, he was probably a former sailor.

The first Swedish settler in Texas about whom no doubt whatsoever exists was Sven or Swante Magnus Svensson or Swenson (1816–96) from Barkeryd Parish in the province of Småland, near the city of Jönköping. He came to New York from Gothenburg in 1836, and via Baltimore he moved to Texas two years later. Like other immigrants he faced a period of hard struggle, but he had a keen business sense and married, moreover, a well-to-do widow. Before long he began to make a fortune in cotton production, commerce, and real estate. His first plantation, not far from present-day Houston, was named Lattarp after the village in Småland, Lättarp, where he was born.

At an early stage Swenson became a friend of Sam Houston, president of the republic of Texas from 1836 to 1844 and later a U.S. senator and state governor. Both had started as store clerks. When the Civil War broke out and Houston was deposed as governor, Swenson's own anti-slavery and pro-union sentiments were well known, and in 1863 he left for Mexico. After the war he established himself in New Orleans as a cotton exporter, and somewhat later he settled in New York as a banker. In Texas, his sons and agents turned much of his land into cattle ranches and introduced scientific breeding and feeding. At the age of 80 Swenson died in Brooklyn, where thousands of Swedish immigrants had then settled. His eldest son, Eric P. Swenson (1855–1945), helped develop the sulphur deposits at Freeport in Texas and became chairman of the board of the National City Bank in New York.

In the late 1840s Swenson made two visits to Sweden, where his American career naturally caused some sensation. Efforts by him to bring about direct trade between Sweden and Texas failed, but he became, on the other hand, the first 19th-century Swedish visitor from America to promote successfully emigration to the United States. As a first result of his activities in northern Småland, 25 relatives, farm laborers and maids left for Texas in 1848, and many groups were formed during the following decades, when Swenson had set up an organization furnishing transportation that was to be paid for by one year's labor in Texas.

Whether the Swedish men and women who left for Texas went in groups or not, Swenson's home parish of Barkeryd remained the focal point of departure. From there, impulses to leave for the American Southwest spread like rings in the water, finally reaching into the provinces adjoining Småland. Of the total Swedish emigration to Texas, the Jönköping district contributed more than two-thirds. In the 19th century no other Southern state attracted permanently a larger number of Swedes, but small groups settled all over the territory south of the Mason-Dixon line.

Among those who accompanied or followed Swante M. Swenson from Sweden in the late 1840s were a sister, two brothers, and two maternal uncles with families, including ten children. His mother also came, after an Atlantic voyage that almost ended in disaster, but she soon went back to Småland and finally retired to a beautiful estate bought by her son. A third uncle, Swante Palm (1815–99), who arrived as early as 1844, was one of the best-educated immigrants to settle in Texas in the 19th century. He has been called a "Renaissance gentleman" of the Southwest.

Sympathizing with the Confederate cause, Swante Palm remained in Texas throughout the Civil War. In 1866 he was appointed its first consul for Sweden and Norway, and during a visit to his native country in 1883 he was received by the Swedish monarch in the Stockholm Palace. Being much more interested in scholarship and literary pursuits than in business or politics, he built up the finest library in Texas, which, for instance, finally comprised the largest Charles Darwin collection in the United States, numerous legal works, a large set of old Swedish Bibles, and an unparalleled assortment of early prints of the Southwest. On his death, 10,000 volumes went to the then 15-year-old University of Texas, where it is known as the Swante Palm Collection. To the same institution Swenson donated a collection of rare coins.

In 1850 Swante M. Swenson had moved to Austin, which then had a population of about 650, and most of the Swedish immigrants brought over by him started to work on his own land. Many built their homes about 20 miles from Austin, in Palm Valley, one of the place-names in Texas that still recall early settlers from Sweden, in this case one of the Palm families. Swenson's ranch near Austin, now part of the city, was called Govalle from the Swedish "god vall" or good grazing.

Many Swedish immigrants have, directly and through descendants, left their mark on Texas, including its larger cities, but the number of Swedish-born people living there never exceeded 5,000. This total was reached about 1910, when the Lone Star State also had attracted Swedish settlers from other parts of the United States. From the beginning the main immigrant stream from Sweden was directed toward the Middle West, which seemed to offer enterprising and land-hungry Scandinavians the best opportunities in a climate and an environment similar to Northern Europe.

The Swedes in Texas have, of course, always been proud of their rich and colorful land. In the old days they used to tell a story about a fellow-countryman of African ancestry who had been taught to speak Swedish and liked to be the first to greet immigrants from Sweden as they got off the train. Invariably the newcomers would express their astonishment upon seeing and hearing him: "But you aren't Swedish, are you?" To which the greeter would answer: "Sure, I'm Swedish, and you'll be as black as I am after having lived for a while under the Texas sun."

Unonius and other settlers in Wisconsin stir a new Swedish interest in emigration

IN 1838, the immigrants from Sweden included Carl Friman or Freeman (1781–1862) and five of his young sons from Varnhem in the province of Västergötland, who took a land claim in what is now Racine County in southeastern Wisconsin. They were in all likelihood the first Swedes to settle in Wisconsin, which became a state ten years later.

Because of failing health Carl Friman returned to Sweden in 1839, taking with him one of his youngest sons, Herman (1829–1913), but three years later the then 13-year-old boy returned to America. After having served in the war with Mexico in 1847–48, when for some reason he assumed the name of Strome, he lived for about 50 years in Kentucky, and then retired to Pasadena, California, where two of his brothers had moved in the early 1870s. The eldest brother, Carl Johan Freeman (1821–70), who had seven children, moved to Nebraska, where descendants still reside. By the middle of the century the four brothers had in Wisconsin helped found Genoa City in Walworth County, west of Racine. Much of the land they bought was paid for by Wilhelm or William Freeman (1823–1911), who had been a relatively successful "forty-niner" in California.

As a young man, Carl Friman had studied at the University of Uppsala, and before his brief stay in America he had for 30 years been an enrollment clerk in an infantry regiment in Västergötland. After his return to Sweden he maintained a lively interest in the United States and carried on an extensive correspondence with his sons. In 1842 he had several letters from Wisconsin published in the popular Stockholm newspaper *Aftonbladet*, while others were printed in local papers. In one of the first letters the sons said that they would welcome additional Swedish settlers, provided that they were well off or able to work hard, but their message must have been misunderstood, for a year later the eldest son wrote to his parental home: "Father, you must not send our letters to the newspapers, because when the Swedes come here and do not find the conditions as ideal as they had expected them to be, they say that it is our correspondence which has lured them to come."

Later the same year a Swedish immigrant in America who had visited the Freeman brothers in Wisconsin wrote to a newspaper at Gävle, the largest Swedish city north of Stockholm, that "their house was far inferior to the charcoal burner's cottage in Sweden." Many more Swedes, however, had read the letters in *Aftonbladet*, in which the southeast of Wisconsin was described as "incredibly beautiful and fertile." On the basis of the Freeman letters, a newspaper in Västergötland expressed the belief that "before long a new Sweden will probably arise on the other side of the ocean," and this prophecy was reprinted in a Stockholm paper.

In the autumn of 1841, a 31-year-old university graduate from Uppsala named Gustaf Unonius (1810–1902) came to Milwaukee in southeastern Wisconsin with his wife Charlotta, a few friends, and a faithful maid-servant. They had traveled from New York via the Hudson River, the Erie Canal, and the Great Lakes, as most people planning to settle in the West did before the construction of railroads. Some 30 miles west of Milwaukee, on beautiful Pine Lake in present-day Waukesha County, the newcomers from Sweden founded a settlement which they hopefully named New Uppsala. Its chances of success were slim, but Unonius himself became an important figure in the early Swedish emigration to the Middle West.

He had several qualities that make a good pioneer, but it was, above all, the dream of a truly democratic society that had led him to America. He was not able to support himself and his family by farming but felt, nevertheless, excited about life in the new country, and in his primitive cabin he started writing enthusiastic letters for the influential *Aftonbladet*. They attracted great attention and were often reprinted by other publications. "The land that has opened opportunities and has given me a home and a feeling of security has become my new fatherland," Unonius said in one of his articles. These were also read in Denmark, and a reprint was circulated in Norway.

Unonius's reports were read by many young men and women who were well equipped to cope with the frontier hardships, and they contributed to the slowly rising tide of Scandinavian migration, helping to turn it toward the Middle West. As a first result of his letters, however, he and his wife were besieged by an odd collection of countrymen, including romantic adventurers and runaways who were totally unfit for the heavy work of breaking ground. A few Swedish immigrants who came from simpler homes fared well as settlers, but the Pine Lake colony soon began to scatter. The Wisconsin countryside never became one of the leading terminals of the Swedish trek to the Midwest. Both Norwegians and Danes settled there in larger numbers.

Among the Swedes who joined the Pine Lake colony in 1842 were an army officer from Stockholm, Polycarpus von Schneidau (1812–59), and his bride, the daughter of a Jewish merchant, for whose sake he had resigned his commission in the ultra-fashionable Svea Artillery Regiment. He was, wrote Unonius, "one of those whom I should least of all have expected to emigrate to America and settle down as a colonist," but he, too, occupies a place of some importance in the history of Swedish emigration to the United States. He and, in particular, his wife were dumbfounded when they saw Unonius's tiny one-room-and-attic log cabin, but at Pine Lake they built an even more primitive hut themselves. Winter came and their first-born child froze to death, but somehow Von Schneidau managed to build a better cottage.

Several of those who passed through Pine Lake failed in their various enterprises, while some enlisted in the U. S. armed forces and others did well in new and sometimes strange occupations. An army officer and chamberlain at the court in Stockholm by the name of Adolf Fredrik Lindsfelt (b. 1806), who seems to have committed some financial irregularity and in 1842 fled from Sweden with his large family and two servants, built the first pretentious mansion at Pine Lake, resembling somewhat his Swedish country estate, but when he did not prosper as a farmer and, moreover, developed a special gift for healing, he moved to Chicago to study medicine. He finally settled at Sheboygan, Wisconsin, to which people traveled for miles to consult him. One of Unonius's companions from Uppsala met a Swedish baron who had gone to California to dig for gold, discovered that he had some mysterious power over snakes and started traveling around the country with a snake menagerie. The most successful Swedish farmer at Pine Lake was a forester, Johan Olof Rudberg (b. 1817), who also became a county surveyor and in 1870 opened a summer resort which was patronized by wealthy Chicagoans.

After a few years Unonius quit pioneering and entered an Episcopalian seminary at Nashotah a few miles southwest of Pine Lake. Ordained as a minister in 1845, he began to serve the Scandinavian and mostly Norwegian settlements in Wisconsin, and both for him and for his wife, who often lived alone with the children, this brought new hardships and great sacrifices. Their first-born son died in 1846, and four more children were buried in America. In 1849 the family moved to Chicago, where Unonius helped organize a Swedish-Norwegian Episcopal congregation, named after St. Ansgarius, the Apostle of the North. He became its first pastor and built a church with financial assistance from Jenny Lind, the famous Swedish soprano whom he got to know well. During a fund-raising tour along the Eastern seaboard in 1849, the year before the celebrated singer arrived in America, he was invited to preach in the Old Swedes churches in Philadelphia and Wilmington, and memories from these occasions he always cherished. The interest in Sweden on the part of his audiences impressed him greatly.

During the nine years he served in Chicago, Unonius and his wife worked tirelessly to render the increasing stream of Scandinavian immigrants aid and comfort. At Uppsala he had studied medicine as well as law, and in 1834 he had been attached to a cholera hospital in Stockholm, experiences which enabled him to take an active part in the fight against the epidemics of cholera which broke out practically every year and raged with particular violence among the poorer population and newly arrived immigrants. Taking care of children who became orphans and placing them with foster parents was, he said later, his most painful problem.

The Unoniuses' best friends in Chicago were Polycarpus and Carolina von Schneidau, who had settled there in late 1844. As soon as the former army officer had recovered from a disability incurred at Pine Lake, he began to offer lessons in fencing, dancing, and gymnastics, and it is said that he shocked the more conservative half of Chicago's population by organizing a class in gymnastics for women, in all likelihood the first in the United States. After having worked for some time as a prospector for copper mines in the Lake Superior region and as a surveyor for a railroad, he studied the art of daguerreotype photography, and with help from Fredrika Bremer, the famous Swedish novelist who toured America in 1849, he opened one of the first daguerreotype studios in Chicago. In 1850 he took a large picture of Jenny Lind in New York, and the next year he won a gold medal from the Chicago Mechanics Institute for excellence in photography. In 1852 he became the first vice counsul for Sweden and Norway in Chicago, and although in failing health he was of great assistance to the Scandinavian immigrants. When he resigned as consul, Unonius was appointed to replace him.

Letters from Von Schneidau to his father in Sweden had, as will be shown shortly, important effects on the emigration to America. Carolina von Schneidau died in 1855, four years before her husband. Their only surviving child, a daughter, became a young woman of considerable wealth and finally married a lawyer in New York.

Unonius returns disappointed to Sweden — Memoirs reflect faith in America's future

AT TIMES Gustaf Unonius felt very critical of political and religious conditions in the United States, and in a diary note of 1849 he went so far as to say that he had "become more and more convinced of the complete evil in the republican system," which in his opinion had degenerated into "mob despotism." In 1853 he and his wife made a visit to Sweden in order to see their relatives and old friends once more, and in press articles and public discussions he turned against those who had nothing but praise for the American republic and in some way or other encouraged emigration. The misery Unonius had seen among the new immigrants in America had, together with his own personal experiences, changed his outlook, but the transformation was not quite as drastic as it had seemed at first.

After having returned to Chicago in the fall of 1853, Unonius and his wife often felt homesick for their old fatherland. Frequent controversies with newly arrived Scandinavian clergymen of the Lutheran faith, moreover, embittered his life, and in the spring of 1858 he resigned his ministry in the St. Ansgarius Parish to move back to Sweden. He hoped to be admitted as a minister into the Swedish state church, but his application was denied because of his Episcopal ordination, and for a while he lived on the edge of poverty. In 1860 the Swedish parliament voted him a sum of money for his work among Scandinavian immigrants in Chicago, and a few years later he became collector of customs in the archipelago northeast of Stockholm, a position his father had held for many years after having returned to his native Sweden when Finland in 1809 was ceded to Russia. After his retirement, Gustaf Unonius and his wife lived on the estate of a wealthy son-in-law. Their only surviving son, Lloyd Gustaf, born at Pine Lake in 1844, emigrated to the United States in 1863. He joined the Union forces the next year but was, after a short time, wounded in battle. Later he became director of a prison or mental hospital in Chicago. One Sunday morning in 1878, when he had gone to church ahead of his family, he disappeared mysteriously.

Shortly after his return to Sweden in 1858 Gustaf Unonius began to write down reminiscences from his 17 years in America, and in 1861–62 these were published at Uppsala in two volumes. They are one of the most valuable sources of information concerning life in the Middle West during the 1840s. An English translation, entitled *A Pioneer in Northwest America* 1841–58, was published in Chicago a century later.

Unonius was, of course, a bitterly disappointed man when he wrote his memoirs, and before he had finished came the shock of the American Civil War, but his basic attitude to the country where he had spent his most vigorous years was, nevertheless, marked by both goodwill and optimism. He still believed, as he had done in his youth, that the American nation, left to itself, would one day reveal to the world "the majesty of the people" and of "the democratic social order." Much false religious display and other errors one certainly found in the United States, but "nevertheless one witnesses there, in the whole general trend, a true practical Christianity."

Unonius's criticisms were often directed against other religious denominations or the new sects, which, he felt, were ready to destroy all freedom except their own. Before his emigration in 1841 he had been, as he also wrote, a zealous advocate of the temperance societies, but in America he soon became convinced that as a means to an end such organizations were a failure. At the bottom of his scale were the agents of the American transportation companies and the baggage and freight handlers, who "in a thousand ways" knew "how to enrich themselves at the poor immigrants' expense." At the middle of the 19th century most newcomers in America, or at least those who did not understand English, seem, in fact, to have been cheated, and not only by transportation agents and ticket-office clerks.

Pine Lake remained close to Unonius's heart, and he could also dream wistfully about the prairies of Wisconsin and Illinois. "When the rolling prairie is settled and cultivated, it offers a cheerful sight indeed, refreshing as cool springs that with a diamond-like clarity glitter here and there on the hillsides. The farms scattered about in the valleys are surrounded by planted locust groves, gardens, and orchards. Some of the high hills seem to shimmer in the air, completely covered with rich, waving fields of grains. Others again are astir with numerous herds of cattle feeding on the lush grass. Above it all is the mild, clear summer sky, from which a special benediction seems to have streamed down over this vast cornucopia heaped up by nature. Undeniably this is among landscape pictures one of the loveliest to behold."

Chicago was called the Garden City, Unonius observed, but when he moved there in 1849 it was more like a vast mud puddle. Ten years later, on the other hand, it was in great part a beautiful garden, and it had, at the same time, become one of the most important business centers of the Union. It will, Unonius continued, "no doubt become one of the most important commercial cities in the world, and the fruitful Mississippi Valley, with the wealth of its resources, will become a dominion outstanding in power, culture and prosperity on a higher plane than any other area that history knows about."

Unonius emphasized in his memoirs that he did not want to encourage emigration, "rather the contrary." What he actually warned against, however, was hasty decisions by young officials, military officers, and poor university students. America had, he wrote, nothing to offer such groups, but it was a land of opportunity for people who were used to hard manual work or possessed special skills, categories which would make up an overwhelming majority of the emigrants from Sweden. Hard-pressed immigrant settlers in the United States, Unonius further said, often "console themselves with the thought that their children will have a better future in the new country, and no doubt they are right," a conclusion that also was apt to make a deep impression. It was typical of a large proportion of the emigrants, from Sweden as well as from other countries, that they gave more thought to the future of their children than to their own. Unonius's own feelings of bitter disappointment when he wrote his memoirs were crystallized in a sentence toward the end which said that he had made two great mistakes in life: one, that he ever emigrated to America, and the other, that after having made his home and found his field of service there, he returned to Sweden.

In June of 1948, when the 100th anniversary of the beginning of sizable immigration from Sweden was celebrated in the Middle West, the pioneering role played by Gustaf Unonius was honored with the unveiling of a memorial stone at Pine Lake, Wisconsin.

Other newcomers, including a trained naturalist, settle permanently in Wisconsin

IN 1843 a group of well-educated Swedish immigrants led by Thure L. Kumlien (1819–88) established a colony in the Lake Koshkonong area in Jefferson County in southeastern Wisconsin, west of the Unonius settlement. Kumlien, the son of an estate owner in Västergötland and the oldest of 15 children, had studied botany at Uppsala under Elias Fries, the most renowned Swedish botanist since Linnaeus, and one of the reasons why he decided to emigrate was that he wanted to marry a girl, Christina Wallberg (1820–74), who was a servant and was considered below him in social status. They were married immediately after their arrival in Wisconsin.

For several years Kumlien divided his time between farming and the study of nature, especially bird life. "Necessity bound his hand to the plow and the hoe," Unonius wrote in his memoirs, "while his natural inclination directed his thoughts to flowers, birds, and insects." A journal which he kept during this periods reveals, as one of his granddaughters has written, a picture of wilderness life "so hard one wonders how the family managed to keep body and soul together." In contrast with her husband, Mrs. Kumlien was used to manual labor. In the early 1850s, when he gave up farming, he began an extensive correspondence with leading naturalists in America and Europe, including the famous Louis Agassiz of Harvard, whom he supplied with collections of natural-history specimens. The Smithsonian Institution in Washington, as well as the British Museum in London and museums in Sweden, Norway, and Holland, also received collections from him.

From 1865 to 1870 Kumlien taught natural history in Albion Academy at Albion, Wisconsin, which became a pioneer institution in the study of ornithology. Later he worked for the University of Wisconsin and other institutions, the last one being the Public Museum in Milwaukee, where he died. He was a large contributor to books about the birds of North America but wrote only one signed article for publication, entitled "The Rapid Disappearance of Wisconsin Wild Flowers." One of his sons also became a noted naturalist.

Other settlers at Koshkonong were Carl Gustaf, or Charles, Hammarqvist (1822–89) from Norrköping in Östergötland, who in 1860 became the first Swedish immigrant to be elected to the Wisconsin legislature; a former school teacher by the name of Gustaf Mellberg (1812–91) from Västergötland, who had studied both at Uppsala and at Lund; and Carl Edvard Abraham Reuterskiöld (1796–1847) from Västmanland, who also had come in 1843 and had brought his wife and seven children. Despite the inscription on his tombstone at Busseyville, Wisconsin, he was not a member of the "Royal Family of Sweden." Koshkonong subsequently became one of the largest Norwegian settlements in Wisconsin.

The most adventurous of the early Swedish settlers in Wisconsin was probably Otto Emanuel Dreutzer (1816–1900), a native of Gothenburg who began his career as a seaman trainee for the Swedish navy. In 1832 he came to America, and four years later he volunteered for service in a military campaign against the Seminole Indians in Florida. He returned to Sweden and served in the navy, but in 1843 he came back to the United States with a large family and settled first in southeastern and then in central Wisconsin, where he became a prosperous lawyer and county judge. Being, as Unonius wrote, in full command of the English language, he had "the ability to push his way to the front in the world." From 1862 to 1867 he served as U. S. consul in Bergen, Norway.

The oldest Swedish settlement in western Wisconsin, Stockholm in Pepin County on the Mississippi, was founded in 1851 by a native of Värmland, Eric Peterson (1822–87) from Immen near Karlskoga. Three years earlier he had left Sweden with two brothers to dig for gold in California, but from Chicago he went instead to Texas, and in late 1850 he started working as a lumberjack and raftsman on the St. Croix River, which forms the boundary between Wisconsin and Minnesota until it enters the Mississippi. Next spring he discovered the beautiful Lake Pepin and decided that the location would be ideal for a settlement. Most of the early settlers came in 1853–54 from Karlskoga in Värmland, which so far had hardly been touched by the Swedish migration to America; they were brought by the founder himself and one of his brothers who returned from brief visits to their native country.

In 1854 a group of about 280 emigrants, a majority of them from Karlskoga and Bjurtjärn parishes, joined Eric Peterson on a trek to the Midwest via Quebec, but 155 died on the way over, or of cholera after their arrival, most of them in Chicago or Moline, Illinois. A ballad beginning "We sold our homes and started out, like birds fly off when summer days are over," was widely published in the Swedish press. One group of survivors proceeded to Stockholm with Eric Peterson, who finally prospered as a farmer and businessman. Over 2,000 people attended the celebration of Stockholm's 100th anniversary in 1951.

In the same section of Wisconsin the names Lund and Narike indicate early settlers from the Swedish provinces of Skåne and Närke. Much farther north is a small town called Falun, after the capital of the province of Dalarna. In 1857 about 100 Swedes lived in Superior City in the northwest corner of Wisconsin. Some Swedish settlers in Chicago are known to have moved to Green Bay in the northeast in 1850.

New Sweden in Iowa oldest existing Swedish 19th-century settlement in America

IN 1845 a group of about 20 persons led by a 55-year-old farmer named Per, or Peter, Cassel (1790–1857) arrived in New York. Most of these immigrants were from Kisa Parish in the southwestern corner of Östergötland, a hilly district· of forests, pastures, and farmland which seemed even farther off the beaten track than it actually was. Polycarpus von Schneidau's father, however, had an estate there, and letters from his son and other members of the Unonius colony in Wisconsin had been copied and circulated about the neighborhood.

Cassel, whose first known ancestor had come to Sweden from Scotland in 1592, was highly respected in his native region because of his personal qualities and progressive political views. He had signed a petition urging a reorganization of the national parliament, and he also advocated temperance and a freer religious life than that sponsored by the Swedish state church. Reading everything he could find about America, he finally became convinced that the New World offered him and his family the best economic future, and if he needed any further incitement, a shipowner in Gothenburg was happy to supply it. Many neighbors and friends seemed willing to follow him, and among these he selected his companions with extreme care. In contrast with Unonius in his younger days, he was unromantic and practical. Since he was the first well-established farmer to leave Sweden for the United States, his decision to emigrate immediately attracted attention in the press.

Peter Cassel had planned to settle in Wisconsin, but in New York he met a countryman, Pehr, or Peter, Dahlberg (1802–93), who had already explored the Middle West and now awaited a ship bringing his wife and seven children. They came in a sailing vessel loaded with iron, after a stormy voyage of two months, and recuperated on board a missionary ship which a Swedish Methodist, Olof G. Hedstrom, had just begun to operate in lower Manhattan. A native of Sweden's southernmost province and granary, Skåne, Dahlberg had been greatly impressed by the quality of the soil in Iowa, and as a result of his accounts Cassel and his friends moved to that area. In the south-east near the Skunk River, in present-day Jefferson County, Cassel in late 1845 established the first Swedish settlement in Iowa, naming it New Sweden. In 1857, when he died, it had a population of about 500. Most of the Swedes were from Kisa, Horn, Oppeby, and other parishes in southern Östergötland. One of Cassel's sons became a member of the Iowa legislature. Another volunteered for service in the Civil War and was killed in combat in Arkansas.

In 1848, or three years after Cassel's arrival, the first Swedish Lutheran church services in the Middle West were begun at New Sweden by a lay preacher, Magnus Fredrik Håkansson or Hokanson (1811–93) from Ronneby in the province of Blekinge; he later was ordained a minister. New Sweden in Iowa is, therefore, regarded as the cradle of the Swedish American Lutheran Church, although An-dover, Illinois, also occupies a special position in its history. At one time Hokanson almost became a Baptist, while Cassel joined the Methodists. New Sweden is the oldest of all existing communities founded in America by Swedish immigrants of the 19th century.

When Peter Cassel had settled in Iowa, he began writing en-thusiastic letters himself, and these, too, were reproduced in Swedish newspapers. The district he and his companions had chosen was not particularly fertile by Iowa standards, being hilly and wooded like their native region in Sweden, but in February of 1846 he wrote in his first letter: "The cornfields here resemble forests rather than grain-fields. . . . If only half of the work that people in our fatherland spend on their land were applied here, the harvest would be incredi-ble." Nearly three years later, in December, 1848, he described condi-tions in Iowa in great detail and made these comments: "No one in Sweden can dream of the advantages America offers temperate, de-pendable, and industrious persons. For people of this type the coun-try is a real Canaan, where the abundance of nature may be called a flow of milk and honey. But those who are neither able nor willing to work, who have other hopes when they depart from Sweden, will here find a Siberia from which they must sooner or later return to the fatherland or find themselves sunk into the deepest misery and pov-erty." Both letters were published by *Östgöta Correspondenten* at Lin-köping, capital of the province of Östergötland. The publisher of this newspaper, which had become one of the leading provincial dailies, was not entirely opposed to emigration but wanted it halted by domestic, agricultural, and political reforms.

Peter Dahlberg, who directed Peter Cassel to Iowa, had been first a shoemaker and fisherman and finally a skipper, before his emigration from Sweden in 1843 at the age of 41. In Iowa he and his family settled in the same section as Cassel and his group, but after having built a log cabin there he was cheated out of his land claim and then earned his living as a carpenter. He also became a student of mathematics, philosophy, and theology. His wife Ingar or Ingrid (1807–90), who has been described as a woman of remarkable personality, became fluent in English and led the congregational singing in a little Methodist chapel. Their five daughters married men who were probably not of Swedish origin, their family names being Le Gresley, Irish, Metz, Mort, and Thomas.

Letters from Iowa lead to new settlements in the Midwest and one in western Pennsylvania

IN SOUTHWESTERN Östergötland and neighboring northern Småland the reports from Peter Cassel and other settlers had a powerful effect, and toward the middle of the century this area was one of the two main centers of Swedish emigration. The other was the southern part of the province of Hälsingland, some 150 miles north of Stockholm. In 1851 or 1852, people from northern Skåne and adjoining Blekinge, from southern and central Småland, and from Västergötland began to arrive in larger numbers.

In 1846, Cassel's emigration and his first letters to relatives and friends in Östergötland caused two groups, together numbering about 100 persons, to leave for New Sweden in Iowa. Most of them, however, failed to reach their goal.

After adventures and heartaches that they could not have dreamed of when they started their journey, members of the first party in 1847 came to Andover in western Illinois, while most of their companions finally settled at Chandlers Valley or, as the township is called, Sugar Grove in northwestern Pennsylvania. On their way to the Middle West, the latter were robbed of their funds in Albany and were left stranded on the waterfront in Buffalo. "Like a flock of frightened sheep, we stood there helpless on the shore," a survivor recalled later. Two countrymen came to their rescue, but for two years the Swedes remained in Buffalo, being unable to earn enough money for their fares further west. As farm workers in the vicinity the men received 50 cents a day.

Most members of the second group of immigrants did reach Iowa, but at first they were not able to find Peter Cassel's New Sweden. They came to the town of Keokuk in the southeast corner of Iowa, where Mark Twain 8–10 years later worked as a compositor in his brother's printing shop, but instead of proceeding farther north and following the Skunk River, a more northern tributary of the Mississippi, they chose by mistake to follow the Des Moines River, through uninhabited land where the Indians were roaming. At Des Moines, then a small fort surrounded by some huts, they were directed farther toward the northwest, and after 25 miles they decided to pitch their tents in the valley of a creek running to the Des Moines River. A former soldier by the name of Charles W. Gaston lived there as a hermit in the wilderness, spending most of his time hunting.

This happened in the fall of 1846, and it was the beginning of a permanent settlement which at first was called Swede Point but later, although still largely Swedish, was renamed Madrid. Having come there by mistake, most of the newcomers joined Peter Cassel at New Sweden, and to begin with only four Swedish families settled at Swede Point. Among them were 54-year-old Anna Larsdotter Dahlander (1792–1854) from Västerlösa Parish in Östergötland, whose husband had died before her emigration from Sweden, and her six children, the youngest of whom was 18. In 1848, one of her daughters married a son of Peter Cassel, this being the first Swedish wedding in Iowa, and another daughter was married to Charles W. Gaston.

The villages of Sugar Grove and Chandlers Valley, where many members of one of the groups that had left Sweden in 1846 finally settled, lie nestled in the hills in northwestern Pennsylvania, 10–14 miles south of Lake Chautauqua in the southwest corner of the state of New York. In late 1846 two young sisters, known as Louise and Josephine, who had first been placed in a poorhouse in Buffalo, were sent to this area for adoption by old settlers, but before long their parents began to miss the children so keenly that they started to walk 90 miles to see them. They not only found their daughters well cared for but were also offered permanent employment. Their father was a crofter from Kisa in Östergötland named Germund Jonsson or Johnson (1815–88).

In the fall of 1848 the Swedes who had been stranded near Buffalo began to arrive en masse at Chandlers Valley, where the men went to work as wood choppers and as soon as possible settled down as farmers. The settlement was first called Swedesburg but was later renamed Hessel Valley, for three brothers from Hässleby in Småland who had been among its founders. The first site for a Swedish church was donated by Germund Johnson, who, however, in 1857 moved to Minnesota with his family. The congregation at Chandlers Valley is still known as the Hessel Valley congregation.

The Chandlers Valley-Sugar Grove area became a base from which Swedes spread to all parts of western Pennsylvania and New York, in particular to Jamestown at the foot of Lake Chautauqua. This small community, which had been founded in 1809, also attracted new immigrants from Sweden and gradually became the largest and most homogeneous Swedish settlement in the state of New York. Many of the Swedes were skilled woodworkers from the highlands of northern Småland, and at Jamestown they gradually built up a furniture industry of nationwide reputation.

The first resident Lutheran pastor in the Chandlers Valley-Jamestown region was the Reverend Jonas Swensson (1828–73), born at Våthult in western Småland and a university graduate from Uppsala; he arrived with his wife in the summer of 1856 and two years later moved to Andover, Illinois. A Methodist church had already been founded at Jamestown by Olof Hedstrom, who was in charge of a missionary center in New York. Jonas Swensson's son Carl Aaron, who was born in the log-cabin parsonage at Chandlers Valley, became one of the best-known clergymen and educators of Swedish parentage in the United States. At Lindsborg, Kansas, he founded Bethany College and started its annual Easter festivals featuring Handel's *Messiah* oratorio.

The two young girls who came in late 1846 are regarded as the first pioneers of the Swedish settlements in the Chandlers Valley-Jamestown district. The inscription on a stone monument unveiled at the centennial celebration in 1946 ends with a quotation from the Bible: "A little child shall lead them."

*Other Swedish pioneers and settlements in Iowa
by the middle 1800s*

SOONER or later all parts of Iowa attracted Swedish immigrants, but by
the middle of the 1800s most of the Swedes had settled either in the
southeast, where New Sweden had been founded in 1845, or in the
central section north of Des Moines, where Swede Point, the present
Madrid, had been established in 1846.

The first Swedish settler at Burlington, in the southeast on the
Mississippi, may have been Fabian Brydolf (1819–97), the son of a
state-church minister at Hällestad in Östergötland, who had come to
America in late 1841 and had first established himself at Cleveland,
Ohio, as a landscape painter. In 1846 he moved to Burlington, the
next year he volunteered for service in the war with Mexico, and
during the Civil War he became Iowa's best-known soldier of Swedish
birth. After some time the Swedes in Burlington were so numerous
that a section of the city was generally called "Swede Town." Many of
them worked in the railroad shops. In 1850 about 200 immigrants from
Sweden are said to have lived in and around Burlington, although
according to the U.S. census the Swedish-born population in Iowa at
that time totaled only 231. Ten years later the Swedes in Iowa numbered nearly 1,500, the beginning of a rapid increase.

At Swedesburg some 30 miles northwest of Burlington, a Swedish
Lutheran congregation was organized in 1866, most of its members
being from southern Östergötland and the others from northern
Småland. About 50 miles farther west, in Wapello County, the first
Swedes arrived in 1847. Most of the early colonists came from Knäred
in southern Halland, where Sweden and Denmark in 1613 signed an
important peace treaty. Munterville in this county was named after a
robust schoolmaster from Sweden, M. Munter, who played a leading
role among the settlers.

The counties north of Des Moines where a great many Swedes
settled included Boone, Webster, and Hamilton. One of the Swedish
centers in this area, about 25 miles northwest of Swede Point, or
Madrid, in Boone County, was named Boxholm by a postmaster who
came from Boxholm in Östergötland. Dayton and Gowrie farther
north were also important. Among the early settlers at Dayton were
John Nels Gabrielson (1826–1908) and his wife Florence (1827–1908)

from Boxholm in Sweden, who came in 1858 via Galesburg, Illinois. Their descendants, who have traced their ancestry in Sweden back to the early 1700s, have for many years held an annual reunion in late September. Among the veteran participants in the 1970s were two grandsons of the first pioneers, Ira N. Gabrielson, a noted biologist and conservationist, and his brother Guy G. Gabrielson, a former lawyer and legislator from New Jersey who in 1949–52 served as chairman of the Republican National Committee.

About 12 miles northeast of Boxholm, where the Des Moines River bends sharply, is a place known as Stratford, which in the old days was called Swede Bend. A clergyman from Dödringshult in Småland named John Linn (b. 1826) and his wife came here about 1850, living under the trunk of a basswood tree while log cabins were being put up for the winter. In 1853 a settler farther south tried to sell him 80 acres of land on the site of the city of Des Moines, but Linn declined the offer, describing the price, 320 dollars, as excessive. Somewhat later he became a Methodist preacher.

Among the many Swedish immigrants who came to New Sweden in 1849 were a crofter from Södra Vi in northeastern Småland, Steffan Steffansson (1807–1855), described as a man of gigantic strength, and his wife and seven children — there had been eight when they left Sweden. In the middle 1850s the family was almost wiped out by cholera and other diseases, but two daughters and a son, Olaus or Oliver, survived. The latter had a son, George M. Stephenson, who became a noted historian and for many years taught at the University of Minnesota. He held academic degrees from Augustana College, the University of Chicago, and Harvard.

Many Swedish settlements and farms in western Iowa were developed in connection with the extension of the railroad system after the Civil War. The largest and most homogeneous of all the settlements grew up in the southwest. In Iowa's northwest corner, on the other hand, the first Swedes arrived in the 1850s, most of them coming from the Boxholm area in Iowa, and in the northeast, along the Mississippi, some Swedes from the northwestern provinces of Jämtland and Härjedalen settled in the forests as early as 1850. One of the counties in the northeast was named Bremer in honor of Fredrika Bremer, a famous Swedish novelist who in the fall of 1850 traveled in the American Middle West. In Bremer County there is, moreover, a community named Frederika and another named Bremer.

The first identified Swedish settlers in Des Moines, P. J. Anderson and Frank Hultman from the province of Östergötland, came in 1856. Two years later Des Moines was selected as the state capital, more and more Swedes settled there, and finally this city became the leading Swedish center in Iowa.

10

In Illinois and its "Prairie Utopia"

First Swedes in Illinois — Many directed there from Methodist base in New York

THE earliest known native-born Swede to settle permanently in Illinois was Raphael Widén, who had been educated in France for the Catholic priesthood but became a businessman and politician. When and how he arrived in America is not known, but in 1814 he was appointed a justice of the peace in St. Clair County in southwestern Illinois, and the next year he was married to a girl of French extraction. Somewhat later he moved to Kaskaskia, the oldest white settlement in the Mississippi Valley, which in the 18th century had been called the "Paris of the West" and in 1818 became the first capital of Illinois. In 1820 Widén was elected a member of the legislature, and in 1826 he became president of the State Senate. Like most Scandinavians he was a strong opponent of slavery, and in 1824 he helped pass a law banishing the system from Illinois. In 1833 he fell victim to one of the recurring cholera epidemics.

The first fully identified Swedish-born farmer in Illinois was Christian Benson (1805–85), a native of Gothenburg, who had gone to sea early and joined the American merchant marine. In 1827, when he had begun to work as a pilot with a freight line between New York and New England, owned by Commodore Cornelius Vanderbilt, he married a Providence girl of Scottish ancestry, and in 1835, after a shipwreck, she persuaded him to quit navigation in favor of farming. He settled in northwestern Illinois, near the present city of Rock Island. In 1849 he took part in the gold rush to California but later returned to his Illinois farm.

Another former sailor from Sweden, Sven Nilsson, settled at nearby Andover in 1840. Among those who joined him there some years later was Captain Pehr Wilhelm Wirström (1816–55), who was born at Vaxholm in the Stockholm archipelago and had come to America in 1845. After having sailed on the Great Lakes he became a real-estate agent and promoter of Swedish settlements in Illinois. In 1850 he and his Swedish-born wife set out for the gold fields of California, but finally moved back to the Middle West.

The most effective agents in directing early Swedish immigrants to Illinois were two Methodist ministers, Olof. Gustaf Hedström (1803–77), who was stationed in New York as a missionary to Scandinavian sailors and other newcomers, and his brother Jonas (1813–59), who settled at Victoria, Illinois, not far from Andover. A third brother, Elias (1816–55), became a cabinetmaker in Detroit. They were born in Nottebäck Parish in Småland. Their father was a corporal in an infantry regiment based at Växjö.

Olof Hedström came to New York in 1826 as a sailor on an over-age Swedish frigate, *af Chapman*, which like another and larger man-of-war was sold there at a public auction. The year before, five naval vessels had more or less surreptitiously been sold by the Swedish government to Colombia and Mexico, which had just won their independence from Spain, but when international complications threatened, in the first place with the Russian Emperor who tried to defend the cause of legitimacy throughout the world, King Carl Johan of Sweden and his advisers decided to back down. The two ships destined for Colombia, *Tapperheten* and *af Chapman*, were auctioned off in New York, and the crews received funds for their return trips to Sweden; but Hedström was robbed of his money and thus found himself stranded. He then started to work as a tailor, married a Methodist relative of his employer, and was, as he wrote himself, "soundly and gloriously converted."

In 1833 Olof Hedstrom returned to Sweden to convert his aged father, and when he came back later the same year, he brought his two younger brothers. After having worked in the Catskill Mountains under the auspices of the American Methodist Episcopal Church, he was, in 1845, summoned to New York as a missionary to Swedish and other Scandinavian seamen and immigrants, and at this post he took charge of a floating chapel, the Bethel ship *John Wesley*, which was moored to a pier in lower Manhattan. The first Swedish or Scandinavian Methodist congregation in America was formed there in 1845. During the next three decades Hedstrom aided thousands upon thousands of newcomers from the North of Europe, serving not only as their spiritual guide but also as an interpreter, postmaster, social worker, and even travel agent. Among Swedes who gave him financial support were Captain John Ericsson, inventor of the *Monitor*, who in 1839 had arrived in New York from London, and Jenny Lind, who in 1850 began her first American concert tour.

As head of the Methodist mission on board the Bethel ship, Hedstrom employed a succession of assistants whom he trained to be Methodist ministers, among them a former Swedish army officer by the name of Peter Bergner, who had arrived in 1832 as a mate on a Swedish vessel, a former curate in the Lutheran state church, the Reverend Carl Petter Agrelius (1798–1881), who came in 1848 with a group of immigrants from the province of Östergötland and was dreaming of a lasting Scandinavian unity on American soil, and a Norwegian, O. P. Petersen, who later became the founder of Methodism in Norway as well as among the Norwegian immigrants in the United States. Agrelius was soon sent to assist Olof Hedstrom's brother Jonas in Illinois, and then he continued as a Methodist preacher among the Scandinavians in Minnesota and Wisconsin. Other graduates or converts from the Bethel ship in New York made their way to Denmark and Finland, and even to Germany, France, and South America.

Olof Hedstrom himself made several extended tours within his adopted country. In the early 1850s he organized the first Swedish Methodist congregations or societies in the Boston area, in the Chautauqua region in the state of New York, and in Chicago, where his former assistant on the Bethel ship, Sven B. Nyman or Newman (1812–1902) from Höganäs in Skåne, was placed in charge. The latter had arrived from Sweden in 1842, and before joining the mission in New York he had been a Methodist preacher in the South.

While obviously not an educated man, Olof Hedstrom must have been an unusually efficient preacher and guide. A professor of theology at Boston University wrote about his early service in the Catskills that he convinced even "those who had come to criticize his broken English," and friends of his in New York said that he seemed to possess limitless energy and enthusiasm, without being a fanatic. In 1863 he made a second visit to Sweden and was then invited to speak from pulpits of the Lutheran state church. Two years before his death in 1877 he retired to Cape May, New Jersey. The present Immanuel Methodist Episcopal Church in Brooklyn is the lineal descendant of the New York congregation headed by him.

Jonas Hedstrom, who was ten years younger than Olof, moved to western Illinois in 1837 to marry an American girl of Dutch colonial descent, whom he had met in the Catskills. Two years later, when he had settled at Victoria as a blacksmith, he was licensed as a Methodist preacher, and in 1846 he established the first Swedish Methodist church in the Middle West. From the beginning, Jonas Hedstrom kept in close contact with Olof in New York, and for many years, or until Jonas's death in 1859, the two brothers carried on a cooperation which helped direct a great number of Swedish and other Scandinavian immigrants to some of the best remaining farmland in Illinois.

When the Swedes began to arrive in that state, large parts of it had already been settled, first mainly by Southerners and then also by people from New England, and villages and towns founded by them attracted many of the newcomers from Sweden. Illinois has, therefore, only a few place-names of Swedish origin, but in Henry County to the northwest there are at least three. The least-known of these communities is Ophiem, which was named by a farmer, Johannes Samuelsson (1815–87), and his wife Maria from the village of Opphem in the province of Östergötland. They came to America in 1849, bringing their five children, all of whom died from cholera during the journey to the Middle West. At Ophiem, however, the parents raised six sons and daughters. They were able to donate considerable funds to churches and schools founded by Swedish immigrants.

A few days before Christmas of 1845, Olof Hedstrom received at the Bethel ship in New York an unusual visitor, Olof Olsson from Söderala in the province of Hälsingland, who with his wife and two children had arrived on a Swedish brig carrying a cargo of iron from Gävle, north of Stockholm. He had come, he said, to look for a large tract of land suitable for a religious colony, and he probably mentioned Illinois, which he and his associates in Sweden already had discussed as their goal in the New World. Like so many other newcomers from Scandinavia he was, of course, advised to go to Illinois, where Jonas Hedstrom would help him.

The two then met at Victoria in northwestern Illinois, where Jonas Hedstrom lived, and in the spring of 1846 Olsson bought for the colony the .first 80 acres about 15 miles farther north, in Henry County. His impressions of America and the Middle West were, he said in a report home, very favorable. "It is a country like the Kingdom of Heaven. It has everything true, good, and free. It is a land for action . . . a land where worker as well as Regent may eat wheat bread." In Sweden, 1845 had been a year of widespread crop failure.

Religious sect from north-central Sweden builds a communal settlement in Illinois

THE largest groups of Swedish emigrants in the 1840s came from provinces north and west of Stockholm. They had decided to leave because they regarded themselves as persecuted for their religious faith, and also because they wanted to escape the threat of recurring famines. They were headed for the same destination, the prairies of western Illinois, where in the spring of 1846 some land had been bought by Olof Olsson. Their leader or "prophet" was a farmer and sectarian preacher named Erik Jansson or Eric Janson (1808–50).

Jansson's relations with the Swedish state clergy were at first friendly, but he became more and more convinced that he had been given a divine mission to restore genuine Christianity, and since he had a magical influence over his followers, he was finally regarded as a sinister fanatic. An edict of the early 1700s which prohibited religious lay meetings was therefore revived. All religious books except the Bible were, according to Jansson, superfluous or harmful, and in 1844, when he had settled in the province of Hälsingland, he organized three public burnings of such literature, which led to riots and intervention by the authorities. Many people were furious with him. After having been locked up and released twice he was to be placed in protective custody at Gävle, but on his way to the prison he was set free by some of his supporters. He then went into hiding in the province of Dalarna, and from there he fled on skis through forests and over mountains to a port in Norway. In the early summer of 1846 he arrived in the United States accompanied by his wife, two children, and a few disciples.

Olof Olsson (1807–46) and his brother Jonas (1802–98), who also spent some time in jail, were Erik Jansson's most influential associates, and they were probably among the first to dream of a religious mass settlement in the New World. Like other dissenters in the same region they had been impressed by Robert Baird, the Presbyterian clergyman from America who in 1840 came to northern Sweden on a temperance crusade. Even more important in prompting migration to the United States was a district judge at Uppsala named Lars Henschen (1805–85), who had become a passionate champion of religious freedom and served as legal adviser to the Jansonists, as the followers of Erik Jansson were called. Henschen was a great admirer of the American constitution, and three of his sons emigrated to the United States. Letters from Swedish settlers in the New World also contributed to the "America fever" which swept through the districts affected by Jansson's sensational preaching. When the prophet himself began to think seriously of moving his followers to the United States, he sent Olof Olsson to scout for suitable land.

The Ljusnan and Voxnan river valleys in the province of Hälsingland were the power centers of the Jansson sect, but there were also large groups in Gästrikland and Uppland to the south, as well as in the neighboring inland provinces of Västmanland and Dalarna. Like the early Christians the believers were to have all things in common, and to finance the resettlement project they sold their belongings, including farms and cattle, and turned the proceeds into a common treasury, from which all travel expenses as well as the cost of the new farmland in America would be defrayed. Quite a few of the emigrants were farmers who had traded in flax and timber and lived in large, artistically decorated houses, but many others did not have sufficient funds to pay for their journey. Several women forsook their husbands, and some men left their wives behind.

During 1846, some 1,200 men, women, and children sailed for the United States in brigs and schooners, most of which carried cargoes of iron. All were overcrowded and the hygienic conditions on board became unspeakable, but frequent religious services and prayer meetings helped to maintain morale. One of the first ships foundered off Newfoundland, and on the others many people died from disease or malnutrition. Several vessels did not arrive in New York until the Hudson was frozen over, and the exhausted passengers had to wait for months before they could proceed up the river to Albany and the Erie Canal. Some of them began to have second thoughts about the Jansonist movement and left to join other Swedish groups in America or settle on their own. The level-headed and energetic people who had organized the migration could not have foreseen all the difficulties.

In the summer of 1846, when Eric Janson had reached his American destination, he and Olof Olsson made additional land purchases, and the new settlement was named Bishop Hill, a literal translation of the name of Janson's birthplace in the Swedish province of Uppland, Biskopskulla, near the city of Uppsala. A meandering stream, large enough to provide power for mills, ran below the wooded slope on which the town was to be built. The Mississippi was only 30 miles away.

The first new settlers arrived in the fall of 1846, after having crossed the prairie on foot or by horse and wagon from Chicago. Olof Olsson had then left the sect to become a Methodist, and before the end of the year he, his wife, and the two children they had brought from Sweden died. Eric Janson's faith in his mission remained unshaken, however, and under his resourceful though despotic leadership the newcomers began to tackle their tasks with all the energy they were able to muster. The joint treasury established in Sweden was retained, and everybody worked for the common good, without acquiring any private property. By the middle of the 19th century there were many experiments of the same utopian or "communistic" type in America. Eric Janson, however, seems to have regarded the communal ownership and organization of labor at Bishop Hill as a temporary arrangement, based on economic necessity.

At first the settlers were sheltered in tents, and from these they moved into dugouts and log cabins. Nearly 150 people, most of whom were in poor condition after the journey from Sweden, died during the first winter, when the food situation became so precarious that certain fast days had to be imposed. Since there were no material provisions for the care of children, celibacy was required of everyone, and the ban on matrimony remained in force until the summer of 1848, when mass weddings took place. A prayer meeting was held every morning at five and lasted two hours.

Farming began in earnest in the spring of 1847, and when summer came Bishop Hill actually began to look like a paradise. The fertility of the land seemed miraculous, and in letters to Sweden the colonists painted life in bright colors. "God has blessed us a hundredfold here on the new earth," one of them wrote. Visitors were impressed by the beauty of the extensive fields, in which the blue of flowering flax alternated with the green or gold of corn and wheat. Flax had for centuries been a specialty in the province of Hälsingland.

More settlers arrived from Sweden but others moved out, as a rule because of opposition to Eric Janson's iron rule, and the population of Bishop Hill during its Jansonist era never reached 1,000. In the fall of 1848 at least 200 members of the colony left to settle in the vicinity, and many of them joined the Swedish Methodist Church. The next blow came in the summer of 1849 when the cholera struck and the number of colonists again was reduced by nearly 150. Eric Janson lost his wife and two of their four children. A month later he found himself another spouse, a Swedish-born woman who had survived three husbands.

The cholera epidemic was immediately followed by the California gold fever, and in the spring of 1850 Jonas Olsson left for the West Coast with eight companions, hoping to improve Bishop Hill's finances. Many other Swedish pioneers in the Middle West had done the same and some had actually struck gold, but on its arrival in California the Jansonist expedition was upset by the news that the prophet, Eric Janson, had been murdered. A Swedish-born veteran of the Mexican War, who had married Janson's cousin, had decided to leave the colony and wanted to take his wife with him, which he had promised not to do. This led to a lawsuit, and during the course of the trial Janson was shot by his opponent.

At first the faithful settlers waited for their leader to rise from the dead, but life soon became normal again, and the religious fervor gradually subsided. For a while the colony was ruled by Janson's widow, with the help of a leading disciple, Anders, or Andrew, Berglund (1814–96) from Alfta in Hälsingland, as proxy for the prophet's 12-year-old son Eric, but when Jonas Olsson came back from California he gained the support of most of the colonists, and together with a popularly elected board of seven trustees he led Bishop Hill for the ten years it had left as a communal settlement.

*Bishop Hill flourishes but in 1860 its leaders decide to
dissolve the commune*

A FEW years after Eric Janson's death, the settlers at Bishop Hill were
widely regarded as model farmers. Not only their cultivated fields but
also their cattle and horses were mentioned by neighbors and visitors
as among the finest in Illinois. Considerable quantities of grains,
broomcorn, and other agricultural products were sold for cash, and
settlers in other parts of the Middle West, including Swedes in Minnesota, obtained seeds from Bishop Hill. The largest land purchases
were made in 1852–55, after which the colony comprised some
10,000 acres.

Flax was grown on a large scale, to be prepared and spun by the
women. In some years the production of linen cloth reached about
30,000 yards. Bishop Hill also had its own tailors, cabinetmakers,
wheelwrights, toolsmiths, clockmakers, and other craftsmen. Carriages and ploughs were shipped to St. Louis and other centers.

As soon as they had solved their most pressing problems, the
colonists began to build more comfortable and durable houses, and by
1855 a whole new town had sprung up from the prairie. Some of the
buildings were the largest in the United States west of Chicago, and all
were unusually sturdy and even beautiful. With a few exceptions they
were built of brick, a material the settlers had never used in Sweden,
and their architectural styles also reflected new ideas and influences.

The largest building was a 200-foot-long four-story apartment
house known as the Big Brick, the ground floor of which contained a
kitchen and dining rooms for the whole colony. It was destroyed by
fire in 1928, and some other units, including the flour mill and the
tannery, have also disappeared, but a dozen structures remain to this
day. They include the impressive Steeple Building, designed as a
hotel but soon turned into a school and dwellings, two apartment
houses, a hotel with ballroom, a large smithy, a wagon shop, and a
dairy. The new hotel became famous among travelers for its excellent
food and beautiful ballroom, and the inhabitants of Bishop Hill regarded it as a good investment.

The prosperity of the settlement continued to increase, and early
in 1857 it was resolved to "send money to help those in need in
Sweden, who, by religious persecution and the rigors of the law, have
been ruined in their goods and conscience." Later the same year,

however, a financial panic spread across the United States, and Bishop Hill met the crisis by contracting heavy debts. A trustee named Olof Jonsson or Johnson (1820–70), who served as business manager, had played a significant part in the colony's economic expansion but also made a number of dubious investments.

The ventures in which Bishop Hill had become involved included banking, trading in stocks and bonds, land speculations and city real estate, meat packing, coal mining, and railroad construction. To outsiders, however, the colony seemed like a prosperous family farm, and in 1857 it opened its doors to more and more Swedish immigrants who were struggling to survive the depression. Toward the end of the year one of the old settlers wrote to Sweden: "Many poor and indigent countrymen, besides widows and fatherless, have this autumn been admitted into our colony, but rarely have any of the rich and well-born offered themselves, for it is as Scripture says, not many of these are called."

The financial situation was not as serious as it had seemed at first, but in 1860 it was decided to dissolve the colony as an organization based on communal ownership. A division of the property was begun, and despite costly lawsuits each member in good standing finally received an impressive allotment. Even without the economic crisis of 1857, Bishop Hill would hardly have been able to survive much longer as a "communistic" enclave in a territory of rising wages and rapidly improving economic opportunities. In particular, members of the younger generations objected to the idea of working without payment in cash.

After the dissolution of Bishop Hill some of the old colonists joined the Shakers of the Pleasant Hill colony in Kentucky, with whom lively contacts had been established at an early stage. Many settled as farmers in the vicinity or made their homes in nearby towns, and others moved to Minnesota.

Descendants of the original settlers soon began to achieve success in new fields throughout the nation. For instance, Eric Johnson (1838–1919), the son of the founder of the colony and an officer in the Union army, became a newspaper publisher and, successively, legislator in Nebraska, Texas, and California. Eric Bergland, whose father, Andrew Berglund, had been one of the leading colonists, distinguished himself both in the Civil War and at West Point, where he was the first Swedish-born cadet. Jonas W. Olsson (b. 1843), whose father bought the first land for Bishop Hill, became the first Swede to be admitted to the bar of Illinois and was also elected to the state legislature. He had come to America as a 3-year-old boy in 1846, and the same year he lost his parents as well as his brother and sister.

One of the Bishop Hill veterans who lived until the early 1900s was Jonas Bergren, who was regarded as something of a technical genius. When he had seen one of Thomas Alva Edison's phonographs he built his own speaking machine and made recordings at Bishop Hill. His recorded interviews, including one with a settler who, at the age of 94, tells about his voyage to America in 1846, are among the oldest in the world.

Self-taught artist depicts life at Bishop Hill, which remains as a unique memorial

A MEMBER of a Jansonist family from Nora Parish in the province of Uppland, who finally became a self-taught artist, is today more widely known than any other Bishop Hill pioneer.

Olof Eriksson or Krans (1838–1916) came to the colony with his parents in 1850. After the Civil War he lived at nearby Galva most of the time, working as a house and decorative painter. As he grew older his memories of Bishop Hill seemed increasingly important to him, and in the 1890s he began an artistic production which resulted in nearly 100 oil paintings. Most of them are portraits, while the others with great authority and power depict scenes from the workaday life of the Swedish settlers. These are, for instance, seen breaking the prairie with plows pulled by six yokes of oxen, or harvesting wheat under a blue sky, or quickly loading their haycarts to escape an approaching rainstorm. The canvases are unique documents as well as genuine works of art. With a few exceptions they belong to the state of Illinois, while a complete set of copies is in the National Gallery of Art in Washington, D. C. Collections have been exhibited in Chicago and New York as well as in Sweden.

After New Sweden in Iowa, Bishop Hill is the oldest of the still existing 19th-century Swedish settlements in America, and it is the only wholly Swedish-built community in the country. Today it has also become recognized as a unique, living memorial of American pioneer life. Most of the original two- and three-story houses, which surround a village square shaded by huge trees, remain intact, and although the architecture is not typically Swedish, the atmosphere is essentially that of a large agricultural-industrial estate or an ironmaking town in north-central Sweden by the middle of the 1800s. In the early 1970s old Swedish customs and practices were still in use among the some 200 inhabitants, and the Hälsingland dialect of around 1850 could still be heard. It was the genuine thing and no window dressing.

Bishop Hill is not only an Illinois state memorial but also a national historic site. Three local organizations contribute to its preservation — the Bishop Hill Old Settlers Association, the Bishop Hill Heritage Association, and the Henry County Historical Society. The neoclassic Steeple Building, which towers over the other structures, is open to the public as a museum, and so is the wooden Colony Church, where the paintings of Olof Krans hang. The original settlers were, according to legend, too busy to note the minutes, and the face of the steeple clock has, therefore, only one hand. The old Oxpojke Trail, along which the ox boys hauled lumber from Bishop Hill's sawmills to the village square for construction of the communal buildings, can still be followed. The second Saturday in September is celebrated annually as Old Settlers' Day, and thousands of persons, chiefly descendants of the pioneers, attend the observance of important anniversaries.

None of the other utopian communities which grew up in the United States in the middle 1800s has the same stately town plan and architecture as Bishop Hill. Pleasant Hill in Kentucky, one of a score of Shaker colonies, is regarded as the nearest equivalent. About 75 miles southwest of Bishop Hill, on a promontory in the Mississippi, is the town of Nauvoo, which Joseph Smith, the Mormon prophet, and his followers founded in 1839. In 1844, when Nauvoo, with a population of nearly 15,000, was the largest city in Illinois, Smith and his brother Hyrum were murdered by a mob in nearby Carthage, and in 1846, when the Swedes founded Bishop Hill, most of the Mormons moved west. Two years later Nauvoo's largest building, the Mormon temple, was destroyed by fire. In the mid-1900s the Mormons began to restore Nauvoo.

Other historic settlements in western Illinois
and in Rockford to the north

IN THE vicinity of Bishop Hill are many communities which, in part, were populated from this colony. They include Victoria, where the first Swedish Methodist parish in the Midwest was organized by Jonas Hedstrom in 1846; Andover, where the first group of Swedes settled in 1847 and a Lutheran congregation was formed in 1850; Galva, which Bishop Hill settlers named for the city of Gävle in Sweden; and Galesburg, where America's first important Swedish-language newspaper was started in 1855 and Carl Sandburg, the poet and Lincoln biographer, was born of Swedish parents.

Other Bishop Hill colonists moved somewhat farther north to Rock Island, where the first Swedish Baptist congregation in America was organized in 1852 by Gustaf Palmquist, a former schoolteacher from Stockholm who five years later returned to Sweden as a missionary. He was born on a farm in northern Småland, in the district where Swante M. Swenson led the emigration to Texas.

Rock Island later became the leading educational and religious center of the Swedish Lutherans, an aspect that will be described in other connections. Immigrants who had first joined the Bishop Hill colony also settled in the adjacent Moline, which grew into an industrial city specializing in farm implements. As mechanics, engineers, and inventors, people of Swedish stock made significant contributions to this development. Many of them came from Karlskoga in Värmland and other communities in central Sweden largely based on the making of iron and steel.

In 1852 some 30 immigrants from Sweden arrived in Rockford in northern Illinois; situated on the Rock River just south of the Wisconsin line, Rockford the following year was incorporated as a city. The newcomers were soon followed by large numbers of fellow countrymen. After only a few years Rockford's Swedish-born population reached 1,000 and at the end of the Civil War 2,000.

Most of the newcomers of 1852 were from Södra Ving in a section of Västergötland which long had been noted for its handicrafts and textile products, and this province remained one of the main sources of the flow of Swedes to Rockford. The others were Småland and its eastern neighbor, the island of Öland in the Baltic. Since its early days

Rockford has had a larger Swedish concentration than any other American city except Jamestown in New York.

In the late 1800s, Rockford, like Jamestown, rose as a leading furniture center but then became known, above all, for its metal products, such as tools and dies, machinery, and hardware. In fact, it grew into one of the largest machine-tool producers in the world. Among the Swedes who came to Rockford in 1852 were six-year-old Pehr August Peterson (1846–1927), who became a leading industrialist, and a 22-year-old carpenter, John Nelson (1830–83), whose inventions of automatic knitting machines helped revolutionize the making of hosiery and laid the foundation for Rockford's important textile industry. Both were born in Västergötland.

The oldest Swedish church in Rockford, the first of seven Lutheran ones, was dedicated in 1856. Later other denominations organized congregations of their own.

First Swedes in Chicago, their future·metropolis, and the growing "Swede Town"

A PRIVATE in the U.S. Army named Peter Holmstrom, who had enlisted at Philadelphia in 1805, seems to have been the first Swedish-born person to set foot in what was to be Chicago. In 1808 he was ordered to the newly established Fort Dearborn for duty.

Chicago became a city in 1837, when it had a population of about 4,000, and its first known Swedish resident, a sea captain named Olof Gottfrid Lange (1811–93), who was a native of Gothenburg, arrived the following year. He had come to the United States the first time in 1825 as a 14-year-old cabin boy on an American brig and continued as a sailor for many years. After settling in Chicago in 1838, he worked in a drug store and gave instruction in English at Fort Dearborn to Norwegian immigrants. In 1841 he moved to Milwaukee, where he met Gustaf Unonius and helped him to select land for his farm on Pine Lake. A period as part owner of a foundry in Chicago ended in failure in 1863, and after that Lange earned his living as an insurance and immigrant agent. He was very active in Swedish societies. In the late 1860s he visited Sweden twice and returned with a collection of 500 books and a number of art portfolios, most of them donations from the royal family.

In the fall of 1846, when the Von Schneidaus and some other

Swedes had settled in Chicago, the first large group of Swedish settlers arrived, and this was the beginning of a constant flow which would be of vital importance to the Midwestern metropolis and make it one of the largest "Swedish cities" in the world. The newcomers were 27 men and women, together with children, from Österunda and Torstuna parishes in the province of Uppland, who on the Atlantic or after landing in America had decided to leave the Eric Janson sect and not proceed to Bishop Hill. Their leader was Anders Larsson (1801–84), an influential and prosperous farmer, who in Chicago earned his first livelihood as a wood sawyer. Later on his economic situation improved rapidly, although a soda-bottling plant which he operated in partnership with another Swede named Charles Sundell had to close down during the panic of 1857. Larsson and his wife Sara Brita (1812–98) became devoted members of the St. Ansgarius Episcopal Church and warm friends of its first pastor, Gustaf Unonius. One of their eight children, Emma Larsson, became a concert singer.

Practically all of the men who came from Sweden started earning their living as laborers or craftsmen, while the women often found employment as servants. Those who arrived in the summer of 1847 included three carpenters and builders, two shoemakers, two wagonmakers, two druggists, one goldsmith and engraver, one instrument maker, one blacksmith, one tailor, one daguerreotypist, one baker, one distiller, and "many seamen."

In an area in the then northwestern outskirts of the city, which became known as Swede Town, the Swedes built their wooden houses, and there they also erected churches, the first one being Gustaf Unonius's St. Ansgarius in 1849–50. A few years later the Swedish Lutheran Immanuel congregation was organized, and Methodist and Baptist churches were also established. The first Swede Town, where Norwegians also lived, was in part identical with the Irish Kilgubbin. In 1853–54 the inhabitants, both Scandinavians and Irishmen, were driven out by the landowners from the section just north of the Chicago River, and by 1860 the center of the Swedish area had shifted toward Chicago Avenue farther north, where German immigrants had settled. In the early 1850s the cholera took a heavy toll among the newcomers, particularly in 1854 when according to some estimates two-thirds of the newly arrived immigrants died.

In 1850, according to the U.S. census, about 200 Swedish-born people lived in Chicago. Seven years later its first Swedish secular society, called Svea, was organized, despite furious assaults from some of the clergymen. The more liberal Gustaf Unonius was elected an honorary member just before his departure for Sweden in 1858. Svea's first chairman was Carl Johan Ståhlbrand, or Charles John Stolbrand, who became one of the best-known Swedish-born officers in the American Civil War. The secretary was the principal founder, Charles John Sundell (1822–92) from Stockholm, who had come to America in 1849 but, after having sought gold in California as well as in Australia and Brazil, had gone back to Sweden. In 1853 he settled in Chicago, and five years later he was appointed Swedish-Norwegian vice consul after Unonius. His efforts during the American election campaign of 1860 were rewarded with an appointment as consul in Stettin, Germany, from where he was sent to Bucharest, the capital of Rumania.

Another politically active member of Svea was John A. Nilsson or Nelson (1829–75) from Forshälla in the province of Bohuslän, the first of numerous successful Swedish-born contractors in Chicago. He was also the first Swede to win an important elective office in that city, being elected sheriff in 1864. The books and art portfolios brought from Sweden by Captain Lange after the Civil War were intended for Svea's library, which, like practically all Swede Town, was destroyed in the fire of 1871. Svea flourished for another 20 years but was then unable to hold its own. During the latter part of the century numerous other and more active organizations were formed by the Swedes in Chicago.

The more prominent Swedes in Chicago in the 1850s included Frans Oscar Malmborg (1820–80), who, after having passed his officer's examination in Sweden in 1845, hurried the next year to America to join the U.S. forces in the War with Mexico. In 1851 he was discharged as a private and then settled in Chicago. Late in 1853 he returned to Sweden hoping to find employment as an engineer in its newly begun railway construction, but instead he started working there as an emigrant agent, the first one to be paid by an American concern. His employer was the Illinois Central Railroad. He had good press contacts, and one of his uncles was an army general. After a few years Malmborg went back to Chicago, from where he continued to write articles for Swedish newspapers, but in 1860 he returned to

Sweden as Illinois Central Railroad's authorized agent for Sweden and Norway. He traveled extensively, advertised in the press, and distributed circular letters, which sometimes were published. In 1861, when he was back in Chicago, he was appointed vice consul there for Sweden and Norway, but he resigned this commission almost immediately and volunteered his service to the Union army.

To immigrants from Sweden and the other Scandinavian countries, Chicago served as a distributing point for the entire Middle West. In northern Illinois not only Rockford 80 miles to the northwest but also the Fox River Valley near Chicago was settled by Swedes in the late 1840s or early 50s. In 1852, for instance, several hundred Swedes, most of them from Västergötland, came to the St. Charles district, drawn by glowing descriptions by a former neighbor who had settled there some years earlier. Immigrants from Sweden also helped populate Aurora, Geneva, and Elgin in the same valley. Quite a few Swedes settled in Illinois's northeastern corner, including Waukegan on Lake Michigan, which became a city in 1859. More and more immigrants went from Chicago to Minnesota, which also attracted Swedes who had started in other settlements in the Middle West, including Bishop Hill.

★ 11

In Minnesota
and Some Other States

Beginnings of the Swedish invasion of Minnesota — The first
settler came with the Indians

IN 1850 Minnesota had only about 6,000 white inhabitants, and according to the U.S. census of that year only four of them were born in Sweden. In the same year Fredrika Bremer, the famous Swedish novelist, wrote prophetically from Minnesota: "What a glorious new Scandinavia might not Minnesota become! Here the Swede would find his clear, romantic lakes, the plains of Skåne, rich in grain, and the valleys of Norrland. Here the Norwegian would find his rapid rivers, his lofty mountains. The Danes might there pasture their flocks and herds and lay out their farms on richer and less misty coasts than those of Denmark." Fifty years later one-eighth of Minnesota's inhabitants consisted of Swedish immigrants, the largest foreign-born group, and in relation to the population of their native country the Norwegians were even better represented.

The first Swede known to have settled in Minnesota, a native of Stockholm named Jacob Fahlström or Falstrom (c. 1795–1859), did not come as an immigrant but as a roving woodsman and trapper from Canada. His parents had died when he was quite young, and he went to sea as a cabin boy on a merchant ship captained by an uncle. During a visit to London the two seem to have become separated, and the boy was hired by Lord Thomas Douglas Selkirk who had begun to sponsor organized emigration from Scotland to Canada. After having sailed into Hudson Bay on a British ship, Jacob went ashore on its southern coast with a hunting party but became lost in the wilderness and was adopted by a band of Chippewa Indians. Because of his blond hair, they called him Yellowhead. This seems to have happened in 1807, or at least not later than 1810.

For many years Jacob Falstrom roamed far and wide with the Chippewa Indians, who were involved in the British and French fur trade, and he also worked directly for the big trading companies. About 1813 he came to Minnesota the first time, and he seems to have gone as far south as the confluence of the Mississippi and Minnesota rivers several years before Fort Snelling, the beginning of Minneapolis-St. Paul, was established there in 1819. At times he lived in the territory that became Wisconsin. Together with another Swede named David Swanson he is listed in the roster of employees of the American Fur Company for 1818–19.

In 1823 Falstrom married a member of the Chippewa tribe, Winona or Margaret Bungo, with whom he had nine children. Four years later he built a log cabin near Fort Snelling, and for some time he carried mail for its garrison through the forests. He spoke the Chippewa language and other Indian tongues with a Stockholm accent and could also make himself understood in English and French. His mother tongue, on the other hand, he did not hear for nearly half a century and cannot have expected to use it again.

The first Swedish-born soldier at Fort Snelling was probably Mrs. Gustaf Unonius's brother Hugo Ferdinand Öhrströmer (b. 1816), who came in 1838 after having resigned from the Swedish army and abbreviated his name to Hugo Ferdinand, but he and Jacob Falstrom can hardly have met. In 1837 Falstrom became the first Methodist convert in Minnesota, and he then worked as a missionary among the Indians and in the newly established lumber camps. After 1850, when his own countrymen had begun to arrive, he preached to them in halting Swedish, and he also served as their counselor and interpreter. Because of his long experience in the wilderness and knowledge of many languages, the "Indian Swede," as he was called, proved to be a great help to other missionaries.

In 1841 Falstrom moved his family to a farm at Valley Creek near Afton on the banks of the St. Croix River, some 20 miles east of Minneapolis-St. Paul in Washington County, and the last part of his life was spent there. In 1964 a granite marker in memory of him and his wife was placed at the Falstrom family burial ground by the Minnesota Methodist Historical Society, more than 30 descendants of the Falstroms attending the dedication ceremony. In 1948, Prince Bertil of Sweden unveiled a memorial plaque on Kellogg Boulevard in St. Paul. Falstrom once owned 80 acres in what is now downtown St. Paul, but he is said to have given up his claim because the land was too hilly.

Margaret Bungo Falstrom survived her husband by more than 20 years, living at the Valley Creek farm with some of her children. When she died in 1880 about 40 Swedish families, most of them from the province of Skåne, had settled in the same district.

Many Swedes were attracted to Washington County and other sections of eastern Minnesota by three young men from the province of Västergötland, Carl Fernström (1831–1908), Oscar Roos (1827–96), and August Sandahl. In the fall of 1850 they built a log cabin at Hay Lake near Marine on the St. Croix River, on a site that since 1902 has been marked by a tall granite monument. The next year they sold their cabin and land holdings to a countryman named Daniel Nilsson from Norrbo in Hälsingland. Fernström then set out for California to dig for gold, Roos moved north into Chisago County where he settled at Taylors Falls on the St. Croix River, and Sandahl returned to Sweden, but within four years about 100 Swedes made their homes in the Marine district in Washington County.

In 1851 a Swedish settlement was founded on far-reaching Chisago Lake, and this was the beginning of an invasion that turned Chisago County, together with its western neighbor, Isanti, into the most Swedish of all districts in the whole of America. In the early 1900s at least 75 per cent of the inhabitants in Chisago County were of Swedish stock, and by the middle of the century older people still spoke Swedish, their dialects generally being those of southern Småland and neighboring Blekinge. Several communities, such as Almelund and Lindstrom, as well as many small lakes were named for Swedish settlers.

The leader of the first Swedes in Chisago County was a relatively well-to-do farmer from Hassela in the province of Hälsingland by the name of Pehr Andersson (1817–81), who with his wife and four children had left Sweden in the fall of 1850. The family first went to western Illinois but the following spring they continued to Minnesota and Chisago Lake. In late summer Pehr Andersson wrote to a young Swedish friend, Eric Norelius, who was studying theology at Columbus, Ohio, that "I hope that the population here will before long increase considerably, for we have room enough for several parishes and a splendid and sound climate." Five or six years later, however, he moved to another Swedish settlement in Minnesota. In 1854, a Swedish Lutheran congregation was organized at Chisago, and within a year it had 350 members. At Taylors Falls, which was the nearest settled place, the Swedes in the beginning became known as "the wooden-shoe people," because of the wooden shoes they always wore.

Several of the early settlers in the Chisago region came from the Bishop Hill colony in western Illinois. Among those who immigrated directly from Sweden was one Carl Andersson from Hovmantorp in southern Småland, who came in 1852 and the next year was joined by two brothers and three sisters. Finally only one sister, out of originally nine children, remained in Sweden, and seven of her children eventually crossed the Atlantic to settle in the New World. In America the members of this Andersson family called themselves Linn, after the name of their parental home in Sweden which was Linnhult. In the summer of 1952 a Linn centennial reunion was held on Chisago Lake, and according to a pamphlet printed for this occasion some 325 Americans could claim descent from the first generation of Linns.

The largest lake in this section of Minnesota, Chisago or Kichi-Saga as the Chippewa Indians and first white colonists called it, plays an important part in an epic work by a Swedish novelist, Vilhelm Moberg (1898–1973), which was published during the years 1949–59 in four volumes and was followed by an English version in the United States and England. The leading characters of the novel, who settled on Chisago Lake, were born in southeastern Småland, and so was Moberg himself who at one time planned to join dozens of relatives in the American Midwest. Emigrants from Småland often embarked at Karlshamn in Blekinge, where a monument inspired by Moberg's narrative was unveiled in 1959. A replica is at Lindstrom on Chisago Lake.

In the United States, immigrants from the same province in Sweden often settled in the same vicinity. A large proportion of the colonists in Isanti County came from Dalarna, historic "Land of the

Valleys." This district in Minnesota has sometimes been called the "Dalarna of America." There was little immigration in the 1850s, but about 100 families from Rättvik, Orsa and other villages in the Lake Siljan region arrived in 1866.

Numerous other settlements in Minnesota founded in the 1850s — Norwegians helpful

IN 1853, a small group of immigrants led by 21-year-old Hans Mattson (1832–93), founded a community that became the main center of the Swedish settlements in Goodhue County on the Mississippi southeast of Minneapolis-St. Paul. It was first called Mattson but was soon renamed Vasa in honor of Sweden's famous 16th-century monarch, Gustavus Vasa. Many of the early settlers came, like Mattson himself, from northern Skåne, but Småland and other Swedish provinces were also well represented. Mattson's first companions were 42-year-old Gustaf Kempe, the son of a clergyman from Västergötland, and 52-year-old Carl Roos from Värmland.

Before settling in Minnesota Hans Mattson had tried his luck in the East, and after a few years of farming at Vasa he moved ten miles east to Red Wing to become a real-estate agent. Financial success came quickly, but he was ruined in the panic of 1857, and after that he studied law and entered politics. In the course of time he helped found three Swedish-language weeklies, all of which reflected his staunch Republican views. In his memoirs, which were published at Lund, Sweden, in 1890 and at St. Paul, Minnesota, the following year, he recalls how he left school and enlisted in the fashionable Vendes Artillery Regiment at Kristianstad in southern Sweden when Prussia attacked Denmark in 1848. One or two years later he realized that a farmer's son would have little chance of promotion in competition with the sons of the nobility, and in 1851 he emigrated to the United States. His memoirs also deal with his Civil War service and subsequent political career. Mattson was born in Önnestad Parish near Kristianstad.

Another of the pioneers of Vasa, Troed Persson or Trued Granville Pearson (1827–1905) from Stoby in northern Skåne, also left an autobiography, which was published in Sweden long after his death. On their way to the Middle West, Mattson and Persson landed in Boston in late June of 1851 with a large group of countrymen, and somewhat later a popular weekly magazine, *Gleason's Pictorial Drawing-Room Companion*, published a story about their arrival, which, when read today, brings back something of the atmosphere in the ports of immigration. "A few days since a party of Swedes, numbering nearly 100, just arrived per Swedish brig *Ambrosius*, marched through Washington Street to Worcester depot, en route for the Great West, where they will establish themselves in colonies. They were entirely of a different class of immigrants from those we are accustomed to seeing, being all well-to-do farmers and mechanics, with their families, who very evidently came to this country to profit by their intelligence and industry . . . The party had a train of 13 wagons, upon the first of which an American flag was hoisted on starting from the wharf, and the men marched side by side of their teams, in single file, carrying muskets." The spirit of the newcomers from Sweden was bolstered by what they heard about their famous compatriot Jenny Lind, who was appearing in the Boston area when they arrived.

Letters from Swedes in Illinois and the fact that the distribution of his father's estate left little for each one of the many children made Troed Persson decide to emigrate, which may be regarded as typical. To begin with he lived in western Illinois, where he married a fellow immigrant from the same region of Skåne, and from where he wrote letters which caused many relatives and neighbors to follow in his footsteps. Among them were his mother, two sisters, and two brothers, and a well-to-do maternal uncle with many children, who came in the company of "a whole little congregation" from northern Skåne. At Vasa, Minnesota, where Trued Granville Pearson settled as a farmer in 1855, he served for more than 30 years as justice of the peace, and was elected a member of the state legislature. In 1900 he visited Sweden accompanied by, among others, his son William Anthony Granville (1863–1943), who, after studies at Gustavus Adolphus College in St. Peter, Minn., and at Yale, became a noted mathematician. He was for many years president of Gettysburg College in Pennsylvania.

At Vasa, the first Swedish Lutheran church in Minnesota was founded in 1855 by the Reverend Eric Norelius (1833–1916), who became one of the spiritual leaders of the 19th-century immigrants from Sweden. A native of Hälsingland like many of the Bishop Hill colonists, he arrived in New York in 1850 at the age of 17 and then for four years studied at a newly founded Lutheran school and seminary at Columbus, Ohio, called Capitol University. In 1857 Norelius established the first Swedish newspaper in Minnesota, called *Minnesota Posten*, in 1860 he helped found the Swedish American Lutheran Church, known as the Augustana Synod, and in 1862 he founded a school at Red Wing which became the beginning of Gustavus Adolphus College at St. Peter in Nicollet County, to the southwest of Minneapolis.

Toward the end of his life Norelius contributed much to the knowledge about Swedish settlements in the Middle West, and his two-volume *History of the Swedish Lutheran Congregations and the Swedes in America* is regarded as a classic in its field. He died at Vasa at the age of 83. His brother Anders or Andrew Norelius (1830–1927), who arrived in America at the same time, became a Baptist clergyman, served as a chaplain in the Union army in the Civil War, and finally settled in Iowa. A grandson of Eric Norelius, Theodore A. Norelius, published for many years at Lindstrom the *Chisago County Press* and was in the middle 1970s still active as a historian of the Swedish immigrants in the lower St. Croix River Valley.

In Nicollet County some 50 miles southwest of Minneapolis, which surrounds Swan Lake, Swedes began to settle in 1855. People from Småland, especially the parish of Vetlanda, went to the newly established town of St. Peter, which in its early days aspired to become the state capital, and a Swedish Lutheran congregation was organized there two years later. Among the first Swedes to settle just north of St. Peter was Gustaf Johnson from southern Östergötland, whom we shall meet again together with his wife and their son John A. Johnson, who became governor of Minnesota and a Presidential candidate. Also in 1855, Scandian Grove was founded about 10 miles northwest of St. Peter, most of its early settlers coming from the Kristianstad district in northeast Skåne. Somewhat farther west, other immigrants in 1858 founded a village they first called New Sweden and finally Bernadotte. In the early 1900s a noted clergyman, Emil Lund (1850–1942) from Falun in Dalarna, who spoke Latin as well as Hebrew, wrote about the village church: "The temple of the parish, its parsonage, churchyard, and its whole estate, in the smallest details, testify to the taste, love of orderliness and artistic aptitudes of the pastor or leader, and to the spirit of sacrifice on the part of the congregation. Everything is so genuinely Swedish: the plantations, the borders of flowers, indeed even the walks of the parsonage and the resting place of the dead. It resembles so very much a well-kept and well-arranged church estate in a fertile Swedish landscape." Some 30 miles southeast of St. Peter, in Waseca County, Swedes began to settle in 1857. Most of them came from the region of Gränna on the east shore of Lake Vättern and had lived for some time in Tippecanoe County and adjoining districts in west-central Indiana.

Farther north, in Carver County some 30 miles southwest of Minneapolis, the first Swedes arrived in 1853 by flatboats on the Minnesota River, and just north of the stream they founded Oscar's Settlement, which later became known as the Union colony. In the summer of 1854 they welcomed a party of 16 people from the district of Herrljunga in central Västergötland, who the same spring had set out from Hartland near Milwaukee, Wisconsin, with three wagons, each drawn by two oxen. Only the small children were allowed to ride in the carriages, while the women walked behind, knitting stockings. In 1858, a Lutheran congregation was founded, and somewhat later the parish was divided into East Union and West Union. The population of the whole region came originally from the forests and plains around Skara and Falköping in Västergötland.

Among the first settlers in the Union colony were Johannes, or John, and Catharina Hult, whose son Andrew Holt (1855–1948) from 1912 to 1942 was an associate justice of the Supreme Court of Minnesota, and Anders, or Andrew, and Maja-Stina Stomberg, whose son Andrew A. Stomberg (1871–1943) became professor of Scandinavian at the University of Minnesota. At the age of about 65 the younger Stomberg wrote that in his youth he had never been able to understand how the steady-going and far from reckless Swedish settlers, whom he knew so well, "had been able to resolve to leave the old home, emigrate to America and, despite almost incredible hardships and anxieties, travel far into the interior where Indians still roamed at will." But, he continued, "On his first visit, at the age of 26, to the community in Sweden whence parents and neighbors had emigrated, the whole phenomenon became quite understandable. The region seemed like a hopeless conglomeration of granite-strewn patches of ground, moorland, shallow lakes, stunted trees, and only here and there small plots of arable land. This, it should be noted, was before reforestation, drainage, dairy farming, and the application of modern methods of agriculture had made the same neighborhood the fair and beautiful place it is today . . . The thoughts of the visitor from the United States went back to the story told by his parents of how they, soon after arriving in Minnesota in 1854, had acquired title to several hundred acres of land as fine and as fertile as may be found anywhere for $1.25 an acre. It now became easier to understand how it had happened that, in this particular section of Sweden, there could hardly be found a family that did not have one or more of its members in America, most of these living in Minnesota. In a distressingly large number of homes, only the parents remained." Large parts of Småland and several other provinces were even less suitable for farming than the section of Västergötland from where the Stombergs came.

Watertown in the northernmost part of Carver County was the northern outpost of a Swedish settlement called Götaholm. A native of Hälsingland, Daniel Justis, came here in the summer of 1856, wandering through the forests. Among those who arrived in 1858 was a former member of the Swedish parliament, Olof Andersson from Värmland, who played an important role in the development of the colony. Before long, its population was increased by the arrival of Swedes from Jamestown, New York, and Sugar Grove, Pennsylvania.

In 1855, Swedish immigrants founded a settlement called Scandia farther north in Carver County, on Clear Water or Waconia Lake. Some came from the region of Galesburg, Illinois, others from Burlington, Iowa. Most of them were Baptists, and their first minister was Fredrik Olaus Nilsson, a former sailor who in 1850 had been expelled from Sweden for "heresy."

In Wright County, north of Carver, most of the early Swedish settlers came from Östmark and neighboring parishes in western Värmland, which probably had been infected with "America fever" from Norway. The first Swedes settled at the present-day town of Buffalo in the middle of the county. In the 1860s, Stockholm and Cokato farther west became other centers of Swedish settlement. In Meeker County, west of Wright, Swedes helped found Litchfield, the future county seat, in 1856. At Rosendale 10 miles southwest of Litchfield, most of the Swedish population came from the parish of Segerstad near Falköping in Västergötland.

Several of the early Scandinavian settlements in west-central Minnesota suffered a serious setback as a result of the Sioux uprising that began in August of 1862, when a large proportion of the men had enlisted in the Union army. The total number of Scandinavians slain was relatively small, but on August 20 thirteen Swedes lost their lives in a massacre about 100 miles west of Minneapolis-St. Paul, in Kandiyohi County, immediately west of Meeker. Almost all were from Vårgårda in the province of Västergötland, and most of them had lived in their frontier homes only a short time. In 1891 their remains were moved from where first interred to a churchyard at nearby New London. The monument erected there became known as "Västgöta monumentet."

At Willmar, the county seat of Kandiyohi, the Swedish and Norwegian elements have always been particularly important, each accounting for approximately 40 percent of the population. Today, however, it is difficult to separate the two, frequent intermarriage being one of the reasons. A two-day Scandinavian coffee festival, with many kinds of home-baked cakes and cookies, takes place at Willmar annually in June. In Douglas County, farther north in west-central Minnesota, Lund and Melby in the northwest, on or near Lake Christina, were named after localities in Skåne, Sweden's southernmost province and granary. Near Nelson in the east stands the church of Fahlun, where the first Swedes arrived in 1866, most of them from western Dalarna.

A shoemaker named Nils Nyberg from Skåne, who came in 1851, seems to have been the first Swedish settler in Minneapolis, which the following year received its present name. When he died in 1890, he is said to have been a wealthy man. Nils Nilson from Östergötland and A. J. Ekman from Gothenburg, who arrived in 1853, are regarded as the first Swedes in St. Paul.

Gradually, Swedish immigrants flowed into all sections of the state, attracted by more and more detailed reports about its farm land, forest resources, ore fields, and industrial possibilities. In 1860, according to the U. S. census, the number of Swedes in Minnesota had increased to nearly 3,200. There were, however, no less than 8,400 Norwegians and 17,500 Germans, most of whom had poured in from already existing settlements in Wisconsin and Iowa. Especially the Norwegians were of great help to the newcomers from Sweden. It was not until the early 1900s that the Swedes became the largest foreign-born group in Minnesota.

Of some 800 place–names of Swedish origin in the United States, about one-fourth are in Minnesota. Cities and towns in Sweden with namesakes in the North Star State include, in addition to those mentioned above, Borgholm, Eksjö, Kalmar, Karlstad, Malmö, Malung, Mora, Ronneby, Uppsala (Upsala), and Vänersborg (Wenersborg). Many other names honor Swedish pioneers, such as Arctander, Bloom, Chilgren, Englund, Enstrom, Knapp, Kost, Lind, Linn, Ogren, Stark, and Strandquist. Jockmock Lake in the northeast corner was not named directly for Jokkmokk in Swedish Lapland but for a pioneer named Gust Hagberg, who became known as "Jockmock." Names of the poetic-patriotic type include Svea, Sveadahl, and Tegner.

Highlights of the early history of the Swedes in Michigan, Indiana, and Ohio

LARGE parts of Ohio and Indiana were already settled when Swedes began to arrive in America in greater numbers, and until the late 19th century Michigan remained in the lee of the flow of Swedish immigrants to the Middle West.

The U.S. census of 1850 showed only 16 Swedish-born residents of Michigan, which undoubtedly was less than the actual number, while in 1860 the total was 266. In the Lower Peninsula the first larger groups of immigrants from Sweden settled in 1853–54 north of Grand Rapids in Kent County, beginning at Lisbon, now known as Kent City. One party came from Säby, near Tranås in the north of Småland. All of its members were used to a hard struggle for life. One, named Gran or Grawn, had a son who became a noted educator and a great-grandson who was elected governor of Michigan. Several other descendants also became well known at least in the Wolverine State.

In the 1850s other Swedes encamped on Lake Michigan north of Muskegon, which subsequently attracted many settlers of Swedish stock and grew into an important sawmill center. Some 70 miles north of Muskegon is the city of Manistee, which became the operating base of one of the most successful of the Swedish immigrants who arrived in the United States by the middle of the 1800s. His name was Lewis

Larsson or Sands (1826–1905), and he was born on a farm at Albro in the province of Södermanland, south of Stockholm and Lake Mälaren. At the age of 24 he emigrated to America, where he started in Chicago. Three years later he began earning his living as a lumberjack at Manistee, where there were few other settlers. After another three years he had, from a daily wage of $1.25–1.50, saved enough money to be able to buy 40 acres of forest land, and in the 1870s he began to build sawmills of his own. These were followed by other business ventures including railroads and saltworks, because of which he was called the "Salt King." He became the leading employer in Manistee, which in 1900 had 14,000 inhabitants, and his fortune was estimated at $6 million. He seems to have been a generous and public-spirited person. During a visit to Sweden in 1880 he is said to have had an audience with King Oscar II in Stockholm.

Some Swedes, such as Elias Hedström, who has been mentioned before, settled in Detroit as early as in the 1830s or 40s, but the cities of southeastern Michigan did not attract larger numbers of Swedish immigrants until the beginning of the automobile era.

In Michigan's Upper Peninsula the first Swedes may not have settled until the 1860s. The mines were then their principal sources of employment, and after them they turned to lumbering, farming, and railroad construction. Ishpeming, in the heart of the Marquette iron-ore region in the northwest, received its first charter in 1857 and became one of the leading centers of the Swedish-born population; few other smaller communities in America have been more important as a mother colony for Swedish settlements and groups in other parts of the country. The city, where also many Finns and Norwegians made their homes, was one of the first ski centers in the United States, and today it is the site of the U. S. Ski Hall of Fame and the Ski Museum. The Upper Peninsula as a whole has been called the "Finland of America."

In the beginning, the Swedish-born population in Indiana grew faster than that of Michigan, or from 16 in 1850 to 330 ten years later. Most of the early immigrants came from the Gränna district on Lake Vättern, in the northern part of Småland, and they settled in or near Lafayette in Tippecanoe County. This migration was brought about by a journeyman tanner named Carl Peter Moberg, who, after a first stay in America, came back to Sweden in 1844 and gave his neighbors in Gränna enthusiastic reports, and a crofter's son by the name of Johannes Petersson, who emigrated in 1849 and settled at Lafayette. A few years later his brother Peter arrived with a large party from Gränna, and other groups followed, including one which was led and financed by a wealthy farmer and traveled via New Orleans. By 1855 some 500 Swedes lived in the Lafayette district, but many of these colonists soon began to move westward. Later on more immigrants from Sweden found their way to Tippecanoe County, but the flow into Indiana was, in the first place, directed toward the areas bordering on Illinois and Michigan, including the southern suburbs of Chicago and Gary, the steel city.

Ohio had 55 Swedish-born inhabitants in 1850 and about 120 in 1860, according to the official reports. Most of the subsequent immigrants from Sweden settled in the Cleveland area, at Youngstown near the border of Pennsylvania, and at Ashtabula farther north on Lake Erie, a major port for iron ore and coal.

One of the first Swedes in Cincinnati had the odd old name Otto Natt och Dag (1794–1865), being a member of a family whose aristocratic traditions go even farther back than to 1280 when the Swedish nobility was first established. In America, however, he called himself Fredrik Franks.

As a young lieutenant in Sweden he had published in 1815 a pamphlet urging a reorganization of the army and military training. Several of the proposed reforms were eventually effected, but the immediate reaction was negative, and Lieutenant Natt och Dag — which means Night and Day — left for Germany and resigned his commission. The next year a Swedish court sentenced him to the loss of life, honor, and property for insulting Crown Prince Carl Johan in a German version of his pamphlet.

Otto Natt och Dag's best friend in Sweden, a young army officer by the name of Johan August Hazelius (1797–1871), stood up for him with such fervor that he came close to being exiled himself. Later he helped raise educational standards in Sweden, military as well as civilian, and his career as an officer finally brought him the title of major general. His son Artur Hazelius (1833–1901) became the founder of the Nordic Museum in Stockholm, which is devoted to Sweden's cultural history, and its sister institution Skansen, which also is a folk park and zoological garden.

In 1819 Otto Natt och Dag is known to have been in New Orleans, and under the name of Fredrik Franks he somewhat later settled in Cincinnati, where he established a museum of natural history and gave popular-science lectures. In the early 1840s one of Gustaf Unonius's traveling companions from Sweden worked for some time in his museum, which then seems to have been able to stir up howling thunderstorms. Two assistants, Unonius wrote in his memoirs, were kept busy "producing thunder, lightning and brimstone" and "keeping the evil spirits in motion."

In 1835, Otto Natt och Dag was finally pardoned by the Swedish government. He had a lively correspondence with his relatives and friends in Sweden and often planned to visit his native country, which, however, he never did. In one of his first letters to Hazelius he described the Americans as self-centered and prosaic, but he seems to have liked the people better and better, although he always thought there was too much "demagoguery" in their politics. In 1841 he married a member of an old family named Adams. Otto Natt och Dag, or Fredrik Franks, lived in Cincinnati for more than 40 years. Today, his descendants in the United States are the only members of the oldest existing branch of the ancient Natt och Dag family.

Another former army officer from Sweden, Carl Gustaf Gyllenberg (1802–49), the son of a cavalry captain, lived for some years in Cincinnati, after having landed in New York in 1836. He worked for some time in Fredrik Franks's museum, and died in Texas. A younger brother, Fritz August Gyllenberg, who was a naval lieutenant, came to America in 1838 but returned to Sweden.

★ 12

In the South, the West, and the Northeast

Swedes in the South in the early and middle 1800s —
Tennessee promoted in Sweden

QUITE a few Swedish immigrants of the early 19th century had settled in the South before the best-known pioneer, Swante Magnus Swenson, came to Texas in 1838. In the 1830s and 1840s there were, at least for some time, vice-consuls for Sweden and Norway at New Orleans, Louisiana; Mobile, Alabama; Savannah, Georgia; Charleston, South Carolina; Norfolk and Alexandria, Virginia; and Baltimore, Maryland. Key West, Florida, and Richmond, Virginia, also seem to have had consular representatives for Sweden and Norway in the early 1800s. The vice-consuls were appointed by the consulate general in New York, which from 1822 to 1858 was attached to the diplomatic mission in Washington. Most of them served in the first place Norway's growing merchant marine.

One of the first Swedes to settle in the South in the 1800s was Peter Hammond (1798–1870), who arrived in Louisiana about 1815 and became the founder of the city of Hammond, some 60 miles northwest of New Orleans. For only a few cents an acre he purchased a large tract of land from the government and began to produce pitch, turpentine, tar, and mast timbers for ships. In 1830 he married Carolina Tucker from Boston, a cousin of Mrs. Ralph Waldo Emerson. During the Civil War he lost most of his property, except the land. An inscription on an official marker in the little private cemetery where he was buried reads in part: "Under this oak is buried Peter Hammond of Sweden, who founded Hammond, La., about 1818." His Swedish family name, which was abbreviated and anglicized when he became an American citizen, may have been derived from the parish of Hammerdal in the province of Jämtland in the northwest of Sweden. He is known to have left his parental home at the age of 14.

In the 1830s New Orleans had a whole little colony of Swedes. Its leading member was a young counselor at law named Gustavus Schmidt (b. 1795), who probably like his older brother Carl Christian Schmidt was born at Mariestad in the province of Västergötland and had studied law at the University of Lund. In New Orleans he married a young American heiress, and among his acquaintances was Edward Livingston, who in the early 1800s practiced law in New Orleans, in 1829 was sent to Washington as a U. S. senator, and two years later became Andrew Jackson's secretary of state. The two brothers became engaged in a lively correspondence. In 1831–32 they discussed an article by Livingston which had appeared in a Swedish legal journal published by Carl Christian Schmidt, then a judge of the Court of Appeals at Kristianstad in southern Sweden and in 1842 named a justice of the Supreme Court in Stockholm. Following the example of his brother in Sweden, Gustavus Schmidt in 1841–42 edited a legal publication called *The Louisiana Law Journal*. Efforts to make him and his family move to Sweden, where, his brother wrote, "one lives happily . . . in a constitutional country under a liberal government among a free, loyal, and noble people," remained unsuccessful.

Other Swedes who lived in New Orleans at this time had such family names as Sneidow, Svenander, and Wollke. A toolsmith named Anderson had left Sweden as early as 1803 but spoke flawless Swedish. André Oscar Wallenberg, the future banker, who came to New Orleans as a seaman in early 1833, spent some time with him and also met many other Swedes. A few days before sailing, he described New Orleans in his diary as "a city of temptation for unreflecting sailors," adding: "Every house has a grog shop, and in many places there are so-called hosts, who coax the men into jumping ship." Sixteen-year-old Wallenberg was, on the other hand, impressed by New Orleans as a city of shipping and commerce. Most of the merchants were, he thought, English or Dutch. In 1844, a Swede named Gustavus W. Schroeder became one of New Orleans's earliest Baptist ministers. In 1851 Carl Ludwig Lybecker settled there as a music teacher, and ten years later he was named Swedish vice-consul.

By the middle of the 19th century, Alabama had more Swedish-born inhabitants than any other Southern state except Louisiana, but little is known about them. A Methodist preacher, Sven B. Nyman or Newman, who later moved to New York and Chicago, lived near Mobile in the early 1840s, and a brother had come to Mobile several years before him. Some 30 Swedes lived in Florida in 1850, according to the U.S. census. One of the best-known early settlers, a former seaman from the Baltic island of Gotland named John Anders Boström or John Andrew Bostrom (1836–1927), arrived seven years later. One of 12 children, he had enlisted as a sailor at the age of 14, and came to the Sunshine State as the result of a shipwreck. After the Civil War, during which he served as captain on a Confederate blockade runner, he and his brother Charles started growing citrus fruits at Ormond Beach, a few miles north of Daytona Beach, where they are said to have been the first settlers. John Andrew Bostrom also became a successful manufacturer of small boats, and as an immigration agent he helped attract Swedish people to Florida.

The best-known Swedish pioneer in Georgia, Paul Romare, was born at Torekov, a picturesque hamlet of fishermen and sailors in the northwest of Skåne. In the middle 1850s he was a bank clerk in Chester, Georgia, and later he moved to Atlanta, where he finally became president of the Atlanta National Bank and one of the state's leading citizens.

In 1850 there was a handful of Swedes at Nashville, Tennessee, including S. J. A. Berg or Burg, who called himself doctor, his mother-in-law, Maria Peterson, and a shoemaker named Carl Fredrik Edman. The year before, a campaign promoting settlement at Walden's Ridge near Chattanooga had been launched in Stockholm by Berg and other Swedish agents, and similar efforts were made in the 1860s with greater success. A pamphlet entitled *A New California*, published in Stockholm in 1849, extolled the climate and the fertility of the land in southeastern Tennessee, while Illinois and Michigan were denigrated. This brochure received an enthusiastic notice in *Aftonbladet*, which called Walden's Ridge "a real little paradise." After the Civil War many other American states conducted similar propaganda. In Mississippi, a mechanic from Sweden, A. P. Petterson, operated a manufacturing business at Water Valley about 1858.

From 1844 and for half a century, the University of Virginia at Charlottesville had a distinguished modern-languages professor of Swedish birth, French maternal parentage and German education, Maximilian Schele de Vere, or simply Schele (1820–98), who had arrived in Boston in 1843 and had been highly recommended by Longfellow and other Bostonians. Extremely popular as an instructor and lecturer, he taught the French, German, Italian, and Spanish languages and literatures, inaugurated a systematic study of Anglo-Saxon, and offered pioneering courses in comparative philology. One of his books, *Americanisms, the English of the New World*, is frequently cited by H. L. Mencken in his famous work *The American Language*. Dr. Schele, who was born at Växjö in Småland, knew Fredrika Bremer from Sweden and guided her through the University of Virginia in 1851.

In the late 1840s a Swede named Gustaf Clemens Hebbe (1804–93), who was an adventurer as well as a man of learning, taught history at a college in Columbia, South Carolina. He had probably taken part in the War with Mexico as a correspondent, and in 1852 he became an unusually active and effective campaign speaker for General Franklin Pierce, the American war hero who was elected the 14th President. After that, Hebbe was often seen in the White House, and in 1854 he was appointed American consul at Aachen in the German Rhineland. Financial problems, however, prevented him from assuming that post; troubles of the same kind had made him leave Sweden and his family in 1839. He came to America the first time in 1842 or 1843, and during the following years he earned his living in New York as a journalist and translator. Most of his larger works — which included translations of Fredrika Bremer and Carl Jonas Love Almqvist, who also came to America — were published by Stiernefeldt and Broadmeadow in New York, a firm in which at least one of two Swedish brothers and noblemen named Stiernefeldt was a partner. Their friend Hebbe finally settled in Norway as a writer and scholar.

In Washington, D.C., a Swedish tailor by the name of Christian Eklöf or Eckloff is said to have been doing a lucrative business in the 1830s, when he enjoyed the support of President Andrew Jackson.

One of the first 19th-century Swedish immigrants to work for a government agency in Washington, G. F. Jochnick, was for many years employed in the Indian Bureau of the Department of the Interior. In 1868 he told a Swedish visitor that he had been there for 30 years. He must have been identical with Gustaf F. Jochnick, who in 1840 enlisted in the U.S. Army for five years and in 1847 reenlisted for the War with Mexico, being discharged the next year because of disability. The Union army records of the Civil War list George F. Jochnick as captain in the Third New York Cavalry Regiment.

Many Swedes at Charleston — Two Hammarsköld families in the Carolinas

CHARLESTON, in South Carolina, was the leading port of entry for immigrants to the Southeast, and during the first part of the 1800s a relatively large number of Swedes made their homes there. As early as 1784–85, Sweden had a vice-consul at Charleston, Adolf Schough.

Nils Fredrik Klint (1772–1842), who was a native of the southeastern province of Blekinge, arrived at the beginning of the century, bought an island on which he lived for nine years, and then settled in Charleston as a merchant. A nephew, Fabian Reinhold Wickenberg (b. 1812), who at Klint's invitation came in 1836, inherited his estate and continued his business successfully. He, in turn, seems to have attracted other people from Blekinge. Three immigrants from the ancient but tiny town of Sölvesborg, where Wickenberg's brother was mayor, arrived in Charleston in the fall of 1847. Other Swedes known to have lived in Charleston at this time include a shipping agent, Niklas Bahr (b. 1808), and a vice-consul named Winthrop. In 1851 two brothers named Myhrman, one of whom died from the yellow fever three years later, came there. Their father was general counsel of the Swedish Ironmasters Association in Stockholm.

Financial problems, caused in part by the need of a structural change in the Swedish iron industry, made two members of the Hammarsköld (or Hammarskjöld) family emigrate to America by the middle of the century, and both settled in the Southeast. Hjalmar Hammarsköld (1817–61) left Sweden in 1844, when the Surahammar ironworks near Västerås in the province of Västmanland, which he had tried to manage for his ailing father, had gone into bankruptcy. Just before his emigration he married 23-year-old Emilie Holmberg

(1821–54), who already had won recognition in Sweden as a pianist, singer, and song composer. Her mother was persuaded to go with them to America.

Early in 1845 the young Mrs. Hammarsköld participated in a concert in Washington, D.C., together with the famous Norwegian violinist Ole Bull, and during the next few years she gave many concerts of her own. After having been based in New Orleans and Montgomery, Alabama, the family in 1849 settled in Charleston, where Hjalmar Hammarsköld became known as an architect. His wife was then engaged as an organist at the St. Peter's Church, and she also taught music and founded a philharmonic society. In 1851 they lived in a charming house of their own, which a Swedish visitor in a letter home described as "a little paradise" and where many music lovers often assembled.

In 1853 the family moved to Columbia, capital of South Carolina, where Hjalmar Hammarsköld had been named "superintending architect" for the construction of the new State House. Several members of the legislature boarded with them, and Mrs. Hammarsköld, according to an eyewitness report, worked "like a slave" in the kitchen. Shortly after the birth of her fifth child, she died early the next year. Somewhat later her husband was charged with want of "practical experience" and other shortcomings as an architect, and he was removed from his post, a decision that aroused him to an indignant protest. Four years later he remarried and finally moved to Memphis, Tennessee. His four surviving children, including his and his first wife's daughter Coralie, who became an opera singer, remained in the United States.

Hjalmar Hammarsköld's cousin and brother-in-law, Carl W. Hammarsköld (1807–60), was a much more experienced and important industrialist in Sweden, and the bankruptcy of his firm, the Skultuna iron and brass works near the city of Västerås, shook the Swedish business world. When it was made public in early 1850, Hammarsköld was already on his way to America, where he first settled at Charleston, South Carolina, and earned his living by making and selling cigars. In his native country he had also been a cavalry captain, and to America he had brought with him his valet, a young man named Wessman, who became his trusted business assistant. Letters show that Hammarsköld almost immediately regretted his flight from Sweden, and later he heard that a bankruptcy could probably have been avoided. After a short time in Charleston he became manager of an ironworks at Cooperville near the border between South and North Carolina, where several newly arrived Swedes were hired as workers.

Carl Hammarsköld's wife, Hedvig (1811–90), was Hjalmar Hammarsköld's sister, as well as his own cousin. In 1851, when she and their two children had joined him, he leased an iron mill at Columbia Furnace in the south of North Carolina, and somewhat later he built up a forge of his own at nearby Spring Hill Forge, where he also operated a flour mill. Although never particularly successful, he gradually overcame his homesickness. After his death in 1860 Mrs. Hammarsköld wanted to return to Sweden with the children, but because of the Civil War their departure was delayed until 1863. Her son, Carl Jacob Hammarsköld, who had become his father's business partner, hastened to join the Confederate forces, but in 1862 he had to resign because of injuries.

Two Swedish maidens report on the antebellum South —
A story of lasting friendship

WHEN Hedvig Hammarsköld came to America in late 1850 she was accompanied by an old friend of the family, Lovisa Mathilda Nettelbladt (1814–67), daughter of a Stockholm merchant, who remained in the South for six years. Traveling extensively, especially in South Carolina but also in North Carolina, she supported herself by teaching and organizing classes in needlework, decorative painting, and the making of artificial flowers. In 1860 she published anonymously in Stockholm a book about her experiences and impressions, a delightful account of the South in the antebellum days.

Several times Miss Nettelbladt met unexpectedly immigrants from Sweden. At Columbia, South Carolina, she found some families from the province of Dalarna who subsisted on selling decorative articles made of hair, an ancient specialty in that part of Sweden. They were remarkably successful but, like most Swedish newcomers at this time, suffered badly from homesickness. A seasoned immigrant, on the other hand, was a 60-year-old Moravian clergyman named Hartvig, who had left Sweden 30 years earlier, served as a missionary in the West Indies, and finally joined a German settlement, Salem, in the northwest of South Carolina.

Wherever Miss Nettelbladt went in the Carolinas she met, according to her travel report, "nothing but good men and women." On many occasions she told pupils and friends about life in Sweden, its holidays, scenery, and changing seasons. Upon her return to her native country she found, at least in the beginning, a less open-hearted and cheerful people.

Of other well-educated Swedes who lived in South Carolina in the early 1850s, three belonged to the teaching staff of a well-known boarding school for girls, Limestone Spring at Gaffney in the north, near the North Carolina line. A young man named Franz Hahr (1825–79) arrived in 1849, and the next year he was followed by his sister Hulda (1828–90), or, to be complete, Jane Hulda Josefina Anna Maria Christina Africana Hahr. Their father had for many years been the Swedish consul general at Tripoli in North Africa, but had moved back to Stockholm. Both Franz and Hulda Hahr married and remained in the United States. Today there are numerous American Hahrs, as well as descendants with other names, and in the 1950s two of them translated a recently published story of the Hahr family from Swedish into English. The clan had its origin in North Germany.

As a result of letters to Sweden from Franz and Hulda Hahr, who at Limestone Spring taught music and drawing, a young woman by the name of Rosalie Ulrika Roos (1823–98) arrived there in late 1851 and soon began to teach music and French. She had been brought up in Stockholm, where her father was a Board of Trade official, as well as on an estate in Västergötland. Despite her lack of experience she felt very happy with her job at Limestone and became a both effective and popular teacher. Her interest in flowers spread like wildfire, and the principal organized botanical excursions. Swedish folk dances and Christmas games, which the girls loved, were also introduced by her.

Among Rosalie Roos's pupils at Limestone were two sisters, Eliza and Annie Peronneau, and early in 1853 she moved to their home, a plantation south of Charleston, to become governess for their younger sisters and brothers. From the beginning she was regarded as a full-fledged member of the family, and although she returned to Sweden after a few years, the warm friendship between her and the Peronneaus never faded. It has, in fact, been continued by their descendants to this day.

At Limestone as well as at the Peronneau plantation, Rosalie Roos conducted a lively correspondence both with her relatives in Sweden and with her new friends in the American South, principally Hedvig Hammarsköld and other members of the two Hammarsköld families. In letters to her parents she wrote with sympathy about life in the South, but she did not share her father's conviction that the United States was an ideal country of freedom and equality, and she dismissed as unrealistic his talk about emigrating or trying to send one of his sons to the New World. One of her leading themes was America as a land of sharp contrasts, such as luxury and misery; or broadmindedness and generosity, on the one hand, and narrow prejudices on the other; or freedom and slavery. Numerous black people in the South were, she once wrote, better off than many crofters and other farm workers in Sweden, an impression that had already been ventilated in the Swedish discussions, but she was convinced that slavery "sooner or later will be abolished, although not without a hard struggle." The bitterness and the hatred between the North and the South, and between slave owners and abolitionists, seemed incredible. Her letters were finally published in Sweden in 1969, after they had just been discovered.

In the spring of 1855 Miss Roos visited Cuba, and from New Orleans she then traveled up the Mississippi and Ohio rivers to Louisville, Kentucky, where she was invited to the home of a Swedish businessman, C. J. Ahlmark, whose wife, adopted daughter, and three assistants or servants also were from Sweden. He had, in fact, also a Swedish partner, Fritz Ahreschoug (1823–57), who had changed his family name to Wood. Via Cincinnati, Chicago, Detroit, Buffalo, and Albany Miss Roos continued her trip to New York, and after visits to London and Paris she returned to Sweden in the fall of 1855, when she was nearly 32 years old. Two years later she married Knut Olivecrona (1817–1905), an eminent jurist who was one of the first advocates of the abolition of capital punishment in Sweden. Inspired by her experiences in America, his wife became one of the pioneers in the movement for improved education and greater opportunities for women. A grandson, Herbert Olivecrona (b. 1891), who in 1919–20 served in a hospital in Baltimore, won international fame as a brain surgeon.

The Peronneau family was shattered by the Civil War, and Eliza, the oldest of the girls for whom Rosalie Olivecrona named her daughter, was the only one of six sisters and brothers to have children of her own. Her third child, a daughter named Clelia, who was the only one to survive the war, was born at Columbia in early 1865, just before the South Carolina capital was shelled by General William T. Sherman and most of it, but not Hjalmar Hammarsköld's State House which was the principal target, was destroyed by fire. In 1884, when Eliza Peronneau's husband had succumbed to war injuries, her 19-year-old daughter Clelia went to Sweden to spend a year with Knut and Rosalie Olivecrona and their children, and some years later she christened a daughter Rosalie Olivecrona. In 1910 Clelia made another trip to Sweden and presented her daughter Olive, as she was called, to her "Swedish family," and in the 1930s Rosalie Olivecrona's son Axel and his daughter Eva visited Clelia at Charleston. Modern transatlantic communications have led to many recent contacts between Eliza Peronneau's and Rosalie Roos's descendants.

Early Swedes in California — One found the gold that years later started the rush

SWEDES came early to the territories on the Pacific Coast, but larger numbers of settlers did not arrive until the 1870s.

The first Swedes in California were sailors, adventurers, gold seekers, traders, and travelers. One of the first visitors during the Mexican era was a mysterious person who called himself Gustavus M. Waseurtz af Sandels (1794–1852). In 1842–43 he traveled up and down the territory, leaving valuable pencil and water-color sketches as well as a well-written report in the English language known as *The King's Orphan* manuscript. The Swedish original has been lost. The English version came to light when a group of California pioneers in New York, including General Johann Augustus Sutter, in early 1878 celebrated the 30th anniversary of the beginning of the gold rush. It was almost immediately published by the *San José Pioneer*. In his monumental *The History of the Pacific States* of 1885 Hubert Howe Bancroft, in whose famous "history factory" a Swede named William Nemos played a leading part, often quoted Sandels and described his activities in California. In 1926 the manuscript was published in the quarterly publication of the Society of California Pioneers, and in 1945 it was republished in a de luxe edition of 300 copies for the same organization and The Book Club of California. Some 30 drawings and water colors by Sandels were included. The traveling Swede had fallen in love with California, and its scenery he described with enthusiasm.

During his travels in 1842–43 Sandels eked out a living as a medical practitioner. His standard prescription was cold or hot baths, and he claimed to have introduced the water cure, combined with faith and rest, in California. He also described himself as a mining expert and naturalist. The best-known person in Upper California at that time was Johann August Sutter, who later became famous for his sawmill at present-day Sacramento where in January of 1848 his chief carpenter discovered the gold that immediately started a local rush and then, in 1849, the historic stampede. Some five years earlier Sandels had told Sutter that he had plenty of gold in his land, but the German-born pioneer answered that he was too busy with his harvest and other matters to be able to do anything about it.

Sandels remains, however, the first discoverer of larger gold deposits in California. In the fall of 1843 he left for Honolulu, and from there he went to Australia. China was also visited. In 1847 he emerged in New Orleans, and there he died five years later.

Before coming to California in the fall of 1842, Sandels had spent 14 years in Mexico, where he seems to have worked for a mining company most of the time. In 1827 he lived in Peru, and before that he had for some years been in charge of a large cattle ranch at Chascomús in Argentina. He had come to South America from Sweden in 1823. At that time he called himself Emanuel Sundels (or af Sandels) Edelhjerta. Under the same name he had lived in Boston and Cambridge, Massachusetts, from Christmas of 1820 until August of 1821, when after strange adventures he was sent home seriously ill. Part of the time he worked as a laboratory or library assistant at Harvard, and both there and in Boston he did drawings and water colors. Upon his return to Sweden he wrote a report on Harvard and a description of Massachusetts, the first in the Swedish language. His family name was originally Sundelius, and he had been given the name Emanuel. He was born in a parsonage at Visnum in the province of Värmland. Before leaving Sweden he studied at Uppsala, and volunteered for military service. A theory that Prince Carl, who in 1809 was elected King of Sweden although Bernadotte soon became the real ruler, was his father is generally regarded as too farfetched. Much of his life, however, remains shrouded in mystery.

In the fall of 1846, when the war with Mexico had begun, Johan Olof Braunesson or, as he had long called himself, John Brown (1799–1859), rode by horseback the 600 miles from Los Angeles to San Francisco in four days, hoping to obtain help for a small American force at Los Angeles — a feat which according to some chroniclers should have made him famous as the "Paul Revere of California." Brown was born in the naval town of Karlskrona, capital of the province of Blekinge in the southeast of Sweden. In 1815 he was on board a ship in Plymouth harbor, England, when Napoleon was brought there as a prisoner of war. Later he fought in many battles in South America under Simon Bolivar, and after having been taken prisoner he managed to escape to California in 1828. There he took part in three more revolutions, the last one being the struggle of 1846. For speed, distance, and endurance, an American expert has written, his ride from Los Angeles to San Francisco has no parallel in world history. He became known by the nickname of Juan Flaco, or Lean John, and toward the end of his life he signed himself "Juan Brown, a native of Sweden, and a true American." In World War II, a Liberty Ship was named for him.

In 1849, when the gold finds in California had become widely known, one of the most frantic migrations of all time began, and hundreds of Swedes joined in the race. Many came from settlements in the Middle West. Johan Olof Liedberg (1822–86) from Jönköping, who had settled in Wisconsin in 1843 and came to California as early as in the fall of 1848, accumulated about 30 pounds of gold in 16 months. In 1852 he returned to Sweden, where he was cheated out of most of his money, and in 1875 he came back to America and settled in Chicago. There he wrote the story of his life, which descendants in Sweden nearly 100 years later had translated into English.

The first Swede to settle as a farmer in Illinois, Christian Benson, found no gold but established an inn or rest house for gold seekers at the junction of the overland trail and the route from Sacramento to San Francisco, and this point is known to this day as Benson's Crossing. Other expeditions emanated from Sweden, where the gold rush as well as California itself received much publicity. In 1849, for instance, the Swedish press reported that the crews of 130 ships in California harbors had deserted for the gold fields, that 8 million dollars worth of gold was being shipped from California in a month, and that 50,000 people had gone overland to the Pacific Coast. The next year many newspapers in Sweden carried interviews with Swedish "forty-niners," and they also ran long articles describing the beauty of California.

Most of the early Swedes in California seem to have anglicized their names, often while traveling or working on English ships. The U.S. census of 1850 listed 162 Swedish-born persons as living in California, and many of these were former sailors who had deserted their ships during the gold rush of 1848–49. Records show that they had adopted such names as Carrol, Green, Jones, Miller, Perry, and Scott.

During the summer of 1852 a Swedish naval frigate, *Eugenie*, visited San Francisco on a voyage round the world. The Swedish-Norwegian consul gave a dinner for the officers, and on one occasion the ship's chaplain held Swedish services on board, which were attended by members of the Swedish colony in San Francisco. While traveling in the Sacramento Valley, one of the officers met a Swede named Ahrenberg, who had been a mill owner in the province of Hälsingland and now, with his wife, was searching for gold.

In 1860, the number of Swedish-born people living in California had, according to the U.S. census, increased to about 1,400. Among permanent or temporary residents of San Francisco mentioned in an account of 1857 were C. W. Lybeck, who served as consul for China, a lieutenant Fleming from the naval base of Karlskrona, a jeweler named Kling who had come from Stockholm, an ore expert who was the son of an admiral in the Swedish navy by the name of Von Sydow, a Count Mörner, a businessman who had changed his name from Forlenius to Edwards, two craftsmen from Västergötland who had adopted the name Armstrong, a brewer named John Lind who had come from Strömstad on Sweden's West Coast, one Samuelson who had a soda factory in Sacramento but lived in San Francisco, Otto and Ferdinand Horn from Östergötland, and one Johnson, who is said to have owned at one time more than two million dollars which, however, he lost on dealings in arms and ammunition during the American Civil War and a conflict in South America. Most of those mentioned were members of well-known Swedish families. Count Mörner and Ferdinand Horn later took part in a gold rush in Brazil.

The more prosperous permanent settlers of Swedish birth were merchants or manufacturers, while others earned their livelihood as fishermen, carpenters, or mechanics. In the growing emigration from Sweden to California, the Baltic island of Öland and the west-coast province of Halland contributed remarkably large numbers of people. Most of the newcomers from these two sections of Sweden worked in the oyster and salmon fisheries or as sailors in the coastal traffic. Others began in the lumber industry or as carpenters and other craftsmen.

A Swedish-Norwegian consulate was established in San Francisco as early as 1850, and the first person in charge was a German by the name of Herrlich, who had served as consul for Sweden and Norway in Brazil. In 1849 he may have had something to do with a shipment of five prefabricated houses from Sweden, which were bought by a Swedish pioneer at Sonoma in the Napa Valley north of San Francisco Bay. In 1856 Herrlich was succeeded by George C. Johnson, who has been described as "an unusually pro-Swedish Norwegian." He became very active as consul and highly successful as a businessman.

In 1860, according to the U.S. census, less than a hundred Swedes lived in the Pacific Northwest. Some of them will be mentioned later.

Swedes in New York and New England — First Swedish settlers there in 1600s

SWEDES have lived in New York almost since it was founded by the Dutch as New Amsterdam. Nearly 200 Scandinavians, most of whom had come as passengers on Dutch ships or in Dutch service, are known to have been residents there around the middle of the 1600s, and thousands of·Danish and Norwegian sailors spent some time there every year. In 1664 the city was renamed New York by the British, but it retained much of its Dutch-German-Scandinavian character down to the time of the American Revolution.

Among the early settlers the Danes and the Norwegians were more numerous than the Swedes, probably because of the Swedish concentration on the Delaware Valley from where, on the other hand, several colonists moved north to the town on the Hudson. Some Swedish and other Scandinavian groups finally settled around Albany, and others moved to Long Island and New Jersey.

In 1639 one Jonas Bronck, a Dane from the Faroe Islands who had arrived via Holland, bought land in the present borough of the Bronx, which was named after him. About 1660, Swedes were among the pioneers who cleared the forest or brush in the area of Harlem. One Mons Pietersen, born in Sweden or in a Swedish-speaking section of Finland, helped lay out the village of Harlem, and then moved to Elizabethtown, New Jersey.

A Swede named Martin Hoffman, born in Estonia which was part of the Swedish realm, arrived in 1657. A saddler by trade, he settled at Albany in 1672. The same year he made a journey to the Swedish settlements on the Delaware to collect money for a Lutheran church in Albany. Hoffman's numerous descendants, listed in a book of nearly 550 pages published in 1899, include some of the Roosevelt families. Many other well-known American families can claim descent from Scandinavians who came to New York in the 17th century.

The immigration from Scandinavia decreased perceptibly after 1664, when New Amsterdam was surrendered to the British, and still more after 1674, when a brief Dutch reoccupation ended, but it never ceased entirely. The total number of Swedes who settled in New York in the 1700s has been described as considerable. In the early 1830s, when a new era was dawning, only about 100 Swedes seem to have lived there, but many others, mostly seamen, may have been about to settle down. In 1836 a group of 22 immigrants formed an organization, called The Swedish Society, for the promotion of mutual assistance and community spirit. It was the first of countless clubs and societies established by Swedes in America in the 19th century, and today it is the oldest Swedish association outside Sweden's borders. Many of its founders were merchants or manufacturers, and some were Swedes from Finland.

The first attempt to publish a Swedish-language paper in America was made in New York in 1851–53 by an adventurer who called himself Anders Gustaf Öbom, while his real name was Napoleon Berger (1812–81). The four-page, four-column sheet he brought out was named *Skandinaven*, and part of it was in the Norwegian language. Napoleon Berger, who was born at Falun in the province of Dalarna, had left Sweden in 1838 after the publication of two pamphlets which were branded as seditious. Before coming to America he had lived in Switzerland for ten years as editor of a German-language paper. Other publishing ventures were launched by him in New York in the 1860s and 1870s.

In 1850 about 500 Swedes lived within New York's present city limits, and ten years later the number had increased to 800. At that time Olof Hedstrom's Methodist Bethel ship was still the only religious center in the Swedish community, but a Lutheran congregation, named after King Gustavus Adolphus, was founded in 1865.

The Swedish-born population in the state of New York increased from about 750 in 1850 to nearly 1,700 in 1860. At least 250 Swedes had then settled at Jamestown in western New York. In 1860 New Jersey had less than a hundred Swedish residents, while in Pennsylvania the total was about 450. Many of these immigrants lived in the Chandlers Valley region and other sections of northwestern Pennsylvania.

The Northeast of America, or New England, also has a long, continuous history of immigration from Scandinavia, although in the 19th century the Swedes were late in settling there in larger numbers. A few Swedish-born people lived in Boston even before New Sweden was founded in the Delaware Valley in 1638, several of the sailors who came in the 1700s remained in New England, and in the Boston area as well as in Rhode Island there were also Swedish settlers during the first part of the 1800s. In 1847 a Swedish quartet gave a concert in Melodeon Hall in Boston, and a Scandinavian society was organized there six years later.

The first group of Swedish immigrants to settle in New England in the 19th century came to Brockton a few miles southeast of Boston in 1851. A shoemaker from Haurida in northern Småland named Daniel F. Larson (b. 1821) began there as a shoeworker in 1844, and after a visit to Sweden seven years later he returned in a company of about 50 people. Most of them had been enrolled for employment in Brockton's shoe factories, whose products were sold all over the United States. In 1868 Larson moved to Minnesota.

One of the first Swedish settlers in Connecticut in the 19th century was a pharmacist from Stockholm, Lorentz Berg (1803–49), who came in 1843 and for J. W. Williams of North Manchester compounded the formula for the first Williams shaving soap. For its production a factory was built at Glastonbury, Connecticut, where Berg in 1849 was fatally injured when repairing a machine.

From 1850 to 1860, according to the U. S. census, the number of Swedish-born in Massachusetts increased from about 250 to nearly 700, but many of those registered moved to the Midwest. Until the latter part of the 19th century New England itself did not attract any impressive numbers of Swedish settlers.

A Look Forward

Three famous descendants of mid-century immigrants:
Johnson, Sandburg, Lindbergh

THE first districts in Sweden to be exposed to the "America fever" included, as already mentioned, those east and southeast of Lake Vättern, that is, the southern section of the province of Östergötland and the adjoining northern part of the province of Småland. In 1851, for instance, Östergötland and northern Småland contributed about two-thirds of the total Swedish emigration to the United States.

Among those who emigrated from northern Småland in 1853 was one Gustaf Jönsson or Johnson, who seems to have been in his early thirties. He had become a proficient blacksmith and woodworker, but a happy-go-lucky and very sociable disposition made it difficult for him to concentrate on his work, and his lively imagination bred dreams about success in America. His passage was paid by friends who also thought that he needed a change of climate. After a year in Chicago he bought land in Nicollet County in south-central Minnesota, and there he also built a smithy. In 1858 he married a 20-year-old Swedish girl named Carolina Christina Hedén or Caroline Christine Hadden, who was born near Linköping in Östergötland. Her parents and one of her brothers had died in a cholera epidemic in Chicago shortly after their immigration, and two of her younger brothers had been adopted by families in Illinois.

Gustaf Johnson seemed about to prosper, but after the Sioux outbreak in 1862 he gave up farming and moved with his family to nearby St. Peter, which probably was a serious mistake. In addition to their first two sons, who were born on the farm, he and his wife had six children, but most of these died in infancy or childhood. After the death of one of his daughters Gustaf Johnson began to drink, poverty oppressed the household, and Caroline took in washing to support her children. One day in 1874 Gustaf sold his blacksmith shop and disappeared for a year, and the second son, 13-year-old John Albert (1861–1909), left school and took the place of his father, who finally was committed to a poorhouse.

After having worked as a store clerk for a dozen years and studied indefatigably in his leisure time, John A. Johnson in 1887 became editor of a newly founded Democratic newspaper at St. Peter, and this was the beginning of an amazing political career. A Democrat in a state with strong Republican traditions, he was elected governor of Minnesota for three successive terms, 1905–11. Among those who took part in the victory celebration after the first election in 1904 was his mother, who died two years later. John A. Johnson was the first native-born governor of Minnesota. Integrity, common sense, verbal elegance, and personal charm were widely regarded as his main assets.

As soon as Johnson in 1906 had been reelected governor in a landslide, Democrats all over the country began to urge him to consider running for the Presidency two years later. In June, 1907, he gave the commencement address at the University of Pennsylvania, which named him an honorary doctor of laws, and after that he was in constant demand as a speaker. Toward the end of the year he was one of the guests at the Gridiron Club dinner in Washington, and his performance on this occasion ensured him national attention as an outstanding personality. Many political leaders and observers finally regarded Johnson as the strongest candidate the Democrats could name, but he remained, of course, much less widely known than William Jennings Bryan, who, despite his defeats in 1894 and 1900, easily won the Democratic nomination in 1908.

"If Johnson had been known a year earlier, he would have been nominated, with every chance for election," an aide to President Theodore Roosevelt was reported to have said. Governor Johnson himself was sufficiently encouraged to begin thinking seriously of 1912. The Republican split that year would, in all likelihood, have assured his election if he had been nominated. His health, however, had been undermined by illness and privation, and in September, 1909, he died after abdominal surgery, only 48 years old. Memorial services were held throughout the nation, and the warships in New York harbor lowered their flags to half-mast. Monuments to Governor Johnson's memory have been raised both in St. Paul and in St. Peter, where he was buried. At the Gustavus Adolphus College in St. Peter, a dormitory has been named in his honor. Another institution close to his heart was the Mayo Clinic at Rochester, Minnesota, where he underwent four operations.

In the spring of 1856 a farm foreman by the name of Daniel Nilsson and his wife Johanna left their cottage at Åsbo in southwestern Östergötland and sailed for America with their seven children. When these grew up they called themselves Danielsson, and one of them, Alfred or August Danielsson (1846–1910), later changed his name to Sandburg. For a quarter of a century he worked as a blacksmith in the railroad shops at Galesburg, Illinois, which since the middle 1800s had been a center for Swedish settlers. In 1874 he married another immigrant from southwestern Östergötland, Clara Andersdotter or Andersson (1850–1926), who had arrived the year before and was employed in a hotel at Bushnell, south of Galesburg. They had seven children, two of whom died shortly after birth. One of their sons was Carl Sandburg (1878–1967), one of America's most beloved poets and an outstanding biographer of Abraham Lincoln.

Sandburg's father never learned to write, and his reading, insofar as his ten-hour working day left him any time and energy for such pursuits, was limited to the Bible and the Swedish weekly *Hemlandet.* He and his wife always spoke Swedish to each other and to their young children, and Carl Sandburg, as he wrote in his autobiographical *Always the Young Strangers*, learned two or three hundred words in Swedish before he learned them in English. He could not, on the other hand, always understand his parents and their friends when they spoke Swedish: "The Swedish language was hurled back and forth, too swift for us children to be sure what they were saying. When they talked of the steerage trip from Sweden, six to ten weeks on a sailing ship, their food only the black bread and cheese and baloney they brought along, we children couldn't quite follow it though we knew it was rugged going."

One of the more sensational emigrations from Sweden before the American Civil War was that of Ola Månsson (1808–92), who had a farm in southeasternmost Sweden, near Simrishamn in the province of Skåne, and for 12 years, from 1847 to 1858, had been a member of the Riksdag. An uncommon political talent and an effective speaker, he won a reputation as one of the most liberal farmers in the Swedish parliament. Later on he became the most influential spokesman for his group, but was then widely regarded as an advocate for the government or even the court. Being stubborn and proud, he made many enemies, who spread rumors about his financial relations with Crown Prince Carl, the future monarch, who was known to be his personal friend. After having become involved in a lawsuit as director of the Bank of Sweden branch office at Malmö, the commercial center of the South, he got tired of what he regarded as more or less personal persecutions, and in 1860 he set out for America with his young second wife and their infant son.

Ola Månsson and family traveled by train and boat to Minneapolis, and from there they trekked behind a team of oxen another 100 miles to a homestead near Melrose, Minnesota. He started calling himself Augustus Lindbergh, the name Lindbergh having already been adopted by a brother in Sweden, and his son, who had been christened Carl August, became known as Charles A. Lindbergh (1859–1924). He taught the boy the three R's, as well as the fundamentals of economics, civics, and government, and further studies led the young man to the University of Michigan law school, after which he began to practice law at Little Falls, Minnesota. As a Republican representative in Congress for five terms, in 1907–16, he established himself as a liberal political reformer, but he became better known as an opponent of his country's entry into World War I. In 1924 he was nominated for governor of Minnesota on the Farmer-Labor ticket, but died during the campaign.

Three years later his son, Charles A. Lindbergh, Jr., made his flight across the Atlantic, and the name Lindbergh was on everybody's lips. The aviator's mother, Evangeline Land from Detroit, had met her future husband while teaching chemistry in the high school at Little Falls, Minnesota. The Lindbergh homestead in Little Falls has been preserved by the State as a historic shrine.

★ 14

Religious Aspects of the Immigration

Lutherans from Sweden begin a national organization —
First college and newspaper

THE Swedish churches in America, whether Lutheran or of other faiths, became an inspiring and steadying force in the existence of the 19th-century immigrants. By immediately taking up the problems of education and health, they also made enduring contributions to their communities and to the nation. All schools and most hospitals and similar institutions established by Swedes in the United States were founded by ecclesiastical organizations. The fact that the first Swedish newspapers in America were published by clergymen is also significant. During the latter part of the 1800s, however, more and more Swedish-language periodicals were issued in the United States, and the many secular ones became particularly important. They played a substantial role in orienting the immigrants in the American environment, and this they could do only because they at the same time met the newcomers' need of constant contact with Sweden, primarily the province or district in which they were born.

The pioneer Swedish Lutheran pastor in America was the Reverend Lars Paul Esbjörn (1808–70), born near Delsbo in Hälsingland, who arrived in New York in 1849 as the leader of a group of nearly 150 immigrants from the same district in northern Sweden. He was then 41 years old, and he had served the Swedish state church for 17 years as an increasingly unorthodox and pietist minister. With his wife and four children — there were six when the journey from Sweden started — he came to Andover, Illinois, in the fall of 1849, and the following spring he formed there a Swedish Lutheran congregation. It was the second such body in the Middle West, the more informal one at New Sweden in Iowa being two years older. In the beginning the new pastor was regarded by the immigrants as an emissary of the Swedish state church, and the Andover congregation had, therefore, only ten charter members. A week later, however, 32 names were added to the church roll. The church built by Esbjörn at Andover was based, in part, on a donation by Jenny Lind, and in 1948 it was officially renamed the Jenny Lind Chapel.

The scattered Swedish population and the poverty of the Swedish-American settlements made Esbjörn's missionary work exceedingly difficult, and to Sweden he wrote numerous letters appealing for pastors to assist him in his mission. After a few years he was able to recruit two unusually able and energetic men, Tuve Nilsson Hasselquist and Erland Carlsson, who, like Esbjörn himself, were given a leave of absence from the Church of Sweden in order to serve as pastors among the Swedes in America. The ecclesiastical authorities in Sweden remained firmly opposed to emigration, but some Lutheran leaders of the new liberal type took a very active personal interest in the religious fate of their countrymen in the United States. In particular Peter Wieselgren, the temperance pioneer, and Peter Fjellstedt (1802–81), whose remarkable career as a missionary had begun in India in 1831, did much to promote Swedish Lutheranism in America, and without influences from them Hasselquist and Carlsson might not have decided to work for this cause.

In 1857 Fjellstedt himself was tempted to accept a call to become the Scandinavian professor at a newly founded Lutheran academy and seminary ambitiously called the Illinois State University, the first president of which, Francis Springer, was a descendant of a Swede who had come to the Delaware Valley in the 1680s. Many Swedish recruits for the Lutheran ministry in the United States were subsequently obtained through Fjellstedt and Wieselgren, but ordained clergymen in Sweden did not, as a rule, want to move to the New World. Down to 1870 the Swedish state church furnished only six pastors, and two of these returned to their native country.

In 1858 Esbjörn moved from Andover to Springfield, where he, when Fjellstedt had decided not to come, had been appointed professor at the Illinois State University. There he became acquainted with Abraham Lincoln, then a lawyer at Springfield, and their sons were schoolmates. In 1860 Esbjörn left the Illinois capital for Chicago, where he founded a seminary which became the beginning of the Augustana College and Theological Seminary at Rock Island, the oldest and foremost educational institution of Swedish origin in America. In 1948 the college and the seminary were separated.

From Chicago the Augustana school was transferred first to Paxton, a settlement on the Illinois Central Railroad about 100 miles farther south, but Esbjörn had no part in this enterprise, which is still regarded as unfortunate, and he was greatly disappointed. He realized, moreover, that his younger colleague Hasselquist was destined to be the leader of the Swedish Lutherans in America. In 1863 after 14 years of preaching and teaching in the Midwest, and after seeing two wives die, he returned to Sweden and became rector in Östervåla Parish near Uppsala, where he had started his career as a curate. In the Civil War two of his Swedish-born sons volunteered in the Union army, and one was killed in action, while the other, who called himself Osborne, was promoted to captain. Later, two other sons became members of the faculty of Augustana College.

Before returning to Sweden, Esbjörn helped bring about a national organization or synod of the Lutheran congregations of immigrants from the then united kingdoms of Sweden and Norway. It was formed in 1860 at a meeting at Jefferson Prairie in southern Wisconsin, near the Illinois border, and was called Augustana, the Latin name of the Augsburg Confession of 1530, the most important Protestant statement of belief on which the Reformation was based. Tuve Nilsson Hasselquist became its first president. Nine years later the Norwegian Lutherans in the United States established a separate organization. The Augustana Synod lasted for more than 100 years, or until 1962, when it was merged with three other church bodies into the Lutheran Church in America.

The Reverend Tuve Nilsson Hasselquist (1816–91) is generally regarded as the ablest and most influential leader in the annals of Swedish Lutheranism in America. He was born at Hasslaröd in northeastern Skåne, and became one of the first graduates of the University of Lund to settle in the American Midwest. In 1852, at the age of 36, he arrived in Chicago with his wife and some 60 immigrants, having accepted a call from Galesburg to become pastor of a church founded by Esbjörn. Early the next year he helped establish Chicago's first Swedish Lutheran church, named the Immanuel, which was to be followed by more than 40 sister congregations. In 1855 he started publishing at Galesburg the weekly *Det Gamla och det Nya Hemlandet* (The Old and the New Homeland), which was the first Swedish-language newspaper of any kind in America, except for a New York gazette which was issued irregularly in the early 1850s.

As president of the Augustana Synod during its first ten years, or until 1870, Hasselquist visited its associated congregations from New York and Jamestown in the East to Minnesota in the Northwest. In 1863, when Esbjörn had returned to Sweden, he also took charge of the Augustana College and Seminary, which in 1875 was moved from Paxton to Rock Island on the banks of the Mississippi, where it still is, and he served as its president until his death in 1891. He adapted himself to American conditions more easily than Esbjörn had done and carried great authority among the Swedish immigrants. From the beginning he was a staunch supporter of Abraham Lincoln and the Union cause.

Like Hasselquist, Esbjörn had been dissatisfied with the state church when he left Sweden, but he was not mentally prepared for the religious free-for-all competition in America, and his letters to Swedish friends at home reflected, almost from the beginning, disillusionment with American religious freedom, which, he maintained, offered no guarantee of genuine Christianity or of higher moral standards, such as the immediate rejection of slavery. Esbjörn began, in fact, to defend the established-church system with such energy that he aroused opposition from Lutheran clergymen in Sweden. Some supporters of religious freedom observed that extremist and subversive tendencies were brought to America by European immigrants, but that they were neutralized by the nation's rich religious life.

In 1853 the Swedish Immanuel Church in Chicago invited as its first pastor the Reverend Erland Carlsson (1822–93), who like Hasselquist was a graduate of Lund University. He was born at Älghult in southern Småland and before leaving he had had four years of pastoral experience. Like both Esbjörn and Hasselquist he had attracted attention in Sweden by temperance lectures, and he also earned his passage across the Atlantic by acting as spiritual guide to a large group of emigrants, in this case some 175 men, women, and children. In Chicago, every conceivable type of Swede had begun to drift into the colony on the North Side, and the services in the Immanuel Church were sometimes interrupted by rowdies who beat tin pans and broke windows, but Carlsson stuck to his guns, denouncing the liquor saloon and the card table, as well as the lodge and the theater. Most of the immigrants were, however, reasonably well behaved, and the powerful pastor helped thousands of Swedish and other Scandinavian newcomers. He was especially active during the frequent cholera epidemics, and in 1884 he became one of the founders of the Augustana Hospital, the first of several such institutions to win a national reputation. After more than two decades as leader of the Immanuel, which after the great Chicago fire in 1871 was rebuilt as a result of his efforts, Carlsson moved to Andover as pastor of the first Swedish Lutheran church. From 1881 to 1888 he served as president of the Augustana Synod.

Esbjörn, Hasselquist, and Carlsson are regarded as three of the "pilgrim fathers" of the Swedish Lutherans in North America. The fourth, and the only one to be educated in the United States, was Eric Norelius, the pioneer pastor in Minnesota. He was president of the Augustana Synod during two periods, 1874–81 and 1899–1911. At the celebration of its 50th anniversary in 1910, when he was 77 years old, he made a moving address, and to guests from Sweden he seemed "like a venerable prophet of old."

In 1870–73 the Augustana presidency was held by the Reverend Jonas Swensson, who in 1856 had come to the Swedish settlement at Chandlers Valley in Pennsylvania and two years later became a pastor at Andover, Illinois. Among the founders of the Augustana Synod was also the Reverend Olof Andrén (1824–70), born at Malmö and like Hasselquist and Erland Carlsson a graduate of Lund University. In 1856 he was named pastor of the Swedish Lutheran church at Moline, Illinois, and four years later he was sent to Sweden to try to raise money for the newly established Augustana College. Two annual church collections were authorized by the government, and the Swedish monarch, Carl XV, donated 5,000 volumes from his private collections as a nucleus for the library at Augustana. Because of his failing health, Andrén decided to remain in Sweden and accept a

Harwardska Universitet i Cambridge

1. The main building of Harvard University as seen in 1821 by a mysterious Swede who called himself Emanuel Sundels Edelhjerta and somewhat later was sent home seriously ill. In 1842–43 he traveled in California, wrote a delightful travel report, and discovered the gold deposits near Sacramento at least five years before the gold rush (pp. 219–220). 2. Broadway and City Hall, New York, as seen by a Swedish naval officer, Baron Axel Klinkowström, who in 1818–20 visited the United States for technical studies (pp. 139–141).

Bradway gatan och Rådhuset i Newyork.

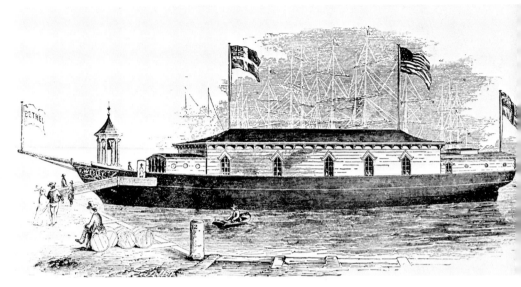

1. The Bethel ship *John Wesley*, moored to a pier in lower Manhattan in New York, played during the period 1845–75 an extremely important part in the Swedish and other Scandinavian immigration. A Swedish-born Methodist pastor, Olof G. Hedstrom, was in charge of the ship, where thousands upon thousands of newcomers from the North of Europe, most of them confused and exhausted, received all possible spiritual and material help, whether they were converted or not (pp. 180–183). 2. An immigrant chest from Bishop Hill, Illinois, brought over from Sweden in 1850. This was typical of the baggage carried by the early immigrants.

1. In the 19th century, many of the Swedish emigrants came from homes similar to this cottage, Snugge near Växjö in Småland, where Kristina Nilsson, who became a famous concert and opera singer, was born in 1843. During the period 1870–83 she made three highly successful American tours (pp. 125, 360–362). 2. "For him there is only the future . . . She cannot help throwing a last glance over her shoulder" — toward her old home in Blekinge or Småland. The Emigrant Monument in the port city of Karlshamn, dedicated on Midsummer Day in 1959, was sculptured by Axel Olsson and inspired by Vilhelm Moberg's emigrant epic, also published in America. Moberg had over 100 relatives in the United States; all of his father's and mother's ten brothers and sisters had emigrated (pp. 199, 791).

IMMIGRANT PARTY OF SWEDES.

1. Swedish immigrants in Boston in the summer of 1851, most of them headed for the Middle West. They had arrived on a Swedish brig which was loaded with iron. One of the leaders of the group was Hans Mattson, who became a great promoter of Scandinavian immigration to Minnesota which he served as secretary of state, a colonel in the Union army during the Civil War, and American consul in Calcutta, India (pp. 200–201, 282–283, 334–337). 2. Immigrant party on the way to California. In 1849–50 hundreds of Swedes joined in the race to the gold fields (pp. 221–222).

This memorial plaque is dedicated to Peter Cassel and his family and companions, all from the province of Östergötland, who in 1845 founded New Sweden, Iowa (pp. 171–173).

IN THIS CHURCHYARD
ARE BURIED MANY OF THE
FIRST BAND OF PEOPLE OF
SWEDISH BIRTH WHO SETTLED
WEST OF THE MISSISSIPPI
RIVER IN 1845.
AMONG THOSE WHO MADE
UP THIS PARTY OF PIONEERS
WERE THE FOLLOWING:

JOHN DANIELSON, WIFE ELIZABETH ANDERSON
AND CHILDREN: A VICTOR, JOHN A.,
MARIA A., MATILDA S. AND FRANK O.

PETER CASSEL, WIFE KATHRINE ANDERSON,
AND CHILDREN: CHARLES J., ANDREW P.,
MATILDA, KATHRINE AND GUSTAVE.

PETER ANDERSON, WIFE
AND THREE CHILDREN.

ERICK AND SARAH ANDERSON

JOHN MONSON, WIFE KATHRINE CASSEL,
AND CHILDREN: MARY AND LOUISA.

ALL CAME FROM KISA AND
VICINITY, SWEDEN.

1. Swante M. Swenson was the foremost Swedish pioneer in Texas, where he arrived in 1838, and became responsible for a large part of the emigration from Sweden to the Lone Star State. After the Civil War he settled in New York as a banker. His initials live on in the SMS ranches in Texas, one of the last great cattle empires in the United States (pp. 159–161, 596–597, 599). 2. Charles A. Lindbergh, Sr., born in Sweden and in 1860 brought to Minnesota as an infant, and his son, the future aviator. This photograph was taken about 1910, when the elder Lindbergh served in Congress (pp. 229, 682–683).

1. Jenny Lind, the "Swedish Nightingale," who in 1850–52 sang herself into the hearts of the American people (pp. 256–261). This daguerreotype was taken in St. Louis, Mo., in 1851 and presented by the singer to Gustaf Unonius, one of the best-known Swedish pioneers in the Midwest (pp. 162–168). 2. Jenny Lind in the 1840s as Marie in the comic opera *La Fille du Régiment*. 3. On September 11, 1850, Jenny Lind gave her first American concert in New York's Castle Garden, a huge auditorium at the southern end of Manhattan, now an open-air theater and known as Castle Clinton. Before sailing for Europe in 1852, she gave 36 concerts in New York alone.

FIRST APPEARANCE OF JENNY LIND IN AMERICA,
At Castle Garden Sept. 11th 1850.
Total Receipts $ 26.238.

1. Before coming to the United States in 1849. Fredrika Bremer had won fame as a novelist. Today she is best known for a book about her two years in America. Minnesota she described prophetically as "a glorious new Scandinavia" (pp. 249–256). 2. Carl Jonas Love Almqvist, poet and novelist, lived in America 1851–65 after having left Sweden to get away from heavy debts and also — probably unfairly — suspected of attempted murder. In this photograph he wears a hat which he said had belonged to a friend he had seen killed in the battle of Gettysburg. His literary production in Sweden ranged from singularly moving, dreamlike poems to realistic folk tales and a novel which was regarded as an attack upon the institution of marriage and rendered his earning a living more difficult (p. 124). 3. No Swedish immigrant made a more notable Civil War career than Charles John Stolbrand, whom President Lincoln finally named brigadier general (pp. 281–282).

1. Captain John Ericsson in 1861, when he designed the *Monitor*. Even before leaving Sweden for England in 1826, he had begun to dream about a turreted ironclad. His development of the propeller brought him to New York in 1839 (pp. 305–327). 2. Battle of the *Monitor* and the *Merrimac* in Hampton Roads on March 9, 1862, after a painting by J. O. Davidson.

pastorate in the state church. His childhood and youth had been full of sacrifices and sorrows.

Lutheran pastors long conservative — Improving education with room for science

THE greatest single influence on the Augustana Synod from the other side of the Atlantic in the 19th century was exerted by Carl Olof Rosenius (1816–68), the lay preacher and evangelist leader who about 1860, when the Swedish Lutheran organization in America was founded, had become the central figure in the religious revivals in Sweden. Born and reared in the far north of the country, he succeeded his friend George Scott when the Wesleyan missionary was forced to leave Sweden after riots in his tabernacle in Stockholm on Palm Sunday, 1842. Rosenius was an orthodox Lutheran, and while he had little faith in the old state church, he was no separatist. As the real leader of the newly formed National Evangelical Foundation he worked for a regeneration within the church organization. The United States, from where he received financial assistance, was regarded by him as the most Christian country in the world, and many of his activities were imbued with American ideas. He had considerable influence also in the other Nordic countries.

The Augustana Synod was, as its founders wanted it to be, a more democratic organization than the state church in Sweden, but it became, at the same time, intensely Lutheran, and a concentrated, orthodox education, followed by the often bitter competition with other denominations, made the average Augustana pastor of the 19th century one of the most conservative Protestant ministers in America. His views were "essentially those of the New England Puritans," according to a leading authority on the religious aspect of Swedish immigration, the late George M. Stephenson, who, on the other hand, immediately added: "It is easy to be unjustly critical of the Swedish-American clergyman if one loses sight of the fact that he was the servant of an immigrant church and that his work was of vastly greater importance as pastor than as preacher." He understood the thoughts and problems of the members of his congregation.

While the Augustana ministers of the 1800s worked to preserve the Swedish language in the United States, many of them seem to have felt that their American patriotism called for family names of the more common English type rather than the ones they had brought from Sweden. Johnson, for instance, became Hamilton, Olson was replaced by Lorimer, and Anderson by Wendell. Later the given name and the surname were often reversed, so that Gustav William Peterson, for instance, was changed to Gustav P. Williams and Lawrence August Person to August P. Lawrence. Among the clergymen who never changed their names were Hasselquist and Erland Carlsson, but they realized at an early stage that the Swedish language could not be permanently maintained in America.

From their homeland the Swedish settlers of the middle 1800s brought to America greater interest in religious than in secular education. Their spiritual leaders understood, moreover, that since their need of educated clergymen could not be met from Sweden, they would have to provide for the training of ministers in their own institutions, and the emphasis everywhere was, therefore, on religious education. In all schools founded by Swedish 19th-century pioneers the instruction offered left much to be desired, but in this case too it is easy to be unjustly critical. Few nationality groups made as great sacrifices for the education of their children as the immigrants from Sweden and the other Scandinavian countries, and there was a gradual and relatively rapid improvement in scholastic standards. At an early stage, consistent support of the public-school system became characteristic of the Scandinavian immigrants, while in higher education they continued to back denominational institutions of their own. From there, many young people went on to other colleges and universities.

After the first difficult period, greater attention was paid to science than was usual at denominational institutions. At Augustana College, for instance, an elective course in botany was given as early as 1877 by Anders Richard Cervin (1823–1900), who was Tuve Nilsson Hasselquist's brother-in-law and had obtained a Ph.D. at the University of Lund. He came to America the first time in 1856, went back to Sweden in disappointment the next year to become a teacher at Kristianstad, his birthplace, but returned to the United States after his ordination as a Lutheran minister in 1864. At Augustana College he taught Greek, mathematics, and the natural sciences. His successor as professor of the latter disciplines was another graduate of Lund, Dr. Joshua Lindahl (1844–1912), who became the real founder of the science department at Augustana. A native of the province of Halland, he had taken part in British as well as Swedish deep-sea expeditions before coming to the United States in 1876 as assistant to the director of the Swedish section at the Centennial Exposition in Philadelphia. After ten years at Augustana he became state geologist of Illinois, and later he moved to Cincinnati, Ohio, as director of its Society of Natural History. At Augustana he was succeeded by one of his own pupils, Johan August Udden, who later directed successful oil explorations in Texas.

When the parochial school founded by the Reverend Eric Norelius at Red Wing in southeastern Minnesota opened in the fall of 1862, only one student turned up; he was Jonas Magnuson from Linneryd in Småland, who later became a noted clergyman under the name of Magny, and who had a son, Clarence R. Magney (1883–1962), who became mayor of Duluth and finally a justice of the Supreme Court of Minnesota. Before the school year was over, the number of pupils had increased to 11. In 1876 the school found a permanent home at St. Peter, and it then acquired its present name, Gustavus Adolphus College. Its first class of seniors was graduated in 1890. Among its early alumni were future political leaders and men of science as well as clergymen and educators.

Early non-Lutheran leaders include intellectuals as well as self-taught people

THE Baptists, Methodists, and other nonconformist denominations in Sweden were not, unlike the Lutheran authorities, opposed to emigration, and several of their leaders even regarded it as a positive blessing to the country. The transatlantic contacts of the non-Lutheran religious movements were always extremely close, and their leading personalities were often active on both sides of the ocean.

The first religious work among larger groups of 19th-century Swedish immigrants in America was done in New York by a former sailor, the Reverend Olof Gustaf Hedstrom, under the auspices of the American Methodist Episcopal Church. Few persons have influenced the lives of Scandinavian immigrants in the United States more than he and his brother Jonas, who, from his base at Victoria, Illinois, offered not only religious counsel but also assistance with the acquisition of land and other practical matters.

Many others of the early Swedish Methodist ministers in the Middle West had been associated with the Bishop Hill colony in Illinois, and as a rule they were, like Jonas Hedstrom, self-taught. Among the pioneers were, however, also two well-educated Swedes, Victor Witting and William Henschen, who belong to the history of the Swedish Methodists both in the United States and in Sweden.

Victor Witting (1825–1906), who was born at Malmö in southern Sweden, had become interested in America from reading the novels of James Fenimore Cooper and by hearing from his father, an artillery captain who was born in Finland, about Gustaf Unonius's departure in 1841. After several years as a sailor and, before long, an officer of the merchant marine, he came to the United States in 1847 with a group of Jansonists, and the next year he married a member of the Bishop Hill colony. He soon became disillusioned with the regime of Eric Janson, however, and after an unsuccessful gold-digging expedition to California with other young Swedes, and an attempt to earn his living by cultivating medical herbs at Victoria, Illinois, he was converted in 1854 to Methodism by Olof Hedstrom in New York.

Witting was then placed in charge of the Swedish Methodist church at Andover, Illinois, from where he was transferred to Rockford in 1859. Three years later he began to publish the first Swedish Methodist weekly, *Sändebudet*, which by the middle of the 20th century, before its expiration, was the oldest Swedish periodical in America. From 1867 to 1876 he was a successful Methodist missionary and organizer in Sweden, and after that he continued his preaching and his editorial work in the Middle West and New England. He died at Quincy, Massachusetts. His memoirs, *Sailor, Emigrant, and Missionary*, was published in 1902 at Worcester, Massachusetts, and another valuable work of 730 pages about Swedish Methodism in America appeared two years later. Witting had a special gift for translating the old Wesleyan hymns from English into Swedish, and wherever Swedish Methodists gather they still sing these songs in his words.

The main burden of educational work among the Swedish Methodists in America was borne for many years by the Reverend Wilhelm, or William, Henschen (1842–1925), whose father, Lars Henschen, a noted judge at Uppsala, helped bring about in the middle 1840s the Erik Jansson sect's emigration to America and served many other religious dissenters in Sweden as their legal adviser. Unusually successful university studies brought his son Wilhelm a Ph.D. degree at the age of 21, and he also studied, but never practiced, medicine. In 1870 he emigrated to Florida with a group of friends and began to plant orange trees. Already in 1872, however, he moved to New York, and for two years he supported himself and his growing family by editing a newly started Swedish-language weekly, *Nordstjernan* (The North Star), which still was published more than 100 years later.

In 1874 William Henschen joined the Immanuel Swedish Methodist Episcopal Church in Brooklyn, which was a direct outgrowth of Olof Hedstrom's Bethel Ship mission, and this was the beginning of a long career as a Methodist preacher, teacher, and editor in the United States and Sweden. In 1875 he was appointed professor at the newly founded Swedish Methodist seminary, which in 1881 was invited to Evanston, Illinois, as a long-term tenant of Northwestern University, and he did not retire until 1911. Four of the intervening years, however, he spent in Sweden as head of its Methodist seminary, and in America he had two periods as a pastor, first at Jamestown, New York, and later at Galva, Illinois. He described himself as "decidedly liberal" and politically independent, and both as an educator and as a publicist he had an unusual influence on his denomination. In 1913 he became one of the first Americans of Swedish birth to receive an honorary doctor's degree from the University of Uppsala.

The foundations of the Swedish Baptist church in the United States were laid by three pastors: Gustaf Palmquist, a former schoolteacher who in 1852 formed at Rockford in Illinois the first Baptist congregation among the Swedes in America, Fredrik Olaus Nilsson, a former sailor, and Anders Wiberg, a former Lutheran minister who, like the other two, also played a leading part in the growth of Baptism in Sweden and actually is regarded as its principal founder.

Gustaf Palmquist (1812–67) was born in the parish of Solberga in northern Småland which, like most other parishes in this province, would become a wellspring of emigration to America. He came to America in 1851, and after having served Baptist churches or missions at Rock Island, Chicago, and New York he returned to Sweden six years later to cooperate with Anders Wiberg in the training of

Baptist preachers. He liked the United States and felt confident that the Swedish immigrants, if they survived the first difficult years, would gradually prosper. The bitter strife among the various religious groups in the Midwest depressed him, however, in the same way as Unonius and Esbjörn, and once he wrote to his friend Wiberg that "America is, like Europe, a vale of tears." Palmquist had two brothers who also became active in the free-church and temperance movements in Sweden and contributed to their American orientation.

Fredrik Olaus Nilsson (1809–91), who was born in Halland, came to America as a sailor, and from 1834 to 1839 he worked for the Methodists in New York. In 1848 he formed the first Baptist congregation in Sweden, but under a law of 1726 he was then sentenced to exile for two years, which caused a heated debate in the Swedish press and sharp comments in religious publications in both England and America. When in 1853 Nilsson came back to New York he was, therefore, received as a martyr to religious liberty. With some fellow immigrants he was sent to the Middle West, where he continued to preach. In 1860, when he had become an American citizen, he returned to Sweden as a Baptist missionary. The law of 1726 had then been repealed, and Nilsson received an engraved royal certificate with the King's signature. After the Civil War he came back to the United States and settled in Minnesota, abandoning the Baptist faith and turning Unitarian.

As a young man Anders Wiberg (1816–87) received strong impressions from the pietism in his native province, Hälsingland, from visiting English and American preachers and temperance promoters, and from religious authors such as John Bunyan. In 1851 he resigned as pastor in the Swedish state church, and the next year he sailed for the United States as chaplain to a group of Swedish emigrants. A series of lectures or travel reports in Stockholm by an extremely pro-American Swedish educator, Per Siljeström, had also spurred his interest in the New World. While the ship stopped at Copenhagen, he was baptized by immersion by the recently exiled Reverend Fredrik O. Nilsson, who then served in Denmark.

After being ordained into the Baptist ministry in New York, Wiberg undertook an extended tour of the Swedish settlements in the Midwest. He next lived in Philadelphia for two years, writing books expounding the Baptist doctrine, editing texts for the American Baptist Publication Society which were distributed both in Sweden and among Swedish immigrants in America, and sending articles to *Aftonbladet*, the influential Stockholm daily. In 1855 he returned to Stockholm with his Philadelphia-born wife, and before long the Swedish capital received its first Baptist church. With American support, Wiberg continued to promote the Baptist denomination in Sweden. In 1863, when the members of his sect had increased to 6,000, he returned to the United States to solicit more funds, and during a three-year stay in America he was able to enlist the services of another highly educated Swedish Baptist, Oscar Brundin, or Broady, who after the Civil War went back to Sweden to begin a 40-year-long tenure as president of the Baptist Bethel Seminary. Many of its students emigrated to the United States and served there as pastors, and some of these eventually returned to Sweden as preachers or teachers, incidentally stimulating emigration.

In his diary, which finally covered 44 years in both Swedish and English, Anders Wiberg once wrote about the Middle West that "it was touching to see the tall Swedes galloping on horseback on the plains of America — their new home." Personally he was all for Swedish emigration to the United States, which to him was the ideal country.

Oscar Brundin, or Broady (1832–1922), who was born at Uppsala, had become a noncommissioned officer in the Swedish navy when he decided to emigrate in 1854. While crossing the Atlantic he lost by death his young wife and was left with a prematurely born child, which survived. The next year he was converted to Baptism by Gustaf Palmquist, and his new American Baptist friends then encouraged him to prepare for the ministry. In 1861 he was graduated from Madison University in Hamilton, New York, which was later renamed Colgate. During the Civil War he served with distinction as a Union officer. When he returned to Sweden in 1866 he brought a new wife, who was a native of Hamilton. He was regarded as one of the greatest preachers of his time, and at the Bethel Seminary in Stockholm he continued to teach for many years even after having left the presidency in 1906, at the age of 74. He always maintained close contact with the United States, and his American alma mater honored him twice with a doctor's degree. His salary came from an American Baptist organization, which is said to have facilitated his leadership in Sweden.

The leading pioneer in efforts to provide academic training for future Swedish Baptist ministers in America was Johan, or John, Alexis Edgren (1839–1908), the son of an estate owner at Älvsbacka in Värmland, who from reading sea stories became so eager to taste the life of a sailor that he at the age of 13 persuaded his parents to let him try. Seven years later, when he had explored large areas of the world, he passed his captain's examination in Stockholm. On his first visit to New York he had met Olof Gustaf Hedstrom, the Methodist missionary, but later he decided, instead, to join the Baptists, and in 1858 he was baptized in New York by total immersion. Between two enlistment periods in the Union navy during the Civil War he attended the Presbyterian Theological Seminary at Princeton, New Jersey, and when the war was over he entered the Baptist Seminary of Madison University at Hamilton, New York. There he married in 1866 a relative of Henry Wadsworth Longfellow. He and his wife were then sent to Sweden with the Reverend Anders Wiberg and Colonel Oscar Broady, both also married to American girls, as Baptist teachers and missionaries. After a few years in Stockholm they moved to Chicago in 1870, and there Edgren founded a seminary for Swedish Baptist ministers in America. Overburdened by work, poverty, and poor health, he resigned his presidency in 1887 and retired to California. From 1892 until 1914 the seminary remained as part of the divinity school of the University of Chicago; it was then merged with the Bethel Academy in St. Paul, Minnesota. Since 1947 the name has been the Bethel College and Seminary.

The Swedish immigrant churches in America did not by any means attract practically all or even most of the settlers born in Sweden. As the flow of immigrants increased, more and more newcomers joined older or newly established American religious organizations, such as the Episcopalians, Unitarians, or Presbyterians, and there were various reasons for such decisions. It was, for instance, not always possible to organize a congregation of Swedes where the settlers lived, and new ties of marriage or friendship also played a part. A majority of the immigrants, finally, never became active members of any church.

★ 15

Flowering Cultural Exchanges

Mid-century a period of historic events in Swedish-American cultural relations

THE very middle of the 19th century became a period of historic significance in cultural and personal relations between Sweden and the United States, primarily because of the impact that Swedish visits to the New World had on both sides of the Atlantic. In the 1840s there were two Swedish women who had won international fame, namely, Fredrika Bremer and Jenny Lind, and at the end of the decade both came to America for extended tours. No Swedish man of the same era had gained anything like the same reputation, but one was well on his way, and he, John Ericsson, inventor of the Civil War *Monitor*, lived in the United States.

In addition, some important Swedish study tours were made in the United States by the middle of the 1800s. One of the travelers was Pehr Adam Siljeström (1815–92), educator and scientist, who probably knew more about education in Europe than any other Swede of his time. Beginning in late 1849, he studied the American school system for about a year, and in Sweden he published a two-volume account of his visit. It has long been regarded as a classic.

For the remainder of his life Siljeström pressed for continued improvements in Swedish education, modeled in part on what he saw on his American trip. A liberal with deep religious interests, he wanted a more democratic spirit in the schools, as well as grade schools that were independent of the church. He also worked, with greater immediate success, for better school buildings and classrooms, like those he had seen in the United States. The first Swedish teachers' college for women was, in part, a result of his efforts, and he managed to establish public libraries in most parishes throughout Sweden. The American people he regarded as "the world's most inveterate readers."

Siljeström was, in fact, full of enthusiasm, not only for American education, but also for the political organization and religious activities in the United States, and he also spread his impressions through public lectures and via the press, including Sweden's first educational journal, which he had helped found. In contrast with the conservatives in Sweden and other European countries, he regarded the American system of government as the product of a long development, which, together with public education and press freedom, guaranteed its stability. He did not want to recommend emigration but believed it was inevitable as long as large groups of people lacked full citizenship in their native Sweden. At the middle of the 19th century no American felt more convinced of the future of the United States as a world power than did Siljeström.

A professor of law at the University of Uppsala, Pehr Erik Bergfalk (1798–1890), received at about the same time as Siljeström a government grant for studies in the United States. At a farewell session with the students he said that he regarded their coming as an endorsement of his decision to travel to America and explore "the miracles which freedom has brought about and which, in fact, freedom alone can produce." A comprehensive report on his study trip was, however, never presented. Bergfalk and Fredrika Bremer, who were old friends, met often in the United States, and during the Civil War, when he lived at Uppsala and she near Stockholm, they exchanged American newspapers and also sent each other telegrams about important events.

In 1853–54 an opera singer, composer, and music critic by the name of Isidor Dannström (1812–87) visited the United States and gave concerts and voice courses, probably influenced by Jenny Lind with whom he had often appeared at the Stockholm Opera. In 1855 he published a pamphlet entitled *From Sweden to America* which a few months later, in a circular letter to the provincial governors, the government recommended for distribution to persons who should know about "the dangers and adventures" awaiting them as immigrants in America. It is true that Dannström's publication contained some information on these subjects, but those who read it can hardly have felt discouraged. Already in the preface, for instance, the author said that by its favorable geographic location, the fertility of its soil and its mineral resources, the industriousness of its inhabitants, and the free spirit of its laws the United States "carries the seed of never-resting progress and boundless development." Immigrants could, therefore, expect many advantages, although they must be prepared for a very sharp competition as well as for class distinctions, even if these were smaller than Europe's. Wisconsin, Iowa, and, in particular, Illinois were especially recommended.

Another well-educated Swede, Baron Axel Adelswärd (1828–1900), who had served in the Swedish navy and fought as a volunteer with the Danes against Prussia in 1848–49, spent seven months in America in 1855–56, traveling south to Charleston and New Orleans, and west to the Mississippi. His diary, which he had planned to publish in a book, was lost during a trip to Cuba, but he also wrote many letters to relatives in Sweden. In his first report home he expressed his deep admiration for the beauty of American women, but added that a Paris lady would "weep tears of blood" if she should be forced to dress in the same way. He liked several of the cities he visited, and perhaps especially Philadelphia and St. Louis. In New York he attended a Scandinavian Methodist meeting where, he wrote, Olof Hedstrom preached "in good English, though with a pure Värnamo accent," shouting, laughing, weeping, or pounding the table "as circumstances demanded." (The Swedish Methodist pioneer was born near the town of Värnamo in central Småland.) The former naval officer also visited the Swedish religious-communal settlement at Bishop Hill in Illinois, which, he said, "as a whole is already prodigiously rich, and will get still richer if they can go on." A son of Axel Adelswärd became a noted industrialist at Åtvidaberg in the province of Östergötland, as well as a liberal and westward-oriented member of the Riksdag and minister of finance.

Nothing that was published in Sweden about America at the middle of the 19th century had a deeper grassroots effect than a book of about 360 pages, which was written by a Lutheran clergyman in Småland, Johan Bolin, who had never been to the United States but read all the literature he had been able to obtain, including a score of works in the German language. Entitled *Description of the United States of North America, With Advice and Information for Emigrants*, and printed at Växjö in 1853, it presented in great detail the American geography, natural resources, cities, system of government, etc. As a rule the author did not express any strong opinions of his own, but his descriptions painted the United States in shining and warm colors. "By many knowledgeable and thoughtful men," he wrote, "its system of government is regarded as the most natural and, for the happiness and self-development of the people, the best in the world." Slavery as applied in the South was, he thought, actually better than its reputation in Europe, but there was good reason to believe that the institution of slavery in America would eventually disappear, as the economic conditions on which it was based were modified or ceased to exist. Bolin's book was followed by many others of the same type.

Both enthusiasm and censure in an American travel book about Sweden

THE few American visitors to Sweden in the 1850s included a young writer and traveler, Bayard Taylor, whose trip resulted in one of the first travel books of importance about the Nordic countries to be published in the United States. He had probably read both Samuel Laing's *A Tour in Sweden in* 1838 and Robert Baird's comprehensive report of 1841.

After having traveled, chiefly on foot, in Great Britain, Germany, Austria, Italy, and France, Taylor published his first book in 1846 at the age of 21. Three years later he went to the California gold fields as special correspondent for the *Daily Tribune* of New York, and his reports, which were republished in a book, added considerable fuel to the gold fever. In 1851 he was again in Europe, and before returning to America in 1854 he visited Egypt, Central Africa, Asia Minor, India, China, and Japan, where he accompanied Commodore Perry on his epoch-making entry. All these travels were also described in popular books. At his death in 1878 he was the United States minister to Germany.

As a quite young man Bayard Taylor read Longfellow's magazine article about Esaias Tegnér's Viking epic *Fritiof's Saga* and became, as he wrote himself, "an enthusiastic admirer of the stirring Scandinavian sagas." His interest in Sweden was further stimulated in 1850, when he met both Fredrika Bremer and Jenny Lind in New York. Six years later he finally had an opportunity to visit Northern Europe.

After a brief stay in Stockholm in early December, 1856, Bayard Taylor and an American friend traveled north to arctic Sweden, first by stagecoach, then by horse-drawn farm carts or sleds, and finally by Lapp pulkas drawn by reindeer. Gradually, the temperature went far below zero, but down to a certain limit Taylor seemed to love every sinking degree of it, observing, for instance, how he could inhale "full draughts into the lungs with a delicious sensation of refreshment and exhilaration."

When the travelers were somewhat more than halfway between Stockholm and the Arctic Circle, Taylor wrote: "The sun rose a little after ten, and I have never seen anything finer than the spectacle we then saw for the first time, but afterwards almost daily repeated — the illumination of the forests and snowfields in his level orange beams, for even at midday he was not more than eight degrees above the horizon. The tops of the trees, only, were touched: still and solid as iron, and covered with sparkling frost crystals. Their trunks were changed to blazing gold, and their foliage to a fiery orange-brown. The delicate purple sprays of the birch, coated with ice, glittered like wands of topaz and amethyst, and the slopes of virgin snow, stretching towards the sun, shone with the fairest saffron gleams. There is nothing equal to this in the South — nothing so transcendently rich, dazzling, and glorious."

Bayard Taylor also liked the people in northern Sweden: "If health and virtue cannot secure happiness, nothing can, and these Norrlanders appear to be a thoroughly happy and contented race." However, in the north of Lapland, where the sun did not rise at all and the temperature sometimes fell to about 50 below zero, his romantic passion for the North was severely tested. There were times when he found "poetry beyond all the sagas and Eddas that ever were written," but for many days he felt deeply depressed: "Everywhere snow, snow, snow, silence and death." Taylor and his companion seem to have been the first Americans to visit northern Lapland in wintertime. In the summer of 1787 an American named William Langhorn, who was famous for his walking, is said to have passed the mountains in Swedish Lapland on his way to Norway, and then returned on his way to Archangel in Russia.

In precisely two months, and after having covered about 2,200 miles some 250 of which were by reindeer, the American travelers were happy to be back in Stockholm, where, however, they "had everything that is disagreeable in winter, without its brisk and bracing qualities." After a closer look, moreover, Taylor came to the conclusion that the beautiful Swedish capital was the most licentious and sinful city in Europe, if not in the whole world. This impression he reported, to begin with, in a letter published in the *New York Tribune*, which later caused objections in some Swedish newspapers. In his book, Taylor retorted that if he had accepted all that had been told him by natives of Stockholm, he would have made the picture even darker. Elsewhere in his opus he deplored, on the other hand, the "spirit of detraction in regard to everything Swedish" that he had often found during his visit to Sweden. During his stay in Stockholm, Taylor enjoyed attending a course of medical gymnastics according to the Swedish Ling system.

At last, spring came sweeping over central Sweden, but the American visitors left the capital "just as it began to be pleasant and lively," and via the Göta Canal they traveled to Gothenburg. On the canal boat Taylor met two or three persons who showed an unusual understanding of America and its institutions, but the captain "betrayed the same general impression which prevails throughout the Continent, that we are a thoroughly material people, having little taste for or appreciation of anything which is not practical and distinctly utilitarian." Nothing, Taylor added, could be further from the truth, "yet I have the greatest difficulty in making people comprehend that a true feeling for science, art, and literature can co-exist with our great practical genius." On the whole, he must have been a good roving ambassador for his country. He had a relatively good knowledge of the Swedish language, and six other foreign tongues he spoke more or less fluently.

Like the Longfellows two decades earlier, Bayard Taylor found Gothenburg "in every respect a more energetic and wide-awake place than Stockholm." The capital, however, made a much better impression on him when he came back there for a quick farewell visit toward the end of September: "In the mild, calm, sunny autumn days which

248

followed [a storm], the beautiful city charmed us more than ever and I felt half inclined to take back all that I had said against the place during the dismal weather of last spring."

Before coming back to Stockholm the two Americans had taken a walking trip through the west-central Swedish provinces of Värmland and Dalarna, and there Taylor was, as he already had been during his winter journey in the North, delighted with the country population. "The more I see of the Swedes," he wrote in conclusion, "the more I am convinced that there is no kinder, simpler, and honester people in the world. With a more liberal school system, a fairer representation [that is, a new parliament and electoral system], and release from the burden of a state church, they would develop rapidly and nobly."

The complete title of Bayard Taylor's book, which was published in New York in 1858, was *Northern Travel: Summer and Winter Pictures of Sweden, Denmark and Lapland*. It was, like his other works, well received but can hardly have had any immediate effect on travel from the United States to Scandinavia. It may, on the other hand, have contributed to the American appreciation of the Scandinavians as immigrants. A Swedish translation was published in Stockholm in 1859.

Among those who read Bayard Taylor's book was Paul du Chaillu, a naturalized American born in Paris. After having written half a dozen books about Africa, he visited Sweden in 1871–72, and ten years later two weighty volumes entitled *The Land of the Midnight Sun, Summer and Winter Journeys through Sweden, Norway, Lapland, and Northern Finland* were published in New York. His work is less a personal travelogue like Taylor's than a natural history of Scandinavia. Among the numerous things that attracted him in Sweden were the cleanliness, the polite manners, and the good food. Du Chaillu was probably the first American writer to describe in detail the smörgåsbord, which in the 20th century became a household word in America. Like most American writers of the modern era, he was greatly impressed by the beauty of Stockholm.

Fredrika Bremer, famous novelist and feminist, spends two rich years in America

FREDRIKA BREMER (1801–65) was the first Swedish writer of fiction to be extensively translated into English, and her novels about family and middle-class life were avidly read in the United States. A Swede who traveled in America in the middle 1840s was startled to hear a newsboy on a train calling out: "Miss Bremer's latest!" The 27-year-old Walt Whitman, who had just become editor of *The Brooklyn Eagle*, wrote that if he ever had children, the first books after the New Testament to be made their household companions would be Fredrika Bremer's novels. No other Swedish writer has won such a universal popularity in the United States.

In the middle 1840s Fredrika Bremer herself wrote that she had long dreamed about visiting America and seeing with her own eyes "that new, rising world." She was born in Finland, where her father, of an old Swedish family, had become a successful businessman. In 1804, when she was three years old, her parents moved to Sweden, making their home in a 17th-century chateau south of Stockholm. Five years later Finland was lost to Russia.

Fredrika Bremer's main purpose in visiting the United States was to study American homes and family life, the status of women, and the influence of democratic government on the development and happiness of the individual. "Yes," she wrote in a letter, "I am going to America to see the human being in the new home, in the free state, and from this point to cast a glance at the future and what we can hope from it, all we people who are going in the same direction as the American people have gone and are going."

She came to New York on October 4, 1849, and during the next two years she traveled far and wide — along the Atlantic coast and in New England, in the South, and as far west and north as St. Paul in the then Minnesota Territory. Only a few days after her arrival a New York newspaper reported that she "has already become the lioness of the town, from her gentleness and great good sense," and before long more or less sentimental poems were composed in her honor. John Greenleaf Whittier, once considered one of the greatest of American poets, wrote an ode beginning "Seeress of the misty Norland, Daughter of the Vikings bold" which was first published in Washington, D.C., and widely reprinted.

Another American poet, James Russell Lowell, who had just scored his first great successes, invited Miss Bremer to his home at Cambridge, Massachusetts, and wrote when she had left: "Fredrika

Bremer stayed three weeks with us, and I do not *like* her, I *love* her. She is one of the most beautiful persons I have ever met . . ." He did not, however, think of physical beauty, but would have agreed with what Nathaniel Hawthorne wrote after having renewed his acquaintance with Fredrika Bremer in Rome in 1858: "She is the funniest little old fairy in person whom one can imagine, with a huge nose, to which all the rest of her is but an insufficient appendage; but you feel at once that she is most gentle, kind, womanly, sympathetic, and true." Hawthorne also said about Miss Bremer that she was "worthy to be the maiden aunt of the whole human race," a judgment which today is rather well known in Sweden although its origin has become obscure.

One of the first literary celebrities Fredrika Bremer met in America was the then 66-year-old Washington Irving, whose books had been translated into Swedish. Miss Bremer wrote that, together with James Fenimore Cooper, Irving "was the first who made us in Sweden somewhat at home in America." During her first tour of New England, in late 1849, large receptions were given for her at Hartford, Connecticut, and Worcester, Massachusetts, where she "shook hands with the whole town." The coming Swedish invasion of this section, and especially of the Worcester area, she did not anticipate. Among the visitors at her hotel in Boston was Henry Wadsworth Longfellow, then professor of modern languages at Harvard, whom she met again numerous times. During her own visit to Harvard she was surprised by the quality and scope of its Scandinavian library. Miss Bremer was also invited to Concord by Ralph Waldo Emerson, whose works she later introduced in Sweden. She seems, in fact, to have been the first person to translate him into a foreign tongue.

In Philadelphia, Fredrika Bremer was much impressed by the activities of the Quakers. In 1850, on June 24, which was Midsummer Day in Sweden, she made a pilgrimage to the Gloria Dei or Old Swedes Church, and there she spoke to several descendants of the early Swedish settlers in the Delaware Valley. Staying in Washington somewhat later she met President Zachary Taylor twice at White House receptions, and on July 9 she was in the Senate when Daniel Webster interrupted the proceedings to announce that the chief executive was dying. She also watched the funeral procession, as well as Millard Fillmore's swearing-in. Both Webster and Henry Clay she met socially several times. Among other members of Congress who made a deep impression on her was Horace Mann of Massachusetts, who had initiated improvements in public education.

Traveling in the Middle West in the fall of 1850 Fredrika Bremer met many Swedish pioneers, but she declined an invitation to Bishop Hill, whose leader and prophet, Eric Janson, had been murdered a few months earlier. At this time, the attention she attracted in the press was often completely overshadowed by the publicity accorded Jenny Lind, who had arrived in the United States on September 1. Three weeks later, when the famous soprano was still in New York, Miss Bremer wrote in a letter from Chicago that it "is so full of Jenny Lind as a city so far remote from New York well can be." For an American literary magazine she had written a long article about Jenny Lind's life, and she had composed a song to be sung by Miss Lind at her first concert in New York, which, if it had been accepted, would have brought her a nice compensation in money. To her friends the Lowells in Cambridge she suggested that they invite Jenny Lind to their home, but Mrs. Lowell answered that while she would gladly do so if Miss Lind needed a rest, it would be like inviting Niagara into her house.

After having sailed down the Mississippi to New Orleans, on a ship she called "Noah's Ark" because of its cargo of more than 1,000 head of livestock, Fredrika Bremer spent the winter and early spring of 1851 in Cuba, which seemed to her "a heavenly oasis between the two hemispheres." She then made a tour of the Southeastern states, some of which she had already visited in 1850. By Maximilian Schele de Vere, whom she had met in Sweden before his emigration, she was invited to the University of Virginia at Charlottesville, and there she heard a graduating student make a commencement address urging freedom and good education for everybody. After a visit to a mental hospital at nearby Staunton, where the inmates sometimes wandered off by themselves, she was mistaken for one of them and, as Professor Schele de Vere reported, escorted back to town "by two sturdy men, who watched her peaceful blue eyes as if they expected a fearful explosion at every moment." Most of the summer of 1851 Miss Bremer spent in Pennsylvania, New York, and New England, and by the middle of September she sailed for Europe. She wrote later that during her two years in America she had experienced more than in an ordinary decade.

Always intent upon seeing America and its people at close range, Fredrika Bremer recorded her observations in 43 long and intimate letters to a younger sister, and shortly after her return to Sweden these were published in three substantial volumes under the title *Homes of the New World*. Reflecting a warm but not uncritical admiration of American society, they made a deep impression and helped stimulate Swedish and other Scandinavian emigration to the United States. In one of her prophetic and often quoted passages Fredrika Bremer said that "a new Scandinavia shall one day bloom in the valley of the Mississippi in the great assembly of peoples there." When published in English in New York even before the last volume in Swedish had appeared, *Homes of the New World* became an instant success. The work was also translated into German, French, Dutch, and Danish, receiving numerous reviews in Europe. A French critic, Edouard Laboulaye, who became an outstanding historian and wrote a comprehensive book about the political history of the United States, said: "By showing us America in all its grandeur, and making us love it, and by imparting to us the secret of that vigor and youth which astonish us, she has served both worlds at once and nobly repaid the debt of hospitality." And Fredrika Bremer herself was happy that she had been able to bring Europeans and Americans closer together, as people to people. "It is hardly credible," she wrote in 1853 to friends in the United States, "how prejudiced against America and Americans a great part of European society yet is."

Among aspects of America which Miss Bremer found inspiring were the democratic form of government, the educational standards, the social-welfare work, and the scientific and technical progress. She reacted, on the other hand, against "the aristocracy of wealth," and slavery, above all, seemed incongruous to her, but she favored a gradual rather than an immediate emancipation, an attitude that caused some sensation both in America and in Europe. The lack of moderation among the abolitionists could only damage their cause, she told William Lloyd Garrison, the Boston firebrand who led the moral crusade against slavery. During the Civil War, on the other hand, Fredrika Bremer sided with the North more consistently than most other leading personalities in Europe, despite a deep sympathy for the South which was based on her own experiences.

The American scenery was one of Miss Bremer's continual delights, and like Gustaf Unonius and other Swedish pioneers in the Midwest she was often stirred by the beauty of the rolling prairie. She wrote, for instance, that "if you have seen the Prairie, in the great valley of the Mississippi, all covered with sunflowers, seen, during a clear autumn day, the sun rising over it, wooing it, as it were a bridegroom his bride, till evening came, and he sank down on the bed of sunflowers to the bosom of the well beloved — have you not seen a vision of the marriage of heaven and earth?" Many of the cities where she stayed for some time, such as Cincinnati and Charleston, she liked, but Chicago, she wrote to American friends, was "one of the ruffest, most bare and brute cities" she had seen in America, and she could not dream of living in New York, where, when out walking and wanting to cross Broadway, "I merely think of getting across the street alive." But thank Heaven, she added, for Brooklyn — which remained a separate city until the end of the 19th century.

On her way back to Sweden, Miss Bremer spent six weeks in England studying political and social conditions, and she summed up her impressions in a series of articles for the liberal *Aftonbladet* in Stockholm. At one time the editor of the newspaper considered discontinuing their publication, since they contained what he regarded as obtrusive socialistic propaganda, but he had, of course, good reason to shy away from such a step. It was the ideas of Christian socialism that Fredrika Bremer tried to propagate, and her interest in these had been stimulated during her tour of the United States. She had, for instance, studied several experiments in communitarian living, similar to the one at Bishop Hill but more intellectual, and in New York she had attended lectures dealing with Christian socialism. Her press reports from England were immediately translated into Danish, Dutch, English, German, and Polish, but in Sweden they were not published in book form until 1922.

By her honesty and compassion, Fredrika Bremer made lasting contributions to Swedish life and culture. After her American tour she helped bring about reforms concerning women's rights and responsibilities, and Sweden's first national women's organization, founded in 1884 or nearly 20 years after her death, was named for her. She also became internationally known as a pacifist. Her novels are now mostly of literary-historical interest, but her travel books may still find grateful readers in large numbers. In the United States, her *Homes in the New World* was issued in condensed form as recently as in 1924 and once more became a best seller.

One of the leading themes in her writings was education as a prerequisite for real, lasting progress, and it seems appropriate, therefore, that at least two public schools in the Midwest were named for her. One of them, in Minneapolis, still bears her name. During her visit to the United States, Fredrika Bremer formed many lasting friendships, and several Americans visited her later in Sweden. One married couple she accompanied from Stockholm to Gothenburg via the Göta Canal, and another she also took sightseeing in Denmark, introducing them to members of the royal family and to Hans Christian Andersen. In Sweden Miss Bremer played an increasingly active role in introducing the works of contemporary American authors, and she encouraged several of her friends to translate such literature.

Fredrika Bremer was a citizen of the world as well as a Swedish patriot and a staunch friend of America — a rare combination at that time. From 1856 to 1861, or the last five years before the American Civil War, she lived or traveled in Switzerland, Italy, Palestine, Turkey, and Greece, and after her return she wrote to a friend in the United States that "I cannot describe how I felt it upon coming home in the high summer of Sweden, when life seems doubled in intensity and beauty. . . . Sweden has advanced wonderfully and is progressing in every way, mentally and materially; I had never seen my country so prosperous and so promising. Indeed, I do not believe any country in Europe is now on a better way and in a better state than just my good land." Remarkable progress had undoubtedly been made, but not enough to stem the coming tide of emigration.

Four years later, when the Civil War was ending and Fredrika Bremer's own life was nearing its conclusion, she wrote in one of her last letters to America: "One of the greatest and most important problems which your people from now will be expected to solve, not only for itself but theoretically for the whole world, is how to turn the Negro population into a free and industrious people, capable of self-government. . . . . North America is at this time the only truly interesting scene on the globe. . . . . Next to my own country none is dearer to me than yours." She died on New Year's Eve the same year.

Jenny Lind's epoch-making American tours in 1850–52

THE most successful and influential tour of the United States ever made by a musical celebrity from Europe began in the fall of 1850 when Jenny Lind (1820–87), the "Swedish Nightingale," arrived from England.

She was the first singer to capture the imagination of the American people and introduced a new era of music appreciation. New music halls were built, singing societies and orchestras were founded in more and more cities, and sales of pianos and other instruments began to soar. In Sweden and the other Scandinavian countries the interest in the United States was stirred by the reports of her triumphs, and Swedes who already had settled in America looked toward the future with a new self-assurance. They were, naturally, immensely proud of her, and she often occupied herself with them and their problems and hopes. Her impact was, however, not limited to the United States and Scandinavia, and their relations. By singing herself into the hearts of the masses, an American historian has observed, she really established an artistic entente between two continents. Her great success led others to organize similar tours, and new ties between America and Europe were thus created.

After eight years of study and work at the Stockholm Opera, Jenny Lind appeared in her first major part, Agatha in Weber's *Der Freischütz*, in 1838 at the age of 17. In 1840 she was appointed singer at the Swedish court and a member of the Academy of Music in Stockholm, and the next year she studied under a highly regarded voice teacher in Paris. She returned to Sweden but left again in 1844 to continue her operatic career in Germany, and before long she was the most celebrated vocal artist in the world. Famous composers became her close friends, queens and princes worshiped her, and English, German, and Austrian poets joined Swedish and other Nordic bards in singing her praise.

In 1849, when Jenny Lind lived in London, she suddenly decided to abandon opera and devote herself to concert singing and oratorio.

Since she always identified herself with the operatic parts she created, life on the stage had become too strenuous for her, but there were also religious reasons for her decision. Phineas T. Barnum, the American showman-promoter, then persuaded the Swedish soprano to come to the United States for a concert tour under his management. Doing his utmost to build her up by advance publicity, he emphasized not only her artistic talents and fabulous European reputation but also her natural goodness, generosity, and modesty.

Upon her arrival in New York on September 1, 1850, Jenny Lind received the most boisterous welcome ever given a visitor from abroad. In the evening she was serenaded by large groups of singers, backed up by 20 companies of firemen bearing torches. The next morning one of the New York papers, the *Daily Tribune*, had four columns on the front page describing her reception, as well as a long and learned poem with 52 footnotes explaining the Scandinavian allusions in it. Another daily, the *Herald*, hailed her appearance as a sign "that the wand of civilization has fallen from the hands of southern nations and passed to the hardy northern races."

On September 11 Jenny Lind with the assistance of two other European artists and an orchestra gave her first concert in Castle Garden, a huge auditorium at the southern end of Manhattan which seated some 7,000 people and later became a municipal aquarium. Her first selection was the famous "Casta Diva" aria from the opera *Norma* by Bellini, and she ended with a somewhat bombastic song called "Greeting to America," which had been written for her by 25-year-old Bayard Taylor, the journalist and poet who later would publish a travel book about the Scandinavian countries. The concert was a grandiose success, and before Jenny Lind left the United States 21 months later, she had made 36 more public appearances in New York.

Bayard Taylor's poem had been chosen as the one most suitable for music of some 750 similar compositions received as a result of a prize contest, and it caused a veritable storm in the press. Most of the other participating versemakers claimed that their own poems were far better, but among these was not Fredrika Bremer, who also had submitted a song. After having met Jenny Lind personally, Bayard Taylor said that "she is the only great, unquestioned genius in woman's form I have ever known, and the more I see her the more I reverence her truth, her purity, her faith in art as the crown and glory of our nature."

From New York Miss Lind went first to Boston for eight concerts and to Providence, Rhode Island. In Philadelphia she also sang to filled pews in the Gloria Dei or Old Swedes Church, and then followed Baltimore and Washington, where President Millard Fillmore called at her hotel and invited her to an evening in the White House. Richmond, Virginia, and Charleston, South Carolina, came next. Early in 1851 the troupe arrived in Havana, where four concerts preceded a much-needed rest. Fredrika Bremer came a few days before the singer was to leave, and the two, who knew each other well, had several happy or nostalgic reunions. During one of them Miss Lind sang for Miss Bremer a popular Swedish song.

Twelve concerts were then given in New Orleans, and from there the company traveled up the Mississippi River, with stops for concerts at Natchez, Mississippi, and Memphis, Tennessee. After five appearances in St. Louis, Missouri, and two at Nashville, Tennessee, the party proceeded to Louisville, Kentucky, Madison, Indiana, and Cincinnati, Ohio, and via Wheeling, West Virginia, and Pittsburgh Miss Lind and her associates returned to New York in May, 1851. They had traveled 4,000 miles, and some of their performances had been severe tests of the prima donna's patience and strength, but 14 concerts were then given in New York. A young German pianist by the name of Otto Goldschmidt (1829–1907) took over as Jenny Lind's accompanist.

When the "Jenny Lind fever," or "Jenny rage" or "Lindomania" as it was also called, reached its height, the name of the "Swedish Nightingale" was on everybody's lips. There were Jenny Lind dolls and other toys for the girls, Jenny Lind gloves, bonnets, shawls, and many other articles for the ladies, and even Jenny Lind cigars for the men. Pianos, sofas, and chairs, as well as sausages and pancakes, were also named for the singer from Sweden. Her portrait could be had on glassware, china, pottery, fans, and in numerous other forms. Baby girls were christened Jenny or Jenny Lind, and at least one boy was given the names Phineas Barnum. On November 8, 1850, the *Boston Liberator* wrote in apparent mental exhaustion: "News-stores and saloons and hotels are christened Jenny Lind; steamboats, locomotives, stages, and all vehicles are 'Jennys'; on the Exchange they sell 'Jenny'-see wheat; the spinning 'Jenny' is eclipsed by the singing 'Jenny', at least for this 'Jenny'-ration; people delight in tracing their 'Jenny'-alogy back into Sweden; all men seem to be studying verbs in the 'Jenny'-tive case; 'Jenny'-rosity is a virtue no longer neglected; even our only Major 'Jenny'-ral has surrendered to the queen; fond mothers call their babes, sportsmen their dogs and horses, farmers their cows and pigs 'Jenny'; in short, 'Jenny' is the 'Jenny'-ric term for all these things . . ."

Practically every newspaper and most magazines in the United States printed, at some time or other, a poetic contribution about the 30-year-old soprano. And in London, *Punch* announced that President Fillmore of the United States was abdicating in favor of Jenny Lind. This humorous weekly, which was founded in 1841 and soon became an English institution, had already honored the "Nightingale" in verse many times. In one poem, for instance, *Punch* said that "thou has bereft me of my wits."

After 95 concerts Jenny Lind terminated her contract with Mr. Barnum, which she was entitled to do. She admired her American impresario but often found it hard to put up with his methods and devices. In many places the choice seats at her concerts had been offered at public auctions, causing an excitement which Barnum regarded as good promotion. In Boston, a singer and entertainer, who must have thought it would be profitable to have his name linked with that of Jenny Lind, bought the first ticket for $625, but a Providence buyer went even higher and paid $650. Miss Lind herself preferred the lowest possible admission prices, and at an early stage she sent Mr. Barnum a letter, asking him to "avoid selling tickets to speculators and at the same time to put the prices within the reach of the people at large." At that time, however, she did not persevere in her objections: a substantial part of her earnings would, she knew, be given to charitable institutions or for the support of religious and educational activities in the United States and Sweden. She was, in fact, almost as interested in helping people who seemed to deserve help as she was in singing.

In the summer of 1851 Jenny Lind began to give concerts under her own management, and these finally totaled about 40. Her business assistants first booked her for Springfield, Massachusetts, and the nearby village of Northampton, for Hartford, Connecticut, and for a number of cities in New York State, including Albany, Auburn, Buffalo, Rochester, Syracuse, and Utica. After several weeks at Niagara Falls she gave three very successful concerts at Toronto, and then she sang in Cleveland and Cincinnati, Ohio, Pittsburgh and Harrisburg, Pennsylvania, Boston and Worcester, Massachusetts, New Haven, Connecticut, and Philadelphia.

Early in 1852 Jenny Lind was married to her pianist, Otto Goldschmidt, who was nine years her junior. The ceremony took place in a private home on Beacon Hill in Boston, and the couple spent their honeymoon in nearby Northampton, where Jenny Lind in a benefit recital on May 6 made her first public appearance as Madame Goldschmidt.

Three farewell concerts were then given in New York, the final one in Castle Garden, and at the end of May Jenny Lind and her husband sailed for Europe. After six years in Germany, where two of their three children were born, they made their home in England. Practically all concerts which Jenny Lind gave or took part in were benefits, and Handel's oratorio *The Messiah* finally became one of her specialties. In Germany, for instance, she helped raise funds for the Beethoven monument at Bonn, for a memorial to Handel in Halle, where he was born, and for a music academy at Leipzig, the birthplace of Mendelssohn, who once said that Jenny Lind was the greatest artist he had known. For some years she taught singing at the Royal College of Music in London. A medallion in memory of the "Swedish Nightingale" was unveiled in the Poets' Corner in Westminster Abbey in 1894.

Jenny Lind never sang in Sweden after her American tours but she was deeply attached to her native country, and she and her family spent happy summer months in the Stockholm archipelago. Her largest single donations established permanent scholarship funds at the Academy of Art and the Academy of Music in Stockholm. In the Swedish calendar her day of birth, October 6, has the name Jenny. In the United States many women's associations of Swedish origin have been named for her. She has also given her name to a few small communities, including one in Arizona and one in California, and there is a Jenny Lind Island in Canada north of the Arctic Circle.

Letters to and by Jenny Lind, souvenir programs, portraits and sculptured busts, at least some of the 40-odd medals struck in her honor in the United States, Britain, Germany, and Sweden, as well as personal belongings and other Lind memorabilia may be found in a large number of museums on both sides of the Atlantic, including the New-York Historical Society, the Museum of the City of New York, the Barnum Museum of Tufts University near Boston and the Barnum Museum of Bridgeport, Connecticut, the American Swedish Historical Museum in Philadelphia, and the Museum of Music History in Stockholm. The collection of the New-York Historical Society, the life work of the late Leonidas Westervelt of New York, includes the contract in which P. T. Barnum guaranteed $187,500 for Jenny Lind's concert tour, more than 250 likenesses of various kinds, and Jenny Lind's gold locket, containing portraits of the two Americans she most admired — George Washington and Daniel Webster. The important collection in the Museum of the City of New York was acquired from William Hildebrand, also of New York. In the 1970s, W. Porter Ware, a former registrar of the University of the South at Sewanee, Tennessee, became known as the foremost private collector of Lindiana. His collection includes several hundred original letters by Jenny Lind, in four languages. Parts of it were displayed in London when the 150th anniversary of the singer's birth was observed in 1970.

The legion of Jenny Lind's more prominent admirers included Longfellow, who attended eight of her concerts in Boston and met her on at least four occasions, and Hans Christian Andersen, the Danish storyteller, who fell in love with her in 1843, when he was 38 and she close to 23. She did not reciprocate his feelings but helped inspire him in several of his fairy tales, including "The Ugly Duckling" and "The Nightingale."

The secret of Jenny Lind's success as a singer was probably not a voice of exceptional glory, but rather the fact that her wonderful art seemed like a genuine expression of an unusual, warm personality. Or, as Longfellow said: "Her power is in her presence, which is magnetic," even if "she sings like the morning star; clear, liquid, heavenly sounds."

16

Inside Sweden

Sweden in 1840–65: economic progress and many reforms, rural overcrowding

IN SWEDEN, the period 1840–65 brought relatively rapid economic advances and a great number of constructive reforms. In many cases, however, the immediate significance of these events was rather limited, and serious economic and social problems remained unsolved.

The modern era in Swedish education was inaugurated in 1840–41 when the Riksdag decided to make elementary-school attendance compulsory. Among those who favored this reform was Crown Prince Oscar (1799–1859), who in 1844 succeeded his father, the former French Marshal Bernadotte, as King of Sweden. In an anonymous article in a semiofficial newspaper, he backed his recommendation of a nationwide public-school system with examples from the United States. The new legislation became effective in 1842, but carrying it through in practice was, of course, another matter. Nearly 1,000 new elementary schools were organized during the first five years, but this was far from sufficient, and even after two decades about three children out of ten remained outside the new system. A dramatic improvement in the educational standards of the Swedish people was, nevertheless, begun by the middle of the 19th century, and this turned out to be of direct importance also from an American viewpoint: among the mass of Swedish immigrants who came after the Civil War, the illiteracy rate was one of the lowest in any nationality.

The old guild system was abolished in 1846, and Sweden's first law about stock companies was enacted two years later. Internal freedom of production and trade was established in 1864, and under the determined leadership of Baron Johan August Gripenstedt (1813–74), a member of the government from 1848 to 1866 and one of the most vigorous exponents of economic liberalism of his age, Sweden opened up greater opportunities for free trade with other countries.

Improved communications were vital to the sparsely populated and mostly forested land, and after lengthy and complicated discussions the Riksdag in 1854 made a historic decision providing for the construction of railroads. The main lines would, as the strong man in the cabinet, Baron Gripenstedt, wanted, be built by the government with the help of foreign capital, while the local lines would be left to private enterprise. Today this outcome is regarded as remarkably progressive for its time. Some historians doubt that the principle of government leadership in railroad transportation would have been accepted a few decades later, when conservative groups had achieved greater influence in a more democratic parliament.

As the leader of the planning and the actual building of the trunk lines the government chose Colonel Nils Ericson (1802–70), who has been called the "Father of the Swedish railways." When he was titled for public services in 1854, he changed the spelling of his name from Ericsson to Ericson, which brought him bitter comments from his brother in America, Captain John Ericsson. He went to work with great energy and determination, but progress was inevitably slow in the beginning, and in 1865 the only trunk line completed was the one between Stockholm and Gothenburg. The southern part of the country was connected with this railroad, but nothing had as yet been done in the northern two-thirds of Sweden, known as Norrland, which soon would be hit by repeated crop failures.

Against the opposition of the farmers, who made up one of the four estates in the old Swedish parliament, the Riksdag of 1853–54 also decided to prohibit private distilleries, which today everybody regards as a great step forward. Another reform enacted around the middle of the century laid the foundations for modern local self-government, and others introduced complete freedom of the press, a large measure of religious freedom, equal rights of inheritance for men and women, and more humanitarian principles in the legislation.

After the February Revolution in Paris in 1848, which was followed by riots in Stockholm where some 30 people were killed, King Oscar I became more conservative, but neither he nor his less gifted but popular son Carl XV (1826–72), who succeeded him in 1859 and was conservative from the beginning, was able to slow down the domestic reform work for very long. The first leader of King Carl's Government Council, in reality prime minister although that office had not yet been established, was Louis De Geer (1818–96), who belonged to the same family as the great Dutch-Swedish industrialist of the 17th century. To the surprise of the monarch, he conducted, with Gripenstedt's support, a moderately liberal, reformist policy.

The new Sweden, able to take its place in the modern industrialized world, was also being fashioned by economic and technological progress. In 1849, the first steam-driven sawmill was set up near Sundsvall some 200 miles north of Stockholm, and such plants were then established all along the Gulf of Bothnia. From 1830 to 1860, lumber exports increased sixfold. The modern Steel Age was ushered in by new production methods, some of which Swedish industrialists helped develop. Cotton mills and looms sprang up in many parts of the country but above all around Borås in the province of Västergötland, largely as a result of the initiative of Sven Erikson (1801–66) whose mother, a poor farmer's wife, was the first woman in Sweden to weave cotton fabrics for sale. Her son, who began by organizing a cottage weaving industry finally employing more than 1,500 women, bought the machinery for his mills from England. Before his death, he saw the beginning of the victorious progress of the Singer sewing machine, the first American laborsaving appliance to win a mass market in Sweden.

New foundations for the modern Swedish metalworking or engineering industry had been laid in the 1830s and 1840s, when such later widely known firms as Eriksberg of Gothenburg, Kockum of Malmö, Nydqvist & Holm of Trollhättan, and Munktell of Eskilstuna were launched. Most of these beginnings were, however, extremely modest. By the middle of the 1800s the Swedish machine shops and similar factories employed only about 1,500 workers, and nearly one-third of these were in the plants of a firm based at Motala on Lake

Vättern, which had been founded in 1822 as part of the preparations for the construction of the Göta Canal.

Sweden's mechanical-engineering industry was, from the beginning, in great part based on Swedish inventions or improvements, and one of its best-known inventors of the middle 1800s, Otto Carlsund (1809–84), was for nearly three decades, from 1843 to 1870, chief engineer of the Motala firm. He had spent several years in London studying and working at shipyards and machine shops, and there he met Captain John Ericsson, who at that time was about to leave England for the United States. Ericsson's invention of the propeller aroused Carlsund's enthusiasm, and already in 1843, when he returned to Sweden, he built the first propeller-driven ship in Scandinavia. Later he improved the original propeller, and after the American Civil War he built the first monitors for the Swedish navy, altering somewhat John Ericsson's design. The first steam turbine for marine engines in the world, as well as the first icebreaker, used from 1858 to 1871 between the Swedish mainland and the Baltic island of Gotland, were built by Carlsund. He is also said to have been first with the designs furthering the aerodynamic efficiency of steamships, but he kept his system secret as his "best patent," and when his principles of construction later were described in the United States, another inventor received the credit.

Under Carlsund's leadership Motala became Sweden's first model industrial concern, as well as a training institution for a new generation of engineers. Quite a few of these technicians would sooner or later emigrate to America, and so would many graduates of the country's technical schools. Two establishments which became Sweden's foremost institutes of technology, at Stockholm and Gothenburg, had been founded in the 1820s. The first president of the Stockholm school was an unusually versatile engineer and scientist, Gustaf Magnus Schwartz (1783–1858), who studied technology in England, France, Germany, and Russia, and made many inventions of his own.

By the middle of the century a modern Swedish banking system began to emerge, and the first great pioneer was André Oscar Wallenberg, who, as already mentioned, as a young man had spent two years in the United States. In 1856, when he had settled in the Swedish capital, he founded Stockholms Enskilda Bank, which became the country's first financial institution of the modern type, successfully channeling savings into industrial and commercial activities. In 1864 he helped establish Skandinaviska Banken, which seven years later was followed by the beginning of Svenska Handelsbanken, which also became one of Sweden's leading banks.

The race between population growth and economic development that had begun during the latter part of the 1700s had not only continued, however, but had gradually become sharper. In the period 1810–50 the Swedish population increased from 2.4 to 3.5 million people. The mortality rate declined steadily, while by the middle of the century the birth rate was more than twice as high as it is today. Agriculture expanded at a faster pace than industry and much new land was added to the cultivated area, but the number of people directly depending on it increased even more steeply. In 1865, the agricultural population had grown by about one million since the beginning of the century, and especially serious was the continued increase in the number of laborers of different categories, with dependents. The landless agricultural population now made up about 40 percent of the whole people, and numerous farms were, moreover, much too small for profitable cultivation. Living conditions varied considerably between good and poor harvest years, but large groups were never above the subsistence level. During long periods the daily fare might consist of, for instance, oat-flour gruel, herring, and potatoes. The cities and towns, on the other hand, did not lack social problems. A steady migration from the rural districts to the urban centers began by the middle of the century.

The progressive legislative work of the middle 1800s was crowned in 1865 with a reform which many liberals had long regarded as more important than anything else, the replacement of the four estates by a parliament of two houses, which, directly or indirectly, would be based on general elections. A bill to that effect was passed by the Riksdag in 1863, but this decision had to be confirmed at the next session. In late 1865, when the final votes were cast, the clergy resolved to await the decision of the nobility. The debate in the magnificent House of Nobles lasted four days, and the reform bill, vigorously defended by Baron De Geer and Baron Gripenstedt, was finally carried by 361 votes to 294. In June of 1866 the Riksdag of the four estates, that is, nobles, clergymen, burghers, and farmers, was dissolved for the last time, and the speaker of the nobles, who had fought against the reform, made a famous farewell address, ending: "Laws may be changed and rights cease to exist, but the duties to our country remain; and if these duties are performed well, the true noble cares little what his position and place in society may be."

The Riksdag reform of 1865–66 was greeted with boisterous celebration in the capital and great satisfaction throughout the country, but it did not by any means result in the introduction of universal suffrage. It was difficult to tell exactly how the new system would work, but because of certain electoral qualifications concerning income and property the great majority of the farm laborers and industrial workers would not yet be able to vote, and they would hardly be able to send representatives of their own to the parliament. Landowning farmers were, on the other hand, favored by the new rules. In the beginning, however, few protests were heard, and the mood in the country was definitely optimistic. A prediction that within the next 50 years well over one million people would leave for the United States would have sounded fantastic, but to the potential emigrants the New World now seemed both closer and more attractive than it had done ten years earlier, before the Civil War.

Sweden and the Civil War: shifting press attitudes, basic sympathies for the North

WHEN the storm clouds of secession gathered over the United States, more grist was brought to the mills of the ultraconservative newspapers in Sweden, which ever since the 1820s had regarded the American republic as a dubious experiment. The more important liberal press, on the other hand, maintained its belief in the United States as a land of the future, capable of overcoming even formidable difficulties and gradually perfecting its democratic institutions. During the Civil War, however, a consistent basic optimism of this type was more common among the people than in the public press.

At the beginning of the war, when few people in Sweden could foresee the long-lived fury of the struggle, Fredrika Bremer expressed an overwhelming feeling of disappointment when she wrote: "Has the New World with its great noble promises, its parliamentary institutions, its enlightened government, its loudly proclaimed ideals of human rights and welfare, no better result to place before mankind

267

than the same blind passions, the same violent struggles, or the same terror which have ravaged and still plague the lands of the Old World?" In a message to all her American friends which was published in the *Daily Tribune* in New York on May 1, 1862, she said that "you cannot know how bitterly I have felt to see a bloody, fratricide war pollute a country gifted beyond all others with all the blessings of this earth." Miss Bremer was, on the other hand, always certain that the North would prevail. "I feel no doubt as to the issue of this war, but much blood and much bitterness may come of it ere it results in peace," she wrote in the summer of 1861 to an American friend, a Southerner who had moved to the North.

Insofar as definite sympathies were voiced in the Swedish press, they were, in general, on the side of the Union, and most commentators doubted that the South would be able to secure its independence, which was not the case in the leading European countries. However, at least one newspaper of importance, *Göteborgs-Posten*, felt that the Southern states should be allowed to go their own way: the Union would do violence to its own ideals of freedom if the Confederacy was subdued by arms.

When the outcome of the battle of Bull Run became known in Sweden in the late summer of 1861, liberal newspapers began to reflect disenchantment with the political leadership and military organization of the North. The public goodwill of the Union cause in Scandinavia was further weakened when, in November, the news came that a Federal warship had stopped the British naval vessel *Trent* to take off two Confederate commissioners, who were on their way to negotiate official British and French recognition of the seceding states. This action was regarded in Sweden as a violation of neutral rights. The Swedish government, as its foreign minister wrote to the envoy in Washington, hoped that the United States would return the prisoners, adding that it would be more dignified "to accomplish this act of justice willingly than to seem to yield to pressure." Essentially, Washington followed this course.

In the fall of 1862, when the Northern armies had suffered further reverses which from Europe seemed even more serious than they actually were, Swedish public opinion as expressed in the press was almost unanimous in questioning the war aims of the Union. Since the North was overwhelmingly superior in numbers and material resources, the Confederates, according to Swedish observers, must be fighting not only with greater military efficiency but also with more moral vigor. Lincoln and his secretary of state had repeatedly declared that slavery was not an issue, and many Swedish liberals, therefore, could see little difference between the Southern struggle for independence and the nationalist movements in Europe, which they consistently supported.

On September 23, 1862, the liberal *Aftonbladet* of Stockholm blamed the defeats and setbacks of the Northern armies on the fact that they were not fighting for the liberation of the slaves. The Emancipation Proclamation had then just been issued in Washington by President Lincoln, but while the Swedish liberals and radicals hailed this as a step forward, the press at first did not seem particularly impressed. As in other European countries as well as in the United States itself, political writers were often inclined to regard the proclamation as wartime propaganda.

At this stage, an end to the carnage in America seemed to many Swedes more important than anything else. In October of 1862, Johan Gabriel Richert, a noted jurist who has been called the "Father of Swedish liberalism," wrote in a letter: "Our friends, the Americans, waste their resources, and what is worse, they slaughter thousands of people hoping to gain something that in reality is out of reach — the loyalty of a people which seems to have both the will and the power to fight to the bitter end for what they call freedom and independence." And in a letter to one of her best American friends, Fredrika Bremer said early in 1863: "Tell me, dear Marcus, where is the chief difficulty from the northern point of view, in allowing a separation between North and South, allowing the South to form, as it requires, a separate republic? . . . Is it the slavery question? Hardly; for slavery would yet be doomed in principle and practice by having a wholly free and to slavery opposed country so near the slave states." After the war, however, Miss Bremer regretted that she had suggested such a solution, writing to the same friend: "For it is sinful to compromise with wrong, especially in a great human cause. Let it be my excuse that I have known many a kind slaveholder and seen happy slaves in the South."

Already in the 1850s Sweden had moved out of the Russian political orbit and into much closer relations with Great Britain and France, a development which inevitably also influenced the Swedish way of thinking concerning the American Civil War. Tension between Denmark and Prussia over the Danish territory south of the Jutland peninsula was, moreover, growing, and Sweden hoped that England and France would back the Danish cause. After the *"Trent* affair" in late 1861 the United States had seemed to be on the brink of war with Britain, and although this particular crisis was settled before the end of the year, other incidents of the same kind could easily take place. An early end to the Civil War seemed, therefore, to be in Sweden's own interest.

After the Emancipation Proclamation, however, the liberal and liberal-conservative leaders and press commentators in Sweden came by degrees to the conclusion that the Union cause had finally been fused with that of human freedom, and after the battles of Gettysburg and Vicksburg in July of 1863 most Swedish observers believed that Lincoln would lead his forces to victory. They were, on the other hand, seldom able to turn their whole attention to the American Civil War, for Sweden's ancient parliament was being recast, and there were also dramatic events close to the country's own borders: first a Polish uprising against Russia, which caused an intense reaction in the Swedish press and at times an almost warlike atmosphere in the country, and then the German-Austrian military attack on Denmark in 1864, which was preceded by Scandinavian discussions about Denmark joining the Swedish-Norwegian union or signing a military alliance with the united kingdoms of Sweden and Norway.

Even during the last years of the Civil War the Confederacy had some ardent supporters in Sweden, but there was a growing note of desperation in their public statements. A newspaper which was published at the cotton-mill center of Borås in the province of Västergötland became more and more friendly to the Confederates as the conflict continued, and the few Swedes who had returned home after having lived in the American South followed its struggle hopefully as long as possible, even if they were opposed to slavery.

An outburst which was full of indignation against the North and nostalgic affection for the Southern civilization, came in the fall of 1863 from Rosalie Roos-Olivecrona, who in the early 1850s had spent three years in South Carolina and there had beloved friends. The South, she wrote in *Tidskrift för hemmet*, a progressive magazine for women which was published in Uppsala, fought for "everything on earth that man holds precious, for its independence, its homes, its existence. The sacrifices it has made for these things, the self-denials it has undergone, the indomitable courage it has shown, the tremendous efforts with which it has, for more than two years, carried on against a superior power in one of the bloodiest wars in history, will in time win the admiration of the world, if not the recognition of the present day." Another articulate but more coldly analytical champion of the Confederate cause, Gustaf C. Hebbe, who in the late 1840s had taught at a college in South Carolina, wrote political articles for a liberal-conservative daily in Stockholm, which, however, did not always back him editorially. An international adventurer and journalist, Hebbe maintained close contacts with national revolutionary movements in Europe. The Swedish monarch, Carl XV, who for years conducted a personal diplomacy, used him as a private emissary in Paris, London, and Copenhagen.

Fredrika Bremer could, like Rosalie Roos-Olivecrona, say that she loved the South, but she always hoped and believed that the North would win the war, if it had to be fought to its bitter end. In early 1864 she wrote to an American friend: "Though every pulse of my being beats for the success of Northern arms and ideas, I do suffer with the South, with its brave men and its much-suffering, self-sacrificing women . . ."

As late as in the fall of 1863 at least one influential journalist, Eva Brag (1829–1913), who was one of the first women in the Swedish press, expressed dissatisfaction with the public support the American Union cause received in Sweden. Swedish opinion had, she thought, been too much influenced by pro-Confederate press comments in other European countries. Her views were first presented in a series of articles for the newspaper she helped edit, *Handelstidningen* of Gothenburg, and a year later these were published in a book entitled *The North American Question*. In the foreword, Peter Wieselgren, the evangelist and temperance pioneer, wrote that since the Civil War actually concerned the existence of slavery in the first place, the whole Swedish people ought to be on the side of the North.

In the fall of 1864 the climate in Sweden had, in fact, already changed, and practically all of the larger newspapers welcomed the approaching Union victory. After the collapse of the Confederacy and the assassination of President Lincoln in April of 1865, the Swedish press devoted more space to American developments than ever before. The liberal organs regarded the outcome of the war and the restoration of the Union as, above all, a triumph for democracy. Those who had been consistent critics of the American republic or of the Union policies in the Civil War did not, on the other hand, reverse their positions, and they had already received new ammunition. Renewed tensions between London and Washington, which claimed indemnity for damage to American shipping inflicted by Confederate raiders built in Britain, and the American ultimatum to the French Emperor concerning Mexico in 1866 made the diplomatic rapprochement between the United States and Russia, the lasting result of which was the American purchase of Alaska in 1867, seem more important than it actually was. For a while, visions of an alliance between democratic America and czarist Russia froze the blood not only of Swedish conservatives but also of many liberal observers.

To the average Swede, the American Civil War must have seemed, above all, far away and confusing, but large groups of people followed the conflict with real interest, and on the whole they were more consistent in their sympathies for the North than the shifting press comments would seem to indicate. An overwhelming majority of the emigrants from Sweden had, after all, settled in the Northern states, and their active participation in the war, based on opposition to slavery and loyalty to the Union, became better and better known in Sweden. Letters from friends and relatives in the American Midwest and East gave many Swedes a growing feeling of direct interest in the fate of the Union, and toward the end of the hostilities hardly anybody was unaware of the fact that a fellow countryman by the name of John Ericsson had made a tangible contribution to its preservation. The tragedy of President Lincoln's death caused general and genuine sorrow in Sweden.

Relations Sweden-U.S.A. friendly throughout war — Rising Swedish emigration

THE governments in Stockholm and Washington maintained friendly relations throughout the Civil War, although there were minor frictions in connection with the "*Trent* affair" and on some other occasions. The appointment of an experienced Swedish diplomat, Count

Edvard Piper (1820–91), as minister to the United States in 1861 was welcomed by the Washington administration, and relations between President Lincoln and the envoy for Sweden and Norway have been described as "most cordial."

Through Count Piper, the President met several of the Swedish officers who came to America to volunteer for service in the Union forces. The Swedish diplomat's personal impressions of the United States were, like those of most of his Scandinavian predecessors in Washington, rather negative in the beginning, but before being transferred in 1864 he came to new conclusions, although he still thought that there was too much skulduggery in American politics. His own political views were conservative.

The European plans for mediation in the Civil War, which also would have meant recognition of the Confederacy, were never supported officially by the Swedish government. When the French Emperor in the fall of 1862 proposed that England, France, and Russia should offer joint mediation and the Congress in Washington passed resolutions stating that the United States would not tolerate the interference of any European powers in the internal affairs of the nation, the Swedish foreign minister wrote to the envoy in Washington that although Sweden would like to see the civil war in a nation, with which she had maintained the friendliest relations, come to an end, "the attitude in the United States regarding European intervention is well known, and, therefore, Sweden would prefer not to take a stand in this question that would be antagonistic to the North."

The Confederacy was never recognized by any European government, but it was able to procure ships and weapons in Europe. Swedish or Norwegian materials were, however, never delivered, and there were never any active Confederate agents in the united Scandinavian kingdoms. At the beginning of the war the Swedish government informed the American minister in Stockholm that it had no intention of permitting activities that were directed against the United States.

The American government showed its appreciation of the attitude of Sweden-Norway several times. In 1863 President Lincoln presented King Carl XV with a pair of cased Colt revolvers of the best American workmanship, which now are on display at the Royal Armory in Stockholm. Swedish officers who came to the United States received special permission to study the progress of naval construction and new ordnance and fortifications.

The emigration from Sweden to the United States fell off sharply in the late 1850s, in part as a result of the American financial panic of 1857, the worst collapse up to that time. In 1861, however, the flow of Swedish emigrants to America grew considerably, and a steady rise followed throughout the Civil War. For the years 1861–65, the number of emigrants bound directly for the United States reached about 12,000, and this was more than twice as many as during the previous five-year period.

One of the new factors behind the increase in emigration was, to begin with, the repeal in 1860 of the remaining Swedish restrictions on travel abroad. Much more important both immediately and especially in the long run was the American Homestead Act of 1862, which promised free land to all aliens who had filed declarations of intent to become U.S. citizens. News of this measure had a magnetic and cumulative impact in Sweden, especially on its large landless farm population, even if the American consul in Stockholm, Benjamin F. Tefft, exaggerated somewhat when he reported to Washington in September, 1863: "I have taken special pains to give publicity to the liberality of our government to emigrants. . . . I consider the Swedes as the best candidates for good citizenship that we have; and I am glad to witness a growing tendency toward emigration. Furnish me with ships, or free passages, and I could take a quarter of the working population of this country to the United States next spring."

While many Swedes must have postponed their emigration because of the Civil War or perhaps even decided to remain at home for good, others wanted to leave in order to get a good start in America while the demand for labor was stimulated by the war, or to join the Union forces. The fact that automatic citizenship would be awarded all immigrants who entered the Union army or navy helped to make enrollment an attractive solution. In November of 1862, when the Emancipation Proclamation had become known in Sweden, the American consul at Gothenburg reported to Washington that he could obtain both trained artillery men and sailors in great numbers, while his colleague in Stockholm wrote that he could supply the Union with up to 1,000 volunteers a month, if he only had the ships to carry them.

The Swedish government finally issued a general warning against emigration in wartime, and in June, 1864, the foreign minister told the American legation in Stockholm that the administration "could not condone solicitation of soldiers by United States consuls in Sweden." The difference between soliciting soldiers and promoting civilian emigration, however, was not sharp. Ordinary emigrants could, of course, become soldiers soon after having reached their destination. It even happened that American recruiting agents crossed the Atlantic on emigrant vessels and, before docking in New York, succeeded in enlisting many of the men on board.

In September of 1864, 25-year-old William Widgery Thomas, Jr. of Maine, who had been one of the 30 young consular agents sent to Europe by President Lincoln to promote emigration to the United States, wrote from Gothenburg that many of the Swedish volunteers in the lost Danish war with Prussia and Austria had returned home much embittered by the defeat and that they were flocking to the American consulates to enlist in the Union armies. "We have forwarded over 30 this week," he continued. "Most of them non-commissioned officers who had served three years in the Swedish artillery before volunteering in the Danish war. Their fare was paid from a purse contributed by 'some good friends in America,' including the consul himself. . . . I am very well aware that as consul I have nothing to do with soldiers but no international law can prevent me from paying a soldier's passage from here to Hamburg out of my own pocket." In 1870 Mr. Thomas founded a Swedish settlement in his home state, Maine, and later he served during three periods as American minister to Sweden and Norway.

During the last years of the Civil War, agents who tried to promote civilian emigration became more and more active in Sweden. The government objected in particular to the efforts of the Reverend Benjamin F. Tefft, former American consul at Stockholm, who had returned from a trip to the United States as an agent for the Foreign Immigration Association of Maine and the Lake Superior Copper Mining Companies, and started advertising for 9,000 miners, lumbermen, and craftsmen. For foreign corporations to come to Sweden and advertise for labor was unfair, the foreign minister said to the American envoy. Tefft chartered a recently renovated passenger vessel, the *Ernst Merck*, which on July 15, 1864, sailed from Stockholm for

Portland, Maine, with 450 men, women, and children on board. About 300 were to go to the Lake Superior copper mines, while the others were under contract with the Foreign Immigration Association of Maine.

The Reverend Benjamin F. Tefft seems actually to have planned to turn over most of the able-bodied men on board to the Maine authorities to help them meet the military quotas during the Civil War, but this scheme was foiled. The passengers went ashore in New York, none of them went to Maine, and only a few seem to have joined the Union army. For a Swedish publication the ship's doctor, Måns Hultin (1830–69), who had planned to emigrate but changed his mind, wrote a series of articles about the voyage and its aftermath, which in 1958 were republished in Sweden in a book. His attitude toward America became rather negative, and he immediately told his readers that they should not expect anything else: "The peculiar people which in a sovereign manner and by God's grace lives and rules in the republic of the United States is a people I did not like, and I may as well say this first as last." The great majority of his immigrants, on the other hand, gradually carved their way in the new country.

The Swedish migration that had been set in motion could not be halted, and in 1864–65 there was a marked quickening of its pace. The largest number of emigrants came from the province of Västergötland, where the textile industry had declined as a result of the American Civil War. In reports to Washington the American minister in Stockholm observed that while the Swedish government frequently expressed its opposition to emigration, it had never placed any obstacle in its way. And its opposition, he said, was "not surprising when we consider the fact that Sweden and Norway cover a larger area of territory than any nation in Europe, except Russia, with the population less than six million."

17

The Swedes in the Civil War

Swedes in the North back Lincoln; most war volunteers from Illinois and Minnesota

MOST of the Swedish immigrants in the American North who were of military age fought for the Union in the Civil War. A relatively large proportion of those who served in the armies earned promotion to the rank of first lieutenant or above. One soldier and four seamen of Swedish birth won the Congressional Medal of Honor, and so did one of the officers who came over from Sweden to join the Union army. Many factors contributed to this overall record.

Events during the last few years before the Civil War had a deep effect on the assimilation of the Swedish immigrants as American patriots and citizens. In the late 1850s more and more of the new-comers in the North began to support the newly formed Republican party, which was against slavery, and in 1858 those in the Middle West took a particularly keen interest in the Lincoln-Douglas debates in Illinois, one of which was held at Galesburg. Three years earlier the first Swedish-language newspaper of any importance in America, known as *Hemlandet*, had been founded there, and through its pages Lincoln was brought close to the settlers from Sweden. Some of their intellectual leaders had also become acquainted with him personally.

In the election campaign of 1860 the Swedes in the Midwest re-garded Lincoln almost as one of their own. Their campaign hymn, which was sung with religious fervor at rallies and parades, contained a reference to King Gustavus Adolphus, who in 1632 fell in what he considered to be a war for freedom of thought and worship, and it ended with an appeal to "vote as one man" for the noble Abraham Lincoln. His victory should, in the opinion of the Swedish immigrants, lead to a gradual but finally complete abolition of slavery, but there were also other serious problems to be tackled. In an editorial on July 4, 1860, *Hemlandet* wrote that a growing feeling of insecurity in America expressed itself in "tyranny, sensationalism, moral decline, ignorance, spread of crime, and fears concerning the safety of life and property." The newspaper had then moved to Chicago, and its circulation was rising.

In the 1860 elections most of the Swedes in the Midwest and the East voted for Lincoln, and in Illinois they were almost solidly for him. In Rockford, for instance, 80 Swedish settlers marched to the polls in a body to cast their ballots for the Rail Splitter. All over the country, the political activities made the immigrants from Sweden feel that they were becoming Americans, and their incorporation in the new nation was further hastened by their participation in the Civil War. In patriotic zeal, quite a few Andersons, Petersons, and Swensons who volunteered for service changed their names to, for instance, Andrews, Peters, and Hawkins.

About 20,000 Swedes, including Swedish-born women and children, lived in the North when the military campaigns began, and during the course of the war at least 3,000 enlisted for service in the Union forces. The largest contingents came from Illinois and Minnesota, where somewhat more than one-half of the Swedish immigrants had settled. Illinois contributed about 1,300 volunteers and Minnesota some 600, not including those who served as home guards. One of the Swedish pioneers in Minnesota, Hans Mattson, issued a flaming appeal via *Hemlandet*, emphasizing that those who had immigrated from Sweden had the same duty as the native-born.

The total number of enlistments in the Union army during the Civil War was about 2,300,000, of which the foreign-born contributed approximately 500,000. The largest contingents of the foreign-born soldiers were the Germans, who numbered over 200,000, and the Irish, nearly 150,000. Among states with Swedish immigrants, it was only Illinois and Minnesota that exceeded their legitimate quotas of volunteers, but newcomers who lived in smaller groups were always less likely to enlist, whatever their national origin. At least one-fourth of the total population of the North was, according to estimates made by modern historians, opposed to the war.

In the only significant Swedish settlement outside the Middle West, Jamestown in the northwest of New York State and nearby Chandlers Valley in Pennsylvania, the proportion of Union volunteers was large. Many Swedes who lived in the coastal cities enlisted in the navy.

The number of Swedish-born officers in the Union army, including those who came over from Sweden to take part in the war and received commissions, was at least 75. In relation to total Swedish enlistments, this was a high figure. According to some historians there were more than 100 Swedish officers in the armies of the North, which seems possible.

Many of the Swedish immigrants in the United States had had military training or even a long period of military service in their native country, and when the Civil War broke out, this suddenly became a valuable asset. "It frequently happens that among the Scandinavians here are several well versed in military tactics from years of constant service in the armies of their country," *The Chicago Tribune* wrote on April 24, 1861. Most of those without military experience could, moreover, quickly be turned into soldiers, for they were robust young farmers or laborers, accustomed to an open-air life, trained in the use of horse and gun, and not unfamiliar with strict discipline.

Swedes who had lived in America only a short time naturally preferred to serve under Swedish commanders, and most of them had a chance to do so. In the largely Swedish units the soldiers sang their own psalms and other songs, had their own musicians, read their own newspapers, and often cooked their own national specialties. There are reports about Swedish companies having begun the march in the morning with songs and kept up the singing all the way, until they were deployed for battle.

In addition to the immigrants who were given or promoted to command posts, Swedish officers came to America to serve the Union or for the purpose of gaining practical experience, as many had done already in the War of Independence. Some of those who took part in the Civil War were at once entrusted with important commands, after having been recommended by President Lincoln, while others preferred to enlist as privates.

The attitude of the Swedish immigrants to the war can hardly be described as enthusiastic, but the volunteers seem to have joined in the firm belief that they were helping to make the United States what it was supposed to be — a land of freedom and equal opportunity for all, regardless of race or creed. Shortly after the attack on Fort Sumter in April, 1861, such sentiments were expressed with eloquent restraint in a letter which a young volunteer, Paul Esbjörn (1837–61), wrote to his father, the Reverend Lars Paul Esbjörn, founder of the Swedish Lutheran Church in the Midwest: "Under circumstances rather strange I write this letter to you. I have come to the conclusion lately to try to do something for my country and for the poor African race. . . . I think this cause is just and a righteous war and should I meet my death on the battlefield I feel I shall die in a glorious cause." A few months later Paul Esbjörn fell in battle at Lexington, Missouri.

In the South, there were Swedes who remained loyal to the Union or at least hesitated to fight against it, but most of the Swedish settlers supported the secession, and younger men who were steeped in the traditions of the South fought with a bravery and a determination matching those of their relatives in the North. The U. S. census of 1860 listed only about 750 Swedes in the states that later seceded, and the number of those who fought in the Confederate forces can hardly have exceeded 50. Most of the Confederate officers of Swedish stock came from the Carolinas and Alabama. Some of the Swedish privates complained, when taken prisoners, that they had been forced by their neighbors to enlist.

Union army units of Swedes or Scandinavians from settlements in the Midwest

SEVERAL immigrant communities in the Middle West furnished predominantly Swedish companies for service in the Union armies during the Civil War, and Scandinavian units were organized both there and in the East.

The first unit to be raised among the Scandinavian element of the population was a New York company which was incorporated in the First New York Volunteers on April 25, 1861, and was called the

Scandinavian Company of New York. A few days before its departure, the Swedes in New York, who were less puritanical than the immigrants in the Midwest, staged an officers' ball, and Swedish women presented the company with a silk American flag. On May 25, a full review of the regiment was held in front of the Astor House, after which the unit embarked for Fortress Monroe.

The most significant Scandinavian contingent was the 15th Wisconsin Regiment, which was composed so largely of immigrants from the North of Europe that it was called the Scandinavian Regiment. In the spring of 1862 it left for the South. The great majority of the 900 men were from Norway, Wisconsin having a larger Norwegian-born population than any other state, but there were quite a few Swedes and also some Danes. One of the captains, Charles Gustafson, was Swedish. Like his Norwegian commander, Colonel Hans Christian Heg, he was killed in the battle of Chickamauga in northwestern Georgia in September, 1863, which became a great Confederate victory. Like all other units engaged there, the Scandinavian Regiment suffered heavy losses. During the war more than one-third of its soldiers were killed on the field or died of wounds.

One of the earliest predominantly Swedish units to get under way was an artillery company which Carl Johan Ståhlbrand or Charles John Stolbrand (1821–94) of Chicago had recruited at De Kalb and Sycamore, Illinois, and which in the fall of 1861 became a battery of the Second Illinois Light Artillery. Some Danes and Norwegians served in this unit. Before the end of the year Stolbrand had been promoted to the rank of major and placed in charge of General John A. Logan's entire artillery force. In May of 1864, when he participated in General Sherman's march through Georgia, he was captured by the Confederates and placed in the ill-famed military prison camp at Andersonville, but in October he was back at his command, having either broken out by himself or been exchanged for two Confederate generals.

During the siege of Savannah in late 1864 Major Stolbrand became disappointed at not being promoted and asked to be relieved of his command. President Lincoln then made him a brigadier general. In the spring of 1865 he was given command of an artillery brigade, but by then the war was over. After a brief period as chief of artillery in the Fort Leavenworth district of Kansas he left active service. General Sherman said about him that "a braver man and a better artillery officer could not be found in the entire army."

In 1866 General Stolbrand settled in South Carolina, where before the war ended he had bought a former slave plantation, and two years later he was an official delegate to the Republican national convention in Chicago, which nominated General Grant. He was also busy designing steam engines and boilers, but suffered a fatal accident during the construction of a submarine. He was buried with full military honors in Columbia, South Carolina, the capitol of which he had once ordered shelled.

No Swedish immigrant made a more notable Civil War career than Stolbrand, who was the son of an unmarried mother near Kristianstad in Skåne. Before his emigration in 1850 he had served the fashionable Vendes Artillery Regiment at Kristianstad for 11 years, the last seven as a sergeant. In 1857 he became the first chairman of the first Swedish secular society in Chicago, and in 1860 he was a highly effective campaign speaker for Abraham Lincoln.

Another veteran of the artillery base at Kristianstad in southern Sweden, Hans Mattson (1832–93), who in 1853 had been one of the founders of the community of Vasa in southeastern Minnesota, became a regimental commander with the rank of colonel, and at times he had command of a whole brigade. When the war began he organized a company of Swedish and some Norwegian volunteers at Red Wing, Minnesota, where he had begun to practice law. In the summer of 1862, when he was home on sick leave, his regiment, the Third Minnesota, was one of the units bluffed into surrendering at Murfreesboro, Tennessee, but early the next year it was reorganized. One of the sergeants of Mattson's original company, John G. Gustafson, finally became lieutenant colonel of the 112th U.S. Colored Regiment.

In 1866 Colonel Mattson was named editor-in-chief of a new Swedish-language newspaper in Chicago, *Svenska Amerikanaren* (The Swedish American), which was published for seven years. The following spring he resigned to work as an immigration promoter for Minnesota, and we shall meet him again in that capacity. In 1869 he was elected secretary of state at St. Paul, Minnesota. His memoirs, which were written in Swedish but also published in an English translation, entitled *The Story of an Emigrant Boy*, give a vivid picture of the life and work of the Swedish pioneers in Minnesota.

Bishop Hill in western Illinois, which Swedish immigrants had founded in 1846 as a religious-communal settlement, was also among the first communities to organize a military unit of its own. Long before the hostilities began, its young men fit for military service were trained by Eric Forsse (1819–89), who, before leaving Sweden with his wife and five children in 1850, had served for 12 years in the infantry regiment at Falun, capital of the province of Dalarna. When their prospects for early action seemed dim, the Bishop Hill soldiers tried to join a special regiment of sharpshooters in St. Louis. They were, at first, accused in Illinois of wholesale desertion, but early in 1862 they participated in the siege of Fort Donelson in western Tennessee. Eric Forsse was still in charge of the company, which belonged to the 57th Regiment of Illinois Infantry Volunteers.

After the battle of Shiloh in Tennessee on April 6–7, 1862, when each side lost about one-fourth of the troops engaged, Forsse was advanced to major, and Eric Johnson, the Swedish-born son of the founder of Bishop Hill, was promoted to succeed him, with the rank of captain. On several subsequent occasions, Forsse commanded the whole regiment and at least twice he had charge of an entire brigade, but being foreign-born and not fluent in English, he was never promoted beyond the rank of major. In the fall of 1864 he resigned his command and returned to Illinois, where he bought a farm near Galva, but five years later he and about 50 other Swedish farmers in the neighborhood moved further west to Kansas. A community founded by them was called Falun in honor of Major Forsse, who became postmaster, justice of the peace, and a member of the Kansas legislature. He was born at Malung in Dalarna and had not settled at Bishop Hill until after the death of Eric Janson in 1850.

Because of illness, Captain Eric Johnson was permanently mustered out of the service in the fall of 1862. After an eventful career in politics and newspaper and book publishing he moved to California, where he died at the age of 81. When he had become ill during the siege of Corinth, Mississippi, the command of the Bishop Hill company was assumed by Per Mattson Wikström or Peter M. Wickstrum (1827–90), who held it throughout the rest of the war. On May 24,

1865, the 57th Illinois, including the Swedish unit, took part in the victory parade at Washington, D.C. Before coming to America in 1850 as a member of the Eric Janson sect, Wickstrum had been a servant in Sweden, and after the war he, too, bought a farm near Galva. He became quite liberal in both his political and religious views, and almost alone of the Swedish-born Civil War veterans he joined the Democratic party. Captain Wickstrum's more practical Swedish neighbors are said to have regarded him as a bit of a dreamer.

Anders Gustaf Verner or Andrew G. Warner (1837–75) of the Bishop Hill company was, like many other Swedish-born soldiers, wounded at Shiloh. In the fall of 1864 he was named captain and placed in charge of a company of the 63rd Colored Regiment, a dangerous post for which he had volunteered. He had never been a member of the Bishop Hill colony, but on his return to Illinois after the war he married the daughter of its founder, Eric Janson. Captain Warner's father, who had brought the family to America in 1850, had been manager of an ancient ironworks in the province of Hälsingland.

Another Bishop Hill officer was Eric Bergland (1844–1918), the son of a leading colonist and a former apprentice in the settlement's printing shop. After the battle of Shiloh he was, at the age of 18, promoted to first lieutenant, and toward the end of the war he was often temporarily in charge of the Bishop Hill company. Then, in the fall of 1864, when the regiment was encamped in Georgia, he suddenly received an appointment to West Point, the first given a native of Sweden. On July 1, 1865, he was formally admitted to the United States Military Academy, and four years later he was graduated at the head of his class. After a few years in the artillery he specialized in military engineering, and at various times he served as an instructor at West Point. His major field assignments included river and harbor improvements in the states of Tennessee, Mississippi, Arkansas, Louisiana, and Texas, and the construction of a number of lighthouses on the Atlantic coast. In 1878 he was married in Washington to a cousin of the wife of Rutherford B. Hayes, at that time President of the United States. Having come to Bishop Hill in 1847 at the age of three, he died in Baltimore at the end of the First World War.

An almost wholly Swedish contingent which was organized in

Galesburg, Illinois, became a company in the 43rd Regiment of Illinois Volunteers, and early in 1862 it was, like the Bishop Hill group, sent south to fight in western Tennessee under General Grant. On Sunday morning, April 6, while encamped near the church at Shiloh, this regiment happened to be one of the few units ready for action when the Confederates launched their surprise attack. The 43rd Illinois held its line for several hours and then retired in good order, but it lost 206 men of the 500 actually engaged. Among the dead was Captain Olof S. Edwall, who had commanded the Galesburg company. His successor was Carl Arosenius, a Swedish-born newspaperman of Galesburg. After Shiloh, the company took part in the siege of Corinth, and then in the Tennessee and Vicksburg campaigns. It was finally sent to Arkansas for clean-up operations, and remained in that state until the end of the war.

"Delay counts everything for us," Carl Sandburg, the most noted American author of Swedish stock, who also was a native of Galesburg, Illinois, quotes General Grant as having remarked while watching a Confederate attempt to take a hill near Pittsburg Landing not far from Shiloh; the hill was guarded by Union gunboats on the river as well as by a First Illinois Artillery battery commanded by Captain Axel Silversparre (1834–1906), who in Sweden had had the title of baron. Born in Strängnäs, he became a lieutenant in the ultra-aristocratic Svea Artillery Regiment in Stockholm; he had later become involved in a night brawl with some civilians in the Swedish capital, and was courtmartialed and dismissed from the service. Early in 1861 he arrived in the United States. By the turn of that year he made a recruiting tour through the Swedish communities in Illinois, and though most of the available young men were already enrolled, he managed to round up a company for the artillery, which under his command was put through intensive training.

After the battle of Shiloh both General Grant and his division commander, General Sherman, congratulated the young Swedish artillery expert, and on other occasions Sherman liked to demonstrate the skill of the Silversparre battery, which remained under his command until the end of the war. In the fall of 1862 Silversparre himself, on the other hand, was ordered to take charge of an artillery park near Memphis, Tennessee, and to train four companies during the coming winter. This assignment he did not like, and while waiting for more exciting duties at the front he was taken prisoner by a band of Confederate guerrillas. After spending nine months in the notorious Libby stockade at Richmond, Virginia, he escaped by bribing a guard, and wearing the latter's uniform he made his way to Wilmington, North Carolina. Via a Confederate blockade runner, on which he worked as engineer, and a British base in Bermuda he came to New York, but by then the war was so nearly over that he never returned to active duty. A syndicate of copper companies in Michigan sent him to Scandinavia to recruit workers for their mines, and early in 1865 he returned with about 150 Swedes, Norwegians, and Finns, many of whom brought their families. In the same year Silversparre became an assistant city engineer in Chicago, and in 1880 he moved to Denver, then a new city.

A company of volunteers which became part of the Sixth Iowa Infantry was organized by Fabian Brydolf of Burlington, Iowa, who had come to the United States as early as 1841 and first settled in Cleveland, Ohio, as a landscape painter. In 1846 he went to Iowa as an interpreter for Peter Cassel and his friends, who also came from Östergötland, and the next year he enlisted for service in the Mexican War, during which he took part in several battles. On April 6, 1862, while leading his company as a captain at Shiloh he lost his right arm. He was then promoted to lieutenant colonel in the 25th Iowa Infantry, where he remained until the end of the war. Brydolf finally returned to his home town in Iowa and continued as a landscape artist, having learned to paint with his left hand.

Among Swedes who at least part of the time served under Stolbrand in the Second Illinois Light Artillery were Frederick Sparrestrom and Andrew Stenbeck (1828–91), who at an early stage were commissioned captains. There were many Swedish-born soldiers in two companies of the 33rd Illinois Regiment. An army sergeant from Sweden by the name of Christian Peterson volunteered for this regiment in 1861 and served for some time as a captain. The Swedish settlers at Jamestown, New York, and Chandlers Valley-Sugar Grove, Pennsylvania, helped recruit several infantry regiments.

Swedish immigrant officers in other units — Several active in postwar relations

SWEDISH-BORN officers and other Civil War volunteers were scattered about in most Midwestern and several Eastern regiments.

The 55th Illinois was led in numerous battles by a professional officer from Sweden, Oscar Malmborg, who, like some other Swedish-born officers of the Union army, was a veteran of the Mexican War. In the 1850s he had divided his life between Sweden and Chicago, where he finally was appointed vice consul for Sweden and Norway. At an early stage of the Civil War the 55th Illinois became known as a model regiment, "the most efficient and most soldierly in the army," according to a letter to the governor of Illinois, and Malmborg received warm commendations from his superiors, including both General Grant and General Sherman. At Vicksburg he was wounded in both eyes, and in 1864, when the intrigues of those who wanted him replaced as commander of the regiment continued, he was assigned to other duties, first as chief engineer of an army corps and then as inspector of posts along the Mississippi. The next year Colonel Malmborg returned to Sweden and settled on the Baltic island of Gotland, where he was born. Gradually his eye injuries made him blind.

An immigrant from Sweden named Ernst Holmstedt, who also had gained experience in the Mexican War and then settled in New York, became a lieutenant colonel of the 41st New York Regiment and finally colonel of the 74th U.S. Colored Infantry. Daniel Anderson entered the war as a member of the First Iowa Cavalry and rose to be its colonel. Adolphus J. Johnson became a captain of the First New Jersey Regiment and later served as colonel of the Eighth New Jersey. Among the captains killed in battle were Axel P. Ekström of the 65th Illinois and Jonas or James Frederick Lembke of the Second U.S. Colored Light Artillery.

Union soldiers with unusual backgrounds included Johan Sandwall (1814–76), who had been an influential liberal journalist in Sweden, first as publisher of a newspaper at Jönköping in northern Småland. There he became so popular among the common people that during street riots after the February Revolution in France in 1848 demonstrators were heard shouting: "We want a republic, and Johan Sandwall as our king!" Later the same year he moved to Gothenburg as publisher of the well-known *Handelstidningen*. In 1851, however, he suddenly left for America after having been accused of embezzlement nine years earlier when he was a bank clerk. He took part with distinction in the Civil War and was promoted to first lieutenant in 1862 after Antietam. When the hostilities ended he became a customs inspector at Norfolk, Virginia, and later he tried his fortune as an immigrant agent in Chicago, where he called himself John A. Fogelberg.

Among the Swedish-born officers in the Union army were also some men who had come to the United States in the 1850s but after the conflict returned to Sweden, where they successfully pursued their careers and contributed much to American-Swedish relations.

Oscar Brundin or Broady, already mentioned as a Baptist pioneer and an influential educator in Sweden for 50 years after the Civil War, enlisted in the Union army immediately after his graduation from Madison University, now known as Colgate, at Hamilton, New York. Before his emigration to America in 1854 he had been an artillery soldier in Sweden and, finally, a noncommissioned officer in the Swedish navy. During the Civil War he entered the 91st New York Regiment with a captain's commission and saw action in 35 engagements, including Gettysburg. In the battle of the Wilderness in early May of 1864 he was transferred to the 61st New York with the rank of lieutenant colonel. At Reams Station in late August, where he was in command of three brigades, he received a wound in his leg. As the war was near its end and he was eager to resume his theological studies, he then submitted his resignation. He was recommended for the rank of brigadier general but declined the honor and retired as a colonel.

Nere A. Elfving (1832–91), the son of a district judge at Växjö in Småland who came to America in 1855 as an engineer with military training, fought with the Union forces throughout the war. Early in 1865 he led a brigade at the capture of Fort Fisher, the formidable Confederate stronghold at the entrance to the port of Wilmington, North Carolina. After having recovered from an amputation, he returned to Sweden in 1866 with the rank of colonel. As an American consul in Stockholm he helped organize Sweden's participation in the Centennial Exposition in Philadelphia in 1876, and as an importer of American machinery he introduced modern harvesters to the Swedish farmers.

Of the six Swedish-born participants in the Civil War who were awarded the Congressional Medal of Honor, the highest American military decoration, one was an army soldier who lived in the United States. His name was Carl Svan or Charles A. Swan, and he received the Medal of Honor in 1865 for bravery in the cavalry raid on Selma, Alabama, on April 2 of the same year. He came from Iowa.

Several immigrants from Sweden were in the medical service of the Union army. A Dr. Finke of Jamestown, New York, joined in the summer of 1861. Dr. G. W. Barck of Galesburg, Illinois, Dr. Charles J. Nordquist of the 83rd New York Regiment, and Dr. John A. Ouchterlony of Louisville, Kentucky, were classified as army surgeons. Dr. J. W. Florine of Andover, Illinois, served as pharmacist and physician.

About 40 officers from Sweden join Union army;
Ernst von Vegesack the best known

THE number of Swedish officers of various ranks who lived or at least were based in Sweden and joined the Northern armies during the Civil War seems to have been about 40. They volunteered either to gain military experience or because of enthusiasm for the Union cause, or both. A few of them may be described as soldiers of fortune, and some must have planned to remain in the United States after the war. The great majority of them became officers in the Union forces, but several did not wait for recommendations from President Lincoln but enlisted as privates, feeling confident that ability and experience would win them promotions. At least six such Swedish officers died in battle, or of wounds, as privates.

"Considering, the size of Sweden and the relative paucity of officers in the Swedish army, the number of officers from that country who secured leave of absence and the number of Swedish volunteers who actually served in the Union army are truly astonishing," Ella Lonn writes in her *Foreigners in the Union Army and Navy*, which was published in 1951. As the foremost of the officers from Sweden she mentions Baron Ernst von Vegesack, citing another American authority according to whom this soldier may be compared with Lafayette of the War of Independence, although the need of the United States for help from abroad was less during the Civil War.

Ernst von Vegesack (1820–1903) arrived in America in 1861 after having resigned his commission as captain in the Swedish regiment based at Falun in the province of Dalarna. He was at once named a captain in the 55th Ohio Volunteers, but this he declined in favor of a post as major on the staff of Major General John E. Wool in

Washington. Early in 1862 he conducted reinforcements to Fort Monroe in Virginia, and in order to take part in General McClellan's peninsular campaign, he then resigned his commission as major and enlisted instead as a private. In the engagement near Hanover Court House in May, 1862, he so distinguished himself that he was once more commissioned a major. He was also appointed a member of the staff of General McClellan himself.

After the battle of Gaines' Mill on June 27, 1862, when his troops covered the retreat of the outnumbered Union forces, Von Vegesack was given command with the full rank of colonel of the 20th New York Volunteers, which was made up chiefly of members of German gymnastic societies. Under its new commander, this unit regained the steadiness it had lost in two recent engagements. In the second battle of Bull Run on August 29–30, 1862, Von Vegesack commanded a brigade. At Antietam on September 17, when more men were killed and wounded than on any other day of the entire Civil War, he at one time carried the banner of his regiment, which helped check the Confederate assault.

Toward the end of 1862 the New York regiment under Von Vegesack took part in the futile Union attack on Fredericksburg, and early in May of 1863 they were in the battle of Chancellorsville, where the Confederates under General Lee won their last great victory. Colonel Von Vegesack was then placed on the staff of the new commander of the Army of the Potomac, General George Gordon Meade, and in that capacity he took part in the battle of Gettysburg. A month later, on August 3, 1863, he resigned his commission and returned to Sweden.

In 1865 Von Vegesack was given the rank of brigadier general by the U.S. government, and in 1893 he received the Congressional Medal of Honor for bravery at Gaines' Mill. He had then risen to the rank of major general in Sweden. For many years he was a member of the Swedish parliament, representing the Baltic island of Gotland, where he was born.

Gustaf Bildstein Helleday (1831–62), who had been a naval officer in Sweden, enlisted as a private in a regiment called the Naval Brigade and gradually reached the rank of lieutenant colonel. He was then appointed commander at Fort Wool on the island of Rip Raps in the Chesapeake Bay area, but died at Fort Monroe in the late summer of

1862. According to obituaries in the press, he was familiar with every species of artillery and was regarded as one of the most accomplished foreign officers in the Union armies.

Fredrick Anton Ulrik Rosencrantz (1825–79), a former captain in a fashionable Stockholm regiment, enlisted in the German Turner Regiment, the 20th New York Volunteers, in 1861 and became a major three years later. He served successively as an adjutant to Generals McClellan, Burnside, Hooker, and Meade. When the war was over he was advanced to lieutenant colonel in the U.S. Army for "gallant and meritorious service during the operations leading to the fall of Richmond." He remained in the United States as an army officer and died at Fort Riley, Kansas. A relative, Palle Rosencrantz (b. 1825), a Swedish cavalry lieutenant who had also been in Danish, French, and British service, was a major in the Fourth New York Cavalry in 1861–63. What then became of him is not known.

Another former Swedish officer, Carl August Rossander (1832–67), who was born at Kalmar in the southeast, enlisted in the Third Rhode Island Artillery early in 1863. Remaining in the United States after the war he became a lieutenant colonel in the Sixth Cavalry in 1867 but died a few months later. The governor and state legislature of Rhode Island honored him with special resolutions. Carl Gustaf von Knorring (b. 1834), who like several other officers had been sent over by the Swedish government to study the new American artillery and fortifications, also served in the Third Rhode Island Artillery, and was finally promoted to lieutenant colonel on the staff of the U.S. commander-in-chief.

Baron Corfitz Ludvig Joakim Staël von Holstein was a young cadet of the Swedish Military Academy when he left for America. He enlisted in the Union army under the name of Charles Holstein and finally became lieutenant colonel of the 52nd Colored Regiment. Baron Jacob Cederström served as a staff officer in 1862–64, beginning with the rank of captain, and so did Adolf Carlsson Warberg (1825–97), who reached the rank of lieutenant colonel.

Elof Oscar Hultman (b. 1837), who had served in the French Foreign Legion in North Africa, became a captain in the 58th New York Regiment in 1862 and a major later the same year. He took part in many battles but then reentered French service in Mexico. Axel Arvid Leatz (1838–1906), who had been a lieutenant in the militia on the Baltic island of Gotland, enlisted in 1863 as a private in the Fifth New York Regiment and was recommended for a captaincy the next year. In the battle of Cold Harbor, Virginia, in early June, 1864, when the Union army in less than one hour lost 6,000 men in killed and wounded, he received a bad wound. After an operation by a Confederate surgeon and gradual recovery, he was carried off to Libby Prison but was soon released in an exchange of prisoners and rejoined his regiment in early 1865, reaching the rank of lieutenant colonel. Carl Rudolph Constantin Weinberg, who had been a lieutenant in the infantry regiment in the province of Hälsingland and like Leatz had enlisted as a private in the Fifth New York, was killed at Cold Harbor.

Herman Isaac Stårck (1839–63), who had been graduated from the Swedish Military Academy in 1861 and become an officer in the Union army, died of wounds received at the siege of Port Hudson on the Mississippi in May, 1863. Pehr Gustaf Bergquist, a lieutenant on leave from a Värmland regiment who had enlisted as a private, also died of wounds. Five other Swedish officers, Adam Hoffkill, Anders August Lindström, Edward Ljunggren, Nils Rosenstjerna, and C. N. Uggla, who also had joined the army as privates, were reported killed or missing. A Swedish volunteer by the name of John C. Ackerström, of the 15th Kentucky Cavalry, fell at Fort Pillow in Tennessee in April, 1864, when a large part of the garrison was killed during a Confederate assault.

Oscar Engelblom, a sergeant in Gothenburg's artillery regiment, seems to have won a reputation for unusual bravery. He served in the Army of the Potomac as an artillery officer, resigned after frictions between two of his superiors, enlisted again as a private, and was finally, when he had become a captain, recommended for the rank of major. A sergeant Grunfelt of the Svea Artillery Regiment in Stockholm, who in America used the name of Roche, became a captain of the 12th New York Cavalry.

Måns Olsson Lindbergh, who had volunteered for British army service in the Crimean War in 1855 and then become a noncommissioned officer in Sweden's southernmost infantry regiment in the province of Skåne, enlisted in the 82nd Illinois Regiment in 1862. After having participated in numerous battles, including Chancellorsville, Gettysburg, Chattanooga, and Lookout Mountain, he was cited by President Lincoln as a brevet captain in the U.S. Army. He is known to have planned to leave for his native country in connection with the Danish-German war of 1864 but did not return home until two years later. He then rejoined his regiment and started planning to lead a group of 1,000 Swedish emigrants to Minnesota, where his father, Ola Månsson Lindbergh, had settled in 1860 with his second wife and an infant son, Charles A. Lindbergh, who became the father of the aviator.

Cadets who left the Swedish Military Academy to take part in the Civil War included Hjalmar Andersson (1843–1916), who in 1863–64 fought with the 48th New York Infantry in South Carolina, Florida, and Virginia. In the battle of Olustee in Florida on February 20, 1864, when one-third of the troops engaged were lost, 21-year-old Andersson had charge of a company. Toward the end of the same year, when he had been promoted to lieutenant, a leg injury forced him to return to Sweden, where he first became an army officer and later a gymnastic instructor as well as the fire chief in the southern port city of Helsingborg. All Civil War veterans in Sweden had, at least in the eyes of the younger generations, an aura of breath-taking adventure, but Hjalmar Andersson became uncommonly popular. His son Harald Hjalmarson (1868–1919), who was a Swedish army officer, organized the military police in Persia and was named a general of its army, and later he became a major general in Finland, where toward the end of the First World War he fought in the national army against the so-called Red Guards. His son Jarl Hjalmarson (b. 1904) became the leader of the Conservative party in Sweden and later one of the country's most successful mediators in labor disputes.

Among the Swedes who came to America to fight for the North were also two young brothers, Herman and Frederic Banforth, who had left Sweden against the wishes of their parents and joined the 56th Massachusetts as privates. A young man by the name of John August Carlstein, who described himself as a student at Skara in the province of Västergötland, was wounded and then discharged.

Most of the officers and other volunteers who came over from Sweden to fight for the Union were members of well-known or well-to-do Swedish families. Among those not mentioned above were John Asker of the 48th New York Volunteers, Carl Ludvig Theodor Berlin of the Ninth New York Cavalry, Carl Olof Oscar Blomberg who rose to major in the First New York Regiment, Carl Fredrik Grevillius who became a lieutenant in the Second New York Volunteers, Axel Henry Grundström, a member of the Swedish legation in Washington who enlisted as a private and almost immediately was promoted to lieutenant, fought in numerous battles, was wounded twice and returned to Sweden after Chancellorsville where he was taken prisoner, Charles Nicolaus Conrad Hamberg, a topographical officer who eventually was named captain, and Otto L. Torslow, who served in the First Rhode Island Light Artillery as a lieutenant.

Comprehensive eyewitness reports from the Civil War are found in a book consisting of letters to relatives and friends in Sweden from Major and finally Lieutenant Colonel Adolf Carlsson Warberg, which was published in Stockholm in two volumes in 1867 and 1871. Warberg, who served as a topographical officer most of the time, was immediately roused by the spirit of freedom and devotion to civic principles in the United States, which, on the other hand, also seemed to him a country of extremes in almost all respects.

Especially in the beginning, Warberg was greatly impressed by the brilliant leadership of the Confederate generals and by the calm courage which their soldiers displayed under fire. The men of the North could, in his opinion, have been just as good soldiers — the material as a whole was, in fact, much better than the military experts in Europe believed — but most of the officers, from the division commander down to the young lieutenant, were during the first years of the war unequal to their tasks. This situation, according to Warberg, was made worse by the constant interference of political careerists and groups, not only in the army organization and the campaign plans but also in promotions and appointments.

Warberg's reaction to the summary execution of deserters from units of the Army of the Potomac that he witnessed in 1862–63 was particularly painful. "I shall never be able to suppress the feeling of abhorrence, the bitter indignation at my own debasement as a human being, which I experienced at the sight of these ghastly spectacles." He believed in the cause for which the forces of the North were fighting but always retained his soldierly respect for the Confederate troops. In the summer of 1864 he described these as "gray-clad like our stockade prisoners, with a plumaged, slouching felt hat pressed down over the forehead, tattered, starving and bronzed like Indians, their bushy hair and wild beards fluttering in the wind around weather-beaten and hardened features."

Warberg's letters to Sweden also contained long and detailed descriptions of the organization in Washington and the war operations. The task of feeding and supplying large armies was, he observed, more difficult than in the cultivated and densely populated plains of Europe, and the lack of good maps, except in the case of Virginia, was also a serious handicap. Several times he voiced a certain pride in the performance of his Swedish brother officers, most of whom were more directly involved in the fighting than Warberg himself, who, however, several times tried in vain to be sent back to the front. In the winter of 1864 he was able to relax at St. Augustine in Florida, "in the bosom of a wonderfully beautiful nature, in a charming climate and among a bleeding people, which has raised so many heroes, and whose women, warm as the country's sun, are as patriotic as its men." Warberg returned to Sweden in 1865 and rejoined his regiment at Borås, the textile center in the province of Västergötland, where the sympathies for the American South probably were stronger than in any other Swedish city. His participation in the war had, in part, been financed by the Swedish government.

The careers of two Civil War veterans: Hjalmar Edgren and John A. Ockerson

FOR at least one of the Swedish officers, participation in the Civil War marked the beginning of a new life which was divided between the United States and Sweden. Hjalmar Edgren (1840–1903), who was the son of a prosperous estate owner in the province of Värmland and a newly graduated army officer, arrived in 1861 to enlist in the Union cause in Virginia. He took part in many engagements, but in 1863 his older brother John Alexis, who served in the Union navy, found him so seriously ill at Yorktown that he advised him to resign.

From 1864 to 1870 Hjalmar Edgren continued his military career in Sweden but also studied in Germany and France. He then returned to America, and after studies at Cornell and Yale he served as an instructor at the latter university, teaching Sanskrit, his foremost specialty, and Romance languages. In 1877 he represented Yale at the 400th-anniversary observance of the founding of Uppsala University in Sweden. In 1880 he moved from Yale to the University of Lund in southern Sweden as an assistant professor, and five years later he accepted a call to a professorship in modern languages and Sanskrit at the newly established University of Nebraska at Lincoln.

The homesickness of his Danish-born wife contributed greatly to Edgren's decision to accept an offer from the University of Gothenburg, where in 1891–93 he was professor as well as the first president. From 1893 to 1901, however, he served again at the University of Nebraska. In 1901, finally, he returned to Sweden as a member of the Nobel Institute of the Swedish Academy in Stockholm.

Edgren was regarded as one of the foremost philologists of his time, and some of his many dictionaries and grammars were for several decades standard works in America. For readers in Sweden he interpreted American institutions and literature, including the poetry of Longfellow, Poe, and Whittier, and prose works by Emerson, Hawthorne, Holmes, and Irving. He also published three volumes of his own poetry. He was buried near his beloved childhood home in Värmland. "His dual loyalty enriched not only his life but that of both Sweden and the United States," writes one of his biographers, Emory Lindquist, president of Bethany College at Lindsborg, Kansas, from 1941 to 1953.

In the spring of 1864 a 16-year-old boy named Johan August Åkesson or John Augustus Ockerson (1848–1924) enlisted in the 132nd Illinois Infantry, giving his age as 18. He was mustered out in late fall but early in 1865 he volunteered again, this time in the First Minnesota Heavy Artillery. His units served mostly in Kentucky and Tennessee.

At the age of three he had come to America with his family from Slättaröd in the province of Skåne, where the Åkessons had been well-to-do farmers. Both his parents as well as his oldest brother died of cholera before they reached their goal, Galesburg, Illinois, the five surviving children were scattered, and John was brought up by guardians. After the Civil War he earned his living in various occupations and continued his studies, and after having won an engineering degree at the University of Illinois in 1873, he gradually became a specialist on the flood-control and navigation problems posed by the Great Lakes and, in particular, the Mississippi.

When the Mississippi River Commission had been established in

1879 by act of Congress, Ockerson was appointed its principal assistant engineer in charge of surveys and physical examinations from the source of the river to the Gulf of Mexico. In 1898 he became a member of the commission, and his technical experience and knowledge made him its dominant figure. He was also recognized internationally as a leading authority on river and harbor improvement, navigation, and related problems, and developed a large practice at home and abroad. One of his greatest individual achievements was the construction of levees to control the flood waters of the Colorado River.

John Augustus Ockerson has been described as an outstanding personality. In the early 1900s he was the United States delegate to international congresses on navigation at Paris, Milan, St. Petersburg, the capital of Russia, and Philadelphia. In 1904 he was one of the leading officials of the Louisiana Purchase Exposition at St. Louis, and he also served as resident commissioner for the Swedish building which finally was taken down and sent to Bethany College at Lindsborg, Kansas, as a gift of William W. Thomas, the American envoy in Stockholm. In 1905 Ockerson and his American-born wife visited Sweden, where they were received at the Stockholm Palace by Crown Prince Gustav and at Marstrand on the West Coast by his father, King Oscar II. They also went to John Ockerson's birthplace in the south. In 1912–13 he served as president of the American Society of Civil Engineers.

Hundreds of Swedes on Union ships — Medal of Honor to four Swedish-born seamen

THE number of Swedes who served on American ships during the Civil War, and in the first place on those of the North, must have been considerable. The demand for trained and experienced seamen was always greatly in excess of the supply. On many Union ships the foreign-born made up about one-half of the complement, and Sweden and the other Scandinavian nations were, as a rule, well represented.

At least 250 immigrants from Sweden who lived in coastal cities and towns served in the Union navy. Other young men came over from Sweden to enlist in the naval forces, and a third category consisted of seamen who had been employed in the American merchant marine and either remained there or transferred to men-of-war. By the middle of the 19th century, as in the 1700s, Swedish sailors were often tempted to desert their native ships and enlist in the American merchant marine, which paid higher wages and offered better working conditions. In the period 1850–64 the number of deserters from Swedish vessels in American waters was about 900, of whom only 26 seem to have been captured and returned.

The Medal of Honor was authorized by Congress in the early 1860s, and on April 3, 1863, it was awarded to sailors and marines for the first time. One of the recipients on that day was a Swedish-born seaman named Alfred Peterson (b. 1838) from the state of New York, who had shown outstanding courage and skill on board the U.S.S. *Commodore Perry* in an attack upon Franklin, Virginia, in the fall of 1862. Before the end of the Civil War, three other seamen of Swedish birth who served in the Union navy received the same decoration. They were Charles A. Read (b. 1837) from Ohio, Olof Smith (b. 1833) from New York, and John Swanson (b. 1842) from Massachusetts. Read, who originally must have had another family name, received his award for gallantry aboard the U.S.S. *Kearsarge* when, in a famous battle outside Cherbourg in France on June 19, 1864, she destroyed the Confederate raider *Alabama*, which had captured and burned 55 Union merchantmen.

The number of Swedish-born officers in the Union navy seems to have been about 25. Alfred Boivie (b. 1833), a native of Stockholm, served as a first lieutenant under Admiral David Farragut and was promoted to the rank of commander.

Johan or John Alexis Edgren, whose brother Hjalmar joined the Union army, had been at sea for ten years and had become an officer in the Swedish merchant marine when he enlisted in the Union navy in 1862, with the rank of ensign. Later on he seems to have been in command of one small warship after another, with the title of sailing master, and finally he had charge of a shore battery in the battles for Savannah and Charleston which ended General Sherman's campaign. He was then offered a promotion if he would continue in the navy, but when the war was over he became instead, as already related, one of the first intellectual leaders of the Swedish Baptists, both in Sweden and in the United States. After his retirement to California he helped found, near Paso Robles, which is halfway between San Francisco and

Los Angeles, a little Swedish settlement which was named Linné after the 18th-century naturalist.

By a strange coincidence, Alexis Edgren was an eyewitness both to the Confederate attack on Fort Sumter on April 12, 1861, when he was a mate on a Swedish brig, and to the re-raising of the American flag over Fort Sumter on April 15, 1865. His brother Hjalmar, on the other hand, on March 9, 1862, saw the historic battle in Hampton Roads between the Confederate ironclad *Virginia* and the U.S.S. *Monitor*, which had been designed by another native of the Swedish province of Värmland, John Ericsson.

Among the thousands of people who observed the naval battle in Hampton Roads was also one of the most competent Swedish officers in the Union army, Ernst von Vegesack, who sent a professional account of what he had seen to Stockholm. He was quite familiar with the activities and inventions of John Ericsson, and he knew also that the artillery on his strange little ship, the *Monitor*, consisted of two Dahlgren 11-inch guns, designed by a native American, John A. Dahlgren, whose father had immigrated from Sweden. Ericsson's and Dahlgren's contributions to the Union during the Civil War seem to have been by far the most significant of those made by people of Swedish stock.

Admiral Dahlgren father of modern ordnance — His brother a Confederate general

MOST of the native Americans of Swedish descent who were actively engaged in the Civil War will never be identified as being in part of Swedish origin, but quite a few are known. Members of the first American-born generation were easily recognized if they retained their Swedish family names, and one of these, Admiral John A. Dahlgren (1809–70), won lasting fame. His father, Bernard Ulrik Dahlgren, who belonged to a Swedish family of scientists and physicians, came to America in 1806 and settled in Philadelphia, where a few years later he was appointed consul for Sweden and Norway.

An inventor as well as a naval officer, John A. Dahlgren introduced the rifling of guns, and he also designed the first heavy artillery and the first accurate gun sights. He is, therefore, regarded as one of the fathers of modern ordnance and gunnery. Most of the Civil War ships, including the *Virginia* (the former U.S.S. *Merrimac*) and other Confederate units, were equipped with Dahlgren guns, but Dahlgren's own activities after the beginning of the hostilities served, of course, only the Union. In land battles, too, his guns often played a decisive part. It has been said about Dahlgren that during the decade preceding the hostilities he laid foundations for Union victory in the Civil War.

In the summer of 1862, after many years as officer and finally commander of the Washington Navy Yard, Dahlgren became chief of the Bureau of Ordnance. One year later he left Washington to assume the command of the blockading South Atlantic fleet, and in the fall of 1864 he helped General Sherman take Savannah by shelling it from the sea. After the war he commanded the South Pacific fleet but then became again Chief of Ordnance and finally, at his own request, head of the Washington Navy Yard where he had designed most of his guns.

Dahlgren was a favorite of President Lincoln, who often turned to him for advice or comments and treated him like a personal friend. The two were born in the same year, and there seems to have been a genuine sympathy and deep understanding between them. A great patriot, Dahlgren was proud of what he was able to do for his country and the Union, but those who knew him well could not fail to see the gentle, sensitive person behind his soldierly, rather austere bearing, or miss the undertone of sadness in his attitude toward his military duties. "War is a curse, and its means of operation can hardly be blessed," he wrote in 1858 while on a warship in the West Indies where his guns were being fired for target practice. "How busy is death — oh, how busy indeed," he wrote some years later during the Civil War. And he reacted, therefore, with unusual force against inefficiency and blunders that prolonged the struggle. When the Union army had suffered one of its bloodiest defeats at Fredericksburg in December, 1862, he exclaimed in his diary: "How terrible to think of so many thousands losing life or limb on such stupid plans! . . . It is an army of postmasters or other civil placemen with arms in their hands. The nation only wants one man — a General!"

John A. Dahlgren's father had died when John was 14 years old. The boy was then encouraged in his studies by Dr. Nicholas Collin, who was one of the last clergymen sent over from Sweden to the old Swedish settlements in the Delaware Valley, and who lived there for

61 years, until his death in 1831. Early in 1839 John Dahlgren married the daughter of a Philadelphia merchant, Mary Bunker. The first few years, when he seemed threatened by gradual loss of vision, they lived on a farm in southeastern Pennsylvania, that is, on territory that had once been Swedish, and in 1843 they moved to Wilmington, Delaware, which had been founded by the Swedes in 1638. On April 1, 1844, when Lieutenant Dahlgren during a cruise in European waters visited a Swedish sloop-of-war in Toulon harbor in France, he confided in his diary: "As I stood on the deck and gazed on the Northern race around me, fair as women, stalwart seamen as they were, it was not forgotten that these were the countrymen of my good father. Amid all the thoughts that crossed his mind, could he ever have imagined that his son would some day stand in the relation of a foreign officer to Swedish men? I asked an officer who stood near me if he had ever met with any of my name. His eyes glistened and his face lit up at the very mention. 'Oh, yes,' said he, 'it is a real Swedish name.'"

In 1961, the centennial year of the Civil War, the U.S. Navy and the Swedish Colonial Society erected a monolith of Swedish red granite on Admiral Dahlgren's grave in Laurel Hill Cemetery in Philadelphia. Widely known memorials to him include the Dahlgren Hall at the U.S. Naval Academy in Annapolis, where the cadets until 1970 held their annual graduation exercises, and the Dahlgren village in Virginia, site of the Naval Weapons Laboratory and the Naval Weapons Factory. Illinois and Minnesota also have communities named Dahlgren, and Alaska has a Dahlgren Peak. Three ships in the U.S. Navy, including a guided-missile frigate, have been named for Admiral Dahlgren.

Admiral Dahlgren's son Ulric (1842–64) became one of the war heroes of the North. Early in 1862 he gave up the study of law at Philadelphia to enlist in the army as a private, and before the end of the year he was commissioned as a captain. In an engagement preceding the battle of Gettysburg in the summer of 1863 he received a bullet through a foot, which required amputation of part of the leg, and at the age of only 21 he retired with the rank of colonel. Early next year, however, he volunteered to lead a desperate cavalry raid to liberate as many as possible of the 22,000 Union soldiers in the Libby Prison and other camps in the Richmond area. "If successful," he wrote to his father before the operation, "it will be the grandest thing on record; and if it fails, many of us will go up."

Caught in a night ambush on March 2, 1864, he and about 20 of his men were shot down and killed, while nearly 100 were captured. After the war, Colonel Dahlgren's remains were recovered and given a public funeral in Washington, which was attended by President Andrew Johnson and the members of the cabinet. Admiral Dahlgren, who had lost his first wife ten years earlier, had then just married Mrs. Madeleine Vinton Goddard, with whom he had three children. Twelve years after his death, or in 1882, she published his diaries with notes of her own. Becoming interested in her husband's Swedish background, she traced his ancestry back to 1593, when the family name was Ericsson.

Admiral Dahlgren's oldest son, Charles Bunker Dahlgren (b. 1839), was an officer in the Union navy. When a Federal warship, the *San Jacinto*, on November 7, 1861, stopped the British naval vessel *Trent* at sea to remove the two Confederate commissioners, and thereby caused an international incident which at first seemed to drive Great Britain into war with the United States, Charles B. Dahlgren was the second officer under Captain Charles Wilkes. His son Ulric, named after the war hero, became professor of biology at Princeton.

Another prominent naval officer of Swedish descent was Charles Gideon Dale (1831–91), who took part in many engagements and actions, including the capture of the Fort Hatteras inlet in August, 1861, and the final assault on Wilmington, North Carolina, in February, 1865. By training a naval engineer, Dale in early 1862 served at the yard at Greenpoint in Brooklyn where John Ericsson's *Monitor* was being created. His father, born in the parsonage at Lysekil north of Gothenburg, had been a naval officer in Sweden and arrived in New York in the 1820s, changing his name from Otterdahl to Dale.

For the Dahlgrens, as for many other American families, the Civil War was a fratricidal war in the fullest sense. John A. Dahlgren, the future admiral, had named his oldest son after his brother, Charles G. Dahlgren (d. 1888), who as a young man was sent to Natchez, Mississippi, as a cashier for the Bank of the United States. When the bank was dissolved he decided to stay in the South, and he bought a plantation, acquired slaves, and became rich. As late as 1859, his nephew

Ulric spent a summer with him on the plantation. In 1861, when the hostilities began, he raised a regiment, the Third Mississippi, of which he became the colonel. In the summer of 1863 he was wounded at the siege of Vicksburg, in which many Swedes took part on the Union side, but he was soon back in service and carried on throughout the war, finally reaching the rank of major general. Ruined by the war and in poor health, he finally moved to Brooklyn, where he died.

A few other Americans of Swedish ancestry achieved prominence in the Confederate army. Brigadier General Roger W. Hanson, known familiarly as "Old Flintlock," who was mortally wounded in the battle of Murfreesboro, Tennessee, early in 1863, was a descendant of the Swedish Hanson family of the colonial era. In the battle of Shiloh in April, 1862, where Union units from Scandinavian settlements in the Midwest suffered heavy losses, the Confederate artillery was under the command of Major J. H. Hallonquist, a graduate of West Point, who was born of Swedish parents in South Carolina. In the summer of 1862 he was promoted to lieutenant colonel, and somewhat later he was made chief of artillery of the Confederate Army of Tennessee.

The foremost soldier of Swedish birth in the Confederate forces was probably August or Augustus Forsberg, who was born in Stockholm in 1831. After graduation from the Institute of Technology and brief service as lieutenant in the engineering corps of the Swedish army, he came to Columbia, South Carolina, in 1855 to assist Hjalmar Hammarsköld in the building of the State House. When a civil war seemed about to begin he is said to have had a fine position somewhere in the North, but he then set out for the South in a fishing vessel and reached Charleston during the bombardment of Fort Sumter on April 12, 1861. To begin with he served as a topographical engineer in the Charleston harbor defense work, but in early summer he was given a regular commission as a lieutenant in the field forces.

During the Civil War, Forsberg took part in some 90 battles and skirmishes and was wounded three times. After an engagement in northern Virginia in 1862, his brigade commander wrote that he "rendered very efficient service in rallying his men and throughout the day distinguished himself for gallantry and acts of daring." Soon after that, the young Swede was promoted to colonel of the 51st Virginia. Under his leadership, a brigade composed of four Virginia regiments became a highly respected unit, earning the popular title of "Forsberg's Brigade." In one of the many engagements at Winchester, Virginia, probably in 1864, Colonel Forsberg was severely wounded, but he seems to have been back in active service in 1865. When General Lee surrendered at Appomattox, he is said to have been made a prisoner of war, but at the special request of the Swedish envoy in Washington, who probably knew his family in Sweden, he was soon released. After the war he served Lynchburg, Virginia, as a city engineer for 21 years. His wife, whose maiden name was Morgan, he had met while he was in the hospital.

Carl Jacob Hammarsköld (1833–84), who in the early 1850s joined his immigrant father in South Carolina and began earning his living as an ironworker, had had military training in Sweden, and according to letters to relatives there he joined the Confederate army with enthusiasm. In the summer of 1862, when he said he had been in command of four regiments with the rank of colonel, he resigned because of an eye disease, and the next year he returned to Sweden. There he began a new career as an accountant for the State Railways, ending as a district traffic manager.

A company of the 52nd North Carolina Regiment had a Swedish-born captain, Eric Erson, who rose to the rank of lieutenant colonel. Carl Ludwig Lybecker (b. 1826), who had served as Swedish consul at New Orleans, is said to have joined the Confederate army in 1862, first serving as captain of the Flying Artillery Corps of the Fourth Division and attaining the rank of lieutenant colonel in late 1863. He retired when the war was over and returned to Sweden five years later.

Swedes also served on Confederate warships and commerce destroyers, which at one time drove the Federal merchant marine from the oceans. After having been captured, several Swedish sailors, who had never been settled in the South, or at least not in the Confederate heartland, appealed to the Swedish legation in Washington on the ground that they had not known their ships were engaged in illegal traffic.

18

The John Ericsson Story

Monitor *versus* Merrimac *on March* 9, 1862 — *First battle between ironclads*

ON MARCH 8, 1862, an absurdly unequal battle was fought in Hampton Roads, the channel through which the James, Nansemond, and Elizabeth rivers flow into Chesapeake Bay. It was a Saturday, there was practically no wind, and in the early afternoon the guns began to boom. Against the Confederate ironclad *Virginia*, which has become generally known in history by her original name, *Merrimac*, the wooden fleet of the Union navy proved helpless.

Two Federal ships were destroyed by the *Merrimac*, and three vessels which attempted to come to their assistance ran aground. Two of these, the steam frigates *Minnesota* and *Roanoke*, ranked among the most powerful men-of-war in existence, displacing 3,200 tons and mounting 44 heavy guns. They were, in fact, sister ships of the old *Merrimac*, which had been burned and scuttled by the Union forces when they abandoned Norfolk in the spring of 1861, and then was raised by the Confederates and sheathed in iron. The falling tide finally saved the stranded ships, but the Confederate ironclad was expected to return the next day and, to begin with, attack the *Minnesota* which was in the worst position. Federal shore batteries had also been hammering the *Merrimac*, but her armor remained intact. Two of her ten guns had, however, been put out of action, and her wounded commander, Captain Franklin Buchanan, who in 1845 had become the first superintendent of the U.S. Naval Academy at Annapolis, had been replaced by his executive officer, Lieutenant Catesby Jones.

At an emergency cabinet meeting in the White House on Sunday morning, Secretary of War Edwin H. Stanton appraised the situation as follows: "The *Merrimac* will change the entire character of the war; she will destroy, seriatim, every naval vessel. She will lay all the cities on the seaboard under contribution. . . . I have no doubt that the monster is this minute on her way to Washington and not unlikely we shall have a cannon ball from one of her guns in the White House before we leave this room." Many people in the North feared that the *Merrimac* would roll up the whole Union blockade of the Southern coasts.

President Lincoln did not share the extreme pessimism expressed by his secretary of war, but he was visibly shaken by the fragmentary reports from Hampton Roads. Anxious to consult Commander John A. Dahlgren as soon as possible, he drove off to the Navy Yard, and there he told the ordnance expert that he had "frightful news." They then joined the conference at the White House, where the secretary of the navy, Gideon Welles, had recovered from the first shock and voiced a staunch optimism: John Ericsson's *Monitor* was already in Hampton Roads and should prove more than a match for the *Merrimac*.

In reality, the *Merrimac* did not directly threaten either the capital and the cities farther north on the Atlantic seaboard, or the Federal blockade of the Confederate ports. She was too heavy to be able to steam from the Chesapeake into the Potomac, and she was not sufficiently seaworthy to venture beyond the Virginia capes. But with the same operational conditions as the Confederate ironclad had had on Saturday, March 8, she would have proceeded to destroy every Federal warship in the lower Chesapeake, and that would have been bad enough. General McClellan's campaign plans on the Yorktown peninsula in Virginia would have collapsed, and the European powers would at least have come even closer to recognizing the Confederacy as a belligerent country, with the same rights to trade with other nations as the North. Major Ernst von Vegesack, who happened to be on a mission conducting troops to Newport News, wrote in his report to Stockholm: "We held everything to be lost and thought Sunday would bring about not only the destruction of the remaining man-of-war [that is, the *Minnesota*], but also drive us from Newport News and maybe Fort Monroe."

When President Lincoln came to see his friend John A. Dahlgren on Sunday, March 9, the historic first battle between ironclads had, in fact, already begun. After hasty repairs, the *Merrimac* returned to Hampton Roads early in the morning to finish off the *Minnesota*, but suddenly she was attacked at close range by the tiny, low-floating *Monitor*, which had arrived the night before. The Federal ship did not seem able to injure seriously her much larger adversary, but the un-wieldy Confederate ironclad was outmaneuvered and halted, and the outcome of their three-hour battle was generally regarded as a tech-nical victory for the *Monitor*. Around noon, the *Merrimac* limped back to her base, and the *Monitor*, whose principal assignment had been to save the *Minnesota* from destruction, made no attempt to pursue.

During the battle, the garrison at Fort Monroe stood on the ram-parts, their eyes trained on the eastern horizon. Farther north, in the middle of the sound, the Federals had built an island fort known as Rip Raps, which was under the command of an artillery expert from Sweden, Lieutenant Colonel Gustaf Bildstein Helleday. The shores were lined with thousands of awe-struck civilians, including many New Yorkers who had seen the *Monitor* towed out of their harbor a few days earlier and then had taken the train to Virginia to watch the contest. The Union vessel looked to some reporters "like a hat set on a shingle," while others thought they saw a cheesebox on a raft. The massive and sinister-looking *Merrimac*, on the other hand, reminded spectators of a drifting barn, submerged to the eaves — in those days a rather common sight during the spring floods. Few of the onlookers could have realized that these two ships would, as Major Von Vege-sack wrote to Stockholm, "give occasion to a total subversion of the navies of all nations." One of them, John Ericsson's *Monitor*, would eventually be regarded as a precursor of the most sophisticated battle-ships.

The *Monitor*'s skipper, Lieutenant John L. Worden, a native-born American of Swedish ancestry, was temporarily blinded during the battle and was replaced by his 22-year-old executive officer, S. Dana Greene. While still in the hospital Worden was promoted to command-er, and he finally reached the rank of rear admiral. His family name was derived from the Swedish word värdig, which means worthy. Two petty officers and at least four members of the *Monitor*'s crew were also of Swedish descent. A seaman of Norwegian birth, Peter Williams from Pennsylvania, who had served as quartermaster during the engagement, in 1863 received the Medal of Honor.

The outcome of the battle brought Captain John Ericsson fame on both sides of the Atlantic. Congress passed a resolution praising the inventor for his enterprise, skill, energy and foresight, and thanking him for the great service he had rendered the country. The highly emotional reaction among the people of the North has been described as "Monitor mania." Popular sheet music inspired by the battle included an "Ericsson Gallop," a "Monitor Polka," a "Monitor Grand March," and a song with the theme, "O give us a navy of iron. . . . and Columbia shall rule the seas."

The *Merrimac* remained in dry dock at Norfolk until April 4, but then she again began to threaten Federal shipping in Hampton Roads. She was kept in check by the *Monitor*, which had become too valuable to be risked again in an open fight. At that time, she was, in fact, the only vessel the Union could not afford to lose. On the other hand, the *Merrimac*'s very existence hampered McClellan's campaign on the Virginia peninsula. On May 6 President Lincoln came to Fort Monroe to discuss this problem, the next day he visited the *Monitor* in Hampton Roads, and a few days later Norfolk was captured by Union forces. Since the *Merrimac* could not be sent out into the ocean and, on the other hand, drew too much water to go up the James River to Richmond, she was destroyed by her own crew. In the following bombardment of the batteries lining the banks of the James, the *Monitor* was hit three times but maintained her reputation for invincibility. At the end of the same year she foundered off Cape Hatteras, but new and better ships of the same type had by then been built. The wreck of the *Monitor* has been found lying in 220 feet of water. In 1975, on the 113th anniversary of the *Monitor*'s launching, the site of the wreck was designated as the first "Unique Marine Sanctuary."

The Confederate officer in command of the *Merrimac* on March 9, Lieutenant Catesby Jones, is reported to have said immediately after the fight that if he had had the *Monitor* instead, he would have sunk the *Merrimac* in 20 minutes. He became known as one of John Ericsson's most enthusiastic admirers. At a meeting of the New York

Chamber of Commerce on March 12, in his only public address on record, Captain Ericsson himself remarked that the *Monitor* would have destroyed the *Merrimac* if it had not been for the fact that her guns were firing too high. The *Monitor's* officers had orders to restrict the powder charges, but a single shot below the *Merrimac's* water line would have been fatal.

If the *Monitor* was inefficiently handled during the battle, the blame for this should be laid to the haste and improvisation under which the ship was produced and turned into a fighting unit, rather than to its officers and men, most of whom were, in fact, inexperienced. Without extraordinary human efforts as well as a large measure of good luck, the *Monitor* would hardly have been able to intervene at all in Hampton Roads on March 9, when she was desperately needed.

U.S.S. Princeton *of* 1844, *first naval propeller, one of the steps toward the* Monitor

JOHN ERICSSON, who called his *Monitor* a "floating battery," seems to have been led into designing this type of warship by a deep concern with the defense problems of his native Sweden, which in his opinion could be defended against Russia or Germany only "by mechanical means." In the 1820s, when the loss of Finland to Russia still weighed heavily upon the Swedish people, he began to dream about a turreted naval vessel for coastal defense, which would have an exceptional firepower and at the same time offer the enemy a minimal target. In 1854 he brought this project up to date and sent a model to France, which, as an ally of Great Britain and Turkey, had just begun to fight Russia in the Crimean War. The answer from Paris, however, was negative.

Another important step toward the *Monitor* of 1861 had been taken in the early 1840s when John Ericsson designed his first ship, an iron frigate of 600 tons named *Princeton*, for the U.S. Navy. Being the first propeller-driven man-of-war as well as the first one with the engine below the waterline, she marked an epoch in naval history and was actually regarded as a marvel of a vessel. Her artillery, the most formidable afloat at that time, consisted of two 12-inch guns, one of which had been designed by Ericsson himself while the other and heavier one, called the Peacemaker, was a replica of it. Other equipment included an optical range finder which had just been invented by the engineer from Sweden.

In February, 1844, the *Princeton* sailed up and down the Potomac, firing her guns again and again until finally one of them, the Peacemaker, blew up. Six people, including two leading members of President John Tyler's cabinet, were killed, and several others were injured. The *Princeton* remained in commission, however, and during the war with Mexico in 1846–47 she saw duty more often than any other naval unit. After that, she was sent on a cruise to Europe without being repaired. Ericsson's gun, the Oregon, is preserved in the park of the U.S. Naval Academy at Annapolis.

At this time John Ericsson was constantly short of money, but his bill for two years' work on the *Princeton* was never paid. A naval officer who had served as his principal contact in Washington was probably to blame for this, but the inventor's relations with the administration remained cool for many years. In September of 1890, the year after his death, the Committee on Naval Affairs of the U.S. Senate tried to answer the question how Ericsson's claim could have been "allowed to sleep so long," writing in part: "Captain Ericsson, though one of the greatest marine engineers that ever lived, if not *the* greatest, was a peculiar man, proud, sensitive, and stubborn, and for a long time he refused to allow his friends to push this claim before Congress."

John Ericsson's claim, however, had actually been pushed by at least one member of Congress, Stephen R. Mallory of Florida, who from 1853 to 1861 served as chairman of the Naval Committee. In the United States Senate on May 14, 1858, he observed in what probably was his last speech on this subject: "There was no experiment in the *Princeton*. The experiment had been made at great cost by Captain Ericsson. He had exhausted every dollar he had on earth in making the experiment. . . . The *Princeton* is the foundation of our present steam marine. It is the foundation of the steam marine of the whole world." At the beginning of the Civil War, Stephen R. Mallory became the first Confederate secretary of the navy, and while he knew that the South could never build a seagoing fleet matching the Federal, he immediately saw the need for ironclads. On May 8, 1861, he wrote to the Confederate Congress that invulnerability might compensate for inequality of numbers, and that it would be both economical and wise to fight "with iron against wood." Two days later his recommendation was accepted. In the North, one of the leading naval architects, John Lenthall, who had designed the original *Merrimac* and many other wooden steam frigates, said that he considered ironclads to be a "humbug."

Converting the old Federal *Merrimac* into a floating fortress proved more complicated than the naval pioneer of the Confederacy had expected, but the work was well under way when the Navy Department in Washington, which had heard of the Confederate project, on August 4 received an appropriation of $1,500,000 for the design and construction of three experimental ironclads. A special naval board spent one month examining some 15 proposals, of which only two, both conventional, seemed to have any merit.

An important role was then played by a New Haven businessman who was responsible for one of the two leading designs, Cornelius S. Bushnell. He had been told to consult Captain John Ericsson, and in the latter's home in New York he was shown a model of the "floating battery." Both the design and the inventor himself impressed him greatly, and toward the middle of September he met in Washington with President Lincoln, the members of the board on ironclads, and other officials. The assistant secretary of the navy, Captain Gustavus Vasa Fox, a New Englander who had been named for a famous Swedish monarch of the 16th century and became Captain Ericsson's most ardent supporter, was immediately enthusiastic, but others had many objections. The President closed the conference by remarking: "All I have to say is what the girl said when she stuck her foot into the stocking. It strikes me there is something in it." On August 29 Ericsson had sent Lincoln plans for a steel-clad ship and a letter offering his services "at this fearful crisis — my life if need be — in the great cause which Providence has called you to defend."

In Washington the resistance to the "floating battery" seemed to increase, but Bushnell managed to persuade Captain Ericsson, whom he later described as "a full electric battery in himself," to come to Washington. After a vivid presentation before the board on ironclads on September 14 the inventor-designer said that he would complete the vessel in 90 days, and that she would cost $275,000. He was finally assured that the contract would be sent to him in New York. Two members of the board, however, remained so skeptical that they inserted a clause requiring Ericsson and his associates to refund the money if the ship did not prove invulnerable to Confederate attacks. Ericsson wrote later in a letter that the *Monitor* could not have been built if he had known of this stipulation at the beginning.

With funds advanced by Mr. Bushnell of New Haven and two manufacturers of Troy, New York, Captain Ericsson immediately gave out the various parts of the construction job to the principal contractors. On October 25 the keel was laid at a private yard in Greenpoint on the East River opposite New York, now in the borough of Brooklyn, where John Ericsson's name lives on in a high school. The inventor himself supervised the work, together with a chief engineer of the U.S. Navy, Alban C. Stimers. As he was bombarded with suggestions and doubts from Washington and there were many other complications, he carried an enormous burden. On January 30, 1862, the *Monitor* was launched, and on February 19 she was turned over to the Navy under the command of Lieutenant John L. Worden, who had only recently been released from a Confederate prison. During her first trial trip neither engine nor steering gear worked properly, and a daily paper published a critical article under the heading "Ericsson's Folly," but after her third test, on March 4, the board on ironclads reported favorably on her performance. Two days later the ship left New York.

Since the *Monitor* had been designed for river and harbor operations in the first place, it was considered prudent to have her towed, rather than let her proceed entirely under her own steam. There were 54 officers and men on board. Chief Engineer Alban C. Stimers, who had volunteered for service at Captain Ericsson's request, was the only one who thoroughly understood the characteristics of the vessel. Encountering rough weather, the *Monitor* shipped so much water that the crew had difficulty keeping her afloat, and at one time, when the engine rooms were filled with gas, the first engineer, Isaac Newton, who had helped build the engine at the De Lamater Iron Works in New York, and his assistants were nearly suffocated. When the ship arrived in Hampton Roads on the evening of March 8, all on board were more or less exhausted, and during the night they had to prepare for the coming battle. However, the *Merrimac's* crew of 355 men was also new and untrained.

The *Monitor* was the first turreted ironclad warship in the world.

Aside from the revolving turret, the principle of which had been known before, she contained numerous technical innovations. According to Isaac Newton, Captain Ericsson could have obtained at least 40 new patents for his various contrivances, but he refused to file the applications.

More monitors built by the United States — Russia and Sweden first to follow

THE $275,000 paid by the United States for the *Monitor* may also be regarded as an investment in the creation of a new weapons system, which helped ensure the naval supremacy of the Union.

Less than a week after the battle in Hampton Roads, Captain John Ericsson received an order for six coastal monitors of an enlarged and improved version. Somewhat later he undertook to build another four of the same so-called *Passaic* class, as well as two much larger monitor ships displacing about 4,500 tons, only one of which, however, was completed during the Civil War.

While under fire from a fort in Georgia, one of the monitors of the *Passaic* class, the *Montauk*, destroyed on February 28, 1863, the Confederate cruiser *Nashville*. The commander of the Union vessel, John L. Worden, took more professional pride in this feat than in his fight with the *Merrimac*. Another monitor of the same series, the *Weehawken*, with a few salvos from her two guns, disabled and captured the ironclad ram *Atlanta*, one of the best Confederate ships. The monitors of the Civil War were, however, often criticized for lack of seagoing qualities. Captain Gustavus Vasa Fox, who like John A. Dahlgren became one of President Lincoln's favorites, heard many such comments but remained enthusiastic.

Smaller river monitors were specially designed for the Mississippi, which was a vital theater of war, and other monitor-type vessels of different sizes were built to the designs of the Navy Department in Washington. The last U.S. monitor was stricken from the navy list as late as 1937, when a total of about 50 monitors had seen commissioned service and another score had been built. Many ships completed after the end of the Civil War were immediately laid up.

After the Civil War two large monitors were sent on long ocean voyages as a demonstration of their efficiency. One of them, the *Miantonomoh*, visited during 1866 ports of the leading naval powers of

313

Europe, creating favorable impressions of American warship design. *The Times* of London, which had long belittled the monitors, wrote of the visitor on July 17: "Round this fearful invention were moored scores of big ships, not all utter antiquities, but modern, and there was not one of them that the foreigner could not have sent to the bottom in five minutes, had his errand not been peaceful. . . . In fact, the wolf was in the fold and the whole flock was at its mercy."

The leader of the *Miantonomoh* expedition was Captain Gustavus Vasa Fox, who had just resigned as assistant secretary of the navy. He and John Ericsson had become close friends, and before sailing for Europe he wrote the inventor on April 23, 1866: "The country never can and never will do you justice pecuniarily for the inventions which have been so useful . . . and which are the results of genius in comparison with other systems which are born of labor and art and long study." What Captain Ericsson earned on the original *Monitor*, and on the other ships he helped build, came to him as one of the contractors, but he received no remuneration for his inventions, or for the experiments connected with them. Toward the end of his life, when some special recognition of his services was discussed both in the press and in Washington, he said that the monitors were intended "as a contribution to the glorious cause of the Union."

During his European tour, Captain Gustavus Vasa Fox also visited St. Petersburg, the Russian capital, to present a resolution which the American Congress, remembering the goodwill shown to the United States by Russia during the Civil War, had passed after an attempt had been made in April of 1866 upon the life of Czar Alexander II. Copies of the drawings prepared for American monitors had then already been furnished to Russia from Washington, and ten ships of this type were included in the ironclad Russian fleet created in 1862–64. Toward the end of September, the *Miantonomoh* anchored at the naval base in Stockholm harbor, where she remained for more than a week, admired by visitors and spectators. Captain Fox and his officers were received by the King, had dinner with the Queen Mother, and made a tour of the Scandinavian Industrial and Art Exhibition, to which Prince Oscar of Sweden, who was to succeed his brother, Carl XV, as monarch, had unsuccessfully invited Captain Ericsson.

One of the officers sent over to the United States by the Swedish government to study naval construction and other military advances during the Civil War was August d'Ailly (1822–77) of the naval engineering corps. He observed the construction of monitors in 1862–63 under John Ericsson's personal guidance and after his return to Sweden supervised the building of such ships for the Swedish navy. The first, christened *John Ericsson*, was commissioned in 1866. Three Swedish monitors and one Norwegian went on a cruise together, and on September 17, 1867, a Norwegian officer wrote to Captain Ericsson: "Honor to him who has placed in the hands of the smaller states a weapon with which they can successfully defend themselves against the aggression of the stronger nations!" The Scandinavian monitors, largely based on Captain Ericsson's drawings, were small vessels of 140 tons, while the original *Monitor* in fighting trim displaced about 1,000 tons. For Sweden, Ericsson subsequently recommended gunboats in place of more monitors.

Another Swedish naval officer, Axel Adlersparre (1812–79), visited New York in 1861 as commander of a Swedish sailing frigate, the *Norrköping*, and later helped direct the modernization of Sweden's naval forces. He and John Ericsson became personal friends and the famous inventor willed a relatively large amount of money to him and his wife. When Ericsson donated two American guns to his native country for its first monitor, Adlersparre wrote to him: "If there is in heaven a special dwelling for patriots, your place will certainly be in the state apartments." In his youth, after having received his commission as a second lieutenant in Sweden, Adlersparre served for three years in the U.S. Navy as a common sailor under Gustavus Vasa Fox. After that, in 1842–43, he continued his voyages in commercial vessels on the Great Lakes.

At the end of the Civil War another Swedish frigate, the *Vanadis*, made two visits to New York. In April, 1865, her officers and crew witnessed the victory celebrations after General Lee's surrender at Appomattox.

Ericsson's first inventions and a tragic romance in Sweden — To England in 1826

JOHAN, OR JOHN, ERICSSON was born on July 31, 1803, at Långbanshyttan near the town of Filipstad in the province of Värmland, where his father was a mining inspector, and where his forebears, both on his father's and on his mother's side, had for generations been associated

315

with the iron industry. Some of his first known ancestors in Sweden were Walloon or Scottish immigrants. His father Olof, who also operated an old silver mine, went bankrupt in 1807, and with his wife Sofia and their three children moved from a beautiful home to a diminutive, peat-thatched crofter's cottage nearby. Three years later he became employed in the building of the Göta Canal through south-central Sweden, which then was considered a much more important waterway than it is today.

John had little conventional schooling but received valuable training first from his parents, then from a governess, and finally from engineers and other specialists working on the construction of the canal. His tutors taught him mathematics, physics, and chemistry as well as English. Solid foundations were laid for his coming mastership as a draftsman, and the canal work itself told him much about the world of engineering. At the age of 14, when he had become a surveyor and learned to handle leveling instruments, he had 600 soldiers working under his direction.

In 1820, John Ericsson entered military service some 350 miles farther north, in Jämtland. Here he became an officer as well as a certified surveyor. He also wrote poems, which reflected a deep feeling for nature, and was widely admired both as a dancer and as a sportsman. At the age of 20 the dashing young lieutenant fell in love with a girl of a distinguished family, whose father, however, refused to give his daughter "to a commoner and a man without a future." John Ericsson's betrothed was sent to Stockholm, and there she bore a son, Hjalmar Elworth (1824–87), who was reared in the home of John's sister, Carolina, with the devoted assistance of his mother. Father and son were not to meet until more than 50 years later, in New York. After having lived in obscurity for ten years, Hjalmar's mother was joined in marriage to a noted Swedish jurist, and the following year, in 1836, John Ericsson married a 19-year-old English girl. She may have reminded him of his Swedish fiancée of 1823–24 insofar as she was beautiful, young, and of good family; she had, moreover, a child who had been born out of wedlock. He and his wife soon began to drift apart, but were never divorced.

While serving as an officer and surveyor in northern Sweden, John Ericsson made his first inventions, including a new rifle and a "flame engine," based on the principle of the expansion of gases from heat. This machine was his first attempt to replace steam by some other and cheaper power, a problem which would occupy his mind most of the time until the end of his life. If he had not become obsessed with it, he would probably have been able to contribute even more to technical and industrial progress than he actually did. Despite his unsuccessful efforts to substitute hot air for steam, he made, on the other hand, numerous contributions to steam engineering.

In 1826, at the age of nearly 23, Ericsson left Sweden for England, on leave of absence from his regiment. Both public officials and personal friends at home had encouraged him to try to develop and exploit his inventions abroad. The next year he received his commission as captain in the Swedish army, and this title he proudly used for the rest of his life, but he never returned to his native country.

Inventor close to international fame at the age of 26 —
Twice in debtors' prison

A PERIOD of intense experimentation began in London. One of Ericsson's first inventions was a pumping engine in which, for the first time, compressed air was used for transmitting power. Then came a tubular steam boiler with artificial draft and a surface condenser, of vast importance for the development of the marine engine. At about the same time the young engineer brought out a self-releasing gun-lock, by means of which naval cannon could be automatically discharged at any elevation regardless of the motion of the ship. In 1833 a hot-air or caloric engine was patented in England, France, the United States, and other countries, and somewhat later Ericsson successfully designed a screw propeller, patented in 1836. A sounding instrument known as "Ericsson's Sea Lead" was patented in England and the United States and came into extensive use in their navies and merchant marines.

Ericsson's new steam boiler was the beginning of the modern steam fire engine. In 1829 the same invention became the basis for his participation in the famous race between locomotives at Rainhill near Liverpool. The 26-year-old Swede entered the competition when only seven weeks of the 22 that were allowed for completing the engines remained, and in contrast with his only real competitor, George Stephenson, he had never before built a locomotive, but the prize was, nevertheless, within his grasp. He finally withdrew from the contest because of minor defects of workmanship in his engine, the *Novelty*, but this locomotive had then proved to be much speedier than even the winner, the *Rocket*. "It was the lightest and most elegant carriage on the road yesterday," *The Times* of London wrote after the first races, "and the velocity with which it moved surprised and amazed every beholder. It shot along the line at the amazing rate of 30 miles an hour! It seemed, indeed, to fly, presenting one of the most sublime spectacles of human ingenuity and human daring the world ever beheld."

While waiting for some of his inventions to pay off, Ericsson often went deep into debt, and in the spring of 1832 he was sent to a debtors' prison. He was still there at Christmas, when his elder brother Nils, who had played an important part in the construction of the Göta Canal and had become a captain in the naval engineering corps, came to visit him. The two brothers, who never saw each other again, discussed the hot-air engine. Two years later John spent a short time in another debtors' prison.

During his 13 years in England, Ericsson completed some 40 inventions and took out 30 patents, but although many people actually believed in him, he regarded the British as largely unreceptive to his ideas, and at times he felt entangled in bureaucratic conventions and antiquated prejudices. In the United States, where he was to spend the last 50 years of his life, he would suffer similar reactions and other disappointments, but he had good reason to believe that the New World would offer him the best opportunities, and this anticipation proved to be essentially justified.

Ericsson's most important invention, the propeller,
introduced in America

JOHN ERICSSON arrived in New York on November 23, 1839. Business relations were almost immediately established with a machine-making and shipbuilding firm, the junior partner of which, Cornelius H. De Lamater, became his closest friend in America. Captain Ericsson's primary objective was to introduce his marine engines, which he continued to develop, and above all his most important invention, the first practical screw propeller. In London, an American naval officer by the name of Robert F. Stockton had given him what he had reason to regard as binding assurances of a government contract for a new warship. His reputation as a remarkable inventor had preceded him to New York, and within the first few months his steam fire engine won him the great gold medal of the Mechanics Institute, which, alarmed by the many destructive fires in the city, had invited inventors to a contest.

The principle underlying the screw propeller had been known before, but Ericsson was the pioneer in applying power directly to the shaft turning the propeller, and that was a revolutionary innovation. "The claim made on behalf of John Ericsson to the honor of substituting the screw for the paddle-wheel has been hotly disputed," his first biographer, Colonel William Conant Church, editor of the *Army and Navy Journal* in New York, wrote shortly after the inventor's death, but, he continued, "in the end, when all the evidence is sifted, his name will be associated with that great advance in steam navigation, as the name of Watt is associated with the steam engine, Fulton's with the steamboat, and that of Morse with the telegraph."

The first ship successfully using the screw propeller was a tiny steamer built in London in 1836–37 which John Ericsson named the *Francis B. Ogden* after an American friend who was U.S. consul in Liverpool. When this vessel steamed up and down the Thames, the boatmen, according to another American shipping expert, "were astonished at the sight of this novel craft moving against wind and tide without any visible agency of propulsion, and, ascribing to it some supernatural origin, they united in giving it the name of the *Flying Devil*."

Even more important in the development of the propeller was the year 1838, when the first direct-acting screw propeller engine ever built was applied by Ericsson to another miniature steamer, the *Robert F. Stockton*, which the following year crossed the Atlantic from England to New York. There, according to her American master who was presented with the freedom of the city, she was "visited by hundreds of curious persons, anxious to realize the possible truth of the nursery story about the 'three men of Gotham' who 'went to sea in a bowl.'"

Little *Robert F. Stockton*, which in fact was the pioneer screw vessel, was employed later for many years as a tugboat on the Delaware River, which had been the main artery of the first Swedish settlements in America. In 1866, when John Ericsson had been widely recognized in England as the real inventor of the propeller, the librarian of the British Patent Office wrote to him that he would like to purchase, if possible, the original engines of the *Robert F. Stockton*, which, however, was then still in service. Seven years later the same librarian sent Captain Ericsson another letter, reading in part: "The benefit you have conferred on the world by the screw propeller is beyond computation. If I could obtain the original engines, in whatever state they now are, I should be proud of them as a trophy, to be placed in the Patent Office Museum in London . . ." At that time, however, Ericsson's engine had been scrapped.

The first American-built ships to use the Ericsson propeller were the *Vandalia*, which in 1841 became the pioneer propeller on the Great Lakes, and the *Clarion*, which was the first propeller-driven ocean steamer, running between New York and Havana. Three of the early vessels were christened *Ericsson*, and an Ericsson Line was established in 1844 to carry passengers and freight between Philadelphia and Baltimore via the Delaware and Chesapeake Canal. It ran successfully for more than 100 years, until truck competition forced it to close down.

In 1842–44 Captain Ericsson designed every part of the first propeller-driven warship in the world, the iron frigate *Princeton*, which has been mentioned above as one of the vessels leading up to the *Monitor*. This was, in fact, the government project that had helped to make Ericsson decide to move to America. The *Princeton* was built at the Philadelphia navy yard under the inventor's supervision, and she carried not only his propeller and semicylinder engine, but also many other of his inventions, including his so-called telescopic smokestack, which could easily be lowered or raised.

As a demonstration of the efficiency of the screw propeller, the U.S.S. *Princeton* was particularly effective, convincing naval leaders and shipbuilders in many countries of its superiority. A Swedish naval officer was able to study her construction and received drawings for a similar man-of-war. This vessel, a steam corvette which was christened *Gefle* after the largest port north of Stockholm, now spelled Gävle, was launched in 1848. Many ships of the British and French navies were built on the same model.

Small hot-air engine commercial success — Final act of solar and torpedo research

ERICSSON's experiments with hot air as a source of power continued after he had moved to New York from London, and in the early 1850s these seemed about to pay off. Some enterprising and wealthy businessmen were so impressed by his caloric engine that they built a paddle-wheel ship driven by such machinery. Christened *Ericsson*, she was intended for transatlantic service, and her caloric engine was, by far, the largest ever designed.

On January 11, 1853, the ship made her trial run, and the next day the papers contained glowing accounts of her success and confident predictions of an early end to the age of steam. The *New York Daily Tribune*, for instance, wrote: "Fulton and Watt belong to the Past, Ericsson is the great mechanical genius of the Present and the Future." There were also skeptics, more or less convinced that a fallacy was involved in Ericsson's reasoning, but in the absence of a clear and satisfactory theory of heat, few of them could explain what the problem was.

In February of 1853 the *Ericsson*, with the inventor on board, made a trip to Washington, where she was visited by President Fillmore, President-elect Pierce, and delegations from both houses of Congress. A few months later, she sank in New York harbor after having been struck by a tornado. "A more sudden transition from gladness and exultation to disappointment and regret is scarcely on record," Captain Ericsson, who had been on board, wrote to one of his friends, and later, in response to a letter of condolence, he added: "You are quite right in thinking that it takes something more to kill me than the sinking of a ship, though it carried down the results of 20 years of labor." The caloric ship may have been one of the great mechanical achievements of its period, but attempts to apply hot air on this scale had to be abandoned.

In 1855 Captain Ericsson wrote in a letter that he was "on the brink of ruin," but the beginning of his rise to prosperity was then not far away. Before the era of electricity there was a great need for a simple foolproof motor, and Ericsson's small caloric engines, which would work without feed water, were found to be very useful for numerous tasks requiring moderate power, from pumping, hoisting, grinding, and printing to the operation of lighthouses, the propulsion of knitting and sewing machines, and the ginning of cotton. Within a few years, thousands of such motors were sold. In the larger cities, the only feasible method of supplying water to the upper stories was to have a tank on the roof and a pumping engine in the basement, and the De Lamater Iron Works is said to have built a total of some 12,000 Ericsson engines for New York alone. Many daily newspapers were printed on presses driven by motors of the same type. As a result of the caloric boom in the farming districts in the Middle West, a little paper called *The Ericsson* was published at Fond du Lac, Wisconsin, then a town of 2,000–3,000 inhabitants. In 1862, the American Academy of Arts and Sciences awarded Captain Ericsson the coveted Rumford medal for his caloric engine of 1858. His hot-air engine is now only a museum piece.

When John Ericsson was old enough to retire, he continued to study defense problems, in particular the possibilities of torpedo warfare. In the 1870s he developed a torpedo boat called the *Destroyer*, which carried a submarine gun which was discharged by compressed air. Having spent a large part of his capital on experiments, he made many attempts to sell this ship, but failed. In 1893, four years after his death, the *Destroyer* was finally sold to Brazil, whose government had lost most of its navy in an uprising. A group of sailors and adventurers, most of them Scandinavians, delivered the vessel at Rio de Janeiro where she helped crush the revolution without firing a shot.

During the latter part of his life Captain Ericsson devoted most of his time to solar research, an activity that was naturally associated with his development of the caloric engine. A motor to be worked by solar heat was produced in some 20 versions, and about 50 fine instruments were invented during the course of these experiments. John Ericsson is, therefore, regarded as one of the leading pioneers in solar research. Among American institutions and organizations which relatively early in the 20th century became interested in his efforts were the University of Arizona and the Association for Applied Solar Energy at Phoenix, Arizona. In the early 1970s his research attracted more attention in connection with the energy crisis and the more active quest for new sources of energy.

Captain Ericsson's laboratory was on the roof of his house at 36

Beach Street in lower Manhattan in New York, which he had bought in 1864 when he moved from Franklin Street in the same section.

John Ericsson dies in 1889 — Remains conveyed to Sweden in 1890 on a U.S. cruiser

JOHN ERICSSON was nearly 86 years old when he died in his home in New York, in 1889 on March 8, the anniversary of the *Monitor's* arrival at Hampton Roads. The next year, upon requests from Sweden, the U.S. government decided to bring his body to his native country as a tribute to the memory of "the most famous representative of the Scandinavian race in America." In New York, on August 25, the casket, wrapped in the American flag which had flown on the *Monitor*, was carried to the hearse by six members of the crew of Captain Ericsson's first "floating battery," and the procession following was led by Rear Admiral John L. Worden.

One of the U.S. Navy's newest ships, the cruiser *Baltimore*, conveyed the casket to Stockholm, where magnificent ceremonies were staged on Sunday, September 14. For the first time in history, the flag at the Royal Palace was lowered to half-mast for a non-royal person. From the capital, and over a railroad built by John Ericsson's brother Nils, the remains were transferred to their final resting place at Filipstad in the province of Värmland, the center of the beautiful mining district where John Ericsson was born.

John Ericsson was, as the U.S. Senate Committee on Naval Affairs observed after his death, not only a great marine engineer but also a peculiar man, combining an aggressive and sarcastic temper with unusual sensitivity and generosity. A rugged physique and enormous will power enabled him to work exceptionally hard, and he allowed himself little time for other matters, including family affairs. Most of the money he earned was spent on new experiments or given away to relatives, friends, and people or institutions in need. In America, his nearest approach to religious observances was in his election to honorary membership in the Swedish Gustavus Adolphus Church in New York, which was founded in 1865; he fully respected the beliefs of other people.

In the spring of 1876, Ericsson wrote: "I have for a series of years led an eccentric life. I never visit anybody, and never receive visits excepting from a few professional persons. . . . In truth, I may be regarded as a stranger, of whom everybody has heard, but whom nobody knows personally." Even at this time, however, at least two personal friends were probably among his regular visitors — Cornelius H. De Lamater and Peter Cooper, the great philanthropist, who, like John Ericsson, at the beginning of his industrial career had built a locomotive. "Knocked together," as he had promised, in 1830, it was the first one operated in America. Peter Cooper was partly of Swedish colonial ancestry.

In 1876, John Ericsson also had a truly remarkable visitor, namely, his 52-year-old son, Hjalmar Elworth, who had reached one of the top posts in the Swedish State Railways, and who had come to America with a commission from his government for the Centennial Exposition in Philadelphia, where Sweden was represented with a large section.

Captain Ericsson's egocentricity increased considerably in his old age. Feeling that he should have been invited to take part in the exposition in Philadelphia, he prepared an expensive volume of 664 pages presenting his inventions and other technical accomplishments. He had always been a prolific and remarkably efficient writer, and his book was largely based on old magazine articles and other material. Entitled *Contributions to the Centennial Exhibition*, it contained magnificent illustrations drawn by Ericsson himself and is regarded as a masterpiece of the printer's and engraver's art. Some 300 copies were printed, and these were distributed to the great scientific libraries of the world and a number of individuals whose opinions the inventor valued. The book weighs 11 pounds.

While Ericsson always had a strong faith in his own capability, he seemed more or less indifferent to rewards and distinctions. Numerous organizations on both sides of the Atlantic elected him an honorary member, but some such nominations he declined as having been made too late. In 1866, the Department of State in Washington offered him the appointment as commissioner to the Universal Exhibition in Paris the following year, which he regarded as a great honor. The Swedish Academy of Sciences elected him an honorary member as early as in 1847, and in 1868 he received an honorary doctor's degree from the University of Lund, which then celebrated its 200th anniversary.

An American citizen since 1848, John Ericsson was grateful for the opportunities the United States offered him and undoubtedly felt at home in his adopted country, but his feelings for Sweden did not by any means cool off as the years went by. He developed, in fact, a profound sentimental affection for his native land, which, despite many appeals from relatives and formal invitations, he never visited. "America," his first biographer wrote, "was to him the land of stern reality — Sweden the home of romance, and he turned from the unrelieved monotony of a loveless life among his machines and his calculations, to draw refreshment from the hidden fountains of youthful recollections."

Although his career as an engineer and inventor would influence many technically gifted Swedes in their decisions to leave for the New World, Ericsson warned friends and relatives in Sweden against emigrating, maintaining that life in America was tougher than his former fellow countrymen realized. He also seems to have felt that his native country actually offered its small population sufficient opportunities within its own borders. While he had no particularly high opinion of the Swede's ability as a soldier — "the stuff is there," the former military instructor said, "but it requires an inconveniently long time to bring it out" — he voiced a deep admiration for "the perseverance, sense of right, and clear heads" of the young farmers' sons and workers in Sweden. When he wrote this, the flow of such young people into the United States had only just begun.

Ericsson collections and monuments — World peace seen as a result of armaments

AT TIMES John Ericsson spoke or wrote in a very sarcastic style about conditions in America, but he often dealt with other subjects in the same vein, especially when he was in a bad humor. In 1888, the year before his death, he received a letter from Artur Hazelius in Stockholm, who had founded both the Nordic Museum and the Skansen folk park and open-air museum, which became the prototype of such institutions in other countries, and who now hoped to be able to establish a John Ericsson collection. In answer, Captain Ericsson sent him a long cable, reading in part: "Accept my cordial thanks, but permit me to inform you that I take no interest in museums which preserve relics of barbarism and ignorance of past generations. . . . I have already destroyed upward of 1,000 drawings, and numerous models, to prevent posterity from supposing that my knowledge was as imperfect as said relics would indicate."

When the inventor died, enough material was, nevertheless, left for several important collections. Two John Ericsson rooms in the American Swedish Historical Museum in Philadelphia contain models of his inventions, personal effects, books by and about him, and a large number of papers and other writings, and the Nordic Museum in Stockholm has a John Ericsson room which, among other things, holds much of the furnishings from his home at 36 Beach Street in New York. The largest collection of letters from John Ericsson is in the Royal Library in Stockholm. In the United States, the Library of Congress in Washington, D.C., and the New-York Historical Society have preserved important source material. Much of Captain Ericsson's business correspondence concerned legal controversies and other fights in which he had become involved. To many people he seemed difficult to deal with, but nobody questioned his honesty and integrity.

A large collection of John Ericsson memorabilia related to the battle in Hampton Roads is in the Mariners Museum at Newport News, Virginia. The Fort Monroe Casemate Museum at Fort Monroe, Virginia, also contains interesting exhibits on the *Monitor* and the *Merrimac*, including colored pictures, models, and maps.

The John Ericsson Society in New York, which was founded in 1907, has been active in furthering interest in John Ericsson's life and work. In New York State, March 9, the anniversary of the battle between the *Monitor* and the *Merrimac*, has traditionally been observed as John Ericsson Day. In 1926, a John Ericsson gold medal was established by The American Society of Swedish Engineers in New York, and it is awarded every other year to a Swedish citizen or an American citizen of Swedish descent, in recognition of eminent merits in the technological or scientific fields. Most of those who have won this award have been or are widely known.

U.S. Navy tributes to the memory of John Ericsson include the naming of a U.S. destroyer for him in the Second World War. The first more important monument to the inventor was unveiled in 1893 in New York's Battery Park. The sculptor, Jonathan Hartley, was, however, not satisfied with his creation, and a new statue, donated by him, was erected in 1903. On May 29, 1926, a monument was unveiled in Potomac Park in Washington, on the bank of the river directly south of the Lincoln Memorial. President Calvin Coolidge and Crown Prince Gustav Adolf of Sweden, the future monarch, were the main speakers. About the engagement at Hampton Roads, President Coolidge said that it "did for the Union cause on the sea what the battle of Gettysburg later was to do for it on land. If some of the European countries had any serious thought of joining the South, such intentions were speedily abandoned." The chief executive further recalled that it was his development of the propeller that brought John Ericsson to America.

Armaments and the art of the war, which Captain Ericsson did so much to develop, he regarded as, fundamentally, a means toward a peaceful end. For instance, in explaining a proposition he made in 1870 to demonstrate the efficiency of his method of underwater attack, he wrote to Captain Gustavus Vasa Fox: "My only object is that of seeing the sea declared by all nations sacred neutral ground. It is the highway of mankind." And in 1866 he wrote to a friend in England: "The art of war, as I have always contended, is positively in its infancy. When perfected, man will be forced to live in peace with man." He underestimated, however, the time needed to achieve this, for he added: "This glorious result, which has been the cherished dream of my life, will unquestionably be attained before the close of the present century."

In his attitude toward war and peace, and also in some other respects, John Ericsson resembled another famous Swedish inventor of the 19th century, the father of dynamite, Alfred Nobel, who once wrote to a noted pacifist: "My factories may make an end of war sooner than your congresses. The day when two army corps can annihilate each other in one second, all civilized nations, it is to be hoped, will recoil from war and discharge their troops." In the early 1850s Alfred Nobel, who was then about 18 years old, spent some time with John Ericsson in New York and obtained from him "certain drawings and information," probably on behalf of his father who had left Sweden and established himself as a manufacturer in St. Petersburg, the capital of Russia.

Another influential Swedish-American engineer — New era in relations Sweden-U.S.A.

SIGNIFICANT contributions to marine engineering in America were also made by another Swedish engineer, Johan Vilhelm Nyström or John William Nystrom (1824–85), who arrived in New York ten years after John Ericsson, in 1849. He was born at Lofta in northeastern

Småland, the son of a toolsmith, and after studies at the budding Institute of Technology in Stockholm, he worked in 1846–49 as an apprentice in the mechanical factory at Motala in the province of Östergötland, which had been established by the founder of the Göta Canal, Count Baltzar von Platen (1766–1829). In his decision to emigrate, he was probably influenced both by John Ericsson's career in England and America and by the migration from Östergötland touched off by Per Cassel, who in 1845 founded New Sweden in Iowa.

Nystrom settled in Philadelphia, and there he almost immediately exhibited a calculating machine, a type of instrument that soon would become one of Sweden's technical specialties, although industrial production was still far away. In the early 1850s, one of the first machines calculating and printing mathematical tables, designed by a Stockholm printer and magazine publisher by the name of Georg Scheutz (1785–1873), was bought for the newly founded Dudley Observatory at Albany, New York. It is now in the Smithsonian Institution in Washington, D.C. Another and more practical machine of the same type was somewhat later designed by a prolific Swedish inventor, Martin Wiberg (1826–1905), who was successfully represented at the Centennial Exposition in Philadelphia in 1876.

Two years later, Willgodt T. Odhner (1845–1905) obtained a U.S. patent for an epoch-making compact calculating machine, which, after improvements, he started manufacturing at St. Petersburg, the Russian capital, in 1890, with assistance from a brother of Alfred Nobel. Instruments of this type, made in many countries under various names, are still known internationally as Odhner machines. A relative of the inventor, the Reverend Clas O. Odhner, married John Ericsson's sister, Carolina, and Captain Ericsson willed part of his relatively modest fortune to their six children, one of whom became a famous historian and a member of the Swedish Academy.

In 1852, John William Nystrom published in Philadelphia a book, *A Treatise on Screw Propellers and Their Steam Engines*, which became widely read by shipbuilders. Three years later came his best-known work, *Pocket Book of Mechanics and Engineering*, which long was a classic in its field, being used by mechanical engineers and shipbuilders on both sides of the Atlantic. Before its author's death at the age of 61, it reached some 20 editions. A Swedish version was printed in Stockhom.

Restlessly active like John Ericsson, Nystrom in 1856–59 lived in Russia, supervising the construction of the railroad along the Volga and Don rivers and designing, among other things, a hydraulic pontoon dock. He then returned to the United States and became an iron and steel manufacturer at Gloucester City in New Jersey, on the Delaware opposite Philadelphia. After that he was for some time a chief engineer with the Department of the Navy in Washington. The years 1866–70 he spent in government service in Peru, studying the exploitation of its mineral resources, and in 1872 he again settled in Philadelphia as a consulting engineer and machine designer. His influence on American engineering was, according to some historians, almost as far-reaching as that of John Ericsson, although today he is much less widely known.

John Ericsson and John William Nystrom were two of Sweden's first international engineers of significance, and together they introduced a new era in their native country's relations with the United States. The activities of Swedish-born engineers and inventors would gradually become a vital contribution to the industrial and technological growth of America, which in turn, would offer technically gifted descendants of Swedish immigrants matchless opportunities.

Fundamentally, countless inventions and technical improvements in the United States have their roots in Swedish history. Sweden entered the modern industrial age relatively late, and one consequence was the prolonged large-scale emigration to America. Most of the emigrants had, to be sure, only a rudimentary education, but they were schooled in the necessity of hard work, strict economy, and resourcefulness. Many had, moreover, like John Ericsson grown up in an atmosphere of educational and technical betterment, or even, like Nystrom, obtained substantial formal training. Without Sweden's old industrial and scientific traditions, and without the early beginnings of comparatively high standards in academic and vocational education, Swedish immigrants would have played a much smaller part in American industry and technology.

Numerous inventions and innovations made by Swedes in America can, in fact, be traced back to some school, study group, factory or ironmaking town in Sweden, or perhaps to some family in which technical skills or an interest in learning had been handed down from generation to generation.

★ 19

The Great Trek Starts

Swedish mass migration after the Civil War sparked by crop failures

DURING the Civil War years, 1861–65, emigration from Sweden had remained relatively modest, totaling about 12,000 people, but shortly after the war a great trek started, and during the next half-century more than one million Swedes moved to the United States. In the same period Sweden's population rose from four million to about 5,800,000. Most of the emigrants were 15–35 years old.

The first mighty emigration waves rolled out from Sweden in the years 1868–73 when more than 100,000, probably as many as 125,000, left for America. Agriculture was the dominant factor in the Swedish economy, and the great majority of those who pulled up stakes were, inevitably, people of the soil. Most of them were laborers and other members of the landless farming population, which since the beginning of the century had increased rapidly and now made up about 40 percent of the country's inhabitants. There were many sons and daughters of relatively well-to-do farmers, but more young men and women came from homesteads which were far too small to provide a decent livelihood, and where subsistence was eked out with forest work or some form of handicraft. Disenchanted landowners also took part in the exodus. Carpenters, tailors, shoemakers, mechanics, and other craftsmen and workers made up most of the nonagrarian minority.

The growth of the landless agricultural groups was largely a result of continued high birth rates together with declining mortality figures, and this development, in turn, was based on better diets and health care. In most larger families, however, the potato was the leading staple. Farm wages and other compensations were still inadequate for a hopeful existence, and in the New World, where many Swedish settlements had already been established, plentiful and cheap land beckoned. During the Civil War the magnetism of America had been augmented by the Homestead Act, which to the Swedish small farmer's son or laborer held out the glorious prospect of owning his own farm in the near future — and not just a tiny holding similar to the great majority of those in Sweden, but one of 80 or 160 acres. The industrial expansion in the United States also opened new opportunities for people who were prepared to work hard. A taste for adventure contributed to many decisions to emigrate, as it had always done.

The heavy emigration from Sweden in the late 1860s and early 1870s may, nevertheless, be regarded as exceptional, for much of it was the effect of temporary economic difficulties. After the middle of the century Sweden for nearly three decades enjoyed an unprecedented prosperity in agriculture, but a financial setback came in 1864, primarily as a result of overspeculation in farmlands. The construction of railroads had, moreover, begun to strain the country's resources, and Denmark's defeat in the war against Prussia and Austria had a sharp psychological impact. This was followed in 1866–68 by repeated crop failures, the result of a succession of severe winters and unusually either wet or dry summers.

The north of Sweden had, in fact, suffered from poor harvests for several years, when in 1867 the crops failed almost completely. In the vast Norrland, or Northland, there were still no railroads, and since the ports became icebound in late fall, it was very difficult to reach the stricken area with relief. The next year the whole of Sweden was hit by one of the longest droughts in the country's history, and the crisis was not relieved until the fall of 1869 when the farmers had gathered a full harvest.

The food situation in Sweden never became as desperate as it was in Ireland during the Great Famine 20 years earlier, but in large parts of the country most homes were reduced to near-starvation. Not only in the north but also in Småland, Blekinge, Värmland, and other southern or central provinces, the bark of trees was often mixed with flour in making bread, and mosses and lichens as well as the roots of flowers and shrubs were also used as food. Many agricultural laborers had to go begging, and the death rate rose considerably. Grain deliveries or financial help arrived from other countries, including the United States, where Captain John Ericsson was the largest single contributor. Thousands of Swedes moved at least temporarily to Denmark or northern Germany, where enterprising agents offered Swedish domestic servants for sale in the newspapers, but the mainstream of emigrants led across the Atlantic.

The leading emigration districts were the provinces of Småland, Östergötland and Värmland, the northeast of Skåne, and Gästrikland and Hälsingland in the north. However, no part of Sweden was left unaffected by the "America fever." There was no province that did not send at least hundreds of emigrants to the United States during the years 1868–73.

By 1870 the Swedish government had become so disturbed by the emigration of so many able-bodied people that the acting minister in Washington, D.C., Count Carl Lewenhaupt (1835–1906), was asked to prepare an account of the conditions of the Swedes in America. In the summer of 1870 he undertook a journey to the Swedish settlements in Illinois and Minnesota, and in the spring of the following year the government in Stockholm published his report as a pamphlet. It was printed in both Swedish and Norwegian, and the authorities obviously believed that it would help to slow down emigration. Lewenhaupt called attention to the cheating and other difficulties the immigrants from Sweden often had to experience, particularly in New York and Chicago, but he found the great majority of the settlers in better circumstances than if they had remained at home. The prosperity of the older Swedish settlements had, in fact, impressed him, and he also mentioned the rapid increase in the value of the land in all regions that had become more densely populated. In the ears of potential emigrants, this was sweet music.

Lewenhaupt's report was published in several Swedish-language newspapers in the United States, and American officials welcomed it as decidedly fair. The Swedish diplomat returned to Stockholm in 1870 after his tour of the Middle West, but in 1876 he was appointed minister to the United States. From 1889 to 1895 he served as foreign minister of Sweden and Norway.

While in the early and middle 1800s most of the emigrants had sailed directly from Sweden to America, the great migration after the Civil War followed an indirect course, primarily via Gothenburg and England. Up to 80 percent of the emigrants sailed from Gothenburg to Hull or Grimsby, and as a rule they then went by train to Liverpool, to board the great steamers bound for New York or Boston. Most of those who sailed from Stockholm, a group that included a great number of emigrants from Finland, went to America by way of Hamburg or Bremen. In the 1880s a direct shipping service was started between Copenhagen and New York, and many emigrants from Sweden's southern provinces traveled by this route. Attempts to establish a direct line from Sweden to America failed because of lack of capital and the increasingly sharp competition on the Atlantic. A direct passenger service between Sweden and the United States was not begun until the First World War.

During the era of mass migration Gothenburg was not only the leading Swedish port but also the foremost center of the emigration industry in Scandinavia. The agents of the steamship companies had their main offices there, many emigrant hotels were built, and special newspapers were published for those about to move to the New World.

Emigration promoters bank on the drawing power
of the Swedish settlers in U.S.A.

LETTERS from Swedes who had successfully settled in the United States were the most effective propaganda for emigration to the New World. After the Civil War, however, organized promotion campaigns were launched in Sweden by the American railroads and other big landowners as well as by the new British, American, and German steamship companies. During periods of high emigration the transatlantic fares were pushed up by cartel agreements among the shipowners, while they were lowered again when business slowed down. The American railroads were naturally eager to attract as many able-bodied men as possible, for they needed labor for the construction work, settlers for their extensive land holdings, and passengers and freight for their trains.

The American authorities also took part in information and propaganda drives. During the Civil War President Lincoln himself had sent 30 special consular agents to Europe to explain the opportunities

333

offered by the Homestead Act, and when the war was over many of the states set up their own organizations to recruit as many settlers as possible and thus increase the population and wealth of their respective areas. This resulted in sharp competition and at times even propaganda wars between various states.

The foremost emigration promoter in Sweden during the first period of mass migration in 1868–73 was Colonel Hans Mattson, the pioneer settler and Civil War veteran from Minnesota. Shortly after the war he had, on behalf of his home state, begun an intensive campaign among the Scandinavians in America, especially in Illinois, Indiana, and New York. As part of these efforts he had written a pamphlet about Minnesota which was printed in the Swedish and Norwegian languages, and on which much subsequent propaganda material published in Scandinavia was based.

In late 1868, 17 years after his emigration, Colonel Mattson returned to Sweden on his first visit. He was then commissioner of immigration for Minnesota and land agent for one of its land-grant railroads, the St. Paul & Pacific, and his main purpose seems to have been to make the resources of the North Star State better known among the farmers and workers in Sweden.

Mattson's first contact of importance was Karl Möllersvärd (1832–1901), the son of an army officer, who after his conversion in America in 1853 had become one of the Baptist pioneers in Scandinavia and now was the editor of a newspaper at Kristianstad, near Mattson's birthplace. A few months later, Möllersvärd was appointed the agent of an American shipping company, the Allan Line, at Kristianstad; in late 1871 he moved to Gothenburg as its general agent, and one year later he also became the chief representative of one of Minnesota's land-grant railroads, the Northern Pacific, whose interests Mattson likewise tried to further.

Before leaving the United States, Colonel Mattson had received reports about an ambitious project for a Swedish colony in Minnesota which had been launched in southern Sweden by Måns Olsson Lindbergh, another Civil War veteran, whose father, Ola Månsson Lindbergh, in 1860 had settled in Minnesota with his second wife and an infant son. The younger Lindbergh, who had been offered the title of captain in the U.S. Army and now was serving in a Swedish regiment as a noncommissioned officer, hoped to be able to lead

1,000 men, women, and children to Minnesota, where they would establish a homogeneous colony with public officials, teachers, and clergymen of their own. When his expedition finally left Sweden in April of 1869, however, only about 200 people were ready to follow him. Conservative newspapers in southwest Sweden had attacked his project from the beginning, and the name of his father, whose sudden emigration from Sweden had caused much criticism, also became involved in this campaign. Måns Olsson Lindbergh returned to Sweden from America in December, 1869, and a few months later he died, probably from tuberculosis.

Colonel Mattson was a shrewder and more experienced promoter. Without engaging in any advertising but using his personal influence at meetings with relatives and old and new friends, he was able to assemble in a few months a group of 441 emigrants, and with these he sailed from Copenhagen at the end of April, 1869, proceeding with the Allan Line from Liverpool a week later. With some exceptions the members of his contingent were relatively well-to-do. Most of them were from Mattson's home district, the northeast of Skåne, but there were also families from other parts of Sweden, primarily the province of Värmland and the city of Örebro, where he had visited relatives of his friends in America. Some 210 of his emigrants went directly to Minnesota, most of them to Red Wing where Mattson still made his home.

Colonel Mattson's successful efforts for an increased immigration to Minnesota led to his election as secretary of state at St. Paul. After somewhat more than one year, in the spring of 1871, he resigned from that post to go to Sweden as a land and emigration agent for the Lake Superior & Mississippi Railroad, which like the other two land-grant railways in Minnesota now belonged to the empire of Jay Cooke, the legendary Philadelphia financier. The famine in Sweden had been followed by a period of general economic upswing, and the emigration was practically bound to decline, but Mattson managed to recruit at least 350 emigrants for the colonization area of the railroad he was working for. The long-range effects of his activities regarding Swedish emigration to Minnesota and other sections of the Midwest were considerable.

A majority of the 350-odd emigrants who went to the railroad land in eastern Minnesota came from Dalarna, while many of the

335

others were from the province of Hälsingland, farther east on the Gulf of Bothnia. Mattson had, in fact, concentrated his activities on these two provinces a great part of the time, and he had done this because of what he had learned about the early Swedish settlers in Minnesota's Chisago and Isanti counties north and northeast of Minneapolis-St. Paul, where large sections fell within the colonization area of the Lake Superior & Mississippi Railroad. He knew, for instance, that in the 1860s many members of Baptist groups at Orsa, Mora, and other communities in Dalarna had emigrated to America, in particular to Isanti County, the "Dalarna of America," and that Isanti therefore had a strong drawing power on relatives and friends in the Swedish Dalarna. Mattson had long realized that there was no more effective emigration promotion than the already existing Swedish settlements in America, and the letters and reports emanating from them.

Colonel Mattson also visited Finland and Norway. His friend Karl Möllersvärd, who had been the first Baptist missionary on Finnish soil, handled a substantial part of the growing emigration from Finland. In 1872 Mattson himself helped organize an American tour for a noted Swedish journalist, Hugo Nisbeth (1837–87), who during the next two years traveled all over the United States, except the South, and spent much time in Minnesota. His articles were published in *Aftonbladet*, the influential Stockholm daily, and widely quoted in the provincial press.

While Mattson conducted little direct emigration propaganda in the Swedish daily press, he became very active in newly founded weekly newspapers, the aim of which was to stimulate emigration to America. In Gothenburg a tabloid called *Amerika* had been published since late 1869, first in close cooperation with a Chicago firm, the Swedish Commercial Company, which promoted emigration to Kansas, Nebraska, and Missouri. Under Mattson's influence, however, it became a wholehearted friend of Minnesota. Discontinued in late 1872, *Amerika* was soon followed by *Nya Werlden* (The New World), with Karl Möllersvärd as editor. Another weekly, *Tidning för Menige Men* (Newspaper for the Common People), was published in Gothenburg in 1872–74. In Jönköping, the largest city in northern Småland, a paper called *Sverige och Amerika* appeared during 1871 and 1872, and in the late 1860s Örebro, capital of the province of Närke, had

Amerika-Bladet, followed in 1870 by a monthly, *Swedish American Review*.

The contents of the emigration newspapers were chiefly letters from Swedish settlers in America, but melodramatic descriptions of the privations suffered by poor people in Sweden were also printed. Most of the first publications of this type went out of business in the early or middle 1870s when the Swedish emigration to America seemed to have lost most of its steam.

Early in 1873, Karl Möllersvärd wrote in a report that as the new general agent of the Northern Pacific Railroad he had encountered an "extreme hostility toward America and emigration." He decided, therefore, not to engage in public propaganda but depend instead on individual persuasion. His Baptist background gave him access to people already leaning toward emigration. In 1874 he became a newspaper publisher at Uppsala.

In May of 1873 Colonel Mattson left Sweden with a group of about 200 emigrants, most of them from the province of Dalarna. A few months later, when he was back in Europe, his employer, Jay Cooke, was ruined by the financial crash, and Mattson himself lost his position as well as most of his property in Minnesota, as he had done in 1857. The next two years he again lived in Sweden, serving as the leader of the Canadian emigration promotion in the Scandinavian countries. At this time there were few Scandinavians in Canada, and it was difficult to enlist new emigrants. In 1876 Mattson returned to Minnesota to begin anew. His subsequent career took him to Calcutta as American consul general and finally again to St. Paul as secretary of state. In the American press he was recognized as an outstanding pioneer and was described, for instance, as "the leading Scandinavian spirit of the Northwest." He died in 1893, survived by his wife Kersti, who came from the same district in southern Sweden, and five of their ten children. Mattson had seen Minnesota's Swedish-born population rise from about 4,000 to over 100,000.

Other emigrant agents in Sweden in the early 1870s were Joseph E. Osborne, son of the Swedish-American pioneer pastor Lars Paul Esbjörn, who promoted the Burlington Railroad land in Iowa and Nebraska, and Captain Gustav W. Schröder (1821–1914), who sent emigrants to a Swedish settlement in Maine which had been founded in 1870 by William Widgery Thomas, Jr. Schröder, who had been converted to the Baptist faith in New Orleans in 1844, had a house in Gothenburg which other emigration promoters as well as religious revivalists used as their headquarters. After having moved first to Chicago, then to San Francisco, and then back to Gothenburg where he became an American consul, he spent the last three decades of his life in New York. He wrote a book entitled *History of the Swedish Baptists in Sweden and America.*

In 1869–77, a veteran of the Civil War, Brigadier General Christopher Columbus Andrews, served as American minister in Stockholm. He was born in New Hampshire but had settled in Minnesota, where his friends expected him to help bring about an increased immigration of Swedes and other Scandinavians. This he seemed determined to do, but his own propaganda activities in Sweden were always conducted with diplomatic restraint. He and Colonel Hans Mattson were good friends. When Andrews left Stockholm in 1877, King Oscar II toasted him with the remark that he had been "the most useful representative the United States had ever sent to Sweden." Relations between the Swedish monarch and William Widgery Thomas, who in 1883 began his first assignment as American minister in Stockholm, became even more cordial.

Migration temporarily checked in 1870s —
Record flood begins in 1879

WHEN the effects of the crop failures in the late 1860s had been overcome the Swedish emigration to America began to recede, and during the five years 1874–78 the average annual flow was only about 4,000, while each year nearly 1,000 former emigrants returned to Sweden. The impulse to emigrate was checked by improving economic conditions and other progress in Sweden, while the attraction of the New World had temporarily diminished as a result of the American financial panic of 1873 and the depression which followed. For the ten-year period 1871–80, the central emigration records list somewhat more than 100,000 people as having left for the United States, while for 1861–70 the official figure was approximately 90,000. The actual totals were probably about 110,000 and 120,000.

From a *political* viewpoint, the decade of the 1870s was not particularly fruitful in Sweden. After the reform of 1865–66, when a modern two-chamber parliament replaced the old legislature based on the four estates, the political power shifted at first toward the farmers, and not toward the urban middle class as the liberals had hoped. As a rule the landowners resisted costly new reforms, but progressive ideas were, nevertheless, represented even among them. In 1870, after a debate marked by the warmest appreciation of the Swedish Jewry, the Riksdag by overwhelming majorities removed all restrictions on the civil rights of Jews and Christian dissenters — a decision which both liberal and conservative newspapers greeted with enthusiasm.

In 1872 King Carl XV died and was succeeded by his brother, Oscar II (1829–1907), who especially in the beginning seemed anxious to restore the declining influence of the monarchy. Two of his principal aims were a strong defense and a closer cooperation with Germany. During the Franco-Prussian war in 1870–71, Sweden's sympathies had been with France, but there were two notable exceptions in the press, the Gothenburg *Handelstidningen* and the likewise liberal Stockholm *Dagens Nyheter*, founded in 1864. During the latter part of the 19th century the great majority of the people became more and more inclined to rule out war as an instrument of foreign policy except in extreme necessity, that is, if Sweden's freedom should be directly threatened. Germany's growing influence, although reflected in many other ways, affected this sentiment only to a small degree.

During most of the 1870s, on the other hand, Sweden enjoyed an *economic* upsurge, with extensive railroad construction, an increasing production of lumber, iron, textiles, and machinery, and a growing foreign trade. Industry attracted more and more workers and thus absorbed some of the agrarian surplus population. Toward the end of the decade, however, emigration again began to rise, and the 1880s brought an unexpected mass movement to America. Neither the authorities nor the great majority of the observers in the press were prepared for it.

In the period 1881–90, about 325,000 Swedes emigrated to America, according to the central statistics. The new waves, however, actually began in 1879 and rolled along until 1893, when Sweden had entered a period of more rapid industrial expansion and the United States again was swept by a disastrous panic. In those 15 years about 490,000 officially registered emigrants, or in reality more than half a million people, were carried over the Atlantic. More than 50,000

Swedes moved to other European countries, and sooner or later many of these ended up in the United States. In some years the direct flow from Sweden to America exceeded 50,000. The lowest annual totals, about 20,000, were recorded in 1884–85 when the demand for labor increased in the Swedish cities and a relatively short-lived financial panic had hit the United States. A few years later, however, emigration from Sweden to America reached about 50,000. In the late 1800s there was also some emigration to Australia and South America.

The forces underlying the Swedish emigration were obviously strengthened by new events in the late 1870s, and the most important one, at least so far as the countryside was concerned, was the beginning agricultural crisis in Sweden and other European countries. In the American Midwest vast wheat fields had been opened up by immigrants, and as a result of the development of railroad transportation and transatlantic navigation, their yield could now be sold in Europe. Fundamentally, of course, this was an advance, but the appearance of cheap American grain in Sweden caused a steep fall in prices, and the farmers were hard hit. Smaller quantities of low-priced grain were imported from Russia. Following the example of other European nations but only after an exceptionally vehement political struggle, Sweden in 1888 imposed agrarian tariffs. The agricultural depression lasted into the 1890s, but it was accompanied by an increasingly rapid modernization of the farming industry, especially in the more fertile sections of the southern and south-central provinces.

The agricultural population in Sweden began to decline in the 1880s, and this was a consequence not only of the emigration to America but also of the increasing drawing power of Sweden's cities and towns. Fundamentally, these two phenomena were closely related, much of the emigration to the New World being one aspect of the growing Swedish movement from farm to city.

To begin with, many of the emigrating farm workers and other inhabitants of the overpopulated Swedish countryside had considered moving to some city in Sweden, but finally the scale was turned in favor of Chicago or Minneapolis, or perhaps the Boston area or Worcester, Massachusetts, where they often expected to feel more at home and also to do better than in Stockholm, Jönköping, or Karlstad: in the cities on the other side of the Atlantic they already had close relatives or friends, who wanted them to come, and who moreover seemed willing to help them over the first difficult period toward some reasonably good employment.

After the setback occurring in 1893–94, the pace of emigration from Sweden remained relatively slow, and the total for the decade of the 1890s came to be about 200,000. The American prosperity which began in 1897–98, however, again helped speed the exodus, and the effects of the financial panic of 1907 were soon offset by a serious labor conflict in Sweden, so that from 1901 to 1910 the emigrants totaled about 230,000. The following three or four years brought little change, but then the outbreak of the World War stemmed the flow. About 80,000 Swedes emigrated to the United States in the period 1911–20.

In 1920, the total of Swedes who had left for America since the beginning of the continuous emigration in the late 1840s reached approximately 1,200,000. Nearly one-fourth had come from the cities.

Low wages and unemployment cause heavy emigration from Stockholm and other cities

DECLINING agricultural prices and wages contributed greatly to the heavy emigration from Sweden in the period 1879–93, but the urge to move was not by any means largely limited to the rural districts. The urban and semiurban population had taken part in the migration to the New World ever since its beginning, and the proportion of nonagrarian emigrants increased constantly during the latter part of the 19th century. During most of the years of mass migration, the emigration intensity was, in fact, higher in the Swedish cities and towns than it was in the countryside.

In the period 1880–93, about 23,000 U.S.A.-bound emigrants said farewell to Stockholm, which accounted for 28 percent of the total urban emigration during this period. By the middle of the 19th century the capital had only about 90,000 inhabitants, but during the decade of the 1880s its population increased from 170,000 to nearly 250,000, that is, by almost 50 percent.

Inevitably, this rapid growth overstrained Stockholm's resources, and periods of recession, unemployment, declining wages, and labor conflicts, which from the end of the 1870s occurred at rather short intervals, were always reflected in rising emigration. In certain years, the emigration intensity was especially high among workers in the metal and building industries, shoemakers, tailors, and dressmakers. Skilled labor often moved out on almost the same scale as unskilled. Especially after 1886, office workers and similar salaried employees emigrated to an extent that almost corresponded to their share in the total working population, and during several periods this was also true of the small manufacturers. Emigrants from other cities and towns included many mining and forest-industry workers.

In Stockholm as well as in other larger cities, and probably also in the country as a whole, no single group reached a higher emigration intensity than the housemaids. The reason must have been that in their case both the drawing power or "pull" of America and the Swedish "push" factors were unusually conspicuous. In Sweden the female servants generally had miserable wages and working conditions. The kitchen, where they worked most of the time, was where many of them slept. In the United States they had, as a rule, their own room and limited working hours, and according to a Swedish newspaper report of 1890, they received a weekly compensation of two to five dollars, which was much more than they could expect in Sweden. Long before 1890, letters from America, organized emigration promotion, and oral reports from visiting former emigrants had produced an enticing picture of life for Scandinavian maids in the New World, and Sweden would not be able to offer serious competition until the housemaid already was headed for almost complete extinction.

The United States also became known as "the country without conscription," and a desire to escape military service probably played some part in many decisions to emigrate.

While most of the emigrants from Sweden were poor or at least in pinched circumstances, people who depended on private charity or aid from public funds were seldom able to join the ranks of the travelers. Convicts and vagrants were also underrepresented in the Swedish migration, and, for obvious reasons, so were the sick and the elderly.

During the 1880s Sweden was flooded with all kinds of activities and material promoting emigration to the United States. Both the Swedish railroads and the transatlantic steamship lines had made travel easier, and the latter stepped up their promotion and sales efforts. An English company, for instance, had a general agent in Gothenburg who, in turn, employed 220 subagents, spread over the whole country.

The Swedish settlers in America remained responsible for the most effective emigration propaganda. The letters they wrote to relatives and friends in Sweden helped spread the "America fever" from parish to parish, and from city district to city district except the more fashionable ones. More and more often the Swedes on the other side offered to send full-paid tickets, and their kinfolk in Sweden were both grateful and impressed. Finally, a substantial proportion of the emigrants traveled to the United States on "prepaids," from Sweden as well as from other countries.

Another potent influence was the circulation in Sweden of Swedish-language newspapers published in the United States. People in remote parts of the country were often more interested in such sheets than in the local journals. The call from the Swedes in the United States was also conveyed by visiting Swedish-Americans, known as "Yankees," who had received a free transatlantic round trip for service as emigration promoters. Before their own emigration, most of them had been hired farm laborers or worked on family farms. If they spoke Swedish with an affected American accent and boasted about their experiences over there, which they often did, many well-educated people dismissed them as comical, but in general their message reached their audiences on village greens or in meeting houses.

In Sweden of the 1880s, emigration to the American Land of Promise was an idea whose time had come, and those who opposed it could offer little effective resistance.

Swedish press opposed to emigration, but fanning it by much of its contents

MOST of Sweden's political, intellectual, and commercial leaders viewed with grieved or indignant astonishment the protracted heavy emigration, which threatened eventual depopulation of large districts. With some exceptions, the newspapers took the same attitude.

In 1887 Count Carl Snoilsky (1841–1903), who two decades earlier had become one of the country's most admired poets, wrote an elegy likening the emigration figures to casualty lists from a war. In the same poem, he finally envisioned the day when Sweden through proper reforms would become a nation whose members would not have to seek their future on the other side of the Atlantic. But four years later, in an ode for the unveiling of the Linnaeus statue in Chicago, he felt so inspired by the rapidly growing strength of the Swedish language in the New World that he admitted having been wrong the first time. Many lesser poets tried to conjure up the cruel disappointment and the desperate homesickness that inevitably would become the lot of the emigrant. Listening to the emigration agent, one rhymer indicated, was the same as listening to the devil. Bards who sympathized with the emigrants or perhaps already lived in America, on the other hand, did not remain silent. In their poems, the United States easily became a land overflowing with milk and honey, as well as with freedom and equality.

The Swedish press played a part in gradually turning the emigration to America into a mass movement, but this was not done purposely. On the contrary, practically all newspapers wanted the Swedes to remain at home. Conservative editorial writers, in particular, mourned the loss of legions of men and women in their best years, and the emigrants were denounced as unpatriotic or even as defectors and traitors. While America had many good friends in Swedish newspapers, especially in those devoted to liberal ideas, the disposition of the press as a whole did not seem particularly amiable. Most of the influential conservative publications remained skeptical toward the United States. In their rather primitive coverage of events and conditions in the New World, several liberal and labor papers paid special attention to the American labor market, which for obvious reasons interested many of their readers, and such press reports often told distressing stories of unemployment or unrest.

At the same time, however, the press contained lots of material that fanned the flames of emigration. Few newspaper readers could, in fact, escape the conclusion that the United States, despite occasional financial panics and other serious difficulties, was moving forward at a fast pace. Radical journalists continued to hold up the American republic as a model for Sweden's own political and industrial progress, as a rule demanding universal suffrage in the first place, while Baptist and Methodist clergymen-writers with American experience emphasized the greater religious freedom in the New World. Many newspapers published accounts from Swedish settlements or portraits of successful Swedes in America; much material of this type was lifted from the columns of the Swedish-language newspapers in Chicago, Minneapolis, and New York. And the emigration propaganda that filled the advertising pages in Sweden was much more effective than the editorial denunciation of the emigrants.

In the late 1800s, the great mass of the Swedish people was anything but nationalistic, and conventional appeals to patriotism met with little response. Most emigrants felt that they simply had to choose between poverty and departure, or, as it was sometimes said, "Swedish skin and bones in Sweden, or Swedish flesh and blood in America."

The most actively pro-American journalist in Sweden was Isidor Kjellberg (1841–95), who had lived in the United States in 1869–72 and brought back feelings of hopeful admiration for practically everything he had seen, except racial discrimination, the agents known as "runners," who always preyed upon arriving "greenhorns," and the Swedish Lutheran church body, the Augustana Synod, and its clergymen. All efforts to try to preserve the Swedish language in the United States he regarded as harmful to the Swedish immigrants.

In St. Paul, Minnesota, Kjellberg had been editor of a Swedish-language newspaper, and in Chicago he had in 1871, before the Great Fire in October, helped publish a radical, muckraking weekly called *Justitia*. In Sweden he became a journalistic pioneer as well as one of the leaders in the struggle for universal suffrage. At Linköping, the capital of the province of Östergötland, he founded in 1872 a liberal daily called *Östgöten*, and there he launched two journalistic techniques which had just been introduced in America, the interview and investigative reporting; the Swedish use of the word interview began, in fact, during this period. On the façade of his newspaper building he placed a miniature reproduction of the Statue of Liberty, which raised its illuminated torch against the originally liberal but then increasingly conservative paper *Östgöta Correspondenten* on the other side of the street, and on national holidays he proudly displayed the Star-Spangled Banner. In particular the workers of Sweden, he felt, ought to look toward the American republic as their ideal, and when he organized the first May Day demonstration at Linköping in

1890, the American flag was carried among the banners at the head of the procession. Kjellberg himself was well aware of the mixed reaction to his activities. In the whole world, he observed, there is no country at once more popular and more abused than the United States.

Economic conditions and the employment situation in the United States were followed with special interest by two Stockholm newspapers, *Socialdemokraten*, which was founded in 1885 by some labor leaders, and the liberal *Dagens Nyheter*. A careful study of their issues from 1886 to 1894 has shown that most of this time their reports gave the impression that it was hard to get a job in the cities of the United States, and that it was almost impossible for the workers to hold their own against the powerful employers. This led to the conclusion that the mass emigration of workers from the Swedish capital was caused, above all, by conditions in Stockholm itself, rather than by the drawing power of America. In the late 1800s a large part of Stockholm's population lived from hand to mouth and was always hard hit by economic recessions.

Time and again, the American society and its economy also seemed largely unattractive. The year 1886, for instance, brought the beginning of a series of reports and comments on the Haymarket Square riot in Chicago, which caused the death of seven policemen and led to seven death sentences. In 1888–89 the American labor market, according to reports to the Stockholm papers, seemed dominated by unsuccessful strikes, wage cuts, and extensive unemployment. Another steady stream of such tidings began in 1891, but nevertheless about 2,500 Stockholmers emigrated to America in that year. In 1892 the long steelworkers' strike at Homestead, Pennsylvania, and the bloodshed that accompanied it loomed on Sweden's western horizon, and yet the emigration from Stockholm reached its highest annual total, about 2,700. In great part, this may be regarded as a protest vote against mass unemployment and social injustices in the Swedish capital. In 1893, when the United States plunged into one of its worst economic crises, some 2,300 citizens of Stockholm crossed the Atlantic, and the record migration from the capital did not end until the next year, when the American bankruptcy seemed almost total.

The conditions pushing the emigrants away from Stockholm and other Swedish cities may often have been more powerful than the pull from America, but disturbing or alarming reports from the other side of the Atlantic could never completely overshadow the fundamental strength of the American economy and the virtual certainty of resumed dynamic growth. Whether they had seen it in Swedish newspapers or heard about it from American promoters, the emigrants also felt more or less convinced that the United States already could offer them better living conditions than Sweden had been able to do. In American cities and towns, for instance, the workers seemed to have more spacious dwellings than in Stockholm, where unbearable overcrowding was very common. About one-third of the income of an unskilled worker's family in the Swedish capital was, nevertheless, spent on rent — a much larger share than in big cities in other countries. Many American states had, moreover, introduced a shorter working day than the one applied in Sweden, although press reports concerning this subject did not always reflect actual conditions.

While the budding labor movement in Sweden was critical of the capitalistic aspects of American society, it was not, on the whole, opposed to emigration. The Social Democratic party favored, for instance, compulsory training in English as a service for those who might be headed for emigration. Sooner or later many of the early leaders of the Swedish labor movement decided to move to the United States, and several did this after they had been blacklisted by their employers. Most of the American labor-market reports that were published in *Socialdemokraten* in Stockholm came from Swedish labor leaders or journalists who had left for the United States. One of the best-known members of this group was Atterdag Wermelin (1861–1907), the son of a Lutheran minister in Värmland, who emigrated in 1887 after having studied at Uppsala and worked as a free lance in Stockholm. Unable to find lasting employment, he finally ended his life by jumping from the Brooklyn Bridge in New York.

Several Swedish socialists of the old school became union or party officials in America, and together with other Scandinavians they formed their own sections within American labor organizations. Especially in the Middle West they also published their own newspapers. Such activities gained new momentum after 1909, when tensions between employers and workers in Sweden exploded in a nationwide conflict.

347

20

More Religious Aspects

Continued religious revivals in Sweden help create new transatlantic ties

THE mainspring of the mass migration from Sweden after the Civil War was the belief or hope that America would offer the immigrants or their children better economic opportunities. Among secondary motives was the dream of a society without class barriers, or at least without high-handed bosses and overbearing bureaucrats. After about 1870, when all legislation concerning dissenters had been made much more liberal, few Swedes decided to move because they were dissatisfied with religious conditions at home, but religion played, nevertheless, an important role in stimulating the desire to emigrate.

For thousands of potential emigrants, the complete religious freedom in the United States remained part of its magnetism. Even people who did not regard themselves as particularly religious were affected by propaganda emanating from the more and more influential free-church groups or using their channels of communication. From the revivalist meetings a stirring breeze from the Promised Land in the West blew over freethinkers and indifferents, as well as over the believers. Sunday schools were set up in parish after parish, and it was no secret that this institution came from America. Many of the emigration agents were free-church men, the main reason probably being that the steamship and railroad companies regarded them as particularly effective.

The spiritual revivals that began in Sweden about 1840 have been described by historians as nothing less than a second religious reformation, just as radical and profound as the one of the 16th century. While the older reformation in Sweden came from above and was of German origin, the younger, pietistic or evangelistic movement was Anglo-Saxon and in its later stages, from about 1870, almost exclusively American. Common people were involved from the beginning, and it helped lay the groundwork for a political and social transformation of Sweden.

The greatest of the religious revivals swept over Sweden in the late 1870s. At that time Paul Peter Waldenström (1838–1917), who like his teacher and predecessor Carl Olof Rosenius came from the far north, had become the foremost pietistic leader in the country. A doctor of philosophy from Uppsala University and then a teacher of Greek, Hebrew, and Christian doctrines at junior colleges, he was in 1864 ordained a minister in the state church. When resigning 18 years later, he had already played a leading part in a growing split between the state church and members of its pietistic wing, the Mission Friends, who in 1878 decided to form the Swedish Mission Covenant. In the weekly *Pietisten*, which he edited for nearly fifty years, Waldenström published in 1872 a vigorous sermon in which he expressed disagreement with the orthodox Lutheran doctrine in regard to atonement. His testimony had reverberations both in Sweden and among the Swedish immigrants in America, where *Pietisten* was widely read.

The Swedish Mission Covenant laid stress on conversion and life rather than on doctrines and institutions, and its leaders welcomed all active Christians who wanted to join. While decidedly conservative in their private code of morals, the Mission Friends have generally been politically liberal and progressive.

Waldenström was one of the greatest evangelistic preachers Sweden has had. For 20 years an influential member of the Riksdag, he introduced the first bill calling for universal suffrage; he also worked for a stronger national defense, which disappointed many of his supporters. He made three trips to America, where he had won many friends. During his first visit, in 1889, he received an honorary doctorate from Yale University. At that time the leaders and ministers of the Lutheran Augustana Synod regarded him as an adversary. Their relations improved in the early 20th century, but Waldenström and other Mission Friends always seemed to have more in common with the American Congregationalists.

Unlike so many of the free-church people, Waldenström was not enthusiastic about America and things American, but during his second visit, in 1901, he became much more impressed than he had been 12 years earlier. In both cases he published a comprehensive, illustrated travel account. His book about the tour in 1889 was, on the whole, marked by reserve and skepticism, while the second report seems to have been written by a both interested and sympathetic observer.

Shortly after his arrival in America in the fall of 1901, Waldenström attended in New Haven Yale University's 200th-anniversary celebration. Among his memorable experiences there was meeting President Theodore Roosevelt, who had acceded to his office only about a month earlier, and who now told the Swedish visitor how much he appreciated everything coming to America from Scandinavia. During a subsequent stay in Washington, Waldenström seems to have discussed with the Swedish-Norwegian envoy a possible audience with the nation's chief executive, but he decided to abstain, having heard that President Roosevelt had said that "the head of a nation of 80 million cannot have time to be one of the country's tourist attractions." The days when foreign visitors of some importance had a good chance to see the President were over.

Quite a few of Waldenström's observations and comments in his second book dealt with the United States as a country of sharp contrasts. Despite its enormous wealth, he wrote for instance, Chicago in the fall of 1901 had to keep its evening schools closed because of lack of funds. Although the Swedish scholar and religious leader in some other connections sounded like an uncompromising conservative, he regretted that not more had been done to tame American capitalism, but in the end he felt decidedly hopeful about the country: "Freedom, used in the light of true knowledge, is the foremost precondition for a people's happy development. Freedom is, therefore, the very core of American life; and the work on spreading knowledge in all fields is certainly greater than in any other country. Oh, I wish that I could take with me something of the industry, the vigor, the perseverance, the endurance that are characteristic of labor in America!"

To an even higher degree than the other denominations, the Mission Friend movement benefited from a constant interaction between religious impulses on the two sides of the Atlantic. In America, many Swedish immigrants of pietist leanings had, to begin with, attended the already established Swedish Lutheran churches, but several mission societies were formed in the late 1860s, and when in 1885 two rival synods were merged into The Swedish Evangelical Mission Covenant in America, its associated congregations numbered 47. Carl August Björk (1837–1916) from Lommaryd in Småland, who had been a shoemaker and a soldier in his native land and in 1868 at Swede Bend, Iowa, had organized the first Mission Friend congregation in America, was elected its first president. He was a great missionary and leader. The name of the association was later changed to The Evangelical Covenant Church of America. A smaller group of Mission Friends, which was organized in 1884 at Boone, Iowa, was first known as The Swedish American Mission Society and finally became The Evangelical Free Church of America. In 1950 it was merged with The Evangelical Free Church Association, which was of Danish-Norwegian origin.

One of the early Mission Covenant leaders, Erik August Skogsbergh (1850–1939), is regarded as one of the greatest preachers the Swedes in America have produced. Born in the province of Värmland, he was driven from home by his father after his conversion and became a student at a religious school for the training of laymen in Småland. In 1876 he left for America to become pastor of a Mission Friend church in Chicago. There he was warmly greeted by the veteran American evangelist, Dwight L. Moody, and at times the two conducted joint campaigns. At the World's Fair in Chicago in 1893, for which Moody arranged evangelistic services in many languages, Skogsbergh was introduced by his American friend as the "Swedish Moody." His most important work was done as a pastor in Minneapolis from 1884 to 1908, and after that he was active in Seattle for five years. In both cities he built mammoth "Swedish tabernacles," as the Mission Friend churches were called. Another outstanding preacher was Gustaf F. Johnson (1873–1959) from Nässjö in Småland, who was called to the Minneapolis Tabernacle in 1914 and served there for 24 years. He had immigrated to Texas with his family in 1883.

The educational system of the Mission Covenant had its beginning in 1884 in a school conducted by Skogsbergh in his home in Minneapolis. Ten years later the first institution was transferred to Chicago and given the name North Park College, while Skogsbergh at Minneapolis founded a new school which the Mission Covenant also finally took over, then calling it Minnehaha Academy. The first president of North Park College was David Nyvall (1863–1946), a native of Karlskoga in Värmland, who, after having interrupted his medical studies at Uppsala, had come to America in 1886. He was admired and respected both as a religious leader and as a scholar. The Chicago Theological Seminary, a Congregational institution, had a Swedish department from 1885 to 1916. A Home of Mercy which the Mission Covenant opened in 1886 grew into the highly regarded Swedish Covenant Hospital. In the early 1900s Dr. O. Theodore Roberg made outstanding contributions as chief surgeon.

David Nyvall's father, Carl Johan Nyvall (1829–1904), had been about to emigrate as a young man but became instead a pioneer Mission Friend and youth leader in Sweden. He visited the United States four times, preaching to Swedish-American audiences. After his first tour, in 1875–76, he wrote in a travel report that "when you hear about all the privations the pioneers have had to endure, you cannot very well advise anyone to emigrate. Many have said that had they known what was in store for them in America, they would never have gone. However, those who have taken homesteads and have successfully braved the first five or six years, are satisfied with their circumstances and do not want to return. . . . Appraising the religious atmosphere in America is an even more difficult thing to do, for that which appears to be ardent religious zeal is often only a profane agitation in favor of certain church groups, and liberal-mindedness and tolerance toward different persuasions are often merely indifference toward all spirituality. And yet I must admit that we have much to learn from America . . ." In the 1880s, Nyvall's home province, Värmland, became one of Sweden's leading mass-emigration districts.

The Mission Covenant Church attracted more members than the Swedish Baptist and Methodist organizations and became the second largest church body among the Swedes in America, after the Lutheran Augustana Synod. In Sweden, the national Mission Covenant also grew more rapidly than the other free-church associations, reaching a membership of 90,000 in 1900. At that time there were about 41,000 Baptists and 17,000 Methodists in Sweden. Large numbers of free-church men and women had moved to the United States.

Salvation Army reaches Sweden from England, new religious sects from America

THE Mormons, or Latter Day Saints, began to conduct missionary work, as well as emigration promotion, in Sweden in 1850. According to Swedish statistics the number of Swedish converts to Mormonism from 1850 to 1909 was about 17,500, of whom nearly 8,000 emi-grated to America, while some 5,000 later withdrew from the church while still in Sweden. Members of all the new religious associations were often subjected to social ostracism in Sweden, and the Mormons also met with strong active opposition.

A Swedish Salvation Army was founded in 1882 by Hanna Ouchterlony (1838–1924), the daughter of a district judge at Vär-namo in the province of Småland. After a religious crisis she had met Bramwell Booth, the eldest son of the founder of the Salvation Army, who came to the forested Värnamo district to improve his health. In the beginning, the militant enthusiasm and new-fashioned methods of the Salvationists aroused opposition, derision, and sometimes even persecution in Sweden, but in ten years Miss Ouchterlony raised an active force of over 10,000. In 1888 she introduced the movement in Norway. In 1892 she visited the Salvation Army units in the United States as a delegate of the international headquarters in London.

One of Hanna Ouchterlony's early associates was a lieutenant of the fashionable Svea Artillery Regiment, Herman Lagercrantz (1859–1945), who in 1889 resigned from the military service to join the Salvation Army. His wife also played an active role in the organi-zation. After a successful career in business, Lagercrantz served as Sweden's minister to the United States from 1907 to 1910 and in 1917.

A Scandinavian branch of the Salvation Army in the United States was begun in 1887 by four women who had been Salvationists in their native Sweden. The first Scandinavian corps was established in Brook-lyn, a young Swedish officer, Mary Hartelius from Helsingborg, being appointed to command it. Jamestown, New York, and Philadelphia followed, and then came Chicago, Moline and Rockford, Illinois, St.

353

Paul, and Minneapolis. At one time the Scandinavian branch had 85 corps and almost as many outposts. Today, it is a wholly integrated part of the international Salvation Army. In 1972, a Swedish descendant from Worcester, Massachusetts, Paul J. Carlson, became National Commander of the Salvation Army in the United States. Erik Wickberg, born in 1904 at Gävle, north of Stockholm, served in 1969–74 as leader of the whole Salvation Army, directing its activities in 71 countries from his headquarters in London.

Another woman, Elisabet Hesselblad (1870–1957) from central Västergötland, became the best known of the few Swedish Catholic converts in the United States in the late 19th century. After her emigration from Sweden in 1888, she began life in New York as a student nurse and was graduated four years later. Her interest in Catholicism was aroused by immigrants from Ireland and other European countries whom she met in the slum districts. After a pilgrimage to Rome in 1903 and a three-year-long study of convents in Europe, she established a new branch of the ancient order of Brigittines, whose nuns were permitted to engage in social work. The original order was founded in the middle 1300s by Birgitta Birgersdotter (1303–73), who after her death and subsequent canonization became known as St. Birgitta, or Bridget. The principal house of the order, at Vadstena on Lake Vättern in the province of Östergötland, played a remarkable part in promoting culture and literature in Scandinavia during the later Middle Ages; today, Vadstena conveys more strongly than any other place in Sweden an impression of the 14th and 15th centuries. Elisabet Hesselblad finally became abbess of a convent in Rome. She has been called a "second Birgitta."

During or shortly after the First World War, the Pentecostal sect became the most rapidly growing church body in Sweden. It had been imported from Norway in 1907, but was originally a California product. An early advance agent was a Swede named Fredrik Franson (1852–1908), born near the ancient mining town of Nora in the province of Västmanland, who came to America with his parents in 1869, at the age of 17, and first settled in Nebraska. In 1875 he became a follower of Dwight L. Moody and started traveling in the United States as an evangelist preacher. After staging a world conference in Chicago in 1881 to prepare for the Second Coming of Christ, he returned to Sweden, and during the next three years he visited more than half of its cities and towns, often preaching to immense crowds. Large meetings were also held in Norway. His appeal was directed at Baptists, Methodists, and Mission Friends primarily, but also to others who were ready to step over denominational boundaries. In 1884 he went to Denmark and from there to Germany, Switzerland, Italy, the Middle East, Russia, and Poland.

Both in the United States and in Sweden, as well as in some other countries, Franson recruited a great many young men and women for missionary work in China, which he visited in 1894 when he also traveled in India and Japan. His enthusiasm survived even the Boxer Uprising in 1900, when 41 Swedish missionaries and 15 of their children were killed. Subsequent extensive travels took him to Australia and South America. About Franson as a preacher George M. Stephenson wrote that "he had only a smattering of English, German, and French, but that mattered none, for he could pray so fervently in the language of his boyhood parish, that his hearers would burst into tears." Franson was one of Sweden's most remarkable religious personalities, and has been called a Swedish Francis of Assisi. At the age of 56, he died at Idaho Springs, Colorado, where he was resting from his whirlwind missionary work.

During the 1870s and 1880s the Swedish temperance movement was also greatly influenced from America, thus becoming much more radical both in method and in spirit. Most of the temperance agitators were absolutists, as they were in the United States. An American promoter, Eli Johnson, visited Sweden in 1876 and was received with enthusiasm by temperance people.

In 1879 the Independent Order of Good Templars was imported to Sweden by Olof Bergström (1841–1910), who nine years earlier had left for the United States. There he preached Baptism, worked as an immigration agent for the Union Pacific Railroad, and helped found the town of Stromsburg in Nebraska. After having set up a score of Good-Templar lodges in Sweden, he returned in 1882 to America, where immigration promotion and land speculations made him one of the founders of Gothenburg, Nebraska. Bergström, who was born at Delsbo in the province of Hälsingland, died in Tennessee. A new temperance organization, the Order of Templars, was founded in the United States in 1883 by an immigrant from the Swedish province of Närke, Adolph Peterson (1853–1923), and in-

355

troduced by him in Sweden the following year. In 1878–83 he had published in New York a Swedish-language monthly for the promotion of temperance. After his visit to Sweden he returned to the United States, where an invention of importance to the weaving of carpets made him rich.

The more active temperance organizations in Sweden continued to grow until 1909–10, when they had a total of about 450,000 members. In 1909, according to a privately sponsored popular vote, 56 percent of the adult population favored prohibition. In 1922, however, prohibition was rejected by a small margin in a consultative public referendum. A liquor-rationing system, which had been introduced in 1917, remained in effect until October 1, 1955. The temperance societies continue to be an important educational influence.

21

New Contacts and Exchanges

Sweden at Centennial Fair in Philadelphia in 1876 —
Expanding imports from the U.S.

IN 1876, commercial and cultural relations between Sweden and the United States were bolstered by Sweden's comprehensive participation in the Centennial Exhibition in Philadelphia.

Among the guests of honor at the celebration of the 100th anniversary of American independence on July 4 was King Oscar II's second son, Prince Oscar (1859–1953), who had arrived as a midshipman on the frigate *Norrköping*, one of two warships sent to Philadelphia by the Swedish government. Prince Oscar, who was the first member of the Swedish royal family to visit America, married in 1888 a Swedish commoner, Ebba Munck, and forsook his rights to the throne. He devoted much of his life to religious and social work, being, for instance, president of the Swedish Y.M.C.A. from 1892 to 1943. One of his sons, Count Folke Bernadotte (1895–1948), became leader of the Swedish Red Cross and lost his life while serving as United Nations Mediator in Palestine.

The Swedish parliament had set aside a considerable amount of money for the preparations for the Philadelphia exposition, and about 500 Swedish firms decided to take part. The fair grounds occupied 60 acres in Fairmount Park, on a high plateau overlooking the Schuylkill — a district which had been settled by Swedish colonists about 1692, after having been purchased from the Indians in 1654 by

Governor Johan Rising of New Sweden. The Swedish exhibits of cutlery, machinery and tools for working metals, wood and stone, agricultural machinery and dairy equipment, ceramic articles and other industrial art, leather goods, wrapping paper, and wood pulp received praise from critics, and Sweden captured 216 awards, placing sixth among the some 30 participating countries. A large Swedish art collection, on the other hand, seems to have attracted little attention, and only two of the exhibiting artists, Georg von Rosen (1843–1923) and Alfred Wahlberg (1834–1906), received medals. Rosen specialized in portraits and in scenes from Swedish history. Wahlberg, who is represented in the Art Institute of Chicago and in the Metropolitan Museum of Art and the Brooklyn Museum in New York, became a pioneer of the modern, French-oriented landscape art in Sweden and all Scandinavia.

Two Swedish sections were specially mentioned by most writers who covered the exposition at Philadelphia, namely, the Swedish schoolhouse with its educational material and the ethnographic exhibit in the Main Building, consisting of groups of plastic figures in provincial costumes. The timbered schoolhouse, which had been sent over from Sweden and erected on the fair grounds near the Main Building, was bought by the city of New York in 1877 and moved to Central Park, not far from West 79th Street. The house was used at first as an outing place for crippled children, and then as a nature laboratory for children and a nature-study center in connection with a "nature trail" no longer existing. Finally it became a storehouse for the Department of Parks.

When the transatlantic trade had recovered after the Civil War, the United States began to achieve an export surplus in its exchange of commerce with Sweden, which had hardly happened during the first part of the 19th century. In some years American exports to Sweden seem to have been about three times as large as the shipments of Swedish goods to the New World. Most of the trade between the two countries went by way of English, German, or other European ports, while the official Swedish statistics listed only the direct shipments. Before 1905, when the Swedish-Norwegian union was dissolved, the American records made no distinction between trade with Sweden and that with Norway.

Throughout the latter part of the 19th century and into the 20th, cotton and refined petroleum were the leading American export articles to Sweden. Scandinavia's long, dark winters resulted in a heavy demand for illuminating kerosene and other petroleum products, and until the 1890s all of Sweden's millions of oil lamps were burning American oil. Fuel from Russia, whose petroleum industry Swedes helped develop, was then introduced on the Swedish market, but the United States remained Sweden's foremost source of refined petroleum.

From the United States, Sweden also purchased large quantities of sole leather and pork. In the late 1800s, American pork became a vital part of the daily fare in every lumberjacks' camp in the forests of northern Sweden, where the calorie need in wintertime was very high. Purchases of American wheat and corn declined after the introduction of protective tariffs in 1888, but with the growth of Swedish industry, new American products began to find a market in Sweden. In the early 1900s, Swedish imports of copper, machinery, and lubricating oil from the United States were exceeded only by those of cotton and refined petroleum. Long before the turn of the century, Swedish sewing machines and harvesters had begun to compete with imports from America. In the early 1900s International Harvester, one of the leading American manufacturers of agricultural machinery, started a manufacturing plant at Norrköping.

Until the early 20th century iron was the only product that the United States purchased from Sweden in larger quantities, and most of it was bar iron: In the late 1880s, American annual purchases of Swedish iron rose to about 65,000 tons, representing a value of nearly 8 million kronor or about $2.3 million. This was approximately twice the quantity shipped from Sweden in the 1830s, but the Swedish iron now accounted for a much smaller part of the American import requirements. After reaching a last peak of about 50,000 tons in the early 1900s, American purchases of Swedish iron steadily declined and finally lost all significance. Instead, the United States imported from Sweden increasing quantities of wire, nails, and steel products. Ore from the rich iron mines in the far north of Sweden was also shipped to America in the early 1900s.

Toward the end of the 1800s, a modest second place in American imports from Sweden was held by wood pulp, which during the second decade of the 20th century would rise to the predominant position in Swedish sales to the United States. At that time, America had also begun to import Swedish newsprint and wrapping paper. During at least part of the late 1800s, safety matches made up the third largest American import from Sweden, followed by separators and some other machinery the total value of which was small.

Direct shipping from Sweden to the United States almost came to an end in the late 1800s, and American ships were rarely seen in Swedish harbors. Both merchant marines were in a period of decline after the advent of the steamship.

After Sweden's participation in the Centennial Exhibition in Philadelphia in 1876, no single event in American-Swedish relations in the late 1800s seems to have attracted greater attention on both sides of the Atlantic than the U. S. government's decision in 1890 to send the remains of Captain John Ericsson to his native land. By the middle of September one of the most modern units of the U. S. Navy, the cruiser *Baltimore*, arrived in Stockholm, and imposing ceremonies followed in the Swedish capital and in the province of Värmland, where the famous inventor was born and finally buried. Today the event as a whole may seem too pompous, but it strengthened the goodwill for America in Sweden and emphasized the basic friendship between the two nations. The Swedes were moved by the honors accorded the memory of John Ericsson, and indirectly the Scandinavian element in America, by the United States. Stockholm received the officers and the crew of the *Baltimore* with a warmhearted hospitality that could hardly have been surpassed.

American-Swedish friendship on the wings of song —
New "Nightingale" in 1870s

TWENTY years after Jenny Lind's triumphant arrival in New York in the fall of 1850, another "Swedish Nightingale," Kristina or Christine Nilsson (1843–1921), came to the United States for an extended tour. She and numerous other visiting vocal artists from Sweden helped enrich the friendship and the cultural exchanges between the two countries, and they also stimulated the Swedish interest in America as a land of opportunities, thus contributing to the flow of emigrants. Swedish settlers have made substantial contributions to musical life in the United States.

Christine Nilsson's career was even more romantic than Jenny

Lind's. The daughter of a crofter near Växjö in the province of Småland, Stina from Snugge, as she was called, had for many years sung and played the violin at parties and country fairs when, at the age of 14, her talents were discovered by a local district judge. Three years later she was ready for concerts in Stockholm, and after four years of studies in Paris she made, in the fall of 1864, a sensational debut at the Théâtre Lyrique in the French capital, as Violetta in Verdi's *La Traviata*. Emperor Napoleon III and Empress Eugénie of France were in the audience. In her first appearance at the Paris Opera three years later, she created the role of Ophelia in Ambroise Thomas's *Hamlet*. As a concert singer she almost always included some old Swedish folk songs or other melodies in her programs, and she even sang such a tune as Ophelia in the opera. The title of the song was "Näckens polka," näcken being a romantic male water sprite.

Highly successful appearances in London followed in the late 1860s. The Swedish soprano won lavish praise as Marguerite in Gounod's *Faust*, a role she also enacted at the Opera in Paris. In 1868 she participated as soloist in the great Handel Festival in the Crystal Palace in London.

In September of 1870, when Christine Nilsson had become a musical celebrity of the first order, she came to the United States. At midnight the first day she was serenaded by Scandinavian singers, and a band played a selection of Swedish folk songs, including "Näckens polka." After her first concert, which was given in Steinway Hall where two other singers also appeared, the critic of the *New York Herald* wrote: "Her voice can only be compared with Jenny Lind's, it has the same combination of strength and sweetness. When she sang the melody of Handel the public knew no bounds. . . ."

Christine Nilsson's fame spread from coast to coast, and during the next two years she gave 261 concerts in 54 cities, among them Boston, Philadelphia, Baltimore, Cincinnati, Chicago, Minneapolis, St. Louis, San Francisco, New Orleans, and Nashville. Her way of dressing and her hairdo stirred up epidemics on the fashion market. Sidney Lanier, the former Confederate soldier, wrote for her a poem titled "Nilsson." At North Bridgewater, now Brockton, Massachusetts, a street was named Nilsson Street. Without giving away money on the same scale as Jenny Lind, she often contributed from her earnings to charity and also gave many benefit concerts. In 1873–74 she made a second tour of America, her appearances finally numbering 157. During the rest of the 1870s London was Christine Nilsson's principal base, and from there she made tours of Austria, Belgium, France, Russia, Scandinavia, and Spain.

In the fall of 1882 the Swedish soprano came back to America for a farewell tour, which began in Boston. On October 22, 1883, she helped dedicate the Metropolitan Opera House in New York, singing Marguerite in *Faust* on this historic occasion. Later on she created the Met's first Gioconda and its first notable Elsa, in Wagner's *Lohengrin.* During her concert tour she was assisted by five servants and by three other singers, including a very popular Swedish tenor, Theodor Björksten (b. 1858), who later became one of New York's leading singing teachers. He was married to a Swedish singer, Hervor Torpadie (1860–1928), who also had many grateful American disciples; their daughter, Greta Torpadie, before moving to Sweden in 1929, began a successful career as a mezzo-soprano and voice teacher. Christine Nilsson herself returned to Europe in the summer of 1884, after having attended a dinner in the White House at the invitation of President Chester A. Arthur. One of the other dinner guests, Senator Joseph R. Hawley, sent her a volume containing the autographs of the President, all the members of his cabinet, all the Justices of the Supreme Court, and all the Senators.

In September of the following year, 20 persons were trampled to death in Stockholm when thousands tried to push their way forward to hear Christine Nilsson sing from a balcony of the Grand Hotel. At that time, her career as a singer was almost over. In 1872 she had married a French banker at a ceremony in Westminster Abbey in London, and five years after his death in 1882 she married a Spanish nobleman, Count de Casa Miranda. Toward the end of her life she spent part of her time near her birthplace in Sweden, where she had bought an estate, and she died at Växjö.

Ever since the days of Jenny Lind and Christine Nilsson, ladies have played a prominent part in musical exchanges between Sweden and the United States. In 1876, the year of the Centennial, a celebrated group known as The Swedish Ladies' Vocal Quartet began a highly successful American tour under the management of a noted impresario who had heard them sing in Holland. In the fall of 1876, concerts were given in New York, Philadelphia, Boston, and Worces-

1. Chicago's Swede Town, rebuilt around Chicago Avenue after the Great Fire in 1871, flourished during the 1880s, when the city's Swedish-born population increased from 13,000 to 43,000 (pp. 372–380). 2. Both at Midsummer and shortly before Christmas, descendants of Swedish settlers in Colorado still gather in the old church at Ryssby, north of Denver (pp. 468–469). 3. The center of the Halland Settlement in southwestern Iowa was in 1870 almost named Halmstad, after the capital of the Swedish province of Halland, instead of Stanton. Swedish traditions, including vocal tributes to the arrival of spring and the Lucia celebration, are still honored in the "Little White City" (pp. 422–425).

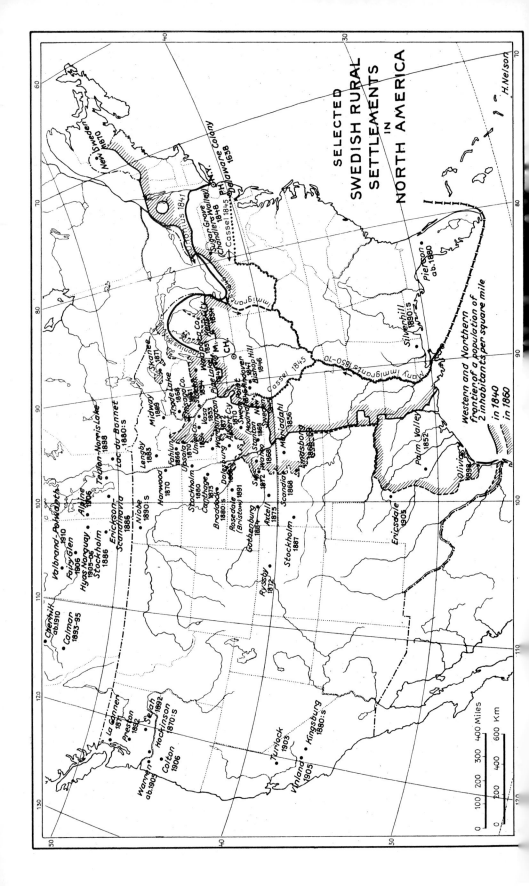

SELECTED
SWEDISH RURAL
SETTLEMENTS
IN
NORTH AMERICA

H. Nelson

Western and Northern
frontier of a population of
2 inhabitants per square mile
in 1840
in 1860

New Sweden ab 1870

Fortius 1841

Sugar Grove 1848
(Chandlers Valley)
Casse 1845
P H
Delaware colony 1638

Pierson ab 1880

Silverhill 1890:s

Skane 1871

Toode Lake 1868

Midway 1869

Svea Dakota Co.

Pine Lake M.
Bishop Hill 1846

New Upsala

Vasa 1853

Swede Point

Stratton New 1863

Mariadahl 1856

Cassel 1845

Many immigrants 1850-70

Lengby 1883

Fahlun 1865

Stockholm 1880

Harwood 1870

Dalarna

Iwanoe 1868

Swede 1872

Kansas City

Marksville 1858

Scandia 1868

Palm Valley 1852

Olivia 1898

Ericsdale 1905

Teulon-Norris Lake 1898

Lac du Bonnet 1880:s

Ericsson-Scandinavia 1886

Niobe 1890:s

Stockholm 1880

Braddock 1880:s

Carthage 1875

Rosedale (Bristow) 1891

Godbenburg 1887

Axtell 1875

Stockholm 1887

Ryssby 1872

Alpine 1906

Hyas-Norquay 1910-05

Stockholm 1886

Valbrand-Polkelbeth 1910

FairGlen 1906

Colmar 1893-95

Cherrhill ab 1910

La Conner 1873

Preston 1892

Warren ab 1905

Selah 1892

Hockinson 1870:s

Colton 1906

Turlock 1903

Vinland 1905

Kingsburg 1880:s

0   100 200 300 400 Miles

0 200 400 600 Km

1. The founder of New Sweden, Maine, William Widgery Thomas, was very fond of the pioneers of 1870 whom he called "mina barn i skogen," or "my children in the woods." Descendants of the early settlers still like to gather at New Sweden on the anniversary of its founding, July 23 (pp. 522–524). 2. The heads of twelve Swedish-language newspapers published in North America. Four of them were still in existence in 1975; the largest, *Svenska Amerikanaren* of Chicago, founded in 1876, *Nordstjernan* of New York, founded in 1872, *Vestkusten* of San Francisco, begun in 1886, and *Musiktidning för Amerikas Svenskar*, founded in 1909 as the official organ of the American Union of Swedish Singers. In 1915, when the Swedish immigrants in America and their children numbered about 1,400,000, there were 70 news weeklies, with a total circulation of 650,000, and some 200 other publications in the Swedish language (pp. 636, 786).

1. John A. Johnson, a son of Swedish immigrants, took his father's place as breadwinner at the age of 13. When he died in 1909 as governor of Minnesota, he was regarded as the beginning of a strong Presidential candidate (pp. 226–228). 2. Minnesota Governor Wendell R. Anderson greets a daughter of former Governor Harold LeVander at Gustavus Adolphus College in St. Peter, Minn., which in 1972 celebrated its 110th anniversary (pp. 202, 237, 787). Partially hidden behind the Governor are Swedish Ambassador Hubert de Besche and Princess Christina of Sweden. In 1975 the Swedish branch of the Vasa Order of America named Wendell Anderson the sixteenth "Swedish American of the Year," an annual award that had previously gone to Dr. Glenn T. Seaborg, chairman of the U.S. Atomic Energy Commission, Elmer W. Engstrom, president of RCA, Admiral Arleigh A. Burke, former Chief of U.S. Naval Operations, and Edwin E. Aldrin, the astronaut (pp. 404, 411–412, 438, 468, 790).

1. The Messiah Festival at Bethany College in Lindsborg, Kansas, held during Holy Week, features the great oratorios of Handel and Bach. Handel's "Messiah" has been performed annually since 1882 by the Bethany College Oratorio Society, the oldest continuous oratorio society in the United States. In 1944, during the Second World War, an entire rendition was transmitted to Europe. Bethany College was founded in 1881 by Swedish immigrants (pp. 460–461). 2. A rear view of Augustana College's Old Main, dedicated in 1889. The Bell Tower was constructed with beams from the first building erected on the campus in 1875, when the college moved to Rock Island, Ill. It was founded in 1860 in Chicago (pp. 232, 236–237, 787).

1. This bust of Pehr August Peterson stands in the lobby of the highly regarded Swedish-American Hospital at Rockford, Ill., which he helped found in 1911. A man of simple and rather eccentric habits, he played a leading part in turning Rockford first into a furniture center and finally into a great producer of hardware, tools, and machinery. Born in the Swedish province of Västergötland, he came to Rockford in 1852 at the age of six (pp. 191–192, 395–398). 2. A grandiose mansion was built in Minneapolis in the early 1900s by Swan J. Turnblad, successful publisher of a Swedish-language weekly. It is now the home of The American Swedish Institute (pp. 415–417).

Swedish holiday traditions, and especially those related to Christmas and Midsummer, are still cherished by Americans of Swedish ancestry, and some have gained popularity even outside such circles.

In Sweden the Christmas season is ushered in on December 13, "Lucia Day." Before daybreak, a daughter of the house assumes the role of Lucia and with her attendants arouses family members and perhaps neighbors, serving them in bed with coffee and fresh-baked buns while she sings a traditional air. Before the current calendar was adopted, the night of December 12–13 was actually the longest of the year, and the Lucia girl, in a white gown and with lighted candles in a wreath of greenery on her head, is still regarded as a symbol of the returning light. Today, Lucia girls also appear in schools, offices, and hospitals. In Stockholm a special celebration is held for the Nobel prize winners.

Christmas Eve is the heart of Swedish Christmas. If customs are strictly followed, the Christmas tree cannot be dressed until that morning. In numerous homes the specially prepared lutfisk and rice porridge is standard fare at the dinner. In homes with children, "Jultomten," the Swedish Santa Claus, arrives in person and distributes his packages. On Christmas Day many rise early to attend the first Mass, "Julottan," which ends before daybreak. The majestic "All Hail to Thee, O Blessed Morn" is traditionally the opening psalm. Many Swedes still remember riding to church in sleighs drawn by horses with small bells. The rest of Christmas Day is quiet, but the following day, also a holiday, is one of visits, parties, and merrymaking.

Aside from the religious traditions, love of nature and of outdoor life marks most holiday celebrations in Sweden. Toward the end of June, during the weekend nearest the solstice, comes the most romantic of all festivals, Midsummer, when cross-barred Maypoles adorned with green garlands and wild flowers are raised, melodious old folk tunes are played, and young people keep dancing until sunrise. In the far north of Sweden, the arctic one-seventh of its territory, the sun, in fact, never sets in June and early July. In the United States, people of Swedish stock may still celebrate Midsummer with enthusiasm, a day in late June often being called "Swedish Day" or "Swedes Day" (pp. 420–421).

Värmlänningarna (The People of Värmland), the most popular Swedish folk play, is given at the Royal Opera in Stockholm. In the late 1800s and early 1900s, it was offered hundreds of times in America, particularly in Chicago and Minneapolis. It was revived on its 100th anniversary in 1946. The play tells a Romeo and Juliet type of story but has a happy ending, and it has brought both tears and laughter, as well as romantic or nostalgic dreams. Audiences were particularly fond of its songs, of the folk dances at the Midsummer festival, and of the closing wedding celebration, with Erik, the son of a proud and wealthy farmer, and Anna, the daughter of a poor cotter, as partners (pp. 375–376).

ter, Massachusetts. The following tour included most of the principal cities and numerous smaller communities in the East and Middle West, and in May of 1878 the ladies reached San Francisco. A tour of the South followed in early 1879. The members of the quartet were Bertha Erixon, Inga Ekström, Amanda Carlson, and Ingeborg Löfgren. Eventually they were all married and remained in America, where today they have many descendants. In 1887, The Swedish Ladies' Octet came to the United States. A third ensemble, The Swedish Düring Ladies Quintet, has also been described as being very successful.

After Christine Nilsson, the first singer of Swedish birth to be heard at the Metropolitan was Johannes Elmblad (1853–1910), a basso profundo, who made his debut in late 1888. Around the turn of the century he belonged to the Stockholm Opera as a director and a singer, and in 1903 he was again at the Metropolitan. He sang 20 times at the annual Wagner music festivals at Bayreuth in Germany, and before turning to opera he had made concert tours in many countries, including Australia and India. A Swedish opera singer of German birth, Conrad Behrens (1835–98), joined the Metropolitan in 1889 and remained a resident of New York until his death. Swedish immigrants invited him to concerts in the Middle West. Behrens, a basso, had studied with three noted masters in Stockholm, and from 1862 to 1870 he was one of the stars of the Stockholm Opera.

The next Swedish singer at the Metropolitan in New York was a soprano of international caliber, Sigrid Arnoldson (1861–1943), who came for one season in the fall of 1893. Her first role was that of Baucis in Gounod's *Philémon et Baucis*. After her debut in Paris she had been hailed by critics as another "Nightingale of the North," and before embarking for the United States she had also scored triumphs in England, Germany, Holland, Hungary, Italy, Russia, and Switzerland. In 1885, Sigrid Arnoldson made phonographic recordings in Paris, being one of the very first artists to take an interest in Thomas Alva Edison's invention of the phonograph.

One of the most popular opera stars of all time was Anna Olivia or Olive Fremstad (1871–1951), who was born in Stockholm of a Norwegian father and a Swedish mother. When she was about 10, her parents emigrated to America and settled in Minneapolis. After vocal studies in Germany she made her operatic debut in Cologne in 1895, and via various other stages in Europe, including the Munich Royal Opera where she sang 70 roles, she came to the Metropolitan in New York in the fall of 1903, first appearing as Sieglinde in *Die Walküre*. Her success was overwhelming, and for 11 consecutive seasons she was one of the Met's greatest attractions. Among her colleagues at the Metropolitan in 1903–1904 was Jennie Norelius or Norelli (1863–1942), who was born at Bollnäs in Hälsingland. Her studies had taken her to Stockholm, Paris, and Italy, and from 1889 she was a member of various opera companies in the United States. In the early 1900s she toured with an opera company in Sweden and also appeared at Covent Garden in London and other famous operas in Europe. From 1920 she made her home in Seattle.

One of the first Swedish opera singers to emigrate to America was Ernst Svedelius (1872–1945), who left Stockholm in 1889 and in 1890–97 worked for Guthrie Moyer's opera company and, as a cantor, for the Holy Name Cathedral in Chicago. In 1897 he returned to Sweden as a soloist of the first Swedish-American chorus to visit Europe, and in Stockholm he accepted an offer of a study fellowship at the Royal Opera, where he later became a great asset. In 1921 he made a concert tour in the United States. He has been described as one of the most magnificent bassos Sweden has produced. Carl Fredrik Lundqvist (1841–1920), who for decades was one of the leading baritones of the Stockholm Opera, came to America for a concert tour in 1893. As a concert singer in Sweden or in Swedish societies in the United States, the uncommonly popular "Lunkan," as he was called, concluded his programs with a serenely patriotic song, written in 1844 but based on an old folk melody from the province of Västmanland, which largely thanks to him finally became Sweden's national anthem.

A virtuoso coloratura soprano, Carolina Östberg (1853–1924), who in the 1870s had become one of the pillars of the Stockholm Opera, gave in 1892–94 greatly admired concerts in America. Another versatile soprano from the same opera company, Anna Oscár (1875–1915), made successful tours in 1903 and 1906, and in 1909 she came back with her husband Martin Oscár (1879–1921), who also was one of the Stockholm Opera's leading artists.

Several Swedes have become known in America as outstanding singing teachers, in addition to those already mentioned. Augusta

Öhrström-Renard (d. 1921), who in the early 1880s was a member of the Royal Opera in Stockholm and then made many successful tours on both sides of the Atlantic, opened a music school in New York in 1897. Others have been active in, for instance, Boston and Worcester, Massachusetts, and in Chicago, Minneapolis, and smaller communities with educational institutions of Swedish origin.

The Swedish enthusiasm for group singing has been abundantly reflected both in the direct exchanges between the United States and Sweden and in the artistic activities of the Swedish immigrants. Swedish university-student choruses and other singing societies have toured America, beginning in 1904 when the University of Lund sent an elite group, and American university glee clubs have visited Sweden. Musical organizations formed by Swedish immigrants began to send choruses to Sweden in the late 1800s, and thousands of concerts have been given in America. Swedish singing clubs have abounded in the Middle West as well as in the East and the West, and quite a few still exist.

In the late 1860s and early 1870s there were male choruses in New York, Brooklyn, Boston, and Chicago. In 1886 a national organization called the United Scandinavian Singers of America was founded, and Scandinavian singing festivals were held in Philadelphia in 1887, in Chicago in 1889, and in Minneapolis in 1891, when the massed chorus numbered over 900 singers. Swedish-born John R. Örtengren of Chicago was the festival director. Frictions between the Swedish and the Norwegian peoples were growing, however, and in 1892, on Thanksgiving Day, November 24, the Swedish singing societies in America formed an organization of their own, the American Union of Swedish Singers. Its first festival was held in Chicago during the World's Fair of 1893, and then followed New York in 1897, Jamestown, New York, in 1901, Chicago in 1905, and New York in 1910. At that time, there were eight well-established Swedish singing societies on the West Coast.

After the singing festival in New York in 1897, a picked chorus of 54 singers toured Sweden, starting at Gothenburg and finishing in Stockholm. The visitors sang at the first important exposition held in the Swedish capital, and King Oscar II invited them to luncheon in the Royal Palace, where he took part in the singing. In 1910 a chorus of 45 men from the Swedish singing societies in America made a triumphal tour in Sweden, and on July 4 they were invited to the Stockholm Palace by King Oscar's son and successor, Gustav V. Their leader, John Örtengren (1862–1939), who from the beginning had played a vital part in the American Union of Swedish Singers, remained in his native country as a voice teacher and choir master. He had emigrated to Chicago in 1888 and taught for nearly two decades at the Chicago Musical College.

When the Lund University Student Singers toured America in 1904, their leading soloist was a temperamental baritone of the Stockholm Opera, John Forsell (1868–1941). Five years later he came back to the United States as a member of the Metropolitan Opera Company in New York. At the end of the first season, in 1910, he was engaged as a soloist at the fifth festival of the American Union of Swedish Singers, and before returning to Sweden he made a concert tour through the United States. Forsell, who had begun his career as an army officer and an elite gymnast, was from 1924 to 1939 director of the Stockholm Opera, which largely thanks to him managed to hold its own as one of the foremost lyrical stages in Europe.

Swedish contributions to American farming, lumbering, and railroad construction

THE first contributions to American economic growth by Swedish immigrants were made in the 1600s by the colonists on the lower Delaware, and during the latter part of the 19th century their leading specialties, agriculture and animal husbandry, became important in the exchanges between Sweden and the United States.

The first more significant contribution from Sweden to American agriculture in the 1800s may have been alsike clover, which long remained an important forage crop in the northern United States. Seed for this plant, which was named after the parish of Alsike in the province of Uppland, north of Stockholm, seems to have been imported to America the first time in the late 1830s.

In 1886, a plant-breeding station which has become widely known abroad was established at Svalöv in southernmost Sweden. During the first two or three decades the main object of the work was to improve the yield capacity, winter-hardiness, resistance to disease and strength of straw, but the scope of the activities was then gradually widened. Chromosome research, among other things, became increasingly important. From Svalöv the United States obtained several new grain varieties. Among the first were Hannchen barley and Victory oats, which was regarded as one of the most valuable imports of its kind.

The first notable director of the Swedish station, Professor Hjalmar Nilsson (1856–1925), studied plant breeding in the United States in 1893, and during his long service at Svalöv he welcomed many American specialists. His successor, Herman Nilsson-Ehle (1873–1949), also won an international reputation for his research on heredity and work on plant improvement, and so did Åke Åkerman (1887–1955), who became Nilsson-Ehle's associate and successor. In 1938, an expert of the U.S. Department of Agriculture, Dr. Eric Englund (1893–1969), who had emigrated from northern Sweden as a young boy, wrote about the plant-breeding station at Svalöv that "possibly no other single institution of a foreign country has contributed more to American agriculture."

In 1877–78 a Swedish inventor, Gustaf de Laval, devised the first practical cream separator, an epoch-making event in the history of dairying, and a number of his machines were soon exported to the United States. In 1885 he invented the lactocrite, which was the first practical milk tester. His other inventions included an emulsifier and one of the first mechanical milkers.

When De Laval made his inventions, American agricultural machinery and techniques had already helped speed up the modernization of the Swedish farming industry. If it had not been for the personal contacts across the Atlantic, the new equipment would have become known in Sweden much more slowly. An increased use of machinery and a more rapid all-round modernization was also furthered by returning former emigrants. Especially after the American financial crash of 1893 and in the early 1900s, many Swedes who had practiced farming in the United States came back to their native country and purchased the farm of their forefathers or perhaps an estate in the neighborhood. In some sections of south-central Sweden, from one-fourth to one-sixth of the farm owners of the early 1900s had been in America.

More important than anything else, of course, was the manpower and the experience that the United States obtained from Sweden for its farming industry. From the virgin lands of the Middle and Far West, the immigrants created thousands of new farmsteads, and the total area cleared and cultivated by Swedish settlers finally exceeded that of the soil tilled by their kinsmen in Sweden. The newcomers had been steeped in traditions of hard work and thrift, and in America they were soon recognized as among the better farmers of their respective communities. Many of their farmsteads were often described as model farms. American agronomists have sometimes voiced regret that the Swedish settlers, who were schooled in a more careful and intensive system of farming, so quickly adopted the extensive methods traditional to America, but, as it has also been observed, they could hardly have acted differently. In the beginning, they lacked adequate transportation facilities and markets.

Farming was the leading occupation of the Swedish immigrants in the 19th century, but they also did a tremendous amount of work on the railroad construction in the Middle West and Northwest. Newcomers from Sweden were to be found in almost every construction gang, and thousands of miles of road, as well as many bridges, were built by Swedish contractors and largely Swedish crews. The railroad workers from Sweden and the other Scandinavian countries often gave an impression of having an excess of vitality and physical strength, and when James J. Hill, the famous railway promoter and financier, started to build the Great Northern, he is supposed to have said: "Give me Swedes, snuff and whiskey, and I'll build a railroad right through hell." Those who had been able to save enough of their earnings usually settled down along the new routes to develop farms. When Hill had built most of his railroads, he pointed in an address to the splendid revenue his company was reaping from typically Swedish and Norwegian settlements.

Another occupation in which Swedes and other Scandinavians easily held their own was lumbering, and there was no need for them to boast, which, however, they often did when they were relaxing with fellow workers. The stories about Paul Bunyan, the mythical hero who was the work giant of American forests, seem to have originated as tall tales exchanged in lumber camps from the Great Lakes to the Pacific in the late 1800s — tales that often were told with a strong Swedish, or perhaps Norwegian or Finnish, accent. In time, many of the lumberjacks built their own sawmills. Others became skilled workers in the building trades and in furniture manufacturing, and perhaps finally owners of their own firms. Wherever Swedish immigrants settled in large numbers, they played, as a rule, a leading part in these two industries. Toward the end of the 1800s there were also thousands of Swedish-born mechanics and engineers in the metal and machine industries, which would attract more and more immigrants of the same origin.

In the Swedish 19th-century migration to America and the building of new homes, many of them on the frontiers of the Middle West or Far West, the women played an epic role. Several historians have paid warm tribute to their economy and efficiency, their love for their homes and their self-sacrificing devotion. Traveling in America in 1875–76, Carl Johan Nyvall, the evangelist preacher, was greatly impressed not only by the farm women but also by the wives of the pioneer clergymen. About the latter he wrote that many of them had to "suffer privations the like of which even a crofter's wife in Sweden knows nothing about." In this case, however, the writer may have gone somewhat farther than he actually intended. In many parts of Sweden the life of a crofter's wife was a struggle for survival most of the time, and so was the existence of the wives of the pioneers in America.

22

In the American Heartland

The drawing power of the Midwest at its height, the East and Far West also beckon

IN THE period 1870–1900 the Swedish-born population in the United States increased from nearly 100,000 to about 580,000, according to the U.S. census reports. In 1870 the Norwegian immigrants were still the largest Scandinavian group, but in the census of 1890 the Swedes had become more numerous than the Norwegians and the Danes combined.

Ever since the 1850s, Illinois and Minnesota had the largest Swedish-born populations, and they became the only states where the total of Swedish settlers reached and exceeded 100,000.

From 1880 to 1890 the Minnesota count jumped from less than 40,000 to about 100,000, and during the next two decades it continued to rise, reaching a maximum of approximately 122,500 in 1910. Illinois's Swedish-born inhabitants multiplied at a somewhat slower rate, from some 42,500 in 1880 to 86,500 in 1890, 99,000 in 1900, and about 115,500 in 1910.

As late as in 1890, Iowa had the third largest Swedish-born population, but in the U.S. census of 1900, New York had moved up to this position, and it was followed by Massachusetts. In the census of 1910, California had also passed Iowa.

The drawing power of the Middle West has never been stronger than during the 1880s, when more than 200,000 Swedes settled there. Most of them went to the regions immediately west of the Great Lakes, where during the Civil War nearly two-thirds of the Swedes in America had lived, but rather large numbers pushed into Nebraska, Kansas, and the Dakotas. Acquisition of cheap land was their primary objective.

Already in the 1880s, however, about 100,000 Swedish newcomers had other destinations than the Midwest, in particular the Middle Atlantic states, New England, and the Pacific Coast, and toward the end of the century these sections became increasingly attractive.

On the whole the Middle West held its own remarkably well, for not only did it receive a smaller proportion of the newcomers from Sweden, it was also bound to lose many of its old settlers and their children as a result of a constant movement toward the west. As soon as a settlement in the old Midwest had attained a certain size, it became the mother colony for new settlements and areas of cultivation farther west, first, for instance, in eastern Nebraska or Kansas. After some time such secondary communities generated their own daughter settlements more to the west, perhaps as far away as in the Rocky Mountain region or on the West Coast. Many families or groups moved directly from the Midwest to the Pacific area. At times there was also a certain migration from the Midwest to the industrial states on the Atlantic.

During the 1880s two-thirds of the emigrants from Sweden were agricultural workers or farmers, but the proportion of industrial workmen was growing. This change in the structure of the migration from Sweden helps to explain the increasing attraction of New England and the Middle Atlantic states. The Midwest had, of course, much to offer even in the industrial field, but technical training and natural inclination made many of the Swedish newcomers particularly fitted for the metal and machine industries, and here the best opportunities beckoned in the East, from Massachusetts to Pennsylvania and New Jersey.

The geographical distribution of the Swedish-born population in the United States, therefore, changed considerably during the late 1800s and early 1900s. By 1870 at least 80 percent of the Swedish settlers lived in the Middle West, but in 1890 this proportion had declined to 70 percent, in 1900 to 65, and in 1910 to 59 percent. The immigrants from Norway remained in the Middle West to a much greater extent.

In the early 1900s, nearly one-fourth of the Swedes lived in New England and the Middle Atlantic states. In 1900, California, Oregon, and Washington accounted for 5.5 percent of the total, and ten years later their share had increased to somewhat more than 10 percent. Less than two percent of the Swedish-born lived in the South.

As the farming areas of the Middle West gradually lost in attraction, an increasing proportion of the Swedes became residents of cities and towns. By the turn of the century more than half of the immigrants from Sweden lived in urban communities. Ten cities had a Swedish-born population of 5,000 or more, namely, Chicago and Rockford, Illinois, Minneapolis, St. Paul, and Duluth, Minnesota, Boston and Worcester, Massachusetts, New York and Jamestown, New York, and San Francisco. They were joined in the early 1900s by Seattle and Los Angeles. In 1900 Rock Island County in Illinois reported 5,653 Swedish-born, most of whom lived in the city of Moline.

During the first period of the 19th-century migration, the great majority of the immigrants from Sweden came in groups, and families with children represented at least 60 percent of the annual total of newcomers. In the wilderness where many of the early immigrants settled, constant teamwork was vital. But during the latter part of the 1800s group expeditions became increasingly rare, and when an increasing proportion of the immigrants aimed at industrial occupations, a family often became more of a handicap than an asset during the first few years. Many breadwinners, therefore, came alone and sent for their families later, and in the early 1900s most of the immigrants were unmarried.

Chicago becomes the hub of the Swedes, the largest "Swedish city" after Stockholm

DURING the last three decades of the 19th century, Chicago solidified its position as the main clearing house of the immigration from Sweden and the leading Swedish center in the Midwest and all America. By 1870, persons of Swedish birth totaled 6,200, in 1880, about 13,000, and in 1890, 43,000. In 1900, when Chicago had 1,700,000 inhabitants, the Swedish-born numbered 49,000, a figure that was exceeded by only three cities in Sweden. And if the 96,000 children of the Swedish immigrants were included, Chicago ranked as the second largest "Swedish city" in the world, after Stockholm, Sweden's capital. The 145,000 persons of Swedish birth or parentage made up about 8.5 percent of Chicago's population. In 1910 the Swedish-born had increased to 63,000. An even higher figure, nearly 66,000, was reached in the census of 1930.

From the beginning, the largest Swedish settlement in Chicago had been on the North Side. Other centers developed on the South Side and in the West, but after the Civil War most of the Swedes lived in Swede Town around Chicago Avenue on the North Side. In 1868–71, when Sweden suffered from repeated crop failures and their aftereffects, the population of this Swedish enclave increased fourfold to about 5,000. In the Great Fire on October 9–10, 1871, the whole settlement was reduced to ashes. Five small churches, five newspaper printing offices, and valuable libraries were wiped out.

Swede Town was, however, soon rebuilt in the same section, and the next two decades became its golden era. Chicago Avenue was now the Main Street of the Swedes, who often called it either "Stora Bondegatan" or "Smålandsgatan," meaning the Big Street of the Farmers or of the People from Småland, a province which, together with the island of Öland, contributed a large proportion of the Swedish settlers. Along this street most signs were in Swedish, and Swedish was practically the only language spoken. There were Swedish general stores, book shops and beer parlors, Swedish tobacco shops stocked with snuff from Stockholm and Jönköping, a Swedish pharmacy, almost inevitably named Kronan (The Crown), a hotel called Norden (The North), which competed with Svea on another street, and Chicago's best-known Swedish restaurant, Walhalla. The atmosphere was similar to that of a bustling market town in Sweden, and to the newcomers the change of milieu from the native countryside did not seem too drastic. Quite a few of the dwellings reflected a certain prosperity, but most of the houses were primitive and overcrowded, and the sanitary conditions were highly unsatisfactory. As in the other Swedish settlements in Chicago, workers of various kinds, maids, and other wage earners made up a majority of the population.

While daily toil claimed most of the vitality of the immigrants, at times many inhabitants of Swede Town engaged in activities of other types. These aimed at some kind of recreation, education, or united action, and their ultimate objective was often to help the immigrants adapt themselves to life in America, and to help make their new land a good home. In the beginning most of the newcomers felt disappointed or somewhat confused, and without banding together for companionship and mutual help they may have lost their bearings. Unscrupulous agents of various kinds were lying in wait for new immigrants, and the police did not always seem convinced that "greenhorns" who did not even understand English were worthy of protection. A majority of the Swedes could probably cope with the cruder tricks, but only a small part of the 19th-century immigrants were able to move ahead without some link with a Swedish base. Whether they had such chances or not, however, many seemed anxious to become Americanized as soon as possible, and this, they often thought, called for new, English-sounding family names, which in several cases also were more practical. Carlson, for instance, was changed to Carson, Charleston or Clancy, Bokstrand to Bookshore, Kraak to Clark, and Grönberg to Greenburg.

By 1880, about 40 associations had been formed among the Swedes on Chicago's North Side, and hundreds followed during the next few decades. They included social and political clubs, singing, music, and art societies, educational organizations, youth and temperance groups, sport and rifle clubs, benefit societies and other fraternal orders, and trade associations. The first organization, founded in 1854, had been open to all Scandinavians, but was disbanded after one year. Even among the Swedes, the club activities seemed at times to express lack of unity rather than cooperation and solidarity, but jealousies among leaders and other frictions were inevitable to some extent. Many of the associations became valuable "schools of citizenship." Two organizations which aimed at better coordination and long-range planning were founded in the 1890s.

The most deep-rooted dissensions of the 19th century split the Swedish immigrants into a conservative church group, often led or supported both by the clergymen of the Augustana Synod and by preachers of the new pietistic movements, and a liberal faction, the members of which sometimes ranged from freethinkers to the leaders of the Episcopalian St. Ansgarius congregation, which had been founded in 1849 by Gustaf Unonius.

Among the liberals of the 1800s were always most of the Swedish immigrants who earned their living as newspapermen. Many regarded the Augustana Synod and other denominations as intolerant and narrowly puritanical in their attitudes toward art and recreation, and perhaps even as a threat to the freedom of thought, but as a rule they did not turn against religion as such. While in the period 1860–70 about one-half of the adult Chicago Swedes seem to have been members of the Swedish congregations, by 1880 the proportion had declined to one-third. Quite a few immigrants affiliated, on the other hand, with American churches. Many who hardly ever went to church were grateful for what the religious associations with Swedish roots had done for medical care and social welfare. The largest hospitals of Swedish origin in Chicago are the Augustana Hospital, which was founded in 1882 by the Lutherans, and the Swedish Covenant Hospital, founded four years later by the Mission Friends.

The oldest Swedish secular society in Chicago, Svea, which had been founded in 1857, organized the first lectures and cultural soirées held under other than church auspices. In 1868 the same association sponsored four dramatic performances in German Hall on the North Side, and this may be regarded as the beginning of the Swedish-language theater in Chicago, which came to full bloom around the turn of the century and lived on until after the Second World War. In the 1880s, when the North Side Turner Hall had become the home of the Swedish theatricals, capacity houses of 2,000 were not rare, and when performances later on were given on Sundays in city theaters, the audience in the Auditorium on some occasions reached 4,000. The Swedes on the South Side had their own facilities. In 1890 two professional actors from Sweden began a visit to Chicago, and in the early 1900s such tours became common. Most of the Swedes in Chicago had never been to a theater in Sweden. In the United States, however, they were not at all exceptional: Swedish-language theatrical ventures were launched wherever there were sizable Swedish settlements.

The Swedish-language theater in Chicago did not reach professional status, and many of the plays were slight farces performed by amateurs, but for several decades there were often productions by schooled and experienced actors. During the 19th century, folk plays and historical dramas became particularly popular, and one composition of the former type, *Värmlänningarna* (The People of Värmland), with music and folk dances, remained foremost in the affections of the Swedes in America. It had had its premiere in 1846 at the Royal Opera in Stockholm, where since then it has been given hundreds of times during the Christmas season. In Chicago and other Swedish centers in America, its leading rival was for decades a folk comedy and allegorical fantasy of 1866 called *Andersson, Pettersson och Lundström*, a title which probably will live for ever in the Swedish language as one of the most familiar quotations. Modern playwrights were, however, also included in the repertoire of the Swedish-language theaters in America. In Chicago, August Strindberg was represented by eight plays, and at least two of the performances seem to have been American premieres.

Without a press of their own, the Swedes in Chicago would hardly have been able to find their way in large numbers to churches, theaters, and club meetings. In 1880, more than a score of weekly newspapers and monthly magazines had already appeared in Chicago, and about half of them, religious or secular, were still being published. After Stockholm and Gothenburg, Chicago was the most important Swedish press center. Books in Swedish were also printed.

Much of the battle between the religious group and the liberals was fought in the press. The leading church organ was *Hemlandet*, which in 1859 had been moved to Chicago from Galesburg in western Illinois. Under the direction of an Augustana layman, Johan A. Enander, it gradually became secularized, but until almost the end of its life, in 1914, its attitudes were close to those of the Augustana Synod. Its foremost liberal opponent was *Svenska Amerikanaren*, which was not identical with a paper of the same name founded in 1866, but had been begun ten years later by Herman Roos (1831–80). Born in Västergötland and the descendant of an old noble family, he had studied both at Uppsala and in Lund and worked for newspapers in Stockholm. He first came to America in 1864. Roos left no children, but many members of the same family, whose complete name is Roos af Hjelmsäter, live in the United States.

After Roos's sudden death in 1880, his friend and associate Magnus Elmblad (1848–88), from Kärda, near Värnamo in Småland, continued to serve *Svenska Amerikanaren* until 1884 when he returned to Sweden. He was one of the most gifted of the many Swedish poets in

America. Shortly after his arrival in 1871 he made one of the best translations into Swedish of "The Star-Spangled Banner," and one of his epic poems was awarded a prize by the Swedish Academy. A comic ballad about the unsuccessful emigration from Sweden of a farmer named Petter Jönsson, who had read in a popular newspaper that "the bureaucrats had ruined his native land," is still widely known among Swedish people, although its author has been forgotten.

As a writer, lecturer, and orator, Johan A. Enander (1842–1910) exerted a vast influence on his fellow countrymen, and in the late 1800s he was generally regarded as one of the grand old men of the Swedes in America. Combining a fervent Swedish patriotism with a genuine pride in the United States, he extolled American law and liberty, and urged everybody to obey the former so that the latter might survive. He was born in a poor farming home at Härja in the province of Västergötland; the promise of free instruction at the Augustana College and Theological Seminary made him decide to emigrate in 1869 at the age of 27. Before long he became first editor and then also owner of *Hemlandet*. In the late 1870s he published a history of the United States in five volumes, and during the years 1880–85 he served on the Illinois Board of Education. In 1889 President Benjamin Harrison appointed him minister to Denmark, but Enander declined for reasons of health.

Enander's fiery patriotism on behalf of the Swedes in America was probably in part a reaction against the national self-assurance and pride manifested both by native Americans and by such immigrant groups as the Germans and the Irish, who were much more numerous than the Swedes. The Swedish and the Irish communities, in particular, often became involved in frictions or conflicts, and a tragic episode occurred in 1893. On the personal level, however, relations seem to have gradually improved. Many fights between Swedes and Irishmen are said to have been caused by rivalry with regard to the fair sex, and in the Middle West as a whole, at least, Swedish-Irish marriages were quite common.

Any sense of inferiority among the Swedes or Scandinavians must be overcome, Enander felt. Speeches celebrating Sweden's long history were, in fact, a standard feature of Swedish festivities in America in the late 1800s and early 1900s, and most of the listeners seemed to like them, even if they were critical of the Sweden they had left. From an American viewpoint such orations probably also served a useful purpose: at times, Swedes like other immigrants needed the stimulation of rousing pep talks.

Some Swedish gala days in Chicago — Swede Town melts away in the late 1800s

THE first great social event in the Swedish immigrant community in Chicago was Christine Nilsson's visit during the Christmas season of 1870.

In the evening of December 22 the famous singer, whom many of the Swedish settlers from Småland had known as little "Stina från Snugge," rode in a long procession from her hotel to a big reception and banquet in German Hall. There were men on horseback bearing torches, carriages with people in colorful folk costumes, and a band playing Swedish melodies. At the reception, the oldest Swedish resident of Chicago, Captain Olof Gottfried Lange, who had arrived in 1838, introduced Christine Nilsson to the audience, another old-timer, Charles John Sundell, the founder of the Svea Society, who during the Civil War period had served as American consul at Stettin in Germany, presented her with a magnificent wreath and other gifts, and Johan A. Enander, the newly appointed editor of *Hemlandet*, read a poem he had written for the guest of honor.

The gala evening had been preceded by a tug-of-war over the sponsorship between the Reverend Erland Carlsson, the vigorous pastor of the Immanuel Church, and the Svea Society, which finally won. This led many of the church people to have nothing to do with the party for the celebrated singer, but the following summer Miss Nilsson returned to Chicago to give two concerts for the benefit of the Swedish congregations, the Svea Society, and the Augustana College and Theological Seminary, then at Paxton, Illinois. A few months later Swede Town was laid waste by the Great Fire.

In 1887, when Chicago celebrated its 50th anniversary as a city, representatives of all the armies in Europe were invited to an international military encampment October 1–20, and Sweden, like Norway and Denmark, sent about 20 officers and men. The leader of the group was Colonel John Lilliehöök (1834–1918), then commander of a regiment at Örebro, who had been in French service and seen action in Austria, Italy, and North Africa. At a large meeting organized by the Swedish societies in Chicago, he and Johan A. Enander were the main speakers, and both seem to have made a deep impression. Enander, who has been called "the most Swedish Swede in America," observed that many Swedish officers had fought as commanders on American soil, "always under, never against The Star-Spangled Banner," and that American freedom had "its oldest roots in the freeborn peoples of the Scandinavian North." The publishers of the Swedish-language newspapers invited the Swedish army team to Minneapolis, and at a reunion there Secretary of State Hans Mattson spoke on behalf of the state of Minnesota and its Swedish population.

Upon their return to Sweden two of the army officers wrote in a report that "for success in America much more is needed than people here generally believe." They probably had met Swedish college or university graduates who had become factory workers or farmhands, and perhaps also adventurers and misfits who had found no useful occupation. Such cases were relatively common, and complaints that there was no place in America for educated immigrants were still heard. Swedish settlers without much schooling answered that what mattered in the new land was not what you had done before coming, but what you were able to do today.

The World's Fair in Chicago in 1893 has been named the Columbian Exposition, being held to commemorate the discovery of America by Columbus 400 years earlier. This aspect of the celebration always angered Enander, who maintained that it was Norsemen who first discovered America, and not "the by Anglo-Americans, Spaniards and Italians almost idolized Columbus," as he said in an address in 1890 when the preparations for the exposition had begun. Sweden, however, was one of 18 countries represented with buildings of their own in the "White City" in Jackson Park. On July 20 the "Swedish Day" was celebrated with meetings, parades, and concerts. The grand chorus of the American Union of Swedish Singers, consisting of 400 male voices, sang repeatedly to enthusiastic audiences of over 10,000 persons, and three Swedish opera stars, Carolina Östberg, soprano, Carl Fredrik Lundqvist, baritone, and Conrad Behrens, basso, took part as soloists. Commissioner for the arts exhibits in the Swedish pavilion was 33-year-old Anders Zorn, who somewhat later achieved a fabulous reputation in America as a portraitist.

Some visitors from Sweden were struck by the large number of Swedish engineers who turned up in Chicago during the World's Fair. Many of them had already tried their fortune in other countries. In 1892 a group of Swedish engineers living in the Chicago area had formed a club of their own, and the newcomers often turned to this organization for assistance with employment. The financial panic of 1893 and the following depression led to its virtual dissolution, but a new and lasting association, The Swedish Engineers' Society of Chicago, was formed in 1908.

In the 1890s the Swedes of Swede Town began to move to more comfortable homes farther north. To begin with they were often replaced by newly arrived countrymen, but in the early 1900s the old Swede Town had been turned into Little Sicily, and two decades later the Italians also moved out. The only remaining monument of the Swedish era was the building of one of the leading Swedish organizations, The Swedish Club of Chicago, which in the 1970s still stood on its old site. The traditions of The Swedish Club date back to 1870.

After the end of Swede Town, the Lake View section around Belmont Avenue, at 3200 North, took on a Swedish character. On the South Side, many Swedes lived in the Englewood district. While there may still be some concentrations of citizens of Swedish stock, Chicago today has no real Swedish center.

Some of the Swedes who helped build Chicago — From laborers to leading contractors

A MAJORITY of the Swedish 19th-century immigrants in Chicago arrived without any real vocational training for industrial and similar occupations, but they were practical, able to work hard, and willing to accept almost any kind of employment. Most of them became laborers. Toward the end of the century the rank and file of the settlers fared relatively well as skilled or semiskilled workers in machine shops and other metal industries, in the clothing factories and in the building trades, or as owners of small businesses. After a heavy influx of unmarried women from Sweden, the Swedish immigrant community had become known as the leading supplier of domestic servants.

Ever since the Civil War period there had been a number of Swedish-born employers, especially in the clothing, woodworking, metal and mechanical industries, and this category increased as the years passed. Several of the first successful immigrants from Sweden were tailors. In the late 1870s the Swedes began to win a reputation as first-rate wood craftsmen and construction workers, more and more of them became contractors, and in the early 20th century the building of houses developed into the leading Swedish specialty. It has, in fact, often been said that "Chicago was built by Swedes," and such statements are not as extravagant as they first sound: a substantial part of the construction work was done by contractors, foremen, and workers of Swedish origin, although it probably never represented more than one-third of the total. Notable contributions to Chicago's development were also made in mechanical and electrical engineering and other fields. Gradually, the number of Swedes in the professions became proportionately larger.

At the end of the Civil War, Captain Charles M. Lindgren (1819–79), was one of the best-known Swedes in Chicago. Born at Dragsmark in the province of Bohuslän, he had gone to sea at the age of 14, and in 1849 he had panned for gold in California. In 1852 he came to Chicago, and there he built up a shipping business on the Great Lakes, finally operating six ships. He was also a Baptist preacher. His son John R. Lindgren (1855–1911) founded, with a partner of Norwegian stock, a banking firm which in 1891 became the State Bank of Chicago. Another pioneer banker of Swedish origin, Henry S. Henschen (1873–1943), was for 30 years connected with the State Bank of Chicago and later became president of the Chicago Bank of Commerce. Both Lindgren and Henschen represented Sweden as consuls. Henschen was born in Brooklyn, his father being William Henschen, who, after brilliant doctoral studies at Uppsala, in 1870 emigrated to Florida and finally became one of the leading scholars of Swedish Methodism.

In the late 1800s, Robert Lindblom (1844–1907), who had come to America in 1864 and had been a grain dealer in Milwaukee, was regarded as the foremost Swedish-born civic and business leader in Chicago. He settled there in 1877, and before the end of the next decade he had made a fortune. He became president of the Chicago Board of Trade and served for some years on the Board of Education. In 1893 he was one of the principal backers of the World's Fair or Columbian Exposition, subscribing half a million dollars to its guarantee fund. Politically he was unique among successful Swedes in

Chicago, being a Democrat and, moreover, leaning toward socialism. Since he was one of the most resourceful advocates of free silver, many people thought that he would have become secretary of the treasury had William Jennings Bryan won the Presidential election in 1896. In 1898–99 he was practically ruined as a result of the famous wheat speculations carried on by Joseph Leiter on the Chicago Board of Trade. The Lindblom High School in Chicago has been named for Robert Lindblom, who was born in Asker Parish in the province of Närke.

One of the first major Swedish building contractors in Chicago was Anders Landquist or Andrew Lanquist (1856–1931), born at Ving in Västergötland, who arrived in 1881. In Sweden he had had some practical engineering experience in the State Railways, and in Chicago, where he started as a bricklayer at 11 cents an hour, he erected in 1891 the first real skyscraper, the Monon Building. In the early 1900s his firm, Lanquist & Illsley, produced a great many well-known structures, both in Chicago and in other cities. Among those in Chicago were the Wrigley Buildings. In the period 1906–10 he produced the U. S. Steel factory buildings at Gary, Indiana.

Two brothers from the vicinity of Moheda near Växjö in Småland, Henry and John E. Ericsson, were at various times associated with Lanquist but also operated their own firms. When Henry Ericsson (1861–1947) arrived in Chicago in 1882 at the age of 21, he had had some technical education as well as practical training in Stockholm. His younger brother John (1868–1934) came to Chicago a few years later, after a spell of farm work in Minnesota, and began by learning how to lay bricks. The two brothers finally became prominent builders of big office structures, banks, theaters, schools, and other public buildings. Both also served as building commissioners in Chicago. Henry Ericsson was appointed to that post in 1911 and John E. Ericsson 20 years later. Their father, who came to America in 1884, had been a farmer in Sweden and also operated a blast furnace.

Henry Ericsson's immediate successor as building commissioner in Chicago was Charles Boström (1882–1945), another successful contractor, who was born in the province of Värmland. He came to America in 1891 and first worked as a carpenter in Michigan. After only two years he started as a builder in Chicago, where he specialized in private housing but also put up several industrial plants. In his spare moments he studied architecture. Being also greatly interested in city planning, he laid out a zoning system for Chicago and then served for many years as chairman of the Zoning Board.

Nils Persson Severin (1861–1945), who came to Chicago in 1888 from southernmost Sweden, erected hundreds of buildings and other structures, most of them in the Chicago area but also including, for instance, the Capitol at Juneau, Alaska, post offices at Honolulu, Boston, and Baltimore, and the central arch of the Arlington Memorial Bridge in Washington, D.C. In 1927 he supervised the remodeling of the White House, and for this work he and his son were personally thanked by President Coolidge. Severin had been a builder in Sweden, and the purpose of his trip to America in 1888 had been to study construction.

A carpenter and cabinetmaker from the northern province of Jämtland, Eric P. Strandberg, who arrived in Chicago in 1882 at the age of 22, became a specialist in hospital and other institutional construction. He built the American Swedish Historical Museum in South Philadelphia. Adolph Lindström, a native of Västergötland, who came in 1901 at the age of 17 and settled at Wilmette, north of Chicago, built apartment houses, hotels, and business buildings. The number of Swedish-born masons and carpenters who worked for him at one time or another finally reached about 10,000. Among other large-scale contractors were Louis M. Nelson, who came from Värmland in 1882 at the age of 15, and Eric E. Skoglund from the central province of Närke, who arrived in 1897, when he was 19 years old, and erected a number of well-known business buildings and apartment houses. Together with other immigrants from Värmland, Nelson helped to build and maintain a children's hospital at Sunne, his birthplace in the beautiful valley of Fryksdalen.

In relation to the population figures, architects of Swedish ancestry have also been remarkably numerous. The first notable Swedish-born architect in Illinois was Lars or Lawrence Gustaf Hallberg (1844–1915) from Vänersnäs in Västergötland, who had been graduated from Chalmers Institute of Technology in Gothenburg, practiced architecture in Sweden, and spent some time in London. In the fall of 1871, after the Great Fire, he hastened to Chicago, and there, as a historian has said, he "became one of the men who built the city literally from the ground up." He was a pioneer in the use of reinforced concrete. Hallberg also became greatly interested in slum clearance and took a leading part in campaigns against air and water pollution. "Sewage," he wrote with reference to Lake Michigan, "should be made a benefit, rather than a source of harm."

John A. Nyden (1878–1932) of Evanston, Illinois, was like the brothers Henry and John Ericsson a native of Moheda in Småland, but his education was principally American. An engineer as well as an architect, he designed and built a large number of hotels, bank buildings, churches, and schools, most of them in Chicago. The American Swedish Historical Museum in Philadelphia was also designed by him, and there he tried, in his own words, "to express the 17th-century architecture of Sweden in American colonial terms." A native of the province of Östergötland, Eric Edwin Hall, who arrived in 1904 at the age of 21, also set his stamp on a great number of Chicago buildings, among them Chicago Stadium, which was the largest indoor stadium in the world. For many years he served as official architect of Cook County. In the 1920s, the number of architects of Swedish ancestry who were authorized to practice in Illinois was about 70.

As assistant city engineer of Chicago from 1886 and city engineer from 1897 until his death, John E. Ericsson (1858–1927) from Skepptuna in the province of Uppland, north of Stockholm, was responsible for a comprehensive modernization of the water-supply system and the construction of about 50 bridges. He emigrated to America shortly after his graduation from the Institute of Technology in Stockholm in 1880. Another Swedish engineer, Julius Soderstam (1859–1942), who for 40 years served the Sanitary District of Chicago, authored the monumental project that reversed the flow of the Chicago River from east to west. He was born at Jämshög in Blekinge. The first two parks in Chicago, the Lincoln and the Union, were laid out and developed shortly after the Civil War by Sven Nelson (b. 1828) and Olof Benson (1837–1909), who had arrived in 1852. Both were from Fjälkestad in northeastern Skåne, a district noted for its ancient chateaux with beautiful gardens.

An immigrant from the parish of Vä in the same part of Sweden, Per Samuel Peterson (1830–1903), became the first professional nurseryman in the Middle West. After emigrating in 1851 and coming to Chicago in 1854, he leased in 1856 a few acres of land just north of the city, which he called the Rose Hill Nursery and expanded into 500 acres. "Rose Hill Peterson," as he was popularly known, also seems to have been the first in the country to master the art of moving large trees successfully. In the early 1900s nearly all of the trees along the streets and in the public squares of Chicago had come from Rose Hill. A street in the city, Peterson Avenue, was named after him. Peterson had learned the elements of his trade in the gardens of one of the largest chateaux in south Sweden, Övedskloster.

The first well-known lawyer and judge of Swedish ancestry in Chicago was Harry Olson (1867–1935), born in Kansas of parents from Filipstad in Värmland. In 1906, when the new Municipal Court was organized, he was elected its first chief justice, a position he held until 1930. He instituted many judicial reforms and was active both in the rehabilitation of criminals and in child welfare work.

In an effort to put a halt to the career of Mayor William Hale (Big Bill) Thompson of Chicago, Judge Olson was twice entered in the Republican primaries, in 1915 and 1919, but he was defeated each time by an immigrant from Västra Tollstad in the province of Östergötland, Frederick Lundin (1869–1947), who has been described as the ablest political manipulator produced by the Swedish element in the United States. Having been brought to Chicago by his parents when he was eleven years old, Lundin started blacking boots and selling newspapers in a tunnel in the Loop. After several years in the milk business he introduced a soft drink called Juniperade, or in Swedish "enbärsdricka," which made him widely known. Up and down the side streets of Chicago he drove with his horse and wagon, accompanied by two black boys playing on banjos. In 1894 at the age of 25 he was elected to the Illinois State Senate. In 1908 he was the first Illinois Swede to be sent to Congress, where he showed little interest in the routine work but tried to advance the cause of pensions for the aged. After his defeat for reelection in 1910, he concentrated on local politics. With the election of William Hale Thompson as mayor in 1915, Fred Lundin became the boss in City Hall. The *New York Times* obituary in 1947 said of him that he had "wielded more political power than any other individual in Illinois for nearly a decade." He liked to call himself the "Poor Swede," while Judge Olson was the "Good Swede."

During the era of Big Bill Thompson, Fred Lundin, and Judge Harry Olson, the most picturesque of many colorful journalists in the daily press in Chicago was Swedish-born Hilding Johnson (1891–1931), who had been brought to America as a child. His family came from Landskrona in south Sweden. For two decades Criminal Courts Building reporter for the *Chicago Herald & Examiner*, he was said to know everybody worth knowing in the political as well as in the criminal world of Chicago. Finally a legendary example of the so-called hard-boiled American newspaperman, "Hildy," as he was called, in 1928 helped inspire a successful melodramatic play, *The Front Page*, by Ben Hecht and Charles MacArthur. There were also popular motion-picture versions, filmed in 1931, 1940, and 1974. The play was revived in the 1970s both in London and in Gothenburg.

In the late 1800s and early 1900s, the best-known woman of Swedish birth in Chicago was probably Othelia Mörk-Myhrman (1859–1936) from Finspång in Östergötland, who had arrived in 1875 at the age of 16 and begun as a nursery maid. She became one of the leaders of the temperance movement and of many other social and cultural activities among the Swedes in Chicago. As director of a cooperative employment bureau for nearly two decades she helped Swedish immigrants by the tens of thousands to find suitable jobs. Later on she organized and conducted study and concert tours of Sweden.

In the early 1900s two young attorneys, Gustaf Bernard Anderson (1867–1949) and Carl R. Chindblom (1870–1956), both graduates of Augustana College and wholly bilingual, began to play prominent parts in the Swedish community in Chicago. Anderson, who was born in Småland but had come to America with his parents a few years later, was also a Harvard graduate and made a distinguished law career. The eldest of 11 Chicago-born children of immigrants from Åsbo in south Östergötland, Chindblom served in Congress from 1919 to 1933 and became a leading figure on the Swedish-American scene. A somewhat younger noted contemporary, Hugo A. Anderson (b. 1887) from Helsingborg in southern Sweden, had begun his career in 1901 as a page in the First National Bank of Chicago, where 25 years later he was named vice president. One of his sons, Robert O. Anderson (b. 1917), became board chairman of the Atlantic Richfield Company, with headquarters in Philadelphia, as well as vice chairman of the John F. Kennedy Center for the Performing Arts in Washington, D.C., a trustee of the University of Chicago and of California

Institute of Technology, and chairman of the well-known Aspen Institute for Humanistic Studies.

Four exponents of medicine in Chicago: Carlson, Magnuson, Hedblom, Dragstedt

FOR obvious reasons it was unusual for members of the first Swedish generation in America, especially the immigrants of the 19th century, to reach prominent positions in the sphere of science and learning, but such careers did occur, mostly in fields where a perfect command of the English language was not vital. One example is provided by Dr. Anton Julius Carlson of the University of Chicago, who for decades was the best-known educator and scientist of Swedish origin in the Chicago area. The second generation became, on the other hand, well represented on the university faculties and in the research institutes. Many of those who spent an important part of their active life in Chicago were born in other sections of the Middle West. Three other health specialists mentioned below came from Minnesota, Iowa, and Montana.

Born on a small farm near Svarteborg in the west-coast province of Bohuslän, Anton Julius Carlson (1875–1956) began working for his living as a sheep herder at the age of seven. In 1891 he joined an older brother in Chicago, who had sent him money for the transatlantic ticket, and after some time there as an apprentice carpenter he began to study for the ministry at Augustana College and Theological Seminary in Rock Island, Illinois. The science teacher at this school, Johan August Udden, who in the early 1900s moved to Texas, made him change the direction of his academic efforts, and after he had won his Ph.D. at Stanford University in California, he served the University of Chicago from 1904 to 1940 as professor of physiology. Popularly known as "Ajax," he was one of the university's most colorful personalities, and numerous stories were told about him. At one time, the university president, a noted educator, suggested that the professorial tenure be abolished, his assumption being that it would "put the faculty on its toes." To this, Dr. Carlson made a retort which soon became famous: "Sir, you are confused about your anatomy. It will put the faculty on its knees."

Carlson's research contributed to a better understanding of most body organs. He became one of the world's leading authorities on the physiology of hunger and the properties of various foods, and made basic advances in determining the cause of diabetes. As a professor emeritus, he devoted much of his study to the physiology of the aged, and articles in popular magazines made him widely known both as a pioneer in this field and as "the man who understands your stomach." During the First World War he had served in the Sanitary Corps, remaining in Europe for a year to help organize relief for under-nourished children. During the Second World War, he assisted the War Department in the development of the "K" ration. In 1937–38 he served as president of the American Association of University Professors and in 1944–45 as president of the American Association for the Advancement of Science. Honorary degrees came to him from eight universities, including that of Lund in Sweden.

Among sons of Swedish immigrants who became medical specialists in Chicago was Paul Budd Magnuson (1884–1968), who first won a reputation as a pioneer in bone and joint surgery. North-western University in Evanston named him professor and department chairman. After the Second World War he became even better known as a crusader for the highest possible quality of the medical care offered millions of veterans by the Veterans Administration, which he finally served as chief medical director in 1948–50. As chairman of President Truman's Commission on the Health Needs of the Nation he answered criticism of the commission's five-volume report by emphasizing that he was an advocate of organization, not socialization, of medicine. In 1946 he had studied a number of modern hospitals and clinics in Sweden. Paul Budd Magnuson was a graduate of the University of Minnesota and of the University of Pennsylvania Medical School. His father, who had arrived from Sweden in the early 1870s at the age of 12, became president of an elevator company in Minneapolis, and his mother was a former schoolteacher from Pennsylvania.

Another member of the same generation, Carl Arthur Hedblom (1879–1934), who was born in Iowa of Swedish settlers, became an internationally known pioneer in surgery of the chest and served during the last nine years of his relatively short life as professor and head of the department of surgery at the University of Illinois Medical School in Chicago. After his doctorate at Harvard in 1911 and three years as professor at the Harvard Medical School of China in

Shanghai, he joined the Mayo Clinic in Rochester, Minnesota, where he soon was placed in charge of the department of chest surgery. In 1924–26 he served as professor and department head in the University of Wisconsin at Madison, and from there he moved to Chicago.

Another eminent surgeon of Swedish parentage, Lester R. Dragstedt (b. 1893), had just for the third time joined the University of Chicago faculty when Dr. Hedblom arrived in Chicago, and later he became professor of surgery and chairman of his department. He served the University of Chicago until 1959, when his achievements in gastroenterology had long been recognized even internationally. In his younger days he had been an assistant professor of physiology under Anton Julius Carlson, and he wrote a biography of the famous "Ajax." We shall meet him again in Montana, where he was born.

The best-known physician of Swedish birth and education in Chicago was probably Anders Frick, born in 1868 at Malmö, who after studies at Lund and the Caroline Institute in Stockholm began to practice in the Windy City in 1897. He taught at Rush Medical College and the University of Illinois, and served for many years as chief physician at Augustana Hospital.

Swedish immigrants who as noted scholars have been connected with the University of Chicago include Oscar T. Broneer, born in 1894 at Bäckebo in Småland, who came to America in 1913. After studies at Augustana College and the University of California at Berkeley, he joined in 1927 the faculty of the American School of Classical Studies at Athens, where he was named professor in 1940. From 1949 to 1960 he was professor of archeology at the University of Chicago, during most of that time directing excavations in Greece. He became an honorary citizen of ancient Corinth.

Some widely known Chicago-based industrialists and businessmen of Swedish stock

AS THE American city with the largest Swedish population, Chicago has had more prominent manufacturers and other businessmen of Swedish birth or parentage than any other community in the United States. Many of those of the second generation came from Swedish settlements in the north or west of Illinois, Minnesota, Iowa, or other parts of the Middle West.

Many of the industrial pioneers of Swedish origin were active in the budding technology industries, with products which at least in part were made of metals. One of the first immigrants from Sweden to make a career in the new field was John Martin Westerlin (1855–1939), born at Fjärås in Halland, who was brought to America in 1868 and, as president from 1890 of the Westerlin Campbell Company in Chicago, became one of the foremost authorities in the refrigeration industry.

Among 19th-century immigrants from Sweden who became widely known industrialists in Chicago were Bror Gustav Dahlberg, John S. Gullborg, Justus P. Seeburg, Alfred Stromberg and Androv Carlson. Sons of Swedish settlers who founded important industries or successful commercial ventures included Vincent Bendix, George William Borg, and Charles R. Walgreen.

In 1894, two Swedish-born engineers in Chicago, Alfred Stromberg and Androv Carlson, formed a partnership which the next year became a company for the manufacture of telephones. Both had been telephone men in Sweden, where in the late 1800s this means of communication reached a higher development than in any other country. In Chicago they produced an excellent instrument, a magneto-operated transmitter and receiver designed along Swedish lines, and with its highly sensitive transmission of sound it became very popular with the farmers, who offered the independent manufacturers their most important market. Listening through the "Farmer's Telephone," as the Stromberg-Carlson product often was called, the subscriber according to contemporary reports could hear not only the conversation at the other end of the line, but also the crowing of roosters outside the door or the bellowing of cows in the barn. Forming mutual telephone associations, rural communities would string their own wire along the highways, and 20 or more telephones would be connected on a single circuit. The isolation of rural life was being overcome.

After having concentrated on rural equipment, the Stromberg-Carlson company started making larger and larger switchboards for cities and towns. By the turn of the century it was a leader among the independent manufacturers, supplying large central exchanges to cities like Kansas City, Missouri, Rochester, New York, and Savannah, Georgia, and also producing specialized instruments, such as hotel, police, and desk telephones. In 1900 the company bought the Dunn

Building on Jackson Boulevard in Chicago, and two years later it employed 1,200 workmen, with sales close to three million dollars.

In the same year, 1902, Stromberg and Carlson sold effective control of their concern to the independent telephone company of Rochester, New York, which had bought all its equipment from the Chicago firm. Other independent telephone manufacturers had already been absorbed by the Bell system. Alfred Stromberg joined the new Stromberg-Carlson Telephone Manufacturing Company at Rochester as its vice president, but in 1905 both he and his old partner, Androv Carlson, returned to Chicago. After the First World War the company they had founded began to make radio equipment as well, and people all over the United States became quite familiar with the Stromberg-Carlson combination. In 1955 the 60-year-old company was turned into a division of General Dynamics.

Alfred Stromberg (1861–1913) was born in Stockholm. In 1876 he became associated with Sweden's best-known telephone pioneer, Lars Magnus Ericsson, and nine years later, when the International Bell Telephone Company had opened an exchange in Stockholm, he was hired by the Bell Telephone Company in Chicago, for which he made a number of inventions. In 1890 he started working for the Chicago Electric Protective Company, where he devised what became known as the "Stromberg system" of burglar alarms. Androv Carlson (b. 1854), who four years later became his partner, was a native of the province of Västergötland and had after his emigration also been employed by the Chicago Bell Telephone Company. He seems to have spent more time than Stromberg working out their own telephone. Both were regarded as unusually competent and dedicated engineers.

The "Stromberg carburetor," once known throughout the automobile field, was named after Alfred Stromberg, but the actual inventor was another Swedish immigrant, John S. Gullborg (1863–1940) from Sandhem in the province of Västergötland. In his father's smithy he took his first steps as a mechanic. Several years later he was hired by the Husqvarna company at Huskvarna in northern Småland, which was founded in 1689 as an arms factory but today specializes in sewing machines, household appliances, and related products, and there he invented an improved method of making guns. Although this brought him recognition and certain advantages, he soon decided to emigrate.

After coming to Chicago in 1886, Gullborg first worked on bicycles and then on telephone devices, finally helping to organize the Swedish-American Telephone Company in 1902. At about the same time he joined the Stromberg-Carlson Telephone Company, where he designed a considerable number of new instruments and helped streamline the operations. After having left the telephone business but still associated with Stromberg, he made numerous other inventions and improvements, including the carburetor, an automatic die-casting machine, which became the basis of a new industry, and the famous grease gun for the lubrication of automobiles. Gradually Gullborg became widely known as an outstanding engineer and inventor.

Two other Swedish-born employees of the Stromberg-Carlson firm, who later launched a manufacturing business of their own, were the brothers Carl D. and Paul J. Bodin, or Bodine, who in 1905 in Chicago began the manufacture of fractional-horsepower electric motors used in electric clocks, dental .drills, moving-picture projectors, and electric refrigerators. Their father, a building contractor at Västra Ämtervik in Värmland, emigrated in 1886 and took along five-year-old Carl, settling at first in Loomis, Nebraska. Mrs. Bodine and four-year-old Paul joined them the next year. Another Swedish immigrant, Albert Ivar Appleton (1872–1951), who was born at Onsala in the province of Halland and in 1903 established himself in Chicago with two employees, also became an important manufacturer of electrical specialties. His products were exported to many countries.

A Swedish Methodist minister at Moline, the Reverend John Bendix from Färgaryd in Småland, and his wife from Östergötland had a son, Vincent Bendix (1881–1945), who ran away from home at 16, held a number of odd jobs in Chicago and New York and never received any formal education but always tinkered with bicycles, motorcycles, and machines. He finally became a widely known industrialist and aviation promoter both in America and abroad. In 1907 he joined the sales force of an automobile company in Chicago, which remained his home base, and the next year he designed and built his own car, the Bendix. While it did not survive, it had a small but vitally important detail, soon known as the Bendix drive, which made practical for the first time the use of self-starters in automobiles. Before this invention, all motor vehicles had to be cranked by hand.

As a relatively young man, Bendix also improved the carburetor and organized the first mass production of four-wheel brakes. After Charles Lindbergh's solo flight to Paris in 1927 he began the acquisition of companies manufacturing aircraft instruments, landing gear, and other accessories, and in 1929 he formed the Bendix Aviation Corporation, which under his direction became a manufacturing concern of international importance. Bendix also showed his interest in aviation by founding in 1931 the Bendix Transcontinental Air Race, which for many years remained a fixed annual event. In 1937 he announced plans for an "aviation city" to bear his name, at Teterboro, New Jersey, where the airport was remodeled and an aeronautical plant erected. In the 1920s Bendix helped finance the Swedish explorer Sven Hedin's expedition to Central Asia in the years 1927–33, in which a large number of Swedish, German, and Chinese scientists took part.

Like Vincent Bendix and many other successful inventors, George William Borg (1887–1960) failed to get a technical education. He was born at West Burlington, Iowa, of Swedish parents who later moved via Rockford to Moline, Illinois. There his father, Charles W. Borg, a former sailor and a skilled mechanic, gradually built a successful machine shop, with a local lawyer and inventor, Marshall Beck, as his partner. Young George Borg, who studied business at Augustana College, took an active part in the operations, and in 1910 he, Beck, and his father's foreman, Gus Nelson, who has been described as a mechanical genius, developed the disk clutch which later was used in many millions of American automobiles. Borg & Beck, which became a leading producer of clutches, moved in 1918 to Chicago, and ten years later the Borg-Warner Corporation was formed by the merging of this firm and three other companies. The elder Borg had then sold out and had become a millionaire. George W. Borg was named Borg & Warner's first president, but he soon preferred being chairman of the board, serving in that post until 1940. His other business interests included a company for the manufacture of automobile and electronic components which he had founded at Delavan, Wisconsin, where he had a 1,000-acre farm. In Arizona he developed one of the most exclusive resorts in America.

Another of the original four in the Borg-Warner Corporation was the Mechanics Universal Joint Company of Rockford, Illinois, formerly known as the Mechanics Machine Company, which had been started in 1890 by four machinists from Sweden and whose products also went into millions of motor vehicles. Following its acquisition by Borg-Warner, a Rockford industrialist of Swedish stock, Eric Ekstrom, became its president. A son of Swedish immigrants in Moline, Gustavus Adolphus Shallberg (b. 1876), who had been George W. Borg's lawyer, served by the middle of the 1900s as executive vice president of the entire Borg-Warner Corporation. From 1944 to 1946 its chief executive engineer was another person of Swedish extraction, Harold T. Youngren, who had previously been associated with General Motors and from 1946 to 1952 served as Ford's chief engineer and vice president in charge of engineering.

Justus P. Sjöberg, or Seeburg (1871–1958), who was born in Gothenburg and after technical studies emigrated to America in 1886, founded in the early 1900s at Chicago the J. P. Seeburg Corporation, which also grew into a large technological manufacturer. It became well known first for its mechanical player pianos and later for its coin-operated phonographs, popularly called "jukeboxes." Seeburg's firm also originated the parking meters, developed ice-cream and soft-drink dispensers, and manufactured a wide range of other products. During the Second World War the company received the Army-Navy E for excellence four times.

A son of Swedish settlers in western Illinois, Charles R. Walgreen (1873–1939), made the name Walgreen widely known. His parents, Carl Rudolf and Ellen Wallgren, lived for many years on a farm 14 miles from Galesburg, where America's first Swedish-language paper had been founded in 1855 and Carl Sandburg, the poet and Lincoln biographer, was born of Swedish parents in 1878. After having started as a worker in a shoe factory, Walgreen in 1901 began his business career with one drugstore in Chicago. In 1939 his son took over the management of a chain which had grown to over 500 stores in 31 different states. More than 100 of the outlets were in the Chicago area. Carl Rudolf Wallgren, who had come to America in 1852, is said to have been more interested in the reading of history than in farming. A granddaughter, and daughter of the drugstore pioneer, Ruth Stephan, wrote two historical novels about Queen Christina of Sweden, daughter of Gustavus Adolphus.

Bror Gustav Dahlberg (1881–1954) was brought to America in

1889 at the age of eight. His father, an artist from Kristianstad in southern Sweden who had been rather well off, died a year or so later in Minneapolis, leaving his widow and five children all but destitute. At 13, Bror Dahlberg began working for his living as an elevator boy. Later he learned the railroad business in the empire of James J. Hill, and from there he moved to an executive position in a large lumber and paper company. This led him into experiments with new, inexpensive building materials, which also would offer insulation against heat, cold, and noise, and he was one of the first to see the potentialities of this field as a new national industry. In 1921 he organized in Chicago the Celotex Corporation for the manufacture of insulating board and other materials. Originally a trademark applied only to Dahlberg's fiberboard, Celotex gradually became a household word and has often been used as a generic term for all kinds of insulating board.

Celotex was made from bacasse, the sugar-cane fiber which is left after the juice is crushed out of the cane. In order to protect and improve the supply of his raw material, Dahlberg invested heavily in Florida and Louisiana sugar lands, and the town of Clewiston in southern Florida was founded by him. Gradually he became convinced that only mass production and mass distribution of prefabricated parts would solve America's low-cost housing problem, and his building materials were used for everything but the framework of a home. Speaking to a Harvard business group in the late 1930s, he concluded as follows: "If the country really bestirred itself to get what people should really have, and what they could create if they would, there should be a call for something like 20 million new homes or family units. Instead of complaining that there is not room for employment, our cry should be: 'So much to do; so little done.'" Dahlberg was a cofounder of the Damon Runyon Cancer Fund.

Swedish industrial enterprise blooms at Rockford — Moline also an important center

OF THE cities in Illinois, Rockford 80 miles northwest of Chicago had the second largest Swedish-born population, and in third place came Moline, on the Mississippi in Rock Island County. In 1930 Rockford had about 10,000 Swedish-born inhabitants. They and their children made up about one-fourth of the city's population.

In Rockford's rise as, first, a leading furniture center and then one of the largest machine-tool producers in the world, Swedish immigrants played highly significant parts. In the 19th century they also founded an important hosiery and textile industry. John Nelson from Kärråkra in Västergötland, who has been mentioned before as one of the first Swedes to come to Rockford, in 1852, was a carpenter and began working in a furniture factory. During a visit to the Chicago Exposition in 1867 he became interested in knitting machinery, and six years later he had constructed a machine making seamless hosiery, an invention that had a lasting impact on the industry. By the middle of the 20th century there were in Rockford alone six large mills producing annually millions of seamless stockings. A bridge, a school, and a hotel in Rockford were named for John Nelson.

To an unusually great extent the Swedes in Rockford founded firms of their own and remained in control, although several companies finally were consolidated with larger corporations. Not only permanent settlers but also thousands of Swedish newcomers who later moved to other communities received valuable vocational training. Even in the late 1920s, immigrants from Sweden started industries which eventually ranked among the largest in the city. In 1930, 72 factories were owned by people of Swedish stock. During the Second World War Rockford was one of America's vital industrial centers.

Until about 1920, furniture manufacture was Rockford's major industry. The principal founder of its machine and tool production was Levin Fast, or Faust (1863–1936), from the Falköping district in Västergötland, who like many other Swedish emigrants had received his first professional training as a machinist in the Motala iron and machine works on the eastern shore of Lake Vättern. In 1890, after having lived in Rockford for three years, he and three other skilled metalworkers from Sweden organized the Mechanics Machine Company, which became an important producer of automotive parts and in 1928, as already mentioned, became one of the first four components of the Borg-Warner Corporation. The founders of 1890 had a capital of only $1,000 but soon received powerful support from Rockford's leading industrialist, Pehr August Peterson, who had arrived in 1852 from Södra Ving in Västergötland and had begun earning his living as a farmhand, as a lumberjack in Michigan, and in Chicago. In Rockford, Levin Faust played a leading role in the founding of several other metalworking firms, including National Lock Company. He also did much for the development of the city's park system. Its largest hotel was named for him.

In the early 1900s the two brothers David Sundstrand (1880–1930), who had come from Stockholm with his parents in 1882, and Oscar Sundstrand (1889–1972), who was born at Rockford, became internationally known as inventors. After having bought a workshop in Rockford, they developed there in 1910–13 a 10-key adding machine of great significance. The name Sundstrand became, in fact, often used for the whole 10-key category of adding machines. In 1915 the elder brother left the office-machine business and started working on machine tools, while Oscar Sundstrand continued to improve the adding machine and also designed accounting and bookkeeping machines. At the end of his life he held some 150 patents. In the 1930s he had moved with the Underwood company to Connecticut.

Among the first Swedish immigrants who came to Rockford in 1852 was a family from Jönköping, the Johannes Magnussons, with one daughter and one son. The latter had a son, Martin Elmer Johnson (1884–1937), who became an internationally noted photographer of wildlife and aboriginal tribes, naturalist, and lecturer. From 1910 to 1920 he and his wife, Osa Helen Johnson, circled the globe by air six times, returning with material, especially from the South Seas, that brought them wide scientific and popular tribute. Later on they made extensive films of the central African jungles for the American Museum of Natural History. Many of their films were seen by millions of people. In 1937, Johnson was fatally injured in an airplane crash in California. His wife, who survived, published in 1940 a best-selling autobiography, *I Married Adventure*.

Rockford has a score of churches of Swedish origin. Even after the middle of the 20th century a Swedish service was conducted in one of them every Sunday morning. At that time there were seven Swedish, or predominantly Swedish, male choruses. The highly regarded Swedish-American Hospital in Rockford was founded in 1911 by a group of private citizens. A new wing was dedicated in 1963 by Prince Bertil of Sweden.

A great many city officials in Rockford have been of Swedish origin, and some of them have served for protracted terms. The leading record holder was August Edward Berggren, or Bargren

(1863–1942), from Axvall in Västergötland, who joined the police department in 1890 and from 1894 until his retirement in 1940 served as chief of the police force. He had come to Rockford with his parents in 1868.

In the early 1950s the Swedish Historical Society of Rockford, which was founded in 1937, turned one of the oldest of the larger houses in Rockford into a museum. Known as the Erlander Home, it was built in 1871 by John Erlander, born in 1826 near Växjö in Småland, who had come to Rockford in 1855 and in 1876 helped found one of its largest furniture companies. In 1952, 100 years after the arrival of the first Swedish settlers in Rockford, the Erlander Home was dedicated as a museum by Prime Minister Tage Erlander of Sweden. In 1954, Carl Sandburg wrote a tribute to the Swedish immigrants which has been cast in bronze and occupies a prominent place in the museum:

"They shared in the making of America. From the wilderness days through storms of war and years of peace, their toils, endurance, valor, their struggles and devotions, are woven as a dark scarlet thread in the Sacred American Story and Dream. Their names and works are worth Remembrance."

A modern museum was built at Rockford in the middle 1970s, and plans for an adjacent "pioneer village" were launched.

Rockford has seen quite a few Swedish-language newspapers. The last one, *Svenska Posten*, founded in 1889, was merged with a Chicago paper in 1918. A semimonthly called *Forskaren* (The Researcher), which emphasized the antireligious element in European socialism, was published in Rockford in 1893–94 and then in Minneapolis until 1924. Another semimonthly of a similar type, *Svenska Socialisten*, began to appear in 1905 but moved to Chicago six years later. Swedish periodicals have also been published in Moline, Rock Island, Batavia, Galva, Knoxville, Paxton, and of course Galesburg, where the first important Swedish newspaper in America was founded in 1855.

Swedes who settled in Moline helped turn this city, together with its neighbor Rock Island, into the greatest center in the United States for the manufacture of farm implements. One of the first firms, the Moline Plow Company, was founded in 1864 with an immigrant from Sweden, a former blacksmith named Anders Friberg, as the superintendent and leading spirit. In the late 1800s most of the workers in this and some other factories were Swedish. Friberg, who was born in 1828 at Skrävlinge in southernmost Sweden and raised in Gothenburg, came to America in 1850. At Moline he invented a famous implement known as the Western Cultivator.

Many notable Americans of Swedish parentage were, like Vincent Bendix, born at Moline or began their careers there, perhaps like George William Borg as burgeoning engineers or inventors. A large proportion of the settlers from Sweden had, before their emigration, been ironsmiths or skilled metalworkers of other kinds, and their sons often seemed to have a special aptitude for engineering and technology.

One of the smiths, Adolf Håkansson, or Adolph Hokinson, who seems to have settled in Moline in the early 1880s and later moved to Mendota 75 miles farther east, had a daughter, Helen Elna Hokinson (1893–1949), who in 1925, as an experienced artist, started working for *The New Yorker* and became one of that magazine's most sophisticated and popular cartoonists. After her death in an airplane accident in 1949, *The New Yorker* wrote in a "final paragraph about an irreplaceable artist," that "the ladies she drew have become perhaps the most widely known and cherished of any characters we have introduced to our readers."

Industries were founded or developed by Swedish immigrants or descendants in several other cities and towns in Illinois. At Kewanee in Henry County, near Bishop Hill, Galva, and other old Swedish settlements, Peter W. Waller became president of a company which, when he died, had glove-manufacturing plants in 15 cities, the largest concern of its kind in the country. During the First World War the firm at one time turned out 300,000 pairs per day, including fireproof gloves for the naval gunners, one-fingered mittens for the laying of mines, and barbed-wire-entanglement gloves. Its low-priced canvas gloves were used by millions of farmers and other outdoor workers. Waller was born in 1868 at Ockelbo in the province of Gästrikland and was brought up in an industrial atmosphere, his father being a master smith and the family hailing from the ironmaking Walloons who immigrated to Sweden in the 17th century. Traveling with an uncle who had visited Sweden, he came to America in 1885 and started working in a factory in Kewanee at $1.25 a day. In the 1920s and 1930s he played a leading part in fund-raising drives for the American Swedish Historical Museum in Philadelphia. Among his Swedish friends was Archbishop Nathan Söderblom, who before his death in 1931 helped trace the genealogy of the Waller family.

Elgin, Illinois, has had at least one widely known citizen of Swedish birth, namely, William H. Samelius (1873–1961), an outstanding horologist and precision expert who from 1921 to 1954 served as dean of the Elgin Watchmakers College. He was born at Belfast, Ireland, where his mother and father, professor of horology in Stockholm, had come on a European study tour, and was brought to Chicago eight years later, in 1881. Collections of watches, clocks, and tools owned or made by Samelius are in Chicago's Museum of Science and Industry, the Smithsonian Institution in Washington, and the Franklin Institute at Philadelphia. A library at Tokyo has been named for Samelius, who during both world wars worked for the U.S. government.

Swedish ancestry on the distaff side is not easily identified, but the achievements of such Americans have been as significant as those of persons with a paternal forebear of Swedish birth. In 1870 Anders Olsson from Svärdsjö in Dalarna moved to America, where two of his daughters already lived. He brought his youngest daughter, 10-year-old Sarah Elizabeth, who later settled with her husband at Table Grove, Illinois. They had a son, Ray Edwin Powell (1887–1973), who became a pioneer in the building of the Canadian and worldwide aluminum industry. From 1937 to 1957 he was president of the Aluminum Company of Canada, remaining as honorary chairman until his death. In 1957–64 he served as chancellor of McGill University in Montreal. He had begun his career as a page boy in the Congress of the United States, where he became acquainted with Andrew Mellon, the financier.

The "Scandinavian" Minnesota — One-third of population hailing from Sweden-Norway

FREDRIKA BREMER'S dream in 1850 about Minnesota as "a glorious new Scandinavia" seemed a few decades later well on its way toward fulfillment. At the end of the century, the Swedish and Norwegian immigrants and their children represented about one-third of the total population. There was also a Danish element. The Swedes had started coming later than both Germans and Norwegians, but in 1900 they were more numerous than the Norwegian-born, and by 1910 they had also passed the settlers from Germany.

The Germans and the Norwegians played an even greater part than the Swedes in bringing the land under cultivation, but it was in Minnesota that immigrants from Sweden and their descendants made their most important contributions to the American farming industry. In 1930 the North Star State reported a Swedish farm population of nearly 90,000, or as many as Illinois, Iowa, Nebraska, and Wisconsin together. At that time, however, only about one-third of the Swedish element in Minnesota lived on farms. In the 1800s a considerable number of Swedes became engaged in lumbering, and of those who arrived around the turn of the century many became miners.

Among the sections of Minnesota where from the early 1870s large numbers of Swedes and Norwegians settled was the fertile valley of the Red River of the North, which separates Minnesota from North Dakota. Much of the Scandinavian colonization was furthered by a Swedish immigrant, Alexander E. Johnson (1840–1918), who worked for the Northern Pacific Railroad as a land commissioner. Johnson, who was born at Karlskoga in the province of Värmland, came with his parents to Chicago in 1854. In 1883 he organized the land and travel firm of A. E. Johnson & Company, which established branch offices in many cities throughout the country, including Minneapolis and St. Paul. In 1906 Mr. Johnson became the first president of The Swedish Chamber of Commerce of the U.S.A., which set up its head-quarters in New York. He also served as Swedish consul for many years.

Minnesota attracted Swedes from other parts of the United States, including the South. Before leaving for Sweden in the spring of 1871, Colonel Hans Mattson received a letter from a Swede in Water Valley in northern Mississippi, who wrote on behalf of about 100 desperate countrymen, most of them from Värmland. They had come to Mississippi in 1870 under the auspices of two brothers, Gustaf and Wilhelm Berglund, who had a construction firm in Water Valley. Conditions there, however, were not what they had expected, and since the summer of 1870 many of the newcomers had died from diseases. Others had managed to move, but most of them were unable to do so. Colonel Mattson and the railroad he was going to serve in Sweden quickly organized a rescue mission, and in early April 73 Swedes arrived in St. Paul, from where they were sent to Rush City in Chisago County. West and south of this community they founded a settlement that later flourished. The president of the Lake Superior & Mississippi Railroad reported to the stockholders: "These people are now comfortably fixed in their new homes, and, with restored health, are writing very encouraging letters to their friends and relatives in Sweden of the climate of Minnesota, the generosity of our company, etc., which will alone no doubt repay all the labor and money expended."

These comments may well have been inspired by Colonel Hans Mattson, who in his memoirs wrote about the same group: "The Northern climate is incomparably the best and most suitable for the Northern people. They had left Sweden as healthy, strong and hopeful men and women, but after having spent only a year in the South they arrived in Minnesota pale and thin, poor and dejected, without strength and energy and almost without hope." In their propaganda wars with other American states, Mattson and other promoters often had reason to discuss the Minnesota climate, which, for instance, a pamphlet of 1865 described as "much more agreeable than the amphibious, half-fluid, half-solid, sloppy, grave-like chill of the East." When the Swedish emigrants whom the Berglund brothers had recruited for Mississippi left Sweden, their number seems to have been about 175. One of the brothers was fined by the Swedish authorities because he was not an authorized emigrant agent.

Toward the end of his life Colonel Mattson founded a bank in Minneapolis. His son Edgar L. Mattson, who was born at Kristianstad in southern Sweden in 1871, one of the years when the Mattsons lived in their native country, rose to leading positions in three different banks in Minneapolis, where he had received his education. He served as president of Minnesota Bankers Association and of two agencies of the American Bankers Association.

First Swede to U.S. Congress in 1886 — Many Minnesota governors of Swedish origin

THE first Swede in the Minnesota legislature was Lars Johan Stark (1826–1910) from Lidköping in Västergötland, who in the early 1850s had settled in Chisago County. He was elected the first time in 1864. In the early 1880s there were seven Swedes and 14 Norwegians in the 147-member state legislature, which was a rather modest representation in relation to the total Scandinavian population. Colonel Hans Mattson, who in 1870 began his first term as secretary of state, was the first Swede in the state administration.

The first Minnesota Scandinavian to play a part in national politics was a Norwegian, Knute Nelson, who in 1882 was elected to the U.S. Congress where he served until 1888. After having been elected governor of Minnesota in 1892 and 1894, he was sent to the U.S. Senate, where he remained until his death nearly three decades later. Nelson began his political career with strong support from Swedish settlers, and relations between the two principal Scandinavian elements remained good on the whole. Swedes and Norwegians often worked closely together in colonization projects, and conjugal unions between members of the two nationalities were common.

The first man of Swedish birth to be elected to the U.S. Congress, in Minnesota and in the whole United States, was John Lind (1854–1930), who also became the first Swede in the governor's chair at St. Paul. Born at Kånna in southern Småland, he came to America with his parents in 1868, a year of famine in Sweden. After studies at the newly founded Gustavus Adolphus College and the University of Minnesota, followed by practice as a lawyer, he was elected in 1886 to Congress, where he served three terms. Being opposed to the gold standard, he swung to the Democratic party during the political upheavals of the 1890s. After one term as governor of Minnesota, in 1899–1901, he was again elected to Congress in 1902. In 1913 President Wilson sent him to Mexico as his personal representative, in an effort to straighten out relations with that country.

John Lind's election to Congress in 1886 marked the beginning of a more active participation in political affairs by the Swedish element in Minnesota. The second governor of Swedish ancestry, John A. Johnson, we have already met in connection with his parents' immigration in the 1850s. He was elected three times, and was widely regarded as the likely Democratic nominee for President in 1912, but in 1909, when he was in his third term as governor, he died. Theodore Roosevelt said that he was "one of those Americans who we like to believe are typical of our people as a whole."

John A. Johnson was succeeded as governor of Minnesota by Adolph O. Eberhart (1870–1944), a lawyer who was born near Karlstad in the province of Värmland. He came to America at the age of 12 and began as a cattle herder on the prairies of northeastern Nebraska. Thirteen years later he was graduated from Gustavus Adolphus College. Despite the Bull Moose defection in 1912, Eberhart was reelected governor on the Republican ticket. Under his direction, the school system in Minnesota was reorganized, and over 300 industrial and agricultural schools were established in the rural districts. A fourth governor of Swedish descent was Joseph Alfred Arner Burnquist (1879–1961), who was born in Iowa of immigrants from Sweden. A lawyer by profession and a member of the Republican party, he served as governor for three consecutive terms, 1915–21.

Floyd B. Olson (1891–1936), the son of a Norwegian father and a Swedish mother from Värmland, was one of the most popular governors in the history of Minnesota. A candidate of the Farmer-Labor party, he was elected three times during the Great Depression, beginning in 1930. He attracted growing nationwide attention but in 1936, after having been nominated for the Senate, he died in office. Olson had begun as a salesman in Canada, and as a stevedore, miner, and fisherman on the Pacific Coast and in Alaska. Before his election as governor, he had been a crusading district attorney in Minneapolis. His middle name, Björnstjerne, was a tribute to one of Norway's best-known literary figures, Björnstjerne Björnson, who in 1859 wrote a poem which became Norway's national anthem.

In the period 1940–75 Minnesota had five governors of Swedish ancestry, namely Luther W. Youngdahl, 1947–51, C. Elmer Anderson, 1951–55, Orville L. Freeman, 1955–61, Harold LeVander, 1967–71, and Wendell R. Anderson, 1971–   . Both Youngdahl and LeVander were graduates of Gustavus Adolphus College. Freeman served from 1961 to 1969 as U.S. secretary of agriculture. His grandfather, who came from Sweden, changed his name from Johnson to Freeman because he found so many other Johnsons in

Minnesota and, moreover, liked the name Freeman. He may have heard a story about one Johnson who came to a famous echo lake in Minnesota and called, "My name is Johnson," the sonorous echo answering: "Which Johnson?"

Luther W. Youngdahl came to the governorship from the Supreme Court of Minnesota, and in 1951 he was named to the U.S. District Court for the District of Columbia. His father, John C. Ljungdahl, or Youngdahl, born in 1860 at Malmö in southern Sweden, emigrated to America in 1886 and began as a commercial fisherman on Lake Superior, later opening a grocery store in Minneapolis. He and his wife, the former Elizabeth Johnson from the Swedish province of Dalsland, whom he had married after the death of his first spouse, sent all their children to Gustavus Adolphus College. One, Benjamin E. Youngdahl, served in 1944–45 with the United Nations Relief and Rehabilitation Administration in Europe and was cited for his work by General Eisenhower. As professor and finally dean of the School of Social Work at Washington University in St. Louis, Missouri, he was elected president of the American Association of Social Workers and two other national organizations in the same field. His brother Reuben K. Youngdahl became nationally known as pastor of the largest Lutheran congregation in the United States and the Mount Olivet Church in Minneapolis. Another brother, Oscar Youngdahl, was elected to the U.S. Congress, and a half brother, Peter Youngdahl, became a lawyer in Los Angeles. John and Elizabeth Youngdahl's daughter Ruth, who began her career as a schoolteacher, married a clergyman, Clarence Nelson, and became widely known as a speaker and author in the field of religion, was in 1973 named American "Mother of the Year."

In 1920, a Swedish-born Republican, Mike Holm (1876–1952), was elected secretary of state of Minnesota, and until his death more than 30 years later he was returned to that office by large majorities, regardless of which party carried the state. Toward the end of his life he was sometimes referred to as "the best-known institution in Minnesota." His parents and their six sons had come to America in the early 1880s, lured by literature from the Great Northern Railway which extolled the virtues of northern Minnesota. Holm's original first name was Mika, and when it was changed to Mike, many Irishmen thought that he was a son of Erin. He was three times elected president of the National Association of Secretaries of State. Born at Ringvattnet in the province of Jämtland, he became an active member of a society in the Twin Cities called Jämtamot.

The only Swedish-born U.S. senator from Minnesota, and in the history of the United States, was Magnus Johnson (1871–1936), who came from Ed Parish in the province of Värmland, southwest of Karlstad. Before his emigration in 1891 at the age of 20, he had worked for two years as a glassblower, and the powerful voice that nature had given him was then developed into a truly stentorian one. He received little formal education but was influenced by the ideas of the new Swedish labor movement. One of his greatest experiences was the arrival of Captain John Ericsson's remains for burial in Värmland, in the fall of 1890, which may have crystallized his decision to emigrate to America.

After two years as a lumberjack in Wisconsin, Magnus Johnson settled as a farmer at Kingston in Meeker County, west of Minneapolis-St. Paul. He served as a justice of the peace and was elected to the state legislature. In 1923, when 80-year-old Senator Knute Nelson had died, a special statewide election was called, and Johnson, who was the candidate of the Farmer-Labor party, won by a wide margin. An able but unconventional man, he became overnight a well-known figure in Washington. His Swedish accent as well as his picturesque ways caused both good-humored and sarcastic amusement, but Johnson remained unperturbed. In the Senate he tried to serve "the farmer, the worker, and the average man," as well as world peace. He was much in demand as a public speaker.

In 1924 Magnus Johnson was defeated by his Republican opponent, and he then stayed out of national politics until 1932, when he was elected to the House of Representatives. In 1936 he ran as an independent for the governorship in Minnesota, but after a motorcar accident early that year his health failed, and in September he died. His "sturdy character and rugged honesty," said the *Minneapolis Journal*, "always commanded respect and admiration even from political opponents," and a columnist in the *St. Paul Dispatch* wrote: "He was a big jovial out-of-doors man who bore the outlines of his storm-stressed Viking ancestors. . . . His real glory was in the fact that he never thought of himself apart from his fellows."

The second U.S. senator from Minnesota of Swedish origin was Ernest Lundeen (1878–1940), who was born of Swedish Mission Friend pioneers in South Dakota and had become a lawyer in Minneapolis. He was elected to the Senate in 1936. In 1917–18 he was a member of the House of Representatives. Like 49 other Congressmen he voted against the United States' entry into the First World War, an act he always noted proudly. In 1898 he had volunteered for service in the Spanish-American War, and he had been a member of an all-American championship rifle team. In the early 1930s he visited Sweden, including the province of Småland where his parents were born. His father had begun there as a teacher, and in the U. S. Senate Ernest Lundeen worked hard for increased aid to education. Swedish-born Charles A. Lindbergh, Sr., who had come to Minnesota as an infant and also was against the declaration of war in 1917, was no longer in Congress when that step was discussed.

The first son of Swedish pioneers in Minnesota to become a prominent jurist was Andrew Holt (1855–1948), who had studied at Gustavus Adolphus College and in 1880 had become the first Scandinavian to complete a course at the University of Minnesota. After many years of legal practice and as a judge in Minneapolis, he was in 1911 elected to the Supreme Court of Minnesota, on which he served until 1942. He was then 87 years old and had long been regarded as the most venerable jurist in the state. His successor was Clarence R. Magney (1883–1962), a former mayor of Duluth. Before university studies in Minneapolis and at Harvard, he had been graduated from Gustavus Adolphus College, where in 1862 his father, born at Linneryd in Småland, had been the first student.

In the 1940s, when a majority of the Supreme Court Justices at St. Paul were of Swedish ancestry, it was sometimes facetiously asserted that when the court tackled really knotty problems of law, it did so in Swedish. In reality, however, the members of Swedish origin had only a skimpy knowledge of the language of their ancestors in Scandinavia. By the middle of the 20th century, according to a special survey, the number of lawyers of Swedish ancestry in Minnesota was nearly 300.

In the late 1800s and early 1900s there had been many Swedish weeklies in Minnesota, but in the 1940s there was none. While Minneapolis-St. Paul, of course, had been the leading publishing center, at one time or another Swedish-language periodicals had also appeared in Cambridge, Duluth, Grove City, Lindstrom, Litchfield, Red Wing, St. Peter, Stillwater, and several other cities or towns.

A young man from Minnesota named John August Lundeen, born at Vetlanda in Småland, who had arrived with his parents in 1853 at the age of five, was the second Swede to enter and complete studies at the U. S. Military Academy at West Point. He came to the academy in July, 1869, two weeks after Eric Bergland, an appointee from Illinois, had been graduated at the head of his class, and he completed the course four years later, fifth in a class of 41 men. After his first tours of military duty, he became in 1876 professor of military science in the University of Minnesota, where he also taught mathematics and the Swedish language. In 1887 he returned to West Point to teach mathematics. Lundeen finally became artillery inspector-general of the Pacific division and was promoted to colonel.

A "lumber king" and the founder of Greyhound among Swedes in Minnesota

THE first widely known businessman of Swedish birth in Minnesota was Carl or Charles A. Smith (1852–1925), the son of a professional infantry soldier from Ekeby in the province of Östergötland; he had come to America with his father in 1867 and had settled in Minneapolis. After university studies and some business practice under the auspices of John S. Pillsbury, who from 1876 to 1882 served as governor of Minnesota, he started in 1878 a lumber yard at Herman in western Minnesota, and before the end of the century he had become one of the "lumber kings" of the Midwest. At Minneapolis his firm erected a giant lumber-manufacturing establishment, while a subsidiary bought vast areas in Oregon and California. Most of Smith's employees were Swedes. Schools that had been founded by Swedish immigrants, including Gustavus Adolphus at St. Peter, Minnesota, Augustana College in Rock Island, Illinois, and Bethany College at Lindsborg, Kansas, received donations from him. He served as a trustee of the University of Minnesota from 1908 to 1913, and during the same period he served as Swedish consul in Minneapolis. His wife, whose maiden name was Johanna Andersson, was the daughter of one of the pioneers in Carver County, Olof Andersson from Värmland, who had been a member of the Swedish parliament.

Andrew A. Stomberg, who for more than three decades was professor of Scandinavian at the University of Minnesota, wrote in 1938 about Charles A. Smith and the other lumbermen from Sweden: "Nowadays one is likely to think first of the ruthless spoliation which the lumber industry wrought, but naturally it had its great economic importance in the building of the Northwest. Lumber in large quantities was necessary for the hundreds of thousands of homes, barns, granaries, and office buildings erected in town and country, and in helping to supply this need, the Swedish immigrant again played an important part in the economic development of the country." Many of the lumbermen from Sweden were, in fact, aware of the dangers of overcutting, and among them was Charles A. Smith, who employed specialists whose efforts were focused on reforestation.

The leading conservationist in Minnesota during this era was General Christopher Columbus Andrews, who also may be regarded as one of the pioneers in the United States. His interest in scientific forestry had been awakened when he served as American minister in Stockholm from 1869 to 1878. At that time Sweden was not as far advanced in conservation measures as the less forested and much more densely populated Germany and Denmark, but progress was being made and there was every reason to expect more determined action. In 1828 the publicly sponsored Forest Institute had been founded in Stockholm by Israel af Ström (1778–1856), who devoted his life to the forests and their preservation, and this is regarded as the beginning of a new era of forest economy in Sweden.

After having studied all aspects of Swedish forestry, General Andrews in 1872 sent to Washington a 64-page report, which immediately was printed as a separate pamphlet for distribution. Nearly three decades later, in 1900, the U.S. Senate decided to have 20,000 copies of an up-to-date version of the report printed for the use of its members. More than 30 other handwritten reports from the American envoy on conditions in Sweden and Norway, ranging from the iron industry to crime and prison discipline, were published by the U.S. government. Forestry remained General Andrews's main interest, however, and without it he would hardly have stayed in Sweden nearly nine years. In 1878 he was succeeded by another Civil War veteran, General John L. Stevens of Augusta, Maine.

In Minnesota, General Andrews wrote and secured the passage of the state's first forestry law, and his initiative also led to the creation of two public forests, aggregating over a million acres. In newspaper articles and lectures he warned against the devastation of the forests and urged the adoption of a rational forest policy.

While farming was the chief occupation of the Swedish-born settlers in Minnesota, thousands encamped from the beginning in the larger cities, Minneapolis, St. Paul, and Duluth, which, with its hinterland of iron-ore ranges, forests, and grain fields, became one of the country's foremost ports.

In 1900, when Duluth's population had reached 53,000, the Swedish-born numbered more than 5,000, and 20 years later, when the city had nearly 100,000 inhabitants, those who had come from Sweden totaled about 7,500. In addition there were thousands of Swedish parentage, and a large group of Swedish-speaking Finns. The latter were active in getting Swedish introduced in a Duluth high school, and quite a few studied at colleges founded by immigrants from Sweden. In northeastern Minnesota as a whole, the immigrants from Finland outnumbered the settlers born in Sweden. The first Swedes and Finns had come to Duluth in the middle 1860s, when wolves, bears, and deer often appeared in the streets.

In Duluth as in other American cities, the Swedish immigrants became represented in most occupations, and they seem to have taken an active part in public affairs. There were several prominent physicians and surgeons, such as John J. Eklund, who at the age of five had come with his parents from the province of Hälsingland, studied at Gustavus Adolphus College in St. Peter, and in 1885 received his medical degree from the Minnesota College Hospital, which two years later became the medical department of the State University. Dr. Eklund helped establish St. Luke's Hospital. Among the lawyers of the early 1900s was a son of Swedish immigrants, Clarence R. Magney, who in 1917–20 served as mayor of Duluth.

Northeastern Minnesota saw the beginning of an enterprise which became one of the best-known transportation companies in the United States. In 1912 a young Swede named Carl Eric Wickman (1887–1954), who in 1905 had begun as a lumberjack in Arizona, joined the miners near Hibbing, 75 miles northwest of Duluth, and two years later he started using a motorcar to carry his fellow workers to and from the mines for a small charge. One of his next steps was to extend operations to Duluth. This was the beginning of the Greyhound Corporation, which when Wickman died operated about 7,000 buses and had some 24,000 employees. He remained as president of the Chicago-based concern until 1946, when he became chairman of the board. His father had been a lumberjack in Michigan in the late 1880s but returned to Sweden to manage a farm near Våmhus in Dalarna. In 1968 a bust of Carl Eric Wickman was unveiled at the Våmhus parish church, whose renovation he had helped finance. Many other Americans of Swedish ancestry have worked for Greyhound, including Orville Swan Caesar (1892–1965), who served as president in 1946–55 and then became board chairman. His father was born at Aneboda in Småland and his mother in Norway.

Many Minnesotans of Scandinavian origin have, like Wickman, made notable or unusual careers extending far beyond the boundaries of their home state. In 1901 a native of Red Wing, Dr. Alexander P. Anderson (1862–1943), who was engaged in research in the New York Botanical Gardens, made a discovery of great importance to the food industry, producing the first puffed wheat and puffed rice. One of the most popular shows in the entertainment world was started by three young men of Swedish parentage, Oscar Johnson and Roy and Edwin Shipstad, who were born and raised in St. Paul. On frozen lakes and ponds they became expert skaters, and after having attracted attention because of their antics on the ice, they launched in 1936 a traveling revue called the Ice Follies which soon reached an annual attendance of millions of people. Oscar Johnson (1899–1970) and Roy Shipstad (1910–75) were also the originators of the skating "horse," which has been imitated by hundreds of other artists. Johnson's parents had come from Småland and Skåne, respectively. The Shipstad brothers were members of a large family hailing from Stockholm.

A remarkably great number of Minnesotans descend from immigrants from the Swedish province of Värmland, a classic mining and ironworking region which in Sweden also is known as the promised land of poetry and imagination. If a Swede were asked to define a true-blue son or daughter of iron-bearing Värmland, he might well suggest one whose father was born at Munkfors and mother at Hagfors, or vice versa, both great producers of quality steels which are exported all over the world. The group of Minnesotans of such

411

parentage includes Elmer W. Engstrom, born in 1901 in Minneapolis, who in 1923 earned a degree in electrical engineering from the University of Minnesota, and later became research director and president of RCA. His parents arrived from Värmland in the late 1880s.

Some early Swedish-born educators and medical experts in Minneapolis-St. Paul

THE Twin Cities in Minnesota, Minneapolis and St. Paul, became next to Chicago the greatest center of Swedish population in the United States, and in Minneapolis the Swedish element was, in relation to the total number of inhabitants, stronger than in any other larger city. In 1900, when Minneapolis had a population of about 200,000, the number of Swedish-born was 20,000, while there were 11,500 Norwegian immigrants and approximately 7,000 Germans. In St. Paul, on the other hand, the Swedes have always been less numerous than the Germans. In 1900 they numbered about 10,000, against approximately 13,000 immigrants from Germany. Even at an early stage, the Swedes in Minnesota showed a greater tendency to settle in cities and towns than the Norwegians and the Germans. In 1930 Minneapolis reported nearly 25,000 Swedish-born and St. Paul 6,400.

The history of the Swedes in Minneapolis and St. Paul is similar to that in Chicago, but since they made up a larger proportion of the total population, their activities and contributions were often both more comprehensive and more noticeable. In the construction industry and in the building of the Twin Cities, their participation was even more important than the one in Chicago. In the teaching profession the Swedish element gradually became well represented, not only in the public schools but also in institutions of higher learning. The University of Minnesota has always had more faculty members of Swedish origin than any other university in the country. Most of them were born in America, but several came from Sweden. By the middle of the 20th century, the number of instructors and professors of Swedish extraction was said to be about 100.

One of the first Swedish immigrants to obtain a doctor's degree at the University of Minnesota was Victor Nilsson (1867–1942), born at Östra Torp in southernmost Sweden, who emigrated to America in 1885. Twelve years later he won his doctorate in Minneapolis, but before that he had begun what would become half a century of enthusiastic and fruitful service to music and song. He was generally regarded as an outstanding pioneer in the development of musical taste in the Twin Cities region. As a music critic and in other ways, he was also very active interpreting Scandinavian music and drama to American audiences.

In 1899, John S. Carlson, born in Småland in 1857 and brought to America when quite young, was called to the University of Minnesota as professor of Scandinavian languages and literature. He had studied both at Gustavus Adolphus and at Augustana College, and then spent two years at Uppsala in Sweden. After a long period of teaching at Gustavus Adolphus, he took in 1895 a doctor's degree at Uppsala, his thesis being a study of the science of philosophy in America. Andrew A. Stomberg, who in 1907 succeeded him as professor of Scandinavian, was born in Minnesota. David F. Swenson (1876–1940), who had come from Sweden at the age of six and received his education at the University of Minnesota and at Columbia University in New York, began to teach philosophy at the University of Minnesota in 1901 and became a full professor in 1917. His translations of Kierkegaard introduced that Danish philosopher to the American public.

Arvid Reuterdahl (1876–1943), who was born in Karlstad, Värmland, and also came to America in 1882 at the age of six, was during 1918–22 in charge of the courses in engineering and architecture at the College of St. Thomas in St. Paul, and from 1922 to 1926 he served as president of the Ramsey Institute of Technology in the same city. He was a graduate of Brown University, and before coming to Minnesota he had taught physics or mechanical engineering and worked as an engineer in many American cities. His leading specialty was bridge construction.

The educational standards of most of the 19th-century immigrants from Sweden left, of course, something to be desired, even if illiteracy was almost nonexistent, and their leaders and spokesmen were, therefore, quite sensitive both to symptoms of submissiveness among the Swedes and to condescending or sarcastic attitudes among other people. In 1901, for instance, one of the Swedish-language newspapers in the Midwest wrote that the newcomers from Sweden often were looked down upon as stupid and meek individuals, who will make excellent stableboys and housemaids but hardly could become, say, doctors or lawyers. At that time, however, Swedes had already made a good start in both professions, in Minneapolis as well as in other cities.

The first Swedish-trained physician in Minnesota was probably Dr. Carl Petter Tigerhjelm, who in 1867 began to practice at Vasa, the little community founded 14 years earlier by Hans Mattson. He had previously followed his profession in the Jämtland and Härjedalen provinces in northern Sweden. Olof Sohlberg from Östersund, the capital of Jämtland, who arrived in 1879 at the age of 20, became four years later the first immigrant to graduate as a medical doctor in Minnesota. In 1884 he began a successful practice at St. Paul, interrupted only by studies in Europe. Erik Mauritz Lundholm, born in 1858 at ancient Venjan in the province of Dalarna, came in 1888 and almost immediately passed his examination before the Medical Board of Minnesota, but returned to Sweden to complete his studies. Having established himself at St. Paul in 1891, he became recognized as one of the ablest surgeons in the Northwest. At Bethesda Hospital in St. Paul, founded in 1882 by a Lutheran association of Swedish origin, he was placed in charge of gynecology and surgery.

Alfred Lind from Tråvad in Västergötland, who emigrated in 1880 at the age of 18, also became one of the leading medical specialists of Swedish birth in the Midwest. For this position he was exceedingly well prepared, having first studied medicine at the University of Minnesota and practiced for two years at Lake Park, then earned a doctor's degree at the University of Berlin, Germany, and practiced for two years in Minneapolis; after that he had taken a course at the Central Institute of Gymnastics in Stockholm in 1897 and again practiced in Minneapolis, and finally studied both at Uppsala and at the Caroline Institute in Stockholm, graduating in 1899. In the same year he began to practice his profession in Minneapolis for the third time.

Other Swedish-born medical pioneers in the Twin Cities were Andrew Soderlind, a graduate of 1889, and Carl John Rignell from Vissefjerda in Småland, who came in 1883 at the age of 18, built up a large practice and also became connected with the University of Minnesota. Around the turn of the century Lind, Soderlind, and Rignell helped bring about the Swedish Hospital in Minneapolis, long one of the largest medical centers of Swedish origin in the United States. In the early 1900s Swedish Baptists and other immigrant groups founded three hospitals in the Twin Cities.

On the whole, the Swedish immigrants and their descendants have been much less active in the city governments of Minneapolis and St. Paul than in the Minnesota state administration. Minneapolis's first mayor of Swedish birth, Eric G. Hoyer, automatically succeeded Hubert H. Humphrey in late 1948, and was then elected to the same post several times. Previously he had been a member of the City Council for many years, six of them as president. Hoyer was born in 1898 in the province of Västergötland.

Swedes in the Twin Cities cherish their heritage — Unusual careers in the press

IN ONE of the more remarkable success stories among the Swedes in Minnesota, the leading part is played by a newspaper publisher. In 1868, when the crops failed in most parts of Sweden, a farmer by the name of Olof Månsson, who lived at Tubbemåla near Vislanda in southern Småland, emigrated to Minnesota with his family and settled at Vasa in Goodhue County. The Månssons had a son, Sven Johan, who soon decided to become a printer and became known as Swan J. Turnblad (1860–1933). In 1883 he invented and patented a letter-writing machine, which sold well. Four years later, at the age of 27, he took over one of the Swedish-language weeklies in Minneapolis, *Svenska Amerikanska Posten*, which had only 1,400 subscribers and was almost bankrupt. Under his leadership and greatly helped by the mass immigration from Sweden, the newspaper quickly reversed its sagging fortunes, and by the turn of the century there were 40,000 names on its subscription lists. At about the same time Swan Turnblad created a sensation by driving around in a new Waverly Electric, the first commercially built automobile in the Twin Cities.

Like other men of wealth and ambition in the late 19th century and early 1900s, Swan Turnblad began to dream of a palatial home of his own, and on Park Avenue, at that time the most exclusive residential street in Minneapolis, he built a turreted mansion which was more grandiose and had more artistic adornments than anyone else's in the Northwest. The elaborate ornamentation of the mahogany and other wood on the first floor and in the stairway was all made by hand, either by local workmen or by expert wood carvers who had been brought from Europe. Most of the large stoves of glazed tile, found in one-third of the 33 rooms, had been made by porcelain specialists in Sweden and assembled by workers sent over from the factories. No two were alike in color and decoration. A huge painting-in-glass on the staircase landing was regarded by experts as one of the finest examples in America of the stained-glass art.

In 1929, when his wife died, Turnblad entrusted his home and some other property to a foundation called The American Institute of Swedish Arts, Literature and Science, and today the Park Avenue mansion remains as The American Swedish Institute. Its activities aim at preserving the Swedish heritage in America, interesting Americans in modern Sweden, and strengthening the ties between the two nations.

Early Minnesota history is reflected in a large collection of furniture, looms, chests, tools, etc. Another permanent display features modern Swedish home furnishings, including crystal, ceramics, silverware, and stainless steel. The first version of this exhibit, called "The ABC of Sweden," was shown in 1949–51 in the public-school system of the City of New York. In 1952 the province of Värmland and its 100-odd parishes sent The American Swedish Institute some 200 choice items, ranging from furniture and textiles to the collected works of Värmland's leading writers, in the first place Esaias Tegnér and Selma Lagerlöf. Among the gifts was also a replica of the bridal crown owned by the Cathedral of Karlstad, capital of Värmland; it has subsequently been often used by Minnesota brides hailing from that part of Sweden. In June, 1953, President Dwight D. Eisenhower made a tour of the building in Minneapolis and its exhibits. He posed for photographers before a large canvas, "Julotta" (the first Mass on Christmas Day), by the Swedish painter Wilhelm Wallander (1821– 88), who specialized in romantic or humorous peasant and genre scenes.

The activities of The American Swedish Institute include loan exhibits, lectures, and other special events. Programs and displays have been offered by many cities and towns in Minnesota with large populations of Swedish ancestry, among them Duluth in the northeast, Rush City, Center City, Chisago City and Lindstrom in Chisago County, Stillwater farther south in Washington County, Cambridge in Isanti County west of Chisago, Vasa in Goodhue County in the southeast, Winthrop in Sibley County and St. Peter in Nicollet, both southwest of Minneapolis-St. Paul, Cokato in Wright County, west of the Twin Cities, and Dassel in Meeker County and Willmar in Kandiyohi farther west.

Minneapolis has been the scene of many of the largest Swedish rallies held in the United States. In 1888, Secretary of State Hans Mattson was one of the principal promoters of the 250th-anniversary celebration of the landing of the first Swedish settlers on the Delaware, which seems to have attracted more Minnesota Swedes than any other festival or meeting in the late 19th century. An industrial exhibition was held in Minneapolis that year, and on September 14 the Exposition Hall was filled to more than capacity by at least 15,000 people. A large picture of the Old Swedes Church at Wilmington, Delaware, was hung in front of the speakers' platform. Thousands stood on their feet until the end of the three-hour-long ceremony when, according to reporters, the vast audience reluctantly dispersed. A souvenir badge was sold for the benefit of the North-Swedish cities of Sundsvall and Umeå, large parts of which had been destroyed by fire.

The program was, of course, overloaded, but the Swedes in Minnesota could hardly have expected to see and hear again so many personalities who would hold prominent places in the history of the Swedes in America. Colonel Mattson himself presided, the leading patriarch of the Swedish Lutherans in America, 72-year-old Tuve Nilsson Hasselquïst, who had come from Sweden in 1852, offered the invocation, and longer addresses were delivered by two persons whom the Swedes in America always welcomed as great orators — William Widgery Thomas, the founder of New Sweden, Maine, and a former American minister in Stockholm, where he would soon be sent again, and Johan A. Enander, the great Swedish-American patriot. Other speakers were the new president of the University of Minnesota, Cyrus Northrop, under whose guidance the small struggling school would grow into a great institution of learning, the Reverend Carl Aaron Swensson, who seven years earlier at Lindsborg, Kansas, had founded a Lutheran school named Bethany College, and Miss Mary A. Brown of Washington, D.C., whose remarks concerned the discovery of America about the year 1000 by Scandinavian Vikings. An address written by Erik August Skogsbergh, the great

417

evangelist and Mission Friend leader, was read by Colonel Mattson. Captain Olof Gottfrid Lange, the first Swede in Chicago and the oldest Swedish immigrant living, was introduced to the audience as an honored guest.

The Seventh New York Regiment Band played, there was also a Swedish chorus, and at least four poems written for the occasion were read. One of the poets was David Nyvall, who later became president of North Park College in Chicago, and another was Herman von Stockenström or simply Stockenstrom (1853–1902), a member of a well-known family in Sweden, who in 1874 had arrived in Philadelphia as a seaman. He had become one of the leading Swedish journalists in Minneapolis, where he finally joined Swan J. Turnblad's increasingly successful *Svenska Amerikanska Posten*. In 1887 Colonel Mattson had named him Minnesota's assistant secretary of state, a post he held for many years. In Sweden he seems to have been the black sheep of the Stockenström family, and his father is said to have practically expelled him from the country. In America, a Swede who met him at Augustana College later said that "he came to America as a social wreck, but when he went through the wash several times, we made a decent person of him."

There were quite a few Swedish newspapermen in Minnesota in the late 1800s. Some of them were, like colleagues in other parts of the United States, decidedly unconventional, and the leading eccentric was Frans Herman Widstrand (1824–91), the son of a Lutheran clergyman in Stockholm. After university studies at Uppsala he became a government employee in the capital, but could not stand it for very long. An enthusiastic but impractical socialist convert, he hated the monarchy as well as the religious establishment.

In 1855 Widstrand emigrated to America and bought land on Lake Constance near Buffalo, northwest of Minneapolis-St. Paul. From there he traveled to a number of communal settlements, including the Shaker colony at Pleasant Hill, Kentucky, where some Swedes had gone from Bishop Hill in Illinois, the Perfectionist community at Oneida, New York, where nearly 300 people lived in a group marriage for almost three decades, and Nauvoo, Illinois, where 500 French Utopians, the so-called Icarians, had moved in after the flight of the Mormons. None of these communistic communes, however, was to Widstrand's liking.

In 1863 he obtained a post in the U.S. Treasury Department in Washington but left after a short time, explaining that he had seen enough misery of various kinds. In 1875 he tried to become a candidate for governor of Minnesota, offering to serve for 500 dollars a year. "No public servant," he said in his platform, "should have more than 1,000 dollars a year, as long as a majority of the people earns less." After having failed grievously in an attempt to develop his homestead into a model commune, and also losing his farm, he concentrated his efforts on newspaper publishing. After moving to Litchfield, the seat of Meeker County which Swedes had helped found in 1856, he produced in the period 1880–86 a sheet called *Rothuggaren* (The Stump Breaker), which was "dedicated to the eradication of poverty, ignorance, malice, lewdness, drunkenness, injustice, and everything evil." A vegetarian and teetotaler as well as a bachelor, Frans Herman Widstrand spent his last few years alone with his books in a cabin at Litchfield.

More influential as a writer and lecturer was Axel Lundeberg (1852–1940), who after university studies and journalistic activities in Sweden and extensive travels in Europe came to America in 1888 as a correspondent for several Swedish newspapers. In his native country he had worked with August Palm, the "Father of Swedish socialism," who was more radical than other Swedish Social Democratic pioneers and was to visit the United States in 1900 and 1906. In Minneapolis, Lundeberg published in 1891–92 a leftist weekly called *Gnistan* (The Spark). He also lectured frequently on scientific, religious, and social subjects. After 15 years in Chicago and a brief stay in Kansas City, where he was ordained a minister in the Swedenborg New Church, he returned to Minneapolis in 1910 and formed a congregation of his own. His huge library included the largest Swedenborg collection in America. A book of his about Theodore Roosevelt in the English language is said to have sold 300,000 copies.

For half a century, from the 1880s and at least until the Great Depression, the area around the intersection of Cedar and Riverside avenues in South Minneapolis, on the west bank of the Mississippi, was the leading Scandinavian entertainment center in the Twin Cities. St. Paul also had a center of its own, Payne Avenue. Cedar-Riverside was a particularly colorful immigrant community, and in the evening the place to go for music from accordions, fiddles or guitars, dancing, vaudeville shows, and other amusements. In the impressive Dania Hall, built in 1886, and other auditoriums, theatrical troupes sometimes offered plays by Ibsen and Strindberg, including, for instance, the latter's brooding and tragic *The Father*, but as a rule the fare was much lighter.

For many years Cedar Avenue's biggest star was Hjalmar Peterson (1886–1960) from Munkfors in the province of Värmland, who arrived in 1906 with three brothers and a few years later, when he toured his native country as a member of the Swedish-American Quartet, picked up the songs and tricks of Sweden's most popular traveling comedians. To these he added melodies and jokes of his own. In Minnesota he adopted the stage name Olle i Skratthult, or "Olle from Laughtersville" — and no Swedish immigrant has, in fact, provoked as many roars of laughter as he. While based in Minneapolis, he became equally well known in other American cities where Swedes had settled in large numbers. Toward the end of his life he joined the Salvation Army and sang only with its band.

In a strange mixture of affection and self-irony, the Swedes and other Scandinavians called Cedar Avenue "Snoose Boulevard," a reference to their taste for "snus," the Scandinavian word for snuff. The same nickname has been used for the main street in other Swedish, Norwegian, or Danish centers in North America. Today, however, the name Snoose Boulevard brings back many melodious or other precious memories, and when people in Minneapolis in the early 1970s started to revive the Cedar-Riverside part of the Scandinavian heritage, they called the celebration "Snoose Boulevard Festival." Olle i Skratthult had then been succeeded by a Swedish-born actress-singer and drama-school teacher, Anne-Charlotte Harvey, who sang many of his songs. A special project began collecting material relating to professional entertainers in the Scandinavian languages in America, to be placed on file with the House of Emigrants at Växjö in Sweden, the American Swedish Institute in Minneapolis, and the Norwegian-American Museum at Decorah, Iowa.

In 1934 immigrants from Sweden and Americans of Swedish descent in the Twin Cities celebrated for the first time a "Swedish Day" or "Swedes Day" (Svenskarnas dag), and a few years later this event was regarded as a permanent institution. Families came from near and far in Minnesota, friends of other national origins joined, and finally from 25,000 to 40,000 persons gathered in Minnehaha Park in Minneapolis. Since the first part of the 20th century, no other festival of Swedish origin in the United States has attracted such crowds. Almost from the beginning it was held on the Sunday nearest June 24, the old Swedish Midsummer Day, and the Minnesotans came to regard it as both a "Swedes Day" and a Nordic Midsummer festival. Many famous or prominent Americans and Swedes have been among the main speakers. The program has always included chorus singing in front of a statue of Gunnar Wennerberg (1817–1901), a Swedish educator and composer, whose enduring popularity is based on a number of patriotic and religious hymns and a book of songs about the often gay life of the university students at Uppsala in the middle of the 1800s.

30,000 *Iowa Swedes in* 1890 — *From farmers to men of learning and public service*

IOWA's Swedish-born population rose in the period 1870–90 from about 11,000 to somewhat more than 30,000, which became the highest figure recorded for this state in a U.S. census. In 1900, however, the number was only slightly smaller. In Iowa as in other parts of the Middle West, immigrants from Sweden turned vast areas of prairie and wildwood into fruitful farmland, while members of the second or third generations often made careers in the learned professions, in public service, or in business and industry.

The first two significant years in the history of the Swedes in Iowa are 1845, when Peter Cassel founded New Sweden in the southeast, the oldest still existing Swedish 19th-century settlement in America, and 1846, when Swede Point, the present Madrid, was established in the central section north of Des Moines. Later on many Swedes settled at Boone, somewhat farther north. The best-known pioneer there was Charles John Alfred Ericson (1840–1910), born at Södra Vi near Vimmerby in northeast Småland, who had come to America in 1852 at the age of 12 and had begun as a farmhand. In 1870 he moved to Boone where he soon prospered as a businessman. He became president of the City Bank of Boone, which he had helped found in 1872, was elected a member of the state legislature, and served six terms as a state senator. The Ericson Library in Boone was built by him. Other institutions in the Midwest, in particular Augustana College at Rock Island, Illinois, as well as Ericson's home parish in Sweden also received donations.

In 1869 Sweden had suffered two crop failures in a row, and Småland had been hard hit. C. G. Sjöstrand from Mörlunda in eastern Småland emigrated with his family and settled on an 80-acre farm in Boone County, northwest of Des Moines. His son Carl Emil Sjöstrand or Seashore (1866–1949) studied at Gustavus Adolphus College and at Yale, became in 1902 professor of psychology at the University of Iowa in Iowa City, and served from 1908 to 1936 as dean of its graduate college. During World War II he was called back as dean and remained in that post until 1946. His psychological research in the fields of hearing, speech, and music gained him an international reputation. A whole battery of psychological instruments were invented by him, and his laboratory at the university in Iowa City was regarded as one of the world's foremost workshops of its kind. Musical aptitude tests which he originated in 1919 and revised 20 years later are still known as the Seashore Measures of Musical Talents. During World War I he helped work out the intelligence and aptitude tests for the U.S. Army, and as an expert on acoustics he developed a new method for locating submarines. He became the first man in Iowa to be elected to the National Academy of Science. In 1911 he served as president of the American Psychological Association.

During the latter part of his life, Dr. Seashore was regarded as one of the most likable and venerable patriarchs in the American world of science and learning. Several disciples of Swedish origin will be mentioned shortly. Of his youth in Iowa, he wrote: "The rich heritage of our family stock in Sweden, health, morals, practical wisdom, and religion, was transplanted in a fast-growing community of immigrants from the same section of the mother country. . . . Father served as director of the school district before he could read or write English, but the first rule he enforced was that English alone should be spoken in the school house and on the school grounds." Many of the pupils were Swedish, and learning English, of course, was vitally important.

The Reverend Bengt Magnus Halland (1837–1902), born at Drängsered in the province of Halland, was one of the most influential Swedish pioneers in Iowa. After graduation from Augustana College and Theological Seminary, he began his career as a clergyman in 1864 at Burlington, destined to be a gateway to the western prairies. A few years later he became a land agent for the Burlington Railroad, and during an inspection tour in southwest Iowa he mapped out a Swedish settlement in the territory between the Nodaway and East Nishnabotna rivers in Montgomery and Page counties. In 1870 he advertised in *Hemlandet* that contracts for this land would soon be offered, the price ranging from 6 to 11 dollars per acre, and that only "non-drinking, God-fearing Swedes" were eligible. Swedish immigrants, most of them from the southeast of Iowa and from Illinois, immediately flocked to the new colony, which became known as the Halland Settlement, and the flow continued for several years. In this as in many other parts of the Midwest, corn was hailed as the king of grains, the priceless gift of a rich soil and a genial climate.

Bengt Magnus Halland himself became pastor at Stanton, the focal point of the Swedish area, which he wanted to call Halmstad after the capital of his home province. His principals in the railroad, however, finally rejected this name as too much of a tongue twister. Gradually nine other Augustana congregations and five Mission Friend societies, all of them using the Swedish language, grew up in the same section. Twelve churches were built, scattered over an area of nearly 200 square miles. Halland, who seems to have been more effective as a pastor and shepherd than as a preacher, resigned in 1883 and moved first to Nebraska, but finally returned to Stanton.

In the early 1900s Stanton was described as "a genuinely Swedish town with a white church crowned by a high steeple on the top of a hill, with white-painted inviting houses, with a Swedish postmaster, stationmaster and physicians, Swedish druggists, shopkeepers and bankers," and "with excellent schools and a high school where Swedish is being taught." Stanton has, in fact, become widely known as the "Little White City." Its foremost modern landmark is the world's largest coffee pot, with a capacity of about half a million cups: it sits at the top of the water tower and is actually a water tank. One of the most popular Swedish phrases in the Stanton area is an old saying that "kaffetåren den bästa är av alla jordiska drycker," meaning that coffee remains the best of all earthly beverages.

Today the people at Stanton have at best a meager Swedish vo-

cabulary, but old traditions from Sweden have been preserved or revived on a remarkable scale. Since the late 1800s, for instance, a
popular Swedish song hailing the arrival of beautiful May, "Sköna
maj, välkommen," has been sung on the streets on the night preceding May 1. A Swedish folk-dance society was organized by the middle
1900s and has performed successfully in other towns and cities. As in
Sweden the Christmas season is ushered in on December 13, or at
least on the Saturday closest to that day, when a young girl is named
Lucia and crowned with a wreath of lighted candles, a symbol of the
returning daylight in the middle of a long winter. Housewives in the
Halland Settlement are still noted for their Swedish food specialties,
especially those served at Christmas, such as lutfisk, a word so well-
known that it has been used in picturesque yells for the Viking teams
of the Stanton High School: "Lutfisk, lutfisk, tack ska ni ha! Stanton,
Stanton, ja, ja, ja!"

Thousands of former and present citizens of Stanton attended the
area's centennial celebration in late June of 1970, which included a
Swedish Heritage Day. Recordings of the settlers' children singing in
the Swedish language "All Hail to Thee, O Blessed Morn" and other
old hymns are in the Library of Congress, Washington, D.C., and in
the University Library at Iowa City.

During the winter of 1889–90 the Reverend Bengt Magnus Halland preached at a place 15 miles north of Miami, Florida, where
some of his relatives and supporters hoped to be able to establish a
daughter colony of the Halland Settlement. The community that
grew up there was named Hallandale. It was incorporated as a city in
1947.

Most of the young people in the Halland Settlement left their
rural homes for careers elsewhere. One of the pioneer families became known as the Ossian clan. Anders Magnus Ossian (1818–75)
from Locknevi in northeastern Småland and his wife Anna Lovisa
from Dalhem in the same district emigrated to America in 1869, and
the following year they were among the first settlers at Stanton. They
left seven children, some of whom had come to America before their
parents, and via their sons they had numerous descendants by the
name of Ossian. In the early 1930s the clan had more than 200 members.

Agnes Samuelson, who was born in the Halland Settlement south of Stanton and had begun as a schoolteacher, served from 1927 to 1939 as superintendent of public instruction in the state of Iowa, which during this period took long strides forward in education. In 1935 she was elected president of the National Education Association, the central organization of all American public-school officials and teachers. Her father, a native of Småland who had arrived in the late 1860s at the age of 12 and had started as a railroad laborer, died when Agnes, the eldest child, was in her middle teens. Five of the seven children received university degrees.

Among the Swedish families who came to Iowa in 1869 were also Hans and Johanna Persson, or Pearson, with children from the small port city of Landskrona in western Skåne. One of their sons, Alfred John Pearson (1869–1939), became professor and dean at Drake University in Des Moines, and in the 1920s he served as U.S. minister first to Poland and then to Finland. Another son, Peter Henry Pearson (1864–1940), became a professor first at Bethany College in Lindsborg, Kansas, and finally at Upsala College, East Orange, New Jersey. Other Iowans of Swedish origin have, for instance, become justices of the Supreme Court of Iowa.

Swedish-language weeklies or other periodicals, most of them religious, have been published in Des Moines, Cedar Rapids, Sioux City, Burlington, Boone, Council Bluffs, Keokuk, and for a short time even at Sheldon, a small town on Floyd River in the northwest. One of the most active collectors of Swedish-American literature in the United States was Gustaf N. Swan (1856–1938) of Sioux City, a native of Östergötland, who in 1870 emigrated to America with his parents and became a businessman, banker, and Swedish consul. His collection of 6,000 books and pamphlets was donated to the library of Augustana College at Rock Island, Illinois.

Noted educational psychologists of Swedish parentage, all influenced by Seashore

CARL E. SEASHORE, the great psychologist of the University of Iowa, was an extraordinary source of inspiration to his students and disciples. Educational psychologists throughout the United States were influenced by him, and many of the leading figures in this field were of Swedish parentage. Three of these were, like Dr. Seashore, elected to the presidency of the American Psychological Association.

J. E. Wallace Wallin (1876–1969), who was born in the Halland Settlement in Iowa, became an internationally known educator and psychologist, with the training of the maladjusted and the handicapped as his foremost specialty. The first American clinics attempting to apply the principles of psychology to educational problems were organized and directed by him, and his pioneer textbooks on the education of handicapped children and on clinical psychology have been used in hundreds of colleges and universities. In some cases he wrote state legislation providing for mentally or physically handicapped children. Wallin taught in a great number of American universities and other institutions, and served on numerous professional and governmental agencies. Augustana College and Yale University had been his principal schools. His father, from Kinneved in Västergötland, who came to America in 1866 and began as a farmer, served for many years as president of the local board of education in Iowa.

Joseph Peterson (1878–1935) became an authority on learning in children and was in the early 1930s elected president of the American Psychological Association. Born at Huntsville, Utah, he received his Ph.D. degree from the University of Chicago. In 1915, when professor at the University of Utah, he was called to the University of Minnesota, and three years later he joined the George Peabody College for Teachers in Nashville, Tennessee. John L. Stenquist (1885–1952), born of Swedish immigrants in North Dakota and in 1922 named director of educational research for the Department of Education in Baltimore, Maryland, developed the Stenquist Mechanical Ability Test, at a time when the efforts to sample and appraise human abilities were still in their infancy.

Louis Leon Thurstone (1887–1956) was born in Chicago, spent six years in Stockholm with his parents in the 1890s and then settled with them in Jamestown, New York. His father's family name was originally Thunström. Dr. Thurstone served for many years as professor of psychology first at Carnegie Institute of Technology in Pittsburgh and then at the University of Chicago, his alma mater. After that he moved to the University of North Carolina as a research professor. In 1954 he was visiting professor at the University of Stockholm. In recognition of his scientific accomplishments in the field of intelligence testing and intelligence theory, he was elected president of the American Psychological Association in 1932.

Another leader in American psychology, John Edward Anderson (1893–1966), born in Wyoming and a Ph.D. at Harvard, was in 1925, when teaching at Yale, called to the University of Minnesota as professor of psychology and director of the Institute of Child Welfare. In 1942–43 he served as president of the American Psychological Association. Willard C. Olson, born in Minnesota in 1899, became in 1935 professor of education and in 1946 also professor of psychology in the University of Michigan at Ann Arbor. His principal interests in psychology were child growth and development. In 1948 he was elected president of the American Educational Research Association. His four grandparents were born in Sweden, and at the University of Minnesota he had studied Swedish language, history, and literature.

One of Dr. Seashore's own students, Harold H. Anderson (b. 1897), became professor of psychology at Michigan State University, lectured at numerous institutions and conferences both at home and abroad, and served as an official adviser on education and youth problems. In 1954 he too lectured at the University of Stockholm. Another Seashore disciple, Everet Franklin Lindquist (b. 1901), served from 1927 to 1969 as professor of education at the University of Iowa and became a leader in the field of "achievement testing." He developed, among other things, the Iowa Tests for Educational Development (ITED), which in 1942 were initiated in 300 high schools in the Hawkeye State and later used throughout the nation. An electronic machine for the processing of the tests was designed by Dr. Lindquist himself. His parents, Jonas Lindquist and Hanna Anderson, were born at Mjölby in the province of Östergötland. In America they first settled at Andover, Illinois, and then moved to the Swedish farming area in Iowa north of Boone. After high school, Everet Franklin Lindquist entered Augustana College at Rock Island, Illinois.

One of Dr. Seashore's sons, Robert Holmes Seashore (1902–51), also became an eminent psychologist, his teaching positions including professorships at the University of Southern California in Los Angeles and Northwestern University at Evanston, Illinois. A younger scholar who also received powerful impressions from Dr. Seashore, Nils Y. Wessell, born in 1914 of Swedish immigrants at

Warren in northwestern Pennsylvania, and a Seashore disciple who became a leader in sound technology, Dr. Harry F. Olson, will be dealt with later.

26,000 *Wisconsin Swedes in* 1900 — *Lenroot the first son to become a U.S. Senator*

WISCONSIN's Swedish population increased from nearly 3,000 in 1870 to about 8,000 in 1880, 20,000 in 1890 and 26,000 in 1900. After that it started leveling off. There were also many Swedish-speaking Finns, who often joined the same congregations or subscribed to the same newspapers. Of the Scandinavian elements, however, the Norwegian was by far the largest. In 1870, Wisconsin had a Norwegian-born population of about 40,000, and in 1920 there were 45,000.

After the Civil War most of the Swedes who came to Wisconsin continued to settle in the northwestern section, between the Minnesota border and Michigan's Upper Peninsula. In 1865 a native of Hudiksvall in the province of Hälsingland, J. W. Forsell, built a cabin on beautiful Trade Lake in Burnett County, and three years later, when he was tired of having only Indians as neighbors, he wrote an article about northwestern Wisconsin for a Swedish-language newspaper in Chicago. A large group of mining workers from Ljusnarsberg in the Kopparberg district in the province of Västmanland, who had left Sweden because of the famine and had arrived in the Green Bay region in Wisconsin, responded to his call, and so did Swedes from Chicago itself. An agricultural district whose population was mainly of Swedish stock finally extended east and south of Grantsburg, and included such small localities as Karlsborg, Freya, Falun, and West Sweden. Most of the immigrants had come from Västmanland, Värmland, and Dalarna. The city of Superior in the far northwest became the home of numerous Swedes. In 1930 they numbered about 2,000.

The proportion of Swedes in the population of southern Wisconsin was always rather small, but in the early 1900s many newcomers became employed in the automotive industry. A well-known executive was John Björn (1861–1939) from Östmark in Värmland, who served as general manager of the Nash Motor Works of Kenosha from 1916 to 1926 and helped develop the successful Nash motorcar. He was also one of the two inventors of the clincher tire, still in use today. His career as a mechanical engineer and inventor had begun in Chicago. The famine in western Värmland drove his father not to America but farther north in Sweden, and John followed, going to school or working in the forests. In the far north, where a railroad was being built for the transportation of iron ore, he improved his knowledge of English as an assistant to English engineers, and in 1890 he emigrated to America. For some years he went from job to job, including one of cleaning sewage pipes in Buffalo. Then he was hired by a well-known Chicago firm making the early-model, high-wheeled bicycles, and later moved with them to Kenosha and into the automobile age.

Many other industries in Wisconsin have given immigrants from Sweden chances to make their way and succeed, benefiting, in turn, from their ingenuity and skills. Hans P. Dahlstrand, born in 1874 at Bosebo in Småland and a graduate of a technical school at Borås in Västergötland, was for decades associated with the Allis-Chalmers company of Milwaukee, and had to his credit more than a score of patents on steam-turbine elements. Gustaf L. Kollberg, born in 1878 at Ljusne in Hälsingland, started working for the same company in 1901 and designed, among other things, a series of large pumping engines for municipal waterworks. Some of them held the world records for economy. Kollberg came to America with his parents as a child but returned to Sweden at the age of 13 and attended a technical school in the province of Dalarna. In 1895 he came back to the United States and continued his education in Chicago.

William Mattsson Bager, born in 1897 in Copenhagen of Swedish parents, emigrated from Sweden shortly after his graduation from the Institute of Technology in Stockholm and joined another large concern in Milwaukee, the Bucyrus-Erie company, where he was in charge of engineering and sales for many years. Some of his inventions revolutionized certain phases of excavating-machinery construction. Technical pioneers of Swedish descent who have been active in Wisconsin include Walter Freeburg, born in 1892 in Kansas, who invented more than 50 automatic machines for the manufacture of electrical control apparatus.

A 30-mile stretch of the Fox River in Eastern Wisconsin, between Green Bay to the north and Neenah on Lake Winnebago to the south, contains the greatest concentration of paper mills in the United

States, and at Neenah the name of Swedish-Norwegian immigrants lives on in the well-known Bergstrom Paper Company. John Bergstrom (1820–88), his wife, and their son Dedrick Waldemar (1847–1928) came in 1852 from Norway, where Bergstrom's hammersmith grandfather and father, like many other Swedes of the same era, had settled. In 1904 Dedrick Waldemar Bergstrom sold his share in a stove factory and purchased a paper mill which became the Bergstrom Paper Company. His eldest son and daughter-in-law, John Nelson (b. 1874) and Evangeline Bergstrom, willed their home to the city of Neenah as a museum, known as the John Nelson Bergstrom Art Center and Museum, which was opened in 1959. Its best-known treasure is a collection of some 700 glass paperweights, said to be the most representative collection of this kind in the world. A nephew of Dedrick Waldemar Bergstrom, George Edwin Bergstrom (b. 1876), became a noted architect at Los Angeles and, as chief consulting architect of the U.S. War Department, the chief designer of the gigantic Pentagon Building in Washington, D.C.

Another and more recent leader in the paper industry in Wisconsin was Folke Becker (1891–1962), a member of a Swedish papermaking family of German origin, who in 1935 became president of Rhinelander Paper Company at Rhinelander in the north, after having been first mill superintendent and then general manager. Born at Jönköping in the province of Småland, he went to school in Norway, where his father was building and operating a paper mill, and became a chemical engineer in Germany. After service as a conscript in the Swedish army, he emigrated to America in 1914, worked for and helped reorganize paper companies in New England and New Jersey, and joined in 1926 the Rhinelander Paper Company, whose operations under his direction were thoroughly modernized and greatly expanded. In the 1930s Rhinelander was one of the few large papermakers that weathered the depression without a shutdown.

Most of the architects, educators, lawyers, and scientists of Swedish origin in Wisconsin in the early 1900s were members of the first American-born generation. Among the exceptions was Gustus Ludwig Larson, born in 1881 at Värpinge near Lund, who, after studies and teaching at the University of Idaho, joined the University of Wisconsin faculty in 1914 and from 1920 to 1943 served as professor and chairman of the department of mechanical engineering. Also an outstanding consulting engineer, he was elected president of the American Society of Heating and Ventilating Engineers. He had come to America in 1890. Vivian Allen Charles Henmon, born in 1877 of Swedish parents in Wisconsin, became in 1927 professor of psychology at the University of Wisconsin, after having held similar posts at Columbia in New York, the University of Colorado, and Yale. He received part of his education at Bethany College in Kansas, which was founded by Swedish immigrants. Charles Joseph Anderson, born in 1880 in Minnesota, was in 1930 named dean of the School of Education at the University of Wisconsin. A noted architect, Herbert W. Tullgren, designed in and around Milwaukee many larger buildings, including cathedrals, theaters, and hotels. He was born in Chicago in 1889 of mixed Swedish and Norwegian parentage.

The first American-born person of recent Swedish ancestry to be elected to the U.S. Senate was Irvine Lenroot (1869–1949) of Wisconsin. His father, Lars Lönnrot, was a blacksmith from Skåne, while his mother, Fredrika, came from Värmland. Arriving in Boston in 1854, they moved the next year to St. Croix Falls in Wisconsin, in the northwest where most of the Swedes settled, and in 1857 to Superior in the northwest corner of the state.

At the age of 14, Irvine Lenroot left school to work in a grocery store. He then became a lumber worker and a court stenographer; in 1897 he was admitted to the bar; and a few years later he was elected to the Wisconsin state legislature. After nine years in the U.S. House of Representatives, he was in 1917 elected to the Senate to fill a vacancy, and in 1920 he was reelected for a full term. In the same year he had been selected by his fellow senators as their candidate for the vice-presidency, but the Republican convention nominated instead Governor Calvin Coolidge of Massachusetts. In 1929 Lenroot was appointed by President Hoover a judge in the U.S. Court of Customs and Patent Appeals in Washington, D.C. His daughter Katharine Lenroot was in 1934 named director of the Children's Bureau in the U.S. Department of Labor and served in that post for many years.

In the late 1800s or early 1900s, periodicals in the Swedish language appeared at Superior and Ashland on Lake Superior in the north, Grantsburg in the northwest, Rhinelander in the northeast, and Marinette farther east on Green Bay. Most of them were short-lived. Many Swedes in Wisconsin subscribed to Swedish-language weeklies published in Illinois or Minnesota.

New Swedish colonies in western Michigan — Engineers and skilled workers in Detroit

THE number of Swedish settlers in Michigan increased sharply in the 1880s, from about 9,500 in 1880 to nearly 27,500 ten years later. This turned out to be the high-water mark, but even in the early 1900s the Swedes came in large numbers, and Michigan's Swedish-born population remained, therefore, almost unchanged until about 1930.

In the middle and late 1800s, most of the Swedes who came to lower Michigan settled in the western section, along or near Lake Michigan. In 1870 an Episcopalian clergyman, the Reverend Josiah P. Tustin of Grand Rapids, Michigan, was sent to Sweden by a railroad agency called the Continental Improvement Company, and he was able to recruit quite a few emigrants, most of whom went to a company colony named Dalarna in Mecosta County, some 40 miles north of Grand Rapids. The next year Tustin went back to Sweden and raised an even larger contingent. Most of its members settled in a community farther north, in Osceola County, which, probably for propaganda reasons, was called New Bleking after the province of Blekinge in southeastern Sweden. More Swedes arrived there in 1872, and New Bleking was then renamed Tustin in honor of its founder.

Among the centers of early Swedish settlement in western Michigan were Lisbon, Sparta, and Alpine north of Grand Rapids, in Kent County. At Lisbon, which later was renamed Kent City, a congregation of immigrants from Sweden was organized in 1866. The year before, Carl Gustaf and Elizabeth Blomström from Svenarum in northern Småland had arrived to join relatives at Sparta, and Blomström established a blacksmith's shop. Their son Charles B. Blomstrom (d. 1923) showed a remarkable aptitude for mechanical engineering, and when still under 20 he built a small engine. Later he became one of the pioneers of the automobile industry.

In 1892, when Henry Ford had not yet started assembling his first "quadricycle" and Charles B. Blomstrom lived at Grand Rapids, he constructed a horseless carriage or automobile, and eight years later, when he had moved to Marquette on Michigan's Upper Peninsula, he built another car which he described as "a buggy with an engine." In 1901 the Blomstrom Motor Car Company was organized in Detroit to build gasoline engines and an automobile named The Queen. For some years this firm operated one of the largest automobile plants in Detroit, employing hundreds of men and making 30-40 cars a week. In 1906 the Blomstrom Manufacturing Company was formed to make a larger car called the Blomstrom. After it had failed to win a sufficient market, Blomstrom helped design several other motor vehicles, including the Frontmobile, the first front-drive car to be made in production lots in the United States. It was produced at Camden, New Jersey. During the first two decades of the 20th century, more than 500 car manufacturers sprang up in America. Many of them turned out experimental models. By the 1920s only about 50 firms had survived.

Among Blomstrom's first Swedish associates was Gustave A. Carlson (1877–1963), born near Västervik in Småland, who came to Detroit in 1892. In 1910 he founded the Acme Manufacturing Company, maker of polishing and buffing machines, which gradually expanded its operations and established subsidiaries in Canada, England, and Germany. Another of the few Swedes who settled in Detroit in the late 1800s was regarded as one of the best marine engineers in America. His name was George Mattson, and he worked for a firm which built boats for the Great Lakes steamship companies.

By the turn of the century Detroit began to attract greater numbers of skilled workers and engineers from Sweden. Some of them had been highly trained in their native country. The total of Swedish immigrants in Detroit has never exceeded 5,000, but their contributions to the city's industry and technology have been much more significant than this figure would seem to indicate. Their activities often centered on the making of tools with which machines, motorcar parts, and other metal products were turned out.

Among those who came to Detroit in the early 1900s was Nels L. Olson (1868–1950) from Hammarlunda in the province of Skåne, who after having learned the blacksmith's trade first went to sea, his journeys taking him to Africa, India, and the Far East. Emigrating to America in 1888, he worked for many years as a smith in California, Oregon, and Montana. Later he was employed by the Bureau of

433

Reclamation as a contractor for the Shoshone irrigation and power project in Wyoming and southern Montana. Keenly aware of the inadequacy of both the equipment and the metals used in excavating, he developed an improved plowshare point which soon proved so popular that methods for quantity production had to be devised. In 1910 he moved to Detroit and with a few associates set up the Swedish Crucible Steel Company. Olson also became president of some other companies and of the Peoples State Bank at Hamtramck.

Otto Lundell (1879–1940) from Floby in Västergötland was gripped by "America fever" after studies at Chalmers Institute of Technology in Gothenburg. He began life in the New World as a factory worker in Rockford, Illinois, at 12 cents an hour, and also worked for a while on a farm in Minnesota. In 1914 he moved to Detroit and became a successful manufacturer of broaches and other tools for automobile production. Together with another native of Västergötland and former Chalmers student, Robert H. Anderson (1883–1923), and Thor M. Olson (1886–1969) from Gothenburg, he began by founding the Michigan Tool Company. Lundell and his associates developed machinery that took the "grind" out of automobile gears and also invented other devices which made motorcars run more smoothly.

Carl Birger Persson or Parsons (1884–1956) from Vinberg in Halland, who at the age of 17 had landed penniless and alone in New York, began as a farmhand. After technical training and studies he became a specialist in designing automobile bodies, and is said to have built the first aluminum body for a motorcar. A successful manufacturer of automobile parts, he served from 1919 to 1924 as the first Swedish vice-consul in the Detroit area. In 1927 he presided when Detroit welcomed its native son, Charles A. Lindbergh, after his solo flight to Paris.

Another Detroit plant serving the automotive industry, Detroit Broach and Machine Company, was founded in 1934 by a group of young Swedish engineers headed by Gustav von Reis (b. 1903), a member of an old Gothenburg family, who, after studies at Chalmers, had come to America in 1926. Numerous other tool and gage companies were founded in Detroit by Swedish immigrants. An oil well in northern Michigan which von Reis developed in 1971, as well as his home in Florida, were named for the ancient town of Marstrand on an island northwest of Gothenburg.

Carl Edward Johansson (1864–1943), who became known as "Measurement Johansson" or "Precision Johansson," did not settle in the Detroit area until 1923, but his influence had begun to be felt some ten years earlier. Born in a cottage at the Frötuna industrial estate in the province of Närke, he emigrated to America in 1882, settling at first in Duluth, Minnesota, where an older brother had preceded him. In 1884 the two Johanssons took a course at Gustavus Adolphus College in St. Peter, and later the same year they returned to Sweden where Carl Edward, after technical studies and intensive on-the-job training, became employed as a supervisor in the rifle works at Eskilstuna, an old Swedish center of fine-hardware and machinery manufacture. Stimulated by impressions during an inspection trip to Germany, he began to dream of a more efficient mass production, based on a uniform standard of measurement so accurate that all parts made in accordance with it would instantly fit together. In 1896 he produced his first set of precision gage blocks, which, in combination with each other, would provide all the measurement figures required in the fabrication of rifles.

France became the first country to adopt the new system on a larger scale. Gradually it was also introduced in the United States, and in 1915 the U. S. War Department declared the Johansson gages standard equipment in all factories manufacturing military material. The war potential of the Allies was thus raised considerably. Later on, the new precision in measurement and control also smoothed the way for mass production in the automotive industry and many other fields. In the fall of 1919 Mr. Johansson began an extended visit to the United States, where he was greeted by the press as the "most accurate man in the world" and the "Gutenberg of the manufacturing industry." In 1923 he moved his American subsidiary company and his Swedish workers from Poughkeepsie, New York, to the Ford engineering laboratory at Dearborn near Detroit, and there he remained for 12 years as Henry Ford's associate, further improving his precision gages. In 1936 he returned to Eskilstuna.

Carl Edward Johansson played a leading part in bringing about conformity, at 25.4 millimeters, between the inch in the United States and that in Great Britain. In 1940 he was awarded the gold medal of The American Society of Mechanical Engineers. A stainless-steel set of his famous gage blocks is in the Smithsonian Institution's Museum of History and Technology at Washington, D. C.

Several Swedish immigrants became executives in the big motor companies. Ernest W. Sjöholm or Seaholm (b. 1887) from Lidköping in Västergötland, who in early childhood came with his parents to Hartford, Connecticut, joined the Cadillac Company in 1913 and became in 1921 chief engineer for the Cadillac division of the General Motors Corporation. Remaining in that post for over 20 years, he was responsible for the development of the Cadillac and La Salle cars. During the Second World War he had charge of making tanks in the Cadillac plant at Detroit. Seaholm had been graduated from the Mechanics Arts High School at Springfield, Massachusetts. One of the largest high schools at Birmingham near Detroit has been named for him. Valentine Y. Tallberg (b. 1901) from Borlänge in Dalarna, who was a graduate of a technical school in the old silver-mine town of Sala in Västmanland, made a similar career in the Ford Motor Company. Working for Henry Ford, German-trained Olof Ljungstrom (b. 1876) from Bedinge in southernmost Sweden designed a new type of electric locomotive, the main features of which were adopted by the leading electrotechnical manufacturers. Tore Franzén from Lund, also in the Swedish south, was for many years an experimental engineer for the Chrysler Corporation.

Descendants of Swedish immigrants who became well known in the automotive industry include Harold T. Youngren, who during the years 1946–52 served as Ford's chief engineer and helped solve the problem of automatic transmission, and Oscar A. Lundin, who started with General Motors in 1933, in 1970 became executive vice president for finance, and finally was named vice chairman of the board. His father, August Lundin (1871–1951), came to America in 1888 from Torne in Småland.

The many Swedish names in education and related fields in the Detroit area have, as a rule, been those of American-born descendants, but an immigrant from Sweden became a pioneering librarian. Adam Ström or Strohm (1870–1951), who was born near Vänersborg in Västergötland, won at 18 a degree from the University of Uppsala and emigrated four years later after a family conflict. In 1911, when he had for ten years been in charge of the public library at Trenton, New Jersey, he came to Detroit, and the next year he began three decades of service as city librarian. Under his leadership, the Detroit Library Commission said in a resolution of 1948, "the library system grew from a small outmoded central library with a rudimentary branch system to a dynamic library system with the beautiful Main Library and 22 branch libraries." The Main Library delivery hall was named the Adam Strohm Hall. Strohm was recognized as a leader in his profession, and in 1930–31 he served as president of the American Library Association. Somewhat later a noted author, Robert L. Duffus, devoted a whole chapter in his book *Our Starving Libraries* to Detroit and its city librarian, writing in part: "The general impression one derives from a visit to Detroit is that the Public Library in that city is animated by a fine, hospitable and generous spirit; . . . and that during the depression it has played a part, which can never be measured, in sustaining the morale of the population."

A son of early Swedish pioneers in the north of Kent County, Charles Theodore Gran or Grawn (1857–1942), helped develop the educational system of Michigan. From 1900 to 1918 he was president of Central Michigan Normal School and Business Institute, now Central Michigan University, in Mount Pleasant, where the Science Hall was named in his honor. Both then and later he was much in demand as a lecturer. In 1912 he studied the educational system in Sweden and other European countries, and 16 years later he again visited the land of his forefathers. He was also regarded as an authority on Swedish literature. One of his grandsons, William Grawn Milliken, became in 1969 governor of Michigan. In the northwest of Michigan's Lower Peninsula, not far from Traverse City which has been called the "World's Cherry Capital," is a town named Grawn, laid out by a relative of William G. Milliken. Charles Theodore Grawn's father, Anders Gran or Andrew Grawn, came from Säby in north Småland, which also was the origin of many other Swedish pioneers in Kent County north of Grand Rapids.

A Scandinavian symphony orchestra, a nonprofessional group, was organized in Detroit in 1930. Today it includes members of many national origins.

Five cities on Michigan's Lower Peninsula have had Swedish-language publications, and they are all in the western section: Battle Creek, Cadillac, Grand Rapids, Manistee, and Muskegon.

Swedes feel at home on the Upper Peninsula, but many depart to form new colonies

DURING the latter part of the 19th century, most of the mining, lumber, and railroad-construction camps on Michigan's Upper Peninsula were full of Swedes and Swedish-speaking Finns. About 1890, nearly half of the workers in the largest mine at Iron Mountain in the southwestern section were Swedes, but this was an unusually large proportion.

At an early stage, Ishpeming in Marquette County on Lake Superior became the leading Swedish center of the Upper Peninsula. As soon as it seemed somewhat crowded, however, the Swedes began to swarm, and many moved to other parts of the United States, where they founded new colonies. For instance, the largest Swedish settlement in rural California, Kingsburg, some 150 miles north of Los Angeles, was in great part populated from Ishpeming.

The first Swede at Ishpeming seems to have been one John Wahlman, who arrived about 1866. Better known is an early newcomer named John Eric Sjöberg or Seaborg, born in 1844, who before his emigration from Sweden in 1867 had been a master mechanic in the ironworks at Hällefors in the west of the province of Västmanland. At Ishpeming he married a girl from the Örebro district in the same section of Sweden, Charlotte Wilhelmina Farrell, whose family name originally had been Andersson, and in 1880 they had a son named Herman Theodore. He, in turn, married Selma Olivia Ericksson from Grängesberg, the leading mining center in the province of Dalarna, and in 1912 they had a son, Glenn Theodore Seaborg, who became an outstanding figure in nuclear science and a Nobel prize winner. When he was 10 years old, the family moved from Ishpeming to southern California.

At Ishpeming, the first Swedish church was founded in 1870. In the early 1880s one Conrad Carlson, said to have been a member of the noble Klingenstierna family, began editing its first Swedish-language newspaper. At that time, the Swedish community at Ishpeming also included Benjamin Owen (1830–89), a noted musician, whose father Samuel Owen, born in England, has been called the founder of both steam shipping and temperance reforms in Sweden. The younger Owen was a cousin of August Strindberg, and he had received some of his musical education from Jenny Lind.

A farming settlement in Michigan's far north, on Huron Bay in Baraga County, was somewhat paradoxically named Skanee after Sweden's southernmost province and granary, Skåne. In 1871, Captain Walfrid Been (d. 1907), master of a vessel on Lake Superior, was so enamored with the beautiful scenery of the district that he settled there and named the place for his home province. People from many other parts of Sweden joined him, and as late as 1930 almost all of Skanee's 300-odd inhabitants were of pure Swedish stock. In this isolated section of the Upper Peninsula, the Swedish language maintained itself unusually well.

Besides Ishpeming, six cities or towns on the Upper Peninsula have had Swedish-language periodicals, namely Calumet, Escanaba, Iron Mountain, Ironwood, Manistique, and Menominee. Escanaba and nearby Gladstone, on the south coast, had one of the largest concentrations of Swedish-born people.

An experienced Swedish observer in the United States has said that the farther north the Swedish immigrants settled, the more colorful they became. One of the pioneers in Upper Michigan used one noble-sounding and one genuine noble name, calling himself Johan Gustaf Runesköld Banér (1862–1938). He was born at Moheda in Småland. One of his American biographers describes him as a former captain in one of Sweden's crack regiments, while according to another he had served as a private in many of Sweden's army units, being sentenced to detention several times for having been absent without leave. Banér came to America in 1885, and after having tried various occupations, including newspaper editing, in other parts of the Midwest, he settled at Ironwood in the northwest corner of Michigan. There he became an unusually prolific poet, taking most of his themes from Scandinavian or Indian mythology. In 1922 he published *Keshena*, a cycle of poems based on Indian folklore as told by members of the Menominee tribe, which he had written in English but later translated into Swedish. According to some of his admirers at that time, it should have brought him the Nobel prize in literature.

One of Banér's daughters, Skulda Vanadis Banér, published in 1944 at Cambridge, Massachusetts, a book of remembrance entitled *Latchstring Out*, which won thousands of happy readers. Crammed with sketches of characters and events, it also describes in loving detail Swedish customs and traditions. In 1959 she produced another book, *Voice of the Lute*, a story for young adults about a woman who comes from the Dakota prairie to find the Sweden of her ancestors even more beautiful and more storied than her beloved father had told her. Miss Banér had visited Sweden in the summer of 1939. She then lost her sight, but, she wrote, the Braille system introduced her to "a wide-horizoned and wonderful world again, my *pekfinger* world — my fingertip world."

A remarkably large proportion of the Swedish immigrants who succeeded as manufacturers or engineers, in Michigan as well as in other parts of the United States, seem to have had some experience as blacksmiths, toolsmiths, or smiths of other kinds before they came, or began their American careers by operating forges of some sort. One of them was Charles G. Janson of Menominee in the southernmost corner of Michigan's Upper Peninsula, about whom the local newspaper wrote in an editorial after his passing in 1955: "The death of Charles G. Janson, at the age of 82, takes a life which exemplifies the strength which America has drawn from its adopted sons. He came from his native Sweden as a young man, equipped only with black-smithing skill and the friendship of his brothers, who had preceded him here. He worked as a smith and wagon maker before those trades used power equipment here, hand-fashioning the sleighs and heavy wagons of industry, welding at the forge before the advent of the torch. . . . His growth was in the tradition of America, for he did not only grow as an individual, but also as a citizen. . . . He was active in civic and fraternal organizations which served the needs of his new country and kept memorable the country that he had left. He was the president of one of Menominee's largest industries, the American Rule & Block Company, and a director of the Commercial Bank. . . . He never lost all of the touch of Swedish in his speech nor his love for his mother country. He was a fine American."

Many other successful industrialists of Swedish birth have begun their careers by learning carpentry or cabinetmaking.

Two farm boys from Småland mature in Midwest, become industry leaders in Michigan

THE city of Niles in the southwest corner of Michigan, near the In-

440

diana border, was long dominated by a single inventor and manufacturer of Swedish birth, Frans Johan Johannison or Francis John Plym
(1869–1940).

Born at Bäckaby in central Småland and brought in 1870 to
America, where his farmer father had preceded him, Plym grew up at
Aledo in northwestern Illinois. As a young man he developed into a
skilled carpenter and cabinetmaker, and by working part time he was
able to enter schools of higher education. In 1899 he finished his
architectural studies at the National Academy of Design in New York,
and began working as an architectural engineer, first at Lincoln, Nebraska, and then in Kansas City, Missouri. In 1907, when he had
patented a ready-made hollow-metal store front, he founded at Niles
the Kawner Company, which later extended its production to bank
and store fixtures, metal-casement windows for ships and lighthouses,
parts for automobiles and airplanes, and escalators. Finally holding
more than a hundred U.S. patents, he also directed plants in Illinois,
California, and Canada. In the 1960s the Kawner Company became
part of the American Metal Climax Company, now known as Amax.

Francis J. Plym made large donations to the city of Niles, which
has a recreational center known as the Plym Park, and to colleges and
other institutions of Swedish origin in the United States. In 1938, he
served as president of the Swedish-American association formed for
the celebration of the 300th anniversary of the founding of the
Swedish colony on the Delaware. For his native parish in Småland he
provided an old people's home as a memorial to his parents.

At Hastings, the seat of Barry County farther to the north in
southwestern Michigan, the largest industries were based on inventions made by another farmer's son from Småland, Emil Tyden
(1865–1951). He was a tall blond boy of 17 when, in 1882, he left his
home at Flisby in northern Småland.

In America, Tyden first worked as a cabinetmaker for an organ
manufacturer at Moline, Illinois, where he had friends from Sweden,
and then moved to a firm of the same type in Chicago. In 1885 he
received his first U.S. patent, and others followed in rapid succession,
so that in 1945 his patents finally numbered 165. After a visit to
Sweden in 1892 he started working for the Union Pacific as a land
agent, trying to bring Swedish settlers to Idaho. Most of them came
from Illinois, Iowa, and Nebraska. In the vicinity of Idaho Falls he

established a colony called New Sweden, and on his advice the settlers planted potatoes as their main crop. Since water was scarce, Tyden formed a company to solve the irrigation problem, and, launching a bold advertising scheme, he started marketing potatoes on a nation-wide scale. He has been called the "Father of the Idaho potato."

While working for the Union Pacific, Tyden invented a self-locking metal clip for the sealing of freight cars. Previously, several men had been required for a long train, but with the new device one person could do the same job. This invention was the beginning of the International Seal & Lock Company, which in 1900 was moved from Chicago to Hastings, Michigan. Before the inventor's death, it produced a million seals daily and had customers all over the world, including almost all railroads of any importance. Tyden's car seal was also adopted by the customs authorities in the United States and Canada and by all express companies. The special automatic machines used in the manufacture of the seals were invented by Tyden himself. At Hastings he also started making the Viking automatic sprinklers for fire protection, and branch factories were established in several large cities throughout the nation. Tyden's interest in agriculture and in the problems of the farmers endured, and in Iowa he operated nine experimental farms.

During World War I Tyden served as production manager of the United States Arsenal at Rock Island, Illinois, and since then he was familiarly known as Colonel Tyden. The Barry County Hospital at Hastings was established by him, and in the same town there is a Tyden Park. The American Swedish Historical Museum in Philadelphia received from him its first donation.

Swedes in the steel center of Gary, Indiana — 7,500 Swedish settlers in Ohio

AMONG well-known industrialists of Swedish birth who lived in Chicago was Albin G. Witting (1873–1950), a native of Lund and a graduate of the Stockholm Institute of Technology, who came to the United States in 1898, began as a clerk in the Homestead Steel Works in Pittsburgh and became chief engineer of the Illinois Steel Company's mills at Gary, Indiana, later the world's largest fully integrated steel plant. Witting was active in many Swedish-American organizations and in relations with his native Sweden. A rather large part of

Indiana's Swedish-born inhabitants, in the early 1900s numbering about 5,000, lived in Gary, just southeast of downtown Chicago, and most of the breadwinners worked in the steel mills.

While Indiana's Swedish-born population about 1910 began a slow decline, Ohio's increased from somewhat less than 4,000 in 1900 to about 5,500 in 1910 and nearly 7,500 in 1920 and 1930. Most of the Swedes lived in the industrial centers of Cleveland, Ashland, Ashtabula, Akron, and Youngstown. Ashtabula on Lake Erie recorded its first Swedish immigrants in 1869, and somewhat later it began to develop into a major port, receiving iron ore and shipping coal. The northern end of the city, Ashtabula Harbor, became known as Swede Town and had its own post office with the official name Sweden. Even about 1930 Swedish newspapers and books were read in most homes of Swedish immigrants. Among those who came in the 1870s was Andrew Swedenborg, who for nearly four decades worked as a dock foreman and secured work for many of his countrymen. He had a family of seven boys and four girls, and four of his sons remained in Ashtabula and became closely identified with the city's industrial development. Thousands of Swedes, on the other hand, stayed for only a few years and then moved to other parts of the country.

In Cleveland, the Swedish-born population reached a high-water mark of about 2,500 in the 1920s. At that time, Emil Forsberg (b. 1872) from Asphyttan in Värmland had become the historian and one of the leaders of the Swedes in the city. Three of its largest construction firms were owned by Swedish immigrants, and there were noted businessmen, manufacturers, engineers, and university professors of Swedish birth or parentage.

A Swedish chemical engineer in Cleveland, Bengt R. F. Kjellgren (1894–1968), became widely known among metallurgists and scientists both in America and abroad. After graduation from the Institute of Technology in Stockholm in 1918 he won a fellowship for further study at the Massachusetts Institute of Technology, and in 1924 he came to Cleveland where he helped develop a refining process for beryllium, a light metal increasingly in demand for modern technology. From 1948 to 1964 he served first as president and finally as board chairman of the Brush Beryllium Company. During the Second World War he participated in the Manhattan Project, which de-

443

veloped the atomic bomb, and in the late 1950s he worked with the U.S. Navy on the Polaris submarine project.

Another noted inventor who was born and educated in Sweden, Nils D. Levin, became chief engineer of the Jeffrey Manufacturing Company of Columbus and held in the late 1930s about 200 patents related to electrical locomotives and various kinds of electrical apparatus. Carl Gunnard Strandlund, who also was born in Sweden and lived at Columbus, became widely known after the Second World War because of his attempts to solve the low-cost housing problem by the use of enameled steel. During the war he had developed in Chicago, with government backing, a method of reducing the processing time on armor plate for tanks from 14 hours to eight seconds, said to be one of the most important ordnance contributions made in the Chicago district. Strandlund had come to America with his parents when he was only four. His father became a development engineer for the John Deere company in Moline, Illinois, makers of agricultural machinery, and in its behalf he developed over 300 patented improvements in agricultural implements. To begin with, his son followed in his footsteps by putting the farm tractor on rubber tires and reducing its weight.

Among the industrial leaders of Swedish extraction in Ohio was Walter G. Nord (1884–1967) of Amherst, whose parents had arrived in 1872, from the provinces of Dalsland and Västergötland, respectively. He invented a variety of machines and devices to serve industry and the household, and directed successfully a number of manufacturing corporations. For nearly two decades he served as president of the American Swedish Historical Foundation.

Swedish immigrants push into Nebraska after the Civil War, total 28,000 in 1890

AFTER the Civil War, Swedes began to move into Nebraska in large numbers. Most of them came from older settlements, especially in Iowa, Illinois, and Minnesota, but immigration also occurred directly from Sweden. From 1860 to 1880, according to U.S. census material, Nebraska's Swedish-born population increased from 70 to about 10,000, and during the 1880s it rose to somewhat more than 28,000, the highest such total on record.

During the first part of the 19th century most Americans believed

444

that the broad treeless plains between the Missouri and the Rockies were, as Zebulon M. Pike had written in 1810, "a sterile waste like the sandy deserts of Africa." Protracted droughts and other trials in Nebraska reminded Swedish pioneers of this notion, and a popular quip suggested that while the buffalo, the Indian, and the rattlesnake had enough sense to leave the state, the Swedes poured in. The German immigrants were, however, even more numerous, numbering more than 30,000 as early as 1880. The railroads conducted aggressive campaigns to attract more settlers, trying to reach Swedish farmers by advertising in *Hemlandet* and other weeklies. The Burlington Railroad published for some time a special news sheet in the Swedish language. Nebraska was often presented as "the best state in the Union."

Omaha, separated from Iowa only by the Missouri River and often called "America's Gateway to the West," has always been a center of the Swedish element in Nebraska. The first Swedes probably arrived in the early 1850s, a few years before Omaha's incorporation as a city, but the oldest identified Swedish resident, Sven Nilsson or Swan Nelson, did not come until 1862. Nels Nelson Windquist, who followed the next year, was named Swedish consul in 1872. Early in 1868 came the Reverend Sven Gustaf Larson of the Augustana Lutheran Church, the first Swedish pioneer pastor in Nebraska. After studies in Stockholm he had emigrated in 1858 at the age of 25, enrolled at the Illinois State University in Springfield, Illinois, where at that time the Reverend L. P. Esbjörn held the Scandinavian professorship, and finally served as pastor at Knoxville, Illinois.

As early as 1864 immigrants from the Swedish province of Dalsland settled on homesteads along Logan Creek about 50 miles north of Omaha, and in 1870 some 200 Swedes lived in this area, where half a century later about 90 percent of the population was of Swedish origin. Oakland is the central point of these prosperous communities, from where in the late 1800s other parts of Nebraska, as well as more distant sections of the United States, were colonized. For instance, at Wausa (Vasa), 75 miles northwest of Oakland, many of the first settlers came from the Oakland district.

In another fertile agricultural region, 30–40 miles west of Omaha in Saunders County, such names as Malmo and Swedeburg tell of early Swedish settlements. Eight families from Minnesota and Moline, Illinois, came to this district in 1867, and they were followed in 1868–69 by at least two groups of immigrants from the province of Skåne, one of them from Hörja in its forested north. These newcomers took up land near the present Swedeburg, where they were joined in 1870 by about 100 families from different sections of Sweden. To begin with, the newcomers lived in holes in the hillside, which they covered with brush and grass. Sven Gustaf Larson, the first pioneer pastor, moved from Omaha to Saunders County, and there he helped establish three Lutheran congregations. He and his wife, born Johanna Carolina Lagerström, and their nine children lived on a homestead near the village of Mead. One of his colleagues, John Torell, wrote about him in 1906, when life on the prairies had become much easier: "Poor himself, with a considerable family to support, he traveled among poor settlers in a poor wagon pulled by poor horses over roads still unbroken. . . ."

The Reverend John Torell (1853–1923), who had come from Sweden in 1875 and after studies at Augustana College succeeded Larson as pastor at Mead, Malmo, and·Swedeburg, spent most of his active life in Nebraska and had a considerable impact on the Swedish settlers. In the early 1880s, when he had moved to Oakland, combined Fourth of July and Swedish Midsummer festivals at Swedeburg attracted more than 1,000 people. At Wahoo, the seat of Saunders County, Torell and two other clergymen founded a Lutheran academy. Torell, who was born near Vänersborg in Västergötland, had studied at a mission-oriented junior college in Uppsala.

Some 50 miles west of Wahoo is Stromsburg, which was founded by Swedes in the early 1870s and became one of the centers of a rather extensive district cleared mainly by settlers from Sweden. Many came from the northern provinces of Gästrikland and Hälsingland, and in the beginning there were sharp religious clashes among them. When Paul Peter Waldenström, the leader of the Mission Friends in Sweden, visited Stromsburg in 1889, the Swedish Baptists already had two churches, and the Methodists and Mission Friends one each.

A few miles northwest of Stromsburg stands the beautiful church of Swede Home, where the first chapel was founded by Swedish settlers in 1873. These pioneers included a large group of people who had come the year before from Illinois, and many of whom were named Hult. Two of these, J. P. Hult and his wife, who had left

Sweden in 1866, died in 1878 in a prairie fire, their son Nels Peter Hult trying in vain to rescue them. In the early 1900s the Hult family and several other settlers moved west to begin pioneering once more in Oregon, but in 1923 Nels Peter Hult attended the 50th anniversary of the Swede Home Lutheran Church. Half a century ago, he said in an address in the Swedish language, "all this field was a wilderness, and so level that one could see nothing but heaven and earth. It was a wonderful sight. . . . Our only capital was youth and joy in work." The church at Swede Home counts a congregation at Colton, Oregon, among its daughters.

About 100 miles southwest of Stromsburg, another agricultural region with a large population of Swedish origin is based at Axtell in Kearney County and Holredge in adjoining Phelps. Here, as in other parts of Nebraska, the harvest was sometimes destroyed by locusts, and in 1876 the settlers would hardly have survived the winter if they had not started to collect and sell the bones of buffaloes, which had been shot for their hides and left on the prairies. Since 1913 the community of Axtell has been the home of the Bethpage Mission for mentally and physically handicapped, which was founded by a Lutheran pastor from Sweden, Kjell Gustaf William Dahl (1883–1917). It has been called the "Miracle of the Prairies." Dahl, who was born at Laholm in the province of Halland, came to America in 1902 to study the paper industry but remained as a minister of the Augustana Synod. As a student at Augustana College in Rock Island, Illinois, he translated into Swedish an English book about a widely known "colony of mercy" at Bielefeld in Germany, and later he visited this institution as part of his preparation for the Bethpage Mission.

Olof Bergström from Delsbo in the Swedish province of Hälsingland, who in the early 1870s had helped found Stromsburg some 90 miles west of Omaha, became in 1881 the founder of a community called Gothenburg about 140 miles farther west, in the valley of the Platte River. A Baptist preacher working as a land agent for the Union Pacific Railroad, he went back to Sweden in the spring of 1882 and induced a number of people to move to Nebraska, telling them that they did not have to know English since Gothenburg was to be a Swedish town. Many of the early settlers were, however, of German and other national origins. The first church was built in 1886 by Swedish Baptists. In the summer of 1960 the city of Gothenburg celebrated the 75th anniversary of its incorporation as a town, as well as the 100th anniversary of the beginning of the famous Pony Express, a private mail service in which riders galloped in relays day and night, each covering 75 miles at a time. The record run over the whole distance of some 2,000 miles, from St. Joseph, Missouri, to Sacramento, California, was made in carrying President Lincoln's inaugural address in 7 days and 17 hours. The overland trail to the Far West followed the Platte River, and Gothenburg, Nebraska, boasts two of the few remaining Pony Express stations.

One of the first children born of Swedish parents at Gothenburg, Louise C. Odencrantz (1885–1969), became a leader in public employment services and in job placement for women and the handicapped. Miss Odencrantz, who spent most of her childhood in Idaho, Texas, and Sweden, studied at Barnard College and the Columbia School of Social Work in New York. In the 1930s she helped plan unemployment insurance in the Department of Labor at Washington, D. C. She lectured both in the United States and at conferences in England, France, and other European countries. Another daughter of Swedish settlers at Gothenburg, Rose Gustava Anderson, became an authority on clinical and counseling psychology. A Ph.D. at Columbia University in 1925, she was elected a division president in the American Psychological Association.

In the middle of the 1880s there were Swedish settlers much farther west, for instance around Chappell, located near Colorado's northeast corner. In 1883 about 150 Swedish families in Illinois had been advised to take up new homes on cheap land in Keith County, just east of Chappell, but when the dry years came, most of them were unable to keep up their payments and lost their farms. The pioneer pastor in this desolate region was F. W. Bergquist, who came in 1888 and built a sod house for his family, including eight children. Finally in charge of eight churches, he helped many of his parishioners find employment in Wyoming coal mines during the economic crisis confronting Nebraska in the 1890s.

The 1880s were, on the other hand, good years in Nebraska. As in other sections of the Middle West, Swedish settlers prospered as farmers in the first place, while success in business as a rule came somewhat later. A venture which became the largest poultry-packing firm in America was founded at Omaha in 1898 by John P. Jerpe (1861–

1942), born at Brunskog in Värmland and an emigrant in 1883. As head of the company he was succeeded in 1929 by his partner Carl A. Swanson (1879–1949), born at Kyrkhult in the province of Blekinge, who had arrived practically penniless in 1896 after having received money for his ticket from two sisters at Omaha. In America he became known as the "Turkey King," and was succeeded by his two sons. Foundations established by Carl and Caroline Swanson and their children have supported Creighton University, the Public Library system, Immanuel Hospital, and other institutions in Omaha.

Immigrants from Sweden who settled at Omaha in the early 1860s included Johan August Åhmanson (1827–91), who began as a grocer, in 1870 was elected to the Nebraska legislature, and finally became a homeopathic physician. He was born at Jönköping in the province of Småland and had started as a bookbinder. By the middle of the century, when the Mormon Church had become active in Scandinavia, he spent a few years in Denmark and Norway, and there he set about organizing a group of Scandinavians for emigration to Utah. In the spring of 1856, he, his Norwegian-born wife, and an infant son sailed from Liverpool to New York with about 100 other Scandinavians, and by midsummer they arrived in Iowa City, the rail terminus, where the Mormons organized "handcart companies" for the 1,300-mile trek via the Omaha area to Salt Lake City.

The fourth of such companies had about 500 members. Misfortune after misfortune encountered the migrants, and early winter storms in the mountains of Wyoming took a heavy toll. Many more, it seems, would have been lost without the resourceful leadership of Johan Åhmanson, or John Ahmanson, who was in charge of the 100 Scandinavians. In Utah, however, he was not satisfied with what he found. The next spring he and his family were reunited in Missouri, and in 1861 they moved to Omaha, Nebraska. His son, William, founded a fire insurance company in Omaha. One of the latter's two sons, Howard F. Ahmanson, became a student at the University of Nebraska's School of Business Administration. In 1927 he moved to California, and there he started building up a business in the insurance, construction and loan fields which finally, before shares were offered to the public in 1972, was regarded as the largest privately held concern in the United States.

The first Swedish church in Omaha was begun in 1868 by the

449

Reverend Sven Gustaf Larson, and more than a dozen followed. In 1887 the Reverend E. A. Fogelstrom of the Immanuel Lutheran Church, who had come to Omaha from Brooklyn, N. Y., founded the Immanuel Deaconess Institute, which three years later admitted its first hospital patients. It also includes a school of nursing, a home for the aged, and a children's home. Fogelstrom left Sweden to become a sailor. After a turbulent youth he had a religious awakening in an English port, and came to America to enter the Augustana Seminary, being ordained in 1879. The Immanuel welfare institutions have received considerable funds from a foundation created in 1952 by Carl A. Anderson, born in 1873 at Hörby in Skåne, who came to Nebraska the first time in 1888. After many years as a machinist, including two in Sweden and four in the U.S. Navy during the Spanish-American War, he founded in 1913 his own, increasingly successful business in Omaha.

Lincoln, the state capital and an important education center, attracted at an early stage hundreds of Swedish immigrants, and more and more of their descendants. Many have served the University of Nebraska in various capacities. Its first Swedish-born faculty member was probably Hjalmar Edgren, already mentioned in connection with the Civil War, who first taught there in 1885–91 and returned in 1893 to become dean of the graduate school. Another noted linguist, Joseph E. A. Alexis (1885–1969), whose father was a well-known Lutheran clergyman in Nebraska, served as professor there from 1919 to 1950, teaching first French and Spanish and later Germanic languages, including Swedish. Among the universities where he had studied were Lund, Sweden, and Madrid, Spain, as well as the Sorbonne in Paris, where he wrote a doctoral dissertation about the Swedish literature in America. Nels August Bengtson (b. 1879) from Mörkhult in Skåne served for decades as professor of geography at the University of Nebraska, beginning in 1908. He was elected president of the National Council of Geography Teachers. Carl Christian Engberg (1872–1929), born at Hyttön in Uppland and an emigrant in 1888, was for many years professor of mathematics and executive dean of the university. A son of Swedish immigrants, Reuben G. Gustavson, served from 1946 to 1953 as chancellor of the University of Nebraska.

The outstanding public building in Lincoln, the State Capitol, has often harbored so many people of Swedish and othe Scandinavian stock that it has been called the "Johnson-Swanson House." A son of Swedish immigrants, Victor E. Anderson (1902–62), served as governor of Nebraska during the period 1955–59. His father came from Svarttorp in Småland, near Lake Vättern, and his mother from Laholm in Halland. Val Peterson, who served as governor from 1947 to 1953 and later became ambassador to Denmark and Finland, was born at largely Swedish-built Oakland, his maternal grandfather's name being Swanberg. The paternal grandparents of Carl T. Curtis, who in 1938 was elected to the House of Representatives and in 1954 to the U.S. Senate where he still served in 1975, were immigrants from Sweden. His grandfather, Carl Swanson from Östergötland, changed his name to Curtis.

Among the Swedish pioneers in Nebraska were several unusual men and women who did not settle there permanently. For instance, John F. Anderson from Jämshög in Blekinge, who had started as a shepherd and paper-mill worker and in 1869 came to the United States as a seaman, began his American career as a foreman working on the construction of the Union Pacific bridge across the Missouri River at Omaha, which was completed in 1872. Anderson's subsequent lifework was regarded of such value that the U.S. Congress by a special act conferred upon him his citizenship "as if born an American."

In Nebraska, people from Skåne seem to have made up larger proportions of the Swedish immigrants than in any other state. Other large groups of settlers in the Beef or Cornhusker State came from Småland and provinces in south-central Sweden.

Nearly a score of Swedish-language weeklies and other periodicals, many of them short-lived, have been published in Nebraska. An immigrant named Oscar Leonard Strömberg (1871–1941), who came to Nebraska the first time in 1895 and from 1912 until his death served as a Methodist minister at Oakland, became the most prolific and popular of all American writers using the Swedish language. Besides hundreds or thousands of poems, short stories, and newspaper articles, he produced about 40 substantial novels. Most of them were printed in Sweden, and at least one was translated into English. Ancient Arboga west of Stockholm, where he was born, and which in the Middle Ages was Sweden's foremost city, served as background for many of his stories. The heroes of his novels personified such virtues as honesty, piety, temperance, and ambition, and they were finally rewarded with both gold and love. Strömberg became particularly popular with free-church and temperance people but found numerous readers even outside these circles.

The trials and contributions of an immigrant school on the Nebraska prairie

LUTHER ACADEMY at Wahoo, 35 miles west of Omaha, which later became known as Luther College, opened officially on November 10, 1883, the 400th anniversary of the birth of Martin Luther. Only five students had registered for the first courses in October, but the number grew rapidly when the corn had been husked, and during the spring term it reached 45. Coeducation assumed an important place in the program, and 12 girls enrolled during the first year.

In 1887 Samuel Magnus Hill, who was not an ordained minister, took over the leadership of the school, and he remained in charge until the early 1900s, a period that was brimful with difficulties and problems. Born in 1851 in Sund Parish in Östergötland, he had come to America with his parents in 1868, graduated from Augustana College at Rock Island, Illinois, in 1879 at the age of 28, taught music and other subjects at Gustavus Adolphus College in Minnesota for three years, and had finally been sent to Salt Lake City as a missionary to win back Swedes who had been converted to Mormonism. From the Mormon Zion he wrote a series of articles for a Swedish-language Augustana publication under the title "Suckar från Sodom," or "Sighs from Sodom," but after a few months he was ready to admit that there were no encouraging results to report. At Luther Academy his approach to religion became increasingly practical, and finally he was in full revolt against the cultural and political conservatism of many Swedish settlers, describing his own attitude as "Christian socialism."

The board, headed by the universally respected Reverend John Torell, paid Hill 700 dollars for the entire school year, but there were times when he and other members of the staff were never sure of receiving their salaries. For the horses stabled on the campus the school always kept a stack of hay, and there were also cows that were milked daily by the manager of the boarding department, as well as pigs that were butchered when meat was required. During a particularly lean ten-year period that began in the late 1880s, the school depended largely on gifts of food from the various congregations, and vegetable soup was then often served as the main meal of the day. At times the end of Luther Academy seemed near, but the principal, Hill, remained an ardent apostle of education. "The more educational institutions, the better. If we can reach our young people, we broaden the culture of the land," he wrote in 1896 in a Swedish-language weekly in Omaha.

The students seem to have been able to live and study at the school in Wahoo for 100 dollars a year. Particularly in the early 1890s, however, money was scarce in the homes of Nebraska, and it was often difficult to raise the cash needed. Toward the end of 1891 the Reverend E. A. Fogelstrom in Omaha, who had helped found Luther Academy, sent his daughters Alma and Hildur, who were students at the school, money for the coming year and a letter reading in part: "I am sending two hundred dollars to keep you two girls at Luther. You must be diligent and good as well as learn much. . . . So now be glad and thankful that God gave you a father who sent you to Luther Academy."

The leading scholar among the teachers of the early period was Per Axel Rydberg (1860–1931), a college graduate from Skara in the province of Västergötland, who had arrived in America in 1882 and two years later, when he had been disabled by an accident in a mine, was called to Luther where he organized the courses in natural science and in the vocational division. Botany was his real specialty, and he frequently conducted excursions for his students, who regarded him as a wonderful teacher. Summers he spent surveying the plant life of Nebraska for the U. S. Department of Agriculture. After leaving Luther in 1893 he continued his studies at the University of Nebraska and Columbia University in New York, where he received his doctor's degree. Later he became curator of the New York Botanical Gardens. He was regarded as the greatest living authority on the Rocky Mountain flora. Among the students at Luther Academy in the early 1900s was Howard Hanson, born in 1896 on a nearby farm, who became a famous composer. His parents had come from Skåne.

A junior college, offering courses in liberal arts, teacher training, commerce, and music, was organized at Luther in 1925. At the school's 50th anniversary in 1933 it was reported that a total of 4,560 pupils had been enrolled and of these 1,305 had been graduated.

453

More than 300 of the students had become teachers, and 85 had entered the ministry. A large proportion of the young farmers among the Swedes of eastern Nebraska had attended Luther for one term, or a few terms. In the 1960s Luther College was merged with Midland College at Fremont farther north, while a new school called the John F. Kennedy College took its place at Wahoo. Luther College was the smallest of the remaining schools of this type which had been founded by Swedish immigrants.

Farmland and railroad construction lure tens of thousands into the Dakotas

IN THE Dakotas, the Swedish immigration reached its maximum later than in Nebraska. In 1910, South Dakota had about 10,000 and North Dakota some 12,000 Swedish-born inhabitants. As a rule, the immigrants settled singly rather than in groups.

The first Swedes to live within the present territory of the Dakotas were probably two or three members of Lord Selkirk's and the Hudson's Bay Company's settlement on the banks of the Red River of the North, which included not only parts of Manitoba and Minnesota but also present-day Pembina in the northeast corner of North Dakota, the first white settlement in that vast area. The tract was settled in 1812 by crofters from Scotland who had been evicted by Highland landowners. A Swede by the name of Michael Hedén arrived in 1812 with Lord Selkirk's first group of settlers, while Einar Holte, who had been a lieutenant in the Swedish navy, came three years later and served as Governor Robert Semple's adjutant. On June 19, 1816, both Semple and Holte were killed in the Battle of Seven Oaks between the staffs of the Hudson's Bay and its rival, the Northwest Fur Company. Michael Hedén escaped, but what happened to him after that is not known. Jacob Fahlström or Falstrom, who had arrived in Canada with one of Lord Selkirk's advance expeditions and has been mentioned before as the first Swede in Minnesota and Wisconsin, may also have lived for some time in the Red River settlement.

When in the late 1860s the homeseekers started coming to the Dakota territory in their canvas-covered wagons, they stopped first at Vermillion in the southeast corner of the present state of South Dakota, where a land office was established. Generous assistance was offered by a clergyman and Civil War veteran by the name of

Daniel Peter Brown, who was born in Stockholm in 1827. His log cabin and schoolhouse just north of Vermillion has been preserved. Many of the Swedish newcomers settled permanently in this area. Their dialects often told of origins in Dalarna or provinces farther north in Sweden, and the log cabins which replaced their first dugouts or sod houses were patterned after the rustic cottages in their native districts. A community near Vermillion was named Dahlsborg, which later became Dalesburg. Some 60 miles farther north, in Minnehaha County, many of the Swedish settlers came from Småland or southern Halland. The province of Närke, in south-central Sweden, was well represented among the farmers near Salem farther west.

Relatively large numbers of Swedes settled in the northeastern part of South Dakota, in or around such communities as Stockholm and Strandburg, and farther north near the North Dakota border, where a village was named Dahlberg. Farther west, in Marshall and Brown counties, much more land was cleared by settlers from Chisago County in Minnesota, practically all of whom had come from southern Småland.

In North Dakota, the Swedish-born population became more evenly distributed over the territory. A community named Harwood, near Fargo on the Minnesota border where nearly half the population is of Norwegian descent, was founded by Swedish railroad workers in 1870–71. At that time the railroad projects lured many Swedes into North Dakota, but the financial panic of 1873 set the migration back for a few years.

Several districts which to a great extent were occupied by Swedes are to be found in the valley of the Sheyenne River in north-central North Dakota, south and southwest of Devils Lake. In one such area near Maddock, the majority of the original Swedish settlers came from Finnskoga in the deep forests in the north of Värmland, while in another area most of the farmers were from the ancient village of Våmhus in Dalarna. In the early 1900s, large numbers of Swedes moved into the northwestern section of North Dakota where extensive areas were opened up to homesteaders.

One of the first Swedish homesteaders at Vermillion in South Dakota, Göran or George Norbeck from the province of Jämtland near the border of Norway, who married a Norwegian immigrant, had a son, Peter Norbeck (1870–1937), who was elected governor of the state and in 1920 a U.S. senator, an office he held until his death. The son of another Swedish pioneer in the same district, Henry Hanson, became a noted bacteriologist, credited with stamping out yellow fever in the Panama Canal Zone. A third member of the second generation, Clinton P. Anderson (b. 1895), who was born at Centerville in southeastern South Dakota, served as secretary of agriculture in the first Truman administration (1945–48) and then as U.S. senator from New Mexico until 1972. In 1933, when he was president of the Rotary International, he visited his father's home at Svärdsjö in Dalarna, finding records of his family dating back more than 200 years.

One of the pioneer surgeons in North Dakota, Eric P. Quain (1870–1962), was born at Sörsjön in Dalarna, near the Norwegian border. Having begun life in America as a farmhand, he studied medicine at the University of Minnesota. His family name, which originally was Kveen, lives on in the Quain and Ramstad Clinic at Bismarck, the capital of North Dakota. Founded in 1905, this institution was the second of its kind in the country. Its reputation was later enhanced by new surgical methods which a famous Swedish specialist, Karl Lennander (1857–1908) from Uppsala University, had taught Dr. Quain at Johns Hopkins Medical School in Baltimore. Dr. Quain helped found the American College of Surgeons. Another M.D. from the University of Minnesota, Leonard W. Larson (1898–1974), who was connected with the Quain and Ramstad Clinic for nearly 50 years, served in 1961 as president of the American Medical Association and in 1966 as president of the American Cancer Society. A third graduate of the same university, Anders Albert Westeen (1860–1926), became a noted physician at Grand Forks, situated on the Red River of the North, where he started practicing in 1893. Born at Linköping in Östergötland, he came to America with his parents in 1868 and studied both at Gustavus Adolphus College in St. Peter, Minnesota, and at Augustana College in Rock Island, Illinois.

In North Dakota the Norwegian immigrants were much more numerous than the Swedes, and many settlers from Sweden spoke Swedish with a strong Norwegian accent. Only Fargo, also situated on the Red River of the North, seems to have had a publication in the Swedish language. South Dakota's largest city, Sioux Falls, was the home of at least one Swedish periodical.

Swedish settlements in Kansas — Lindsborg, famous music center, founded in 1868

THE first Swedes known to have settled in Kansas came from Galesburg, Illinois, in 1855–56, when soldiers, missionaries, and tradesmen made up the newly organized territory's white population of little more than 1,000. During the California gold rush of 1848–51 some 90,000 people had traveled through Kansas along the Santa Fe Trail.

In 1855 came John A. Johansson or Johnson (d. 1893), who had been a farm laborer near Galesburg, and the following year he was joined by his elder brother Nils P. Johnson (d. 1911) with wife and children, who had traveled from Galesburg in a "prairie schooner" pulled by two yokes of oxen. The two brothers had left their home in Horn Parish in southern Östergötland in 1852. On the eastern shore of the Big Blue River in northeastern Kansas, about 20 miles north of the present-day city of Manhattan, they built the first sod huts and started farming, and in 1859 they sent for their mother, three brothers, and four sisters in Sweden. The mother, Maria Johnson, died the next year, and somewhat later the growing settlement was named Mariadahl, or Maria's Valley. The Johnsons were great pioneers, and the two older brothers became so successful that they were able to will considerable sums to educational and charitable institutions.

In the early 1900s the Mariadahl district had 14 Lutheran congregations. The historic Mariadahl Church, which was the oldest Swedish Lutheran church west of the Missouri River, was razed by earthmoving machines in the summer of 1961, to make way for water impounded by the Tuttle Creek Dam at the mouth of the Big Blue River near Manhattan. Founded in 1863, it had been ready for services in 1867 and completed four years later.

A large Swedish settlement grew up at Axtell farther north, near the Nebraska border. Peter Froom (d. 1894) from Ockelbo in the province of Gästrikland seems to have been the first pioneer. Another Swede who holds a place in the history of Kansas, Anders Palm from Killeröd in Skåne, came in 1858 to Lawrence on the Kansas River, 30 miles west of Kansas City, and there he built a windmill with machinery which was brought over from Sweden and mounted by Swedish mechanics. A foundry was also set up.

In 1857, an ambitious project for establishing a Scandinavian colony in Kansas was launched by C. H. Gran, a medical practitioner at Andover, Illinois, who received vigorous support from the Reverend T. N. Hasselquist, pioneer Swedish Lutheran pastor at Galesburg and editor and publisher of the weekly *Hemlandet*. The results of the campaign were disappointing, but the year 1858 brought several Swedes to the new territory. One of them, L. O. Jäderborg from Gästrikland, homesteaded not far from Abilene, the future seat of Dickinson County in the northeast of central Kansas, and after the Civil War he gradually increased his holdings to 1,100 acres of fertile land.

Hemlandet's early enthusiastic support for Kansas was followed by a series of articles describing the strife there and the dangers for its settlers. In the spring of 1859, a letter from Louis Lybecker, who two years earlier had been on a surveying mission in Kansas and now lived at St. Louis, warned the Swedes in Illinois against moving there, asking them if they were prepared for "an endless prairie with its eternal monotony." The example set by the Johnsons and other hardy pioneers, however, proved encouraging, and after the Civil War more and more Swedes flowed into Kansas. Toward the end of the 1860s special efforts were made to attract immigrants from Sweden, which then seemed headed for real starvation.

Anders Bengtson Carlgren (1819–1905), a former estate owner who came in 1864 and returned to Sweden in 1892, seems to have been the first Swede to settle in the valley of the Smoky Hill River, near the site of what would become the best-known Swedish center in Kansas. His first dwelling was a hollow tree trunk, while his diet often consisted of wild turkey, prairie chickens, and other game, the supply of which at that time was abundant. In 1866, 17 Swedes homesteaded in the same region.

In the spring of 1868, a group of Swedish newcomers in Chicago organized a corporation known as the First Swedish Agricultural Company of McPherson County, Kansas, the main purpose of which was to acquire a large tract of land in Kansas for a Swedish and Lutheran colony. The leaders were Sven A. Lindell from Barkeryd Parish in northern Småland and John Ferm from Storfors in Värmland. In the valley of the Smoky Hill River in northern McPherson and southern Saline counties in central Kansas, some 13,000 acres were bought from the Union Pacific Railroad, and before the end of 1868 members of the company in Chicago began to settle there. In

Sweden they had been farmers or farm laborers, ironsmiths, lumber workers, carpenters, or tailors, and all had been reared in an atmosphere of piety.

For Lindell and other leaders of the Swedish settlers, with such names as Lindh, Linde, and Lindgren, the colony on the Smoky Hill River was named Lindsborg. This village was to become the center of a settlement district of about 500 square miles where the population was mostly of Swedish stock. Members of another land company, which finally had been formed at Galesburg, purchased land north and west of the group from Chicago.

The conclusive factor in Lindsborg's early history was the decision of a young pietistic pastor of Sweden's Lutheran church, Olof Olsson (1841–1900) of Sunnemo in the province of Värmland, to move to the new settlement in Kansas with a large group of followers. His section of Sweden had been little touched by the early migration to the New World but in the late 1860s, under the combined influence of the crop failures and reports from relatives and friends in the American Midwest, Värmland too was gripped by "America fever." Through studies in Sweden and Germany, Olsson had prepared himself for work as a foreign missionary, and in the spring of 1869 he set out from Värmland with about 200 men, women, and children. Half of them were from the Sunnemo and Ransäter areas. Before crossing the Atlantic they split into two groups, and the 100-odd members of one party never came to Kansas: a railroad agent persuaded them to settle instead in Linn County in northern Missouri, whose county seat had been named Linneus. In June of 1869 the others, led by Olof Olsson, joined the colonists at Lindsborg. All were Lutherans by confession, but in conflict with the state church in Sweden.

Living at first in sod houses or dugouts, the newcomers started breaking the prairie. In a letter to a friend in Sweden in the fall of 1869, the Reverend Olof Olsson wrote: "The advantage which America offers is not to make everyone rich at once without toil and trouble. . . . The difficulties are so great at the outset that not every person has the courage to overcome them. The best plan is for several acquaintances to settle in the same tract, where they can encourage and help each other. That is the situation here."

Lindsborg became the last of the religious Swedish mass settlements in America. From the beginning there was a strong atmosphere

459

of puritanism in the colony. After the village in Palestine where Christ according to the Bible raised Lazarus from the dead, the first congregation was named the Bethany Swedish Evangelical Lutheran Church. It was founded in 1869 and was accepted into the Augustana Synod the next year. A religious controversy over the doctrine of atonement, which had begun in Sweden, flared up in the early 1870s, and one group left Olof Olsson's fold to form a Mission church of its own.

Shortly after his arrival in 1869, Olof Olsson organized both a church choir and a brass band, which was a significant beginning, and he also set up a school for the children. For several years he was a member of the Kansas state legislature, but in 1876 he moved to Rock Island, Illinois, as professor of theology at the Augustana College and Seminary. After the death in 1891 of Tuve Nilsson Hasselquist, he became president of this institution.

In 1879 one of the early graduates of Augustana, the Reverend Carl Aaron Swensson (1857–1904), who was born in the Swedish settlement at Chandlers Valley in Pennsylvania (near Jamestown, New York), came to Lindsborg as pastor of the Bethany Church, and two years later he founded a Lutheran school named Bethany College. As its first teacher he engaged a graduate of Augustana College, Johan August Udden, who later became a noted geologist and oil pioneer in Texas. When the new school at Lindsborg opened on October 15, 1881, in the sacristy of the Bethany Church, the two teachers were there and ten pupils assembled. When farm work was over later in the fall, Swensson rounded up more young men, and the first-year attendance finally reached 27. While Swensson taught Swedish and religion, Udden took over all other subjects. By 1891, the first baccalaureate degrees were conferred upon four graduates.

Inspired by Olof Olsson, who had heard Handel's "Messiah" in London and then assembled an oratorio choir at Augustana, Swensson and his wife Alma in 1881 organized the Bethany Oratorio Society, consisting of 50 men and women from the Lindsborg district. At Eastertide the following year, on March 28 to be exact, this group gave its first performance at Lindsborg, and there were also concerts at the neighboring communities of Salemsborg, Freemount, Salina, and McPherson. The same organization, which gradually grew into 500 voices and a large orchestra, has ever since presented the "Messiah" as part of Lindsborg's Holy Week Festival. On Good Friday, the Oratorio Society sings Bach's "St. Matthew Passion," a tradition which goes back to the 1920s. Many families have been represented in the chorus from the beginning, sometimes by three generations, and famous singers and instrumentalists have appeared as soloists.

The state of Kansas and the whole Southwest have obviously benefited greatly by Lindsborg's Handel festivals. Concerts have occasionally been given outside the Lindsborg area, in Kansas City, Wichita, or Oklahoma City. Radio broadcasts have sometimes sent the "Messiah" to nationwide audiences, and in 1944, during the Second World War, an entire rendition was transmitted to Europe.

From 1897 to 1909 the Bethany Oratorio Society received inspirational leadership from Samuel Thorstenberg (1875–1938), who was born in Kansas and had studied at Lindsborg, in Stockholm, and in New York. He was also founder and director of the Jamestown Conservatory of Music at Jamestown, New York. A graduate of the Academy of Music in Stockholm, Hagbard Brase (b. 1877), was then in command of the chorus for three decades, from 1915 to 1946.

After Carl Aaron Swensson's death in 1904 at the age of 47, his assistant, the Reverend Ernst F. Pihlblad (1873–1943), who was born in Kansas City, succeeded him as president of Bethany College, a post he held until just before the Second World War. His father, born at Finnerödja in Västergötland, was of unmixed Walloon stock. His wife, Marie, a native of the province of Värmland, was a sister of Victor Sjöström or Seastrom, one of Sweden's first great moving-picture directors, who in 1923–30 worked for Metro-Goldwyn-Mayer in Hollywood. As president of Bethany, Pihlblad was succeeded by Emory K. Lindquist, a native of Lindsborg and a former Rhodes scholar at Oxford, England.

Today Lindsborg has a population of only about 2,500, but because of its traditions of musical and other artistic achievement it has become widely known. In the American press it has sometimes been called the "Oberammergau of the Plains," in reference to the village in the Bavarian mountains in Germany where for centuries a Passion play has been performed every ten years. Other forms of artistic activities, such as wood carving and painting, were also part of life at Lindsborg almost from its inception. At Bethany a school of art was established in 1890. It was long directed by an immigrant from the

461

province of Västergötland, Birger Sandzén, of whom we shall hear more.

In the Lindsborg area and particularly in the farm homes, Swedish remained the dominant language for three or four decades. In the largest congregations the clergymen preached in Swedish most of the time as late as the early 1920s, and even by the middle of the century a divine service was occasionally offered in Swedish for the benefit of the older people. Outside Bethany Church on a Sunday morning, an elderly woman was heard saying that "salvation seems hardly possible in any other language than Swedish."

People hailing from Värmland are still in the majority in some sections of the Lindsborg district, but such place-names as Smolan and Falun tell of immigration from Småland and Dalarna, and Västergötland, Blekinge, and other Swedish provinces also helped populate central Kansas. A Swedish Civil War veteran, Major Eric Forsse, was one of the founders of Falun. Ten miles south of Lindsborg is a community called New Gottland, which has nothing to do with the Baltic island of Gotland but means "a new good land." Some 80 miles north of Lindsborg, near Nebraska, a Swedish colony named Scandia was founded in the late 1860s, and 10–15 years later the settlers numbered at least 1,000. A Swedish farmer and his wife who in the 1880s settled south of Scandia had a son, Frank Carlson (b. 1893), who served as a congressman in Washington from 1935 to 1946 and then as state governor until 1950, when he was elected to the U.S. Senate.

Of the larger cities in Kansas, Salina, some 20 miles north of Lindsborg, has the greatest proportion of citizens of Swedish origin. Immigrants from Sweden also contributed to the development of Kansas City and, in particular, the adjoining Kansas City, Missouri. In 1870, only five of the larger cities in the United States, namely, Chicago, New York, Brooklyn, San Francisco, and Boston, had a greater number of Swedish-born people than Kansas City, Missouri. which reported about 600 such inhabitants. With a few exceptions, however, Missouri never attracted Swedes in larger numbers, the main reason probably being that it already was relatively well populated when the Swedish immigration began in earnest.

An immigrant from Vimmerby in Småland, Godfrey G. Swenson (b. 1876), who arrived in 1896 and began his career as a mason, became one of the most successful building contractors in Kansas City. He completed about 150 major projects, including some of the largest structures in Kansas City and the adjacent territory of Oklahoma, as well as in Kansas. During his lifetime Kansas City grew from less than 70,000 to over 600,000 inhabitants.

The Swedish-born population in Kansas reached its peak before the end of the 1800s. The U.S. census figure for 1890 was about 17,100. Missouri attained its highest level in 1900 with some 5,700, while in Kansas's neighbor to the south, Oklahoma, the Swedish element culminated in 1910 with somewhat more than 1,000. In the early 1900s, Oklahoma had more Swedish-born inhabitants than any other Southern state except Texas.

Swedish inventors at Lindsborg, a pioneer journalist, and immigrants who returned

AMONG the immigrants from the Swedish province of Värmland who came to the Smoky Hill River Valley in central Kansas in 1869 were Anders Erickson, his wife Anna Maria, and at least one child, 3-year-old John Erickson (1866–1943), born at Långbanshyttan, which also was his famous namesake Captain John Ericsson's birthplace. Another son, Charles J. Erickson (1870–1954), was born the next year at the Erickson homestead, three miles northwest of Lindsborg.

Anders Erickson, the father, had an unusual talent as a mechanic and became recognized in the entire area for his skill as a blacksmith, as well as a fine craftsman in both metal and wood. When the two brothers were growing up, they often watched their father in his workshop, and together with a friend, Frank A. Lundquist (1868–1954), who had come from Galva in Illinois, they started tinkering with their own machinery. As many other inventive boys, they tried, for instance, to solve the problem of perpetual motion.

When they were in their early thirties and late twenties, respectively, the Erickson brothers became pioneers in the development of modern telephony. In their efforts in this field they were greatly influenced by their friend Frank Lundquist, who as the employee of a telephone company had observed the operation of a hotel telephone exchange in Salina, and said to himself that some day all these connections would be made automatically. It became, in other words, apparent that an electromechanical, or automatic, switching system would have to be devised in order to provide rapid and economical inter-connections of telephone lines.

With financial support from two Swedes who were grain dealers in Lindsborg and Salina, the Erickson brothers started working on this problem. After some time they moved to Chicago, and toward the end of 1893 they were contacted there by two other inventors, Alexander E. Keith and Almon B. Strowger. A system for electrical switching of calls had been patented in 1889 by Strowger, but this was only the beginning. In 1896, the subscriber station with a finger wheel for dialing was invented by the Erickson brothers and Keith, and a patent was granted two years later. In 1897, the same three inventors applied for the patent for the 1,000-line electromagnetic switching system, which was granted in 1901.

John Erickson was finally credited with 115 patents, while his brother, Charles, had a total of 35. Both received an award for distinguished service in telephony. Outstanding contributions were made by them not only concerning the dial telephone but also in the invention of the piano wire switch, the automatic selection of an idle trunk, and the preselection of trunk lines. Frank Lundquist also obtained numerous telephone patents.

In the spring of 1879 a keen-eyed and well-schooled immigrant from Sweden, Ernst Teofil Skarstedt, came to Lindsborg, and after having worked first as a farmhand, at 10 dollars a month, and then as a carpenter, he began to publish a Swedish-language weekly called *Kansas Stats Tidning*. It was intended as a liberal counterweight to a Swedish periodical, *Svenska Härolden*, which had been founded at Salina somewhat earlier. But the liberals among the Swedish pioneers in central Kansas, as Skarstedt later wrote, were not numerous enough to be able to support a newspaper, and in late Feburary of 1880 he gave up, after having produced ten issues. His competitor soon moved to Kansas City but went out of business a few years later. Skarstedt, on the other hand, became one of the best-known Swedish newspapermen in America, and we shall meet him again in his favorite section of the country, the Pacific Northwest.

Skarstedt's impressions of Kansas in 1879–80 had obviously not been particularly favorable. There were, he thought, hardly any signs of progress. The older Swedish pioneers in the Lindsborg area had formed a conservative power center, and on many questions they held "the most one-sided, fanatical and bigoted opinions." Several of them maintained that there was no genuine Christian spirit or morality in Sweden, a belief that the newcomer scorned as preposterous. Even in Kansas there were Swedes who, like Skarstedt himself, remained outside the religious groups. While many of these immigrants seemed headed for at least moderate success, the newly arrived liberal journalist observed, others reflected varying degrees of frustration, often trying to drown their troubles in rum.

When Skarstedt came back to Kansas for a brief visit in 1884, however, he found all conditions greatly improved. "Of the cities and towns," he wrote, "Lindsborg had changed the most. When I thought of its appearance in the spring of 1879, such a development in the short span of five years seemed almost incredible." The Reverend Carl Aaron Swensson had, according to Skarstedt, meant more than any other person in the Swedish settlements in Kansas, and "his name will for all time shine as one of the foremost in the history of Swedish-American culture." While born in America, which he regarded as "the hope of the nations," Carl Swensson was fluent in Swedish and proud of the land of his ancestors. Many people at Lindsborg called him "Prästa-Kalle," a nickname reflecting playful affection rather than devout respect. There were, however, also persons, including colleagues of Swensson in the Augustana Lutheran Church, who felt disturbed by his boundless energy and exuberance.

In the spring of 1870 a group of well-educated and formerly rather prosperous people, all of whom had lived in the fertile farming district in the southeast of the province of Skåne, came to Manhattan, the seat of Riley County in northeastern Kansas. Among them were Gustaf Lindgren (1821–88), his wife, Ida Nibelius Lindgren (1829–1909), and their five children, who ranged in age from two to 16. Mrs. Lindgren's mother came from a well-known family by the name of Billing. A first cousin of hers, Gottfried Billing (1841–1925), became, as bishop of Lund and a member of the Riksdag for many years, one of Sweden's best-known religious and political leaders.

It was after a series of misfortunes, including crop failures and a damaging fire, that Gustaf Lindgren had decided to move to America and settle in Kansas. Their new home a few miles from Manhattan he and his wife named Lindesfrid, after a farm in Skåne where they had lived happily for many years. Life in Kansas, they soon found, was also full of hazards, such as droughts and locusts, and during the first winter Ida Lindgren had to borrow flour for the baking of bread. After that, she worked as a seamstress in several homes in Manhattan. In 1875, however, one of their sons, 20-year-old Hugo Lindgren, was invited by an uncle to return to Sweden and join him in his business, and six years later the rest of the family, except the oldest daughter who had married a neighbor, Robert Harding, moved back to Skåne.

In the same year, 1881, about 550 Swedish immigrants in America returned to Sweden, and from then on this figure would increase considerably, often reaching 4,000 to 5,000 a year. Decisions to move back were, as a rule, based on a number of factors, but a sense of isolation in the new country often contributed, as it probably did in the case of the Lindgrens. Although both alert and convivial, they do not seem to have had any contact at all with the Lindsborg colony, which was 80 miles distant, or even with the Swedes of Mariadahl, who were only 20 miles away.

The Lindgrens may, on the other hand, have moved back anyway, for Gustaf Lindgren was already nearly 50 years old when he came to America, and young Hugo Lindgren's growing success as a businessman offered the family a good chance to return to Sweden, where they had many other well-established relatives. Hugo Lindgren served from 1903 to 1913 as American consul at Malmö, Sweden's third largest city. Ida Lindgren, who survived her husband by 21 years, often told family members and friends of her trials and joys on the prairie farm some 5,000 miles away. Her letters home from the Kansan Lindesfrid during the years 1870–81 were published in 1960 by an association called Riksföreningen för svenskhetens bevarande i utlandet, which was founded at Gothenburg in 1908. A sister organization in America, Svenska kulturförbundet or the Swedish Cultural Society of America, was founded two years later.

★ 23

In the Rocky Mountains

Pioneers in agriculture, mining, and science among Swedish settlers in Colorado

MOST of the early Swedish settlers in the Rocky Mountain territories were attracted by their mineral wealth, but subsequently more and more immigrants turned to agriculture and cattle ranching, forest industries, and urban occupations. As scientists or artists, several Swedes helped explore the Rocky Mountains without settling there. Utah was the first mountain state to draw Swedes in larger numbers, but in the 1880s Colorado took over the leading role. Its Swedish-born population continued to increase until the early 20th century, reaching about 12,500 in 1910.

A Swede, who acquired an Indian wife and became known as Cross Eagle, is said to have lived in Colorado in the 1830s and perhaps even earlier. According to local legends and reports he was a Swedish nobleman, Hjalmar Adlercreutz, whose German-sounding family name actually means "eagle cross." (Another Adlercreutz, Fredrik Tomas, who was an army officer, fought in the 1820s with distinction in the Columbian army, and later served as Swedish consul general in Venezuela.) In the late 1850s, when gold had been discovered in the plains near the present site of Denver, Swedes were among the thousands of people who came to Colorado. The first immigrants from Sweden known to have settled there were Anders P. Björkegren and Peter Magnes, who arrived in 1859.

Peter Magnes (1824–1902), who was born near Eksjö in northern Småland, became Denver's first outstanding citizen of Swedish origin. While he had first arrived because of the gold rush, it did not take him long to see that his future lay in agriculture. From Illinois, where he had settled in 1852, he brought fruit trees, bushes, and seeds of many kinds, and his crops soon became known for their high quality. He is regarded as the father of Colorado's important sugar-beet industry, and was also a pioneer in cattle raising. Along the old Santa Fe trail, which skirted his property, he laid out a village that was named Petersburg in his honor, and now is a southern suburb of Denver. "Honest Peter," as he was called, served as county commissioner for several years.

Anders P. Björkegren or Augustus G. Burke (1834–1908), born in Hudene Parish in the province of Västergötland, was left behind in Sweden when his father and two sisters emigrated to America in the middle 1840s, but in 1857 he landed in Boston, and from there he worked his way to the Middle West, mostly as a baker. Because of the difficulty Americans had in pronouncing the name Björkegren, he changed it to Burke. In 1858 he came to Colorado with a military expedition but then went to Chicago and planned to return to Sweden. An immigrant from Denmark, however, persuaded him to go back to Denver, which in the meantime had become an infant boom town, and there he and his Danish friend established a bakery and built Colorado's first brickhouse. Burke soon married a girl named Mary Harding.

After having sold the bakery and engaged in mining, Burke sometimes earned his living as a fiddler at dances and entertainments. Finally he prospered as a farmer near Boulder, north of Denver. A grandson, Arleigh A. Burke (b. 1901), who was born on the same farm, became an outstanding naval officer and served from 1955 to 1961 as Chief of U.S. Naval Operations. During visits to Sweden, he was welcomed to his ancestral home in Västergötland by numerous relatives. An exhibit room in the American Swedish Historical Museum in Philadelphia was named the Dahlgren-Burke Room in honor of Admiral John A. Dahlgren and his son Colonel Ulric Dahlgren, both of Civil War fame, and Admiral Burke.

In 1869–70 a group of Swedes founded a settlement near the city of Longmont, north of Denver, naming it Ryssby after a parish in

Småland. Other immigrants, many of whom came from Halland, joined them, and a "Vermland settlement" was established somewhat farther east. The church at Ryssby, on a hill eight miles northeast of Boulder, was dedicated on Midsummer Day in 1882. No regular services have been held since 1906, but descendants of Swedish settlers in Colorado still gather there both at Midsummertime and shortly before Christmas, when part of the observance is in the Swedish language. The first pastor at Ryssby was Fredrick Lagerman, who came in 1877 from Augustana College at Rock Island, Illinois. In the old days the farmers worked as a cooperative unit and divided their earnings. The harvests were secured by artificial irrigation.

In other sections of Colorado most of the Swedish immigrants became miners or railroad workers. During the years 1867–76 the three brothers Anders, Hans, and Daniel Recén left their home in the vicinity of Leksand on Lake Siljan in the province of Dalarna, and in 1876 they came together in Colorado. About 60 miles southwest of Denver, at an altitude of about 10,000 feet, they began to prospect for gold and silver, other miners joined them, and the town of Recen soon had several hundred inhabitants. After three years the youngest of the brothers, convivial Daniel (1853–1917), found a silver mine, called the Queen of the West, and the other two, now known as Andrew (1842–1912) and Henry Recen (1848–1914), did relatively well. Their mother Kari (1813–1900) came in the late 1880s at the age of 75 to help Henry, who had become a widower, with his children. Today nothing remains of the town of Recen. Its post office was named for nearby Kokomo.

In 1880 some 300 Swedes lived at Leadville, 75 miles southwest of Denver, where rich lead and silver ores had been discovered and the population of which reached 35,000. Aspen and its silver mines 30 miles farther southwest also attracted hundreds of Swedes. After the big rush in the 1870s and 1880s, a Swedish engineer, Charles Anderson from Fellingsbro in the province of Närke, was for decades in charge of the principal mines at Aspen, including the famous Mollie Gibson and Smuggler. A railroad pioneer named Hagerman, who financed the construction of a railway over Hagerman Pass to Aspen, is said to have been Swedish by birth. Before his death he donated the 200-mile grade to the state for an auto road.

No locality had a greater drawing power than Cripple Creek, 20 miles southwest of Colorado Springs, which in the 1890s became known as the world's greatest gold-mining camp and by the middle of the 20th century had yielded about 800 million dollars worth of gold.

An American scholar of Swedish extraction wrote in 1949 about the Swedish miners in Colorado that they were "extremely individualistic, impatient of any restraints by society or any higher moral agency, yet paradoxically enough friendly, extremely generous, and having a high sense of social responsibility and democracy."

In Denver as in many other American cities, Swedes played a leading part in the construction of homes and larger buildings. One of the best-known Civil War veterans from Sweden, Captain Axel Silversparre, came to Denver from Chicago in 1880. While never particularly successful, he seems to have laid out some of the early streets and helped survey the first part of the route for the Denver, Pacific and Rio Grande Railroad which ultimately was to penetrate the Rockies on the way to Salt Lake City, Utah. He is also credited with having made one of the first authentic maps of Colorado.

The first highly successful Swedish-born building contractor in Denver was Frank Anderson (1858–1936) from Ryssby in Småland, who came to America in 1879 and to Denver three years later. He erected the city's first 8-story building and became one of its leading businessmen. Arvid Olson (1864–1930) from Kävlinge Parish in the province of Skåne, who arrived in 1888 after two years in Minnesota, produced in the early 1900s more notable buildings than any other contractor in Colorado. Among his creations were the Denver Auditorium and St. John's Cathedral.

The best-known Swedish name in engineering and manufacturing in Colorado is probably that of Carl August Norgren, born in 1890 in South Dakota where his parents, Gustavus Norgren from Husby in Dalarna and Caroline Anderson from Mjölby in Östergötland, had settled. After engineering practice in Omaha, Salt Lake City, Seattle, and Chicago he went in 1920 to Colorado for his health, and six years later he organized at Denver the C. A. Norgren Company, which became a widely known manufacturer of pneumatic accessories and by the middle of the 1900s had licensed branch factories in Sweden and England. Carl A. Norgren himself invented many of the devices and obtained some 50 patents. His other interests ranged from cattle breeding to youth activities, music, and natural history. As president of the Norgren Company he was succeeded in 1962 by his eldest son, Neil Norgren.

Some of the Swedish engineers in Colorado, among them Nils Weibull who in the early 1900s also participated in a large electric-power project in Arizona, went back to Sweden to pursue their careers there. David Wermelin, who before his emigration had begun to study medicine at Uppsala, designed at Denver a number of labor-saving mining and other machines, but left the patenting of them to his employers. It may have been because of him that Atterdag Wermelin, who has already been mentioned as one of the early socialists in Sweden and an emigrant in 1887, came to Colorado. He is said to have been offered an important job in the large steelworks at Pueblo, 110 miles south of Denver, but regarding himself as unfit to handle a whole army of men, he declined. In 1895 Wermelin sent from Denver to his good friend Hjalmar Branting, the leading founder of Sweden's Social Democratic party, a letter which has been described as that of a restless soul who could not adjust to life on either side of the Atlantic.

The first 19th-century immigrant from Sweden to win a prominent position in education and science in Colorado was probably John B. Ekeley (1869–1951), who from 1902 to 1937 served as professor and head of the department of chemistry at the University of Colorado. Born at Örebro in the province of Närke and brought to America at the age of three, he studied and taught in the 1890s at Colgate University in Hamilton, New York. Together with another scientist he invented a method for extracting tungsten, a metallic element with a Swedish name ("heavy stone"), from its ores, and his laboratory manual for inorganic chemistry was issued in several editions during the years 1912–34.

George Norlin (1871–1942), who was born of Swedish immigrant parents in Kansas, became professor of Greek at the University of Colorado in 1899 and served from 1919 to 1940 as president of the same institution. In public addresses he often underlined the need for free-thinking individuality. In the early 1930s he was Theodore Roosevelt professor of American history and institutions at the University of Berlin in Germany. A son of Swedish settlers at Denver, Reuben G. Gustavson (1892–1974), also became a distinguished university administrator, as well as a nationally known chemist. After having served in Denver for many years, finally as president of the University of Colorado, he moved in 1945 to the University of Chicago as vice president and dean of faculties, and the following year, as already mentioned, he was elected chancellor of the University of Nebraska. His father came from the city of Luleå in northern Sweden and his mother from Uppsala. Alfred C. Nelson, born in 1898 at Salt Lake City of parents from the province of Skåne, became professor of chemistry at the University of Denver, dean of its graduate school, and acting chancellor.

In the early 1900s a health center for tuberculosis patients, called the Swedish National Sanatorium, was established at Englewood, near Denver, by Swedish immigrants under the leadership of Dr. Charles A. Bundsen (1872–1956) from Holma in the province of Bohuslän, who, after some years at sea, had gone ashore in Canada and via Chicago came to Denver in 1898. Religious and fraternal organizations of Swedish origin in the United States offered the sanatorium project their enthusiastic support. Considerable funds have also been raised by the annual sale of a small token, an artificial anemone called the "Mayflower," which a group of Swedish men and women at Providence, Rhode Island, began to manufacture and distribute in the early 1920s. In 1931 a new building named the Mayflower Pavilion was inaugurated at Englewood, and among the guests of honor on this occasion was a visitor from Sweden, Mrs. Beda Hallberg (1869–1945), who in 1907 had launched the "Mayflower" in the fight against tuberculosis in her native country. About 8 million such emblems are sold annually in Sweden, and the proceeds are now used for aid to medical research, preventive health care, and disabled or retarded children. A similar change has been made in the activities of the institution at Englewood, which today is known as the Swedish Health Center.

At Cortez in Montezuma County in Colorado's southwest corner, the Johnson Hospital was founded in 1917 by Dr. Emil Enander Johnson, born in 1882 on a farm near Ljungby in southern Småland. He emigrated with his parents in 1897, and some years later he began to study medicine in Chicago. His hospital at Cortez became known all over the Four Corners area, where Colorado, Utah, Arizona, and New Mexico meet. In 1926 he showed his institution to Crown Prince

Gustav Adolf and Crown Princess Louise of Sweden, who from Cortez went to visit the Mesa Verde National Park and its famous cliff ruins. In 1891 some of these had been scientifically excavated by a young Swedish archeologist, Baron Gustaf Nordenskiöld, whom we shall meet again.

Colorado's first governor of Swedish stock was George A. Carlson (1876–1926), who served from 1915 to 1920 and was highly regarded. He was born in Iowa of immigrants from the province of Halland. His father came to America in 1871. Another son of Swedish pioneers, Edwin C. Johnson (1884–1970), served as governor from 1933 to 1937 and was then a member of the U.S. Senate until 1955, when he returned to Colorado to serve a final term as the Centennial State's chief executive. He was born on a farm near Scandia, Kansas, of parents who had come from Skåne and later settled in Nebraska. Originally a railroad worker, Edwin C. Johnson moved to Colorado to improve his health.

The first Swedish-language newspaper at Denver was published in 1880–84, and the second was founded in 1888. The latter's traditions were continued from 1924 to 1941 by *Westerns Nyheter*, which then was converted into English and renamed *The Western News*. For nearly fifty years it was published by Enoch Peterson, born in 1893 at Persberg in the province of Värmland, who retired in 1974 and was succeeded by a son. Among the numerous Swedish journalists of an older generation was Ninian Waerner (1856–1905), a native of the city of Norrköping, who before coming to America in 1884 had studied law at Uppsala and music in Germany. Wherever he worked as a newspaper editor, in Chicago, at Denver in 1889–91, in Minneapolis, and finally from 1896 in Sweden, he became known above all as a bizarre humorist and a somewhat sentimental poet.

First Swede in Utah in 1847 — Copenhagen center of Mormon missionary activities

THE first Swede in Utah was John Eric Forsgren (1816–1890), who was born in the port city of Gävle and went to sea at the age of nine. In 1832 he made his first landing in the United States, eleven years later he was baptized by the Mormons at Boston, and the next year he helped construct the Mormon Temple at Nauvoo in Illinois. When

Joseph Smith, the Mormon leader, had been murdered in 1844, Forsgren went to California in the famous Mormon Battalion, and in October of 1847 he came to the site of Salt Lake City where Brigham Young and his company of pioneers had settled three months earlier. In 1849 he volunteered and was sent to Sweden as a missionary but was banished from the country after a short time.

A Scandinavian mission was, however, established in Copenhagen in 1850, and when Forsgren returned to Utah three years later he had with him a group of about 300 converts, including a small number of Swedes. Most of them were tenant farmers or farm laborers from Skåne, the southernmost province, which continued to supply a large proportion of the Swedish converts to Mormonism. Another leading source was Stockholm. Many of the Scandinavian newcomers of the early 1850s were assigned by Brigham Young to the development of the Sanpete Valley on the western slopes of the Wasatch Mountains, south of Salt Lake City, a region that became known as the "Granary of Utah." New groups of Mormons came from Sweden, and Swedish immigrants who were not members of the Mormon Church also settled in Utah, especially in the 1880s.

One of the best-known Mormon pioneers of Swedish birth was Ola Nilsson Liljenquist (1826–1906) from Ignaberga in Skåne, who came to Utah in 1857 with his Danish-born wife, after pushing a handcart some 300 miles from Iowa City to eastern Nebraska and then driving an ox team about 1,000 miles to his destination. After less than two years he went back to Scandinavia as a missionary, and when leaving again in 1862 he was in charge of 484 converts. In Utah, Hyrum in Cache County in the north became under his leadership a thriving cooperative town. Later on, many other immigrants from Sweden played leading or important parts in their communities. August William Carlson (1844–1911) from Karlskrona in southeast Sweden, who came in 1871 and some years later translated the Book of Mormon into the Swedish language, became a successful banker and businessman as well as a member of the Salt Lake City Council and a regent of the University of Deseret, now the University of Utah.

On the whole, the Swedes in Utah merged rapidly with the other groups, and family names were often changed to more common ones of the English type, including both Brown and Smith. The Mormon Church wanted all members who did not speak English to learn that language as soon as possible, and it made no distinction between the Swedes and other Scandinavians.

The Danes, however, were more numerous and seemed more influential than the Swedes, and around the turn of the century a Swedish journalist, Otto Rydman (1867–1934) from Gränna in northern Småland, led a revolt against what he regarded as the Danish supremacy and for the establishment of a Swedish auxiliary within the church organization. The gazette he published, *Utah Korrespondenten*, had been founded in 1890 to serve the Church, but four years later he had become its sole owner. The first Swedish paper in Salt Lake City was issued during the years 1885–92. Two anti-Mormon papers, both unsuccessful, have also been published.

Gradually, the Mormon Church modified its attitude toward foreign languages and traditions. Its leaders realized that a command of some Scandinavian language, for instance, was valuable in its missionary work, and that the Swedish "julotta" service early in the morning of Christmas Day, which at one time caused opposition, could well be observed with official approval. In 1915 the leader of the "Swedish insurrection," Otto Rydman, sold his paper to another Swedish-language publication, *Utah Posten*, which was supported by the Mormon Church and managed to exist until 1935.

The most influential Swedish-born person in the Mormon Church was Janne Mattson Sjodahl (1853–1939) from Karlshamn in the province of Blekinge, who had been a Baptist minister of note in Sweden and Norway before he, in 1886, emigrated to Utah and joined the Mormon Church. After visits to Palestine and Switzerland on behalf of the Church, he joined the staff of the *Deseret News* in 1890, and from 1906 to 1914 he served as editor-in-chief of that important daily. Returning to Utah in 1919 after an assignment in England, he became editor of the Swedish *Utah Posten* as well as of three other foreign-language papers issued by the Mormon Church, one Danish-Norwegian, one Dutch, and one German.

Sjodahl translated three Mormon scriptural works into Swedish, including the Book of Mormon which 57 years earlier had been translated by August W. Carlson, and he authored a number of ecclesiastical works, some of which are still used extensively in the Church today. In 1897 he was selected by the Church authorities to present on behalf of the Scandinavians in Utah a copy of the Book of Mormon

and an onyx casket to King Oscar II and his consort, who then celebrated the 25th anniversary of their accession to the thrones of Sweden
and Norway.

While most Swedes in Utah learned English at an early stage, the
Swedish language, as elsewhere, lived on for a considerable time. In
1966 a Swedish dialect-research expedition from the University of
Uppsala interviewed the nearly 107-year-old Hilda Erickson (1859–
1968), born at Ledsjö north of Skara in the province of Västergötland. As a nearly seven-year-old girl, together with her mother and
two brothers, she had come to Salt Lake City on October 22, 1866,
after a 1,000-mile trek on foot and by ox cart across the Great Plains
and over the Rockies from Omaha. After 100 years in Utah she was,
of course, fluent in English, but she also spoke a perfect Swedish, or
rather the dialect heard in the 1860s on the plains around Skara. The
trip from Omaha in 1866, she told the Swedish researchers, took ten
weeks, but "to us children it was intensely interesting and pleasant the
whole time." Mrs. Erickson, who was the oldest Swede in the world, also
captivated the Swedish TV audience. There were other Swedes in Utah
who reached an advanced age. One of them is reported to have said in
answer to a question concerning the number of his years: "A man's
got to live a long time for two countries."

In 1910 Utah had about 7,200 Swedish-born inhabitants. The
immigrants from Sweden were, like other inhabitants, heavily concentrated east and southeast of the Great Salt Lake. In Salt Lake City
itself, about six percent of the population was of Swedish origin. Even
by the middle of the 20th century, its suburb North Salt Lake was
called "Swede Town." There were, however, Swedish settlers almost
all over the state. In the northernmost counties the proportion of
Swedes was relatively large. In the sparsely populated northwest
corner a small community was named Lynn for a Swedish farmer,
Lind, who had come there about 1880. Grantsville, south of the Great
Salt Lake, was in part developed by Swedish immigrants. In 1892 a
Swede from Utah by the name of Carl Johan Lundgren founded the
settlement of Lund in the southeastern part of Idaho, which was first
brought under cultivation by Mormons. Scandinavian Mormons also
helped colonize parts of Wyoming, Colorado, New Mexico, Arizona,
and Nevada.

In regard to Utah as well as other states, many sons and daughters
of immigrants made careers in new fields and largely in other parts of

the country. A couple by the name of Sundwall at Fairview in central Utah, where settlers from Sweden were rather numerous, had a son, John Sundwall (1880–1950), who won a Ph.D. degree at the University of Chicago and an M.D. from Johns Hopkins at Baltimore. After having held professorships at the universities of Utah, Kansas, and Minnesota from 1907 to 1921, he served for about 25 years as professor of hygiene and public health in the University of Michigan at Ann Arbor. He also became a hygiene expert in the U.S. Public Health Service in Washington, and was elected president of the American Student Health Association and the American School Health Association. A professor of mechanical engineering at Utah State University in Logan, Dan Arthur Swenson, and his wife Margaret had a daughter, May Swenson (b. 1919), who became a noted poet, and the recipient of many awards and fellowships. Works by modern Swedish poets, including Werner Aspenström, Gunnar Ekelöf, Erik Lindegren, Harry Martinson, and Tomas Tranströmer, have been translated by her into English. Her own poetry has, in turn, been rendered in the Swedish language. One of Brigham Young's many sons married a Swedish girl, Anna Marie Rosberg or Roseberry, and they had a son, Kimball Young, who became a noted sociologist, beginning his academic career at the University of Oregon and ending at Northwestern University.

By the middle of the 20th century some small groups of Swedish immigrants joined their fellow believers in Utah. Today, even many people in Sweden who know little or nothing about modern Mormonism have heard or read about the world's largest collection of family records, preserved on microfilm in vaults in the granite cliffs of Little Cottonwood Canyon, 20 miles southeast of Salt Lake City. Microfilm copies of the same materials, along with other sources, are available for research at the library and archives of the Church's Genealogical Society in downtown Salt Lake City. Interested persons may also use microfilm copies in branch libraries throughout the United States, as well as in Canada, Mexico, Australia, and New Zealand.

The records include microfilm rolls of all Swedish parish registers and many other official documents from olden times until the modern era. The most ancient ones are from the 1300s. Every day the archives have Swedish-speaking visitors, who go through records written by hand by the old parish pastors. The purpose of building up a complete registry of this type is connected with the religious beliefs of the Mormon Church, or, as it is officially named, the Church of Jesus Christ of Latter-Day Saints.

20-year-old "uncut" immigrant becomes governor of Montana four decades later

WYOMING, Idaho, and Montana received their first Swedish settlers in the 1860s. In Wyoming the Swedish-born population reached its high in 1910 with some 2,500, while Idaho and Montana reported their top figures in 1920, about 5,100 and 7,200.

Most of the pioneers engaged in mining, farming or animal husbandry, and cattle breeding was often conducted on a large scale. A Swedish-born woman named Margaret Carlston became, for instance, one of Montana's greatest ranchers, with the assistance of four sons. After having run a boarding house for miners since 1878 she bought her first ranch in 1903, lost her fortune in a bank failure in the early 1920s, but became successful again before her death in 1931.

In Idaho, the first Swedish congregation, which belonged to the Lutheran Augustana Synod, was organized in 1884 at Moscow, which had been founded a few years earlier in the heart of a fertile district near the Washington border. Most of the early Swedish settlers in this section of Idaho came, either directly or via Minnesota, from Östmark and neighboring parishes in the province of Värmland. In the late 1800s and early 1900s people from western Värmland played a particularly important part at Troy, 10 miles east of Moscow. Relatively large numbers of Swedes also settled farther north in Idaho, as well as in the south at Boise, the capital, and near Idaho Falls. In the vicinity of Idaho Falls, as already mentioned, a Swede named Emil Tyden, who later became a prominent industrialist in Michigan, helped found a settlement called New Sweden, which specialized in growing and marketing the Idaho potato.

At Kellogg in the Coeur d'Alene lead, silver, and zinc mining district of the Bitterroot Mountains in northern Idaho, a Swedish mining expert, Julius Bernhard Haffner (d. 1967), was for 15 years in charge of the Bunker Hill mines. Born at Dagstorp in the province of Skåne and a graduate of the Institute of Technology in Stockholm, he came to the United States in 1910 after having worked in England, France, Germany, and Russia. He became a director of the Lead Industries Association, the Idaho Mining Association, and the American Institute of Mining and Metallurgical Engineers. The University of Idaho at Moscow, whose mining students he served as an adviser, awarded him an honorary doctor's degree in 1956.

In Montana, most of the Swedes lived in the mountain region. Of the cities, Great Falls and the mining center of Butte attracted the largest flocks, while Anaconda and Helena, the capital, had the greatest proportions of Swedish-born people. A young man named Axel Vilhelm Löfgren from Östmark in Värmland came to Helena in 1890, and during the years 1895–1909 he was followed by three brothers and five sisters. All of them traveled singly, having decided to emigrate as soon as they felt old enough. All five sisters married and remained in the Helena district.

One of the Swedish settlers at Anaconda, John Dragstedt from the city of Kungsbacka, south of Gothenburg, had come to America with his parents at the age of 16. In Iowa he married Caroline Seline from Stockholm, who had been brought to the United States as an infant, and at Anaconda they had two sons who became outstanding specialists in the medical field. Lester R. Dragstedt (b. 1893) was in 1923–25 professor of physiology at the Northwestern University Medical School, and after that he served the University of Chicago for 35 years as professor of surgery. After decades of research he introduced in 1943 a new surgical technique which greatly improved the treatment of duodenal ulcers and became known in some European countries as the "Dragstedt operation." He has also discovered a new hormone. In 1959 he moved to the University of Florida in Gainesville as research professor of surgery. Numerous professional associations, including the Royal College of Surgeons of England and the Swedish Surgical Society, elected him an honorary member. He visited Sweden several times. His younger brother, Carl Albert Dragstedt (b. 1895), served from 1926 to 1968 as professor of pharmacology at the Northwestern University Medical School in Evanston, Illinois, and made significant contributions to that science. Like Lester R. Dragstedt, he became chairman of his department. At Anaconda, their father had charge of a large repair shop and designed mining machinery that was used in the frozen ground of Alaska.

In the fall of 1911 a 20-year-old Swede named J. Hugo Aronson (b. 1891), raised on a ten-acre tenant farm at Gällstad in the province of Västergötland, landed in Boston and, without knowing any English whatsoever, went to work for a secondhand furniture store near that city. The next two-and-a-half years he saw America on the tramp, picking up temporary work where he could, and in the summer of 1914 he arrived in Montana, where he was put off a freight train by a brakeman. A year later he was a landowner, and after army service in France during the First World War followed by a few years in Wyoming, he settled again in Montana and made a successful career as an oil-rig builder, trucker, rancher, and banker. Becoming known as the "Galloping Swede," he founded a community named Gallop City in northern Montana.

After many years as a member of the state legislature, Aronson served as governor of Montana from 1953 to 1960. Magazine articles made him nationally known, and in Europe the Voice of America broadcast the story of his life. During one of his visits to Sweden, in 1959, he had a long audience with King Gustav VI Adolf, who remembered well his tour of Montana and the Yellowstone National Park in 1926 when he was crown prince.

Some of those in Montana who were opposed to Hugo Aronson as governor said that his greatest asset as a politician was his being rough and uncut. In an autobiography that was published in Montana in 1971, Aronson wrote: "My life has been a rough and rugged road. Without formal education, I have been in some very embarrassing positions. But taking a long over-all look backward and thinking about how good America has been to me, I think I'd choose the same route." In 1925–33 Montana had a governor of Swedish parentage, John E. Erickson, who had grown up in Kansas and before his election served as a district judge. In 1969–72 Forrest H. Anderson served as governor, after having been attorney general for many years and, before that, an associate justice of the Supreme Court of Montana. His father was born in Sweden and his mother in Ireland, a combination that has been relatively common.

In Idaho, Donald W. Samuelson, of Swedish extraction, served as governor from 1966 to 1970. He was born in Illinois and went to college at Galesburg.

The Swedish-born populations of Nevada, Arizona, and New Mexico were concentrated in the mining towns and the irrigation centers. In 1920, according to the U.S. census, 860 Swedes lived in Arizona, which had the highest total. In 1910, Nevada reported some 700 Swedes and New Mexico 365. In 1970 Arizona had increased its count to nearly 1,000.

24

On the Pacific

The migration to the Northwest comes alive in 1880s, culminates in early 1900s

THE influx of Swedes into the Pacific Northwest did not assume larger proportions until the 1880s, when the transcontinental railroad had been completed, and it did not reach its highest level until the early 1900s. For the state of Washington, the U.S. census reports showed about 650 Swedish-born people in 1880, more than 10,000 in 1890, nearly 13,000 in 1900, and about 32,000 in 1910. After that, the number rose further to nearly 35,000 in 1920. At that time the Swedes made up 14 percent of the foreign-born population. Most of the settlers in the Northwest did not come directly from Sweden but had lived for some time in other parts of the United States, in particular the Middle West.

The first Swedes in the Northwest were trappers and traders in the service of the Hudson's Bay Company or the Russian American Company. Many of the 90-odd Swedish-born who according to the U.S. census of 1860 lived in the present states of Washington and Oregon had come from California after the gold rush by the middle of the century. Others had trekked to the Pacific Coast from the Midwest over the Oregon Trail. Quite a few Swedish sailors jumped ship in the ports of the Northwest.

The Puget Sound country, with its long coastline and numerous islands, and the lower Columbia River Valley attracted most of the

19th-century Swedish settlers. To begin with, they played particularly important parts in farming, fishing, and lumbering. Many of the first model farms in the Northwest were built by immigrants from Sweden, and commercial fishing on the Pacific Coast was largely developed by Swedes and other Scandinavians. Toward the end of the 1800s the Swedish immigrants began to contribute more as mechanics and engineers, builders, and businessmen, while their sons and daughters to an increasing extent turned toward the learned professions or public service.

One of the first Swedish pioneers in the state of Washington, Nicholas Delin, practically founded the city of Tacoma. Other early settlers were Peter Friberg, who after an adventurous life as a sailor built a cabin at Puget Sound in the late 1850s, and Fredrik Landsten or Fred Landstone, who came from San Francisco to Port Discovery in 1861 and later made his home at Poulsbo on Liberty Bay in Kitsap County, west of Seattle and Puget Sound. On the same shore are the communities of Scandia, where three brothers from the north-central Swedish province of Medelpad were among the first settlers, and Pearson, named after a Swede who was its first homesteader. The state of Washington has some 50 place-names of Swedish origin.

The first Swedish-born shipbuilder on record in the Northwest was Ole Engblom (1823–90) from Attmar in Medelpad. After nearly 20 years at sea, finally as captain of a schooner on the Pacific, he came to Puget Sound in 1864 and began to build ships first at Port Orchard and then at Port Blakely. In 1870 he moved to Seattle. In the early 1900s, shipyards owned by immigrants from Sweden were to be found in nearly all seaports in Washington. In Seattle, ships of many types were built at a yard owned since 1909 by Charles Fryberg, who in 1874, when he was three months old, had been brought to the West Coast by his parents from Sweden, and his younger brothers William and Henry.

In the early 1870s, immigrants from the province of Halland in southwestern Sweden, including Carl Johan Kilberg or Chilberg (b. 1818) and Olof Pålsson or Polson (1833–1903), were among the first settlers near present-day La Conner in the delta of the Skagit River in northwestern Washington. Chilberg had come to America with his family as early as 1846, and before moving to La Conner he had lived at Ottumwa, Iowa, most of the time. Polson had been a leader in his home district in Halland and had emigrated after having lost his farm in a fire; he first settled at Ottumwa, where he was joined by his wife and seven children.

Other immigrants from all parts of Sweden, most of whom had already been farming in the Middle West, joined Chilberg, Polson, and other pioneers at La Conner. A number of highly productive farms were developed, and the Skagit Valley became an important agricultural area as well as the largest Scandinavian settlement in the Evergreen State. The city of Mount Vernon was, and remains, its commercial center. Somewhat farther south lies Cedarhome, the hub of a district where about half of the population was of Swedish stock, while most of the other settlers had come from Denmark and Norway. One John Anderson from the island of Hisingen at Gothenburg came there in 1879 and was followed by other Swedes, many of whom were born in the northwestern province of Jämtland. To settlers who had come directly from Sweden the fertility of the Skagit area seemed like a fairy tale.

By the middle of the 1870s the Swedish settlers in the Pacific Northwest had become so numerous that the Augustana Synod sent out two ministers to study their religious needs. The first Swedish Lutheran congregation in Washington was organized in 1881 at La Conner on the Skagit River. The Swedish Baptists, Methodists, and Mission Friends also established their first churches during the 1880s. An attempt to start a Swedish-language newspaper was made in 1885 in Seattle by Hans Lagerlöf, a relative of Selma Lagerlöf, who in 1909 became Sweden's first Nobel prize winner in literature. Ventures of the same type followed at Tacoma, Spokane, and Bellingham. In 1934 four newspapers were combined under one name, *Svenska Posten*, which was still published at Seattle in the 1970s.

One of the legendary pioneers of the Northwest, K. O. Erickson (1864–1954), had been only 12 years old when he left his home near Mora on Lake Siljan in the province of Dalarna. First he became a sailor, and later on a gold miner in Australia and New Zealand. En route to Alaska in the spring of 1888, he came to the Olympic Peninsula, and there he settled as a fur trader among the Indians on the Quillayute River, near the Pacific. In four different villages he established fur stores, calling the central one Mora in honor of his birthplace. He learned the Indian language and became an honorary chief of the Quillayute tribe. At Port Angeles on the north shore of the peninsula he founded one of the first successful savings and loan associations in the country. Erickson finally became widely known in Sweden, which he visited twice in his old age. He donated considerable amounts to the Swedish Boy and Girl Scout Association and to the town of Mora.

In the Puget Sound country, the Swedish-born population gradually became concentrated in and around the larger cities, Seattle, Tacoma, Everett, and Bellingham. In eastern Washington most of the immigrants from Sweden settled in the Spokane area, and in the south-central section many chose the Yakima Valley, now famous for its apples and other fruits. At one time the greater part of the population of the town of Selah, just north of the city of Yakima, was of Swedish birth. Among prominent businessmen of Swedish origin in Yakima were Alexander Miller (b. 1856) from Rönås in Skåne, who arrived in 1887, and A. E. Larson (1862–1934) from Minnesota, who had started as a lumberjack in the 1880s and in the early 1900s was one of the most successful citizens in central Washington. Larson became president and Miller vice president of the company owning the famous Sunshine silver mine at Kellogg, Idaho. Both took an increasingly active part in community affairs.

Among the early Swedish settlers in Seattle were three sons of the above-mentioned Carl Johan Chilberg, Andrew, James P., and Nelson, who in 1875 established a grocery business there. Andrew Chilberg (1845–1934), who was born at Knäred in Halland and the following year came to America with his parents, played a notable part in Seattle's development as a banker and city treasurer, and was named consul for Sweden and Norway. Nelson Chilberg (b. 1840), who spent many years in Alaska, had a son, John Edward Chilberg, born in 1867 in Iowa, who became engaged in banking, mining, and transportation in Alaska. One of Seattle's leading citizens, he served in 1909–10 as president of the Alaska-Yukon-Pacific Exposition, held on grounds which became part of the University of Washington campus. Much of the preparatory work was done by another Swede, Otto Godfrey Killander or Chealander (b. 1868), who was a native of the city of Kalmar. The exhibition included a small Swedish building, whose contents were regarded as better than its exterior.

Another business pioneer in Seattle, Nils B. Nilsson or Nels B.

Nelson (1854–1907), arrived in 1891, two years after the Big Fire, and opened a small furniture store which became the beginning of one of the largest department stores in the West, known as Frederick and Nelson. Nelson, who was born near Kristianstad in the province of Skåne, had come to America in 1873 and had first settled on a farm in Colorado. In the early 1900s one of the leading attorneys in Seattle was Carl Johan Smith, who had come to America in 1883 at the age of 18 and had first practiced law in Butte, Montana. In Seattle he became state chairman of the committee on constitution and citizenship of the American Bar Association.

An immigrant from Emmislöv in Skåne, Niles Henry Nicholson, who had come to America in 1889 and begun as a stonecutter, cabinetmaker, and janitor in the East, became a prominent physician and the founder of the Seattle Pediatric Society. The foremost welfare institution of Swedish origin in the state of Washington, the Swedish Hospital in Seattle, was founded in 1908 by Dr. Nils August Johansson (1872–1946). Coming from Lund, the university town in south Sweden, he arrived in America in 1893 to visit the World's Columbian Exposition in Chicago, and remained to attend the medical school at the University of Colorado. He moved to Seattle in 1906.

A Swede named Charles J. Erickson (1852–1937), born in Hudene Parish in Västergötland, was for many years the leading contractor in the Pacific Northwest, where he arrived in 1889 after nine years in Chicago. He erected buildings of all kinds as well as railroads and sawmills, graded miles of streets in Seattle, and laid sewers and water mains. In 1909–11 he built four dry docks for the U.S. Navy at the Bremerton yard near Seattle, and during the First World War the ten largest steel ships produced in the Northwest during the war period. About 1910 he owned an 18th-century estate in Sweden, Lindö, some 40 miles south of Stockholm.

Several contractors of Swedish birth specialized in the construction of railroads. With the help of 5,000 men, Axel Holman built the Chicago, Milwaukee, St. Paul and Pacific Railroad across the Cascade Mountains. Alone or in partnership with others, Charles J. Johnson, who had started as a pick-and-shovel man, constructed over 300 miles of railroads. They included 80 miles through the Cascade Mountains, two-thirds of which had to be built through rock, involving the blasting of four long tunnels and the construction of many bridges.

Among persons of Swedish descent who have been elected to Congress was Monrad C. Wallgren, born in Iowa, who was a member of the House from 1933 to 1941 and then served in the Senate until 1945 when he resigned to become governor of the state of Washington. Warren G. Magnuson, who became a U.S. senator in 1944, was born in Minnesota of Swedish-Norwegian farmers.

The Swedish Club of Seattle, founded in 1892, is one of the most active organizations of its kind in the United States. In the early 1970s it had about 7,000 members, including many who hailed from Norway, Denmark, Finland, and Iceland. Since 1946, consistent efforts have been made in Seattle to gather material and other information about the Swedish pioneers in the Northwest. The collection, called the Swedish Archives, is based at the library of the University of Washington.

Swedish pioneers in the forest industry of the Northwest, including six brothers

IN THE Pacific Northwest, immigrants from Sweden have played a particularly important part in the development of the forest industry.

A Swede from the island of Gotland in the Baltic Sea, Nikolaus Dalin or Nicholas Delin, became by the middle of the 1800s the first white man to settle on land within the present city limits of Tacoma, which has been called the "Forest Products Capital of America." In 1852 he built a water-powered sawmill there, but the outbreak of an Indian war three years later drove him and his family away. He had come to California in 1849 by way of Cape Horn and had then continued to Puget Sound.

In the late 1800s and early 1900s, Swedish immigrants developed many of the sawmills and other forest industries in the Tacoma area south of Puget Sound. The first Swedish secular organization in the Northwest, now known as Valhalla, was founded at Tacoma in 1884.

Nils Anderson (1860–1941) from Ursviken in northern Sweden, now part of the city of Skellefteå, arrived in the late 1870s as a sailor, began to operate his own logging business and became a recognized leader in the life of Puget Sound. He logged successively with oxen, horses, overhead cables and motor trucks, using more modern methods as they became available. His daughter, Pearl Anderson Wanamaker (b. 1899), became state representative and senator, introducing or sponsoring progressive legislation concerning education and social welfare, and she then served for many years, 1941–57, as state superintendent of public instruction. She was elected president of both the National Education Association and the National Council of Chief State School Officers.

To some extent, at least, Nils Anderson must have been responsible for the arrival of six of his nephews from Ursviken, who together made industrial history in the state of Washington. First came Ossian Anderson (1891–1942), who was to play the leading part. He arrived in Seattle in 1910, and after a few years of training he joined his uncle in the logging business. His elder brothers, Arthur (1888–1939) and Sten (1890–1925), had come to New York in 1906 but did not settle in the Northwest until 1919–20. Edward (b. 1893) and Karl (b. 1895) arrived at about the same time, after several years in Iowa, and so did the sixth brother, Olof (b. 1898), who traveled from Sweden without any intermediate stops. Their two sisters, Amy and Lilly, also came, and in 1920 both parents, Anton and Matilda Anderson, followed their children to America. A seventh brother remained to look after the family's lumber interests in Sweden, but he took part in reunions of the Anderson clan in the American Northwest.

In 1919 Ossian Anderson and two of his brothers, who had settled at Olympia, bought a modest sawmill above Tumwater Falls somewhat to the south, which was the beginning of the far-flung Anderson Brothers organization. After having launched more extensive logging operations, they built a new and larger sawmill farther south of Olympia, and in 1922 they began the production of prefabricated houses, known as Tumwater Ready-Cut Homes, which were sold all over the United States and also shipped abroad.

In the 1920s the six brothers helped develop the rapidly growing cellulose industry in the Pacific Northwest. Enlisting the aid of ten other men in Olympia, they built a sulphite-pulp mill at Anacortes on Fidalgo Island in Puget Sound, 70 miles north of Seattle. It was the first producer of chemical wood pulp on the Pacific Coast to use waste wood, and also the first to ship pulp out of the Northwest. In 1926 the same stockholders built a larger plant at Bellingham farther north, and the two pioneer mills were later merged into the Puget Sound Pulp and Timber Company, which built a big bleached-pulp plant at Everett, 20 miles north of Seattle. Ossian Anderson, who was the principal organizer of the new ventures, became president of Puget Sound Pulp and Timber Company and a director of many other companies and organizations. In 1936 he built the first bleached-kraft mill at Tacoma and in 1937 a new sulphite mill at Bellingham. By 1940 the plants built under his leadership produced 45 percent of the large pulp production of Washington State.

Importing equipment from Sweden, the Anderson brothers in 1928 built the first gang-saw mill in the Northwest. The Swedish gang-saw mill operation made it profitable to process logs which formerly were either left to rot on the ground or burned as scrap, thus proving a boon to conservation. Ossian Anderson himself was a staunch advocate of conservation of natural resources and often served as spokesman for the whole pulp and paper industry. In 1933 he sent a letter to President Franklin D. Roosevelt on the conservation of forests and their use in the fight against unemployment.

The Swedish gang-saw equipment was gradually adopted by many mills in the American Northwest, as well as in British Columbia. In introducing it, the Anderson brothers cooperated with two engineers from Sweden. One of them, David Dalin (1892–1975), lived in the United States from 1911 to 1938 and then became president of the Swedish company making the equipment, Svenska Maskinverken at Södertälje, south of Stockholm. His wife, the former Ebba Dahlin (1896–1956), had from 1928 to 1936 been an assistant professor of history at the University of Washington, and in Sweden she became known as an interpreter of American literature and ideas.

At Enumclaw, 20 miles east of Tacoma, an immigrant from Borgstena in Västergötland, Carl Magnus Hanson (d. 1906), and his three sons founded in 1898 the White River Lumber Company, which became one of the largest lumber concerns in the state of Washington. In 1930 about one-third of the town's 2,000-odd inhabitants were of Swedish stock, the forest province of Ångermanland being particularly well represented. Carl Magnus Hanson and his two eldest sons had come to America in 1883, homesteading near Seattle two years later. An immigrant from the city of Sundsvall in the province of Medelpad, Edward Emil Westman (b. 1887), who arrived in 1909 and started as a sawmill worker in Tacoma, moved to Olympia in 1921 and helped build up the plywood industry in the Northwest.

The most legendary businessman of Swedish origin in the forest industry of the Northwest, Alfred H. Anderson (1854–1914), was born at La Crosse, Wisconsin, where his father, Måns or Mons Anderson, prospered as a manufacturer of clothing for lumberjacks. A graduate of the University of Wisconsin, he married the daughter of a prominent lumberman, Agnes H. Healey, and in 1885 they moved to the Pacific Northwest. As a member of the second Washington legislature in 1890–91 he played a leading part in establishing the present campus of the University of Washington, and he later helped improve its resources. "It was his vigorous support that was very largely responsible for the fact that the University of Washington is today one of the largest in America," a spokesman for the university has observed. In the panic of 1893 Alfred Anderson lost most of his wealth, but in the early 1900s he had become the most prominent individual lumberman in the Northwest. He was a huge, flamboyant man, weighing about 300 pounds. A gigantic bathtub ordered by him for his mansion in Seattle was duplicated for the benefit of President William H. Taft. His widow donated a new building, named the Alfred H. Anderson Hall, to the University of Washington as a home for the College of Forestry, now known as the College of Forest Resources.

An outstanding teacher and research professor at the College of Forestry was Bror H. Grondal, born in 1889 of Swedish settlers in Texas and a graduate of Bethany College at Lindsborg, Kansas, where his six brothers and sisters also studied. He became president of the National Forest Products Research Society, and was one of the few American citizens who held life membership in the Swedish Society of Foresters. Among Swedish-born forest experts in the Northwest was Axel J. F. Brandstrom (1898–1968) from Umeå in the far north, who, after teaching at the College of Forestry in Seattle, became a senior forest economist in the U.S. Forest Service and then the chief forester of one of the largest forest industries. A graduate of the Stockholm Institute of Technology, Lage Wernstedt (1878–1959), who came to the United States in 1902 and studied forestry at Yale, spent most of his active life in the U.S. Forest Service in the Pacific Northwest. Inventions of new instruments gave him a place among the pioneers in aerial photogrammetry.

Among noted specialists in other fields than forestry at the University of Washington were Carl Edward Magnusson, born in 1872 of Swedish immigrants in Minnesota, who in 1906 became professor and head of the department of electrical engineering and from 1917 to 1929 served as dean of the College of Engineering; and George A. Lundberg, born in 1895 of Swedish settlers in North Dakota, who, after many years at Bennington College in Vermont, from 1945 to 1953 served as professor and head of the department of sociology. He was elected president of the American Sociological Society and of the Sociological Research Association.

Two Seattle Swedes in industry and technology, and a journalist-philosopher

IN 1889 a native of the province of Värmland, Charles S. Johnson from Hammarön at Karlstad, who had been in America since 1881, settled in Seattle where he became engaged in the building trade. He married Hanna Gustavson from the tiny city of Åmål in the neighboring province of Dalsland, and they had a son, Philip Gustav Johnson (1894–1944), who became one of the industrial leaders in the Northwest.

Already as a young boy, Philip Johnson seemed fascinated by machinery. While still studying engineering at the University of Washington, he was in 1917 recruited by William E. Boeing who had just established a small shop on Lake Union. By 1920 Johnson was named plant superintendent, and from 1926 to 1933 he served as president of the company. In 1931–33 he was also president of United Air Lines, the first transcontinental operator of planes flying passengers, mail, and freight on a regular schedule.

After having helped organize the Trans-Canada Airlines, Philip Johnson resumed in 1939 the presidency of the Boeing Corporation, which was headed for a rapid expansion during the Second World War. In recognition of his services to the community he was in 1943 voted Seattle's leading citizen. In 1944, when he died at the age of 49, he was awarded posthumously the President's Certificate of Merit for outstanding services in the design and mass production of the B-17 Flying Fortress and the B-29 Superfortress. Thousands of people of Swedish birth or parentage worked for Boeing. Even by the middle of the century quite a few engineers came over from Sweden to help staff its research and development laboratories and factories.

In 1904, a 29-year-old Swede named John Isaksson or Isaacson (1875–1939) came to Seattle. He had worked for some years in his

"I had to pinch myself in the arm to make certain I was not dreaming," Crown Prince Gustav Adolf said about the "Swedes Day" and New Sweden Tercentenary celebration at Minnesota State Fair Grounds on Sunday, July 17, 1938. Some 100,000 Minnesotans were assembled, and the future monarch addressed them in Swedish (pp. 420–421, 705, 790).

1. "Most Americans knew Gustav V of Sweden as the ramrod-straight old man who played tennis," a New York newspaper observed when the monarch passed away in 1950 at the age of 92. In the world of sport he was known as "Mr. G." He played tennis until he was 88 (p. 747).
2. The Triton Pool, with sculpture by Carl Milles, at Cranbrook Academy of Art, Bloomfield Hills, Mich. Cranbrook, where Milles served in 1931–50, has the largest collection of Milles's work in the world, outside of Millesgården in Stockholm, now a national museum (pp. 719–723).

1. Carl Sandburg, his wife, Lillian, and Swedish Ambassador Erik Boheman (right) in Chicago on Sandburg's 75th birthday in 1953. From 1945 until his death in 1967, Sandburg lived in North Carolina on Connemara Farm, once described by him as "a helluva baronial estate for an old socialist" and now a national historic site. The main goat barn was called the "Swedish House," while two large oak trees were named for Abraham Lincoln and Robert E. Lee. Sandburg's parents came from Sweden (pp. 228, 645–647, 748). 2. In 1948 President Truman awarded Prince Bertil of Sweden the Legion of Merit, Degree of Commander, "for exceptionally meritorious conduct in the performance of outstanding services to the Government of the United States." Prince Bertil had come to America as leader of a delegation to the Swedish Pioneer Centennial (pp. 704–705, 790–791).

Instead of trying to attract attention to itself, the Swedish pavilion at the World's Fair in New York in 1939 had been designed so as to place the chief emphasis on its contents. The pavilion as a whole evoked enthusiastic comments in American newspapers and magazines. At one corner stood a white marble statue of Engelbrekt, medieval champion of national independence, sculptured by Carl Eldh in 1935 for the tiny city of Arboga where Sweden's first national assemblies were held in the 1400s (pp. 706–708).

The international reputation of Swedish crystal and other industrial arts was established in the 1920s. The engraved bowl, the "Bacchus Festival" from Orrefors, is of that period. Designed by Simon Gate, it won one of Sweden's 35 Grand Prix at an international exhibiton in Paris in 1925. An American collector ordered a replica in 1975. Most Swedish glassworks, including Kosta, Boda, and Strömbergshyttan, are in the province of Småland (pp. 689–691).

The Sofia Girls, a gymnastic team from Stockholm, performing at Rockefeller Center Plaza in New York in 1967. During the period 1939–71 they made eight tours of the United States. Other Swedish groups that have toured America include the Malmö Girls and the Idla Girls, both led by refugees from Estonia. Both appeared on the popular Ed Sullivan TV Show. In the late 1800s and early 1900s Boston was the leading center of Swedish gymnastics in America (pp. 534–537).

Not many emigrants were able to bring looms with them to the New World, but they did bring their skills and their interest and joy in handwork. In the basic American literature on handweaving today, the influence of traditions from Sweden, particularly in the patterns, is obvious. The recent increase of interest in weaving in America draws heavily on Swedish traditional techniques but is also much influenced by contemporary Scandinavian work. In Sweden, handwoven fabrics and rugs are common in the homes and also found in many public buildings.

1. This self-portrait was painted by Anders Zorn in Paris in 1896, when he was about to make the second of his seven trips to the United States. Among Americans who sat for him were three Presidents, many captains of industry and finance, and many elegant ladies. Zorn was born and died at historic Mora on Lake Siljan in the province of Dalarna (pp. 660–661). 2. Carl Milles at work on *St. Martin of Tours*, or the William Volker Memorial Fountain, which a few years after his death in 1955 was dedicated in the new Cultural Center at Kansas City, Mo. Nearly all of Milles's 100-odd monuments and fountains are in the United States and Sweden (pp. 721–722).

1. A somewhat weather-beaten replica of the New Sweden Monument at Wilmington, Del., is in Gothenburg harbor. The first Swedish ships bound for America sailed from Gothenburg in late 1637 (p. 40). 2. A granite monument at Sunne in Värmland, shaped like that province, is dedicated to kinsmen overseas. It stands on land belonging to Rottneros Manor which Selma Lagerlöf, in 1909 winner of the Nobel prize for literature, in her best-known novel, *Gösta Berling's Saga*, renamed Ekeby (pp. 668–670).

1. Gustaf de Laval, who in 1878 produced the first centrifugal cream separator and in the 1880s developed the first practical steam turbine (pp. 367, 612–613). 2. Alfred Nobel, who invented dynamite and other high explosives, and in a will of 1895 donated funds for the Nobel prizes (pp. 604–608).

Ernst F. W. Alexanderson came to America in 1901 and died in 1975 at the age of 97. In 1906 his high-frequency alternator made possible the first voice radio broadcast, and in 1927 he gave the first home television demonstration in his home in Schenectady, N.Y. Like numerous other immigrants from Sweden he was a graduate of one of that country's institutes of technology (pp. 580–582).

father's smithy at Indal in the province of Medelpad, and then spent 12 years as a blacksmith in railroad and mining-machinery repair shops in Montana. In Seattle he established a metal shop of his own, with one employee. This was the beginning of the Isaacson Iron Works, which before long became one of the largest steel industries on the Pacific Coast, employing 400–500 men and making equipment for ships, such as anchors and propeller shafts, structural steel, bulldozers, and other heavy machinery. In 1944, when several thousand men were employed and the founder had been succeeded by his son Henry, one of the Liberty ships of the Second World War was named in his honor.

One of the first Swedish immigrants to take an active interest in the history of the Swedes in the Pacific Northwest was Ernst Teofil Skarstedt (1857–1929), one of the most colorful and gifted of the hundreds of Swedes in America who became journalists and writers in their mother tongue. He wrote three books about Oregon, Washington, and their Swedish populations, and these as well as his numerous newspaper and magazine articles helped attract many Swedes to the Northwest. The states of Washington and Oregon he liked better than any other section of the country.

Skarstedt was the son of a Lutheran minister in the western province of Bohuslän, who finally became professor of theology at the University of Lund. His relations with his father, who in the first place wanted a more resolute ambition in the young man, were often strained — a not uncommon condition which contributed to many emigrations from Sweden at that time. After unfinished studies at the Institute of Technology in Stockholm, he came to the United States in early 1879, planning to settle as a farmer and philosopher as soon as possible. From Minnesota he moved to Kansas, and there, as already mentioned, he tried to publish a Swedish-language weekly at Lindsborg. The next year, 1880, he began as a newspaperman in Chicago.

After that, Skarstedt worked for one Swedish-language publication after another, from San Francisco and Seattle to New York. Like many if not most of his colleagues, he offered newly arrived immigrants and visitors from Sweden invaluable help. But he also earned his living as a farmer, shipyard worker, music teacher, or photographer in the Pacific Northwest, and in California he spent some time as a student of agriculture, bookseller, and chorus conductor. He was a productive author on a variety of subjects as well as a poet, and he has been described as a good husband and father, a philosopher and hermit, a great nature lover, a talented violinist, and an apostle of reason and justice. Tolstoy's Christian radicalism seems to have been one of the lasting influences on him. A large book collection, the beginning of which had been destroyed in the San Francisco fire of 1906, was his only material asset of importance. He spent his last years at Friday Harbor on San Juan Island, north of Puget Sound. A son, Marcus Skarstedt, became professor of mathematics in Whittier College at Los Angeles.

Together with his first wife, Anna, who had come over from Bohuslän to marry him, and their children, Skarstedt in 1885–86 spent seven months in his native country. He met many interesting people and gathered other pleasant memories, but his main impression was that Sweden in most respects was lagging far behind the United States. "And therefore," he wrote in an autobiographical book, *Vagabond och Redaktör*, which was published in Seattle in 1914, "nothing made me as mad as when I heard people, who knew nothing at all about America, make cocksure comments on its cultural conditions, deplore the Swedish emigrants, and denigrate the advantages these had gained by moving to the New World." Thirty years later, in 1916, Skarstedt visited Sweden as a member of a large group of Swedish-American newspapermen who had been invited by the government, and he then found the country decidedly more progressive, despite the strains of the First World War. One day the journalists were received in audience by the monarch. King Gustav V, Skarstedt wrote, must have been surprised by my unconventional dress, but he "spoke to me in the same friendly way as to the others, all of whom were in tails, with white tie."

Portland the hub of the Oregon Swedes — Large sawmills built on the Pacific

THE Swedish-born population in Oregon also increased sharply first in the 1880s, from less than 1,000 to nearly 4,000, and then during the years 1900–1910 when it rose from about 4,500 to more than 10,000. In the early 1900s, the Lewis and Clark Exposition of 1905 and the activities of the Oregon State Commission of Immigration helped attract Swedish immigrants in growing numbers. The commission's promotional efforts seem to have been beamed primarily to the Scandinavian and German peoples.

The first Swede known to have settled in Oregon was a shoemaker by the name of Carl Magnus or Charles M. Wiberg, born in 1820 in the city of Norrköping in Östergötland. After having lived in London for three years, he arrived in New York in 1845 and settled at Milwaukee, Wisconsin, but lost his business in a city fire and came in the summer of 1852 to Portland, which had just been incorporated as a town. He reached Oregon after an arduous journey via the Isthmus of Panama. Another early Swedish settler was John Nasburg (b. 1839), who came from Illinois and in late 1852 reached The Dalles on the Columbia River, which was the end of the Oregon Trail. In 1854 one Andrew Johnson was cast away from a vessel outside Coos Bay, and the next year he helped build a fort at nearby Empire.

In 1875 a Swede from Kansas, N. F. Palmquist, came to Powell Valley, 14 miles east of Portland, which became the first more important Swedish settlement in Oregon. In 1906 an Oregon Swedish land company bought 2,000 acres some 25 miles southeast of Portland for the purpose of establishing a Swedish colony to be called Carlsborg, now commonly known as Colton, and within ten years the Swedish land holdings had increased to 11,000 acres. A Lutheran minister in Portland, Carl J. Renhard (1870–1946) from Höreda in Småland, was the moving spirit in this project. He won the support of many Swedish settlers in eastern Nebraska, including relatively well-to-do Nels Peter Hult and his family.

Warren in the Columbia River Valley, some 20 miles northwest of Portland, is the center of another agricultural region, which in the early 1900s was populated by Swedes and Swedish-speaking Finns. Its leading promoter, C. J. Larson, had had to give up his farm in western Kansas during the drought years of the 1890s. Several settlements which specialize in fruit farming were also developed by immigrants from Sweden. In the wheat-growing country in north-central Oregon, some of the largest farms were owned and operated by Swedes who started arriving there in the 1870s.

For decades the forest industry teemed with Swedes, ranging from lumberjacks to sawmill operators. By the turn of the century,

Carl or Charles A. Smith, who had come to Minneapolis in 1867 at the age of 14, extended his rapidly growing business activities to the Pacific Coast. He then built three sawmills in the Coos Bay area in Oregon, one of which was the largest in the world at that time. Box factories and other wood-processing plants were established at Bay Point in California, 40 miles north of San Francisco. From Coos Bay, sawn lumber was carried to Bay Point by ships named *Nann Smith*, *Adeline Smith*, and *Myrtle Smith* after Charles A. Smith's daughters. Nothing in the nomenclature was reminiscent of Sweden, yet the family was wholly Swedish. Mrs. Smith's maiden name was Johanna Anderson. The name of Mr. Smith's father in Östergötland was Wild, which in Swedish calls to mind a humble but valiant soldier of the old school.

In 1930, no less than 44 percent of the some 11,000 Swedes in Oregon lived in its largest city, Portland. From the beginning, a large proportion of the Swedish settlers there became engaged in the building and wood-working trades, while others entered various engineering fields. Three bridges over the Willamette River in Portland, for instance, were built by contractors from Sweden employing Swedish labor. A Swedish-trained engineer named Gustaf Bernhard Hegardt, born in 1859 at Domö in Västergötland and an emigrant in 1880, came to Oregon from Chicago in 1888, helped build the jetties at the mouth of the Columbia River, and played in the period 1909–26 a leading part in the creation of Portland's modern port facilities. In the late 1920s and early 1930s he led the construction of the modern port at Oakland, California, and the pioneering Oakland Municipal Airport. In 1928 he became president of the American Association of Port Authorities.

In Portland as in several other American cities, one of the early Swedish leaders was also an emissary of Swedish song and a widely known authority on music. Johan Ludwig Wallin (1875–1936), who was born at Helsingborg in south Sweden, came to Portland with his parents in the late 1880s and began earning his living as a typesetter and journalist. His main interest was music, and as the leading critic of the *Oregon Journal* and a promoter and organizer of musical activities he wielded influence and spread inspiration throughout the Pacific Northwest. The old Portland Opera Association as well as the Portland Junior Symphony Orchestra, which won national recognition, received much valuable assistance. Wallin worked consistently for the musical education of the youth, and was largely responsible for the development of many noted or outstanding artists.

Another influential figure in the Swedish colony at Portland, Torgny Zakrison, was born at Gothenburg in 1850 and became a lawyer before his emigration in 1878. Via Central America, where an older brother had a coffee plantation, and San Francisco he came to Portland in 1880. He also developed business interests in the city of Astoria, near the Columbia River mouth. One of the Swedish pioneers there, Gustaf Holmes (b. 1845) from the province of Värmland, had emigrated from Sweden in 1867 and via Iowa and a homestead in Kansas came to Oregon in 1875. After five years as a fisherman on the Columbia he began operating canneries in Oregon and British Columbia, acquired real estate in Astoria and Portland, and became president of the Scandinavian American Bank.

Other Swedish immigrants, who when they arrived were young enough to receive a thorough education, made careers in the worlds of learning and science. Olof Larsell was only five years old when he came with his parents in 1891, from Rättvik on Lake Siljan in the province of Dalarna. After studies at a college in Oregon and at Northwestern University in Evanston, Illinois, followed by some temporary professorships, he served from 1921 to 1952 as professor of anatomy in the University of Oregon Medical School at Eugene. For many years he was also dean of the graduate division of the Oregon State System of Higher Education. Being actively interested in cultural relations with Sweden and a member of a learned society at Uppsala, he published biographical sketches of such Swedish anatomists as Olof Rudbeck, Anders Retzius, and the latter's son, Gustaf Retzius (1842–1919), who also won international fame and in 1893 received an honorary doctor's degree at Harvard University. In 1934, Larsell published in Baltimore a translation of the autobiographical notes of Jöns Jacob Berzelius, the famous chemist. In 1952 he moved to the University of Minnesota as professor of neuroanatomy, the nervous system being his leading specialty.

One of the first Swedes on the Pacific Coast to reach high public office was Albin Walter Norblad of Astoria, born at Malmö in the province of Skåne, who in 1929 as president of the State Senate became governor of Oregon by succession when the incumbent died.

During the First World War he was, like many other immigrants, gripped by an intense nationalism, and in the Oregon legislature he pushed through a bill that made it illegal to print practically anything in any language except English. The law was later declared unconstitutional.

The first Swedish congregation in Oregon was organized in 1879 at Portland by members of the Lutheran denomination. The Emanuel Hospital, today one of the largest medical centers of Swedish origin in America, was founded in 1912 by the Reverend Carl J. Renhard. The Reverend A. M. Green, who as superintendent for 21 years until 1938 was responsible for much of its success, had come to America in 1892 and had begun as a dishwasher in a hotel in Tacoma, Washington.

The first attempt to issue a Swedish-language newspaper in Oregon was made in Portland in 1890, but the beginning of lasting success did not come until 1908 when F. W. Lönegren, from Vederslöv near Växjö in Småland, founded *Oregon Posten*. Before leaving Sweden in 1889 at the age of 29, he had studied at the universities of Lund and Uppsala, and after his immigration he worked first as a teacher and then for Swedish-language newspapers in Minnesota. While most of the Swedish immigrants in Oregon in the early 1900s were moderately conservative Republicans, Lonegren's editorial policy leaned toward an anticapitalist attitude. Despite a constant need of more income, he always refused to accept liquor advertising. *Oregon Posten* played a part in raising educational standards in the Swedish immigrant community.

All of Sweden's 25 provinces were represented among the Swedish settlers in Oregon. One of the largest groups hailed from Värmland, whose dialects also were often heard in the state of Washington.

Swedo-Finnish governors in Russian Alaska — Historic gold strike in 1898

ALASKA, which is almost twice as large as the Scandinavian peninsula, has lured thousands of adventurous and robust Scandinavians to its shores. Sweden and Norway contributed some of Alaska's early white settlers, and Swedish Finns were among the very first pioneers there. Even in the 20th century the Nordic peoples have been well represented in Alaska. According to a census in 1939, Norwegians then made up its largest foreign-born group, followed by Swedes, Canadians, and Finns.

A Swede, Sven Waxell was, as previously mentioned, one of the discoverers of Alaska. Its recorded history began in July of 1741, when members of a Russian expedition led by Danish-born Vitus Bering, with Waxell as second in command and about to replace his ailing chief, landed on an island in the southeast of Alaska. Long newspaper articles about Waxell, "Alaska's forgotten man," appeared in the Alaskan press in the early 1970s. A canvas showing Vitus Bering, Sven Waxell and crew aboard their ship viewing the mountain they named St. Elias has been painted by one of Alaska's best-known artists, M. C. "Rusty" Heurlin, born at Kristianstad in south Sweden and in 1971 an honorary doctor of fine arts at the University of Alaska. It is part of a series of 18 paintings called *The Great Land*.

One of the leading pioneers in Alaska during its Russian era was a noted explorer, Baron Ferdinand von Wrangel, who from 1829 to 1835 served as governor of the territory and later, in 1840–49, as director of the Russian-American Company. At that time Sitka in southeastern Alaska, which had been established in 1799 as a fort and trading post, was by far the largest of the few white settlements. Its official name as the capital of Russian Alaska was Novo Archangelsk, or New Archangel.

Wrangel's foremost assistant in the 1830s was a Swedish Finn, Captain Adolph Etholén, who in 1840 took over as governor of Alaska. The ship on which he returned to Sitka after a visit to Finland also brought a dozen other Swedish-speaking Finns, including Etholén's young wife, born Margreth Sundvall, and a clergyman named Uno Cygnaeus (1810–88), who later became known as the father of Finland's modern school system.

In the early 1800s Sitka had become the principal port of the Pacific coast in America, and during the five years that Captain Etholén served as governor, Russia's American colony reached its fullest flowering. Steamships were built at the shipyard in Sitka, plows, spades, and other tools were made for the Spanish farmers in California, and bells were cast for the California missions, where many of them are still in use.

In 1840 a Lutheran mission was established at Sitka, and a school followed. In 1853 the congregation had about 150 members, most of them Swedish-speaking Finns and Indians. Even toward the end of the 1800s there were Indians in Alaska who could speak Swedish, having been taught this language in the Lutheran school at Sitka. A hospital was also built by Governor Etholén, who in 1845 returned home via Siberia and became an admiral in the Russian navy.

Among the Swedish Finns in Russian service who came to Sitka in the early 1850s was a naval officer named Hampus Furuhjelm (1821–1909), who, like other members of the same family, was descended from a Lutheran minister at Enköping west of Stockholm. After a few years he became chief of the Russian naval base at Ayan in the Sea of Okhotsk, north of Japan, and in 1858 he was appointed governor of Alaska.

To begin with, Hampus Furuhjelm returned to Finland and married Anna von Schoultz, the daughter of an adventurous Swede from Finland, Nils von Schoultz (1807–38), and his wife Ann Campbell (1813–62), born at Calcutta of Scottish parents. Before their marriage Von Schoultz had begun a career in the Svea Artillery Regiment in Stockholm, joined the Poles in their struggle against Russia, and served in the French Foreign Legion in Africa. After their wedding at Florence in Italy, Nils and Ann von Schoultz lived for two years, 1834–36, at Karlskrona in southeastern Sweden. He had then become a chemist, and in 1836 he went to the United States, probably hoping to market his inventions. At Salina, near Lake Onondaga in the state of New York, now part of the city of Syracuse, which in the 19th century supplied most of the salt used in the United States, he introduced new salt-refining methods. During a visit to Washington, D.C., in 1837, he declared his intention of becoming a U.S. citizen. The following year he joined "The Upper Canadian Rebellion," having been led to believe that the Canadian people were anxious for freedom and independence from Britain. After having commanded a small invading force in the legendary Battle of the Windmill, he was captured, condemned to death, and executed. A book about Nils von Schoultz, *Soldier of Fortune* by Ella Pipping, a great-granddaughter, was published in Boston in 1971.

In the summer of 1859 the Hampus Furuhjelms arrived at Sitka, and there they were welcomed by the new governor's younger brother Hjalmar Furuhjelm (1823–86), who was a mining engineer,

498

and the pastor of the Lutheran congregation, Gustaf Winter (1817–83), who had been named to that post in 1852. The first child in the Furuhjelm family, a girl who was christened Annie Fredrika (1859–1937), was born toward the end of the same year, and two boys came within the next few years. The roster of specialists at Sitka does not seem to have included a dentist, for when the Furuhjelms needed dental treatment, they traveled the 1,500 miles to San Francisco. Among the many seamen and other visitors from Finland who came to Sitka, most of them Swedish-speaking, were a young skipper, Lars Krogius (1832–90), and his wife, born Qvist. The name Krogius later became widely known in international shipping circles.

In the early summer of 1864 the Furuhjelms sailed from Sitka, and before returning to Finland, Hampus Furuhjelm served for several years as governor at Nikolayevsk on the Sea of Okhotsk, the capital of Eastern Siberia. Annie Fredrika Furuhjelm became, like her namesake Fredrika Bremer, a pioneer in the women's rights movement. One of her autobiographical books deals in part with life at Sitka, where she was born, and for which she often felt homesick. Her literary works found many readers also in Sweden. Among her best friends there were Selma Lagerlöf, Nobel prize winner in literature, and Ellen Key (1849–1926), who as a progressive educator and author had a deep influence on Swedish public opinion in the early 1900s. At the beginning of the century she denounced the Russification policy in Finland, which remained a Russian grand duchy until 1917. In 1918, Annie Furuhjelm's Alaskan-born brothers were executed by "Red Guards" during the war for independence in Finland, which also was a civil war.

In the Lutheran church at Sitka, service was conducted in English for the first time on October 13, 1867. Five days later Alaska was officially turned over to the United States which had purchased it from Russia for $7.2 million.

A native of the Baltic island of Gotland, Captain Ferdinand Westdahl (b. 1843) of San Francisco, was the first person born in Sweden to enter the interior of Alaska. In 1866 he was first mate on the barque *The Golden Gate* in an expedition to the distant Northwest. Three years later he made another journey to Alaska and was then able to travel up the Yukon about 1,500 miles.

In 1886 the Mission Friends in Sweden decided to begin missionary work in Alaska, and the following year the first two missionaries arrived in its northern wilderness. One of them, Axel E. Karlson (d. 1910), went to Unalakleet, a small Eskimo village on Norton Sound, south of Seward Peninsula in northwestern Alaska. Before coming to America he had worked for two years as a missionary in northern Russia, been arrested by the Russian police and brought to prison in Moscow but finally released after official Swedish interventions. In 1889 he was joined at Unalakleet by another missionary, August Anderson. At about the same time the whole Alaskan mission, which included five missionaries, was turned over by the Mission Friends of Sweden to their affiliate in America, the Evangelical Mission Covenant. In 1893 August Anderson and a missionary sent by the American Covenant, a Swede by the name of Nels O. Hultberg, established a station of Golovin Bay in the south of Seward Peninsula, 75 miles east of the site of Nome. The next year Hultberg was joined by his wife, who also was Swedish, and in 1897 by a former student at North Park College in Chicago, Peter H. Anderson, who began to teach in a mission school but soon, like Hultberg, was infected with gold fever.

In 1895 Hultberg had begun to search for gold on the Seward Peninsula, together with a miner by the name of George Johanson, and they had found traces of the yellow metal. Other expeditions were organized, but Hultberg himself seems to have made the first more remarkable find, in August of 1898. Somewhat later, however, he left Chinik for a year's furlough because of failing health.

Then, on September 22, 1898, three amateur prospectors from Sweden made a spectacular gold strike on Anvil Creek, a tributary of the Snake River, four miles inland from the beach on which the city of Nome later was built. The leader of the group was John Brynteson from Ärtemark Parish in the province of Dalsland, and the other two were Erik O. Lindblom from Dalarna, who had been a tailor in San Francisco and had come to Alaska on a whaler, and 20-year-old Jafet Lindeberg, one of the young men in charge of the reindeer imported to Alaska to augment the food supply. They soon became known as the "Three Lucky Swedes." Claims were also staked for Brynteson's traveling companion, John L. Hagelin, the teacher at Chinik, Peter H. Anderson, and two of the missionaries, Nels O. Hultberg and Axel E. Karlson. The latter and his wife left Alaska in 1899, but in 1901 they returned to Unalakleet where they worked as missionaries for nine years.

News of the Anvil Creek strike and other gold finds in the same section spread like wildfire, first through northern Alaska and then to other parts of North America. As soon as navigation opened in the spring of 1899, hundreds of people joined the first successful prospectors, and during the summer of 1900 the bleak Snake River area was the destination of Alaska's greatest gold stampede. Within seven weeks nearly 20,000 men, and several women, swarmed into Nome.

The Swedes who had made the first important gold strike in northern Alaska aroused bitter envy and were accused of having staked too many claims. Later they became involved in a costly legal battle, which jurists characterized as unparalleled in the history of American jurisprudence. Judge James Wickersham, who became one of the leaders in Alaska's development toward statehood, paid in his diary a warm tribute to the "independent vigorous character" of the three men who had located the rich Anvil Creek mines, and who, he added, despite their foreign birth and education were able to put up a successful fight for their rights.

John Brynteson (1871–1959), who led the triumphant expedition to Anvil Creek, had left his home in Sweden in 1887 at the age of 16. Working as a miner at Ishpeming, Michigan, he heard rumors about gold finds in Alaska, and after having arrived there he joined the mission of the Evangelical Mission Covenant of America. As a prospector for gold he was, like most others, at first disappointed. After having left Alaska in 1900, he married a Swedish-born girl and bought a fruit farm near San José, California. Six years later he returned to Sweden with his family and settled on an industrial estate, Svaneholm in southern Värmland, near the place where he was born. The people in the district, which soon began to prosper, called him the "Gold King."

The Evangelical Mission Covenant of America also became involved in protracted litigation, but some of the Anvil Creek gold helped it to expand and improve its educational and welfare activities. North Park College in Chicago, which had begun as an extremely modest school in Minneapolis, was able to construct three modern buildings, and a new Swedish Covenant hospital was built in the same city. In San Francisco, John Brynteson donated a property to the Covenant's seamen's mission. The first building was destroyed in the earthquake of 1906, but Brynteson then decided to erect a larger and better structure, known as Scandinavian Sailors' Home.

Hundreds of gold hunters from Sweden have tried their luck in other parts of Alaska, as well as in the Klondike area in the Yukon Territory, and several are still there. The most famous one was Karl Johan Andersson or Charles John Anderson (1859–1939), generally called Charlie and widely known as the "Lucky Swede," who in 1896 bought the legendary claim Number 29 on Eldorado Creek near Klondike River for 800 dollars, from three gentlemen who regarded their stake as worthless, and during the next three years took out gold valued at nearly 1.5 million dollars. Charlie Anderson, who has also been called the "Midas of the North" and the "Matador of Eldorado," paid the highest wages in the Klondike area. After having invested his wealth in real estate in San Francisco, he lost everything in the earth-quake and fire of 1906. Somewhat later he moved to Vancouver, British Columbia, and started working in a sawmill. He had emigrated from Sweden in the 1880s and lived in the United States for several years. Another Swede, John Erickson, who later spelled his name Erikson, was also among the successful pioneers in the Klondike region. He became a banker and newspaper publisher in Seattle, also operating mines in Nevada. He often visited Sweden, and in Värmland, where he was born, he bought an estate, Odenstad. Most of the Swedes who came to Klondike took part in the stampede of 1897–98. Both there and in Alaska the gold seekers from Sweden were widely regarded as hard-working and vigorous but somewhat comic and easily duped. Strangely enough, several of them became unusually successful.

Both the Klondike stampede and several of the gold rushes in Alaska were recorded by an itinerant photographer named Eric A. Hägg or Hegg (1867–1955), who was born at Bollnäs in the Swedish province of Hälsingland and had been brought to the United States as a child. His unique material is in the library of the University of Washington at Seattle. Books about the Alaska and Yukon gold hunts have depended on it for their illustrations.

At Goodnews Bay in the southwest of Alaska, Swedish explorers, who had come from the province of Jämtland, helped discover the most important platinum mine in North America. Most of the Swedes in Alaska became, however, farmers or fishermen. In 1934 the Federal government proposed group settlements as part of an emergency relief program, and the following year about 200 families sailed from Seattle to the Matanuska Valley, northeast of Anchorage. The settlers who remained there permanently were almost all of Scandinavian origin, and most of them had come from farms in the Middle West. In the 1960s Matanuska contributed about 70 percent of Alaska's total agricultural production, primarily milk, eggs, and vegetables. Among its first pioneers was Victor Falk with family, who came from Long Beach, California, in 1931 when the valley was a wilderness. His father had immigrated from Sweden and settled at Rock Island, Illinois.

A native of Värmland named Conrad Freeding (1869–1916), who came to Alaska the first time in 1897, became mayor of Nome and, in 1913, a member of Alaska's first territorial legislature. Fairbanks, Alaska's second largest city, had at one time a strong Scandinavian flavor. In the 1930s and 1940s one of Alaska's best-known citizens was Colonel Otto Fredrick Ohlson (b. 1870) from the Swedish west-coast province of Halland, who served as general manager of the government-owned Alaska Railroad. He has been described as "economic czar" of Anchorage, Alaska's largest city. In 1945 he was succeeded by another Swede, Colonel John F. Johnson, who in 1941 had been sent by the U.S. Army to Iran to organize its transportation system and also had important commissions in the Pacific area during the Second World War. In the 1950s Anchorage became a regular stop on the Scandinavian Airlines transpolar flights between Copenhagen and Tokyo.

Swedish fruitgrowers in California — A legendary shipowner in San Francisco

AFTER the Civil War the Swedish-born population of California grew slowly at first, reaching about 2,000 in 1870 and 4,200 ten years later, according to U.S. census figures. At the turn of the century it was about 14,500, and then it jumped to more than 26,000 in 1910 and nearly 42,000 in 1930. At that time, almost 40 percent of California's Swedish-born inhabitants lived in San Francisco and Los Angeles, and this proportion would rise considerably if the suburban areas were included. San Francisco and its suburbs hold a prominent place in the history of the Swedes in California, but in the 20th century the Los Angeles district has attracted greater numbers of Swedish people. Most of them came from the Middle West or the East.

The largest Swedish settlements in rural California grew up around Kingsburg, about 150 miles north of Los Angeles and 20 miles south of Fresno, and at Turlock some 75 miles east of San Francisco. The first Swede to settle at Kingsburg was Frank D. Rosendahl (1843–1915), who also contributed much to its continued development. A native of the central province of Närke, he became a land surveyor and an expert gardener, in 1868 laying out the city park at Umeå in the far north of Sweden. He then emigrated to America, and after having worked for New York's Central Park and Golden Gate Park at San Francisco, he settled in 1878 at Fresno as a fruitgrower and moved to Kingsburg in 1885.

At about the same time Swedish immigrants at Ishpeming on Michigan's Upper Peninsula organized a colonization society with the intention of securing land in California, and a member of this group, Andrew Erikson (1857–1941), who in 1886 came to the West Coast as a scout, recommended Kingsburg. The following year the Swedes there were already numerous enough to found a congregation of their own. In the early 1900s five of Kingsburg's seven churches had been built by Swedish settlers, and almost all of its businessmen were, like the members of the local government, of Swedish origin. Today the Swedish descendants make up only about one-third of the population, but the people of Kingsburg honor its Swedish traditions by turning the community into a "Swedish village," with half-timbered houses painted in bright colors and street decorations in the form of blue-and-yellow flags and gay Dala horses. This handicraft article, which has been carved out of wood, is often regarded as a symbol of Dalarna, a Swedish province which boasts industries of international significance but also has preserved a flavor of the past. Each year on the third Saturday in May Kingsburg stages a Swedish Festival featuring maypoles and Swedish folk costumes, a parade with floats, and a Swedish smörgåsbord. About 125 miles south of Kingsburg is a community of a similar type but of Danish origin, Solvang.

Kingsburg lies at the center of the grape belt in the San Joaquin Valley. Its raisin-processing plant, Sun-Maid Raisin Growers, is the largest of its kind in the world, handling a substantial part of California's raisin production of 250,000 metric tons annually. Swedish immigrants and their descendants have played a leading part in developing and marketing this specialty.

The Turlock settlement in the northern part of the San Joaquin Valley, which became famous for its melons, was practically founded by Nels O. Hultberg (b. 1865), whom we have already met as a Mission Friend missionary and gold digger in Alaska. Most of the other Swedish settlers in the Turlock area, including those at Youngstown, who had come from Youngstown, Ohio, were also Mission Friends, and their first congregation became one of the largest in North America, but other denominations were also represented. The Swedes at Youngstown had been led there by the Reverend Jonas Bodén (1856–1942) from Järvsö in Hälsingland.

Hultberg, who was born at Torrlösa in Skåne, came to America in 1887 at the age of 22 and had been a blacksmith, a farm laborer, and a railroad worker when he went to Alaska in 1893. In Turlock, where he settled in 1903, he built the first dairy, two lumber mills, a hotel, and a large office building, and he also had a model fruit plantation, with a vineyard, and was interested in numerous other activities. One of his principles in his dealings with other settlers was never to allow a family to leave because of want.

By 1870, wine growing had already become one of California's foremost agricultural resources. Among Swedes known to have been engaged in the wine business in the Sonoma or Napa valleys northeast of San Francisco were C. W. Lybeck, J. G. Wilson, and John Lind, who were, or at least had been, residents of San Francisco. The Inglenook Vineyards at Rutherford, one of the leading wineries in California, were founded in 1879 by a Swedish-speaking Finn, a former sea captain named Gustaf Nybom or Gustave Niebaum (1842–1908), who had gone to sea early and in 1868 sailed into San Francisco with a valuable shipload of furs from Alaska. Before planting his first vines in the Napa Valley he explored the wine industries in France, Germany, Hungary, Italy, Portugal, and Spain.

Around the middle of the 1800s many people in Scandinavia dreamed about a much closer Danish-Norwegian-Swedish cooperation, and the Scandinavian immigrants in San Francisco seemed determined to put this idea into practice in their own community. A

Scandinavian Society was organized there in 1859, and George C. Johnson (d. 1872), the Swedish-Norwegian consul, and C. W. Lybeck (d. 1892), a merchant from Gothenburg who must have been one of the leading Swedish businessmen on the West Coast, seem to have been the principal founders. Most of the other charter members were skilled craftsmen. The association grew rapidly and became, in fact, a center for the Scandinavians in the San Francisco area, maintaining a reading room with newspapers and books, promoting lectures, staging well-attended parties, and giving receptions for such famous visitors as Christine Nilsson, the Swedish opera singer, Ole Bull, the Norwegian violinist, Adelina Patti, the Italian soprano, and her countryman Enrico Caruso. Christine Nilsson came twice, in December of 1873 and in December of 1882. She received enthusiastic welcomes and sang to houses that were packed to suffocation.

The Scandinavian Society, whose president was usually a Norwegian, also helped bring about a Scandinavian Lutheran congregation and a Scandinavian singing club, the Orpheus. A Scandinavian newspaper, the *California Skandinav*, was founded in 1873, but its editor, Hugo Nisbeth, gave up the next year. He had come to the United States as a correspondent for *Aftonbladet* of Stockholm, and in Sweden he published an entertaining book about his two years in America.

The first historian of the Scandinavian Society of San Francisco, August Wetterman (1828–1917) from Västerås, has been described as one of the leading characters among the Swedes in California in the early days. After becoming a musician in the Swedish army, he sailed in 1850 for California via Cape Horn. His company played in San Francisco, tried gold mining, and broke up, but Wetterman became a popular musician and music teacher, and was for many years the organizer of Swedish or Scandinavian festivals and concerts. For the benefit of the Scandinavian Society he staged in 1863 a three-act comedy by August Blanche, entitled *Stockholm, Västerås och Uppsala*, the first theatrical play given in the Swedish language in San Francisco.

When George C. Johnson, the Swedish-Norwegian consul, died in 1872, he was succeeded by the Danish consul in San Francisco, Gustav O'Hara Taafee, who had been a merchant in China, and for two years the three Scandinavian countries were represented in California, and the whole West Coast area, by one man. After 1875, however, the

Scandinavian Society began to decline in importance, and the Swedes, Norwegians, and Danes in San Francisco formed their own national organizations. Some had, in fact, already been launched, in part under the auspices of the Scandinavian group. The first Lutheran congregation in the Bay area had been organized in 1860 by Swedish immigrants, including C. W. Lybeck and another wealthy merchant, Captain Carl J. Janson or Charles J. Johnson (d. 1879), who had arrived in 1850. The still existing Swedish Ebenezer congregation was formed in 1882 by the Reverend Johannes Telleen, who came from Denver, Colorado, and its first church was dedicated three years later.

One of the more remarkable Swedes in San Francisco in the 1870s and 1880s was Stockholm-born William Nemos (1847–1933), who came there from Australia, where he had tried his luck as a gold digger, and before that had lived in London for seven years, most of the time working for one of the leading houses trading with India. After a short period as a railway engineer in Oregon he was in 1873 hired for the famous "history factory" operated by Hubert Howe Bancroft, who left 39 volumes mostly dealing with the "Pacific states" — Central America, Mexico, and the Far West of the United States and Canada. Nemos, who seems to have been a great linguist, authored an impressive number of volumes and finally became supervisor of Bancroft's workshop as well as of his invaluable library, which in 1905 was donated to the University of California. He resigned his post in 1888 and spent the rest of his life in Scandinavia, writing and studying the history of the Vikings. His name was originally Wilhelm Roos. The name Nemos was a pathetic allusion to the fact that he was born out of wedlock ('nemo' is the Latin word for nobody).

The best-known enterprise of Swedish origin in California, the Matson Navigation Company, was founded by Wilhelm Mattson or William Matson (1849–1917), who was born at Lysekil, a fishing port in the rock-bound province of Bohuslän. He began life as a sailor at an early age and in 1867, when he was 18 years old, he landed in San Francisco. At 21 he became the captain of a small ship, setting out for the North Pacific, and 12 years later, in 1882, he commanded as part owner a 200-ton schooner, the *Emma Claudina*, which carried cargoes of supplies from San Francisco to the Hawaiian Islands and, on the return trip, raw sugar, pineapples, coffee, and hides. A few years later he built the brigantine *Lurline*, the first in a series of ships named after his daughter.

The trade prospered and Captain Matson added ship after ship. In 1901 he had a fleet of about ten, and his company was incorporated. Somewhat later he decided first to change to steam transportation and then to convert his steamships to oil. His first steamship, bought in 1902, was the first on the Pacific to use wireless telegraphy, and a third, built in 1917, was the first to use a gyro pilot and compass.

Captain Matson's use of oil as fuel put him in conflict with the railroads, and he then built the first California pipeline from his own oil wells at Santa Maria to the coast. He also helped organize the commercial development of the Hawaiian Islands. His trade routes were gradually extended to the Orient and the Indian Ocean. During the First World War three of his ships were used as transports, carrying about 100,000 American soldiers and huge cargoes to France. The *Wilhelmina*, for instance, made 15 round trips. Among its officers was Charles Arthur Berndtson (b. 1894) from the island city of Marstrand near Gothenburg, who became senior captain of the Matson Company and one of the most popular skippers on the Pacific. Many other immigrants from Sweden worked for Matson as sailors or officers.

Captain Matson is regarded as one of the most dynamic and picturesque figures in the history of trans-Pacific shipping. He seems to have shunned publicity almost as scrupulously as a Swede who came to California eight years after his death, Greta Garbo, but he became president of the San Francisco Chamber of Commerce, and in 1908 the Swedish government named him consul general for the Pacific Coast area. In the mid-1900s the Matson mansion in San Francisco was bought by the Swedish government and became the residence of the Swedish consul general, who also has his offices there. Captain Matson's daughter Lurline and her husband William P. Roth, who became head of the Matson Line, had a son, William Matson Roth, who served as the chief United States representative in the Kennedy round of tariff negotiations, completed in 1967 in Geneva.

Another legendary San Francisco Swede, Erik O. Lindblom (b. 1857), whom we have met as an unusually lucky gold prospector in Alaska, was born in the province of Dalarna and had worked as a tailor both in Sweden and abroad, including London where he stayed for six years, when he sailed for America in 1886. After stopovers in New York and at Butte, Montana, he came to San Francisco in 1893 and continued as a tailor but also began to study the science of mining. Five years later he jumped ship in Alaska, and after the gold strike he helped found a large mining company there. Later he made investments in mines, public utilities, real estate, and banks in California and the state of Washington.

Among the first successful Swedish building contractors in San Francisco were S. Persson (b. 1858) from Ivetofta in Skåne, who came in 1882, and Gottfrid Petterson (b. 1863) from Älghult in Småland, who arrived in the late 1880s via Rockford, Illinois. Their firm, Petterson & Persson, erected numerous buildings, both large and small. For some time they had an associate, N. A. Trubeck (b. 1870), who had been a laborer on his father's farm near Tomelilla in Skåne and then, among other things, a shipyard worker in Denmark, a carpenter in Rockford and Chicago, a fruit picker in Oregon and Washington, a real-estate speculator in Chicago, a copper miner in California, a marine electrician, and finally a ship's carpenter sailing to China and Japan. Jonathan Anderson (b. 1860) from Bärby in Västergötland, who came to San Francisco in 1885 via Minnesota, Oregon, and Idaho, built, like Petterson & Persson, whole blocks and town sections. After the earthquake and fire of 1906, Swedish contractors and workers contributed much to the new San Francisco.

The Swedes in California as well as the country of Sweden took a very active part both in the California Midwinter Fair of 1894, which was held in San Francisco's Golden Gate Park and was designed to call attention to the city's year-round temperate climate, and in the Panama-Pacific International Exposition at San Francisco in 1915, which commemorated the completion of the Panama Canal. On both occasions, the editor and publisher of the newspaper *Vestkusten*, Alexander Olsson (1868–1952), who like many other Swedish settlers in California had come from the Onsala peninsula in northern Halland, was one of the driving forces among the Swedes in San Francisco. In 1915, when William Matson offered Sweden's official participation strong support, the large Swedish building had been designed by a leading architect, Ferdinand Boberg (1860–1946), whose powerful styles were influenced both by Spanish architecture and by two outstanding Americans, Henry Hobson Richardson and Henry Sullivan.

Boberg was also responsible for the Swedish buildings at several other exhibitions, including the pavilion at the Louisiana Purchase Exposition at St. Louis in 1904.

One of the first more remarkable Swedes in the Los Angeles area, Sven Pålsson or Swan Paulson (b. 1860), had emigrated in 1879 from Kattarp in Skåne. After having worked as a lumberjack and miner in Pennsylvania, in a foundry in Chicago and coal mines in Illinois, and on railroad construction in Iowa, Minnesota, the Dakotas, and the Pacific Northwest, he came in 1885 to Los Angeles, where, to begin with, he earned his living in the sewage system. After seven years as a foreman in an ice plant, he was able to buy 200 acres at Chatsworth, now in the northern part of Los Angeles, but three consecutive drought years reduced him to poverty, and his five daughters were sent to a children's home. By 1910, however, he was one of the most successful farmers in southern California, known as the "King of Chatsworth." His wife Anna, who died shortly after the farm had been bought, came from Värmland.

At Pomona in the Los Angeles area, a paper mill was established in 1926 by Fritz O. Fernstrom (1886–1956) from Falun in Dalarna, who had come to America in 1911, and his younger brother Erik. The mill, which was built by Swedish workers and used Swedish machinery, specialized in tissue paper and wrappers for oranges and other fruits, and part of its production was exported to South America, Australia, and New Zealand. In 1952 the company, known as the Fernstrom Paper Mills, was sold to a larger forest-industry operator. Today, Los Angeles occupies an important place in shipping and trade relations between the United States and Sweden.

The Farmers Market at the corner of Fairfax Avenue and Third Street in Los Angeles, which has become a commercial success as well as a world-famous tourist attraction, was founded in 1934 by Roger Dahlhjelm (1881–1950), whose paternal grandfather, Claes Dahlhjelm from Vallerstad in Östergötland, in the early 1850s had been one of the first settlers on Chisago Lake in Minnesota. To begin with, Roger Dahlhjelm invited 17 depression-stricken farmers to come to his lot in Los Angeles and make their sales to the public, provided that they could guarantee a high standard. After some time, first-rate meat, fish, and other produce were added to the morning-fresh vegetables and fruits, and in the 1970s practically anything could be bought at the Farmers Market, which comprised some 160 shops and stalls. Members of the film colony had been among its first customers. Dahlhjelm was, according to his biographers, an outstanding personality and left a permanent impression upon life in Los Angeles.

California has had one governor of partly Swedish parentage, namely, Earl Warren (1891–1974), a native of Los Angeles, who served from 1943 to 1953, being elected three times with unprecedented bipartisan support. The first time, in 1942, he defeated the Democratic incumbent, Culbert L. Olson, whose father had come from Denmark and settled in Utah as a farmer. Earl Warren's father was born in Norway, while both his mother and his wife were born in Sweden.

The Swedish-language weekly *Vestkusten*, founded in 1886, was still published at San Francisco in the 1970s. Los Angeles has also had its quota of Swedish publications, and one of them, in part written in English, was among the survivors of the 1970s. Other Swedish periodicals have been published in Oakland, Turlock, and Eureka, a lumbering center in northern California.

Some more notable California Swedes — Nobel laureates and others of Swedish stock

AN IMMIGRANT from Pjätteryd in southern Småland, John Elof Boodin (1869–1950), who taught philosophy in Los Angeles for many years, was one of the first widely known university professors of Swedish birth in California. His educational foundations were laid in a school at Uppsala. Arriving in America in the late 1880s, he studied first at the universities of Colorado and Minnesota, and then at Brown and Harvard, where, as one of the first immigrants from Scandinavia, he obtained his doctorate in 1899. His professional career then took him to Grinnell College in Iowa, University of Kansas, Carleton College in Minnesota, University of Southern California, and finally to the University of California at Los Angeles, where he served as professor of philosophy from 1928 to 1939. He is said to have been an inspiring teacher. Both in his lectures and in his books, one of his leading themes was the wholeness of things, which the modern age of specialization has tended to neglect. During a European tour before coming to California, he gave lectures in universities at London, Oxford, Cambridge, Paris, and Leipzig.

Another native of Sweden, Axel Ragnar Olson (1889–1954) from Helsingborg in the south, who was brought to the United States at the age of three, became a noted chemist and was in 1930 named full professor in the University of California at Berkeley. Olof Lundberg (1901–52), born in Stockholm and raised at Härnösand in the north, emigrated to America at the age of 28, when the Great Depression was about to begin, and finally became comptroller of the whole University of California system, which he had joined as a certified public accountant in 1938.

From 1917 to 1946 Gustaf Stromberg (1882–1962), a native of Gothenburg with a doctor's degree from Lund, was one of the leading astronomers at the Mount Wilson Observatory near Pasadena. He became so well known that at the New York World's Fair in 1939–40 his name was listed on the "Wall of Fame" as one of the Americans of foreign birth who had made "outstanding contributions" to American civilization.

Several Swedes have inscribed their names in the annals of physical education and sports in California. Among the first was Signe Hagelthorn, who, after graduation from the Boston Normal School of Gymnastics in 1909, became director of physical education at Mills College in Oakland. In 1911–13 she organized courses in gymnastics at the schools in Los Angeles. During another three years in Oakland she opened 42 playgrounds and gave courses for instructors, and she also conducted summer courses in the University of California at Berkeley. Before moving to New York in 1925, she led physical-education activities for the children and young people of San Francisco.

For over two decades Ernst M. Brandsten (1883–1965), a native of Karlskoga in Värmland who emigrated from Sweden after the Olympic Games at Stockholm in 1912, served as a swimming instructor at Stanford University in Palo Alto. In the Olympic Games at Antwerp in Belgium in 1920 the U.S. divers began to dominate international competition, and this supremacy has been credited to Brandsten and a few other coaches, including his wife Greta, an Olympic champion of 1912, who also became a swimming instructor at Stanford, and a Swede named Hjalmar Johanson, who for many years worked as a coach on the Pacific Coast. Brandsten's foremost contribution, according to the *Encyclopaedia Britannica*, was "his thoroughness in teaching fundamentals and his success in standardizing equipment." After the Olympic Games in Paris in 1924 he became the chief U.S. swimming coach.

Sven Rickard Lokrants (1892–1940) from the island of Munsö near Stockholm, who had begun to study medicine before his emigration in 1914, became in 1924 director of health for the Los Angeles schools, and in 1932 he was the medical director of the Olympic Games. One of the official surgeons, Fritjof Emil Berge, was also born in Sweden. Dr. Lokrants was elected president of the American Association of School Physicians, and has been called the "Father of corrective physical education in the schools of America." He had continued his medical studies at Boston, where many physical-education specialists from Sweden settled.

One of the first Swedes in Hollywood was Linda Arvidson, who in 1907 collaborated as a writer with the moving-picture pioneer David W. Griffith, who was her husband. In 1911 an attractive blonde named Anna Q. Nilsson (1888–1974), who was born at Ystad in southernmost Sweden and had been an artist's model in New York, began a screen career which in 20 years brought her more than 200 roles. Another member of the first generation of Hollywood Swedes, Olga Knutson or Celeste who had been the youngest of 12 children in a family at Lund, came to Chicago in 1907 when she was still in her early teens. After a few years of circus life she settled in the American film capital and became a highly successful animal trainer and daredevil, known as "the leopard woman." The legendary Gloria Swanson, who also became a stage actress, came from Chicago, her father, an army captain, being of Swedish parentage.

A few immigrants from Sweden have become leading bankers in California. In 1907 a two-year-old boy, Rudolph A. Peterson (b. 1904), was brought to California by a childless uncle and aunt, who during a visit to his parents' home, a farm at Svenljunga in the province of Västergötland, had obtained permission to adopt him. He grew up near Turlock southeast of San Francisco, where two-thirds of the population was of Swedish origin, and after having worked his way through the University of California's College of Commerce, he began a career in banking. In 1936 he joined the Bank of America as its district manager in Fresno. After having served as president of the Bank of Hawaii at Honolulu from 1956 to 1961, he was called back to the Bank of America as vice chairman, and in 1963 he became president and chief executive officer of the world's largest private banking organization. After his retirement at the end of 1969 he served as chairman of President Nixon's 16-member task force on foreign aid, and in 1972 he became head of the United Nations Development Program, succeeding Paul G. Hoffman who in 1948–50 had been the U.S. administrator for the Marshall Plan.

Eric Hallbeck (1897–1970), who was born at Höör in southern Sweden and in 1920 began what he regarded as a study trip to America, also saw the Bank of America, where in 1952 he was named a vice president, grow into the world's largest bank. In 1948 he helped bring about a San Francisco office which later became The Swedish-American Chamber of Commerce of the Western United States. From 1965 to 1971 Louis Billings Lundborg, who had begun his career as a research chemist in sugar refineries in Hawaii, served as chairman of the board of the Bank of America. He was born in 1906 at Billings, Montana, of parents who had come from the vicinity of Kisa in the Swedish province of Östergötland.

Among well-known Californians of Swedish birth was also Carl M. Fridén (1891–1945) from Alvesta in the province of Småland, who developed the Friden calculating machines. As a young laboratory apprentice and student in a technical school in Stockholm he met an inventor of calculating machines, Karl Rudin, and conducted experiments for him. In 1911 he became a traveling engineer for a Swedish match company, and via Australia he came in 1917 to California, where he began as a draftsman. His first calculating machine was sold to a well-known manufacturer but in 1934 he established his own firm in Oakland, which at that time had about 3,000 Swedish- born inhabitants.

The most prominent scientists of recent Swedish ancestry in California are two Nobel prize winners, Glenn T. Seaborg, who has already been mentioned in connection with his birthplace, Ishpeming on Michigan's Upper Peninsula, and Carl David Anderson of the California Institute of Technology at Pasadena.

Seaborg, who came to southern California with his parents in 1922 at the age of ten, made his scientific career in the University of California at Berkeley, where in 1958–61 he served as chancellor. In 1951, at the age of 39, he and his Berkeley colleague Edwin M. McMillan received the Nobel prize in chemistry for their work on the transuranium elements, including plutonium. Later he helped discover more chemical elements, among them nobelium, which was named for Alfred Nobel. For ten years, 1961–71, he was chairman of the U.S. Atomic Energy Commission. Seaborg's father was born at Ishpeming of Swedish immigrants, while his mother had come from Sweden at the age of 17. His forebears in Sweden were master machinists for two generations, and so was his father who was born in the United States. He has taken part in several family reunions in Sweden.

In 1936, when he was 31 years old, Carl David Anderson became co-winner of the Nobel physics prize, chosen for his discovery of the positron four years earlier. He was born in 1905 in New York. Both his parents came from the province of Östergötland, his mother from Tjärstad where her father, a soldier named Ajax, had been given a cottage and a few acres of land, and his father from the vicinity of Vreta, whose beautiful parish church dates from the early 1100s, and where the ruins of an adjoining nunnery were excavated 800 years later. Ajax's daughter, Emma Adolfina, did unusually well at school, but in 1893 she emigrated with an older sister at the age of 15. In New York she started working in the home of a Columbia University professor, and several years later she married Carl David Anderson, who was earning his living as a chef in a restaurant. They moved to Los Angeles in 1912, when their son Carl David was seven years old. In 1923 he entered the California Institute of Technology, and there he began to teach physics four years later. In 1962 he became chairman of the division of physics, mathematics, and astronomy.

Among the Swedes or children of Swedish immigrants who lived at Kingsburg about 1910 were Olof A. Carlson and his wife Ellen, whom he had met in Minnesota. He was a barber by trade and was probably born in Minnesota shortly after his parents' arrival from Sweden in the early 1880s. Via Arizona and Mexico, whose climate attracted them, they then moved to Riverside, east of Los Angeles, which like Kingsburg had received many Swedish settlers, and where their son Chester, born in 1906 in Seattle, went to school. Both Olof and Ellen Carlson had become crippled by illness, and Chester supported the family by odd jobs or, during his junior-college years, as a sample boy in a cement factory. Working six weeks and then attending school for six weeks, he completed the two college years in four.

Finally he was admitted to the California Institute of Technology at Pasadena, which offered him a loan, and in 1930 he was graduated with honors in physics.

Both parents had died by then, and Chester Carlson moved to New York, where during the Great Depression in the early 1930s he is said to have suffered more on his few dollars per week than he had ever done in California. Toward the end of the 1930s he invented the xerography dry-copying process, and while he had great trouble launching a product based on his system, he was finally transformed into a multimillionaire and one of the greatest donors of his era. A few years later, in 1968, he died in New York.

A first cousin, Roy W. Carlson, who was born in 1900 in Minnesota and also studied at the California Institute of Technology, became a noted physicist, holding teaching or research positions in the University of California and the Massachusetts Institute of Technology. A number of widely used electrical instruments for measuring stress, strain, temperature, and pressure were invented by him. The Carlson family came from the Malmö area in the province of Skåne, and Chester Carlson's mother also hailed from southernmost Sweden.

One of the best-known family names of Swedish origin in California is that of Ahmanson. The already mentioned founder of the American family, Johan August Åhmanson from Jönköping in Småland, who came to Salt Lake City in 1856 and five years later settled in Omaha, had a son, William H. Ahmanson, who tried his fortune in the insurance business. His son Howard F. Ahmanson (1906–68) developed the Los Angeles-based Home Savings and Loan Association into the largest institution of its kind and became, according to the obituary in *The New York Times*, "one of the least-known but wealthiest of the nation's financial magnates." His philanthropies included the Ahmanson Foundation, established to provide financial encouragement in education, the arts, and medical research, the Ahmanson Center for Biological Research at the University of Southern California, and the Los Angeles County Art Museum, whose main gallery was named for him. The Music Center, which opened in 1964, has an Ahmanson Theater. As leader of the Ahmanson group of companies Howard Ahmanson was succeeded by a nephew, William H. Ahmanson. The latter's brother and associate, Robert Ahmanson, has done much research concerning the history of the Ahmanson family.

Among the leading architects in California in the early to middle 1900s was George Edwin Bergstrom, born in Wisconsin of Swedish extraction, who in 1902 settled in Los Angeles, in 1916 became president of the Los Angeles Housing Commission, and in 1939–41 served as president of the American Institute of Architects.

Some examples of fruitful exchanges California-Sweden
via Swedish immigrants

IN 1873 a 26-year-old naturalist named August Gustav Eisen (1847–1940), who had just been made an assistant professor at the University of Uppsala, received an official traveling scholarship for zoological studies in the United States. He spent the winter of 1874 on Santa Catalina Island south of Los Angeles, and remained in the Golden State for the better part of his life. In America he called himself Gustavus A. Eisen.

At Fresno, in the heart of the St. Joaquin Valley, Eisen started one of the largest nurseries in America and carried on research which became of basic importance for Californian fruit farming, in particular fig culture and the raisin industry. He was also one of the pioneers in promoting the national-park idea in the United States. During expeditions in the Big Tree regions of California he had become deeply concerned over the destruction wrought by the lumber industry, and in September of 1890 the Sequoia National Park, the second in the United States, was created as a result of his efforts. Even then he wanted to save all the remaining sequoia groves, but the next step was not taken until much later.

In part, Eisen conducted his conservation campaigns under the auspices of the California Academy of Sciences at San Francisco, and from 1892 to 1900 he served as the zoology curator of this institution. It was in the realm of zoology that he made his most significant scientific contributions, and his leading specialty was the Oligochaeta, a large order of worms which includes the earthworms. Some of his conclusions anticipated modern research concerning the structure of the chromosomes and the nature of the genes. American zoology, which had not yet gained a leading position, was stimulated by his activities and findings.

From 1910, when he first spent five years in Europe and Egypt and then settled in New York at the age of 68, Eisen was equally

517

productive in the fields of archeology and the history of art, but on the whole less successful from a scientific viewpoint. In 1932 he published a three-volume work about the portraits of George Washington. He died in New York and was buried on the slope of a Sequoia National Park mountain. One of its peaks was named in his honor.

The first scientist he met after his arrival in America in 1873 was Louis Agassiz, the famous Swiss-American naturalist and Harvard professor, who died a few months later and was buried in Mount Auburn at Cambridge, Massachusetts. Many of Eisen's scientific and practical activities in America can be traced back to his studies in Sweden. One of his first important teachers, for instance, was an archeologist on the Baltic island of Gotland who also became known as a pioneering conservationist. During his first year in California he collected organic material from the Pacific for one of Scandinavia's first specialists on the marine fauna, Sven Lovén (1809–95), who was professor at the Museum of Natural History in Stockholm and in 1877 established a station on the Swedish West Coast, at Kristineberg in the province of Bohuslän, where many biological oceanographers from other countries, including the United States, have carried on research. The American stations at Woods Hole, Massachusetts, and at La Jolla in San Diego, California, have become well known in Swedish circles.

In 1870, a 24-year-old Swede by the name of Carl Olof Swanberg (b. 1846) came to San Francisco. He was born at historic Kalmar in southeastern Sweden and had gone to sea early with his father, a skipper, whom he assisted as a cook for six years. At the age of 15 he began to operate on his own, and it was via South America that he worked his way to San Francisco. Like many other young immigrants from Scandinavia in the middle 1800s he started in the oyster fisheries, and within two years he had an oyster bed of his own. His rapidly growing business interests in California remained focused on shellfish, but at the same time he became a large-scale farmer in Sweden.

In 1887–88 Swanberg bought two large farms in the Kalmar district, and by the turn of the century he added a third estate, Engeltofta near the city of Ängelholm in northwest Skåne. The latter had become a model farm in the early 1800s, and somewhat later it was purchased by King Carl XIV Johan, the first Bernadotte on the Swedish throne. Swanberg visited his Swedish farms at least every two years, directing a number of important experiments in animal and plant breeding, and also concerning the prevention of cattle diseases. One of his farms specialized in purebred Jersey cattle, while another developed a crossbreed of Jersey and Holstein. Most of his plant experiments concerned alfalfa, one of the most important forage crops, which at that time was little known in Sweden. At one of his estates, Svartingstorp north of Kalmar, production increased eightfold in 30 years. Many farmers and agronomists in Sweden learned from him, as fruit farmers in California had picked up new ideas from Gustavus Eisen.

Swedish settler in Hawaii becomes pioneer publisher and champion of native culture

THE first notable Swedish settler in the Hawaiian Islands was Abraham Fornander (1812–87), who lived there for nearly half a century. He became a champion of Hawaiian language and culture and made significant contributions to the knowledge and understanding of the Polynesian people.

Abraham Fornander was born in the parsonage at Gärdslösa on the Baltic island of Öland, where Sweden's most gifted Romantic poet, Erik Johan Stagnelius (1793–1823), had begun his brief life two decades earlier. Fornander's father was a well-known clergyman. After a short period of studies at Uppsala and Lund, he shipped out as a sailor in the early 1830s, and for many years nothing was heard from or about him. He probably visited America, and must have traveled widely throughout the Pacific area. In 1842 he went ashore in Hawaii, then ruled by the liberal-minded Kamehameha III. In 1847 he married a lady chief from the island of Molokai, Pinao Alanakapu, and became a plantation owner. A few years later he yielded to the call from the newly discovered gold fields in California, but he returned to Hawaii in 1852, deeply disillusioned. His wife died five years later.

From 1852 to 1864 Fornander was active as a pioneering newspaper or magazine publisher, beginning with the *Weekly Argus* which is reported to have been established to oppose government restrictions on free speech. During his student years in Sweden, a publication named *Argus* had been a mouthpiece of the liberal opposition. In Hawaii he seems to have enjoyed rising respect, and in 1864 King Kamehameha V appointed him circuit judge of Maui, the second largest island. The next year he was named inspector general of the Hawaiian school system, six years later he was reappointed circuit judge, and 15 years later, at the age of 74, he became one of the four judges of the Supreme Court of Hawaii.

The most important single source of Hawaiian mythology and folklore today is a collection which Fornander brought together in the 1860s and 1870s when he had a team of native Hawaiians roam every part of the islands in order to record for posterity the songs, chants, legends, and rites of the people. After his death in 1887, Charles R. Bishop purchased the collection of manuscripts from his estate and later gave them to the Bishop Museum of Polynesian Ethnology and Natural History in Honolulu. This material became the basis for a nine-volume edition of the Hawaiian folk tales published by the Bishop Museum during the years 1916–20. Tapping the same rich source, the University of Hawaii Press in 1959 published an illustrated volume containing seven Hawaiian folk legends. Fornander's personal papers in the Fornander Collection at Honolulu include several of his father's hand-written sermons, delivered in the medieval church at Gärdslösa during the years from 1810 to 1822.

Another huge project of great importance for Hawaii led to the publication in London in 1878–85 of a three-volume work entitled *An Account of the Polynesian Race; its origin and migrations and the ancient history of the Hawaiian people to the times of Kamehameha I.* Fornander here tells the history of the Polynesian people and the Hawaiian language by placing them in relationship to other cultures and linguistic families. The third and last volume he dedicated to his daughter Catherine, as follows: "To my daughter Catherine Kaonohiulaokalani Fornander this work is affectionately dedicated as a reminder of her mother's ancestors and as a token of her father's love."

Toward the end of his life Fornander reestablished his contacts with Sweden. When the Swedish frigate *Vanadis* called at Honolulu in 1884 during its circumnavigation of the globe, Judge Fornander offered the officers and crew valuable assistance, and for this as well as for his contribution to scholarship he received a royal Swedish decoration. When another naval vessel from Sweden, the *Eugenie*, visited Honolulu in the summer of 1852, during the first Swedish circumnavigation of the globe, Fornander, who returned from California the same year, does not seem to have been on hand. On July 1, the commander of the ship, Captain Christian Virgin, signed on behalf of the united kingdoms of Sweden and Norway a treaty of friendship, commerce, and navigation with the kingdom of the Hawaiian Islands. Nothing that happened in the direct relations between Scandinavia and Hawaii, however, could match in importance the activities of one of the few Scandinavian 19th-century settlers on the islands, the long unknown Abraham Fornander.

From 1922 to 1942 a Stockholm-born physician, Nils P. Larsson or Larsen (1890–1964), was medical director of Queen's Hospital in Honolulu, which under his leadership was raised from the fourth to the first rank. His ceaseless campaigns for better health standards throughout the islands resulted in a greatly lowered infant mortality rate, adequate diets, and an improved control of epidemics. He was elected president of the Hawaii Medical Association and of the Honolulu Academy of Science. In Sweden he became well known, first as a host to Crown Prince Gustav Adolf and Crown Princess Louise during their visit to Hawaii in 1926, and later as a visiting lecturer in his native country. His father, a tailor from Brunskog in Värmland, had in 1893 brought his large family to Peekskill, New York. After graduating from the Cornell Medical School in New York in 1916, Nils P. Larsen served as a medical officer in the American Expeditionary Force during the First World War. As medical director of Queen's Hospital in Honolulu he was succeeded by Dr. Gustaf W. Olson, who had had his medical training in Minnesota and California.

25

In New England

New England immigration heavy in late 1800s — New Sweden, Maine, founded in 1870

SWEDISH immigration to New England did not assume large proportions until about 1880, when Sweden's industrialization was already under way. During the 1880s the stream of immigrants was particularly heavy, and tens of thousands followed during the next quarter-century.

In 1910 about 40,000 Swedish immigrants lived in Massachusetts, some 18,000 in Connecticut, 7,500 in Rhode Island, and less than 6,000 in Maine, New Hampshire, and Vermont. In Connecticut the Swedish-born population increased somewhat in the 1920s, reaching 18,500 in 1930. On the whole, the Swedish population in New England has always been concentrated in cities and other industrial areas. Maine was the most significant exception.

Swedish immigration to Maine was to a great extent the work of one single man, William Widgery Thomas (1839–1927), who was born in the Pine Tree State. As an American consular agent at Gothenburg in 1863–65 he had become fond of Sweden and had learned the Swedish language. Five years later, when Maine's population had begun to show a decline and Thomas was appointed its commissioner of immigration, he went back to Sweden in order to recruit settlers, and after a vigorous campaign he returned with the first, hand-picked contingent. In the summer of 1870, 50 men, women and children came with him to Maine and settled in the wilderness of Aroostook County in the extreme north. All the men and women, Mr. Thomas later observed, "were tall and stalwart, with blue eyes, light hair, and cheerful, honest faces. There was not a physical defect or blemish among them."

The Swedish immigrants paid their own fares but in Maine each family received 100 acres of virgin forest land. Like the Swedish 17th-century colony in the Delaware Valley, their settlement was named New Sweden. The first boy born there was christened William Widgery Thomas, his family name being Persson. More immigrants arrived even before the end of 1870, the rugged land was gradually cleared, and the settlers soon became at least self-sustaining in grains, meat, and dairy and poultry products. After some time they started specializing in potato growing, helping to make Aroostook County one of the leading producers in the United States.

The colony's first school was established in 1871. During the winter many of the children came on skis, some having to travel five miles through the woods. Throughout 1872, a newly started weekly at nearby Caribou, *The North Star*, ran a column in the Swedish language. The founder of New Sweden, who became known there as "Father Thomas," lived among the settlers in a log cabin until 1873, watching over his "children in the woods," as he affectionately called them. The difficulties of the first few years may have been even greater than he anticipated, but in retrospect he regarded his experiment as successful. New Sweden, he observed, was the only lasting agricultural settlement in New England founded since the colonial era with immigrants from across the ocean. A steady increase in Maine's population began in the 1870s, and the Swedish immigration as well as the attention New Sweden aroused in America must have helped.

New Sweden's first church building was dedicated on July 23, 1880, the 10th anniversary of the founding of the colony. At that time the settlement had nearly 800 inhabitants of Swedish stock, and other immigrants from Sweden lived beyond the 36 square miles of its township. A sub-colony called Stockholm, which gradually became industrialized, was formed to the north. Other localities were named Westmanland and Jemtland after provinces in Sweden. The propaganda for the settlement in Sweden was, as a rule, directed at the northern sections of the country, whose population was considered best fitted for life in the north of Maine.

Gradually most of the Swedish farmers' sons and daughters moved to the cities, and New Sweden thus served as a distributing center for the second generation to the industrial communities of New England. Descendants of the settlers are now scattered all over the United States, but many like to gather at New Sweden on the anniversary of its founding, July 23. In 1970, when the first 100 years were celebrated, people came from the Middle West, Florida, and even California. A public building known as the Capitol, which had served as the first church and schoolhouse and had been preserved as a museum, was destroyed by fire the following summer, but its contents, including handmade furniture and tools, were saved. A replica of the building was completed in 1974.

At Caribou, the largest town in the vicinity of New Sweden, the Nylander Museum was built in 1938 to house the geological collections of Olof O. Nylander (1864–1943), a Swedish-born house painter who had become a self-educated geologist and discovered the first fossil specimens unearthed in Aroostook County. He received an honorary degree from the University of Maine.

In the late 1800s William W. Thomas became a Republican-appointed minister at Stockholm, serving under four Presidents, in 1883–85, 1889–94, and 1897–1905. In 1887 he married a Swedish woman. He was a popular orator and took part in many celebrations on both sides of the Atlantic. In 1891 he published a two-volume work entitled *Sweden and the Swedes*. As a young man he had translated into English a large historical novel, *The Last Athenian*, by Viktor Rydberg (1828–95), one of Sweden's leading liberal authors of the 19th century.

In New Hampshire, a southern section around the Merrimack River, including the state capital, Concord, and the town of Merrimack, attracted a large part of the Swedish immigrants. At Concord, home of a famous white marble, most of the young pioneers from Sweden became stonecutters. In 1884 John Swenson from Falkenberg in the province of Halland, who had arrived in 1871, founded a granite company which became the largest concern of its kind in the state.

In the early 1870s a Swedish settlement began to grow up around the marble quarries at Proctor in west-central Vermont. The first Swede there was a husky young man, Lars Larson, whom the founder and owner of the marble industry, Redfield Proctor, had met in New York and persuaded to work in the quarries. He left after a few years to take up potato farming in New Sweden, Maine, but many other Swedes came to the Proctor marble center. A section of the town which was settled mostly by Swedes became known as "Paradiset," or the Garden of Eden. Beginning in 1899, a prolonged strike at the quarries in Quincy, Massachusetts, caused many Swedish granite cutters to move from there to Barre and Montpelier, Vermont. At Barre, said to be the largest granite center in the world, 15 granite plants were at one time owned by immigrants from Sweden.

Vermont, which never reported more than some 1,300 Swedish settlers, is the only state in the East which has had a governor who was born in Sweden. Joseph B. Johnson, who served in 1955–58, was born in 1893 at Helsingborg in Skåne while his mother was home on a visit from America, and her Norwegian husband was trying to ride out the economic crisis in the United States. Mrs. Johnson returned to America with her children the next year.

Swedish concentration in Boston area — Industrial and other leaders in the Bay State

ONE of the Swedish group emigrations by the mid-1800s had been aimed at Brockton, the shoe center in Massachusetts, but it was not until the 1880s that the flow of Swedes into the Bay State built real momentum. From 1880 to 1910 its Swedish-born population increased more than eightfold to about 40,000, and in the early 1900s Massachusetts ranked fourth among the states in number of settlers from Sweden. Rhode Island's Swedish-born population multiplied from 1880 to 1910 nearly ten times. Its textile mills attracted thousands of Swedish immigrants, especially from the province of Västergötland which long has been noted for excellence in weaving. Such parishes as Böne, Dalum, Hössna, and Timmele, all north of Ulricehamn, were well represented.

The Swedish immigrants in Massachusetts and Rhode Island did not plan to become farmers but were inclined to settle in cities or towns as workers or artisans. From their native country most of them brought some kind of industrial experience or special training, and as American settlers they naturally tried to build on these foundations. In the long run their contributions to the steel, metalworking, and toolmaking industries became particularly important.

Religiously, too, the attitudes of the New England Swedes differed somewhat from those of the older immigrants. On the whole, they lacked the zeal of the more pietistic settlers in the Middle West, while, on the other hand, they seemed to have more natural liking for the Church of Sweden. The Lutheran congregations in New England, like those in most other parts of the East, were also more sensitive to the new currents within the established church in Sweden, although the 20th century brought leaders with a new outlook in the Midwest. Swedish festivals and rallies in Boston and Worcester, the two leading centers in Massachusetts, have in proportion to population gathered as many participants as similar events in the Middle West. Both cities have had many Swedish newspapers, most of them short-lived.

Nearly one-half of the Swedes in Massachusetts settled in the Greater Boston area, and in Rhode Island there was an even more pronounced concentration in and around Providence. In the late 1800s most of the Swedish workers in the Boston district obtained employment in the shoe and textile industries. Among communities with large Swedish groups in the vicinity of Boston were Beverly, Lynn, Malden, Everett, Waltham, Dorchester, Newton, Quincy, Natick, and Norwood.

One of the first 19th-century Swedes to make a successful career in business and industry in Massachusetts was Ludvig Sjöström (1831–1910), a graduate of the Institute of Technology in Stockholm, born at Kristianstad in the province of Skåne where his father had a garment factory. After a visit to the International Exhibition in Paris in 1867 he decided to move to the United States, where he worked for some years in textile mills in Massachusetts. He then started a business of his own which later became known as the U.S. Worsted Company and helped make Lawrence, 25 miles north of Boston, one of the world's most important centers of worsted and woolen-goods production. Until 1897, when he turned the management over to his sons, Ludvig Sjostrom was one of the most active and respected leaders of the Swedish community in Boston, where he spent much of his time.

The Swedish colony in Boston received a younger leader in 1893 when Dr. Richard Hogner (1852–1930), an experienced physician and surgeon, arrived from Sweden. He had left because he regarded himself wronged by the medical authorities in an appointment, and in Boston he was received with open arms and built up a flourishing practice. He was also a great promoter of Swedish gymnastics, songs, and customs, and to a museum in Stockholm he sent much ethnographical material. Whimsically eccentric as well as a splendid athlete, he once walked, for instance, around a whole city block on his hands. Dr. Hogner, who was born in Stockholm, returned to Sweden in 1929 at the age of 77. One of his sons, Pierre Richard Leonard Hogner, born in 1884 at Överkalix in northernmost Sweden, studied architecture at Harvard and in Paris and began practicing at Portland, Oregon, in 1910.

For over 50 years, 1896–1950, one of the best-known architects in Boston was Harry Johan Carlson, born in 1869 of Swedish parents at St. Paul, Minnesota. He designed numerous college and office buildings, churches, and residences, including a famous estate built by the industrialist Thomas W. Lawson of "Frenzied Finance" fame. Jens Fredrick Larson, who was born in Boston in 1891 of Swedish-Danish parents and studied at Harvard, designed a great number of college and university buildings in the United States and abroad, and served from 1928 to 1950 as advisory architect for the Association of American Colleges. He then moved to North Carolina, continuing as an architect.

Working for two of the largest construction companies in the country, Andrew H. Peterson, who was born of Swedish parents in East Boston, had charge of the building of the impressive Field Museum and the well-known Palmer House in Chicago, the General Motors Building in Detroit, and scores of other commercial, educational, and industrial structures in the Midwest, New England, and the Middle Atlantic States. During the Great Depression he was head of the Public Works Administration in Massachusetts. A fourth American of Swedish parentage, Eugene C. Hultman, born in 1875 at Boston, was also in the 1920s and 1930s regarded as "one of the foremost Swedes in Massachusetts." His appointment as police commissioner in 1930 was welcomed by members of all factions, and before that he had served as fire commissioner, building commissioner, and postwar food and fuel administrator. His father was a former sailor from Gothenburg, while his mother came from an old Boston family.

In the rapidly growing mechanical industry in Massachusetts, one of the first successful Swedish inventors was Carl Oscar Hedström, born in 1871 at Lönneberga in Småland, who at the age of nine had come to America with his parents, first settling in Brooklyn. After school he became an expert toolmaker, and in the 1890s, when there was a bicycle craze in America as in many other countries, he built many of the racing machines used by the champions. In 1901, after having joined a bicycle manufacturer at Springfield, Massachusetts, he built the first Indian motorcycle, the forerunner of the modern motorcycle industry in the United States. Another vehicle of the same type, which also incorporated a number of important inventions, was named for Hedstrom himself. On the Florida sands, the inventor rode a mile on one of his Indian machines in 1 minute and 3.2 seconds, a new record. One of the early models made by Hedstrom in a small shop in Springfield is permanently exhibited at the Smithsonian Institution in Washington, D.C.

Much better known than Hedstrom, who at 42 retired to a country estate in Connecticut, was Frank Mossberg (1858–1953) from Blomskog in the province of Värmland, who arrived shortly after his graduation from the Chalmers Institute of Technology at Gothenburg in 1882 and began as a janitor and workman. In the early 1890s he founded the first of several mechanical-engineering firms at Attleboro, 30 miles south of Boston, and there he also became more and more productive as an inventor, finally holding more than 200 U.S. and other patents. These covered such subjects as roller bearings, textile machinery and tools of various kinds, a braider carrier which became used in braiding machines all over the world, and automatic fog signals for ships and lighthouses. Another invention revolutionized the process of rolling cigarettes by machinery. Before Henry Ford launched his internal-combustion engine, Mossberg produced an electric automobile that could go 60 miles at 20 miles an hour on a single battery charge, but when he appealed for an investment of 10,000 dollars, the faith in the future of such a vehicle proved to be lacking. The inventor then turned his mind toward other projects. His pressed-steel company, founded much later, became one of the largest in the East. At the World's Fair in New York in 1940, a special gold medal was cast in his honor, and when it was presented to him as the "Nation's Oldest Inventor," on "Frank Mossberg Day," a large portion of the citizens of Attleboro came to New York by special train to take part in the celebration.

A young Swedish engineering student, Stockholm-born Carl R. Hellström (1895–1963), studied in Paris during the First World War and was then sent by the French government to the United States as a consultant to the French Engineering Commission. At 22 he was assistant superintendent of all Allied shell production in America. In the early 1940s he became first chief engineer and then general manager of the old Smith & Wesson revolver firm of Springfield, Massachusetts, and in 1946 he was named president. He is said to have saved the historic but dying firm, and enabled it to play a vital role as an arms manufacturer during the war. In 1949 Hellstrom hit the front pages of many American newspapers when he lifted the veil from a bomb- and gas-attack-proof plant he had built for Smith and Wesson.

In the Boston area as in New Hampshire and Vermont, many Swedish immigrants earned their living in the marble quarries. A stonecutter at Quincy had a son, Kenneth D. Johnson (1898–1958), who became president of the New York State Welfare Board and dean of Columbia University's School of Social Work in New York. He was a graduate of Brown University and Harvard Law School.

An entirely new specialty was developed at Providence, Rhode Island, by George F. Berkander (1879–1937), who had come from Böne in Västergötland with his parents in 1888 and about two decades later introduced plastic jewelry to America and the world. His products were finally sold in stores all over the country, and his designers produced over 50 designs a day. The Berkander plant also made the little "Mayflowers" or celluloid wood anemones which, as already mentioned, were sold to raise funds for the Swedish National Sanatorium at Englewood near Denver, Colorado, today known as the Swedish Health Center. The "Mayflower" movement originated in Sweden, but the one in America was started by Swedish immigrants at Providence, Rhode Island, where George Berkander was one of the leaders.

*Pioneering industries in Worcester largely staffed
by workers from Sweden*

BUILT in part along beautiful Lake Quinsigamond, about 40 miles
west of Boston, is the city of Worcester, which, in relation to total
population, acquired one of the largest concentrations of Swedish-
born people in the United States. Its development into an industrial
and cultural center in New England had begun long before the first
Swedes arrived, but immigrants from Sweden made vital contributions to its continued growth. Worcester also became an experimental
and vocational school for Swedish engineers and workers, and a focal
point of mutually rewarding interchange between the United States
and Sweden.

The first Swede to settle in Worcester was a young musician from
Uddevalla in the west-coast province of Bohuslän, Carl or Charles F.
Hanson (b. 1849), who came in 1866, probably attracted by the city's
growing reputation as a music center. Before the end of the decade
he was followed by a small group of immigrants from the clay and
pottery district at Höganäs in the northwest of Skåne.

Two of the newcomers from Höganäs, Sven Pålson or Swen Pul-
son (1847–1929) and his brother-in-law John Jeppson (1844–1920),
developed the first ceramic grinding wheel, which is regarded as an
important part of the beginning of the Norton Company, founded in
1885, and long since the world's largest maker of grinding machinery
and abrasives, with affiliated plants in many other countries. Its position as an American key industry became more widely known during
the Second World War, when its work force rose to some 20,000.
John Jeppson's son George N. Jeppson (1873–1963), who in the late
1890s had completed his technical education at the School of Mines in
Stockholm, was then president of the company. He took an active
interest both in community affairs and in relations with Sweden. His
son John Jeppson (b. 1916) served as president of the Norton Company in 1967–71 and after that as chairman of the board.

At first all of the men in Norton's shop at Worcester were
Swedish, most of them from Höganäs and friends of John Jeppson.
Year by year they were joined by relatives and friends. As late as 1914
about 75 percent of the workers were of Swedish origin, a majority of
them still hailing from the pottery district in the northwest of Skåne.
In the Swedish-American vernacular, the Norton plant in the north-

ern section of Worcester was often called "Höganäs-shopet" or "Skåninga-shopet."

Worcester was also one of the first centers of the American steel industry, and several leaders in this field visited Sweden for studies of its iron and steel mills or at the School of Mines in Stockholm. A number of Swedish engineers and metallurgists were persuaded by them to emigrate, and these, in turn, inspired foremen and workers to follow suit, so that during the last two decades of the 19th century thousands of Swedes, most of them from the old mining and iron-making districts in Värmland, Dalsland, Västmanland, and other central provinces, came to Worcester and started working for its steel manufacturers.

The largest employer was Washburn & Moen, later known as the American Steel and Wire Company. In 1880 this concern engaged two young specialists from Sweden, Jacob or James Forsstedt (1851–1929) and Wilhelm Bildt (1854–1906), who both became chief engineers and made inventions or improvements furthering the development of the American steel industry. Forsstedt was also the first Swede to hold an elective office in Worcester. A man of unusual eloquence, he was sometimes called the "Swedish Demosthenes." Born at Avesta in the province of Dalarna, where his forefathers ever since the 1600s had been copper masters, he returned to Sweden in 1898 and then helped modernize its metal industry by introducing American production methods. His son Ralph S. Forsstedt, who was born in Worcester in 1881, followed him after graduation from the Worcester Polytechnic Institute, and he too broke new ground in Sweden with American technology, including an electrical time recorder invented by Alfred Stromberg, the Swedish telephone pioneer in Chicago. Wilhelm Bildt, born at Onsala in Halland, returned to Sweden in 1899, when one of his inventions had been purchased by many of its iron and steel companies.

Another Swedish steel engineer, and graduate of the Institute of Technology in Stockholm, Emanuel Trotz (1860–1925), who came to America in 1887 on a government grant, served from 1888 to 1901 as superintendent of the same steel mills in Worcester, and after their absorption by the U.S. Steel Corporation he remained until 1904 as chief metallurgist. After five years as a consulting engineer in Worcester he returned to Sweden and became president of an increasingly important steel and metalworking company in the province of Blekinge. In America he had helped design and build large steel and rolling mills at Roebling, New Jersey, and a steel mill with wireworks at Philipsdale, Rhode Island.

Many skilled iron and steel workers from Sweden found jobs in other Worcester industries, and more and more immigrants founded their own manufacturing firms, the main initial investment often being their technical ingenuity.. Hjalmar G. Carlson, born at an industrial estate in Östergötland, who had come to Worcester as a young boy, invented new steel-pressing methods. For one such invention, which during the First World War greatly facilitated the making of artillery shells, he received in 1921 the Medal of The American Society of Mechanical Engineers and in 1924 the Holley Medal. An early settler named Ivar Johnson started to manufacture firearms and sporting goods in Worcester. In 1891 he moved his rapidly growing industry to Fitchburg 20 miles farther north.

Among the industrial pioneers at Fitchburg was also Carl H. Hedstrom from Kloster near Hedemora in the province of Dalarna, who came in 1901 at the age of 20 and was joined by two brothers. A mechanic from the industrial town of Trollhättan in Västergötland, Claus O. Johnson, who in 1903 started working for Ivar Johnson at Fitchburg, organized ten years later in Worcester a firm, Hollander & Johnson, which became a noted manufacturer of tools and specialized equipment. Charles H. Oslund, a machinist and smith from the ancient ironmaking town of Forsbacka in the province of Gästrikland, who came to Worcester in 1893 with his wife and two sons, obtained nearly 100 patents for machinery of various kinds. His seven sons — five were born in America — formed a company making bottling machines that were used throughout the world. Like practically all other manufacturing firms founded by Swedish immigrants in New England, it was converted to war production in the early 1940s. One of the Swedish-born industrialists at Worcester, Pehr G. Holmes (1881–1952), served as mayor in 1917–19 and in the U.S. House of Representatives from 1931 to 1947. Born at Mölnbacka in Värmland, he came to America with his parents at the age of five.

An unusual career was made by Oscar N. Sohlberg or Solbert (1885–1958), born at Karbenning in the province of Västmanland, who in 1893 came to Worcester with his father, an axmaker, and started earning his living as a newsboy. In 1906 he graduated from the Worcester Polytechnic Institute and four years later from the United States Military Academy at West Point, standing number 6 in a class of 83 members. After several years as an instructor of engineering at West Point and as a colonel serving in the First World War, he was sent to London as a U.S. military attaché. In 1924–26 he was military aide to President Coolidge, and in 1924 he was appointed the official travel escort to the Prince of Wales. Both in 1926 and in 1938 he performed the same duty for Crown Prince Gustav Adolf and Crown Princess Louise of Sweden. In 1926 he had left active service to join the Eastman Kodak Company of Rochester, New York, but during the Second World War he was named chief of special services in Europe, retiring with the rank of brigadier general.

In Worcester as in many other American cities and towns, the Swedish settlers organized their own congregations, welfare institutions, and associations of many different kinds, including, for instance, numerous singing societies, and gradually they became engaged in almost every aspect of the community's life. The Fairlawn Hospital was founded in 1921 by a group of citizens of Swedish and other Scandinavian extraction.

For many years Worcester had an immensely popular Swedish clergyman, Johannes or John Alfred Hultman (1861–1942), who on both sides of the Atlantic became widely known as a traveling, singing evangelist, called "Solskenssångaren" or the "Sunshine singer." From 1897 until his death in 1942 after a church concert at Burbank, California, he conducted, principally as a singer, about 7,000 divine services in the United States and more than 5,000 in his native Sweden, to which he returned the first time in 1901 and where he and his family lived from 1909 to 1913 and again from 1919 on. In 1869 he had come to the United States with his parents, who settled in Iowa. After beginning as a shepherd boy, he first studied and later taught music in Chicago, and in Omaha, Nebraska, he spent 14 years as a pastor and composer-singer of gospel songs. From 1900 to 1906 he served as pastor of the Salem Square Swedish Congregational Church in Worcester, where he and his family also lived during the First World War. His mission was to impart joy, and his gentle, sunny

personality had a magical effect on his listeners. The house at Är-
nanäs near Sävsjö in Småland where he was born became a memorial
in 1948.

In the late 1800s, a weekly called *Skandinavia* was the largest and
most ambitious Swedish-language newspaper in New England. In
1918 it was absorbed by another Worcester weekly, *Svea*, which four
decades later was combined with *Nordstjernan* of New York. In its
early days, the Swedish community in Worcester had seen some
strange publications. One called *Byrackan*, or The Cur, was published
in 1885, and three years later came *Orkanen*, or The Hurricane, both
typical scandal sheets. Of radical leanings were *Blixten* (The Lightning) and *Dundret* (The Thunder), both appearing in 1894 and then
consolidated into *Arbetarens Vän* (The Workman's Friend), and *Nya
Sverige* (New Sweden), which was published in 1915–20, the place of
printing sometimes shifting to Boston. One of its 1915 issues contained a satirical piece on the average New Englander's image of
Sweden: a kingdom about the size of South Boston, with a king who
lives in an igloo and whose wife makes stockings out of yarn imported
from Worcester, and with a people who are uncommonly ignorant, not
being able either to play baseball or to speak English, though they
chew snuff remarkably well.

In 1910, Worcester had about 8,000 Swedish-born inhabitants. Of
its present population of nearly 200,000, approximately one-sixth is
of Swedish origin.

Boston an early center for Swedish gymnastics and handicrafts

AN ENTHUSIASTIC interest in physical education was typical of quite a
few Swedish immigrants in New England, and Boston in particular
became an early leader in this field in America. From there, Swedish
gymnastics spread to other sections of the country. Many Swedish and
other pioneers in the Midwest and on the West Coast had spent some
time studying or practicing in Boston. New York City played a somewhat similar role. In Chicago, Polycarpus von Schneidau, who in 1842
had joined Gustaf Unonius at Pine Lake, Wisconsin, began to introduce Swedish gymnastics a few years later.

A young former army officer and graduate of the Central Institute of Gymnastics in Stockholm, Baron Nils Posse (1862–95), who
arrived in 1885, helped launch Swedish gymnastics in Boston. In

1890 this stystem was introduced in the city's public schools, and under the direction of a Boston physician, who had studied gymnastics in Stockholm, it soon became obligatory. The Boston Normal School of Gymnastics was established in 1890 by a wealthy lady who had become keenly interested in Swedish gymnastics, and Posse became its first leader. The next year, however, he began to train instructors in his own gymnasium. In 1893 he helped organize exhibitions by a troupe of elite gymnasts from Stockholm at the World's Columbian Exposition in Chicago.

As instructor at the Boston Normal School, Posse was succeeded by Claes Enebuske, who had come to the United States in 1887. Before receiving an M.D. degree from Harvard and retiring from gymnastics, he taught during summers at the Chautauqua Institute near Jamestown in western New York, which attracted students from all parts of the country and where somewhat later a large gymnasium was built on the Swedish pattern and with Swedish equipment. It was named for Jakob Bolin, who in the early 1890s had begun his American career as an instructor at the Brooklyn Normal School of Gymnastics; he had then moved to Chautauqua, and in 1910, four years before his death, he became professor of physical education at the University of Utah. His work at Chautauqua was continued by Carl Gustaf Carlström, a graduate of the Central Institute in Stockholm, who had begun in Chicago in 1907. In 1923 Carlstrom was appointed president of the American College of Physical Education.

At the Boston Normal School, Enebuske was succeeded by another graduate of the Central Institute of Gymnastics in Stockholm, Carl Collin (b. 1864), who taught there and at Wellesley College for many years. He too took a medical degree at Harvard, but continued as an instructor of physical education at Battle Creek, Michigan, and in Chicago. Among the students at the Boston Normal School during his time was Carl G. Anderson, who had come to America after graduation from a gymnastic institute in Stockholm, and who in 1910 moved to New Jersey where Swedish gymnastics were introduced in the Newark high schools and other institutions. An all-round athlete as well as an outstanding gymnast, he later became athletic director or coach at Harvard and Rutgers universities and of the Newark Athletic Club.

Most of the Swedish pioneers in physical culture in America were graduates of institutes in Sweden. One of the few notable exceptions was Wilhelm Skarström or William Skarstrom (1869–1951) from Stockholm, who had begun as a sailor and come to America in 1889. After work as a gymnastic instructor in New York and Brooklyn and studies at the Boston Normal School of Gymnastics, he taught in 1897–99 physical education at Groton School, where Franklin D. Roosevelt was one of his pupils. In the early 1900s, when he too became an M.D. at Harvard, he served successively at the Massachusetts Institute of Technology, the University of Southern California in Los Angeles, and Columbia University in New York. From 1912 and until his retirement two decades later he was professor of hygiene and physical education at Wellesley College near Boston, which has honored his memory with the William Skarstrom Fund for physical culture. He wrote two books about the Swedish Ling system of gymnastics.

Skarstrom's predecessor Carl Collin had among his pupils at Wellesley College a young Swedish-born woman, Signe Hagelthorn, already mentioned above, who was a graduate of the Boston Normal School of Gymnastics. Having arrived in Boston at the age of 13 to visit relatives, she became one of the most active pioneers in physical education and health promotion in America. Beginning at Oshkosh, Wisconsin, she organized teacher-training courses and health instruction in the schools, and after that she spent 16 years in Los Angeles, Oakland, and San Francisco, engaged in activities ranging from the opening of numerous playgrounds to lecturing in the medical school of the University of California. From 1925 to 1932 she served as professor of physical education at New York University. After a three-year visit to Sweden she became in 1935 dean of Adelphi College at Garden City, Long Island.

One of the early leaders in the field of Swedish gymnastics in New York was Captain Theodor A. Melander, born at Sigtuna near Stockholm and a graduate of the Central Institute of Gymnastics. Thoroughly familiar with the history of Swedish gymnastics in the United States, he regarded the brothers George and Charles Taylor, both physicians in New York, as two of the first pioneers. The former introduced the Swedish exercises at his hydropathic institute in New York in 1855. The following year the younger brother made a study trip to Stockholm. His son Per Henrik Taylor, who also became a physician, was named in honor of Per Henrik Ling, the "Father of Swedish gymnastics."

In 1865 a medico-mechanical institute was opened in Stockholm by Dr. Gustav Zander (1835–1920), who had developed his own system of health exercises and designed numerous machines for mechanical physiotherapy, and during the next half-century about 200 such institutes were established in other countries. In the early 1870s an elaborate Zander Institute was founded in New York by a Russian immigrant, and in the beginning it met with great success. Zander-type machines were also installed in many American hospitals, but in the early 1900s their use began to diminish. An internationally known Swedish pioneer of lasting importance was Viktor Balck (1844–1928), by profession an army officer, who is regarded as one of the fathers of the modern Swedish sports movement. His enthusiastic attitude toward gymnastics and sports was greatly influenced by British ideas and practices. In 1911 he was, in return, awarded a high English decoration for the value of his suggestions in the training of British soldiers and sailors.

In an article about gymnastics written in 1938, Theodor A. Melander of New York ended on a note of pessimism and resignation, admitting that Swedish health gymnastics, despite hard and time-sacrificing work by many, had not succeeded in establishing itself in the United States. Swedish-type massage and physiotherapy, on the other hand, had gained appreciation both from the medical profession and from the population in general. Today, however, the old Ling system of gymnastics has been thoroughly revised even in Sweden, and the new Swedish form of rhythmic gymnastics has won widespread recognition and practice in the United States.

Swedish handicrafts and manual training became, like physical education, known in the United States via immigrants and travelers, and the Swedish word *slöjd* was gradually incorporated in the English language as 'sloyd.' When a special Sloyd Training School was established in Boston in 1888, a Swedish expert, Gustaf Larsson (1861–1919), who had been educated at the Normal School of Sloyd at Nääs in his native province of Västergötland, was invited to teach there, and after a few years he became the principal. Hundreds of teachers were sent out from the Boston school all over the United States, and Larsson established subsidiary centers as far away as in Cuba and India.

Folin of Harvard, Lindgren of MIT, Edgren and Rudolph J. Anderson of Yale

MOST of the 19th-century Swedish immigrants who became noted university or college professors, in New England as in other sections of the country, were specialists in the field of natural science.

Otto Folin (1867–1934), who in 1907 accepted a call to the Hamilton Kuhn chair of physiological chemistry at the Harvard Medical School, was regarded as one of the foremost biochemists of his time. For the study of changes in the nature and concentrations of chemical substances within human beings during metabolism, he developed unique analytical procedures which in the scientific world became known as the "Folin methods." In a memorial adress in 1934, Dr. Henry A. Christian, professor of medicine at Harvard and physician-in-chief to the Peter Bent Brigham Hospital in Boston, said: "You, my younger colleagues and students, scarcely can vision medicine without the methods of blood analysis perfected by Folin and his pupils and those inspired by Folin's own accomplishments, so completely have these micro-methods of quantitative analysis become a factor integrated into the web and woof of the fabric of clinical-medical and surgical lore."

The son of a tanner and the district midwife at Åseda in the province of Småland, Otto Folin came to America in 1882 at the age of 15, joining an older brother at Stillwater, Minnesota, and working his way toward a higher education. After studies at the University of Minnesota followed by a trip to Europe, he received his doctor's degree in 1898 at the University of Chicago. His European tour in 1897 included Sweden, and there his principal teacher was Olof Hammarsten of Uppsala, who had won international recognition as a pioneer in biochemical research. In 1918 Otto Folin received an honorary doctor's degree from the then 250-year-old University of Lund.

From 1912 to 1933 Waldemar Lindgren (1860–1939), the son of a district judge at Vassmolösa near Kalmar in southeastern Sweden, served as professor of economic geology at the Massachusetts Institute of Technology in Boston, and he too was one of America's leading specialists in his field. After substantial schooling in Sweden and Germany, he came to America in 1883 and almost immediately started working for the U.S. Geological Survey, where he finally became chief geologist. Most of his explorations and a majority of his numerous scientific publications concerned the geology and ore deposits of the Rocky Mountains and the Far West. In 1923 he was elected president of the Geological Society of America, and ten years later, when he retired from his professorship, other geologists presented him with a memorial volume, *Ore Deposits of the Western States*. His textbook about mineral deposits was published in several editions.

During the period 1966–72 the Massachusetts Institute of Technology had a president of Swedish ancestry, Howard W. Johnson, born in Chicago in 1922, who had previously served as dean of the Sloan School of Management at M.I.T. and in 1972 became chairman of the M.I.T. corporation. His paternal grandfather, who came to America in the 1860s as a young man, was born in Stockholm, and his paternal grandmother was also of Scandinavian origin. At Tufts University in Medford, a Boston suburb, a son of Swedish immigrants, Nils Yngve Wessell (b. 1914), served as professor of psychology for many years and as president from 1953 to 1966. His father was born at Kåseberga, at Sweden's extreme southeastern corner, and his mother in Stockholm. An immigrant from Sweden, Nils G. Sahlin, born at Stockholm in 1900 and raised on the island of Öland, served in 1956–68 as president of Quinnipiac College in Hamden, Connecticut. He came to America at the age of 21 and earned his doctor's degree at Yale 16 years later.

The first Swedish-born faculty member at Yale University in New Haven, Connecticut, was not a scientist but an eminent linguist. Hjalmar Edgren, who has already been mentioned, started teaching French in 1874, and in 1878–79 he served as an instructor of Sanskrit and comparative philology. Edgren also taught at Gothenburg and Lund universities in Sweden, and during two periods at the University of Nebraska in Lincoln. At Yale, the son of a Swedish pioneer pastor in the Middle West, Gustav A. Andreen (1864–1940), was appointed to the chair of Scandinavian languages in 1900, but the next year he assumed the presidency of Augustana College at Rock Island, Illinois. In 1920, Adolph B. Benson (1881–1962), whose father, a blacksmith from northern Skåne, in 1892 had settled in Connecticut with his large family, became an assistant professor of German and Scandinavian, being named full professor 12 years later. He also made significant contributions to historical research concerning relations between America and Sweden.

Another Swedish immigrant, Rudolph John Anderson (1879–1961) from Härna in Västergötland, who arrived in 1893, served from 1927 to 1948 as professor of chemistry at Yale. He had studied at Tulane University in New Orleans and at Uppsala and other institutions in Europe, finally obtaining his doctorate in biochemistry at Cornell University in Ithaca, New York. Anderson became internationally known in the world of science as an authority on the chemistry of bacteria, particularly tubercle and leprosy bacilli. He was for many years president of the American Society of Biological Chemists. In 1947 he received an honorary degree from Lund University in Sweden. In 1970 Yale's chemistry department inaugurated a new type of colloquium program exploring new and emerging fields of chemistry, named The Rudolph Anderson Symposia in Chemistry.

Carl O. Johns (1870–1942), who came to America in 1879, started teaching chemistry at Yale in 1904, and in 1930, when he had been director of research of the Standard Oil Company, he was elected president of the Yale Chemical Society, which meets in Berzelius Hall. He received his first more advanced education at Upsala College, which was founded in 1893 in Brooklyn by Swedish immigrants, and studied later at Bethany College in Lindsborg, Kansas. A few more recent Swedish immigrants, who became professors at Yale or other universities in New England, will be mentioned later.

By the middle of the 1900s, Yale faculty members of recent Swedish ancestry included a professor of engineering, Philip G. Laurson, born in northwestern Illinois; a professor of surgery, Gustaf E. Lindskog, who was born of Swedish parents in Boston; a professor of pediatrics, Grover F. Powers, a native of Indiana whose father's name was originally Johnson, and a professor of modern European history, Harry R. Rudin, whose parents, immigrants from Sweden, had lived in Vermont. A graduate of Gustavus Adolphus College at St. Peter, Minnesota, Sydney E. Ahlstrom, joined the Yale faculty in 1954 and was ten years later named professor of American history and modern church history. His book *A Religious History of the American People* won a National Book Award in 1973. His paternal grandparents came from Korsberga and his maternal grandparents from Jät, both in the province of Småland.

"Rose King" as well as numerous tool and machine makers among Connecticut Swedes

IN CONNECTICUT the Swedish-born population increased from about 2,000 in 1880 to more than 18,000 in the early 1900s.

The first sizable influx of Swedes began about 1870, when Portland with its sandstone quarries, on the Connecticut River south of Hartford, was the principal destination. Owners of quarries often hired Swedish immigrants on their arrival in New York. Many of the newcomers were later employed in the silk mills at Middletown on the other side of the river.

A mile or two north of Middletown is the little town of Cromwell, which became noted for the magnificent nurseries and greenhouses of A. N. Pierson, where for some decades most of the employees were Swedish. Anders Nils Persson or Andrew N. Pierson (1850–1925), born at Håslöv in Skåne, was the son of a flower-loving schoolteacher who also moved to the United States. At the age of eight he was apprenticed to a florist in Sweden, and in 1866, after having come to America by steerage, he started as a gardener in Connecticut where some of his brothers had already settled. At Cromwell his activities finally were so extensive that he became widely known as the "Rose King of America." Many new varieties of roses were developed by him, and he was one of the first promoters of flower shows in the country. The little town of Pierson, near Lake George in Florida, was named for one of his brothers, who became a successful citrus grower.

A number of Swedes settled as farmers in the valley of the Connecticut River, and in the northeastern corner of the state, in Thompson and Woodstock townships, there was an agricultural district where in the early 1900s one-fifth of the population was of Swedish origin. The first Swedes arrived there in 1871. The great majority of the Swedish immigrants in Connecticut, however, settled in urban areas.

In the 1880s the factories in Hartford began to attract Swedes in great numbers. Among those who came in 1895 was a man from the province of Bohuslän, Bengt M. W. Hanson (1866–1925), who had arrived five years earlier and became one of the leading figures in

Connecticut's industrial life. In Sweden he had had some college education as well as technical experience. In Hartford he began at the bench in the small-tool department of the Pratt & Whitney Company, which had been founded in 1864 by two American toolmakers and through them had begun to pioneer in the production of machine tools, especially for the production of ordnance. Hanson, who finally became vice president and general manager of the company, followed in their footsteps, inventing and building an amazing number of new tools and machines for the mechanical industries. During most of the First World War he had charge of the gun production of the Colt Fire Arms Company, also serving as an adviser to the Federal government. At the same time he helped bring the Swedish SKF Ball-Bearing Company, which decided to establish a subsidiary in the United States, to Hartford. The factory built there was later consolidated with a plant in Philadelphia. After Hanson's death, his business associate Clarence E. Whitney said: "The world has lost one of its most brilliant mechanical engineers. Our country has lost one of its most patriotic citizens."

Many other Swedes worked for Pratt & Whitney, among them Charles G. Johnson from Vånga in Västergötland, who had come to Providence, Rhode Island, in 1890 at the age of 20. His specialty was precision-gaging and measuring equipment. In 1921 he formed his own company, which nine years later was acquired by Pratt & Whitney.

The metal and hardware manufacturers of New Britain, south of Hartford, obtained large groups of Swedish immigrants from the city of Eskilstuna, located southwest of Stockholm and long known for its fine hardware, and from Finspång in Östergötland, a metalworking town with traditions from the early 1500s. In 1903 the Reverend J. E. Klingberg, born near the ironmaking town of Hällefors in Västmanland, founded at New Britain a children's home which became one of the largest and best-equipped institutions in New England. A Lutheran church which was completed at about the same time is regarded as one of the most beautiful churches of Swedish origin in America. At Thomaston, some 40 miles farther west, a Swedish immigrant from Halmstad in Halland, Karl W. Halldén (1884–1970), who had come to America at the age of nine, founded in 1916 his own machine company. His patents finally numbered more than 50. One of his inventions made possible the continuous strip-mill process in producing sheet metal. Halldén helped establish the department of engineering at Trinity College in Hartford, and its engineering laboratory was named for him.

Among the Swedes who came to New Haven in 1896 was Gustaf Swebilius (1879–1948), the son of a watchmaker at Vingåker in Södermanland, who immediately went to work for an arms manufacturer and soon became a competent toolmaker. Later he made important inventions. During the First World War he solved the problem of synchronizing machine-gun fire with the airplane propeller, so that bullets could be fired between the blades. In 1926 he established his own factory at Hamden, just north of New Haven, where during the Second World War some 5,000 workers were employed. Swebilius, who was known to them as Gus, is said to have known more about automatic weapons than any other man in America. Most of his large estate was willed to research on cancer and epilepsy. Among his many Swedish assistants was Herman B. Carlson, born in 1881 at Motala on Lake Vättern and trained in its machine works.

In Bridgeport, Connecticut's second largest city and foremost industrial producer, Swedish immigrants and their descendants have played a significant part as founders and leaders of tool and machine companies. An immigrant from Gothenburg, Axel Hilmer Nilson (1849–1928), who arrived in 1880 when he was a highly skilled machinist, is regarded as the first important pioneer. After having worked in a large factory which employed many Swedish hardware-men and mechanics, he founded in 1892 his own machine company. He was succeeded by his son Jacob Nelson, born at Karlstad in Värmland. In the 1880s the Swedes in Bridgeport received powerful support from P. T. Barnum, the great showman, who cherished fond memories of Jenny Lind and had a high regard for the skills of the Swedish immigrants. As mayor of Bridgeport in 1875–76, he did much for the improvement of the city. In return, the Swedes in Bridgeport have always taken an active part in the annual Barnum Festival. In the 1950s the program began to include a Jenny Lind contest which was coordinated with a similar event in Sweden, finally enabling two young "Jenny Linds" to exchange visits across the Atlantic.

At Groton, noted for its shipbuilding works, the Electric Boat Company has had several eminent Swedish engineers, including Eric

H. Ewertz (1873–1950) from Karlskrona, the naval base in southeastern Sweden, who in the late 1800s had been responsible for the construction at Elizabethport, New Jersey, of the famous *Holland*, the first submarine commissioned in the U.S. Navy and regarded as the prototype of the modern submersible. From 1934 to 1950 he worked for Electric Boat as a consulting engineer. As a works manager, Carl A. Franzén (1887–1949) from Kalmar also made significant contributions to the building of submarines during the Second World War. He had started with the company in 1916. A machinist at Electric Boat, Kaleb Jansson, born at Örebro in 1878 and an emigrant in 1917, won a wide reputation as an amateur botanist; a brother in Sweden, Anton Jansson, began as a journalist and became an outstanding entomologist.

One of the Swedish industrialists in Bridgeport, Rudolph F. Bannow (1897–1962) from Gothenburg, became in 1960 the first foreign-born president of the National Association of Manufacturers. He had come to America at the age of 13 and begun as a patternmaker. In 1929, at the beginning of the Great Depression, he and another Swedish immigrant, Magnus Wahlström (1903–72) from Surahammar in Västmanland, founded a company making a high-speed milling machine which became known as the "Bridgeport miller." Shortly after the expiration of Bannow's term, the National Association of Manufacturers decided to have a full-time rather than an honorary president, and the first person named to this post was Werner P. Gullander, whose father, a Lutheran missionary and pastor, was born at Gullåkra near Lund in southernmost Sweden.

Four cities in Connecticut have had Swedish-language weeklies or other periodicals, namely, Bridgeport, Hartford, New Britain, and New Haven.

26

In the Mid-Atlantic States

New York third largest "Swede state" by 1900 — *Jamestown an industrial center*

THE Middle Atlantic states, New York, New Jersey, and Pennsylvania, had in 1870 less than nine percent of the Swedish-born population in the United States, but this proportion then increased constantly, reaching about 13 percent at the turn of the century and 15 percent in 1930.

The Swedish-born population in New York State increased almost tenfold from 1870 to 1910, from about 5,500 to nearly 54,000. The highest point, more than 61,000, was reached in 1930. From 1900 New York ranked third among the states in the number of Swedish-born settlers.

Already in the late 1800s or early 1900s, more than two-thirds of the Swedes in New York State lived in the New York metropolitan area. Of the other cities, Jamestown had by far the largest Swedish-born group, and then came Buffalo and Rochester.

Situated some 60 miles southwest of Buffalo at the southern end of Lake Chautauqua, Jamestown is surrounded by an area of dairy farms, orchards, and vineyards, but the city itself is an industrial center with numerous manufacturing establishments. Most of these were founded by Swedish immigrants or their descendants.

The first Swedes had come to Jamestown in 1849 from nearby Chandlers Valley in Pennsylvania, which the early immigrants from

Sweden called Hessel Valley after Hessleby in the province of Småland, and thousands of men, women, and children arrived during the
decades after the Civil War. In 1930 the Swedish-born numbered
nearly 8,000. Today about half of Jamestown's some 40,000 inhabitants are of Swedish origin.

The first Swede to have a business of his own in Jamestown was
John Gelm, who in 1850 at the age of 10 had come to Chandlers
Valley from Hessleby and settled in Jamestown in 1866. His son
George E. Gelm (1870–1944) became a naval officer. During the First
World War he was assigned to the command of the battleship *Kearsarge*, and later to that of the *Florida*. By 1870 several Swedes in
Jamestown began to make furniture or other articles of wood, and
scores of countrymen founded larger factories during the next few
decades. In 1935, when many of the woodworking firms had converted to metal, a furniture specialist of Swedish parentage received
an order for the furnishing of the new U.S. Supreme Court building
in Washington, D. C., calling for 211 pieces of furniture in 20 different styles, including the chairs used by the nine Justices.

Gradually wood was replaced more and more by metal, and a
variety of other goods such as tools, automobile parts, kitchen equipment, and metal furniture were made. A Swedish immigrant who
arrived in 1890, Charles P. Dahlstrom (1872–1909) from the island of
Gotland, built the first fireproof metal door, and in the 1930s the
company founded by him delivered more than 50,000 such doors for
the Rockefeller Center buildings in New York City alone. Another
immigrant, Karl Peterson, founded a small-tool company whose products were sold all over the United States and in many foreign countries. In the early to middle 1900s, Oscar A. Linné or Lenna (1876–
1951) from Helsingborg in southern Sweden was one of Jamestown's
foremost industrialists and civic leaders. When he was seven years old,
his father left for America, intending to dig gold in California, but
was never heard from again. At 18, however, the son followed
him across the sea, first supporting himself in America as a lumberman and a Great Lakes seaman. In 1914 he organized a company
in Jamestown which, to begin with, specialized in the manufacture of
automobile radiators and became one of the largest of its kind in the
country, with the Swedish motorcar industry among its customers.
For many years he visited Sweden almost every summer.

The first more important metalworking company in Jamestown

was founded by a native American. Among its many Swedish employees was Charles Gustav Peterson, who had arrived from Värmland at the age of four. His son Roger Tory Peterson (b. 1908), who became a famous ornithologist and has been called a "modern Audubon," began his career as a young boy watching birds around Lake Chautauqua. Many of his books have been published also in Sweden.

One of Jamestown's mayors, Samuel A. Carlson, born in 1868 of parents from Askeryd in Småland, became known far beyond the borders of New York State. From 1908 to 1938 he served almost continuously as the city's chief executive. Early in his career he had to make a hard fight for a city-owned electric-power plant, which many regarded as a "socialistic innovation." Charles A. Beard, the American historian, called his autobiography "a living document in the history of popular government."

Samuel Carlson had been editor of one of the early Swedish-language weeklies in Jamestown, where at least one such newspaper was published from 1874 until the Second World War. Numerous secular organizations and quite a few singing societies and choirs were formed by the Swedes, and ten churches were built. In the early 1900s Dr. Julius Lincoln (1872–1954), born at Lindsborg, Kansas, was regarded as the city's leading clergyman. For over two decades he was in charge of the First Swedish Lutheran Church, first served in 1856 by the Reverend Jonas Swensson whose son, Carl Aaron Swensson, born at Chandlers Valley, in 1881 founded Bethany College at Lindsborg. In the 1930s Julius Lincoln played one of the central parts in the preparations for the New Sweden tercentenary celebrations.

At least one of the 19th-century Swedish immigrants who settled in New York State and remained there became a distinguished scholar and university professor, namely Nathaniel Schmidt (1862–1939), a native of Hudiksvall in the northern province of Hälsingland, who after a few years of university studies in Stockholm left for America in 1884. After further studies he served from 1888 to 1896 as professor of Semitic languages and literature at Colgate University in Hamilton, New York, and from 1896 to 1932 as professor in the same subjects at Cornell University in Ithaca. In 1904–1905 he was director of the American School of Archeology in Jerusalem, and later he became a member of the American School of Oriental Research in Jerusalem and Baghdad. In 1931–32 he was president of the American Oriental Society. A younger brother, Emanuel Schmidt (1868–1921), who emigrated from Sweden two years later, became a Ph.D. at the University of Chicago and a leader or teacher at Baptist schools in Seattle and St. Paul, Minnesota.

Early Swedish settlers in Buffalo included Lars Gustaf Sellstedt, who arrived in 1846, after many years as a seaman, and became a successful portraitist as well as the principal founder of the Buffalo Fine Arts Academy. We shall meet him again. A typographic designer named Axel Edvard Sahlin (1887–1956) from Lund in south Sweden came in 1911 to the Roycroft Shops at East Aurora near Buffalo, a socialistic colony of artisans and artists, and during the next 15 years he established the Roycroft style of printing, which gave a pronounced impetus to artistic printing in America. His work won many international honors and awards for its excellence of typography. In 1927 he set up his own typographical business in Buffalo. He also became widely known for his volumes of *Sahlin's Typography*. His elegant Christmas publications are now rare collector's items. For many years he was president of the Swedish Club in Buffalo. A younger brother, Emil Georg Sahlin, joined The Roycrofters in 1914 and his brother at Buffalo in 1928.

Industrial concerns have been established by Swedish immigrants in New York State even outside the Jamestown and New York areas. Since 1925 precision gages have been made at Poughkeepsie by the Standard Gage Company, which was founded by a native of Gothenburg, Erik Aldeborgh (b. 1886), and after his retirement has been run by his two sons. He started at Poughkeepsie in 1919 as an associate of Carl Edward Johansson, widely known as "Precision Johansson," who later joined Henry Ford at Detroit.

Several persons of Swedish parentage have been members of the New York State legislature, while few seem to have served in more prominent positions in the state administration at Albany. In 1969 Ewald Berger Nyquist, born in 1914 as the seventh of nine children of Swedish immigrants in Rockford, Illinois, was named commissioner of education.

35,000 Swedes in New York City in 1910 — Many U.S.-born from homes in other sections

FOR the Swedes as well as for other immigrants, New York City was above all the great gateway to America. At the same time it became a symbol of the dynamic progress and the boundless opportunities of the New World. The great majority of the newcomers could not dream of settling there, but sailing toward and passing through this throbbing metropolis was, despite the unpleasant surprises in the form of cheating and robbing that often lurked, a mystically inspiring experience. If the city's dimensions struck them with awe, they often reacted with a certain ironic sense of humor. Of all the stories told by Swedes in America, one of the most popular was about a man and his wife who had just come over from the Old Country and landed in New York. More and more amazed, the husband finally exclaimed, "If this is New York, what must Lindsborg be like!" Or Lindstrom, Minnesota, or Galva, Illinois, if the couple were headed there.

After the Civil War, however, a rapidly growing number of Swedes settled in New York, including Brooklyn, which remained a separate city until 1898. From less than 3,000 in 1870, according to the U.S. census, the Swedish-born population increased to about 6,000 in 1880, nearly 16,500 in 1890, over 28,000 in 1900, and about 35,000 in 1910. After a slight decline during the next ten years, the number of Swedish-born rose again to more than 37,000 in 1930, the highest such figure on record. For decades, about half of the Swedish-born population lived in Brooklyn, but this proportion began to decline in the early 1900s. Increasing numbers of immigrants were, like the younger, American-born generations, attracted to the new residential sections in the suburbs.

Because of its geographical location, its direct transatlantic communications, and its concentration of cultural, commercial, and industrial activities, New York with its suburbs has played a more important part in relations between the United States and Sweden than any other American city. No urban center except Chicago had more Swedish-born inhabitants than New York, but their share in the total population, on the other hand, was always quite modest. By the turn of the century, residents of Swedish birth represented about 0.8 percent of New York's 3.4 million people. Many prominent New Yorkers of Swedish parentage were born in other parts of the United States, in particular its principal Scandinavian powerhouse, the Middle West.

The first widely known Swede in New York was Captain John Ericsson, whose *Monitor* was launched at Greenpoint in Brooklyn in 1862, and who lived in Manhattan from 1839 until his death 50 years later. The first Swedish organization in New York, still known as The Swedish Society, had been founded three years before his arrival, and without taking an active part except as a donor in several cases, he could follow the rapid expansion of the Swedish community's activities after the Civil War.

The first Lutheran congregation, named for Gustavus Adolphus, was formed in 1865, 20 years after Olof G. Hedstrom had begun his Scandinavian Methodist mission on the Bethel Ship in New York harbor, and it was followed two years later by the Swedish Immanuel Methodist congregation in Brooklyn, actually an offshoot of the Bethel Ship work which Hedstrom continued until 1875. In the late 1800s and early 1900s, scores of churches were founded by Swedish immigrants in the New York area. A Swedish hospital was inaugurated in Brooklyn on Midsummer Day, June 24, 1906, and other welfare institutions were also established.

Attempts to publish Swedish-language periodicals were made in New York in the 1850s and 1860s, but the first one crowned with lasting success began in 1872 with the publication of *Nordstjernan* (The North Star), which still appeared more than 100 years later. One of its first publishers was an immigrant of 1869 from the city of Kalmar in southeast Sweden, Håkan Johansen (1829–1910), who became a leader among the Swedes in New York, and who as owner of the newspaper was followed first by his son and then by a grandson. A socialist weekly called *Arbetaren* (The Worker) was published from 1896 to 1928.

The unveiling of the second John Ericsson statue at the Battery in New York in the summer of 1903 became the beginning of improved cooperation among the Swedish groups in New York. A central organization, later known as The United Swedish Societies of Greater New York, was formed the same year. Its first president was an immigrant from Floby in the province of Västergötland, Emil F. Johnson (1864–1953), who had come to New York in 1887 shortly after his graduation from the Institute of Technology in Stockholm. As an analytical chemist operating his own business, he served from 1895 to 1915 as a public-health inspector and devised an effective system of milk control for New York as well as for other cities. In 1891 he had helped found an organization called the Swedish Aid Society, which during its 15 years procured employment for about

20,000 Scandinavian immigrants, and in 1906 he was one of the founders of The Swedish Chamber of Commerce of the United States. At the age of 83 he moved back to Sweden.

In 1888 a group of younger Swedish engineers formed an organization known as The American Society of Swedish Engineers. It was regarded primarily as an association for mutual improvement and support, and as such it played an important role for several decades. Close contacts were maintained with similar societies in other cities, particularly the one in Philadelphia. The first president was Carl J. Mellin, who did pioneering work for the Navy Yard in Brooklyn. One of his successors of the 19th century, Victor H. Hybinette, is still regarded as one of the foremost metallurgists of his era.

In the early 1900s, the Swedish central organization and the engineers' association helped welcome many prominent Swedish visitors to New York. In 1906, for instance, came Otto Nordenskjöld (1869–1928), a polar explorer who was in the United States on a lecture tour; in 1908 Oscar Montelius (1843–1921), who had won fame as an archeologist and also was very active as a lecturer; in 1911 Svante Arrhenius, one of the founders of the modern science of physical chemistry and in 1903 Sweden's first Nobel prize winner, who had been invited to give lectures at Yale; and in 1912 Gunnar Andersson (1865–1928), botanist and geographer, who had been invited to America as an expert and adviser on forest management.

The leaders of the Swedish central association were particularly proud of their participation in the welcome-home festivities offered by the City of New York for the American Olympic team on August 24, 1912. Helped by a complete representation in the various contests, Sweden had managed to win the unofficial top score in the Olympic Games in Stockholm, which were regarded everywhere as a great organizational success and also had been favored by glorious summer weather. In the parade on Fifth Avenue the American athletes and their leaders were followed by Swedish flag-bearers in historical costumes, marshals in blue-and-yellow sashes, and members of Swedish associations, including the Swedish-American Athletic Club of Brooklyn. Women in colorful Swedish folk costumes also took part in the procession. The crowds on the sidewalks often seemed to applaud the Swedish troupe as much as their own team. The ceremony at City Hall and a large Terrace Garden banquet in the evening also became memorable occasions for the Swedish participants. Never before, some of them said, had Sweden basked in such limelight and been honored with such warmth in New York.

The American sports fans knew that most of the members of Sweden's Olympic team, as well as several of the American track-and-field stars, had been trained by Ernst or Ernie Hjertberg (1867–1951), who, before being invited to Sweden in 1910, had been a highly successful coach of the New York Athletic Club and the Irish-American Athletic Club. He is, in fact, regarded as a pioneer in coaching in America. A native of the city of Jönköping, he had come to the United States at the age of four. After the Olympic Games in Stockholm he remained in Sweden until 1922, when he became Holland's Olympic coach. Returning to America after the Amsterdam Games in 1924, he served for 12 years as athletic director of Rice Institute in Houston, Texas. He finally worked again in New York, one of his principal goals being to recruit workers and office employees for active participation in sports. His daughter, Adèle Heilborn (b. 1899), served from 1938 to 1966 as managing director of the Sweden-America Foundation in Stockholm.

Of the Swedish engineers in New York, one named David L. Lindquist (1874–1944) made inventions of particular importance to the city's development. A native of Stockholm and a graduate of its Institute of Technology, he had spent some years with the Asea electric company in Västerås and had after that both studied and practiced in Germany. In 1902 he came to the United States to study high-voltage power transmission, but instead he went to work for the Otis Elevator Company in New York, whose founder in 1853 had exhibited his first elevator at the World's Fair in the Crystal Palace. In 1905 Lindquist developed the gearless-traction elevator, which became the standard for all buildings requiring elevators of high rise and great speed, and actually revolutionized the whole system of vertical transportation. In 1911 he was named Otis's chief engineer, and four years later he introduced the automatic system of self-leveling elevators. In 1922 came the automatic signal-control system, which requires the operator only to press a set of buttons and made such structures as the Empire State Building commercially practicable. At about the same time, the escalator was completely redesigned under Lindquist's direction. Many safety devices were among the 64 U.S.

patents granted him as sole inventor and the 56 he received as joint designer. He was very modest about his achievements and has not always received proper credits. Technical experts, however, have called him one of the greatest analytical engineers of his time, as well as the "Father of the New York skyline," or even "of the American skyline unlimited." He employed so many assistants trained in Sweden that it was said that every engineer had to know Swedish in order to work for the Otis Company.

Another immigrant, Alexander F. Victor (1878–1961) from Bollnäs in the province of Hälsingland, who came to America in 1901 after having received his education in Sweden, has been called the "Father of amateur movies," and his inventions also meant much to the educational film. In 1923 he designed and manufactured the first 16-millimeter cameras and projectors, which brought new impetus to educational films for schools, churches, clubs, public institutions, and industrial organizations. Five years earlier he had introduced the so-called safety standard film, which permitted or facilitated the use of motion pictures in education, industry, and home. Victor, who had started in America as a traveling magician, lived in New York for many years but also spent much time at Davenport, Iowa, where he had a factory. He bequeathed his estate to activities promoting birth control in overpopulated countries, and his name lives on in funds serving that purpose.

One of the more far-reaching American inventions of the middle 1900s was Chester Carlson's development of the xerographic copying process, which revolutionized copying methods around the world, made many types of information more readily available and gradually had even political repercussions. The basic work was done in the late 1930s at Astoria in Queens, in a tiny room which the inventor had turned into a laboratory. Exploiting the new method, however, proved to be very difficult. One after another, some 20 major companies came to the conclusion that the invention had no commercial future, but in the 1960s Chester Carlson, who in his youth had known extreme poverty, finally became a very wealthy man. A few years after his death, in 1968 at the age of 62, the securities he had given away anonymously were said to be worth more than 100 million dollars. The causes of education, public health, and world peace had been particularly close to his heart. In a written tribute at the memorial service in Rochester, New York, United Nations Secretary General U Thant said about Chester Carlson that although his invention of xerography "was an extraordinary achievement in the technological and scientific field, I respected him more as a man of exceptional moral stature and as a humanist." Carlson was born in Seattle and grew up in California. Despite his origin, he had little or no contact with Swedish immigrants or organizations in the United States.

In New York the Swedes have been less prominent as general contractors and architects than in the Middle West, but have specialized more in foundation work and such details as flooring. The city's first steel skyscraper, or at least the metal frame, was designed by a Swedish immigrant named Emil Swensson (1858–1919), who was born in Denmark, grew up at Varberg on Sweden's west coast, and was graduated from Chalmers Institute of Technology in Gothenburg. After having worked for a Carnegie company in Pittsburgh from 1887 to 1901, he became an independent consulting engineer. The first more significant building contractor of Swedish birth in New York was probably Gustave A. Sandblom (1867–1948), a graduate of a technical school in Stockholm, who had come to the United States in 1890. He did the steelwork for the old Manhattan Life Building, erected in 1893, and other early skyscrapers. Eight years later an immigrant named John A. Johnson (1865–1938) from Södra Lundby in the province of Västergötland, who had arrived in 1888, founded a business of his own, which his two eldest sons helped develop into one of the biggest building firms in the New York area. For the World's Fair in 1939–40 it put up or did the woodwork for a majority of the buildings, including the Trylon and Perisphere, the theme center of the exposition. The successful Swedish pavilion, designed by Sven Markelius of Stockholm, was entirely built by the Johnson firm. During the Second World War the Johnsons built a number of military camps and training stations, including Camp Dix in New Jersey, and a large part of the Oak Ridge atomic experimental station in Tennessee. Veterans hospitals and public housing projects followed after the war.

A Swedish immigrant named Werner Nygren, who had begun his engineering work in Boston in 1898, was an outstanding specialist in the heating and ventilation of large buildings. In New York, he designed the heating and ventilating systems for the Woolworth Building, the American Telephone and Telegraph Building, St. Patrick's Cathedral, Hunter College, the R. H. Macy department store, and the Columbia-Presbyterian Medical Center. His commissions in other cities included the Travelers Insurance Building in Hartford, Connecticut, and the Los Angeles Public Library. Nygren became president of the New York Heating Board of Trade and of the New York Association of Consulting Engineers.

Many of the workmen who ran up the frames of the skyscrapers or worked on other steel structures were former sailors or other immigrants from Sweden. A large group took part in the building of the Brooklyn Bridge, opened in 1883. John F. Anderson (1848–1927), who had begun as a sheep herder in his native Blekinge, had come to America as a sailor and in the early 1870s had been employed on the construction of the Union Pacific Bridge across the Missouri River at Omaha, worked from 1879 to 1882 as a foreman on the first Hudson River tunnel, from Hoboken, New Jersey, to Morton Street in New York. After having built a bridge across the Atchafalaya River in Louisiana, he founded in 1884 a firm in New York which built or did the foundation work for many large bridges in the United States, England, and Australia. Later he started mining operations and built railroads in Cuba. After the turn of the century he spent most of his time in Sweden and Copenhagen, where he served as American deputy consul general, but in 1922 he moved to San Diego, California. During his travels he collected valuable ethnographical material, most of which was donated to museums in Sweden.

Some Swedish-born architects were active in New York in the early 1900s. One of the first noted architects of recent Swedish ancestry was Harrie Thomas Lindeberg (1880–1959), who was born in New Jersey of Swedish parents from Stockholm where his forebears on the paternal side, with few exceptions, had been silversmiths for two centuries. In 1906 he began practicing in New York, and at an early stage he also established a base in Chicago. His production, finally extended to 26 states, included a great number of sumptuous suburban homes. Art critics called his style "distinctly American," and while no two units were exactly the same, the term "Lindeberg house" became widely used. College buildings and monumental public structures, including American embassy buildings abroad, were also designed by him.

One Swedish immigrant of the 19th century became a successful banker in New York, namely, Swante Magnus Swenson from Barkeryd in Småland, whom we have mentioned before. He had settled in Texas in 1838 and had become a wealthy businessman. After the Civil War he founded in New York the banking firm of Swenson, Perkins and Co. Its name was later changed to S. M. Swenson and Sons. After his death, his sons carried on the business.

Quite a few immigrants from Sweden have founded manufacturing companies or other business organizations of their own in the New York area. An immigrant from Karleby in Västergötland, Andrew G. Hagstrom (b. 1890), who came to New York in 1909 and seven years later started to build a career in the map business with a capital investment of 85 dollars, was by the middle of the century widely known as the "Map King." His production included automobile maps, tourist guides, subway charts, and numerous other special maps. A "profile" in The New Yorker magazine in 1949 described him as "an authority on metropolitan geography." Immigrants as well as members of the first American-born generations have become executives of larger corporations. A graduate of Chalmers Institute of Technology in Gothenburg, Ragnar A. Hummel (1887–1959) from Torsjö in Småland, who emigrated in 1909, helped develop the Lone Star Cement Corporation and became chairman of its board. He also served on many organizations devoted to the improvement of relations between the United States and Latin America. From a background of research, engineering, and technical management, Elmer W. Engstrom in the early 1960s rose to the position of president of RCA. His Swedish parents had emigrated in the late 1880s from steel towns in the province of Värmland and settled in Minneapolis.

An immigrant from Malmö in southern Sweden, John Aspegren (1876–1924), who arrived in 1899, began in the same year a career in the cottonseed-oil business in New York. In 1912, at the age of 36, he became the first foreign-born president of the New York Produce Exchange. He also helped organize the importation of wood pulp from Scandinavia. In 1916 he was elected president of The Swedish Chamber of Commerce of the U.S.A., succeeding Alexander E. Johnson, who had been a land and immigration agent in Minnesota; he held that position until his death. Aspegren had been enrolled as a student at Lund University and had studied business in Germany, England, France, and Belgium. As president of the Swedish Chamber of Commerce he was succeeded by the U.S. managing director of the Swedish American Line, G. Hilmer Lundbeck (1870–1949), who became a leader of the Swedish business community in the New York area and served for two decades, until 1944. He was born at Uppsala, Sweden, and had come to America with his parents in 1881.

In the late 1800s and early 1900s there were many Swedish tailors along Fifth Avenue, usually trained in London as well as in Stockholm. One of them, Carl Victor Backstrom, used to regard his tailoring of the suit Woodrow Wilson wore when inaugurated President as his crowning achievement. One of New York's best-known barbers of the mid-1900s, Charles De Zemler, was born at Uppsala in 1887 and emigrated to America in 1914. In 1935 he set up three shops in Rockefeller Center.

In 1903 a Swedish physician who was born in Finland, Johannes Hoving (1868–1954), and his wife Helga, a Danish-born actress who had made her career in Sweden, arrived in New York. In its Swedish community he became widely known also as a lecturer, popular writer, and leader. One of his sons, Walter Hoving, born in Stockholm in 1897, became the best-known retail executive of Swedish origin in New York. A vice president in Macy's department store in 1928, he later was named president or board chairman of Lord & Taylor, Bonwit Teller, and Tiffany's, all on Fifth Avenue. For many years he played a leading part in the Fifth Avenue Association. His son, Thomas Hoving, became director of the Metropolitan Museum of Art in New York. The first Hovings in Sweden were 17th-century immigrants from Holland.

The best-known advertising executives of recent Swedish ancestry in New York were probably Alfred W. Erickson (1876–1936), one of the founders of the McCann-Erickson Agency, who was born at Farmers Mills, New York, where his Swedish father was an engineer, and Sigurd S. Larmon (b. 1891), who became president and board chairman of Young & Rubicam. At Erickson's death in 1936, *The New York Times* called him "a dominant figure in the American Association of Advertising." Larmon was born of Swedish parents at Stanton, the center of the Halland Settlement in southwestern Iowa.

A native of Sweden, born at Linköping in Östergötland, was William Axel Warn (1868–1947), who worked for *The New York Times* for 38 years, beginning in 1902, and became the dean of the legislative and political correspondents at Albany. Governors and legislators as well as colleagues affectionately called him the "Baron," a title that probably had something to do with his dignified manner. Before settling in New York in 1895, he had practically covered the globe as a seaman. Writing for Swedish-language publications was his first experience as a journalist. Another native of Linköping, Oscar E. Cesare (1883–1948), became associated with the *Times* as a cartoonist. In 1922 he had one of his first celebrated cartoons, a portrait of Lenin which he had drawn in Moscow, published in its Sunday magazine. He had come to America at the age of 18 and first lived in Buffalo and Chicago. Swedish-born Godfrey N. Nelson (1878–1954), who had been brought to America in his infancy, became, as a legal expert, secretary and vice president of *The New York Times*.

A Peterson, a Johnson, and a Nystrom in science and education in New York

A PHYSICIAN named Frederick Peterson (1859–1938), who came in 1883 from Buffalo where he had been a university professor of pathology, was one of the most original and resourceful persons of Swedish parentage in New York in the late 1800s and early 1900s. He was born in Minnesota of Swedish immigrants.

Primarily a specialist in the treatment of nervous diseases, Peterson served as attending physician at various hospitals in New York, and in 1903 he became clinical professor of psychiatry in Columbia University. At the same time he was a great connoisseur of art, a poet, a translator of Swedish poetry, an author of educational and medical works, and an authority on Oriental plants, use of colors, and mysticism. When a book of poetry called *Chinese Lyrics* appeared in 1916, no one suspected that the pseudonym Pai Ta-shun concealed an American Swede named Peterson from Minnesota. As an art collector he also was greatly attracted to China. A large collection of paintings from the Ch'ing period which, under a gift from William Bingham, was distributed among Princeton University and colleges like Amherst, Bowdoin, Dartmouth, and Williams, had originally been collected by Frederick Peterson.

His book *Mental Diseases* went through nine editions, and another entitled *Creative Re-education* also found many readers both in America and in other countries. When Mark Twain and his daughter Jean in the fall of 1899 came back to New York from Sweden, where they had spent the summer months receiving treatments from a physical-culture specialist at Sanna near Jönköping, Jean was placed under the care of Dr. Frederick Peterson. In Sweden the famous American writer had become so enthusiastic over his daughter's improvement that he began to take the treatments himself, and after his return to the United States he ,recommended the system to his friends.

Another honored Swedish name in education and learning was that of Henry Johnson (1867–1953), who taught history at Teachers College, Columbia University, from 1906 until his retirement in 1933 and became known to many as the "Dean of American history teachers." By the middle of the century it was estimated that about 5,000 of his former students were teaching history in schools and colleges throughout the United States. He was born in the village of Norra Rörum in central Skåne, where his father, Jöns Jönsson, seems to have been a relatively well-to-do farmer. In the late 1860s the family moved to America, settling first in the Sauk Lake area of Minnesota and then at Sauk Centre itself, which in Sinclair Lewis's *Main Street* became Gopher Prairie.

Jöns Jönsson, or John Johnson as he soon called himself, and his wife were remarkably reticent about their life in Sweden, according to Henry Johnson's autobiographical *The Other Side of Main Street* which was published in 1943, and the children, who finally numbered eight, felt anything but pride in their ancestry. As a student at the University of Minnesota, young Henry Johnson, in fact, refused to join the Scandinavian Club on the ground that such organizations were un-American. Later on he traveled twice in Europe without even a thought of visiting Sweden, but during his third tour he suddenly realized the full meaning of national origin and, in his case, native soil. "The visit to Sweden left me proud of my native country. . . . Had I been trained to facility in my mother tongue and in some knowledge of its literature, things might have been different."

An eminent theoretician of retailing and marketing was Paul Henry Nystrom (1878–1969), who from 1926 to 1950 served as professor in the Graduate School of Business of Columbia University and often was called the "Dean of American business economists." As an author, he earned for himself a place in the history of business economics, some of his books becoming well known also in business schools in Sweden and other European countries. He always took a lively interest in the activities of the Swedes in New York and in American-Swedish relations. Paul Nystrom was born on a farm in western Wisconsin, of a father who had come from Byarum in northern Småland and a mother from Norway.

Few Swedes or Swedish descendants have been of the Catholic faith, but one, Edward E. Swanstrom, who was born in 1903 in New York of a Swedish father and an Irish-American mother, attained the rank of bishop. In 1947 he was named executive director of the Catholic Relief Services in New York. His father came in the late 1800s from Skövde in Västergötland.

The first Swedish immigrant who eventually became a celebrated actor and film star was Johan Verner Ölund or Warner Oland (1879–1938) from Bjurholm near Umeå in the north of Sweden, who with his father, a student of forestry, landed at Boston in 1892 at the age of 13. Around the turn of the century he made his stage debut in New York, and later he operated his own theaters and tours. Several plays by August Strindberg, including *The Father*, *Easter*, and *Miss Julie*, were produced by him and his wife, Edith Gardener Shearn by birth. In 1916 Warner Oland went over to the movies, and in the early 1930s his Charlie Chan, the Chinese master detective, became a world-famous film character.

Arthur Donaldson (1868–1955) from Norsholm in Östergötland began his career in Swedish-language companies and later became a versatile opera singer and actor in the English language. It was he who made famous an immigrant named Yon Yonson, the leading character in a comedy based on a Swedish greenhorn's oft-ridiculed difficulty of distinguishing between a 'j' and a 'y.' "Yumping Yimminy, wat a yump!" exclaimed Yon Yonson after some successful stunt, and the audience roared. The part that made Donaldson himself widely known, however, was that of the hero in the operetta *The Prince of Pilsen*, in which he appeared more than 1,000 times at the Broadway Theater, under the management of Henry W. Savage and beginning in March of 1903. Early in 1926 Donaldson became the first actor to appear in a sound film, a short play in Swedish called *The Verdict* which had been written for the experiment by an immigrant from

Sweden and made in a studio at Third Avenue and 48th Street in New York. The picture was shown later at the Brooklyn Academy of Music, and being regarded as "a remarkable achievement" it was re-sounded and played in English under the title of *The Retribution*.

In the early 1900s, Swedish-born Carlotta Nillson (d. 1951) played in several leading roles on Broadway. She had come to America with her mother in the early 1890s at the age of ten. On September 20, 1912, an actress named Martha Hedman (1883–1974), born at Öster-sund in the province of Jämtland and brought to bloom in Finland, made her successful debut in New York. Charles Frohman, the theatrical manager, had met her in England and persuaded her to come. Numerous other appearances followed, and in 1915 David Belasco cast her in the role of Xelva in *The Boomerang*, an immediate and long-lasting success which won Martha Hedman a national reputation. She was regarded as one of the most beautiful women on the American stage, and her clothes and manners were copied by thousands of girls. After many years of absence she made a successful comeback in New York in 1942.

In 1913 a Swedish opera singer, Julia Claussen (1879–1941), made her first appearance in America at one of New York's famous morning musicales, and while practically unknown to most of the listeners, she sang seven encores before they let her leave the stage. After the concert she immediately left for Chicago to fill an engagement with the Chicago Opera Company. On November 23, 1917, she began the first of 15 seasons with the Metropolitan Opera Company in New York, singing Delilah to Caruso's Samson. Among her colleagues was Marie Sundelius (1882–1958), who had arrived from Karlstad in Värmland at the age of ten, received her musical education in America and joined the Metropolitan in 1916. For many years she was one of its leading sopranos. She also sang at the Royal Opera in Stockholm and at numerous Swedish singing festivals in the United States. In 1932 she started teaching at the New England Conservatory of Music in Boston.

Swedes in the service of the City of New York or its various institutions

MANY of the Swedish descendants in public service in New York have been native New Yorkers. In the old city of Brooklyn, an attorney named J. Edward Swanstrom (d. 1911), who was the son of a

Swedish-born clergyman, became president of the Board of Education, and after the consolidation of the other boroughs he was reappointed as head of the school system for all New York. In 1901 he was elected president of the Borough of Brooklyn, which had over a million inhabitants.

In 1936, after 35 years of teaching in New York, Johanna M. Lindlof (1872–1954) became the first woman teacher, and the second woman, on the city's Board of Education. From 1912 to 1936 she had taught in a public school in Manhattan, and in 1971 a school in the Bronx was named for her. Her father, Johan Erik Sjöberg from Finspång in Östergötland, came to America in 1870, when her mother, a native of Värmland, had already arrived. Her husband, Oscar Ferdinand Lindlof from Skåne, who died in 1911, was for many years president of The Swedish Society in New York. In 1945 an accountant named Andrew G. Clauson was appointed a member of the Board of Education, and for several years he served as its president. He was born in 1895 on Staten Island of Swedish parents, from Västergötland and Värmland, respectively.

In 1945 New York's Fusion mayor, Fiorello La Guardia, appointed Arthur W. Wallander, who was born in 1892 in Manhattan and had begun as a patrolman in 1914, to the post of police commissioner. He was continued in the office by the new Democratic mayor, William O'Dwyer, but resigned early in 1949. Wallander's father came from Växjö in Småland and his mother from Svenljunga in Västergötland. In 1927 he served as a special guard to Charles Lindbergh at the young aviator's triumphant homecoming after his New York-Paris flight.

One native of Sweden has become a judge in New York City, namely Peter B. Hanson, who was born in 1877 at Helsingborg in the south and in 1900 was graduated from the New York Law School. From 1927 to 1937 he served as a justice of the Children's Court of Brooklyn, later known as the Domestic Relations Court. One of his greatest interests outside his legal work was the Big Brothers' organization.

One of the best-known librarians of Swedish extraction was Edwin H. Anderson (1861–1947), a native of Indiana, who in 1906–1908 served as director of the New York State Library and Library School at Albany and from 1913 to 1934 was director of the New York Public

Library. In 1913 he was elected president of the American Library Association. A Harvard graduate named Axel E. Landerholm, born in 1887 of Swedish immigrants in Portland, Oregon, served from 1915 to 1952 New York Public Library's science and technology division, and after that he helped the Merchant Marine Library in New York build up what has been described as the most comprehensive nautical library in the United States. Aksel Gustav Salomon Josephson (1860–1944) from Uppsala in Sweden, who came to America in 1893 at the age of 33 and continued his studies at the Library School in Albany, was in 1894–96 connected with the institution which in the early 1900s became the New York Public Library. He then moved to Chicago, where the Bibliographical Society of America was founded by him. Among librarians he became known as the "Dean of cataloguing and bibliography."

An eminent Swedish botanist, Per A. Rydberg from the ancient cathedral and school town of Skara in Västergötland, who in the 1880s had been one of the first teachers at the Swedish immigrant school in Wahoo, Nebraska, served from 1907 to 1931 as curator of the New York Botanical Garden in the Bronx. He became internationally known as an expert on the North American flora, especially that of the Rocky Mountains and the adjacent plains. The Rydbergia genus of plants was named for him. Rydberg took his doctorate at Columbia University, supporting himself by teaching at Upsala College in New Jersey.

A Swedish gardener and landscape architect of brilliant parts but with a somewhat bizarre disposition, Knut Malte Forsberg (1829–95), helped in the early 1870s Frederick Law Olmstead and Calvert Vaux landscape Central Park and seems to have made rather important contributions to this work. The son of an ambitious footman at the royal court in Stockholm, he had studied gardening and landscape architecture both in Sweden and abroad. An international competition for the design of Bois de Boulogne at Paris seems to have been won by him, and in Stockholm he designed at least two parks. Both in Europe and in America he was, at times, extremely extravagant. He finally earned his living as a draftsman in the office for public works in Brooklyn, but in his special field, city gardening and landscaping, he is said to have been ahead of his time. Before his emigration in the late 1860s he had started dreaming about a Scandinavian republican union, and in a procession at the World's Fair in Chicago in 1893 he carried the flag of the republic of Scandinavia, one of the few times such a banner has been displayed. Another Swede who much later joined New York's park service and seems to have become a chief gardener, Nils Jönsson or Jonsson-Rose (b. 1862) from Ottarp in Skåne, was cast in a different mold. In 1899 he built greenhouses in Central Park which sometimes attracted 25,000 visitors in one day. Frustrations in his work made him return to Sweden, but he came back to New York and started working for his old employer. He was also a painter and a poet.

Many Swedish-born residents of the New York area were seafaring men or engaged in the activities of the port of New York. Five sea captains and one chief engineer, all of them sons or other descendants of a fisherman named Johan Simon Klang at Lysekil in the province of Bohuslän, made the name Klang widely known. Captain Gustaf Klang (b. 1878), who came to America in 1898, was in command of four successive editions of Vincent Astor's luxury yacht *Nourmahal*, also used for scientific expeditions. Captain George Fried, born in 1877 at Worcester, Massachusetts, of parents from Åbygården 'at Klippan in Skåne, became famous as commander of vessels which performed extremely difficult rescues at sea. After one such action, on January 22, 1929, when Fried was in command of the S.S. *America* and a crew of 32 was rescued from a sinking Italian freighter in the middle of the Atlantic, the rescuers as well as the rescued were tumultuously received in New York. Captain Fried was welcomed by the mayor at the City Hall, and the U.S. Congress recessed in his honor. After having been named a supervising inspector in the Bureau of Navigation and Steamboat Inspection in New York, he contributed much to the efforts to improve safety at sea. He had served in the U.S. Army during the Spanish-American War and in the U.S. Navy from 1900 to 1918.

In the early 1900s a Swedish skipper, Andreas P. Lundin (1869–1929) from Härnösand, who had sailed the seven seas for two decades, settled in New York as a marine engineer. A new, decked lifeboat had been designed by him. In America he started manufacturing on license a davit invented in England by a Swedish engineer, Axel Welin (1862–1951), which immediately became part of the equipment on all new American ships. Davits designed by Welin were later used on many of the world's largest passenger vessels.

On December 27, 1915, in the midst of the First World War, the Swedish American Line's first steamship, the *Stockholm*, came to New York on her maiden voyage under the Swedish flag. Many Swedes in America and others who were actively interested in relations with Sweden regarded this as the beginning of a new era. Among the ship's passengers was a group of Swedish journalists, and her cargo included a Swedish art exhibit which in early 1916 opened in the Brooklyn Museum and became a great success. Swedish music was featured at concerts in Carnegie Hall and other auditoriums.

The *Stockholm*, which had previously run between Rotterdam and New York as the *Potsdam*, had been purchased from the Holland America Line, the Swedish American Line having had to pare down its program because of the war. In 1917, the unrestricted submarine warfare and the entrance of the United States into the war forced the Swedish company to suspend operations until the fall of 1918.

24,000 Swedish-born in Pennsylvania in 1900 – New Jersey had 13,500 in 1930

THE Swedish-born population in New Jersey increased twentyfold from 1870 to 1910, from 550 to about 10,500, while the number of Pennsylvania Swedes rose from 2,300 to 23,500. In the Keystone State the greatest number of Swedish-born inhabitants, more than 24,000, was recorded in 1900, while those in New Jersey did not reach their highest point, nearly 13,500, until 1930. After that, the decline was relatively slow, so that by the middle of the century New Jersey had more Swedish-born people than Pennsylvania, and also more than, for instance, Iowa and Nebraska, where Swedish immigration had long been a closed chapter. Commercial relations with Sweden may still help maintain the numerical strength of the Swedish element in New Jersey. In the Garden State, Sweden's industry is well represented with manufacturing and sales subsidiaries.

In New Jersey as in New York State, more than two-thirds of the Swedes settled in the New York City metropolitan area. Other Swedish concentrations were in the Red Bank district and around Camden on the Delaware River opposite Philadelphia, where colonists from Sweden had lived in the 1600s.

Since 1924 East Orange, New Jersey, has been the home of Upsala College, which was founded in 1893 by the New York Conference of the Augustana Lutheran Synod. That year marked the 300th anniversary of a meeting at Uppsala, Sweden, which declared the allegiance of the Swedish people to the Protestant Reformation, and the school was, therefore, named Upsala. The first schoolroom was in the basement of the Bethlehem Church on Pacific Street in Brooklyn, where 16 students attended classes, and the principal was a brilliant young scholar who had just won a Ph.D. degree from Yale, the Reverend Lars Herman Beck. He was told by friends that he would "starve to death" if he accepted the post, but he remained for 17 years. After a period of trials and disappointments at Kenilworth, New Jersey (1898–1924), the school made rapid progress at East Orange, where another holder of a Ph.D. degree from Yale, the Reverend Carl G. Erickson, who had become president in 1920, remained in charge until his death in 1936. Upsala of today is a coeducational college of liberal arts and science. Situated only 15 miles from New York, its campus covers 45 acres in the heart of the residential area of East Orange. It was designed by Jens Fredrick Larson, the noted college architect, whose creations in New Jersey also include the Institute for Advanced Study at Princeton.

At Princeton, both Princeton University and the Institute for Advanced Study has had several Swedes among its professors or members. The first Swedish-trained scholar at Princeton may have been Thomas Hakon Gronwall (1877–1932), who taught higher mathematics there in 1913–15, and became editor of the *Annals of Mathematics*, published at Princeton. After scientific and technical work in connection with the American war effort and four years as a mathematical expert in the Ordnance Department in Washington, D.C., he spent his last ten years in New York as a successful consulting mathematician. He also taught at Columbia. His published papers, many of which belong to the field of physics, became well known among specialists. Born at the Dyltabruk industrial estate in the Swedish province of Närke, Gronwall won his doctorate at the University of Uppsala and was later graduated from the Institute of Technology in Berlin.

In 1900 about half of the Swedish-born people in Pennsylvania lived in the largely agricultural districts in the north and northwest, where the Chandlers Valley settlement in Warren County just south of the New York State line had been the first more significant Swedish colonization. Among the leading Swedish centers in this part of

Pennsylvania were Warren, Sheffield, Ludlow, Kane, and Wilcox. In some of these towns, many of the Swedish immigrants became glass-blowers or tanners. By the turn of the century most of the people at Ludlow, Kane, and Wilcox were of Swedish stock. The mixture of English and Swedish spoken by Upsala College freshmen from Ludlow in the 1920s became known as "Ludlow Swedish." Farther south in Pennsylvania, as well as in the Wilkes-Barre area in the northeast, many Swedes worked in the coal mines.

In relation to total population the Swedish element at Pittsburgh in the southwest has always been insignificant, but it was relatively large in Braddock and McKeesport, also important steel-producing towns, in the same section. Many of the Swedes in the Pittsburgh district were engineers or skilled workers, and their contributions to the steel industry were out of proportion to their numbers. A well-edited Swedish news weekly, *Svenska Veckobladet*, was published at McKeesport from 1890 to 1918, and Braddock and Pittsburgh have also had Swedish-language periodicals of some kind.

One of the Swedish settlers at McKeesport, Frans Oscar Carlson (1856–1929) from Ankarsrum in northeast Småland where a still-existing industrial estate was founded in the 1600s, and his wife Matilda Sofia (1861–1935) from the same section of Sweden had a son, Gunard Oscar Carlson (1895–1969), who became a pioneer in the development of stainless-steel plate and plate products. His company, G. O. Carlson, Inc., of Thorndale in Chester County in southeastern Pennsylvania, not far from Philadelphia, became one of America's leading producers of stainless-steel, nickel-alloy, and titanium plate. In memory of his only son he established the Gunard Berry Carlson Memorial Foundation, which supports educational, religious, and scientific undertakings, and he was the first American citizen to become a life member of the Swedish-Italian Archeological Society in Rome. In his honor, the Chester County airport has been named the Chester County G. O. Carlson Airport. His parents came to America in 1880.

In the late 1800s and early 1900s a little more than 2,000 immigrants from Sweden lived in the Philadelphia area, large parts of which two centuries earlier had been owned by farmers and businessmen of Swedish birth or parentage. The most important relics from the Swedish era are two "Old Swedes" churches, Gloria Dei on Delaware Avenue near Christian Street in South Philadelphia, constructed in

1700, 45 years after Sweden lost political control of its colony, and St. James, on Woodland Avenue and 69th Street in West Philadelphia, built in 1762 by a congregation led by a clergyman from Sweden.

Approximately every fifth Philadelphia family with roots in the Delaware Valley of the 17th and 18th centuries is of Swedish ancestry, according to semiofficial estimates. Several such families have already been mentioned. Among those who by the middle of the 1800s made Philadelphia a literary center were members of a family named Peterson, who claimed descent from one Erick Pieterson of New Sweden. Henry Peterson (1818–91) became in the late 1840s editor and publisher of *The Saturday Evening Post*, the old weekly which developed into an American institution, and for 25 years he remained its dominating personality, increasing its emphasis on fiction and verse. His son Arthur Peterson (1851–1932), who for some time served as editor of the magazine, published several books of poetry. One entitled *Songs of New Sweden* was first published in 1887, the year before the 250th anniversary of the landing of the first colonists from Sweden on the Delaware. He must have read practically everything about New Sweden that was available at that time, but the Swedish settlers he saw in a romantic light. All of them, "fair-haired, sturdy children of the north," lived in red-painted log cabins, as in Sweden where, however, the red paint from the ancient Falun copper mine was not used by the farmers until the late 1700s, and each one was "wearing the dress of his native parish." Even when the 300th anniversary of the coming of the Swedes was celebrated in 1938, some writers and illustrators in America seemed to have been influenced by such romanticism. Others of Arthur Peterson's poems were inspired by the old Norse mythology and sagas. Obviously proud of his ancestral roots in Scandinavia, he maintained that Great Britain owed "her centuries of maritime supremacy" to the restless, seafaring Vikings and their descendants in the British Isles. Three cousins of his father established in Philadelphia the noted publishing firm T. B. Peterson Brothers, and their elder brother Charles Jacob Peterson (1819–87) edited for 47 years *Peterson's Magazine*, first called *Lady's World*, which reached a circulation of 150,000.

In the early 1700s Jesper Swedberg of Skara in the province of Västergötland presided as non-resident bishop over the old Swedish congregations in the Delaware Valley, where his son Jesper served as a schoolmaster for nine years, and at the end of the same century Philadelphia became the American center of the missionary activities for the theology of Bishop Swedberg's famous son Emanuel Swedenborg.

In 1876, Swedenborgians who, in contrast to the parent sect, regarded Swedenborg's theological writings as authoritative divine revelations, founded at Philadelphia the Academy of the New Church, and since the turn of the century this movement has had its headquarters at Bryn Athyn, a beautiful place near the Pennypack Creek, which the Swedish and Dutch settlers of the 17th century called Penickpacka Kill. Bryn Athyn's Welsh name is translated officially as "Hill of Cohesion." Today Bryn Athyn, on Philadelphia's northern outskirts, is one of the centers of the New Church in the United States, as well as a unique Swedenborgian community. The nucleus consists of the Cathedral, which was completed in 1919 and has been called "the most beautiful Gothic building in America," and the adjoining Choir Hall and Council Hall, both in the Romanesque style. On the hillsides and in the valleys nearby are schools, dormitories, a library which contains all of Swedenborg's scientific and religious works, a community hall and other buildings, as well as the homes of New Church members. Local craftsmen played a leading part in the creation of Bryn Athyn, which has managed to preserve an atmosphere of harmony and patriarchal simplicity. Its schools supply a complete education from kindergarten to a degree in theology. Music holds an important position.

Best known of the few Swedish-born residents of Bryn Athyn was Carl Theophilus Odhner (1863–1918), a member of the family into which Captain John Ericsson's sister Anna married. Emigrating from Sweden in the early 1880s, he specialized in Swedenborg research and became in 1898 professor of church history and theology at Bryn Athyn. He was one of the founders of the Swedenborg Scientific Association. His niece Cyriel Odhner, who in 1952 had a book entitled *The Swedenborg Epic* published in New York, married a Swedish sculptor, Thorsten Sigstedt (1884–1963), who came to America in 1928 and almost immediately joined the Bryn Athyn community. His production included in the early 1950s some 40 wood sculptures for the new Court Building at Harrisburg, Pennsylvania, where another state building had already been adorned by the best-known 20th-century sculptor of Swedish birth, Carl Milles. Carl T. Odhner's nephew Hugo Ljungberg Odhner (1891–1974) came to America at the age of 15, studied at Bryn Athyn, became active as a missionary in Canada and South Africa, and joined the Swedenborgians at Bryn Athyn in 1928.

Amandus Johnson (1877–1974), who became a leading authority on the Swedish contributions to American history, spent most of his active life in Philadelphia. Born at Långasjö in the province of Småland, he came to Minnesota with his maternal grandparents as an infant. His interest in the history of the Swedes in America was aroused in 1903 when, as a student at Gustavus Adolphus College in St. Peter, he heard an address by Johan A. Enander, the veteran writer and orator. In 1908 he won his doctor's degree at the University of Pennsylvania with a thesis about the New Sweden colony of the 17th century, and after studies in archives in Sweden, Finland, England, and Holland he published in 1911 a two-volume work, *The Swedish Settlements on the Delaware*, which remains the most important of his many books about Swedes in America. In the early 1920s he spent two years in Africa, having practically given up his main pursuit, but in 1924 he started activities which led to the construction of the American Swedish Historical Museum in Philadelphia.

By the middle of the 1900s, Thorsten Sellin (b. 1896), sociologist and criminologist, was the internationally best-known Swedish-born citizen of Philadelphia. A native of the city of Örnsköldsvik in the northern province of Ångermanland and emigrating to America in 1913, he continued his studies at Augustana College in Rock Island, Illinois, and the University of Pennsylvania, where in 1922 he won his doctor's degree with a thesis on marriage and divorce legislation in Sweden, as well as an assistant professorship. Criminology then became his leading specialty, and he studied it with noted scholars in Europe. From 1930 to 1967 he served his alma mater as professor of sociology, being head of the department 1944–59, and for many years he also gave lectures at Columbia in New York. In 1946 he spent a year lecturing in three Swedish universities and participating in the work of the Swedish Penal Code Commission, and in 1959–60 he lectured at Cambridge in England. In the United States he was active in advising on the preparation of legislation. In 1950–51 he was secretary general of the International Penal and Penitentiary Commission at Berne, Switzerland, and in 1961 he presided over the International Congress of Criminology at The Hague. For four decades, 1929–68, he was editor of *The Annals*, published by the American Academy of Political and Social Science. His scientific works deal with such subjects as the methods of the science of criminology, the criminality of youth, and the death penalty. Two sons became university professors.

Numerous Swedish steel engineers in Mid-Atlantic states —
Many return to Sweden

IN THE late 19th and early 20th centuries, when technical education in Sweden had been improved considerably at all levels, Swedish engineers made particularly important contributions to American industrial and technical growth and became at the same time responsible for a rapidly expanding exchange of ideas and experience between the United States and Sweden. Many returned, in fact, to their increasingly dynamic native country, or spent at least several years there. Of those active in shipbuilding, railroad transportation, and mechanical and electrical engineering, quite a few were permanently or in part based in the New York area, on both sides of the Hudson River. Schenectady, New York, and Princeton, New Jersey, were other important centers, and Pittsburgh, Pennsylvania, became the adopted home of numerous steel engineers and metallurgists from Sweden.

One of the foremost Swedish metallurgists in America was not a steel expert but a nickel specialist. Victor Hybinette (1867–1937), who in 1899–1900 served as president of The American Society of Swedish Engineers in New York, was the son of a blacksmith at the old copper-mining center of Falun in the province of Dalarna, and the descendant of a Walloon ironworker who came to Sweden in the early 1600s. After graduation from Chalmers Institute of Technology in Gothenburg and practice in Sweden and Norway, he emigrated to America in 1892. Building a new nickel smeltery for a metal company at Bayonne, New Jersey, he invented a method for electrolytic refining of nickel which a few decades later contributed about 75 percent of the world's nickel production. A few years in New York as the International Nickel Company's chief metallurgist were followed in 1906–1908 by the building of copper, nickel, and cobalt works for the

North American Lead Company at Fredericktown, Missouri, in 1908 by a long period of industrial activities in Norway and Sweden, and in 1931 by the founding of two metal companies in the United States, one at Wilmington, Delaware, and the other at Jackson, Michigan. As a consulting engineer for International Nickel, Hybinette conducted a study that in the middle 1930s led to the exploitation of Europe's richest nickel deposits at Petsamo in northernmost Finland, which during the Second World War was ceded to the Soviet Union.

In the Pittsburgh district, many Swedish-trained engineers and inventors have been identified with the growth of the American steel industry almost from its beginning. One of the first and greatest was Per Torsten Berg (1853–1926), born at Rogslösa in Östergötland and a graduate of the Stockholm Institute of Technology in 1878. The next year he began life in America as a laborer in a rail mill near Pittsburgh, and ten years later he became chief engineer of Andrew Carnegie's huge Homestead mill. There he introduced a long series of inventions and improvements of his own, and sooner or later most of these were adopted in other countries. By the turn of the century his work force numbered some 18,000, and he employed about 60 Swedish engineers, many of them as draftsmen. In 1902 he returned to Sweden as European representative of the newly formed U.S. Steel Corporation, and in 1909 he was appointed a deputy consul general for the United States. As minister of education, his brother Fridtjuv Berg (1851–1916) sponsored important reforms, including one which simplified the spelling of the Swedish language.

When Berg returned to Sweden one of his young employees, A. W. Söderberg, was named assistant chief engineer of the Homestead Works, and in 1915 he became chief engineer. He too made several important inventions, also devoting much time to volunteer work in public education. In 1938 he was, in turn, succeeded by another Swede, Anders G. Ericson, born in Finland in 1895 and a graduate of the mining school at Filipstad in the Swedish province of Värmland; he had come to America in 1920. His domain included several steel mills and other works in or near Pittsburgh. In the early 1940s he directed a gigantic plant expansion, required by the American war effort.

George Knut Hamfeldt (1870–1949), born in Finland and a graduate of a technical school in the Swedish city of Norrköping, came to America in 1890, began as a lathe operator and draftsman, was put in charge of a Carnegie Steel blast-furnace plant in Pittsburgh, and helped found the Midland Steel Company of Pennsylvania, where he served as general manager and director in 1905–1907. The following year he returned to Europe, and after a period as consulting engineer and director of a French steel company in German Lorraine, he became in 1913 one of the founders of the Oxelösund iron and steel works on the Baltic south of Stockholm, now among the largest in Sweden and owned by the Gränges company. He served as general manager of the Oxelösund plant until his retirement in 1930.

Emil Swensson, already mentioned as designer of the first steel skyscraper in New York City, also designed the first steel-hopper-bottom freight car and the first hot-metal bridge, carrying molten metal over the Monongahela River in Pittsburgh. For several years he served as chief engineer and finally general manager of the Keystone Bridge Works, another Carnegie company, which he had joined in 1887 as a draftsman. He had many opportunities for cooperation with another Swedish engineer, John Brunner (b. 1866), a graduate of the Stockholm Institute of Technology, who built bridges for the city of Pittsburgh and served as chief of its Bureau of Engineering and Construction, before moving to the Illinois Steel Company in Gary, Indiana, in 1902. A steel-treating process which substantially prolongs the life of railway rails was perfected by him. Gustav L. Fisk, born in 1887 at Uttersberg in the province of Västmanland and a graduate of a technical school at Örebro, became chief engineer of the Mesta Machine Company at Pittsburgh and invented numerous modern rolling-mill-machinery units. Ragnar Berg, chief engineer of the Koppers Company at Pittsburgh, developed a number of labor-saving devices in the coke-oven field. Born and educated in Stockholm, he came to America in 1911 at the age of 25.

William C. Oberg, born in 1888 at Karlskrona in the province of Blekinge, began his career in 1911 as a worker in the Carnegie Steel Company and finally became manager of the nine Pittsburgh plants of the Carnegie-Illinois Steel Corporation, employing about 55,000 men. Claes Sigurd Landen (b. 1897) from Grängesberg in Dalarna, who came in 1920 after studies at Örebro and in Germany and began as a locomotive repairman, became in 1948 chief engineer for the

Chicago district of the Carnegie-Illinois Steel Corporation, with head-quarters in Pittsburgh. Oscar Nathaniel Lindahl from Stockaryd in Småland became in 1941 a vice president and director of the same company. In 1949 he was named executive director of the General State Authority and of the Bridge and Highway Authority of the state of Pennsylvania.

There were also Swedish steel experts in other sections of Pennsylvania as well as in New York and New Jersey. Casimir von Philp (1853–1917), whose first ancestor in Sweden had immigrated from Scotland in the early 1600s, became chief engineer of the Bethlehem Steel Company and made inventions which improved the rolling-mill machinery. Waldemar Dyrssen (1886–1928), member of a Swedish family of German-Frisian origin, was also an experienced engineer when he arrived in America, with degrees from the Institute of Technology and the School of Mining in Stockholm. He worked in 1913–15 for the Bethlehem Steel Company at Bethlehem, Pennsylvania, from 1915 to 1924 for the U.S. Steel Corporation in New York, and the last three years of his life, as chief engineer and partner, for a firm at Pittsburgh manufacturing equipment for the steel industry. A number of inventions which became used in most industrial countries were made by him. One of the first Swedish immigrants to pilot his own aircraft, Dyrssen was killed by a hit-and-run driver near his home, Bredablick, outside Pittsburgh. After the death of his American-born wife a few years later, their two sons moved to Sweden, where one became professor of chemistry at the University of Gothenburg, the other an officer in the Swedish Air Force.

Another graduate of the Stockholm Institute of Technology, Axel Paulsson (1889–1944) from Malmö in the Swedish south, came to America in 1916 as a fellow of the Swedish Ironmasters Association and Board of Trade but remained for 14 years, most of the time as a metallurgist and finally assistant general manager of the Ludlum Steel Company of Watervliet near Albany, New York. In the early 1920s he built a steel mill in Brazil for a Ludlum subsidiary. In 1930 he became chief engineer of the Avesta steel company in the Swedish province of Dalarna.

One of the Swedish steel specialists in Pittsburgh, Oscar R. Wikander (1876–1956) from Gothenburg, observed in 1950 in a magazine article that not all of the hundreds upon hundreds of

574

Swedish immigrants who landed in the American steel industry could become captains of industry or noted engineers. They lived, he continued, "quiet and unspectacular lives, working as skilled or unskilled laborers, technicians, clerks, timekeepers, inspectors, foremen, and what have you. They are known for their industry and ability in their jobs and for their practice of good citizenship and civic responsibility in community life."

Two Swedish engineers who were graduated from the Institute of Technology in Stockholm during the First World War, Karl Sundberg (1891–1939) from the northern province of Hälsingland and Hans T. F. Lundberg (1893–1971) from Malmö, did pioneering work in geophysical prospecting, and their techniques of locating new deposits of metal ores and petroleum became widely used in the United States, Canada, and many other countries. At Boliden in northern Sweden they found in 1924 pyrite ores yielding copper, silver, gold, and other metals. Sundberg remained a resident of Sweden, but the company he headed had a United States subsidiary, and many of his scientific papers were published in American magazines. In 1923 Lundberg settled in New York, which remained one of his bases even after he had moved to Canada three years later. In his prospecting activities he made wide use of aircraft. In the late 1950s, the worth of the ore deposits discovered by him in 28 countries was estimated at five billion dollars.

Several Swedish shipbuilders succeed first in the United
States, later in Sweden

CARL J. MELLIN (1851–1924), born at Hagelberg in the province of Västergötland, who in 1888 became the first president of The American Society of Swedish Engineers in New York, began a new era in ship propulsion when he designed the triple-expansion engines for the U.S. battleship *Texas*, which was built at the Navy Yard in Brooklyn. He was also a leading pioneer in machine-controlled firing of naval guns, with his turret controls and gun-operating gear first installed on the U.S. cruiser *Vesuvius*.

A young graduate of Chalmers Institute of Technology in Gothenburg, Hugo Hammar (1864–1947), who for some years had practiced shipbuilding in England, began in 1890 at a yard in Boston. The next year he helped construct the decks for the battleships *Maine* and *Massachusetts* in Philadelphia, not far from the "Old Swedes" church Gloria Dei, and then followed four years in the engineering section of the Brooklyn Navy Yard, where he directed the construction of the cruiser *Cincinnati* and the rebuilding of some inadequate units.

In Brooklyn there were two other Swedes in responsible positions, Fredrik Lilliehöök (1860–1930), who in 1911 became professor of shipbuilding engineering at the Institute of Technology in Stockholm, and Carl E. Richson (1857–1925), who after ten years in the United States returned to Sweden in 1897 and, like Hugo Lilliehöök (1845–1912) who from 1867 to 1872 had practiced as a naval architect in New York, played a significant part in the building of a modern Swedish coast-defense navy. One of the ships Lilliehöök and Richson helped build was the cruiser *Fylgia* which in 1907 came to New York. Among the cadets on board was a member of the Swedish royal family, Prince Wilhelm.

Before returning to Sweden in 1896, Hugo Hammar was employed in the huge shipyard at Newport News, Virginia, which placed him in charge of the engineering work on five warships, including the *Kearsarge* and the *Kentucky*. Among the other engineers were several Swedes, at least one of whom returned to Sweden and joined the naval materiel administration. Hammar himself became chief engineer of a shipyard in Gothenburg and in 1910 managing director of another, soon known as Götaverken, which grew into one of the world's leading shipbuilders. In a book about his seven years as an immigrant in America, published in 1938, he wrote that "the growth of the Swedish industrial economy since the turn of the century has without doubt been greatly affected by Swedish American initiative and aggressive energy," and that "our Swedish engineers have accomplished beautiful things in the United States." In the 1890s Hammar had been one of the most active members of The American Society of Swedish Engineers in New York. Born on the Baltic island of Öland as the seventh of 12 children, he had had to work his way toward a higher technical education. Even at the height of his career in Sweden, when he was regarded as one of the country's foremost industrial leaders, he often described himself as a "plate worker."

The eagle boats built by the Ford Company for the U.S. Navy

during the First World War became famous for performance and for their high-efficiency noiseless power transmission, utilizing the system of reduction gears from turbine to propellers. This system was invented by a Swedish engineer named Gustave Fast, then residing in Baltimore and also a member of the Engineers' Society in New York. A self-aligning coupling, used on steam turbines and in steel mills where high speeds and great power capacities are required, was likewise invented by him. Fast was born in 1884 at Kristinehamn in Värmland and studied at Chalmers Institute in Gothenburg.

Carl J. Mellin became known not only for his marine engines and gun controls but also for outstanding improvements in locomotive design. As chief engineer of the Richmond Locomotive Works in Virginia he achieved such an increase in the pulling capacity of steam locomotives that he has been said to have laid the groundwork for a new period in American railroad history. The new type of engine earned him in 1901 the highest award at the Pan-American Exposition in Buffalo and in 1904 a gold medal at the St. Louis Exposition. In 1902 he became consulting engineer for the newly formed American Locomotive Company at Schenectady, where he lived until his death in 1924.

Many other Swedish engineers helped improve American railroads. Karl F. Elers, first employed by Westinghouse at Pittsburgh and later a consulting engineer in the same city, created equipment which had a cushioning effect on the starting and stopping of trains, as well as on jolts due to bad track conditions. His type of elastic coupling found many other uses, including the operation of the locks in the Panama Canal. The electric locomotives used to pull ships through the Panama Canal were designed by C. W. Larson, one of the pioneer engineers of the General Electric Company, who specialized in locomotives for mines and industrial plants. An unusually versatile inventor, Wilhelm B. Bronander (1889–1956), developed a track-joint tester that helped make the roadbed safe for the modern high-speed trains. He was also an authority on packaging machines and lightweight Diesel engines, and obtained some 200 patents. Born at Lidköping in Västergötland, he came to America in 1907, completed his studies at the Pratt Institute in Brooklyn, and then settled in New Jersey.

577

The "Lindstrom" hand brake and other devices used in American railroad cars were designed by Charles Lindstrom (1854–1921) from Stockholm, who had arrived in 1876. After having been employed by the Pennsylvania Railroad for many years, he became chief engineer for the Pressed Steel Car Company of Pittsburgh. Carl A. W. Brandt from Stockholm, who arrived in 1902 and became chief engineer for the Superheater Company, was both an inventor and a writer of books on locomotive boilers. In 1940, two years before his death in New York, he was awarded the Melville Gold Medal of The American Society of Mechanical Engineers.

Many Swedish engineers who came to America in the late 19th or early 20th centuries specialized in power-plant equipment. Oscar Junggren (1865–1935), born at Landskrona in southern Sweden and a graduate of a technical school in Malmö, emigrated in 1889 and became the chief designer of electric power plants for the General Electric Company in Schenectady. He obtained about 130 patents, most of them relating to steam turbines, and in the period 1924–32 he designed 30 different turbine units. "Nearly one-half of all the electric power in the world created by steam turbines comes from those manufactured by General Electric under Mr. Junggren's guidance," said a company statement in 1938. In 1931 he received the Charles A. Coffin award as a "designer and creator of large turbine units and especially for his invention of the triple compound turbine, a distinct advance in the art."

In 1903 an immigrant from the Swedish province of Uppland, Carl W. E. Wallin, was employed as an engineer at the Westinghouse company's generator works at Pittsburgh, and three to four decades later he had charge of the mounting of its gigantic generators at the Boulder, or Hoover, Dam in the Colorado River and the Grand Coulee Dam in the state of Washington. In 1946 the Westinghouse company's highest distinction, the Order of Merit, was awarded him for "his skill in testing."

A noted developer of new electric motors was Sven Robert Bergman, born in southernmost Sweden and a graduate of the Institute of Technology in Stockholm, who joined General Electric in 1902 and in 1934 received the company's Charles A. Coffin award for his contributions to rayon-spinning machinery. Another of the many graduates of the Stockholm Institute of Technology who emigrated to

America, Carl F. Norberg (1899–1959), became president of the rapidly growing Electric Storage Battery Company, now known as ESB, Inc., with headquarters at Philadelphia. He was born at Klavreström, an ancient industrial community in the province of Småland. His older brother Rudolph C. Norberg (1881–1958) had led the company before him.

New office machines have been developed by Swedish engineers in the East, as well as in the Midwest and on the West Coast. Carl Gabrielson of Syracuse, New York, was the chief designer of the L. C. Smith typewriter, being also responsible for the machinery needed for its manufacture. He was born at Gothenburg in 1869 and came to America at the age of 18. Gunne Lowkrantz (1902–64), who came from Sweden at the age of 20, became director of the International Business Machine Corporation's electrical laboratory at Endicott, New York. During the Second World War he helped develop long-range navigational instruments for aircraft at Binghampton, New York, and later he also worked on undersea exploration devices.

Few Swedish engineers have achieved a greater financial success than Gideon Sundback (1880–1954) of Meadville, Pennsylvania, who invented or at least perfected the zipper fastener and also designed much of the machinery used in its manufacture. He was born at Ödestugu in Småland and came to America in the early 1900s.

Revolutionary ways of dealing with cement were invented by Karl P. Billner (1887–1965), during the last 25 years of his life a resident of Philadelphia. His methods became used throughout the world. Born at Billesholm in the province of Skåne, he was graduated from Chalmers Institute of Technology in 1906 and came to America the same year. After having designed and supervised the construction of the first concrete bridges across the Columbia River in Oregon in 1913–14, he returned to Sweden and developed at Stockholm a lightweight concrete called aerocrete, which was launched on an international scale. In the 1930s this was followed by a method of extracting excess water from newly-poured concrete with a vacuum pump, thus considerably increasing the strength of the concrete. From 1926 to 1940 Billner lived in New York, then moving to Philadelphia. His innovations in concrete construction won him the Frank P. Brown Medal of the Franklin Institute in Philadelphia in 1947, and the American Concrete Institute's Turner Medal in 1962.

579

Ernst Alexanderson, an immigrant of 1901, and other pioneers in electronics

ERNST F. W. ALEXANDERSON (1878–1975), best known for his contributions to radio and electronics, is regarded as the most prominent of all Swedish engineers who came to the United States in the late 1800s and early 1900s.

Born in the ancient university town of Uppsala, where his father was professor of classics, Ernst Alexanderson was graduated from the Stockholm Institute of Technology in 1900 and then did postgraduate work in Berlin. The achievements of Thomas Alva Edison and German-born Charles F. Steinmetz of the General Electric Company spurred his decision to emigrate to America, where he arrived in 1901. Early the next year he obtained a position with General Electric in Schenectady, New York, and there he remained with a brief exception, doing pioneer work in electrical engineering and obtaining more than 300 U.S. patents. Among the many fields covered were electrical machinery, electric traction and ship propulsion, power transmission, radio telegraphy and telephony, radio broadcasting, and television.

Alexanderson's first great invention was a high-frequency alternator, or alternating-current generator, which for the first time put the human voice on the air. On Christmas Eve in 1906 it was successfully tested in a music and voice transmission from Reginald Fessenden's experimental station at Brant Rock, Massachusetts. The program was heard by wireless operators on ships within a radius of several hundred miles, and this was the beginning of radio broadcasting. One of those who heard it wrote later: "Had the spirit world suddenly made itself vocal, there could have been no more amazement."

In 1914–18 Alexanderson's inventions laid the foundation for the first great transoceanic radio-communication system. A powerful Alexanderson transmitter installed in the Marconi station at New Brunswick, New Jersey, was used toward the end of the World War for the sending of orders to the U.S. Navy and the forces in Europe, and for conveying President Wilson's Fourteen Points to Germany. Within ten years there were radio transmitters with Alexanderson alternators in many countries, including Sweden.

After the war General Electric organized the Radio Corporation of America to exploit Alexanderson's inventions and related developments, and it loaned the Swedish-born inventor's services to RCA, where he served as chief engineer in 1920–24. At a meeting of The American Society of Swedish Engineers in New York in 1956, David Sarnoff, then board chairman of Radio Corporation of America, observed that "when the history of RCA is written it must begin with Alexanderson for without him and his alternator there would be no RCA today."

On June 5, 1924, Alexanderson transmitted over the RCA stations the first transatlantic facsimile, a handwritten greeting to his 83-year-old father, who already in 1879 had moved with his family to Lund, the university town in southern Sweden. "It is a great pleasure to be able to write my first radio letter to you," his son said in this message. "It makes the distance seem shorter."

One of Alexanderson's inventions in radio broadcasting made possible the modern selective receiver. As early as 1927 he conducted successful television experiments in and around Schenectady, achieving the first significant home reception. In 1930 he demonstrated a complete television system, including the projection of a large picture on a theater screen.

Alexanderson also made important contributions to electric ship propulsion and railway electrification. New methods of operating induction motors at variable speeds had been among his first innovations in Schenectady, and during the First World War these were embodied in the design of the electrical equipment for the battleship *New Mexico*. The same system was later installed on American aircraft carriers and other warships. During the Second World War, Alexanderson accomplished much in the application of electronics to modern warfare.

In 1919 Alexanderson received the gold medal of the Institute of Radio Engineers, and in 1938 he became an honorary Ph.D. at the University of Uppsala. Toward the end of the Second World War, in January of 1945, the Edison Medal of the American Institute of Electrical Engineers was given him "for his outstanding inventions and developments in the radio, transportation, marine and power fields." In his address at the presentation ceremony he recalled the scientific progress made during the war, and continued, "It is a paradox that it takes a war to permit the creative talent of the nation to function in its full and natural way. This creative talent could be employed in peacetime in the creation of new industries that would provide employment and prosperity for the people. In the electrical industry alone there are great new possibilities." Among these he mentioned heating and cooling of houses by electric power.

An enthusiastic yachtsman, Alexanderson in summertime set sail on Lake George, where his Swedish craft, *Nordic*, became well known. He has been called the "Father of yachting on Lake George." His first paternal ancestor in Sweden was a sea captain from Germany who in the late 1600s settled on the Baltic island of Gotland. His mother was a member of the Von Heidenstam family.

Another Swedish-born engineer, Nils E. Lindenblad (b. 1895), who in 1915 was graduated from a technical school in the city of Norrköping where he was born, joined in 1920 the research laboratories of the newly formed Radio Corporation of America at Princeton, New Jersey, first cooperating with Ernst Alexanderson in antenna research and development. In 1954 he developed the first electronic refrigerator and two years later the first electronic air conditioner.

In 1928 Harry F. Olson, born in 1902 in Iowa of immigrants from southernmost Sweden, started working in the RCA research center at Princeton, New Jersey, and in 1945 he became director of its acoustical laboratory. At the University of Iowa, where he received his Ph.D., he had studied with Swedish-born Carl E. Seashore, whose psychological research in the fields of hearing, speech, and music achieved international fame. One of Harry Olson's early contributions at Princeton was the velocity microphone, which soon became the standard equipment for motion-picture sound and radio broadcasting. This was followed by several other types of microphones, improvements in radio and phonograph loudspeakers as well as in pickup and recording equipment, talkies, and public-address systems, and an electronic music synthesizer able to generate any tone produced by human voice or musical instrument, as well as tones beyond human or instrumental capabilities. During the Second World War Dr. Olson was, like Carl E. Seashore during the first conflict, engaged in acoustical research concerning submarines. Some of his books about acoustical and musical engineering are regarded as basic texts in their fields. He has been called "Mr. Sound."

Elmer W. Engstrom, who, as mentioned before, was born of

Swedish parents in Minneapolis and finally became president of RCA, joined the company in 1930 and was later for many years in charge of the research laboratories at Princeton, New Jersey. In 1949 he received an honorary doctor of science degree from New York University, the citation reading: "His personal contributions to radio and electronic development, notably the incredible progress of television, command the respect of his scientific peers." Both Engstrom and Harry Olson have maintained close contact with Sweden, which they visited together at least once and where their accomplishments became well known in scientific circles.

Among other engineers of Swedish stock who specialized in telecommunications and electronics was Liss C. Peterson (1898–1952), a graduate of Chalmers Institute of Technology who in 1930 became associated with the Bell Telephone Laboratories in New Jersey. He contributed to the development of the transistor and to research on coaxial cable systems. In 1950 he was elected a fellow of the Royal Society of Science and Letters in Gothenburg.

27

In the South

Swedes spread all over the South — Some unusual careers in Washington, D.C.

OF THE Southeastern states, only Florida has had a Swedish-born population of more than 1,000. The most surprising feature of the Swedish-born population in the South was perhaps its wide dispersal. In 1930, for instance, there were Swedes in 73 of Virginia's 124 counties, in 22 of South Carolina's 46, and in 35 of Alabama's 67 counties. No less than 55 of Florida's 67 counties had Swedish-born settlers.

Delaware, where the first government was organized by Swedish colonists who started coming in 1638, had in 1969–72 a governor of Swedish parentage, Russell W. Peterson. He was born in 1916 in Wisconsin, the seventh son of an immigrant barber from Sweden, and had made his business career in Delaware's largest city, Wilmington, the old Swedish Fort Christina. Both his parents had come from the vicinity of Eksjö in northern Småland. During a visit to Sweden in 1971, Governor Peterson was presented with records concerning his ancestors. In the 20th century Delaware never had more than about 300 Swedish-born inhabitants. In 1970 both Maryland and Virginia reported higher totals than before, about 850 and 600.

In the early to middle 1900s, 250 to 500 people of Swedish birth lived in the District of Columbia; American-born residents of Swedish origin were, naturally, much more numerous. One of the occupants of the White House was of relatively recent Swedish ancestry, namely,

Mrs. Dwight D. Eisenhower, whose maternal grandparents, Severin and Johanna Maria Carlson, were born and raised in the province of Halland. They emigrated to America in 1868–69, probably influenced by the crop failures of that period. Mrs. Eisenhower was, like her mother, born in Boone, Iowa.

Several senators and some congressmen of Swedish 19th-century birth or parentage we have already met in the various states where they were born or elected, and a number of legislators or political leaders with family roots in the distant Swedish era on the Delaware have also been mentioned. Well-known Washington veterans who belonged to the latter group have included Thomas F. Bayard from Delaware, who served as senator from 1869 to 1885 and as secretary of state from 1885 to 1889; Claude A. Swanson from Virginia, who served in the House for 12 years, as governor of Virginia for four, in the Senate for 23 years, and finally, from 1933 until his death six years later, as secretary of the navy under President Franklin D. Roosevelt who also claimed Swedish colonial ancestry; and Harold L. Ickes, who served as secretary of the interior from 1933 to 1946. Senator Bayard wanted a monument to the New Sweden colonists 62 years before such a memorial was erected at Wilmington, Delaware, in 1938. When Crown Prince Gustav Adolf visited Washington in 1926, Senator Swanson pointed out to the future monarch his descent from one of the first Swedish colonists on the Delaware. After having attended the annual banquet of the Swedish Colonial Society at Philadelphia in 1940, Secretary Ickes wrote in his diary that both the envoy from Sweden and the minister of Finland had claimed him as a descendant of his own country, and that probably both were right.

For many years there have always been some descendants of 19th-century immigrants from Sweden in the U.S. Congress. By the middle of the 1970s both the Senate Republican Conference and the House Republican Conference had a chairman of recent Swedish ancestry. They were Senator Carl T. Curtis from Minden, Nebraska, who was elected in 1975, and Congressman John B. Anderson from Rockford, Illinois, elected in 1969.

Earl Warren, who from 1953 to 1969 served as Chief Justice of the United States, was of Norwegian-Swedish parentage, his father having been born in Norway and his mother, whose maiden name was Chrystal Hernlund, in the province of Hälsingland in Sweden. Mrs.

Warren was born on the Swedish island of Gotland in the Baltic Sea, in a Baptist church where her father, Nils P. Palmquist, had been the first pastor, and which was built with funds donated by an American skipper in honor of his Gotland foster mother. In the summer of 1953, when Earl Warren was governor of California, he and his family spent three weeks touring Sweden. Governor Warren also studied the Swedish social-welfare system and civil defense. The wife of his successor as Chief Justice, Warren E. Burger, is of Swedish extraction, her maiden name being Elvera Stromberg. Justice William H. Rehnquist (b. 1924), who was appointed to the Supreme Court in 1972, also has Swedish antecedents. His paternal grandparents, or at least one of them, came from the area around Linköping in the province of Östergötland, arriving in America in the late 1800s and first settling in Chicago. His grandfather came with two or three brothers, and they immediately changed their family name from Andersson to Rehnquist, one of the few examples of immigrants from Sweden going from one Swedish-type name to another.

Two Americans of recent Swedish ancestry, Clinton P. Anderson and Orville L. Freeman, have, as already mentioned, served as secretary of agriculture, Anderson in 1945–48 and Orville L. Freeman in 1961–69. Some other cabinet members have also been, in part, of recent Swedish descent. A legal expert by the name of Carl E. Bagge (b. 1927), who in 1962–64 served as special assistant to the President of the United States, was born of Swedish immigrants in Chicago. In 1965 he was named to the Federal Power Commission in Washington, and five years later he became president of the National Coal Association. His studies of law had taken him to the University of Uppsala in Sweden. Clark Raymond Mollenhoff, a noted journalist and jurist who in 1969–70 served as special counsel to the President, was born in 1921 in Iowa, where his paternal great-grandparents, Hans Hansson Möllenhoff and the former Maria Sophia Andersdotter, had settled with their children in 1881. Hans Möllenhoff came to America in 1851 and lived at first in Andover, Illinois.

When new world trade negotiations opened in Geneva, Switzerland, in early 1975, Harald B. Malmgren, then the President's Deputy Special Representative for Trade Negotiations, was the leader of the U.S. delegation. Another descendant of Swedish immigrants, William

M. Roth, whose maternal grandfather, William Matson, had become a famous shipowner in California, led the American delegation at the Kennedy round of tariff negotiations in Geneva in the middle 1960s.

A remarkable trade-union and government career was made by Mary Anderson (1872–1964), who for 25 years was head of the Women's Bureau in the Department of Labor. Born on a small farm near Lidköping in the province of Västergötland, she emigrated with an older sister in 1889 at the age of 16, worked for a year as a domestic in Michigan and then began as a stitcher in a shoe factory in Chicago. Remaining as a shoe operator for nearly two decades, she gradually broadened her education and became increasingly active as a trade-union member and finally leader. The first woman to sit on the executive board of the International Boot and Shoe Workers Union, she was, at the beginning of the First World War, drafted into the Women-in-Industry Section of the Council of National Defense. After the war she became the first director of the Women's Bureau of the U.S. Department of Labor. She had then represented the American women workers at the Versailles Peace Conference, and other international conferences followed. In 1941 Smith College awarded her an honorary LL.D. degree as "a leader in the field of industrial relations who has devoted her life to improving conditions for working women throughout the country." When she retired in 1944 at the age of 71, President Franklin D. Roosevelt called her work "a monument of constructive achievement in the best interest of millions of wage earners." In late June of the same year she had been one of the principal speakers at the "Swedes Day" celebration in Minnehaha Park in Minneapolis. Mary Anderson became well known in Sweden.

State Department officials of Swedish extraction include U. Alexis Johnson (b. 1908), who in 1966–69 served as U. S. ambassador to Japan, in 1969 was named under secretary of state for political affairs, and in 1973 became the chief American negotiator at the talks with the Soviet Union on limitation of strategic arms. He was born at Falun, Kansas, which was founded in the late 1860s by one of the best-known Swedish Civil War veterans, Major Eric Forsse, and other immigrants from Sweden. Mr. Johnson's mother's maiden name was Ellen Forsse.

In 1952–58 John M. H. Lindbeck (1915–71), born in China where his parents were missionaries, was public-affairs adviser on Chinese affairs to the Department of State. A graduate of Gustavus Adolphus College at St. Peter, Minnesota, and a Ph.D. at Yale, he served Columbia, Harvard, Princeton, and Yale during various periods as an expert on China, and took a leading role in major national organizations helping to promote scholarly Chinese studies. Testifying before the Senate Foreign Relations Committee in 1966, he said it was time to start thinking about how to bring China into the mainstream of world affairs. He was then chairman of a joint committee on contemporary China formed by the American Council of Learned Societies and the Social Science Research Council. A younger brother, George A. Lindbeck, also born in China and a graduate of Gustavus Adolphus College, became in 1951 professor of philosophy and theology at Yale, and in 1960 professor of theology. During the Second World War he taught mathematics and meteorology at Augustana College under the Army Special Training Program, and later he taught for some time logic and philosophy at Upsala College. Their father, John Walter Lindbeck (1883–1958), was born in Skede Parish near Vetlanda in Småland, studied at Augustana Theological Seminary in Rock Island, Illinois, and served in China from 1912 to 1949. Their mother, Magda Hallquist by birth, was born in Minnesota, to a family hailing from Bitterna in Västergötland.

A third graduate of Gustavus Adolphus College, Norman Albert Carlson, who was born in 1933 of Swedish parents in Iowa, was in 1970, at the age of 36, appointed director of the Federal Bureau of Prisons. He came to Washington in 1960, working as project director for a program permitting selected inmates to live in a community center during the last 60 days of their sentence.

A Swedish-born physician and surgeon in Washington, Robert Oden, became widely known, and was consulted even by patients who came over from Sweden. He was born at Gothenburg in 1882, came to America in 1907, and received his M.D. degree from George Washington University in 1919. After advanced studies in medical schools and hospitals on both sides of the Atlantic, he began practicing internal medicine in Washington in 1927. His research had then helped lay the foundations for modern brain surgery. In 1938–39 he served as president of the Washington Medical and Surgical Society.

Swedish engineers help build the vigorous pulp and paper industry of the South

DURING the early to middle 1900s, Swedish-trained chemical engineers and businessmen played important roles in the building of the pulp and paper industry in the South as well as in the Northeast, in the Middle West, and on the Pacific Coast. Some of the foremost contributions were, in fact, made in the Southern states, which were able to develop an abundant supply of fast-growing pine and where the sulphate or kraft industry, which in contrast to the sulphite mills could use pine wood as raw material, therefore became heavily concentrated. Its final product is kraft paper and other packaging materials of various kinds. The sulphate process was developed in Sweden and Germany in the early 1880s, but it took its time in crossing the Atlantic. The first successful kraft mill in North America began producing in 1907 at East Angus, Quebec.

Among the Swedish newcomers in New York in the spring of 1906 was 26-year-old Elis Olsson (1880–1959), the son of a blast-furnace owner at Karlskoga in the province of Värmland and a graduate of the technical school at Örebro. He had come to America to study the bleaching of wood pulp, and after having practiced in two mills in the state of New York he went back to Sweden. Within less than a year, however, he returned to the United States, and after some time with a paper company at Rumford, Maine, he moved in 1908 to East Angus, Quebec, where the pulp mill had just been converted to sulphate operation. After having had a Swedish consulting engineer, Henning Helin of Quebec, report on the equipment and prospects of a small pulp and paper company at West Point, Virginia, he joined in 1918 this firm, eventually known as The Chesapeake Corporation of Virginia, which under his leadership became one of the most advanced units of the American forest industry.

Unlike most pulp and paper mills, the plant at West Point, on the York River and thus near Chesapeake Bay, kept running on a more or less normal schedule throughout the Great Depression. By the middle of the 1960s, when Elis Olsson's son Sture was president of the company, the daily production of the pulp mill, as well as that of the two huge paper and board machines, exceeded 1,000 tons, while in 1919, when the engineer from Sweden had taken over the management, the entire mill turned out less than 20 tons per day. Elis Olsson was also active promoting good forestry practices. His private stands of pine at the Romancoke estate, which in the 1700s was owned by George and Martha Washington and later passed to the family of Robert E. Lee, became a showplace of forest management.

For a program of constant improvement and expansion Elis Olsson needed able engineering assistance, and the first engineer he hired was a Swedish friend, John Paul Ekberg (1884–1960), who had worked with him at East Angus, Quebec. A graduate of the Institute of Technology in Stockholm, Ekberg had come to America in 1907, and in 1915–16 he had directed the construction of two kraft mills in New England, one at Wilmington, Vermont, and the other at Van Buren, Maine. At West Point he became chief engineer and technical superintendent, and finally vice president. Another Swedish engineer, Karl T. Thorsen (1889–1957), was made chief chemist and pulp-mill superintendent. In 1928 he was succeeded as chief chemist by Elis Olsson's nephew Erik Zimmerman, who had studied at the Institute of Technology in Stockholm and was vice president in charge of production when he retired in 1971.

Significant contributions to the growth and rising technical standards of the pulp and paper industry in the American South have also been made by Gunnar W. E. Nicholson. Born in 1893 in Älmeboda Parish in Småland, where his father, Alfred Niklasson, was a farmer and sawmill owner, he graduated in 1916 in chemical engineering from the Chalmers Institute of Technology in Gothenburg. Having worked in six different pulp and paper mills in Sweden, he planned to spend two years studying the industry in the United States, where he arrived in 1921. Via six plants in Maine, Ohio, and the provinces of Quebec and Ontario in Canada he came in 1927 as general superintendent to the Bogalusa Paper Company at Bogalusa, Louisiana, at that time the largest pulp and paper operation in the United States. After ten subsequent years as superintendent and manager of International Paper Company mills in Arkansas, Alabama, Mississippi, Florida, and South Carolina, he became in 1941 resident manager of Union Bag & Paper Corporation at Savannah, Georgia, and four years later he moved to New York as vice president and a director of the same company. From 1956 to 1967 he served as president of the Tennessee River Pulp and Paper Company, in the founding of which he had played a leading part. The company's pulp and kraft-linerboard plant at Counce, Tennessee, which represented a new high level of efficiency, was built under his direction, and modern forest-management methods were introduced throughout its timber-land. Since the beginning of organized conservation in the 1930s Nicholson had always felt optimistic about the future of forestry in the South, which by 1970 supplied two-thirds of the pulpwood required by the American pulp and paper industry.

In 1946 Gunnar Nicholson became president of the Technical Association of the American Pulp and Paper Industry, and in recognition of his technical and educational efforts he was in 1954 awarded the same organization's gold medal. For outstanding contributions to international pulp and paperboard technology he was elected an honorary member of the Swedish Association of Pulp and Paper Engineers, and he also became a member of the Swedish Academy of Engineering Sciences. Both in the United States and in Sweden, in particular his home parish of Älmeboda, a great number of young people were helped by him to continuing education.

A graduate of the technical school at Örebro in central Sweden, Richard Låftman of Laftman (1886–1961), worked during the period 1911–31 for several pulp and paper companies in the South, including the one at Bogalusa, Louisiana, where he served as manager and technical director from 1923 to 1931. After an engagement in the forest industry in Sweden he served from 1938 to 1951 as general manager and vice president of National Container Corporation. For that concern he built a kraft mill in Jacksonville, Florida.

Among Swedish-born leaders in other industries in the South was Oscar Nelson (1879–1953) from Vena in Småland, who became a driving force in the development of carbon black, vitally important in the manufacture of artificial rubber for automobile and airplane tires and also used in printer's ink, paints, and many other products. He came to America at the age of 19 and worked for ten years in one of the first carbon-black plants to be built, at Kane, Pennsylvania, where many Swedes settled. In 1925 he consolidated a number of natural-gas and carbon-black companies in West Virginia, Kentucky, and Louisiana and became president of the new organization. During the Second World War his firm built nine plants in Texas. Near Lewisburg in the valley of Greenbrier River in West Virginia he owned a

591

stock farm which became widely known for its purebred Hereford cattle. It was named Morlunda after Mörlunda in Småland.

In Kentucky, the best-known early Swedish settler was a physician and educator, John A. Ouchterlony (1838–1905) from Småland. Coming to America in 1857 at the age of 19, he served during the Civil War as an army surgeon at Louisville, Kentucky. After the war he began private practice and also taught medicine, finally as professor at the University of Louisville. In 1885 he was received in audience by Pope Leo XIII in Rome and admitted into the knighthood of the Order of St. Gregory the Great. Among his relatives in Sweden was the founder of the Swedish Salvation Army, Hanna Ouchterlony. The Ouchterlony family was originally Scottish.

Kentucky never had more than some 200 Swedish-born inhabitants, while its neighbor to the south, Tennessee, reported about 350 as early as 1870 and a somewhat higher total in 1910. A campaign promoting emigration to Tennessee was conducted in Sweden by the middle of the 1800s. At the University of Tennessee, Axel Brett, born in 1886 at Nättjebacka in the Swedish province of Dalsland, served for many years as professor and head of the department of philosophy and psychology, beginning in 1923. He had studied at Gustavus Adolphus College in St. Peter, Minnesota, and, as a fellow of The American-Scandinavian Foundation, at the University of Uppsala in Sweden.

In North Carolina and South Carolina the Swedish-born population never reached 200, according to the census figures, while Georgia reported about 300 in 1910 and 1920. Duke University at Durham, North Carolina, has had some Swedish-born faculty members. A botanist named Hugo Leander Blomquist (1885–1964), born at Sorsele in the province of Lapland, came to Duke in 1920, and from 1935 to 1954 he served as chairman of the department of botany. He had come to America with his parents in 1892 and had begun earning his living on a farm in North Dakota.

Swedes among the citrus-fruit pioneers in Florida and Alabama

IN FLORIDA, the number of Swedish-born increased without interruption during the century following the Civil War, a development not equaled by any other state. From about 30 in 1870, its population of Swedish birth rose to 560 in 1900, and then to over 2,000 in 1930 and

1940, about 3,500 in 1950, some 6,300 in 1960, and 6,600 in 1970. The continued increase was caused by a constant flow of retired people from other sections of the United States. Most of the Swedes settled in Miami, Jacksonville, St. Petersburg, and other rapidly growing cities.

Among the Swedish pioneers in the Sunshine State during the first period after the Civil War was Wilhelm or William Henschen, one of the best educated 19th-century emigrants from Sweden, who in 1870 near Sanford in Seminole County in central Florida, together with a group of friends, began an agricultural settlement called New Upsala. This venture was reminiscent of the New Upsala founded in 1841 at Pine Lake, Wisconsin, by Gustaf Unonius. The Swedes cleared the land and planted orange trees, but in the beginning most of them earned their living as carpenters, blacksmiths, or tailors, or at whatever jobs they could find.

Two brothers of William Henschen, Esaias and Joseph, helped recruit laborers in Sweden for General Henry S. Sanford, who gave his name to the town of Sanford. Attracted by glowing reports of the citrus industry, several groups of Swedes found their way to central Florida. Sanitary conditions there, however, still left something to be desired, and fearing for the health of his wife and children, William Henschen pulled up stakes and moved to Brooklyn, New York. In 1873–74 he supported himself and his rapidly growing family by editing the newly founded Swedish-language newspaper *Nordstjernan* in New York, and later, as already described, he became one of the leaders of Swedish Methodism in America. One of his sons, Henry S. Henschen, became a noted banker in Chicago, and another, Gustave Esaias Henschen (1874–1945), settled at Georgetown, Texas, as a medical practitioner.

William Henschen's brother Joseph Henschen (1843–1930), who had studied medicine at Uppsala, remained in Florida and became a large citrus grower and landowner, as well as a trusted adviser to newcomers from Sweden. He seems to have been involved in the naming of the town of St. Petersburg, observing during the discussion that "my name, Henschen, would not be good, for no one could spell it." A brother who made his career in Sweden, Salomon Henschen (1847–1930), won international fame as a neurologist and was in 1923 called to Lenin's deathbed near Moscow. In the late 1860s he had studied botany with Dr. Anders Fredrik Regnell in Brazil, who had emigrated from Sweden to improve his health and became a famous surgeon, botanist, and donor. The father of the Henschen brothers, Lars Henschen, was a noted judge at Uppsala, a champion of religious freedom, and a great admirer of American democracy. In the 1840s he served as adviser to followers of Eric Janson, the religious leader and zealot who founded the "Prairie Utopia" Bishop Hill in western Illinois.

In the northwest of Volusia County, north of Seminole, the town of Pierson was named after Per Persson or Peter Pierson (1857–1926), who arrived in 1876 after having been associated with his brother Andrew N. Pierson of Cromwell, Connecticut, later known as the "Rose King of America." Two other brothers and three cousins were among the early settlers in the same section of Florida. At one time all the members of Pierson's town council were of Swedish origin. Among the founders of Ormond Beach and Daytona Beach, on the Atlantic coast in Volusia County, was John Andrew Bostrom from the Baltic island of Gotland, who had come to Florida as a sailor in 1857, and later was joined by one brother and two sisters. Bostrom, who became a successful citrus grower and also worked as an immigration agent, served for 15 years as mayor of Ormond Beach. Both he and Peter Pierson have many descendants and other relatives in Florida.

One of the finest orange groves in Orange County, in central Florida south of Seminole, was developed by Olof Larson, a native of the province of Värmland who came in 1877 from the coal regions of Pennsylvania with his wife and two sons. Many other Swedes moved into the same area, which was called Piedmont and now is part of the city of Apopka. In the Vero Beach section farther south large citrus orchards were built up by Axel Hallstrom (1870–1966), who had begun his working life on his parents' farm in the province of Skåne, studied horticulture in Germany and England, and had for some time been in charge of the extensive gardens of James J. Hill, the railroad promoter and financier, at St. Paul, Minnesota. In Florida he became president of the Orange Growers' Association and of the Florida Citrus Exchange. A science room in the American Swedish Historical Museum in Philadelphia was created by him in the late 1950s.

The city of Hallandale on the Atlantic Ocean 15 miles north of Miami was founded in the late 1800s as a daughter colony of the

Swedish Halland Settlement in southwest Iowa. Today there is a relatively large number of people of Swedish extraction both at Gainesville and in Tallahassee, the state capital in the northwest. Many of them are associated with the large universities or other educational institutions. One of the first Swedish immigrants in the academic world in Florida, Hasse Octavius Enwall (1873–1948) from Tuna in eastern Småland, served from 1921 to 1945 as professor of philosophy at the University of Florida in Gainesville. He came to America in 1891. Florida has had one Swedish-language newspaper, *Florida-Posten.*

In Alabama, the Swedish-born population increased almost constantly until 1910, when it reached about 750. Its principal centers were Birmingham, the leading steel and machinery producer of the Southeast, and the tiny community of Silverhill in the state's southwestern corner, Baldwin County east of Mobile Bay, where an agricultural colony was founded by Swedish immigrants in 1897. Most of the pioneers came from Chicago. In the early 1900s Oscar Winberg, a native of Västergötland who also had lived in Chicago, became one of the leading members of the settlement, introducing modern farming methods and becoming a recognized world authority on the cultivation of oranges. In the 1930s he had 60 varieties of oranges under cultivation in his experimental groves at Silverhill. For decades, Swedish Midsummer Day, June 24, was celebrated with dancing around Maypoles and the playing and singing of old folk tunes. A periodical in the Swedish language was published at Silverhill in the early 1900s.

In Birmingham there were quite a few Swedish engineers. Jöns or John Elias Fries (1876–1932), born at Frinnaryd in Småland, a graduate of the Institute of Technology in Stockholm and an emigrant in 1903, was from 1920 until his death 12 years later chief engineer of the U. S. Steel subsidiary at Birmingham, where he built the first electrically operated steel mill.

In 1870 Mississippi reported a Swedish-born population of nearly 1,000, which was more than any other Southern state had at that time. Most of the Swedes lived in Lafayette, Yalobusha, and Chickasaw counties in the north, but large numbers moved, as already related, to Minnesota and other parts of the Middle West, and in 1880 only about 300 were left in Mississippi. In Louisiana, the Swedish-born population reached its high point, somewhat more than 500, in the census of 1920. Many of the settlers were former sailors.

Texans of Swedish stock celebrate the anniversary of
S. M. Swenson's arrival in 1838

THE most important Swedish settlements south of the Mason-Dixon line were in Texas, where the Swedish-born population in 1910 reached a top level of about 4,700.

After the arrival in 1838 of Sven or Swante Magnus Swenson, a 22-year-old native of Barkeryd Parish in northern Småland, and the coming in 1848 of a group of some 25 people from the same district, the most significant year in the history of the Swedes in Texas was 1867 when about 100 immigrants, most of them from the north of Småland, came at the same time. Swante M. Swenson, who had left Texas during the Civil War, moved from New Orleans to New York in the same year, but he believed in the future of the Lone Star State, where he retained extensive business interests. Cooperating with an uncle in Austin and a brother in Småland, who there became known as "Johan i Långåsa," he organized an agency promoting the migration of young Swedes to Texas. Their fare was paid by Swenson, but they had to pay off their debt by working for him or some Swedish farmer in Texas. Later most of them developed their own farms, and as a rule prospered on the raising of cotton.

The Swedish immigrants in Texas were an unusually homogeneous group, and a majority of them settled within an area of 700 square miles in Williamson and Travis counties, near the capital of Austin. Georgetown was its northernmost center. In Travis County one village was named New Sweden and another Lund. Gradually, the Swedes spread to practically all parts of Texas. In 1930 there were Swedish immigrants or at least members of the first American-born generation in 230 of the state's 254 counties.

Of the cities, Austin in 1930 had the largest Swedish-born population, about 380. In Houston the count was about 280 and in Galveston 270. In the 19th century many Swedish sailors settled down in Galveston. As in other parts of the United States, an active interest in education was typical of the immigrants in Texas. For two decades, 1911–31, the Swedish Methodists owned Texas Wesleyan College at Austin, and from 1906 to 1929 the Swedish Lutherans in Texas had a similar school, Trinity College, at Round Rock, 17 miles north of the capital. A Swedish-language newspaper founded in 1896 was still published at Austin in the 1970s. Elgin and Georgetown have had periodicals in the Swedish language.

To celebrate Swedish Midsummer as well as the anniversary of the arrival of Swante M. Swenson in 1838 and of a large group of Swedish immigrants in 1867, Texas Swedes and descendants assemble annually in late June in Zilker Park in Austin under the auspices of the Texas Swedish Pioneers Association. The day of this reunion is known as Old Settlers Day or, in Swedish, Banbrytaredagen. Zilker Park has a Swedish log cabin, which was built in 1849 on S. M. Swenson's ranch "Govalle," now part of the city of Austin.

In 1938, when the 100th anniversary of Swenson's arrival in Texas as well as the 300th anniversary of the first Swedish settlement in America were observed in Austin, about 6,000 people of Swedish extraction took part in the celebration. A businessman named Carl T. Widén (b. 1884) presided, the beginning of more than three decades of service as president of the Swedish Pioneers Association. Born in Iowa of Swedish parents who had arrived in the Midwest in 1867, he had become fluent in the Swedish language and an authority on the history of the Swedes in Texas. Stockholm-born Sigurd N. Ekdahl, from 1920 to 1951 a member of the University of Texas faculty as a specialist on physical education, served for many years as president of an organization formed in 1951 to promote cultural relations between Texas and Sweden. He came to Worcester, Massachusetts, in 1902 at the age of 16 and attended in Boston the Posse Normal School of Gymnastics.

Among the Swedes who came to Texas shortly after the Civil War was Gustav Vilhelm Belfrage (1834–82), a member of a well-known Swedish family of Scottish origin, who became an unusually active naturalist of the American frontier, with entomology as his specialty. In 1868–73 he sent valuable collections of insects to educational institutions in Boston, Stockholm, London, St. Petersburg, and other cities, and at his death in Texas he left over 36,000 "pinned specimens in good order." A Swede from Hudiksvall in the north, John Peter Sjolander (1851–1939), who had received part of his education in Britain and had come to America in 1871, became in Texas a farmer, a writer of poems and stories, and a great patriot. Two of his best-known songs were inspired by the San Jacinto battleground, where Texas in 1836 had won its independence from Mexico, and by the blue bonnet, the state flower. Sjolander finally became known as the "Sage of Cedar Bayou."

In the early 1900s the best-known Swede in Austin was a geologist, Dr. Johan August Udden (1859–1932), who conducted oil explorations as a result of which the financial position of the University of Texas was greatly improved. Born in Lekåsa Parish in the province of Västergötland, he was brought to America at the age of two. The family settled in Minnesota, and Udden received his education there and at Augustana College in Rock Island, Illinois. After teaching natural science at Bethany College in Lindsborg, Kansas, and at Augustana, he began in 1903 his first period of service in Texas. He was one of the first to voice deep concern about soil erosion.

Dallas and Fort Worth received their first Swedish settlers in the early 1870s. John Tomson, who came to Dallas in 1871 and lived there until his death in 1918, became a well-known businessman. A member of the first American-born generation, J. Erik Jonsson, served as mayor of Dallas in 1964–71, when he had played a significant part in the industrial life of the city. Coming to Dallas in 1934 from New Jersey where he had been superintendent of a technical laboratory, he helped lay the foundations for a corporation called Texas Instruments, which became one of the more successful manufacturers in the field of electronics, and which in 1951–58 he served as president and then as board chairman. A number of universities and other educational institutions elected him one of their trustees, and he received many honorary doctorates and awards. His father, John Peter Jonsson, who seems to have been born in the industrial village of Hammar at the northern end of Lake Vättern, and his mother, who was born in Stockholm, met and married in Brooklyn, where they operated a cigar store. Their son John Erik was born there in 1901.

Another prominent citizen of Dallas who retained the Swedish spelling of his name was Alfred Oscar Andersson, who was born in 1874 at Liverpool, England, of Swedish parents and brought to America in 1888. After studies at Princeton he became a newspaperman in the Middle West. In 1906 he moved to Dallas where he established the *Dallas Dispatch*, and later he also founded a newspaper in Houston.

In the lower Panhandle region in the northwest of Texas, the heirs of Swante M. Swenson and his second wife, born Cora Susan McCready, own four ranches totaling about 260,000 acres, which make up one of the last great cattle empires in the United States. Their famous SMS brand, derived from the founder's initials, was one of the earliest registered in Texas. The SMS ranches were developed by the pioneer's two sons, Eric and Swen Albin Swenson. Their uncle Johan's son Andrew John Swenson, who had come to Texas in 1881, became manager of the ranches in 1922, and he was succeeded by two sons, William G. (Bill) and A. M. G. ("Swede") Swenson. They, in turn, were followed by other members of the same family. At Stamford, some 300 miles northwest of Austin, the Swenson company every Fourth of July sponsors a "cowboy reunion" which features the biggest amateur rodeo in America. In 1867 Swante M. Swenson had established a banking firm in New York. It was finally merged with the National City Bank, where the pioneer's eldest son, Eric P. Swenson, became chairman of the board.

28

Sweden: A Great Transformation

*Sweden of the late 1800s: Widespread gloom but a
growing faith in progress*

IN A LONGER perspective, the large-scale emigration from Sweden toward the end of the 1800s may be seen as a reflection of the national
mood of that era. The 1880s, in particular, were a period of widespread pessimism and gloom, but also of growing impatience, new
ambitions, and greater realism. The forces of conventional tradition
and pompous conservatism seemed to be in effective command, but
they were, in fact, being challenged at more and more points. The
vision of a more dynamic society and a richer individual life drove a
substantial part of the population to the New World, but it also began
to stir those who remained, and a Sweden of more rapid change was
widely regarded as both necessary and possible. The United States
itself was often held up as a model.

The regenerated belief in progress nourished the interest in better education, and during the 1880s both farmers and workers were
reached by new forms of instruction and civic training. In 1868 the
farmers, in cooperation with university men, had organized the first
folk high schools, or people's colleges, on the Danish model, and
many institutions of the same type, about half of them agrarian, were
established during the next few decades. The first folk high school
affiliated with the labor movement was not started until 1906, but
in the late 1800s more and more workers took part in study groups and

attended popular lectures. The interest in adult education was also furthered by the temperance societies and by the new church societies.

In literature a new era was introduced by August Strindberg, whose first novel, published in 1879, lampooned established injustices and prejudices in a fresh vein of robust humor and social realism. There were, however, also other literary currents. The 1890s brought, above all, a poetic renaissance, full of beauty and color, imagination, the lore of the past, sparkling gaiety, and at times tender sadness. It was obviously also a Romantic revival, but it had little in common with the Romanticism of the early 1800s. Its patriotism was, on the whole, far removed from a sentimental or arrogant chauvinism. The leading figures were Verner von Heidenstam (1859–1940), winner of the Nobel prize for literature in 1916 when, because of the First World War, no other award was made; Gustaf Fröding (1860–1911), generally regarded as Sweden's greatest lyric poet since Carl Michael Bellman of the late 1700s; and Erik Axel Karlfeldt (1864–1931), who in 1931 was posthumously awarded the Nobel literature prize. To the same epoch belongs another Nobel prize winner, Selma Lagerlöf, who developed the prose tale and attained a worldwide fame none of the poets could dream of.

Around the turn of the century, these and other literary personalities became sources of inspiration to numerous Swedes both at home and abroad, particularly of course in the United States. And so did several of the great painters who appeared during the same period, including Carl Larsson (1853–1919), Bruno Liljefors (1860–1939), and Anders Zorn (1860–1920), as well as the new composers, such as Hugo Alfvén (1872–1960). In 1903 he wrote his *Midsummer Vigil*, which, in an adapted version, is often heard on the radio in America under the title *Swedish Rhapsody*.

In the Swedish parliament, a member of the Liberal party named Sven Adolf Hedin (1834–1905) fought with brilliance for democratic and social reforms, as well as for a stronger national defense. The rapid progress of the United States he regarded as one of the most hopeful of all developments abroad. At the beginning of his political career, in 1867, he wrote that "our corner of the world, that is, Western Europe, must be Americanized, or its civilization will be overwhelmed . . . from the East." Among his friends in the press were

Isidor Kjellberg, the radical journalist who after a few years in America founded a dramatically pro-American newspaper at Linköping in Östergötland, and Ernst Beckman (1850–1924), a successful newspaperman and for many years a member of the Riksdag. The latter visited the United States several times, spending his last few years in California where he died. Both Kjellberg and Beckman said that Sweden ought to become as alike America as possible, and Sven Adolf Hedin again hinted at this goal in a bill calling for workmen's old-age insurance, which he submitted to the Riksdag in 1884. It did not lead to more significant legislation until 1913, but Hedin, who is Sweden's first politician of the modern type, is regarded as one of the pioneers of the country's social-welfare system.

The first important architect of social reforms in Europe was Bismarck in Germany, who in the early 1880s devised a comprehensive scheme of insurance against accident, sickness, and old age. Even the Swedish monarch, Oscar II, was impressed by this, and like Bismarck he hoped to be able to divert the workers from socialism by a national system of social security. The social reforms in Sweden, however, did not begin in earnest until the labor movement had become strong enough for active participation. At that time, considerable industrial progress had already been made.

The first real trade unions in Sweden were organized in the 1870s but it was not until the 1880s that they began to grow with any marked speed. The first major strike occurred in 1879 at Sundsvall, the center of the largest forest-industry district in the north, from which thousands of workers emigrated during the next few decades. The Social Democratic Labor party was founded in 1889, and its first objective was to obtain full voting rights for its members and supporters. The call for universal suffrage was also raised by the temperance societies and by the nonconformist religious movements, both of which owed much to influences from America. By the turn of the century only about six percent of the Swedish people were able to vote in the general elections to the Riksdag.

The actual leader of the Social Democratic party from the beginning was a young scientist and newspaperman, Hjalmar Branting (1860–1925), who in 1889, the year when his party was founded, was sent to jail for radical propaganda in a press controversy concerning religious freedom. As a young political agitator he may not have ruled out the eventual need for a revolution in Sweden, but even at their first congress in 1889 the Social Democrats aimed at peaceful, gradual reforms, and this direction was firmly established under Branting's official leadership. In 1896 he became, with the assistance of the Liberal party, the first labor member in the parliament, and in 1920 he formed Sweden's first Social Democratic government.

In an editorial article in the late 1860s, when the emigration from Sweden reached its first high-water mark and Hjalmar Branting was a young boy, a Jönköping newspaper mentioned as one of the many causes of the exodus "the unrest that comes from the fact that our social reformers do not drive onward with high pressure like a steamboat on the Mississippi." In retrospect, the progress made during the following decades may indeed seem inadequate, but the absence of more determined action was not only due to lack of foresight and initiative among the ruling classes. Paradoxically, the emigration itself contributed to the sluggish pace of the reform work by relieving the load of overpopulation in the rural districts. Without the large-scale exodus the need for reforms would have become much more obvious, but it is, on the other hand, far from certain that it could have been met without violent clashes. The emigration to America served, in other words, as a human safety valve, and this helps explain the fact that the industrial revolution in Sweden never brought about any social upheavals.

Fundamentally, the main reason why no sweeping social reforms were effected in Sweden during the latter part of the 1800s was the same as the principal cause of the emigration, namely, the lack of adequate economic resources. In a report commenting on the flow of emigrants from Västergötland and Dalsland in 1879–80, an unusually active but politically conservative provincial governor, Count Erik Sparre (1816–86), wrote: "The only effective means of combating emigration is to move America over here — its national economy, and everything that makes its greatness. It is by developing this life, by the rearing of the kingdom's children to usefulness, initiative, and self-confidence through opportunities for labor and visions of progress, that one can hope to persuade them to remain in the homeland."

This was, to be sure, an ambitious program, and in 1880 it must have seemed almost utopian to a large part of the Swedish people, but foundations for its realization were, in reality, already being laid. Many young engineers, scientists, and businessmen were among those who believed that a much more productive Sweden could be achieved in the relatively near future. They were, at least, working on it.

Explosives invented or tamed by Alfred Nobel speed
the industrial revolution

THE inventions of Alfred Nobel (1833–96), which began in the 1860s with an epoch-making percussion cap and a "safety blasting powder" called dynamite, helped open the door to the international industrial revolution. Iron ore and other minerals needed for the manufacture of machinery and transport equipment became available in rapidly increasing quantities, and the construction of railroads, tunnels, canals, and highways was substantially facilitated. In Sweden, Alfred Nobel also made other contributions to the industrial and technological development. He and his brothers were among the first Swedes who became successful international industrialists, and they thus played a part in bringing Sweden closer to the outside world.

Alfred Nobel was born in Stockholm. At the age of nine he was taken by his mother to St. Petersburg, then the capital of Russia, where his father, Immanuel Nobel (1801–72), who after a disastrous fire had become bankrupt in Sweden, had preceded them and started a foundry and machine shop. Encouraged by the Russian military authorities he overexpanded his plant during the Crimean War, and when the conflict was over and he received no more government orders, he again became bankrupt. In 1859 he returned to Sweden.

In 1850, at the age of 17, Alfred Nobel was sent by his father on a foreign study trip that included a brief visit to New York. There he called on Captain John Ericsson, presumably to obtain copies of the inventor's drawings for his caloric or hot-air engine.

In the early 1860s Alfred Nobel began his experiments with nitroglycerin, an explosive liquid chemical that had been discovered in 1846 by an Italian chemist, but had so far been used only as a medicine. After having invented and patented an igniter, which for the first time made nitroglycerin explode at the right time and place, he founded his first two factories, one at Stockholm and the other near Hamburg, Germany. In 1864 the new explosive was used for blasting a railway tunnel under the southern heights of the city of Stockholm. Careless handling of the nitroglycerin, however, involved serious risks, and in the same year the factory at Stockholm blew up, killing five people including Alfred Nobel's youngest brother, 20-year-old Emil Nobel. To begin with, the manufacture was moved to a lighter anchored in the sea approaches to Stockholm.

On April 15, 1866, when a whole series of nitroglycerin disasters had begun to frighten the American people, Alfred Nobel came to New York for the second time. The following day a nitroglycerin explosion wrecked a warehouse in San Francisco, killing at least 15 people, and somewhat later came reports of an even worse disaster in Panama. Nobel then called on the mayor of New York, identifying himself as the inventor of a safe way to make nitroglycerin explode under control. At the same time he invited the New York newspapers as well as scientists to a public demonstration. It was staged on May 4 in a quarry on West 83rd Street in upper Manhattan, and proved successful.

Nobel had come to the United States to defend priority rights to his inventions, but these efforts did not meet with long-range success. In 1866 a company in which he held 25 percent of the capital stock built a small nitroglycerin factory at Little Ferry, a village on the western shore of the Hackensack River, close to Ridgefield, New Jersey. Early in 1870 it was wrecked by three successive explosions.

On his way back to Europe at the end of July, 1866, Nobel tried to work out a solution to the nitroglycerin problem, and before long he made the liquid safer to handle by mixing it with an absorbent substance, kieselguhr. This product, which he called dynamite, was first patented in England on May 7, 1867, and in Sweden four months later. After that he continued to improve his explosives and organized production companies in practically all European countries, except Russia. The demand for the new blasting materials was so great that in ten years the inventor became wealthy. In 1873 he established himself in Paris, and in 1890 he moved to San Remo, Italy.

The worldwide explosives industry which Alfred Nobel founded was to a great extent built up by Swedish chemical engineers, among them his close friend and associate Alarik Liedbeck (1834–1912). In 1868–70 a dynamite factory was built near San Francisco, in what now is Golden Gate Park. It was thanks to dynamite that in 1869 it became possible to complete the first American transcontinental railroad through the Rocky Mountains and Sierra Nevada.

Nobel's American business caused him many difficulties, however, and despite the enormous use of dynamite in the New World, it contributed little or nothing to his growing fortune. In a fit of depression in 1885, he sold practically all his American holdings. Swedish chemists and technicians contributed, on the other hand, considerably to the development and manufacture of the new explosives in the United States. Historical reviews of the American explosives industry are full of the names of Swedish immigrants, including many who never worked for Nobel. Deliveries of dynamite for the construction of the Panama Canal began during Nobel's lifetime and finally reached 30,000 tons.

In Sweden, Alfred Nobel encouraged and supported quite a few young engineers. Toward the end of his life he conducted experiments on new chemical products, such as artificial silk, rubber, and leather. In 1894, two years before his death, he bought the Bofors company at Karlskoga in the province of Värmland, a small town which furnished a total of nearly 5,000 emigrants to the United States, including hundreds of ironsmiths and other skilled workers who in the late 1800s already were at work in Moline, Illinois, Worcester, Massachusetts, and Pittsburgh.

The Bofors company had been formed in the 1870s, but was rooted in ironmaking traditions dating back to the early 1600s, and under Alfred Nobel's leadership the steel mills and gun factories in southeastern Värmland began their development into one of Sweden's best-known industrial concerns. During the Second World War, Bofors' 40-mm. anti-aircraft gun became the most widely used type of artillery in the Allied forces, more than 100,000 such pieces being made in the United States. Today Bofors turns out more products for peaceful uses than for military purposes. Like many other Swedish firms it has licensing agreements with a number of U.S. companies.

When Alfred Nobel died in 1896, after a truly cosmopolitan life, explosives and accessories invented by him were manufactured in hundreds of factories all over the world. Early the following year a Stockholm newspaper published his will, according to which the bulk of his estate should be converted into a fund, the income from which should be distributed annually in the form of prizes for work that had been of "the greatest benefit to mankind" in physics, chemistry, physiology and medicine, literature, and peace promotion. The first Nobel prizes were awarded in 1901.

With financial assistance from Alfred Nobel, his two elder brothers, Robert (1829–96) and Ludvig (1831–88), developed the dormant Russian oil fields in the Caucasus, which became the basis for an industry of worldwide significance. Most of their engineers were Swedish. In the late 1870s they started using Swedish-built steam tankers, regarded as the first serviceable such ships in the world. Taking advantage of the spring floods, the vessels traveled across Russia to the Caspian Sea along the canal-and-river route, which about 1,000 years earlier had been used by the Swedish Vikings. In 1903 the Nobels built for the Caspian Sea the first motor ship of any importance, using an internal-combustion engine to generate electricity for the main drive. It was also the first time that electric propulsion was tried in a commercial vessel.

Ludvig Nobel, who lived at St. Petersburg most of the time, also helped develop the Russian mechanical industry. His son Carl Nobel (1862–93) introduced Gustaf de Laval's inventions in Russia, first of all the separator. In 1893 his older son Emanuel Nobel (1859–1932) became the leader of all the Nobel enterprises in Russia, and gradually won great respect as an unusually able and decidedly progressive captain of industry. He was named a member of the directorate of Russia's central bank. At first, his uncle Alfred Nobel's final will caused him disappointment as well as complications with regard to his Russian business interests, but his subsequent cooperation became of decisive importance for the acceptance of the testament and the establishment of the Nobel Foundation.

In Russia, Emanuel Nobel finally controlled industries whose total value was several times larger than Alfred Nobel's wealth. He was in the Caucasus during the revolution in 1917, but the next year he managed to escape, and then lived in Sweden until his death.

The Nobels were descendants of a family of farmers at Östra Nöbbelöv near the small city of Simrishamn in southeasternmost Sweden. The first member of the family who was able to get a university education took the name Nobelius, which two generations later was shortened to Nobel. Among Nobel's ancestors was also Olaus Rudbeck of Uppsala, Sweden's greatest scientist of the 17th century.

Sweden's industrialization led by forest industries and advances in steelmaking

DURING the last few decades of the 19th century highly significant technical innovations were achieved in the rapidly growing Swedish forest industry as well as in the making of iron and steel.

The industrialization of Sweden, which had begun by the middle of the 1800s, was led by the steam-driven sawmills, and lumber soon became the country's foremost export article. Mechanical wood pulp or groundwood was also produced at an early stage. In 1872 a new era dawned, for in that year the first chemical-pulp factory in the world started operation at Bergvik in the old emigration district in the province of Hälsingland. Its production was based on the so-called sulphite method, which had been worked out by a young engineer, Carl Daniel Ekman (1845–1904). This development greatly increased the value of Sweden's forest resources and also helped revolutionize the forest industry in other countries. Ekman himself, in fact, left Sweden a few years later to establish sulphite mills in England, France, and Italy, and his method was introduced in the United States as well. In the 1880s a number of Swedish engineers helped develop the sulphate method for the making of kraft pulp and, finally, kraft paper, "kraft" being a Swedish word meaning strength. The stage was thus set for a rapid expansion of Sweden's pulp industry which in the early 20th century became the country's leading exporter. Gradually, more highly developed products, above all paper and board, became increasingly important.

During the 19th century, as economic historians have observed, Sweden's ironmasters, metallurgists, and ironworkers wrote one of the most glorious pages in the country's economic history. At times the very existence of its tradition-rich iron and steel industry seemed threatened by the discovery abroad of cheaper production methods, especially in view of the fact that there were virtually no domestic coal supplies. Gradually, however, the Swedish mills managed to overcome the difficulties by adopting and developing the new processes and, in part, by specializing in high-quality grades.

The first successful experiments of Henry Bessemer of England, whose process for mass production of quality steel ushered in the Steel Age, were undertaken in 1858 at Sandviken in the old iron-making district in Gästrikland; ten years later the acid open-hearth process was introduced in Sweden, and in the 1880s the first basic open-hearth furnaces were installed. The basic process made it possible to produce steel from phosphoric ores, and this meant that Sweden's largest supplies of iron ore, at Grängesberg in the province of Dalarna and in the north of Lapland, could be opened up. From the Grängesberg mine, which is owned by the Gränges metal and shipping company, ore was first exported in 1892, and five years later the first export shipments were made from the rich arctic fields, the beginnings of a trade that in the 20th century turned Sweden into a leading supplier of iron ore on the international market. In 1900 a Swedish engineer, Fredrik Kjellin (1872–1910), built the first practical induction furnace for the smelting of steel. Since then, the production of electric steel has increased almost constantly.

The largest steel mill in Sweden, Domnarfvet at Borlänge in the province of Dalarna, was inaugurated with the Bessemer process in 1878, and replaced 19 minor ironworks scattered throughout the same district. It is owned by the Stora Kopparberg company, which traces its beginnings to miners who about the year 1080 started working a huge copper deposit, for centuries the largest source of the red metal in the world, in what is now the city of Falun, the capital of Dalarna. Today the company produces not only steel of many types but also wood pulp, newsprint, and chemicals, all based on its own forests, mines, and power stations. Stora Kopparberg is regarded as the oldest industrial corporation in the world, and it has been the subject of numerous articles in the American press, dealing not only with its unique traditions but also with its contributions to modern technology and industrial progress. Its oldest document, a stock certificate dated June 16, 1288, was exhibited in the Swedish pavilion at the New York World's Fair in 1964–65, the first time that it was displayed outside of Sweden. In remarks on the Senate floor, Senator Hubert H. Humphrey of Minnesota welcomed the action as "evidence of the continuing bonds of friendship and trade between our two countries."

Another large industrial concern of the same structure as Stora

Kopparberg is Uddeholm. Its steel, pulp, and paper mills as well as its chemical factories and hydroelectric plants are concentrated in Värmland, south of Dalarna, and most of its forests and mines are also in this province which during the era of emigration lost a greater part of its population than most other sections of Sweden, in part as a result of its many small ironworks dying out. Uddeholm dates back to 1668, when the first iron mill was built, and became a stock company in 1871. By the middle of the 19th century it was Sweden's leading exporter to the United States. New economical smelting processes were developed by its ironmasters in the 1860s, and in the late 1880s cold-rolling was introduced by two of its engineers, one of whom, Gustaf Jansson (1850–1934), in 1876–80 had practiced the rolling technique in Worcester, Massachusetts. Cold-rolled steel then became one of Uddeholm's specialties, and the company was a pioneer in the manufacture of one such product, razor-blade steel. When Gillette introduced the safety razor in America in 1904, the blades were made from cold-rolled Uddeholm steel. Stainless razor-blade steel was developed by the same company. Some other Swedish steelmakers have been active in the same field almost from the beginning.

In 1862 an iron and steel center by the name of Sandviken began to rise in the province of Gästrikland, a fountainhead of early emigration to the American Middle West, and the founder was Göran Fredrik Göransson (1819–1900) who four years earlier had been the first man in the world to put the epoch-making Bessemer steelmaking process to practical use. In 1876 the Sandviken company, or Sandvik as it is now called, participated in the Centennial Exposition at Philadelphia, and exports to the United States started the following year.

At that time Sandvik had already launched rock-drill steel which was to become one of its specialties; in 1883 it was one of the pioneers in the production of cold-rolled steel strip, and two years later it built a saw factory which grew into the largest in Europe. The first springs for clocks and watches were made before the end of the century, and this was another development of lasting significance. Similar devices were later used on American space ships. Today, Sandvik makes a wide range of high-quality steel products, most of which are employed in industrial processes or end up as vital parts of finished equipment, being sold in almost all industrial countries. It is the world's largest producer of tungsten or wolfram carbide, used for the rotary bits of rock drills and other cutting tools. In the United States it has a number of manufacturing facilities besides its sales organization. A tube plant in the Hanford area in the state of Washington, which was established in cooperation with an American company, serves the nuclear and aerospace industries.

Another steel center in the ancient mining and ironmaking district north and northwest of Stockholm is Fagersta, which lies within the provincial boundaries of Västmanland. Its modern era began in 1873, when a stock company named Fagersta was founded. Three years later its steel won high praise at the Centennial Exposition in Philadelphia, and during the next few decades new plants, processes, and products were added in rapid succession. Fagersta was then led by Christian Aspelin (1830–1919), who became legendary because of his concentration on high quality, and Johan Brinell (1849–1925), who was his chief engineer. The first Swedish high-speed steel was developed by Brinell. By the turn of the century he devised a hardness test for steel and other metals which was adopted in all countries, and even today such terms as Brinell hardness and Brinell number are used wherever steel is made or tested. "Few metallurgists have done so much toward the advancement of the metallurgy of steel as Mr. Brinell," an American expert, Belgian-born Albert Sauveur of Harvard, wrote in 1904.

The SKF ball-bearing company owns two steel mills, at Hofors in Gästrikland and Hällefors in Västmanland, and is a leading producer of specialty steels. A steel mill at ancient Garphyttan in the province of Närke makes high-quality drawn wire and is the largest manufacturer of valve-spring wire in the world.

Inventors of mechanical and electrical equipment help found vital industries

PRODUCTS wholly or in part made of metal, and ranging from small tools and fine instruments to aircraft and heavy machinery, are the leading specialties of today's industrial Sweden, and vital parts of the foundation were laid during the late 19th century not only by the nation's steelmakers but also by inventors specializing in mechanical and electrical engineering. Their designs and constructions gave rise to highly specialized and export-oriented metalworking establishments, which today are among Sweden's best-known manufacturers. Machinery that was invented or improved by Swedish engineers also contributed greatly to the founding or growth of industries not producing metal articles. Other important inventions were made in the early 1900s. The history of Swedish inventions teems with contacts with the United States and other countries.

One of Sweden's first significant new industries of the 1800s was based on the safety match which by the middle of the century was developed by Gustav Pasch (1788–1862), who had been a pupil of Berzelius, the famous chemist, and Johan Lundström (1815–88), who built a factory at Jönköping, the principal city in one of Sweden's foremost emigration districts in the province of Småland. Ingenious machines were invented by Alexander Lagerman (1836–1904), and in the 1870s the match factory achieved an advanced automation which was most unusual in industrial production at that time. Toward the end of the 19th century the safety match became one of Sweden's leading export articles. In 1917 the country's match factories were merged in the Swedish Match Company, which today has some 110 subsidiaries in 25-odd countries, including the United States. One of its Swedish affiliates, the Arenco company, was founded in 1880 to make newly invented equipment for the match industry. In the 20th century, laborsaving equipment for other industrial activities, from cigar making to food packing, became more important. In 1920 Arenco produced the world's first cigarette packer, and by 1930 about three-fourths of all American cigarettes were packed in Arenco machines.

Sweden's most prolific inventor of the late 1800s was Gustaf de Laval (1845–1913), the son of an army officer and land surveyor at Orsa in Dalarna, who after engineering studies in Stockholm took a doctor's degree in chemistry at Uppsala. In 1878 he designed the first centrifugal cream separator, which was followed by other inventions which also helped revolutionize the dairy industry, and in 1883–89 he developed a fast-running steam turbine which added greatly to his international reputation. He was often called the "man of high speed." The first turbine shipped to America was exhibited at the Chicago World's Fair in 1893, where it attracted tremendous interest. At that time De Laval employed over a hundred engineers in his engineering shop in Stockholm, and many of these continued their careers abroad. His major inventions became an important part of the foundation for two of Sweden's world industries, Alfa-Laval of Stockholm, which specializes in equipment for the food industry, and Stal-Laval of Finspång, manufacturer of steam and gas turbines and ship-propulsion machinery. De Laval gave his name to two companies in the United States, a manufacturer of separators at Poughkeepsie, New York, and a steam-turbine specialist at Trenton, New Jersey.

Some of the first telephones used in Sweden were made in the United States, and in 1880–81 the International Bell Telephone Company opened exchanges in the three largest cities, Stockholm, Gothenburg, and Malmö. At about the same time, the world's first stand-up telephone was designed by Lars Magnus Ericsson (1846–1926); other inventions were made by him and his part-time associate Henrik Cedergren (1853–1909), and in the late 1800s Sweden ranked as the leading telephone country. Cedergren also built telephone exchanges abroad and operated, for instance, telephone nets in Moscow and Warsaw. A workshop which Ericsson had set up at Stockholm in 1876 became the beginning of the L. M. Ericsson Telephone Company, which in the early 20th century developed the Russian telephone system and gradually grew into one of Sweden's largest industrial concerns, with subsidiaries throughout the world.

The productive activities of another pioneer in electrical engineering and the father of Sweden's high-voltage technology, Jonas Wenström (1855–93), coincided with the record emigration wave of 1879–93. In theory, he solved the problem of the incandescent lamp at about the same time that Thomas Alva Edison did it in practice, in late 1879. Continuing his experiments in a flour mill at Örebro in south-central Sweden, he produced a dynamo-electric machine, exploited in America through a company formed at Baltimore, and a magnetic ore separator, which became widely used in the United States. In 1888 Wenström himself visited America, and somewhat later a younger colleague, Ernst Danielsson (1866–1907), spent two years there, at first working for the Wenstrom Dynamo and Motor Company at Baltimore. During the last few years before his death in 1893 at the age of 38, Wenström played a leading part in developing the three-phase alternating-current system which until the middle of the 1900s was the only method of long-distance electrical transmission. His equipment and techniques, which were completed by

Danielsson, were soon successfully tested by the Asea company, which had been formed in 1883 to exploit Wenström's inventions. Today, Asea ranks among the major electrical manufacturers of the world. It is also active in the atomic-energy field. Its head office and principal factories are at Västerås in the province of Västmanland.

In the southern part of Östergötland, one of the first centers of Swedish emigration to America, there is an industrial town by the name of Åtvidaberg where copper mining began in the 1300s and reached its highest point by the middle of the 19th century. In 1889, when the mines were almost exhausted and the district seemed destined for lasting depopulation, the leader of the mining company decided to start making office furniture, and he arrived at this decision after having seen American roll-top desks exhibited in Paris and established contacts with an American manufacturer of woodworking machinery. This was the beginning of the modern era at Åtvidaberg, which in the 20th century became the headquarters of Sweden's largest office-machine industry and one of the world's leading exporters of such equipment, known as the Facit group. In the early 1930s Facit started making the first 10-key calculating machine in the world, which was based on an invention by Karl Rudin. Ten years later it absorbed a company formed to exploit the inventions of Willgodt T. Odhner, who had started his career at Ludvig Nobel's factories in St. Petersburg and in 1875 designed the first commercial calculator. In 1966 Facit joined forces with another important Swedish manufacturer of business machines, the Addo company. Under the pressure of severe international competition, the Facit-Addo group was merged in 1971 with the Swedish Electrolux company, manufacturer of household appliances, which also sells the bulk of its output abroad.

A company founded at Stockholm in 1873 and named for Atlas, the Greek Titan who carries the earth on his shoulders, lives on in the Atlas Copco concern which by the middle of the 20th century became the world's largest organization specializing in compressed-air equipment, such as compressors, rock drills, and industrial and contractor's tools of many kinds. Its oldest parent company, maker of locomotives and railway rolling stock, began at an early stage to take an interest in compressed air as a tool of modern technology. The new tunneling methods developed in Sweden by the mid-1900s attracted great attention in North America.

Two vitally important hand tools, the universal pipe wrench and the adjustable wrench, were invented in the late 1880s and early 1890s by Johan Petter Johansson (1853–1943), a crofter's son from Vårgårda in Västergötland who at one time had decided to emigrate to America where his parents and several other close relatives settled. In 1887 he built a workshop at Enköping, northwest of Stockholm, which may be regarded as the beginning of the Swedish Bahco company, today the largest manufacturer of adjustable wrenches outside the United States and also a specialist in ventilation equipment. Altogether Johansson obtained about 100 patents. The first persons to start manufacturing the adjustable wrench in the United States were two Swedish immigrants, who had brought a set of tools produced at Enköping. Another inventor named Johansson who also was born in a small cottage, Carl Edward Johansson, has been introduced in connection with his 12-year stay in Detroit, Michigan. His precision gages helped make modern mass production possible.

Thorsten Nordenfelt (1842–1920), who in 1885–88 constructed four types of steam-driven submarines and produced one of the first practical torpedo tubes, is still regarded as one of the leading pioneers in submarine design, although part of the credit should go to an associate, Helge Palmcrantz (1842–80). His first submersible was built in Stockholm and the other three in England, where Nordenfelt had moved in 1869. He was one of the founders of a large English industrial company, Vickers and Maxim. In 1903 he moved back to Sweden. Another Swede who settled in England, John Gjers (1830–98), became an internationally noted metallurgist and made inventions which were widely used in America. Christer Sandberg (1832–1913), who moved to London at the age of 36, became a leading expert on railroad rails and helped develop the international standard.

In the 1890s a naval engineer and army officer, Wilhelm Unge (1845–1915), developed a military rocket and made, in fact, many contributions to modern rocket technology, although today his work is almost forgotten. Among those who joined the board of his engineering firm, prophetically named the Mars company, was Gustaf de Laval, and at one time his supporters included Alfred Nobel, who witnessed at least one test at Bofors. Unge obtained patents in several European countries and also in the United States. The Swedish military authorities, however, took no interest in his inventions. In 1908 the German Krupp concern bought his patents and remaining stock of "aerial torpedoes," but actual production was never begun by them.

Among other engineers whom Alfred Nobel backed financially were two young brothers, Birger Ljungström (1872–1948) and Fredrik Ljungström (1875–1964), who later became well known for their inventions. Their father had exhibited geodetic instruments at the Centennial Exposition in Philadelphia in 1876. In 1912 they completed a new type of steam turbine, known in the English-speaking countries as the Ljungstrom compound-reaction turbine. Their other inventions included an air preheater or fuel-saving device, which was adopted by many steam-power plants in America, and an electrothermal process for the extraction of oil from shale. One of the components of the already mentioned Stal-Laval company of Finspång was founded by them in 1913.

In 1896, the year when Henry Ford unveiled his first "horseless carriage," the first Swedish-built automobile was tested at Surahammar in the province of Västmanland. It had been constructed by Gustaf Erikson (1859–1922), an engineer from a mining district northwest of Stockholm, who worked for a carriage-making firm at Södertälje, south of the capital; the firm much later became part of the Saab concern. In the early 1900s, however, Sweden's industrial resources were too modest for successful auto making. In 1927 the first Swedish passenger car of lasting significance was presented by Volvo, which had been founded in 1915 as a subsidiary of the SKF ball-bearing company in Gothenburg. Its leaders studied automobile manufacturing in several countries, in particular the United States. By the middle 1970s Volvo had larger sales than any other Swedish manufacturing company. Saab, also known as Saab-Scania, which was founded in 1937 and started as an aircraft manufacturer, began making automobiles in 1950. Its production also includes space equipment, computers, and control systems.

Sweden's first more important aircraft designer was Carl Nyberg (1858–1939), a self-taught mechanical genius. His craft, built before the advent of the internal-combustion engine, never became airborne, but his experiments were valuable contributions to technical progress. A wind tunnel made by him was one of the very first of its kind, Gustaf de Laval being responsible for another. The first flights with a Swedish-built airplane were made in 1910. Saab's production of planes designed in Sweden began in 1941. In this as in other industrial fields there are numerous ties with industry and technology in the United States and some other countries.

Gustaf Dalén (1869–1937) seemed at one time destined for successful farming, on the family farm in Västergötland, but encouraged by Gustaf de Laval he entered instead Chalmers Institute of Technology in Gothenburg, at the age of 23, and two decades later he was Sweden's best-known inventor and one of its foremost industrial leaders. In 1912 he received the Nobel prize in physics for his invention of an automatic "sun valve," based on the difference in the heat radiation from a reflecting body and that from a blackened one. By combining such valves with improved gas accumulators, Dalén constructed new types of beacons and buoys which functioned automatically, being turned on by darkness and turned off at dawn, and thus eliminated the need for permanent lighthouse keepers. They were rapidly introduced all over the world and became of immense importance to navigation.

In 1909 Dalén helped found a manufacturing company now known as Aga, which he led until his death. Even today many of its products, including airport and railway signals, surveying instruments and medical apparatuses, are in one way or another linked to the founder's inventions, although continued research-and-development has been vitally important. In the year when Gustaf Dalén received the Nobel prize he was literally drenched in flaming acetylene gas during an experiment, and his elder brother Albin, who had become one of Sweden's leading eye specialists, operated in a frantic effort to save his sight, but failed. In 1945 the Swedish Academy of Sciences issued a Dalén commemorative medal with a Latin inscription which reads: "When the day vanishes, he bids darkness light the beacons."

In 1907, when Gustaf Dalén invented the automatic sun valve, 30-year-old Sven Wingquist (1876–1953), who after technical schooling in Sweden had studied for a while in the United States, produced the first self-aligning ball bearing and thus laid a foundation for the newly formed SKF ball-bearing company. In its first workshop at Gothenburg 12 people produced some 100 bearings a day, while in the early 1970s SKF and its affiliated companies in other countries employed about 62,000 workers who made nearly two million bearings daily. Ball and roller bearings occupy a key position in modern industrial production. A factory at Philadelphia which was related to the German ball-bearing industry was purchased by SKF in 1916 and considerably enlarged. Sven Wingquist, who from 1907 to 1919 served as SKF's managing director in Gothenburg and later as board chairman, received in 1921 an honorary doctor's degree from Stevens Institute of Technology at Hoboken, New Jersey. One of his leading themes as a Swedish industrialist was the vital need of the highest possible quality.

In 1918 two students at the Stockholm Institute of Technology, Baltzar von Platen (b. 1898) and Carl Munters (b. 1897), invented a new refrigerator based on the absorption system, which, after improvements, was launched by the Electrolux company of Stockholm under the leadership of Axel Wenner-Gren (1881–1961), who already had started making a fortune on vacuum cleaners. He had come to the United States the first time in 1907, a year of financial panic, when he took a job in a New Jersey factory paying 15 cents an hour. Later he became well known on both sides of the Atlantic as a "mystery millionaire" or "international capitalist." The Bahamas and Mexico were among his bases of operations. In 1941 he helped set up an aeronautical laboratory at the University of Kentucky, and a larger donation established a foundation for anthropological research in New York. Stockholm has a Wenner-Gren research center.

Beginnings of modern banking and a merchant marine serving international trade

THE growing industrialization called for a modernization of Sweden's old-fashioned banking system, and considerable progress was made in the late 1800s and early 20th century. Among the leaders was André Oscar Wallenberg, who during two years as a seaman and stevedore in the United States in the 1830s had become interested in economics and finance, and after that continued his studies in various European countries. Stockholms Enskilda Bank, which he founded in 1856, became Sweden's first financial institution of the modern

"'You have made your visit to Sweden a mission of real friendship and good will," Prime Minister Tage Erlander said to General Dwight D. Eisenhower at the end of the former President's visit to Stockholm in the summer of 1963. He is seen here with a miniature model of a cannon from the Swedish man-of-war *Vasa*, which sank in Stockholm harbor in 1628, was salvaged in 1961, and now is preserved in a museum of its own (pp. 749–750).

Senator Hubert H. Humphrey of Minnesota, Mayor Willy Brandt, West Berlin, oarsman Walter Reuther, the American labor leader, and Swedish Premier Tage Erlander met in the summer of 1963 at Harpsund west of Stockholm, the official country residence of Swedish prime ministers.

August Strindberg's career as a writer began in 1869 when he was 20 years old, and from that time on, life and art were inseparable to him. His world reputation is based, above all, on his dramatic writing, which as a rule was the child of his sorrow (pp. 662–668). — Below: Inga Tidblad and Ulf Palme in *Long Day's Journey into Night* at the Royal Dramatic Theater in Stockholm, where Eugene O'Neill's posthumous drama, called "the greatest play written by an American," had its world premiere in 1956. Three other posthumous plays by O'Neill were first produced in Stockholm. Like the American playwright, August Strindberg was no prophet in his own country (pp. 763–764).

When Charlie Chaplin visited Sweden in 1964, he and Ingmar Bergman talked film for one and a half hours. At that time Ingmar Bergman was director of the Royal Dramatic Theater in Stockholm. He won international fame as a producer of motion pictures (pp. 767–769).

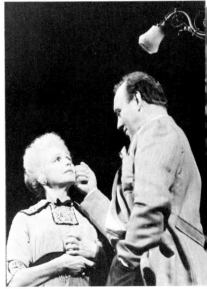

Greta Garbo, seen here in *Queen Christina*, the 18th of the 24 films she made in the United States, was for many years the "First Lady of Hollywood." She was also called "The Divine," as well as the "Swedish Sphinx" (pp. 670, 683–684, 687).

Birgit Nilsson, for many years the most generally admired opera star, made her debut at the Stockholm Opera in 1946 and her American debut in 1956, at a concert in the Hollywood Bowl. In 1959 she came to the Metropolitan Opera in New York (pp. 754–755).

Ingrid Bergman was, like Garbo, schooled and discovered in Sweden, while Hollywood and Broadway made her a star. Five years after her American film debut in 1939 she received her first Academy Award. In 1946 she was voted America's number one box-office attraction. Her third Oscar came in 1975 (pp. 671, 727–728).

1. Because of long wars and the consequent exhaustion, the construction of the Stockholm Royal Palace took more than 50 years, ending about 1750. Nicodemus Tessin the Younger was the architect. 2. In early 1966 some 50 black youngsters from Chicago visited Stockholm, under the auspices of a program called "Learning for Life." 3. An immigrant from Yugoslavia trying to learn Swedish. Sweden, which in the late 1800s, in proportion to population, was one of the leading countries of emigration, became after the Second World War a country of immigration. In 1975 nearly eight percent of its inhabitants were foreign-born, compared to five percent in the United States.

1. King Gustav VI Adolf and Dag Hammarskjöld, Secretary General of the United Nations 1953–61, photographed before the annual meeting of the Swedish Academy in Stockholm in 1957. 2. Professor Wassily Leontief of Harvard, winner of the Alfred Nobel memorial prize in economic science, receiving his award from King Carl XVI Gustaf at the ceremony in the Stockholm Concert House in 1973 (p. 718).

1. Former patternmaker Rudolph F. Bannow from Bridgeport, Conn. (right), born in Gothenburg and the first American immigrant to become president of the National Association of Manufacturers, and former toolmaker Arne Geijer, president of the Swedish Confederation of Trade Unions and of the 55-million-member International Confederation of Free Trade Unions, met in Stockholm in 1960 to discuss labor-management problems (p. 544). 2. Film stars Liv Ullmann and Max von Sydow, who played the leading parts in the Swedish films *The Emigrants* and *The New Land* which received high praise in the United States, discuss the history of the pioneers with a descendant of early settlers at Bishop Hill, the Swedish "Prairie Utopia" in western Illinois (p. 791).

"Sweden will have to choose between exporting merchandise and exporting people," it was said when the emigration to America again increased in the early 1900s. Today, Sweden exports nearly one-fourth of its total output of goods and services. The port of Gothenburg is the largest in Scandinavia. Its Scandia Harbor was specially built for container traffic and other modern methods of handling goods. As a rule, Sweden buys from the United States more than it sells (pp. 807–815).

Of the Swedish economists who began their careers in the 1920s, Gunnar Myrdal (above) and Bertil Ohlin became best known in America. In 1938–43 Dr. Myrdal conducted a study under the auspices of the Carnegie Corporation which resulted in a famous work, *An American Dilemma: The Negro Problem and Modern Democracy* (pp. 702, 713–715).

1. Making use of the most modern machines and the latest techniques, the Kockum shipyard at Malmö in southernmost Sweden became one of the world's leading shipbuilders. The large gantry crane was completed in 1974, its lifting capacity representing a new world record. 2. The high-voltage techniques developed in the laboratories of the Asea company at Ludvika in the province of Dalarna have been introduced in many countries, including the United States and Canada. Asea shipments to America in the late 1960s included equipment for the Pacific Intertie, the country's first high-voltage direct-current system (pp. 810–811). 3. Scandinavian Airlines navigators studying the Polar Path Gyro, developed by Bendix Corporation, founded by a son of immigrants from Sweden. In 1954 SAS made aviation history by opening an arctic route between Scandinavia and the Pacific coast of America (pp. 392–393, 748).

type, successfully channeling savings into industrial and commercial activities. Seven years later he helped establish Skandinaviska Banken, which in 1871 was followed by the beginning of Svenska Handelsbanken.

The bank which André Oscar Wallenberg founded and led until his death remained under the direction of his descendants until 1971, when it was merged with Skandinaviska Banken. His son Marcus Wallenberg (1864–1943) played a leading part in the founding or reorganization of a number of important industrial undertakings in Sweden and Norway, and after the First World War he made significant contributions to European economic reconstruction. By the turn of the century his older brother, Knut Agathon Wallenberg (1853–1938), secured continued Swedish ownership of the rich ore fields in northern Lapland, and in 1917 he and his wife created Sweden's largest private foundation for the promotion of education and scientific research.

The last few decades of the 1800s also brought new enterprise in shipping and foreign commerce, and two initiatives, which at first seemed insignificant, would have particularly far-reaching consequences. In 1873 a retail-shop assistant from Jönköping by the name of Axel Johnson (1844–1910) founded a firm in Stockholm which to begin with principally imported coal but soon also became a successful exporter of steel and lumber. In 1883 Johnson helped reorganize the Avesta ironworks in Dalarna, which carried on traditions from the 1300s and in the 20th century became Sweden's foremost stainless-steel manufacturer. Two years later he bought his first steamer and in 1890 he formed his own shipping company, Nordstjernan or the Johnson Line, which in 1904 began regular traffic with Buenos Aires and other ports on the east coast of South America.

The rapid expansion continued under Axel Johnson's eldest son, Axel Ax:son Johnson (1876–1958), who in 1914 as leader of the shipping company opened direct services to the west coast of South and North America, first via the Strait of Magellan and then via the Panama Canal. Later he built Sweden's first oil refinery and added construction, shipbuilding, and the manufacture of heavy industrial machinery and other equipment to his business interests. Products which have become known in the United States include stainless steel from Avesta in Dalarna, paper machines and controllable-pitch propellers from Karlstad, and hydraulic presses made at Motala. A continuous pulp digester developed by Kamyr of Karlstad, partly owned by the Johnson group, has had an enormous impact on pulping operations in the United States. Large foundations for the promotion of science and culture have been established by Axel Ax:son Johnson and his wife, who was born in America, and by other members of the Johnson family.

At Kristinehamn, a port in the old mining district in southeastern Värmland, a former railroad brakeman by the name of Axel Broström (1838–1905) in 1865 borrowed money to buy a small sailing vessel for traffic on Lake Vänern and via the Göta River down to Gothenburg. In 1870 he started skippering a steamer of his own, and in 1882 he settled in Gothenburg where eight years later he founded the Tirfing Steamship Company. Under the powerful and visionary leadership of his son Dan Broström (1870–1925), Tirfing in the early 20th century became the central component of a shipping and shipbuilding empire still known as the Broström group. It includes the Swedish American Line, which was founded in 1914 when another Swedish shipping pioneer, Gunnar Carlsson (1887–1967), also played an important role.

Around the turn of the century many if not most Swedes must have regarded Gothenburg as, above all, the chief port of embarkation for Swedish emigrants to America. The city had, however, a long history of commerce and shipping and there were numerous signs of rapid progress, even if few could foresee that before the middle of the 1900s the country's "Gateway to the West" would be one of Northern Europe's leading industrial and maritime centers, with services and other economic activities all over the world.

The discovery of the Northeast Passage and other celebrated explorations

IN 1878–79 a Swedish scientific expedition led by Adolf E. Nordenskiöld (1832–1901) discovered the long-sought Northeast Passage, bringing a ship from the Atlantic to the Pacific through the arctic waters and ice fields north of Europe and Asia. His ship, a bark with an auxiliary engine named *Vega*, was frozen in at the end of September, 1878, near the Bering Strait, but completed the voyage successfully the following summer. The long trip back to Sweden via

Japan, Hong Kong, Singapore, Italy, Portugal, England, and France became a triumphal tour, and in Stockholm the people went wild with enthusiasm. April 24, when the expedition arrived, is still known in the Swedish calendar as Vega Day.

Nordenskiöld was born in Finland, then part of the Russian empire, and had been compelled to leave for political reasons. After the *Vega* expedition, however, he and his wife, the former Anna Mannerheim, were invited to dine with Czar Alexander in St. Petersburg. From 1858 to 1875 Nordenskiöld had taken part in eight Swedish expeditions to the arctic areas. The first two were led by Otto Torell (1820–1900), who is regarded as one of the founders of modern polar research. In the summer of 1876 the Nordenskiölds visited the Centennial Exposition in Philadelphia and also spent some time in New York. Among his associates in Stockholm was Erik Dahlgren (1848–1934), who became an internationally noted expert on the history of explorations in the Pacific area, including the Hawaiian Islands. A great-grandson of Nordenskiöld, Gustaf Arrhenius, became professor at the Scripps Institution of Oceanography at La Jolla, California. The first biography of Adolf Nordenskiöld in the English language, written by Hungarian-born George Kish, professor of geography at the University of Michigan, was published in 1973.

Adolf Nordenskiöld's eldest son, Gustaf Nordenskiöld (1868–95), carried out important research in widely separated fields but died at the age of 27. Hoping to improve his health he went to America in 1891 and conducted archeological and geological studies in Florida, Kentucky, Colorado, and Arizona. In the Mesa Verde canyons in Colorado he also made excavations, and in 1893 he published a large work entitled *The Cliff Dwellers of the Mesa Verde*, which became of great importance for subsequent archeological research concerning the American Southwest. His rich collections from Mesa Verde belong to the University of Helsinki in Finland and the Museum of Cultural History in Gothenburg.

A younger son of the famous explorer, Erland Nordenskiöld (1877–1932), studied the ancient culture of Latin America during six expeditions and carried Sweden to a 20-year-long leading position in this branch of ethnography. In 1924 he organized the 21st International Congress of Americanists at Gothenburg, where his outstanding Latin American collections were displayed, as they still are, in the

Museum of Cultural History. Two years later he gave a series of lectures at the University of California in Berkeley. A first cousin of the Nordenskiöld brothers, Otto Nordenskiöld (1869–1928), explored Alaska and the Yukon in 1898 and later made notable contributions to polar research, including an expedition to the antarctic regions in 1901–1903. Many other members of the Nordenskiöld family have also become noted for their ability. One, Otto Henrik Nordenskiöld, fought with distinction on French ships in the American War of Independence and later led the Swedish navy in a war against Russia. All the Nordenskiölds descend from a noncommissioned officer, Erik Mattson of Nordanåker in the province of Uppland, who died in 1700 at the age of 103.

The successful completion of Adolf Nordenskiöld's great expedition in 1879 fired the imagination of a 14-year-old boy named Sven Hedin (1865–1952), who seven years later made his first trip to Asia and later opened up the vast interior of that continent to modern geographical research, exploring and mapping spaces that until his entry had remained unknown. In 1927–35 his explorations were crowned with a Sino-Swedish expedition to the northwestern provinces of China, in which 45 specialists in various fields took part. Hedin gave numerous lectures in the United States, especially in 1923 and 1932, his books about China were always received with great interest, and hundreds of articles about him appeared in the American press. After the Second World War the U.S. Army Map Service took over the publication of a large atlas of Central Asia which is regarded as one of the permanent monuments to Sven Hedin's initiative and energy. Photographs from space were also used in the preparation of the maps. In 1925 Hedin published a book about the Grand Canyon, with his own color illustrations.

During some of his Asian expeditions Sven Hedin received invaluable assistance from a Swede named August Larson (1870–1957), who in 1893 had arrived in Mongolia as a missionary for the American Bible Society and the Christian Missionary Alliance in New York. Four years later he married an American missionary, Mary Rodgers, and during the Boxer Rebellion in China in 1900 he and his wife rescued many American and Swedish colleagues. After the Chinese revolution in 1911 he was appointed adviser to the Chinese government on Mongolian affairs, and in 1920 the religious leader of Mongolia gave him the title of duke. In 1939, when eastern Mongolia and northern China had been invaded by Japanese forces, he moved to the United States and settled at Vista in California, where he died. "Duke Larson of Mongolia," as he often was called, was the son of an agricultural laborer near Västerås in the province of Västmanland. The title of duke had actually been given to him by a Living Buddha at Da Khure, now Ulan Bator.

While Sven Hedin was exploring central and eastern Asia, a linguist named Bernhard Karlgren (b. 1889), the son of a schoolteacher, laid new foundations for Western sinological research, that is, the science dealing with the Chinese language, literature, and culture. In his doctor's thesis, published 1915–26 in four volumes in the French language, and subsequent works he reconstructed the development of the Chinese language since long before Christ and clarified phonetic and grammatical problems which the Chinese themselves had not yet solved. He is said to have been the first person of our time who was able to speak the Chinese which Confucius, the famous philosopher, spoke about 2,500 years ago. Like many of his other works, Karlgren's dissertation was translated into Chinese, and in China it became the basis for modern dialect research. A volume entitled *The Chinese Language, an Essay on its Nature and History*, was published in New York in 1949, and other books were also first issued in English. Japanese translations appeared in Tokyo. Karlgren made his first research expedition in China in 1910–12. From 1918 to 1939 he served as professor of East Asiatic linguistics and culture at the University of Gothenburg, and from 1939 to 1959 as director of the Museum of Far Eastern Antiquities in Stockholm.

The collections of the Museum of Far Eastern Antiquities in Stockholm were largely built up by Osvald Sirén (1879–1966), born at Helsinki, Finland, who for many years served first as professor at the University of Stockholm and then as curator in the National Gallery of Art. In the period 1917–35 he undertook four extensive research expeditions in China. Parts of his collections were acquired by the Philadelphia Museum of Art. Most of his books about Chinese painting and sculpture were published in the English language.

In 1876, a young graduate of the Stockholm Institute of Technology named Samuel August Andrée (1854–97) worked as an attendant in the building which contained the Swedish educational exhibits at the Centennial Exposition in Philadelphia, and which later was moved to Central Park in New York. In Philadelphia, Andrée met an enthusiastic and experienced balloonist, John Wise, who gave him his first lessons in flying. After his return to Sweden he studied aeronautics and began to work out a plan for crossing the North polar region in a balloon. In the summer of 1897 he and two Swedish companions, Nils Strindberg and Knut Fraenkel, started from Spitzbergen in a balloon called *Örnen* (The Eagle), and were never again seen alive. The three men survived the crash of the balloon but died a few months later, probably of trichinosis which they had contracted by eating polar-bear meat. In the summer of 1930 their remains, as well as diaries and other records including some films, were found by a Norwegian sealer on an island in the Arctic Ocean, and in the fall of the same year they were brought to Stockholm on a naval vessel. The events of 1930 caused a great sensation both in Europe and in America, and before the end of the year two books about Andrée were published in New York.

Pioneering work in physics, meteorology, physical chemistry, and biochemistry

FROM the middle of the 1800s and until his death three decades later, the grand old man of the natural sciences in Sweden was Elias Fries, the "Linnaeus of the 19th century." In 1877 his oldest son Thore (1832–1913) was named professor of botany and practical economy at Uppsala. He had then already taken part in the botanical exploration of the arctic regions and had become widely known in botanical circles for pioneering work in lichenology, the study of lichens. Linnaeus's summer home at Hammarby near Uppsala, which the government bought in 1879, was restored by Thore Fries and remains today largely as it was in the late 1700s. Two of his sons also became eminent botanists, extending their investigations to South America and Africa. Other descendants of Elias Fries have contributed to a unique family tradition of important research in botany and related sciences.

The traditional Swedish interest in botany and its practical applications has been carried over to America along numerous lines. Among Swedish botanists who helped explore the North American flora in the early 1900s was Sven Johan Enander (1847–1928), a clergyman from Lillhärdal in the northwestern province of Härjedalen, who won an international reputation as a specialist on the large Salix genus. Speaking only Swedish and Latin he traveled all over the northern hemisphere, visiting the United States for the first time in 1913. In 1928, after having sailed up the Yukon River in Alaska and visited the Aleutian Islands at the age of 81, he died at Victoria, British Columbia, poisoned by gas from a leaking pipe. A younger Swedish botanist, Eric Hultén (b. 1894), became a specialist on the flora of the Aleutian Islands, Alaska, and the Yukon.

Several of Sweden's leading physicists of the 19th century, including Anders Ångström of the University of Uppsala (1814–74), Janne Rydberg of Lund (1854–1919) and Bernhard Hasselberg (1848–1922), made significant contributions to the science of spectroscopic phenomena, that is, the radiations from a luminous source separated into their constituent colors or wavelengths. Ångström, the son of a Lutheran minister in the province of Medelpad, is regarded as one of the founders of spectrum analysis — the analysis of substances or bodies by means of their spectra, which became of epoch-making importance for the natural sciences. The atomic theory of Niels Bohr, the Danish physicist, resulted from a consideration of spectroscopic data. In a work of 1868 about the solar spectrum, Ångström expressed the wavelengths in units of one ten-millionth of a millimeter, and this unit is still known as the Ångström unit or the angstrom, often abbreviated Å.U. or simply A.

Janne Rydberg, born at Halmstad in the province of Halland, was also one of the numerous links in the methodical research that laid the foundations for modern nuclear science. In 1889 he made a famous investigation of the spectra of chemical elements, for the serial numbers of which he introduced the term atomic number. His name lives on in the designation of a universal wavelength constant, Rydberg or Rydberg's constant, which like the Ångström unit is found in American and English dictionaries. Bernhard Hasselberg, a native of Västergötland, established his international reputation in Russia. In 1888 he became professor of physics at the Academy of Sciences in Stockholm.

Anders Ångström's brother Carl (1821–96) became a successful inventor and served as one of the referees for the machinery section at the Centennial Exposition in Philadelphia in 1876, and his son Knut (1857–1910), who like his father became professor of physics at Uppsala, won international recognition for research concerning the radiation of heat and energy from the sun. He also devised various delicate instruments, including one that was adopted by many scientific expeditions and by observatories all over the world. Knut Ångström's son Anders (b. 1888) took part in an American solar expedition to Africa in 1912 and led an expedition to Mount Whitney in California the next year, and another son, Tord (b. 1892), became one of Sweden's aviation pioneers.

Hugo Hildebrandsson (1838–1925), in 1878 named professor of meteorology at Uppsala, became one of the founders of the international science of meteorology. Much of his research concerned the upper air. Among the young meteorologists in Stockholm toward the end of his life was Carl-Gustaf Rossby (1898–1957), who had begun his scientific career as a pupil of one of Sweden's internationally best-known mathematicians of the early 1900s, Ivar Fredholm (1866–1927). In 1926 the Sweden-America Foundation gave Rossby a fellowship to go to the United States, where he was hired by the Daniel Guggenheim Fund for the Promotion of Aeronautics and sent to California to establish the first airway weather-reporting system, which became the model for the U.S. airlines. In 1928 Rossby was invited by Massachusetts Institute of Technology to develop its department of meteorology, which he headed until 1939. Rossby's service and contributions during the Second World War will be described later. In 1947 he returned to Stockholm to take up a professorship at the university and organize the International Meteorological Institute, which became one of the leading centers for meteorological research in the world. Rossby's own work, which included discovery of the "Rossby waves," laid the basis for a good deal of modern meteorology.

From about 1875 important contributions to oceanographic studies and methods were made by a Swedish chemist and hydrographer, Otto Pettersson (1848–1941), who designed widely used instruments, organized the first international hydrographic conference at Stockholm in 1899, and three years later helped found the International Council for the Study of the Sea. His son Hans Pettersson (1888–1966) led in 1947–48 a Swedish oceanographic expedition of 45,000 miles, mostly through equatorial regions. It was equipped with instruments never before applied to deep-sea research, including a piston core-sampler to raise cylindrical cores of sediment up to 70 feet long. Hans Pettersson's account of the deep-sea expedition, *Westward Ho with the Albatross*, which was published in New York in 1954, received long reviews in American newspapers.

A series of discoveries of new chemical elements by Jöns Jacob Berzelius and other Swedish scientists during the first part of the 19th century was completed in 1879–80 by two professors of chemistry at the University of Uppsala. Lars Fredrik Nilson (1840–99) identified scandium, named after Scandinavia, the existence of which had been predicted by a Russian chemist. During studies of the rare earths, Per Cleve (1840–1905) discovered holmium, from Holmia which is Latin for Stockholm, and thulium, after Thule, an old name for the Scandinavian North of Europe. Cleve's daughter Astrid Cleve (1875–1968) also became an eminent chemist, and her husband of 1902–12, German-born Hans von Euler-Chelpin (1873–1964), who had come to Stockholm in 1897 to work with Svante Arrhenius, became in 1929 cowinner of the Nobel prize for chemistry. Their son Ulf von Euler (b. 1905) shared in 1970 the prize for physiology and medicine with one American and one English scientist.

Among the pioneers in international biochemical research was Olof Hammarsten (1841–1932), whose originally extremely modest institution at the University of Uppsala attracted students from many countries, including Swedish-born Otto Folin who in 1907 became professor at the Harvard Medical School. Hammarsten's comprehensive guide to a study of physiological chemistry was translated into English, German, Russian, and Italian. Biochemistry, that is, the chemical study of plant and animal life, has remained one of Sweden's leading scientific specialties.

In 1903 Svante Arrhenius (1859–1927) became Sweden's first Nobel laureate, being awarded the chemistry prize for the services he had rendered that science by his electrolytic theory of dissociation. The first draft of this theory had been published as early as in his doctoral thesis of 1884, which contained the results of his studies of the electrical conductivity of solutions. Arrhenius helped build a bridge between chemistry and physics and is regarded as one of the principal founders of the modern science of physical chemistry. In 1895 he was named professor at the University of Stockholm, and in

1905 he became the first director of the newly established Nobel Institute for Physical Chemistry, which attracted young scientists both from Sweden and from other countries. In 1904 Arrhenius gave a series of lectures at the University of California in Berkeley, dealing among other things with the problem of immunity, and seven years later he was invited to Yale. To the American public he was known chiefly for his speculations in the field of cosmic physics. Gustaf Arrhenius of the Scripps Institution of Oceanography at La Jolla is his grandson. He and a noted Swedish physicist, Hannes Alfvén, who had left Sweden for California in the late 1960s, were among the first scientists to receive lunar material brought back to earth by the Apollo spaceships.

One of Sweden's internationally best-known astronomers, Knut Lundmark (1889–1958), was in 1921–22 associated with the Lick Observatory in California and in 1922–23 with the Carnegie Institution in Washington, D.C. Working with the American astronomers Harlow Shapley and Edwin Powell Hubble, he pioneered in the study of nebular and metagalactic systems.

Swedish Nobel laureates in the sciences include Manne Siegbahn (b. 1886) who in 1924 received the physics prize "for his discoveries and investigations in X-ray spectroscopy," and The Svedberg (1884–1971), winner of the chemistry prize in 1926. Dr. Siegbahn is prominent among Swedish scientists who have created their own schools. Dr. Svedberg was in 1923 visiting professor at the University of Wisconsin, an experience that, he said, helped him greatly in his continued research. In 1949 the Franklin Institute in Philadelphia gave him the Franklin Medal, its highest award, for his development of the ultracentrifuge, an indispensable aid in studying high molecular substances, and "his inspiring leadership of others in the field of colloid chemistry."

29

The End of Mass Migration

New Swedish emigration reaches top in 1902–1903 *and, after a general strike, in* 1910

SWEDEN'S growing determination to rule out war as an instrument of national foreign policy, except in extreme necessity, was tested in 1905 when the Norwegians declared the Swedish-Norwegian union dissolved. This step had provocative aspects, and many believed that war was inevitable. Military preparations were made in both countries. Powerful voices urging moderation and conciliation, however, were heard, and finally a peaceful agreement was reached. King Oscar II died two years later at the age of 78 and was succeeded by his oldest son, Gustav V (1858–1950).

Like Sweden's loss of Finland a century earlier, the dissolution of the union had on the whole a stimulating effect on the Swedish nation, which again needed all the vitality and fundamental unity it could muster. Since the middle of the 1800s the value of Sweden's foreign trade per head of population had, in real terms, increased tenfold; in banking and finance the country had also become much more outward-looking, and it was therefore directly affected by the international economic crisis which began in late 1907 and seemed to have been caused by a financial panic in the United States. In Sweden the recession lasted longer than in America, and a period of sagging wages and growing labor unrest culminated in the summer of 1909 in a series of lockouts and a general strike, in which nearly 300,000 workers became involved. The unions lost the strike and suffered a serious setback, but the discipline and solidarity of their members had been proved, and the labor movement was soon ready for further advances.

Another step toward universal suffrage was taken in 1907–1909 under a Conservative government, and nearly 20 percent of the population, or twice as many as previously, were then able to vote in the general elections. At this time the Liberals and the steadily growing Social Democratic party worked in unison to a great extent, and it was a government based on these two factions that in 1917–18 brought the problem of universal suffrage for both men and women to its final solution. The Conservatives had then given up their resistance and took part in the decision, thus contributing to the tradition of cooperation or compromise that has often been regarded as typical of Swedish politics.

During the first decade of the 20th century Sweden saw more people leave for America than during any other such period except the 1880s. The driving force was, as before, the belief or conviction — frequently bolstered by reports and invitations from relatives or friends — that the New World would offer better economic opportunities. The highest annual emigration figures of the early 1900s, about 35,000–40,000, were recorded in 1902 and 1903, when the United States found itself in a period of booming prosperity, while Sweden's accelerating industrial growth was accompanied by relatively serious labor conflicts and the harvests in the northern provinces, always meager at best except perhaps for the grasslands, failed completely. Then came more labor unrest and finally the general strike of 1909, which, together with the higher American wage level, made thousands of industrial workers decide to move to the United States, or at least played a part in such decisions. In 1910 the number of emigrants was about 25,000, the third highest figure of the decade.

In 1908, on the other hand, only about 9,000 Swedes left for America, one of the lowest figures since the emigration seemed about to peter out in the middle 1870s, and in the same year over 6,000 former emigrants returned to Sweden. Behind this turn of events was the aftermath of the 1907 financial panic in the United States, which had made a deep impression in Sweden and other European countries. In the Swedish press there was little or nothing of the malicious "rejoicing" that some American writers of Swedish extraction believed they had seen, but critical comments were made and conditions in the United States were often painted grimly.

In the Conservative *Svenska Dagbladet* 42-year-old Gustav Cassel, who would become one of Sweden's first internationally known economists, wrote in the fall of 1907 that "Europe has good reasons to complain of having its whole economic life time and again subjected to violent dislocations only because the great republic of the West is unable to organize its banking system according to rational principles and administer it in a reasonably honest way." Several newspapers published long reports dealing with the power of the American trusts, speculative excesses in Wall Street, or the seamy side of life in the big cities, but there were also articles of other types. At the height of the American panic in late 1907, *Socialdemokraten*, the leading labor organ, wrote that the crisis was actually international, and that the capitalistic development had brought both increased prosperity and greater risks of financial crashes.

A lasting increase in the reimmigration of Swedes from America may have seemed likely at one time, but the high level of 1908 proved temporary. In the early 1900s and until the First World War, the number of former emigrants who celebrated Christmas in Sweden with parents or other relatives seems to have been close to 10,000, which naturally impressed the Swedes at home. In the fall of 1907 many Swedish newspapers reported that money orders from former emigrants to relatives and friends in Sweden during the last 15 years totaled nearly 100 million kronor, also an impressive figure. In the period 1901–16, Swedes in America sent over 50 million dollars to their native country.

Among the more remarkable transatlantic travelers from Sweden in the early 1900s was August Palm (1849–1922), who visited the United States in 1900 and 1906. A tailor by trade, he had been a Socialist agitator in Denmark and Germany, which expelled him in 1877, and later became Sweden's first Socialist pioneer as well as the founder of the newspaper *Socialdemokraten* in Stockholm. In a report on what he sarcastically called his "incendiary tour" of 1900, published in Stockholm the following year, he found much to criticize in America but regarded it nevertheless as "the great land of the future," where he undoubtedly would have tried his fortune if he had been 32 instead of 52 years old. The things that had impressed him included the housing standards of the workers and the humane treatment of the inmates in the Minnesota state prison.

While the large-scale migration to America had aroused strong opposition in Sweden even in the 1800s, the unexpectedly heavy exodus after the turn of the century caused a more articulate and deep-searching reaction. That a sparsely populated land, which had just begun to develop some of its most valuable natural resources and seemed to need all its manpower, year after year should ship vigorous men and women by the tens of thousands to the richest country in the world, more and more people regarded as absurd. In 1902–1903 the emigration from Sweden, with a little more than five million inhabitants, exceeded that from Germany, which had a population of about 60 million. German commercial exports, it was observed, had on the other hand increased greatly: Sweden too had to choose between exporting merchandise and exporting people.

Swedish conservatives, in particular, denounced the continued outflow as a threat to the national defense. Efforts to tighten the restrictions on the emigration of military conscripts did not, however, meet with success. Compulsory military service helped stimulate emigration, but a closer study of the statistical material shows that few men moved out only because they wanted to escape their duties under the colors.

Migration, first halted by the war of 1914–18, *spurts in* 1923 *but ends in* 1930

TWO private bills which were introduced in the Swedish parliament in 1904 urged determined measures against emigration. The author of one of them was Ernst Beckman, who had visited the United States several times, had married an American, and finally retired to California. To him, as he had said before, the only constructive way to stop emigration was "to move America over to Sweden," that is, national production must be raised substantially, universal suffrage must be introduced, more and more citizens must become owners of their own homes, and, last but not least, the school system must be modernized, so that the public school, as in America, would become the basic school for everybody. Education, including vocational training, had, according to Beckman, been one of the richest wellsprings of the economic and industrial vigor of the United States.

In 1907 a commission of inquiry appointed by the government started working on the emigration problem, and six years later its director and moving spirit, Gustav Sundbärg (1857–1914), who had become Sweden's first professor of statistics, submitted a 900-page report and a score of supplements dealing with various aspects of the exodus. Much space was devoted to the farming industry, which still supported nearly half of the country's population. Its productivity had increased substantially since the beginning of the mass migration, but imports contributed a considerable part of Sweden's food supply.

The findings and recommendations of the emigration commission were soon completely overshadowed by the First World War, which finally brought transatlantic travel to a virtual standstill. In 1915–19 Swedes who returned from America were almost as numerous as the new emigrants. The economic depression that followed in the wake of the war, however, hit Sweden hard, and widespread unemployment, coupled with stimulating reports from America, led to a relatively large emigration, particularly in 1923 when it reached 25,000. The total for the 1920s was about 90,000. The agrarian population contributed a substantial proportion, but there were many industrial workers and a remarkably large number of engineers.

In the 1920s the emigration, however, was losing its momentum, and 1923 became the only year when the number of emigrants from Sweden headed for the United States exceeded the immigration quota for Swedes under the new American legislation restricting the flow of newcomers. In 1921 the maximum for Sweden was set at 20,042, in 1924 at 9,561, and in 1929 at 3,314. Even the latter quota was never filled.

The decade of the 1920s in Sweden was largely a period of recovery and reorientation after the experiences of the First World War and under the impact of the growing industrialization. The 48-hour week had finally become a reality in 1919. In the general elections of 1921, universal suffrage for men and women was practiced for the first time. Both as a modern democracy and as a so-called welfare state, Sweden is of comparatively recent vintage.

In 1920 Sweden joined the League of Nations, and immediately became involved in the first major dispute submitted to the new security organization. It concerned Åland, an archipelago of thousands of small islands situated in the Baltic Sea at the entrance to the Gulf of Bothnia, just outside Stockholm. Supported by the principle of national self-determination, the islanders, who are of Swedish origin and Swedish-speaking, declared their wish to be reunited with Sweden. The League of Nations, however, ruled in 1921 that both historically and geographically the islands formed a part of Finland and should remain under that country's sovereignty, with express guarantees for their local autonomy and military neutralization. The decision caused profound disappointment in Sweden but was loyally accepted. Hjalmar Branting, who at this time was Sweden's foremost spokesman at international conferences and consistently pleaded the cause of reconciliation and pacification, shared in the fall of 1921 the Nobel peace prize with a Norwegian historian and pacifist. He had then just formed his second government, based on the Social Democratic party. During the First World War his sympathies had been with the Allies.

In 1924 Sweden recognized the Soviet Union officially. In 1925 the high hopes attached to the League of Nations by the Swedish people were reflected in a Riksdag decision providing for a drastic reduction of the national defense. At that time the Social Democrats were in charge of the government with the support of the Liberals, and the three cabinets which followed, two Liberal and one Conservative, were also based on a minority in the Riksdag, thus needing the votes of some other faction than their own. In 1928 collective labor agreements were, in accordance with established practice, officially recognized as legally binding, and a special Labor Court was set up for the adjudication of disputes concerning contracts already in force.

In Sweden as in many other countries a period of rising prosperity ended in 1929–30, when a financial crash in the United States again was the principal harbinger of an international depression. Swedish emigration had already reached its final act, but the economic crisis in America brought it to a sudden halt. In 1931 the number of emigrants was less than 1,000, and it then declined to even lower levels. The reimmigration to Sweden, on the other hand, showed a sharp increase in the early 1930s, and for the decade as a whole it was almost three times as large as the emigration. Other countries in Europe had the same experience.

At the height of the economic crisis, in the spring of 1932, the death of the Swedish "Match King," Ivar Kreuger (1880–1932), by apparent suicide caused consternation on both sides of the Atlantic, as well as heavy losses to stockholders. The effects of the collapse of Kreuger's financial empire on the Swedish economy, on the other hand, were not at all as serious as many had feared. After general elections in the fall of the same year, a Liberal cabinet was succeeded by a Social Democratic ministry with a much broader base in the parliament, and an ambitious program to combat unemployment, assist the distressed farmers, and stimulate industrial production was launched with the support of the Agrarian party. Greatly helped by a growing demand for its leading export products, Sweden by the middle of the 1930s entered a period of rapidly declining unemployment, accelerating industrial expansion, and improving social-security benefits.

When emigration came to an end, Sweden had seen nearly 1,300,000 men and women leave for America since the trek started by the middle of the 19th century. More than 200,000 had, however, returned to their native country, their reasons ranging from failure or disillusionment to financial success combined with homesickness. Many of those who came back had decided to retire, while others were in their active years and brought both capital and ideas by which the Swedish economy benefited. In numerous cases they contributed to a broadening of relations between the two countries. Thousands of repatriates, however, met with unexpected difficulties, which sometimes led to a new decision to emigrate. There is, on the other hand, no doubt that among the Swedes in America the desire to return to Sweden was greater than the actual reimmigration figures indicate. Many of them lacked the funds for a trip back and a new start, or were too proud or stubborn to admit what they regarded as defeat.

30

Swedish-American Zenith, and World War I

665,000 Swedish-born in America in 1910, 300 periodicals, 2,000 churches

THE Swedish immigrant community in the United States reached its zenith in 1905–15, although in some respects it continued to grow until about 1930. Its strength led some enthusiasts to believe that the Swedish language would flourish forever in America.

In 1910 there were 665,000 Swedish-born people in the United States, the highest total recorded in an official census. Nearly 550,000 American-born had parents who were natives of Sweden, and in addition there were more than 200,000 with a Swedish-born father or mother. The Swedish element, including the first generation born in the United States, thus numbered over 1,400,000. The total was higher in 1920 and 1930, but the number of Swedish-born had then begun to decline.

Most of the immigrants from Sweden and many members of the first American-born generation participated in Swedish-language activities of some sort. During the period 1905–15 there were about 60 weekly newspapers and 230 biweekly or monthly publications, 130 of them denominational. The news weeklies had about 250,000 subscribers, and in 1915 the total circulation of the 72 more significant newspapers and other periodicals seems to have reached 650,000. Hundreds of books in the Swedish language were produced by publishing houses owned by Swedish immigrants. During the years

1906–10, for instance, Augustana Book Concern at Rock Island, Illinois, which had been founded in 1884, published 151 Swedish titles, while those in the English language numbered 31. In Chicago, books in Swedish were printed by more than a dozen establishments. Many volumes contained poetry. Both Swedish immigrant song and the Swedish theater prospered.

Service in the Swedish language was conducted in about 2,000 churches and chapels, and on the great religious holidays the total attendance is said to have reached 700,000. The Lutheran Augustana Synod had nearly 200,000 active adult members, and then there were the Swedish Mission Friends, Baptists, Methodists, Episcopalians, Adventists, and Salvation Army units. Most of these denominations continued, in fact, to grow until about 1930. At that time the Augustana Synod had more than 1,000 churches, about 1,200 congregations, and nearly 250,000 adult members.

In all cities and towns where Swedes lived in larger numbers, the immigrants had formed societies and clubs of various kinds. Both Chicago and Minneapolis–St. Paul had several hundred. The largest Swedish organizations in the country were the still existing Vasa Order of America, the Independent Order of Vikings, and the Independent Order of Svithiod, which offer sick benefits and similar assistance, and at the same time take an active interest in recreational and cultural activities, including exchanges with Sweden. The Vasa Order, which in 1929 attained a membership of 72,000 and also has branches in Canada and Sweden, was founded in 1896 in Connecticut. Its central archives are at Bishop Hill, Illinois, in a building dedicated in 1974. The Order of Svithiod, in ancient times the name for Sweden, was organized in Chicago in 1880, and the Order of Vikings was founded there ten years later. Unsuccessful attempts to bring about a central "umbrella" organization for all the Swedish societies in the United States were made in New York in the early 1900s.

In 1915 most of Sweden's provinces had supplied America with contingents of immigrants which, in relation to their populations, were quite impressive. About 210,000 had come from Småland, which in 1900 had a population of 560,000; almost 160,000 from Västergötland, including the city of Gothenburg (600,000 inhabitants in 1900); approximately 130,000 from Skåne, Sweden's breadbasket in the south (630,000 in 1900); some 100,000 from Värmland (270,000); about 75,000 from Östergötland (280,000); and 60,000 from Halland (140,000). From west-central Dalsland, a sparsely populated province which in 1900 had a population of about 70,000, the flow had reached nearly half that figure. The Baltic island of Öland, with about 30,000 inhabitants at the turn of the century, had lost some 18,000 by emigration to America, although several thousand finally returned. The emigrants from Stockholm, which from 1870 to 1900 increased its population from 135,000 to 300,000, numbered about 60,000.

The Swedish immigrants in the United States were often more conscious of their old provincial home than of their national origin, and those hailing from the same province had warm feelings of kinship. Especially in the 1920s, Swedish-American societies in which membership was based on provincial origin sprang up like mushrooms. Chicago and Minneapolis finally had such associations representing all the Swedish provinces, except perhaps Uppland, north of Stockholm and Lake Mälaren, which like Södermanland to the south always had a low rate of emigration.

Most of the immigrants knew little about Sweden's past, and few of them had taken an active part in the celebration of great national events. In the United States, however, they encountered many manifestations of a strong national spirit of various types, and gradually they developed an immigrant nationalism of their own, which mixed a romantic pride in Sweden's and all of Scandinavia's history and culture, a hearty appreciation of Swedish achievements in the United States, and a deepening love of their adopted country. One of the first great champions of this special Swedish-American nationalism was the previously mentioned Johan A. Enander of Chicago, who wanted to mold the Swedish heritage "into a harmonious whole with all the beautiful, the noble, the true, which the new fatherland has so freely offered the immigrant. Our nationality should be not only at the receiving end, but also able to give." Like leaders of other ethnic groups, Enander maintained that to make a good American, an immigrant must be surely rooted in his own culture. For the Swedes, love for America as the chosen bride, and for Sweden as the dear old mother, was the only natural solution.

Enander died in 1910 at the age of 68, after having been editor of the oldest Swedish-language weekly, *Hemlandet* of Chicago, for 35 years, but others carried on in the same spirit, although as a rule in a lower key. Among the leading newspapermen were Alexander J. Johnson (1850–1930) from Stockholm, who in 1888 had begun to turn one of Chicago's comic Swedish-language papers into a successful news weekly, *Svenska Kuriren*, and published it until 1929; Jakob Bonggren (1854–1940) from Bergane in the province of Dalsland, who served the still existing *Svenska Amerikanaren* from 1883 to 1936 and also became known as a poet; and Oliver A. Linder (1862–1939) from Gylle in Skåne, who in 1880 had begun in America as a farmhand and in 1908 succeeded Bonggren as editor of *Svenska Amerikanaren*. In the heyday of the Swedish-language press, two of the weeklies reached a circulation of 70,000–80,000.

Swedish-American nationalism was a somewhat paradoxical phenomenon, and it did not by any means save the country of Sweden and its leaders from castigation or maltreatment in the columns of the Swedish-language press. After the 50th-anniversary celebration of the Augustana Synod in 1910, a Swedish clergyman and Riksdag member wrote in a travel report that Swedish-American papers had given him the impression that Sweden was "the most miserable country on earth." Sensationalism, he thought, had misled them. Among the visitors from Sweden who attended the Augustana jubilee were also a bishop of the state church and the president of the University of Uppsala, Henrik Schück (1855–1947), who won fame in Scandinavia as a literary historian.

Like the Norwegians and the Danes, the Swedish immigrants adjusted themselves on the whole with relative ease to their adopted country and became in a remarkably short time Americanized. That, at least, is the conclusion of numerous observers and scholars, including many without any Scandinavian background. In the 1800s most Scandinavians moved to the Middle West, where they often became farmers and landowners, but large numbers of other immigrants also took natural and sturdy root, whether they lived in farm districts or finally settled in cities, which 60 percent of the Swedes had done as early as 1910.

"The Swedish-American has a certain sense of ownership in the glorious heritage of American soil," Colonel Hans Mattson of Minnesota wrote in his memoirs, "and he feels that the blessings which he enjoys are not his by sufferance, but by right." He believed in the virtues of hard work, self-improvement, and self-reliance, and at the same time he had a strong sense of community and cooperation. With many exceptions the immigrants from Sweden were not well educated, but there was little illiteracy, and the bumpy road toward a good command of English proved relatively short. The great majority of the Swedes and other Scandinavians were also eager to obtain American citizenship. As a rule, however, the process of assimilation involved both birth pangs and growing pains. The Swedish immigrant literature is full of them.

The belief in a relatively quick Americanization of the Swedish immigrants has been questioned by modern scholars in Sweden, who pay special attention to their manifold secular and religious activities in the Swedish language, the relative longevity of this language wherever Swedes settled in greater numbers, and the low rate of intermarriage among the Swedish settlers. The same authorities realize, on the other hand, that the societies, churches, and publications of the Swedish immigrants have not only helped to preserve or underline their national identity, but also facilitated their adjustment to conditions in the new country. Many of the associations have schooled their members in the technique of meetings and conferences, and several have offered instruction in English.

It is true that many Swedish immigrants never became adjusted, but such exceptions were inevitable. As for the rate of intermarriage among the Swedes in America, it did remain low as long as the immigration continued. Those who married outside their own nationality preferred Norwegians, followed by Danes and Germans. Swedish-Irish marriages, however, were also relatively common, one reason being that many members of the two groups settled in the same areas. The local supply of eligible partners was, of course, always an important factor.

Some Swedish-American writers who have been quite proud of the comparatively quick Americanization of their fellow countrymen have actually been inclined to think that the adjustment to some extent, and perhaps even from an American viewpoint, was too rapid and comprehensive. In the early 1900s one such critic observed, for instance, that there were few if any traces of Swedish individualism or traditions in the homes of immigrants from Sweden: "All are furnished in American style and bear the same hopeless uniformity." And when in the 1920s and 1930s Sweden's progress in the field of industrial art and design attracted a rapidly growing interest in the United States, people of Swedish birth did not, on the whole, take an active part. American-born people of Swedish descent often seemed more engaged.

The comment about the monotony of Swedish homes in America may have hit the mark in many cases, but it was actually too sharp and sweeping. The great majority of the immigrants could not afford fashionable furnishings, but all over the country, and particularly in the rural districts and smaller towns, Swedish homes were known not only for their cleanliness and good husbandry but also for their warm and hospitable atmosphere. The ceilings may have been low and the furniture simple and timeworn, but there were cheerful curtains and brightly wrapped pots of flowers in the windows, and colorful rag carpets on the newly washed floors. Numerous Americans of Swedish parentage have described their old homes in terms reflecting both gratitude and nostalgia.

The attitudes that Swedish immigrants and their descendants in America took or still take to Sweden and things Swedish have on some occasions been analyzed and explained along the following lines. The immigrants themselves were too busy getting established to have time for great concern with their native country, in particular its continued transformation and modern aspects. When they thought of Sweden, they thought mostly of their parental home, their old relatives and neighbors, and the scenery of their native region. And they did cherish Swedish food specialties and the old holiday traditions, above all the Midsummer celebration and the Christmas festivities. The first American-born generation, on the other hand, was anxious to be universally accepted as 100 percent American, and therefore tended to ignore or perhaps even look down upon the Swedish immigrant heritage, including the language. It is not until the second American-born generation that a more active and thoughtful interest appears, and it is often directed both toward the Swedish family origin and toward Sweden's modern progress, sometimes even toward the Swedish language.

To all such generalizations there are, of course, numerous exceptions. Today it may, in particular, be almost impossible to draw a clear line between the attitudes of the first and second American-born generations.

The trials of "Swedish America" during the First World War, and the Great Depression

FOR the Swedish immigrants as for the other ethnic groups in the United States, the First World War was a period of bitter trials. In the beginning they were widely regarded as pro-German, which, in so far as this impression was justified, undoubtedly had something to do with the old Swedish attitude toward Russia. Finland was still part of the Russian empire, its constitutional rights had been restricted, and attempts were being made to convert the people to Russian ideals and practices.

As long as possible the Swedish-language newspapers stressed the importance of the neutrality of the United States. After the American declaration of war on April 6, 1917, on the other hand, they rallied to the support of their government. Among political leaders of Swedish extraction who always wholeheartedly backed President Wilson were Governor J. A. A. Burnquist of Minnesota and former Governor John Lind, who was born in Sweden. Charles A. Lindbergh, Sr., who left the House of Representatives in early March, 1917, had worked hard against intervention but after the declaration of war he wrote to his daughter that "we must all be foolish and unwise together, and fight for our country."

After the outbreak of war in Europe in 1914, Sweden, Norway, and Denmark proclaimed their strict neutrality, and public opinion in Sweden overwhelmingly supported this policy, which also was anchored in a determined rearmament. The period of military training was extended to 340–365 days for ordinary conscripts, and to 485 days for junior-college graduates. Germany tried to induce Sweden to enter into an alliance against Russia, but the Swedish government firmly refused. Some incidents, however, made its policy of neutrality appear as less strict or more pro-German than it actually was.

One of the episodes, the so-called Luxburg affair which involved German abuse of Swedish diplomatic cable channels from Argentina to Europe, caused a sharp reaction even among the Swedes in America, in particular New York. This happened in September, 1917. The official organ of the Lutheran Augustana Synod, published at Rock Island, Illinois, claimed that Sweden had, after all, honorably maintained its neutrality, but it also wrote that "America is our country, for which we would not hesitate to offer our lives even if it came to a battle against our old fatherland." Such a turn of events was, however, hardly even a remote possibility.

Sweden's deviations from neutrality during the war included important concessions to the Allies, and these were induced by an extreme shortage of vital supplies toward the end of the conflict, a shortage that was aggravated by an exceptionally poor harvest in 1917. Already in the spring of the same year food riots occurred in many Swedish cities and towns, and the winter of 1917–18 became as difficult as those in the late 1860s, when mass emigration to America began. In the spring of 1918, however, a newly established and less formalistic Swedish government reached an agreement with the Allies providing for permits to import considerable quantities of foods and other supplies. In return, Sweden leased out half of its remaining merchant tonnage to the Allied powers, promised to curtail drastically its exports to Germany, and extended considerable credits to the Allies. The year before, shortly after the United States had entered the war, a Swedish delegation had been sent to Washington to try to bring about import facilities, but these negotiations proved fruitless.

The ultranationalism that was whipped up in the United States during the First World War, and which numerous leaders and historians later deplored, led to restrictions on all kinds of foreign-language activities. In a score of states, for instance, English was finally the only language permitted in public and private school instruction, and many "hyphenated Americans," as they had been called, did not dare show that they subscribed to a foreign-language paper. During the Second World War the attitude toward the immigrant press in the United States was entirely different.

In the late 1910s the use of Swedish by the immigrants and their descendants was about to taper off anyway, and the long-range effects of the wartime pressure were limited. After the war the decline of the Swedish-American press continued at a quicker pace, and in the early 1930s the Great Depression brought a new direct setback. In 1932 its total circulation had fallen to less than half the figure in 1910–15. Numerous congregations and societies had then begun to give up the Swedish language, in many cases after emotion-filled debates. In an-

swer to those who opposed the switch to English, pastors of the immigrant churches sometimes answered that their function was to save
souls rather than to preserve the Swedish language. To begin with,
most churches became bilingual, but after that they offered Swedish
services only on special occasions. Hundreds of clubs and lodges,
however, upheld the Swedish language almost until the middle of the
century.

The Swedish immigrants may have been in a better position to
weather the economic storm of the early 1930s than many other national groups, but the crisis was nevertheless a bitter and disillusion-
ing experience. Great numbers of skilled building, machine, and tool
workers were among those particularly hard hit. All over the country,
numerous immigrants lost at least part of their savings. In Chicago,
for instance, a dozen banks closed on the same day in 1931. In
Rockford, Illinois, only two of eight banks and in Lindsborg, Kansas,
only two out of three remained open for business. In the elections of
1932, a substantial part of the immigrants from Sweden voted Democratic for the first time. Their old party allegiance had, however, been
tested both in the political storms of the 1890s and in the Bull Moose
election of 1912, when Theodore Roosevelt was favored by many
voters of Swedish origin.

Primarily for the sake of brevity and convenience, the Swedish
immigrant community in the United States, with its churches,
societies, and newspapers, has in Sweden often been called "Swedish
America." As a rule the term does not include those who remained
outside practically all activities organized by and for Swedish immigrants in America. How large a proportion they represented is difficult
to tell. The Swedish-born settlers and their children who belonged to
the immigrant churches never made up more than about one-fourth
of the total, at least not after the beginning of the mass migration.
The others either did not become church members or enrolled in
religious organizations of non-Swedish origin. In 1962 the Augustana
Synod itself ceased to exist as a separate organization: it joined the
Lutheran Church in America, which also included German, Finnish,
and Danish Lutherans. A Lutheran consolidation had, in fact, for
many years been Augustana's goal.

31

Swedes in American Arts

*Sandburg and Hanson, midwesterners of Swedish parentage,
excel in letters and music*

MANY Americans of Swedish parentage have contributed to American letters, and the most eminent one is, of course, Carl Sandburg. His father, August Danielsson, had come to America in 1856 at the age of ten, and his mother, Clara Andersdotter or Andersson, had arrived in 1873 when she was 23 years old. Both were from southwestern Östergötland, one of Sweden's first emigration centers, and they lived at Galesburg, Illinois, where one of the first 19th-century Swedish Lutheran churches in America had been founded in 1851 and the first Swedish-language newspaper of any importance had appeared four years later. August Danielsson, a poor, hard-working blacksmith, could hardly sign his own name but was able to "read his Bible after a fashion."

Carl Sandburg always felt close to the working-class people from whom he had come. As a young man he became, in turn, a milk driver, a bootblack, a soldier in the Spanish-American War, a hobo, a farmer, a door-to-door salesman, a journalist, and several other things. There were times when he did not want to admit being of Swedish parentage, but fundamentally, and particularly in his mature years, he was proud of his origin. A great storyteller, he loved racy anecdotes about his immigrant kinsmen.

While not particularly familiar with Swedish art and literature,

Sandburg developed, for instance, an affectionate admiration for Albert Engström (1869–1940), whose production, ranging from short stories and travel books to caricatures and etchings, has often been described as too Swedish to be understood by anyone but a Swede. In Sweden he has become a legend like no other literary figure except Carl Michael Bellman of the 18th century.

For many years Sandburg collected material for a book about Engström who, it has been said, "learned the Swedish people to laugh in Swedish." As a caricaturist and storyteller he specialized, to begin with, in his native, poverty-striken northern Småland with its hardy breed of small farmers, crofters, railroad workers, and revivalist preachers. Later he also became fascinated by the picturesque peasant-fisherfolk of the island-studded Roslagen district northeast of Stockholm, and at the same time he created his most popular cartoon character, a bizarre but genial bum from the Stockholm waterfront, the incarnation of freedom from more or less stupid conventions. Modern literary research has shown that Engström not only was influenced by Mark Twain and other American writers but also drew inspiration from American cartoonists, which came as a surprise to the Swedish people.

At one time Sandburg also seems to have played with the idea of writing a biography of Charles XII, Sweden's warrior king of the early 1700s. Instead, he started working on his monumental biography of Abraham Lincoln, according to one authority "the greatest study of an American ever written by another American." Lincoln's family background was in some ways similar to Sandburg's and in the latter's home town, Galesburg, he had had one of his historic debates with Stephen A. Douglas. On February 12, 1959, the 150th anniversary of Lincoln's birth, Sandburg addressed a joint session of the U.S. Congress in Washington. His last book of poetry, entitled *The People, Yes*, which was published in 1936, has often been called his greatest poetic work. An American literary historian has observed that "a foreigner will find more of America in *The People, Yes*, than in any other book we can give him."

Perhaps no single event brought out the Swede in Carl Sandburg to a higher degree than the Swedish Pioneer Centennial of 1948. At the largest celebration, on June 4 in Chicago Stadium where some

18,000 people were assembled, President Harry S. Truman, Prince Bertil of Sweden, and Carl Sandburg were the main speakers.

Carl Sandburg visited Sweden twice, first as a newspaper reporter in 1918–19 and the second time in 1959. During his second visit, when he was in his 82nd year, he looked up the places in Östergötland where his parents were born and discovered nine cousins. Until then he had been in doubt about the part of Sweden his father had come from. In Stockholm he was received in audience by King Gustav VI Adolf. His public appearances, especially on television and as the main speaker at the Sweden-America Day celebration in the Skansen folk park and open-air museum, were highly successful. He also called on the University of Uppsala, which in 1950 had awarded him an honorary doctor's degree. Many Swedish poets and novelists have been influenced by Carl Sandburg.

The great majority of the Swedish immigrants with literary talents or ambitions wrote, naturally, in their mother tongue. Among the notable exceptions was Gösta Larsson (1898–1955), born in a workingman's home in Malmö in southern Sweden and finally trained as an engineer, who came to America in 1922. In New York, where he lived for many years, he worked as a stevedore, snow shoveler, movie extra, etc., and also attended courses at Columbia University, before devoting himself to writing. His first novel was rejected by a Swedish publisher, and he then decided to try to master the English language instead. In 1934 he made his debut with *Our Daily Bread*, a novel about the life of a workman's family during the general strike in Sweden in 1909, which was well received by the reading public both in the United States and in Sweden, where a Swedish translation was published. It was followed by *Fatherland, Farewell!*, *The Ordeal of the Falcon*, and *Ships in the River*, which was sold to be filmed.

The foremost American composer of Swedish parentage, Howard Hanson, was born in 1896 at Wahoo, Nebraska, where he studied at Luther College. His parents and grandparents came from Lund in southernmost Sweden. He has been called a modern romanticist and the "American Sibelius."

In the early 1920s, when Hanson lived in Rome, he wrote his first, or Nordic, symphony, which has been played all over the United States as well as in Rome, Paris, London, and Berlin. The last movement includes a Swedish folk song from the 12th century. For the tercentenary of the first Swedish settlement in America, celebrated in 1938, he composed his third symphony, to express his reverence "for the spiritual contribution that has been made to America by that sturdy race of northern pioneers who were in later centuries also to constitute such a mighty force in the conquering of the West." A symphonic poem, *North and West*, into which the composer also poured his love for his ancestral and native countries, was conceived when he was traveling in Sweden as a tourist in 1922.

A unique achievement in Hanson's career was *Merry Mount*, an opera depicting Puritan Massachusetts of 1625, based on a tale by Hawthorne, and written on request for the Metropolitan Opera Company in New York. It had a brilliant premiere in 1934, requiring some 50 curtain calls, and was also carried over the NBC broadcasting system. All the reviewers stressed the often recurring massive choral writing, which according to the composer was a direct echo of the Swedish hymns he had heard as a boy in Luther College, and of "All Hail to Thee, O Blessed Morn" sung in Swedish prairie churches on Christmas morning.

Howard Hanson, however, was much more active as an educator than as a composer. From 1924 to 1964 he served as director of the Eastman School of Music at the University of Rochester in Rochester, New York, which became a leader in musical education in the United States. In 1925 he inaugurated a series called the American Composers Concerts, and in two decades he presented approximately 900 works by some 400 American composers, nearly half of whom had been students of the Eastman School of Music. Hanson has often been guest conductor of orchestras both in Europe and the United States. He became a fellow of the Academy of Music in Stockholm.

Another composer of Swedish descent, Arne Oldberg (1874–1962), was born at Youngstown, Ohio, where hundreds of Swedes settled. After studies in Vienna and Munich he served from 1897 to 1941 as professor in the School of Music at Northwestern University in Evanston, Illinois. His compositions, wrote one music critic, "show sincerity, warmth, and excellent technical workmanship." Two symphonies won national prizes. His son Eric Oldberg (b. 1901) served from 1936 to 1971 as professor and head of the department of neurology and neurological surgery at the University of Illinois College of Medicine. He also became president of the Chicago Board of Health. His great-grandfather, Anders Oldberg, was the Lutheran pastor at Alfta in the province of Hälsingland, in the 1840s one of the leading centers of the Erik Jansson sect which was responsible for the first large group migration from Sweden to America and the founding of Bishop Hill in western Illinois. The Reverend Anders Oldberg fought against the "Erik Jansson heresies" and tried to avert threatening family tragedies, often without success. His emigrating son, who became the composer's father, belonged to the Swedenborg church.

Leroy Anderson, who was born in 1908 at Cambridge, Massachusetts, of Swedish parents, became a successful composer of popular music. At Harvard he studied Swedish, Norwegian, Danish, Icelandic, and German with the intention of becoming a teacher, but he was also director of the Harvard University Band. In 1936 he began making orchestral arrangements for the Boston Pops Orchestra, and in 1950 he started conducting his own recording orchestra. His *Blue Tango* was the first purely instrumental composition to reach the No. 1 position on America's Hit Parade. *Irish Suite* and three suites of carols are among his numerous other works. His father was born at Övarp in Skåne. His mother, who came from Stockholm, became the first organist of the Swedish Covenant Church in Cambridge.

Many immigrant careers in American painting, mostly from humble beginnings

WHILE few Swedish immigrants were able to contribute to American letters in the English language, quite a remarkable number sought and found artistic outlet in the pictorial art form. Their more or less successful careers were often marked by hardship, adventure, self-study, and growing opportunities, but there was always a great variation. Newcomers with schooling in the arts were far from rare. Most of the immigrants with artistic talents brought from their native country a deep love of nature, and many of them became devoted interpreters of the beauty of America.

One of America's first Swedish-born artists in the 19th century was Lars Gustaf Sellstedt (1819–1911), who in 1831 at the age of 12, in a revolt against his stepfather, left his home at Sundsvall in northern Sweden and went to sea as a cabin boy. In 1834 he came to America but continued as a seaman, in 1837–40 in the U. S. Navy and later on the Great Lakes. There he met a naval trainee from Sweden, Lieutenant Axel Adlersparre, who told him to concentrate on his favorite pursuit, portrait painting. In 1846 he settled in Buffalo, and though largely self-taught he gradually became a highly regarded portraitist. His wife, born Caroline Scott, helped him into the leading circles in the culturally active city, and among his friends were President Millard Fillmore, whose portrait he painted three times, and President Grover Cleveland, who also sat for him. In 1862 he was the principal founder of the Buffalo Fine Arts Academy, which in 1905 opened the Albright Art Gallery, now the famous Albright-Knox Gallery. In 1875 he was the first Swedish-born artist to be elected to full membership in the National Academy of Design. In 1904 he published a remarkable autobiography, *From Forecastle to Academy*, and in 1910, when he was 91, *Art in Buffalo*. Sellstedt visited Sweden three times, and in 1853–54 he painted his mother's portrait. In 1962 a memorial exhibition was held in Buffalo.

Art studies in Buffalo also helped launch John F. Carlson (1874–1945) from Ukna in Småland, who came with his parents in 1880 and as an artist won warm recognition for his woodland scenes and other landscapes. After a tour of England, France, and Holland he joined the artist colony in Woodstock, New York, where for many years he led his own school for landscape artists. Samples of his art are found in the Corcoran Gallery in Washington, D.C., and many other museums in the United States. Carl O. Lindin (1869–1942), from Fellingsbro in the province of Närke, was also for decades a member of the Woodstock colony. Before leaving Sweden at the age of 18 he had been a farm and railroad laborer, but in Chicago, where he first settled as an immigrant, generous supporters enabled him to study at a local art school and later for four years in Paris. During this period, 1893–97, he spent the summers painting in Sweden. Lindin took part in many exhibitions in America and Europe, including Paris and London. He became known especially for his interpretations of the prairie landscape in the haze of summer.

Another Woodstock artist, Henry Mattson (1887–1971) from Gothenburg who came to America in 1906, started as a factory worker at Worcester, Massachusetts, where he studied briefly at the school of the Art Museum. By hard self-study and bold experimenting he finally reached a prominent position in American painting. A noted critic called him "a giant figure." His dramatic marines and landscapes are represented in many of the country's finest collections, including the Metropolitan Museum of Art and the Whitney Museum of American Art in New York, the Carnegie Institute in Pittsburgh, and the White House. The Pennsylvania Academy of Fine Arts in Philadelphia awarded him two gold medals, and in 1952 he received full membership in the National Academy of Design.

After having sailed the seven seas and the Great Lakes for 17 years, Carl or Charles E. Hallberg (1855–1940) from Gothenburg settled down in Chicago as a janitor in 1890 and gradually became a successful marine painter. In 1900 he was encouraged by the famous Anders Zorn, who then made one of his many visits to Chicago, and in 1904 he was represented in the American art collection at the Louisiana Purchase Exposition in St. Louis, Missouri. Works by him are found in several American museums as well as in the National Gallery of Art in Stockholm and the Gothenburg Art Museum. Alfred Jansson (1863–1931), a farmer's son from Kil in Värmland, studied art in Stockholm and Paris, came to America in 1889 and settled in Chicago, where he painted a number of frescoes in the Swedish pavilion at the Columbian Exposition in 1893. His realistic landscapes, many with motifs from the Chicago area, won critical acclaim and were shown at exhibits from New York and Philadelphia to San Francisco. In Sweden he is represented in the National Gallery of Art.

Bror Nordfeldt (1878–1955), a farmer's son from southernmost Sweden, emigrated with his parents in 1891, studied painting at the Art Institute of Chicago, and won his spurs at exhibitions in Paris and London in 1901. As an etcher he was represented in displays of American graphic art both in the United States and abroad. He gave art courses or lectures at the Minneapolis School of Art, the University of Texas in Austin, and other institutions. Marines or other works by him are in the Metropolitan Museum in New York, the Corcoran Gallery in Washington, and the Toledo Museum of Art at Toledo, Ohio. J. Lars Hoftrup (1874–1954), who was born on a farm at Hofterup in the Swedish South and emigrated with his parents in 1881, became a self-taught artist. He lived near Elmira, New York, in the valley of Chemung River, whose tranquil mood inspired many of his canvases. His home and studio, which he called Arts Torp (meaning a cottage or small farmhouse), became a mecca for water-color enthusiasts, and for several years he also taught painting at Elmira College. He is represented in the Cleveland Museum of Art, Phillips Memorial Gallery in Washington, D.C., and the Brooklyn Museum. A third native of Skåne, Carl Ringius (1879–1950), specialized in paintings of the New England coast. In 1910 he helped found the Connecticut Academy of Fine Arts at Hartford.

August R. Franzen (1863–1930), born on a farm at Drothem in Östergötland, came twice to America as an immigrant, the second time in 1891 when he had studied art in Gothenburg and Paris. Settling in New York as a professional painter, he drew his motifs mostly from common people and everyday life, but after another round of studies in Europe he became one of America's most fashionable portraitists, with many celebrities as his customers. Among his best-known works is one of President William H. Taft, since 1913 owned by Yale University. In 1906 he helped establish an art center in New York, the Gainsborough Studio, which became a model for other cities. Franzen was the second Swedish-born artist to enter the National Academy of Design as a full member, being elected in 1920.

Carl Fredrik von Saltza (1858–1905) and Arvid F. Nyholm (1866–1927) had much in common: both studied at the Academy of Art in Stockholm as well as in Paris, both were friends and disciples of Anders Zorn, and both came to America in 1891 and specialized in portrait painting. Saltza, who was born at the Sörby chateau in Östergötland and whose father was chief of protocol at the Swedish court, taught for several years at the Museum of Fine Arts in St. Louis and then at the Art Institute of Chicago. The last six years of his life he led the schools of painting at Columbia University and Teachers College in New York. Nyholm, a Stockholmer by birth, lived first in New York and later in Chicago. In the National Gallery in Washington he is represented by a portrait of Captain John Ericsson, while one of Governor A. O. Eberhart of Minnesota, done in 1914, hangs in the State Capitol in St. Paul. He became a member of the National Academy of Design.

Knut or Knute Heldner (1877–1952) was raised in poverty at Vederslöv in Småland, from 1906 fought his way in the American Midwest as a lumberjack, mineworker, paver, and cobbler, and won in 1914 his first gold medal for painting at the Minnesota State Exposition. As an artist he was particularly successful in depicting hard-working or toilworn people and domestic animals. One of his creations was purchased for President Warren G. Harding by the Republicans of Minnesota. He spent his last years in New Orleans.

Carl Sprinchorn (1887–1971) from Östra Broby in Skåne came to America in 1903 and studied art in New York and Los Angeles. In numerous oils, water colors, and drawings he depicted both the hectic or sophisticated life in the big cities, in America as well as in Europe, and the peaceful or rugged landscape in Maine, which for half a century he regarded as his real homeland. Works by him were acquired by a score of American museums, including the Metropolitan Museum, Whitney Museum and Brooklyn Museum in New York, Philadelphia Art Museum, and the Phillips Memorial Gallery in Washington. In 1972 the University of Maine presented a memorial exhibition.

Leading Western artists often taught or studied at Lindsborg in Kansas

MANY Western artists of Swedish birth or parentage taught or studied at Bethany College in Lindsborg, Kansas, the settlement founded in the late 1860s by immigrants from Sweden. A school of art was organized there in 1890, and one of its first directors was Olof Grafström (1855–1933), the son of a farmer at Attmar in Medelpad, the "Middle Path" province of northern Sweden. Before leaving his native country in 1886, he had studied successfully at the Academy of Art in Stockholm and had become one of the artistic discoverers of the mountains of Jämtland and Lapland. In America, he first lived in Portland, Oregon, and Spokane, Washington, winning recognition as a painter of landscapes. In 1897 he moved from Lindsborg to Rock Island, Illinois, as head of the art department of Augustana College. For Swedish immigrant churches in America he painted nearly 200 altarpieces. A few years before his death he returned to his native parish in Sweden. A daughter became a successful fashion illustrator in New York.

As an art center of significance far beyond the borders of Kansas, Lindsborg owes more to Birger Sandzén (1871–1954) than to any other artist. In 1894, after having studied art in Stockholm and Paris, he happened to read about Bethany College in his parental home, a parsonage at Blidsberg in Västergötland, and to Carl A. Swensson, founder and president of the college, he sent the following inquiry: "Can you use a young Swede who can paint, sing tenor, and teach French?" Swensson replied, "Come immediately," and for Sandzén this was the beginning of a lifelong and fruitful association with Lindsborg and its cultural activities. An active leader of the art school and often teaching other subjects as well, Sandzén at the same time developed an independent and powerful artistic production, including paintings, woodcuts and dry-points, inspired by the grandeur of the prairie landscape and, above all, the colorful mountains of the West. By lecturing in universities and other institutions, he also did much to make the Midwest and the Southwest more art conscious. He had or took part in many exhibitions in America and Europe. Canvases or prints by him are found in, for instance, the Metropolitan Museum in New York, the Library of Congress in Washington, the British Museum in London, and the National Gallery of Art in Stockholm. Carl Milles, the sculptor, was an admirer of Sandzén's art and is represented in the Birger Sandzén Memorial Gallery at Lindsborg, dedicated in 1957.

An artist named Carl Gustafson Lotave (1872–1924), born at Jönköping in Småland and educated in Stockholm and Paris, was for two years in the late 1890s an associate of Sandzén at Lindsborg. He then moved to Colorado Springs, where he produced notable landscapes, portraits and frescoes. Toward the end of his life he painted in New York the portraits of King Albert of Belgium, General John J. Pershing, and Marshal Foch and Marshal Joffre of France. In 1925 his remains were entombed in Colorado's Hall of Fame on the top of Pikes Peak near Colorado Springs. Gustav Natanael Malm (1869–1928), who had come to Lindsborg in 1894 and studied with Sandzén, painted 37 altarpieces and frescoes for churches in Kansas. In 1909 he published a book entitled *Charlie Johnson, Svensk-Amerikan*, about a character who moves among the Swedish immigrants of Kansas and Nebraska and speaks their hybrid dialect. Later he started collecting wood carvings by a famous Swedish artist, Axel Petersson of Döderhult in Småland.

Among Birger Sandzén's first disciples at Bethany College was also Oscar Brousse Jacobson (1882–1967), a farmer's son from Västrum on Småland's Baltic coast, who came to America in 1890 and after

Lindsborg studied art in Paris and at Yale University. After some years as an art teacher in Minneapolis and at Pullman, Washington, he was in 1915 engaged by the University of Oklahoma at Norman and served as professor there until 1945. Under his leadership the school of art became an important institution, and the art museum, which in 1953 was named Jacobson Hall, received valuable European, Oriental, and American Indian collections. Jacobson also lectured at numerous other universities and museums. As a practicing artist he painted primarily landscapes, and his works, including some done in the Sahara desert, were exhibited in many American institutions as well as in Paris and Sweden. Two books about Indian art by him and his wife, born Jeanne d'Ucel, were published in France.

Indian art and folklore also became a source of inspiration for another Swedish immigrant, Carl Oscar Borg (1879–1947). The son of an indigent soldier at Grinstad in the province of Dalsland, he landed in Norfolk, Virginia, in 1901 and came to Los Angeles two years later. In 1910 William Randolph Hearst's mother sent him to Europe, and during the following years he painted in France, Italy, Spain, and Egypt, and had works exhibited in Paris and London. After 1914, when he settled in San Francisco, he spent much of his time with the Indians of the Southwest, and his vividly colored depictions of Pueblo Indian and Arizonan cowboy life became known and admired in art circles throughout the United States. The Academy of Sciences in Stockholm awarded him the Linnaeus Medal for his research among the Hopi and Navajo Indians. In 1949 a memorial exhibition was held in the Art Museum in Gothenburg, where Borg lived during the Second World War. His canvases and etchings are widely distributed in Sweden, France, and the United States, especially in California and Arizona.

Gunnar M. Widforss (1879–1934) also had an unusual career. A graduate of a school of design in his native Stockholm, he had already traveled extensively in eastern and southern Europe when he first came to the United States in 1905. He returned disappointed to Sweden, scored his first real success as an artist in Paris in 1912, and continued painting in southern Europe as well as in the archipelagoes of Gothenburg and Stockholm. En route to the Far East in 1921 he was struck by the beauty of California, and in a subsequent rich production of water colors he depicted fondly the magnificent scenery of the West, including the Yosemite National Park and the coast at Monterey, the Mesa Verde National Park in Colorado, Grand Canyon in Arizona, and the Yellowstone National Park in Wyoming, Montana, and Idaho. In 1924 a collection of his works was shown in the National Gallery of Art in Washington. Widforss, who has been called the "Painter of the National Parks," finally settled at Grand Canyon, and died there. In 1938 a mountain top in the Grand Canyon National Park was officially named Widforss Point.

Two painters of American battle scenes, and some
noted sculptors and carvers

TWO Swedes who came to America during the latter part of the 1800s, but were not carried to its shores by the surging migration from Sweden, began as magazine illustrators and had exceptional but remarkably similar careers as painters.

Thure Thulstrup (1848–1930), whose father for many years was a cabinet minister in Stockholm, had served as an officer in the Swedish army, in the Foreign Legion in North Africa, and in the Franco-German war of 1870–71 before he came to Canada in 1872, at the age of 24. Tired of warfare, he worked at first as a topographical engineer, but after having settled in New York in 1874 he became instead one of America's leading magazine and book illustrators. Although wholly self-taught as a painter, Thulstrup made a name for himself in this field too, especially by large, colorful, and detailed battle scenes of the Civil War which were based on visits to the battlefields, interviews with old soldiers, and the artist's own recollections from the war in France. Many of these works are in the State Capitol at Atlanta, Georgia, the Soldiers and Sailors Memorial Hall in Pittsburgh, and the Seventh Regiment Armory in New York. Society life in New York and the American South in peacetime also furnished Thulstrup with many motifs. His best-known monumental painting, often reproduced in history books, is *The Cession of Louisiana*. It hangs in the Cabildo in New Orleans where the Louisiana Purchase was consummated in 1803 and which now is part of the Louisiana State Museum.

Henrik or Henry Reuterdahl (1870–1925), a native of Malmö in southern Sweden who came to Chicago in 1893 as illustrator for a Stockholm magazine and decided to stay in America, became known as a marine artist during the Spanish-American War when he accompanied the U.S. Navy. In 1908 he aroused much greater attention, both in the United States and abroad, by severely criticizing what he regarded as unsatisfactory conditions in the naval service, and it is said that he thereby contributed to its efficiency. In 1913 he was twice invited to join a naval squadron on an international cruise, and in 1917 he again went to war with the U.S. Navy as a marine artist. Reuterdahl also executed wall paintings for several battleships. His large canvas, *The Combat between the Monitor and the Merrimac*, belongs to the National Gallery in Washington, and ten of his marines are in the Naval Academy at Annapolis, where he is known as Lieutenant Commander Henry Reuterdahl. Many paintings and drawings are in Swedish museums.

America has had many other draftsmen of Swedish origin. Gustaf Henning Lindström or Gus Higgins (1863–1909), who after art studies in his native Stockholm emigrated to America in 1879, began a stormy career in Chicago helping the French artist Felix Philippoteaux paint large battle scenes from the Civil War. His rich talent was often mistreated, but as a political cartoonist for *The Chicago Tribune* and other publications he established his reputation of being one of the best in his field. He was also a popular decorator, as well as a poet and musician. Abian Anders Wallgren (1892–1948), who was born in Philadelphia of Swedish immigrants, became famous during the First World War as "Wally" of *The Stars and Stripes*. According to an obituary, he "was credited by General John J. Pershing with keeping up the morale of thousands of doughboys by his travesties of officers and his humorous treatment of the difficulties and problems of the soldiers."

Gustaf Tenggren (1896–1970) from Magra in Västergötland, who was an experienced artist when he arrived in 1920, became one of America's most popular magazine and fairy-tale illustrators, as well as a successful painter in oil and water color. His book *The Tenggren Mother Goose*, published in 1940, was hailed by one critic as "perhaps the loveliest Mother Goose of all time." In 1936–39 he served as art director for the Disney studios in Hollywood, making important contributions to the highly successful films *Snow White and the Seven Dwarfs* and *Pinocchio*. Tenggren made his home first in Cleveland, Ohio, then in New York, and finally in Maine.

The first American immigrant from Sweden to become a widely

known sculptor was David Edström (1873–1938), the son of a tailor and nonconformist preacher at Vetlanda in Småland, who started earning his living as a farmhand and slaughterhouse worker in Iowa where his parents had settled in 1880. After having sailed to Stockholm as a coal stoker in 1894, he almost immediately produced an unusually promising piece of sculpture, and a Swedish banker and art patron, Ernest Thiel (1859–1947), then enabled him to study for four years at the Academy of Art. Among contemporary students of sculpture in Stockholm was Carl Milles. In 1915, when Edström had won recognition also in Paris and London, he returned to America, settling in Los Angeles five years later. His second wife, who was a native American, had already introduced him to Christian Science, and much of his sculpture was allegorical, psychological, and symbolistic.

In 1925 the State University of Iowa at Iowa City built a museum called the Edstrom Building, where some 70 of his creations were assembled. His many busts include one of King Gustav V of Sweden and one of Abraham Lincoln, which is in the State Capitol at Springfield, Illinois. In 1937 his Florence Nightingale monument, *Protecting the Flame of Life*, was placed in Lincoln Park at Los Angeles. Edström is well represented in Swedish museums, especially the Thiel Gallery of Art in Stockholm. His life was full of contrasts and drama. An extraordinary autobiography, *The Testament of Caliban*, was published in New York and London just before his death.

Karl Fredrik or Frederick Skoog (1878–1938), a soldier's son from Väse in Värmland and an emigrant of 1902, created a number of notable sculptures, including the First World War monuments at Cambridge, Massachusetts, and Cromwell, Connecticut, and *The Giant's Last Stand*, a bison's fight with mountain lions, in the State Capitol at Topeka, Kansas. Agnes Fromén (1868–1956), the daughter of a sea captain from Östergötland, came to Chicago in the early 1900s via Australia and Paris and won her first prize in 1912 with a fountain. Works by her are on display in the United States, Sweden, and China. Francis Peter Hedlund (d. 1945), who was born in Worcester, Massachusetts, of Swedish parentage, helped Gutzon Borglum, who was of Danish extraction, design both the Rushmore Memorial in the Black Hills of South Dakota, with its colossal heads of Presidents Washington, Jefferson, Lincoln, and Theodore Roosevelt, and the Stone Mountain Memorial near Atlanta, Georgia. Hedlund also did considerable work in England, Ireland, and Sweden.

Carl or Charles Haag (1867–1933), a native of Norrköping in Östergötland and a watchmaker's apprentice at the age of 12, arrived in America in 1903, after having studied art at Gothenburg and in five countries on the European mainland. In New York, where he lived before moving to Chicago and Winnetka, Illinois, the Metropolitan Museum in 1906 bought one of his sculptures, the first by an immigrant from Sweden. Misfortune or tragedy was often portrayed in his creations, but some of his later wood sculptures reflected, on the other hand, a keen sense of humor. He was influenced by Sweden's master carver, Axel Petersson "Döderhultarn" (1868–1925), whose art was shown in New York, Chicago, and San Francisco in 1913–15 and who today has two museums of his own at Oskarshamn on Småland's Baltic coast. One of Sweden's most original artists, Petersson turned log after log into vividly expressive figures, most of them representing country folk who, in fact, often seemed more real in wood than they did in actual life.

Another noted Swedish-American wood sculptor, Carl Hallsthammar (b. 1894) from the vicinity of Hallstahammar in Västmanland, came as an immigrant in 1924. Six of his life-sized figures in wood adorned the General Motors Building at the Century of Progress Exposition in Chicago in 1933, and after an extended study of the Red Man, he carved a group of Indians which gained high acclaim. A work called *Spirit of the West* is in a museum in Los Angeles. Like many other artists from Sweden, Hallsthammar settled in Chicago, where in 1934 he opened a school for wood sculpture. Before leaving Sweden he spent a few summers studying with Anders Zorn at Mora in the province of Dalarna.

Chicago the leading art center — Zorn influential in exchanges U.S.A.–Sweden

BY THE turn of the century Chicago had become the leading center of the Swedish-born artists in America, even if many were active in other parts of the country. The first Swedish painter to settle there was Peter M. Adamsson or Almini (1825–90) from Småland who, after some training in Stockholm and a visit to Russia, arrived in 1852. He decorated many churches and assembly halls, opened the city's first art gallery and became known as a great promoter of artistic activities. Since 1905 Chicago's Swedish-American art associations have sponsored at least one annual show.

The first large display of art from Sweden in the Middle West was held at the World's Fair or Columbian Exposition in Chicago in 1893. Commissioner for the art exhibits in the Swedish pavilion was Anders Zorn (1860–1920), who already had established a reputation in Europe. From the beginning he felt at home in the United States, and during seven visits, the last one in 1911, he became widely known as an ambassador extraordinary from Sweden and was greatly admired as a portraitist. Among Americans who sat for him were Presidents Grover Cleveland, Theodore Roosevelt, and William H. Taft, Mrs. Grover Cleveland and other ladies, and many captains of industry and finance. American art museums and families own most of these portraits, as well as a considerable number of other canvases. The Taft portrait, executed in 1911, hangs in the White House. Zorn, who also won fame as an etcher and sculptor, traveled extensively in the United States, and among his friends were not only celebrities and millionaires but also many educators and younger artists.

In Sweden, Zorn became known as a warm friend of America. His interest in an ever-growing exchange of scientific, other cultural, and practical experience between Sweden and the United States was reflected in a large donation to the Sweden-America Foundation when this organization was founded in Stockholm immediately after the First World War.

Throughout his cosmopolitan and often hectic life, Anders Zorn remained a devoted son of his native province, Dalarna, whose people, scenery, customs, and music inspired much of his production. He was born at historic Mora on Lake Siljan, the son of a farmer's daughter and a brewer from Bavaria, and this town is now full of Zorn relics and monuments. They include his and his wife's home and a museum building of 1939 in which many of his paintings hang, an open-air museum of some 30 structures created by him, his statue of Gustavus Vasa as the future "Builder of the Realm" appeared in 1521, and a folk high school which Zorn established in 1907. The museum building was designed by Ragnar Östberg, who first met Anders Zorn in 1893 at the World's Fair in Chicago and today is remembered, above all, as the architect of Stockholm's Town Hall. No small town in Sweden has attracted as many visitors from America as Mora, which also has become known abroad as the base of the 55-mile Vasa ski race, held annually early in March in honor of King Gustavus Vasa.

In 1920 a Swedish-American art exhibition, which had been organized by The American-Scandinavian Foundation, was shown in leading museums in Sweden. Many of the participating artists were old friends of Anders Zorn, who died in the same year. American painters and draftsmen of Swedish origin were also well represented at a large exposition in Gothenburg in 1923, again helping to stimulate interest in cultural exchanges over the Atlantic. In late 1924 an exhibition comprising 60 works by Zorn opened in Carnegie Institute at Pittsburgh, and it was then shown in Minneapolis, Baltimore, Washington, D.C., Buffalo, and New York.

No other Swedish artist could, of course, match Anders Zorn's fame in the United States in the early 1900s, but several had become relatively well known as a result of exhibitions or the activities of Swedish-American painters and art teachers. Among them were the previously mentioned Carl Larsson, who often specialized in home and family life, and Bruno Liljefors, interpreter of wildlife and nature, as well as Richard Bergh (1858–1919), a leading portraitist, and John Bauer (1882–1918), who created a charming and mystic fairy-tale world. August Hagborg (1852–1921), who won fame in Paris with coastal fisherfolk scenes, is well represented in American collections. Today, Ernst Josephson (1851–1906) and Carl Fredrik Hill (1849–1911), who anticipated modern expressionism and surrealism, are widely regarded as Sweden's most significant artists of the 19th century. Via exhibits, lectures, magazine articles, and books, both have gradually become better known in American art circles. August Strindberg, the writer, has also become recognized as an unusually interesting Swedish painter of the late 19th and early 20th centuries.

★ 32

From Strindberg to Lagerkvist

*Strindberg introduced on the American stage
in the early* 1900s

AUGUST STRINDBERG (1849–1912) has been called the "Titan of Swedish literature," as well as "a man of a thousand contradictions." A writer of prodigious productivity, he authored about 60 plays, nearly a dozen novels, more than 150 short stories, several volumes of poetry, and scores of historical, critical, and polemical essays. Virtually all of his works are autobiographical, that is, they deal in one way or another with his storm-swept inner life and transform into great literature his personal experiences, including attacks on his literary talent by detractors, his prosecution for alleged blasphemy in 1884, his three marriages which all ended in divorce, his periods of humiliating poverty, and the mental depressions from which he suffered sporadically. The most harrowing one of these, the so-called Inferno Crisis, which culminated in 1896, finally brought about a rebirth of Strindberg's poetic powers.

Strindberg's dramatic production is his most important contribution to literature, but much of his literary talent and even some of his essential human qualities, such as his basic common sense, his warmth, his humor, and his love of nature, only intermittently found outlet in his dramas. A good-humored novel set in the Stockholm archipelago, a world of lush or rugged rocky islands, became his most popular book in Sweden. Entitled *The Natives of Hemsö*, it was, like many of his other works, written abroad.

While borrowing little or nothing from other writers, Strindberg was influenced by many literary figures in other countries, including Mark Twain and Edgar Allan Poe among those in America. In the late 1870s he translated a selection of American humorists for a Stockholm publisher. As a young man Strindberg looked to the United States as a leader in cultural and political progress, and a careful study of his writings has shown that this attitude by and large remained unchanged throughout his life. During the Inferno Crisis, Swedenborg became one of Strindberg's most powerful influences.

Strindberg's fame as a dramatist was established in Germany, where during the years 1900–25 his plays were given much more often than in Sweden. In the United States he has enjoyed periods of popularity, and after the middle of the 1900s there were signs of a lasting revival. His dramas have, on the whole, aroused greater interest among university teachers and students, and in the experimental theaters, than on Broadway and in commercial playhouses. American playwrights influenced by Strindberg include first of all Eugene O'Neill, as well as Tennessee Williams, Edward Albee, and Thornton Wilder.

Of Strindberg's plays, the one best known universally is probably *Miss Julie*, which the author himself called "the first naturalistic tragedy in Swedish drama." It was produced in Copenhagen in 1889, in Berlin in 1892 and, more successfully, in Paris in 1893, while Stockholm had to wait for its first performance until 1906. Already in 1905 it was given in New York in the Russian language, with Alla Nazimova, who later became a famous American stage and motion-picture actress, in the leading part. In 1913 it was offered by the 48th Street Theater in New York, and another production followed. In 1947 the German actress Elisabeth Bergner toured the United States with *Miss Julie* for six months, but failed to reach Broadway. Several critics described the play as "somewhat old-fashioned." It was then produced by the Alley Theater in Houston, Texas, and by a black ensemble from Howard University in Washington, D.C. The McCarter Theater in Princeton, New Jersey, and the Theater of the Living Arts in Philadelphia gave it in 1966.

663

A TV production in 1960, first broadcast January 25–31 by Channel 13 in New York, contributed much to a better understanding of Strindberg's tragedy. In *The New York Times*, Jack Gould wrote after the opening that "the evening is one of the most powerful and absorbing in the history of television drama. Strindberg could well have written with TV in mind. His probing characterization, his searching psychological emphasis and his uncompromising realism are made all the more stark by their introduction into the home." Strindberg's one-acter *The Stronger* was presented at the same time and described by Gould as "a pure gem on TV." The two plays were given in translations by Arvid Paulson, born in 1888 at Helsingborg in southern Sweden, who in 1910 made his debut as an actor on the American stage and later took a particularly active part in translating and interpreting Strindberg's works to Americans.

Miss Julie's standing as the Swedish dramatist's best-known play has also been enhanced by several motion-picture adaptations, in particular one directed by Alf Sjöberg (b. 1903) of Sweden, which in 1951 won the Grand Prix at the Film Festival in Cannes, France, and became an international box-office success. The film critic of *The New York World-Telegram & Sun* wrote that the introduction of Strindberg to American movie screens "comes as a ringing triumph for everyone concerned in *Miss Julie*. This somber tragedy with its brooding air of doom will ring powerfully and lastingly through every movie memory it enters."

The Father, another naturalistic drama of the late 1880s, was the first Strindberg play to be performed in English in America and to attract any greater attention. In a translation by Edith and Warner Oland, who himself played the Father, it was presented in April, 1912, at the Berkeley Lyceum, an intimate theater on 43rd Street just west of Fifth Avenue. The critics were divided, but the play would probably have lasted longer than it did if it had not been for the sinking of the *Titanic* a few days after the opening. In 1919–20 a Jewish ensemble offered the play in New York and Detroit. After a mediocre production in 1928, Robert Loraine, who had successfully played in *The Father* for many months in London, gave the drama in 1931 at the 49th Street Theater in New York. Again the critique was mixed. Brooks Atkinson of *The New York Times* wrote: "In the completeness of its expression and passion of an idea it is, in fact, one of the great works of the modern drama. . . . Being a genius, Strindberg turns his drama into a hurricane of the furies. It is a dance of death of the evil forces of the world."

In 1949, when the 100th anniversary of the Swedish author's birthday was celebrated, *The Father* ran for 69 performances at the Cort Theater on Broadway. In answer to unimpressed colleagues, the famous George Jean Nathan wrote in *The New York Journal-American*: "In its almost every detail . . . the play remains more modern than any of the numerous later ones it has inspired. And not only more modern but infinitely superior." Beginning in late 1949, the same play had a six-month run at the Provincetown Theater in New York, and it was also given in Boston. Yale University followed in the early 1950s. In 1962 both *The Father* and *Miss Julie* were presented at the Cort Theater in New York by a Swedish-speaking ensemble from the Royal Dramatic Theater in Stockholm, which had begun its American tour at the World's Fair in Seattle. The Swedish company's visit revealed, according to the critic of *The New York Times*, "the consistent standards and ensemble spirit of one of Europe's most venerable national theaters." It was the first time that an ensemble from Sweden's national stage visited the United States. *The Father* was, like *Miss Julie*, revived in New York in the 1970s.

Another marriage drama, *Creditors*, had its American premiere in the spring of 1912 at the Stage Society in Boston. The well-established experimental Little Theater in Chicago reproduced it in 1913–14. In 1922 the Greenwich Village Theater was first to offer the play in New York, and in 1949–50 the Cherry Lane Theater presented a more important production, which was well received by the critics and ran for 108 performances. A score of performances followed in another theater.

Of Strindberg's short one-act plays written in the late 1880s, the previously mentioned one-acter *The Stronger* was given in 1911–12 in Milwaukee and Madison by the Wisconsin Dramatic Society. The first of several notable New York performances was staged in 1913 at the 48th Street Theater, which at the same time gave another one-acter, *Pariah*, which has only two speaking roles. A third one-act play, *Simoom*, set in an Arab burial vault in North Africa and by Strindberg himself called "a brilliant Edgar Poe piece," began its professional American career in Chicago in 1911. Four years later it was staged by Arvid Paulson at the Professional Women's League in New York. It was given as an opera at Tanglewood, Massachusetts, in 1949.

A fairy-tale play by Strindberg, *Lucky Per's Journey* of 1882, was produced in 1923 by the Pasadena Community Players in California. Much later, Strindberg wrote another delightful play, a medieval fantasy called *Swanwhite*, which was inspired by a romance which led to his third, brief marriage. It contains his only conventionally romantic love story. In 1908 Jean Sibelius wrote the music for its world premiere at the Swedish Theater in Helsinki, Finland, which became one of the leading Strindberg centers in Europe. Both *Swanwhite* and *Lucky Per's Journey* have been heard on the radio in America.

A new epoch in the history of the theater began during or shortly after the First World War when plays written by Strindberg after the Inferno Crisis received masterly performances. Producers and directors had then begun to realize their new significance. The famous Austrian-born producer Max Reinhardt, who later moved to America, came to Stockholm with German versions of *The Ghost Sonata, The Pelican*, and *A Dream Play*, and critics and theatergoers were overwhelmed by the power of these dramas. In New York in the 1920s, when Eugene O'Neill and the Provincetown Players staged *The Ghost Sonata* and *A Dream Play*, O'Neill hailed Strindberg as "the precursor of all modernity in our present theater."

Strindberg's first drama after the Inferno Crisis, the first part of the *To Damascus* trilogy, which was written in Paris in 1898, is regarded as one of his greatest works. It was given at the Auditorium in Chicago in 1914–15. In March, 1958, when an International Theater Month was celebrated, it was produced by the experimental theater at Vassar College in Poughkeepsie, New York. The three parts of the cycle were then condensed into one. In *To Damascus*, Strindberg introduced the theme of atonement which is echoed in much of his post-Inferno production.

Easter, another drama of penitence and written in 1900, had its American premiere in 1913 at the Little Theater in Chicago, in the Swedish language. The following year it was offered as a reading performance at the Professional Women's League in New York, and other presentations followed in 1916 and 1926. The theater at the University of Minnesota gave it in 1950. Under competent, imaginative directors, *Easter* has proven itself to be one of Strindberg's most successful dramas.

In 1900 Strindberg also wrote *The Dance of Death*, a new study of marital misery, in two parts. Outside of Sweden, the first part has become one of Strindberg's most frequently produced creations. In the United States, a traveling company presented it as early as 1912. The first more significant production came in 1920 under the auspices of the Theater Guild in New York, and in 1935 the Federal Theater in New York played the drama during three weeks. A Broadway version early in 1948 closed after eight days, despite excellent acting. Recent revivals have included an interesting production mounted in 1974 by the New York Shakespeare Festival at Lincoln Center. The translation used was by Elizabeth Sprigge.

Strindberg called *A Dream Play* of 1901 "my most beloved drama, the child of my greatest torment." O'Neill, who produced it in New York in 1925, was obviously impressed by it. In late 1948 it was given at the University of Minnesota as a prelude to the Strindberg centennial. Two other universities, Columbia and Illinois, as well as the Goodman Theater in Chicago, followed some ten years later. In 1960 it was staged in a primitive off-Broadway theater in New York, and in 1964 it had a one-month run at the Vanguard Playhouse in Detroit. Sweden's internationally best-known stage directors, Olof Molander (1892–1966) and Ingmar Bergman, have tackled the fascinating *Dream Play* as one of their greatest challenges.

In 1907 Strindberg turned out some "chamber plays" for his and his partner August Falck's Intimate Theater in Stockholm, including *The Ghost Sonata*, which is regarded as his most enigmatic drama but also as a work of art of demonic beauty, and the even more gruesome *The Pelican*, his last great dissection of Woman, which the author said he had written against his will. The Provincetown Players' presentation of *The Ghost Sonata* in New York in 1924 became historic. In 1940 this play, together with a work by Shakespeare, was given at the inauguration of the University of Wisconsin's magnificent new theater. Several experimental stages, including those at Vassar College and Yale as well as the Pasadena Playhouse, followed suit. In 1929 *The Pelican* was played by a youthful ensemble in the MacDougal Street Playhouse in New York, and in 1957 it was produced at Northwestern University in Evanston, Illinois.

Of Strindberg's historical plays, *Erik XIV* has become particularly popular abroad, probably because of the Swedish 16th-century monarch's resemblance to Hamlet. Another post-Inferno drama of the same type, *Charles XII*, had in 1957 its American premiere at Yale's experimental theater in New Haven. *Gustavus Vasa*, widely regarded as Strindberg's foremost historical play, was in 1912 given in the Swedish language in Chicago. It was directed by a noted visitor from Sweden, August Lindberg (1846–1916), who also acted the leading role. Strindberg's historical plays were translated into English in the 1950s by Walter Johnson, then chairman of the department of Scandinavian at the University of Washington in Seattle. Others have translated some of the plays.

In his last drama, *The Great Highway* of 1909, Strindberg mixed cruel castigations, sweet but melancholy memories, humorous satire, and tender lyrics. Although in this play director and actors face unusual problems, it was successfully produced at the Pasadena Playhouse in 1952.

Like Ibsen and Tolstoy, Strindberg never received the Nobel prize for literature. In 1911 a sum of money was raised by public subscription in Sweden and given to him as an "Anti-Nobel prize."

In 1936 Eugene O'Neill, who that year was awarded the Nobel prize for literature, acknowledged in a message to Stockholm his debt to "that greatest genius of all modern dramatists," August Strindberg. The American playwright continued: "It was reading his plays when I first started to write, back in the winter of 1913–14, that, above all else, first gave me the vision of what modern drama could be. . . . If there is anything of lasting worth in my work, it is due to that original impulse from him, which has continued as my inspiration down all the years since then."

Selma Lagerlöf enjoys larger circulation abroad than any other Swedish author

WHEN Selma Lagerlöf (1858–1940) in 1909 became the first Swede and the first woman to win the Nobel prize for literature, she had already begun to win worldwide fame. Her books were gradually translated into some 40 languages, including Arabic, Armenian, Hebrew, Japanese, and Russian. They reached larger circulations abroad than those of any other Swedish writer.

While still a schoolteacher, Selma Lagerlöf made her literary debut in 1891 with *Gösta Berling's Saga*, a collection of stories of seemingly lighthearted manor-house life in her native Värmland, which were told with an unusually lively imagination and in a new lyric prose style. Her next major work, *Jerusalem* of 1901 1902, is in its first part a monumental study of the clash between an ancient conservative farmer traditionalism and modern religious sectarianism in the province of Dalarna, and the ensuing emigration to Jerusalem. In the late 1800s a number of farmers in the "Land of the Valleys" had actually sold their ancestral farms and followed a returned Swedish-American sectarian preacher to the Holy City. There they joined an American colony which had been founded by a lawyer, Horatio G. Spafford, and his wife, Norwegian-born Anna Spafford. In 1873 the latter had been one of a score of passengers rescued from a sinking transatlantic ship, while more than 400, including her four daughters, had been lost. The second part of Selma Lagerlöf's novel deals with the life of the colony in or near Jerusalem.

In 1902 the National Association of Teachers in Sweden commissioned Miss Lagerlöf to write a schoolbook that would present in story form the geography, folklore, flora, and fauna of the various Swedish provinces. The work she produced, *Nils Holgerssons underbara resa genom Sverige* or *The Wonderful Adventures of Nils*, published in 1906–07, became a children's classic not only in Sweden but also in many other countries. The first American edition, published in two volumes in 1907 and 1911, was used as supplementary reading in public schools. Selma Lagerlöf's authorized American translator, Velma Swanston Howard, who was born in Sweden and went back to work on a newspaper in Stockholm, contributed much to her early success in the United States and other English-speaking countries.

The Nils Holgersson of the book is the disobedient and mischievous son of a small farmer in the south of Sweden, who is turned into a thumbling and carried off on his mother's tame gander, lured to follow the wild geese on their flight to the North. Nils now understands the speech of animals, and being a good-natured boy at heart he soon becomes their devoted friend. As the geese fly from the deep

South to northern Lapland and back, with many side trips to the east and west, the whole country unfolds before the readers who also are introduced to many local legends and other folklore. At the end the boy regains normal size.

Selma Lagerlöf wrote many other books, one of which, *The Ring of the Löwenskölds*, became a Literary Guild of America selection in 1931. Despite the gentle religious faith that runs through several of her works, she was not spared from inner struggles, and at times the growing burden of work, together with her worldwide popularity, threatened to crush her. The old Mårbacka manor in Värmland, where she had lived until her 24th year but which the family then had to sell, was bought back as soon as she could afford it, and later she built a larger manor house on the same spot. Two years after her death, Mårbacka was opened to the public as a museum.

Like Strindberg, Selma Lagerlöf had faith in America. In early 1933, during the Great Depression and two weeks after Hitler had assumed power in Germany, she made a long address to radio listeners in the United States, under the auspices of an international radio forum. The voice now heard, she began, "belongs to an old Swedish woman who has never been in America, but who throughout her long life has received from it lessons and gifts." Darkness has now descended upon the world, but, she continued, the belief in human goodness and a growing sense of solidarity must one day return, and "I have the feeling that it is in the great daughter country of the West that Mother Europe's most beautiful dream will reach its fullest bloom." Esaias Tegnér, the great poet, had had the same vision 116 years earlier.

During the years 1916–23, which are regarded as the "golden age" in Swedish films, several of the best moving pictures produced were based on books by Selma Lagerlöf. The first one, *The Girl from Stormyrcroft*, directed by Victor Sjöström or Seastrom (1879–1960) who later spent seven years in Hollywood, called attention to the continued plight of the agricultural laborers in Sweden. The other leading Swedish film-maker, Mauritz Stiller (1883–1928), who at the age of 27 had arrived from Finland, directed *Gösta Berling's Saga*, released in 1924. For the role of an Italian girl who reforms Gösta Berling, a defrocked minister, he cast a young Swedish actress named Greta Garbo. The following year, after Louis B. Mayer had seen the film in Berlin, Stiller and Greta Garbo left for Hollywood.

Hjalmar Bergman and Pär Lagerkvist also have their followers in the United States

HJALMAR BERGMAN (1883–1931) is regarded as Sweden's foremost playwright after Strindberg. He was also an outstanding novelist. In Europe he is much better known than in the United States, although the American interest in him has been growing. Altogether, his dramas have reached a far larger audience than those of Strindberg.

Of Bergman's first more significant plays, the one-acter *Mr. Sleeman Is Coming* (1916) has won appreciation among drama students and university-theater directors on both sides of the Atlantic. His first resounding success as a dramatist came in 1925 with *Swedenhielms*, also known in the United States as *The Nobel Prize*, a sparkling comedy with a double purpose, which has had thousands of performances in ten languages. Before his death in 1931, Bergman adapted for the theater his two most popular novels, *His Grace's Last Will*, presented thousands of times in Germany alone, and *The Markurells of Wadköping*, or *God's Orchid*, which also has scored many successes abroad. Both are comedies with more or less tragic undertones. A novel entitled *Granny and Our Lord* was dramatized after the author's death.

Hjalmar Bergman was born at Örebro, one of the centers of the ancient Bergslagen ironmaking and mining district which became the locale of many of his works. He lived in Italy for several years and spent much time traveling in other countries. In late 1923 he went to Hollywood, invited by Samuel Goldwyn to author film scripts, but soon began to feel depressed and returned to Europe. His first new creation there was a comedy about seven Europeans and an unknown, wealthy American woman, thrown together in a ski hotel in northern Sweden. A subsequent film version brought a young Swedish actress named Ingrid Bergman one of her first successes on the screen.

Bergman's last work was a fragmentary novel entitled *Jac the Clown*, a biting commentary on the Hollywood mentality and at the same time a moving, ironic exposition of one side of his own literary development. His view of life, often disguised by glittering humor or irony, was fundamentally one of tragic fatalism. Blind instincts rule in his world of fiction, and no instinct has more fatal consequences than the lust for power.

Another of the central figures in 20th-century Swedish literature, Pär Lagerkvist (1891–1974), made his debut in 1912, and practically every year thereafter he produced a volume of essays or short stories, a novel, a play, or a book of poetry. Many of these works won high critical acclaim. The general public, however, was not fully aware of his existence until 1933, the first year of the Third Reich in Germany, when he published a short novel entitled *The Hangman*, which was dramatized by the author himself and was produced both in Sweden and abroad. A study of the ancient and stubbornly surviving mysticism of violence and terror, this work was in reality, as an American literary critic wrote after the Second World War, "one of the strongest and most farseeing condemnations of totalitarianism." Lagerkvist remained an uncompromising adversary of the modern dictatorships.

During the Second World War he wrote a novel of strange and disturbing beauty entitled *The Dwarf*, which quickly gained national fame. It appeared in English in 1945. His next novel and best-known work, *Barabbas*, was published in Stockholm in 1950 and was subsequently translated into at least a score of foreign languages. The first American edition was brought out in New York in 1951, and for some time it figured in the best-seller lists, a rare feat for an author who always has seemed to refuse to make concessions to public taste, and whose works on the whole have little popular appeal.

In 1951 Lagerkvist was awarded the literary Nobel prize "for the artistic power and deep integrity with which he seeks an answer in his writings to Man's eternal problems." Four subsequent novels, among them *The Sibyl* and *The Death of Ahasuerus*, were also published in the United States. Several of his plays, including *The Man Without a Soul* and *Let Man Live*, are available in English and have been produced on experimental stages in America.

Pär Lagerkvist was born at Växjö in Småland. The piety of his parental home, a growing feeling of alienation and direct contacts with French expressionism were among his early influences. Despite his constant search for new answers to his questions, as well as for new forms of expression, there is in his production a deep continuity. A number of tender poems, with a shimmering background of the mysteries of life and nature, helped endear him to Swedes everywhere.

The Stirring 1920s

*A new era of growing understanding and exchanges
over the Atlantic*

A NEW era of greater understanding and expanding cultural, scientific, and economic relations between the United States and Sweden began after the First World War. The changes may hardly have been noticeable at first, but the decades of the 1920s and 1930s became full of more or less important milestones.

Despite the protracted emigration from Sweden and the myriads of transatlantic family and friendship ties existing at the end of the world conflict, the United States remained to the great mass of the Swedish people a distant and strange land. It had come out of the war with increased prestige and its potential for industrial and cultural growth seemed almost boundless, but its final refusal to subscribe to the League of Nations and a new world order caused, on the other hand, profound disappointment. Sweden's problems during the war had, on the American side of the Atlantic, left a residue of doubt or mistrust, much of it obviously due to a lack of insight into Swedish conditions and motives.

Gradually, advances in communications and transportation helped strengthen and multiply the old ties over the Atlantic. Radio and film, a more extensive as well as a more up-to-date press coverage, and new ships on the transatlantic run made constant contributions to a process which brought the American and Swedish peoples closer to each other.

In 1919 the keen Swedish interest in better contacts and more active exchanges was reflected in the establishment of a special organization in Stockholm, the Sweden-America Foundation, to promote the scientific, cultural, and practical relations between the two countries, primarily by sending qualified young men and women to the United States for study and training, but also by furthering the knowledge of American achievements in Sweden. Among the founding fathers were Svante Arrhenius, the scientist and Nobel prize winner, Hjalmar Branting, the political leader, Nathan Söderblom, the archbishop, Dan Broström and Axel Ax:son Johnson, both successful shipowners of the modern type, Jacob Wallenberg, one of the leading bankers, Anders Zorn, the famous artist, and J. Sigfrid Edström, a prominent industrialist.

Because of his active participation in transatlantic relations as well as his leadership of Swedish and international business and sports organizations, J. Sigfrid Edström (1870–1964) became widely known in the United States, where he had worked as a young man and where his wife was born. In 1913 he founded the International Athletic Federation, and in 1920 he became a member of the International Olympic Committee, serving as its president from 1946 to 1952 and being succeeded by Avery Brundage of the United States. From 1939 to 1944 he was president of the International Chamber of Commerce. Two of the first four scholarship funds of the Sweden-America Foundation were brought about by Mr. Edström, who from 1932 to 1952 served as president of the organization, and by the Asea company, which he led as managing director in the period 1903–33. Other funds were created by Anders Zorn and by the central organization of the Swedish consumer cooperatives.

From the beginning, the activities of the Sweden-America Foundation were greatly facilitated by the existence of a similar but larger organization in the United States, The American-Scandinavian Foundation, which had been founded in 1910 by an immigrant from Denmark, Niels Poulson (1843–1911). Its main objective is to advance the intellectual relations between the United States and the Scandinavian countries through a variety of programs, including fellowships for American students and scholars, the publication of books and a quarterly magazine, and placing so-called trainees with American firms.

In 1975, The American-Scandinavian Foundation had published about 125 translations of Scandinavian authors and books about the Scandinavian countries. It is the oldest institution active in the field of international education in the United States, and cooperates closely with associated organizations in all Scandinavia. In 1912–21 Dr. Henry Goddard Leach (1880–1970), born in Philadelphia of "old New England stock" and educated at Princeton and Harvard, was executive secretary, and later he served as president for two decades. A rare combination of imagination and common sense he regarded as characteristic of the Scandinavians.

The greatest single addition to the endowment of The American-Scandinavian Foundation came in 1964 in the form of a bequest valued at about 2.5 million dollars from the estate of Mrs. Ivar Thord-Gray, the former Winnifred Ingersoll of Canton and Chicago, Illinois. The income from the fund thus created, known as the Thord-Gray Memorial Fund, is used for scholarship exchange between the United States and Sweden and for other projects of educational and cultural significance. Mrs. Thord-Gray's interest in furthering American-Swedish relations had been stimulated by her husband, General Ivar Thord-Gray (1878–1964), who was born in Stockholm and whose family name was originally Hallström. He went to sea at the age of 17, jumped ship in South Africa, became a farmhand, and joined the British forces in 1897. After that he spent many years fighting or working as a farmer or businessman, in Africa, in the Philippines with the American army 1907–1908, in Indochina and Sumatra, with the Chinese army during the rebellion of 1913, in France with the British during the First World War, when he also served as a military instructor in the United States, and in Siberia and the Far East with the British or White-Russian armies in 1918–19. In 1925 he settled at Greenwich, Connecticut. In his later years, when he still spoke flawless Swedish with a Stockholm Southside accent, he turned to writing, archeology, and primitive languages. He compiled the only known dictionary for the language of the Tarahumara Indians of Mexico, with whom he fought in the Mexican revolution in 1913–14. A work of more than 1,000 pages, it was published by University of Miami Press.

The Swedish circles which in 1919 had established the Sweden-America Foundation created somewhat later another privately financed organization, which in New York set up an information service known as The American-Swedish News Exchange. By the middle of the 1930s, a noted American journalist, Marquis W. Childs, called it "an authentic medium of international understanding." Its first mission, according to an announcement early in 1922, was "to tell the truth and to increase the volume of news from Sweden of legitimate interest to this country, as well as to increase the volume of news from this country to Sweden." In stressing the importance of a mutual exchange, the Swedish information office was probably unique at that time. In the early 1920s well-informed Swedes felt that numerous Swedish press reports concerning the United States were melodramatic or superficial, not doing justice to the country and its institutions. A Swedish newspaper correspondent in America was a rare bird indeed, and there were no American correspondents in Sweden. The American-Swedish News Exchange was led from 1926 to 1946 by an American journalist and Harvard graduate, Naboth Hedin (1884–1973), who was born at Reftele in Småland and had come to America in 1900.

In 1923 the city of Gothenburg, after a two-year delay caused by the war, celebrated the 300th anniversary of its first city privileges with a large exposition. Several displays and events were devoted to relations with America, as seemed natural in Sweden's "Gateway to the West" where a special friendship with the English-speaking world has always been a leading theme. An "American Week" culminated on the Fourth of July. Among the ships in the harbor was the battleship *North Dakota*, which en route to the Mediterranean had been redirected to Gothenburg. It was probably the first time that the midshipmen from Annapolis visited Sweden's foremost port and second largest city. Other memorable occasions of the same type included one in the summer of 1936, when 1,250 midshipmen came to Sweden on an extensive voyage and, according to reports in the American press, agreed that "the squadron's visit to Gothenburg was the unqualified success of the cruise."

During the "American Week" at Gothenburg in 1923, Congressman Carl R. Chindblom, who was making the first of numerous visits to Sweden, appeared as spokesman for the Swedish societies in the Chicago area. Minnesota had sent an official delegation, headed by Edgar L. Mattson, a Minneapolis banker and son of Colonel Hans Mattson, the pioneer who became one of the first great promoters of Scandinavian immigration to Minnesota. The son of another famous Swedish pioneer in America, Eric P. Swenson, had visited Sweden a few months earlier as a member of a group from the National City Bank of New York, where he was chairman of the board. His father, Swante M. Swenson, who came to Texas in 1838, was responsible for a substantial part of the Swedish immigration to the Lone Star State.

In the same year, 1923, several Swedes came to the United States for lecture tours, among them Sven Hedin, the famous explorer, and Elsa Brändström (1888–1948), who during the First World War had become internationally known for aiding prisoners of war and refugees. Later on her welfare work extended to new fields, including aid to refugees in the Second World War, but she was best known as the "Angel of Siberia," a title bestowed by German and Austrian war prisoners in Siberian camps to whom she, under unspeakable difficulties, ministered as a volunteer nurse of the Swedish Red Cross in 1915–20. In America she raised funds for homes for war invalids and orphans in Germany. From 1934 she and her husband, German-born Robert Ulich, made their home in Cambridge, Massachusetts, Dr. Ulich having been named professor of education at Harvard. Elsa Brändström-Ulich was born in St. Petersburg, where her father, an army officer, served at the Swedish legation. At least one of the many books written about her tells how before leaving Germany she was invited to a conference by Adolph Hitler and answered with a telegram of one word: "Nein."

Archbishop Söderblom touring America in 1923 — Winner of Nobel peace prize 1930

IN THE fall of 1923 Dr. Nathan Söderblom (1866–1931), archbishop of Uppsala since 1914 and Sweden's greatest religious leader of the modern era, made one of the most concentrated and strenuous tours of the United States ever undertaken by a visitor from Sweden. He was accompanied by his wife, Anna Söderblom.

He lectured at numerous universities, such as Columbia, Yale, Harvard, Clark, Pennsylvania, Johns Hopkins, Chicago, Minnesota, and Berkeley, preached in a great number of churches of Swedish or other origin, including the Episcopal Cathedral in New York and Gloria Dei in Philadelphia, and gave interviews wherever he went. In Washington he had long conversations with President Calvin Coolidge, Secretary of State Charles Evans Hughes, and Secretary of Commerce Herbert Hoover. "For seven weeks," he said later, "I was able to speak with voice, and during the last two weeks without voice."

An immigrant from Sweden, who had studied at Harvard and heard Dr. Söderblom preach both there and, in Swedish, in Boston, wrote later: "To tell the truth, my expectations were not high. . . . But I soon had my awakening. . . . The Archbishop had hardly spoken his first sentence, before I could feel that he had the entire crowd as though hypnotized. . . . 'What a political spellbinder he would have been,' I reflected."

Archbishop Söderblom had been invited by the Lutheran Augustana Synod, founded in 1860 by Swedish immigrants, and on November 6, the anniversary of King Gustavus Adolphus's death in 1632 on a battlefield in Germany, he attended the dedication of new buildings at Augustana College and Theological Seminary in Rock Island, Illinois. In relations between the established church in Sweden and the national organization of the Swedish Lutherans in America his visit marked a turning point, or at least underscored the fact that a new era had begun. The late George M. Stephenson of the University of Minnesota, who long had a tendency to be skeptical of almost everything coming from the Church of Sweden, praised Söderblom as "a liberal, catholic, ecumenical man, a man of the world in the best sense," whose "attitude toward the Augustana Synod transcended all nationalistic, denominational, and creedal barriers. . . . Upon his visit to the United States in 1923, pastors and laymen found in him a man after their own hearts. He was more democratic and informal than many Augustana dignitaries." One of Dr. Söderblom's American disciples and friends, Dr. Conrad Bergendoff, born in 1895 in Nebraska of Swedish parents, became in 1935 president of Augustana College and Theological Seminary and served until 1962, the last 14 years as president of the college alone. Gustaf Albert Brandelle (1861–1936), who served as president of the Augustana Synod from 1918 to 1935, was also an advocate of greater religious solidarity or unity.

Söderblom was, of course, proud of the Augustana Synod, "the largest association of Swedes beyond Sweden's borders." The Swedes in America and their accomplishments were, he felt, not at all as well known in Sweden as they should be. At times, however, the continued flow of emigrants filled him with sadness. "Our extended, northern and sparsely populated country," he wrote, "is giving away its carefully reared sons and daughters to the world's richest nation. . . . Rear and give away has been our involuntary lot. . . . When we consider our nation's destinies through the ages, the emigration to America can no longer cause bitterness and lamentation." Sweden had contributed "durable and tested timber to the building of vitality's young world dominion and mankind's most universal nation."

In newspaper interviews Dr. Söderblom deplored the United States' decision not to join the League of Nations, which reminded him of a father deserting his offspring. Such comments were, with some exceptions, not popular in the press. On other occasions the visitor warned his audiences of the temptations inherent in neutrality. The lure of a self-righteous attitude, which existed during the World War, is even worse today, he said in a Swedish sermon in Chicago. "May we whip out of us the little devil known as self-satisfaction, which easily sneaks into a protected corner behind our sorrow and agony over world events." But, he added, "it is an absolute although painful duty to condemn, without hesitation, things that our conscience tells us to reject."

After his return to Sweden Dr. Söderblom wrote a book about his American preaching tour, entitled *From Uppsala to Rock Island*, and Mrs. Söderblom also published a travel report. At home he remained an eloquent champion both of the United States and of its Swedish element. Although he never liked hearing the phrase "biggest in the world" while traveling in America, he said in an address in Stockholm, there was one thing that certainly deserved that description, namely, American idealism.

Nathan Söderblom's consuming interest was achieving the goal of spiritual unity in the world through cooperation among the churches. In the United States he had, therefore, a special penchant for the Presbyterians, whom he regarded as the most broad-minded of all the religious communities.

Born in a parsonage in the province of Hälsingland, Söderblom was at an early age influenced by the religious revivals of the 19th century. His taste for international activities was aroused during a visit to America in 1890, when he attended one of the first international Christian student conferences at Northfield, Massachusetts, and was invited to the home of Dwight L. Moody, the famous revivalist, whom he greatly admired. He also visited both Harvard and Yale. "The summer I spent in New England in 1890 was of fundamental importance to my life and spiritual activity," he wrote later. In 1894–1901 Söderblom served as pastor of the Swedish church in Paris. At the beginning of this period he won Alfred Nobel's friendship, and at about the same time he was able to raise money for August Strindberg, who, destitute and ill, had sought a refuge in the French capital. Studies in the history of religion at Sorbonne then led to a doctor's degree and an international reputation in the world of learning. From 1901 to 1914 Söderblom served as professor at Uppsala, and in 1912–14 also as professor at Leipzig in Germany.

Dr. Söderblom's work for Christian unity culminated in 1925 when he brought about the most impressive ecumenical gathering the world had seen up to that time, the Universal Christian Conference on Life and Work in Stockholm. It was attended by more than 600 delegates from the Protestant and Orthodox Church communities in 37 countries, including all major ones except the Roman Catholic Church.

One of the many newspapermen from abroad who covered the Stockholm conference, William H. Stoneman of the *Chicago Daily News* who later lived for some time in Scandinavia, wrote in one of his final reports: "When Dr. Söderblom rose to the pulpit in old Uppsala Cathedral on the closing morning, he gave the most extraordinary exhibit of versatility which has been seen in the history of the Swedish church. He opened with St. Paul's greeting in Greek, followed with the prayer 'Veni, Sancte Spiritus' in Latin, and then proceeded to talk to the congregation in English, French, German, and Swedish." The feeling he inspired as a leader of the ecumenical movement was briefly expressed by an English clergyman who made the oft-quoted remark that if it were possible for Protestant Christendom to have a pope, the choice would fall on Söderblom. In 1930 the Nobel committee of the Norwegian parliament awarded him the Nobel peace prize.

Among Swedes who visited the United States in 1924 were three outstanding medical specialists, Karl Petrén (1868–1927), Einar Key (1872–1954), and Gösta Forssell (1876–1950), a noted art historian, Johnny Roosval (1879–1965), and an eminent astronomer and mathematician, Carl Charlier (1862–1934). All five were well known in professional circles on both sides of the Atlantic, and the group as a whole was part of a steadily growing interchange of ideas and experience. Upon his return to Sweden, Dr. Roosval published a book about American art, while Dr. Charlier the next year issued his lectures at the University of California at Berkeley. In interviews in Sweden, all five urged much closer contacts and, if possible, the establishment of regular exchange professorships between the universities of the two countries.

Erik Nelson, on flight round the world in 1924, *and other pioneers of aviation*

IN 1924 one of the pioneers of American aviation, Erik Henning Nelson (1888–1970), who was born and educated in Stockholm, won international fame in the first flight round the world.

On April 6, four two-seater, open-cockpit Douglas World Cruisers of the Army Air Service took off from Seattle on the first leg, and on September 28 two of them, one piloted by Lieutenant Erik H. Nelson, completed the flight, after having covered about 26,000 miles. Nelson, who also was the engineering officer of the flight, had worked closely with the manufacturer in the design, adaptation, testing, and construction of the planes. Douglas Park at Santa Monica, California, the site of the Douglas factory where the World Cruisers were built, was dedicated to the pioneers of 1924.

After two years of technical studies in Stockholm, Erik Nelson spent five years at sea, first on a training ship and then on commercial sailing routes all over the world. He landed in New York in 1909 and became, in turn, a rigger in a shipyard, a swimming instructor, a spear carrier at the Metropolitan Opera, a professional billiard player, an automobile salesman and test driver, assistant to a stunt flier in Florida, a mechanic and draftsman in aircraft factories, and, after flight training during the First World War, a flying instructor, to be finally in charge of teaching aerial acrobatics.

After the war Nelson made important contributions to the techni-

681

cal organization of military aviation, but became best known for his part in a series of trail-blazing flights. On a 4,000-mile expedition between the Mexican Gulf and the Pacific in 1919, he carried a photographer into the Grand Canyon for the first aerial pictures of this area, and the same year he led a squadron on a 7,000-mile recruiting tour of 32 cities. In 1920 he was the engineering officer of an 11,000-mile New York-Nome mission, designed to open an air route to Alaska. After the round-the-world flight and some years as an Air Corps representative at the Douglas factories in Santa Monica, Nelson in 1928 joined the Boeing company in Seattle, then led by Philip G. Johnson who was a son of Swedish immigrants, and there he became a vice president and director, taking an active part in the creation of the Boeing 247, a forerunner of the large warplanes. An adviser to the war-production effort in 1940–41, he returned after Pearl Harbor to what had become the Army Air Force. After having retired as a brigadier general, he became technical adviser for Scandinavian Airlines System on transatlantic and transpolar routes. In 1955 he moved to Hawaii, where he called his home Villa Stockholm. His large collection of aviation memorabilia was donated to the Museum of Technology in the Swedish capital.

Other immigrants from Sweden who have been mentioned among the aviation pioneers of the 1910s and 1920s include Hugo Sundstedt (1886–1966). Born at Örebro in central Sweden, he received his pilot's certificate in 1909. In 1914, when he was studying aircraft construction in France, he flew from Paris to Stockholm with only one intermediate landing for refueling. In 1916 he seems to have received an invitation from American interests to come to New York to build a flying boat for a flight over the Atlantic, but after the United States' entry into the war the plane was sold to the Navy. Another seaplane, the *Sunrise*, was built in 1919 but crashed during a trial flight. Captain Sundstedt then concentrated on engineering and manufacturing. During the Second World War he built transport planes of his own design.

No American of Swedish ancestry has created a greater sensation and won more fame than 25-year-old Charles A. Lindbergh did when on May 20–21, 1927, he flew his *Spirit of St. Louis* from Roosevelt Field, Long Island, New York, to Le Bourget near Paris. His pioneer flight began a new era in aviation. In the fall of 1933 Charles A.

Lindbergh and his wife visited Sweden and met several of his relatives in the province of Skåne. His grandfather was born there, at Gårdlösa near the city of Simrishamn, while his father was born in Stockholm and was brought to America in 1860 as an infant. Their ancestors had been farmers for many generations.

Another American of Swedish parentage, Colonel Bert R. J. Hassell (1893–1974), was the first pioneer aviator of the Great Circle route over the Atlantic, which most commercial airliners now use. He was born in Wisconsin of parents from the province of Värmland, who later moved to Rockford, Illinois. Around the turn of the century the family spent several years in Sweden, where the boy went to school at Karlstad. Though Colonel Hassell crashed in Greenland on his projected flight from Rockford to Stockholm in 1928, he and his companion pilot returned to America convinced that the northern route could be made safe. During the Second World War he was placed in charge of the Army Transport Command base at Goose Bay in Labrador. In 1971 he was named to the Aviation Hall of Fame.

Greta Garbo to America in 1925 *— More opera stars — New Swedish American liners*

IN 1925, on July 6, Greta Garbo arrived in New York aboard the *Drottningholm* of the Swedish American Line. She was traveling with her mentor and friend, Mauritz Stiller, who had been offered a three-year contract as a director by Metro-Goldwyn-Mayer, and had accepted on the condition that his protégée also be invited to Hollywood. The welcoming party in New York consisted of an M-G-M employee and a free-lance photographer. In December of 1928, when six of the 24 films she was to make in Hollywood had been shown, Greta Garbo sailed from New York on a Christmas and vacation trip to Sweden, and she was then pursued by a swarm of reporters and photographers. Both in Gothenburg and at Stockholm a cordon of police had to protect her from her curious and enthusiastic countrymen.

Born in 1905 on Stockholm's Southside, Greta Garbo, or Greta Lovisa Gustafsson as her name was at that time, began earning her living in a neighborhood barbershop. The next year, 1921, she made her first appearance before a motion-picture camera in an advertising film made for a department store in Stockholm. In 1922–24 she

683

studied at the academy of the Royal Dramatic Theater in Stockholm, and in 1923 she earned 3,000 kronor, or about 700 dollars, for her part in the film *Gösta Berling's Saga*, which was directed by Mauritz Stiller. The dramatic school in Stockholm, which was founded in 1787, has turned out a great number of first-rate actors and actresses, among them Ingrid Bergman.

The first Swedish audience had seen a motion picture flicker on a screen at an industrial exhibition at Malmö in 1896, the year after the movie debut in the United States. The first permanent movie theater in Sweden was opened at Gothenburg in the summer of 1902, a few months after Los Angeles had opened the first one in America, and in 1906 Stockholm boasted no less than 23 motion-picture theaters, while New York, which naturally soon took over the lead, had only 16. At an early stage Sweden thus became relatively well prepared both for a film production of its own and for a rapid expansion of imports. One of the first American pictures to be shown was *The Great Train Robbery*, made in 1903. Two decades later the Swedish people had already begun to receive a constant flow of entertainment and influences from the capital of the new art form, Hollywood, while the first "golden age" in Swedish films was drawing to a close. Victor Sjöström and Mauritz Stiller were the leading directors, and Sjöström left for Hollywood in 1923.

On February 4, 1924, Karin Branzell (1891–1974), who is regarded as one of Sweden's greatest contributions to opera art in America, made her debut at the Metropolitan as Fricka in Wagner's *Die Walküre*. She remained as a regular member of the New York company until the end of the 1944 season, and returned for several appearances in 1950–51. In 1946 she joined the voice faculty at the Juilliard School of Music, and this was followed by other teaching assignments in New York. Miss Branzell had made her debut at the Stockholm Opera in 1912. A successful Swedish tenor, Martin Öhman (1887–1967), joined the Metropolitan in the fall of 1924 but returned to Europe after a short season, the New York climate not agreeing with him. At that time the Metropolitan roster included Julia Claussen, who went back to Sweden in the early 1930s, and Marie Sundelius, who had arrived from Sweden at the age of ten.

684

Early in 1925 Nanny Larsén-Todsen (b. 1884), who had been with the Stockholm Opera for 16 years, appeared at the Metropolitan, and despite difficulties in becoming acclimatized she remained for two seasons. In Europe she was regarded as one of the greatest Wagner singers of her time. William Gustafson, an eminent bass singer who made his debut at the Met in 1921, was born in Boston but spoke Swedish without an accent. His untimely death in 1931 cut short a fine career. A brother, Paul Gustafson, became a noted obstetrician and a member of the Harvard Medical School faculty.

After resumption of full transatlantic service shortly after the end of the First World War the Swedish American Line started planning for the first liner designed and built especially for the company, and on November 30, 1925, the M.S. *Gripsholm* arrived in New York on her maiden voyage. She was also the first motor-driven passenger vessel on the Atlantic. Three years later the somewhat larger M.S. *Kungsholm* entered service, being welcomed in New York on December 3, 1928. Among her passengers on the trip back to Gothenburg was Greta Garbo.

The *Kungsholm* and the *Gripsholm* became two of the most celebrated commercial vessels afloat, and they and their successors did much to stimulate travel and other contacts between Sweden and America. During the latter part of the 1920s the tourist trade grew so rapidly that it soon exceeded the peaks of the emigrant traffic, for which the Swedish American Line had been developed in the first place. The flow of emigrants was dwindling, and the number of passengers traveling in each direction became, therefore, practically the same. Former emigrants and their families made up a substantial proportion of the American tourists headed for Sweden. During the period of mass emigration Sweden had had no passenger line of its own to America.

During the Second World War the *Kungsholm* was purchased by the U.S. government which used her as the troop transport *John Ericsson*. The *Gripsholm* and a third Swedish American liner, the *Drottningholm*, made 33 voyages repatriating diplomats, wounded soldiers, women, and children under the sponsorship of the Swedish Red Cross and the International Red Cross.

*Future King and Queen of Sweden on ten-week tour of
the United States in 1926*

IN THE summer of 1926 Crown Prince Gustav Adolf and Crown
Princess Louise toured the United States for ten weeks on an official
visit. Their hosts as well as the general public and the press were impressed by their "democratic qualities," and they were received everywhere with a warm friendliness and hospitality.

In Washington they were guests of President Coolidge at the
White House, and participated on May 29 in the unveiling of a
monument to John Ericsson, father of the U.S.S. *Monitor*, on the
banks of the Potomac. A chorus of about 600 members of the American Union of Swedish Singers sang at the ceremony. President
Coolidge was serenaded before leaving the White House. The Crown
Prince and Crown Princess also made a visit to the Congress. From
the floor of the House they were welcomed by Congressman Carl R.
Chindblom from Chicago, one of the few American-born sons of
Swedish immigrants who spoke English and Swedish with the same
ease and eloquence.

In Philadelphia the Crown Prince laid the cornerstone for the
American Swedish Historical Museum, planned as a memorial to
John Morton, signer of the Declaration of Independence, whose
great-grandfather, Mårten Mårtensson or Morten Mortenson, had
joined the Swedes on the Delaware in 1654. Their descendants were
represented at the ceremony by a widely known physician from Minneapolis, Dr. Howard McIlvain Morton (1868–1939), born at Chester,
southwest of Philadelphia, which the Swedes, who founded it, had
called Upland.

At East Orange, New Jersey, the Crown Prince and Crown Princess visited Upsala College and at West Orange they called on
Thomas Alva Edison, who surprised them by saying that he, too,
probably was of Swedish descent. Being of Dutch-English ancestry on
his father's side, he believed he was of Swedish descent via Holland.
At Princeton the Crown Prince received his first American honorary
degree. Yale, Clark, and Chicago followed suit, while Harvard waited
until 1938. In 1926 the 43-year-old future monarch had already become known as an archeologist and collector of Oriental art. At
Harvard he arranged for an exchange of archeological artifacts between the Peabody Museum and the National Gallery of Art in Stockholm.

In New York the 600-voice chorus of the American Union of Swedish Singers gave two gala concerts in the Metropolitan Opera House, which was filled to capacity by enthusiastic audiences. Two Swedish-born stars at the Met, Julia Claussen and Marie Sundelius, were soloists. The second concert was attended by the royal guests, and Crown Prince Gustav Adolf, who was president of the Singers' Union in Sweden, made a speech which was greeted with ovations and vocal tributes. During the day the Crown Prince visited the Metropolitan Museum of Art five or six times, and his discussions there led to an exhibit of modern Swedish decorative arts in early 1927.

To the U.S. Military Academy at West Point as well as to New Haven, Connecticut, the visitors from Sweden traveled on board John Pierpoint Morgan's yacht *Corsair*, which had been cruising in Swedish waters. In Massachusetts they took part in two Midsummer festivals, one at Worcester, attended by 30,000 people, and the other at the Swedish old-people's home in Newton near Boston, where 15,000 were assembled.

The tour proceeded west via Buffalo, Niagara Falls, and Detroit. The many events in the Chicago area included an open-air rally at the Swedish old-people's home in Evanston, where according to the police at least 50,000 had gathered. One day was spent at Rock Island, Illinois, the cultural center of the Swedish Lutherans in America.

In Minnesota the Swedish travelers visited Red Wing and Vasa, both important in the history of the Swedes in America. In Minneapolis-St. Paul the authorities had proclaimed a holiday in honor of their royal guests, and 40,000 filled the stadium of the University of Minnesota, where the main ceremony was held. With many intermediate stops the tour moved on to Gardiner, Montana, the north entrance to Yellowstone National Park, and from there it went south via Salt Lake City and Zion National Park in the southwest of Utah to Arizona and the Grand Canyon, finally turning west toward southern California.

In Hollywood, Louis B. Mayer gave a luncheon attended by Greta Garbo, Lars Hanson, and the latter's wife, Karin Molander. Like Miss Garbo, Lars Hanson (1886–1965) worked for Metro-Goldwyn-Mayer, but after two years he returned in 1927 to the Royal Dramatic Theater in Stockholm, finally becoming Sweden's foremost dramatic artist. Karin Molander (b. 1890) had been one of Sweden's leading actresses during the "golden age" in the films, 1916–23. Other Swedes in Hollywood at this time were Nils Asther, who played twice with Greta Garbo, and Einar Hanson, who was killed in an automobile accident in 1927. At a concert in the Hollywood Bowl, Anna Q. Nilsson, a native of Ystad in southernmost Sweden who had begun her American screen career in 1911, paid homage to the royal visitors in an address in English and Swedish.

En route to San Francisco, where the tour ended, the travelers stopped at Turlock. A new high point of informality was reached during two days in the Bohemian Grove, the summer camp of the Bohemian Club of San Francisco, where the club members traditionally opened the summer season with a ceremony known as the "Burning of Care," and where "high jinks" of various kinds followed.

Early in August Crown Prince Gustav Adolf and Crown Princess Louise left for the Far East on board a Japanese steamer. It was said that they had seen more of America than any other official visitors, and that their successful tour had given its Swedish element a powerful injection of self-confidence and optimism. Less than a year later the spirit of Americans of Swedish origin was bolstered spectacularly by one of their own, Charles A. Lindbergh.

Early in 1927 Crown Prince Gustav Adolf's younger brother, Prince Wilhelm or William (1884–1965), came to the United States for a lecture tour which took him to some 50 cities and towns. In Sweden he had already published a dozen books, including travel reports, short stories, plays, and poetry, and many more would follow. "Tall as a Maypole," as one of his many literary friends in Sweden described him, he had become widely known as a big-game hunter, but while he told his American audiences of some such expeditions, he had actually become much more interested in exploring and studying. "The more one hunts, the more one becomes a game preserver," he said in an interview. "One prefers seeing the game to shooting it." Upon his return to Sweden he wrote a series of articles about America for leading newspapers in Stockholm, Helsinki, Oslo, and Copenhagen. Europe, he observed, must for its own sake become much better acquainted with the United States. Prince Wilhelm visited the New World the first time in 1907, when he came as a lieutenant on the cruiser *Fylgia*.

★ 34

More Cultural Exchanges

"Swedish Modern" arrives, scoring in America in 1927 *and at Stockholm Fair in* 1930

THE exhibition of modern Swedish arts and crafts at the Metropolitan Museum in New York opened on January 17, 1927, and closed on March 20, after having been extended for three weeks because of the great interest shown. It was the first time a European country had been invited to present products of this type. From New York the exhibition moved to Detroit and Chicago. Art critics have described it as the beginning of a new era in American attitudes toward applied arts and industrial design.

In New York the exhibits were seen by some 60,000 people, which does not seem impressive by today's standards but was regarded as remarkable at that time. Art critics and commentators, designers, interior decorators, and museum experts came in large numbers. In the press, numerous advance articles with sumptuous illustrations had explained the new Swedish styles in glass, ceramics, pewter, wrought iron, precious metals, tapestries and rugs, book bindings, and furniture.

The exhibition came about as a result of an artistic renaissance in Sweden, which was based on a new cooperation between artists and manufacturers. Teamwork of that type had for about ten years been actively promoted by the Swedish Society for Industrial Design, founded as early as 1845; this organization had also been important in developing a sense of style and quality among the people. A Home Exhibition in Stockholm in 1917, which included 23 interiors created by young architects and special sections for glass and china, is regarded as the first milestone.

"More beautiful things for everyday use" became the slogan of the new movement, which obviously aimed at better household goods but also led to the production of large, engraved pieces of glass, unique ceramics, and other truly artistic products. The first great success abroad came at an international exhibition in Paris in 1925, when Swedish glassware, furniture, lighting fixtures, and other industrial-art objects won an outstanding number of prizes, including 35 Grand Prix and 46 gold medals.

Glass contributed more than anything else to the international reputation of Sweden's industrial arts, and some of its producers in this field, in particular Orrefors and Kosta, became widely known. Orrefors had been founded in 1726 as an ironworks; glass manufacturing did not begin there until the late 1800s and the first significant artists were not engaged until 1916–17. Today, huge Orrefors chandeliers and other decorative articles are found in several public and private buildings in the United States, including the Kennedy Center for the Performing Arts in Washington, D.C., and the General Motors Building in New York. The Kosta works, on the other hand, began producing crystal as soon as it had been established in 1742. Other noted producers include Boda, Reijmyre, and Strömbergshyttan. Most of the glassworks are in southeast Småland. Sweden's oldest ceramic-art specialist, Rörstrand, started in 1726 at Stockholm, but its factory is now at Lidköping, a small idyllic town in Västergötland. Rörstrand creations in the United States include a monumental stoneware relief called "Growing Land" on the main floor of the Commerce Trust Company building at Kansas City, Missouri, completed in 1964. It was designed by Carl-Harry Stålhane (b. 1920), who in 1960 had received the International Design Award of American Decorators.

The main objectives in the new applied arts in Sweden were simplicity, beauty, and, in the case of products intended for everyday use, functional utility. Textiles were, as a rule, clear in color and had cheerful patterns. A genuine feeling for the nature of the material used was evident in most of the products; much of the furniture, for instance, had a natural finish. During the 1930s these styles became known in the United States as "Swedish Modern." A typical description of the new products was "simple, good-looking, unpretentious, and serviceable." Other critics summarized their impressions in two words: "Elegant simplicity." In the new Waldorf-Astoria Hotel in New York, a large suite of rooms was furnished in the "Swedish Modern" style.

American interest in Swedish applied arts reached a second height in 1930 with an exposition in Stockholm which was devoted to the modern way of living. While most of the critics offered warm praise, others voiced a certain disappointment or skepticism, observing, for instance, that some displays were too extremely functionalistic, and that the Swedes should pay more attention to their rich heritage in the decorative arts. However, the exhibit's concentration on the modern, or ultramodern, did not mean that the old handicrafts were neglected everywhere in Sweden: the homecraft movement had, in fact, also been revived in the early 1900s.

As a whole, the Stockholm Exposition left a good or even powerful impression in American art circles. In 1936, when the Museum of Modern Art in New York staged a retrospective exhibit of exposition architecture in preparation for the coming World's Fair in New York, it was found that the Stockholm show had been the best planned and most effective of its kind. Enlarged pictures of it dominated the photographic displays. In Sweden, and all Scandinavia, the Stockholm exhibition laid the foundation for new thinking about housing, and it introduced new, unconventional furnishings and more practical art-industry products. Many years later an American architect, G. E. Kidder Smith, wrote in one of his books, entitled *Sweden Builds*: "The aim of this exposition was to point the way to a new architecture and a new life. . . . The architecture itself was of a festive freedom with a light and airy grace . . . but the 'message' of the fair did not end there. For part of the reason for the exhibition was to explore the new ways architecture might socially serve man."

The men primarily responsible for the Stockholm Exposition were Gregor Paulsson (b. 1889), head of the Swedish Society for Industrial Design, who also had been in charge of the art-industry exhibitions in

Paris and New York, and the architect Gunnar Asplund (1885–1940). The latter designed a number of modern, matter-of-fact buildings, but the Forest Cemetery at Stockholm, with three burial chapels, is regarded as his foremost work, and as one of the principal architectural creations of the 1930s in Sweden. "If there is to be a 'monumentality' in contemporary architecture," G. E. Kidder Smith wrote, "it can begin with this, a truly poetic conception."

Despite the growing American interest in modern architecture, a product of the national-romantic temper in Sweden, Stockholm's magnificent Town Hall, which had been completed in 1923, claimed for many years a large part of the attention that writers and photographers accorded Swedish creations. In Sweden, too, it came to be regarded as a symbol of Stockholm. Its architect, Ragnar Östberg (1866–1945), received in 1934 the gold medal of the American Institute of Architects, which was presented to him by President Franklin D. Roosevelt at the White House on May 17, in the presence of a gathering of American architects and representatives of the fine arts. "I take particular pleasure in presenting this medal for I am, I believe, the only President of the United States to have Swedish blood in my veins," said President Roosevelt, who obviously did not realize that two presidents of the 19th century, the Harrisons, also had some drops of "Swedish blood" in their veins. The ceremony took place in connection with a convention of the American Institute of Architects. Östberg also received a prize at Yale University.

In 1933 Chicago celebrated its 100th anniversary with a world's fair, called the Century of Progress Exposition, and Sweden was represented with a pavilion of its own where products of its art industry were displayed. Despite the Great Depression the fair proved immensely popular and was held over for another year, the total of paid admissions reaching about 40 million. The exposition may not have taken place at all if it had not been for the energy and enthusiasm of Charles S. Peterson (1873–1943), who at a critical stage had pushed the preparations and was vice president of the fair corporation. Born at Daglösen in the Swedish province of Värmland, he started in America at the age of 14 and became a successful businessman in the printing trade. He was named a member of the Chicago Board of Education in 1913 and served as city treasurer in 1927–31.

*Swedish interest in American literature fanned by its
new tone of self-searching*

MANY American classics and other books of the 19th century were still
widely read in Sweden in the early 1900s, and in several cases up-to-
date editions set new circulation records. Imports of recently published American novels and books of poetry brought from the other
side of the Atlantic a new note of self-searching and self-criticism, and
especially in literary circles in Sweden this helped to stimulate interest
in the letters of the New World.

In 1930 Sinclair Lewis, the author of *Babbitt* and *Main Street*, became the first American to be awarded the Nobel prize for literature.
He was given it, the Swedish Academy said, "for his vigorous and
graphic art of description and his ability to create, with wit and
humor, new types of people."

While a number of critics in the United States welcomed the
award, many others were inclined to regard it as a left-handed com-
pliment to American culture. In private discussions, people of
Swedish origin often expressed embarrassed disapproval. *Main Street*
had, after all, become known as a satiric characterization of a typical
American town, and the name *Babbitt* was being used as a derogatory
synonym for a businessman who worships material success and is
insensitive to other values.

During the discussions in Stockholm another American novelist,
Theodore Dreiser, whose *An American Tragedy* had made a deep impression, had been weighed against Sinclair Lewis, and when the
Swedish Academy finally decided in favor of the latter, it was
influenced by a desire to recognize the significant contributions to
modern literature made by American humor. *Babbitt*, which was published in 1922, became that year's best seller in England, and in 1923
appeared in a Swedish translation, was regarded as particularly important. Among other American writers whom many, including
Sinclair Lewis himself in his Nobel lecture in Stockholm, considered
to be worthy of the Nobel prize was Willa Cather. In Sweden, however, she remained relatively little known, even if she had won some
devoted admirers. She had grown up in a Scandinavian district in
Nebraska, and in two of her novels, *O, Pioneers!* and *The Song of the
Lark*, the heroines are of Swedish stock.

In Sweden, the characters in Sinclair Lewis's *Babbitt* and *Main*

Street can hardly have been regarded as exclusively American, but rather as more or less familiar in many countries. Long before Lewis received the Nobel prize, Sweden's first expert on modern American literature, Ruben G:son Berg (1876–1948), had written: "As a human being Babbitt is a standard product, with a standard family and standard friends, and his life is a standard life with standard virtues and vices. We Swedes ought to remember this type from the United States and its history, for we already have him in our midst, preaching the extraordinary merits, economic advantages and spiritual solidity of standardization. . . . He has replaced a romantic back number known as individualism and a classical relic called intellectualism."

In the early 1920s Ruben G:son Berg studied literature in the United States. Upon his return to Stockholm he lectured about his impressions and conclusions in an adult-education society for workers, and in 1925 he published a book entitled *Modern Americans*. Self-dissecting and self-criticism had, he felt, become more common in American letters than in the literature of any other country, and this seems to have been one of the main reasons why his interest had turned to the United States. Like many other literary men in Sweden, as well as in other European countries, he could hardly be described as pro-American in the conventional sense.

Another pioneer interpreter of modern America to Swedish readers, Gustaf Hellström (1882–1953), who today is remembered primarily as a novelist, served in 1918–23, after several years in London and Paris, as the U.S. correspondent for the Stockholm daily *Dagens Nyheter*. In 1919 he published, in a book, a sympathetic account of Woodrow Wilson's peace plans, together with a generally favorable discussion of American politics, life, and mentality. A novel of the following year, entitled *A Letter of Recommendation*, reflected on the other hand an unhappy disenchantment with postwar America. Among its leading subjects were an allegedly cynical big business, an ineffective trade-union movement, and a double standard concerning sex. During the 1930s and 40s, Hellström's sympathies were always with the democracies of the West.

The more or less skeptical attitude toward American society in literary circles in Sweden was nourished by such phenomena as the "comstockery," a term coined by George Bernard Shaw and meaning an aggressive and narrow-minded professional prudery of the type successfully represented in the late 19th and early 20th centuries by Anthony Comstock. A spectacular American event with a negative impact was the Scopes or "monkey" trial in 1925, when a biology teacher in Dayton, Ohio, John T. Scopes, was convicted of breaking a state law prohibiting teachings contrary to the biblical story of creation. Swedish intellectuals who wrote the most scathing comments, and seemed to have enjoyed themselves greatly doing it, can hardly have realized that reactions of a similar type were expressed on a much larger scale in the United States.

The reading habits of the rank and file were, to a great extent, different from those of the literary elite. In the early 1900s Jack London, who combined romantic adventure, breath-taking violence, and socialistic ideas, was not only the most sought-after American writer, but the most popular of all authors, at least in the public libraries. He became the third American to have his collected works published in the Swedish language, the first one being James Fenimore Cooper and the second Theodore Parker, a Unitarian clergyman and antislavery reformer of the middle 1800s. Influences from the United States remained unusually strong in the Swedish free-church movement. Another American who became widely read, particularly in labor circles, was Upton Sinclair, whose novel *The Jungle*, a report from Chicago's meat-packing industry, was translated immediately after its publication in 1906. Books for children and young people, perhaps in particular girls or young women, were almost always among the most popular American products. Warnings from literary critics, who often described such books as artificial and insipid, had little effect.

In the early 1900s, the Swedish people's feelings for Bret Harte and Mark Twain were as warm as they had been when these authors were first introduced. Some 40 of Harte's books have been published in Sweden. Mark Twain's volumes number only about 20, but *Tom Sawyer* and *Huckleberry Finn* remain among the four or five best-known American books. At the beginning of the century Swedish boys often learned large parts of *Huckleberry Finn* by heart. Only *Uncle Tom's Cabin*, which during the first quarter of the 20th century appeared in quite a few editions in Sweden, has undoubtedly been more famous. The Swedes also continued to read older American classics, including James Fenimore Cooper and Washington Irving, who had been received with enthusiasm in the early and middle 1800s. Henry David Thoreau, whose *Walden, or Life in the Woods*, had appeared in 1854, did not attract wider attention in Sweden until the third decade of the 1900s. Herman Melville's *Moby Dick* does not seem to have been translated into Swedish until 1943.

Longfellow, who by 1925 had been translated into Swedish more often than any other American bard, was still being rendered in the Swedish language, but literary critics and connoisseurs had already begun to discover such new poets as Edgar Lee Masters, Vachel Lindsay, Robert Frost, and Carl Sandburg. A growing interest in Walt Whitman, who had issued his first *Leaves of Grass* in 1855, was another indication of the dawn of a new era. The lyrical modernism in Sweden has been greatly influenced by Whitman, whom a number of the country's best-known modern poets have translated. In the main lobby of the headquarters of the Workers Educational Association in Stockholm, completed in 1961, are two large reliefs by a noted painter and sculptor, Bror Hjorth (1894–1968), both symbolizing humanism and inspired by a poem by Whitman, "The Base of All Metaphysics," as well as a Swedish translation of part of that rhapsody.

Modern Swedish lyrics were already in the 1920s influenced by such American poets as Ezra Pound, Hilda Doolittle, and Amy Lowell. Two young poets translated much of their work in two volumes of *Verse from the West*, which appeared in 1922–24.

The Swedish library system was greatly improved in the early 1900s, in part as a result of a government-financed study trip that Valfrid Palmgren, now better known as Valfrid Munch-Petersen (1877–1967), made to the United States in 1907. The next year she introduced American-type courses in library science in Stockholm, and in 1911 she established in the Swedish capital Scandinavia's first library for children and young people. Her book *Libraries and Popular Enlightenment*, written upon her return from the United States, was translated into many languages. Charles Lorentz Larson, who was born in 1894 in New Jersey but became an educator in Sweden, studied in 1929 the American school system on a scholarship from the city of Stockholm and later helped modernize the school libraries in Sweden.

35

The Extraordinary 1930s

In the United States of the 1930*s Sweden is looked upon as the "Middle Way"*

IN THE 1930s Sweden reached a place in the sun in the American public-opinion arena, a position which its people could not possibly have dreamed of ten years earlier. More and more Americans discovered Sweden and learned of its modern progress, but this does not by any means explain everything. Without the Great Depression and the search for, or dream of, effective and acceptable remedies, Sweden would not have attracted the same attention. From a Swedish viewpoint, the sunshine seemed, to a great extent, both too brilliant and too sudden. Most Americans knew so little about Sweden that they were bound to misunderstand much of what they read or heard.

Many Americans were drawn to Sweden simply because they liked it, or because they had established some close contacts with Swedish people. Among the scores of writers who visited the country in the early 1930s were Edna Ferber, who had had many novels, including *Show Boat*, translated into Swedish; Marc Connelly, whose play *The Green Pastures* in 1932 scored a great success at the Royal Dramatic Theater in Stockholm; Pearl Buck, whose *The Good Earth* was translated into Swedish immediately after its publication in 1931, and who was to win the Nobel prize for literature; and Russell Crouse, a journalist who was to become a successful playwright and producer and already had sung the praises of Sweden in the press.

In the fall of 1934 Will Rogers, the humorist, who has been called the most popular American of his day, visited Stockholm, and to *The New York Times* he sent a brief dispatch which read in part: "These Swedes are so hospitable they don't give you time to write or hardly even to read the papers. They are the healthiest-looking people you ever saw. . . . The King does not have much time to practice with a sword, but he swings a right smart tennis racket." At that time King Gustav V was 76 years old and he would, as "Mr. G.," play tennis until the age of 88. Few Europeans had their pictures published more often in the American press.

Throughout the 1930s American writers took a very active interest in the Swedish art industry and the "Swedish Modern" style in interior decoration, which often were featured or mentioned in department-store or specialty-shop advertising. Sweden's old rustic styles and its primitive household arts also became increasingly popular, and many families turned their homes, or at least guesthouses, into colorful "Swedish peasant cottages."

The first social reform or experiment in Sweden to arouse wide attention in the United States was the liquor rationing system, which had been introduced during the First World War. In the early 1930s, Sweden's economic advances and policies became the principal leading theme, and American coverage grew into an ever-flowing stream of newspaper reports, magazine articles, pamphlets, and books.

One of the first indications of what was to come was a series of articles in *The Christian Science Monitor* in early 1932, according to which Sweden seemed "halfway to Utopia." In the summer of 1933 news stories about a surprising Swedish recovery from the depths of the depression began to appear in the press, and in late fall came one of the most important magazine articles about Sweden that has been published in the English language.

The author was a 30-year-old journalist, Marquis W. Childs, who in 1930, the year of the Stockholm Exposition, had made his first visit to Sweden as a feature writer for the *St. Louis Post Dispatch*. His article, entitled "Sweden: Where Capitalism Is Controlled," appeared in the November issue of *Harper's Magazine*. The first and the last two sentences summed up the essence of his message: "If one were compelled to select in the present moment of flux and chaos a certain area of the earth's surface in order to show the highest good that Western civilization had up to the present achieved, one might go farther and do worse than choose Scandinavia. . . . It is possible that if world capitalism now gains a breathing space, there may be completed in Sweden the gradual and orderly transition from one type of economic life to another. The very fact that such a transition may be possible is enormously heartening."

The article was hailed by a New York newspaper, *The Sun*, as "a big splash in the pool of current economic discussion." Many writers traveled to Sweden to see for themselves, and their conclusions were largely the same as those of Marquis Childs: without going to extremes Sweden had succeeded remarkably well in setting its house in order, and continued wise policies were now lifting the country out of the economic slump. In 1933 the Swedish government had introduced a scheme of public works, a venture which many American observers regarded as important. It did not, in fact, bring about recovery but must have helped reduce the number of unemployed.

In the spring of 1934 the first more significant American book about the intrinsic charm of Sweden, *Sweden, the Land and the People* by Agnes Rothery, was published in New York, and this gave a new injection to those who had begun to look toward the Scandinavian North with new expectations. The *Brooklyn Eagle*, for instance, reviewed the book under the caption "Sweden Must Be Eden." Later the same year the moribund *North American Review*, which nearly 100 years earlier had published a long article by Longfellow about ancient Sweden and Esaias Tegnér's Viking-inspired poetry, presented an essay entitled "The Garden of Sweden."

On May 25, 1935, Secretary of State Cordell Hull signed a reciprocal trade agreement with Sweden, which thus became the second European nation to come to terms with the United States under the new trade-agreements program, and the first to sign a new complete commercial pact. The agreement had a stimulating effect on American-Swedish commerce, and the greater opportunities for free trade were warmly welcomed in Sweden. Sweden's economic revival in the 1930s was, in fact, greatly facilitated by its commercial policy, which successfully bucked the dominant trend toward increased restrictions on foreign trade.

Encouraged by Yale University Press, Marquis Childs decided to unfold his "controlled capitalism" theme in a book, and early in 1936

Sweden — The Middle Way was published. Capitalism in Sweden he regarded as wholesomely modified by government ownership of the service utilities and most of the larger power plants, by government planning for adequate employment and, to an increasing extent, low-cost housing, by a strong trade-union movement, and by consumer cooperatives which played, and still play, a particularly important part in food distribution. They had also established their own manufacturing industries, some of which had been able to break international monopolies. The highly significant roles of private enterprise and ownership were, on the other hand, hardly covered at all. An overemphasis on the cooperative movement was later admitted by the author.

While the book was received with the keenest interest, most reviews seemed balanced or realistic. One critic called it "the best political news in years," adding that the "method of sane compromise and steady progress, each step tested by the sole criterion: does it work?", had also been practiced in America. Another reviewer observed that Sweden, after all, was not quite a Utopia, her prosperity being tied to that of other nations. Childs himself, however, had indicated that he did not regard Sweden as "even an approximation of Utopia." Later the *New York Daily News* devoted its whole editorial column to "Sweden — The Middle Way": "We'd be the last to advocate a hysterical Sweden cult in this country. . . . But we do believe Americans can learn a few things, gather a few hints, from the way in which Sweden handles the contradictions of capitalism."

The first edition of *Sweden — The Middle Way*, which in February of 1937 went into its ninth and last printing, reached a circulation of 25,000 copies. A second edition attained five printings in 1938–44, and in 1947 came a third edition, later followed by paperbacks. The book's circulation in the 1930s may not seem particularly impressive, but it was read by numerous political leaders, including President Roosevelt and his Republican opponent in the elections of 1936, Governor Alfred M. Landon, as well as by a great many government officials, economists, university professors, newspaper and magazine publishers, and journalists. It resulted, moreover, in a new and larger stream of American newspaper and magazine writers to Sweden. Many of them wrote whole series of articles, and it was these and other reports, rather than the book itself and the first reviews, that created the impression of a real "Middle Way" boom in the United States. Headlines and single phrases, in particular, were often extravagant.

On June 23, 1936, when the Democrats opened their national convention at Philadelphia, President Roosevelt announced that he had appointed a commission to study producer and consumer cooperatives in Europe, and that he was particularly interested in the situation in Sweden. He had, in fact, a copy of *Sweden — The Middle Way* before him when he made the announcement. The commission presented its report in November, being divided three to three on the question of assistance to the cooperatives. The Swedish cooperatives had never asked for any special help from the government.

Swedes don't like "being put in a glass bowl" — Many problems remain to be solved

IN 1937, when the number of unemployed in the United States again rose to ten million, the Swedish "Middle Way" seemed to attract new interest. A number of small newspapers published an editorial with the caption "Let's All Go to Sweden." There were, however, also symptoms of a beginning surfeit. In late fall, for instance, *The Saturday Evening Post* ran an editorial entitled "Spoiling the Norsemen," and reading in part: "Isn't it almost time to stop saying nice things about Sweden? So thick and fast come the laudatory books about the Swedes and their neighboring kinsmen that friends' must feel like knocking on wood. It is not that the praise is undeserved. It is richly deserved. But perhaps it is not the wisest thing to speak out while the child is listening."

The one who wrote that article seems, however, to have misunderstood the situation somewhat, in two respects. First, many of the "nice things" said in America were obviously not directed at Sweden, but rather intended for domestic consumption and the promotion of economic and social reforms in the United States. And second, while the Swedes were glad to have won American friendship and goodwill and at times even felt flattered by the praise, they took the more extravagant comments and conclusions with many grains of salt. Economists, in particular, offered outright objections.

The adulation in the United States and other countries "should surely have turned the blonde head of the Norsemen," H. B. Elliston, then financial editor of *The Christian Science Monitor* and later editor of *The Washington Post*, wrote in an article in the December, 1937, issue of *The Atlantic*. But, he continued, the opposite has actually happened. "In a visit that I paid to Sweden this summer, I found the Swedes somewhat irritated, if anything, by the praise that has been bestowed upon them. . . . They simply don't like being put in a glass bowl by the world's reformers." Mr. Elliston agreed with the objectors that much that Sweden had done to meet the depression had been misunderstood abroad, but what was happening there remained, he observed on the other hand, "of great interest to other countries engaged in making democracies function progressively in a complex economic world. It can furnish more lessons than the Swedes in their present state of mind are prepared to admit."

That the Swedish people should take a decidedly reserved attitude toward the "Middle Way" boom in America and some other countries was, after all, to be expected. Neither the Liberal and Conservative parties nor private business and industry could, for instance, be pleased by Sweden being described abroad as a Social Democratic and cooperative heaven-on-earth. The Social Democrats, on the other hand, were bound to react against the impression that Sweden already had solved most of its problems, and that there was little need for further reforms. Some young party members were, in fact, so disturbed that they wanted parliament to set aside funds for a propaganda campaign in the United States which would illuminate the seamy side of Swedish society. In the summer of 1937, Finance Minister Ernst Wigforss (b. 1881), who was the leading Socialist theorist of the Social Democratic party, observed that the government's economic measures in great part represented a continuation of the policies of its Liberal predecessors, and that it was many "cooperating circumstances" that had helped Sweden overcome the depression in a remarkably short time.

In articles on both sides of the Atlantic, one of Sweden's leading younger economists, Bertil Ohlin, observed that Sweden unfortunately had not found "a safe middle way," and that many serious social problems remained to be solved. Another, Gunnar Myrdal, said that singling out the good or excellent phases of Swedish life may seem all right, but that this undoubtedly would inspire others to emphasize Sweden's failures and shortcomings — a prophecy that was fulfilled to a greater extent in the 1960s and early 1970s than it was in the 1930s. In press interviews in the United States in 1938, a third economist, the veteran Eli F. Heckscher, emphasized that an unusually keen demand for Sweden's export staples more than anything else accounted for the country's prosperity. Among the things that many American writers, and at least one famous economist, had misunderstood was the Swedish money policy. Americans had, Dr. Heckscher added, become "far too romantic about Sweden," and he also stated bluntly: "Unfortunately neither America nor any other large country can learn anything from Sweden's recent period of prosperity." In the final chapter of his book, Marquis Childs had actually said practically the same: "The significance that Sweden's achievement may have for the world at large is debatable. It may be extremely limited."

In retrospect, the publication of Marquis Childs's book about the "Middle Way" remains an event of considerable practical importance. It aroused a wide American interest in Sweden and brought Scandinavia thousands of visitors who were anxious to learn more about that part of the world. Today it also seems possible to regard the book and its repercussions as a positive contribution to the spiritual climate in the America of the 1930s: together with many much more significant factors, it may have helped in keeping alive the faith in a future of economic common sense and political freedom.

Future monarch heads large Swedish delegation to New Sweden Tercentenary in 1938

THE New Sweden Tercentenary in the summer of 1938, which recalled the arrival of the first Swedish colonists on the Delaware in 1638, was the most comprehensive and impressive celebration observed jointly by the United States and Sweden. While focusing attention on a single ethnic element in the American nation, it helped stimulate new interest in all the cultural backgrounds of America.

From Sweden came the most representative delegation the country had sent abroad in modern times, numbering 80 persons all told. Headed by Crown Prince Gustav Adolf, who was accompanied by his wife, Crown Princess Louise, and his third son, Prince Bertil, it included two cabinet ministers, the speakers of both houses of the Riksdag, church dignitaries, leaders in education, industry, social-welfare work and other fields, and special representatives of the farmers and industrial workers. The descendants of Governor Johan Printz through his daughter Armegott, said to number about 1,000, were represented by the chief judge of the city of Stockholm, Gunnar Fant. Finland, which in the 17th century furnished a number of colonists for New Sweden, had sent a delegation led by its minister for foreign affairs. On the American side were engaged President Franklin D. Roosevelt, Secretary of State Cordell Hull, the governors of Delaware, Pennsylvania, and several other states, and the mayors of Wilmington, Philadelphia, and many other cities.

At the presentation of Carl Milles's New Sweden Monument in Wilmington on June 27, President Roosevelt and 26-year-old Prince Bertil, a successful pinch hitter for his ailing father, were the main speakers. The sculpture was a gift from the people of Sweden. A Swedish select chorus of 70 voices, led by Hugo Alfvén, the composer, and the Swedish Royal Horse Guards Band made their first appearances in the United States. The festive spirit was able to withstand even torrential rain. Wilmington had been founded by the Swedish colonists in 1638 as Fort Christina. It was there that law and order, the Christian religion, education, European agricultural methods and commerce were first introduced permanently into much of the areas now embraced by Delaware, western New Jersey, and southeastern Pennsylvania.

In Philadelphia the following day, June 28, the Swedish delegates were greeted by lavish decorations in blue and yellow, the city's own colors as well as Sweden's, and by an electric sign on City Hall which in letters several feet high said: "Welcome Swedish friends!" Speaking by radio from his cabin on the Swedish American liner *Kungsholm*, Crown Prince Gustav Adolf formally dedicated the American Swedish Historical Museum, for which he had laid the cornerstone during his visit in 1926. Both the chorus from Sweden and a choir composed of 1,000 members of the American Union of Swedish Singers sang in the Concert Hall.

Prince Bertil also made a tour of New Jersey. At a celebration in Central Park in New York, Mayor Fiorello La Guardia introduced him as "this representative from a democracy within a kingdom, of an ancient race but of a young people, of a cold climate but with warmth in their hearts, and this individual who, if he stays with us 48 hours longer, we shall be calling Bert." During a following long series of visits to the United States, Prince Bertil became, in fact, widely known as Bert.

Crown Prince Gustav Adolf was able to carry out the latter part of his program, including large celebrations in Boston Garden, in Chicago on Soldiers' Field, and in Minneapolis-St. Paul at the Minnesota State Fair Grounds, where according to some estimates over 100,000 people were assembled. "I had to pinch myself in the arm to make certain that I was not dreaming," the future Swedish monarch said later. Before sailing for Sweden on July 22 he visited Washington and gave, from New York, a radio address that was carried by the national networks. Prince Bertil and other members of the Swedish delegation made extensive tours of their own. New Sweden festivals were held even in Texas and on the West Coast.

The New Sweden Tercentenary celebrations had actually begun in the fall of 1937 when an exhibition of Swedish decorative and fine arts, spanning 8,000 years, opened in New York and then was sent on a tour of ten other cities. During the academic year 1937–38 a number of leading Swedish scholars appeared as special lecturers before American university and college audiences, the first one being Dr. The Svedberg, winner of the 1926 Nobel prize for chemistry. Their lectures finally totaled 270. Correspondence between American and Swedish school children was promoted by special postcards, and especially in the state of Delaware the schools offered instruction in the early history of the Swedes in America. In 1938 special New Sweden postage stamps were issued both in the United States and in Sweden, and there were also commemorative coins. Several books about Sweden or Scandinavia were published in America in the late 1930s.

On his return to Sweden, Crown Prince Gustav Adolf told the press how impressed he was by the American hospitality and active interest, but he added a word of caution: Sweden had for some time been in the spotlight in the United States, and it was not only pleasant but also risky to occupy such a position. Much, it seemed, was expected from Sweden in the future, and the country might not always be able to live up to such expectations.

Some members of the Swedish delegation observed that the highly successful celebration in the United States, together with other events

in recent years, had placed on Sweden a special responsibility: after all
the extensive hospitality and the genuine interest that the American
leaders and people had offered, new measures must be taken from
the Swedish side to further develop the friendly relations between the
two nations.

More could have been done in Sweden, especially toward a wider
understanding of the American people and its everyday life, but the
fact that the Swedish advances in the United States actually remained
modest when compared with the American impact on Sweden, was
also important. After having visited Sweden in 1936, an American
banker of Swedish parentage, Henry S. Henschen from Chicago, who
in 1885–89, when his father temporarily returned to Sweden as a
Methodist leader, had gone to school in Stockholm and Uppsala,
wrote in an article for a Swedish newspaper: "The Americanization of
Swedes in the United States seems natural, but the same metamor-
phosis in Sweden is hard to explain. During my last visit I saw nothing
but American movies, heard American slang and sport terms, found
the bookstore windows full of American authors in translation,
traveled in American motorcars, and read advertising about all possible American gadgets. Some people even seemed to think that the
Fourth of July should become the national day. Why not form an
association for the preservation of Swedish culture in Sweden?"

*Sweden a hit at New York Fair in 1939 — American interest
in cooperatives, labor relations*

IN THE summer of 1939 Sweden took part in both the New York
World's Fair in Flushing Meadow and in the Golden Gate International
Exposition on man-made Treasure Island at San Francisco. The
participation in the World's Fair was comprehensive and became
highly successful.

The aim of the exhibit in New York was to show briefly how
Sweden had exploited its rather limited natural resources, how it had
tried to provide a more even distribution of the national wealth, and
how it had developed its decorative and industrial arts to make both
homes and public buildings more attractive and convenient. The
Swedish pavilion, which had been designed by Sven Markelius, consisted of several one-story buildings, grouped about a central garden
or court, but the chief emphasis was on the contents. The decorative

arts were displayed in a high-ceilinged hall which led into a series of five homelike interiors.

Enthusiastic comments were printed in many American newspapers and magazines, including *The Architectural Forum*: "Completely assured and unpretentious, the Swedish pavilion is unquestionably the most civilized piece of modern architecture in the entire Fair grounds"; *The New Yorker*, where Lewis Mumford had wielded the pen: "The Swedish building is a miracle of elegant simplicity"; and *The Nation*: "The gay little Swedish pavilion *is* civilization!" Talbot F. Hamlin, a noted architect, observed in one of several articles that Sven Markelius had, above all, created an atmosphere of quiet peace and relaxation. One of the chief artistic memories of many visitors to the World's Fair would, he thought, be that of the Swedish pavilion's charming court, "with its flowers, its blue-gray pavement dotted with comfortable chairs, its quiet pool and the glittering glass fountain, and the delicate white birches with their tracery of branches and fluttering leaves, seen against the slim supports and the broad, light, sheltering roofs which the architect has designed. Here is an architecture of today, without the clichés of stylism."

Of the Swedish displays, the collection of crystal, ceramics, silver, pewter, and textiles, as well as much of the furniture, excited the highest praise. The revival of the Swedish art industry had continued and, in fact, even been refreshed during the 1930s, and from an international viewpoint it reached its height toward the end of that decade. According to Swedish designers and art critics, however, this style had to some extent become misrepresented in the United States. At the World's Fair in 1939, the Swedish art-industry section was launched under the slogan "Swedish Modern, a movement toward sanity in design." Commissioner general of the Swedish pavilion, which included an uncommonly popular restaurant named Three Crowns, was Count Folke Bernadotte, who on many occasions was accompanied by his wife, the former Estelle Manville.

It was the Swedish pavilion at the New York World's Fair that made Sven Markelius (1889–1972) internationally known as an architect. Already in 1937 he had become an honorary corresponding member of the Royal Institute of British Architects, and in 1948 he was elected an honorary fellow of the American Institute of Architects. In 1947 he served on the advisory committee for the United Nations headquarters in New York, and ten years later he was a member of an international committee called in for consultation on the plans for Lincoln Center. In 1949 he was a visiting professor at Yale, where he received the Howland Memorial Prize, and in the early 1960s he accepted invitations from the Massachusetts Institute of Technology and the University of California at Berkeley. On his return to Sweden he said in interviews that the United States had much to offer in the field of theater architecture. In the cultural life of America, he added, the college and university theater is an inspiring phenomenon.

In 1962 Markelius became the third Swedish recipient of the gold medal of the Royal Institute of British Architects, the first two being Ragnar Östberg, creator of the Stockholm Town Hall, and Ivar Tengbom (1878–1968), who designed the Concert House in the Swedish capital. From 1944 to 1954 Markelius had been in charge of town planning in Stockholm, and plans for a thorough modernization of the city's downtown area and for the construction of some of the new largely self-contained suburbs, such as Vällingby and Farsta, had been drawn up or begun during that period. Vällingby, in particular, was lavishly praised abroad. In America, G. E. Kidder Smith wrote that it was "the embodiment of Sweden's intimate relationship between architecture and the land on which it stands." Some other new town sections in Sweden were, on the other hand, severely criticized by Mr. Smith.

In a lecture in London in 1962, Markelius said that in the center of large cities, pedestrians and motor vehicles must if possible be separated. "If the cities are becoming inhuman, the foremost reason is the catastrophic increase in traffic. Goals that we should always cherish are safety, silence, and privacy." One of Markelius's last major creations in Sweden was the magnificent Trade Union Center in Stockholm, completed in 1960.

In the information booth of the Swedish pavilion at the New York World's Fair there were more inquiries concerning the cooperative movement than about any other aspect of Sweden. The interest had been aroused by Marquis W. Childs's book of 1936, *Sweden — The Middle Way*, and the numerous press reports resulting from it, and also by President Roosevelt's decision the same year to send a study commission to Sweden and some other European countries. The Swedish consumer cooperatives had become known, above all, for their battles against cartels and price rings in the 1920s and 1930s. Their leader was Albin Johansson (1886–1968), who served until 1957 and won many friends and admirers in the United States. Cooperation was regarded by him as a means of raising economic productivity by efficient competition. He was frankly skeptical of nationalization, distrusting a state monopoly as much as a private one. Under his leadership the Swedish cooperatives helped introduce modern, bright, and cheerful shop design as well as the self-service supermarket. Today they handle about one-sixth of all retail sales. Their factories account for about four percent of Sweden's industrial production.

In the summer of 1939 Sweden had also attracted some attention as a country where a long period of bitter conflicts between workers and employers had been succeeded by increasingly peaceful labor relations. In the summer of 1938 President Roosevelt had sent commissions to England and Sweden for a study of their industrial relations, including the activities of employers and trade unions, and the report on conditions in Sweden was published in late September. A book entitled *This Is Democracy — Collective Bargaining in Scandinavia*, and written by Marquis W. Childs, was brought out by Yale University Press at about the same time.

At the end of the same year, 1938, the unions and the organized employers in Sweden had reached an agreement which laid the groundwork for relations based on close personal contacts and group responsibility without government interference. The discussions, which had started in the fall of 1936, had been held in a hotel at Saltsjöbaden, near Stockholm, and the text agreed upon became known as the Saltsjöbaden Agreement. It attracted considerable attention in the American press as well as in industrial circles. In the spring of 1939, for instance, *The New York Times* published a three-column letter-to-the-editor from the president of General Electric, Gerard Swope, who had been chairman of the study commission to Sweden and had carefully studied the new labor-market pact. The Swedish agreement, he ended by saying, "reflects the conviction, born of long experience, that persuasion by voluntary mediation should be used to the fullest extent and that compulsion by law or even by arbitration should be avoided."

Swedish labor experts who discussed the Saltsjöbaden Agreement in America in 1939 observed that while the pact might well be described as epoch-making and obviously evidenced a great deal of common sense and self-control on both sides, it was neither as sensational in character as had sometimes been indicated nor likely to be as effective in pacifying Swedish labor relations as most observers abroad seemed inclined to believe. Labor conflicts did, indeed, become relatively rare in Sweden but strikes and lockouts may still occur.

36

Economics: A Case in Point

*Cassel, Myrdal, Ohlin, and other Swedish economists
become known in America*

DURING the 1930s, the practical importance of the science of economics became more obvious than before. Contacts between the United States and Sweden in this field increased constantly. A new and more numerous generation of Swedish economists made significant contributions to theoretical research and took, at the same time, an active part in public affairs. Both in Sweden and abroad it was often called the Stockholm School.

Of the new Swedish economists, Erik Lindahl, Gunnar Myrdal, and Bertil Ohlin became particularly well known abroad. The somewhat younger Erik Lundberg and Ingvar Svennilson, as well as Dag Hammarskjöld, were also regarded as members of the Stockholm School. What the economists of this group had in common was certain methods of analysis, rather than new theories. In the early 1930s their interest focused on the use of public-policy measures against depression and unemployment. To some extent they anticipated the theories of John Maynard Keynes, still known as the "new economics."

Erik Lindahl (1891–1960), whose academic career ended at Uppsala, was in 1956 elected president of the International Economic Association. He built in great part on the pioneering work of Knut Wicksell (1851–1926), who is regarded as the founder of modern economics in Sweden and has influenced economists all over the world. At the age of 50, after publishing three important works, Wicksell was named professor at the University of Lund. Two decades later he became an honorary member of the American Economic Association. The first treatise to deal systematically with his works, *Economic Doctrines of Knut Wicksell* by Carl G. Uhr, was published in 1960 by University of California Press. Its author, born in Sweden in 1911 and an emigrant of the late 1920s, had joined the University of California at Riverside in 1954 and became full professor in 1963. He has several times been invited to teach graduate courses and seminars at universities in Sweden and Finland.

Wicksell was deeply concerned with political and social issues, but to the universities and authorities of his time he seemed too radical. Education, he maintained, should be free of charge at all levels. In 1909 he spent two months in jail for alleged blasphemy. His program for economic progress called for a substantial expansion of the public sector, partly at the expense of private enterprise but also for the benefit of its future health. Lindahl emphasized that planning by public authorities is not only compatible with but also necessary for the efficient functioning of a market economy.

Another Swedish pioneer was Gustav Cassel (1866–1944), who for 30 years served as professor at the University of Stockholm. Also an elected honorary member of the American Economic Association, he was an authority on monetary problems and international economic relations. After the First World War he played a prominent part at international conferences and served as adviser to several European countries. In 1928 the Banking and Currency Committee of the House of Representatives in Washington invited him to give a report on the stabilization of the dollar. When he visited Congress and appeared in the gallery, the House gave him a standing ovation. Toward the end of the 1920s Cassel called attention to a threatening shortage of international means of payment and the consequent risk of deflation. He felt less at home in the 1930s, but much of what he said was "news" even in the United States. Many of his numerous newspaper and magazine articles reflected a conviction that the capitalistic system must be preserved if economic and social progress were to continue. A planned economy, he maintained, would always tend to develop into bureaucracy and dictatorship.

Eli F. Heckscher (1879–1952), from 1909 to 1944 a professor at the School of Economics in Stockholm, was convinced that a modified system of economic laissez faire, including low or gradually disappearing customs duties, would serve the peoples much more efficiently and painlessly than comprehensive government regulations. He was skeptical of public measures against the depression, but advocated social reform and wanted a more even income distribution. Applying economic theory to history, he became a pioneering economic historian, and the last two decades of his life were devoted to the writing of a monumental four-volume work, the economic history of Sweden from 1500 to 1815. A more concise work entitled *An Economic History of Sweden* was published in 1954 by Harvard University Press, one of Dr. Heckscher's former students, Göran Ohlin (b. 1925), being responsible for the translation. After having won his doctorate at Harvard in 1956, Ohlin served for six years first as an assistant professor at Stanford University in California and then as associate professor at Columbia in New York. In 1961 he was visiting professor at Yale. In 1969 he was named to a chair at the University of Uppsala.

Bertil Ohlin (b. 1899), who began his studies with Wicksell in Lund and Cassel and Heckscher in Stockholm, spent a year in the early 1920s at Harvard as a fellow of the Sweden-America Foundation in Stockholm. He studied with Frank W. Taussig and J. H. Williams and wrote a thesis on the theory of international trade, the field in which he was to win international fame. His *Interregional and International Trade*, first published in 1933 by Harvard University Press, remains a standard work in its field. Being unable to accept an invitation from Harvard in 1934, he came in 1937 to the Univeristy of California as a visiting professor and in 1959 to the University of Virginia. Lectures given at Columbia University in 1947 were published under the title *The Problem of Employment Stabilization*. In late 1959 he was invited to address the Harvard Economics Department, where he was welcomed as "one of the world's great economists," and one of the few who had successfully been able to combine economic theory with political reality.

From 1929 to 1965 Bertil Ohlin held a chair at the Stockholm School of Economics. In 1944–45 he served as minister of commerce in the wartime government, and from 1944 to 1967 he was the leader of the Liberal party, which became the largest opposition party in Sweden. In the early 1930s he had been one of the first advocates of an active policy against the depression. Somewhat later he coined a new term, "social-liberal," to express what, in his opinion, the Liberal party was and ought to be. A socially progressive policy of any scale, he emphasized, is possible only on the basis of a continuously rising prosperity and sound accumulation of capital in a decentralized economic system based chiefly on private ownership.

A doctoral thesis presented by Gunnar Myrdal (b. 1898) in 1927 helped usher in the so-called Stockholm School. The English translation, which did not appear until 1953, is entitled *The Political Element in the Development of Economic Theory.* In 1929–30, at the beginning of the Great Depression, Myrdal studied and traveled in the United States as a fellow of the Rockefeller Foundation. In 1933 he succeeded Cassel as professor at the University of Stockholm. In 1936 he and his wife Alva Myrdal (b. 1902) stirred up an animated debate in Sweden with a book about the country's population problem. Lectures given by him at Harvard in the spring of 1938 were later collected under the title *Population, A Problem for Democracy.*

In the fall of 1938 Dr. Myrdal returned to the United States to direct a comprehensive study of the American Negro "in a wholly objective and dispassionate way as a social phenomenon." Among his assistants was Ralph Bunche, then professor at Howard University and in 1950 winner of the Nobel peace prize for mediating in 1949 the Palestine conflict between Israel and the Arab nations. In 1944 the Carnegie Corporation published Myrdal's report and conclusion, *An American Dilemma: The Negro Problem and Modern Democracy.* A noted American sociologist, Robert Lynd, described this work as "the most penetrating and important book on our contemporary American civilization that has ever been written." It has also been called "a book that changed American life." The Supreme Court of the United States cited the book in 1954 in its decision that declared school segregation illegal. Dr. Myrdal himself said he knew of "no other country where such a thing could have happened," meaning that only in America could a foreigner have been invited to make a frank appraisal of the nation's most sensitive problem.

In 1941 Gunnar and Alva Myrdal published in Stockholm a book

714

entitled *Contact with America*, an enthusiastic interpretation of American democracy. It helped bolster morale in Sweden, which had been practically isolated from the West by Hitler's military might. Studying the American economy in 1943–44 Dr. Myrdal came to the conclusion that the war period would soon be followed by a great depression, especially as "political development in America is likely to be away from planning, rather than toward it." He added that he was well aware of the uncertainty of this prognosis, as of all other economic forecasts. His book, *Warning Against Peace Optimism*, was translated for publication by the National Planning Association. In 1945–47 Myrdal served as minister of commerce in Stockholm, in 1947–57 as executive secretary of the U.N. Economic Commission for Europe, and in 1960–67 as the first head of the Institute for International Economic Studies at Stockholm University. In 1968 his *Asian Drama*, the fruit of a decade of research and writing on South Asia, was published in New York by the Twentieth Century Fund. In 1973 he and his wife Alva, who since 1967 had been a member of the Swedish government and its top disarmament negotiator, were appointed research professors for a one-year term at the Center for the Study of Democratic Institutions at Santa Barbara, California. He planned to start a new study on racial conflict in America, while Mrs. Myrdal would write a report on the problems of disarmament from an international viewpoint. In 1974 the Myrdals moved their base to New York. Gunnar Myrdal has received more honorary degrees from American universities than any other Swedish scholar. Like Bertil Ohlin, he was elected an honorary member of the American Economic Association.

Erik Lundberg (b. 1907), whose doctor's dissertation of 1937 dealt with the theory of economic expansion, studied in 1931–33 on a Rockefeller fellowship at various American universities. For many years he taught at the Stockholm University, later joining the faculty of the School of Economics. In 1957 a significant work entitled *Business Cycles and Economic Policy*, a revised version of the Swedish original, was published in London. In his concluding remarks the author said that "an economy based largely on a highly decentralized market economy with a fairly freely functioning price system" seemed to offer greater advantages than any other known system. Lundberg had come back to America as a visiting professor in 1950, when he lectured first at

Princeton and Harvard, and finally at the University of Washington in Seattle. In 1960–61 he was a visiting research professor at the University of California.

In 1961 Erik Lundberg also lectured in Harvard's Economics Department, where he was introduced as representative of Sweden's chief exports to the United States, movie stars and economists. However, while Swedish economists obviously make frequent visits to the United States, so far only a few have actually settled there. These include Danish-born Bent Hansen (b. 1920), who earned his Ph.D. in Sweden where he became a university professor and director of the National Institute of Economic Research. In 1966 he was named to a chair at the University of California at Berkeley.

Another example is Hans B. Thorelli (b. 1921), who in 1959 became professor at the University of Chicago and in 1964 moved to Indiana University at Bloomington. His dissertation, presented at the University of Stockholm, bears the title *The Federal Antitrust Policy — Origination of an American Tradition*. Before leaving Sweden, Thorelli served as managing director of the Industrial Council for Social and Economic Studies, a privately financed nonpartisan organization which was founded in 1948. Known in Sweden as SNS, it was modeled after the Committee for Economic Development in the United States. The leading founder was Axel Iveroth (b. 1914), who had served as industrial attaché at the Swedish Embassy in Washington and later became president of the Swedish Industries Federation. In 1970 he became chairman of the board of the Sweden-America Foundation in Stockholm. Axel Leijonhufvud (b. 1933), who took his first degree at Lund University and received his doctorate from Northwestern University in 1967, joined the faculty of the University of California at Los Angeles in 1964 and was in 1971 named professor of economics. He has also served as department chairman and has lectured at many universities in the United States, Scandinavia, and England.

Like many other Swedish economists, Tord Palander (1902–72) studied in America on a Rockefeller Foundation fellowship. In 1952–53, when he had moved from the Gothenburg School of Economics to a chair at Uppsala, he was visiting professor at The Johns Hopkins University in Baltimore. Ingvar Svennilson (1908–72), who completed his doctor's thesis, *Economic Planning*, in 1938, became active both as a university professor and as a leader of official economic long-range investigations in Stockholm. In 1959–60 he served as Irving Fisher professor at Yale.

Sune Carlson (b. 1909) won his doctor's degree at the University of Chicago in 1936, with a thesis that has become part of the international standard literature on the theory of production. After a period as professor at the Stockholm School of Economics and some years with the United Nations in New York, he joined the faculty at Uppsala in 1958. Harald Dickson (b. 1912), professor at Gothenburg from 1955, wrote his doctor's thesis about the housing market in the United States and Sweden, which he began to develop at the University of Wisconsin. Folke Kristensson (b. 1914) studied in America in 1936–37, became professor at the Stockholm School of Economics in 1949, and was a visiting professor at the University of California in 1954 and 1961. Hugo Hegeland (b. 1921), who has served as professor at Gothenburg, Lund, Uppsala, and Umeå in the far north, studied for two years in America, mainly at Duke University in Durham, North Carolina.

Assar Lindbeck (b. 1930), who in 1971, after several years as professor at the Stockholm School of Economics, was named head of the Institute for International Economic Studies at Stockholm University, conducted research in the United States in the late 1950s. He was invited to the University of Michigan as a visiting professor in 1958, to Columbia University in 1968–69, and to the University of California in 1969. Dr. Lindbeck is regarded as a supporter of the Social Democratic party in Sweden but has often expressed his faith in a decentralized market economy. A paperback entitled *The Political Economy of the New Left*, largely based on lectures given by Dr. Lindbeck in America in 1969, was published in New York in 1971. One of its objectives was to facilitate a dialogue between the New Left and academic economists. Staffan Burenstam Linder (b. 1931), a member of the Stockholm School of Economics faculty since 1961, was visiting professor at Columbia University in 1962–63 and at Yale in 1966. Columbia University Press has published his book *The Harried Leisure Class*. Dr. Linder is one of the leaders of the Moderate party in Sweden.

Economists who have been employed by the Swedish trade-union movement include Rudolf Meidner (b. 1914), who in the early 1950s wrote a dissertation about the Swedish labor market under full employment, and Gösta Rehn (b. 1913), who later for many years served as director for manpower and social affairs in the Organization for Economic Cooperation and Development in Paris. Dr. Ernst Wigforss, a Social Democrat who served as minister of finance in several governments, retiring in 1949, became an exceedingly well-read economist, although he had started his academic career as a linguist.

The leading American economists have, as a rule, become even better known in Sweden than their Swedish colleagues are in the United States. They do not visit Sweden as lecturers on anything like the same scale, but their books are, on the other hand, widely read by graduate students, and several of them have been used as textbooks. A celebrated series of lectures in Stockholm which honors Knut Wicksell has been dominated by American scholars, such as Robert Triffin, Paul A. Samuelson, Robert M. Solow, and Richard N. Cooper. American economists who have studied in Sweden include Leonard Silk, who became a noted economic journalist. A popular version of his doctor's thesis of 1948, published by Duke University Press, is entitled *Sweden Plans for Better Housing*.

In 1968 the then 300-year-old Bank of Sweden instituted an Alfred Nobel memorial prize in economic science, to be awarded annually, like two of the prizes established by Nobel, by the Swedish Academy of Sciences. Dr. Bertil Ohlin became the first chairman of the Academy of Sciences committee for the economics award. Among the nine laureates of the first six years were three economists of Harvard University and one member of the faculty of the Massachusetts Institute of Technology.

The many American-Swedish ties in the field of economics are by no means unique. Similar contacts and exchanges have been developed in many other spheres of science, such as the various branches of medicine, biochemistry, physics, astronomy, genetics, sociology, and archeology. In the field of technology the relations have also been very close.

37

Swedish Artists in America

Carl Milles moves to Detroit area — His sculptures are spread over America and Sweden

CARL MILLES (1875–1955) was one of the first mature European artists to settle in the United States, which he did in 1931, and become an American citizen. He was already regarded as the most creative and imaginative sculptor of his era, and the vitality of American life stimulated him to new efforts. His physique was delicate, and at times his eyesight seemed threatened. Altogether he finished more than 100 monuments and fountains, several consisting of ten or more large figures, and nearly all of them are in the United States and Sweden. His American base was the Cranbrook Academy of Art at Bloomfield Hills near Detroit, which has many of his sculptures.

His productions were strongly rooted in life, and he derived inspiration from many sources — the body and soul of man, the animal kingdom, the beauty and power of nature, folklore, mythology, and history. Much of what he did looks magnificently robust, but he was also capable of subtlety and tenderness. A sense of humor was another leading characteristic. Since childhood he had been inclined to mysticism, and several of his works reflect a belief that everything that lives is immortal.

Milles's sculpture was, as a rule, designed to be viewed against sun and sky or together with rushing, rippling, or spraying water. Fountains playing with water became, in fact, his foremost specialty, and he has been called the greatest designer in this field since Bernini in the 17th century, from whom he drew inspiration. More tritons, mermaids, dolphins, and fishes were created by Milles than by any other sculptor.

In 1927 two American architects saw Milles's Diana Fountain in the courtyard of an office building in Stockholm, a copy was ordered for the Michigan Square Building in Chicago, and in 1929 the sculptor came to the United States for the first time. In 1931–32 a large exhibit was shown in several cities. The first work conceived and executed in the new studio at Cranbrook was the Jonah Fountain, showing the famous biblical character as he is being ejected from the mouth of the whale. In 1936 a towering statue of an Indian, holding the symbolic pipe of peace, was unveiled in the City Hall of St. Paul, Minnesota. It is made of Mexican onyx. In the same year, at 6 o'clock on a summer morning, one of the sculptor's most widely known creations, the Orpheus Fountain, on which he had started work before coming to the United States, was unveiled outside the Concert House in Stockholm. Richly illustrated reports were published in the American press.

In 1938, Milles's New Sweden Monument, crowned by the ship *Kalmar Nyckel* under full sail and made of Swedish black granite, was dedicated at Wilmington, Delaware, near the rocks where the first Swedish colonists stepped ashore in 1638. At Harrisburg, Pennsylvania, six bronze doors, each consisting of two wings and all designed by Milles, were installed in the State Finance Building. On three of the doors the artist had depicted man's struggle with nature and the agricultural interests of the Keystone State, while the other three were devoted to its industrial activities. This little-known work, completed in less than a year, was described by an American art critic as "stupendous," and "convincing of the sculptor's poetic understanding of the fundamental spirit of America."

Much of the sculpture displayed at the New York World's Fair in 1939 showed influences from Carl Milles. The master himself was represented by a large statue called *The Astronomer*, by a group of three figures including one representing a Pony Express rider, and, in the courtyard of the Swedish pavilion, by the striking equestrian statue of Folke Filbyter, a replica of the original which crowns the fountain in the central square at Linköping, capital of the province of

Östergötland. Another replica is in the St. Louis Art Museum. The statue was inspired by a medieval legend about Folke Filbyter, a mythical member of the powerful Folkung family, who traveled on horseback all over Sweden, seeking his only grandson who had been carried away by monks. A model for *The Astronomer* is in the Philadelphia Museum of Art.

The first monumental fountain Carl Milles designed for America plays since 1940 in Aloe Plaza in St. Louis, Missouri. Officially known as the *Meeting of the Waters* but often called the *Wedding of the Rivers*, it celebrates the confluence of the Mississippi and the Missouri. The former, a 12-foot male figure escorted by four rowdy tritons, rides on the back of a dolphin to meet his bride, who is attended by four sea nymphs. There are nine other water sprites, and the bronzes are enveloped in clouds of spray. Objections were heard when the design was published — some people said it looked like a "wedding in a nudist colony" — but they seem to have melted away when the fountain was dedicated. The *St. Louis Post Dispatch* called it "an oasis of green and silver, a group of statuary that radiates gaiety and humor," and an art expert in Chicago hailed it as "one of the masterworks of modern times." Reports of the sculptor's brief address at the dedication vary somewhat, but he seems to have admonished the tritons and naiads in the pool to enjoy life but behave well at the same time: "Remember that at every sunrise you have to be here."

In 1952 Carl Milles finished another work of heroic dimensions, the Fountain of Faith in the National Memorial Park, a private cemetery at Falls Church, Virginia, near Washington, D.C. In 28 figures he portrayed the joyful reunions after death of people he had known, in America, France, and Sweden. All were cast in bronze in an art foundry in Stockholm, then coated with a soft green and placed in the fountain pool of green granite. About 12,000 people attended the dedication in the fall of 1952.

Early in 1955, eight months before he passed away in Stockholm, Carl Milles completed the final figure in his work, *St. Martin of Tours*, and three years after his death this group, known as the William Volker Memorial Fountain, was dedicated in the new Cultural Center at Kansas City, Missouri. Its central figure, Bishop St. Martin of Tours, is represented in the episode for which he is best known, sharing his cloak with a beggar. A horse scratches his head in bewilderment over this good deed, his hind legs folded about him in comic abandon.

In the United States there are many other works by Milles. In 1941 a group of three mural sculptures in wood, called *Man and Nature*, was unveiled in the lobby of the Time and Life Building in New York's Rockefeller Center. The central figure is a hunter on horseback pausing in a forest to listen to the song of a bird. One of the sculptor's last fountains, *The Arts*, is in the court of the restaurant of the Metropolitan Museum of Art, which also owns a head of Orpheus. Ever since 1931 the Art Institute of Chicago has had the Fountain of Tritons. It also has the Small Triton Fountain and a sculpture called *Angel*.

In the courtyard of the Art Center at Des Moines, Iowa, man's fantasy flies through space with Pegasus, the winged horse, as it does in a park at Malmö in south Sweden. At Allerton Park, belonging to the University of Illinois and situated between Decatur and Champaign, the *Sun Singer*, which also graces the Stockholm waterfront near the Royal Palace, lifts his eyes and arms to the skies from a prairie knoll. The Detroit Institute of Arts displays, in reduced size, both the Folke Filbyter statue and a fountain called *Europa and the Bull*, which Milles designed for the central square in Halmstad in southwestern Sweden, and it also owns a small fountain known as *Sunglitter*. Ann Arbor, Michigan, has a fountain called *Sunday Morning in Deep Water*.

For the Art Museum of Worcester, Massachusetts, Milles designed a small fountain in silver pewter, a column decorated with small fishes and topped by a large fish from the mouth of which the water spouts. In Fairmount Park in Philadelphia, three bronze angels, which were copied from the originals at Stockholm, float since 1972 atop high columns. The Virginia Museum of Fine Arts at Richmond features in front of its building Milles's Small Triton Fountain, showing a triton seated on waves and holding a conch shell to his lips. Since 1951, a fountain called the *Tree of Paradise* has been at the Museum of Fine Arts in Houston, Texas.

Carl Milles was born on a small country estate near Uppsala. His father, a Swedish army officer, had served in the French army during the Franco-German War, and his mother was of mixed French and Swedish ancestry. After elementary school and some technical training in Stockholm young Milles left in 1897 for Chile, to join a friend of his father's who was conducting a school of Swedish gymnastics. However, he stopped over in Paris, and remained there for seven years. After continued studies in Munich, Germany, and in Italy, he settled in 1908 at Lidingö, a city on an island in Stockholm's immediate vicinity, and during the next 20-odd years he produced, with an almost unbelievable creative energy, a long row of sculptures and monumental fountains. Among his first important commissions were a monument to Sten Sture, a Swedish national hero of the 1400s, which was placed near Uppsala, and a colossal wood statue of Gustavus Vasa, "Builder of the Swedish Realm" in the early 1500s, which is in the Nordic Museum in Stockholm.

In 1920 Carl Milles was named to a professorship at the Academy of Art in the Swedish capital. In his decision to move to the United States in the early 1930s he may have been influenced by Eliel Saarinen, the eminent Finnish architect, who had joined the Cranbrook Foundation in 1925. After the Second World War, and especially in the early 1950s, Milles spent much of his time in Sweden and in Rome, where the American Academy placed a studio at his disposal.

Millesgården, Milles's home and studio at Lidingö, was given by the artist to the Swedish nation and has become one of the most treasured attractions in the Stockholm area. It overlooks an inlet from the Baltic Sea and is a little world of its own, with beautiful buildings, quaint walls broken by niches, pergolas, tiled walks and flagged steps, ponds, terraces, two shrines built for Austrian-born Olga Milles, and lots of sculptures, numerous works by Milles himself as well as his collections of antiques. In one of the gates at the entrance, these words are inscribed in wrought iron: "Låt mig verka medan dagen brinner," that is, "Let me give my best while the day is glowing."

Jussi Björling, Kerstin Thorborg, and other Swedes on American operatic stages

NO OPERATIC tenor since Caruso has been acclaimed with warmer enthusiasm on both sides of the Atlantic than Jussi Björling or Bjoerling (1911–60). His first adult performance in the United States took place on November 28, 1937, when he was soloist on a nationwide radio broadcast that originated in Carnegie Hall in New York. In December he sang at the Chicago Opera, and early in January he gave a recital of his own in New York, which was followed by concerts all over the country. At the Metropolitan Opera he made his debut on Thanksgiving Day, November 24, 1938, as Rodolfo in Puccini's *La Bohème*. He was then 27 years old, the youngest artist ever to receive a guest contract to sing principal roles at the Metropolitan Opera. During the following two seasons he was heard in Verdi's *Il Trovatore*, *Rigoletto*, and *Un Ballo in Maschera*, and in Gounod's *Faust*. He specialized in Italian and French repertories.

After America's entry into the war Björling remained in Sweden, singing at the Stockholm Opera where he had begun his operatic career in 1930. The Hitler regime refused to grant him permission to cross Germany on his way to New York. In 1945 he returned to the Metropolitan, and save for several gaps in the late 1950s, he sang there until his death. He also appeared with the Chicago, San Francisco, and San Antonio operas. His concert tours took him to scores of American cities, and he was very active in the recording studios, leaving behind him over 300 discs including complete recordings of many operas. At one time or another, music critics on both sides of the ocean characterized his art as "vocal velvet," or as a voice of great natural beauty coupled with rare refinement and taste. After a recital in Carnegie Hall in New York on March 4, 1958, a *New York Times* critic wrote: "One could not help reflecting that it will be something to tell our grandchildren that we heard Björling at the height of his powers." The *New York Herald Tribune* called him "the world's greatest tenor."

Jussi Björling was born at Stora Tuna in the province of Dalarna, which has been called the "Heart of Sweden." His father, who at the turn of the century had been "discovered" as a singer in New York and studied at the Metropolitan Opera school, organized at the end of the First World War himself and three of his four sons, including eight-year-old Jussi, into the Björling Quartet, and in 1919–21 this group toured the United States, singing in folk costumes for Swedish and other Scandinavian churches and community gatherings.

In the 1930s Jussi Björling became the leading tenor at the Stockholm Opera, and guest appearances in Vienna, Prague, Dresden, Salzburg, Paris, and London helped build up his international reputation. His first recital in Copenhagen's Tivoli became a booming success, and after that his fame in Denmark was matched only by his popularity in Sweden. At practically every concert in his native country he sang a patriotic ballad, "Land, du välsignade" (Thou blessed land), which remained closely associated with him in the hearts of the Swedish people. He died at his summer home in the Stockholm archipelago.

On the distaff side Sweden was throughout the 1930s well represented at the Metropolitan Opera, first of all by Karin Branzell who had arrived in 1924 and withdrew in 1944. Julia Claussen, who had joined the Chicago Opera in 1913 and the Met in 1917, left in 1932 on a European tour. On January 25, 1931, Göta Ljungberg (1893–1955) made a sensational debut at the Metropolitan as Sieglinde in Wagner's *Die Walküre*. Among her best parts were also the title roles in Strauss's *Salome* and Puccini's *La Tosca*. After leaving the Metropolitan in 1935 she sang with other American opera companies. Another star from the Stockholm Opera, Gertrud Pålson-Wettergren (b. 1897), made her debut at the Metropolitan on December 26, 1935, as Amneris in Verdi's *Aïda*, and early the next year she sang, at short notice, Carmen in the Swedish language. She also came to the Metropolitan in 1938. Before appearing in New York she had been a member of the Chicago Opera Company.

Kerstin Thorborg (1896–1970), who after appearances at Covent Garden in London had been called "the greatest Wagnerian actress of the present day," made her debut at the Metropolitan on December 21, 1936, as Fricka in *Die Walküre*. In 1938, when Austria's incorporation into Hitler's Germany made her leave the Vienna State Opera, she became a regular member of the New York company, where she remained until 1950. Her repertory included Verdi and Strauss operas. She gave many performances on other operatic stages in America, as well as concerts throughout the country. After having appeared in 1950 at the Stockholm Opera, where her career had begun, she retired to the town of Hedemora in Dalarna, her native province.

Shortly after the Second World War, not only Jussi Björling and Kerstin Thorborg but also several other Swedish opera singers appeared at the Metropolitan. On December 4, 1945, Torsten Ralf (1901–54), a lyric-dramatic tenor from the Stockholm Opera with a well-established European reputation, made his debut in the title role of Wagner's *Lohengrin*. On January 9, 1946, Joel Berglund (b. 1903), the leading baritone of the Stockholm Opera, sang Hans Sachs in Wagner's *Die Meistersinger*. He remained until 1949, when he was named director of the Royal Opera in Stockholm. On November 16, 1946, came a celebrated tenor, Set Svanholm (1904–64), as Siegfried in Wagner's opera by that name, and during the following ten years he appeared in many other Wagner roles, as well as in *Aïda* and other operas. From 1956 to 1963 he served as director of the Stockholm Opera. On February 15, 1947, Hjördis Schymberg (b. 1909), leading soprano from Stockholm, was heard at the Metropolitan for the first time, as Suzanna in Mozart's *Le Nozze di Figaro*. An impressive basso from the Stockholm Opera, Sven Nilsson (1898–1970), who had established his international reputation at Dresden in Germany, appeared at the Metropolitan in 1950–51. He was followed in 1952–53 by a baritone with a wide international experience, Sigurd Björling (b. 1907), who had made his debut at the Stockholm Opera in 1936 and in 1950 had been associated with the San Francisco Opera. Several of the Swedish stars at the Metropolitan took part in the company's tours of the country.

A tenor who was born in Wisconsin of Swedish parents, Eyvind Laholm, sang in 1939–40 at the Metropolitan. He had won his reputation on stages in Germany and had also, in 1934, appeared at the Stockholm Opera. His name was originally John Edwin Johnson. Even more widely known as a tenor was Gustav Harald Lindau or Aroldo Lindi (1889–1944) from Tuna in the northeast of Småland, who had come to America at the age of 14. A patron of the arts who heard him at Swedish concerts in Boston sent him to Italy for voice studies, and in 1923, as Aroldo Lindi, he made his debut at La Scala in Milan under Toscanini. Covent Garden and many other opera houses in Europe, including Stockholm, followed. Lindi then joined first the operas in Chicago and Philadelphia, and finally the touring San Carlo Grand Opera Company. At times he was acclaimed as "a second Caruso." He died during a performance of Leoncavallo's *I Pagliacci* in San Francisco.

A Swedish-born soprano of Hungarian parentage, Astrid Varnay, was in 1941–53 a member of the Metropolitan Opera Company where she held a leading position among the Wagner specialists, and she returned in 1956 and 1974. Blanche Thebom, who was born near Pittsburgh of parents from Sandviken in Sweden, made a triumphant debut on December 14, 1944, as Fricka in Wagner's *Die Walküre*, and became one of the most versatile stars at the Metropolitan. There and on tours she sang Amneris in *Aïda* more than 80 times. In 1950 she appeared at the Stockholm Opera and visited Sandviken, the steel center in the province of Gästrikland, which her parents had left in 1894. At the railroad station, where large crowds had gathered, the mayor welcomed her with a speech and flowers. A concert by Miss Thebom in the evening became a tremendous success. At a subsequent party the managing director of the Sandvik steel company presented her with a family chronicle which showed that her ancestors since about 1500 had lived on a farm named Vika in the same part of Sweden.

Ingrid Bergman, a newcomer of 1939, and other actresses and actors from Sweden

IN 1939 a new film star from Sweden appeared on the American horizon in the form of Ingrid Bergman, who soon sparkled with distinctive brilliance and turned her light also upon the stage. Her debut was made in a Hollywood version of the Swedish film *Intermezzo*, in which she played the leading female part. Other roles, including that of Maria in *For Whom the Bell Tolls*, followed in rapid succession, and in 1944 Miss Bergman won her first Academy Award, or Oscar, for her performance in *Gaslight*. Her first stage success came in 1940 in Ferenc Molnar's *Liliom*, which was presented in New York. In 1941 she played the title role in Eugene O'Neill's *Anna Christie*, first at Santa Barbara, California, then in San Francisco, and finally at the summer stock theater in Maplewood, New Jersey. In 1946 she again played on Broadway, in Maxwell Anderson's *Joan of Lorraine*, which ran for 11 months. She was voted America's number one box-office attraction. Among her many awards was one from the Teachers Diction Society which honored her for having the best diction of any actress on stage and screen.

In 1949 Miss Bergman left Hollywood and turned to acting in Italy and elsewhere in Europe. She came back in 1957 to pick up the New York Film Critics Award for her performance in *Anastasia*, an American-produced film which also won her a second Oscar. While her career had become decidedly international, more films were made in Hollywood. After 21 years she returned to the American stage in 1967 in Eugene O'Neill's *More Stately Mansions*, which in 1962 had had its world premiere in Stockholm in the Swedish language and now was produced in the United States for the first time. It opened at the new Los Angeles performing-arts center, in the 2,100-seat Ahmanson Theater which was named for the son of a Swedish immigrant, and then moved to New York. The reviews were mixed.

In 1972, when Ingrid Bergman lived in France, Senator Charles H. Percy of Illinois read into the *Congressional Record* an apology for a "bitter attack" that had been made on her in the Senate in 1950 because of her romance in Italy with the film director Roberto Rossellini, who became her second husband. Senator Percy described the actress as "one of the world's loveliest, most gracious and most talented women" and "a true star in every sense of the word," adding that he knew that across the land millions of Americans would wish to join him in his tribute. In the same year, 1972, Miss Bergman was invited to address the National Press Club in Washington, where she drew a record attendance.

Ingrid Bergman, who was born in Stockholm in 1915, lost her German-born mother at the age of two and her father when she was 12. Her father, a photographer and portrait painter, had in 1927, shortly before his death, toured the United States as a member of a Swedish singing society. In 1933–34 Ingrid Bergman studied at the school of the Royal Dramatic Theater in Stockholm, interrupting her training after having been offered a contract with Sweden's leading film producer.

Two Swedish actresses who were graduates of the Dramatic Theater School in Stockholm and had considerable experience back of them, both on the stage and the screen, came to America during or shortly after the Second World War. Signe Hasso (b. 1915), who arrived in 1940, spent the first ten years in Hollywood and then settled in New York. She has appeared in numerous motion pictures, stage plays, and radio and TV programs. Several guest performances in Sweden gave evidence of her popularity in her native country. Viveca Lindfors (b. 1920), who came in 1946, also began her American career in Hollywood and immediately starred in a number of films. In the 1950s she became active on the stage, and her performance in the title role of the Broadway production of *Anastasia* won her the Drama League award. She was one of the founders of the

Berkshire Theater Festival at Stockbridge, Massachusetts, and in 1966–69, as head of a professional company called the Strolling Players, she brought creative theater to college and high-school audiences all over the country. Her keen interest in August Strindberg has been reflected in several productions.

People of Swedish birth or parentage have contributed artistry and fine workmanship to the American film industry almost from its beginning, not only as actors and actresses, but also as cameramen, engineers, designers, architects, and writers. The first significant actress was Anna Q. Nilsson from Ystad on Sweden's south coast, who began her screen career in 1911. Another immigrant, Johan Verner Ölund or Warner Oland, began making movies a few years later but did not become widely known until the 1930s, when he created Charlie Chan, a Chinese detective. He did this so well that when traveling in China or Japan he was mobbed by admiring fans. Oland died during a visit to Sweden in 1938 and was buried at his native Burholm near the city of Umeå in the north.

In the 1920s Hollywood was literally invaded by Swedish stars and directors, and among those who remained in the United States was, of course, Greta Garbo. After the middle of the century there were not so many new immigrants in the American film world, but several actors and actresses from Sweden worked for some time in the United States. Among them were Max von Sydow (b. 1929), Bibi Andersson (b. 1935), and Ingrid Thulin (b. 1929), all of whom had been introduced to American audiences in films directed by Ingmar Bergman. After her Broadway debut in 1973, Bibi Andersson was hailed as "a superlative actress." Norwegian-born Liv Ullmann (b. 1939), who came to Hollywood in 1972 and was received in the American press as a full-fledged star, had scored her first great successes as a screen actress under Bergman's auspices.

American screen actors and actresses of Swedish parentage, or with one Swedish parent, include Gloria Swanson, who was born in Chicago, Susan Hayward, who came from Brooklyn, Myrna Loy, whose mother hailed from Sweden, Richard Widmark, who was born in Minnesota, and Jean Rogers, once called "the most beautiful natural blonde in California," whose father had come from Malmö and mother from nearby Lund in southern Sweden. Her name was originally Elinor Lovgren (b. 1916). Many other performing artists of

Swedish origin have also adopted Anglo-Saxon stage names. For instance, Ragnar Gottfrid Lind, born near Worcester, Massachusetts, became in the late 1930s Hollywood's Jeffrey Lynn. Peggy Lee, the famous singer and actress, whom Duke Ellington, "King of Jazz," called "The Queen," began her colorful career as Norma Jean Engstrom. She was born in North Dakota. In 1970 she was invited to sing in the White House at a state dinner for President and Mrs. Pompidou of France. In the late 1950s and the 1960s, two movie actresses who were born in Sweden, May Britt Wilkens and Ann-Margret Olson, became known under their given names.

For many years the leading name of Swedish origin in American radio was that of Edgar Bergen, born in 1903 in Chicago as John Edgar Berggren, of parents from the city of Hässleholm in the south of Sweden. Ventriloquism, it has often been said, was elevated by him from vaudeville to fine art. His famous dummy Charlie McCarthy's original name was "Kalle," the Swedish diminutive of Karl or Charles. A tough Irish newsboy, as well as Tom Sawyer and Huckleberry Finn, have been mentioned as models. In many radio or TV programs, Charlie McCarthy teased Bergen about his Swedish origin. Once, for instance, they were together visiting Elsinore in Denmark, the scene of Shakespeare's *Hamlet* and separated from southern Sweden only by a narrow sound. Almost inevitably, Edgar Bergen quoted the Bard: I think "something is rotten in the state of Denmark," and Charlie was heard squeaking: "But Bergen, it's blowing over from Sweden!" When Charlie seemed to become overimpressed with his own importance, however, Bergen deflated him by asking, "What would you be without me?" and Charlie knew the answer: "Speechless." Edgar Bergen has taken an active interest in cultural relations between the United States and Sweden. His daughter Candice became a noted screen actress.

38

The Second World War

*Sweden "a fortress within a fortress" in World War II,
also a source of relief*

IN THE LATE fall of 1939, a few months after the outbreak of the
Second World War, Finland was attacked by Soviet forces. In the
spring of 1940 Denmark and Norway were invaded by the Germans.
In the summer of 1941 Finland again became involved in war with the
Soviet Union, this time on the side of Germany. Alone among the
Nordic countries Sweden was able to preserve its peace throughout
the armed struggle.

One of the main reasons was probably Sweden's geographic position: with the war events taking the course they did, its territory did
not assume the same strategic importance as the adjoining areas. The
fact that an occupied and ravaged Sweden would have been of little
value to Germany as a trade partner was also important. If, moreover,
the Germans had also attacked Sweden in the spring of 1940, their
relations with the Soviet Union, still officially friendly, would probably have suffered. On some occasions Sweden's determined rearmament and a high state of mobilization may have helped save the country from the fury of a blitz attack. A defensive force was always vital to
Sweden's foreign policy, which fundamentally aimed at Sweden's survival as a free country.

After the Russian assault on Finland in the fall of 1939, a national
coalition government was formed in Sweden with the Social Demo-

cratic leader, Per Albin Hansson (1885–1946), as prime minister and a career diplomat, Christian Günther (1886–1966), as minister for foreign affairs. At that time national unity was actually subject to great strains, for many Swedes were in favor of armed aid to Finland in its lone struggle with the Soviet Union. Finnish requests for regular troops were refused but large quantities of military equipment and other supplies, including 300 pieces of artillery, were sent. A Swedish volunteer corps reached the front just before the peace was signed in Moscow on March 12, 1940, after three and a half months of fighting.

When the war in Finland began, the Swedish authorities hoped to be able to make extensive purchases of military equipment abroad, and after some time these hopes centered on the United States. In early 1940 a Swedish trade delegation headed by Prince Bertil spent nearly two months in Washington and New York, and the discussions concerned both immediate deliveries of defense materiel and successive shipments of, in particular, airplanes, motor torpedo boats, and artillery. Knowing that naval leaders in Sweden were anxious to obtain at least one armored cruiser, Prince Bertil mentioned this to President Franklin D. Roosevelt, and his reaction, according to Gunnar Hägglöf (b. 1904), a former cabinet minister who was a member of the Swedish delegation, was more favorable than expected. After having studied various naval units that might be suitable for Sweden and the Baltic Sea, the President suggested the cruiser *Pensacola*. Secretary of State Cordell Hull seemed to think that Sweden ought to have this ship, and two influential members of the Senate Foreign Relations Committee were inclined to agree, but later the project ran into stiff opposition. The delegates from Sweden returned home without the *Pensacola*, and they were actually not sorry. Fundamentally, the transaction had always seemed unrealistic even from a Swedish defense viewpoint.

On April 9, 1940, less than a month after the end of the so-called Winter War in Finland, Denmark and Norway were invaded by the Germans, and the Swedes, who militarily were not at all prepared for a threat from the south, tried to brace themselves for a possible onslaught. The number of men under arms was immediately increased from about 90,000 to 375,000. Repeated demands from Berlin for the transit of war materials to the German forces in northern

Norway were rejected by the government, and the highest state of combat readiness was imposed along Sweden's western and southern borders. The morale among the troops was good, but training and equipment left much to be desired. Vital military supplies had been seriously depleted by the shipments to Finland. Political as well as military leaders were praying that Sweden would be given a chance to gain time for all-out rearmament.

The fact that the situation of the German units in the north of Norway never became hopeless may have helped save Sweden from a German assault in the spring of 1940. Early in June the last Allied troops, as well as the Norwegian government, left Norway. Paris fell a week later, and France asked for an armistice. Stockholm naturally also followed with the utmost attention developments on the other side of the Baltic Sea, where by the middle of June the Russians invaded Lithuania, Latvia, and Estonia. Finland was again subjected to Soviet pressure.

At one swoop Sweden had been cut off from the West. Three-fourths of its normal foreign trade had been lost, and for its economic survival as well as for its rearmament the country had become dependent on commercial relations with Germany. Some kind of modus vivendi had, therefore, to be worked out with Berlin, and after difficult negotiations, during which the first demands were whittled down considerably, Sweden agreed to let unarmed German soldiers on leave travel via certain Swedish railway routes to or from Norway. The transit of war materials was also permitted. These concessions caused bitterness and indignation in Sweden, but they were not by any means regarded as even the beginning of surrender. The determination to resist a German aggression was not affected, and the ability to offer such resistance improved as the months went by.

In the United States, Sweden's policies during the Second World War were better understood than those of 1914–18, but the transit-traffic concessions of 1940 gave many people the impression that the Germans had, for all practical purposes, gained control of the Swedish railroad system, and that German soldiers perhaps soon would be able to move freely in Sweden. When voiced in public, such misconceptions were, however, not left uncontested. Some American newspaper correspondents in Europe emphasized that the transiting German troops were, in fact, unarmed soldiers on leave, and that they traveled under the control of Swedish military, who did not let more soldiers go into Norway than went out. On some occasions, however, the transit traffic was abused by the Germans for the transfer of new troops. A special Swedish concession in June of 1941, after Germany's assault on the Soviet Union, resulted in the passage of one German division from Norway to Finland, which officially supported this action. A subsequent German request to send one division from Germany via Sweden to Finland was, on the other hand, immediately rejected by the Swedish government. Berlin then became extremely critical of Sweden's attitude toward the war in Russia.

Sweden's extraordinary position was sometimes described by American writers as that of "a fortress within a fortress." In early 1941 the Swedish nation was encouraged in its isolation by the arrival of the first so-called safe-conduct ship from the West, the beginning of a traffic which required repeated permissions from both the belligerent parties and was interrupted several times, but which in four critical years brought Sweden a substantial quantity of vital supplies, including oil, from the other side of the Atlantic. In the fall of 1943 the Germans halted the traffic after having found out that speedy British motorboats were carrying ball bearings and similar products from a Swedish port through the German blockade to Britain. Following an established route, the Swedish safe-conduct ships traveled across the ocean fully lighted from stem to stern, the blue-and-yellow colors painted on their sides and decks. The Germans, in particular, naturally insisted that balance be maintained between outgoing and incoming tonnage. A large part of the Swedish merchant marine, totaling 600,000 gross tons, had been cut off from Sweden by the German blockade and served the British and Allied war effort.

One of the largest Swedish mobilizations of the Second World War was ordered by the government early in 1942, when the Russians had launched their first offensives against the invading Germans and Hitler seemed to fear a British attack in northern Norway, in which, he thought, Sweden would take part or at least become involved. The equipment and deployment of the military units functioned smoothly, despite an unusually severe winter, and Swedish self-confidence was bolstered. One year later Sweden was, of course, even better prepared, and the government began to chart a more rigorous course in its relations with Germany. In late summer of 1943 about

300,000 men were under the colors, and the transit concessions were finally canceled. The Germans, whose military difficulties had increased steadily, did not seem particularly surprised.

Sweden's decision in 1943 did not mark a return to strict neutrality. The Allies began, in fact, to demand some kind of "non-belligerency" in their favor, and the great majority of the Swedish people seemed ready to support all reasonable assistance that could be offered without dramatic gestures. At one time the United States wanted Sweden to break off its diplomatic relations with Germany, but this subject was dropped. Swedish trade with Germany was, on the other hand, gradually reduced until it finally, at the end of 1944, came to a complete standstill, except for a few relief shipments.

From the beginning, Sweden's wartime commercial exchanges with Germany had been maintained on a strict barter basis, Swedish iron ore being directly balanced against German coal as to both price and quantities. The iron ore remained valuable to the Germans even after they had secured the Lorraine and Luxembourg ore fields. Sweden, in turn, could hardly operate without coal and coke, and Germany was the only source of supply. At the end of the war there were no outstanding Swedish credits — Sweden, in fact, ended the war in a unique position among those trading with the Nazis, owing them money — and at no time were either arms or ammunition shipped to Germany. Sweden was, on the other hand, able to buy weapons, and German steel products and machinery were imported on a large scale.

On April 15, 1945, when the war in Europe was near its end, Prime Minister Winston Churchill wrote to his secretary of state for foreign affairs: "Few questions are more important than bringing the Swedes into the war to liberate their Norwegian brother State. In this way Sweden would assume an honourable position among the Allies, her previous neutrality having a strong foundation in the great danger she ran until quite recently from the German power." British military leaders, however, remained skeptical, and the Swedish government and Riksdag took an entirely different attitude, fearing that even the threat of a Swedish intervention in Norway would make an orderly liquidation of the German occupation more difficult. And the Swedes saw no honor in a last-minute leap into the war.

As one of the few neutrals, Sweden was able to offer humanitarian and other constructive assistance. In the fall of 1943, when a Nazi plan to deport Denmark's Jewish population had been leaked to Danish leaders by a German consular official in Copenhagen, the Danish underground and Danish fishermen smuggled nearly 8,000 fellow countrymen of the Jewish faith across the sound separating Denmark and Sweden, a distance of 2.5 to 17 miles. In the fall of 1944 shipments of vital supplies helped the Finns free themselves from the German grip and obtain a new armistice with the Soviet Union. In the north of Finland retreating German troops laid the towns and villages waste, and 55,000 men, women, and children, with horses and cattle, fled across the border to Sweden. At about the same time 30,000 refugees arrived from the Baltic countries, where the German occupation had been succeeded by a second Russian occupation. About 7,000 Estonian Swedes, or practically this whole ethnic group, had already settled in Sweden. In early 1945, during the last months of German resistance, the Swedish Red Cross under the leadership of Count Folke Bernadotte sent convoys of ambulances to the various German concentration camps, and some 20,000 inmates, about half of them Danes and Norwegians, were brought safely to Sweden. Another 10,000 former inmates, all seriously ill, came somewhat later.

During the war about 1,000 Americans of the U.S. Air Force made forced landings in Sweden, where they received the welcome and care of a friendly nation. Most of them were able to return to their bases in Britain before the war was over. Some of the fallen Flying Fortresses were made available to Sweden for remodeling and use as transport planes. They were then employed for test flights across the Atlantic to New York, which enabled Scandinavian Airlines to introduce commercial service in the fall of 1946.

In the spring of 1945, when the war seemed near its end, the United States began delivery of 50 fighter planes to the Swedish Air Force, which had been expanded and improved many times over since the war started. Almost all of its some 800 first-line planes, as well as engines and armaments, had been made in Sweden, but at least as far as many of the engines were concerned, indirect American assistance had been important. Sweden's aircraft-engine specialist, Flygmotor of Trollhättan, had, in fact, copied Pratt & Whitney's Twin Wasp engine, and since this had been done without access to blueprints or production data from the company at East Hartford, Connecticut, it was regarded there as "an uncommon display of engineering virtuosity." Visiting the United States in the fall of 1945, a Swedish Air Force delegation headed by General Bengt Nordenskiöld (b. 1891) offered to pay royalties on the engines, which also came as a surprise to the American company. In 1952 the U.S. Air Force Chief of Staff, General Hoyt S. Vandenberg, visited Sweden, and upon his return he said in a press conference in Washington that he was impressed by "the excellence of the Swedish Air Force."

In the summer of 1946, after a unanimous decision by the Riksdag, Sweden applied for membership in the United Nations. In the Security Council, Sweden was unanimously recommended for membership, after warm words by many delegates, including Herschel V. Johnson of the United States, who in 1941–46 had served his country as chief of its diplomatic mission in Stockholm. On November 9, the General Assembly unanimously elected Sweden a member, and a week later Foreign Minister Östen Undén (1886–1974) signed the instruments of adherence in New York. Responding to welcoming remarks by the President of the Assembly, he said in part: "Because of the temperament of its people, its historical experience and geographical situation, Sweden is inclined to be tolerant in its judgments and disposed to see what is justifiable in mutually opposed points of view, no matter how sharply conflicting these may seem to be." The Swedish people, he added, would not find it hard to obey the simple but important U.N. principle "to practice tolerance and live together with one another as good neighbors."

Sweden's national coalition government had been dissolved in the summer of 1945, a few months after the end of the war in Europe, and a Social Democratic ministry had been formed under the leadership of Per Albin Hansson, who, except for a few months in 1936, had been prime minister since 1932. He was the son of a bricklayer at Malmö in the south. In the fall of 1946 Mr. Hansson died from a heart attack, and the minister of education, 45-year-old Tage Erlander, became his successor.

Americans from Sweden in World War II — Swedes in the industrial war effort

THE American military records of the Second World War contain a large number of Swedish names, most of the best-known ones being those of sons of immigrants.

General John H. Hilldring (b. 1895) of the U.S. Army, who was born of Swedish parents in New Rochelle, New York, served in 1941–42 for six months as assistant chief of staff in charge of personnel and was then, as major general, in command of the 84th Infantry Division. Before his retirement in 1946 he served first in the War Department in Washington and finally as an assistant secretary of state in charge of occupation affairs. His parents had come to America in the 1880s, his father from Hilldringsberg and his mother from Blomskog in the province of Värmland. General Hilldring was fluent in the Swedish language.

General John E. Dahlquist and General Henning Linden were both born in Minneapolis, and both had studied at the University of Minnesota, where they took courses in Swedish language and literature and played active parts in Swedish theatrical and literary activities. Henning Linden (b. 1892), who became a brigadier general in 1943, served during the war both in the Pacific area and in Europe. His father came from Västra Stenby near Motala in Östergötland, and his mother from Gräsmark in Värmland.

John E. Dahlquist (b. 1896) was in 1942 made deputy chief of staff to Lieutenant General Dwight D. Eisenhower, commander of the U.S. Army forces in Europe. From the summer of 1944 he was, as a major general, in command of a division, including the one to which Hermann Goering surrendered. In 1949 he was announced as the new commander of the First Infantry Division, called the "backbone of the occupation forces in Germany," and in 1954 he was appointed Continental Army Commander. His father had come from the parish of Grinstad and his mother from Ryr, both in the province of Dalsland. Dahlquist's first known ancestor in Sweden, Ingevald of Berga, died in 1564, and his farm, Berga not far from the church of Öre in Dalsland which in part dates from the 1200s, is still in the same family. His descendants, who now number nearly 5,000 in Sweden and Norway and several thousand in the United States, have become known in Scandinavia as the Ingevald clan. The first widely known member of the clan was Johan Olof Wallin, who became one of Sweden's foremost poets and hymnologists, and finally archbishop of Uppsala.

Another army officer from the Midwest, Earl Clarence Bergquist (b. 1902), took part in the campaigns in Europe and was named a major general in 1955. His younger brother Kenneth Paul Bergquist (b. 1912) served in the Air Force where he became one of the leading specialists on air-defense techniques. In 1944–45 he took part in several combat missions against the Japanese. In 1954, at the age of 41, he was promoted to major general. After that he served, among other things, as director of operations at Air Force headquarters in Washington, D.C., and commander of the Air Force Command and Control Development Division. He helped develop air-defense systems for Canada, Alaska, and Greenland and was a consultant for the establishment of the NATO air-defense system. His recreations included the cooking of Swedish dishes. The father of the two generals had come in 1898 from Nedre Ullerud and their mother from Övre Ullerud in Värmland, settling first in Minnesota and later moving to North Dakota.

A young man named Chesley Gordon Peterson, whose paternal grandfather, Solomon Peterson, had come to Utah from Sweden in 1864 and married a Norwegian girl, became in 1940, at the age of 20, commander of the Eagle Squadron of the Royal Air Force, an all-American volunteer fighter unit in England. Holding different commands first in Europe and later in the United States, he advanced through the grades to major general. Another Utah family of Swedish-Norwegian origin, the Alben Borgstroms of Thatcher in the north, lost in 1944 four sons within six months — one at Guadalcanal, one in Italy, a third on a bomber mission over Europe, and the fourth in the invasion of France.

Major Richard I. Bong, born in 1920 at Superior, Wisconsin, became the best-known fighter pilot of Swedish origin. When receiving the Medal of Honor in late 1944, he had destroyed 36 Japanese planes in aerial combat and thus set a record for the Second World War. His father, born in the Swedish province of Dalarna, had been brought to Wisconsin in 1897, when he was six years old. Major Bong's mother was of Scottish, Irish, and English stock.

One of the first American aces in the Pacific, Edward Robert Sellstrom, who had survived the sinking of the U.S.S. *Lexington* and also served on the carriers *Saratoga* and *Yorktown*, lost his life in 1942, and the next year a 1,300-ton destroyer escort was named *Sellstrom* in his honor. His parents had come from Sweden, and he was a graduate of Gustavus Adolphus College at St. Peter, Minnesota. Two large Air Force bases in the United States have been named for pilots of Swedish extraction, the Bergstrom Air Field at Austin, Texas, in honor of Captain John A. E. Bergstrom of Austin, who on December 8, 1941, the day after Pearl Harbor, was killed during a Japanese attack in the Philippines, and the Malmstrom Air Force Base at Great Falls, Montana, in honor of Colonel Einar A. Malmstrom, born of Swedish parents in Chicago, who crashed in 1954 near Great Falls where he served as deputy commander of the 407th Strategic Fighter Wing.

Brigadier General Carl E. Nathorst or Charles E. Nathurst (1862–1945) became in 1942, when he was 80 years old and the Japanese occupied the Philippines where he lived, a prisoner of war, and in 1945 he as well as his wife and daughter met death in their burning barracks at Manila. He was born at Dagsholm in the Swedish province of Dalsland, came to America in 1881, went to the Philippines with the 13th Minnesota Volunteer Infantry in 1898, and remained there when the Spanish-American and Philippine-American wars were over. After a period as a gold digger he joined the newly organized Constabulary forces and was named their chief in 1927. An older brother in Sweden, Alfred Nathorst (1850–1921), became an eminent geologist, botanist, and polar explorer. Three members of the Nathorst family, sons of a noted agricultural pioneer, had emigrated to America in the mid-1800s.

Among Americans of Swedish origin who served in the naval forces during the Second World War was Arleigh A. Burke (b. 1901), whose paternal grandfather, Anders P. Björkegren from Hudene in the province of Västergötland, had been one of the first Swedish settlers at Denver, Colorado. After his first combat assignment in the Pacific in the fall of 1943, when he commanded a destroyer squadron, he became popularly known as "31-knot Burke." In 1944–45 he was chief of staff of the famous Carrier Task Force 58, and in 1955–61 he served as Chief of U.S. Naval Operations, a four-star admiral. When Admiral Burke visited Sweden in 1960, he met more than a hundred relatives who had gathered for a special service in the church of Hudene northeast of Gothenburg. The pastor bade the Burkes welcome in English, and Admiral Burke read a brief address in Swedish, the first speech he had made in the language of his forefathers. The members of the Björkegren clan formed a permanent association with Arleigh Burke as an honorary member.

When Admiral Arleigh A. Burke was Chief of Naval Operations,

Rear Admiral Clarence E. Ekstrom was in command of the Sixth Fleet. He was born in 1902 in Wisconsin, and his father, John Ekström, had come from the city of Ängelholm in south Sweden. Roy Stanley Benson (b. 1906), whose parents had come from Sweden and when married settled in New Hampshire, was during the Second World War in charge of two submarines. In 1957–58, when he had been promoted to rear admiral, he served as commander of a cruiser division, and somewhat later he was in command of the submarine force of the Pacific Fleet. Admiral Benson's father was born at Helsingborg, the southern port, and his mother at Jönköping in Småland. His paternal grandfather had worked for one of the largest and oldest estates in Sweden, Krapperup in the "chateau country" in the south.

Rear Admiral Theodore C. Lonnquest (b. 1894), whose parents also were born in Sweden, served throughout the war as director of engineering of the Bureau of Aeronautics, in charge of the design and development of the Navy's wartime aircraft. After the war he was assigned to the development of the aviation applications of atomic energy. His father was born in Stockholm, received technical training in the L. M. Ericsson Telephone Company, settled about 1890 at Lynn, Massachusetts, where the family name through a clerical error became Lonnquest instead of Lonnquist, and made his career in the General Electric Company. His forefathers had for generations been farmers or ironmasters in Småland and Värmland. Vice Admiral William Renwick Smedberg III (b. 1902) was a descendant of an early Swedish immigrant, Charles G. Smedberg, who was born at Stockholm in 1784 and became a wealthy businessman in New York. In 1944 he served as chief of staff of a cruiser-destroyer task force in the Solomons and mid-Pacific campaigns. After the war he became commander of the battleship *Iowa*, superintendent of the U.S. Naval Academy at Annapolis, and commander of the Second Fleet. His father, William R. Smedberg, Jr., was a brigadier general.

A naval officer who was born in Chicago of Swedish parents, Charles E. Rosendahl (b. 1892), became the country's leading expert in lighter-than-air dirigibles. When the first American rigid airship, the *Shenandoah*, in 1925 crashed in a squall in Ohio, he managed to land safely with one section several miles away. Later he was named commander of the Naval Air Station at Lakehurst, New Jersey, the most important of the American airship bases, which also served as a landing place for the transoceanic Zeppelins from Germany. During the Second World War he was returned to sea duty and attained the rank of rear admiral. In the last major sea battle for Guadalcanal in 1942, he was in command of the U.S.S. *Minneapolis*. During the later years of the war he was in charge of naval-airship training and experiment at Lakehurst. "His faith paid dividends to his country in the war in helping clear the German submarines from our coast and eventually from the Western Atlantic," *The New York Times* wrote editorially when he nominally retired in 1946. Admiral Rosendahl's father came from the province of Västmanland and his mother from Dalarna.

Lieutenant Commander and finally Rear Admiral Carl E. Anderson, born at Stockholm of a Swedish father and an Irish mother, was regarded as one of the most picturesque and spirited naval officers of the Second World War. At numerous landings on islands in the Pacific, including those at Iwo Jima where one of the fiercest battles of the war was fought in 1945, he was responsible for the disembarkation of troops, munitions, and other supplies, being widely regarded as "the world's champion beachmaster." In a magazine article he was said to possess "a voice like a tired foghorn, yelling in a jargon changing from English to Swedish in direct proportion to the heat of his ready anger." His men called him "Squeaky." As a boy he had sailed in Swedish training ships, and in 1909 he had deserted a British vessel in Hawaii. Years of hard work as a sailor, skipper, fisherman, and canner in the Pacific area, including Alaska, followed. Since the First World War he had been in the naval reserve.

A medical officer of Swedish parentage, Clifford Anders Swanson, born in 1901 at Marquette, Michigan, served with naval units during the war and in 1946–51 as surgeon general of the Navy. He retired with the rank of rear admiral. Both his parents came from the province of Dalsland. In 1943–48 an immigrant from Sweden, Captain Erik G. Håkansson (1886–1950), commanded the Naval Medical Research Institute at Bethesda, Maryland, near Washington. He was born at Madesjö in Småland, went to school at Vadstena and Linköping in Östergötland, emigrated in 1909, and began studying medicine at the University of Illinois, earning his living by offering Swedish massage and health exercises. During the First World War he began specializing in tropical diseases. He was at Pearl Harbor on December 7, 1941, treating some 250 men for burns and other injuries.

Most of the factories founded by Swedish immigrants or their sons, as already shown, turned out precision tools of various kinds, instruments, machine or automobile parts, machinery and other products of metal, and they were, therefore, able to play an immediate and effective role in the industrial war effort. In other sections of American industry vitally important contributions were made by engineers, inventors and business executives of Swedish birth and education, as well as by thousands of members of the first American-born generation. An outstanding example in the latter category was Philip G. Johnson, born in Seattle of Swedish parents, who when the war began returned to his post as head of the Boeing Aircraft Company. Exhausted by overwork, he died in 1944 at the age of 50.

Among the inventions made in Sweden which proved of great value to the American war production was the self-locking or elastic stop nut, which Ture Gustaf Rennerfelt (1862–1950) had produced in the middle 1920s and later was developed by Swedish engineers in the United States. It had a built-in vulcanized fiber collar, which made it hang onto its bolt under all conditions of vibration. About 2.5 billion such nuts, of some 2,500 types and sizes, were made in America in 1943, and while they were used in implements of war of many different kinds, the aircraft industry was by far the largest customer. The number of lock nuts in a heavy bomber like the B-29 is said to have been about 50,000. The inventor, Ture Gustaf Rennerfelt, was a graduate of the Stockholm Institute of Technology and had spent many years, 1888–89 and 1901–1907, in the United States as an engineer and inventor. His cousin Ivar Rennerfelt (1874–1949), who in 1901–1909 had been a successful engineer in America, invented in Sweden an electric melting furnace which became used in most steel-making countries.

In 1940 a Swedish inventor named Boris Hagelin, born in 1892 at Baku in the Caucasus where his father worked for the Nobel enterprises, brought to the United States an electrically operated coding and decoding machine, which during the war was used by all American armed forces. About 140,000 units were produced. Best known of the war implements emanating from Sweden was the Bofors 40 mm.

743

antiaircraft gun, the American war production of which totaled about 100,000 pieces. Gage blocks based on Carl Edward Johansson's invention at Eskilstuna in 1896, and now measuring down to one-millionth of an inch, helped make possible the rapidly organized mass production of guns, tanks, and airplanes. The hardness of steel was tested with high accuracy by a method originated by Johan August Brinell about 1900, at Fagersta northwest of Stockholm. The high-speed steam turbine which Gustaf de Laval had begun to develop at Stockholm in the 1880s had, in combination with helical reduction gears, helped revolutionize marine propelling equipment.

Dr. Carl-Gustaf Rossby, the Swedish weather expert who had come to the United States in 1926 as a fellow of the Sweden-America Foundation and somewhat later established America's first airway weather-reporting system, organized and directed the training of unprecedented numbers of meteorologists for the U.S. Air Force. Traveling from his base as head of the department of meteorology at the University of Chicago, he set up branch units at New York University, University of California in Los Angeles, California Institute of Technology, and Massachusetts Institute of Technology. He also visited most of the theaters of war where his meteorologists were stationed, including those charged with the forecasts for Overlord, the Allied invasion of the European mainland in the summer of 1944. In 1944–45 Dr. Rossby served as president of the American Meteorological Society. Two years later he returned to Sweden.

Carl L. Norden, inventor of a precision bombsight which during the war was one of the military top secrets of the United States, seems to have been of Swedish origin, as his name indicates, but he was born in Java in the Dutch East Indies (in 1880), raised in the Netherlands and Germany, and received his engineering education in Switzerland. In 1915 he established himself as a consulting engineer in Brooklyn. In late 1944 The American Society of Mechanical Engineers awarded him the Holley Medal "for his invention and development of the Norden Bombsight and other valuable devices which should hasten the peace." His many inventions included an automatic pilot. Carl Norden was a devoted student of Swedenborg.

39

From the Early Postwar
Years to Vietnam

*Postwar boom for U.S. exports to Sweden, the Marshall Plan,
the North Atlantic Pact*

WHEN THE Second World War was over, Swedish relief activities were
extended to include nearly every war-ravaged country in Europe, and
considerable credits were granted for reconstruction. Immediate help
was often vital. Because of the four-year-long drastic reduction in
imports, Sweden itself was in great need of supplies from abroad, but
its industries were intact and relatively large foreign-exchange re-
serves, earned in great part by merchant vessels in Allied service,
enabled it to make extensive purchases, particularly in the United
States.

In 1945 no single country delivered more goods to Sweden than
the United States. Even coal and coke were shipped. Sweden's exports
to America also seemed to recover rapidly, but this was largely due to
accumulated stockpiles of wood pulp. In 1946 Sweden's imports from
the United States increased nearly fivefold, while its exports declined.
Because of the shortage of dollars and other foreign currencies the
Swedish government early in 1947 introduced import restrictions, but
these did not prove as effective as expected. In 1947 imports from the
United States, which included vitally needed fuels, raw materials, and
machinery, showed a continued sharp increase and accounted for no
less than one-third of Sweden's purchases abroad. Its total foreign

trade resulted in a record import surplus. Industrial production, on the other hand, was already much larger than before the war.

In 1947 the United States launched the Marshall Plan, aimed at promoting European economic recovery, and from the beginning Sweden took a wholehearted part. Sweden never asked for nor received any gifts, but its dollar situation was improved considerably as the result of an American loan of $20.4 million and the so-called conditional and similar aid, totaling approximately $90 million, that paid in dollars for Swedish shipments to other countries. Study trips were also organized under the Marshall Plan. In early 1949, for instance, Swedish labor leaders toured American industrial centers to study labor relations and production methods. Sweden's loan from the United States was fully repaid in 1963, many years earlier than stipulated.

"The general European recovery that the Marshall Plan has made possible is, so far as Sweden is concerned, the most significant aspect of this unique American initiative," Prime Minister Tage Erlander said in the fall of 1951 when the aid operations were coming to an end. "It is our opinion that the cooperation developed in this connection between the United States and Sweden has further strengthened the bonds of friendship between the two countries."

Early in 1949, when preparations for the North Atlantic Pact were far advanced, Sweden offered to enter into an independent defensive alliance with Norway and Denmark. This was a more drastic departure from Sweden's traditional foreign policy than was generally realized abroad, the country being willing to abandon its neutrality in war sufficiently to share unlimited mutual responsibilities for the defense of Scandinavia. The negotiations failed, however, and, instead, Norway and Denmark joined the North Atlantic Treaty Organization, which enabled them to begin their military rearmament with American assistance. Sweden has never asked for any military aid from the United States. Much equipment has, on the other hand, been purchased from American firms.

Most American press commentators who expressed an opinion on the subject thought that Sweden ought to join NATO. Among the exceptions was Walter Lippman who believed that if Sweden took such a step, Finland's position as the Soviet Union's neighbor in the North would become more difficult. A diplomatic correspondent for

1. Kalmar Castle in southeastern Sweden was for many centuries an important border fortress and known as the "Key to Sweden." The ship that in 1637–38 carried the first Swedish colonists to the Delaware Valley was named for it (p. 20). 2. The "Old Swedes" Church in Wilmington, Del., consecrated on Trinity Sunday, June 4, 1699, as Helga Trefaldighets Kyrka, or Holy Trinity Church, is the oldest surviving church built by a Swedish congregation in the Delaware Valley. The earliest religious services of the New Sweden colony were held in 1638 at Fort Christina, the beginning of the city of Wilmington. Holy Trinity was built near the site of the fort, where a cemetery had been laid out by the first colonists (p. 35).

"God has blessed us a hundredfold here on the new earth," wrote one of the pioneers at Bishop Hill in northwestern Illinois, which was founded in 1846 by a religious sect from Sweden and existed as a communal settlement until 1860. Its settlers were the vanguard of the mighty tide of Swedish immigration in the 1800s. Around the turn of the century, life in the "Prairie Utopia" was recreated by a self-taught artist, Olof Krans, who had arrived there at the age of 12. Today, Bishop Hill is a unique, living memorial of pioneer life in the Middle West (pp. 183–190).

Gustavus Hesselius, who came to the Delaware Valley from Sweden in 1712, became the first notable artist of the colonial period in America and has been called the "Father of American painting." Among those whose portraits he painted was Lapowinsa, an Indian chief (pp. 52–53).

Large parts of rural Sweden are much more productive than in the late 1800s when in some years tens of thousands of young farmers and farm laborers left for the American Midwest. This picture provides a glimpse of the plains between Skara and Lidköping in the province of Västergötland, near Lake Vänern. Today, five percent of Sweden's population live by farming, compared to 70 percent in 1880. The area Swedish immigrants put under the plow in America was as large as the whole cultivated territory in Sweden (pp. 366–368).

On Göta Canal, which was built in 1810–32 and continues chiefly as a tourist attraction, tiny steamboats cross lake-dotted south-central Sweden. Canal engineers and participation in the canal work gave John Ericsson, father of the *Monitor*, a substantial part of his technical education. Among early American travelers on Göta Canal were Henry Wadsworth Longfellow and his wife Mary, who in 1835 sailed from Stockholm back to Gothenburg (pp. 122–123, 130, 316).

In 1758 Linnaeus bought the small country estate of Hammarby, six miles southeast of Uppsala, which became his beloved summer retreat. Today it is a place of pilgrimage for Swedes and visitors to Sweden who are interested in the great naturalist. Flowers that Linnaeus loved are grown in the garden. The many plant names he contributed to the English language include bromeliad, forsythia, gardenia, kalmia, rudbeckia, and zinnia. Some of the largest collections of books by and about Linnaeus are in the United States (pp. 71–72, 77–80, 624).

1. Near the city of Borgholm on the island of Öland in the Baltic is the ruin of a castle, built on a site where a fortress stood some 2,000 years ago. Öland has been called Sweden's "American island." In 1970 at least a tenth of the some 20,000 islanders had lived in the United States. Most homes have American relatives. 2. This photograph was taken at an old-homestead museum near Halmstad in Halland. Hundreds of parishes in Sweden had their own colorful folk costumes, used on Sundays and on festive occasions, but these began to disappear in the early 1800s. Today they may be seen mostly in the province of Dalarna, and in some other sections where the homecraft movement has furthered a renaissance. In America, Swedish folk costumes have often been worn by folk-dance groups and on the Midsummer holiday.

1. The Swedish-American sculptor Carl Milles's old studio and home, with numerous specimens of his own art and a large antique collection, has become one of the most treasured attractions of the Swedish capital. There, as Milles himself wanted, art and nature work together, and the North and the South of Europe have been united. The large figure in this picture is Milles's *Poseidon*, in Greek mythology the lord of the sea. The sculpture on the column is Milles's *Man and Pegasus*, the original of which is in the Art Center at Des Moines, Iowa. Works by Milles are found in many cities in the United States and Sweden (pp. 719–723). 2. The Grand Foyer of the Kennedy Center for the Performing Arts in Washington, D.C., has 18 huge chandeliers and 22 wall brackets from the Orrefors glassworks in Sweden. Fourteen of the chandeliers are a gift from the Swedish government (p. 690).

Stockholm's Town Hall, completed in 1923, is widely regarded as the masterpiece of the national-romantic architectural school in Sweden, as well as a symbol of the capital. A national leader named Birger Jarl, who founded Stockholm about 1250, is remembered with a symbolical gilt tomb at the base of the tower. At noon and at 6 p.m., a carillon plays the strains of the Ballad of Saint George (Göran, or Örjan, in Swedish), which became popular in Sweden toward the end of the 1400s. The building's architect, Ragnar Östberg, was honored by President Franklin D. Roosevelt at a ceremony in the White House in 1934 (p. 692).

1. Since 1914, ships of the Johnson Line, which is based at Stockholm, have maintained direct services between Sweden and western ports of the United States and Canada, first via the Strait of Magellan and then, from 1915, via the Panama Canal. Here two modern Johnson liners meet in the Golden Gate at San Francisco (p. 619). 2. M.S. *Kungsholm* in New York Bay, under the Verrazano-Narrows Bridge. The white ships of the Swedish American Line, always named *Kungsholm* and *Gripsholm*, were among the most celebrated transatlantic vessels afloat. During the 1920s and 1930s, and also after the Second World War, they did much to stimulate travel and other contacts between Sweden and America (p. 685).

The Washington Post wrote in the spring of 1952 that while the United States a few years earlier had tried to nudge Sweden into the Atlantic Pact, "officials here now think Swedish neutrality is not such a bad thing for the West after all." Dorothy Fosdick, who for several years served on the Policy Planning Staff of the U.S. State Department, wrote somewhat later about Sweden's refusal to join the pact: "What looked to some like a defeat, however, turned out not to be one. For determined, self-respecting neutrals, with stable governments, in strategic positions, can be as useful as allies; indeed, they may be more helpful than some outright allies."

In Sweden, an overwhelming majority of the newspapers favored a continued alliance-free policy. The most notable exception was *Dagens Nyheter*, the leading Liberal paper, which under the editorial direction of Herbert Tingsten (1896–1973), a former professor of political science who had begun his comprehensive American studies with the system of government, consistently advocated Sweden's adherence to the Atlantic Pact. The United States, he wrote, had half reluctantly shouldered its mission as the central force and defender of the democracies, and its efforts to build up a badly needed system of solidarity deserved all possible support. Dr. Tingsten, who was a forceful but not uncritical interpreter of American ideas and developments, retired in 1960 as editor-in-chief of *Dagens Nyheter*, which then seemed to move further left. Especially in connection with the war in Vietnam, the newspaper became outspoken in its criticism of the United States.

In 1950, no event in Sweden received more space in the American press than the death of King Gustav V (1858–1950) at the age of 92. Hundreds of editorials paid tribute to the monarch, who had occupied his post for 43 years, the longest reign in Sweden's history. The largest of many memorial services in the United States was held in New York in the Cathedral of St. John the Divine, which was filled to capacity. Many American newspapers observed that the new King, Gustav VI Adolf, had a better firsthand knowledge of the United States than any other crowned head and many chiefs of state in Europe. He had also become widely known as an archeologist and art collector. Among his close American friends was Bernard Berenson, the famous art expert. In 1966 the King chose for display in the United States, beginning at the National Gallery of Art in

Washington, 150 masterworks from his vast collection of Oriental art. Gustav VI Adolf died in 1973 and was succeeded by his grandson, Carl XVI Gustaf (b. 1946).

In 1952 Prime Minister Tage Erlander made a two-week unofficial tour of the United States, stopping at New York, Washington, Detroit, Chicago, Rockford and Rock Island, Minneapolis, and Ashland, Wisconsin, where he had first cousins. It was the first time a Swedish prime minister visited America. "Relations between the United States and Sweden," he said in an address in Washington, "have always been characterized by the greatest cordiality. No serious controversy has ever arisen between our two countries, and I am confident that none ever will. Any other situation would be unnatural, for we have so much in common — in basic ideals, in government, in outlook."

In 1954 Mr. Erlander as well as the prime ministers of Denmark and Norway took part in Scandinavian Airlines' inauguration of its polar route between Scandinavia and Los Angeles, an event that made aviation history and brought the North of Europe and the Pacific Coast of North America much closer to each other. In Washington the three Scandinavian heads of government were invited to lunch with President Eisenhower in the White House.

From 1948 until 1958 the Swedish Embassy in Washington was headed by Erik Boheman (b. 1895), who during the Second World War had been under secretary of state in Stockholm. As ambassador in Washington he traveled to all parts of the United States and spoke at hundreds of meetings. In a farewell address before a largely Swedish audience in New York he said that if he had stayed longer he would have "run the risk of becoming the one who explains and defends the American point of view to Sweden, rather than the other way around." *The Washington Post* observed in an editorial that "Mr. Boheman has been one of the few persons in this capital with the time and inclination to think freely about the challenges of the free world." As Swedish chief of mission in Washington Mr. Boheman was succeeded by Gunnar Jarring (b. 1907), who since 1956 had served as ambassador and permanent representative to the United Nations. In 1967, when he served as Sweden's ambassador to the Soviet Union, he became the "special representative" of the United Nations Security Council for the promotion of peace between Israel and the Arabs.

On September 17, 1961, Dag Hammarskjöld, Secretary General of the United Nations since 1953, was killed in an airplane crash during a peace mission to Africa, and on September 29 he was honored with a state funeral at Uppsala, the first of its kind since 1896 when Louis De Geer, an aristocrat and statesman who had led the forces of political reform to significant victories, was laid to rest. The delegation from the United States was headed by Vice President Lyndon B. Johnson and Ambassador Adlai Stevenson. In an address welcoming the American delegates to Sweden, Prime Minister Tage Erlander observed that aside from the other Nordic countries, Sweden felt a closer affinity to the United States than to any other country. Adlai Stevenson returned to Sweden three years later to speak at the annual spring festival of the university students at Uppsala, the first visitor from abroad to be the main speaker on that occasion.

In the summer of 1962 General and Mrs. Dwight D. Eisenhower visited Sweden. Addressing a conference of teachers from 80 countries, the former President said he was "especially happy that this convention is held in Sweden, the country that my wife proudly points to as the birthplace of her maternal grandparents. Moreover, it was my good fortune to know and admire two of the world's modern leaders for justice and peace, both of whom lost their lives in the service of the United Nations, Count Folke Bernadotte and Dag Hammarskjöld, both citizens of this nation." At a press conference immediately after his arrival in Stockholm, General Eisenhower mentioned a remark about Sweden that he had made in Chicago in 1960, which, he said, "was based on what I had read in an American magazine." He added: "Since then, I have had many friends who have returned from Sweden and told me that I was wrong. I admit it and apologize for my error." These words were deeply appreciated in Sweden.

In a pep talk to Republicans at the start of the election campaign in 1960, President Eisenhower had said that ambition had declined, drunkenness increased, and the suicide rate gone up "almost unbelievably" in a certain very friendly country with a predilection for socialism. Many observers, both in America and in Sweden, had from the beginning seen a connection between the President's remarks and an article in an American magazine, or rather two magazines, which gave the impression that alcoholism and suicide had become unusu-

749

ally serious problems in Sweden and that the country's comprehensive social-welfare system was the root of the evil. The Swedish suicide rate has, in fact, always been relatively high. Statistically speaking it is not higher today than it was in the early 1900s, when the rural population and the younger generations, where the incidence of suicide is comparatively low, made up a considerably larger proportion of the people than they do today. About 1,800 suicides are committed in Sweden each year, and not one of them can be ascribed to health or pension insurance and other social benefits.

"President Kennedy personified some of mankind's brightest and most beautiful dreams," Prime Minister Erlander said in a brief address over the Swedish radio and TV systems on the evening of November 22, 1963, shortly after the death of the President had been reported. Eighty-one-year-old King Gustav VI Adolf drove to the residence of the U.S. ambassador to offer his condolences. Prince Bertil, Prime Minister Erlander, and Olof Palme, newly appointed cabinet minister, flew to Washington to attend the funeral.

After 23 years as prime minister, a record in a democratic country, Tage Erlander resigned in the fall of 1969. Several years earlier, a widely known witty Englishman, Malcolm Muggeridge, had written that he deserved some international award as a man who had been prime minister for so long "without becoming pompous, arrogant, or oracular." As leader of the Social Democratic party and prime minister he was succeeded by Olof Palme (b. 1927), who since 1967 had been minister of education. He had for some years been Mr. Erlander's personal secretary and assistant. Prior to that, in 1947–48, he had studied at Kenyon College in Gambier, Ohio, which in 1970 awarded him an honorary doctor's degree.

From the Korean war to the struggle in Vietnam:
How the Swedish people reacted

IN THE Korean war that began in the summer of 1950, Sweden supported the action of the United Nations, in which the bulk of the military strength was provided by the United States. The conflict in Korea, Foreign Minister Östen Undén said in an address, concerned the whole world. The aggression was directed not only against South Korea, but also against the whole policy which the United Nations had pursued in the Korean question. Sweden had given its moral support to the endeavors to halt the aggressor, Mr. Undén added, and as an immediate material contribution it was sending a field hospital. Later on, Sweden, Norway, and Denmark jointly equipped and staffed a full-fledged hospital for the training of Korean physicians, surgeons, and nurses.

In the fall of 1950, when the U.N. forces were driving the invaders back, the Stockholm *Dagens Nyheter* wrote that the democratic world "owes the United States the greatest respect and gratitude for its sacrifices, and must realize more than ever before that America's might is the one certain guarantee of the rights of the democracies and the freedom of the individual. . . . A new wave of confidence sweeps the world."

In 1948–49 an overwhelming majority of the Swedish people had followed with increasing hopes the Berlin airlift, an air-supply operation mounted by the United States, Britain, and France to counter the Soviet blockade of the western sector of Berlin. "It is primarily the firmness and strength of the United States that has forced the Soviet Union to retreat," *Dagens Nyheter* wrote when the blockade was raised. In 1956 the Swedes were greatly aroused by the armed Soviet intervention in Hungary, and the Red Cross and other private organizations, as well as the government, took immediate action to bring relief. "Even we Swedes, who for a century and a half have been spared wars and revolutions, have been shaken to the marrow by this drama," wrote the Conservative *Svenska Dagbladet*. Social Democratic leaders and groups, among others, issued statements denouncing the Russian Communists and voicing solidarity with the Hungarians. A similar reaction occurred in Sweden when Soviet forces were sent into Czechoslovakia in August of 1968.

In the 1960s and early 1970s, the Swedish people felt greatly disturbed by the growing or continued American involvement in the war in Vietnam. The nation seemed largely united in this reaction, but there were always more or less noticeable differences of opinion. Many citizens thought, for instance, that some protests made by leading members of the Swedish government were too drastic. Youthful demonstrations which were directed against the war but also seemed anti-American were widely deplored, the more noisy ones being denounced by spokesmen for the government.

There were many reasons for the exceedingly strong Swedish reaction, and it is hardly possible to list them in order of importance. A deep-rooted conviction that war is a self-defeating method of settling international disputes was mixed with a keen awareness of the suffering inflicted upon the people of Vietnam. Radio and in particular television brought the struggle into practically every home in Sweden, and not only the suffering and devastation but also the disparity of resources available to each side were seen in sharp relief. Most of the TV films shown in Sweden emanated from American networks, just as a great majority of the pictures published in the press were of American origin. Swedish journalists were, on the other hand, often sent to Vietnam, and their reports, while unable to do justice to the official American attitude concerning the war, helped keep the people informed of what was happening.

In Sweden the war in Vietnam was never regarded as a repetition of the Korean war, which had successfully halted a Communist invasion, but as part of the Vietnamese struggle for national independence and social justice, with its roots in the colonial era. When the American large-scale intervention was launched, a new eruption of compassion for ill-treated or poor peoples in the old colonial areas had just begun in Sweden, and this helps explain the intensity of the reaction against the war in Vietnam. Another component was disappointment with the course pursued by the United States, which seemed different from what the Swedes thought they had good reason to expect. From the beginning they were also influenced by the American antiwar movement. A feeling that Sweden in its own self-interest must stand up for the independence of the Vietnamese nation added fuel to the Swedish reaction. Dissenters questioned the kind of freedom that would have been achieved without an American intervention. Among them was a radical Socialist maverick, Ture Nerman (1886–1969), who during the Second World War had published a violently anti-Nazi newspaper.

Few reasonably well-informed Swedes saw improper motives behind the American action. Both Prime Minister Olof Palme and his predecessor, Tage Erlander, said in public addresses in 1969 that the United States' engagement in Vietnam, although turned into a tragedy, seemed to have been dictated by a wish to further a democratic government and social progress. During the war Sweden offered North Vietnam humanitarian aid in the form of medicine, hospital equipment, milk products, and schoolbook paper, and considerable help to reconstruction followed.

A scathing denunciation by Prime Minister Palme of the resumption of the American bombings of the Hanoi-Haiphong area at Christmas in 1972 caused a protracted diplomatic rift between the United States and Sweden, which did not again exchange ambassadors until the spring of 1974. No other area of relations between the two countries was affected. Even the two embassies continued to function, as normally as they possibly could without having a chief of the highest rank.

In the early 1970s Prime Minister Palme said repeatedly that he did not worry at all about relations between the United States and Sweden once the "frightful war" in Vietnam was over. The basic friendship between the two peoples was, of course, not in doubt, but there were observers who thought that the war period with its frictions and excesses might have left some long-lasting scars. During the most formative years of their lives, many members of the younger generations in Sweden had heard or read little about America except news and comments related to the war in Vietnam and the immediately following so-called Watergate affair, and they could, therefore, easily have become prejudiced. Circles of the New Left, moreover, seemed to have come to the conclusion that one of the more effective ways of promoting socialistic ideas was to dwell upon the internal problems of the United States.

Insofar as anti-American feelings had been aroused in Sweden, the Swedes tackled that problem directly. One of the country's foremost foreign correspondents, Sven Åhman (b. 1907), who was sent to New York by *Dagens Nyheter* in 1946 and established a solid reputation for objectivity, said in a farewell interview in 1973: "The United States has never been either heaven or hell. After the Second World War, America enjoyed in Sweden an outright adulation, and we who lived there often had reason to point out that everything was not perfect. Today we have, instead, good reason to maintain that everything is not as corrupt as many in Sweden seem to believe." Among the many Swedes who even during the most difficult years voiced a deep optimism concerning the future of the United States was Dr. Gunnar Helén (b. 1918), who in 1969 succeeded Dr. Bertil Ohlin as leader of the Liberal party. While Sweden had developed her political democracy in undisturbed peace, he said on one occasion, America had reached its present position after one civil war, two world wars, and several bilateral conflicts.

40

The Constant Interchange

Birgit Nilsson, legendary dramatic soprano, and a new cluster of Swedish stars

"IN 76 years of Metropolitan Opera House history, few debuts have matched the one of a Swedish soprano named Birgit Nilsson," a leading American critic wrote after Miss Nilsson's huge success as Isolde in Wagner's *Tristan und Isolde* at the Metropolitan Opera in New York on December 18, 1959. Both the *Times* and the *Herald-Tribune* began their reviews under two-column heads on the front page, a rare occurrence. The ovation after the last curtain was described as "hysterical."

When Birgit Nilsson came to New York, she was already well known among opera buffs and music lovers on the West Coast and, above all, in Chicago. She had made her North American debut on August 9, 1956, at a concert in the Hollywood Bowl with the Los Angeles Philharmonic Orchestra, singing excerpts from *Tristan und Isolde* and *Die Götterdämmerung*. On October 5 she sang Brünnhilde in *Die Walküre* at the San Francisco Opera, and a few weeks later she repeated this role for her debut with the Chicago Lyric Opera. During the 1958 and 1959 seasons in Chicago she sang four different roles, including Isolde and Princess Turandot in Puccini's *Turandot*.

Miss Nilsson made her formal debut at the Stockholm Opera in 1947, and ten years later she had appeared on most of the major opera stages in Europe. At La Scala in Milan, she scored one of her greatest successes, as Princess Turandot, on the opening night of the 1958–59 season. The critic of *Corriere della Sera* wrote: "To have lived, one must have heard this voice at least once." From 1959 to 1966 she sang 162 performances at the Metropolitan in New York, as well as 22 as a member of the touring company, and many have been added since then. "Empires can rise and fall, but not Miss Nilsson," the *New York Times* critic wrote after a new *Tristan und Isolde* in the fall of 1971. She was then regarded as the undisputed queen of Wagnerian singers, as well as an outstanding Aïda, Elektra, Salome, Tosca, and Turandot. Her wide range of soprano roles has not often been matched. Numerous critics have commented on her apparently tireless, infallibly on-pitch voice, able to soar even over the fortissimos of a 106-piece orchestra. Her most passionate fans became known as Nilssonites. She has also given recitals all over the United States.

Birgit Nilsson (b. 1918) grew up on a farm at Västra Karup on the southwestern coast of Sweden, and as the only child she often did a boy's or young man's work. A local church organist and choirmaster was her first and probably most important vocal teacher. In 1941–45 she studied at the Academy of Music in Stockholm. There she received a scholarship from a fund established by Christine Nilsson, who in 1870–72 made her first American tour and in 1883 helped dedicate the Metropolitan Opera House in New York. At the gala farewell in the old Met in 1966, Birgit Nilsson was wearing a gold wreath that had been presented to Christine Nilsson at the opening by an unknown admirer.

During the 1959–60 season, when Birgit Nilsson made her debut, there were four other stars from the Stockholm Opera at the Metropolitan: Jussi Björling, who had not appeared since 1957, another tenor, Nicolai Gedda, who had joined the American company in 1957, and two sopranos, Elisabeth Söderström and Norwegian-born Aase Nordmo-Lövberg, both of whom came in the fall of 1959.

Nicolai Gedda, who was born in Stockholm in 1925 of a Swedish mother and a Russian father, started his career as a bank teller. At the Academy of Music he won, like Birgit Nilsson, the Christine Nilsson fellowship. A lyric tenor, he made a sensational debut at the Stockholm Opera in 1952. The next year he began a highly successful international career, and since then he has only made guest appearances in Sweden. At the Metropolitan he made his debut on

November 1, 1957, in the title role of Gounod's *Faust*, and this was the beginning of hundreds of performances, primarily in the Italian and French repertories. In 1972 Gedda was said to be the most widely recorded tenor in history, having completed well over 100 albums.

After her debut at the Metropolitan in the fall of 1959 as Susanna in *Le Nozze di Figaro*, Elisabeth Söderström (b. 1927) was welcomed in the press as a great and captivating singer and an actress of the first rank. During her years at the Metropolitan, 1959–64, she also gave many concerts in the United States. She became one of the greatest assets of the Stockholm Opera, which she joined in 1950, and her talents and experience brought her numerous successes throughout Europe. Aase Nordmo-Lövberg won an international reputation for her parts in Verdi operas.

On October 29, 1960, Kerstin Meyer (b. 1928), then the leading mezzo-soprano of the Stockholm Opera, made her debut at the Metropolitan as Carmen. She has also made concert tours in the United States. Another mezzo-soprano from Stockholm, Barbro Ericson (b. 1930), appeared at the Metropolitan in 1967–68. Among Swedes at the San Francisco Opera in the 1960s was Berit Lindholm (b. 1934), a dramatic soprano of the Stockholm Opera. During the 1974–75 season she made her debut at the Metropolitan.

A tenor from the same stage, Helge Brilioth (b. 1931), whose father and grandfather, Nathan Söderblom, had been archbishop of Uppsala, came to the Met on December 12, 1972, as Siegfried in the Wagner opera, and according to the *New York Times* critic gave "the finest impersonation of that killing role New York has seen since the postwar days of Set Svanholm." Another tenor, Norwegian-born Ragnar Ulfung (b. 1927), who had joined the Gothenburg Opera in 1955 and the Stockholm Opera three years later, made his first appearance at the same time, and was also praised. Ulfung had previously sung at the operas in Chicago and San Francisco, and in particular at the summer opera in Santa Fe, New Mexico, where people regarded him as one of their own. On January 29, 1973, a lyric baritone, Ingvar Wixell (b. 1931), a member of the Stockholm Opera in 1955–67 and then of the Deutsche Oper in Berlin, sang the title role of Verdi's *Rigoletto*, a debut that critics described as "very impressive." He had previously been a guest at the San Francisco Opera during four seasons. A Swedish bass, Bengt Rundgren (b. 1931), who in

1969 had moved from the Stockholm Opera to the Deutsche Oper in Berlin, followed at the Metropolitan in the spring of 1974. Other Swedish opera singers who in the early 1970s became known in operatic circles in the United States include Catarina Ligendza (b. 1937), the daughter of two long-time members of the Stockholm Opera. Her international career took her not only to Vienna, Bayreuth, Covent Garden in London, and La Scala in Milan, but also to the Metropolitan Opera in New York. Well-known American opera and concert singers of Swedish parentage include Theodor Uppman, born in 1920 in California, who made his debut at the San Francisco Opera in 1948 and at the Metropolitan in 1953. In early 1974 Brooklyn-born Klara Barlow, whose mother had immigrated from Sweden, made a successful debut at the Met as Isolde.

During the years 1883–1974 a total of at least 29 opera singers who had been born and educated in Sweden appeared at the Metropolitan Opera in New York. Two other singers were born in Sweden but had received their training in the United States, some were naturalized Swedes, and several were born in America of Swedish parents. Many Swedish opera stars sang on stages in Chicago, San Francisco, and other cities.

As director of the Stockholm Opera, Set Svanholm was succeeded in 1963 by Göran Gentele (1917–72). He took his company on tours to the other Scandinavian capitals, and to Hamburg in 1965, Montreal in 1967, and Munich in 1969. In 1970 he was appointed general manager of the Metropolitan as successor to Rudolf Bing from 1972, but was killed in a motor accident in Italy in the summer of the latter year. Observers in the press agreed that even before his first season began, he had made an auspicious start. His plans provided, among other things, for inviting his friend Ingmar Bergman to the company as a director, and for a gradual "Americanization" of the venerable Metropolitan. In 1961, after Bergman's debut at the Stockholm Opera with a production of Stravinsky's *The Rake's Progress*, critics had called him one of the few great opera directors of the day, and the composer himself said that he had never seen a better production of *The Rake*. It also aroused a great deal of attention in the American press.

English-born Antony Tudor, who joined the American Ballet Theater in 1939 and later became ballet director of the Metropolitan

Opera in New York, served in 1949–50 and 1962–64 as director of the Royal Swedish Ballet in Stockholm. In 1972 the assistant ballet master of the American Ballet Theater, James Moore, was named artistic director of the Royal Swedish Ballet which he served for some years. In November of 1973 the Swedish Ballet celebrated its 200th birthday in the Royal Opera with a program that spanned the two centuries. In the fall of 1974, when the Stockholm Opera was closed for renovation, the Royal Ballet made its American debut with a tour that included the Middle West, the Pacific Coast, and the Atlantic seaboard. The critique ranged from favorable to mixed.

From 1963 to 1973 a former chief conductor and music director of the Stockholm Royal Opera, Sixten Ehrling (b. 1918), served as music director of the Detroit Symphony Orchestra, conducting more than 700 concerts. In 1967 he became the first conductor to lead the so-called Big Five orchestras in the United States within a single year. In 1973 he took over the leadership of the Juilliard orchestras in New York and then also appeared as a conductor at the Metropolitan Opera as well as in Sweden.

Among Swedish composers whom Sixten Ehrling introduced both in Detroit and in New York was Karl-Birger Blomdahl (1916–68), who wrote three symphonies and in 1959 the music for the modernistic science-fiction opera *Aniara*, based on a volume of verse by Harry Martinson, which has been called "the first great poetry of the Atomic Age." The scene is the space-ship *Aniara*, which, after evacuating thousands of humans from the earth, is thrown off its course within the solar system and plunges on in the direction of the distant constellation of the Lyre, while its passengers receive reports of the step-by-step destruction of their old planet. Fundamentally, the poet deals with man's situation on earth.

An opera entitled *Journey to America* was completed in 1932 by one of the first great pioneers of modern music in Sweden, Hilding Rosenberg (b. 1892). It describes a Swedish emigrant's experiences in the New World, and his return to his native land and his sorrowing sweetheart. As part of the celebration of the Swedish Pioneer Centennial in the Middle West in 1948, Rosenberg conducted the Chicago Symphony Orchestra in its presentation of his most powerful work, *The Revelation of St. John*, an oratorio which had been inspired by the events of the Second World War. The Swedish Choral Club of

Chicago also took part. An opera with a title in the English language, *Love, Love, Love*, was completed in 1970 by Eskil Hemberg (b. 1938). In the late 1960s and early 1970s he took the Academic Choral Club of Stockholm on three concert tours in the United States, including Alaska. The Lund University Student Singers, who toured America the first time in 1904, made their fourth visit in 1974. In the fall of the same year the Uppsala University Chorus, known as O.D., made its second tour and was also praised, the *New York Times* critic describing it as "a virtuoso group."

Glimpses of American-Swedish interchange in literature, drama, and other arts

THE VITALITY and originality of the leading American novelists and other writers of the late 1920s and the 1930s made a deep impression in Europe, and at the end of the latter decade Sweden had become as receptive to literary influences from America as any other country outside the English-speaking orbit. John Dos Passos, William Faulkner, Ernest Hemingway, John Steinbeck, and Thomas Wolfe seemed to represent the New World in a more immediate and, from an artistic viewpoint, more rewarding way than Theodore Dreiser, Sinclair Lewis, Upton Sinclair, and other members of the preceding generations. Hemingway, in particular, and Faulkner became models to a much greater extent than Edgar Allan Poe and Mark Twain had been. For modern Swedish fiction, Hemingway has meant much more than, for instance, Pär Lagerkvist, Sweden's only literary Nobel prize winner of the mid-1900s. Sinclair Lewis and Theodore Dreiser had little or no influence on Swedish novelists.

Of the new American prose writers, Faulkner was in 1950 awarded the Nobel prize for 1949, while Hemingway was given the 1954 prize and Steinbeck the one for 1962. When William Faulkner received his prize in Stockholm, Gustaf Hellström of the Swedish Academy, who had spent many years in England and America, described him as the unrivaled master of all living American and British novelists.

The first Swedish critics to take an active and consistent interest in the new American literature were Artur Lundkvist (b. 1906), a self-taught prodigy whose wide-ranging production of poetry and prose carried him into the 18-member Swedish Academy in 1968, and Thorsten Jonsson (1910–50), who began as a poet and short-story writer, in 1943–46 lived in New York as U.S. correspondent for the Stockholm *Dagens Nyheter*, and died a few years later after he had become his newspaper's cultural editor. Lundkvist's first book dealing with the American literary scene, entitled *Atlantvind* (Atlantic Wind), was published in 1932. Thorsten Jonsson provided brilliant translations of Hemingway and Steinbeck, in 1942 a collection of critical essays on six American novelists, including Erskine Caldwell, James T. Farrell, and William Saroyan, and in 1946 a personal report on the United States, *Sidor av Amerika* (Aspects of America). The fact that William Faulkner became a Nobel prize winner in 1950 may in part be regarded as a result of his work. His own style as a writer in Swedish, although a model of lucidity and precision, reflected strong American influences. Thorsten Jonsson, in turn, had numerous followers in Sweden, both in literature and in journalism.

In 1946, during one of his many visits to Sweden, John Steinbeck said in an interview that "Selma Lagerlöf's romantic novel, *The Story of Gösta Berling*, might almost be described as my Bible," and he added that his own novel *Tortilla Flat* was "a child of *Gösta Berling*." Miss Lagerlöf, who in 1909 became Sweden's first winner of the Nobel prize for literature, may in fact have had a greater influence in America than any other Swedish novelist or short-story writer. Swedish authors of the early to middle 1900s who have had novels published in the United States include, besides the already mentioned Hjalmar Bergman, Pär Lagerkvist, and Vilhelm Moberg, Frans G. Bengtsson (1894–1954), who rendered Thoreau's *Walden* into Swedish and whose numerous scholarly specialties included the American Civil War; Eyvind Johnson (b. 1900), a literary internationalist who became one of Swedish literature's most consistent opponents of Nazism and other forms of totalitarianism; Harry Martinson (b. 1904), cited elsewhere as a poet, who for many years earned his living as a seaman and in 1949 became the first author of proletarian background to occupy a chair in the Swedish academy; Stig Dagerman (1923–54), widely regarded as a literary wonderchild who perhaps ripened too rapidly; and Sara Lidman (b. 1923), whose first novels won universal acclaim, and who later played one of the leading parts in the Swedish agitation against the war in Vietnam. In

1974 Eyvind Johnson and Harry Martinson shared the Nobel prize for literature.

In the early 1970s two Swedish authors were listed in *Who's Who in America*, namely Pär Lagerkvist and Astrid Lindgren (b. 1907), the latter a very productive and popular writer of children's books, with spectacular but relatively good-natured mischief as one of her leading themes. Her *Pippi Longstocking*, translated by Swedish-born Florence Lamborn, was published in the United States in 1950, and a dozen titles followed, including *Mischievous Meg*, *The Children of Noisy Village*, and *Emil in the Soup Tureen*. In 1970 her books had been translated into 30 languages, including Swahili, and had sold nearly four million copies. Her characters have also become known via films, radio, and television. Astrid Lindgren was born at Vimmerby in Småland. More sophisticated is Tove Jansson (b. 1914), a Swedish Finn and creator of the bizarre world of the Moomin trolls, who have become widely known even outside the North of Europe.

The most popular Swedish writer of children's books before Astrid Lindgren was Elsa Beskow (1874–1953), who specialized in texts of the fairy-tale type and also was an excellent illustrator. Her stories and songs, many of which were set to music by Alice Tegnér (1864–1943), became popular in many countries, including the United States. The first great writer of books and stories for young people in the Swedish language was a Swedish Finn, Zachris Topelius (1818–98), who by the turn of the 19th century was more widely read in Sweden than any native author. A few years later came *Nils Holgersson's underbara resa genom Sverige* (The Wonderful Adventures of Nils), Selma Lagerlöf's enormously successful geography book, which immediately was translated into English and published in America. In the early 1900s Sweden also had one of the world's great illustrators of fairy tales, John Bauer, who in 1918 at the age of 36 drowned with his family in Lake Vättern, near the city of Jönköping where he was born. He is represented in art collections in the United States. A new era of American-type mass production of storybooks and other influences dawned in Sweden in the middle 1930s, when three short films by Walt Disney were followed by cheap picture books. Numerous translations of American adventure books had been issued in the 19th century, and more followed in the 20th.

In the 1930s and the following decades, many Swedish poets found inspiration in Walt Whitman, Carl Sandburg, and St. Louis-born T. S. Eliot, who in 1948, by then a British citizen for 20 years, received the Nobel prize. Most Swedes with deep literary interests read American and English poetry in the original, but although verse often seems to defy translation, Swedish versions have become available on a relatively large scale. The number of Swedes who are familiar with the most modern American poetry is naturally small, but their expertise, on the other hand, is remarkable, and a similar situation, in reverse, exists in the United States. American translators of modern Swedish poetry include two of the country's best-known modern poets, May Swenson, who was born of Swedish immigrants in Utah, and Robert Bly, who in 1968 received the National Book Award in poetry. Of Norwegian ancestry and familiar with the Swedish language, he had in the early 1960s produced a partly new translation of Selma Lagerlöf's *The Story of Gösta Berling*. Both May Swenson and Robert Bly have translated a Swedish poet named Tomas Tranströmer (b. 1931), who in the early 1970s toured the United States and read his poetry to academic audiences. In 1974 W. S. Merwin, described as the most puzzling of America's significant modern poets, read some of his poems in Stockholm. Modern American poets of Swedish birth include Siv Cedering Fox, born in 1939 at Överkalix in the far north and brought to America at the age of 14, and Lennart Bruce, who was born in Stockholm in 1919 and lives in San Francisco. Being truly bilingual he writes his poems in two versions, one American and one Swedish.

The late Gunnar Ekelöf (1907–68) is widely regarded as Sweden's most important 20th-century poet. Parts of his 15 volumes of poetry have been translated into several languages, including English.

At the universities in Sweden, pioneering contributions to the organization of American studies were made by Bodvar Liljegren (b. 1885), professor of English at Uppsala in 1939–51, who in the 1940s built up its American Institute, and Lars Åhnebrink (1915–66), an associate professor at the same university, who somewhat later initiated a widespread revival of the interest in American letters. As the thesis for his doctorate he wrote *The Beginnings of Naturalism in American Fiction*, and in the early 1960s he came to the University of Washington in Seattle to lecture on American literature. His wife became a specialist on the same subject. Lars Åhnebrink served as chairman of the Nordic Association for American Studies and as executive member of the European Association for American Studies. Among those who had stimulated his interest in American literature was Kenneth Ballard Murdock, professor of English at Harvard, who in 1946 was American-Scandinavian Foundation lecturer on American literature and ideas to Scandinavian universities, including Uppsala. In 1947 a businessman in New York, David Samuel Gottesman, established a five-year program enabling Uppsala University to invite American and other cultural leaders to lecture on humanistic subjects. The project was, he said, an expression of gratitude for the help Sweden had given the Jewish people during and after the Second World War. In 1934, American English seems to have been first taught in Sweden at the Anglo-American Center at Mullsjö in the province of Småland, which had been founded in 1924 by English-born Charles Allwood and was continued by his son Martin S. Allwood. Many American plays have been performed there in the original language.

In his Nobel lecture in Stockholm in 1930, Sinclair Lewis mentioned Eugene O'Neill among other Americans who might have received the literature prize. O'Neill, he said, "has done nothing much in American drama save to transform it utterly, in ten or twelve years, from a false world of neat and competent trickery to a world of splendor and fear and greatness." At that time O'Neill had already made an auspicious start on the Swedish stage, and in 1936, when he became the second American to win the Nobel prize for literature, he was regarded as one of the most significant playwrights of the new century.

O'Neill's *Anna Christie*, which was published in 1922, had been produced at the Royal Dramatic Theater in Stockholm in 1923, and *Strange Interlude*, which came in 1928, was given the same year. In 1933, both *Desire under the Elms* and *Mourning Becomes Electra* were offered in Stockholm. *The Iceman Cometh* was produced at the Royal Dramatic immediately after its publication in 1946.

O'Neill's four posthumous plays were donated by the author's widow, Carlotta O'Neill, to the Royal Dramatic Theater, where they had their world premieres. They had been unearthed with the assistance of Dr. Karl Ragnar Gierow (b. 1904), poet and playwright, who

763

in 1951–63 served as director of the Royal Dramatic and in 1961 was elected a member of the Swedish Academy. The first drama, *Long Day's Journey into Night*, which has been called the greatest play written by an American, opened in Stockholm on February 10, 1956. Then came *A Touch of the Poet*, which began its run on March 29, 1957, and the one-act *Hughie*, billed together with O'Neill's *Emperor Jones*, which opened on September 18, 1958. The last posthumous play, *More Stately Mansions*, had its world premiere at the Royal Dramatic on November 9, 1962. The performance, including two intermissions, took about five hours, while the original version would have required nine or ten. When this work was given to the Swedish theater, Mrs. O'Neill said that "my husband always felt that Sweden had done his plays better and with greater interest and enjoyment than any other country." Including *More Stately Mansions*, fourteen of O'Neill's dramas had by then been produced at the Royal Dramatic in Stockholm.

The sums accruing from the successful productions of O'Neill's posthumous plays in Stockholm are set aside in a fund which awards O'Neill grants to talented actors and actresses at the national stage. In 1963, when the Royal Dramatic celebrated its 175th anniversary, the American ambassador to Sweden expressed his country's gratitude for the theater's part in introducing O'Neill. A large collection of books by and about the American playwright was presented to the Royal Dramatic's library. Eugene O'Neill had on several occasions expressed his sense of obligation to August Strindberg, whose works first had given him "the vision of what modern drama could be." Strindberg, as already shown, has influenced many other American playwrights, and several of his dramas are often performed in the United States.

Other American playwrights who are well known in Sweden include Edward Albee, Maxwell Anderson, Erskine Caldwell, William Inge, Arthur Miller, Clifford Odets, Thornton Wilder, and Tennessee Williams. During the Second World War about a score of American plays were given by the Royal Dramatic in Stockholm and the city theaters in Gothenburg and Malmö. A national organization that had been established in 1933 as part of the educational system and manages most of the touring companies offered several plays, including John Steinbeck's newly published *The Moon Is Down* about the resistance movement in a Nazi-occupied country. The companies which in summertime appear in Sweden's municipal recreation parks offer, as a rule, lighter fare. Most successful American musicals become hits also in Stockholm and other Swedish cities.

After the Second World War, Sweden's industrial arts, widely known as "Swedish Modern," remained one of its most valuable cultural assets in the United States. Even before the war ended a comprehensive photographic exhibit opened at the Architectural League in New York, and during the next two years it was shown in many of the country's leading museums, including the Art Institute of Chicago, the Minneapolis Institute of Arts, the M. H. de Young Memorial Museum in San Francisco, and the Seattle Art Museum. Richly illustrated articles were published in leading design magazines, and the design editor of *The New York Times* wrote: "For almost five years war brought the outward flow of Swedish goods and ideas practically to a standstill. The first inkling of what has been going on there comes from an exhibit portraying Swedish design 1940 to 1945, presented by The American-Swedish News Exchange and now touring United States Art Centers. An imposing array of some 300 photographs of home exteriors and interiors, furniture, fabrics, ceramics and crystal has met with somewhat the same eager appraisal as the first fashion sketches out of liberated Paris." The exhibition and its extensive American tour were organized by Holger Lundbergh, born in Stockholm in 1897, who had come to America in 1919 and joined The American-Swedish News Exchange in 1927.

In 1949 the Board of Education in New York invited Sweden to provide a traveling exhibition largely consisting of modern decorative and industrial arts, and for five years such a show circulated among the city's high schools. "Viewing this exhibit," a leading school official said at the opening, "will help cultivate the taste not only for what is useful, but also for what is beautiful." A similar collection was shown in Minneapolis. During the following decades the pace of change in Swedish industrial arts became more rapid, and among the significant trends was one toward greater individualism or originality. Sweden's designers and producers worked in close contact with their colleagues in the other Nordic countries, and the most important exhibit in America in the 1950s was a joint one, called "Design in Scandinavia." Comprising some 800 objects ranging from furniture to jewelry, it opened on January 15, 1954, at the Virginia Museum of Fine Arts in Richmond, Virginia. During the next three or four years it was seen by more than half a million people in the United States and Canada.

One of the outstanding cultural events in Sweden toward the end of the Second World War was an exhibition of American architecture, entitled "America Builds," which on June 14, 1944, opened at the National Gallery of Art in Stockholm. It had been arranged by the Sweden-America Foundation as the main project in the celebration of its 25th anniversary, with The American-Scandinavian Foundation in New York and the Office of War Information in Washington, D.C., as cosponsors. The exhibition consisted of about 400 photographs, selected by the Museum of Modern Art in New York. A leading Swedish art critic, Gotthard Johansson (1891–1968), who in 1951–60 was chairman of the Swedish Society for Industrial Design, welcomed it as "the best architectural exhibition I have ever seen."

The largest collection of American arts and crafts shown in Scandinavia, entitled "Objects: USA," was displayed in Stockholm in the early summer of 1973, after having first toured the United States for some years and then visited Paris, Madrid, Milan, Zürich, and Hamburg. The exhibit, which comprised 242 objects by 221 artists, was described in the Swedish press as a fantastic collection of objects of clay, wood, metal, textile, glass, and plastics, most of it advanced, challenging, and free from all thinking in terms of utility. "Those who might believe that the United States is a nation wanting in artistic activities will get that impression thoroughly revised when they visit the current exhibit," wrote one art critic.

In the fall of 1973 a group of American art patrons and artists, with some support from the Swedish government, donated a collection of modern American paintings and sculpture to Stockholm's Museum of Modern Art (Moderna museet), which in the 1960s had been the first museum in Europe to exhibit the new American art. The 31 works had been selected by Pontus Hultén (b. 1924), since 1960 director of the Museum of Modern Art in Stockholm and in 1973 director-designate of the Museum of Modern Art in Paris. In Stockholm he had organized a whole series of exhibits showing the new American art, including "Four Americans" in 1962, "106 Forms of Love and Despair," also known as the Pop Exhibition, in 1964, and a separate Claes Oldenburg exhibition in 1966.

The 31 works received in 1973 made the Swedish museum's already extensive holdings of contemporary American art the most comprehensive public collection of such art outside the United States. Among the artists represented, both in the old collection and in the new works, are Claes Oldenburg, born in Stockholm in 1929 and raised in Chicago where his father, a Swedish career diplomat, served as consul general for Sweden; James Rosenquist, born in 1933 at Grand Forks, North Dakota, of Swedish immigrants; and Öyvind Fahlström, born in 1928 at São Paulo, Brazil, of Swedish parents, who by the middle of the 1900s had begun to divide his life between Stockholm and New York.

Claes Oldenburg, who was brought to America the first time as an infant, became in the 1960s one of its best-known artists. He was called the "Picasso of Pop," but was also hailed as a master draftsman in the classic tradition. In the fall of 1969 the Museum of Modern Art in New York offered a huge and highly successful retrospective exhibition. Long articles about Oldenburg and his art were published in leading newspapers and magazines, and even people who were not particularly interested in art remembered him as the creator of "soft" sculptures and "giant" objects, including, for instance, such American food specialties as a cheeseburger, a baked potato, and a banana sundae. While Claes Oldenburg had studied at Yale, his younger brother Richard, born at Stockholm in 1933, went to Harvard. Richard Oldenburg, who had begun his career in publishing, was in 1972 named director of the Museum of Modern Art in New York.

Ingmar Bergman boom begins in America in 1958 — *Sweden's foremost film-maker*

IN THE late 1950s and throughout the 1960s and early 1970s, a motion-picture producer and stage director named Ingmar Bergman aroused more interest and discussion abroad than any other Swede. In the United States his films were seen by millions, he was interviewed on radio and television, books were written about him and his art, and the newspaper and magazine articles would fill many volumes. Not since the middle of the 1800s had a Swedish artist been the center of such concentrated and largely fascinated or rapt attention in America.

The Ingmar Bergman boom or mania, as it also was called, lasted much longer than the Jenny Lind craze but was, on the other hand, more limited in its scope. It did not, as the adulation of the famous singer, directly affect everyday life. There were, of course, many other differences between the two phenomena, but both Miss Lind and the decidedly "intellectual" Ingmar Bergman fitted in some way into the spirit or cultural context of the times.

In the American press Ingmar Bergman was hailed as "a poet with the camera," "a magician," "perhaps the greatest film-maker of all time," and "Sweden's mysterious genius." He was also called the "Bunyan of show business," and that description did not refer to the Superman of the forests, Paul Bunyan, but to John Bunyan, the English religious author and preacher, who, while in prison, wrote the autobiographical *The Pilgrim's Progress*, an epic of a lonely pilgrim's inner life. The leading themes of Bergman's own work as a script writer and film director were God and the Devil, Life and Death, the drama of Man and Woman, or just Woman, and the tragic solitude of all human beings. He could, however, also be lighthearted.

Neither in America nor in other countries did Ingmar Bergman impress everybody. Several critics and many moviegoers found him pretentious or obscure. Bergman himself has, in fact, admitted that at times he has been too obscure, but, he added, "my function is not to explain everything." He has also observed that "my philosophy is not to have any basic philosophy," that "all my films are dreams," and that in many cases the meaning of a certain scene may vary with his own mood or other conditions. Some of his pictures, including at least one which has been much admired, he would, it seems, rather forget. In 1971 a writer in *Life* magazine, Richard Meryman, made this observation: "In a tiny, sunny corner of himself, Bergman is bemused by being Bergman. It is a niche where he does not take himself and his art so very seriously."

Ingmar Bergman has undoubtedly helped explore new artistic frontiers. More international prizes have been awarded him than anyone else in motion-picture history. He has hardly ever produced a film without first-rate acting, and an astounding ability to bring out the very best in his actors seems, in fact, to be one of his secrets. His photography, for which Sven Nykvist, a native of the old emigration center of Moheda in Småland, has often been responsible, has also won high praise.

In the United States, Ingmar Bergman first became widely known in 1958–59 for his *Smiles of a Summer Night*, a both romantic and cynical comedy which in 1973 was adapted for the Broadway musical stage (with the title *A Little Night Music*), *The Seventh Seal*, an allegorical tale set in the Middle Ages, *Wild Strawberries*, which like other Bergman products reflects influences from Strindberg's dream plays, and *The Magician*, a burlesque study of the susceptibility of the human mind to the sway of illusion. Among the high points of his rich production in the 1960s and early 1970s were *Through a Glass Darkly*, a passage from the Bible which as a result of the film became a familiar quotation, *Persona, The Passion of Anna, Cries and Whispers*, and *Scenes from a Marriage*. Bergman's first English-language film, *The Touch*, which was produced in Sweden and opened in 1971, disappointed many of his admirers.

Bergman was born in 1918 in a parsonage at Uppsala. The stage has always been his foremost love, and at the age of 26 he was placed in charge of the city theater at Helsingborg in south Sweden. In 1946–61 he directed many stage productions in Gothenburg, Malmö, and Stockholm, including the Royal Opera. In 1963–66 he headed the Royal Dramatic, where he later again worked as a stage director. His first guest appearances outside Scandinavia were made in 1959 when he took an ensemble from the Malmö City Theater both to London, where Goethe's *Faust* was given in the Swedish language, and to the International Theater Festival in Paris.

Other film-makers who have contributed to what has been called the second "golden age" in Swedish films include Alf Sjöberg, who in 1925 began his long career as a stage director at the Royal Dramatic. In 1944 he directed a movie which in English was called *Torment*, and which in 1946 won the Grand Prix at the International Festival in Cannes, France. In 1947 it opened in New York and brought Ingmar Bergman, who had written the script, his first press notices in America. A member of Bergman's own generation, Arne Sucksdorff (b. 1917), specialized in lyric but realistic films about nature and a way of life largely untouched by modern civilization. One of a different kind, *Symphony of a City*, received the American "Oscar" for the best short subject of 1948. Sucksdorff's first full-length feature, *The Great Adventure*, a study of two boys and the teeming wildlife around a farm in central Sweden, for which the International Film Festival at Cannes honored him in 1954, was received with enthusiasm when it came to America the following year. New York critics called it a "masterpiece." The General Federation of Women's Clubs selected it to be shown at their national convention in 1955, and early in 1956 it was presented twice on a nationwide TV program.

Sweden has always imported more moving pictures from the United States than from any other country. Even by the middle of the 1970s more than half of the films shown were American.

Sweden the "social laboratory" attracts interest in America — Ombudsman new word

DURING THE latter part of the 20th century the United States remained Sweden's foremost source of more or less useful new information and impulses. The fields of science, engineering, industry, business, and entertainment were probably particularly important, but hardly any sphere was excepted.

The year 1950, for instance, marked the beginning of a period of far-reaching changes in Swedish education, and it was both preceded and accompanied by studies of the American school systems. Other countries were also included in the Swedish surveys. Today there are numerous educational similarities between Sweden and the United States, but there are also significant differences.

In 1963 the Swedish government introduced press conferences of a new type, similar to those given by the President of the United States, which were regarded as the principal model. When a fact-finding committee has been appointed to prepare some new legislation, considerable attention is almost always paid to efforts to solve the same problem in the United States. And, for instance, when a district council plans to build a new hospital or modernize an old one, a small group of delegates may be sent to America for studies. The final product in Sweden is likely to have at least some important features that have been adopted from American institutions or blueprints, although they have also been adapted to local conditions.

In some special fields, America seems to have absorbed even more from Sweden than vice versa. Especially in the 1930s this was true of industrial art and design. Swedish social programs, especially those relating to health, pensions, and the care of the aged, have often attracted much more attention in the United States than the American schemes have aroused in Sweden. For many years the average Swede has had a tendency to underestimate the scope of social welfare in the United States. American writers and experts have, on the other hand, often described modern Sweden as an interesting social laboratory. For social research in the United States, Swedish specialists as well as political and industrial leaders have a deep respect.

Swedish labor-management relations and employment policies have attracted interest in the United States ever since the 1930s, and this American inquisitiveness reached one of its peaks in the early and middle 1960s. In the fall of 1962 three Swedish top officials, representing the trade unions, the employers, and the government, appeared before the President's Advisory Committee on Labor-Management Policy in Washington and then took part in other meetings all over the country. In the summer of 1963 the same group accepted an invitation from the U.S. Senate Subcommittee on Unemployment and Manpower.

The first invitation had come from Secretary of Labor Arthur J. Goldberg who visited Sweden in 1961 and in a subsequent interview in Washington observed that Sweden had both a strong private-enterprise system and a strong trade-union movement, being in that sense "very comparable" to the United States. On both sides of the bargaining table in Sweden, responsibility seemed to be the rule. Mr. Goldberg did not know whether the Swedish way of tackling labor-management problems would work in the United States, but some ideas might well be tried, and this seemed to apply especially to the retraining of workers who were being displaced in industry.

In 1963–64 a comprehensive report on Sweden's unemployment programs was prepared in Washington for the Joint Economic Committe of the U.S. Congress. It dealt in particular with two schemes which were said to be "among the most ingenious devised by any Western country to cope with the problem of unemployment": labor productivity and mobility were consistently furthered by the retraining and relocation of displaced workers, and during economic downturns investments in plants and equipment were stimulated by funds that private industry, induced by special benefits, had built up during the booms. During the first quarter-century after the Second World War Sweden enjoyed virtually full employment most of the time, but in the late 1960s the number of unemployed increased unexpectedly, although without assuming massive proportions. Sweden as other industrial countries had to cope with a new combination of unemployment and inflationary pressures. Gunnar Myrdal's word for it, stagflation (stagnation and inflation), also became used in America.

Swedish labor legislation does not provide for compulsory arbitration, but in one case the employers and the trade unions have voluntarily agreed on such a solution as a last resort. Since 1937, a special "peace pact" between the newspaper publishers and the mechanical craft unions has ruled out strikes and lockouts. The agreement is based on recognition of the fact that a free public discussion is one of the foundations of a democratic society. In America the Swedish "peace pact" has aroused considerable attention in the press, especially during or immediately after periods of protracted newspaper shutdowns.

In the 1960s an old Swedish word, ombudsman, became accepted as English and found its way into more and more U.S. dictionaries. The first indications of its coming popularity in America could be observed in 1959–60, when the Swedish institution of *justitieombudsman*, usually called JO, reached the age of 150 years. American interest was also stimulated when campaigns for the establishment of an ombudsman, or several ombudsmen, began in Canada and other English-speaking countries. The first ombudsman outside Scandinavia was appointed in New Zealand in 1962.

The Swedish *justitieombudsman* is a special, independent parliamentary commissioner who keeps watch over the way in which the administrative agencies, the courts, the police systems, the prisons, the state-church ministers, the social-welfare services, and to a certain extent the local authorities apply the laws and regulations to the public. The ombudsman's sources of information include his own inspections, tips from the press, and private complaints. In his investigations he enjoys complete access to all official documents and records. The strongest weapon in his arsenal is his power to prosecute, but the sanction most commonly applied is an official admonition and the ensuing publicity.

In America the Swedish *justitieombudsman* has been described as a "grievance man," a "people's watchdog," and a "protector of the citizen's rights against bureaucratic blunders and abuses." Today, Sweden has three ombudsmen of this type. Since 1954 the country also has an antitrust ombudsman and since 1971 a consumer ombudsman, both of whom are appointed by the government. A press ombudsman who was established in 1969 is named by a special committee.

In 1966, when bills calling for a U.S. ombudsman had been submitted to the U.S. Congress, Sweden's 31st *justitieombudsman* testified before the Senate Subcommittee on Administrative Practice. Even then American and Swedish legal scholars seemed to agree that in the United States ombudsmen might work more effectively at the state level and, in particular, at the local levels. In 1974 at least five American states had ombudsman offices, and in three of these, Hawaii, Nebraska and Iowa, the officials were, as in Sweden, named by and responsible to the legislature. Dozens of American cities had ombudsmen and scores more had legislation pending that would create them.

Hawaii appointed an ombudsman in 1969, and before taking office he visited Scandinavia to see how the rights commissioners functioned there. In some parts of the United States the word ombudsman has been used for investigators and mediators in landlord-tenant disputes. In the middle 1970s there were newspapers with special ombudsmen, and at many university and college campuses the students had their own ombudsmen.

Sweden and the United States among leaders in environmental protection drive

A NEW era with a more active interest in the quality of human life on earth, and with concerted efforts to halt the pollution of air and water and other disruptions of the ecological balance, seemed to dawn in the late 1960s or early 1970s. Swedish antipollution efforts became known in the United States, and American attitudes and actions were reported and discussed in the Swedish press. An American biologist, Rachel Carson, whose book *Silent Spring* of 1962 had been

773

immediately translated into Swedish, is regarded as one of the leading generators of the international movement.

Swedish authorities were the first to recognize the dangers of mercury poisoning, and the year 1966 brought a ban on the agricultural use of mercury. Industry aimed at reducing mercury discharges by about 90 percent. In the spring of 1969 Sweden became the first nation to impose a total ban on the use of DDT and its chemical relatives. American observers described Sweden's program for pollution control as particularly ambitious. In the summer of 1970 a group of American industrialists, organized through the New York Board of Trade, visited Sweden to observe the coordination of industrial and government efforts. Such projects as the revival of polluted lakes with compressed air and the conversion of sludge to fertilizer were also studied. The chairman of the House Subcommittee on Conservation and Natural Resources, Congressman Henry S. Reuss of Wisconsin, also took part in the tour. An exchange of study visits had begun.

The Swedes themselves, however, were not at all certain that they were doing enough. In the spring of 1971 the Stockholm *Dagens Nyheter* published long articles which reported the United States as having taken the lead in environmental activities, while Sweden lagged behind.

Already in 1968 Sweden had called for a worldwide conference under United Nations auspices to focus attention on the environmental problems, to stimulate national and regional action and to explore the need for international antipollution measures, and before the end of the year this proposal was accepted by the U.N. General Assembly without opposition. Stockholm was chosen as the meeting site. In the final debate in the Assembly, Ambassador Sverker Åström (b. 1915) of Sweden warned of the dangers of continued neglect: "Even if we avoid the risk of blowing up the planet, we may, by changing its face, unwittingly be parties to a process with the same fatal outcome." Ambassador James Russell Wiggins of the United States offered the Swedish resolution enthusiastic support: "We have not much time left in which to learn to proportion our population to available resources and to become good enough trustees of our inherited wealth of air, water, earth and forms of life so that our posterity may hope to survive in a condition better than bestial struggle." In preparation for the convocation in Stockholm, an international conference called "International Organization and the Human Environment" was held in 1971 at Rensselaerville, New York. It was made possible by a grant from a foundation established by Robert O. Anderson, a noted industrialist who was born in Chicago of Swedish parents.

The United Nations Conference on Human Environment was held in Stockholm June 5–16, 1972. The 1,500 delegates representing 113 nations assembled in an atmosphere of skepticism, in part because of the absence of countries like the Soviet Union, East Germany, and Poland, and the results were not up to the original expectations. A series of resolutions which have been described as historic were, however, produced and subsequently endorsed by the United Nations as a whole. Gradually, a number of important or promising environmental actions, including a bilateral agreement between the United States and the Soviet Union, grew directly or indirectly out of the Stockholm conference. June 5, the day when the conference opened, is now observed annually as World Environment Day.

In the United States, a relatively large number of people of Swedish or other Scandinavian origin have always played leading or active parts in efforts concerning the conservation of nature and the preservation of wildlife, and the new environmental movement has received vigorous support from the same circles. Charles Lindbergh was an enthusiastic conservationist. Roger Tory Peterson, the "modern Audubon," whose father also came from Sweden, played a leading part in bringing about a new attitude toward nature and wildlife. In 1971 the World Wildlife Fund's gold medal was presented to Governor Russell W. Peterson of Delaware, whose parents had come from Sweden. He was chosen for helping to pass a ban on new heavy industry along the entire 100-mile Delaware Bay coastline. In 1973 he was made chairman of the U.S. Council on Environment Quality, and he was also, like Robert O. Anderson, named to a study commission called the National Commission on Critical Choices for America. Ira Noel Gabrielson, a noted biologist whose paternal grandfather had come from Sweden in the 1850s, was then president of the World Wildlife Fund in America. Another widely known veteran naturalist and wildlife expert, Sigurd Ferdinand Olson, was born in Chicago of parents who came from the Mora district in Dalarna and the city of Malmö in south Sweden. Dr. Gustav Adolph Swanson, born in 1910, has taught hundreds of professional wildlife conservationists at four universities, Maine, Minnesota, Cornell, and, finally, Colorado State. All four of his grandparents came to Minnesota from Sweden.

"We are entering a new phase of the scientific age, a scientific-humanistic era," Dr. Glenn T. Seaborg, in 1961–71 chairman of the U.S. Atomic Energy Commission, said in an address at Pittsburgh in 1968. Mankind is beginning to realize that "we do not conquer nature, we coexist with her — or, even more correctly, within her realm."

In the late 1960s and early 1970s, a new concern for such other basic matters as the quality of life at places of work and job satisfaction also appeared in many industrial countries, and this development was immediately reflected in the exchange of ideas and experience between the United States and Sweden. American newspapers and other media began to publish reports on Swedish efforts to apply modern methods of industrial democracy and give the workers both greater freedom and more responsibility. The Swedish auto makers, Saab-Scania and Volvo, were the first such manufacturers in the world who tried to do away, at least in part, with the conventional assembly line and instead divide the work forces into assembly teams with decision-making powers. Similar experiments were made in some industries in the United States, and other antimonotony efforts were undertaken in both countries. In their search for new techniques that should result in more job satisfaction, Swedish industrial leaders and managers studied the new American research on worker alienation and job enrichment, which was regarded as particularly advanced.

A worker exchange program designed to determine the effect of work enrichment on American blue-collar employees was begun in late 1974 when six production workers from the big three auto manufacturers spent four weeks in Sweden working in three-man teams assembling engines at the Saab-Scania plant in Södertälje south of Stockholm. Only one of the Americans had an unqualified positive reaction to the new Swedish system, but an immediate acceptance was hardly expected by experienced observers. The exchange program was organized by the New York State School of Industrial and Labor Relations, a division of Cornell University, while funding was provided by a grant from the Ford Foundation. Swedish efforts to humanize working conditions continued.

Biochemistry illuminates close links between Swedish and American science

MANY OF Sweden's internationally best-known scientists of the modern era are to be found in biological chemistry or biochemistry, that is, the study of the chemical aspect of the physiology of living organisms, and the neighboring fields of science.

One of the leaders in the rapid expansion of biochemical research was Einar Hammarsten (1889–1968), a nephew of Olof Hammarsten who is regarded as the principal founder of biochemistry in Sweden. The younger Hammarsten became in 1928 professor at the Caroline Institute in Stockholm and was greatly stimulated and helped when the Rockefeller Foundation at about the same time began to support the schools of medicine in Scandinavia. The financial basis for large-scale research was also broadened by substantial grants from the Knut and Alice Wallenberg Foundation for the promotion of science and education, established in 1917 by a prominent Stockholm banker and his wife.

It was in Dr. Hammarsten's laboratory at the Caroline Institute that Dr. Torbjörn Caspersson (b. 1910), the first Swedish cancer-research specialist to become widely known in scientific and medical circles in America, in the early 1930s developed the microspectrophotometer, which enabled scientists to see what goes on within a living cell without the traditional dissecting and staining operations. Today, the results of the investigation are automatically recorded and processed in a built-in automatic computer in the ultramicrospectrograph. The weight of the things that could be observed was finally brought down to one-thousandth of a millionth of a milligram. In 1945–50 Dr. Caspersson told medical conventions and scientific societies in the United States about his instrument. A number of American scientists working full-time in his cell-research laboratory at the Caroline Institute, which forms part of the Medical Nobel Institute, have been subsidized by the U.S. government, and the U.S. Public Health Service, the Rockefeller Foundation, and the Damon Runyan Memorial Fund for Cancer Research have supported his work with direct grants. Dr. Caspersson helped found and edit the leading scientific journal in his field, *Experimental Cell Research*, which is printed in Sweden and published in the United States.

As a result of the research activities launched by Dr. Hammarsten with support from the Rockefeller Foundation, Hugo Theorell (b. 1903) in 1932 managed to crystallize myoglobin, a pigment in the muscles, and with the aid of a Rockefeller Foundation grant he began in 1933–35 at Berlin advanced enzyme studies which had a bearing on cancer research. In 1955 he was awarded the Nobel prize in physiology or medicine. Under his direction the biochemistry department of the Medical Nobel Institute in Stockholm developed into what scientists have called a "Mecca of biochemistry." Among his closest associates were two prominent American scientists, Britton Chance of the Johnson Institute of Research in Philadelphia, who in 1946–48 had studied biochemistry in Stockholm, and Linus Pauling, winner of the Nobel prize for chemistry in 1954.

It was, moreover, as a direct continuation of research work at the Rockefeller Institute in New York that Dr. Erik Jorpes (1894–1973) of the Caroline Institute in 1935 helped establish the chemical composition of heparin, which became widely used for the prevention and treatment of blood clots. Another Stockholm-based scientist, John Runnström (1888–1971), who from 1939 to 1955 headed the Wenner-Gren Institute for experimental cell research, became a pioneer in zoophysiological research in Sweden and was, like his Swedish colleagues, elected an honorary member of American academies of science.

As a "Mecca of biochemistry" Uppsala University has often competed with Stockholm. Its biochemical research was in the period 1938–68 led by Arne Tiselius (1902–71), a pupil of The Svedberg who had developed the ultracentrifuge. Dr. Tiselius's introduction of the electrophoresis method for the study of blood serum and other biological material, which in 1948 helped bring him the Nobel prize for chemistry, is regarded as a milestone in the history of biochemistry. Two instruments devised by him to separate proteins into many chemical compounds became known as the "Tiselius apparatus" and used by scientists throughout the world. The globulin found in blood serum he divided into three distinct fractions named alpha, beta, and gamma, the latter containing the chemical substances which help fight disease caused by invading bacteria and viruses. To the biochemical institution at Uppsala the Rockefeller Foundation contributed 100,000 dollars for the purchase of special American instruments. Dr. Tiselius studied at Princeton in 1934–35 as a fellow of the Rockefeller

Foundation, and in 1939 he conducted research at the Rockefeller Institute in New York.

A group of Uppsala biochemists led by Anders Grönwall (b. 1912), later professor of clinical chemistry, managed in 1943 to synthetize dextran, which became widely used as a blood-plasma substitute at transfusions. A Swedish product called Macrodex, made from crude dextran, was launched on the market in 1947, and in the early 1950s, when large-scale production had begun in the United States, it was used with success during the war in Korea.

Few Swedish scientists have aroused as much attention in American news weeklies and daily newspapers as Dr. Holger Hydén (b. 1917), Gothenburg University specialist on the chemistry of the cells and especially the nervous system, did during tours of the United States in the 1960s. His and his colleagues' research, based on extraordinarily delicate microscopic dissection of single brain cells, was said to open the door to an understanding of how man learns and retains what he learns, and thus, for better or for worse, to a significant degree of control over the development of memory and other intellectual capacities.

In the early 1970s an estimated 500 laboratories around the world were working on prostaglandins, a group of hormones produced by virtually all tissues of the body, which were expected to provide the basis for a series of new and highly effective medicines. These would, for instance, lower blood pressure and control the reproductive process. The term prostaglandin had been coined in the middle 1930s by Ulf von Euler-Chelpin of the Caroline Institute in Stockholm, who in 1970 shared the Nobel prize in medicine with two other scientists, and while it turned out to be a misnomer, the name became part of the medical nomenclature. A younger colleague at the Caroline Institute, Sune Bergström (b. 1916), was encouraged by Dr. Euler to try to isolate prostaglandin and determine its structure, and in 1957 Bergström succeeded in isolating two different prostaglandins, which was regarded as a major breakthrough. In the middle of the 1960s three laboratories, including that of the Caroline Institute and one in America, discovered how to produce prostaglandins by biosynthesis.

In the early 1940s Dr. Sune Bergström conducted biochemical research in the United States, to begin with at Columbia University in New York as a fellow of the Sweden-America Foundation. Results of his work were presented at a meeting of biological chemists at Chicago in 1941. American recognitions for his pioneering achievements in prostaglandin research include the John Gamble Kirkwood Medal at Yale University, which was given to him in 1973.

A Swedish master photographer, Lennart Nilsson, may well be mentioned in a survey of American-Swedish interchange in biochemistry and physiology. In 1965 an extraordinary sequence of photographs showing a live baby inside the womb was published by *Life* magazine. In 1974, in a book entitled *Behold Man* and published in Boston, Nilsson made a photographic journey of discovery inside the body: with 350 stunning photographs, magnifications up to 45,000 times and most of them in color, as one reviewer wrote, he "presents the human body as a series of interior landscapes in a way that has never been seen before." Lennart Nilsson, who was born in 1922, started photographing nature when he was 12 years old. He has received awards from the American Heart Association and other American institutions. His unique art is also regarded as a contribution to cancer research.

From the middle 1920s to the 1960s, when this type of activity in Europe was discontinued, fellowships from the Rockefeller Foundation enabled nearly 150 Swedish scientists and scholars to study and conduct research in the United States. About 50 of them were specialists in medicine or physiology, while 25 were biochemists. In addition, 16 institutions in Sweden received considerable amounts for their research. Generous support of vitally important research has also been offered by other American foundations as well as by public authorities.

The largest single grant awarded a Swedish scientist by an American organization, 500,000 dollars, came in 1963 from the Ford Foundation to Dr. Egon Diczfalusy (b. 1920) of the Caroline Institute for research on human reproductive endocrinology. Part of it was used for inviting research fellows from America and other countries to the hormone laboratory at the Caroline Hospital in Stockholm. Dr. Diczfalusy was born in Hungary. Two other members of the Caroline Institute faculty who were born at Budapest in 1925, Georg Klein and his wife Eva Klein, became as specialists on tumor biology widely known in professional circles in the United States. In 1960 they received in Chicago the Ann Langer award for cancer research, and lecture tours in the United States followed.

Nuclear research and engineering is another field where there are many direct links between Sweden and the United States. After Hannes Alfvén, the 1970 Nobel laureate in physics who a few years earlier had also begun to work at the University of California in San Diego, Sweden's internationally best-known research specialist in the field of plasma physics is Bo Lehnert (b. 1926), professor at the State Council for Nuclear Research in Stockholm, who in the early 1970s often was described as one of the leaders in efforts to produce controlled nuclear-fusion reactions and thus harness hydrogen power for peaceful uses. Sigvard Eklund (b. 1911), who for many years was associated with the Nobel Institute of the Swedish Academy of Sciences and later became one of the leaders of the Swedish Atomic Energy Company, was in 1961 named director general of the International Atomic Energy Agency at Vienna, Austria. In 1968 he and two other scientists of IAEA received in New York the eighth Atoms for Peace award for their contributions in promoting international cooperation in the non-military development of nuclear energy.

The decidedly cosmopolitan orientation of Swedish science has been furthered by the Nobel prizes. The annual distribution of the awards for physics, chemistry, and physiology or medicine calls for detailed and careful surveys of contemporary research. These, in turn, are apt to stimulate Sweden's own scientific activities. The rapid progress in the United States is reflected in a dramatic increase in the number of prize winners: in the years 1901–31 only five Americans won science prizes, while for 1932–74 the number was 95.

In the period 1901–74 the five prizes established by Alfred Nobel, for physics, chemistry, physiology or medicine, literature, and peace efforts, were given to 440 persons, institutions, and organizations, and 34 countries were represented. The American prize winners totaled 117 and the Swedish 21.

A rich flora of scholarship programs, student exchanges, and summer courses

THE ANNUAL total of American scientists conducting research in Sweden in the middle 1970s was about 150. Swedish research workers in the United States, not including visiting professors and lecturers, numbered about 250. In 1974 the number of American university and college students in Sweden was estimated at about 200, while the Swedish count in America seemed to be approximately 400. Trainees are also exchanged on a relatively large scale, the flow of young Swedes to the United States being particularly lively. The leading institutions in the exchange of scholarship students and trainees between Sweden and the United States are the already mentioned Sweden-America Foundation in Stockholm and The American-Scandinavian Foundation in New York, whose activities also concern Denmark, Finland, Iceland, and Norway.

The Fulbright scholarship program, which sends Americans abroad for graduate study, teaching, lecturing, or advanced research and enables foreigners to visit the United States for the same purposes, was initiated by the U.S. Congress in 1946 and begun in Sweden in 1952. In 1960–73 the total number of Fulbright scholars in Sweden was 174, of whom 74 were senior scholars. The Swedes sent to the United States, who received travel grants only, numbered 309. Fulbright scholars may, like other exchange visitors, receive financial support from more than one program. For instance, Dr. Steven Koblik from Pomona College at Claremont, California, who in the early 1970s conducted historical research at Lund University and then published a book about Sweden's neutrality policy during the First World War, was supported by four grants: a Thord-Gray fellowship from The American-Scandinavian Foundation, a scholar enrichment grant from the Swedish government, a travel grant from the Fulbright exchange program, and a publication grant from a Swedish research council.

In 1965, a Swedish Kennedy Scholarship Fund was established in memory of the late President John F. Kennedy through a joint grant by the Swedish government and private industry, and the first awards were made in 1973. The program is focused on the field of research and study of political institutions and public administration in Sweden and the United States.

American donors of special scholarship funds for Scandinavian students have included the late Thomas E. Brittingham, Jr., of Greenville and Wilmington, Delaware, who served as investment adviser to the Nobel Foundation in Stockholm, and his family. In

1953–63, 78 students from Sweden, Norway, Denmark and Finland, including 24 from Sweden, were given one free year at the University of Wisconsin.

In 1947 an international graduate school for English-speaking students, now known as the Institute for English-speaking Students, was organized at the University of Stockholm, and by 1974 a total of about 1,000 young men and women, most of them Americans, had studied there. In addition, several hundred students had attended the language courses. The emphasis is on graduate studies in government, economics, sociology, and international relations. There is also a "junior year" for younger college students.

Since 1949, a program of higher education in Sweden and the other Nordic countries has been offered by Scandinavian Seminar in New York. Over 1,000 Americans have spent a year of language learning and independent study under its auspices in Sweden, Norway, Finland, or Denmark. Each student is placed in a residential school for young adults called folk high school or people's college, which is peculiar to Scandinavia. The first folk high school was established in Denmark in 1844, and today Sweden has about 100 such schools. In the early 1970s each annual contingent sent to Scandinavia comprised more than 100 students from 60–70 universities and colleges in the United States.

Under the auspices of the American Field Service, a large number of Swedish boys and girls between 16 and 18 have spent a year in the United States, living with an American family and studying at a high school. The same organization, which is based in New York, offers Americans a summer program in Sweden. Family living is combined with group travel.

Other organizations active along the same lines include Experiment in International Living of Putney, Vermont, Youth for Understanding of Ann Arbor, Michigan, and Rotary Student Exchange. In Sweden, work camps are organized by International Voluntary Service, Chicago. The Anglo-American Center at Mullsjö in Sweden near Lake Vättern has a summer camp of its own. Teachers' tours have been organized by the American Federation of Teachers in Washington, D.C.

For language students, the extension divisions of Sweden's five universities, from Lund in the south to Umeå in the far north, offer free Swedish-language instruction during the summer. Special summer programs in the English language are always offered at some universities and other schools, in part under American auspices. California State University at Long Beach, California, has for many years had a summer program at Uppsala University, and New York University has sponsored a graduate program in health education at Uppsala. For students with a good knowledge of Swedish or Norwegian, the University of California has offered a whole academic year of full-time study at Lund University in Sweden and Bergen in Norway. At Uppsala University and at a folk high school at Grebbestad on Sweden's west coast, the Swedish Institute offers a summer course in the Swedish language which may be described as an introduction to Swedish life and culture. Courses in music and singing for international students are offered at Vadstena; in 1974 an international orchestral-music camp was organized near Arvika in the province of Värmland. Summer courses in arts and crafts are offered on the Baltic island of Öland, and handweaving courses are given at Insjön in Dalarna as well as in Stockholm.

American-Swedish exchanges in the field of science have been furthered by two youth organizations, Young Researchers in Sweden, which was founded in 1963, and its American model, the Science Youth Movement.

41

The Immigrants and Their Descendants

*Swedish-born in USA: from 665,000 to 127,000 in 60 years —
A new cultural era*

IN THE absence of extensive immigration from Sweden, the number
of Swedish-born people in America has declined rapidly ever since
the census of 1930. In 1970 the total was about 127,000, against
214,000 in 1960, 325,000 in 1950, 445,000 in 1940, 595,000 in 1930,
and the all-time high of about 665,000 in 1910. Even the first
American-born generation, that is, those with either both parents
or one parent of Swedish birth, had in 1970 begun to shrink
considerably, numbering about 680,000, compared to 830,000 in 1960,
967,000 in 1930, and 753,000 in 1910.

In 1970 California for the first time had the largest number of
Swedish-born residents, about 18,500. Illinois was a close second with
some 18,000. New York came third with about 13,500, and Minnesota, which in the early 1900s boasted nearly 125,000 Swedish-
born, was fourth with some 13,000. Minnesota, however, still had the
largest number of residents of, wholly or in part, Swedish parentage,
nearly 102,000. Then came California, 85,000, Illinois, 80,000, and
New York, 38,000.

In 1970 Chicago remained the largest "Swedish city" in the United
States, its count of Swedish-born being 7,000. New York reported
about 6,100, Minneapolis 3,900, Los Angeles 3,300, Seattle 2,400, and
Rockford, Illinois, nearly 2,000. The largest concentrations of the

first two generations of Swedish origin were in the Chicago metropolitan area, about 66,500, the Minneapolis-St. Paul area, 56,000, and Los Angeles-Long Beach, 36,000. Then came the following metropolitan areas: New York, about 30,000, Seattle-Everett, 22,000, and San Francisco-Oakland, 20,000.

The history of the mass immigration from Sweden, subsequent migrations within the United States, and the structure of the recent influx from Sweden help explain the changing geographical distribution of the Swedish-born. California, for instance, was doing well because its Swedish-born population reached its highest point as late as about 1930, and also because the Golden State, like Florida, attracted elderly people from other parts of the country. California as well as New York and some other states benefited, moreover, from the composition of the new immigration from Sweden.

By the middle of the 20th century and during the following decades, when the annual immigration of Swedish people averaged first about 2,000 and then some 1,500, an overwhelming majority of the immigrants came from the cities, and it was made up of engineers, technicians, scientists and other professionals, young businessmen or university graduates, and a rather large proportion of young women. Before the new American immigration legislation in 1965, women were, in fact, in the majority, and many of them went to California. Whether there or in other parts of the country, quite a few remained in the United States with American husbands. A minority of the new immigrants would work for Swedish business interests in America.

In the census reports of 1970 Swedish was given as the mother tongue for no less than 626,000 American citizens and other residents, but the number of those with a good command of the Swedish language must have been much smaller. In the middle 1970s only six Swedish-language weeklies were left, and most of them were fighting for their survival. A total of about 20,000 copies were printed, while 60 years earlier Swedish-language newspapers and similar journals had had a circulation of at least 650,000. In the religious field, the 102-year-old Augustana Lutheran Church, by far the largest among the denominations of Swedish origin in America, had in 1962 merged with other church bodies into the Lutheran Church in America. Many of the still existing secular associations lived on not because they served an obviously useful purpose but because their members wanted to carry on an old tradition as long as possible and still liked to get together once in a while. A significant reactivation occurred, however, in several cases.

Among the well-established institutions built by immigrants from Sweden were many hospitals and six undergraduate colleges, Augustana in Rock Island, Illinois, Gustavus Adolphus at St. Peter, Minnesota, Bethany in Lindsborg, Kansas, Upsala at East Orange, New Jersey, and North Park College, Chicago, and Bethel College, St. Paul, which have other religious roots. The main task of the colleges is, of course, to prepare young men and women for creative and rewarding careers, and in this respect they have been so successful that it is hard to believe that none of them has had a regular enrollment of more than about 2,000. At the same time the colleges continue to be, in varying degrees, centers of Swedish traditions and of new efforts to further contacts and exchanges with the land and people of Sweden.

A wealth of material on the Swedish element in the United States has been accumulated at Augustana, and the college has both a Historical Society, founded in 1930, and a Swedish Institute, set up in 1940 to promote intellectual relations with Sweden and a better understanding of Swedish culture. Gustavus Adolphus College has repeatedly expressed its interest in closer ties with modern Sweden. Its Alfred Nobel Hall of Science, the first American memorial to Nobel, was dedicated in 1963 by Dr. Glenn T. Seaborg, then chairman of the U.S. Atomic Energy Commission and in 1951 cowinner of the Nobel chemistry prize. Among those present were 25 other winners of Nobel prizes. It was the third largest gathering of Nobel laureates in history. In 1950, when the 50th anniversary of the Nobel Foundation was celebrated in Stockholm, 22 former prize winners were gathered as eight new laureates received their awards. This total of 30 was exceeded on April 29, 1962, when 49 laureates attended a dinner at the White House upon invitation of President and Mrs. John F. Kennedy. Dr. Edgar M. Carlson, born in Wisconsin of Swedish parents, served as president of Gustavus Adolphus College from 1944 to 1968. His father had come from Linneryd in Småland.

Various efforts and tendencies in the colleges of Swedish origin were, in fact, among the forerunners of a new era in the cultural history of the Swedes in America — an era when the Swedish element

787

has become less easily identifiable and has lost much of its sentimental attachment to the old country but, on the other hand, looks more deeply into its own history, takes a more realistic interest in Swedish and Scandinavian culture, and engages in a new constructive cooperation, which does not have to be limited to people who have family roots in Sweden or some other Scandinavian country. An interest in things Swedish or Scandinavian can be just as genuine and deep without any blood relationships.

In this new era, the historical societies and cultural institutes founded by Swedish immigrants and their descendants are expected to play an increasingly important role. In 1973 three major groups, the Swedish Pioneer Historical Society of Chicago, the American Swedish Historical Foundation in Philadelphia, and the American Swedish Institute in Minneapolis launched a new coordinating organization, known as Swedish Council of America. It planned "to bring into cooperative relationship all groups and individuals whose purpose is to promote knowledge and understanding of the Swedish heritage in American life and to strengthen the cultural ties between America and Sweden." Dr. Nils Yngve Wessell of New York, since 1968 president of the Alfred P. Sloan Foundation, was elected the first chairman, and Dr. Nils William Olsson of Minneapolis, who has made significant contributions to Swedish immigration research and to American-Scandinavian cultural relations, was named coordinator. He was born in Seattle, went to school in Sweden, and became fluent in the Swedish language.

In the same year, 1973, a group of scholars and other specialists, under the auspices of the Center for Northwest European Studies at the University of Minnesota and Scandinavian Airlines System, discussed the ethnic and cultural future of the Scandinavian-American community in the United States, and one of the conclusions was that programs in Scandinavian studies at colleges and universities, as well as ethnic organizations which have introduced educational activities, have proved particularly effective. The participants agreed that ethnic awareness can be a powerful creative force.

By 1970 about 5,000 American university and college students were studying Scandinavian subjects at various levels. Complete programs in Scandinavian languages and literatures were conducted at five institutions, namely, the universities of Washington, Minnesota, and Wisconsin, and the University of California at Berkeley and at Los Angeles. Two other universities, Chicago and Harvard, were very strong in some areas. A total of 43 universities had Scandinavian courses, while for the colleges the number was 12. Enrollments in social-science courses were making headway at the expense of language studies, reflecting a growing interest in Scandinavian society. Most of those who take a doctor's degree have no family ties with Scandinavia. Since 1911 a nationwide association, The Society for the Advancement of Scandinavian Study, has been promoting interest in and study of the Scandinavian languages and literatures. It publishes a quarterly, *Scandinavian Studies*.

The establishment of direct air traffic between Scandinavia and the United States, begun by SAS in 1946, and the subsequent development of cheap air travel has had a greater direct impact on relations between America and the Scandinavian countries than any other chain of events after the Second World War. An air bridge was built over the ocean, and not only millions of passengers and huge quantities of cargo but also dreams and hopes, experience, ideas, and plans have been shuttled over it. New or stronger family bonds, new cultural or commercial contacts, broader horizons and deeper understanding are among the results.

In the flow of travelers from the United States to Sweden, Americans of Swedish descent have always accounted for a considerable share. In recent decades tens of thousands have for the first time visited the farms, cottages, or at least parishes from which their parents or other emigrant ancestors came, and legions have made repeated trips. In the 1950s and 1960s a building contractor from Chicago named Ragnar Benson, born in 1899 at Virestad in southern Småland and an emigrant at the age of 12, became widely known in Sweden as a particularly active and grandiose air traveler. At times he brought not only relatives but also many friends and employees, numbering up to 70 persons. American-born descendants of Swedish immigrants have been able to mobilize hundreds of relatives for family reunions in Sweden.

Numerous Americans of Swedish origin have made the journey hoping to be able to trace their ancestry, if possible hundreds of years back, and most of those who have prepared themselves properly before leaving the United States have, as a rule, been more or less successful. The opportunities for genealogical research in Sweden are, for various historical and technical reasons, good. In special cases expert assistance is given without request. When the astronaut Col. Edwin E. Aldrin, Jr., who in 1966 had established a world endurance record for "walking" in space and in 1969 during the Apollo 11 flight became one of the first two men to walk on the moon, visited Sweden in 1970, it was already widely known that his paternal grandparents, Johan and Anna Aldrin, had in 1892 emigrated to Worcester, Massachusetts, from Nykroppa in the province of Värmland, one of the ancient ironmaking centers of the Uddeholm company, and that his first known Swedish ancestor was born in 1708. His grandfather had been an ironsmith in Värmland, while his father, Edwin E. Aldrin Sr., became an officer of the U.S. Army Air Corps and a founder of the Aeronautical Engineering School, now the Air Force Institute of Technology.

The Swedes in America have never organized annual parades, at least not in the larger cities, but there have, on the other hand, been many mass meetings. Even in the 1970s the "Swedes Day" festival in Minneapolis, always held toward the end of June, gathered from 20,000 to 40,000 participants, the largest reunion of people of Swedish and other Scandinavian origin in the United States. Among the speakers in the 1950s and 1960s were President Lyndon B. Johnson, Vice Presidents Richard M. Nixon and Hubert H. Humphrey, and Chief Justice Earl Warren.

The Swedish Pioneer Centennial in 1948, which commemorated the beginning of a sizable Swedish immigration to the Middle West and, if it had not been for the war, perhaps would have been held a few years earlier, is generally regarded as the last far-reaching Swedish-American manifestation, and the largest after the New Sweden Tercentenary in 1938. Commemorative stamps were issued both in the United States and in Sweden. In the huge Chicago Stadium, where the festivities opened on June 4, President Harry S. Truman, Prince Bertil of Sweden, who headed the Swedish delegation, and Carl Sandburg were the main speakers. On a giant screen were shown pictures from the life of the Swedish immigrants, accompanied by orchestral music and choirs totaling nearly 2,000 voices.

Celebrations were also held in Rockford, Rock Island, and Moline,

Illinois, Minneapolis-St. Paul, Des Moines, Iowa, Omaha and Lincoln, Nebraska, Detroit, Michigan, and many other cities and communities, such as Pine Lake, Wisconsin, and Andover, Bishop Hill, and Galesburg, Illinois, which are important in the history of the Swedish pioneers of the 19th century. On King Gustav's 90th birthday, June 16, an address by him was broadcast to America and heard over national radio networks. The Swedish delegation of 10 persons ended its tour in Philadelphia and New York, where Prince Bertil's farewell address was sent out via radio. In Chicago, President Truman had awarded Prince Bertil the Legion of Merit, degree of Commander, "for exceptionally meritorious conduct in the performance of outstanding services to the Government of the United States."

*On both sides of the Atlantic, a deeper interest in the
history of the Swedes in America*

THE Swedish Pioneer Centennial in 1948 made Swedish and other immigrants more conscious of their old heritage, and in Sweden it helped activate the interest both in the history of the emigration and the Swedes in America, and in the American nation as a whole. Similar stimulating effects had a great epic on the Swedish migration to America which one of Sweden's most popular novelists, Vilhelm Moberg, already had started working on in 1948, but the last volume of which was not published until 1959. It describes the lives and adventures of a group of small farmers and farm laborers from the province of Småland who in the early 1850s emigrated to Minnesota Territory, where they settled on Lake Chisago. In 1949–64 the first volume, *The Emigrants*, sold 344,000 copies in Sweden. In 1954 the second volume issued in America, *Unto a Good Land*, became one of the monthly selections of The Literary Guild. In particular, the first of two Swedish films based on Moberg's work, directed and photographed by Jan Troell (b. 1931), received high praise in the United States. The critic in *Life* magazine wrote in the fall of 1972 that "*The Emigrants* is one of the great movies about this country, about America as an idea, America as an experience."

Immediately after the Pioneer Centennial, an organization called the Swedish Pioneer Historical Society was formed in Chicago, to preserve and publish materials bearing on the history of the Swedes in America. An association of the same type, Swedish Historical Society of America, had been in existence from 1905 until the early 1930s, when it faded away. The Norwegians in America, on the other hand, had long been both determined and successful. The Norwegian-American Historical Association, which was founded in 1925, had in 1970 published more than fifty volumes with source material and surveys.

In Sweden so-called "Sweden-America Days" had been held before 1948, but now this celebration, dedicated to the friendship and close personal relations between the two countries, became firmly established. In 1948, in fact, the last Sunday in September was set aside as Sweden-America Day all over the country. Prime Minister Tage Erlander spoke on the radio about the Swedish element in the United States, and Vilhelm Moberg, the author, was heard in a radio address from Iron Mountain, Michigan.

At the universities the interest in the Swedes in America began to increase, and in 1962 Uppsala became the center for an intensive study of Swedish emigration under the direction of Sten Carlsson (b. 1917), professor of history. The establishment of a department of American history at Uppsala was made possible by a five-year grant from the American Council of Learned Societies. Students and scholars at other universities, particularly Lund and Gothenburg, also turned to various aspects of the emigration to America. At the Institute for Dialectology and Folklore Research in Uppsala, headed by Folke Hedblom (b. 1908), accounts of old Swedish pioneers and the Swedish dialects still spoken in America in the 1960s and 1970s, as recorded on hundreds of tapes, became available for research.

A study and service center of national and international scope is the Emigration Institute at Växjö, capital of the Kronoberg district in the province of Småland, where much material concerning Swedish emigration, such as letters, newspapers, and church records, has been deposited. It began its activities in 1966 although its building, the House of Emigrants, was not officially opened until 1968, when a large exhibit called "The Dream of America" was shown. The first international emigration symposium in Scandinavia was held at Växjö in 1967. A "Minnesota Day" is celebrated there annually in early August.

By the middle of the 1900s a growing interest in the Swedish emigration to America appeared on the local level in Sweden, in provinces, regions, and parishes. Of the provinces, Värmland and Småland made particularly rapid headway. Most of the some 100,000 emigrants from Värmland have been registered in a card-index system at Karlstad. The anniversary of John Ericsson's birth, July 31, is observed annually in Värmland.

A book of nearly 1,000 pages entitled *En smålandssocken emigrerar* (A Småland parish emigrates), is one of the most impressive works on the emigration published in Sweden. It was brought out in 1967 by a group of people in Långasjö, which at that time had about 1,400 inhabitants. In 1850–1930 approximately the same number of people had emigrated to America, and the book deals with many of these, their local background, and their adventures and activities in the New World. Sooner or later about 225 former emigrants from Långasjö returned to their home parish, and one-third of the farms in the area were bought by them.

In 1962 some 90 persons from Långasjö chartered an SAS plane from Copenhagen to visit the United States and tour some of the regions settled by emigrants from the same part of Småland. Near Center City in Chisago County they found a farm named Långasjö, which had been started in 1854 by the first farmer to emigrate from Långasjö, Carl Abrahamsson or Charles Abraham (1820–1914), and now was owned by a grandson. The members of the new generation had never been to Sweden but spoke fluent Swedish with a Långasjö accent. The local school had long been known as the Långasjö School.

Since most Swedes still are aware of having relatives in the United States, a growing interest in the history of emigration is often accompanied by some form of genealogical research. Långasjö offers one example. In the north of Sweden two schoolteachers, Alfred and Ebba Zingmark, spent a great part of their time tracing the descendants of Erik Andersson and his wife "Spinnel-Anna," who in 1765 had founded a village named Storsandsjön 35 miles northwest of Umeå, and 150 miles south of the Arctic Circle. During an American tour Alfred Zingmark visited about 300 families, and later he published a book listing more than 5,000 descendants in Sweden and the United States. By the middle of July, 1965, the 200th anniversary of the beginning of the family story at Storsandsjön was celebrated by nearly 3,000 members of the clan, then the largest Swedish-American family reunion ever held. Vårgårda in Västergötland is the base of another far-flung clan; it claims descent from a farmer named Andreas Andersson who by the middle 1700s married Anna-Maria Nicander. Sweden's most legendary progenitor, Margareta Burea (1594–1657), who when married lived in the parsonage at Leksand on Lake Siljan and became known as "Stormor i Dalom" (The Great Mother of Dalarna), has thousands of descendants, many of them in America.

The new Swedish interest in the history of emigration, together with the growing social concern of the younger generations both in Sweden and in the United States, led shortly after the middle of the 20th century to the rediscovery of Joe Hill (1879–1915), whose memory had been kept alive in some labor circles in both countries but otherwise had been forgotten. He was born as Joel Emanuel Hägglund, at Gävle north of Stockholm, left for America in 1902, and first changed his name to Joseph Hillstrom. At San Pedro, California, he joined the newly formed local of International Workers of the World, a radical trade union, and began writing stirring labor songs in the English language, which could be sung to the tunes of popular ballads or Methodist hymns. In 1913, after spending a month in jail for a crime which was not proved, he went to Salt Lake City, and the next year he was charged with the murder of a former police chief and his son, and sentenced to death. According to his friends he had been "framed" because of his strike actions.

President Woodrow Wilson and other prominent Americans, including Jane Addams and Helen Keller, implored the governor of Utah to reduce the sentence to life imprisonment, and the Swedish envoy in Washington also intervened. Hill, who maintained he was innocent, was still a Swedish citizen. On the evening of November 18, 1915, he wrote his last, gently lyrical song, "My Last Will," and the next morning he was executed. Some 30,000 mourners took part in a procession in Chicago, where the funeral was held. Hill's songs became part of America's folk-music heritage. On May 7, 1970, a song entitled "I Dreamed I Saw Joe Hill Last Night" was sung during the funeral service for Walter Reuther, late president of the Congress of Industrial Organizations. Joe Hill has often been called the "Man Who Never Died." His fame has been nourished by books, newspaper and magazine articles, recordings of his songs, musicals, and a Swedish film directed by Bo Widerberg (b. 1930), which was shown in the United States about 1970 when its director had become internationally known for his *Elvira Madigan*.

The Swedes in America and their children have not by any means, as some writers believed, played a dominating part in cultural relations between the United States and Sweden, but thousands of them have made extremely important contributions. Impressive examples not already mentioned include Alrik Gustafson (1903–70), born in Iowa of Swedish immigrants, who for three decades was professor of Scandinavian literature at the University of Minnesota, became a leading expert on such Swedish authors as August Strindberg and Pär Lagerkvist, and whose monumental *A History of Swedish Literature*, published by University of Minnesota Press in 1961, was welcomed by the most exacting critics in Sweden. It was, in fact, considered to be so good and significant that a Swedish edition was published in Sweden, where there was no shortage of literary histories.

Several American newspaper correspondents in Sweden have been of Swedish birth or parentage, among them Alma Luise Olson (1883–1964) from Lindsborg, Kansas, who worked for *The New York Times* for 12 years, returning to the United States in 1940. She wrote hundreds of articles on literature, art, drama, and other topics in Sweden and the other Scandinavian countries. The Swedish literary scene has never been as well covered in an American daily newspaper as it was in the 1930s.

42

New Links in Science, Technology, Trade

Swedes who came to work in America in 1919–70, mostly in science and education

THE SOME 90,000 Swedes who came to the United States during the first ten years after the First World War had, on the whole, received a more substantial education than the immigrants of the middle to late 1800s and the early 1900s, and among them were many trained engineers and other professionals who had been at least on the verge of unemployment. During the following decades, when the immigration from Sweden had been reduced to a trickle, the proportion of professionals of various kinds became much larger. Most of the specialists who came had left Sweden not because they had reason to fear unemployment but because they wanted new experience, a new mental climate, higher incomes, or perhaps the unsurpassed research facilities that the United States could offer. Several were, in fact, invited to come. Many of the new immigrants kept in close contact with developments in Sweden, and sooner or later quite a few returned to that country.

The "brain drain" in Sweden has never approached the same proportions as in some larger European countries, but in the early 1960s the migrations of all university graduates, including those with advanced degrees and training, were studied by a committee. Except for a few categories, Sweden at that time was gaining more university graduates than it was losing. The United States was the leading importer of Swedish scientists, followed by England, Switzerland, and France.

Practically all of the persons mentioned below have been selected from the fields of education, science, and technology. Since 1965, the composition of immigration from Sweden to America has been affected by the new Immigration Act, which abolished the old national-origins quota system. The preferences established include one for professionals or persons of exceptional ability in the sciences and the arts.

Scientists of Swedish birth in America who are widely known in professional circles include Bengt Stromgren, who was born at Gothenburg in 1908, and in 1938 became professor of astronomy at Copenhagen, where his father, a noted astronomer, had served for many years. The younger Stromgren had then already taught and done research at the University of Chicago, where he later served as professor and director of its observatories. In 1957 he became a member of the Institute for Advanced Study at Princeton, New Jersey. At that time the famous research center for eminent scholars already had among its members Arne Beurling, born at Gothenburg in 1905, who had joined in 1954 and before that for many years had been professor of mathematics at Uppsala. In Stockholm during the Second World War, Dr. Beurling helped break the ciphers used by the Germans for secret messages to military and diplomatic posts and units abroad. Another Swedish mathematician, Lars V. Hörmander (b. 1931), was a member of the Institute for Advanced Study in 1964–68. He was then invited to a chair at his alma mater, the University of Lund. In 1963–64 he had served as professor at Stanford University in California.

Einar Hille (b. 1894), who for four decades taught mathematics at leading American universities and in 1947–48 served as president of the American Mathematical Society, was born in New York of Swedish parents. After studies and a doctorate at the University of Stockholm he came to the United States in 1920 as one of the first fellows of the Sweden-America Foundation, became an instructor at Princeton, transferred to Harvard and served Yale from 1933 to 1962 as a full professor. He lectured at Stockholm, Uppsala, Paris, Bombay, India, Canberra, Australia, and ten universities in Japan.

Significant contributions to scientific contacts and exchanges between Sweden and the United States have been made by Professor Per-Olov Löwdin (b. 1916), of the University of Uppsala and the University of Florida at Gainesville. In 1955 he became leader of an international research group in quantum chemistry at the University of Uppsala, where he was named to a chair in 1960. Since that year he has combined his work at Uppsala with similar activities at the University of Florida, spurring one of the most successful scientific exchanges Sweden has had with another country. The quantum chemistry groups at Uppsala and Gainesville have sister groups both in the United States and in other countries, including Denmark and Norway.

One of Sweden's leading physicists and nuclear-research scientists, Hannes Alfvén (b. 1908), who from 1940 to 1973 held professorships in electronics and plasma physics at the Stockholm Institute of Technology, has lectured or conducted research in the United States during several periods. In 1967 he was named professor at the University of California at San Diego. In 1970 he became Nobel prize winner in physics "for fundamental work and discoveries in magneto-hydrodynamics with fruitful applications in different parts of plasma physics."

Olof Rydbeck (b. 1911), professor of electronics at Chalmers Institute of Technology in Gothenburg, accepted in 1957 a call from Cornell University at Ithaca, New York, to be the first Victor Emanuel research professor. He returned to Sweden the following year. A doctor of science at Harvard in 1940, he was during three periods a visiting professor at Rensselaer Polytechnic Institute in Troy, New York, and became in 1967 a member of the Graduate School of Arts and Sciences of Pennsylvania State University. Another expert in electronic engineering, Henry Wallman (b. 1915), received his doctorate at Princeton in 1937, did research or taught at its Institute for Advanced Study and at the universities of North Carolina and Wisconsin, conducted radar research at the Massachusetts Institute of Technology in 1942–46 and then taught mathematics there until 1948, when he returned to Sweden as a visiting professor at Chalmers Institute in Gothenburg. In 1955 he was named professor of applied electronics at Chalmers.

No person of Swedish birth and training has made greater contributions to the modern development of American engineering education than C. Richard Soderberg (b. 1895), who in 1938 joined the

Massachusetts Institute of Technology as professor of applied mechanics, in 1947 became head of the department of mechanical engineering, and in 1954–59 served as dean of engineering. He has also designed and invented steam turbines and generators for both land and marine applications. For pioneer work in turbojet aircraft engines he received in 1955 the Exceptional Service Award from the U.S. Air Force. In the 1960s he remained associated with M.I.T. and also helped launch a joint American-Swedish effort in industrial gas turbines, the companies involved being United Aircraft in the United States and the Asea company's Stal-Laval subsidiary at Finspång in Sweden. One of eight children of a Baltic-herring canner at Ulvöhamn in northern Sweden, Richard Söderberg was the only member of his family to leave his native island and make his living elsewhere. After graduation from Chalmers Institute of Technology in Gothenburg he came to the United States in 1919 as a member of the first group of fellows of the Sweden-America Foundation. In 1922–38 he worked for Westinghouse at Pittsburgh, finally as chief turbine engineer, except for the years 1928–30 when he was head of the turbogenerator division of the Asea company at Västerås in Sweden.

Karl Uno Ingård (b. 1921) took his first degrees at Chalmers in Gothenburg and his doctorate at the Massachusetts Institute of Technology, where he began teaching physics in 1952 and became a full professor in 1966. His specialties include physical acoustics and plasma physics as well as aeronautics and astronautics.

Hundreds of Swedish medical experts have studied, done research, or lectured in the United States, and quite a few have remained there for long periods or indefinitely. A member of the faculty of the Caroline Institute in Stockholm, which awards the Nobel prize for physiology or medicine, Fritiof F. Sjöstrand (b. 1912), was in 1960 named to a chair in the department of zoology at the University of California in Los Angeles, where he had been a visiting professor the year before. His leading specialty is electron microscopy of cells and tissues, for which he has developed new techniques and instruments. A radiologist from the Caroline Institute, Erik Carlsson (b. 1924), came in 1957 to Washington University's Institute of Radiology at St. Louis and later joined the University of California Medical Center at San Francisco, where he was appointed professor of radiology in 1968. Jörgen Fex (b. 1924), who also began his career at the Caroline Institute, came in 1966 via Canberra, Australia, to the National Institute of Mental Health at Bethesda, Maryland, and in 1969 to Indiana University as a professor of neurology. A fourth M.D. from the Caroline Institute in Stockholm, Johannes Rhodin (b. 1922), served in 1958–63 as professor of anatomy at the New York University School of Medicine, and in 1964–74 as professor and chairman of anatomy at New York Medical College. He was then called to a professorship at the University of Michigan Medical School at Ann Arbor, Michigan, where he became chairman of the department of anatomy. Göran Bauer (b. 1925) from the University of Lund served in 1962–69 as professor of orthopedic surgery at Cornell University Medical College in New York, and was then called to a chair at Lund University. Anders Otterland (b. 1920), who studied at Gothenburg and served as professor of social medicine at the University of Umeå in the far north, was in 1968 appointed professor at the Graduate School of Public Health at the University of Pittsburgh.

The Harvard Medical School had in the 1970s four faculty members from Sweden, all of whom had taught or conducted research at schools of medicine in that country. Torsten N. Wiesel (b. 1924) from the Caroline Institute began his American career in 1955 at The Johns Hopkins University Medical School in Baltimore and became in the late 1960s professor first of physiology and then of neurobiology at Harvard. Claes H. Dohlman (b. 1922), an eye specialist who received his doctorate at Lund, came in 1958 to Boston where he built up the cornea service at the Massachusetts Eye and Ear Infirmary and the cornea center at the Retina Foundation for ophtalmological research. In 1969 he was named an associate professor at Harvard Medical School and in 1973 professor and chairman of the department of ophtalmology. Sven Paulin (b. 1926), who was raised in Germany, after his father's death joined his mother in Sweden and earned his M.D. at the University of Gothenburg, was in 1966–67 a visiting professor at the University of Florida and at Stanford, and became in 1970 professor of radiology at Harvard. Karl E. Åström (b. 1919) left the Caroline Institute in 1966 and was in 1971 named associate professor of neuropathology at Harvard. Cissela Bok, the daughter of Gunnar and Alva Myrdal and wife of Derek Curtis Bok, the president of Harvard, received her Ph.D. from Harvard, became a specialist on medical ethics, and has lectured on that subject.

Swedish-trained medical specialists who have served in Minneapolis include Dr. Hilding Berglund (1887–1962), who during most of the period 1925–32 was head of the division of general medicine at the University of Minnesota and then returned to Sweden, and Dr. Wilhelm Stenström (1891–1973), who came to America in 1919 for studies at Harvard as a fellow of the Sweden-America Foundation in Stockholm. His long career at the University of Minnesota began in 1926 when he was named an associate professor of biophysics and head of the radium and roentgenotherapy departments at the Medical School.

At the University of Washington Medical School in Seattle, Karl Erik Hellström (b. 1934) was in 1969 named professor of pathology, and three years later his wife, Ingegerd Hellström (b. 1932), became professor of microbiology and nursing. Both have specialized in experimental cancer research, dealing with the body's immunological defense against tumors. Before leaving Sweden in 1966, they were associate professors at the Caroline Institute in Stockholm. Swedish-born medical specialists who received at least most of their education in America include Orwar Swenson, born at Helsingborg in 1909, who obtained his doctor's degree at Harvard in 1937 and in 1960 was named professor of surgery at the Northwestern University Medical School.

A noted Swedish expert on cell research and biophysics, Hans G. Borei (b. 1914), who in 1951 came to the University of Pennsylvania and the California Institute of Technology as a visiting professor, was a few years later named professor of zoology and general physiology at the University of Pennsylvania. His specialties include marine biology, and in 1965 he was placed in charge of the Swans Island Marine Station in Maine. Lennart Roden (b. 1929) from the Caroline Institute in Stockholm was in 1970 named professor of pediatrics and biochemistry at the La Rabida-University of Chicago Institute in Chicago, which he had joined in 1961. Some years later he moved to the department of biochemistry at the University of Birmingham in Alabama.

A research geologist of the University of Stockholm, Ernst V.

Antevs (1888–1974), came to North America in 1920 with a scientific expedition led by Baron Gerard De Geer (1858–1943), the pioneer Swedish geo-chronologist. He remained in the United States and was for some time connected with Harvard. The subjects of his many books include the recession of the last ice sheet in New England and the alpine zone of the Mount Washington range. He finally settled in Arizona. Another noted geologist, Sture Landergren (b. 1897), served in 1963–68 as a senior research professor at the University of Miami, and then returned to Sweden. A plant biologist from Stockholm University, Lars Gunnar Romell (b. 1891), served in 1928–34 as research professor of forest soils at Cornell University at Ithaca, New York, and also returned to Sweden. Dr. Bengt G. Rånby (b. 1920) from the University of Uppsala moved in 1956 to America, where he first worked as a research specialist for an industrial corporation and then, from 1959, as professor of pulp and paper technology and head of the Empire State Paper Research Institute at the State University of New York in Syracuse. In 1961 he returned to Sweden as professor at the Institute of Technology in Stockholm.

Georg A. Borgström (b. 1912), who during his last eight years in Sweden was head of the National Institute for Food Preservation Research, came to the United States in 1956 as professor at Michigan State University in East Lansing, first of food science and nutrition and from 1960 also of geography. He is a leading international authority on food utilization and world feeding. In articles and books, published in several languages, he has underlined the inadequacy of the resources on an earth with a rapidly growing population. In 1974 he also began lecturing at the University of Gothenburg.

In the fields of archeology and the study of the antiquities and the arts, relations between Swedish and American scholars and institutions have long been close. Olov Janse (b. 1892), who began his academic career at Uppsala and later held a professorship in Paris, led in the 1930s important French-American excavations in Indochina and the Philippines. In 1940–43 he served as professor of East Asiatic archeology at Harvard, and in 1943–55 he worked for the Department of State at Washington, D.C. Erik Sjöqvist (b. 1903), who obtained his doctorate at Uppsala and then for many years headed the Swedish Institute in Rome, served from 1951 to 1969 as professor of classical archeology at Princeton University where he had been a visiting professor in 1948–49. Another Uppsala Ph.D., Åke W. Sjöberg (b. 1924), who specialized in assyriology, came in 1963 to the University of Chicago and in 1966 as full professor to the University of Pennsylvania at Philadelphia. Carl A. Nordenfalk (b. 1907), who in 1958–69 served as director of the National Gallery of Art in Stockholm, was in 1969 named to a research post at the Institute for Advanced Study at Princeton.

Swedes can hardly be expected to come to the United States to teach English, but in 1944 a Swedish-educated scholar, Helge Kökeritz (1902–64), was appointed to a full professorship in English at Yale University. An associate professor at the University of Uppsala, he came to America in 1939 on a traveling scholarship from his alma mater, and the following years he did research or taught at five universities, Wisconsin, Harvard, Yale, Iowa, and Minnesota. As professor at Yale he became an internationally recognized authority on Shakespeare's and Chaucer's pronunciation. In 1954, when his monumental *Shakespeare's Pronunciation* had just been published, he had the cast of a Shakespeare production at Yale pronounce the words in the Elizabethan fashion, an event that aroused wide attention. In Shakespeare's plays he discovered many new puns that had amused or perhaps shocked the dramatist's contemporaries. Kökeritz was born on a farm on the Baltic island of Gotland.

Another associate professor at the University of Uppsala, Gunnar Boklund (b. 1919), who in 1953–56 served as a lecturer of Swedish at Harvard, was in 1963–68 professor of English at the University of Denver in Colorado. He was then named to a chair at Uppsala but returned to Denver in 1973. Birgitta K. Steene (b. 1928), who took her first degree at Uppsala and her doctorate at the University of Washington in Seattle, served in 1967–73 as professor of English at Temple University in Philadelphia and then moved to the University of Washington as chairman of its department of Scandinavian languages and literature. Her doctor's thesis is entitled *American Drama in Sweden 1895–1958.*

Other Swedes who have taught or teach Scandinavian languages and literature at American universities include Gösta Franzén (b. 1906), a former associate professor at Uppsala who in 1944–74 held a professorship at the University of Chicago, Assar Janzén (1904–71), a former associate professor at Gothenburg and Lund, who from

1949 until his death served at the University of California at Berkeley, Eric O. Johannesson (b. 1923) from Lund University, who in 1955 joined the faculty at Berkeley, Nils Hasselmo (b. 1931) from Uppsala University, and with a doctorate from Harvard, who in 1965 joined the University of Minnesota, and Leif Sjöberg (b. 1925) from Uppsala, who in 1958–68 led courses at Columbia University in New York and then was named professor of comparative literature and Scandinavian studies at the State University of New York at Stony Brook, Long Island. All have been among the most active promoters of American-Swedish exchanges in the literary and artistic fields.

A Swedish psychologist, Helge Lundholm (1891–1955), who received his Ph.D. at Stockholm in 1919 and the same year became a member of the first group of fellows of the Sweden-America Foundation, in 1930 joined the faculty of Duke University at Durham, North Carolina. In 1938 he became chairman of the department of psychology after William McDougall, a noted English-born psychologist who had previously held a professorship at Harvard University.

Hans Zetterberg (b. 1927), a graduate of Uppsala University and for some years a member of the Columbia University faculty, was in 1967 appointed chairman of the department of sociology at Ohio State University in Columbus. He has spent much of his time in Sweden directing the Swedish Institute of Public Opinion Research at Stockholm.

Several outstanding Swedish theologians have pursued their careers in the United States or served there for some time. Krister Stendahl (b. 1921), who received his doctorate from the University of Uppsala in 1954 and then was called to Harvard as professor of New Testament studies, was in 1968 named dean of the Divinity School at Harvard. He has been described as one of the top New Testament scholars in the United States, as consistently concerned with the struggle against social ills, and as a champion of the essential unity of the Christian churches. Among his ancestors in Sweden was Samuel Owen, a Methodist and industrial pioneer, who had immigrated from England in the early 1800s. Dr. Stendahl was in 1967 one of three leading candidates for the post of archbishop in the Church of Sweden, and by far the youngest.

Another theologian who also had studied at Uppsala, Nils Ehrenström (b. 1903), served from 1955 until his retirement in 1969 as professor at Boston University, teaching the history of ecumenicity. Gösta W. Ahlström (b. 1918), who had been a member of the Uppsala faculty, came to the University of Chicago as a visiting professor in 1962 and was the following year named to a chair in Old Testament studies. A fourth Uppsala theologian, Bertil E. Gärtner (b. 1924), served in 1965–69 as professor of New Testament studies at Princeton Theological Seminary, and then returned to Sweden. In 1970 he was named bishop of the Gothenburg diocese. Bengt R. Hoffman (b. 1913), who had been a rector in Sweden and also worked abroad for the World Council of Churches and other international organizations, was in 1967 appointed professor of ethics and ecumenical studies at the Lutheran Theological Seminary in Gettysburg, Pennsylvania.

Some other Swedes who became noted scholars received at least most of their higher education in the United States. Nels F. S. Ferré (1908–71), who arrived at the age of 13, studied both at Uppsala and Lund universities and at Harvard, where he obtained his doctor's degree. He served for many years as professor of philosophy and theology at Vanderbilt University in Nashville, Tennessee, later at the Andover-Newton Theological School at Newton Center, Massachusetts, and finally at the College of Wooster in Wooster, Ohio. In 1951 he went to England as a Fulbright lecturer at Oxford University, and in 1957 he was president of the American Theological Society. In some of his books he explained modern Swedish theology. A younger brother, Gustave Adolf Ferré (b. 1918), who was brought to America at the age of six, obtained his Ph.D. at Vanderbilt University, served as a Baptist minister and professor of philosophy, and was in 1971 named vice president of North Texas State University at Denton. An older brother, George Ferré (b. 1904), who came to America at the age of 15 and earned his M.D. in Boston, became a noted surgeon at Miami, Florida. One of their four sisters, Margaret V. Ferré (1913–65), received her Ph.D. from the University of Pennsylvania and became chairman of the department of foreign languages at Eastern Baptist College at St. Davids, Pennsylvania. Another sister, Thyra Ferré (1905–75), who arrived at the age of 19, became three decades later a successful writer of fictional accounts of her family life in Sweden and America. Described as "warm, friendly, entertaining books," they were translated into several foreign languages as well as into Braille. The father of the Ferrés, Frans Ferré, was a Baptist minister in Sweden who moved frequently about the country and in 1924 answered a call to the First Swedish Baptist Church in Springfield, Massachusetts.

One of the more colorful careers is that of Gösta Wollin, born in 1922 at Ystad in southern Sweden, who described himself as an oceanographer, inventor, and criminologist, and also is an educator and youth leader. He came to the United States in 1942 and joined the Army, served as a paratrooper in the invasions of Normandy and Holland, returned to Sweden and wrote two novels, and came back to America in 1950 to enter Columbia University's School of Social Work in New York. In 1958–60 he served as executive director of the Big Brothers of America and in 1960–67 as project director of the National Council on Crime and Delinquency. He has done significant research on deep-sea sediment. His inventions include a snowmaking machine.

An unusual contribution to science and technology in America was made in the 1930s by a Swede named Harry Söderman (1902–56), who did not settle in the country but became widely known. In the Police Academy Building in New York he set up a research laboratory designed to apply modern science to the field of crime detection and criminal identification. It was dedicated in June 1934. In the same year Söderman spent six months with the Manhattan Homicide Squad, and together with Chief Inspector John J. O'Connell he wrote what turned out to be a classic book on modern criminal investigation. In 1924–26 he had studied crime and police techniques in Asia, including China, and in 1926–28 he both studied and lectured at the University of Lyons in France, where he received his doctorate. In 1930 he was named professor of police science at the Stockholm University Law School and in 1939 also director of the National Technical Institute of Criminal Police.

During the Second World War Harry Söderman secretly helped train 15,000 Norwegians and nearly 5,000 Danes in police techniques, so that they would be ready to serve in their countries immediately at the war's end. When the Germans capitulated in the spring of 1945, he became police chief ad interim in Oslo and, with tears streaming down his cheeks, told the Norwegian political prisoners that they were free. In the early 1950s he helped the authorities at Bonn organize the new German criminal and political police. Söderman was also one of the founders of Interpol, the international police organization. In an American magazine article in 1953 he was called "the world's smartest detective." A friend of his was reported to have said that he often wondered whether Harry was quite real: "You keep waiting for him to step into the pages of a mystery novel."

Best known of the Swedes who have served international organizations based in the United States is, of course, Dag Hammarskjöld (1905–61), Secretary-General of the United Nations in 1953–61. Two Swedes have been managing directors of the International Monetary Fund in Washington, D.C. Ivar Rooth (1888–1972), a former governor of the Bank of Sweden, served in 1951–56, and Per Jacobsson (1894–1963), an international financial expert, succeeded Rooth and served until his death in 1963. Dr. Jacobsson was regarded as one of the main architects of international monetary cooperation. "His role in international affairs," said President John F. Kennedy, "has been unique both in the building of a strong international monetary system and in the creation of a broad public understanding to support and strengthen it."

Two high-technology economies linked by trade, investments, and many other ties

TRADE BETWEEN Sweden and the United States, both typical high-technology countries, has to an increasing extent become an exchange of technology — both products and know-how. Royalties and fees for patent licenses, formulas, manufacturing processes, product designs, and the like are not included in the official trade figures but represent a relatively impressive total. The two economies are also linked by a host of other ties, such as investments both ways, joint enterprises, banking connections, shipping and air services, and an exchange of personnel in research, engineering, and management.

From the American colonial era until the early 1900s, iron and steel constituted the bulk of Swedish exports. They were followed by wood pulp and other forest products, which by the end of the 1930s made up 80 percent of Sweden's shipments to America and held their own even during the first postwar period. In return, the United States for many years shipped to Sweden large quantities of cotton and petroleum products. Since then, commercial exchanges between the two countries have become more and more diversified, and in both directions the emphasis is now on the more advanced products of the engineering, machine, and metals industries, ranging from the finest specialty steels, measuring and control instruments and tools to heavy industrial equipment, jumbo aircraft, and huge supertankers.

The impact of a rapidly growing foreign trade transformed Sweden from one of Europe's poorer rural societies into a modern and prosperous country, and a flourishing commerce remains vital. Sweden's high degree of industrialization and continued economic advances make heavy imports necessary, and these can be maintained only by corresponding exports. For many years about one-fourth of the country's production of goods and services has been exported, and nearly one-half of the output of its manufacturing industry is sold abroad.

In the early and middle 20th century, a substantial import surplus with the United States was regarded in Sweden as almost inevitable. Even in the 1960s there were years when the Swedes bought from America more than twice as much as they sold. The trade balance between the two countries gradually improved, however, and in the early 1970s Sweden even achieved a small temporary export surplus. More important, however, was the fact that the commercial interchange as a whole seemed promising and capable of continued expansion.

At the turn of the 19th century Sweden's exports to the United States represented only 0.1 percent of its sales abroad, while about two percent of Sweden's imports came from the United States. By the early 1970s, on the other hand, both of these shares had grown to at least six to seven percent. It is true that they had been considerably larger in the late 1930s. Comparisons with that period, however, must take into account both the changed structure of American-Swedish commerce and the prodigious growth of inter-Scandinavian and inter-European trade. In the 1930s, Sweden's exchanges with the other Nordic countries were extremely modest. But in the early 1970s, Denmark, Norway, and Finland supplied one-fifth of Sweden's imports and received one-fourth of its exports.

The steady expansion of Sweden's exports of manufactured products to the United States has been the result not only of industrial and technological advances at home but also of a growing familiarity with the American market and improved marketing techniques. The popularity of Sweden's compact motorcars, Volvo and Saab, has also played an important part. These were introduced in the United States by the middle of the 1950s, and before long they had become Sweden's foremost dollar earners.

The United States has, in turn, shown an increasingly active interest in Sweden as a trading partner and has made special efforts to boost its exports. In 1963, for instance, an official American trade-promotion program was launched in Sweden. President John F. Kennedy issued a message recalling how "the old Kingdom of Sweden became one of the young American Republic's first trading partners," adding that "Sweden is now a supplier of quality products to our homes and industries, as well as a valued customer of the United States." In 1965 a U.S. Trade Center, serving the whole North of Europe, was opened in downtown Stockholm. At that time, American business had begun to regard Sweden, with its dynamic economy and keen competition, as an excellent test market for exporters planning to introduce their products in the larger European countries. A country which, for instance, in 1950–65 had gone from 250,000 to 1,800,000 motorcars, and where the economic forecasters figured on at least 2,600,000 units by 1975, appealed to sales-minded Americans. An impressive growth had also taken place in Denmark, Norway, and Finland, which together with Sweden represent a prosperous market of about 22 million people.

On a per-capita basis, Sweden is second only to Canada as the best market for American products. Among its imports are machinery and machine tools of many kinds, computers and associated data-processing equipment, nuclear reactors, electronic and teletechnical components, and instruments, as well as chemicals and plastics, metals, dried, canned, and fresh fruits, tobacco, textiles, and clothing. Sweden's own industry produces about 85 percent of its military hardware, but the United States has long been its foremost foreign supplier of such equipment.

Direct imports of motorcars from the United States, which before the Second World War were considerable, have been largely replaced by purchases from American-owned factories in West Germany and England. Together with Denmark and Norway, on the other hand,

Sweden has spent huge amounts for commercial aircraft, engines, and ground-support equipment made in the United States. Since the beginning of its transatlantic passenger and cargo service in 1946, Scandinavian Airlines' outlays in America have, in fact, been larger than its American gross earnings. SAS, which is partly owned by the Swedish, Norwegian, and Danish governments but entirely unsubsidized, has played a vital role in the dramatic increase in travel between America and Scandinavia.

Swedish engineering exports to America include generating and transmission equipment for the power industry, process machinery for the forest industries, other machinery of different kinds, office machines, packaging machines, rock drills, engines, sewing machines, refrigerators, tools, and instruments. Swedish specialty steels, such as spring steel, tubing, and welding wire, have one of their best markets in the United States. Other American imports from Sweden are clothing, mink furs, crispbread and canned food items, furniture, crystal, and ceramics.

One of the best examples of advanced engineering exported from Sweden is the technology by which alternating-current electricity is converted into high-voltage direct current (HVDC) for economical transmission over long distances, and then is reconverted into alternating current for transformation to lower voltages suitable for distribution to consumers. The first HVDC system, which transmits power from the Columbia River basin in the Pacific Northwest to Los Angeles, a distance of about 850 miles, was commissioned in the summer of 1970. In the dedication ceremony at the northern terminal, Celilo on the Columbia River, Secretary of the Interior Walter Hickel paid tribute to Swedish "technical ingenuity" which had enabled Asea to solve the problem of HVDC transmission. Among those present was the developer of the conversion equipment, Dr. Uno Lamm (b. 1904), former electrotechnical director of Asea, who by then lived in California and had served as chairman of the steering committee for the joint venture in which General Electric, Asea's partner in a licensing agreement, also was represented.

Experts had long known that the use of direct current for power transmission would be the most economical solution under certain conditions, but it was not until 1954 that the first HVDC line, running from the Swedish mainland to the Baltic island of Gotland, was completed. The same system was then applied to the transmission of electricity across the English Channel, and was used in similar projects in Italy, Japan, New Zealand, and Canada. A link of the same type connects the coordinated Scandinavian power grids with those of the European mainland. Officials of the U.S. Department of the Interior and the Federal Power Commission visited Sweden in 1962 to acquaint themselves with the technique, which had first been developed in Asea's laboratory at Ludvika in the province of Dalarna. Dr. Lamm, whose father was professor of electrotechnics at Chalmers Institute in Gothenburg, and his team of assistants had started their experiments there in 1929.

Another agreement between Asea and American Electric Power Company, the largest investor-owned distributor of electricity in the United States, provides both for Swedish participation in the development of new alternating-current power transmission networks and for joint research. In 1973 the two companies decided to build in Indiana an experimental station for AC transmission at ultrahigh voltages, over one million volts — an evolution of a technology which Asea and the Swedish State Power Board had pioneered soon after the Second World War.

In the middle 1970s, other projects involving American-Swedish technological partnership included an agreement between Asea and United Aircraft Corporation covering the development of large industrial gas turbines for stationary power plants, and an agreement between Asea and General Motors to exchange technology on thyristor power conversion and to build as a joint venture two all-electric locomotives for demonstration to U.S. railroads.

In 1974 the U.S. Department of the Interior and a Swedish agency signed an agreement outlining a program of cooperation in rock tunneling, including rapid excavation. The goal was to achieve a maximum exchange of experience in a number of specified areas, including efforts to increase the excavation rate, improve safety, and reduce costs. Sweden has long been noted for advanced rock-tunneling techniques.

In the pulp and paper industry, there has long been a rewarding exchange of technology between the United States and Sweden. Equipment made or designed in Sweden is used in America on a large scale. With a few exceptions, such as shipbuilding in which field Sweden for several years has been next to Japan, the world leader, Swedish industrial-production figures can hardly be impressive by American standards, but substantial parts of the pulp and paper production in the United States is, somewhere along the line, handled or helped by equipment or techniques of Swedish origin. Many of the new efforts focus on heat economy, energy conservation, and environmental protection.

Sweden-based inventors who have become widely known in industrial circles in the United States include Norwegian-born Johan C. F. C. Richter (b. 1901), a pioneer in the development at Karlstad in Värmland of the Kamyr continuous digester which in America is used in sulphate mills producing more than half of the national output of sulphate pulp, and Arne Asplund of Stockholm (b. 1903), whose defibrator method has made fiberboard one of the cheapest and most used building materials in existence. Asplund studied technology at the University of Wisconsin, graduating in 1927, and after that he worked some time for a successful American inventor. Upon his return to Sweden he helped establish its first hardboard plant.

Household appliances have played a part in American-Swedish trade ever since the Singer sewing machine was introduced in Sweden in 1865. The Swedish Husqvarna company at Huskvarna in the province of Småland, which had started in 1689 as a royal arms factory, began making sewing machines in 1872, and in the 20th century it became one of the world's leading exporters of such products. In the early 1970s an annual total of nearly 50,000 American homes added Husqvarna's Viking sewing machine to their technical equipment. A racing motorcycle by the same manufacturer has also become widely known. Husqvarna started making motorcycles in 1903, two years after an emigrant from Småland, Carl Oscar Hedström, had built the first Indian and helped lay the foundation for the modern motorcycle industry in the United States.

Of cameras and other photographic materials, Sweden imports much more from the United States than vice versa, but a Swedish camera, the Hasselblad, has become highly respected among American professionals and advanced amateurs. Hasselblads have, in fact, been part of the equipment on all the American-manned space flights since 1962 and have taken some 40,000 color and black-and-white photographs. The camera was developed during the Second World

War for aerial photography, under the leadership of Victor Hasselblad (b. 1906) of Gothenburg, whose interest in nature also played a part. Both in Sweden and in the United States, various members of the Hasselblad family of cameras have been widely used by bird photographers. One of the first was Crawford H. Greenewalt, who in 1960, when he was president of E. I. du Pont de Nemours & Co., published a lavishly illustrated book about hummingbirds.

Another minor but significant Swedish specialty is an artificial kidney, made at Lund and in the early 1970s imported in growing numbers to the United States. Work on a manufacturing plant at Newport News, Virginia, began in 1974.

Wanting to be closer to a market that already absorbed 25 percent of its output, Volvo, Sweden's leading automobile manufacturer, in 1974 started building a car factory at Chesapeake, Virginia. It was the first time that a foreign automobile company had decided to manufacture cars in the United States. The decision was welcomed not only in the Old Dominion but also by newspapers in other parts of the country and by trade-union leaders. *The New York Times* observed in an editorial that the flow of American investment abroad had helped to diffuse the high productivity and the fruits of research and development conceived in the United States, and that Volvo also might have something new to offer. After a visit to Sweden, Leonard Woodcock, the president of the United Auto Workers, said that he had been impressed by the cleanliness and safety of its automobile plants. In 1974, Volvo also had factories in Canada, Belgium, Iran, Malaysia, Australia, Indonesia, and Peru.

The SKF ball-bearing company was, as already mentioned, one of the first Swedish exporters to start a manufacturing subsidiary in the United States. At Worcester, Massachusetts, Sweden's leading pharmaceutical company, Astra, built a plant largely concentrating on a local anesthetic named Xylocaine, which went into production in 1951. Before the end of that decade the Astra group had become the largest producer of local anesthetics in the world. In 1952 a Swedish-owned match factory was started at Kenner, Louisiana, 15 miles up the Mississippi from New Orleans. Many of the Swedish sales and manufacturing subsidiaries in America are based in New Jersey, New York, and Connecticut.

In 1970 the number of people employed in Swedish-owned companies abroad was about 250,000, representing about one-fifth of the total employed in Swedish manufacturing and mining at home. More than half of the Swedish subsidiaries were located within the European Common Market. In the United States, employees in Swedish-controlled companies totaled less than 10,000. American investments in Swedish business and industry are considerable. In 1970 the American-owned companies in Sweden employed 27,000 people. More than 3,000 worked for IBM's subsidiary in Sweden, where an important part of the whole IBM concern's development of health-care and medical applications is being done. At an early stage Swedish hospitals became pioneers in medical-data processing.

American-Swedish joint ventures include an iron-ore mining operation in Liberia in Africa, which is managed by the Swedish Gränges company; petrochemical plants at Stenungsund north of Gothenburg on Sweden's West Coast, which are based on American licenses and in which two Swedish and two American concerns participate; a Swedish company for the development, manufacture, and marketing of pressure vessels and other heavy components for the nuclear power industry, in which an American corporation holds a 25 percent interest; and a tube plant in Washington State, which serves the nuclear and aerospace industries.

The American and Swedish industries are also linked by numerous licensing agreements and arrangements providing for other types of cooperation in the exchange of technology. Private inventors are active along the same lines. For instance, when Waloddi Weibull (b. 1887) in 1953 retired from a professorship at the Stockholm Institute of Technology, he started serving as a consultant to the U.S. Air Force for the promotion of the safety and economy of its aircraft. Two decades earlier he had embarked on a study concerning the reliability, fatigue-life, or fracture of metals and aircraft parts. In 1973 he received the Medal of The American Society of Mechanical Engineers.

The United States has long been the Swedish merchant marine's foremost customer. In 1970 it contributed about nine percent of its gross freight receipts. A substantial part of Sweden's commercial tonnage operates chiefly between foreign ports, while, on the other hand, only a small part of its own exports and imports is carried in Swedish bottoms.

Sweden's role in future commercial and technological exchanges with the United States will to a great extent depend on a continued successful specialization in Swedish industry and its ability to develop and market new products, methods, and systems. Such contributions are being made not only by Sweden's leading exporters but also by its small-scale industry, which plays a vital part in the country's economy. In relation to population, large sections of Sweden may, in fact, boast more individual industrial ventures than any other similar areas in the world. The old emigration districts in Småland, Västergötland and other provinces, where poverty and further depopulation once seemed inevitable, have thus become as prosperous as any other part of Sweden, or of Europe, for that matter. At Gnosjö in Småland, for instance, about 8,000 people make a living in 270 factories with a work force ranging from a handful to about 150. At nearby Anderstorp, 130 of the 3,500 inhabitants operate their own factories. Many of the firms export a large part of their production. The Swedish Northland does not have the same traditions of small-scale manufacturing, but in the 1960s and early 1970s the industrial growth there was more rapid than in the central and southern provinces. Subcontracting has assumed great importance.

Sweden's foremost trading partners are, naturally, in Europe. In the early 1970s the European countries received about 80 percent of Swedish exports, and only four percent of this went to Eastern Europe including the Soviet Union.

Illustrations

Philadelphia. Gloria Dei, Philadelphia: Historical Society of Pennsylvania. Axel Oxenstierna: Swedish Portrait Archives, National Gallery of Art, Stockholm. Johan Printz: Esther Chilstrom Meixner, Philadelphia. Swedenborg: Painting by Per Krafft the Elder, Portrait Gallery, Gripsholm. Swedish Information Service (SIS), New York. Bryn Athyn Cathedral: Michael Pitcairn, Bryn Athyn. Linnaeus: National Gallery of Art, Stockholm. Scheele: ATA, Sören Hallgren. George Washington, by Wertmüller: National Gallery of Art, Stockholm. Treaty of 1783: SIS.

Section II, between pages 234 and 235

Harvard: Uppsala University Library. Broadway and City Hall, New York, by Klinkowström: Royal Library (KB), Stockholm. Bethel Ship: ATA, Sören Hallgren. Immigrant chest: North Park College, Chicago. Cottage: Erik Liljeroth. © Allhems förlag, Malmö. Monument, The Emigrants: Werner K. Djerwig, Karlshamn. Swedish immigrants in Boston, and immigrants on way to California: Library of Congress. Memorial plaque, New Sweden, Iowa: Emigration Institute, Växjö, Sweden. Swante M. Swenson: Texas Historical Society, through Carl T. Widen. Charles Lindbergh, father and son: Minnesota Historical Society. Jenny Lind: Gustaf Unonius, Chicago. Jenny Lind in an opera: Coulson Studio, Cowan, Tenn. Jenny Lind in Castle Garden: New-York Historical Society. Fredrika Bremer: FLT-telefoto, Stockholm. Almqvist in America: SIS. General Stolbrand: Emigration Institute, Växjö. John Ericsson and *Monitor* versus *Merrimac*: Library of Congress.

Section III, between pages 362 and 363

Swede Town, Chicago: Emigration Institute, Växjö. Ryssby Church, Colorado: Evadene B. Swanson, Fort Collins, Col. Stanton, Iowa: Zenith Pictorial Advertising Co. Map of the United States, with Swedish rural settlements: from Helge Nelson, *The Swedes and the Swedish Settlements in North America.* © Kungl. Humanistiska Vetenskapssamfundet, Lund. Memorial plaque, New Sweden, Maine: Nils William Olsson, Minneapolis. Newspaper heads: Emigration Institute, Växjö. John A. Johnson: Minnesota Historical Society. Wendell R. Anderson: Gustavus Adolphus College, St. Peter, Minn. Bethany College Oratorio Society: Bethany College, Lindsborg, Kansas. Augustana: Augustana College, Rock Island, Ill. Pehr A. Peterson: Swedish American Hospital, Rockford, Ill. American Swedish Institute, Minneapolis: Gabriel E. Jabbour. Midsummer: Swedish Tourist Traffic Association, Stockholm. *Värmlänningarna* at Stockholm Opera: Studio Järlås. Lucia: Gullers, Stockholm.

Section IV, between pages 490 and 491

Minnesota State Fair Grounds and Crown Prince Gustav Adolf: American Swedish Institute, Minneapolis. Gustav V: Karl Sandels, Stockholm. Milles sculpture at Cranbrook: Harvey Croze, Cranbrook. Carl Sandburg and Ambassador Boheman: Wide World Photos. President Truman and Prince Bertil: Acme Newspictures. Swedish Pavilion at New York World's Fair: SIS. Crystal bowl by Simon Gate: Orrefors. Swedish girl gymnasts: John Pedin, New York Daily News. Weaving: Nordiska Kompaniet, Stockholm. Zorn self-portrait and Milles at work: SIS. New Sweden Monument, Gothenburg: Stanley Pretorius, Västkustens Turisttrafikförbund, Gothenburg. Monument with eagle: John Hyltskog, Swedish Tourist Traffic Association. De Laval: Museum of Technology, Stockholm. Nobel: SIS. Ernst Alexanderson: Thyra Alexanderson, Schenectady, N.Y.

Section V, between pages 618 and 619

General Eisenhower in Stockholm and the rowboat at Harpsund: Pressens Bild, Stockholm. Strindberg: Royal Library (KB), Stockholm. Chaplin and Ingmar Bergman: Pressens Bild, Stockholm. Greta Garbo: Museum of Modern Art, New York. Birgit Nilsson: SIS. Ingrid Bergman: Arthur Cantor Associates, New York. Stockholm Palace: Bror Karlsson. Chicago girl and Stockholm Palace, immigrant from Yugoslavia, and Gustav VI Adolf and Dag Hammarskjöld: Pressens Bild. Carl XVI Gustaf and Nobel laureate: Reportagebild Stockholm. Rudolph Bannow and Arne Geijer: Jan Strämberg, Gothenburg. Liv Ullmann, Max v. Sydow and Bishop Hill veteran: SIS. Gothenburg harbor: Bewe, Gothenburg. Myrdal: Harald Borgström, Stockholm. Ohlin: Bror Karlsson. Shipyard: Kockum, Malmö. Electric laboratory: ASEA, Västerås. SAS pilots: Scandinavian Airlines.

★

Bibliography

Most of the source material has been listed chronologically as far as possible, or at least under the respective chapter headings from 2 to 42. The following eight works, all dealing with the emigration from Sweden, the history of the Swedes in America, or the history of Sweden, have been consulted so often that they actually belong to many if not most of the chapters, and they will be mentioned again only in special cases.

Benson, Adolph B., and Hedin, Naboth, *Americans from Sweden*. Philadelphia 1950.
Benson, Adolph B., and Hedin, Naboth (ed.), *Swedes in America 1638–1938*. New Haven 1938.
Nelson, Helge, *The Swedes and the Swedish Settlements in North America*. Lund 1943.
Olsson, Nils William, *Swedish Passenger Arrivals in New York 1820–1850*. Chicago 1967.
Westman, Erik G. (ed.), *The Swedish Element in America*. I–IV. Chicago 1931, 1934.
   (Volumes I and IV contain articles about the Swedish element in various states and cities. Volume II contains articles about Swedish churches, organizations, and cultural activities.)
Andersson, Ingvar, *A History of Sweden*. Stockholm and London 1956.
Carlsson, Sten, Rosén, Jerker and others, *Den svenska historien*. I–X. Stockholm 1966–68.
Fleisher, Eric W., and Weibull, Jörgen, *Viking Times to Modern*. The Story of Swedish Exploring and Settlement in America, and the Development of Trade and Shipping from the Vikings to Our Times. Stockholm and Minneapolis 1954.

The following books, also difficult to place in a certain chapter, have been consulted more or less frequently:

Babcock, Kendric Charles, *The Scandinavian Element in the United States*. Urbana, Ill., 1914.
Backlund, J. Oscar, *A Century of the Swedish American Press*. Chicago 1952.
Benson, Adolph B. (ed.), *The Will to Succeed, Stories of Swedish Pioneers*. New York 1948.
   (This collection was chosen from more than 2,000 essays which were entered in a

contest sponsored by the Swedish American Line for the Swedish Pioneer Centennial of 1948. In addition, about 600 essays were bound in 10 unpublished volumes, and we have had access to one such set.)

Gustafson, Alrik, *A History of Swedish Literature*. Minneapolis 1961.

Heckscher, Eli, *An Economic History of Sweden*. Cambridge, Mass. 1954.

Hildebrand, Karl, Fredenholm, Axel (red.), *Svenskarna i Amerika*. I–II. Stockholm 1926.

Janson, Florence E., *The Background of Swedish Immigration 1840–1930*. Chicago 1931.

Ljungmark, Lars, *Den stora utvandringen*. Sveriges Radio, Stockholm 1965.

Morison, Samuel Eliot, *The Oxford History of the American People*. New York 1965.

Nelson, O. N., *History of the Scandinavians and Successful Scandinavians in the United States*. I–II. Minncapolis 1904.

Norelius, Eric, *De svenska luterska församlingarnas och svenskarnes historia i Amerika*. I–II. Rock Island, Ill., 1890, 1916.

Nyblom, Gösta (ed.), *Americans of Swedish Descent*. Rock Island, Ill., 1948.

Swedish-American Historical Society, *Yearbook* 1905–1926, and *Bulletin* 1928–1932.

Augustana Swedish Institute, *American Swedish Handbook* I–VIII. Rock Island, Ill., 1943–73.

The following American and Swedish biographical reference books have often been consulted: *Who's Who in America* 1899–1973, *Who Was Who in America* (4 volumes), *Encyclopedia of American Biography, Dictionary of American Biography, American Men and Women of Science, Physical and Biological Sciences*, 1971. *Svenska män och kvinnor* I–VIII, *Svenskt biografiskt lexikon* I–XX, *Vem är det, Svenskar i utlandet* 1929, 1959, 1969, *Allhems konstnärslexikon* I–V (Dictionary of Swedish Artists). Also, Ernst T. Skarstedt, *Pennfäktare*, Stockholm 1930 — which lists 575 Swedish-American writers, the vast majority of whom wrote in Swedish.

The following bibliographical aids have been used:

Ander, O. Fritiof, *The Cultural Heritage of the Swedish Immigrant*. (About 2,000 books and booklets, some 1,000 newspapers and magazines, and many magazine articles.) Rock Island, Ill., 1956.

Larson, Esther Elisabeth, *Swedish Commentators on America 1638–1865*. An annotated list of selected manuscripts and printed materials. New York 1963.

Lundstedt, Bernhard, *Svenska tidningar och tidskrifter utgifna inom Nordamerikas Förenta Stater*. Bibliografisk översikt. Stockholm 1886.

Frequently used source material includes bound sets of the "News from Sweden" bulletins issued in 1941–64 by The American-Swedish News Exchange in New York. The same organization's scrapbooks for the 1920s and 1930s have supplied some valuable information; the scrapbooks compiled after the Second World War, unfortunately, have not been able to survive the new era. We have also had access to the *Bulletin* of The American Society of Swedish Engineers (ASSE) in New York for the years 1901–73, to the material files of Swedish

Information Service in New York and of the American Swedish Historical Museum in Philadelphia (ASHM), and to the *Bulletin* of The American Institute of Swedish Arts, Literature, and Science (later The American Swedish Institute) in Minneapolis for the years 1941–63. Four important sources will be listed often below, with the following abbreviations:

ASM: *The American Swedish Monthly*, published by The Swedish Chamber of Commerce of the U.S.A., New York, 1934–65.

SP: *The Swedish Pioneer Historical Quarterly*, published by Swedish Pioneer Historical Society, Chicago, 1950–74.

YB: The *Yearbook* of American Swedish Historical Foundation, Philadelphia, 1944–73.

ASR: *The American-Scandinavian Review*, published by The American-Scandinavian Foundation, New York, 1934–74.

2. The Scandinavian Vikings

Stenberger, Mårten, *I vikingarnas spår*. Sveriges Radio, Stockholm 1967.
Arbman, Holger, *The Vikings*. New York 1961.
Sellman, R. R., *The Vikings*. New York 1959.
Sawyer, P. H., *The Age of the Vikings*. London 1962.
Jansson, Sven B. F., *The Runes of Sweden*. Stockholm 1962.

3. Swedes on the Delaware

Here, *Americans from Sweden*, by Benson-Hedin, already mentioned, was one of the more important sources.

Johnson, Amandus, *The Swedish Settlements on the Delaware* 1638–1664. I–II. Philadelphia 1911.

Ferris, Benjamin, *A History of the Original Settlements on the Delaware*. Wilmington, Del. 1846.

Paxson, Henry D., *Where Pennsylvania History Began*. Philadelphia 1926.

Ahnlund, Nils, *Nya Sverige. De historiska huvuddragen*. Stockholm 1938.

Ryden, George H., 'The Story of New Sweden.' ASR 1938 March.

Stevens, C., 'John Campanius: Linguist and Missionary.' ASR 1958 Autumn.

New Sweden tercentenary issue. ASM 1938 June. About New Sweden: ASM 1937 Aug., Oct., Dec., 1938 July, 1943 May, 1954 Nov., 1955 June, 1956 Dec., 1963 Jan., 1965 Nov. About Johan Printz: ASM 1938 May, 1943 July.

Meixner, Esther Chilstrom, *The Governor's Daughter: The Story of Armegott Printz*. Philadelphia 1965. (Also, ASM 1962 July.)

Leiby, Adrian C., *The Early Dutch and Swedish Settlers of New Jersey*. Princeton, N.J. 1964.

Eckman, Jeannette, *Crane Hook on the Delaware* 1667–1699. An Early Swedish Lutheran Church and Community. With the Historical Background of the Delaware River Valley. Newark, N. J. 1958.

Clay, Jehu Curtis, *Annals of the Swedes on the Delaware*. Fourth edition, Chicago 1938.

Springer, Courtland B. and Ruth L., 'Charles Springer of Christina.' YB 1949.

Meixner, Esther Chilstrom, *Swedish Landmarks in the Delaware Valley*. Bridgeport, Pa., 1972. (Also, ASM 1960 Oct., 1962 Sept., SP 1956: 21–34.)

Ferris, Robert G., *Explorers and Settlers*. Historic Places Commemorating the Early Exploration and Settlement of the United States. Washington, D.C. 1968. (About Gloria Dei: ASM 1957 May.)

Wallick, Raymond G., *St. Gabriel's Church*. 1720–1970. Douglasville, Pa.

BIBLIOGRAPHY

About place-names in the Delaware region: SP 1957: 60–62, 124–136.

Acrelius, Israel, *A History of New Sweden*. Philadelphia 1874.

Norberg, Otto, *Svenska kyrkans mission vid Delaware i Nordamerika*. Stockholm 1893.

Jacobsson, Nils, *Svenska öden vid Delaware 1638–1831*. Stockholm 1938.

— *Bland svenskamerikaner och gustavianer*. Stockholm 1953.

Hesselius, Andreas, *Journal 1711–1724*. Philadelphia 1947.

Anderson, Carl Magnus, *Pastor Wrangel's Trip to the Shore*. New Jersey History. 1969 Spring.

Benson, Adolph B., 'A Swedish Officer of Charles XII in Colonial Louisiana,' *American Scandinavian Studies*, selected and edited by Marshall W. S. Swan. New York 1952.

4. The Linnaean Age

Andersson, G. Gunnar, *Svenska snillen. Från Stiernhielm till Scheele*. Stockholm 1964.

Lindroth, Sten, *Kungl. Svenska Vetenskapsakademiens Historia 1739–1818*. Stockholm 1967.

Lindroth, Sten (ed.), *Swedish Men of Science 1650–1950*. Stockholm 1952.

Johnson, William A. (transl.), *Christopher Polhem, The Father of Swedish Technology*. Hartford, Conn. 1963.

Toksvig, Signe, *Emanuel Swedenborg, Scientist and Mystic*. New Haven 1948.

Block, Marguerite Beck, *The New Church in the New World*. New York 1932.

Sigstedt, Cyriel Odhner, *The Swedenborg Epic*. New York 1952.

Seaborg, Glenn T., and Valens, Evans G., *Elements of the Universe*. New York 1958.

Hagberg, Knut, *Carl Linnaeus*. New York 1953.

Blunt, Wilfrid, *The Compleat Naturalist*. A Life of Linnaeus. New York 1971.

Buckman, Thomas R., *Ad Memoriam Caroli Linnaei*. Catalog of an exhibition commemorating the 250th anniversary of Linnaeus's birth. Lawrence, Kansas 1957.

Waxell, Sven, *Vitus Berings eventyrlige opdagerfaerd 1733–1743*. Copenhagen 1948.

Bell, Olive Joslin, 'Sven Waxell, Alaska's Forgotten Man.' *The Alaskana*, 1972 April.

Benson, Adolph B., 'The Beginnings of American Interest in Linnaeus,' *American Scandinavian Studies*. New York 1952.

Kalm, Peter, *Travels in North America*. Ed. by Adolph B. Benson I–II. New York 1966. (Also, ASM 1938 Feb.)

Smith, A. W., *A Gardener's Book of Plant Names*. New York and London 1963.

Hylander, Nils, 'Växtsläkten uppkallade efter svenskar,' *Svenska Linné-Sällskapets årsskrift* 1967.

Information about Linnaeus and Linnaeus collections has been obtained from Dr. Wilhelm Odelberg of the Swedish Academy of Sciences, Stockholm, and from Dr. Olof Selling, Djursholm, Sweden.

5. The Gustavian Era and the American Revolution

Here, *Den svenska historien* and *Viking Times to Modern*, both already mentioned, were important sources.

Johnson, Amandus, 'The American-Swedish Treaty of 1783.' ASR 1958 Summer.

— 'Sweden Was First to Offer a Trade Treaty.' ASM 1950 July.

Fleisher, Eric W., 'Dating America's First Treaty with Sweden.' SP 1958:43–47.

About St. Barthélemy: ASM 1959 Oct. (Also, information from Rolf Lamborn, Winter Park, Florida.)

About John Hanson: YB 1959. John Morton: ASM 1953 July.

BIBLIOGRAPHY

Benson, Adolph B., *Sweden and the American Revolution*. New Haven 1926.
Johnson, Amandus, *Swedish Contributions to American Freedom* 1776–1783. I–II. Philadelphia 1953, 1957.
Fahlman, Erik, *General Döbeln*, Stockholm 1915. Also, *Några anteckningar om och av General von Döbeln*, 1–3. Stockholm 1850.
About John Paul Jones: ASM 1935 Sept., YB 1959.

6.   In America: Bridging Two Epochs

Johnson, Amandus, *The Journal and Biography of Nicholas Collin*, 1746–1831. Philadelphia 1936.
Scott, Franklin D., *Artist and Immigrant Farmer* (Wertmüller). Chicago 1963. (Also, SP 1955: 34–54, YB 1964.)
Keen, Gregory B., *The Descendants of Göran Kyn of New Sweden*. Philadelphia 1913. (About Dr. W. W. Keen, ASM 1949 April.)
Rambo, Jr., Ormond, 'The First Pioneers: The Rambo Family.' YB 1948.
Sturgis, Samuel B., 'The Story of My Swedish Forefathers.' YB 1958.
McRaven, William Henry, *Life and Times of Edward Swanson*. One of the original pioneers who with General James Robertson founded Nashville, Tenn., 1779. Nashville, Tenn. 1937.
Genealogical material in the New York Public Library was also consulted.
Olsson, Nils William, 'Extracts from Early Swedish Consular Reports from the United States.' YB 1967.
Anderson, Florence, 'The First Swedish Consul in Boston.' YB 1958.
Mulliner, LaMar D., 'A History of the American Consular Office at Göteborg.' YB 1947.

7.   The Era of Bernadotte and Berzelius

Den svenska historien and Ingvar Andersson's *A History of Sweden* were important. Also, Alrik Gustafson's *A History of Swedish Literature*, *Swedish Men of Science*, and Sten Lindroth's book about the Swedish Academy of Sciences.

Hilen, Andrew, *Longfellow and Scandinavia*. New Haven 1947.
Longfellow, Henry Wadsworth, 'Fritiof's Saga.' *North American Review* 1837 July.
Benson, Adolph B., 'A List of English Translations of Fritiof's Saga,' *American Scandinavian Studies*. New York 1952.
Jorpes, J. Erik, *Jac. Berzelius, His Life and Work*. Stockholm 1966.

8.   Growth of Relations and American Influences in Sweden

To begin with, *From Viking Times to Modern* was important.

Burr, Aaron, *Private Journal*. Ed. by Matthew L. Davis. I–II. New York 1938.
Benson, Adolph B., 'Aaron Burr in Sweden.' YB 1953.
Elovson, Harald, *Amerika i svensk litteratur* 1750–1820. Lund 1930.
Runeby, Nils, *Den nya världen och den gamla. Amerikabild och emigrationsuppfattning i Sverige* 1820–1860. Uppsala 1969.
Scott, Franklin D. (ed.), *Baron Klinkowström's America* 1818–1820. Evanston, Ill. 1952. (Also, SP 1952 Winter.)
Scott, Franklin D., and Lundblad, Jane, 'Gosselman on North America in the 1830s.' SP 1960: 99–107.

Key, Helmer, *A. O. Wallenberg*. Stockholm 1916.
Westin, Gunnar, *George Scott och hans verksamhet i Sverige*. I–II. Stockholm 1928, 1929.
— 'George Scott's Journey to America in 1841.' *Swedish-American Historical Bulletin* 1932.
Baird, Robert, *Visit to Northern Europe*. New York 1841.
Norton, John E., 'Robert Baird, Presbyterian Missionary to Sweden of the 1840s.' SP 1972: 151–167.
Laing, Samuel, *A Tour in Sweden in 1838*. London 1839.

9. Swedish-American Pioneers of the 1840s and 1850s

First, important sources include Olsson's *Passenger Arrivals in New York 1820–1850*. In the following, and in many stories concerning Swedish immigrants that have been organized by states, Nelson's *The Swedes and the Swedish Settlements in North America* was a leading source. It gives a detailed geographical analysis of Swedish settlement patterns, including secondary migrations. Runeby's *Den nya världen och den gamla* and Benson-Hedin's *Americans from Sweden* were again consulted.

Olsson, Nils William, 'Swedish Enlistments in the U. S. Army Before 1851.' SP 1951 Winter, Spring.
Westin, Gunnar, 'Background of the Swedish Pioneer Immigration.' YB 1948.
Hokanson, Nels, *Swedish Immigrants in Lincoln's Time*. New York 1942.
Rosenquist, Carl M., 'The Swedes of Texas.' YB 1945.
Widen, Carl T., 'From Småland to Palm Valley in Texas.' SP 1967: 128–131.
Ransom, Harry, 'Swante Palm and His Books.' YB 1949. Also, YB 1958.
About S. M. Swenson: ASM 1955 Aug., 1962 Oct., YB 1958.
Friman, Axel, 'On the Trail of Early Wisconsin Swedes.' SP 1961: 10–16. (Information about the Frimans also directly from Lt. Col. Axel Friman, Gothenburg, Sweden.)
Unonius, Gustaf, *A Pioneer in Northwest America 1841–1858*. I–II. Minneapolis 1950, 1960.
Stephenson, George M., 'Pioneering in Wisconsin a Century Ago.' ASM 1941 Nov.
Freeburg, Victor O., 'A Lieutenant and His Lady' (v. Schneidau). ASM 1941 Nov.
Main, Angie Kumlien, 'Thure Kumlien, Swedish-American Naturalist.' YB 1960.
Gustafson, Henning, 'Stockholm, Wisconsin, A Century Old.' SP 1951 Autumn.
Johnson, E. Gustav, 'An America Letter in 1854 from a Värmlänning.' SP 1967: 93–100. (Also, SP 1961: 35–38.)
'Per and Ingar Dahlberg,' *Annals of Iowa*, 1928 July. (Iowa, also ASM 1948 June)
Lawson, Evald Benjamin, 'Chandlers Valley Pioneers.' ASM 1941 July. (Also, ASM 1958 Sept.)
Stephenson, George M., 'An America Letter of 1849' (Steffan Steffansson). *Yearbook of the Swedish Historical Society of America* 1926.

10. In Illinois and Its Prairie Utopia

Bergendoff, Conrad, 'The Beginnings of Swedish Immigration into Illinois.' ASM 1948 June.
Lawson, Evald Benjamin, 'Olof Gustaf Hedstrom — Pioneer Leader of Swedish Methodism.' YB 1945. (Also, YB 1962)
Isaksson, Olov, *Bishop Hill, Ill. — A Utopia on the Prairie*. Stockholm 1969.

— 'Discover Bishop Hill.' SP 1968: 221–233. (Also, Bishop Hill, ASR 1970 June.)

Widén, Albin, 'Bishop Hill.' ASR 1942 Sept.

Lindstrom, David E. 'The Bishop Hill Settlement.' YB 1945.

Nelson, Ronald E., 'The Bishop Hill Colony and Its Pioneer Economy.' SP 1967: 32–48.

Westerberg, Wesley M., 'Bethel Ship to Bishop Hill.' SP 1972: 55–70.

About Bishop Hill and Eric Janson: ASM 1946 Oct., 1951 Sept., SP 1950 July, ASR 1959 March. About Olof Krans: ASM 1948 May, 1953 March, YB 1961.

Beijbom, Ulf, *Swedes in Chicago*. A demographic and social study of the 1846–1880 immigration. Uppsala 1971.

Johnson, Gustav E., *The Swedes of Chicago*. Typewritten dissertation. Chicago 1940.

Johnson, E. Gustav, 'Chicago Swedes Organized Svea.' SP 1957: 115–128.

11.   In Minnesota and Some Other States

Norelius, Theodore A., 'The First Swede in Minnesota' (Jacob Falstrom). SP 1957: 107–115. (Also, ASM 1938 Dec., YB 1960, SP 1965: 119–121.)

Swanson, Roy W., 'Frontiersmen of Minnesota.' ASM 1948 June. 'Swedes in Minnesota.' ASM 1958 May.

Norelius, Theodore A., 'Swedes Pioneer A New Land' (Chisago). SP 1957: 49–56.

Olsson, Nils William, 'The Arrival in Boston June 27, 1851 of the Swedish Brig Ambrosius' (Hans Mattson, Troed Persson). SP 1961: 47–57.

Bjerking, Arvid, *En skånsk banbrytare i Amerika* (Trued Granville Pearson's autobiography). Oskarshamn 1937.

About Vasa, Minn., and Hans Mattson: ASM 1954 April, SP 1960 July, 1966 Oct.

Swanson, Roy W., 'Scandinavian Place-Names in the American Danelaw.' *Swedish-American Historical Bulletin* 1928.

Albinson, Grace G., 'An Early Swedish Settlement in Michigan.' YB 1947.

About Otto Natt och Dag: Larson's *Swedish Commentators in America 1638–1865*.

12.   In the South, the West and the Northeast

The sources include Hokanson's *Swedish Immigrants in Lincoln's Time*.

Lovel, Isabel N., 'Hammond, La., and Its Swedish Founder.' SP 1967: 221–226.

Norby, Reidar, '8 Advance Skillings' (Gustavus Schmidt). YB 1968.

Varg, Paul A., 'Maximilian Freiherr Schele de Vere.' SP 1950 Oct.

Hebbe, Brita, *Wendela* (Gustaf Clemens Hebbe). Stockholm 1974.

Olsson, Nils William, 'An Early Pioneer Letter from South Carolina,' SP 1953 July.

Hammarskjöld, Nina, *Ätten Hammarskjöld*. Stockholm 1915. (Also, information from the State House, Columbia, S.C.)

Olsson, Nils William, 'The Elusive Anonym of a Swedish Lady in Ante-Bellum South' (Miss Nettelbladt, Hahr family). SP 1958: 60–68.

Nettelbladt, L., *En svenska i Amerika*. . . . af -m -n. Stockholm 1860.

Roos, Rosalie, *Resa till Amerika 1851–1855*. Stockholm 1969.

Paulin, Axel, and Odelberg, Wilhelm, *Edelhjertas öden*. Stockholm 1961. (Also, SP 1962: 82–85.)

G. M. Waseurtz af Sandels, *A Sojourn in California by the King's Orphan 1842–43*. San Francisco 1945.

Swan, Marshall W. S., 'A California Pioneer: John Brown.' YB 1948.

Lindberg, Ruby, 'Some Swedes in Early California.' SP 1953 Jan.

Ekman, Ernst, 'Swedish Consular Reports from San Francisco A Century Ago.' SP 1968: 162–173.

Evjen, John O., *Scandinavian Immigrants in New York 1630–1674*. Minneapolis 1916.

Olsson, Nils William, 'Was Napoleon Berger the First Swedish Journalist in America?' SP 1952 Winter.

13. A Look Forward

Helmes, Winifred G., *John A. Johnson, The People's Governor*. Minneapolis 1949.
Sutton, William A., 'The Swedishness of Carl Sandburg.' ASR 1972 June. (Also, ASR 1938 March, ASM 1946 Feb., 1952 Dec., 1956 May, 1959 July, 1960 Jan., SP 1961 July, 1962 April, 1967 Oct.)

14. Religious Aspects of the Immigration

Stephenson, George M., *The Religious Aspects of Swedish Immigration*, Minneapolis 1932.
Rönnegård, Sam, *Utvandrarnas kyrka*. Stockholm 1961.
Olson, Oscar N., 'Augustana, A Century of Religious Service.' ASM 1948 June.
Arden, G. Everett, *Augustana Heritage*. A History of the Augustana Lutheran Church. Rock Island, Ill., 1962. (Also, ASM 1935 June)
About Augustana College: ASM 1940 June, 1947 May, 1950 Dec., 1953 June–Aug., 1960 June. Gustavus Adolphus College: ASM 1950 May, 1953 Dec., 1954 Jan., Feb.
Thörnberg, E. H., *Sverige i Amerika, Amerika i Sverige. Folkvandring och folkväckelse*. Stockholm 1938.
Westin, Gunnar, 'Emigration and Scandinavian Church Life.' SP 1957: 35–49.
Liljegren, N. M.; Westergreen, N. O.; and Wallenius, C. G., *Svenska methodismen i Amerika*. Chicago 1895. (Also, ASM 1945 May).
Olson, Adolf, *A Centenary History* (Baptists in America). Chicago 1952. (Also: ASM 1952 May, SP 1952 July. Bethel College: ASM 1953 Oct., Nov.)

15. Flowering Cultural Exchanges

First, Runeby's book about views of America and attitudes toward emigration in Sweden 1820–1860.

Scott, Franklin D., 'Glimpses from Travel Letters of Baron Axel Adelswärd,' 1855–56. SP 1960: 145–154.
Bolin, Johan, *Beskrifning öfwer Nord-Amerikas Förenta Stater*. Jemte Upplysningar och Råd för Utwandrare. Wexjö 1853. Facsimile reprint Stockholm 1970.
Taylor, Bayard, *Northern Travel*. New York 1859.
Benson, Adolph B., 'Bayard Taylor's Interest in the Scandinavian North,' *American Scandinavian Studies*. New York 1952.
Johnson, E. Gustav, 'America's Laureate of the Gilded Age and His Interest in Scandinavian Culture' (Bayard Taylor). SP 1972: 207–220.
Rooth, Signe A., *Seeress of the Northland*. Fredrika Bremer's American Journey 1849–1851. Philadelphia 1955. (Also, ASM 1950 Sept., SP 1951 Spring, Autumn)
Dana, Henry Wadsworth Longfellow, and Hawthorne, Manning, 'The Maiden Aunt of the Whole Human Race.' Fredrika Bremer's friendship with Longfellow and Hawthorne. ASR 1949 Sept.
Horn, Vivi, *På sångens vingar* (Jenny Lind). Stockholm 1945.
Benson, Adolph B., 'Bayard Taylor's Jenny Lind Prize Poem.' SP 1956: 61–70.
— 'Jenny Lind in English and American Verse.' YB 1957.
About Jenny Lind: ASM 1945 Nov., 1961 Aug., SP 1951 Spring.

Information about Jenny Lind was also obtained from W. Porter Ware, Sewanee, Tenn.

BIBLIOGRAPHY

16.   Inside Sweden

First, the already mentioned books about the history of Sweden.

Bondestad, Kjell, 'The American Civil War and Swedish Public Opinion.' SP 1968: 95–115.

Ekman, Ernst, 'Sweden and the Beginning of the American Civil War.' YB 1961.

17.   The Swedes in the Civil War

Here, *Americans from Sweden*, by Benson-Hedin, and *Swedish Immigrants in Lincoln's Time*, by Nels Hokanson, were important sources.

Ander, O. Fritiof, 'Lincoln and the Founders of Augustana College.' SP 1960: 45–72.

Lonn, Ella, *Foreigners in the Union Army and Navy*. Baton Rouge, La., 1951.

Ness, Jr., George T., 'Swedish-born Graduates of West Point.' ASM 1946 Dec. (Also, information from the U.S. Military Academy)

Warberg, A. C:son, *Skizzer från nord-amerikanska kriget 1861–65*. Stockholm 1867–71.

Lindquist, Emory, *An Immigrant's Two Worlds*. A biography of Hjalmar Edgren. Rock Island, Ill. (Also, ASM 1940 Nov.)

Ockerson, John Augustus, *An autobiography*. Typewritten, ASHM Philadelphia.

Medal of Honor 1863–1968. Prepared for a U.S. Senate Committee. Washington, D.C. 1968.

Dahlgren, Madeleine Vinton, *Memoir of John A. Dahlgren*. Boston 1882. (Also, ASM 1962 March)

Johnson, Amandus, 'Colonel Ulric Dahlgren.' YB 1961.

Lonn, Ella, *Foreigners in the Confederacy*. Chapel Hill, N.C., 1940.

Widén, Carl T., 'Texas Swedish Pioneers and the Confederacy.' SP 1961: 100–107.

18.   The John Ericsson Story

Church, William Conant, *The Life of John Ericsson*. I–II. New York, 1906–07.

Goldkuhl, Carola. *John Ericsson, Mannen och uppfinnaren*. Stockholm 1961.

Noven, John, *Gideon Welles, Lincoln's Secretary of the Navy*. New York 1973.

Eller, E. M., *Monitors of the U.S. Navy 1861–1937*. Washington, D.C. 1969.

Yellett, John E., 'Captain John Ericsson: Pioneer in Solar Energy.' Newsletter of the Association for Applied Solar Energy, Phoenix, Ariz., 1956 Sept.–1957 June.

About John Ericsson: ASM 1937 March, 1939 Nov., 1953 March, April, 1957 Oct., 1962 March, 1965 Nov.

Johnson, Amandus, 'Svenska stormän i amerikanska teknikens historia' (William Nystrom). *Industria*, Stockholm, 1948 May.

19.   The Great Trek Starts

Moberg, Vilhelm, 'How the America Legend Was Born in Sweden.' ASM 1948 Dec.

Ander, O. Fritiof, 'Reflections on the Causes of Emigration from Sweden,' SP 1962: 143–154.

Brattne, Berit, *Bröderna Larsson*. En studie i svensk emigrantverksamhet under 1880-talet. Uppsala 1973.

Ljungmark, Lars, *For Sale — Minnesota*. Organized Promotion of Scandinavian Immigration 1866–1873. Stockholm 1971.

Nilsson, Fred, *Emigration från Stockholm till Nordamerika 1880–1893*. Stockholm 1970.

Stephenson, George M., 'Isidor Kjellberg, Crusader,' *Swedish-American Historical Bulletin* 1928.

Nilsson, Nils Gunnar, 'Isidor Kjellberg journalist.' *Sydsvenska Dagbladet* Sept. 22, 1974.

828

BIBLIOGRAPHY

20.   More Religious Contacts

Again, Stephenson's *Religious Aspects of Swedish Immigration*, and *Americans from Sweden*, by Benson-Hedin.

Olsson, Karl A., *By One Spirit*. The Evangelical Covenant Church of America. Chicago 1962. (Also, ASM 1935 June, North Park College: ASM 1954 July)
Waldenström, P., *Genom Norra Amerikas Förenta Stater*. Stockholm 1890.
— *Nya färder i Amerikas Förenta Stater*. Stockholm 1902.
Nyvall, C. J., *Travel Memories from America* 1876. Kristinehamn 1876. Chicago 1953.
'The Scandinavian Branch of the Salvation Army in the United States,' in *The Swedish Element in America* (mentioned above).
Tjader, Marguerite, *Mother Elisabeth* (Elisabeth Hesselblad). New York 1972.

21.   New Contacts and Exchanges

Johnson, Amandus, 'Sweden at the Centennial, 1876.' ASM 1939 Oct.
Benson, Adolph B., *Prince Oscar at the U.S. Centennial*, 1876. SP 1953 July.
Thomas, W. W., *Sweden and the Swedes*. Chicago 1892.
Löfgren, Mia Leche, *Kristina Nilsson*. Stockholm 1944. (Also, ASM 1943 Aug.)
Benson, Adolph B., 'Famous Singers from Sweden' (Ladies Vocal Quartet). ASM 1952 Jan., Feb.
Edwards, Everett E., 'Their Road Led West.' How Swedish Pioneers became American Farmers. ASM 1948 June. (About Eric Englund, ASM 1943 April)

22.   In the American Heartland

Again, several already mentioned books, including Nelson's *The Swedes and the Swedish Settlements in North America*, Benson-Hedin, Beijbom, and Gustav E. Johnson's dissertation *The Swedes of Chicago*.

Beijbom, Ulf, 'Chicago's Swede Town.' SP 1964: 144–158.
Naeseth, Henriette C. K., *The Swedish Theatre of Chicago* 1868–1950. Rock Island, Ill., 1951.
About Anton J. Carlson: *Time* Feb. 10, 1941, *Saturday Evening Post* Sept. 13, 1947, ASM 1944 March, 1950 Jan. P. B. Magnuson: ASM 1949 March. Alfred Stromberg, Androv Carlson: *Dynamic America* (General Dynamics), New York 1961. A. I. Appleton: YB 1952. Vincent Bendix: ASM 1937 Nov.
Casey, Robert Jr., *Mr. Clutch*. The Story of George William Borg. New York 1948.
Oursler, Will, *From Ox Carts to Jets* (Borg Warner). Englewood Cliffs, N. J. 1959.
About J. P. Seeburg: ASM 1945 Feb., 1954 Jan. C. R. Walgreen: ASM 1938 Oct., 1951 June. B. G. Dahlberg: ASM 1940 Feb.
Nelson, Herman G., 'Rockford, Ill. retains its Swedish flavor.' ASM 1948 June. Also: ASM 1939 Jan., 1952 Jan., Feb., 1954 Aug., 1957 Dec.
Carlsson, Sten, 'Scandinavian Politicians in Minnesota Around the Turn of the Century,' *Scandinavian-American Interrelations*, by Harold S. Ness and Sigmund Skard (ed.). Oslo 1971. (Also, Sten Carlsson, *Skandinaviska politiker i Minnesota* 1882–1900. Uppsala 1970)
About Floyd B. Olson: ASM 1935 Feb. Luther W. Youngdahl: ASM 1947 March, 1958 May. Benjamin E. Youngdahl: ASM 1946 Feb. Mike Holm: ASM 1940 May. Magnus Johnson: SP 1965: 122–136. Ernest Lundeen: ASM 1938 March. Charles A. Smith: *Vestkusten* Panama Pacific International Exposition issue, San Francisco 1915.

BIBLIOGRAPHY

Andrews, Alice E., *Christopher C. Andrews, Pioneer in Forestry Conservation in the United States*. Cleveland, O., 1928.

Swanson, Evadene Burris, 'A New Hampshire Yankee in King Oscar's Court' (C. C. Andrews), SP 1965: 18–25. (Also, SP 1970: 84–104)

About C. E. Wickman: ASM 1943 Nov. Alexander P. Anderson: ASM 1941 Feb. Johnson & Shipstad: ASM 1941 March, 1943 Jan., 1958 May. Elmer W. Engstrom: ASM 1951 Oct.

Gump, Gertrude, *The Story of Swan Johan Turnblad*. The American Swedish Institute, Minneapolis 1974. (Also, ASM 1942 Jan., 1954 Oct., 1958 May)

Mattson, Hans, *Souvenir*. 250th Anniversary of the First Swedish Settlement in America. Minneapolis 1889.

About Iowa and Des Moines: ASM 1951 July, Nov., 1956 Oct. Stanton: Centennial 1970, official history and program. Agnes Samuelson: ASM 1936 March.

Wessell, Nils Yngve, 'Some American Scandinavian Psychologists.' YB 1947. (Also, Dean Seashore: ASR 1938 Dec., ASM 1939 Feb. Everet F. Lindquist: ASM 1955 April)

Also, information about Stanton from Sigurd S. Larmon, New York. About Wisconsin, from Stig G. Wiren, Kenosha, Wis., Bergstrom Paper Co., Neenah, Wis., and John Becker, New York.

Olsson, Nils William, 'The Swedish Settlement of Tustin, Mich.' SP 1962: 109–117.

Rylander, Andrew E., 'Detroit Swedes.' ASM 1948 June.

About Gustave A. Carlson: YB 1960. Nels L. Olson: ASM 1950 Oct. Otto Lundell: ASM 1938 Nov. Carl B. Parsons: ASM 1943 April.

Althin, Torsten, *C. E. Johansson 1864–1943*. Stockholm 1948.

About Adam Strohm: ASM 1941 June. Johan R. Banér: ASM 1952 June. Skulda Banér: ASM 1944 Nov., 1957 Aug., 1959 Aug., 1962 Oct. Francis J. Plym: ASM 1935 Dec. Emil Tyden: ASM 1946 July, YB 1952, 1964.

Information about Michigan from Signe Karlstrom, Bloomfield Hills, Mich., Nils R. Johaneson, Grosse Pointe, Mich., Governor William G. Milliken, and Glenn T. Seaborg, Berkeley, Cal.

Dowie, James Iverne, *Prairie Grass Dividing*. Rock Island, Ill., 1959.

Olson, James C., *History of Nebraska*. Lincoln, Neb., 1955.

Alexis, Joseph, 'Pioneers in Nebraska.' ASM 1948 June.

About Omaha Swedes: ASM 1952 May. Carl A. Swanson: ASM 1945 Dec. Joseph Alexis: ASM 1947 Aug. Leonard Strömberg: SP 1972: 169–184. Luther College: ASM 1955 Feb.

Also, information from Einar Viren, Omaha, Neb., and Robert H. Ahmanson, Los Angeles, Cal.

Sherriff, Florence Janson, 'The Swedish Settlements in North Dakota.' SP 1953 Jan.

About Daniel Peter Brown: SP 1954: 56–61. Peter Norbeck: ASM 1936 Oct. Clinton P. Anderson: ASM 1945 Sept. Eric P. Quain: ASM 1955 April, and information from the Quain and Ramstad Clinic, Bismarck, N.D.

Lindquist, Emory, *Vision for a Valley*. Olof Olsson and the early history of Lindsborg. Rock Island, Ill., 1970.

— *Smoky Valley People; a History of Lindsborg, Kansas*. Lindsborg 1953.

About Lindsborg, Bethany College, and the "Messiah" tradition: ASM 1936 April, 1941 Nov., 1948 June, 1955 Oct., Nov., 1961 April, YB 1945, SP 1952 July, 1958: 111–123.

About Mariadahl Church: ASM 1952 June, 1961 Nov. Carl A. Swensson: SP 1966: 184–190. Frank Carlson: ASM 1940 April.

Lindquist, Emory, 'The Invention and Development of the Dial Telephone.' *The Kansas Historical Quarterly*, 1957:1.

Skarstedt, Ernst T., *Vagabond och Redaktör*. Seattle 1914.

Lindgren, Ida, *Från nybyggarhemmet i Kansas 1870–1881*. Göteborg 1960. (Also, SP 1965: 3–17.

Also, information from Emory Lindquist of Wichita, Kansas, and Hugo Lindgren, Stockholm.

23. In the Rocky Mountains

Carlson, Elmer, 'The Earlier Swedes in Colorado.' YB 1949.
About Swedes in Denver: ASM 1953 Jan-June. Ryssby Church: ASM 1959 Dec. Reuben G. Gustavson: ASM 1946 April. Swedish National Sanatorium: ASM 1948 Oct. Emil E. Johnson: ASM 1941 June. Edwin C. Johnson: ASM 1939 Dec.
Information from Harald Millgård about the Recen family (including articles in *Borlänge Tidning*), and from Egon and Glenn D. Peterson, Denver, Neil Norgren, Denver, and Admiral Arleigh A. Burke, Washington, D.C.
Benson, Adolph B., 'New Light on the Swedish Mormons.' YB 1958.
Mulder, William, 'Mother Tongue, "Skandinavisme," and "The Swedish Insurrection" in Utah.' SP 1956: 11–20. (Also, SP 1958: 33–35)
Lindgren, Raymond E., 'The Swedes Come to Utah.' YB 1949. (Also, ASM 1949 Sept., 1951 April)
Lärn, Hubert, 'Fantastic Hilda — Pioneer History Personified.' SP 1964: 63–76.
Aronson, Hugo, and Brockman, L. O., *The Galloping Swede*. Missoula, Mont., 1970. (Also, ASM 1956 Nov., 1959 Aug.)

Also, information from the Church Historian, Salt Lake City, Utah.

24. On the Pacific

Skarstedt, Ernst T., *Washington och dess svenska befolkning*. Seattle, 1908.
Pollard, Lancaster, *A History of the State of Washington*. I–IV. New York 1937.
Lofgren, Svante, 'The Early Swedish Settlements of Washington.' YB 1946.
— 'Some Swedish Business Pioneers in Washington.' YB 1947.
About Swedes of Northwest: ASM 1952 Aug., 1957 Jan. Swedish Gangsaws: ASM 1952 March. Philip G. Johnson: ASM 1938 Aug., 1944 April.
McDonald, J. J., 'Ossian Anderson, Industrial Leader.' *Americana Illustrated* 1941:2.
Reed, Mark E., 'Alfred H. Anderson, A Personal Tribute.' University of Washington *Forest Club Quarterly*, 1925 Nov.
'Lage Wernstedt: Pioneer in Photogrammetry.' *Journal of Forestry*, 1945 Feb.
Skarstedt, Ernst T., *Oregon och Washington, samt deras skandinaviska inbyggare*. Portland 1890.
— *Oregon och dess svenska befolkning*. Seattle 1911.
Smith, William Carlson, 'The Swedes of Oregon.' YB 1946.
Also, information from the University of Washington, College of Forest Resources, Bror L. Grondal and Harry Fabbe, Seattle.
Furuhjelm, Annie, *Människor och Öden*. Helsingfors 1932.
Pipping, Ella, *Soldier of Fortune* (Nils v. Schoultz). Boston 1971.
Carlson, Leland H., 'Swedish Pioneers and the Discovery of Gold in Alaska.' YB 1948.
Wharton, David B., *The Alaska Gold Rush*. Bloomington, Ind., and London 1972.
Nicpon, Philip, 'Scandinavian-Americans in Alaska.' ASR 1974 Sept.
Skarstedt, Ernst T., *California och dess svenska befolkning*. Seattle 1910.
Fjellström, Phebe, *Swedish-American Colonization in the San Joaquin Valley*. Uppsala 1970.
Björk, Kenneth, 'Scandinavian Experiment in California.' SP 1954: 67–78, 100–116.
Lindberg, Ruby, 'August Wetterman — California Pioneer.' YB 1959.
Green, Erik, 'Herbert Howe Bancroft and Wilhelm Roos (alias Nemos).' *Lychnos Yearbook* 1950–51. Uppsala and Stockholm.
About California Swedes: ASM 1954 Feb.-June, 1957 Jan. Oakland Swedes: ASM 1952

Sept. William Matson: ASM 1938 April. Roger Dahlhjelm: *Encyclopedia of American Biography*, ASM 1942 Feb., 1949 March, 1951 Nov. John Elof Boodin: *Faculty Bulletin*, University of California, 1951 Dec. Gustaf Stromberg: ASM 1950 Feb. Sven R. Lokrantz: ASM 1940 Feb. Rudolph A. Peterson: ASM 1964 Feb. Carl M. Friden: ASM 1944 Feb. Glenn T. Seaborg: ASM 1947 Sept., 1955 Dec. Gustavus A. Eisen: ASM 1935 Nov. Carl O. Swanberg: *Vestkusten* exposition issue 1915.

Dessauer, John H., *My Years with Xerox* (Chester Carlson). New York 1971.

Olsson, Nils William, 'Abraham Fornander — Swedish Pioneer in Hawaii.' SP 1962: 71–76.

Ekman, Ernst, 'Swedish-Hawaiian Relations in the 19th Century.' YB 1963. About Nils P. Larsen: ASM 1953 June, 1960 Oct.

Also, information from Kingsburg, Cal., Eric C. Bellquist and Roy W. Carlson, Berkeley, Franklin D. Scott, Claremont, Cal., and Mabel Johnson, New York.

25. In New England

Wieden, Clifford and Marguerite, 'The Beginnings of a New Sweden in Maine.' YB 1946.

Menton, Arne S., 'Children in the Woods.' ASR 1953 Dec.

Kalijarvi, Thorsten, 'The Stonecutters of Concord, New Hampshire.' YB 1946.

Harvey, Dorothy Mayo, 'The Swedes in Vermont.' YB 1960.

About Joseph B. Johnson: ASM 1955 May. Brockton, Mass.: ASM 1942 April. Swedes in Boston: ASM 1951 Nov., Dec. In New England: ASM 1960 Aug.

Peterson, Bernard, 'Swedish Pioneers in the Greater Boston Area.' SP 1951 Summer.

Widén, Albin, *Svenskar som erövrat Amerika*. Stockholm 1937.

Trulson, Anton H., Ekblaw, W. Elmer, *Who's Who in Viking Industry and Craftsmanship in Northeastern United States*. Worcester, Mass., 1946.

About Carl R. Hellstrom: *Saturday Evening Post* August 13, 1949. George F. Berkander: ASM 1937 Jan. Swedes in Worcester: SP 1953 April, October, 1954: 117–124, 1959: 105–117. ASM 1958 Oct.

Hedin, Naboth, 'George N. Jeppson' (and Norton Co.). YB 1963. (Also, ASM 1941 Feb., 1960 May)

About Signe Hagelthorn: ASM 1937 April. Otto Folin: ASM 1935 Sept. Nils Y. Wessell: ASM 1954 March. Adolph B. Benson: SP 1963 Jan., YB 1964. Gustaf Swebilius: ASM 1941 July, 1943 Nov.

About Swedes in Connecticut: ASM 1935 July, YB 1953. Rudolph Bannow: ASM 1954 Dec., 1960 Feb.

Information from General Dynamics, Electric Boat Division, and other sources.

26. In the Mid-Atlantic States

Several previously mentioned sources, including *Americans from Sweden, Swedes in America* and *The Swedish Element in America*.

About Samuel A. Carlson: ASM 1936 July, YB 1961.

Berger, Vilhelm, *Svenskarna i New York*. New York 1918.

Hoving, Johannes, *Sextio år, Mitt livs dagbok*. Uppsala 1928.

'Olympic Champions Cheered and Dined.' *The New York Times*, August 25, 1912.
Green, Sophie F., 'Father of the American Skyline Unlimited.' ASSE Bulletin Winter, 1949–50. (Also, ASM 1940 Sept.)
About Alexander F. Victor: ASM 1939 April. Harrie T. Lindeberg: ASM 1940 July. Andrew G. Hagstrom: ASM 1948 July. W. Axel Warn: ASM 1948 Feb.
Johnson, Henry, *The Other Side of Main Street*. New York 1943. (Also, ASM 1947 Oct.)
About Paul H. Nystrom: ASM 1949 Sept. Arthur Donaldson: ASM 1940 May. Johanna M. Lindlof: ASM 1936 July. Arthur W. Wallander: ASM 1945 Nov. Klang brothers: ASM 1939 Sept. George Fried: ASM 1936 Jan.
About Upsala College: ASM 1939 June, 1943 Oct., 1950 June, 1953 Sept., 1960 Feb., ASR 1952 Sept. Old Swedish families in Philadelphia: *Philadelphia* (mag.), 1946 Jan. Amandus Johnson: ASM 1936 Aug., 1957 Nov., YB 1963, 1967. Thorsten Sellin: ASM 1955 Sept., YB 1963. Bryn Athyn: YB 1957.
Peterson, Arthur, *Songs of New Sweden*. Chicago 1912.
Wikander, O. R., 'Steel's Right Hand Men.' *Industria International*, Stockholm 1949–50.
Smith, Julian F., 'Swedes in the American Navy.' ASSE *Bulletin* Winter 1948–49.
Hammar, Hugu, *Som emigrant i USA*. Stockholm 1938.
About Hans Lundberg: ASM 1949 Aug. Ernst Alexanderson: ASM 1940 Jan., 1945 March, 1948 May. Harry F. Olson: ASM 1956 Jan.
Information from Lennart O. Alfelt, Academy of the New Church, Bryn Athyn, Pa., and from Sven L. Wahlström, Stockholm and other steel experts.

27. In the South

About Eisenhower's mother-in-law: ASM 1952 Oct., 1960 May.
Anderson, Mary, *Woman at Work*. Minneapolis 1951. (Also, ASM 1935 Aug., 1943 Nov., 1960 March)
Information about the Lindbeck brothers from *The New York Times* and Gustavus Adolphus College, St. Peter, Minn.
Dill, Alonzo Thomas, *Chesapeake — Pioneer Papermaker*. Charlottesville, Va., 1968.
Information about Elis Olsson: ASM 1953 July. Oscar Nelson: ASM 1946 June. Swedes in Florida: SP 1966: 191–196, 1967: 132–147. Joseph Henschen: SP 1968: 194–200. Axel Hallstrom: YB 1966. Oscar Winberg: ASM 1939 Dec. Carl T. Widén: ASM 1961 April. Texas Swedish Cultural Foundation: ASM 1952 Feb. John P. Sjolander: YB 1960. Johan A. Udden: YB 1962.

28. Sweden: A Great Transformation

First, the books about the history of Sweden, and Florence Janson's work about the emigration from Sweden, also mentioned above.

Schück, H., etc., *Nobel — The Man and His Prizes*. New York 1962.
Tjerneld, Staffan, *Nobel*. Stockholm 1972.
Benson, Adolph B., 'Swedish Leaders in the American Industry of Explosives.' YB 1959.
Strandh, Sigvard, 'Wilhelm Teodore Unge, A Swedish Pioneer in Rocketry.' *Daedalus* 1964 (Yearbook of the Museum of Technology, Stockholm).
Rynell, Sven, 'J. P. Johansson — Inventor of Products and Ideas.' *Daedalus* 1965.
Kish, George, *North-east Passage*. Adolf Erik Nordenskiöld, his life and times. Amsterdam 1973.
Odelberg, Wilhelm, *Swedish Scholars of the 20th Century*. Stockholm 1972.
'Weatherman Carl-Gustaf Rossby.' *Time*, Dec. 17, 1956.

Also, information from paper and steel experts and other specialists in Sweden.

29. The End of Mass Migration

Here, the sources include *Svenska Dagbladet* and *Socialdemokraten* during October-November 1907, a period of financial crisis in the United States.

Kälvemark, Ann-Sofie, *Reaktionen mot utvandringen.* Emigrationsfrågan i svensk debatt och politik 1901–04. Uppsala 1972.
Palm, August, *Ögonblicksbilder från en tripp till Amerika.* Stockholm 1901.
Sundbeck, Carl, *Svensk-amerikanerna, deras materiella och andliga sträfvanden.* Rock Island, Ill., 1904.

30. Swedish-American Zenith, and the First World War

Skarstedt, Ernst T., *Svensk-amerikanska folket i helg och söcken.* Stockholm 1917.
Lindmark, Sture, *Swedish America 1914–1932.* Uppsala 1971. (Also, SP 1965: 216–232, 1968: 3–31, 1969: 25–41)
About the assimilation of Swedes in America: SP 1956: 47–61 (George M. Stephenson), SP 1956: 136–147 (Adolph B. Benson), SP 1968: 143–157 (Conrad Bergendoff).
Nystrom, Daniel, *A Ministry of Printing* (Augustana Book Concern), Rock Island, Ill. 1962.
About Vasa Order: ASM 1940 Oct., 1944 Sept., 1952 Dec. Order of Svithiod: ASM April 1953. Order of Vikings: ASM 1941 Feb., 1952 Oct.
Pehrsson, Per, 'Svenskarna i Amerika.' Riksföreningen för svenskheten, *Årsbok* 1910.
Hasselmo, Nils, *Amerika-svenska.* Språkutvecklingen i Svensk-Amerika. Rock Island 1962.
Larson, Bruce L., *Lindbergh of Minnesota.* A political biography. New York 1973.
Koblik, Steven, *Sweden: The Neutral Victor.* Sweden and the Western Powers 1917–1918. Lund 1972.

31. Swedes in American Arts

Literature about Carl Sandburg was mentioned under 13. For painters and sculptors, Allhems *Konstnärslexikon* (Dictionary of Swedish Artists), was an important source.

About Gösta Larsson: ASM 1941 Jan. Howard Hanson: *Christian Science Monitor*, Oct. 14, 1944, ASM 1934 March.
About John F. Carlson: ASM 1936 May. Henry Mattson: ASM 1952 March. Carl Sprinchorn: ASM 1950 July, ASR 1974 June. Birger Sandzén ASM 1937 Jan., 1957 Aug., ASR 1954 Dec. Oscar Jacobson: ASM 1938 Dec. Carl Oscar Borg: ASM 1935 Jan., SP 1955: 84–86, ASR 1956 June, YB 1962. Thure Thulstrup: SP 1962: 9–19. Henry Reuterdahl: SP 1962: 39–44. Gustaf Tenggren: ASM 1946 Jan. Charles Haag: ASR 1946 Sept. Anders Zorn SP 1956: 3–10.

32. From Strindberg to Lagerkvist

Here, Alrik Gustafson's *A History of Swedish Literature* was again an important source. Also, information from Arvid Paulson, New York.

Ollén, Gunnar, *Strindbergs dramatik*. Stockholm 1961.
Paulson, Arvid, 'The Father.' Critical opinion and leading American performances during the past half century. *Scandinavian Studies*, presented to Dr. Henry Goddard Leach on the occasion of his 85th birthday. Seattle 1956.
Gustafson, Alrik, 'August Strindberg 1849–1949.' ASR 1949 June.
Linder, Erik Hj., 'Hjalmar Bergman in Hollywood — A Sad Chapter.' YB 1972.
Lagerlöf, Selma, 'Vädjan till Amerika.' Radio address in Swedish Feb. 13, 1933.

33. The Stirring 1920s

About Sweden-America Foundation: ASR 1939 Dec. American-Scandinavian Foundation: ASM 1951 Jan.

Söderblom, Nathan, *Från Upsala till Rock Island*. Stockholm 1924.
— 'The American Idealism.' Address, Swedish-American Society, Stockholm. April 30, 1924.
About Elsa Brändström-Ulich: ASM 1947 July. Conrad Bergendoff: ASM 1940 Jan. Swedes in American Aviation: ASM 1936 Sept. Erik H. Nelson: ASM 1938 April. Hugo Sundstedt: ASM 1942 Oct. Bert Hassell: ASM 1945 Feb.
Bainbridge, John, *Garbo*. Garden City, N.Y. 1955. (Also, ASR 1938 March, ASM 1939 Jan., "Sweden's Hollywood")
Wayner, Robert J. (ed.), *What Did They Sing at the Met?* New York 1971.
Henrikson, Fritz, *Med Sveriges kronprinspar genom Amerika*. Stockholm 1926.

34. More Cultural Exchanges

Here, the scrapbooks of The American-Swedish News Exchange were important. Also, information supplied by Anders Österling in *Nobel — The Man and His Prizes*.

Berg, Ruben G: son, *Moderna amerikaner*. Stockholm 1925.

35. The Extraordinary 1930s

Without the above-mentioned scrapbooks, the survey of the "Middle Way" period could hardly have been written.

Henriksson, Fritz, *Sweden's Participation in the U.S. Celebration of New Sweden*. Stockholm 1939. (Also, ASM 1938 June-Aug., ASR 1938 Sept.)
About Sweden at World's Fair in New York: ASM 1939 March, June-Sept., Dec., ASR 1939 June. Albin Johansson: ASM 1946 March. Roosevelt Commission on industrial relations in Sweden: ASM 1938 Oct.

36. Economics: A Case in Point

This survey is largely based on magazine articles, news reports, and interviews with Swedish and American economists.

Landgren, Karl-Gustaf, *Economics in Modern Sweden*. Library of Congress, Washington, D.C., 1957.

37. Swedish Artists in America

The Carl Milles story is, in part, based on personal interviews (including one with Anne Hedmark of Millesgården) and on correspondence with American museums and other institutions.

Rogers, Meyric R., 'Carl Milles in America.' ASR 1941 Sept. (Also, ASM 1951 Oct.)

Arvidsson, Karl Axel, *Millesgården*. Stockholm 1953.

About Jussi Björling, Kerstin Thorborg: ASM 1940 Dec., 1951 Dec. Karin Branzell: ASM 1945 March. Aroldo Lindi: ASM 1937 Jan. Ingrid Bergman: ASM 1940 May, 1941 April, Sept., 1943 Aug., 1947 Jan., ASR 1946 June. Signe Hasso: ASM 1949 Dec. Viveca Lindfors: ASM 1946 Aug. Jean Rogers: ASM 1940 June. Jeffrey Lynn: ASM 1939 Nov. Edgar Bergen: ASM 1937 Sept., 1949 Feb.

38. The Second World War

Carlgren, Wilhelm M., *Svensk utrikespolitik* 1939–1945. Stockholm 1973.

Hägglöf, Gunnar, *Sveriges krigshandelspolitik under andra världskriget*. Stockholm 1958.

Fox, Annette Baker, *The Power of Small States*. Diplomacy in World War II. Chicago 1959.

'Irriterad Churchill: Sverige måste slåss.' (Churchill to Anthony Eden April 15, 1945). Ulf Brandell, *Dagens Nyheter* Dec. 10, 1973.

About John H. Hilldring: ASM 1942 May, 1946 April. John E. Dahlquist: ASM 1942 Sept. Henning Linden: ASM 1944 Jan. Kenneth P. and Earl C. Bergquist: *Current Biography* 1961 March, *Sydsvenska Dagbladet* Dec. 12, 1960. Chesley G. Peterson: ASM 1943 Nov. Borgstrom brothers: ASM 1944 Nov. Richard I. Bong: ASM 1944 Feb. Charles E. Nathurst: ASM 1942 Aug. Arleigh A. Burke: YB 1967. Charles E. Rosendahl: ASM 1937 June. Carl E. Anderson: *Saturday Evening Post* May 13, 1945. Erik G. Håkanson: ASM 1944 Feb. Ture G. Rennerfelt: *Fortune* 1945 March. Boris Hagelin: ASM 1946 Aug. Swedish inventions: ASM 1944 July. Carl-Gustaf Rossby: ASM 1942 July.

Also, correspondence with many of those mentioned, including Admirals Roy Stanley Benson, Theodore C. Lonnquest, and Clifford Anders Swanson, and with Bertel Rennerfelt, Stockholm.

39. From the Early Postwar Years to Vietnam

First, the news bulletins of The American-Swedish News Exchange down to 1964 were important.

Fosdick, Dorothy, *Common Sense and World Affairs*. New York 1955.

About Sweden and the Korean War: ASM 1950 Aug. About Vietnam in 1969: Olof Palme at the Gumaelius Reunion in Malmö in November, and Tage Erlander in Oslo in late November or early December.

40. The Constant Interchange

This chapter is largely based on news reports, magazine and newspaper articles, correspondence and interviews.

BIBLIOGRAPHY

Thompson, Lawrence S., 'Sweden Likes American Literature.' ASM 1939 March, May.
'American Books Abroad,' in *Literary History of the United States*, by Robert E. Spiller, etc. New York 1969.
Anderson, Carl L., *The Swedish Acceptance of American Literature*. Stockholm 1957.
Scott, Franklin D., 'American Influences in Norway and Sweden.' *Journal of Modern History*, 1946 March.
Boström, Wollmar F., 'Swedish-American Cultural Relations, 1925–1945.' YB 1945.
Sjöberg, Leif, 'Gunnar Ekelöf, Poet and Outsider.' ASR 1965 Winter.
Lindahl, Mac, 'American Plays in the Swedish Theater.' ASM 1945 Dec.
Meryman, Richard, 'Ingmar Bergman,' *Life*, Oct. 15, 1971. (Also, *Current Biography* 1960 April)
Dolan, Paul, 'Creating State Ombudsmen: A Growing Movement.' *National Civic Review*, 1974 May. (Also, 'The Two Kinds of Ombudsmen — One Is Tough,' by Michael T. Kaufman, in *The New York Times*. November 17, 1974)
For the section about biochemistry, the article about Einar Hammarsten in *Svenskt biografiskt lexikon* was important. Also, *Nobel — The Man and His Prizes*, magazine articles, and material from The Rockefeller Foundation.
Robinson, Donald, *The 100 Most Important People in the World Today* (Torbjörn Caspersson). Boston 1952. (Also, 'He looks at life,' by Sven Åhman, ASM 1956 Nov.)
About Holger Hydén: 'The Search for the Memory Molecule.' *The New York Times Magazine*, July 7, 1968. (Also, *Time*, Feb. 10, 1961, *New York Herald Tribune*, Sept. 9, 1962) Sune Bergström: ASM 1941 July. Prostaglandins: *New York Times Magazine*, Dec. 5, 1971.

41. The Immigrants and Their Descendants

Bergendoff, Conrad, 'On the Occasion of the Centennial of Augustana College.' SP 1960: 35–44.
Carlsson, Sten, 'Some Aspects of the Swedish Emigration to the U.S.' SP 1969: 192–203.
About Ragnar Benson: ASM 1951 April, 1959 May. Swedish Pioneer Centennial: ASM 1948 July, 1950 Dec., SP 1969: 161–191.
Olsson, Nils William, *Tracing Your Swedish Ancestry*. Uppsala 1974.
Moberg, Vilhelm, 'Why I Wrote the Novel about Swedish Emigrants.' SP 1966: 63–77.
Hedblom, Folke, 'Swedish Speech and Popular Tradition in America.' SP 1965: 137–154, 1967: 76–92.
En smålandssocken emigrerar (Långasjö Parish). Växjö 1967.
Sima, Jonas, 'Joe Hill — The Man Who Never Died.' YB 1965.

42. New Links in Science, Technology, Trade

The section about Swedish scientists and scholars in the United States is largely based on personal interviews and correspondence.

About Bengt Stromgren: ASM 1955 Oct. G. Richard Soderberg: ASM 1949 July, 1957 March. Helge Kökeritz: ASM 1944 June, 1954 June, 1958 Dec. Harry Söderman: *Saturday Evening Post*, May 16, 1953.

The survey of commercial and technological exchanges is also largely based on interviews and correspondence. Other sources include memoranda from the Swedish Export Council and the Swedish Board of Trade, and numerous articles in *The American Swedish Monthly*.

'Sweden's Trade with the USA.' *Index*, Stockholm 1968:8.
'Sweden: Top Market for U.S. Goods.' *International Trade Review* 1964 May.
'Scandinavia today is billion dollar U.S. market.' *International Commerce* April 3, 1967.
About Swedish Match U.S. subsidiary: ASM 1952 Aug. American Astra: ASM 1959 Nov.

The following books, booklets, and articles, not mentioned above, have also been consulted:

Benson, Adolph B., 'Swedish American Leaders in Education.' ASM 1936 Jan., Feb., April.
— 'Swedish Contributions to America.' SP 1953 April.
Brook, Michael, 'Radical Literature in Swedish-America.' SP 1969: 111–132. Brook's sources included *Skandinaver på vänsterflygeln i USA* (Scandinavians on the Left Front in the United States), authored by the late Henry Bengston, then a resident of Chicago, and published in Stockholm in 1955. It deals with the Socialist movement among Swedish and other Scandinavian workers in America, especially in Chicago and the Midwest. Bengston himself was a moderate Socialist.
Dowie, J. Iverne, and Tredway, Jr. Thomas (ed.), *The Immigration of Ideas*. Essays presented to O. Fritiof Ander. Rock Island, Ill., 1968.
Dowie, J. Iverne, and Espelie, Ernest M. (ed.), *The Swedish Immigrant Community in Transition*. Essays in honor of Conrad Bergendoff. Rock Island, Ill., 1963.
Furer, Howard B., *The Scandinavians in America* 986–1970. Dobbs Ferry, N.Y., 1972.
Johnson, Amandus, *Contributions by Swedes to American Progress*, 1638–1921. New York 1921.
Landfors, Arthur, 'Swedish-American Poetry.' SP 1970: 153–162.
Måwe, Carl-Erik, *Värmlänningar i Nordamerika*. Säffle 1971.
Widén, Albin, *Nybyggarliv i Svensk-Amerika*. Stockholm 1972.

Addendum, page 575, after the paragraph about Karl Sundberg and Hans T. F. Lundberg, ore and oil prospectors:

A third graduate of the Stockholm Institute of Technology, Folke Kihlstedt (1901–56), was also regarded as one of the world's foremost ore and oil prospectors. After the Second World War, when he was in charge of the U. S. Steel Corporation's ore prospecting in Venezuela, he played a leading part in discovering one of the world's richest iron deposits, Cerro Bolívar. During the latter part of his life, Kihlstedt made his home at New Market, Maryland. (In its September 30, 1950 issue, *The Saturday Evening Post* carried, as its leading feature, an article titled "Ten-Billion-Dollar Mountain," with a subhead beginning "In one of the great ore strikes of our time, a Swede named Kihlstedt found 'the world's richest iron deposit'.")

Index of Personal Names

There are, in the beginning, separate sections for Presidents of the United States, for U. S. senators and state governors of at least partly Swedish ancestry (not including descent from immigrants of the 1600s and 1700s), for the Delaware settlements of the 17th and 18th centuries, for Swedish officers who fought in the War of Independence in America, and for the Kings of Sweden mentioned in the text. In alphabetizing, the diacritical marks of the Swedish letters å, ä, and ö have been disregarded.

INDEX OF PERSONAL NAMES

Rehn, Gösta 718
Rehnquist, William H. 586
Reinhardt, Max 666
Renhard, Rev. Carl J. 493,
 496
Rennerfelt, Ivar 743
Rennerfelt, Ture Gustaf
 743
Retzius, Anders 495
Retzius, Anders Jahan 68,
 69, 128
Retzius, Gustaf 495
Reuss, Henry S. 774
Reuterdahl, Arvid 413
Reuterdahl, Henry 656–7
Reuterskiöld, Carl Edvard
 Abraham 169
Reuther, Walter 794
Rhodin, Johannes 800
Richert, Johan Gabriel 132,
 269
Richson, Carl E. 576
Richter, Johan C. F. C. 812
Rignell, Carl John 414
Ringius, Carl 652
Rinman, Sven 65
Risberg, Gustaf 116
Roberg, O. Theodore 352
Roden, Lennart 801
Rodgers, Mary 622
Rogers (b. Lovgren), Jean
 (Elinor) 729
Rogers, Will 698
Rolander, Daniel 74
Romare, Paul 212
Romell, Lars Gunnar 802
Roos, Carl 200
Roos, Herman 376
Roos, Oscar 198
Roos (m. Olivecrona),
 Rosalie 217–9, 270–71
Roos, Wilhelm, see Nemos,
 William
Roosval, Johnny 681
Rooth, Ivar 807
Roseberry (Rosberg), Anna
 Marie 477
Rosenberg, Hilding 758
Rosenblad, Mathias 147
Rosencrantz, Fredrick
 Anton Ulrik 291
Rosencrantz, Palle 291
Rosendahl, Charles E.
 741–2
Rosendahl, Frank D. 504

Rosenius, Rev. Carl Olof
 150, 151, 235
Rosenquist, James 767
Rosenstjerna, Nils 292
Roslin, Alexander 87
Ross, Betsy 36
Rossander, Carl August 291
Rossby, Carl-Gustaf 626,
 744
Roth, William Matson 508,
 586–7
Rothery, Agnes 699
Rothman, Georg 74
Rudbeck, Olaus 57, 71, 77,
 495, 608
Rudbeck the Younger, Olof
 77
Rudberg, Johan Olof 164
Rudin, Harry R. 540
Rudin, Karl 514, 614
Rundgren, Bengt 756
Runeberg, Johan Ludvig
 98, 119
Runnström, John 778
Rush, Benjamin 107, 146
Russell, Jonathan 133–4
Rydbeck, Olof 798
Rydberg, Janne 625
Rydberg, Per Axel 453, 563
Rydberg, Viktor 524
Rydman, Otto 475

S

Saarinen, Eliel 723
Sahlin, Axel Edvard 548
Sahlin, Emil Georg 548
Sahlin, Nils G. 539
Samelius, William H. 400
Samuelson, Agnes 425
Samuelson, Paul A. 718
Samuelsson, Johannes 182
Samuelsson, Maria 182
Sandahl, August 198
Sandberg, Christer 615
Sandblom, Gustave A. 554
Sandburg (Danielsson),
 August 228
Sandburg, Carl 228, 398,
 645–7, 696, 762, 790
Sandels, Johan August 44
Sandgren, Charles 116
Sands (Larsson), Lewis
 206–7
Sandwall, Johan 287

Sandzén, Birger 462, 653–4
Sanford, Henry S. 593
Sarnoff, David 581
Saroyan, William 760
Scheele, Carl Wilhelm 66,
 67–8
Scheffer, Henrik Teofilus
 65
Schele de Vere, Maximilian
 213, 252
Scheutz, Georg 328
Schmidt, Carl Christian 211
Schmidt, Emanuel 547–8
Schmidt, Gustavus 211
Schmidt, Nathaniel 547
Schough, Adolf 214
Schröder, Gustavus W. 212,
 337–8
Schück, Henrik 639
Schwartz, Gustaf Magnus
 265
Schymberg, Hjördis 726
Scopes, John T. 695
Scott, Rev. George 146–51
Seaborg, Glenn Theodore
 438, 514–5, 776, 787
Seaborg, Herman
 Theodore 438
Seaborg (Sjöberg), John
 Eric 438
Seaholm (Sjöholm), Ernest
 W. 436
Seashore (Sjöstrand), Carl
 E. 422, 425–8
Seashore, Robert Holmes
 427
Seastrom (Sjöström), Victor
 461, 670, 684
Seeburg (Sjöberg), Justus P.
 390, 394
Sefström, Nils Gabriel 127
Seline, Caroline 479
Selkirk, Thomas Douglas
 196, 454
Sellin, Thorsten 570–71
Sellstedt, Lars Gustaf 548,
 649–50
Sellstrom, Edward Robert
 739
Semple, Robert 454
Senf, John Christian 95
Sergel, Johan Tobias 87
Severin, Nils Persson 383
Shallberg, Gustavus
 Adolphus 394

★

Selected Subject Index

★

Index of Swedish Place Names

This index lists the places of origin of immigrants from Sweden — cities, towns, villages, or parishes — that are mentioned in the text. The two largest cities, Stockholm and Gothenburg, have sections of their own. In numerous cases only the provincial origin — Skåne, Småland, Västergötland, etc. — is mentioned in the text, and these are not included in the index. Stockholm and Gothenburg are, therefore, overrepresented in relation to many of the provinces.